Nostradamus

John Hogue has spent 23 years studying the work of
Nostradamus and this, his third book on the prophet, is
the sequel to Nostradamus and the Millennium *and*
Nostradamus – The New Revelations.

by the same author

Nostradamus and the Millennium
Nostradamus – The New Revelations
The Millennium Book of Prophecy: *Visions and Predictions*

Nostradamus
The Complete Prophecies

JOHN HOGUE

ELEMENT

Shaftesbury, Dorset • Boston, Massachusetts • Melbourne, Victoria

Cover design by The Bridgewater Book Company
Designed and typeset by Footnote Graphics, Warminster, Wilts

Printed and bound in the USA by
Edwards Brothers, Inc.

British Library Cataloguing in Publication
data available

Library of Congress Cataloging in Publication
data available

ISBN 1-86204-388-4

Mississippi Mills
Public Library

Table of Contents

Introduction:
A History of the Future

My journey into the world of Nostradamus began decades ago with the celluloid tattoo circulating in a worn film projector in shuttered darkness. The year was 1967, and my sixth-grade social studies class was watching a documentary on the Nazi takeover of Germany called *The Crooked Cross*. Serried ranks of blood-red flags emblazoned with swastikas marched across the screen in the silver and black footage of a nightmare.

"Over four centuries ago," declared the narrator, "a Frenchman named Nostradamus predicted a day when the German child would 'know no law' and follow the banner of the 'crooked cross . . .'"

Nostradamus . . . The name quickened energies up and down my spine. The unguarded moment was filed away in my young mind and soon lost in a crowd of other sensations of youth. I remained blissfully unaware of the seed that had been planted beneath the surface of my mind which would secretly germinate in my subconscious for seven years.

Then in 1974, at the end of high school, a friend handed me a paperback copy of a pulp-fictionalized examination of Nostradamus. John Bole augured that this "prophecy stuff" was right down my alley.

He was right.

As I began to read, the seed sprouted and I was caught in the Nostradamus phenomenon, although the flypaper was a third-rate, sensationalized examination filled with historical inaccuracies. Even the cover illustration of the 16th-century doctor from southern France, with his curly shoulder-length tresses and waxed mustache, better resembled a composite of Louis XIV and Cardinal Richelieu from a later century. From this book I learned my first lesson in Nostradamian lore: no matter how mediocre the examination, no matter how vicious the skeptical attack, Nostradamus' legacy is like Teflon. No homily or hatchet job can repress our fascination with his nebulous prophecies, much less retain its hold on us.

The life and work of this 16th-century Renaissance Man was an enigma to even his contemporaries and has fascinated generations in the centuries since his death. Still today, Nostradamus – "celestial scientist," seer, doctor of medicine, herbalist, and creator of cosmetics and fruit preservatives – attracts both praise and blame and provokes controversy.

His ten-volume work *Les Propheties*, containing the greater part of his

1,110 prophecies written in four-line stanzas called quatrains, is one of
the few works that has remained continuously in print for over 440 years.
Efforts to unravel its obscure verses have gathered their own momentum
and, in these pivotal times as we approach the millennium, interest in his
predictions is now mounting to a climax. Many are convinced that his
auguries reveal the final years of the 20th century and the first few
decades of the next to be a time of unprecedented social strife, disease,
ethnic wars, ecological disaster, and change on a scale never known before.

But did Nostradamus really foresee all this, or are his interpreters
speaking for him?

Bias is the dust that covers everyone's magic mirror into the future.
Projections becloud the vision of the authentic prophetic genius as well
as the psychic-hotline quack. To project is human. Prophets deposit the
first layer of dust when they translate their paranormal visions into the
dialectics of words. On top of that settle the dust motes of commentaries
from those more psychically challenged mortals – the interpreters of a
prophet's subjective poetries. The desires and expectations of 15 generations of interpretators have obscured Nostradamus' looking glass. Can
anything be clearly seen?

Commentators of each new generation struggle with this question and
split into camps of supporters and debunkers. Believers in Nostradamus
suffer the slings and arrows of skeptics' claims that his prophecies are so
open to interpretation as to render them almost impotent, notwithstanding the fact that a number of clear predictions name people, dates, and
intimate details of tomorrow's events with an uncanny accuracy that will
forever disturb the peace of skeptics.

Thirty years have passed since I first felt chills at the utterance of his
name. Much of the last 23 years I have spent in the study of Nostradamus'
prophecies and controversies. While on this journey of discovery I have
written three books on the subject and watched my own views change
from those of an admiring dilettante to what I hope are more balanced
observations of the Nostradamus phenomenon. As I see it today, one must
doubt Nostradamus in the way indicated by the meaning of the original
Indo-European root from which we get the English word *doubt*. One must
stand as a witness not clinging to either support or skepticism. Rather than
being a "no-sayer" or a slavish "yea-sayer" with little discrimination, one
must encounter the mysteries of Nostradamus and say "perhaps."

Perhaps more is going on between the cryptic lines of Nostradamus
then the controversy suggests. Are we overlooking the obvious? Maybe
the calculated obscurity of Nostradamus serves a higher purpose than mere
prediction of events? As each new generation engages in the heated debate about whether he was a fraud or a mystic, Nostradamus' prophecies
indirectly bring the present to our attention. When else than in the

present can we decipher warnings of future challenges and make changes in our destiny? The past is gone, the future is not yet.

Whether you praise or calumnize the man, how many figures in history are still the source of hot controversy after 440 years. Only one thing seems to be certain about Nostradamus: he isn't going away. And despite all the hype and hubbub for and against his writings, they compel most of us to reflect upon where our current actions are taking us.

My reflections at this time – teetering as it is on the edge of a new millennium – have compelled me to present you with the first full examination in 36 years of all Nostradamus' propecies.

Nostradamus: The Complete Prophecies contains a number of innovations. The commentary will examine multiple future potentials of prophecies, from interpretations set down in earlier centuries, to those of our time, and finally to those that speculate on destinies humanity may access thousands of years in our future. This will also be the most in-depth examination yet undertaken of Nostradamus' epic prose prophecy letters, the *Preface* and *Epistle to Henry II*. Unfolding before you is a chronicle reaching far into the distant future. The "latter days" of our difficult era are used as a springboard into the coming peace and harmony of the Third Millennium. Then Nostradamus' vision propels us even farther ahead to the destruction of Earth near the end of the Fourth Millennium. But the story of humanity doesn't end there. Nostradamus is one of the few prophets in history to glimpse the coming galactic civilization of humanity.

In my previous books I touched upon the theory that we might find the prophecies obscure or incomprehensible either because they are about events so far in the future that we can't decipher their coding, or because they forecast futures we can *never* access because humankind's free will has taken it down a different path of destiny.

Consider a few of the good and evil futures we have missed:

- What kind of king would Edward VIII have been if the British had accepted Wallis Simpson as his wife? Apparently a far better ruler than the current line of Windsors.
- Did you know that Nostradamus foresaw the *Anschluss* not only of Austria but also of Switzerland into Hitler's Reich? Is this a failed prediction? A close examination of the Nazi movement in Switzerland reveals just how close this prophecy came to fulfillment.
- What if Rommel's panzers had pushed the Allied invasion of Normandy back into the sea in June 1944? Strong clues in the prophecies indicate that the Soviets could have shaken hands with American GIs on the Rhine river rather than the Elbe! The Cold War's iron curtain might have fallen between France and a communist united Germany, instead of a communist East Germany.

- What if President Kennedy hadn't been assassinated? Would the Cold War have ended 30 years earlier and forestalled today's dangerous breakup of the Soviet Union?

These and many other alternative futures will be examined along with hundreds of astonishingly accurate predictions for the centuries after Nostradamus' death in 1566. In his progress through his future and our past we examine Christendom's struggle with the Barbary Corsairs, the reigns of Henry de Navarre and Louis XIV, and the last words uttered by Louis XVI as the guillotine blade fell. We stare into the prophet's oracular porthole in time to see and hear images of the English Civil War, the ascent of the United States, the songs and chaos of the French Revolution, and the evil destinies of three Antichrists: Napoleon, Hitler and a third yet to threaten peace on Earth. We follow the seer's account of many wondrous and terrible inventions, from radio, satellite dishes, and submarines, to the oxygen masks of "half-pig" men in their jet "air fleets." We see him describe the atomic bomb, Hiroshima and Nagasaki, man walking on the moon, the Challenger disaster, the Reagan assassination attempt, the rise and fall of communism, and the fire and fury of cruise missiles in the Gulf War.

We look as well at Nostradamus' visions of a future that is also our own. We are threatened with a Third World War that could start any time from 1999 through the 2020s – a war we can avoid if we wake up and stop the population explosion and ecological degradation of this planet. In the next millennium humanity will recreate itself. Genetic revolutions will produce androgynous beings. Religions as we have known them will disappear. A golden age is coming. Paradise on Earth will last for a thousand years, then falter after the turn of the next millennium in AD 3000. Earth is destroyed by the expanding Sun in AD 3797. Long before and after this, the exodus of humanity into space will launch a second golden era. Human colonies will thrive ever after upon worlds orbiting the stars in the constellation of Cancer.

Once we have encountered the complete canvas of Nostradamus' 7,000-year history of the future, with all its dark and dire brush strokes, its all-too-rare flashes of human enlightenment – and after we have peeled off the layers of restoration by four centuries of commentators – we might better educate ourselves about all the intimate and detailed reasons why our history so far has been consistently a disaster in the making.

The canvas is not finished. And it can be changed.

By understanding Nostradamus' chronicle of, as he writes, the "sad and prodigious" events of tomorrows past and tomorrows yet to be born, we of the present day, poised upon the threshold of a new millennium, have the choice and ability to change our behavior. And by so doing we can direct destiny towards a future history of peace, love, and understanding.

The Life of Nostradamus

Although scholars agree that Michel de Nostredame was born in 1503 to recently "Christianized" Jews in the town of St Rémy, Provence, the finer details of his family's background and economic status are still debated. Some believe he was the son of a Jewish grain dealer called Jaume, while others say his father was a prosperous notary by the name of Jacques.

His sympathetic biographers tell us that Michel's mysterious talent for prophecy was first encouraged by his grandfathers, both learned men of the Renaissance, who in younger days were the personal physicians to the most free-thinking king of the time, Réné the Good of Provence, and his son, the Duke of Calabria. Their eager pupil showed a superior aptitude for math and the celestial science of astrology.

His paternal grandfather deemed him ready at 14 to study the liberal arts at Avignon, the papal enclave of Provence. There Michel angered his priestly teachers by openly defending astrology and Copernicus. At 19 he was sent to study medicine at the University of Montpellier. He breezed through his baccalaureate examinations in 1525. Soon afterwards his schooling was disrupted for a few years by an outbreak of the bubonic plague: 16th-century France suffered from seasonal bouts of *le charbon*, the black death. So severe was this new outbreak that Montpellier University closed its doors, and faculty and students alike fanned out through southern France to battle the disease. With a license to practice medicine in hand, Michel de Nostredame saddled up his mule, packed up his medical and astrological books and astrolabe, and set off on the open road on the trail of the plague. The emergency had liberated him from the fundamentally primitive views of his teachers and provided him with the freedom to put his medical theories to the test.

Nostradamus followed the plague's shadow westwards through Montpellier, Narbonne, Toulouse, and all the way to Bordeaux, never leaving a town until the danger had passed. He honed his skills and availed himself of the knowledge and teachers of the Renaissance's mystical underground of alchemists, Moorish medicine men, Jewish Cabalists, and pagans. Some of his ideas on bleeding and hygiene were quite progressive and controversial for the times. By 1529 he returned to Montpellier, where he received his doctorate degree and adopted the Latinized name Nostradamus. He remained a professor of medicine there for the

following three years until friction over the rigid and conservative cur-
riculum became unbearable for him, and he left to set up a practice in
Toulouse.

In 1534 he moved to Agen, where he became friends with the volatile
Julius-César Scaliger, one of the great minds of the Renaissance. In Agen
Nostradamus fell in love and married. Strangely enough, he made no
mention of the young woman's name in his writings, nor does his supportive
biographer, Chavigny, who can tell us only that she was "of high estate,
very beautiful and very amiable." Some biographers believe her name
was Adriète de Loubéjac. Skeptics have theorized that these biographers
mistake Nostradamus' bride for that of Scaliger, whose wife's name was
Andriète de Roques-Lobéjac. At 46 Scaliger married her when she was
apparently newly orphaned aged only 16. There is a third possibility –
that Nostradamus' "Adriète" was a relation of Scaliger's wife, perhaps a
cousin or even a half-sister. Be that as it may, it is known that she bore
him a beautiful boy and girl. For the next three years Nostradamus eased
into an idyllic family life and a flourishing medical practice. Thanks to
Scaliger, his patients were the rich and beautiful of Agen.

In 1537 tragedy struck with such brutal intensity that the young doctor's
spiritual and mental well-being was shattered. In that year plague returned to Agen. The healing hands that had cured thousands must have
wrung themselves helplessly over the cooling corpses of his wife and
children. Friends and family turned against him, holding him responsible
for their deaths. Scaliger, who was prone to violent argument and breaking his friendships, chose this moment to castigate the young doctor. His
wife's family sued him for their dead daughter's dowry, and won. His
patients abandoned him, since their superstition convinced them that a
doctor who can't save his own family must be in league with the devil.
Next he was questioned by Church authorities for making a chance
remark years before. He had seen an inept workman making a bronze
statue of the Virgin and commented that he was "casting demons." After
receiving the summons to face the Inquisition at Toulouse, Nostradamus
packed up his mule with a few belongings and stole away into the night.

Little can be found in history's records about the next six years of his
life. It is at least known that he traveled as far north as Lorraine, as far
east as Venice, and lived for a time as far south as Sicily. One can suppose
that he wandered through western and southern Europe to avoid the
Church Inquisitors while trying to pick up the shattered pieces of his life on
a pilgrimage of self-discovery. It is during this dark night of Nostradamus'
wandering soul that the first legends of his awakening prophetic powers
began to emerge.

A group of Franciscan monks traveling one day along a muddy road
near the Italian town of Ancona suddenly saw the solitary doctor walking

towards them. As they approached he stood aside to let them pass, but on seeing Brother Felice Peretti he immediately bowed, then knelt in the mud before him. The friars, knowing that Peretti had previously been a swineherd and was of lowly birth, were puzzled by this homage and asked Nostradamus to explain. He replied: "I must yield myself and bend a knee before His Holiness." The friars were highly amused at the explanation but, 40 years after his chance meeting, Brother Peretti became Pope Sixtus V, 19 years after the death of Nostradamus.

Another legend chronicles Nostradamus' stay at the Château de Florinville where, on a stroll with his lordly host around the grounds, the conversation turned to prophecy. Florinville wanted to put the prophet's powers to the test. They had stopped before a corral containing two suckling pigs, one black, one white. When Florinville asked Nostradamus which pig would provide dinner that night, he replied without hesitation, "We will eat the black pig, but a wolf will eat the white."

Florinville secretly ordered his cook to slaughter the white pig. The cook dressed the pig for the spit and left the kitchen on an errand, forgetting to close the door. On his return, he found Florinville's pet wolf cub happily devouring the white pig. The horrified man shooed it away and ran to the corral to fetch the black pig. At dinner that night all mouths watered as the cook set the roasted pig before Lord Florinville, who smiled at Nostradamus across the table.

"We are not eating the black pig as you have predicted. And no wolf will touch it here."

Nostradamus was so adamant that this was the black pig that Lord Florinville eventually summoned the cook. Florinville was stunned, and his guests entertained, when the cook admitted everything under the penetrating gaze of Nostradamus gray eyes.

All legends aside, what we do know is that Nostradamus resurfaces in history in 1544 in Marseilles,where he sets up a practice in this ancient crossroads of the French Riviera.

The November rains that year began the winter of 1544–45, during which Provence suffered one of its worst floods on record. The swollen rivers were dotted with the bloated corpses of animals and people. By spring the rains and flood waters receded, leaving one of the most devastating pestilences of the century in their wake. Hysteria and death spread over most of southern France for several years. By 1546 Nostradamus was summoned to Aix, the capital of Provence, to combat the most severe outbreak of le charbon. Nostradamus worked around the clock for the next 270 days ministering to the sick.

With the assistance of an apothecary named Joseph Turel Mercurin, Nostradamus produced fragrant herbal and rose-petal lozenges. He admonished his patients to keep these "rose pills" under their tongues at all times without swallowing them. Other surviving fragments of his medical journals imply that bleeding his plague patients was avoided (although he seems to allow bleeding for other remedies). Nostradamus advised patients to make sure their drinking water and bedding were clean, and to open the windows of their foul-smelling bedrooms to fresh air. He suggested they eat a balanced diet low in animal fat and get a moderate amount of exercise. These regimens of diet, exercise, and hygiene, along with his legendary health and fearlessness when facing disease, may have helped more to cure his patients than the rose pills themselves.

Once the danger had passed, the city parliament gave Nostradamus a pension for life, and the citizens of Aix showered him with gratitude and awards. It is said that he gave many of the gifts to the families and dependents of those he had not been able to save.

The hero of Aix next received a call for help from the City Fathers of Salon. He had no sooner cured the plague there when he received an urgent call from Lyons. Many stories and legends of questionable accuracy arise from his stay at Lyons, but it is historically noted that he eradicated a plague of whooping cough through mass prescriptions filled by one pharmacist René Hepiliervard.

He returned to Salon in 1547 to settle there for the rest of his life. He was enchanted by the little town's beauty and dry, sunny skies. It is believed that he stayed with his brother Bertrand in his home. Bertrand is purported by some biographers to have introduced Nostradamus to an attractive and intelligent young woman of a wealthy and respected Salonaise family. Anne Ponsarde Gemelle, who was made a widow by the untimely death of a certain Jean Baulne, became Nostradamus' second wife.

For the next eight years Nostradamus gradually withdrew from medical practice to engage himself in a highly successful cosmetics cottage industry.

At this time he also plunged wholeheartedly into the occult. A room on the top floor of his house was transformed into a secret study, and he started writing an annual almanac that made a few cautious stabs at prediction. He was so encouraged by the reaction to his prophecies that he embarked on an ambitious project: the future history of the world, told in 1,000 enigmatic quatrains (four-line poems), using a polyglot smattering of French, Latin, Italian, Hebrew, Arabic, and Greek. This masterpiece has had interpreters of prophecy (including myself) scratching their heads ever since.

He began work on *Les Propheties* on the night of Good Friday 1554. A total of ten volumes, or "Centuries" of one hundred quatrains each, was planned.

The first three Centuries were published in May 1555. They open with a *Preface* dedicated to his infant son, César. This letter contained confessions and descriptions of his prophetic techniques, and a prose prophecy that stretched his vision all the way to the year AD 3797. Nostradamus cranked out Centuries 4 through an incomplete Century 7 by 1557. The final three Centuries were composed in 1557 and 1558, along with an ambitious prose prophecy letter known as the *Epistle to Henry II*, written in a macabre and psychedelic prose rivalling the biblical *Book of Revelation*. A few special copies of the *Epistle* and the last 300 quatrains were printed and found their way to the French court, but it was Nostradamus' wish to delay general publication until after his death to protect his growing family from the mounting popularity and controversy of his prophecies (Nostradamus and Anne would eventually have six children).

By 1556 Nostradamus' *Les Propheties* was the rage at court. After Queen Catherine de' Medici was shown a quatrain predicting the death of her husband, King Henry II, in a jousting accident, Nostradamus was summoned to Paris. His royal audience was a success and he became an intimate occult friend to the Queen. Nostradamus was safely ensconced in his Salon study when Henry II fulfilled that prophecy in 1559. Following quatrain 35 of Century 1 to the letter, Henry sustained a wooden splinter from the jousting shaft during a tournament; it rammed through his helmet's golden visor and plunged behind his eye into his brain. On the night of his death, crowds gathered before the Inquisitors, burning Nostradamus in effigy and demanding the priests burn him in earnest. Only Nostradamus' friendship with Queen Catherine saved him. This was the first of several successful prophecies that would make Nostradamus' prophecies the talk of the courts of Europe.

Persecution followed fame. During the early 1560s France was lurching towards the first of nine civil wars fought over religion and Nostradamus was being tormented by street ruffians in Salon. Though he outwardly practiced Catholicism, many Catholics viewed the Christianized Jew as a Calvinist heretic, while the Protestants and Calvinists of Salon cursed him as a papist.

With greater dangers came greater supporters. The Duke and Duchess of Savoy became his patrons. It is said he cast an accurate astrological forecast for their newborn son, who later became Savoy's greatest ruler, Charles-Emmauel "the Great." It is during this time that Nostradamus played with writing Centuries 11 and 12, but only fragments remain. From 1550 until his death he continued to crank out highly popular annual almanacs containing prose prognostications, and later, annual bundles of quatrains predicting the events of the coming year. Little from these original almanacs survive except for 141 quatrains published from 1555 through 1567, which are known as the *Presages*.

In 1564, while on a "tour of pacification" through the French realm,

Catherine de' Medici (now the Queen regent) and the adolescent King Charles IX made a point to visit the aging prophet of Salon. Before resuming their tour, Catherine had Charles IX honor Nostradamus with the title Counselor and Physician in Ordinary, with the privileges and salary this implied.

Nostradamus reached the high point of his prophetic career with only a year and eight months left to live. His noted robust health underwent a rapid collapse in 1566. In June, upon returning from the royal Embassy of Arles as a representative of the king, Nostradamus had a severe attack of gout, which soon developed into dropsy. He asked his family and disciples to move his deathbed into his beloved secret study where, in great physical pain but spiritual serenity, he awaited his end. His last prediction concerned his own approaching death:

> On his return from the Embassy, the king's gift put in place. He will do nothing more, He will be gone to God. Close relatives, friends, brothers by blood [will find him] completely dead near the bed and the bench.

At daybreak on 2 July 1566 family and friends found him dead in his bed with his swollen leg propped on a bench, exactly as he predicted.

Anne carried out her husband's final request that his coffin should be standing upright, enclosed within an inside wall of the Church of the Cordeliers of Salon. On his tomb was inscribed the following epitaph in Latin:

Here rest the bones of the illustrious Michel Nostradamus, alone of all mortals judged worthy to record with his near divine pen, under the influence of the stars, the future events of the entire world. He lived sixty-two years, six months and seventeen days. He died at Salon in the year 1566. Let not posterity disturb his rest. Anne Ponsarde Gemelle wishes her husband true happiness.

Guidelines for reading Nostradamus

I was willing to hold my peace by reason of the injury, not only of the present, but future time as well, and refrain from writing because if the present kingdoms, sects and religions were to see the future kingdoms, sects and religions to come, and see how diametrically opposed they are to their pet fantasies, they would condemn that which future centuries will know to be true . . . Later . . . [I] decided to relinquish withholding my tongue and pen from paper by declaring in dark and cryptic sentences the causes of the future changes of mankind . . . by clouding them in obscure but, above all, prophetic language.

Michel Nostradamus 1555

I made up my mind, but I made it up both ways.
Casey Stengle: Manager of the New York Yankees (circa 1955)

If Nostradamus was ever to be reincarnated as a baseball manager, the thought- and tongue-twisting Casey Stengle of the New York Yankees and New York Mets would be my first choice. Like Stengle, Nostradamus turns his native tongue into his own language, fashioning and discarding syntax and grammar rules one sentence at a time. Stengle's retrograde thinking and dyslexic words of wisdom revolutionized baseball. Nostradamus' peculiar pen has made him the unsurpassed king of prophets. In the dross of absurdities and calculated insanities Nostradamus hides the gold nuggets of authentic and unrivaled prophetic inspiration. Stengle's fractured figures of speech were innocent utterances, whereas the seer of Salon, Provence, shaped his ambiguous messages with great care and forethought.

And Nostradamus' obscurity conjures many results. For one thing, his writing is muddled enough to be taken any way one wishes. It befuddled the Church Inquisitors to the extent that Nostradamus accomplished something rare for authentic seers of his day – he avoided torture and execution as a magician and died peacefully in his bed. His ambiguities have kept the controversy of his prophecies alive, and even enhanced his stature as a seer in the centuries following his death (just as he predicted).

What Casey Stengle once said about managing a baseball team can be applied to Nostradamus' success as an obscurer: "The secret of managing is to keep the guys who hate you away from the guys who are undecided."

Nostradamus' cryptic chronicle of the future has succeeded in distancing his attackers from the majority of his undecided readers. Defining his nebulous narrative is not unlike lying on your back in the grass and gazing at the shapes of puffy clouds. You see a giraffe. Your friend sees an elephant. You can argue with him. Your success at convincing the other depends on your eloquence, not on the reality of the cloud. People keep playing the same game with the misty mentality of Nostradamus. He understood that people love to project their prejudices onto the canvas of the obscure, and that this passion in human nature for giving shape to ambiguities will always survive a skeptic's attack. Nostradamus ensures his cloudy credibility by injecting moments of brilliant clarity that occasionally burn an opening in the general overcast of his narrative. We suddenly see names, dates, and intimate details of events as they happened – or will happen.

Nostradamus' 36,200 weird words of prophecy are the molecules that compose the dark surface of his magic looking glass. On rare occasions we can peer into its surface and see the seeds of humanity harvested in to-morrow's field of dreams. But the magic doesn't end there. Nostradamus' "glass" reflects both ways. His strange language, symbols, barbarisms, and insights can also be used as a projector of the hidden secrets of his inter-preters, be they the commentators or the readers of his oracular opus. A study of Nostradamus is more than just another examination of fulfilled and yet-to-be-fulfilled prophecies; it can be an exploration into how we project our thoughts, feelings, hopes and fears on the future.

Before beginning a journey through time and our projections, it would be advisable to study some of Nostradamus' grammar rules (or lack thereof), decoding techniques, and interpretive pitfalls uncovered during 400 years of scholarship. In this way we can rub some of the fog off his looking glass to better see who or what is gazing back at us.

CLASSICAL GRAMMAR RULES

Nostradamus' poetry uses a number of classical Greek and Latin gram-matical devices.

- **Aphaeresis**: Elimination of one or more letters and sounds from the beginning of a word – as in *paroir* for *apparoir* (to appear).
- **Apocope**: Omission of the last sound or syllable or a word – for example, *Orl.* for *Orléans*. Nostradamus sometimes takes further liberties and omits the rest of a phrase. For example, *corn* for *corne d'abondance* (a cornucopia).
- **Ellipsis**: Exclusion of words and phrases that are understood or taken for granted by the 16th-century reader. When possible I will enter these words to the text in square brackets, for example: *Friends, relatives,*

brothers of the blood [will find him] completely dead between the bed and the bench.

- **Epenthesis**: Insertion of a letter or syllable into a word – for example: *Timbre* for *Tibre* (the Tiber river).
- **Hyperbaton**: Transposition or inversion of the natural order. Nostradamus consistently scrambles the natural order of his sentences and verse lines.
- **Metathesis**: Transposition within a word of letters, sounds, or syllables. For example, the Old French *mezan* is transposed from the Latin *mensa* (month). Nostradamus often does this to preserve rhyme.
- **Metonymy**: A figure of speech in which an idea is evoked or named by means of a term designating some associated notion. The name *Mars* has a metonymical designation for *war*; *scepter* can imply a *king*; *hunger*, can mean a *general famine*.
- **Prosthesis**: Insertion of an extra letter or syllable at the beginning of a word. For instance, *expectacle* (*ex* added to *spectacle* [spectacle]).
- **Synecdoche**: A grammatical trick in Greek and Latin to make the part represent the whole. For example: *Paris* stands for *France*; *Boristhenes* for the *Ukraine* or perhaps even *Russia*.
- **Syncope**: Shortening of a word by the omission of a sound, letter, or syllable from the middle of the word. For example, Nostradamus abbreviates a number of his future-tense verbs: *donra* for *donnera*; *lairra* for *lairrera*; *monstra* for *monstrera*; and so on.

ANAGRAMS

Words and phrases are scrambled to construct other words and phrases using the same letters – for example: *rapis* becomes *Paris*; *chyren* is Henry II's Latinized name, *Henryc*. Phonetics allow for V to become U or Y to become I; S to become C; or I to be J; and so on.

Nostradamus made his own variations for switching or replacing letters. One or two letters can be dropped – for example, *Noir* becomes *roi* = "king." Letters can be added and or changed: *Hister* becomes *Hitler*; *Hadrie* becomes *Henrie*, finally Henry de Navarre.

So we might translate the anagrams for a future Antichrist emerging from the Middle East thus:

- **Mabus** > mABUs, dropping the first letter *m* and the last letter *s*.
- **Adaluncatif** > *Cadafi*, where the *t* is dropped and the word *Luna* stands for the crescent moon, symbolizing Islam. From this you derive the decoded name "Cadafi Luna" = *Qadaffi of the Crescent* [Islam].
- The Palestinian terrorist (or freedom fighter) Abu Nidal considers Qadaffi of Libya one of his closest allies. The anagram *Adaluncatif* can also reveal his name: (A)dal(u)n(cat)i(f) = Nidal. Drop the *c* and the

remaining letters: *a-u-a-t-f* can phonetically spell *fatau* for Fatah, the militant branch of the Palestine Liberation Organization to which Abu Nidal once belonged.

At this point you might be wondering whether a monkey is as capable of throwing significant light on Nostradamus' anagrams as a mystic, given enough time. One primary "rule" of this word play is to keep that question open to interpretation.

PUNCTUATION PORTENTS

Many scholars wonder if Nostradamus is punctuationally challenged or openly is disregarding the rules as a calculated device to cloud his writing. Grammar and spelling rules in late Renaissance France were less systematic than those of today. Nostradamus' French flows thick with arcane words and meanings. Alien spellings of ancient and medieval words vie for dominance with chaotic grammatical devices. Paragraphs were almost nonexistent. Nostradamus' prose seems to follow whatever is his whim, and he blithely uses commas for periods, periods for colons, and colons for commas and periods. The punctuation of the quatrains is slightly more systematic – and I repeat "slightly."

His spelling reflects his times. French in the 16th century was not the majority language of France. Its usage was undergoing a transition from being one of several languages and dialects spoken in the realm to becoming the official national language of state and commerce. It was only beginning to be systematized. You will see in Nostradamus' writings the first signs of modern spelling blended with older spellings of the same word.

One cannot even rule out the possibility of Nostradamus' picking up some future grammatical habits from his trance sessions. Nor can one prove it.

NAMES, LOCALITIES

Places appear under their historical or classical names. For clarity I will sometimes place the modern name in brackets alongside the classical – for example: Aquitaine [France] and Boristhenes [Dnieper river region] Similarly, a nationality or religious group can be hidden in classical names: Cimbrians – an ancient Teutonic tribe – stands for the Germans.

THE POLITICS OF ANIMAL NAMES

Countries may be characterized as animals, in the form of heraldic or mystical symbols associated with them. For example, *Cock* for France, *Bear* for Berlin or Russia, or *Wolf* for Italy.

PROPER NAMES IN UNCOMMON PLACES

Proper names can be hidden in normal words and phrase, and vice versa. For example, *de Gaulle* can indicate *of* or *from Gaulle* or the French leader Charles de Gaulle; *Pasteur* can either mean a church *pastor* or, more literally, *Louis Pasteur*. It all depends on corresponding clues in the quatrain. Even verbs and adjectives can hide a name. *Abas* meaning "put down" can stand for the future Antichrist *Mabus*, or for *Abbas*, a common Arabic name. In line 1 of quatrain 6 of Century 3, *abas* could stand as a double-pun for *putting down*, or figuratively stand for *Abu Abbas*, the Palestinian terrorist who hijacked the Italian ocean liner *Achille Lauro* in the mid-1980s.

INSIGNIAS AS PORTENTS

You will see plays on words and phrases identifying people and movements through their insignias, coats of arms or other emblems: The *crooked cross* – the swastika; *swarms of bees* – probably Napoleon, whose family coat of arms featured swarms of bees; the *eagle* – the eagle standards carried by Napoleon's armies.

REMOTE VIEWING

Geographically speaking, the predictions that apply to France and its neighbors are clearer and more numerous than those about distant lands.

TIME: QUATRAIN INDEXING AS PROPHECY

In hundreds of cases the quatrain numbers appear to correspond to the predicted events in the quatrains themselves. For instance, a prophecy mentioning the forest of the Ardennes in Luxembourg as an attack route used in the ultimate destruction of an empire is numbered Century 5, Quatrain 45 (5 Q45). The forest was used twice as a German attack route, once for the fall of France in 1940 and later for the fall of Hitler's Nazi empire in 1945! Sometimes the quatrain indexing also seems to represent specific dates corresponding to the subject of the particular quatrain. A clear example is the famous prophecy describing in detail the attempted escape from France of Louis XVI and his family during the French Revolution. The royal party escaped from Paris on the night of 20 June 1791. The quatrain is numbered Century 9, Quatrain 20 (9 Q20).

NO SEQUENCE OF TIME

The prophecies rarely follow any logical sequence. The events they describe are frequently scrambled out of chronological order – even within a quatrain itself – requiring the interpreter to find key phrases and words linking the events into some understandable order.

ALTERNATIVE FUTURES

To the modern reader most of Nostradamus' predictions seem obscure tangles of syntax and jumbled meaning. Of his known 1,110 quatrains, over 800 are little more than augury-babble. They may be just his prophetic mistakes, or perhaps some seem nonsensical to us because their details concern events in our unknown future. But, in my opinion, many of the incomprehensible quatrains are accurate chronicles of events which might have been if history had taken a different turn – predictions for a parallel universe, in fact.

SUGGESTED WAYS TO UNTANGLE THE OBSCURITY

Nostradamus intentionally obscured his prophecies, setting the stage for interpreters to attempt to untangle them for centuries to come. Whether a given interpretation for a quatrain is the one he intended or whether his wildly obscure crabbed poetry was meant to unlock the interpreter's own second sight cannot be resolved.

I will apply the age-old argument used against Nostradamus – that his predictions are open to all kinds of interpretation – to support their strength rather than illuminate their weakness. The obscurity by its nature cannot prove or disprove that our interpretations of Nostradamus are the correct ones; nevertheless, this book will provide dozens of historical examples of commentators accurately foreseeing future events reflected in the obscurity even when their slant on a prophecy, in my opinion, was not aligned with Nostradamus' intent.

A deep and careful examination of his prophecies will reveal evidence supporting the argument that Nostradamus had many layers of intentions for the use of his prophecies. One important one is that each generation can use them to see how the infinite potentials of the future reflect the positive and negative consequences of our present actions. If these potentials are interpreted correctly they can help us change ourselves for the better, *today*, because we can never live in the future. It has always been and it will always be *today*.

With this said, there are six interpretive slants one can use to unlock a quatrain. They are:

1 **A fulfilled prophecy:** One that is universally accepted by scholars to have one clear meaning.

2 **A partially fulfilled prophecy:** Complete fulfillment depends on our choices in the present.

3 **A alternative or quantum future prophecy:** One that could have been fulfilled if individual and collective decisions had directed future destiny down a different course.

4 **A near-future prophecy:** These will get a special flagging if they are dire, such as the famous July 1999 prophecy, or those that warn of a Third World War that stems from the stresses of overpopulation, famine, and ecological breakdown in the 2020s and 2030s.

5 **Distant-future prophecy:** A number of seemingly unintelligible quatrains could describe a distant future event, such as an account of the thousands of years of extraterrestrial human history to come.

6 **A gibberish prophecy:** You will see several hundred of these. They are quatrains that could be simply beyond my capacity to interpret – a fact I will always readily admit. My own limitations aside, there could be a number of reasons why a quatrain is unintelligible:

   a) It is an incorrect prediction or deliberately made to mislead the uninitiated.

   b) It is a personal prophecy that only Nostradamus and his immediate friends and family could decipher.

   c) It describes clues and details that would be clear only to those of Nostradamus' immediate time and locality. These will never be decoded because historical records of those times are lost or never existed.

   d) It is a past alternative-future event that I invite the reader to unravel. Or you can wait for a future interpreter better versed in the intimate historical details than myself.

   e) It describes a near or distant future event that will make sense to us only when the future draws nearer to the present and more clues to the riddles appear.

COMMON MISTAKES MADE BY INTERPRETERS

LATTER-DAY DILETTANTES

The mounting millennial and New Age hysteria of the 1990s has produced a number of recent interpretations of Nostradamus unrivaled in their poor research and fantastic claims. One of the more entertaining revelations is logged in the works of Dolores Cannon, who claims to know someone who talks to the ghost of Nostradamus. When Ms Cannon appeared opposite me on NBC's *Ancient Prophecies I*, she confidently described Nostradamus' study as "cold, dank and dark, and completely made of stone." To me, such declarations reveal that neither Cannon nor her "ghost" has ever set foot in Nostradamus' real study – as anyone who has visited his house, which still stands in Salon, Provence, will know. It seems that Ms Cannon and her ghost are also unaware of Nostradamus' well-documented search for ever drier climates to alleviate his sensitivity to dampness. He spent the final 19 years of his life at Salon because the climate there was even more arid than his birthplace, St Rémy.

PREDATORY DEBUNKERS

Some modern skeptics (James Randi being the best example) attack Nostradamus with opportunistic relish. Like any good predator, they stalk the weaker quatrains in the herd of Nostradamus prophecies, but they avoid encountering the horns of a solid prophetic success. (See the Index for my rebuttal to James Randi's ten debunkable quatrains as well as my list of ten debunker's nightmares.)

"NOSTRADAMUS SAYS . . ."

While doing radio interviews I am often asked, "What does Nostradamus say about . . .?"

To which I reply, "Nostradamus hasn't said anything for a long time. He's been dead for nearly 500 years. What is true is that I'm saying something according to my understanding of Nostradamus."

I wish more latter-day diviners of the long-departed prophet would make this distinction.

Beware of the interpreter's ego. I always try to keep this in mind.

But it would be redundant to tag "in my opinion . . ." to every interpretation I make, so let me say up front that anything I write about Nostradamus' prophecies is my interpretation. I won't hide behind the etheric cop-out that I'm "channeling" his ghost, some New Age angel, dolphin or space alien-leprechaun. If I get it wrong it is *my* fault, not someone or something else's.

NOSTRADAMUS, THE DARLING OF THE TABLOIDS

One thing is certain – when Nostradamus is quoted in the purulent perusals of current events by tabloid reporters, they will never log the quatrain's index number so you can check their translation against the original. For instance, the tabloids have consistently quoted the great Nostradamus predicting "the worst winter in history" for the last three years. If they keep trying, perhaps they'll get it right.

CODE-BREAKING NOSTRADAMUS

Contrary to the claims of many imaginative dilettantes and a few sincere theorists, no one has yet found the key to any single all-encompassing code that unlocks his secrets. After 22 years of study I conclude that a magician of Nostradamus' intelligence would not be so stupid as to forge a weak link in the chain of his future legacy. At best there may be random devices and codes, but as we will see, even unlocking a random code conjures up more questions and mysteries than answers. It seems to be Nostradamus' rule to keep 'em guessing.

Some of the most entertaining books on Nostradamus boast about discovering some secret code. For instance, in 1991 authors Peter Lorie and V. J. Hewitt boldly claimed that they had made a complete scientific decodification of the prophet, from his chapeau of anagrams down to his syllable toes. With such a marketing hook I wondered why the promised "detailed" and scientific instructions were tucked away in the back of the book. The instructions brazenly asked the reader to comprehend Hewitt and Lorie's "scientific" theories by taking a leap of faith beyond objectivity. The back cover boldly declares that Hewitt herself was foreseen by the prophet as the one who would unlock his secrets. So far, their book is remarkable only in its remarkably detailed failures, such as Prince Charles' failing to become King of England in 1993, George Bush's failing to win a second term as president of the United States, and California's not sinking into the Pacific Ocean at exactly 7 pm on 8 May 1993.

Since that time Hewitt has struck out on her own, and her declarations are far more cautious and open to interpretation. One no longer sees the dates for "decoded" prophecies listed on the cover of her books. There is much more use of "could" than "will" in her declarations these days.

I would cordially suggest to Hewitt, Lorie, and any future code-busters that they submit their claims to an impartial test. Anyone who believes he or she has decoded Nostradamus' quatrains should send a selection of decoded quatrains, with down-to-the-day-and-minute declarations for the coming year, to a reputable metaphysical organization such as the American Society for Psychical Research. After one year those interpretations can be unsealed before an audience of debunkers, journalists, and true believers to test their veracity. Once predictions are verified, then, and only then, should that author publish his or her book claiming to decode Nostradamus.

Rather than play hide-and-seek for some code to dispel all mystery, future translators might consider that Nostradamus may have intended that we apply the perspectives of our own era to his prophecies.

His own astrological makeup indicates that Nostradamus was not an ego wishing to be found out. But he was an alchemist of controversies. His obscurity has worked to keep alive for centuries what may be a practical joke or a true prophetic gift, or some combination of the two. Debunkers and blind believers alike ought to be aware that attempting to make the prophet fit their own preconceived ideas and prejudices and calling it his "real" intention is futile.

A WORD ON THE OLD AND MEDIEVAL FRENCH AND MY TRANSLATION

1 **The Preface, Epistle and the 10 Centuries**. Most of the text of Nostradamus used in this book comes from the 1568 Benoist Rigaud edition, the version closest to the original edition of his first ten Centuries, with Nostradamus' grammar and spelling (see the Bibliography for details).

2 **The duplicate and extra quatrains (from Century 6, 7, 8, 10, 11 and 12) and the Presages**. Most of this extra material attributed to Nostradamus was taken from the earlier Ménier edition of *Les Propheties* (1589) and from *Janus Gallicus* (1594) by Jean-Aymes de Chavigny. These found their way into the famous unnamed 1605 edition, which possibly was published by Pierre Duruau of Troyes. It is safe to say that 30 to 35 years had passed from the the time the ink of Nostradamus' pen dried on these extra manuscripts until they first went to press in 1589–94, raising some doubt as to their authenticity. They are generally accepted as original (albeit heavily edited) works by Nostradamus because they more or less follow his odd literary style. The 1605 edition also uses a spelling and punctuation style different from the Benoist Rigaud. In some cases I have restored spelling and punctuation to better match this principal edition of the first ten Centuries.

3 **Fraudulent prophecies.** The 58 Sixians, the two Anti-Mazarin propaganda quatrains, and the Prophecies of Orval are not included in this book because their composition and style strongly suggest quackery falsely attributed to Nostradamus.

4 **The index numbers for the quatrains**. For easier reference, all quatrain indexing will be presented in Arabic numerals rather than the original Roman numerals. For instance: 3 Q22, means Century (Volume) 3, Quatrain 22. Duplicate quatrains will have "dp" tagged to the end, such as 10 Q100dp.

5 **New index numbers for the Preface and Epistle.** This may be the first English edition to restore the *Preface* and *Epistle* to their original Old French spelling and punctuation as they appeared in the Benoist Rigaud edition. I have taken the liberty of indexing phrases for better cross-referencing. *Preface* numbers will be cited as PF1, PF2, etc; *Epistle* indexing will be EP1, EP2, etc.

6 **New Presages indexing.** The 141 *Presage* quatrains will be referenced as P1, P2, etc.

7 **Translation footnotes.** When an explanation of the variations in translation is warranted, the footnotes will appear immediately below each French-to-English translation of a quatrain.

8 **Old French abbreviations.** Be forewarned that Nostradamus uses the symbol ~ over the vowels *a, e,* and *o* to abbreviate *an, en,* and *on.* Sometimes he abbreviates *que* or *qui* with a ~ over the *q.*

IMPORTANT   POINTS   OF   STYLE

1 When I refer to a word from Nostradamus' original text, I will always enter it in *italics.* When commenting on my English translation I will always enter words from the quatrain in ***bold italics.*** Quotes from other quatrains will usually be followed by their index numbers; for example: ***Mabus will soon die*** (2 Q62).

2 Whenever an astrological prediction is inserted into a quatrain, see the paragraph entitled *Astrological Time Window* at the end of my interpretation. It will examine the astrological configurations of a quatrain and plot potential windows in the past, present, and future for the events described in the quatrain.

3 On the several hundred occasions when the indexing of a quatrain can be decoded as a date see the paragraph below the interpretation that is titled **Quatrain Indexing Date.**

4 A number of themes recur in the prophecies. A reference paragraph will appear at the bottom of each quatrain that introduces a new theme. It will refer you to the Index for a detailed list of all cross-references.

5 A General Prophecy Index for all subjects and names in the prophecies will list each item by their index number only. I will not make a distinction between my references and those that supposedly are directly from Nostradamus, because in most cases it is a question of interpretation rather than empirical fact.

6 Other quirks from the quill of Nostradamus will be described as they appear.

Now we are ready to take the plunge into Nostradamus' vision of the future. I wish you good luck on your journey – or better, *bonne chance,* as Nostradamus might have said.

THE
PROPHECIES

1555

The Preface
of M. Nostradamus to his Prophecies

Before we plunge into Nostradamus' Preface to *Les Propheties*, a few observations. Nostradamus' prose narrative style rivals the psychedelics of St John the Divine in the book of *Revelation*. His thoughts rush along in a wild stream-of-consciousness, in chaotic rhythm, with run-on sentences that meander down clausal detours that can continue for half a page.

Translators and interpreters have tried to tidy up his writing to make it read in a more linear and rational flow. I believe that if Nostradamus had wanted his Preface to be logical and rational he would have written it so. Certain mystics use an unusual cadence or a nebulous and turgid writing style as a device to shake us out of our usual mental habits so we can look beyond the words to that which cannot be said. By editing Nostradamus for the sake of comfort and clarity, his well-intentioned interpreters may be doing him a disservice. Yes, his labyrinthine sentences and circular thinking are made more bearable to the rational mind – but at the sacrifice of the occult narrative devices set to trigger the reader's subconscious mind. I therefore feel compelled to render my English translation as close as possible to the original Old French narrative, with all its odd punctuation (or lack of it) and its jungle of endless clausal diversions and run-on sentences.

I would like in addition to suggest a reading meditation technique that has helped me better enjoy and absorb the essence of the Preface. First find a quiet place to sit in a chair, or lie down comfortably on the floor. Close your eyes, relax your body, and watch your breathing for 15 minutes, letting go of all the cares of the day with each exhalation of the breath. Then take up the English translation of the Preface and read it straight through. Reading out loud is best. Suspend your left brain, rational mind's resistance to Nostradamus' odd grammar and sentence construction. He is talking to your right brain, the seat of subjective, intuitive experience. Flow through the words in the way that a kayaker paddles with the current of the river. Let the rush of his words take you down their own path of sound and rhythm. Feel free to repeat the reading more than once. I would suggest reading the Preface translation up to three times before investigating my interpretation.

I find that the experience of reading – or watching movies – is enhanced if I remember myself in the act of observing the flow of words on a page or images on the screen. The senses become sharper and my body and breathing relaxes. By remembering myself while engaged in an action, I feel energized and nourished by whatever activity is being observed. I suggest you try it when surfing the Nostradamus wave.

Here we go.

PF1   *PREFACE*
OE M. MICHEL
NOSTRADAMVS
à *ſes* Propheties.
Ad Cæſarem Noſtradamum filium,
Vie & felicité

PREFACE
OF M. MICHEL
NOSTRADAMUS
to his Prophecies.
To Caesar Nostradamus my son,
Long life and happiness.

PF2   *Ton tard aduenement Céſar Noſtradame mõ filz, m'a faict mettre mon
long temps par continuelles vigilations nocturnes reſerer par eſcript toy
delaiſſer memoire, apres la corporelle extinction de tõ progeniteur*

**Thy late arrival, César Nostradame, my son, has caused me to devote a
great deal of time in continual nocturnal watches so that – by putting it
in writing – you may be left a memorial after the corporeal extinction of
your father**

PF3   *au cõmun proffit des humains de ce que la Diuine eſſence par
Aſtronomiques reuolutions m'ont dõné cognoiſſance.*

**[that will be] to the common benefit of the human race, [the source
being] that divine essence – drawn out of astronomical revolutions –
which has been given to my understanding.**

PF4   *Et depuis qu'il a pleu au Dieu immortel que tu ne ſois venu en naturelle
lumiere dans ceſte terrene plaige, & ne veux dire tes ans qui ne ſont*

**And since it has pleased immortal God that you should have come to the
natural light of this earthly shore but recently, and your years cannot yet
be said to**

PF5   *encores accompaignez, mais tes mois Martiaux incapables à receuoir
dans*

**be matured [or coupled, formed] – [and since in] your martial months
[you] are incapable of receiving [my message]**

PF6   *ton debile entendement ce que ie ſeray contrainct apres mes iours definer:
veu qu'il n'eſt poſsible te laiſſer par eſcrit ce que ſeroit par*

[because of] your weak understanding – [I see] that that which I am

PF1–3   The opening turgid sentence is self-explanatory. César, though, is only a few months old at the time. These writings of prophecy will be delivered to the safekeeping of his first-born son, to be shared at large for the common benefit of the human race.

PF4–5   Now the river of his writing flows down a contradictory path, expressing some doubts about his son's future guardianship of the prophecies. Nostradamus resigns himself to the fact that as a new father at 50, it is almost certain he will die long before seeing his son mature, given that life expectancy at the time was 38 to 45 years.

PF6   César's **weak understanding** of the prophecies may extend into adulthood. Nostradamus makes it quite clear that his son will not inherit his father's prophetic gifts. The seer admits the impossibility of explaining his prophecies. Time will injure more than the memory and corporeal form of the prophet.

forced to designate after my passing is not possible to leave you in writing because it would be

PF7   *l'iniure du temps obliteré: car la parolle hereditaire de l'occulte prédiction ſera dans mon eſtomach intercluſe: conſiderant auſſi les*

obliterated by the injury of time – indeed, the voice of my hereditary gift of occult prediction will be entombed with me. There are also grounds to consider

PF8   *auentures de l'humain definement eſtre incertaines, & que le tout eſt regi & gouuerné par la puiſſance de Dieu ineſtimable, nous inſpirant*

that events of human origin are uncertain, but all is regulated and governed by the inestimable power of God, inspiring us

PF9   *non par bacchante fureur, ne par limphatique mouuement, mais par aſtronomiques aſſertions.* Soli numine diuino afflati præſagiunt & ſpiritu prophetico particularia.

not by drunken ecstasy, nor by the spirit of a deep melancholic process, but by the evident influence of the stars: Only those divinely inspired can predict particular things in a prophetic spirit.

PF10   *Combien que de long temps par pluſieurs fois i'aye predict long temps au parauant ce que depuis eſt aduenu, & en particulieres regions,*

For how long a time and how often have I predicted what has come to pass, and in the particular regions,

PF11   *attribuãt le tout eſtre faict par la vertu & inſpiration diuine & autres felices & ſiniſtres aduentures de acceleree promptitude prononcees, que*

acknowledging all to have been accomplished through divine power and inspiration and [how often have I foreseen] other joyous and sinister events which with increasing promptness

PF12   *depuis ſont aduenues par les climats du monde: ayant voulu taire & delaiſſer pour cauſe del'iniure, & nõ tant ſeulement du tẽps*

have later come to pass throughout other climates and regions of the world. I was willing to keep silent by reason of the injury – and not only in the

PF13   *preſent, mais auſſi de la plus grãde part du futeur, de mettre par eſcrit, pource que les regnes, ſectes & religions feront changes ſi*

PF7   Nostradamus will explain a little later that he experiences time not as a linear phenomenon but as a continuum. It is impossible, therefore, to use a language of dialectics to describe a truth and an eternity that contain the past, present, and future, with all their contradictions. In short, the *injury of time* stems from the way we normally perceive it. It is this limited perception, tied to the constraints of the written word, that injures his ability to communicate the nondual and transcendental state of the continuum.

PF8   Nostradamus believes that the divine consciousness of God transcends human uncertainty. Divine providence forges a clear destiny above and beyond mere human habits and actions, which are accidental and unconsciously motivated.

PF9   He claims here that God's divine consciousness can shine its light down upon an all-too-human prophet who, in turn, can communicate the vision by means of some yet-unexplained astronomical calculations. For now, Nostradamus will present himself as a calculating celestial scientist and not some melancholic soothsayer. Expect him to contradict this claim later on.

PF10   He takes a moment to give us some background on his earlier prophetic experiments and successes. Nostradamus began publishing his prophecies in almanacs four years earlier, in 1550. By 1554 he was widely read across France.

PF11   This is the first of many times he is compelled to declare his religious correctness to the Church authorities. He must convince the Inquisition that God alone inspires him to see the evil and wondrous visions of tomorrow.

PF12   The success of his early experiments in prophecy made him meditate long and hard over what harm his history of the future might do to himself, his family, and to the future at large if he were to publish the things God had shown him.

PF13   This was his dilemma. The majority of readers want reality to conform to their beliefs. Yet, if he wrote down events in a straightforward narrative, most people would see their fantasies destroyed and reshaped on the lathe of tomorrow's events.

present time, but also for the future time as well – and refrain from
writing because the [present] kingdoms, sects and religions will make
changes so

PF14   *oppoſites, voire au reſpect du preſent diametralemēt, que ſi ie venois à*
reſerer ce qu'à l'aduenir ſera ceux de regne, ſecte, religiō,

diametrically opposite to the present view, that if I came to reveal what
will happen in the future those [present] kingdoms, sects, religions

PF15   *& foy trouueroyēt ſi mal accordāt à leur fantaſie auriculaire, qu'ils*
viendroyent à dāner ce que par les ſiecles aduenir on cognoiſtra eſtre veu
& apperceu.

and faiths would find [the future] so little in accord with the fantasies
they would like articulated that they would damn that which future
centuries will know and have seen to be true.

PF16   *Conſiderant auſſi la ſentence du vray Sauueur:* Nolite ſanctum dare
canibus, nec mittatis margaritas ante porcos, ne conculcent pedibus
& conuerſi dirumpāt vos.

Also consider what the true Savior said: Give not that which is holy
unto dogs, nor cast your pearls before swine, lest they trample them
under their feet and turn and rend you (Matthew 7:6).

PF17   *Qui a eſté la cauſe de faire retirer ma langue au populaire, & la plume au*
papier, puis me ſuis voulu eſtendre declarant pour le commun

Later, [I] decided to withhold my tongue, and pen from paper, because
of foreseeing the advent of the common people.

PF18   *aduenement par obſtruſes & perplexes ſentences les cauſes futures,*
meſmes les plus vrgentes, & celles que i'ay apperceu, quelque humaine
mutation qu'aduienne ne ſcandalizer l'auriculaire fragilité, & le tout

[Therefore I wrote] in dark and cryptic sentences the events of the future
evolution of human kind, especially the most urgent ones, and the ones I
perceived, [doing so] without scandalizing and upsetting fragile
sentiments

PF19   *eſcrit ſoubs figure nubileuſe, plus que du tout prophetique, combien que,*
Abſcondiſti hæc à ſapientibus, & prudentibus, id eſt potentibus &

by clouding my writing in obscure but, above all, prophetic language,
inasmuch as: Thou hast hidden these things from the wise and the
prudent, that is, from the powerful and

PF14 Rather than thank him for his compassion, they would damn their own future and probably incite the Inquisition to kill the messenger.

PF15–16 Nostradamus must therefore, find a writing style that will keep the mob and the mediocre (the **dogs** and **swine**) at bay. At the same time he must take care to leave clues for those who are willing to face the truth about tomorrow's changes so that they can recognize and decode the **pearls** of insight carefully hidden in his cryptic writings.

PF17 In the end he could not contain the need to share his vision of future history. He was a royalist and class-bound 16th-century man plagued with powerful impressions of a coming dark age when the mob would bring down their kings and rule the Earth (**the advent of the common people**) – something we "commoners" of today know and accept as democracy.

PF18 Nostradamus resolved that, come what may in negative reactions from readers of his own time, he had a spiritual responsibility to share his findings with both his contemporaries and all humanity in times to come. Here we have his clearest admission that he consciously chose to write about future human evolution in an obscure and calculatedly nebulous style so that the ignorant and prejudiced would deem him a fool and leave him alone, while the more openminded might pass beyond the verbal roadblocks to glimpse future human potential for good and evil.

Nostradamus establishes some important ground rules.

1) He deals only with significant events that could – or did – change the course of history.

PF19 2) All the bad grammar, the enigmas, anagrams, the mix of several languages, the bald-faced absurdities, and the general cloudiness of his writing are devices to hide truths from those who want the future to mold itself around their hopes and fears. It may even be done to hide the prophecies from future tyrants, who might recognize their mistakes in the prophecies, change their decisions, and perhaps create a worse future than Nostradamus had foreseen. Imagine what would have happened if in 1990 Saddam Hussein had recognized himself in the prophecies and decided to attack Kuwait in 1996 when his missiles were tipped with nuclear weapons? A man who can see tomorrow has a great karmic responsibility.

3) Obscurity works as a pacifier. The mediocre-minded can project their own ideas onto Nostradamus' opacity and satisfy themselves that either he is a charlatan or he supports their **fragile**, or airy-fairy, **sentiments**.

PF20   regibus, & enucleaſti ea exiguis & tenuibus: *& aux Prophetes par le
       moyen de Dieu immortel, & des bons Anges ont receu l'eſprit de
       vaticination, par lequel ils voyent les choſes loingtaines, & viennent*

**from kings, and hast revealed them to the small and the weak (Matthew
11:25) and also to the Prophets, by means of the Immortal God, and his
good Angels, they receive the spirit of prophecy, by which they behold
distant things and**

PF21   *à preuoir les futurs aduenemens: car rien ne ſe peut paracheuer ſans luy,
       auſquels ſi grande eſt la puiſſance, & la bonté aux ſubiects, que pendant
       qu'ils demeurent en eux, toutefois aux autres effects ſubiects pour la
       ſimilitude de la cauſe du bon genius, celle chaleur & puiſſance*

**future events; for nothing can be accomplished without Him whose great
power and kindness to his creatures is so great that as long as these
dwell in them, much as they may be exposed to other influences, on
account of their good genius this prophetic heat and power**

PF22   *vaticinatrice s'approche de nous: comme il nous aduient des rayons du
       Soleil, qui viennent iettans leur influence aux corps elementaires & non
       elementaires.*

**approaches us: it comes to us like rays of the sun casting influences on
bodies both elementary and nonelementary.**

PF23   *Quant à nous qui ſommes humains ne pouuons rien de noſtre naturelle
       cognoiſſance & inclination d'engin, cognoiſtre des ſecrets abſtruſes de Dieu
       le Createur* Quia nõ eſt noſtrum noſcere tempora, nec monẽtra, *&tc.*

**As for ourselves who are but human, we can discover nothing by our own
natural notions of our ingenuity about the obscure secrets of God the
Creator. It is not for you to know the times nor moments, etc.
(Acts 1:7).**

PF24   *Combien qu'auſſi de preſent peuuent aduenir & eſtre perſonnages, que
       Dieu le createur aye voulu reueler par imaginatiues impreßions, quelques
       ſecrets de l'aduenir, accordéz à l'Aſtrologie iudicielle comme du paſſé,*

**However, in the present or in the future there may be persons to whom
God the Creator might wish to reveal through fanciful impressions, some
secrets of the future, according to judicial astrology, in much the same
manner that in the past**

PF25   *que certaine puiſſance & volontaire faculté venoit par eux, comme flambe
       de feu apparoit, que luy inſpirant on venoit à iuger les diuines & humaines
       inſpirations.*

PF20 The *prophetic language* is written for the **weak** – or better, the "humble" – in spirit, who are willing to move beyond their own conditioned and egoistic projections to experience Nostradamus' hidden secrets.

Now he launches into the first essay on his prophetic techniques. First he hints at the magical route the divine messages take from the hierarchy of spirits down to the mortal prophet. Nostradamus, standing in his magic circle in his secret study, may have used ancient Cabalistic techniques to conjure up good Angels rather than the more elemental and lower denizens of the astral plane known as daemons.

PF21 Whenever Nostradamus makes a controversial occult statement he will remind us that his work is inspired by God and his accepted spiritual messengers alone, and operates within accepted Catholic ideas of his time.

The divine ones, or **Angels**, that sit at his side (see 1 Q1,2) bring to him the prophetic heat and visions.

PF22 This divine fire of prophecy descends upon the prophet's stilled mind and heart like the brilliance of the sun. It guides the spectral emissaries to influence the mortal medium to prophesy.

PF23 He takes a step back to remind us that normal human consciousness cannot tap in to the divine secrets or gauge the time of their happening. This famous biblical disclaimer is another smokescreen to mollify the Church censors. Even evangelists of our time use Acts 1:7 when pressured to predict the time for the fulfillment of their prophecies.

PF24 Judicial astrology is known today as political astrology. It encompasses the plotting of astrology charts for countries, state leaders, and the birth of constitutions and governments. Here and elsewhere Nostradamus implies that the astrology discipline objectively translates his *fanciful* visions into writing.

PF25 Nostradamus reveals his heavy reliance on the neo-Platonist magician Iamblinchus (AD 330). No doubt, he had a copy of Marsilio Ficino's translation of *De mysteriis Aegyptiorum*, the famous book on Egyptian, Chaldaean and Assyrian magic rituals that is often cited to be Nostradamus' instruction manual on prophecy (see 1 Q1,2).

a certain power and voluntary faculty came over them like a flame, inspiring them to judge human and divine inspirations alike.

PF26   *Car les œuures diuines, que totalement font abfolues, Dieu les vient paracheuer: la moyenne qui eft au milieu, les Anges: la troifiefme, les mauuais.*

For the divine works, those which are totally absolute, God accomplishes; those which are median, the angels; and the third kind, by evil [spirits].

PF27   *Mais, mon fils, ie te parle icy vn peu trop obftrufement: mais quant aux occultes vaticinations qu'on vient à receuoir par le fubtil efprit du*

But, my son, I speak here a little too obscurely; as for the hidden prophecies which come to one by the subtle spirit of

PF28   *feu, qui quelquesfois par l'entendement agité contemplant le plus haut des aftres, comme eftant vigilant, mefmes qu'aux prononciations, eftant*

fire, sometimes through the judgment being disturbed in contemplating the remotest of stars, while remaining alert and watchful, the pronouncements, we [can]

PF26 One could define the occult philosophy of this Greek mystic from ancient Syria in the following way. Humankind lives in the visible or physical world. Above this exists the higher vibratory dimension of the invisible and eternal world of the gods. The former is changeable, whereas the latter dimension is ever constant and perfect. Between the worlds of Eternity and Mortality is an astral dimension that links the divine with the physical. Our prophet, initiated in the mysteries, uses his own centering and consciousness – his soul force, if you will – to contact the spirit media of this twilight dimension to forge a conduit between the physical world and the divine and timeless perfection of the world of Eternity. Iamblinchus describes an elaborate hierarchy of astral messengers for this task, starting with the rare accomplishment of direct contact with a god by the magician and going on to the more frequent conjuring of archangelic, angelic, heroic and daemonic astral emissaries.

PF27 Iamblinchus believed that the divine world of Eternity contains all the potential destinies, causes and effects, and archetypes expressed in the physical, time-bound world. A mortal man, by nature, is limited to the rules of time and space. His sense of time is linear. He is like a man at the fork of many crossroads who cannot look beyond the horizon of the present to see which road is the right one to travel. But through magical meditations and with the assistance of divine messengers and lower elemental spirits, he can enter within himself, to access the invisible, latent flame of divinity sleeping within everyone. For brief moments he can tap into the divine ecstasy of the Ever Now state of eternity, and from this higher state of awareness, his soul can gaze down at the same crossroads stretching beyond the physical present and see potential future events on various paths of destiny radiating from the present. It is as if these divine spirits, in union with his own expanded consciousness, take him to a much higher vibration from where he can view the faraway bumps and turns down various crossroads of destiny.

PF28 Now comes the hard part. How does one bring such an experience back to the mortal and linear time-bound mind so that this eternity beyond dialectics can be explained through the dialectics of the written word?

Basically it is impossible. One cannot bring a flame under the water without changing it. Perhaps a flash can be seen before the water douses its light, and some ashes will remain floating there to hint at the fire that once was. At the very least, Nostradamus' written prophecies are the cinders left from that divine blaze.

PF29 *furprins efcrits prononcant fans crainte moins attainct d'inuerecunde loquacité: mais quoy tout procedoit de la puiffance diuine du grand Dieu eternel, de qui toute bonté procede.*

surprisingly take them down in writing and pronounce them without fear or shame and with the minimum of verbiage. But why [you ask]? Because all things proceeded from the divine power of the great eternal God, from whom all goodness proceeds.

PF30 *Encores, mon fils, que i'aye inferé le nom de Prophete, ie ne me veux attribuer tiltre de fi haute fublimité pour le temps prefent: car qui*

Furthermore, my son, though I have been attributed the name of "prophet," I do not wish to attribute to myself a title so sublime for the present. For

PF31 Propheta dicitur hodie, olim vocabatur videns: *car Prophete proprement mon fils, eft celuy qui voit chofes loingtaines de la cognoiffance naturelle de toute creature.*

He who is called a prophet now was once called a seer. For a prophet – strictly speaking, my son – is one who sees things remote from the natural perception of all creatures and men.

PF32 *Et cas aduenant que le Prophete, moyennant la parfaicte lumiere de la Prophetie luy appaire manifeftement des chofes diuines, côme*

And for instance it can happen that the prophet, by means of the perfect light of the prophecy manifestly appearing before him, [can see] things which are divine as well

PF33 *humaines, que ce ne fe peut faire, veu q̃ les effects de la future prediction s'eftedent loing.*

as human; which he cannot yet understand, for the effects of predicting the future extend far.

PF34 *Car les fecrets de Dieu incomprehenfibles, & la vertu effectrice contingent de longue eftedue de la cognoiffance naturelle prenãt leur*

For the incomprehensible mysteries of God and their effective power belong to a dimension very remote from natural human knowledge, taking their

PF35 *plus prochain origine du liberal arbitre, faict apparoir les caufes qui d'elles mefmes ne peuuent acquerir celle notice pour eftre cogneues, ne*

PF29   He will never openly state the above. He will claim instead that he can communicate the subjective fire of these trans-temporal visions through the dialectics of linear time and its written words. But I wonder if he's pulling our leg here when he says **with the minimum of verbiage**.

PF30   After another politically correct genuflexion to the Church, Nostradamus takes us spinning on his merry-go-round definition of **prophet**. He would like the Church censors and the religiously intolerant to believe that, strictly speaking, he is not a prophet.

PF31   I think his logic is similar to that of the woman who says she is "strictly speaking" almost pregnant. His protests aside, this definition adequately characterizes his own occult work.

Nostradamus is accutely aware of how **remote** such a glimpse into divine eternity is to the **natural perception** of man and animal.

PF32   He is well aware of the limits of his own 16th-century perceptions when faced with the events of the distant future. He intimates that the mortal mind of the prophet, when beholding the perfect vision from the world of Eternity, can misread Eternity's symbols.

PF33   I find it interesting that he uses the word **effects** of future prediction. Perhaps he means the effect is always future to the cause of events born in the present. We give birth to our future in the present. The future never comes, at least as far as mortal time and space are concerned. A prophecy is at best an abstract hint at possible outcomes or directions our present actions will manifest.

PF34-35   He claims that divine nature transcends all time and illusions of natural human perception. The divine mysteries are beyond human ego or the borrowed personalities and knowledge we gather and presume wrongly to be reality. The divine state is ephemeral, subtle, and invisible to time, the ego, and to the mortality of man. It is the very essence of **free will**. In other words it is nirvana, liberation itself.

immediate origin from the free will. They bring about the appearance of
events which of themselves could not acquire enough attention to become
known, neither

PF36   *par les humains augures, ne par autre cognoiſſance, ou vertu occulte,*
       comprinſe ſoubs la concauiſé du Ciel meſme, du faict preſent de la totale
       eternité, qui vient en ſoy embraſſer tout le temps.

       by human augury, nor by any other hidden knowledge or virtue
       comprised under the concavity of heaven, not even by the contemporary
       fact of all eternity, which comes to embrace all time in itself.

PF37   *Mais moyennãt que que indiuiſible eternité, par comitiale agitation*
       Hiraclienne, les cauſes par le celeſte mouuemẽt ſont cogneues.

       But through some indivisible eternity and by means of Heraclian
       agitation, the happenings are made known by celestial movements.

PF38   *Ie ne dis pas, mõ fils, àfin que bie l'entedez, que la cognoiſſance de ceſte*
       matiere ne ſe peut encores imprimer dans ton debile cerueau, que

       I do not say, my son, that the knowledge of this matter cannot yet
       impress itself upon your tender mind, nor

PF39   *les cauſes futures bien loingtaines ne ſoyent à la cognoiſſance de la creature*
       raiſonnable: ſi ſont nonobſtãt bonnemẽt la creature de

       [do I say] that very distant events are not within the understanding of
       reasoning man, much less those which are simply the extrapolation

PF40   *l'ame intellectuelle des choſes preſentes loingtaines ne luy ſont du tout ne*
       trop occultes, ne trop reſerees: mais la parfaicte des cauſes

       by an intellectual person of current events – these are by no means too
       carefully hidden from him, but on the other hand nor can they be said to
       be obvious. But a perfect

PF41   *notices ne ſe peut acquerir ſans celle diuine inſpiratiõ: veu que toute*
       inſpiratiõ prophetique reçoit prenãt ſon principal principe mouuãt de Dieu
       le createur, puis de l'heur & de nature.

       knowledge of events cannot be acquired without divine inspiration, since
       all prophetic inspiration receives its principle motivating force from God
       the Creator, then from good fortune and from nature.

PF36 We return to Iamblinchus' view that our lives in mortality and time are embraced by the divine Eternity, which is the invisible source of the cause of phenomena and time in the physical world. Notice that he says the state of Eternity embraces **all** time, not just time in general. This implies that many alternative, or quantum futures are available to us depending on our individual or collective actions in the present moment.

PF37 *Hiraclienne* is a term derived from the Greek essentially meaning "epileptic". The modern sense of the word brings to mind a soothsayer, gone rigid and foaming at the mouth. But there are a number of older meanings. "Herakleie" may find its roots in the person of the Greek mystic Herakleitos (*c.*540–*c.*480 BC), who was also unfairly known as "the dark" or "the obscure" because his philosophy was nondualistic. He called this philosophy the Hidden Harmony. If we take the words of Herakleitos as a guide, someone in a **Heraclian agitation** would experience a state of transcendent consciousness in which "God is day and night, winter and summer, war and peace, satiety and want ... the way up and the way down are one and the same. Even sleepers [the unconscious and sinful ones] are workers and collaborators in what goes on in the universe. In the circle the beginning and the end are common."

PF38 The narrative takes a breath and dives into the stream of consciousness once again.

PF39 He is not saying that the nondual dance of opposites or **Heraclian** view is beyond his son's – or others' – grasp. Nor is the shape and quality of distant future events beyond the understanding of a reasoning man.

PF40 Now Nostradamus makes a few circular (Heraclian) statements. First he says imperfect human reasoning can project its own intellectualism on a future vision, while at other times it has the potential to comprehend the divine and eternal revelations of God. The normal human mind can think about things and conclude the essential. But thinking about swimming is impotent compared with the experience of getting wet and paddling. In short, what he's saying awkwardly is that one must go beyond thinking to directly experience a revelation.

PF41 Authentic prophetic vision comes from awakening the correct psychic instincts, achieving union with and direct experience of one's God-source, and last but not least, encountering a bit of good luck (**good fortune**).

PF42   *Parquoy eſtant les cauſes indifferentes, indifferentemēt produictes, & non produictes, le preſaige partie aduient, ou a eſté predit.*

For which reason, a presage may be fulfilled in part or be correctly predicted [only] in proportion to the extent to which comparable events have manifested themselves similarly or have failed to manifest themselves.

PF43   *Car l'entendement creé intellectuellement ne peut veoir occultement, ſinon par la voix faicte au lymbe moyennāt la exigue flāme en laquelle partie les cauſes futures ſe vendrōt à incliner.*

For human understanding, being intellectual, cannot see hidden things unless aided by a voice coming from limbo by means of the slender flame showing what direction future events will incline toward.

PF44   *Et auſſi, mõ fils, ie te ſupplie que iamais tu ne vueilles employer ton entendement à telles reſueries & vanitez qui ſechēt le corps &*

Furthermore, my son, I beg that you will never want to employ your understanding on such dreams and vanities as dry up the body.

PF45   *mettent à perdition l'ame, donnant trouble au foible ſens: meſme la vanité de la plus qu'execrable magie reprouuee iadis par les ſacrees*

put the soul in [peril of] perdition and give trouble to weak senses. [I caution you] especially against the vain and more than execrable magic, long condemned by the Holy

PF46   *eſcritures, & par les diuins canons, au chef duquel eſt excepté le iugement de l'Aſtrologie iudicielle: par laquelle, & moyennāt*

Scriptures and by the divine Canons [of the Church]. However, judicial astrology is excepted from this judgement. For it is by means of

PF42   He implies indirectly here that the accuracy of his prophecies depends in part on his ability to suspend his psychic, mental, and emotional projections and limitations. His degree of clarity is a reflection of how deeply he can let go and let God shower his visions. Perhaps he is admitting here that some of his predictions are more biased than others.

PF43   This is a good place to describe the pitfalls of prophetic bias. A divine vision is like pure water passing through the tea strainer of one's intellectually conditioned mind. It is impossible that the pure waters will drain themselves into the phenomenal world without being tainted by the flavor of the tea leaves of one's cultural and religious programming.

With this in mind, our prophet is indirectly describing how he rinses the strainer of his mind clear of leafy mental hopes, fears, and expectations. He applies magical techniques to empty his mind of all intellectual debris. But he approaches his secrets cautiously in print because his confessions run dangerously close to heresy.

The **voice coming from limbo** is that of a conjured angelic or daemonic spirit. It seems that many of Nostradamus' prophecies were visualized through a number of magical tools, such as a consecrated bowl of water or a finely polished metal mirror lit indirectly by the soft glow of sanctified candles.

The key to unlocking his powers is the *exigue flãme*. This is Old French for a "very small [or slender, or thin] flame." The exact nature of this flame is prudently kept secret. It might refer to a key letter that unlocks the Cabalistic arcana, or it may be the peculiar and paranormal light that fills Nostradamus' secret study preceding the entry of an angelic or daemonic messenger; it could even stand for the nearly invisible light of one's innate and hidden divine consciousness.

Once this spark of godliness within the prophet is awakened, he can best interpret the direction of future events. Note that Nostradamus uses an indirect word **incline**. This verb implies that at best he can predict the apparent rather than the actual directions or outcomes of a given action. If Nostradamus experienced the future as preordained he would have used a verb like "take" or "adopt" or "grasp."

PF44   Now he begins a long digression.

PF45   He puts on the mask of a religiously correct magician and warns his son against burning out his mind and body by delving into the seductive and evil reveries of black magic.

PF46   Judicial astrology is exempt from this caveat because certain

PF47   *inſpiration & revelation diuine par continuelles ſupputations, auõs nos propheties redigé par eſcrit.*

[such] inspiration, divine revelation, and continual nightly watches and calculations, that we have drafted our prophecies into written words.

PF48   *Et cõbien que celle occulte Philoſophie ne fuſſe reprouuee, n'ay onques voulu preſenter leurs effrenees perſuaſions cõbien que pluſieurs volumes qui ont eſté cachez par longs ſiecles me ſont eſté manifeſtez.*

Although such occult Philosophy might not have been condemned, I had no desire to make freely public all its unbridled assertions. I had at my disposal several volumes that had been hidden for a great many centuries.

PF49   *Mais doutant ce qui aduiendroit, en ay faict, apres la lecture preſent à Vulcan, que cependant qu'il les venoit à deuorer, la flamme leſchant*

But dreading what might otherwise become of them, I made a present [of them] to [the God] Vulcan, and even as he began to consume them, the hungry flame

PF50   *l'air rendoit vne clarté inſolite, plus claire que naturelle flamme, comme lumiere de feu de clyſtre fulgurant, illuminant ſubit la maiſon,*

lent the air an unusual brightness, clearer than that of natural flame – bright as lightning – suddenly illuminating the house

PF51   *comme ſi elle fuſt eſté en ſubite cõflagration.*

as if in a sudden conflagration.

practices were sanctioned, or at least tolerated, by the Church as
long as one could prove they were used by the patriarchs of the
Old Testament. It is a well-known fact that the Jewish priesthood
used this astrological technique to prophesy. The Church also
allowed occultists some room to practice the Hebraic magical
techniques recorded by King Solomon (?973–?933 BC), whose book
The Keys of Solomon the King, it is safe to say, was Nostradamus'
second occult source for rituals after Iamblinchus. Latin translations
of it were in circulation at the time.

PF47   One can picture Nostradamus gazing at the stars in Salon, standing in the modest observatory he had cut into his roof, practicing
the secret calculations of his Jewish ancestors, the priests at
Solomon's Temple. According to Smith and Fuller's *Dictionary of
the Bible*, they had an "understanding of the times." For them the
cycles of the stars and planets and the inclination of the months
and feast days, along with the trajectory of comets and meteors
and other stellar phenomena, spoke together a language communicating the pattern of future events. Nostradamus says that
we have drafted the prophecies into written words. Is he using
the polite first-person plural, or does he include in the credits for
his book of prophecy the labors of his disciple, Jean-Aymes de
Chavigny, or those of his spirit guides?

PF48   Nostradamus doesn't answer. He brushes the Jewish celestial
science aside as **unbridled assertions** (perhaps to satisfy the
Church censors) and admits to possessing several volumes of treatises on Jewish magic, implying that perhaps these are family
heirlooms passed on and recopied in Hebraic letters down the
centuries. Nostradamus may have consulted an ancient scroll of
the *Keys of Solomon* in Hebrew.

PF49   Now Nostradamus launches into his famous (and possibly apocryphal) tale that he burned all his books on Jewish magic,
ephemerises, and treatises on black magic (no doubt, after
committing them to memory) because of their heretical views.

PF50   He puts on the mask of a responsible scholar serving as his own
Church Inquisitor, saving others from evil by burning these
witches of print and parchment on the stake of his own bonfire in
the enclosed courtyard of his house. I doubt if the real Inquisitors
were fooled, but the admission satisfied the social rule of the day.
We of modern times would be surprised at the extent the Church
priests and upper classes dabbled in pagan and heretical magic.

PF51   The most Christian Queen Catherine de' Medici of France herself had an army of astrologers, magicians, and ladies-in-waiting
playing priestess in her apartments at St Germain-en-Laye and

PF52   *Parquoy à fin qu'à l'aduenir ne feußiez abuzé, perscrutant la parfaicte transformatiõ tant séline que solitaire, & soubs terre metaux incorruptibles, & aux ondes occultes, les ay en cendres conuertis.*

Thus, so that in the future you might not be led astray in a search for the perfect transformation of silver, or of gold, or of incorruptible metals under the earth, or hidden in the waves, I have reduced [these books] to ashes.

PF53   *Mais quant au iugement qui se vient paracheuer, moyennãt le iugemēt celeste, cela te veux ie manifester: parquoy auoir cognoissance des*

But [beyond this] it is that judgement that comes by means of discernment obtained through reference to the heavens, that I want to reveal to you. By this [insight] you may have knowledge of

PF54   *causes futures, reiectãt loing les phantastiques imaginations qui aduiendront, limitant la particularité des lieux par diuine inspiration*

future events while rejecting completely the fanciful imaginations [of things] that will occur. By limiting the descriptions of the locations by means of harmonizing divine and supernatural inspiration

PF55   *supernaturelle: accordant aux celestes figures, les lieux & vne partie du tēps de proprieté occulte par vertu, puissance, & faculté diuine, en*

with astronomical computations, one can accurately name places and specific times, with an occult accuracy, authority, and a divine faculty. Through

PF56   *presence de laquelle les trois tēps sont cõprins par eternité, reuolution tenãt à la cause passee, presente & future: quia omnia sunt nuda, & aperta & c.*

this [faculty], the cycles of time – the past, present and future – become incorporated into one eternity: For all things are naked and open. (Hebrews 4:13).

PF57   *Parquoy, mon fils, tu peux facilemēt nonobstant tõ tendre cerueau, cõprendre que les choses qui doiuent aduenir, sepeuuent prophetizer*

In this way, my son, notwithstanding your tender mind, you will easily be able to understand that things that are bound to happen can be prophesied

PF58   *par les nocturnes & celestes lumieres, qui sõt naturelles, & par l'esprit de prophetie: non que ie me vueille attribuer nomination ne*

by the lights of the sky at night, which are natural, coupled with the spirit of prophecy. Not that I would assume the title

the Château Chaumont on the Loire. It was particularly important in Nostradamus' day that you kept your liaisons with heresies,
as with your mistresses, discreet. By declaring in print that these
magical books are **unbridled assertions** and then burning them,
Nostradamus is showing discretion.

PF52　Even so, that said, it is often the case that the strange and lurid
light of truth burns brighter than fiction. Maybe Nostradamus did
have this paranormal experience. Then again, the binding glue,
ancient inks and parchments, and the bright colors of hand-
illustrated books may have fed brilliance and unholy color to the
bonfire. We will never know if the nervous scholar projected evil
on the light and colors of the fire because he repressed his feelings
of guilt for burning his family's most hallowed treasures.

PF53　Nostradamus, with scarcely a literary pause, returns to the
mechanics of future gazing.

PF54　Whatever these calculations are, he claims to have found a state
of balance from which to interpret the future by using them to
stay centered on his own projections (**fanciful imaginations**) and
the awe-inspiring and nonlinear insights stemming from an
unleashed **supernatural inspiration**.

PF55　Judicial astrology is therefore used in tandem with Nostradamus'
strong sensitivity towards geography to translate the divinely
inspired vision of a time continuum into specific places and cycles
of time.

PF56　He clearly indicates that his visions arise from outside of time as
we know it. Through divine inspiration the present embraces
events of the past and the future as one eternity. As we will see,
some of Nostradamus' prophecies appear to be retroactive.

PF57　Skeptics of the seer believe he was cheating his readers by cloak-
ing past events in the guise of prophecy. It is, however, equally
possible that Nostradamus in a trance state is **naked and open** to
whatever the divine spirits reveal to him, whether it is an event
in the past or the future.

PF58　For his angelic messengers everything is happening in the Eternal
Now. Our mortality and linear concept of time are the real
cheats.

PF59 *effect prophetique, mais par reuelee inſpiration, comme hõme mortel, eſloigné nõ moins de ſens au Ciel, que des pieds en terre.*

or quality of a prophet, for revealed inspiration, like a mortal man, is no less distant in knowledge and sense from Heaven than his feet are from the ground.

PF60 Poſſum nõ errare, falli, decipi, ſuis pecheur plus grand que nul de ce mõde, ſubiect à toutes humaines afflictiõs.

I cannot fail, err, or be deceived, although I am the greatest sinner in the world, subject to all human afflictions.

PF61 *Mais eſtãt ſurprins par fois la ſepmaine limphatiquant, & par longue calculatiõ, rendant les eſtudes nocturnes de ſoueſue odeur, i'ay composé*

But many times a week I am overtaken by a prophetic ecstasy – and by means of exhaustive calculation, having undertaken my nocturnal studies within an agreeable fragrance – I have compiled some

PF62 *liures de propheties contenãt chacun cent quatrains aſtronomiques de propheties, leſquelles i'ay vn peu voulu rabouter obſcurement: & ſont perpetuelles vaticinations, pour d'icy à l'annee 3797.*

books of prophecies, each containing one hundred astronomical quatrains composed of prophecies which I have desired to render a little obscurely. They are perpetual prophecies, and extend from now to the year 3797.

PF63 *Que poßible fera retirer le front à quelques vns, en voyant ſi longue extenſion, & par ſoubs toute la concauité de la Lune aura lieu &*

It is possible, that some will raise their brow at seeing such a far-reaching extent of time and a treatment of everything under the vault of the moon that will happen and

PF64 *intelligẽce: & ce entendãt vniuerſellement par toute la terre les cauſes mõ fils.*

[will be] universally perceived all over the earth, my son.

PF65 *Que ſi tu vis l'aage naturel & humain, tu verras deuers tõ climat, au propre Ciel de ta natiuité, les futures aduẽtures preuoir.*

But if you attain the natural span of human life, you will come to see, under your own native skies, the [surprising] future events [I have] foreseen.

PF59 Nostradamus leaves the repetitive account of his prophetic process, and his insistence that he is not really a prophet, to enter a new disclaimer peppered with humility about his own human sins and failings.

PF60 But then he contradicts himself, perhaps to present the complete truth about his process. He claims, albeit in a very roundabout way, that a mortal man who is opening his prophetic eye becomes aware that he is big enough, by the grace of prophetic light, to contain all contradictions.

PF61 Most translations of this introductory clause translate the word *odeur* as a poetic reference to our seer's attaining the appropriate mood for his nocturnal studies. He is actually describing a special incense used in his magical rituals. The pleasing aroma contains powerful herbs that free him from his mind and emotions and stimulate the prophetic fire.

PF62 After he describes the form of his book of prophecy as Centuries, or volumes of 100 astronomically composed quatrains, he flings before us an interesting concept, that his prophecies are **perpetual**. In other words, they are quantum-future oriented. It depends on one's point of view and consciousness. For us, the possible futures born of this moment flow along in a line. To the divinely inspired, all actions of all times happen simultaneously – or in perpetuity.

The date 3797 makes this the most distant-dated prediction in history. Later he will train his prophetic eye far beyond to a date set 1,800 years ahead of our own time.

PF63-64 Even Nostradamus must pause to reflect upon this ambitious forecast.

PF65 He promises his infant son that he will see many of his father's prophecies come to pass in the natural span of his life. By the time César died at the age of 77 in 1631 a number of Nostradamus' prophecies had been fulfilled. Some were even widely known, such as the death of Henry II in a jousting accident (1 Q35), the death of his heir, Francis II (10 Q39), the accession of Henry IV (2 Q55, 10 Q18), and his assassination (3 Q11).

PF66   *Combien que le ſeul Dieu eternel, ſoit celuy ſeul qui cognoiſt l'eternité de ſa lumiere, procedant de luy meſmes, & ie dis franchement qu'à ceux*

Although the eternal God alone knows the eternity of the light proceeding from himself, I say frankly to all those

PF67   *à qui ſa magnitude immẽſe, qui eſt ſans meſure & incõprehenſible, a voulu par longue inſpiration melancolique reueler, que moyennant*

to whom he wishes to reveal his immense magnitude – immeasurable and unknowable as it is – after long and melancholic ecstasy, that it is

PF68   *icelle cauſe occulte manifeſtee diuinement, principalemẽt de deux cauſes principales, qui ſont cõprinſes à l'entendement de celuy*

a hidden thing divinely manifested to the prophet by two principal means, which are contained in the understanding of the

PF69   *inſpiré qui prophetiſe, l'vne eſt que vient à infuſer, eſclarciſſant la lumiere ſupernaturelle, au perſonnage qui predit par la doctrine des*

inspired one who prophesies. One comes by infusion, which clarifies the supernatural light in him who predicts by the doctrine of

PF70   *Aſtres, & prophetiſe par inſpiree reuelation, laquelle eſt vne certaine participatiõ de la diuine eternité, moyennant le Prophete viẽt à*

the stars, making [it] possible to predict by divine revelation; the other comes by means of an authentic participation with the divine eternity, by which means the prophet can

PF71   *iuger de cela que ſon diuin eſprit luy a dõné par le moyen de Dieu le createur, & par vne naturelle inſtigation: c'eſt à ſçauoir que ce que*

judge what is given to him from his own divine spirit through God the Creator and a natural instilling; so that what is

PF72   *predict eſt vray, & a prins ſon origine etheréement: & telle lumiere & flãme exigue eſt de toute efficace, & de telle altitude no moins*

predicted is true, and has an ethereal origin. This light and the slender flame [one's inner spark of God] are altogether efficacious, and of exalted origin no less

PF66   From PF66 through PF74 we enter the next-to-last examination of
        Nostradamus' prophetic gift. In this case he is less obscure than
        before, and much of what he says is self-explanatory. I will add
        only a few extra assertions.

        He explains again how a vision is conjured, and mentions the
        attributes required of a prophet.

PF67   God in his omnipotence and eternal time continuum chooses
        those to whom he wishes to reveal his magnitude – which is with-
        out measure in its perfect knowing that transcends the mortal,
        conditionally limited and linear-time bound ego of man. A
        melancholic ecstasy in Old French terms may describe the stern,
        gloomy-eyed gape of Nostradamus reflected in the waters of his
        brass divining bowl. He will describe this state in more detail in
        the second preface written for the final three Centuries, the
        Epistle to Henry II.

PF68   Nostradamus is about to describe two principles, **infusion** and
        authentic participation, which a prophet must master to access
        the invisible and subtle light of a divine manifestation. The first
        requires self-understanding attained through meditation.

PF69   In other words, one attains a distance from the disturbing quali-
        ties of thoughts, hopes, fears, and emotions through witnessing
        them without judgement. A quietude settles upon the prophet
        until he becomes an empty vessel for transmission, what some
        Eastern mystics have called a hollow bamboo flute, played by the
        invisible presence of the divine.

PF70   Working with the first principle of *infusion* one achieves dis-
        identification from the moral mind, emotions, and projections
        about time. Through the second principle of **authentic participa-
        tion** one attains to a total and ecstatic trance state. Nostradamus
        reiterates that the correct interpretation of visions received while
        in these states is accomplished with the aid of astronomical
        calculations.

PF71   He makes a clear declaration that divine spirit is not outside the
        prophet. Iamblinchus expressed that a mortal magician's soul
        energies are used in the twilight dimension between the lower
        physical and higher eternal plane as a conduit for prophecies. It is
        open to interpretation whether Nostradamus physically conjured
        spirits into his secret study, or whether they impressed themselves
        upon his consciousness while he was in the trance.

PF72   If we were to spy on his nocturnal sessions we might see him
        sitting alone on his brass tripod within the magic circle. His eyes
        are stern and feverish, and he is speaking and responding to an
        invisible partner. We might feel a chill in the air from an astral

PF73 *que la naturelle clarté & naturelle lumiere rēd les Philofophes fi affeurez,*
que moyennāt les principes de la premiere caufe ont attainct

than natural clarity and the natural light that renders philosophers so
sure of themselves which by means of the principles of the first cause
they have attained

PF74 *à plus profondes abyfmes des plus hautes doctrines.*

to the innermost cores of the most exalted doctrines.

PF75 *Mais à celle fin, mon fils, que ie ne vague trop profondement pour la*
capacité future de tō fens, & außi que ie treuue que les lettres

But an end to this, my son, for I must not stray too far from the future
capacity of your senses. I find that letters

PF76 *feront fi grande & incomparable iacture, que ie treuue le mōde auāt*
l'vniuerfelle cōflagration aduenir tant de deluges & fi hautes

will suffer a very grand and incomparable loss. I find also that before the
future universal conflagration the world will see so many floods and such
high

PF77 *inundations, qu'il ne fera guiere terroir qui ne foit couuert d'eau & fera*
par fi lōg tēps q̃ hors mis enographies & topographies, que le

inundations, that there will remain scarcely any land not covered by
water, and this will last for so long that outside of the topography of
earth and the races which inhabit it,

PF78 *tout ne foit pery: außi auāt & apres telles inundatiōs, en plufieurs cōtrees,*
les pluyes feront fi exigues, & tōbera du Ciel fi grande

everything will perish. Furthermore, before and after these floods many
nations shall see very little rain and there will fall from the sky such a
great

PF79 *abondāce de feu & de pierre candentes, que n'y demeurera rien qu'il ne*
foit cōfommé: & cecy aduenir en brief, & auāt la derniere conflagration.

amount of fire and flaming meteorites that nothing will remain
unconsumed. All this will happen a short time before the final
conflagration.

PF80 *Car encores que la planette de Mars paracheue fon fiecle, & à la fin de*
fon dernier periode fi le reprendra il: mais affemblez les vns en Aquarius

presence filling the room, but no more. Each time Nostradamus returns us to a theme, such as the slender flame, his turgid narrative grudgingly exposes more clues. The slender flame burns in the being of the true initiate in divine mysteries.

PF73-74   The vision is therefore not a projection from his own mortal mind and emotions. It is from God, or so he claims. Moreover, the genuine initiation into the divine mysteries is comparable to that of great classical philosophers and spiritual seekers who use the first principle of infusion or meditation.

PF75   Enough of this esoteric roller-coaster ride, says Nostradamus, who implies here that there is much more to say to César but he already knows that more than this even as a full grown man his son will not understand.

PF76   Now begins the first pole vault into the future. One might reason that in Nostradamus' dyslexic writing style it is sensible to start his history of the future with a glimpse of events from the far end.

PF77   He is distressed with what he sees as the coming loss of learning and education. Perhaps he views a future trend for the 21st century in which humanity is in danger of becoming even more technically headstrong, robotic, and culturally illiterate than it is today.

PF78   Nostradamus hurtles over millennia to give a blow-by-blow account of what modern astronomers believe will happen to Earth billions of years from now, when the sun exhausts its nuclear fuel and swells into a red giant, eventually devouring Mercury, Venus and perhaps even planet Earth. As we will see later in the quatrains, between the years 3755 and 3797 tremendous gravitational disturbances make Earth's climate go haywire, making the coming climatic chaos of global warming in the 21st century look pale in comparison.

PF79   These are the first symptoms of what he calls **the final conflagration**. Great tidal waves taller than continents roll over Earth's antiquities and ancient-future civilizations. Then a meteor shower of debris from the remains of Venus and Mercury reduces the surface of our planet to a scorched wasteland. The oceans evaporate and our home planet is consumed. Nostradamus believed Mars would continue its orbit after the death of Earth. He may find grudging agreement among astronomers who believe the aging sun has enough mass to expand at, or slightly beyond, the Earth's orbit when it expands into a red giant. Nostradamus and the astronomers differ on the timing. He believed it would occur 1,800 years from now. They see it several billion years later.

PF80   Even among the embers of this last conflagration the human race will survive to colonize space. Nostradamus not only reports on

For although the planet Mars will finish its cycle, at the end of its last age, it will start again. Some will assemble in Aquarius

PF81   *par plufieurs annees, les autres en Cancer par plus longues & côtinues.*

for several years, others in Cancer for a longer time and for evermore.

PF82   *Et maintenãt que fommes conduicts par la Lune, moyennant la totale puiffance de Dieu eternel, qu'auant qu'elle aye paracheué fon total circuit, le Soleil viẽdra, & puis Saturne.*

And at present, we are conducted by the Moon – by means of the total power of the eternal God – when she will have completed her entire cycle [1889–2250], the Sun [the 20th century] and then Saturn [the Aquarian Age] will come.

PF83   *Car felon les fignes celeftes, le regne de Saturne fera de retour, que le tout calculé, le mõde s'approche d'vne anaragonique reuolution: & que*

According to the celestial signs the reign of Saturn will return a second time [the Age of Capricorn], so that as it is all calculated, the world then approaches its final death-dealing revolution. From this

the survival of Mars but uses its astrological cycle to define a window of time. In Julian calculation an era of Mars lasts roughly 700 years. With this in mind he is possibly dating the period it takes a number of "arks" to travel the great distances of the galaxy to colonize other star systems.

Tonight, when you step out of your home to behold the vault of the heavens, train your eye upon the distant stars of the constellations of Aquarius and Cancer. There you will see your future home, perhaps even your future incarnation walking upon a new Earth warmed by the sunlight of distant stars.

PF81 Nostradamus gives some indication that the exodus to Aquarius will not be as fruitful as the mission to the stars of Cancer, where it seems mankind will build its permanent home. The Old French meaning for *continuel* is "uninterrupted" and thus **evermore**. Another translation would have our descendants dwelling in worlds around the stars of Cancer **for a longer and uninterrupted time**. Perhaps they will live conscious of the eternity of the present, and therefore live beyond the interruptions of time itself.

PF82 The narrative circles back several thousand years, to our times at the threshold of the New or Aquarian Age.

Esoteric astrology explains that the influence of the Aquarian Age over the current Piscean Age began several centuries ago. Nostradamus sees human consciousness dominated by the Aquarian epoch of science and humanism by AD 2250, around the end of the current lunar cycle (1889–2250). In the next 250 years we could make contact with other galactic civilizations and enter a new era in human evolution as part of a wider galactic community.

PF83 Saturn co-rules the Age of Aquarius and the succeeding Age of Capricorn. The latter is symbolized by a great mountain peak penetrating deep into the sky. The mountain signifies the highest peak of evolution possible on this physical plane. By the 37th century, humanity will begin to adapt its evolution to the first influences of the coming Age of Capricorn. The key words for Capricorn are "utilize" or "restrict." The human race will need to apply all its hard-earned lessons from the past or be destroyed by its godlike power over mind, matter, and time. The Capricorn Age will be heralded by the physical destruction of the Earth from a cosmic source, the final **death-dealing** conflagration. Perhaps the sun will explode into a nova much sooner than astronomers calculate because of some interstellar weapon or through the tinkering of a cosmically exploitive future humanity. Fortunately there will be warnings, and it seems that humanity will escape Earth like seeds from a dying flower blown to freedom.

PF84   *de preſent que cecy i'eſcrits auant cent ſeptanteſept ans trois mois vnze*
       iours par peſtilence, longue famine, & guerres, & plus par les

       present moment I can write that before 177 years, 3 months and 11
       days, by pestilence, long famine and wars, and most of all by

PF85   *inundations le monde entre cy & ce terme prefix, auant & apres par*
       pluſieurs fois, ſera ſi diminué, & ſi peu de monde ſera, que l'on ne

       floods, the world between now and the end of this predestined term, [as
       had happened already] several times before and [will again] after, be so
       diminished, and so few remaining, that no one

PF86   *trouuera qui vueille prendre les champs, qui deuiendront libres auſſi*
       longuement, qu'ils ſont eſtex en ſeruitude: & ce quãt au viſible

       will be found willing to work in the fields, which will become wild for as
       long a period as they had been tilled. And according to the visible

PF87   *iugement celeſte, qu'encores que nous ſoyons au ſeptieſme nombre de mille*
       qui paracheue le tout, nous approchãt du huictieſme, où

       judgement of the stars, although we are in the seventh number of the
       millenary – which finishes all – we are approaching the eighth sphere
       [cycle], which

PF88   *eſt le firmament de la huictieſme sphere, qui eſt en dimenſion latitudinaire,*
       où le grand Dieu eternel viendra paracheuer la reuolution: ou les images
       celeſtes retourneront à ſe mouuoir & le

       is in the firmament of the latitudinary dimension of the eighth sphere,
       whence the great eternal God will come to complete the revolution and
       the heavenly bodies will return to their motion, and the

PF84   Dating a future event is the hardest feat in prophecy. If the future were preordained it would be otherwise. In this case Nostradamus' claim doesn't fit the facts. If you count 177 years, 3 months, and 11 days from March 1555 you get 11 June 1753. This was a relatively peaceful year in world history. Events in that year certainly do not match any of the apocalyptic prophecy in PF84–86. In the quatrains we will see Nostradamus' remarkable successes with dates and cycles of time.

PF85   Although his time calculations and natural disaster prediction are wrong, the terrible images of war and pestilence could be partially correct. He might have been seeing visions of wars, famine, and pestilence soon to beset France in nine religious wars between 1562 and 1598. His prophecies also chronicle the mayhem and destruction from eight decades of war in the Netherlands between the Spanish and the Dutch (1568–1648) and the great central European apocalypse of the Thirty Years War of 1618–1648. It is estimated that one-third to one-half of the population of the devastated German and Bohemian principalities perished. Chroniclers of the times say that much of the German Palatinate was a desert of untended fields dotted with the burnt smudges of ransacked villages and towns.

PF86   This level of devastation would not return to Central Europe until World Wars I and II. And since Nostradamus is dipping into a time continuum, I wouldn't rule out a case of temporal overlap – a phenomenon in which the seer witnesses several events from different times mingled together at the same locality. He could have seen images from 16th, 17th, 20th, and even future 21st century wars and ecological disasters and misinterpreted them for the time window of 1555 through 1753.

PF87   The *visible judgement of the stars* is his poetic way of describing how the movements of the stars serve him as a mode of communicating future events through judicial astrology.

    In the *Epistle* (EP42–50 and EP142–159), Nostradamus gives two divergent time lines of history, which would put the seventh millennium between either AD 1242–2242 or 1826–2826, rather than the more conventional AD 1000–2000. Dated prophecies in the body of the quatrains support the conventional time line.

PF88   The *eighth sphere* or cycle of time most likely stands for the third millennium (AD 2000 through 3000), a time collectively foreseen as a Golden Age. Between 1993 and 2012 most of the cycles of time plotted by ancient civilizations and native peoples will *complete the revolution* and *return to their motion* again. This happens only once in roughly 26,000 years! In the third millen-

PF89   *mouuement superieur qui nous red la terre stable & ferme* non
inclinabitur in seculū sæculi: hors mis que son vouloir sera

**superior movement will render the earth stable and secure for us, not
deviating from age to age (Psalm 94:5) unless He wills it to be;**

PF90   *accomply, mais non point autrement: combien que par ambigues opinions
excedantes toutes raisons naturelles par songes*

**His will be done and not otherwise. How many [are] the ambiguous
opinions beyond all genuine reason through Muslim dreams,**

PF91   *Mahometiques, auβi aucunesfois Dieu le createur par les ministres de ses
messagiers de feu, en flamme miβiue vient à proposer aux sens*

**and also even sometimes by God the Creator by means of fiery missives
brought by his angels of fire, there come before our exterior senses,**

PF92   *exterieurs mesmement à nos yeux, les causes de future prediction
significatrices du cas futur qui se doit à celuy qui presaige manifester.*

**even our eyes, the events of future prediction, and that which is
significant to future circumstances. These ought to manifest themselves
to one who presages anything.**

PF93   *Car le presaige qui se faict de la lumiere exterieure vient infailliblement à
iuger partie auecques, & moyennant le lume exterieur:*

**For the presage which is made by the exterior enlightenment comes
infallibly to be judged together with and by means of the exterior light.**

PF94   *combien vrayement que la partie qui semble auoir par l'œil de
l'entendement, ce que n'est par la lesion du sens imaginatif, la raison*

**Truly, the part that seems to come by the sight of understanding comes
only by the lesion [opening?] of the imaginative sense. The reason**

nium humanity will welcome the return of the divine law of God establishing order in the cosmos.

PF89   Many mystical paths around the world define the law of godliness as essentially a state of balance (*stable*), union, and harmony. From this centering comes love and conscious actions. The greatest revolution in history would be one that established harmony between all men, women and children of all races, religious persuasions and personal preferences.

PF90   The narrative in PF90–98 circles back one last time to the theme of magical rituals. It is essentially the same discourse as before, so this may be a good place to insert a condensed overview of the occult rituals and tools Nostradamus used to call down the divine fire of prophecy.

Nostradamus fashioned his own composite ritual from Hermetic, neo-Platonist, Chaldaean, Egyptian, Assyrian, and Hebraic magical traditions, chiefly derived from the works of Iamblinchus, King Solomon, and a rare treatise in Greek by the noted Byzantine historian Michael Psellus (1018–1078), entitled *Of Daemons According to the Dogma of the Greeks*. He would prepare himself by fasting for three days to disconnect from the corporeal energies of the body. He would also abstain from sex to build his psychic energies and direct them upwards towards the ethereal plane. Night is preferable for the conjuration of spirits. The weather should not be stormy, too windy, or disturbed by the shadows of moving clouds. Great care must also be taken to astrologically plot the right hour for conjuring each specific class of spirit messenger: the archangels, angels, heroes, and elemental daemons.

PF91-93   Before entering his secret study he would bathe himself in consecrated water, don a simple robe, and take up a laurel branch as his magic wand. He would enter a consecrated circle drawn in the center of the wooden floor and perhaps illuminated by candles. The circle protected him from the divine emissaries about to be conjured. The passage that runs from PF91 to 97 focuses primarily on the angelic and daemonic messengers of fire and their different qualities of divine *exterior* (ie, nonphysical) light, although Iamblinchus and King Solomon also describe the invocation of spirits of water, earth, air, and ether. Nostradamus was known to love the hot and dry climates of his native Provence; perhaps he had his best success with the *fiery missives* of angelic spirits.

PF94   His incantations for spirit communication are mostly derived from the *Keys of Solomon*. It is possible he uttered them in Hebrew rather than Latin. The magical tools and disciplines he may have used within the circle to bring himself into a trance

PF95 *eſt par trop euidēte, le tout eſtre predict par afflation de diuinité, & par le moyen de l'eſprit angelique inſpiré à l'homme prophetiſant,*

is very evident. All is predicted through divine inspiration, and by means of the angelic spirit inspiring the man who is prophesying,

PF96 *rendāt oinctes de vaticinations le venāt à illuminer, lui eſmouuant le deuant de la phantaſie par diuerſes nocturnes apparitions, que par*

rendering him anointed with prophecies, illuminating him, moving him before his fantasy through diverse nocturnal apparitions. By

PF97 *diurne certitude prophetiſe par adminiſtration Aſtronomique, conioincte de la ſanctißime future prediction, ne conſiderant ailleurs qu'au courage libre.*

daytime he can certify the prophecy through astronomical calculations, combining the most holy future prediction with nothing more than free courage.

PF98 *Viens à ceſte heure entendre, mon fils, que ie trouue par mes reuolutions qui ſont accordantes à reuelee inſpiration, que le mortel*

See now, my son, that I find by my calculations, which are according to revealed inspiration, that

were varied, although most of them required the discipline of scrying – gazing on certain objects without blinking. Some believe he sat in his observatory gazing at the reflection of stars in a dark bowl of water, whereas it is clear that he used hydromancy extensively when in the magic circle of his study (for details see 1 Q1,2) and to a lesser extent may have gazed at a flame or peered into the deep and polished surface of a lead or pewter mirror.

PF95 The most famous and controversial Assyrian technique comes from his study of Psellus, who wrote:

> Thus those about to prophesy take a basin full of water which attracts the spirits creeping stealthily in the depths. The basin then full of water [to the brim] seems ... to breathe as with sounds; it seems to me that the water was agitated with circular ripples as from some sound emitted below.

PF96 > Now this water diffused through the basin differs but little in kind from water out of the basin, but yet it much excels it from a virtue imparted to it by the incantations which have rendered it more apt to receive the spirit of prophecy. For this description of spirit is peevish and earth-bound and much under the influence of composite spells.

PF97 > When the water begins to lend itself as the vehicle of sound, the spirit also presently gives out a thin, reedy note but devoid of meaning; and close upon that, while the water is undulating, certain weak and peeping sounds whisper forth predictions of the future.

At sunrise our seer would cease his magical and subjective communications with spirits to the testing and interpretation of the previous night's visions with judicial astrological calculations.

PF98 At first light he would move from the magic circle over to his writing desk where he would set to work translating his visions into prose, using consecrated paper and a pen made from the third feather of the right wing of a white male gosling, ceremoniously plucked.

Only on the first rewrite would Nostradamus cloak his notes into obscure and coded four-line poems. He made sure the prophecies were out of sequence. Legend states that he wrote each quatrain on a single piece of paper and had Chavigny, his disciple, toss them in the air to be gathered in whatever order they fell. Although many Nostradamians down through the centuries want to believe he hid his original notes for later discovery, it is more likely he consigned them to the flames of his alchemical furnace once the quatrains were written.

PF99 *glaiue s'approche de nous maintenant, par pefte, guerre plus horrible qu'à vie de trois hommes n'a efté, & famine, lequel tombera en terre, &*

the sword of death is approaching us now through plague and war more horrible than has been seen in the life of three generations, and famine, which will fall upon the earth, and

PF100 *y retournera fouuent, car les Aftres s'accordant à la reuolution, & außi a dict:* Vifitabo in virga ferrea iniquitates eorum, & in verberibus percutiam eos.

return there often, according to the cycles of the stars, and likewise to the saying: I will visit their iniquities with a rod of iron, and will strike them with blows (adapted from Psalm 89:32)

PF101 *car la mifericorde de Dieu ne fera point defpergee vn temps, mon fils, que la plufpart de mes Propheties feront accomplies, & viendront eftre par accompliffement reuolues.*

For the mercy of God shall not be extended at all for a time, my son, until most of my prophecies will have been accomplished, and will by accomplishment have become resolved.

PF102 *Alors par plufieurs fois durant les finiftres tempeftes* Conteram ego, *dira le Seigneur,* & confringam, & non miferebor, *& mille autres*

Then several times during the sinister tempests, I will trample them, the Lord will say, and break them, and not show pity (adapted from Isaiah 63:3). And thousands of other

PF103 *aduentures qui aduiendront par eaux & continuelles pluyes, comme plus à plain i'ay redigé par efcrit aux miennes autres Propheties qui font*

events will come to pass, because of floods and continual rains, as I have set forth more fully in writing my other Prophecies, which are

PF104 *compofees tout au long,* in foluta oratione, *limitant les lieux, temps & le terme prefix que les humains apres venus verront, cognoiffant*

drawn out at length in prose, defining the places, times and appointed duration so that men coming after will see them, knowing

PF105 *les aduentures aduenues infailliblement, comme auons noté par les autres, parlant plus clairement: nonobftant que foubs nuee feront*

PF99   In PF99 through PF101 Nostradamus uses his *free*, or liberated
       courage to delve one last time into the future.

    A generation lasts from 20 to 30 years. **Three generations'**
time, therefore, covers between 60 and 90 years. His vision of terrible wars and famines may best describe the 90 years of religious
wars approaching France, the Netherlands and Central Europe a
little less than a decade after this was written. They were the
Wars of Religion, 1562–1598; the Eighty Years War, 1568–1648;
and the Thirty Years War, 1618–1648, respectively.

PF100 Other 90-year windows of war and famine may also apply. Our
       own times better match his lurid forecast of catastrophic wars and
       global famine. One could place the window from 1914 through
       2004 and cover both world wars and the 16 million to 20 million
       people so far slaughtered in regional conflicts fought during the
       Cold War. Or one could move the window forward and start count-
       ing from World War II (1939) to the global wars Nostradamus
       and other prophets warn will roil across the world in our over-
       populated, famine-stretched civilization of the 2020s. As we will
       see later, Nostradamus gives indications that we might not be
       smitten with the **rod of iron** of World War III until the 2020s.

PF101 Here Nostradamus uses the word **resolved** rather than "fulfilled."
       This, together with the reference to the **accomplishment** of
       prophecies, intimates to me that there is more than mere fulfill-
       ment involved here. The prophecies and their obscurity are a
       device for conjuring a response in the reader far more subtle than
       foreseeing events.

PF102 But this mystery and the enigma of thousands of other events
       await further clarification once we begin our examination of
       his 1,109 quatrains and second prophetic letter, the *Epistle to
       Henry II*.

PF103 Nostradamus is coy with his grammar, making it unclear whether
       these **other prophecies**, which are **drawn out at length** in prose,
       are from his prognostications in the early almanacs of 1550–1555,
       or whether he is describing the original prose notes written after
       magical sessions in his secret study.

PF104–105   Well, the claim of infallibility is a stretch. This may be
       another return of the not-too-subtle snake-oil pitch we find in his
       medical confitures and recipe books. If by prose prophecies he is
       speaking of just his almanac prose predictions, this could refute
       the theory expressed by many scholars that his almanac prose
       prophecies and the 141 Presages in his later almanacs limit them-
       selves only to the near-future events of Nostradamus' day.

the events to have occurred infallibly; such as those others we have noted, speaking more clearly – for although they are written under a cloud

PF106   *comprinſes les intelligences: ſed quando ſubmouenda erit ignorantia, le cas ſera plus eſclarci.*

the meanings will be understood. When the time comes for the removal of ignorance, *the situation will be cleared up still more*.

PF107   *Faiſant fin, mon fils, prens donc ce don de ton pere Michel Noſtradamus, eſperant toy declarer vne chacune Prophetie des quatrains icy mis.*

I make an end here, my son. Take then this gift of your father, Michel Nostradamus, who hopes to make known to you each prophecy from the quatrains introduced here.

PF108   *Priant au Dieu immortel, qu'il te veuille preſter vie longue, en bonne & proſpere felicité.*

I beseech the immortal God, that he will be willing to bestow upon you long life, in good and prosperous happiness.

PF109   *De Salon ce 1 de Mars, 1555.*

From Salon this first of March, 1555.

PF106 Nostradamus closes the Preface by promising that his cloudy prophecies will be understood at the appropriate time, when a new spiritual understanding embraces humanity. Perhaps this will come as soon as the next century when the Golden Age of Aquarius is expected to bring down the dogma-bound religions of the world. Rather than being a member of a religion, people of the Aquarian Age will simply be religious.

Those of the coming eighth millenium (AD 2000 through 3000) will understand the devices, metaphors and, in some cases, the prophetic practical joke of Nostradamus' writings. By that time the human race will be more in balance in its objective and subjective natures, and will be able to weave the opposites of magic and science into complementaries rather than feeling split by them as polarities.

PF107–109 Before he signs off with a parental blessing, Nostradamus expresses the hope that, to his son – and perhaps all the "sons" and "daughters" of future generations who study his prophecies – his spirit will *make known* the secrets of his 36,000-word history of the future.

Century I

1 Q1

Estant afsis de nuict fecret eftude
Seul reposé[1] fur la felle d'ærain:
Flambe exigue[2] fortant de folitude
Fait profperer qui n'eft à croire vain.

Being seated at night in secret study
Meditating alone upon the brass tripod:
A minute flame comes forth from the
solitude
Making successful that which should
not be believed in vain.

[1]To repose, to pause; to settle; (poetic) to contemplate, meditate.
[2]*Flambe exigue*: (conventional) Latin *exiguus* = very small, minute, slender, or thin; minute flame (occult) one's spark of divine consciousness witnessing existence from the center of the cyclone of one's emotions and thoughts.

The first two quatrains launch the *Les Propheties* with a cryptic story of Nostradamus' nocturnal occult ritual in which he sets aside his normal mental and emotional limitations to awaken his prophetic powers.

The ritual is similar to the rite of the ancient Greek sibylline oracles of Branchus. He is alone at the dead of night in his secret study on the top floor of his house in Salon, sitting in deep meditation on a brass tripod. At last he becomes aware of the gap of consciousness, the slender flame of divine witnessing. The many days of purification, fasting, and magical preparation have not been endured in vain.

See Index: minute/slender flame.

1 Q2

Laverge en main mife au milieu de
BRANCHES[1]
De l'onde il moulle & le limbe[2] & le
pied:
Un peur & voix fremiffent par les
manches:
Splendeur diuine. Le diuin pres s'afsied.

The divining wand in hand is placed in
the middle of Branchus;
With water he moistens the hem (of his
robe) and foot.
Fear! A voice quivers through his long
sleeves:
Divine splendor. The divine one sits
near by.

[1]**BRANCHES**: a) the three legs, or branches, of the tripod; b) indirect reference to the sibylline oracles of Branchus; c) (myth.) Branchus, son of Apollo, the sun god patron of poetry and prophecy. He entered mortal life through his mother's mouth and later met his divine father in a forest. Upon kissing his father he attained the gift of divine prophecy. The Brachidae, his legendary descendants, were the priests and priestesses of the oracle at the temple of Apollo at Didyma near Miletus in Asia Minor.
[2]Latin *limbus* = the hem of a garment.

The following words within Nostradamus' magical bible *De mysteriis Aegyptiorum*, best describe the customized ritual used here. He has taken the role of the prophetess being possessed by a god and has incorporated aspects from the oracular traditions of both Delphi and Brachidae (note the underlined words that parallel those he uses in 1 Q1 and 1 Q2):

> . . . the prophetess of Delphi, whether she gives oracles to mankind through an attenuated and fiery spirit, bursting from the mouth [or sulfuric vent] of the cavern, or whether being seated in the adytum on a <u>brass tripod</u> . . . becomes sacred to the God . . . she entirely gives herself up to a <u>divine</u> spirit, and is illuminated with a ray of divine fire. And when . . . fire ascending from the mouth of the cavern circularly invests her in collected abundance, she becomes filled from it with a <u>divine splendor</u>. But when she places herself on <u>the seat of the God</u>, she becomes coadapted to his stable prophetic power: and from both these preparatory operations she becomes wholly possessed by the God. And then . . . he is present with and illuminates her in a separate manner, and is different from the fire, the spirit, the proper seat, and, in short, from all the visible apparatus of the place, whether physical or sacred.
>
> The prophetic woman too in <u>Brachidae</u> whether <u>she holds in her hand a wand</u>, which was at first received from some God, and becomes filled with a <u>divine splendor</u>, or whether <u>seated on an axis</u>, she predicts future events, or <u>dips her feet or the border of her garment in the water</u>, or receives the God by imbibing the vapor of the water; by all these she becomes adapted to partake of a metaphysical illumination of the God.

Our prophet sits upon a tripod in front of a brass bowl filled to the brim with steaming water made pungent with stimulating oils and perhaps lightly narcotic herbs. This is done to imitate the vapors from the volcanic fissure that the Delphic oracle imbibed to prepare for her possession by a god. Between deep inhalations of perfumed vapor he chants magic incantations and feels the minute flame of divine fire penetrate his soul. At the right moment, Nostradamus dips his wand, a laurel branch, into the brass bowl. He anoints his foot and the hem of his robe. A sudden rush of paranormal energy into his body is at first frightening, but he surrenders himself to it and is transported by ecstasy. The voice of a higher entity vibrates inside him. Is it his own inner consciousness, or is it the spirit of Branchus himself, come to do our prophet's bidding? The prophet does not record an answer. He lowers a consecrated pen to parchment and begins to write a history of the future, as it is told by the hushed voice of his divine messenger.

1 Q3

Quand la lictiere du tourbillon verſee,	**When the litter is overturned by a whirlwind**
Et ſeront faces de leurs manteaux couuers:	**And the faces are covered by their cloaks,**
La republique par gens nouueaux vexée,	**The republic will be troubled by new people:**
Lors blancs & rouges iugeront à l'enuers.	**Then whites and reds will judge wrongly.**

Many of Nostradamus' finest predictions are about the period of the French Revolution. We can feel, in the language and tone of Revolution quatrains the prophet's horror and disbelief as well as his struggle to understand the vision of chaos and blood that has come to him. Twice he refers to it as a *whirlwind*, a description that may not be just a metaphor but an attempt to date the Revolution. On 13 July 1788, exactly one year before the storming of the Bastille, France was visited by a violent windstorm, one of the worst ever recorded. Named the Great Tornado of 1788 by contemporary journals, this cyclonic storm rained hail the size of acorns and unleashed a phalanx of tornadoes that cut a swath of destruction from Tours, Chartres, and Paris, through Lille and into Belgium.

If Nostradamus had intended the meteorological and social whirlwind to be one and the same, he can be excused for blending two events into one. His vision of the *common people* (PF17) overturning the litters of the aristocracy was recorded 235 years earlier.

The irresistible storm of revolution would force the aristocracy to leave France as refugees, their faces covered by cloaks on the windy passage across the English Channel, or leave life with their heads *covered by cloaks* carried away from the guillotine within a bloody wicker basket. *Whites* are the Bourbons, whose cockade was white. They ignored the needs of their people and brought disaster upon themselves. *Reds* signifies the revolutionaries, for that color was as symbolic of rebellion in Nostradamus' time as it is in our own.

See Index: French Revolution.

1 Q4

Par l'vniuers¹ sera faict vn monarque,	In the whole world there will be one monarch,
Qu'en paix & vie ne sera longuement,	Whose life and peace will not be for long,
Lors se perdra la piscature barque,²	Then the fishing bark [of Peter?] will be lost,
Sera regie en plus grand detriment.	It will be ruled to its greater detriment.

¹Old French *univers* = the whole world, the universe.
²Latin *piscatura* = a) fishing bark; the bark of St Peter, symbolic of Pope and Vatican; b) Peter of Rome, the last pope before doomsday, as predicted in 1139 by the Irish prophet St Malachy. This appears to be a shared vision recorded by St Malachy and Nostradamus, though separated by four centuries. It is doubtful Nostradamus ever saw Malachy's manuscript, as it was only rediscovered in the Vatican library in 1595, 40 years after the prophet published this quatrain.

The monarch is a pope. Not of Nostradamus' time but of ours, and he could be the last pope before doomsday. His reign is short and his portion of inner peace far shorter. The *fishing bark* symbolizes the papacy. It is the *bark* of the first pope, the fisherman from Galilee, St Peter. In this case it could stand for the Vatican or indirectly clue us in to the name of the last pope, named after the first, who will steer the ship of the Holy See into the rocks of the Apocalypse in our near future. This is the first of several prophecies in which Nostradamus echoes a medieval seer he never met or read, St Malachy of Ireland. The tone of this quatrain written in 1554 parallels a prophecy recorded 415 years earlier, when St Malachy was on the last leg of his pilgrimage to Rome in 1139. On first sighting the Eternal City stretched out below, he immediately fell to the ground in an ecstatic trance. He lay there for hours murmuring cryptic Latin phrases, which his attendant recorded for posterity. Each of Malachy's phrases signifies either the name, heraldic device or background of all the 111 popes, from his contemporary, Celestinus II, until Judgement Day. He closes with a paragraph on the tragic reign of the final pope, of whom he said:

> During the last persecution of the Holy Roman Church, there shall sit Petrus Romanus [Peter of Rome], who shall feed the sheep amid great tribulations, and when these have passed, the City of the Seven Hills shall be utterly destroyed, and the awful Judge will judge the people.

After Pope John Paul II passes away, only two popes will follow, according to Malachy's list. Nostradamus, writing at a time a little closer to the latter days perhaps uncovers one more important detail: Peter of Rome is partly responsible for guiding the papacy to its ruin (*it will be ruled to its greater detriment*).

See Index: Peter of Rome (the last pope).

1 Q5

Chaſſés ſeront pour faire long combat,	They will be driven away on account of a long battle;
Par le pays ſeront plus fort greués:	
Bourg & cité auront plus grand debat,	They will be very much overpowered in the countryside,
Carcaſ.[1] Narbonne auront cœur eſ prouuez.	Town and city will have the greater struggle,
	Carcassonne and Narbonne will have their hearts tested.

[1] Apocope of *Carcassonne*.

Although the prophecies *Les Propheties* are out of time sequence, Nostradamus would have ensured that his contemporary readers would soon encounter the visions he had risked his life to publish. **They** are the French people, who are a few years away from fighting the first of nine civil wars known as the Wars of Religion. This conflict would pit Huguenots (French Protestants) and Catholics in a **long battle** for the sacred throne of God and the temporal throne of France from 1562 through 1598. *They* in line 2 are his contemporary readers, the literate and upper-class country gentry, who will not be able to travel safely in the countryside without risking their life and limb as well as their goods from roving bands of Catholic or Protestant thugs. *They* are also his readers and their children in cities throughout France who in the years to come would suffer a **greater struggle** in which many would die in waves of nationwide massacres.

In the final line Nostradamus accurately cites Carcassone and Narbonne as targets for future civil strife. These are the same cities where as a young man he healed the sick. History tells us that when the Catholic majority in Carcassonne declared itself for the Catholic League, the Huguenots seized part of the town. Narbonne would become another center of religiously inspired massacres.

See Index: Wars of Religion; St Bartholomew's Day Massacre.

1 Q6

L'œil de Rauenne fera deſtitué,	**The eye of Ravenna will be impoverished,**
Quand à ſes pieds les ælles failliront:	**When the wings will give way at his feet:**
Les deux de Breſſe auront conſtitué,	**The two of Bresse will have made a constitution,**
Turin, Derſeil que Gaulois fouleront.	**For Turin, Vercelli, which the French will trample.**

Nostradamus offers here a geography lesson in the French occupation of Italian kingdoms. Ravenna has belonged to the Papal States since 1509. All the other localities were under French occupation in 1555, although they belonged to the Duke of Savoy. Bresse was occupied from 1535, lost in 1559, recaptured in 1595, and finally ceded to France in 1601. Turin found itself a captive host of the French 1506–62, 1640, and 1798–1814. Vercelli was occupied 1553–56, 1704, and 1798–1814. With all this data repeated by numerous Nostradamus scholars, still living and long dead, not much more can be made of it, except that Edgar Leoni believes the *eye* of Ravenna must be whoever was pope in 1555. This makes things more confusing because the year contained three popes: Julius III died in March, Marcellus II lasted 26 days from 9 April to 1 May before dying of a stroke, then Paul IV was chosen on 23 May.

1 Q7

Tard arriué l'execution faicte,	**Arrived too late. The act already**
Le vent contraire lettres au chemin	**done.**
prinſes:	**The wind was against them. The**
Les coniurez xiiij. d'vne ſecte:	**letters intercepted on the way:**
Par le Rouſſeau ſenez les entreprinſes.[1]	**Fourteen conspirators of a party,**
	By Rousseau [the red-haired one] the
	enterprise will be undertaken.

[1]Enterprise, undertaking; (negative) usurpation, encroachment.

Before America had its Watergate, France had its "Dreyfus-Gate." In 1894 the noble mask of French chauvinism slipped, revealing its anti-Semitic face in the sensational conspiracy and trial of the unjustly accused Jewish army officer Alfred Dreyfus. The conspiracy, which haunts the French legal system to this day, haunted Nostradamus 340 years before it happened. He gives an accurate account of the trial and was a better judge of Dreyfus' innocence than the avowed anti-Semite judge of the case, Waldeck Rousseau, whom the prophet names outright.

We can only wonder what Dreyfus' staunch defender, the eminent writer and thinker Émile Zola, would have thought of this quatrain had he been aware of it and had he been as avid a fan of Nostradamus as his near-contemporary, Victor Hugo.

After the first trial convicted Dreyfus of espionage and treason and sent him to the notorious prison on Devil's Island, new evidence arrived that proved Dreyfus had not sent secret documents to Germany. Zola and others pressed for a retrial and eventually, in 1899, the government appointed Waldeck Rousseau to reexamine the Dreyfus Case.

Details of the second conspiracy, or "Waldeck-Gate," surface in the lines of this quatrain. Line 1: **Arrived too late. The act already done.** The evidence had come too late to save Dreyfus from Devil's Island. Both trials were famous for their anti-Semitic overtones. There may be a hidden pun in the first phrase **arrived too late**. It implies a missed "schedule," namely a *bordereau*, as the infamous letter disclosing French military secrets to the German military attaché in Paris was called.

Line 2's cliché describes the difficulties of his defense attorneys: **The wind was against them.** Waldeck Rousseau found Dreyfus guilty a second time, but on the strength of Émile Zola's crusade for justice, Dreyfus was pardoned by President Loubet. A new investigation uncovered the true criminals and proved the letters incriminating Dreyfus were forgeries.

Line 3 may refer to the number of conspirators (14), although it is not known exactly how many there were. In line 4, Nostradamus, the Christian-ized Jew and prophet, may be accusing the noted anti-Semitic judge of being part of the conspiracy: **By Rousseau the enterprise will be undertaken.**

1 Q8

Combien de fois prinſe cité ſolaire[1]	How often will you be captured, O city
Seras changeant les loys barbares &	of the sun?
vaines:	Changing the laws that are barbaric
Ton mal s'approche. Plus ſeras tributaire,	and vain:
La grand Hadrie[2] recourira tes veines.	Evil times approach you. No longer will
	you be enslaved,
	The great Hadrie will revive your veins.

[1]cité solaire (the City of the Sun) always means Paris.
[2]Anagram: ad Henri = Latin towards or to Henri. Anagram rules allow the i to be replaced by
y and the letter n to be added to H-e-(n)-r-y.

Paris, the City of the Sun, as it would be named a century after the grim event foreshadowed by this quatrain, has known many conquests and sieges. In 1590 it faced the most crippling siege of any city in Europe since the siege of Constantinople in the 15th century. Between May through August royalist forces under Henry IV surrounded the city. Within a week bread disappeared from the diet. Contemporaries estimate that 5,000 to 12,000 people died of starvation. Some people were reduced to eating candle wax; others considered milling bones from cemeteries to make their bread. There were reports of cannibalism.

The gift of foresight may allow the melancholy prophet to see that evil times eventually do pass. He correctly forecasts the end of Parisian suffering when the **barbaric and vain** laws belonging to the Seize (sixteen) Parliamentarians are overturned. In the 1580s the ministers of the sixteen districts of Paris joined together to make the first of several attempts in Parisian history to establish a cult republic by commune – a concept the royalist prophet found horrifying. Good fortune would come for Paris and all of France in the double meaning of **revive your veins**. Towards the end of the six-month siege, Henry – pained by the suffering of its starving citizens – sent food into Paris. Later, as undisputed king, he would **revive** the French people with peace and prosperity.

See Index: Hadrie/Henry IV.

1 Q9

De l'Orient viendra le cœur Punique[1]	From the East will come a treacherous
Faſcher Hadrie & les hoirs Romulides	act
Accompagné de la claſſe[2] Libyque	To vex Hadrie and the heirs of
Temples Mellites[3] & proches iſles vuides.	Romulus [Italy].
	Accompanied by the Libyan fleet,
	The temples of the Maltese
	[trembling] and its islands emptied.

[1]La coeur Punique = the Punic heart, (16th-c. col.) treachery.
[2]Latin classis = fleet, army.
[3]People of Malta.

Interpreters target this dual prophecy for various times. The near-contemporary would view the **treacherous act** in the **East** to be the fall of Famagusta, the Cypriot capital, to the Ottoman Turks in 1573, 18 years after this quatrain was published. **Hadrie** in that case is a cryptogram for the Adriatic Sea, and by extension Venice, whose galleys, along with those of other seafaring Italian kingdoms, will end their war with the Turks in 1573. The final two lines move backwards to events eight years closer to the publication of this quatrain, when the Ottoman Turks laid siege to Malta in 1565. Much of their fleet and transports were galleys supplied by their allies the Barbary (**Libyan**) Corsairs.

Nostradamus diviners of the following French generation would pin this quatrain to Henry IV sometime betweeen 1589 and 1594 during the climax of the ninth and final War of Religion. This time the eastern threat is not against the Adriatic Venice but against **Hadrie**, the seer's anagram for Henry IV, who is forced to lift the siege of Paris in 1590 to face a Spanish relief army marching from the east out of Flanders, commanded by the Duke of Parma. This Spanish maneuver annoyed at least one heir of Romulus, the pope, who was warming to the idea of Henry IV on the French throne. But even the future generation agree that the final two lines fit with the siege of Malta in 1565.

Modern Nostradamus watchers would stretch his prophetic reach much further. A number of them – such as Jean-Charles de Fontbrune – see a future Muslim invasion coming from the East that will trigger World War III. However, the idea that great hordes of neo-Ottoman Turks and neo-Barbary/Libyan Corsairs will invade European Christendom in the early 21st century seems a little far-fetched.

In my interpretation I would at least agree that the eastern threat should remain Middle Eastern, since the Old French meaning for *Orient* denoted the lands of the Eastern Mediterranean. But as far as I see it, no Islamic fundamentalist hordes are amassing to vex future popes or deposit millions of soldiers on the shores of the Adriatic Sea. Rather, the invasion is less ambitious, less pan-Arab and monolithic, and more the activity of a handful of fanatics armed with weapons of mass destruction. In modern terms this **Libyan fleet** consists of several Soviet-style submarines in Muhammar Qadaffi's navy making a nuclear terrorist attack on Italy's shores. Nostradamus' astrological clues set this potential event for either 1996 or 1999 or in the 2020s and 2030s, when the sun and Saturn are undergoing their annual opposition – a pretty general call which has already missed several predicted windows in time.

See Index: submarines.

1 Q10

Serpens[1] tranſmis dans la caige de fer, | The serpent's coffin is put in a vault
Ou les enfans ſeptains[2] du Roy ſont pris: | of iron,
Les vieux & peres ſortiront bas de l'enfer, | Where seven children of the King are
Ains mourir voir de fruict mort & crys. | held:
| Their ancestors will rise from the
| depths of hell,
| Before dying lamenting at seeing the
| fruits of their line dead.

[1]Serpent: a) *sarpos* = derived from Greek meaning coffin; b) symbolic for Catherine de' Medici.
[2]Latin *septeni* = the seven.

After the death of her husband, Henry II, in 1559, Catherine de' Medici changed her heraldic emblem to a serpent with its tail in its mouth. Ever the occult student, she was aware of the symbolic message of the serpent ring of power. If great power corresponds to temperance and wisdom balanced, the serpent holds its tail – but if the balance is lost, the serpent devours itself. By choosing this emblem Catherine showed herself aware of the dangers ahead as matriarch of her seven notorious children:

Francis II (1543–60): Francis died of the fainting sickness six weeks before his eighteenth birthday.

Elizabeth (1545–68): Married to Philip II of Spain, she showed signs of being a great queen but died while giving birth at 22.

Claude (1547–75) This hunchbacked princess also died in childbirth at 28.

Charles IX (1550–74): A king who delighted himself during royal hunts by hacking off the heads of donkeys and pigs with a single blow. He transferred his cruelty to humans by sanctioning the St Bartholomew's Day Massacre two years before his death at 24 from a cold. During the massacre he was seen shooting fleeing Protestants for sport.

Henry III (1551–89) He was King of Poland as well as France. The universally unpopular bisexual ruler was assassinated in his bed-chamber by a Franciscan monk named Clément.

Marguerite (1553–1615): "Little Margot" grew up in disgrace. Her husband Henry de Navarre spurned her for her rampant nympho-mania. She died childless at 53, thereby extinguishing the House of Valois.

Hercules (1554–1584): The brutish Duc d'Alençon was the laughing-stock of Europe for courting the "virgin" Queen Elizabeth I of England. He conspired to kill his brother Henry but died – to even his mother's relief – from a sudden illness.

1 Q11

Le mouuement de ſens, cœur, pieds &
    mains,
Seront d'accord Naples, Lyon, Sicille:
Glaiues, feux, eaux puis aux nobles
    Romains,
Plongez tuez mors par cerueau debile.
	The motion of sense, heart, feet and
	    hands,
	Will be in accord [between] Naples,
	    Leon, Sicily:
	Swords, fires, waters, then the noble
	    Romans,
	Drowned, killed or dead because of a
	    feeble mind.

A contemporary interpretation has Naples, Leon and Sicily all belonging to the Spanish Habsburg Empire. Spanish and Sicilian troops exploit the feeble-brained leadership of the pope and launch an attack on Rome. This is an example of what we often find in Nostradamus: an essentially accurate prophecy cloaked in exaggerations. The Duke of Alva would make a demonstrational march on Rome a year after the publication of this quatrain, but the magnitude of death and destruction is more the product of Nostradamus' melancholic mirror-gazing than what actually happened.

An interpretation that better suits the exaggerations is Fontbrune's application of this quatrain to Garibaldi's attack on Rome via Naples in 1867, and his defeat by the hands of the **noble Romans** of the Franco-Papal Army at Mentana. Fontbrune makes this work by turning *Lyon* into the British "Lion" who was in accord with Garibaldi's failed invasion. The "feeble-minded" fellow is Francis II, the last king of the Two Sicilies (consisting of the Kingdom of Naples and of Sicily), who was banished from Naples in 1860. After his exile, the Kingdom of Italy annexed the Kingdom of Two Sicilies in 1861.

1 Q12

Dans peu dira[1] faulce brute fragile,
De bas en hault eſleué promptement:
Puis en iſtant deſloyale & labile,
Qui de Veronne aura gouuernement.
	In a short time a false, frail brute will
	    lead,
	Elevated quickly from low to high:
	Then in an instant disloyal and
	    slippery,
	He who will have the government of
	    Verona.

[1]Old French *duire* = to lead, to govern.

This is about Verona. The generalities can embrace the intrigues of this Italian town from 1555 until terrestrial doomsday in AD 3797. We know that one Jacopo San Sebastiani held the post of captain of Verona from 1539 to 1562. This time frame would place him in Verona during any of Nostradamus' travels through Italy. Perhaps this opinion of Captain

Jacopo is more personal than prophetic. Was he an early debunker of our prophet? Nostradamus sometimes foretells doom and gloom for those who have slighted him; in most of these cases anger gets the better of his augury. We will see him castigate and prophetically pummel John Calvin, but he hardly ever scores a knockdown.

1 Q13

Les exilez par ire, haine inteſtine,	**The exiles because of anger and**
Feront au Roy grand coniuration:	**internal hatred**
Secret mettront ennemis par la mine,[1]	**Will inflict a great conspiracy against**
Et ſes vieux ſiens contre eux ſedition.	**the King:**
	Secretly they will place enemies as a
	threat,
	And his own old ones, sedition
	against them.

[1]Latin *mina* = threat.

Another prophecy fulfilled in Nostradamus' lifetime, five years after publishing *Les Propheties*, is that of the Conspiracy of Amboise in 1560. There was no love lost between France's three most powerful clans – the Bourbons, Montmorencys, and the Guise. The Bourbons, being a greater-noble house equal to the Royal House of the Valois, were in direct line by blood for the throne. The sudden death of Henry II left them licking their lips in expectation as the sickly heir, Francis II, limped into the new decade. The lesser-noble house of Montmorency plotted with the Bourbons and the king, hedging their bets to become chief advisor to whichever grand noble family – whether the current Valois or the ambitious Bourbons – triumphed in the power struggle. Both the Bourbons and Montmorencys detested the even-lesser-noble clan of Guise which, through luck, guile, and a commoner's touch, had acquired the most influence on the young king as his protectors and advisors. The Guise were best positioned and least qualified by royal bloodline to take the throne if Francis should fall victim to the fainting sickness. Before that happened the Guise must be physically removed from his side.

The Montmorencys and Bourbons joined in a conspiracy to send an army of several hundred selected men to seize the Château Amboise, capture Francis II, and murder the Guise to "save France". An informant in their camp leaked the plot, allowing François de Guise, the Lieutenant-General of France, to summon French military forces to "protect the king from seditionists." Many of the leaders of the conspiracy were rounded up and executed. An exultant François de Guise decorated the Château walls with their corpses.

The Queen Regent, Catherine de' Medici, who was no friend of the

Bourbons or Montmorencys, was equally threatened by the swaggering Guise. She pardoned many of the key perpetrators, such as Antoine de Bourbon, King of Navarre, and the Prince de Condé. Now they were beholden to her for their lives, and she could use this new allegiance to offset the power of the Guise.

1 Q14

De gent eſclaue[1] chanſons, chants & *requeſtes,*	**From the enslaved people, songs,** **chants and demands,**
Captifs par Princes & Seigneur aux *priſons:*	**The princes and lords are held** **captive in prisons:**
A l'aduenir par idiotz ſans teſtes,	**In the future by such headless idiots**
Seront receus par diuines oraiſons.	**These [demands] will be taken as** **divine utterances.**

[1]Old French *esclave* = a) enslaved; b) *Esclavonia*, or Slavonia, an ancient name for Russia, the land of the Slavs.

Étienne Jaubert (1656) thought this was a near-contemporary prediction of the Huguenots' attempt during Nostradamus' time to revolutionize the Catholic ritual, which brought upon them a string of massacres. Anatole Le Pelletier (1867) is the first to apply it to the French Revolution. Leoni and other latter-day scholars, including myself, see this as an intriguing double prophecy for both the French and Russian Revolutions.

It appears that Nostradamus heard and saw the tattered Paris mob of a distant century marching through the narrow streets, yelling popular slogans or singing *La Marseillaise*. Their contemporary rivals called men like Danton and Robespierre maniacs. To Nostradamus they are **headless idiots**, a pun on their character and on their violent fate. Add to this the indexing of the quatrain as 14, which could stand for the date the Bastille was stormed, 14 July 1789.

In the steaming waters of his prophetic bowl, Nostradamus saw the locations changing but the themes of history repeating themselves. Narrow Parisian streets and alleys gave way to the frozen boulevards of Moscow, and the song of revolutionary fervor changed from *La Marseillaise* to the *L'Internationale*. *Esclave* in the first line now means "enslaved" or, more literally, "Slav."

Once again a monarchy and aristocracy is under threat, and a new breed of "headless idiots" imprison and kill a royal family. The new revolutionary leaders – Lenin, Trotsky and other Bolsheviks – are later purged themselves in a new Reign of Terror masterminded by a modern Napoleon/Robespierre, Josef Stalin.

Quatrain Indexing Date: Sometimes the quatrain number can represent a compound date. On 14 July, the Bastille was attacked, launching the French Revolution of 1789–1799. In the year (19)14, Imperial Russia entered World War I, setting in motion the disasters that would lead to the Russian Revolution of 1917.

See Index: French Revolution; Russian Revolution; communism, fall of.

1 Q15

Mars nous menaſſe par la force bellique,[1]	**Mars, you menace by the force of**
Septante foys ſera le ſang eſpandre:	**war,**
Auge[2] *& ruyne de l'Eccleſiaſtique,*	**Seventy times will he cause blood to**
Et plus ceux qui d'eux rien voudront	**be shed:**
entendre.	**Increase and ruin for the Clergy,**
	And more for those who will desire to
	hear nothing from them.

[1]Latin *bellicus* = warlike.
[2]Latin *auge*, from *augere* = to increase.

In early 1995 the Worldwatch Institute reported that the planet has endured 148 wars since the end of World War II. In 1995, there were 34 to 36 wars being fought simultaneously. And the number is increasing. Nostradamus seems to predict a future year when 70 wars will plague Earth at the same time. The pressures these conflicts place upon the priesthood of the Catholic Church will be overwhelming. The last line intimates that the demands for assistance will fall even harder on the Protestant missions in Russia and the developing world, and also sorely tax the charity missions of other mainstream and non-Christian priest-hoods of the Hindus, Buddhists, and Muslims.

Astrological Time Windows
Wars often erupt on Earth when Mars is in either Aries (the god of war) or in Leo (the god of megalomania if in negative aspect). The possible windows for World War III as a plague of 70 ethnic wars on Earth are:

World War III for the 1990s and the Millennium: (Aries) April–May 1996 [China threatened Taiwan, Israel attacked Lebanon]; (Leo) October 1996; (Aries) March–April 1998 [with Saturn!]; (Leo) August–October 1998; (Aries) February–March 2000; August–September 2000; and so on.

World War III in the early 21st century: In the 21st century I would expect the highest potential for war when Mars enters Aries at the same time Saturn enters its two-year transit of Leo (2005–2007), and again when Mars is in Leo in June–July 2006, and in Aries again at the end of the Saturn transit of Leo in May–June 2007.

World War III window for 2020s–2030s: The next time Mars aspects Aries
and Leo several times during a Saturn–Leo transit (August 2034–October
2036) is during the final degrees of Neptune's transit of Aries. In my
opinion, this is the most dangerous time for a Third World War in the
next century because it would come when the planet's ecological food
and water sustainability reached a critical stress point due to pollution
and overpopulation. This final and deadly scenario can be avoided if
humanity gets serious *now* about pollution control and zero population
growth. See 4 Q67, 4 Q84, 5 Q14, 5 Q25, 5 Q91.

See Index: future conflicts (21st century).

1 Q16

Faulx à l'eftang[1] ioinct vers le Sagitaire,	**Saturn joined with (Scorpio)**
En fon hault AVGE[2] de l'exaltation,	**transiting toward Sagittarius,**
Pefte, famine, mort de main militaire,	**At its highest ascendant,**
Le fiecle[3] approche de renouation.	**Pest, famine, death through military**
	hands,
	The century as well as the Age
	approaches its renewal.

[1]Old French *étang* = a pond; (astrol.) a water sign. Saturn can leave Scorpio only to enter
Sagittarius.
[2]AUGE, from Latin *augere* = to increase.
[3]*siecle*: double meaning – "century" as well as an "era" or "age."

The themes of plague, famine, drought, war, and renewal are repeated
throughout *Les Propheties*. This is the first of 14 quatrains that have one
or two lines unfolding this apocalyptic sequence, which also sounds like
a present-day and near-future prophecy.

This quatrain, along with 4 Q67 and 2 Q62, provides clues to the start
of the final countdown of Nostradamus' years of tribulation prior to the
new age of peace. The countdown will be triggered by the simultaneous
occurence of three factors on what is a clearly predicted date:

1) the transit of Saturn from the constellation of Scorpio to Sagittarius,
a fire sign (see 1 Q16);

2) the transit of Mars through a fire sign (Aries, Leo, or Sagittarius) at
the same time (see 4 Q67);

3) both Saturn and Mars perform their transits when a great comet
appears at the end of a century or when an astrological epoch is approaching its renewal with the onset of the new Aquarian Age (see 2 Q62).

Saturn transits any constellation once every 29.5 years and Mars every
two years. The comet is the key that links these quatrains together.
Saturn moved into Sagittarius on 17 November 1985. Halley's Comet
became visible in the skies a few days later. Mars **joined** Saturn in
Sagittarius from 2 February to 29 March 1986, when the comet was at its

brightest. This does not rule out a future visitation of a still-unknown comet during Saturn's next transit from Scorpio on 24 December 2014 or again on 22 February 2044.

Nostradamus may be telling us to watch for apocalyptic warning signs during this countdown period. We will begin to see world plague, famines and droughts of unparalleled intensity, many wars and raids (perhaps referring to terrorist attacks), the hidden fires of volcanoes, and the invisible fire of the greenhouse effect (the **hot wind** of 4 Q67). All these began to exert their terrible influence from late 1985 through the spring of 1986. The great Ethiopian famine and a rash of some of the world's worst cases of drought in Africa, Asia, southern Europe, and the North American grain belts all peaked at the sighting of Halley's Comet in 1985–86. During that time the Third World was suffering from over 50 wars, the worst being the Iran–Iraq conflict, and the AIDS plague was recognized as a threat to world health. The years 1985–86 saw many terrorist raids. Civilians were gunned down by terrorists in two international airports; the United States replied with two retaliatory **raids** (see 4 Q67) on the terrorist-sanctioning state of Libya.

See Index: Apocalyptic sequence of events.

1 Q17

Par quarante ans l'Iris n'apparoiſtra.	**For forty years the rainbow will not appear;**
Par quarante ans tous les lours ſera veu:	**For forty years it will be seen every day:**
La terre aride en ſiccité croiſtra,	**The arid earth will grow more dry,**
Et grans deluges quand ſera aperceu.	**And great floods when it will be seen.**

Nostradamus may be applying to excess a biblical metaphor from Genesis, borrowing from the 40-days-and-40-nights theme of Noah's Ark in the Deluge. He predicts a 40-year cycle of drought followed by 40 years of rains, perhaps for France and most likely for Nostradamus' native Provence. The final two lines are another lurid description of the climatic extremes expected in the 21st century due to global warming.

1 Q18

Par la diſcorde negligence Gauloiſe,	**Because of French discord and negligence,**
Sera paſſaige à Mahommet ouuert:	**A passage to Muhammad will be opened:**
De ſang trempé la terre & mer Senoiſe,	**With blood soaking the earth and sea of Siena,**
Le port[1] Phocen de voilles & nefz couuert.	**The port of Marseilles covered with the sails of ships**

[1] *Phocen* = a) Phocaeans, the founders of Marseilles; b) Phocis, central Greece; c) Phocaea, ancient Greek colony of west Anatolia, Turkey; d) Phoenician, general metaphor for modern-day Beirut, Lebanon, or other Phoenician centers along North Africa and the Middle Eastern coast.

Jaubert applies the first interpretation of this prophecy to events of the Hapsburg-Valois Italian Wars in 1555–56. He has Henry II chumming it up with his Turkish "ally," Suleiman the Magnificent, to send Barbary Corsairs on a raid against the island of Elba to divert the Habsburgs while he continues his invasion of northern Italy. It is more likely that the attack was launched to take advantage of the warring Christian states. Whatever the motivation, the Corsairs do besiege Piombino, near to Siena, which itself was a French ally. A French garrison would surrender to the Florentines at Siena on 22 April 1555, just days before publication of *Les Propheties* in May. Jaubert adds a dubious explanation to line 4: that a fleet of ships had gathered at the docks of Marseilles to receive supplies for French troops holed up on Corsica.

A whole bevy of latter-day Nostradamians navigate through the prophet's grammatical ambiguities in the final lines to predict a future invasion of Marseilles, Toulon, and the French Riviera by a huge Muslim armada. This **passage to Muhammad** leads notable scholars such as André Lamont, Peter Lemesurier, Fontbrune, and a number of fly-by-night Nostradamians of the tabloids, as well as a few other pot-boiler bookies, to gamble their reputations on a theme that, in my observation, just doesn't wash – not even the gunwales of a Corsair's poop deck. History records that there weren't enough galleys in the sultan's fleet to deposit an army that could march up the Rhône valley to conquer France, Spain, Italy, and western Germany in the 16th century, or any other century of the Ottoman Empire's existence. However, Fontbrune believes Islam in our near future will somehow build a fleet that can carry a great military horde that will not only conquer much of western Europe, but do what Hitler never could and cross the English Channel to threaten London. And, somehow, the European Union, NATO and the United States will look the other way, cap the switch of their overwhelming nuclear, chemical, and conventional missile arsenals, and just let the Muslim make a sea passage for Muhammad in broad daylight around the Millennium.

What is more feasible is that those **sails** covering the port of Marseilles were intended for an earlier time. And like so many of Nostradamus' vagaries in grammar, the fleet of line 4 can be equally Muslim or non-Muslim. It depends on the interpreter's drift, which often suffers from an a lurch in projections. I believe this and hundreds of other quatrains attributed by my colleagues to a Muslim invasion of Europe in World War III can all be applied to past historical events. A few may be Nostradamus' exaggerations for far smaller, and perhaps far more lethal, invasions by small bands of nuclear terrorists.

1 Q19

Lors que ferpens viendront circuir l'are,[1]
Le fang Troyen[2] vexé par les Efpaignes:
Par eux grand nombre en fera faicte tare.
Chef fruict, caché aux mares[3] dans les
    faignes.[4]

When the serpents will come to
    encircle the altar,
The Trojan blood is vexed by the
    Spanish:
Because of them a great number will
    be made to suffer.
The chief flees, hidden in the swamp
    within the swamp.

[1]Latin *ara* = altar.
[2]*Sang Troyen* – ie the French. France in the 16th century enjoyed a popular myth that their kings were descendants of surviving Trojan royalty.
[3]Old French *mares* = marsh.
[4] Old French marsh, swamp.

Jaubert claims that Coligny escaped the flaming wreck that was his command, the besieged town of St Quentin, and was later pulled out of the surrounding swamp by the victorious Spanish and taken prisoner.

Actually he was caught in the flaming wreck of the bombarded town by an overwhelming attack from a Spanish force of 64,000 men. His garrison only numbered 1,000, the majority of them survivors who had swum through the swamps from the rout of the French relief army 17 days before on 10 August 1557. It is a fact that Coligny's second-in-command, his gallant brother Andelot, did swim through the swamps to escape capture.

See Index: St Quentin (battle of); Andelot/TOLANDAD.

1 Q20

Tours, Orleans, Blois, Angiers & Reims,
    Nâtes,
Cites vexées par fubit changement:
Par langues eftranges feront tendues
    tentes,
Fleuues, dards Renes, terre & mer
    tremblement.

Tours, Orléans, Blois, Angiers,
    Reims and Nantes,
Cities shaken by sudden change:
Tents will be pitched by those of
    foreign tongues,
Rivers, javelins at Rennes, land and
    sea trembling.

The vision in the brass bowl is of towns along the Loire River (except for Reims) that will suffer a recurring of wars and occupation by foreign troops. First their cobblestone streets feel the tramp of Prussian boots when Napoleon falls from power in 1815. The grandsons of those Prussians would return again in 1871 after France's defeat in the Franco-Prussian War. By the early 20th century, Prussian bluecoats give way to American khaki; the sharp staccato of Prussian commands are replaced by a mix of mid-Western twangs and Southern drawls echoing off the old walls and streets. The year is 1917, and the Loire towns and the city of Reims open themselves to a friendly occupation of American "doughboy" soldiers come to help France win World War I. Then with the suddenness of a lightning war, the Germans return in 1940 to Reims and the Loire, this time as occupiers from Hitler's Greater Germany. They would remain for the next four years.

Scholars of Nostradamus could go wrong if they think the last line describes a natural earthquake shaking Rennes. Perhaps it is the quaking thunder of tank treads and motorized artillery of the returning Americans on the cobblestone streets and echoing through the bivouacs outside these towns along the Loire. The final line could picture the day when elements of Patton's Third Army would break out of Normandy in the summer of 1944, in their own lightning war, sweeping the Germans out of Rennes and other cities of the Loire for one last and benevolent occupation of the region.

1 Q21

Profonde argille blanche nourrit rochier,	**Deep white clay nourishes the rock,**
Qui d'vn abiſme iſtra lacticineuſe:	**Which from an abyss will go out milk white:**
En vain troublez ne l'oſeront toucher,	**Needlessly perplexed they will not dare to touch it,**
Ignorans eſtre au fond terre argilleuſe.	**Unaware that the earth at the bottom is of clay.**

André Lamont believes Nostradamus is giving Europeans clues to their future discovery of how to make porcelain. In 1704, Boetcher – a Saxon alchemist – would find a way for them to manufacture china plates, thus ending Europe's sole reliance on Chinese imports.

1 Q22

Ce que viura & n'ayant aucun ſens,	**That which will live without any senses,**
Viendra leſer à mort ſon artifice:	**Will come to injure itself to death through artifice:**
Auſtun, Chalon, Langres & les deux Sens,	**Autun, Châlon, Langres and the two Sens,**
La greſle & glace fera grand malefice.	**Hail and ice will cause great evil.**

One could describe a machine as a thing that lives without senses. It destroys itself by thoughtlessly following its own motive machinations. The French towns listed in line 3 will be affected by its demise. The dead yet living thing brings on a sudden climatic change, if not a new ice age.

Several lifelike-though-unliving things could cause this. Any of today's nuclear cruise or intercontinental ballistic missiles can senselessly drive themselves via the artifice of rocket engines to their target and death and, if numerous enough, can cause enough dust and smoke to rise into the stratosphere to cause a nuclear winter.

A comet or meteor can also run itself into the ground by the artifice of gravitational attraction and injure itself in a collision with Earth. The result could be a nuclearlike winter, from all the dust hurled into the atmosphere by its impact.

There are a number of quatrains following down these missile/meteor slants.

See Index: comet/meteor strike; nuclear winter.

1 Q23

Au moys troifiefme fe leuant le Soleil,
Sanglier, Liepard au champ Mars pour
   côbatre:
Liepard laiffé, au ciel extend fon œil,
Vn Aigle autour du Soleil voit s'esbatre.

In the third month, the sun rising,
The Boar and the Leopard meet on
the battlefield:
The fatigued Leopard looks up to
heaven,
And sees an Eagle playing with the
sun.

On 18 June 1815, in the third month after retaking power, Napoleon prepared to do battle with the era's other great general, the Duke of Wellington, on the rain-soaked fields of Belgium. Napoleon had defeated the Prussian army under Field Marshal Blücher two days before at Ligny. He had sent a third of his army in pursuit, gambling that Marshal Grouchy's 30,000 men would pursue the Prussians and prevent them from surprising his right flank while he engaged the British.

By dawn on the 18th, the Emperor had endured another long and terrible night of suffering from a chronic urinary infection. The pressures of sustaining his Empire and fighting 50 pitched battles in 20 years had burnt him out. Still he was expecting victory at Waterloo. The red orb of the summer sun rising over the muddy campgrounds reminded him of an autumn sunrise many years before at Austerlitz, the place of his greatest victory. While watching the 3,480th sunrise after Austerlitz, Nostradamus' older and war-weary First Antichrist wanted to believe it was an omen of victory – Napoleon desperately needed the sun that had shone on Austerlitz in December 1805 to rise in June, in the approaching winter of his career.

The rising sun of Waterloo could not dry out the mud. As the light increased it was clear that Napoleon's cannons and troops could not maneuver at dawn as they had done at Austerlitz. Precious time would be lost. And no one knew where Grouchy or the Prussians were.

The battle began at exactly 11:30 am. One hour and several thousand lives later, keen-eyed junior members of Napoleon's general staff spotted a great mass of men on the distant eastern horizon. One sweep of his spyglass told Napoleon they were not Grouchy's returning forces but Blücher's Prussians coming to the aid of Wellington. Time was running out. If Napoleon couldn't give Wellington's army the *coup de grace* by sundown, his own right flank would be overrun by 30,000 Prussians.

Wellington's men held on to the ridge of Mont St Jean all that bloody afternoon, beating back wave after wave of French cavalry and infantry assaults. By sundown Napoleon committed his final reserves – his own Imperial Guard. The grenadiers swept across the trampled and corpse-strewn fields propelled with the irresistible confidence of 20 years of victory. A thin red line of British soldiers crouched in the tangled wheat upon Mont St Jean, poised for the collision. Wellington rolled his eyes and said, "If Blücher doesn't come now, they will break every bone in my body."

In that terrible moment, Wellington could not have known how close he was to victory.

As he watched the eagle standards of the Imperial Guard crest the ridge before the setting sun, a prophecy written 261 years before was coming true: **The third month** (June 1815), **the sun rising** (Napoleon's omen of Austerlitz), **the Boar** (this is Napoleon), **and the Leopard** (what Napoleon called the heraldic lion, symbolizing England, here referring to the Duke of Wellington, on the **battlefield** of Waterloo).

The vision of Nostradamus becomes reality for the exhausted Duke as he sees the brass eagle standards of the French playing in the sun, just as the British line discharges the first of several deadly volleys into the advancing enemy.

The vision in Nostradamus' bowl of water grows faint and will not complete the prophecy until later in 1 Q38.

See Index: First Antichrist (Napoleon); Waterloo.

1 Q24

A cité neufue penſif pour condemner,	**The new city contemplating a condemnation,**
L'oiſel de proye au Ciel ſe vient offrir:	**The bird of prey offers itself to the heavens:**
Apres victoire à captifs pardonner,	**After victory pardon [given] to the captives,**
Cremone & Mantoue grãs maux aura ſouffert.	**Cremona and Mantua will have suffered great evils.**

A number of European towns have names that mean "new city". The most notable candidates are Naples (from the Greek, *nea-polis*) and Cittanova. The **bird of prey** is a synonym for the Imperial Eagle of Napoleon Bonaparte. General Bonaparte made one large step toward his imperial dreams by winning another Italian campaign in 1796. At one time during the campaign, some of his forces were garrisoned at Cremona. He laid a protracted siege to General Würmser's Austrian garrison of 16,000 at Mantua, which later surrendered to Napoleon on 14 January 1797. Würmser's men underwent a parade surrender ceremony in which they were disarmed of their weapons and 1,600 cannons and paroled (*pardon given*).

Modern-day Cremona also has a nuclear power plant. The **great evils** could be a nuclear disaster or an act of terrorism set to take place there.

1 Q25

Perdu trouué, caché de ſi long ſiecle,	**The lost thing is found, hidden for so many centuries,**
Sera Paſteur[1] demy Dieu honoré:	**Pasteur will be honored as a demigod:**
Ains que[2] la Lune acheue ſon grand ſiecle,	**This happens when the moon completes her great cycle,**
Par autres vents[3] ſera deshonoré.	**He will be dishonored by other rumors as foul as farting.**

[1]*Pasteur* =a) Pastor of a church; b) Louis *Pasteur*, the pioneer of immunology and microbiology. Nostradamus only uses the word twice: here and in 6 Q28, where the latter is clearly for the pope, "the great Pastor" of Rome.
[2]Old French *Ains que* = before.
[3]Winds (16th-c. col.) the foul farts of evil rumors.

To combat the plague, Nostradamus used medical techniques that were centuries ahead of his time. One prophecy in particular has caused much speculation as to whether or not the 16th-century doctor utilized his prophetic skills to save lives. Louis Pasteur's discovery that germs pollute the atmosphere was one of the greatest milestones in medical history, and he was called a **demigod** by his contemporaries. Until his theories were proved beyond doubt, he endured vicious attacks from influential colleagues in the medical academies of his time. Pasteur is not only named by Nostradamus, but the prophet also correctly dated the establishment of the Institute Pasteur. He achieved this by reference to the last great lunar cycle in astrology, which began in 1535 and ended in 1889, the year the institute was created.

A century after his death in 1895, a new scandal threatens Pasteur's posterity. Princeton historian Gerald Geison, in his book *The Private Science of Louis Pasteur*, finds a self-serving and sloppy scientist hiding behind this legend of scientific discovery and altruism. His source is a careful reading of Pasteur's original lab books. Pasteur's notes do show that he tested his rabies vaccine on a 9-year-old boy bitten by a rabid dog, as is popularly believed, but they also overturn his public claim that he had done thorough tests before making a child his lab mouse for experimental treatments. Whether Pasteur will be **dishonored** or this book will be viewed as *foul rumors* is left for the future to decide.

See Index: ten debunker's nightmares.

1 Q26

Le grand du fouldre tumbe d'heure diurne,	**The great man will be struck down in**
Mal & predict par porteur[1] poftulaire:[2]	**the day by a thunderbolt,**
Suiuant prefage tumbe d'heure nocturne,	**The evil deed predicted by the bearer**
Conflit Reims, Londres, Etrufque	**of a petition:**
peftifere.	**According to the prediction another**
	falls at night time,
	Conflict in Reims, London, and
	pestilence in Tuscany.

[1]Bearer – but Modern French can see *porteur* stand for a tramp on the railway track. Many Kennedy assassination conspiracies try to unravel the unsolved mystery of five men masquerading as tramps who were arrested in the Dallas, Texas, railway yard adjacent to Dealey Plaza where the assassination took place.
[2]Latin *postularius* = demanding, claiming, petitioning.

With his remarkable sensitivity to major upheavals in our future history, Nostradamus would have been unlikely to miss the assassinations of President John F. Kennedy (JFK) and his brother, Senator Robert Kennedy (RFK), which so shocked the world. With the president's assassination in 1963, the American post-war age of innocence ended and the nation faced the new realism of war in Vietnam and turbulent protest at home. But in 1968 hopes were renewed by the political rise of Robert Kennedy, who won a decisive victory in the California primary. The Kennedy charisma was back and, riding on a wave of political support and public euphoria, Robert seemed destined for the White House. A few minutes after delivering his victory speech Robert Kennedy was assassinated.

A plethora of plausible but controversial assassination theories have circulated since the 1960s, ranging from an underworld conspiracy to kill the Kennedy brothers to a state-sanctioned assassination of President Kennedy by Fidel Castro, Cuba's Marxist dictator. Such conspiracy theorizing was given a new lease on life first by Bill Kurtis' critically acclaimed documentary The Men Who Killed Kennedy (1988) and later in the 1990s by Oliver Stone's blockbuster movie JFK, which proposes that a rogue element in the United States government assassinated the president in a coup d'état. Stone's dramatization has us believe that the assassination was carried out to forestall Kennedy's efforts to pull American forces out of Vietnam and end the Cold War 30 years earlier. There is no denying that the deaths of John Kennedy and his brother directed the world down a new prophetic pathway of chance. Their assassinations may have aided those with a vested interest in the continued expansion of a military-industrial complex with its highly profitable business of armaments and weapons development. If Kennedy had lived, there may never have been a Vietnam and 60,000 American and 2 million Asian deaths would have been prevented.

Now to the specifics of this quatrain. President John Kennedy was shot shortly after 12 noon in Dallas, Texas, on 22 November 1963. Senator Robert Kennedy was assassinated a few minutes after 1 am, moments after his victory speech in the 1968 presidential primary. Jeane Dixon, one of the foremost prophets of modern times, earned international notoriety for predicting JFK's assassination as early as 1956. The *bearer of a petition* could be Dixon. Nostradamus may have chronicled her unsuccessful attempt to forewarn the president, and later, Senator Kennedy, who was her friend. The last line dates RFK's murder through events occurring around that time – student riots in France and London during 1968–69 (**Reims** is a synecdoche for France), and the 1966 Florence flood, when authorities feared that pestilence in Tuscany would follow the disaster.

See Index: Kennedy assassinations.

1 Q27

Deffouz de chaine Guien du Ciel frappé,
Non loing de la eſt caché le treſor:
Qui par longs ſiecles auoit eſté grappé,
Trouué mourra, l'œil creué de reſſort.[1]

Beneath the mountain chain of
 Guienne struck from the heavens,
Not far from there is the treasure
 hidden:
That which for long centuries has
 been gathered,
When found, it will perish, its eye put
 out by a spring.

[1]Spring; elasticity; energy; motive.

Guienne gives us the general location of the treasure hidden somewhere in south-western France (see 9 Q7). The butter of many interpretations has been spread across these lines. To me, this treasure sounds like a device that has recorded information over the eons. The articles in this quatrain can just as easily translate to "he" as they do to "it," which would make this device something potentially sentient. The day its examination of man is discovered, it is destroyed. The powers that light its observant eye are shut off.

1 Q28

La tour de Boucq¹ craindra fuſte² Barbare,³	**Tobruk will fear the low-drafted Barbarian boat,**
Vn temps, long temps apres barque heſperique:⁴	**For a long time, much later by the Western Fleet:**
Beſtail, gẽs, meubles tous deux feront grãd tare,	**Cattle, people, chattels, both [fleets] cause great waste,**
Taurus & Libra quelle mortelle picque?⁵	**What a deadly quarrel in Taurus and Libra!**

¹Tower of Boucq = Tobruk.
²A low-draft galley; (poetic) a low-draft German U-boat.
³*Barbare*: either Barbary Corsairs or Barbarossa. The latter is sometimes Nostradamus' code name for Adolf Hitler.
⁴Latin *Hesperia* = Land of the West (Leoni); *Hesperus/Hesperos*, the evening star. In classical mythology the Hesperides were the daughters of Atlas and Hesperus. They lived on the extreme western edge of the known world. The ancient Romans called modern-day Portugal and Spain by this name (Kidogo). Nostradamus, however, seems to extend its meaning farther west to embrace the New World in general and contemporary America in particular. The land of the evening star stands for the stars of the American flag.
⁵? = misprint for *!*

The Libyan port of Tobruk has one of the finest harbors in North Africa. It was an important supply port for Axis and Western Allied forces during World War II. In the first phase of the North African campaign it was captured from the Italians in a combined British land, air, and sea assault on 22 January 1941. The British supply ships which safely nestled in Tobruk's harbor would have feared the low silhouette of "Barbarossa's" boat – not the low-riding galleys of the "Barbary" pirate but Nostradamus' other "Barbarossa" – the name he gives Adolf Hitler after the code-name of Hitler's invasion of the Soviet Union, Operation Barbarossa. This makes the barbarian boat a German submarine, or U-boat. Throughout most of the war (**for a long time**) several of these barbarian boats were usually on station outside the safety of the harbor, waiting to torpedo any Western Allied ships venturing into the Mediterranean.

In the end Field Marshal Erwin Rommel's Afrika Korps could not defeat the Allies because the Axis fleets of U-boats and the Italian surface navy were defeated by the superior Anglo-American (**Western**) fleets in their struggle to dominate the Mediterranean. Most of Rommel's desperately needed supplies were sent to the bottom of the sea. Even the well-sheltered 40-foot-deep harbor of Tobruk was clogged more than once with the wreckage of scuttled Axis and Allied cargo ships packed with supplies.

The final line is a remarkable dating of two battles fought over Tobruk. The first **deadly quarrel** sees Rommel's stormtroopers beaten back by General Morshead's Australian garrison at Tobruk on 30 April 1942, when the sun was in its annual transit of the constellation of Taurus. One year later, during the next transit of the desert sun through Taurus, Rommel unleashed a second Axis offensive, driving the British out of Libya. In the following month a British force of 33,000 men and mountains of supplies (*people, chattels*) surrendered at Tobruk after heavy fighting.

Tobruk fell again to the British after their decisive victory against the Afrika Korps at El Alamein. This most **deadly** of desert **quarrels** began with a horrendous British artillery barrage lighting up the desert night in the early hours of 23 October 1942, shortly after the sun finished its transit of Libra!

1 Q29

Quand la poiſſon tereſtre & aquatique,	**When the fish [that is both]**
Par force vague¹ au grauier ſera mis:	**terrestrial and aquatic,**
Sa forme eſtrange ſuaue & horrifique,²	**Will be put upon the beach by a**
Par mer aux murs bien toſt les ennemis.	**strong [cruising] wave:**
	Its form [is] strange, attractive
	(smooth) and horrific,
	From the sea to the walls [they]
	instantly reach the enemy.

¹It usually stands for "wave," but if we apply the classical Latin *vagus* (wandering, roving, roaming) or the nautical term *vage* (cruising), perhaps we have a "cruise missile" described here.
²Latin *horrificus* = frightful.

What future image has impressed its alien shape upon the 16th-century mind of the prophet? Is it the broad duck-billed prow of an amphibious armoured *fish* grinding its chin into the graveled beaches of Normandy? A gurgling, sputtering roar is heard when air and diesel meet as the great amphibian rises laboriously from the waves, displaying its round and rolling feet. The olive-drab polliwogs in helmets, holding fast to its back, spring onto the sand. They hop, leap, dive for cover, and run towards the chalky cliffs. Many fall and do not rise again. Was Nostradamus seeing the Normandy beach landings of June 1944, or something closer to home? Is it a *monstre* from his own native shores in the Gulf of Fréjus, where infernal metal water bugs race out of control? They do not heed the signaled commands of their magicians and cause schools of metal amphibians to swim out of their way. Was Nostradamus viewing the smooth and frightful drone boats, filled with high explosives, that the Allies intended to drive over the German beach obstacles during the Allied landings on the Riviera in August 1944? Their signals were jammed by the Germans on the shore sending them out of control in all directions. Only two speeding drones mounted the beach in a great wave to explode on target.

But the Riviera landings witnessed other strange amphibians. Are these the amphibious Sherman tanks rolling from the water across the beaches into the steep, pine-covered hills of the Riviera in search of their favorite Nazi prey? Are more frightful amphibians foreseen? Does Nostradamus witness the flaming eye of Satan's sea-to-air missile riding the column of a great wave just before it leaps from beneath the sea ? Its cauldronlike lungs suck in the air with an ear-splitting roar, faster than the speed of sound, the cyclops beast of deep fathoms now slips across an invisible carpet of air a few feet above the waves. Its nose and body is graceful, its electronic eye emotionless and frightful. The Iraqi soldiers in their cement pillbox on the Kuwaiti shore do not see it coming. Suddenly it plows through their four-foot cement walls, which become fire.

See Index: missile themes.

1 Q30

La nef eftrange par le tourment marin,	Because of the tormented seas, the strange ship,
Abourdera[1] pres de port incongneu:	Will arrive [or land] at an unknown port:
Nonobftant fignes de rameau palmerin,[2]	Notwithstanding the signals from the branch of palm [radar dish?],
Apres mort pille bon auis[3] tard venu.	After death, pillage: good advice [or birds] arriving late.

[1]Alternative: will land (poetic), denoting a ship or submarine landing, but also the landing of an aircraft or spaceship.
[2]Latin palmarius, of palm.
[3]Either for "advice" or Latin avis = bird.

Out of a churning ocean, whether of water or of cosmic ions, we see a **strange ship** landing at an unknown port. Is this uncharted haven a pirate's lair in the 16th century? Is it a secret rendezvous site where a container submarine deposits nuclear terrorists and their atomic device on a lonely stretch of Italian shoreline sometime around the dawning of a new millennium (see 2 Q5)? Could this be a landing at the end of the next millennium with a floating "ship" arriving from distant skies to deposit the first colonists on a new world orbiting a star in the constellation of Cancer or Aquarius?

The answer hides somewhere under the veil of Nostradamus' nebulous poetry. A man shimmies up a palm tree to wave the "all clear" signal and Barbary Corsairs begin dragging their plunder down into the waves. A terrorist extends his microwave dish to signal his commander, Nostradamus' Third Antichrist after Napoleon and Hitler, lurking offshore in a submarine. In the distant future, human beings beyond our imagining extend a retractable metallic shaft and open the parabolic umbrella towards a sky filled with alien stars; they signal their mothership that landfall is attained.

Any one of these images is possible.

The final line displays another of Nostradamus' cryptic apocalyptic themes of a holocaust followed by a new era (from **death, pillage,** to **good advice ... arriving late**). A word play on the Latin *avis* against the French word for "advice" links this quatrain to the mystical message of the "rare birds" crying "Now!" which is written in the *Epistle* (see EP212). They give the world this cryptic message (**advice**) just before the global apocalypse begins. Perhaps they are extraterrestrials making contact with humanity before it destroys itself, or they are the spiritual catalysts – the new Christs and Buddhas – preparing humanity to make the next great spiritual step in evolution.

Quatrain Indexing Date: AD 2030, 2130, 2230, 3030 ... ad infinitum?

See Index: space colonies, travel.

1 Q31

Tant d'ans les guerres en Gaule dureront,	**For too many years the wars in France will last,**
Outre la course¹ du Castulon² monarque:	**Beyond the course and momentum of the monarch of Castulon:**
Victoire incerte trois grands couronneront,	**Uncertain victory will the three great ones crown,**
Aigle, coq, lune, lyon, soleil en marque.³	**The eagle, cock, moon, lion, sun in its mark.**

¹Direction, (fig.) course of life, the momentum or life of a country, a war, or a man, etc.
²Ancient Iberian city, synecdoche for Spain.
³ Latin *incertus* = uncertain.
⁴*Soleil en marque* = the sun in Leo.

Nostradamus had tried hard to warn his countrymen of the coming Wars of Religion (1562–98) seven years before they began. It seems we have a prophecy about their completion after running the course of 36 blood-soaked years. Line 2 makes a double pun out of **course** which in Old French would describe the momentum or trajectory of King Philip II of Spain, who cannot stay the course of war with France because of the slackening momentum of the Spanish economy. In other words, the **course** of Spanish fortunes ended in 1596 with Philip's empire in bankruptcy, effectively taking Spain out of the conflict with France, or **beyond the course** of Philip's ambitions to prosecute the war to a victorious finish. Though he became increasingly enfeebled with financial woes and age, he wouldn't sue for peace with Henry IV of France for another two years, until he sensed that he was himself beyond the **course** of his natural life and death was near.

The three rulers in **uncertain victory** would be Elizabeth I of England, the newly crowned Henry IV of France, and Pope Clement VII. Spain was checked by France, which would indirectly benefit England, but Spain would fight her until 1604. The pope could celebrate Henry IV's conversion to Catholicism, and his victory over the Huguenots, but Henry's Edict of Nantes gave far more freedom of worship to the Huguenots than the pope would have liked. The factions in France had ended their conflict more out of exhaustion than from a clear winner, so the feeling of uncertainty was strong in the devastated land. However, Henry IV would go far to heal the wounds and rebuild France.

The final line returns us to a staccato of astrological data and double-puns of animals representing nations. The eagle in this case represents Philip and the Spanish Habsburgs, who have an eagle in their coat of arms; the cock is the ancient Gallic symbol of France; the Moon is the crescent symbol of the Ottoman Turks; and the Lion is Elizabethan England. The final phrase may be a near miss at astrologically dating the death of Philip II of Spain when the sun is in its astrological **mark** (constellation) of Leo. According to the Gregorian calendar, the advent of which was predicted by Nostradamus (see 1 Q42), the sun is in Leo every year between July 22 to August 21. The death watch for Philip may have begun just as the sun finished its transit of Leo – but he didn't actually die for another three weeks.

1 Q32

Le grand empire ſera toſt tranſlaté	**The great Empire will soon be**
En lieu petit qui bien toſt viendra	**exchanged**
croiſtre:	**For a little place, which will soon**
Lieu bien infime d'exigue comté,	**come to increase in size:**
Ou au milieu viendra poſer ſon ſceptre.	**A very petty and tiny place [for a]**
	county,
	In the middle of which he will come
	to lay down his sceptre.

After defeat at Waterloo in 1815 (see 1 Q23, 1 Q38), Napoleon was exiled to the tiny island of St Helena in the South Atlantic. He who once ruled an empire covering most of western Europe now sat in a modest house upon a **little place** of a few square miles, mostly of rock. The tropical climate and idleness conspired to kill him by 1821. Thus fell the first of Nostradamus' three predicted Antichrists.

Earlier interpreters liked to pin this transferral from great holdings to small upon another European Emperor, Nostradamus' contemporary, Charles V, who at 55 retired, handing over an empire equal in size to Napoleon's. His brother Ferdinand took the Imperial power of the Holy Roman Empire, and his son, Philip II, received sovereignty over the

Netherlands and Spain. Once having abdicated all responsibilities, Charles V exchanged his far-flung empire to settle as a guest in a much smaller place, the monastery of Yuste, in the province of Extremadura, Spain, where he died in 1558. The publication of this quatrain would have predated the event of Charles' abdication by several months, making both interpretations authentically fulfilled prophecies.

1 Q33

Prés d'vn grand pont de plaine ſpatieuſe,	Near the great bridge of spacious plain,
Le grand lyon par forces Ceſarées:	The great Lion with Imperial forces:
Fera abbatre hors cité rigoureuſe,	Will cause a felling outside the austere city,
Par effroy portes luy ſeront reſerées.	Because of fear the gates will be opened to him.

Just as Hitler's propaganda minister, Josef Goebbels – blinded by the myth of the Führer's invincibility – would have had difficulty finding a prophecy assuring ultimate victory for Germany, so Nostradamus – blinded by his bias against John Calvin – could not pen a correct prophecy about the fall of Geneva (*the austere city*), which was the headquarters of John Calvin from 1541 through 1564.

In this spin-doctored prophecy Nostradamus sees a great, lionized warrior hunting Calvin down. Perhaps this warrior is Nostradamus' friend and astrological client, the Duke of Savoy. Whoever he was supposed to be, this **Lion** was expected to assemble Imperial forces of the Holy Roman Empire near the spacious plain on the city's western approaches, which was (poetically speaking) their **great bridge** through the steep Alpine terrain into Geneva. These forces would make preparations for laying siege by felling many trees on the verdant foothills. But the fearful inhabitants would first renounce Calvin, their heretical religious leader, and surrender the city to **the great Lion**.

1 Q34

L'oyſeau de proye volant à la ſeneſtre,[1]	The bird of prey flying to the left [for six months],
Auant conflict faict aux Françoys pareure:	Before the conflict preparation made by the French:
L'vn bon prendra l'vn ambigue ſiniſtre,	One will take it for good, another for a sinister mixed bag,
La partie foyole tiendra par bon augure.	The weak country will hold it as a good omen.

[1] Old French *semestre* = a) semester, six months; b) Latin *sinistre* = left; alternatively, *fenestra* = window. A complex pun for a "something flying from the left during a time window of six months."

Implied here is the German condor or eagle symbols of Hitler's Luftwaffe. The rich layers of meaning personalize this **bird of prey** as Hitler, represented by his high-altitude Dornier reconnaissance planes circling over Paris, six months before the Battle of France. The word *semestre* can give us roughly the length of the six-month lull on the western front between the fall of Poland in early October 1939 and the invasion of France in May 1940. *Semestre* also means "left." Paris was "left" or west of German airbases at that time. *Semestre* can also represent *fenestra*, or "window." Put all these layers together and we get a **bird of prey flying to the left** (over Paris and the French lines) sometime during a time window of six months.

The French did prepare for a second war with Germany by building an extravagant fortress system called the Maginot Line. Behind this wall they nurtured their illusions of invincibility (**good omen**). In terms of men and material, France had the most powerful military land force in western Europe, but their tactics and their equipment were behind the times. The **good omen** may also be a long pause in fighting. The French press could propagate the idea that the Germans were too frightened of the Maginot Line and of French élan. This was nothing more than the boasting of the weak. The French government was politically leftist (*sinistre*), divisive (**mixed bag**), and impotent.

At least one Nostradamian scholar, Max de Fontbrune, saw France's Maginot mentality as a **sinister mixed bag**. He risked vilification on a national scale by declaring to the French that a vast redoubt of concrete fortresses and subterranean garrisons built at astronomical expense would be a useless defense against a German invasion in the coming war. The fierce debate over Max de Fontbrune's interpretations ended when Hitler went sightseeing beneath the Eiffel Tower with his generals.

Quatrain Indexing Date: Q34 = 1934. Perhaps another general attempt to zero in on World War II for 1937, 1941, 1942, and 1945 (see EP174–175).

See Index: Maginot Line.

---

1 Q35

Le lyon ieune le vieux furmontera,	**The young lion will overcome the older one,**
En champ bellique[1] par fingulier duelle:	**On the field of combat in single battle:**
Dans caige d'or les yeux luy creuera,	**He will pierce his eyes through a golden cage,**
Deux claffes[2] vne, puis mourir, mort cruelle.	**Two wounds made one, then he dies a cruel death.**

[1]Latin *bellicus* = of battle.
[2]Usually Latin *classis* = fleet, or army. In this case, however, allegedly from Greek *klasis* = a break, a fracture. Prieditis adds that *klasis* is a term used in geology for a fault-line, implying a double meaning: the fatal wounding of the King of France caused by the fractured lance would cause an earthquake in European politics.

The quatrain foretelling the death of King Henry II of France in a jousting accident is one of the most famous, predocumented, and successfully fulfilled prophecies in history. It can be paralleled in our time only to Jeane Dixon's documented forecasts of the rise of John F. Kennedy to the presidency and his assassination.

At the end of June 1559, Henry II ignored all warnings against ritual combat from Nostradamus and his queen's court astrologer, Luc Gauricus, and decided to celebrate the dual marriage of his sister Marguerite to the Duke of Savoy, and his daughter Elizabeth by proxy to King Philip II of Spain, by staging a three-day tournament. Thousands gathered from all over France along rue St Antoine outside of Paris to see the athletic French king compete in jousting tournaments. On the final day the king's attire and that of his horse were in the heraldic colors of his mistress, Diane de Poitiers. He was resplendent in full gilded armor, wielding a great lion-decorated shield. The excitement of the crowds on rue St Antoine paralleled the festive joy of those tens of thousands lining the streets of Dallas, Texas, four centuries thereafter, who watched the resplendent motorcade carrying President Kennedy and his lovely wife turn into Dealey Plaza.

On two festive days in two different centuries, two psychically gifted women tried to hide their premonitions of doom. One was Queen Catherine de' Medici, sitting in the place of honor on the festooned platform in front of the tournament lists. The other was Jeane Dixon, a 20th-century US psychic who, at around half-past noon on 22 November 1963, was sitting at lunch with friends at the Mayflower Hotel in Washington DC – the very moment Kennedy's motorcade was turning into Dealey Plaza in far-off Dallas.

Queen Catherine had just seen her husband's final bout with Garbriel de Lorge, Comte de Montgomery, end in a draw, and for a moment she could secretly sigh in relief. The prophecy documented three years before in the 35th quatrain of Century I, which foretold Henry's death in a jousting accident, seemed a destiny unfulfilled. Then she noticed a heated conversation between the two ritual warriors. The king had lifted his gilded visor and was leaning over his horse to speak more forcefully to the younger man. Montgomery's manner betrayed nervousness at what the king requested. At last he bowed his head and drew up his own lion-embossed shield. Both *lions* reached for a new lance. Catherine bit her hand in dismay. It was obvious now that Henry had demanded another match. The terrible suspense of the last three days would be drawn out a few minutes more. The future's inclination toward the two destinies described in Nostradamus' prophecies for Henry would remain in doubt a little longer. Would Henry live to become a second Charlemagne, or would he be overcome with a mortal wound on the ritual field of combat?

Just as Catherine pondered her husband's quantum futures in the 16th century, Jeane Dixon, in the 20th, suddenly became so distraught that she couldn't touch her food. "Something dreadful is going to happen to the president today," she declared. Throughout the month, Dixon's friends had noticed her increasing concern about a premonition of doom for the young President Kennedy. She had been making accurate and documented predictions about him for over a decade. She had attained notoriety for her vision recorded in 1956 by Jack Anderson, publisher of *Parade Magazine*, in which she saw the White House with the shimmering numbers *1-9-6-0* hovering above it. Pulled like a magnet, her consciousness floated toward the main door, where a young man with striking blue eyes stood upon the threshold. An inner voice impressed upon her that this young man, a Democrat, would be elected President in 1960 and was destined to die violently while in office.

In two different centuries the cry of horror bursts from festive throngs. A shattered lance mortally wounds a French king in the head and throat. A rifle cracks in Dealey Plaza, fatally wounding an American president in the head and throat.

A great splinter of ragged wood rams through the gilded visor and impales the king's eye. He reels in the saddle. Catherine shrieks and faints.

Jeane Dixon and her friends look up as the orchestra at the Mayflower suddenly stops playing and the conductor announces that someone has just taken a shot at the president. Her friends try to comfort her, saying that he must have avoided danger. "No," she replies, "The president is dead ... You will learn that he is dead."

Catherine de' Medici's ladies-in-waiting cannot console their revived queen, for she knows the future has inclined towards that end she had tried so hard to forestall: *The young lion will overcome the older one.* Both men that day had held shields embossed with lions. Montgomery was six years younger than Henry, who was 41. *On the field of combat in single battle.* A tournament is a *field of* ritual *single combat. He will pierce his eyes through a golden cage.* During the final bout Montgomery failed to drop his lance in time. It shattered, sending a large splinter through the king's gilded visor (*golden cage*). *Two wounds made one, then he dies a cruel death.* Along with multiple minor punctures in the face and throat are two mortal wounds. One splinter has destroyed the king's eye; the other has impaled his temple just behind the eye. Both have penetrated his brain (*two wounds made one*). Bacterial infections spreading through Henry's brain drained his life away. He lingers for 10 agonizing days (*then he dies a cruel death*).

We have seen the prophetic paths of Jeane Dixon and Nostradamus cross again in 1 Q26.

See Index: Henry II, alternate future; Kennedy assassinations.

1 Q36

Tard le monarque ſe viendra repentir,	**Too late the monarch will repent,**
De n'auoir mis à mort ſon aduerſaire:	**Of not having put to death his**
Mais viendra bien à plus hault conſentir,	**adversary:**
Que tout ſon ſang par mort ſera deffaire.	**But he will come to consent to a**
	much higher thing,
	Than for all his blood through death
	to waste.

Henry III has his chief rival Henry de Guise, and Henry's brother Cardinal Louis, assassinated in 1588. But one obstacle pruned means that a dozen leaves of trouble grow in its place. By killing the very popular Guise, rather than his more troublesome brother, the Duc de Mayenne, the king has made an enemy out of his own Catholic camp. He will be chased from his throne and later knifed to death by a Catholic priest. Mayenne, the surviving brother, takes over the Catholic League and wages one more bloody War of Religion against the new and rightful heir to the French throne, the Protestant king of Navarre (now Henry IV of France). Eventually Mayenne will concede all powers to Henry IV, especially when the king converts to Catholicism, recanting the heresy that had been Mayenne's reason to continue the fight. Mayenne will sheathe his sword rather than keep fighting and see the House of Lorraine completely annihilated by war and irrelevancy.

See Index: Henry de Guise assassination; Henry III assassination.

1 Q37

Vn peu deuant que le ſoleil s'eſconſe,	**A little before the sun sets,**
Conflict donné grand peuple dubiteux:	**Battle is given, a great people in**
Profligés, port marin ne faict reſponse,	**doubt:**
Pont[1] & ſepulchre en deux eſtranges	**Dashed to the ground, the marine**
lieux.	**port makes no answer,**
	Bridge [Sea] and tomb in two strange
	places

[1]Latin *pontus* = bridge; Greek *pontos* = the high sea.

The marine port makes no answer because it is dashed to the ground by an atomic attack. The two entombed places are Hiroshima and Nagasaki. A little before the **sun** of the Japanese Empire sets, the final major battle of World War II is waged at Okinawa. The **great people** could be the Japanese or the Americans. After Okinawa is invested, both sides are in doubt about the future. Okinawa was a test battle for the planned invasion of the Japanese home islands, and after its bloody conclusion America is **in doubt** that it can afford the estimated million casualties fighting in

Japan itself. The bomb clears the way for a new and brutal era in military history, and a new world peace.

So much for a 20th-century interpretation. Here's one for the early 19th century.

Napoleon's Imperial Guard advances across the blood-soaked fields of Waterloo just before sunset on 18 June 1815. They are repulsed by the British, and the French army breaks ranks in a full rout (**dashed to the ground**). Napoleon would be exiled to inactivity and slow death on the island of St Helena in the South Atlantic. From this strange tropical rock in the middle of a tepid blue nowhere, Napoleon's bones would later be removed across the sea to Paris and placed in a grandiose sepulchre beneath the golden dome of another exotic place, the Hôtel des Invalides.

See Index: Waterloo

1 Q38

Le Sol[1] & l'aigle au victeur paroiſtront,
Reſponce vaine au vaincu l'on aſſeure:
Par cor ne crys harnois n'arreſteront,
Vindicte paix par mors ſi acheue à
    l'heure.

The Sun and the Eagle will appear to the victor.
The vanquished is reassured with an empty message:
Neither bugle nor cries will stop the soldiers,
In time peace is vindicated if achieved through death.

[1]Latin Sol = sun.

We return again to the Duke of Wellington watching the French Imperial Guard's eagle standards playing with the setting sun at Waterloo, just as they disappeared in the fire and smoke of a shattering British volley (see 1 Q23). Now the lines of the second Waterloo prophecy written 261 years before the event spring from potentiality to reality. **The Sun and the Eagle will appear to the victor. The vanquished is reassured with an empty message** ...

Before the Imperial Guard advanced, Napoleon passed a false message among his regular troops that the men massing on their left flank were Grouchy's French troops and not the Prussians. The weary sun of Waterloo illuminated an unbelievable sight to the French regulars of the Imperial Guard emerging from the smoke of British volleys in full retreat off the ridge. In the waning light they also saw the battle flags and slate blue uniforms of Prussians on their right flank. The truth behind Napoleon's **empty message** registered on the minds of tens of thousands of exhausted Frenchmen. His army broke ranks and ran.

Neither bugle nor cries will stop the soldiers. In time [liberty and] *peace is vindicated if achieved through death.* No bugle call or command could stop the stampede. Only the retreating Imperial Guardsmen held their ranks, forming battle squares to face the advancing English and Prussians and buy time for Nostradamus' First Antichrist to escape the ignominy of capture. Within 15 minutes thousands of Guardsmen lay dead and dying.

Peace descended on Europe like the gathering darkness to cloak the bodies of 47,000 dead and wounded men.

1 Q39

De nuict dans lict le ſupreſme[1] eſtrangle,	**The night, in bed, the highest one**
Pour trop auoir ſeiourné, blond eſleu:	**strangled,**
Par troys l'empire ſubroge exancle,[2]	**For having tarried too long, the blond**
A mort mettra carte, & pacquet ne leu.	**elect:**
	By three substitutes the empire is
	enslaved,
	Put to death, paper and packet
	unread.

[1]Supreme, highest one. *Supresme* can also mean "the last one".
[2]Latin *exanclatus* = enslaved, suffered.

In 1830 the last of the Condé Bourbons, and a supporter of the Royalist claim to the French throne, was found hanging by the neck in his bedroom (*the highest one strangled*). Conspiracy buffs of the 19th century claim that he was strangled to death because he supported the Duc de Bordeaux's claim to the throne. His assassins strung him up to hide the telltale bruises made by the hands that twisted his neck. The *three substitutes* in line to rule France are Louis Philippe (1830–48), followed by Louis Bonaparte (Napoleon III) and the Second Empire (1848–71), and finally a string of French Republics starting with the Third Republic of Louis Adolphe Thiers and Maréchal Patrice de MacMahon. A second interpretation of *three substitutes* could allude to the three enemies of Condé. Charles X, the Duc d'Angoulême, and the Duc de Bourgogne. Nostradamus, the royalist sympathizer, sees the Second Empire, enslaved again by the nephew of his First Antichrist, Bonaparte.

The chief author of this conspiracy theory, Le Pelletier, insists that Condé was blond and had written a will (*paper and packet*) in favor of Bordeaux. Not long after his lifeless feet drew circles in the air, his assassins are said to have destroyed and replaced the will with one in favor of the Duc de Aumale, the son of Louis Philippe. The real wishes of Condé would forever remain *unread*.

1 Q40

La trombe fauffe[1] diffimulant folie,	**The false trumpet concealing madness,**
Fera Bifance vn changement de loix:	**Will cause Byzantium a change of laws:**
Hyftra d'Egypte qui veut que l'on deflie,	**From Egypt there will go forth one who wants withdrawn,**
Edict changeant monnoyes & aloys.	**[The] Edict [that makes] money and metal standards unstable.**

[1]*trombe fauffe* – Joseph Robert Jochmans suggests as an intriguing interpretation for *false trumpet* an attempt by Nostradamus to describe modern day loudspeakers and radio broadcasts, etc., used in a future Islamic revolution in Turkey and Egypt.

One can walk through the thought processes of several modern interpreters to train this quatrain on modern Turkey. Erika Cheetham bids us to consider this as portraying the political climate between Egypt and the Ottoman Empire during the time Napoleon returns from Egypt, from his military expedition in 1799, bringing along artifacts and archeological discoveries that would trigger Napoleonic France's infatuation with all things Egyptian. Jean-Charles de Fontbrune targets this for the early 20th century after the collapse of the Ottoman Empire, when Turkey lost its Egyptian province and gained a new republic through the Turkish Revolution of 1920. We then move ahead into our own future, with Jochmans' interpretation that this quatrain foretells a call to Islamic revolution in Turkey and Egypt through the **false trumpet** or modern loudspeakers from the muezzin's minaret.

1 Q41

Siege en cité eft de nuict affaillie,	**City besieged – a night assault,**
Peu efchapé: non loin de mer conflict:	**Few escaped, conflict not far from the sea:**
Femme de ioye,[1] retours fils defaillie,	**The whore on the return of her son faints for joy,**
Poifon & lettres cachees dans le plic.	**Poison and letters hidden in the fold.[2]**

[1]*Femme de joye* = woman of joy, (col.) a prostitute.
[2]Alternative: *Poison hidden in the fold of the letters.*

At least one hundred besieged cities must have suffered a night assault at some time between 1555 and today. The list gets shorter if the city is **not far from the sea.** This frosting of specifics ladled over a quatrain cake of generalities is easy to sweeten with all kinds of projections. Jaubert frosts it with the contemporary invasion of Italy by the French in 1556–57. Rolfe Boswell (1941) picks the fall of Dunkirk in 1940 (even though Dunkirk isn't near but right on the sea). Boswell's **whore** is the Third Republic, and the *poison and letters* are poetic for the Nazi indoctrination of prisoners.

When in doubt, Fontbrune usually applies any obscurely predicted battle, maneuver, or siege to a future world war. Back in the mid-1980s when the Cold War was still chilling our interpretations, he had Paris (which, by the way, is not very near the sea) under siege by the Russians and the *whore* became the Fifth French Republic falling to communism. Now that the Cold War is over, Lemesurier has Marseilles under the gun of a huge – and nonexistent – Muslim invasion fleet sometime in our near future.

1 Q42

Le dix Kalende d'Avril de faict Gotique,
Refufcité encor par gens malins:
Le feu eftainct affemblee diabolique,
Cherchant les os du d'Amant[1] & Pfelin.

The tenth of the Calends of April, in
  Gothic count,
Revived again by evil people:
The fire [of insight] extinguished,
  diabolical assembly,
Seeking the bones of the Daemon of
  Psellus.

[1]Perhaps Nostradamus scrambled *Démon* into *d'amant* to placate the Church censors.

Here is another quatrain the debunkers of Nostradamus avoid challenging. Nostradamus seems well aware of the change that would take place 28 years later in 1582, when most Catholic countries adopted the reformed Gregorian calendar of Pope Gregory XIII over the Julian calendar of his time. Each year of the Julian calendar contained 365 days and six hours, and by 1582 the extra time had gradually moved the vernal equinox from 21 March to 11 March. Pope Gregory rectified the error by making 10 days vanish. October 5 became October 15, 1582. The change was quite unpopular; most Europeans demanded their ten days back.

The tenth day of the **Calends of April** is April 10, for the Calends signified the first day of the Roman month. The new Gregorian system would subtract 10 days from the **Gothic count** making it April 1, or Good Friday, a date regarded as the best day for magical invocations. Some believe that Nostradamus is clueing us in to the day he began conjuring and writing *Les Propheties*, around the end of March, 1554.

I believe the last two lines give us an account of the final moments of his first session with the devas and daemonic messengers of prophecy. The slender flame of his trance is extinguished along with the **diabolical**, or daemonlike, assembly of spirit familiars. At dawn's first light they poetically retreat with the darkness, seeking the resting place of Michael Psellus, the noted neo-Platonist who wrote a book on demons and Hellenistic magical practices.

1 Q43

Auant qu'aduienne le changement d'empire,	Before the change of empire occurs,
Il aduiendra vn cas bien merueilleux:	There will occur one very marvelous event:
Le champ mué, le pillier de porphire,[1]	The field moved, the pillar of porphyry,
Mis tranſlaté ſus le rocher noilleux.	Placed, transferred onto the gnarled and knotty rock.

[1]Porphyry: a kind of red and white crystallized feldspar.

The **change of empire** might link this to **the great empire** of the Third Reich **falling** through the Ardennes in 5 Q45. However, many empires have **changed** in Europe since 1555. The "Reich" most likely described here is the First Reich, or the Holy Roman Empire. A mere five months after the publication of this quatrain, Charles V handed over his imperial powers to his brother Ferdinand and sovereignty in the Netherlands and Spain to his son Philip II in an opulent formal ceremony (**marvelous event**) in the Hall of the Golden Fleece in Brussels. The following year Charles would leave the fields and palaces of the Spanish Netherlands and sail to Spain, where he would live out his days as a guest in a monastery in the gnarled and arid province of Estremadura. The building of his tomb is at least indirectly implied by the **pillar of porphyry**.

1 Q44

En bref ſeront de retour ſacrifices,	In short sacrifices will be returned,
Contreuenans ſeront mis à martire:	Transgressors will be put to martyrdom:
Plus ne ſeront moines, abbez, ne nouices,	No longer will there be monks, abbots or novices,
Le miel ſera beaucoup plus cher que cire.	The honey will be much more expensive than wax.

A general commentary on religious revolution for the modern era, covering anything from the French Revolution to the present, and perhaps far beyond. At first glance the quatrain fits the disbanding of Catholic monasteries and Church properties, and the banishment of priests and nuns during the French Revolution. The wax candles disappear in church windows and, metaphorically at least, the **honey** anointing Louis XVI during his coronation may see him pay the ultimate expense – losing his life through execution. The new pagan sect is the Cult of Reason. A similar treatment can be applied to the atheistic cult of communism banishing Russian Orthodox priests, abbots, and nuns during the Bolshevik Revolution of 1917. But these are only the first vulgar examples of the changes coming in the new age.

Line 1 is poetic for the return of paganism, perhaps even the neo-paganism and return to earth religions during the latter days of the 20th century. The transgressors are the early pioneers of new religious thinking which the mainstream religions usually depict as cult members or "gurus" and then persecute. In some cases they are martyred for their beliefs. In line 3 Nostradamus adds, with some regret, his vision to that of many prophetic traditions that see an end to the Piscean religions of superstition and faith during the new and scientifically oriented Aquarian Age. The 21st century will find the monks, abbots, and novices of Christianity and many other mainstream religions fading away. Within a century or two they will be replaced by a new, nondogmatic, and scientific religiousness: one that applies theory and meditation techniques in an inner search to scientifically understand human and divine consciousness. In other words, one doesn't blindly believe a religious mystery. In the Aquarian Age one searches, doubts, observes the subjective, and then later analyzes what is witnessed. Then you either know, or accept, that you do not yet understand a religious mystery.

1 Q45

Secteur[1] de sectes grand peine au delateur,	**Cutter of sects great punishment to the informer,**
Beste[2] en theatre, dressé le ieu scenique,	**Beast in the theater, erects the scene [for the] play,**
Du faict antique ennobly l'inuenteur,	**The ancient fact exalts the inventor,**
Par sectes monde[3] confus & schismatique.	**Because of sects the world confused and schismatic.**

[1]Latin *sector* = cutter: he who cuts a sect is its founder.
[2]Beast: a cryptogram of, and an editorial jibe at, John Calvin's chief disciple, Theodore de Bèze (who signed his own name as *Besze*).
[3]*Monde* = world, universe; (fig.) abbreviation for *tout le monde* = everybody.

Leoni believes this is less a prophecy and more a diatribe against John Calvin, but I think that is not completely fair. If one dusts off the anger and takes a second look, **Beast** is a close match to *Besze*, the Old French spelling one finds on the letters and religious pamphlets signed by Calvin's right-hand man, Theodore de Bèze. A **theater** of sorts was set up for him in the summer of 1561 to explain Calvinism to the French National Council (see P63). Catherine de' Medici invited de Bèze in a desperate bid to nurture a dialogue between Protestant French Huguenots and Catholics, and thus avoid a religious civil war. All went well with his performance until he began arguing against the sanctity of the Holy Eucharist (**the ancient fact**). The **beast** from Geneva soon made a hasty retreat, and Europe, especially France, slipped ever deeper into a religious-war fever.

1 Q46

Tout aupres d'Aux, de Leftore &
  Mirande,
Grand feu du Ciel en trois nuicts tumbera:
Cauſe aduiendra bien ſtupende &
  mirande,
Bien peu apres la terre tremblera.
	Very near to Auch, Lectoure and
	  Mirande,
	Great fire in the sky for three nights
	  will fall:
	A very stupendous and marvelous
	  event will happen,
	Very soon after the earth will
	  tremble.

This quatrain describes a celestial event in the département of Gers in south-west France that lasts for three nights and is followed shortly thereafter by an earthquake. UFOs have been reported on the eastern approaches of Gers, outside of Toulon. UFO researcher Jacques Vallée cites an incident on page 282 of *Passport to Magonia*: In August 1961 "five persons observed a luminous yellow sphere, 8 meters in diameter, flying about 10 meters above the road. Horizontal and vertical bands of darker tone gave the impression of 'windows.' The object flew up very fast when the car reached [Toulouse]."

The early 1960s were noted for great earthquakes in Morrocco (1960), Bali (1963), and the great Alaskan quake of 1964. If this celestial event is still in the future, the three towns in Gers may witness significant UFO sightings before an earthquake rumbles out of the nearby Pyrenees Mountains.

1 Q47

Du lac Leman[1] les ſermons faſcheront,
Des iours ſeront reduicts par les ſepmaines:
Puis moys, puis an, puis tous
  deffailliront,
Les magiſtrats damneront leurs loix
  vaines.
	The speeches of Lake Leman become
	  angered.
	The days drag out into weeks:
	Then months, then years, then all
	  will fail,
	The authorities will damn their
	  useless powers.

[1]Latin *Lemannus* = Lake Geneva.

Early interpreters have identified this quatrain as another diatribe by Nostradamus against the Protestant John Calvin, and his theocratic city-state of Geneva. Twentieth-century interpreters claim it for the League of Nations, which disbanded in 1946 and became the United Nations. (Note the quatrain enumeration.) Today the same city is the scene of further debates between US and former Soviet diplomats over nuclear disarmament, as well as the site where much endless and impotent discussion drones on about how to stop the global plague of ethnic cleansing and ethnic wars, primarily the one raging in the Balkans over Bosnia-Herzegovina.

Since the Strategic Arms Reduction Treaties (START I and II) of 1988. Geneva has been and remains one of the major locations for negotiation regarding the 75 percent reduction of United States and Russian nuclear arsenals by 2003. At the time of writing (early 1996), Worldwatch reports that around 40,600 nuclear warheads remain undestroyed, and dozens of nuclear warheads from the collapsed Soviet empire are unaccounted for. Both START treaties will have to be reratified by the new and unsteady nuclear powers of Ukraine, Belarus, and Kazakhstan. If this cannot happen, then START I and II are useless. The Ukraine shows signs of keeping a few of its strategic nuclear weapons while shipping most back to the Russian Federation, and the same hoarding could happen between now and 2003 if the five former Soviet republics in Central Asia go through with their dream of forming a confederation or even a new state of their own called Turkestan. The security measures that kept nuclear weapons safely inside the borders of the Soviet Union have evaporated with its dissolution. Qualified intelligence reports in 1993 mention at least two nuclear-tipped Soviet missiles surfacing in Iran.

Prophetically speaking, START is like having hamburger "buns" without the "beef" of the unilateral nuclear disarmament of all states. The lack of a solid global proliferation control policy has helped set the stage for the entry of Nostradamus' third and final Antichrist, and his war of Armageddon.

Quatrain Indexing Date: Q47 = 1947, a near miss for 1946, the ratification year of the United Nations Organization, which has New York City and Geneva as its two primary capitals.

1 Q48

Vingt ans du regne de la Lune paſſez,	**When twenty years of the Moon's reign have passed,**
Sept mil ans autre tiendra ſa monarchie:	**Another will take up its reign for 7,000 years:**
Quand le Soleil prendra ſes iours laſſez,	**When the exhausted Sun gathers up its days,**
Lors accomplit & mine ma prophetie.	**Then my prophecy and threats will be accomplished.**

The Nostradamus controversy (whether he is a prophet or a practical joker) is approaching 450 years in running. This quatrain might clue us in to the length of the prophet's legacy. Roussat believes the astrological lunar cycle mentioned above is that of 1535 to 1889. Twenty years after 1535 is *Les Propheties'* publication day, 1555. This could extend Nostradamus' chronicle of human history beyond the ninth millennium.

1 Q49

Beaucoup auant telles menees, Ceux d'Orient par la vertu lunaire:[1] L'an mil fept cens feront grands emmenees, Subiugant prefque le coing Aquilonaire.[2]	Very much before such intrigues, Those of the east by virtue of the Moon: The year 1700 will cause the great ones to be carried away, Nearly subjugating a corner of the northern land.

[1]lunaire = of the moon; symbolic of the crescent battle flag of the Ottoman Turks.
[2]Latin aquilonaris = northern.

On assuming the crown of Sweden in 1697, Charles XII faced a three-way threat to Swedish supremacy of the Baltic from the neighboring kings (**great ones**) of Denmark and Poland and Peter the Great of Russia. Diplomatic intrigues developed into open conflict by the year 1700. The Great Northern War lasted 21 years. Charles XII managed briefly to get the Turks (**the moon**) into the fray against Russia.

In the end Charles' expansionism was checked and the war all but ended when he was shot through the eyes at the siege of Fredrikshald in Norway in late 1718. By the treaties of Stockholm (1709–20) a number of territories changed hands in the Baltic. Sweden delivered the duchies of Bremen and Verden to Hanover for a large war indemnity and gave the city of Stettin and parts of west Pomerania to Prussia. Denmark gave up its war prizes, except for Schleswig. Russia received the largest prizes – Livonia, Ingermanland, part of Karelia, and a number of Baltic islands and Finland ceded from Sweden (**nearly subjugating a corner of the northern Land**).

1 Q50

De l'aquatique triplicité naiftra, D'vn qui fera le jeudy pour fa fefte: Son bruit, loz, regne, fa puiffance croiftra, Par terre & mer aux Oriens tempefte.	Out of aquatic triplicity will be born, One who will take Thursday for his feast day: His [its] renown, praise, reign, and power will grow, By earth and sea the East [is] turbulent.

The list of leaders born with three planets in a water sign can be narrowed down to Americans, whose feast day is the national holiday of Thanksgiving Day, held every year the fourth Thursday of November. The third party hopeful, in the 1992 American presidential elections, Ross Perot, was born with a Jupiter–Sun conjunction with near conjunction of the Moon in Cancer. The winner, Bill Clinton, has no water aspects in his birth chart, but the Clinton/Gore administration, which was in effect **born** on election night (3 November 1992), not only has the

Sun, Pluto, and Mercury in the water sign of Scorpio, but also possesses a grand *triplicity* of planets in three water signs. This augurs a two-term presidency that plants and waters the seeds of a new, post-Cold War America. This administration promotes and nurtures a new vision of internationalism on all levels of diplomacy, economy, and military policy. It may be hard for us now to imagine it, but people in the 2050s may look back on three 20th-century American presidents as the leaders most responsible for bringing the world out of nationalistic wars, cold wars, and ecological wars and into a new and global society. These presidents will be Franklin Delano Roosevelt, Richard Nixon, and William Jefferson Clinton.

Line 4 implies that future Gulf or Middle East wars will plague Clinton in his second term. Even a crisis over Hong Kong, Taiwan or Korea may yet burden him with a military crisis from 1996 through 1999. Century 4, Quatrain 95, however, implies that the victor is born on American soil.

1 Q51

Chef d'Aries,[1] Iupiter, & Saturne,	**Head of Aries, Jupiter and Saturn**
Dieu eternel quelles mutations?	**Eternal God what changes!**
Puis par long fiecle fon maling temps	**Then the bad times return after a**
retourne	**long century,**
Gaule, & Italie quelles efmotions?	**What turmoil in France and Italy.**

[1]The head of Aries: (astrol.) the constellation of Aries.

Several windows in time are possible in relation to line 1's astrological conjunction of Jupiter and Saturn in Aries. Leoni cites Dr Christian Wöllner's calculations for the conjunction: on 19 October 1583, and 13 December 1702, and again on 2 September 1995. One could agree with Leoni that 1702 seems to be a fulfillment of the prophecy since Italy and France were fighting in the War of the Spanish Succession in 1702. But there are two problems. One is that Wöllner's computations are notoriously inaccurate; the other is Leoni's prejudice against astrology, which often dilutes this fine scholar's research when it comes to checking astrological interpretation of Nostradamus.

The next Jupiter–Saturn conjunction will be in February 1999. This is a very significant year in Nostradamus' prophecies. The survival or destruction of human civilization hinges on what actions we take, individually and globally, during the last year of this millennium. Imagine what awe-inspiring and terrible visions we would experience if a divine spirit stirred an oracle's bowl of water to conjure visions for humanity 441 years from today. Would we not cry out as Nostradamus has in the second line? The things we take for granted, like cars, commercial jets, commercials themselves – whether on billboards or the boob tube – would appear miraculous to the 16th-century mind. Alas, despite all these marvels, mankind does not balance technological discoveries with new revelations in spiritual consciousness. After the long 20th century is finished, the bad times return with a new conjunction in the sign of Aries, whose god, Mars, is that of war. But occult teachings tell us there are two sides to every aspect. Mars, if he strives for consciousness and compassion, becomes the sacred magician, the spiritual teacher; he holds the firebrand of awareness, not war.

The higher aspect of Mars tells us that if there must be turmoil in France, Italy, and the world, let it be a war against ignorance, superstition, and stupid habits. Let it be a war against the conditioning of each new generation that causes them to unconsciously cling to fossilized moralities. Mars the Magus tells us that the new millennium will require that we become a new humanity.

Astrological Time Window

The Jupiter–Saturn conjunction in Aries takes place only twice in the 20th century: 21 December 1939 through 21 March 1940, and 14 February through 2 March 1999 (see 10 Q72). The dating implies that the **bad times** similar to those of World War II return again at the end of the 20th century. With the new millennium comes the new challenge of an exploding birth rate and plummeting food and water reserves, added to the uncertain ecological consequences of global warming. If 1999 does not see a dramatic global resolve to change ourselves and tackle these problems, Armageddon may yet visit us in the 2020s and 2030s.

1 Q52

Les deux malins de Scorpion conioinct,	**Two wicked ones conjoined in Scorpio,**
Le grand feigneur meurtriy¹ dedans fa falle:	**The great lord murdered within his hall:**
Pefte à l'Eglife par le nouueau Roy ionct,	**A pestilence to the Church, from the king newly united,**
L'Europe baffe & Septentrionale.²	**Europe decadent and the North.**

¹Old French *meurtrir* = to murder. In modern French it means only "to bruise."
²Adjective from Latin *septentrio* = [the constellation] of seven stars [near the pole star]: Ursa Minor. Fontbrune believes it is an allusion to the "Russian" bear.

The maliciously aspected planets are Saturn and Mars conjunct in Scorpio. Selim III of the Ottoman Empire was deposed in 1807 during a Mars–Saturn conjunction in Scorpio, but he wasn't strangled until the following year. The year 1807 saw Pope Pius VII a prisoner of Napoleon. It was also the year that most of Europe came under his domination and Czar Alexander I of Russia struck up an alliance with Napoleon against the British.

Astrological Time Window
The next Mars–Saturn conjunctions in Scorpio are October 2012 (the year time ends in the Mayan calendar), July–September 2014, September–October 2042.

1 Q53

Las qu'on verra grand peuple¹ tourmenté,	**Alas! How much one will see the great people tormented,**
Et la Loy ſaincte en totale ruine:	**And the sacred law in total ruin:**
Par autres loix toute la Chreſtienité,	**By other laws all of Christianity [is governed],**
Quand d'or d'argent trouue nouuelle mine.	**When gold and silver is sought through a new source.**

¹Thanks to Nostradamus' Gallic pride, any time one sees **great people** it most often stands for the French.

This may be a continuation of 1 Q51 when the **great people** of France will be tormented in a future time, perhaps as soon as 1999. Imagine the perplexity of Nostradamus viewing our far-looser interpretations of Christianity. Or his bewilderment at our modern electronic economies in which one can draw cyber-coded gold and silver from one's Internet bank. No doubt the prophet had a hard enough time comprehending earlier advances such as the paper money innovation, the Assignats of the French Revolution, the **new source** of which depended on wealth stolen from the clergy.

But for the 21st century this **new source** for silver-and-gold-grubbing may imply a new resource such as Arab oil and the dangers of the Christian world's depending on an ever more militant Islam as a source of wealth. Equally possible is a new source of wealth coming from developed countries who will profit from their grain reserves in an overpopulated world as much as the petrol states of the Middle East will use its oil reserves as a political weapon in an energy-starved world.

Quatrain Indexing Date: 1953, perhaps a near-miss in dating the first significant Pan-Arab resistance against the West when Egypt's Colonel Nasser nationalized the Suez Canal in 1956.

See Index: Jupiter–Saturn conjunctions.

1 Q54

Deux reuolts faicte du maling falcigere,¹	**Two revolutions caused by the evil scythe-bearer,**
De regne & ſiecles faict permutation:	**Making a complete change in reign and centuries:**
Le mobil ſigne à ſon endroict ſi ingere,	**The mobile sign [of Libra] in its place so mettlesome,**
Aux deux egaux & d'inclination.	**Equal in favour to both sides.**

¹Latin *falciger* = carrying a scythe.

Conventional wisdom would tag the *scythe-bearer* as Saturn, which exerted its negative influence in the French and Russian Revolutions. However, Saturn also has constructive ways of reflecting uncompromising change by being the planet of reality checks. In the light of Saturn's positive utility, the two revolutions mentioned here not only concern the rise and fall of Marxist communism, but also point to the revolutions taking place at the beginning and end of the 20th century. The first Russian Revolution of 1917 was Saturn's reality check on the corruption of the Czar's autocratic rule. In August 1991, 74 years later, a second Saturnian revolution exposed the social and political bankruptcy of the Bolshevik Utopia, signaling the disintegration of the Soviet bloc.

The quatrain indexing (Q54) could be interpreted as a fulcrum in time, the midpoint in the pendulum's swing from one extreme revolution to the advent of another. The death of Stalin made 1953 (a near-miss for Q54) a pivotal year in the Cold War and for communist hegemony, through the election of Nikita Khruschev as First Secretary of the Central Committee. In this powerful position Krushchev could begin the de-Stalinization of Soviet society.

The mobile sign is Libra's scales of Justice and Balance, which Nostradamus in other quatrains uses as a symbol for democracy. Perhaps this prediction hints that the kind of *change* Nostradamus is referring to here is a form of democratic government which affirms that all people are created equal (*equal in favor to both sides*).

A wider interpretation of the two revolutions of the hammer and sickle (*scythe*) sees them as disclosing the fates of the Russian and Chinese communist revolutions. Communism in those countries will completely collapse as a result of Chinese and Russian efforts to democratize before the coming millennium, *making a change in reign and centuries*.

If America or democracy is implied by the *mobile sign* of Libra, it could also foretell a time of chaos and crisis for global democracy in the near future. The strain on Earth's finite resources and food made by an increasingly voracious horde of humanity will require that democracy, like communism, undergo revolutionary changes. One solution may be a blend of the best aspects of democracy and communism. In other words, line 1's Saturn reality check in the 21st century may intimate to us that a true and lasting social revolution cannot come from the extremes of the right and left wing but through balance (*equal in favor of both sides*), through a synthesis of East and West, communism and democracy, socialism and capitalism.

Quatrain Indexing Date: 1954, which misses Stalin's death by one year; or, 2054, marking a new global civilization operating under a political-economic system that is a synthesis of democracy and communism, and socialism and capitalism.

See Index: Russian Revolution; fall of communism.

1 Q55

Soubs l'oppofite climat Babylonique,[1]   **Under the opposite Babylonian**
Grande fera de fang effufion: **climate,**
Que terre & mer, air, Ciel fera inique,   **There will be great shedding of blood:**
Sectes, faim, regnes, peftes, confufion.   **Heaven will appear unjust both on**
                                                     land and sea and in the air,
                                                   Sects, famine, kingdoms, plagues,
                                                     confusion.

[1]Latin *Babylonicus* = Babylonian; in this case "the place opposite Babylon" is poetic for the city of Paris, Nostradamus' other *Babylon*.

The first line is puzzling. It may apply to Paris, France, which sometimes Nostradamus described as the Mesopotamia of Europe, for the city is geographically defined by two rivers, the Seine and the Marne. The phrase can be applied equally to the region of modern-day Mesopotamia (Iraq), where the Tigris and Euphrates rivers flow. It is safe to say that the fates of both "Mesopotamias" are at least poetically intertwined. French forces played a large part in Operation Desert Storm. The massive allied airstrikes and the funeral shroud of burning Kuwaiti oil fields torched by retreating Iraqis did indeed make the heavens appear unjust on the land, sea, and in the atmosphere people breathed. The neighboring **kingdoms** of the Gulf Sheiks, Jordanians, and Saudis suffered terribly from the war and its ecological disasters. At the time of writing, five years after the Gulf War, the cessation of hostilities has left only political uncertainty (**confusion**) in the Gulf, thousands of malnourished Iraqi children (**famine**), and a future legacy of health problems and shortened life expectancy (**plagues**) due to petroleum pollution.

The future may look upon the blackened Mesopotamia of the Middle East taking its revenge on Paris, the Mesopotamia of Europe. In December 1994 Algerian terrorists held a dress rehearsal. On Christmas Eve Algerian terrorists hijacked Air France Flight 8969, with its 227 passengers, at Algiers' Houari-Boumédienne International Airport. During the tense siege three hostages were killed before the plane was permitted to fly to Marseilles. When they landed in the early hours of 26 December, the hijackers demanded 27 tons of fuel to fly to Paris (a flight to Paris requires only 10 tons). Later that afternoon they were overpowered and killed when anti-terrorist gendarmes hurled concussion grenades into the cockpit.

Some of the hostages had overheard the terrorists talk about their plan to detonate the plane over Paris. They saw them check and recheck 20 sticks of dynamite set behind the pilots' seats and the passenger seats in the central portion of the plane between the gas tanks in the wings. If they had succeeded in flying out of Marseilles for Paris, the 42-ton Airbus with 15 tons of highly volatile jet fuel would have erupted into a giant gasoline bomb over central Paris, creating a conflagration as catastrophic as a detonation of a tactical nuclear weapon. The tons of flaming jet fuel would have set large areas of the city on fire.

See Index: Algerian plane hijack.

1 Q56

Vous verrez toſt & tard faire grand change,	You will see, sooner and later, great
Horreurs extremes & vindications:	changes made,
Que ſi la lune conduicte par ſon ange,	Extreme horrors and vengeances:
Le Ciel s'approche des inclinations.	For as the moon [of Islam] is thus led by its angel,
	The heavens draw near to the reckoning.

Gabreel (Gabriel) is the avenging angel of the Christian and the Islamic Apocalypse. As suggested in 10 Q72, the terror of the Middle Eastern Antichrist comes from the skies (*the heavens*). This could therefore mean that nuclear *fires from the skies* (from 10 Q72) will descend on the Western democratic powers as early as July of 1999. The quatrain indexing may target the year 1956, which witnessed the first successful victory of Pan-Arab Nationalism against the West during the Suez Canal incident, when Egyptian President Gamal Abdel Nasser nationalized the Suez Canal and forced French and British forces to withdraw.

Quatrain Indexing Date: Q56 = 1956, the year of the Suez Canal crisis.

1 Q57

Par grand diſcord la trombe tremblera	By great discord the whirlwind will tremble
Accord rompu dreſſant la teſte au Ciel:	Broken accord, lifting the head to heaven:
Bouche ſanglante dans le ſang nagera,	Bloody mouth will swim with blood,
Au ſol la face ointe de laict & miel.	The face once anointed with milk and honey lies in the soil.

This remarkable prophecy was written 239 years before the event. Louis XVI mounted the scaffold, his eyes sweeping over the jeering mob below. Under his piercing gaze the drums and crowd fell silent and the deposed king began to protest his innocence in clear, steady tones. But the drums started to roll again and the executioner Sanson proceeded. As he raised the blade, witnesses heard the king reciting the third verse of the third psalm, "Thou, O Lord, are my glory, and lifter of my head . . ." until his voice was silenced by the falling blade. Sanson then lifted the king's severed head high in the air in front of the crowd.

The **whirlwind** of the French Revolution did tremble with the death of Louis XVI, setting into motion the lunacy of the Reign of Terror. Louis had promised to remain in Paris but was caught escaping (**broken accord**). The prophet describes the executioner displaying the king's severed head to the mob and, in a double pun, echoes Louis' last words from the third psalm (**lifting the head to heaven**), which he recited as the blade fell. Line 3 gives a vivid description of beheading (**bloody mouth will swim with blood**).

In considering the last line, Steward Robb, in *Prophecies of World Events By Nostradamus*, gives us an ingenious interpretation that dates the beginning and end of Louis' life as king. Louis had been crowned on the feast day of St Agnes, 21 January, and in honor of that day his face was anointed with milk and honey. The holy offices of St Agnes contain the key words to line 4: *Mel* [honey] *et lac* [milk] *ex ore* [mouth] *ejus suscepi, et sanguis* [blood] *ejus ornavit oras* [face] . . . Louis was guillotined 19 years after his coronation, on St Agnes' Day, 21 January 1793.

See Index: flight to Varennes.

1 Q58

Tranché le ventre naiſtra auec deux teſtes,	Cutting the belly, [it] will be born with two heads,
Et quatre bras: quelques ans entiers viura:	And four arms: A few years it will live whole:
Jour qui Alquiloye¹ celebrera ſes feſtes,	The day which Aquileia will celebrate its feasts,
Foſſen, Turin, chef Ferrare ſuyura.	Fossano, Turin, chief of Ferrara will follow.

¹There were ten cities called Aquileia in the Roman Empire. Ancient Venice may be intended here. Le Pelletier suggests Latin *Aquilae lex* = eagle's law.

It is difficult for any interpreter to read the entrails of this quatrain. I place it as a French prophet's biased synonym for the monster **born with two heads** sired by Charles V when he split his vast empire between his brother Ferdinand and his son Philip II six short months after this quatrain was published. One could say that these **two heads** later became the empires of the Spanish and the Austrian Habsburgs. The Austrian Habsburgs would eventually adopt the two-headed black eagle as their emblem.

The **four arms** of this monster wrap Nostradamus' France in their embrace. They are the routes of potential dangers and invasions: the first **arm** is in the Pyrenees through Navarre, the Spanish Netherlands is the second; the invasion routes through Savoy and Italy are the third **arm**; and those through the ports of the south of France the fourth. The final line lists those Italian and Mediterranean kingdoms and states that will follow the new world order after Charles V's retirement. The intimation that Philip and Ferdinand would unite the empire again and add Venice/Aquileia to the alliance never became reality.

1 Q59

Les exilez deportez dans les iſles,
Au changement d'vn plus cruel monarque
Seront meurtris: & mis deux les ſcintiles,[1]
Qui de parler ne ſeront eſtez parques.[2]
	The exiles deported to the isles,
	At the advent of an even crueler
	    monarch
	Will be murdered: and two put to the
	    sparks,
	Who had not been sparing with their
	    speech.

[1]Latin scintilla = spark.
[2]parques, from Latin parcus = sparing, moderate.

A general augury for history's endless file of people being deported to prison camps. The word "isolation" is etymologically connected with **isles** (islands). If I were to pick the most notorious penal archipelago in history, I would choose Josef Stalin's island chain of concentration camps spread across the vastness of the Soviet Union, described by Russian author Alexander Solzhenitsyn as the Gulag Archipelago. Few **monarchs** were as cruel, or sent more millions to oblivion than Stalin.

With this interpretation in mind I wish to translate ſcintile with a more modern application – literally **sparks** representing the flash of modern guns as they cut down the political enemies of Stalin by firing squad.

1 Q60

Vn Empereur naiſtra pres d'Italie,
Qui a l'Empire ſera vendu bien cher:
Diront auec quels gens il ſe ralie,
Qu'on trouuera moins prince que boucher.
	An Emperor will be born near Italy,
	He will cost his Empire very dearly:
	They will say that from the sort of
	    people that surround him,
	That he is less a prince than a
	    butcher.

Nostradamus foresaw the coming of three tyrants whom he called Antichrist. These men, he warned, could move mankind towards total world destruction sometime shortly after the year 2000. The first of these is identified in this quatrain. He is a man who was to critically influence the military and political course of modern European history – Napoleon Bonaparte, born near Italy on the island of Corsica.

Nostradamus envisioned a bloody reign of a commoner dictator (**common advent of the people**) beginning in 1792 (see EP167). This man was destined to force the crowned heads of Europe to adopt his laws and strategies so they could defeat his revolutionary empire, an empire that would cost France 2 million men, to make and to lose. As a consequence, the united Europe that defeated Napoleon became ever more Napoleonic. Moreover, the First Antichrist succeeded in steering European history towards the demise of monarchies, a development that set the geopolitical stage for the two future Antichrists. Nostradamus predicted that they would emerge in the 1940s and 1990s.

See Index: Antichrist – the First (Napoleon), Second (Hitler), and Third (future).

1 Q61

La republique miferable infelice,[1]	The miserable, unhappy republic,
Sera vaftee[2] de nouueau magiftrat:	Will be ruined by the new magistrate:
Leur grand amas de l'exil malefice,	Their great amassing of the wicked exile,
Fera Sueue rauir leur grand contract.	Will cause the Swiss to carry off their great contracts.

[1]Latin infelix = unhappy.

An orthodox slant would construe this as another attack by Nostradamus on John Calvin, who was shepherd to the Protestant citizens of Geneva and de facto **magistrate** of a theocratic city-state. Rather than stay with the mainstream theory I will pin this quatrain on the near-future destiny of the Palestinian state, under its new (and first) president, Yasser Arafat. Those doing all the **amassing** (or better, "Hamassing") against Arafat are the anti-Zionist Palestinian faction, Hamas. The subjects of my interpretation will suffer either from my correct insight or from my prophetic bias, as I am tainted by the conditioning of a Christianity-challenged Westerner. This said, I sense that Yasser Arafat's presidency will be a bust. Perhaps he is assassinated. There seem to be few good leaders to replace him, but then my eyes are filled only with images of Arafat, thanks to the bias of the Western press.

My decoding hinges on whether the French word for "amassing," amas, is in fact a cryptogram for (H)amas, whose operatives may perform some act of terrorism so heinous that it derails the efforts of peacemakers from the Middle East all the way to the peace tables of Geneva.

This interpretation hinges on **Swiss** representing a Geneva that is more than Calvinist – a Geneva that is the capital of 20th-century diplomacy. Otherwise this quatrain remains better suited to a time and a bias far closer to Nostradamus' heart.

1 Q62

Le grand perte las que feront les lettres,	A great loss, alas! there will be of learning,
Auant le cicle de Latona[1] parfaict:	Before the cycle of Latona [the moon] is completed:
Feu grand deluge plus par ignares fceptres,	Fire, great flood more through ignorant rulers,
Que de long fiecle ne fe verra refaict.	How long the [lunar] cycle will not see itself restored.

[1]The mythological mother of Apollo and Diana; the Moon. The Latonan cycle is based on lunar months and lasts roughly 354 years.

A society that abandons its higher arts is like a tree that cuts off its own flowers. That society becomes impoverished and the tree will eventually come to a disaster. Nearly all great civilizations have begun their decline by throwing the pearls of their highest understanding into the maw of its swinish collective mind, its lowest common denominator of values. Today the Pax Americana spreads across the world its materialism and the all-hallowed market-value and Mickey-Mouse mentality. Hokum is holy. Excellence becomes a hostage of the majority vote. Soon the world will watch tabloid shows like *American Journal* and forget to read the *Journal American*. Art, music and literature will become democratic. Popularity, not aesthetics, will dictate funding. The Grammies and the Oscars will be the only diploma respected. MTV will be our grandchildren's professors and mentors. Whatever challenges our values or rattles our rationales will be deemed antisocial. Soon after that, it will be forgotten altogether. As Lynda S. Clary of Bethesda, Maryland, wrote in the Letters section of *Time* Magazine, "Killing cultural funding will leave future generations with an educational, aesthetic and spiritual deficit far greater than the financial one we currently face."

Not only has American society degraded and thrown away the wisdom of native cultures (along with the natives), it will also soon deny its own hard-won lessons when history departments shut down for lack of funding, or worse, are downsized in intellectual excellence to match the students' waning capacity. The consequence is an even dumber generation succeeding the last, ruled by those chosen by the mobocracy because they are predictable, and lower in quality than the mob itself.

If we do not turn back to the value of excellence, the current grand lunar cycle – which began in 1889 with a puff of coal-industry smoke during the high industrial revolution – will host an ecological disaster of biblical proportions before the Latonan cycle ends in AD 2243.

Astrological Time Window

Lunar cycles are based on lunar rather than solar months. They last roughly 354 years. The lunar cycle mentioned here is 1889–2243. This means that a loss of respect for learning and the lessons of the past will create a mediocrity explosion to parallel the exploding birth rates and pollution, until the climate and the seas rise up against us at the onset of the 23rd century. This date is close to the actual date inaugurating the full influence of the Aquarian Age, a time when the worship of excellence and consciousness will return.

1 Q63

Les fleurs[1] paſſés diminue le monde,	**Pestilences extinguished, the world becomes small,**
Long temps la paix terres inhabitées:	**For a long time the lands will be inhabited in peace:**
Seur marchera par Ciel, terre, mer & onde:	**One will travel safely by air, [over] land, sea and wave:**
Puis de nouueau les guerres ſuſcitées.	**Then wars will start anew.**

[1]Misprint for *fléaux* = the "ring" of inflammation around the "roses" of pestilential boils.

No prophecy could better describe the Cold War era. By 1963 (Q63), advances in medical science had almost eradicated the great killer diseases such as yellow fever, polio, and smallpox. The dawning jet age following the war paved the way for countless millions to travel safely through the skies, to every continent, over every ocean. Airline companies transported 1.3 billion passengers in 1995. Developments in communications technology facilitated contact between different peoples and cultures.

For nearly half a century fear of the atomic bomb has prevented the power brokers of the world from punishing Earth with a third global war. The struggle between the superpowers has been played out in the developing countries of the Third World.

Superpower disagreements have boiled to the surface during a string of wars after 1945: Korea, Suez, Vietnam, and a dozen other confrontations between the Arab nations and Israel, or India and Pakistan. With the end of the Cold War, tensions are on the increase in the Third World, as are a series of vicious wars arising out of the ethnic hotbeds in the former Communist bloc, the Second World. More people flew around the world in 1995 than in any previous year, but the year also produced an increase in wars across the world. Between 30 to 32 conflicts are raging at the time of writing, the majority of them civil wars within national boundaries.

The technological and medical advances foretold by Nostradamus have their darker consequences. A drastic cut in infant mortality has spawned overpopulation. Record growth in industrial production has improved the quality of life, but pollution threatens Earth's fragile ecosystem. Computers, which have revolutionized our lives, are capable of transmitting a message of peace – or global nuclear destruction – at the stroke of a key.

Quatrain Indexing Date: Q63 = 1963?

See Index: inventions foreseen.

1 Q64

De nuict Soleil penſeront auoir veu,	**They will think they have seen the**
Quand le pourceau demy homme on	**sun at night,**
verra:	**When they see the half-pig man:**
Bruict, chant, bataille, au Ciel battre	**Noise, chants, battles seen fought in**
aperceu:	**the sky:**
Et beſtes brutes à parler lon orra.	**And one will hear brute beasts**
	speaking

Leoni's tongue-in-porcine-cheek interpretation that Khrushchev is the *half-pig man* might fit with the indexing to reveal a date (1964); however, I see this as another example of the uncanny accuracy of Nostradamus in forecasting future technology. He records future battles of great air fleets, piloted by *half-pig* men (masked pilots). He hears their radio transmissions to match his own wild poetry, with foreign tongues and coded gibberish: **Noise, chants . . . brute beasts speaking.**

In my previous books I have applied this quatrain to the Battle of Britain, but it could easily be applied to the jet pilots in the Korean, Vietnamese, and Yom Kippur wars, Desert Storm, and unfortunately, coming airbattles in the next few decades of the 21st century.

Quatrain Indexing Date: 1964 as a near enough date for Krushchev – or airbattles over Vietnam.

1 Q65

Enfans ſans mains[1] iamais veu ſi grand	**Child without [power] never was seen**
foudre,	**so great a thunderbolt,**
L'enfant royal au ieu d'œſteuf[2] bleſsé:	**The royal child, at the game of**
Au puy[3] briſes[4] fulgures[5] allant mouldre,	**revenge, wounded:**
Trois ſouz les chaines[6] par le milieu	**On the summit fractures, lightning**
trouſſés.	**flashes going to soundly thrash,**
	Three in chains trussed up around
	the middle.

[1]Latin *manus* = hand force, strength, powers.
[2]Old French *éteuf* = either ball (for tennis) or (fig.) "a game of revenge."
[3]Old French *puy* = summit, hill.
[4]Old French = breaks, fractures.
[5]Latin *fulgur* = lightning strike.
[6]Old French *chêne* = oak; however, "chain" is possible.

During his incarceration in the Temple prison, Louis XVII, the Bourbon heir to the throne, was taken away from his mother and placed into the grubby hands of Simon the Cobbler. He suffered lightning flashes of pain from numerous whippings and beatings. Simon was instructed to humble the young Dauphin and seemed to exult in the abuse, as if it were a game. The context of the word Nostradamus uses, *oesteuf*, suggests that the quatrain figuratively describes a game of revenge. Circumstantial evidence points to the Dauphin's injuries as the cause of death in 1795. The last line could be either a representative image of aristocrats tied together by the waist being led to the guillotine, or it specifically points to the three most important aristocratic victims of the Reign of Terror: Louis XVI, Louis XVII and Queen Marie Antoinette. The description would then be poetic rather than factual, since the king and queen were not tied in this way, and the Dauphin died in prison.

1 Q66

Celuy qui lors portera les nouuelles,	He who then will bear the news,
Apres vn peu il viendra respirer	After a short while he will come to rest
Viuiers, Tournon, Montferrant & Pradelles,	Viviers, Tournon, Montferrand and Pradelles,
Grefle & tempeftes les fera foufpirer.	Hail and tempests will make them gasp.

A quatrain with a clear though private message. Because the recipient and the messenger have long since returned to dust, it is pointless to decipher it except to say that Pradelles is in Haute-Loire in east-central France; Montferrand is in the Puy-de-Dome; Viviers is on the west bank of the Rhône in Languedoc; and so is Tournon, about seven miles upstream from Valence.

1 Q67

La grand famine que ie fens approcher,	The great famine which I sense approaching,
Souuent tourner, puis eftre vniuerfelle:	Will often turn [up in various places] then become universal:
Si grande & longue qu'on viendra arracher,	It will be so vast and long-lasting that [people] will grab
Du bois racine, & l'enfant de mammelle.	Roots from the trees and children from the breast.

I once watched a documentary called The Birth of Europe. The segment portrayed the travails of the 13th century, when European society suffered terrible plagues and wars because its numbers had swelled beyond the agricultural sustainability of the times. The first half of the century welcomed a series of bountiful harvests and good weather that instituted a sudden population increase. Then an abrupt climate change called the Little Ice Age visited Europe, causing skies to be darkened with unremitting rain for three straight years. Europe suffered continental crop failures, followed by a great famine, and finally by the Black Death, the bubonic plague. Society was disrupted and the land was vexed by fundamentalist religious extremism and numerous wars over dwindling resources. The beleaguered all across the continent were convinced that the Apocalypse was at hand. One empirical fact supports the prophetic vision of St John the Divine: the Black Death alone killed off one-third of the European population, and wars and famines reduced it further by half.

The documentary made me wonder. Will history repeat itself? Will the 21st century repeat the horrors of the 13th because a little global warming – rather than a little ice age – disrupts our overwrought agriculture and technology? Will half the expected 8 billion of us by 2020 die of famines, plagues, and wars?

As we approach the 21st century, each day 250,000 people are born, more than 90,000 new motor vehicles hit the road, more than 160 square miles of tropical rain forest are destroyed, 57,000,000 metric tons of carbon dioxide contaminate the air, and 40,000 children under the age of 5 die from hunger or bacteria-infested water.

With the end of the Cold War the world becomes ever more enamored with the market-side, high-waste-producing American lifestyle, yet our current global technologies and infrastructure and food sustainability can support a population of only 2.5 billion living the American Dream. By 1997 the world population will exceed 5.7 billion. Ninety million hungry and thirsty new consumers are born each year. By the new millennium this will increase to 100 million each year. In 20 years the population will reach 8 billion; in 50 years, 14 billion. Zero Population Growth reports that the United States – the land of 3,000 calories a day per capita – is undergoing a baby boom even greater than the one after World War II. The country that consumes the most energy and spews out the most pollution (one-sixth of the population using one-quarter of the world's energy) will roughly double in numbers to 500 million by 2050, and be responsible for half the world's current energy consumption rate! By 2030 China could by itself eat up the world, since it will require *all* the current grain exports of the world. By 2025, we will have to build a nuclear power plant every week to keep up with the energy demands of nearly a dozen billion people!

Thirteenth-century hell hath no fury like the one we are concocting for ourselves in the 21st century – that is, if we don't heed the warnings of our prognosticator and today's insightful pundits.

The plagues, famines, and droughts predicted by Nostradamus have already begun and continue to be right on astrological schedule, as I correctly forecast in my first book in 1986. The growing world drought and the spread of famine and hunger, especially in early 1990s Africa, continues to remind a foot-dragging new world order that the greenhouse effect cannot be ignored.

Quatrain Indexing Date: Q67 = 1967, the year dating the beginning of the future worldwide famines. This is the year grain production in Africa began its current, and disastrous, decline.

See Index: Global famine.

1 Q68

O quel horrible & malheureux tourment,	Oh what a horrible and ill-starred torment,
Trois innocens qu'on viendra à liurer:	Three innocent ones whom one will come to hand over:
Poifon fufpecte, mal gardé tradiment,	Poison suspected, evil treason preserved,
Mis en horreur par bourreaux enyurez.	Put in horror by intoxicated executioners.

I agree with Lamont that upon first impression this could be about the brutal murder of the Czar Nicholas and his family by Red Guards in Ekaterinburg, Siberia, in 1917. Similar word links to poisoning exist in other Romanov murder quatrains, such as 4 Q71. Sometimes it is prudent to avoid the habit of scholars who pin meanings of a quatrain to their own century. Perhaps this one is about the 16th.

In line 1 Nostradamus could be playing with words again to make a compound pun – if we can replace the letters left out of *tourment*. If one adds an n and e to *tourment* the line could also read **Oh what a horrible and ill-starred** tournament. Henry II suffered the **torment** of a mortal wound in a tournament in 1559 (see 1 Q35). With the addition of letters to one word the fog is burned away and this quatrain starts to make a lot of sense. The **three innocent ones** are his young sons, François, Charles, and Henry, who are burdened with adult responsibilities and kingship far too soon. Novelists enjoy saying that Charles IX was poisoned, but no definite proof exists; Francis II died from the fainting sickness shortly after the death of his father; and Henry III was assassinated.

The last two lines may suddenly change the subject, as Nostradamus commonly does. From the three Valois kings he jumps to the plots of Henry III against Henry de Guise, his chief rival. Perhaps the last line pictures Guise walking into the king's bedchamber to find the king's bodyguards waiting for him with drawn swords and the sour and rapid breath of drunken assassins poised for murder.

Even so, I cannot help but ride the waves upon Psellus' wishing bowl back to the royals of the 20th century, the Romanovs. It is a documented fact that while the Czar, his family, and retainers waited in the basement, their executioners, sitting upstairs, were drinking heavily to fortify themselves while they loaded their pistols. The Czar's jailkeeper kept him in the dark, telling his family that they were only going to be moved to another location. His jailers had known for a while about the treasonous *act*, or order for their execution, and they preserved the secret until the very last moment when the guards appeared at the door with barrels raised and pistol hammers ready to fall.

1 Q69

La grand montaigne ronde de ſept ſtades,[1]	**The great mountain, 4,247 feet in**
Apres paix, guerre, faim, inondation:	**circumference,**
Roulera loin abiſmant grans contrades,[2]	**After peace, war, famine, flooding:**
Meſmes antiques, & grand fondations.	**[The impact] will spread far,**
	drowning great countries,
	Even antiquities and their mighty
	foundations.

[1]A *stade* is 606 feet 9 inches, so seven stades amount to a circumference of 4,247 feet 3 inches. That could give us an asteroid of between 500 and 1,000 feet in diameter, similar to the diameter of Asteroid 1989C which makes a dangerous fly-by past the Earth every 13 months for the next 30 years.
[2]Provencial *contrada* = country.

An asteroid strike seems to be hidden in the cloudy lines of several quatrains – not in some distant future but perhaps as a clear and present danger every 13 months for the next 30 years. The interloper will come in the shape of a shadow-mountain from space, a chunk of refuse labeled by author Jane Blosveld in *Omni* magazine as "rocky placenta left over from the solar system's birth." Each year it orbits closer to Earth, and it may eventually collide with either this planet or the Moon.

In March 1989, retired geologist-turned-asteroid-hunter Dr Henry Holt studied photos taken by the 18-inch Schmidt telescope at Mt Palomar Observatory in California and discovered an asteroid between 500 and 1,000 feet in diameter which he labeled 1989FC. The asteroid hurtled past Earth at a distance of a mere 450,000 miles – a very close shave in cosmic terms. Dr Holt estimates that "sooner or later," it will hit something.

According to Clark Chapman, a researcher at the Planetary Science Institute in Tucson, Arizona, "This asteroid passed closer to the Earth than any asteroid or comet ever observed." Fortunately a rock as big as 1989FC has a 1:20,000 chance of making this interpretation of Nostradamus correct this year or any other. Still, many scientists believe Asteroid 1989FC or a cosmic fragment of similar proportions will eventually score a hit. If it does, Bevan French, a program scientist at NASA's Solar System Exploration Division, says its 2,000-megaton impact would unleash blast waves and firestorms, flattening everything in a 50-mile radius.

See Index: asteroid strike in the Aegean Sea.

1 Q70

Pluie, faim, guerre en Perſe non ceſſée,	**Rain, famine and war in Persia will**
La foy trop grand trahira le monarque:	**not cease,**
Par la finie en Gaule commencee,	**A trust too great will betray the**
Secret augure pour à vn eſtre parque.	**monarch:**
	For the end was planned and conceived
	in France,
	A secret sign for one to be more sparing.

Ayatollah Khomeini captured world attention in 1963 when his Iranian followers staged a series of demonstrations against the Shah of Iran's government. Khomeini was subsequently exiled to Iraq, where he began his 15-year struggle to forge his fundamentalist movement. After being removed from Iraq in 1978 he directed the Iranian revolution from Paris (**planned and conceived in France**) instructing them not to hesitate "to shed your blood to protect Islam and overthrow tyranny." The **trust** the Shah of Iran had in America and its CIA operatives, who had helped him gain power decades before, was indeed **too great**. President Carter balked at the request for overt or even covert military support of the Shah's collapsing regime. The final line is reflective. Perhaps the Islamic revolution that followed was a sign to the Shah that he had pushed his people too hard and too fast into the modern world.

Since 1979, the Iranian people have suffered continued deprivation, natural disasters, and the loss of a million people in wars and revolution. A 1990 earthquake in northern Iran killed 45,000, injured 100,000, and left nearly a half-million people homeless.

Quatrain Indexing Date: Q70 = 1970, when the Shah of Iran is at the height of his power and his trust of his American allies. The Shah's **trust** which was nurtured by President Nixon's administration, would be **too great** a trust during the Carter administration.

1 Q71

La tour marine trois fois prise & reprise,	**The marine tower three times seized**
Par Heſpagnols, Barbares, Ligurins:	**and recaptured,**
Marſeille & Aix, Arles par ceux de Piſe,	**By Spaniards, Barbary raiders, and**
Vaſt,[1] feu, fer, pillé Auignon des	**Ligurians:**
Thurins.	**Marseilles and Aix, Arles by those of**
	Pisa,
	Devastation, fire, steel, Avignon
	pillaged by the Turinese.

[1]Latin *vastus* = devastated.

Cheetham found this one irritating and undecipherable. Lemesurier and Fontbrune fling it on their heaped pile of "Asiatic/Muslim invasion of the

French Riviera" themes. I would meet them halfway. There is no doubt this quatrain points to an invasion of the southern French coast, but the chances of Islamic nations' uniting and creating the naval and armed forces required to invade Europe in some future Normandy-like World War II landing are quite slim. It is a ludicrous prophetic posit equal to the belief of Christian evangelists that China will invade the West with "200 million horsemen."

Most likely we have here a failed alternative future for an invasion of the Ottoman Turks in or close to Nostradamus' time. The prophet saw Spain and Genoa, allied with the Turks and Barbary Corsairs, embarked on an expedition against Provence. I don't doubt he peered through the mists and shadows of his vapour-beclouded bowl of water and saw ships invading the Riviera, or Italian troops plundering Avignon. But at what time? I think Nostradamus would sometimes misread the images when coming out of a trance. The process of moving from a subjective experience to objective writing made it easy for his mind to cloak what he experienced in more familiar garb. He probably saw an invasion of southern France but projected Muslims, Genovese, and Spaniards onto a vision that more adequately describes Provence during its occupation by the Axis and during the Allied landings of World War II. The Italians pillaging Avignon were not Turinese mercenaries but Mussolini's Italians, who marched through Avignon, Aix, and Arles in November of 1942 to assist German troops in occupying Vichy-controlled southern France. For the next year the Italians occupied the French Alpine regions as far west as the Rhône river and as far south as Avignon. Later, in August 1944, the Allied invasion fleet did set sail from bases in Italy. One could say by synecdoche that they are **those of Pisa**. Marseilles in particular, Aix, and Arles endured vicious street fighting or **devastation**, **fire** and **steel**, during the Allied invasion

See Index: Allied invasion of the French Riviera.

1 Q72

De tout Marſeille des habitans changee,	**The inhabitants of Marseilles completely changed,**
Courſe & pourſuitte iuſqu'au pres de Lyon,	**Flight and pursuit right up to the approaches of Lyons,**
Nalbon, Tholoze par Bourdeaux outragee,	**Narbonne, Toulouse outraged by Bordeaux,**
Tuez captifs preſque d'vn million.	**Killed, captives almost a million.**

In 1940 the French government fled Paris for Bordeaux, leaving the capital to Hitler's panzers. The **outraged** towns later belonged to the hated Vichy puppet government. It appears that Nostradamus foresaw the peaceful town and hills of his native Provence become a battlefield in a distant, future war. In 1944, the great steel monsters firing and making tumult landed on the shores of Provence in Operation Dragoon. The forces of the Free French initially pushed the Germans out of Marseilles and all the way back to Lyons. Official French casualty estimates for World War II put their losses at 863,145.

1 Q73

France à cinq pars par neglect affaillie,	**France on five fronts is assaulted**
Tunys, Argel¹ efmeuz par Perfiens:	**because of negligence,**
Leon, Seuille, Barcelonne faillie,	**Tunis, Algeria stirred up by the**
N'aura la claffe par les Venitiens.	**Persians:**
	Leon, Seville, Barcelona having
	yielded,
	[They] will not have the fleet from
	[or for] the Venetians.

¹Anagram for *Alger.* = Algeria.

First let us examine this as a prophecy for our time. The subject is France's resistance to European Union. It might even cover Chirac's international blunders of brazenly perforating a South Pacific atoll with nuclear detonations in the mid-1990s at a time when nuclear test-ban efforts were showing promise. Line 2 covers the threat of Islamic fundamentalism to France in the guise of Iranian-supported Algerian terrorists who nearly detonated an Air France passenger jet over Paris. Line 3 is Spain after having surrendered (**yielded**) its national identity to join the EU. Line 4 is either some vague reference to Italy (home of the **Venetians**) backing out of NATO, or it becomes a roadblock to my interpretation, detouring us back to the 16th century for another try at this quatrain.

The detour takes us to 1557, a few short years after the publication of this quatrain, when the forces of Henry II faced a military disaster at St Quentin.

One botched adventure followed another, and France was under assault on five fronts. The Spanish threatened her from Savoy, the Spanish Netherlands, and the Pyrennees. Spanish fleets harassed her from the west coast, where their English allies held a foothold on the continent at Calais. Italy was the fifth front, and had been the main theater of war between the Valois and Habsburgs for 50 years.

North Africa was definitely **stirred up** during this period by numerous pirate raids on European and Venetian holdings in Rhodes and Cyprus and raids along southern Europe's shores. But these Barbary Corsairs were hardly **stirred up** by the Persians, unless North Africa indirectly stands for the entire Ottoman Empire during its civil war in 1559. Even so, the

Persians waited on the sidelines, delivering the Sultan's rebel son to his executioners.

The Persians (Iranians) of today are definitely stirring the pot of North African Islamic extremism in our time. This may be another example of a time fluctuation in Nostradamus' vision that causes him to converge events from widely distant centuries into one vision in one time.

Quatrain Indexing Date: Q73 = 1573, the year the Turko-Venetian war ended. Possibly 1973, the opening year of the 27-year war of the Third Antichrist (1972–99), which depends on North African bases for terrorist attacks.

1 Q74

Apres feiourné vogueront en Epire,[1]	*After tarrying they will move forward*
Le grand fecours viendra vers Antioche:	*by rowing for Epirus,*
Le noir poil crefpe tendra fort à l'Empire,	*The great relief effort will be toward*
Barbe d'ærain fe rouftira en broche.	*Antioch:*
	The black curly-haired one will strain
	hard for the Empire,
	Brazen Barb[arossa] will be roasted
	on a spit.

[1]Epirus, north-western Greece

There was no second crusade to Antioch in Nostradamus' time. The future shoe I'd try to fit on this gnarly foot of a quatrain are actions in Greece and the Middle East in 1940–41. Italian forces crossed the Adriatic to conquer Albania early in the war. From there they attacked western Greece (**Epirus**) in October 1940. The Free French and British Commonwealth forces successfully invaded Vichy-held Syria (**Antioch** is right on the Turkish–Syrian border). They mostly advanced from Iraq towards the west.

Here's where our interpretation rubs a bunion. Nostradamus gives us two Barbarossas. The conventional version is his contemporary, the pirate leader of the Barbary Corsairs. The unconventional one is Adolf Hitler, after his favorite medieval German king, Frederick Barbarossa. The first Barbarossa would die in 1557, a few years after this quatrain was published. He was not burned on a spit, whereas the second **Barbarossa** came pretty close to being. After his suicide, Hitler's body was cremated in a shallow pit outside his bunker in Berlin. The man with the black curls is either Don Juan of Austria, mistakenly pitted against Barbarossa in the battle of Lepanto in the 1570s, or the wiry-haired commander of the Vichy French forces in Syria, General André de Verdilhac – but the latter is a stretch.

This could be a future strategic attack on the Middle East via Greece through Turkey contemplated as an alternative by Hitler. Acting on it depended on the Turks joining the Axis Alliance, which they never did.

See Index: Battle of Lepanto.

1 Q75

Le tyran Sienne occupera Sauonne,	**The tyrant of Siena will occupy Savona,**
Le fort gaigné tiendra claſſe marine:	**The stronghold gained will hold the marine fleet:**
Les deux armees par la marque d'Anconne.	**The two armies by the standard of Ancona.**
Par effrayeur le chef s'en examine.	**Because of terror the chief self-searches.**

This has something to do with the Italian intrigues of Henry II during the mid-to-late 1550s. Siena was a free city, allied to France against its chief adversary, the Florentines. The garrison sent by the French to Siena capitulated in April 1555, about a week before *Les Propheties* were published and well after this quatrain was written. The standard of the city of Ancona was that of the Papal States, to which it had belonged since 1532.

1 Q76

D'vn nom farouche[1] tel proferé ſera,	**Of a ferocious name such will be proclaimed,**
Que les trois ſeurs auront fato[2] le nom:	**That the three sisters will possess for destiny his name:**
Puis grand peuple par langue & faict dira,[3]	**Then to a great people [the French] he will speak in words and deeds,**
Plus que nul autre aura bruit & renom.	**More than any other man [he will have] fame and renown.**

[1]*Nom farouche* = a) ferocious name; b) Greek *neapolluon* = certain destroyer; c) Greek *ne(o)apolluon* = new destroyer; d) Apollyon, the angel of the abyss (Revelation 9:11).
[2]Latin *fatum* = fate, destiny.
[3]*Dira* = a) will speak; b) Old French *duire* = to lead, govern.

Clues to unlock a quatrain can come in surprising places. One can imagine Le Pelletier on a stroll through the Place de Vendôme sometime in the 1860s, stopping at the great column of Napoleon's memorial. He pauses to study the inscription "NEAPOLIO. IMP. AUG." Eureka! the key to a Nostradamus mystery is found. Le Pelletier is the first one to unravel the **ferocious name** of the man foreseen here. "Neapolio" is a play on the Greek word *neapolluon*, which means "new" (neo-) or "certain" (ne-) "destroyer" (-apolluon).

Le Pelletier sees this as an apt, poetic description of the destiny of

Nostradamus' First Antichrist. Expanding on his interpretation, I see the **three sisters** are a double pun for the Three Graces of classical Greek mythology and the three sisters of Napoleon – Caroline, Pauline, and Elisa – to whom he gave crowns and titles. The **ferocious name** they immortalize for destiny is also "(N)apollyon," immortalized in Revelation 9:11 of the New Testament as "the angel of the abyss, whose name, in Hebrew, is Abbadon, and in Greek, Apollyon, the Destroyer".

Of the three Antichrists, Napoleon was correctly foreseen as the most obsessed with **deeds** of glory and his immortal **destiny**. To this day more books have been written about Napoleon than any other despot, except perhaps for the fierce mid-20th-century German warlord, Nostradamus' Second Antichrist.

1 Q77

Entre deux mers dreffera promontoire,[1]	**Between two seas stands the promontory,**
Que puis mourra par le mords[2] du cheual.	**A man will later die by the bit of a horse:**
Le fien Neptune[3] pliera voille noire,	**For his own man Neptune unfurls a black sail,**
Par Calpre[4] & claffe aupres de Rocheual.	**Through Gibraltar and the fleet near Rocheval.**

[1]This describes the Rock of Gibraltar, which stands between the Atlantic and the Mediterranean (**between two seas**).
[2]Old French *mords* (modern French, *morsure*) = bite.
[3]*Neptune*: Classical god of the oceans. This can be applied generally to England and less frequently to other sea powers, such as the Ottoman Turks.
[4]*Calpre* = Classical name for Gibraltar.

In 1805 the British Fleet, commanded by the legendary Lord Nelson, defeated the French and Spanish fleets under Admiral Villeneuve off the Spanish coast near Cape Trafalgar, which is between Cape Roche (Rocheval) and Gibraltar. Napoleon could not proceed with his planned invasion of England. This would create a fatal strategic setback. England remained unbeaten and safe from his victorious armies and was free to invade occupied Spain and incite the Russians to break Napoleon's continental blockade of England. This led to his disastrous war with Russia in 1812. By 1814 his empire collapsed.

Lord Nelson died in the Battle of Trafalgar. On his flagship, HMS *Victory*, black sails were unfurled for her homeward voyage. The hapless Villeneuve was captured in the battle. When he was returned via a prisoner exchange, Napoleon had him strangled to death by one of his Mameluke bodyguards, who used a horse's bridle (*a bite* or **bit of a horse**). Nostradamus saw the executioner's weapon 250 years prior to the crime.

1 Q78

D'vn chef vieillard naiftra fens hebeté	To an older chief will be born one
Degenerant par fçauoir & par armes:	with dull senses
Le chef de France par fa fœur redouté,	Degenerate both in knowledge and in
Champs diuifez, concedez aux gendarmes.	weapons:
	The chief of France feared by his
	sister,
	Fields divided, conceded to the
	soldiers on horses.

I dedicate this one to La Reine Margot, the lusty and ill-starred daughter of Catherine de' Medici.

The **older chief** is Henry II. Charles IX is the child in question. As a fully grown **chief** (king) **of France** he was **feared by his sister** Marguerite. Charles, a dull and easily manipulated monarch, had permitted the massacre of her husband's wedding guests on St Bartholomew's Day (August 1572). Her marriage to the Huguenot King Henry de Navarre had worked as wedding bait to entice the Huguenot leadership into the Catholic lion's den of Paris. Marguerite was further compromised by her sometime lover, the **chief** of the Catholic Leaguers, Henry de Guise who plotted against her new Huguenot husband while scheming against her degenerate brothers, Charles IX and the Duc de Anjou (the future Henry III). The final line is a good general description of the nine Wars of Religion: it suggests the Catholic and Huguenot nobility jockeying for territory and influence during the long lulls between civil war's sharp and short-term military actions. Many of these battles were won or lost by cavalry attacks (**soldiers on horses**).

1 Q79

Bazaz, Leftore, Condon, Aufch, Agine,	Basas, Lectoure, Condom, Auch and
Efmeus par loix querelle & monopole:	Agen,
Car Bourd. Toloze Bay mettra en ruine.	Affected by laws, quarrel and
Renouueller voulant leur tauropole.[1]	monopoly:
	For Bordeaux, Toulouse, Bayonne
	[it] will ruin.
	Wishing to revive their sacrifice of a
	bull.

[1]Latin *taurobolium* = the sacrifice of a bull.

All these towns are in south-west France and are watered by the Garonne river except for Bayonne. According to Leoni there is a widely disputed theory that the town of Condom, like the inventor Thomas Crapper, had its name immortalized for its association with a naughty bit or two. The rest of the quatrain describes a prophylactic defense of another kind. The

quatrain is so general that it could be as much about a Huguenot rebellion in Nostradamus' time as the French farmer and produce drivers'
revolt against EU regulation of French agricultural perks in the 1990s.

The final line either metaphorically describes the desire of some
French farmers to return to the old and conservative ways rather than go
forward with the EU, or is another of the prophet's odd comparisons: of
Hugenots to Jove-worshipping pagans.

1 Q80

De la ſixieſme claire ſplendeur celeſte,	**Of the sixth bright celestial splendor,**
Viendra tonner ſi fort en la Bourgongne:	**It will come to thunder very much in**
Puis naiſtra monſtre de treshideuſe beſte,	**Burgundy:**
Mars, Auril, May, Iuin grand charpin¹	**Then a divine portent of a very hideous**
& rongne.	**beast will be born,**
	March, April, May, June, great
	bandaging [of wounds] and
	decapitating.

¹*monſtre* = *monster* or Old French for a *divine omen* delivered by a daemonic messenger.
²Old French *charpin* = the rags used to dress wounds. Derived from Latin*carpere* = to tear.

The constellation of Virgo is implied in line 1. Burgundy is the scene of too
many wars to make a definite interpretation, although conflicts that **thunder**
could apply to artillery barrages of the 20th century. Now all we need is to
find a modern battle harvesting death in the hills of Burgundy during the
month of harvests, September (zodiacal Virgo). This leaves us only one
choice. In September 1944 the German Nineteenth Army had made a fighting withdrawal through Burgundy. Patton's US Third Army from the Normandy landings linked up with General Patch's Seventh Army to advance
up the Rhône river valley from the Riviera at Dijon on 11 September.

The final line takes us into the first half of 1945, where Nostradamus
may have foreseen the final titanic battles of World War II: the Ruhr
Pocket, Berlin, and Okinawa.

1 Q81

D'humain troupeau neuf ſeront mis à	**Nine will be set apart from the human**
part,	**flock,**
De iugement & conſeil ſeparez:	**Separated from judgement and counsel:**
Leur ſort fera diuiſé en depart,	**Their fate to be determined on departure.**
Kappa,¹ Thita,² Lambda,³ mors⁴ bannis	**Kappa (κ), Thita (θ), Lambda (λ)**
eſgarez.	**dead, banished and scattered.**

¹Greek *Kappa*, tenth letter of the Greek alphabet.
²Greek *Theta*, eighth letter of same.
³Greek *Lambda*, eleventh letter of same.
⁴Old French *morts* = dead.

In 1961, around the time the United States was hurling its first Mercury astronaut into space on a Redstone rocket, Edgar Leoni first published his belief that this quatrain could have a modern, space-oriented application – one that indicated a future fatal voyage in space. A decade later Erika Cheetham boldly went where Leoni had never gone before, firing off the hypothesis that this quatrain is about the death of the three Soviet cosmonaughts of Soyuz XI. However her idea that the three Greek letters **Kappa**, **Thita** and **Lamda** are the initials of the three cosmonauts, Dobrovolsky, Patsayev and Volkov, however, is – unfortunately – a crash of another kind.

Still, I believe Leoni was on the right track: a space disaster is foretold here. I recall the terrible day I saw on TV a visitors' stand at Cape Canaveral crowded with images of mothers, fathers, and other beloveds of seven American astronauts, and the moment reflected in their disbelieving eyes when the spacecraft exploded.

On 28 January 1986, 71 seconds after lift-off, the US space shuttle *Challenger* exploded. The tragedy, witnessed by shocked millions around the world, was caused by the leakage of volatile gases from the left solid rocket-booster. Seven astronauts were killed in the explosion. In an era when space flight would have been the stuff of fairy tales to Nostradamus – apart from a mistake in numbers (nine rather than seven killed) – he makes an uncannily accurate description of this disaster.

During the months of investigation following the explosion, the National Aeronautics and Space Administration (NASA) came under close scrutiny. The inquiry revealed flaws in the shuttle itself and in command decision-making (*separated from judgement and counsel*).

The final line with its riddle of Greek letters has puzzled interpreters for centuries. I would venture that they are an anagram for some of those involved in the *Challenger* scandal: K, TH, L = TH(io)K(o)L = Thiokol. This could stand for the rocket manufacturer, Morton Thiokol Inc., which designed and built the faulty solid rocket boosters. Neither management nor NASA officials took much interest in the doubts expressed about the booster design by junior engineers at Morton Thiokol Inc. In the scandal many company heads and engineers, along with a number of senior NASA officials, were fired (*banished and scattered*).

1 Q82

Quand les colomnes de bois grande tremblee,	**When the columns of timber tremble greatly,**
D'Auſter[1] conduicte couuerte de rubriche:	**Led by the South Wind covered in red:**
Tant vuidera dehors grande aſſemblee:	**Such a great multitude will be drawn off:**
Trembler Vienne & le Pays d'Auſtriche.	**Vienna and the country of Austria will tremble.**

How does one unravel the riddle of columns of timber trembling? Are they wooden-walled fortresses under an artillery barrage? Are they logging convoys or forests trembling from an earthquake? I personally experienced a large-scale forest temblor while camping in California's Sierra Nevada mountains. The quake's shock wave moved across the mountains from the north, and in the sultry, windless night it sounded like ten thousand logs rolling down a hill. When it passed over our camp the trees swayed as if they were bent by a gust of gale-force wind, even though the air was still. The log thunder rolled off to the south, leaving us in peace.

If this is a prophecy in past tense for us, the trembling timbers could be the oars of Turkish galleys on the move, or the earth trembling under a great army of Turks emerging from the Austrian forests near Vienna in 1683 to lay a second siege on a city that had been a Christian outpost of eastern Europe since 1529. In both cases they failed to win the city.

But if we move into prophecy, future tense, the shivering timbers are from future earthquakes in central Europe. Around the turn of the century chaotic weather patterns caused by the greenhouse effect introduce a string of droughts across southern Europe. The hot Mistral (*south wind*) blows through a desiccated Provence. The wind is colored by the red smoke of catastrophic forest fires along the Riviera all the way down through Spain.

A great multitude **drawn off** may be the same victims of the global plague described in the Epistle, which **carries off** two-thirds of humanity. Perhaps it is the **blood** plague described in several quatrains that is caused by HIV, the Ebola virus, or radiation from widening ozone holes in the atmosphere. Perhaps Mother Nature is using a number of ways to **draw off** a rodentlike population explosion of humans in the first half of the 21st century.

This is not a future scenario I would like to encounter.

1 Q83

La gent estrange[1] diuisera butins,	**The alien race will divide the booty,**
Saturne en Mars son regard furieux:	**Saturn in Mars his [its] gaze furious:**
Horrible estrange[1] aux Tosquans & Latins,	**Horrible slaughter to the Tuscans and Latins,**
Grecs qui seront à frapper curieux.	**Greeks who will take part [in] a careful strike.**

[1]Latin *strages* = defeat, slaughter; rather than Old French *estrange* = alien, foreign.

The alien race are the Muziks and Mongolian troops of Zhukhov's Siberian soldiers, rummaging through the snow-covered wreckage of the Italian Eighth Army outside of Stalingrad. **Saturn in Mars** represent the cabalistic colors black into red. A contemporary slant would take these to represent the Spanish. For the 20th century it could stand for the fascists of Mussolini (the black shirts) against the Red Soviets. On 16 December 1942, three Soviet armies charged across the frozen Don river, along a 60-mile front guarded by the Italian Eighth Army. Over half of the 225,000 men from Tuscany and Rome were killed or wounded, and 60,000 survivors were captured.

The last line could chronicle the successes of Greek communist (red) and noncommunist guerrillas against the Italian and German occupation forces when they coordinated *careful strike(s)* of sabotage, culminating in the destruction of the vital Gorgopotamos railway bridge on 25 November 1942.

1 Q84

Lune obfcurcie aux profondes tenebres,[1]	**The Moon obscured in profound shadows,**
Son frere paffe de couleur ferrugine:[2]	**His brother becomes the color of stained blood:**
Le grand caché long temps foubs les tenebres,	**The great one hidden for a long time in the shadows,**
Tiedera fer dans la plaie fanguine.	**Will hold the blade in the bloody wound.**[3]

[1]Old French *tenebres* = darkness, night, gloom, shadows, hiding place.
[2]Latin *ferruginus* = rust-colored.
[3]Alternatively: *Will cool the blade in the bloody wound.*

One of Nostradamus' prophetic strong suits is identifying the murders of various members of the French royal line. This is the first of three quatrains that give a relatively clear, but unheeded, warning for the near-perfect dating of the assassination of the Duc de Berri outside the Paris Opera.

The murder of the Bourbon heir-apparent is accurately foreseen in 3 Q96 as taking place on the night of 13 February 1820. This date is supported by the astrological information in line 1 of this quatrain. The Moon was indeed in a *profound shadow* on that night; according to American astrologer Dan Oldenburg there occurred a new moon at 9pm (Paris time) on February 13!

Line 2 concerns Charles X, the father of the Duc de Berri and the brother of Louis XVI, who was executed by guillotine in the French Revolution (*his brother becomes the color of stained blood*). The phrase *profound shadows* could also be a description of the assassin, Louvel, waiting outside the Paris Opera in the shadows, dagger in hand. Louvel leapt upon de Berri as he was helping his wife into the carriage. As the grooms quickly dragged the assassin away, the duke looked down in horror at his own hand gripping the dagger buried up to the hilt. "I am dead!" he cried, "I am holding the hilt of the dagger!" Nostradamus was apparently intimating the parting words of the Duke as he clutched the blade (**Will hold the blade in the bloody wound**).

See Index: House of Bourbon, Duc de Berri (assassination)

1 Q85

Par la refponce de dame Roy troublé,	**The King is troubled by the Queen's reply,**
Ambaffadeurs mefpriferont leur vie:	**The fearful ambassadors take their lives into their own hands:**
Le grand fes freres contrefera doublé,	**The greater of the brothers will double disguise his action,**
Par deux mourront ire, haine, enuie.	**Two of them will die through anger, hatred and envy.**

Nostradamus first introduces part two of his prophecy on the assassination of Henry de Guise by Henry III. (Turn to 3 Q51 for part one.)

On the stormy night of 22 December 1588, Henry III's Mignons – a dozen of his best male friends, male lovers, and bodyguards – pounced on Henry de Guise with swords bared. His cries of "My friends!" were drowned out by the steady drumbeat of a downpour. His sword and scabbard were entangled in his cloak and he could not reach them in time. Quick hands darting in and out of the lightning flashes caught hold of his arms and neck; other hands thrust five poniard blows into his chest, neck, and groin. Yet with an extreme effort he carried his attackers across the room, pounding and scraping their boots on the floorboards, to fall in a heap in front of the king's bed. So violent was the storm that the 70-year-old ailing mother of the king, Catherine de' Medici, sleeping in a bedroom one floor below, didn't hear a single footstep or body-fall.

The next day she awoke from her afternoon nap to see her son by her bedside, consulting with her physician, Dr Cavriana, who was assuring him that she was doing well and taking her medicine. The king turned to her and asked, "How do you feel, Madame?" "Oh, my son, fairly, fairly," she replied in a tone that might gain her some sympathy. His reply would give her cause to go to her grave. "As for me, Madame, I am extremely well," he declared. "Excuse me. Monsieur de Guise is dead. He will be heard of no more. I have had him killed."

One can only speculate on what was going on inside Catherine's mind that moment as she stared at him, while the king rambled on excitedly, rejoicing in his revenge for the Duke's insolence and many offenses. Did her mind turn back the pages of her life to all the warnings and prophecies of doom for the House of Valois? Did she think again of her occult heraldic device of the Serpent clasping its tail in its teeth? The serpent ring stands for ultimate power, such as that she wielded often down through the years as regent, preparing her boys for the throne. So far Francis II and Charles IX had been weaklings, disasters. The power they held was unbalanced, like the serpent that, in devouring his own tail, eats itself up completely. Now as she heard her favorite and final son finish explaining his actions, one can only wonder if she thought her son was yet another power-mad and hungry serpent beginning a feast of himself.

"My Lord, have you well ordered your affairs?" she asked darkly. "Monsieur de Guise has many friends." He assured her that he had, to which she replied fatefully, "I pray to God that all will turn out well." She collapsed back into the pillow and fell silent. At the time the king scarcely acknowledged her response and revitalized by the elixir of revenge, left the room. But a short time later he would be at great pains to remember her warning to set his affairs in order, for his actions, as foreseen by Nostradamus, would see him assassinated in the following year.

The King is troubled by the Queen's reply. Catherine de' Medici sees herself as a pawn in her son's terrible blunder and is furious. Not only did Henry III murder the Duc de Guise, but after his conversation with her that morning he would have the Duke's brother, the Cardinal de Guise, murdered, effectively cutting off the head of the Catholic leadership against the Huguenots. This completes a deed so dastardly that Catholic France unites against their own Catholic king. Catherine's exasperation is so acute it brings on her death soon afterwards.

The last three lines tell of the consequences of Henry III's blunder.

The fearful ambassadors take their lives into their own hands. The ambassadors of the Estates-General denounce Henry III for the murder of Guise and his brother, the Cardinal Louis. They direct all their support to the surviving brother Charles, the Duc de Mayenne.

The greater of the brothers will double disguise his action. Mayenne accomplishes the *double disguise* by taking both titles held separately by his brothers: Lieutenant General of France and Commander of the Catholic League.

Two of them will die through anger, hatred and envy. The two are Henry de Guise and Cardinal Louis, murdered by their jealous king.

See Index: Henry III assassination.

1 Q86

La grande royne quand ſe verra vaincue,	**The great Queen when she will see herself conquered,**
Fera excés de maſculin courage:	**Will be excessive in masculine courage:**
Sur cheual, fleuue paſſera toute nue,	**Upon a horse, totally vulnerable, she will pass over the river,**
Suite par fer: à foy fera outrage.	**Pursued by the sword. She will outrage her faith.**

Mary Stuart had thoroughly outraged her Catholic subjects through her affair with the notorious Bothwell. She escaped prison only to see her army defeated at the Battle of Langside. Mary fled across the Solway Firth to England to seek refuge in Queen Elizabeth's court. She became the English queen's prisoner and eventually met her death at Fotheringay in 1587.

Quatrain Indexing Date: Q86 may be a near-miss attempt at predicting the year of her beheading in 1587.

1 Q87

Ennofigee[1] feu du centre de terre.
Fera trembler au tour de cité neufue:
Deux grands rochiers long tẽps ferõt la
    guerre,
Puis Arethufa[2] rougira nouueau fleuue.

Earth-shaking fire from the center of the Earth.
Will cause the towers around the New City to shake:
Two great rocks for a long time will make war,
And then Arethusa will color a new river red.

[1]Latin *Ennosigaeus* = the Earth-shaker, a kenning for Neptune. This implies a submarine quake and tsunami.
[2]Arethusa is also the name of a town in the ancient Roman province of Syria.

This quatrain may reinforce others heralding 1987 as the earliest year for superquakes. The two great rocks stand for Earth's continental plates grinding (*will make war*) against one another. In my first book on Nostradamus, published in 1987, I stated that this quatrain stood for the next time San Francisco or Los Angeles could suffer the long awaited "big one," the next great quake on the San Andreas Fault. I pinpointed the time window for the late 1980s during which the Whittier quake (1987) and the Loma Prieta–San Francisco quakes (1989) occurred.

Fortunately neither was the "big one," but these, and the great California quakes of July 1992 and January 1994, may certainly be a dramatic prelude. Volcanic eruptions corresponding with earthquakes are also hinted at in the last line of this quatrain. Arethusa is a classical Greek nymph who in legend changed herself into a spring. By describing Arethusa as **red** Nostradamus warns us of lava flows. This may indicate that huge volcanic eruptions will hit major First World population centers from 1996 through the spring of 2000. We may see Mt Rainier in Washington State explode and threaten the city of Tacoma with lahars and superheated mudflows. Serious eruptions of Mt Vesuvius and Etna in Italy and Mont Pélé on the Caribbean island of Martinique cannot be ruled out for the same period. At the time of writing a major eruption is expected near Martinique on the island of Montserrat.

Quatrain Indexing Date: Q87 = 1987, which did see several massive quakes east of Los Angeles in Whittier and the Mojave Desert. However, these cannot be compared to the long-awaited superquake expected from the San Andreas Fault. One cannot rule out 2087 as the date for this quake. The year 1987 also hosted a quake of a different kind. The **two great rocks** at war were Iran and Iraq in their seventh year of a bloody World War I-style trench war. In 1987 Iran unleashed a 500,000-man offensive into southern Iraq, which stalled to a gory halt at the approaches of Basra. **Arethusa** may have a double meaning for the earthquake of war, near what was once a Roman province of Syria. If so, perhaps we missed this terrible quatrain's fulfillment.

1 Q88

Le diuin mal furprendra le grand prince,	**The divine wrath will surprise the great Prince,**
Vn peu deuant aura femme efpoufee.	**A short time before he will have married a woman.**[2]
Son apuy & credit[1] *à vn coup viendra mince,*	**Both support and credit will suddenly diminish,**
Confeil mourra pour la tefte rafee.	**Counsel, he will die because of the shaven heads.**

[1]Credit; trust; authority, influence, esteem, etc.
[2]Alternative: *A short time before he will have had a married woman.*

This quatrain pinpoints the beginning of troubles for Charles I of England as well as their outcome many years later. In 1625 Charles I declared on his wedding day that the persecution of Catholics in England should stop. In its divine "Puritan" wrath Parliament, already estranged by the king's disregard of its powers, openly refused him by vetoing his request for subsidies (**credit**) for his war against Spain. His marriage to a Catholic princess further rubbed their Puritan noses in what they condemned as his papist intrigues (**divine wrath** again). Twenty-four years later communication between king and Parliament broke down and civil war ensued. The day came when the king's own court (**counsel**) would sentence him to die because of pressure from the victorious Roundheads (**shaven heads**).

1 Q89

Tous ceux de Ilerde[1] *feront dans la Mofelle,*	**Everyone from Lerida will be in the Moselle,**
Mettant à mort tous ceux de Loire & Seine:	**Putting to death all those of the Loire and Seine:**
Le cours marin viendra pres d'haute velle,[2]	**The marine current will come up to the high wall,**
Quand Hefpagnols ouurira toute veine.	**When the Spanish will open every vein.**

[1]Latin *Ilerdia* = for Lerida, a city in Spain.
[2]Latin *vallum*, = wall, ditch.

If this predicts the conquest of France by Spain, then it is a complete failure. Several modern scholars have tried to piece together a complete teacup prophecy out of a few broken fragments. Cheetham tries to make one fragment imply the Duke of Wellington's peninsular campaign – this overlooks the minimal contribution of Spanish contingents in the expedition into southern France in 1814. Fontbrune grabs another broken shard and by extension turns Spanish Habsburgs into Prussian soldiers surrounding Bazaine at Metz during the Franco-Prussian War in 1870. He reasons well that the war was fought over the Spanish succession, but no Spanish soldier fired a shot at a Frenchman, much less slaughtered an appreciable proportion of the population.

James Laver's attempt is the most thought-provoking. He translates *haulte velle* ("high valley") as "High Well(ington)." The Duke of Wellington did lead a mostly British force with a few Spanish units into France to win the irrelevant Battle of Toulouse (irrelevant because it was fought after Napoleon had abdicated his throne). But Toulouse is well south of Nostradamus' Loire–Seine axis of slaughter, and in my opinion James Laver does no better than the others in salvaging this quatrain.

1 Q90

Bourdeaux, Poitiers au ſon de la campane,	**Bordeaux, Poitiers at the sound of the bell,**
A grande claſſe[1] ira iuſques à l'Angon:	**A great army will go as far as Langon:**
Contre Gauloys ſera leur tramontane,	**The north wind will be against the French,**
Quand monſtre hydeux naiſtra pres de Orgon.	**When a hideous monster [or divine omen] will be born near Orgo**

[1]Latin *classis* = fleet, or in some cases, army.

The description of a divine omen visiting France through the medium of a two-headed and generally hideous newborn babe is similar to the monster in 1 Q80. Langon is 30 miles south-east of Bordeaux, on the Garonne river. Orgon is a dozen miles north of Salon. Invasion! The alarm is sounded across Provence and south-western France. But who is the invader?

In 1815 Napoleon Bonaparte escaped from Elba and landed near Cannes with a band of 1,000 men. It is known that an effigy of Napoleon was burned in the public square at Orgon to protest his return. After taking power Napoleon was defeated at Waterloo in June. Bad weather played a role in his defeat (**the north wind will be against the French**). The summer of 1815 is known as the summer that never came. A volcanic eruption in Indonesia was responsible for cooling the climate just enough to treat Europe to soggy and cold weather throughout the summer months. A muddy battlefield at Waterloo had upset Napoleon's timetable. He was forced to wait six precious hours before the sun dried the field well enough to initiate a battle. If the June weather had been sunny, he could have defeated the Duke of Wellington's Anglo-Belgian army in ample time before the Prussian army came to their rescue. (See Waterloo quatrains 1 Q23, 1 Q38.)

1 Q91

Les dieux feront aux humains apparence,	**The gods will make it appear to the humans,**
Ce qu'ilz feront auteurs de grand conflict:	**That they will be the authors of a great conflict:**
Auant ciel veu ferain efpee & lance,	**Sword and lance [fly] before heaven is observed as serene,**
Que vers main gauche fera plus grand afflict.	**So that on the left hand there will be great affliction.**

Who are the gods? Are they merely the flotsam of poetic license or do they describe a future godlike human or alien race responsible for a war in the **heaven** of space. Let's take the question from another angle. Are these sky gods partly responsible for some of the wars we humans wage in our times? Are they providing technology to certain terrestrial guinea-pig governments as one of many steps towards preparing humanity for open contact with an extraterrestrial civilization? Let's hope whoever sits on the left hand of these gods, such as the CIA or Saddam Hussein, does not get the information and hardware to curtail human freedom.

Quatrain Indexing Date: Q91 = 1991, the year of the Gulf War against Iraq.

1 Q92

Souz vn la paix par tout fera clamee[1]	**Under one man peace will be proclaimed everywhere**
Mais non long temps pillé[2] & rebellion:	**But not long after there will be looting and rebellion:**
Par refus ville, terre, & mer entamee,	**Because of a refusal, town, land and sea will be broached,**
Mors & captifs le tiers d'vn million.	**A third of a million dead or captured.**

[1]Old French *clamer* = to proclaim.
[2]Old French *piller* = to pillage.

Some quatrains are handed down from one application to another through the centuries. This one has suffered such a fate. Jaubert pins it on the Wars of Religion (1562–98), the refusing town being the Huguenot stronghold of La Rochelle, which fought off a vigorous siege in 1572. But the casualties are too inflated for that day. This tempts Boswell and

Henry C. Roberts to place it nearer to their times. Roberts applies his national bias, making this one sing to his American point of view. He designates the third of a million dead as the American GIs who fell as a result of the Japanese attack in World War II. Boswell, his contemporary, has launched modern scholars on the most plausible interpretation – that it has something to do with the fall of Louis Napoleon and the Second French Empire during the Franco-Prussian War (1870–71).

Aided by the collective machinations of his scholars, Nostradamus foretells the tragic and sudden fall of Napoleon III, the **one man** who called the Second Empire the "empire of peace" (**peace will be proclaimed everywhere**). The second line aptly describes the rebellion and bloodshed of the Paris Commune of 1871. The refusal is the Prussian Kaiser Wilhelm I's rejection of Napoleon III's humiliating demands concerning the Hohenzollern candidacy for the Spanish throne. The result of this refusal was that France found itself plunged into a war it was not prepared to fight. The Prussians and their German allies made rapid and deep incursions into French territory (**land and sea will be broached**), and historians estimate that French losses in those killed and captured were around 300,000 (Nostradamus is 33,000 casualties over the mark.) This estimate is conservative, however, because it takes no account of inadequately recorded civilian deaths.

The latest fashion dresses this quatrain in desert camouflage for Operation Desert Storm, in 1991. Jochmans has American president George Bush as the leader proclaiming an end to the Cold War and the beginning of a New World Order. From the city of La Rochelle we move to Paris resisting involvement in the alliance against Iraq. Although French president Mitterand tried harder than Bush to negotiate with Saddam Hussein of Iraq, when the shooting began, the French were shoulder to shoulder with their post-colonial partners. The **dead or captured** are either Iraqi casualties or the same number of Iraqi children *imprisoned* by the sanctions, or dying of dysentery caused by the bombing of water purification systems across the nation.

Quatrain Indexing Date: Q92 = 1992, a near miss for the end of the Gulf War, that is, if Jochmans' interpretation is the one intended.

1 Q93

Terre Italique pres des monts tremblera,	**The Italian land near the mountains will tremble,**
Lyon & coq non trop confederez:	**Lion and Cock not too well confederated:**
En lieu de peur l'vn l'autre s'aidera,	**Instead of fear the one will aid the other,**
Seul Catulon[1] & Celtes moderez.	**Only liberty and Celts [the French] restrained.**

[1]Old French *Catulon* from Latin *castula* = the Roman tunic worn by the Republican goddess of liberty.

This does sound like Napoleon's Italian campaigns. At that time Britain was at war with Republican France. The quaking mountains are poetic for the Alps, which **tremble**(d) at the victory after the three-day battle of Rivoli in January 1797, and later in 1800 when the French army marched over the Alps to win the battle of Marengo. These two victories brought a political and social earthquake to the states of Italy, changing them forever. *Catulon* in this case may refer to the classical tunic worn by the Republican symbol of the French Revolution, Marianne. One can even imagine her smiling face – and perhaps a smiling breast or two falling over her castulon – painted on the battle banners fluttering over the shaggy heads of Bonaparte's tattered but rough-and-ready veterans.

Quatrain Indexing Date: Q93 comes close to the year that launched Napoleon's first Italian campaign: 1796.

1 Q94

Au port Selin[1] le tyran mis à mort,	**At Port Selin the tyrant is put to death,**
La liberté non pourtant recouuree:	**Liberty is not completely recovered:**
Le nouueau Mars par vindicte & remort,	**The new Mars because of revenge and remorse,**
Dame par force de frayeur honnoree.	**The lady through force of terror [is] honored.**

[1]*Port Selin* = Port of the Crescent Moon – usually Constantinople but sometimes the port of Genoa.

This is definitely not about Lepanto. Arthur Prieditis proposes that it concerns the assassination of the Turkish tyrant Abd-el-Aziz on 4 June 1876. Leoni has it down for a failed prophecy of the assassination of Andrea Doria, the tyrant of Genoa and admiral of the Imperial Fleet (Genoa also has a crescent as its symbol). A third possibility is the Young Turks' Rebellion of 1908–1909, when General Mustafa Kemal, later known as Kemal Atatürk, led an army of liberation into Constantinople **(Port Selin)**. This **new Mars** (god of war) deposed (rather than killed) Sultan Abdul-Hamid II with the approval of Muslim clerics, and named his brother Muhammad V Reshid as ruler in a Committee of Union and Progress (CUP)-run government. The identity of **the new Mars** of line 3 doggedly remains less readily apparent, but I would like to check the history of Atatürk. The lady of line 4 still remains a mystery.

1 Q95

Deuant mouſtier trouué enfant beſſon,
D'heroic ſang de moine & veſtutiſque:
Son bruit par ſecte langue & puiſſance ſon,
Qu'on dira fort eſleué le vopiſque.

Before the monastery a twin child is
found,
Of the heroic and ancient blood of a
monk:
His fame, through a mode of language
and powerful sound,
Such that one will say elect the
healthy survivor of the prematurely
born twins.

[1]Old French *Veſtutiſque*, from Latin *vetustus* = ancient.
[2]Old French *Vospiſque*, from Latin *vopiscus* = the healthy survivor of prematurely born twins.

Nostradamus could be waxing poetic for the first set of twin-named popes in Catholic history, John Paul I (1978) and John Paul II (1978–).

The final two lines are open to all kinds of papal interpretations, but the gist is well suited to both John Pauls. The first shook the Church with his surprisingly strong language of drastic reform, but he died suddenly, and suspiciously. He was replaced by a far more healthy John Paul "twin" from Poland, who at the beginning of his reign promised to carry on the reform but has used his **mode of language** and the **powerful sound** systems used in large-scale public masses to promote and enforce a far more conservative message than the first John Paul.

1 Q96

Celuy qu'aura la charge de deſtruire
Temples, & ſectes, changez par fantaſie:
Plus aux rochiers qu'aux viuans viendra
nuire,
Par langue ornee d'oreilles reſſaſie.

A man who will be charged with
destroying
Temples and sects altered by fantasy:
He will harm the rocks rather than
the living,
Ears filled with ornate speeches.

The idea that traditional religions are a fantasy or a shadow of their original living teaching is a recurring theme for Nostradamus. The man mentioned here must be a pioneering mystic who will strike out against old rocklike dogmas, earning the unified wrath of the world's organized religions. We will know him as an eloquent and compelling speaker. The Indian mystic Osho was put in chains in America in 1985. Unification Church leader Sun Myung Moon was vilified. He was first imprisoned by the North Koreans and later served a term in prison in the United States. Bahá'í mystic 'Abdu'l-Bahá and his father before him (Bahá'u'lláh) spent much of their lives in exile or in prison for their beliefs and teachings.

Quatrain Indexing Date: Q96–1996 is the beginning of the end of orthodox religions. In a century they will have completely faded away or changed beyond recognition.

The Founders of the Coming Spiritual Revolution

A number of Nostradamus' prophecies seem to chronicle today's new spiritual teachers and their movements. The pattern of these prophecies indicates the unique historical phenomenon we call the Human Potential or New Age movement.

Within this movement there are many groups (both fraudulent and genuine) that experiment with alternative lifestyles, philosophies, and religions, often Eastern in origin, and that practice new psychological and physical therapies. These groups, although not always in agreement over details, are mostly concerned with discovering new paths to world peace and ecological balance. All strive to awaken humankind to its potential for higher consciousness.

These prophecies can be gathered into eight specific categories. They are the prophet's eight clues to the character of the coming new religion, to its nondogmatic and individualistic teachings, and to the identification of its visionaries.

The eight clues (and their corresponding quatrains) are:

- **A man from the East at home in the West:** a spiritual catalyst finds his teachings welcomed in the West, primarily in Europe and North America. (See 2 Q29, 10 Q75.)

- **The Rod of Hermes** (after the caduceus wand of Hermes implying that the teaching is non-dualistic). (See 2 Q29, 5 Q54, 10 Q75.)

- **The outlawed teacher:** the status quo religions will try to prevent such teachers from traveling freely around the world. (See 1 Q96.)

- **The mystic rose:** the *rose* or *red* color, along with all the red shades of sunset, symbolizes teachings from the East and is applied to the colors worn by disciples of the Eastern teachers. (See 5 Q96, 9 Q51.)

- **Mars and flame.** The new religious rebellion against the dogmas of the past is symbolized by a **red** and rebellious **flame**. Many prophets foresee a purification of humanity **by fire**. It is for us to choose whether this fire is one of global warming and world ethnic wars, or a fire of new religious self-awareness and consciousness. (See EP104–105, EP139.)

- **Diana *Dhyana*: the Moon and meditation.** The science of self-observation is one of the main tenets of the new religion. The Moon applies either to the feminine and intuitive aspects of the new religion or to the name of one or more of the spiritual catalysts. (See 2 Q28, 4 Q31, 9 Q12.)

- **The infuriating traveler:** the more controversial and globe-trotting the spiritual catalyst is, the more likely he or she is a visionary. No spiritual teacher in history has been accepted yet by the mainstream religions. They are called gurus and cultists today just as Buddha, Muhammad and Jesus Christ were called when they walked upon the Earth. (See 2 Q28.)
- **strange birds crying "Now!"** The strange birds are the spiritual teachers themselves calling upon humanity to wake up *now* before it is too late. (See EP212.)

Twelve men have been in the forefront of a spiritual revolution during the 20th century. Let us consider these personalities in the light of the prophet's eight clues. These are certainly not the only candidates possible, but the parameters set by Nostradamus narrow the list to those either coming from the East or drawing most of their inspiration from Eastern, nondualistic teachings. A third requirement is that the teacher is a rebel, even in the eyes of his own Eastern religious roots.

SWAMI PARAMAHANSA YOGANANDA
(1893-1952)
Indian Mystic, Founder of the Self-Realization Fellowship

Yogananda, who introduced Kriya Yoga to the West, taught that the mind and heart could be raised from a limited moral consciousness into union (*yoga*) with the consciousness of God. Yogananda and his disciples sometimes wore orange robes in the Eastern tradition of the seeker.

MEHER BABA
(1894-1969)
Indian Sufi Mystic

Meher Baba, a Parsee, born in Pune, India, was a master of the devotional path of Sufism. He was opposed to religious hierarchy, ritual, and ceremony, and his motto was, "Don't worry, be happy." His followers set up "Baba Lover" centers all over the world and, in the United States alone, Baba's teaching attracted an estimated 6,000 disciples.

SWAMI PRABHUPADA
(1896–1978)
Founder of the Hare Krishna Movement

This Indian mystic came to the West to spread the message of Krishna Consciousness. One symbol of the consciousness is flame, represented by shades of red. His followers sing and dance and wear the orange robes of ancient Krishna devotees.

L. RON HUBBARD
(1916–1986)
Author of Dianetics™, *Founder of the Church of Scientology*

Scientology aims to help people recover spiritual health after suffering psychic and mental traumas, guiding them on the path towards reestablishing a "clear" mental and spiritual state. The creator of Scientology, and his "new" religion itself, have encountered opposition around the world and fought many legal and political battles. His Church has an estimated 5 million adherents and is considered dangerous by many established religions. One of its symbols is a flaming volcano.

ABDU'L-BAHÁ
(1844–1921)
Leader of the Bahá'í faith

The eldest son and successor of Bahá'u'lláh, upon whose death he assumed full authority for the Bahá'í movement. He interpreted teachings that pave the way for a synthesis of all religions in a spiritual global village. Throughout much of his adult life he spread the faith from his new religious seat on Mt Carmel in Israel. Like his father, he had a prodigious correspondence with believers and enquirers around the globe, and endured long years of prison life. He made extensive tours to Europe and America and was a prophetic advocate for a League of Nations.

J. KRISHNAMURTI
(1891–1986)
Indian philosopher and meditator

Theosophists claimed Krishnamurti to be the incanation of Maitreya – the returned Buddha – but he publicly denied this title and dismantled the organization which had been created to spread his Messianic message. He then traveled and lectured widely in America, England, Switzerland and India for over 70 years. His concept of meditation was related to "witnessing," which he taught could offer each individual complete and absolute freedom.

G.I. GURDJIEFF
(1877–1949)
Master of "The Fourth Way"

Gurdjieff was born in Alexandropol in Russian Armenia. For some 20 years, his obsession to understand life's strange and mysterious phenomena drove him to travel throughout the remotest regions of Tibet, Central Asia, and the Middle East. Leaving Russia after the Bolshevik takeover, he established a communal spiritual campus outside of Paris in 1922, and later set up a Gurdjieff school in the United States. His teachings are a revolutionary synthesis of Sufi, Central Asian and South Asian techniques of meditation and awareness training which he called "The Fourth Way" – the other orthodox paths being the way of the yogi, the devotee, and the *sadhu*. In 1924 he disbanded the Mystery School and devoted himself to recording his teachings in three volumes: *Beelzebub's Tales to his Grandson*, *Meetings with Remarkable Men*, and finally *Life is Real Only Then When "I Am."* From 1933 onward he lived almost exclusively in Paris.

S W A M I   S A T Y A   S A I   B A B A
(1 9 2 5 –)
Siddhi Yogi

This man proclaims himself to be the reincarnation of the Muslim mystic Sai Baba (1856–1916). He is a noted miracle worker, with millions of disciples in India and a more modest following in the West. In the Hindu tradition of *sanyas* (seeker and follower) he wears orange robes and, while he currently shows little interest in traveling to the West, that may change in the future.

S U N   M Y U N G   M O O N
(1 9 2 0 –)
Founder of The Unification Church

Sun Myung Moon's Church has come into conflict with the authorities on numerous occasions and, as a result, Moon has spent a period in jail. His claim is that he is the personification of Jesus Christ in the foretold Second Coming, and his last name phonetically coincides with Nostradamus' prediction that the leader will be associated with the moon.

O S H O   (F O R M E R L Y   K N O W N   A S   B H A G W A N   S H R E E   R A J N E E S H)
(1 9 3 1 – 1 9 9 0)
Indian Philosopher

A former philosophy professor from India, this man was front page news all over the world in his last few years, especially during the 1980s. His red-clad followers, called sanyasins, have taken part in his experimental communes in India and in the United States, and political, local and religious controversy surrounds him. Osho's spontaneous daily discourses on love and meditation embrace a wide range of subjects, from sex to superconsciousness. His merciless, humor-filled insights into man's unconscious and conditioned behavior, and his uncompromising critical view of political and religious institutions, have earned him unanimous rejection by all mainstream religions. In the mid-1980s Osho was jailed and deported from the United States. After his departure, his attempt to go on a world religious tour met with strong political and theological pressure, and he was expelled or denied entry to 21 countries in the space of only five short months.

His followers allege that pressure from the Christian fundamentalist-controlled Reagan government used threats to pressure other governments to keep their borders closed to the mystic. An example of this reported in investigative reporter Max Brecher's book *A Passage to America*, Osho was one step away from being granted permanent residence in Uruguay when, according to Brecher's highly-placed sources, the Uruguayan president Sanguinetti received a phone call from the American Ambassador Malcolm Wilkey, who said, "You are a free country. You can do what you want. But you owe the United States 6 billion dollars. And this is the year for re-negotiating a new loan. If you do not make your payments on time, we will raise the interest rates."

Sanguinetti discovered that the thinly-veiled threat hinged on Uruguay's granting Osho permanent residence. The Uruguayan government decided not to grant permanent residence to the mystic and he was "invited to leave." Not long afterward Sanguinetti was invited to the Reagan White House, where it was announced that Uruguay's loan would, after all, be extended, and that his country would be the location for the next round of GATT (the General Agreement on Tariffs and Trade) talks.

In 1986 the movement reestablished itself in Pune, India. Osho died of heart failure in 1991. His followers claim that he died from complications after being poisoned by the US government while he was in prison in the El Reno Penitentiary in Oklahoma in November 1985. No clear evidence of poisoning was found by doctors who examined him prior to his death, although it is a known fact that thallium is an assassination poison of choice for organizations like the CIA because symptoms of damage appear only after two years – by which time the poison itself cannot be found in the victim's body.

ADI DA SANTOSHA
(1939–)
American mystic

Adi Da Santosha (previously known as Bubba Free John, then Da Free

John, and Da Avabhasa) continues to draw a growing following. Currently resident in the Fiji Islands, this unpredictable American mystic
calls himself a Master of the Heart. He teaches self-transcendence or
union with God, otherwise known as Divine Consciousness. This is a
Hermetic teaching that works through self-observation of each moment
– "now." Adi Da Santosha has suffered considerable persecution from
organized religions and governments.

S W A M I   M A H A R I S H I
M A H E S H   Y O G I
(1 9 1 1 -)
Founder of the Transcendental Meditation (TM) Movement

A former physicist, born in northern India, this leader founded the
highly successful Transcendental Meditation Movement, now
practiced by millions in the West as a technique for personal stress
reduction and the attainment of inner tranquillity. He has also
traveled widely and provoked considerable controversy, especially
during the 1960s.

A final evaluation of each candidate in the prophecies follows the
last entry of the "Eight Clues" quatrains in 10 Q75.

A   V I S I O N A R Y   L E A G U E   T A B L E

The Clues	east	Hermes	outlawed	red	Mars	Moon	travels	bird
The visionaries:								
Yogananda		*			*			*
Meher Baba		*						*
Prabhupada		*	*	*				*
Hubbard		*					*	
'Abdu'l-bahá		*	*	*				*
Krishnamurti		*	*			*		*
Gurdjieff	*	*	*		*		*	
Sai Baba	*			*				
Moon	*		*	*		*	*	
Osho	*	*	*	*	*	*	*	*
Adi Da Santosha		*		*	*	*		*
Maharishi		*	*	*	*			*

See Index: Eight clues to the catalysts of the coming spiritual revolution.

1 Q97

Ce que fer, flamme n'a ſceu paracheuer,
La douce langue au conſeil viendra faire:
Par repos, ſonge, le Roy fera reſuer,
Plus l'ennemy en feu,[1] ſang militaire.

That which fire and sword did not
   know how to accomplish,
Will be managed by a sweet-speaking
   tongue in council:
The King will be made to contemplate
   the dream seen while sleeping,
Moreover, the enemy at [his own]
   hearth, in warlike blood.

[1]Figurative: Latin focus = a) the fireplace, esp. the hearth; b) the altar fire; c) the funeral pyre. All meanings applicable in a complex, layered image of the hearth burning and the king reading the letter in its light when Clément pulls the dagger.

By 1589, Henry III's position was precarious in the extreme and calls for his death issued from all sides. After conspiring to murder Henry de Guise, he was forced to flee with his Mignons to the camp of his enemy, Henry de Navarre. The instrument of revenge was to be Brother Clément, a Dominican friar, who obtained a private audience in the king's bedchamber at St Cloud on 2 August. Clément's mild manner and gentle speech threw the king off guard and, as he stood near the cosy fire of his hearth to read the letter, he noticed the young friar motioning him to come close for a whispered message. As the king drew close the friar stabbed him in the belly with a concealed dagger. When loyal bodyguards responded to the king's cries, it is said that Clément met their sword blades with arms outstretched like a crucified Christ.

It was well known that Henry III, still a relatively young man at 38, was morally and physically spent, and that three days before death he had foreseen his demise in a dream and related to his Mignons its nightmare vision of the crown and scepter of France being trampled by a monk-led mob (see P58).

1 Q98

Le chef qu'aura conduit peuple infiny,
Loing de ſon Ciel, de meurs & langue
   eſtrange:
Cinq mil en Crete & Theſſalie finy,
Le chef fuyant ſauué en marine grange.

The chief who will have conducted
   [the] infinite people,
Far from the skies of their own,
   consisting of alien customs and
   tongues:
Five thousand (AD?) finished in Crete
   and Thessaly,
The chief fleeing, saved in a seagoing
   barn.

Infinite people can refer to the French, but it could also fit a future human race that lives in physical and spiritual harmony. A people of the infinite, both at home in outer and inner space.

I take line 2 literally to mean alien skies of another world, perhaps in some distant planet of the Cancerian or Aquarian star systems mentioned in the Preface as humanity's future home. Line 3 could date this quatrain for AD 5000. The reference to regions around the Aegean Sea being *finished* might pinpoint the meteorite strike described elsewhere, or Nostradamus may be seeing this as a precursor to final conflagration of the planet Earth by the sun in the year 3797. In the final line our prophet tries to describe the technology of a distant millennium when the captain of the first mission to a remote world is plucked off the surface of an alien sea by a space vehicle that can only be described as a seagoing barn by someone from the 16th-century. Perhaps *barn* describes this cosmic Noah's Ark?

See Index: end of the world (AD 3797).

1 Q99

Le grand monarque que fera compagnie,	**The great monarch who will make company,**
Auec deux Roys vnis par amitié:	**With two Kings united by friendship:**
O quel souspir fera la grand mesgnie,[1]	**Oh what a sigh will the great household make,**
Enfans Narbon à l'entour quel pitié.	**Children around the environs of Narbonne, how pitiful.**

[1]Old French *mesnie* = family, household, troop.

The *two Kings* in friendship might be another link to the Brothers of the North (Russia and United States) theme. If we are talking about modern times, the great monarch need not be a blueblood but a great French president. Perhaps it is Jacques Chirac, who is certainly a major player in European and Russo-American diplomacy. The *great household* could be that of the European Union.

Something terrible happens near Narbonne. It may be either a nuclear disaster or an act of nuclear terrorism at the nearby reactor plants at Cruas and Tricastin in the lower Rhône River valley. Children are the most vulnerable victims of radiation poisoning, but prophecies of global famine in the 21st century may point to a sad vision of children starving in and around Narbonne.

Quatrain Indexing Date: Q99 = 1999, the year Nostradamus sees all hell breaking loose if we don't change our present course to something more positive and life-affirming.

See Index: Brothers of the North theme.

1 Q100

Long temps au Ciel fera veu gris oifeau,	**For a long time a gray bird will be**
Aupres de Dole[1] & de Toufcane terre:	**seen in the sky,**
Tenant au bec vn verdoyant rameau,	**Near Dôle and Tuscan land:**
Mourra toft grand & finera la guerre.	**Holding in its beak a verdant branch,**
	Soon will die the great one and the
	war will end.

[1]Either Dôle or an apheresis of Mirandole, Mirandola.

Most interpreters assume that the gray bird is a dove of peace. Dôle is in Burgundy, but Mirandola is intended by apheresis since it is 30 miles north of Tuscany. The quatrain is general enough to fit any peace ending a Franco-Italian conflict shortly after the death of a great leader. Cheetham thinks it was the son of the Duchess de Berry, the Comte de Chambord, who was known as the Dove of Peace. One cannot rule out American President Roosevelt as the **great one.** He died shortly before the end of hostilities between France and fascist Italy during World War II.

Century II

2 Q1

Vers Acquitaine par infuls Britãniques
De par eux mefmes grãdes incursiõs
Pluyes gelées ferõt terroirs iniques,
Port Selyn[1] fortes fera inuafions.

Toward Aquitaine [France] the British
  make assaults,
By these same partners great incursions:
Rains and frosts will make the terrain
  unsafe and uneven,
Against the port of those of the Crescent
  they will make mighty invasions.

[1]Port Selyn = Port of the Crescent: Istanbul [port + Greek seléné = moon]; variant: port of the crescent flag of Turkey.

Nostradamus warns future generations of the great evils of modern warfare. World War I inspired a prophecy of huge battles fought by vast armies (the size of a whole country's population in his day), and stretching across thousands of miles. Instead of knights in dazzling armor and baggy-sleeved pikemen, Nostradamus sees the hell of the Western Front with its perverse and uneven lunar landscape sculpted by the rain of countless artillery shells, where the terrified soldiers of the future, surrounded by swollen corpses, die like rats in a barbed-wired wasteland. In the final line he transports us 1,000 miles east, to the approaches of Istanbul (port of . . . the Crescent), where the sun beats down on soldiers scrambling up the steep cliffs of the Dardanelles to die under the rasping tattoo of Turkish machine-gun fire.

2 Q2

La tefte bleu[1] fera la tefte blanche,[2]
Autant de mal que France a faict leur
  bien,
Mort à l'anthene[3] grand pendu fus la
  branche,[4]
Quand prins des fiens le Roy dira
  combien.

The blue [turbaned] head will inflict
  upon the white [turbaned] head,
As much evil as France has done them
  good,
Death from the great antenna hanging
  from the branch,
When [he is] seized the king will ask
  how many of his men have been
  captured.

[1]Blue head = a) blue turban of Islamic extremists, such as the Afghan leader, Heckmediyhar, or a Shi'ite in general; b) blue cap of the United Nations, implying a United Nations leader.
[2]White head implies either a white man, a man with a white head of hair, or a man wearing a white shawl or turban – a Sunni Muslim.
[3]Old French antenne = aerial, antenna, antennae.
[4] To hang (a person) etc. on a branch; to divide into branches; modern French to connect electricity, to plug in.

Would we of the 20th century be able to describe the unfamiliar media tools of the 24th century as well as Nostradamus conveys the link between modern-day imaging antennas and information gathering implied in this quatrain? He describes here a near-future event, perhaps a coup d'état in the year 2002 (Q2). Similar references in other quatrains to **blue head** could imply a coup by a blue- or black-turbaned Shi'ite Ayatollah of Iran against a Sunni Muslim leader (**white** [turbaned] **head**). It could stand for either the blue-turbaned Afghan rebel leader, Heckmediyhar, or the blue-turbaned Taliban guerillas who have extended their Islamic holy war beyond Afghanistan. A third possibility is of the blue-capped United Nations forces inflicting some military reprisal on the white-headed or white turbaned leader. A death is broadcast on television (**antenna . . . from the branch** – ie from a tower or aerial). Nostradamus is perhaps trying to describe this strange image suspended before his eyes in the oracular bowl of Branchus (**branch**[us]). A number of national European television stations in France and Greece call themselves *Antenna*.

Quatrain Indexing Date: Q2 = 2002? Other astrological prophecies point to the early years of the new century as a prime window for a climactic showdown with Islamic terrorists.

2 Q3

Pour la chaleur folaire fus la mer,	**Because of heat like that of the sun upon the sea,**
De Negrepont[1] les poiffons demi cuits:	**Around Negroponte the fish will become half cooked:**
Les habitans les viendront entamer,	**The inhabitants will come to make the first slice into them,**
Quand Rhod, & Gennes leur faudra le bifcuit.	**When [in] Rhodes, and Genoa their [food] will fail.**

[1]Negroponte: Venetian name for Euboea, their colony in Greece (modern Evvoia).

Sunrise in the afternoon. That is how the citizens of Athens in the next millennium might have described what happened if they had lived. At 3 o'clock the eastern horizon glowed brighter than daylight, flash-burning the retinas of dwellers along the Aegean coast. Minutes later, Athenian ear drums would be perforated by an explosion as loud as 2,000 one-megaton hydrogen bombs. Next, the deafened citizens of Athens would behold a new mountain range rising into the sky and falling in the form of sea water over the eastern hills.

The day the asteroid fell, the ocean fell upon Athens from the sky!

If an asteroid spears the Aegean, the waters off Evvoia would flash-boil all marine life, sending a plume of steam higher than Earth's mountains *because of the . . . sun upon the sea*. The resulting cloud of dust could block out the sun's rays for many months, or a few years, causing global crop failures and a catastrophic famine that could kill billions (*their [food] will fail*).

2 Q4

Depuis Monach iufque aupres de Sicile,	**From Monaco as far as Sicily,**
Toute la plage demourra defolée:	**All the coast will remain desolated:**
Il n'y aura fauxbourg, cité, ne ville,	**There will remain there no suburb,**
Que par Barbares pillée foit & vollée.	**city or town,**
	Which the Barbarians have not
	pillaged and violated.

Initially I tended to support Lamont's view – written in 1942 – that this is for south France and the shores of Italy, soon to be ravaged during invasions of Europe. In the subsequent year Anglo-American forces would land on Sicily, and in the following year invade the Italian coast with devastating effect at Messina, Salerno, and Anzio.

Nostradamus admits that his vision of future events is clouded, so he may have mistaken the Allied invasion of Italy and France during World War II for some future raid of Barbary Corsairs closer to his own time. This does not rule out a future application – perhaps a nuclear terrorist attack by the Algerians or Libyans following the same attack route.

Another important clue to the identity of Nostradamus' Third and final Antichrist is the proper interpretation of the Nostradamian word *Barbares*, which can be read either as **Barbarians** or Barbary, ie the regions of Algeria, Tunisia, and Libya where the Barbary Coast pirates had their ports (at Algiers, Tunis, and Tripoli). Drop the letter *b* and *barbare* becomes an anagram for the word "Arrabe" or "Arabe". As we will see in other quatrains, who or what that word represents is another key to the trigger of Armageddon. Currently, the most likely candidate for a *barbare* or
Barbary leader is Libyan strongman Muhammar Qadaffi. Although he has been relatively inactive on the terrorist scene since 1986, prophecies forewarn us not to ignore this terrorist or his large-scale Pan-Arab ambitions.

See Index: nuclear terrorism, south and south-east Europe.

2 Q5

Qu'en[1] dans poiffon,[2] fer[3] & lettre[4]	**When weapons and plans are enclosed**
enfermée,[5]	**in a fish,[7]**
Hors fortira qui puis fera la guerre:	**Out will come a man who will then**
Aura par mer fa claffe[6] bien ramée,	**make war:**
Apparoiffant pres de Latine terre.	**His fleet will have traveled far across**
	the sea,
	To seem to appear at the Italian shore.

[1] Nostradamus' error for *Quand* = when, at which.
[2] Double meaning: either = fish (submarine) or Pisces.
[3] Double meaning: either = weapons or Mars.
[4] Double meaning: either = letters, papers or Mercury.
[5] Double meaning: either = enclosed or in conjunction.
[6] Latin *classis* = fleet.

[7]Variant: **When Mars and Mercury are in conjunction with Pisces.**

This continues the terrorist theme of the last quatrain. In several places Nostradamus makes it clear that there's a Libyan (Barbary) connection to a future (terrorist) invasion of southern Europe. Muhammar Qadaffi, an admitted protector and supporter of Abu Nidal and other terrorist organizations, also possesses five Soviet-made Foxtrot Class diesel-powered attack submarines in his fleet. Whoever the man is with plans and special weapons to **make war**, his underwater journey to destiny may be dated in the hidden double meaning of the first line: **When Mars and Mercury are in conjunction with Pisces.** This astrological conjunction took place 5–6 April 1994 and again on 23–25 March 1996, just as the two planets left the sign of Pisces within a day of each other and Mars (the god of war) entered Aries, the sign of war. In both cases, fortunately, no terrorist incident took place. The latter conjunction saw a threat of war between mainland China and Taiwan over the latter's democratic elections.

Astrological Time Window

Conjunctions of Mercury and Mars in Pisces take place frequently: February–March 1998, February 2000, April 2007, March 2009, February–March 2011, February 2013, and so on. The next most likely time window for world conflict will be during Neptune's transit of Aries (2025–2038). During that period the conjunctions of Mercury and Mars in Pisces will be: March–April 2026 and March 2028.

2 Q6

Aupres des portes & dedans deux cités
Seront deux fleaux & oncques n'apperceu
  vn tel:
Faim, dedans pefte, de fer hors gens
  boutés,
Crier fecours au grand Dieu immortel.

Near the harbors within two cities,
There will happen two scourges the
  like of which was never before
  seen:
Famine, pestilence within, people put
  out by the sword,
Cries for help to the great immortal
  God.

In other quatrains Nostradamus may reveal the date(s) when a new and terrible nightmare weapon would obliterate two port cities: 6 August 1945, the day Hiroshima was irradiated, and perhaps even 9 August, the day Nagasaki suffered the second nuclear attack. Turn the 6 upside down and you get the date for the bombing of Nagasaki three days later on 9 August. The words of this quatrain capture some of the prophet's horror while witnessing the two Japanese ports sacrificed on the altar of the dawning nuclear age.

It cannot be ruled out, however that this is the third quatrain in sequence describing a nuclear terrorist attack from North Africa by submarine, rather than the bombing of Hiroshima and Nagasaki – in which case the indexing could stand for 2006 or 2026.

Quatrain Indexing Date: Q6 = 6 August 1945, or 6 upside down is a 9 for 9 August 1945, the two dates American attacked Japan with atomic weapons. Alternative date: 2 Q6 = 2006 or 26 for 2026, a potential window for another atomic detonation.

2 Q7

Entre plufieurs aux ifles deportés,
L'vn eftre nay à deux dents en la gorge:
Mourront de faim les arbres esbrotés,
Pour eux neuf Roy nouuel edict leur forge.

Between several carried away to the
  Islands,
One to be born with two teeth in his
  throat:
Dying of famine, the trees stripped of
  leaves,
For them the new King, novel edict
  hammers out.

For centuries islands off the southern French coast were used as penal colonies for criminals as well as political prisoners. It is also alleged that Louis XIV was born with two teeth already formed.

Perhaps he wasn't the only one.

A mystery about a man of noble birth forced to wear an iron mask has intrigued people for centuries. The identity of this man has never been revealed, leaving many to speculate that he was Louis XIV's twin brother, who was kept hidden from the public eye. Voltaire in his *Siècle de Louis XIV* states that upon taking the throne in 1661 Louis XIV had a young prisoner of above average height and of "extremely handsome and noble appearance conveyed with the utmost secrecy to the castle on the island of St Marguérite in the sea off Provence."

Voltaire continues: "On the way there this prisoner wore a mask, the chin-piece of which had steel springs to allow him to eat with it on, and the order was to kill him if he took it off. He stayed on the island until 1690, when a trusted officer named Saint-Mars, the governor of Pignerol, was made governor of the Bastille and went to St Marguérite to get him and conduct him to the Bastille, still wearing the mask."

This mysterious prisoner is said to have died in 1703.

The last two lines describe a significant event in the first half of Louis XIV's reign, the revocation of the Edict of Nantes in 1685.

2 Q8

Temples¹ facrez prime² façon Romaine, | Temples consecrated in original
Reiecteront les goffres³ fondements | Roman fashion,
Prenant leurs loix premieres & humaines, | They will fling back the rude
Chaffant, non tout des faincts les | foundations
    cultements. | Taking their first and human laws,
  | Chasing, almost all the cults of the
  | Saints.

¹*Temples*: the name Huguenots gave to their churches.
²Latin *primus* = first.
³Old French *goffe* = fat, rude, disorderly, unmannerly.

Three possibilities for a religious revolution are brewing within these lines.

The first takes us back to Nostradamus' own time when the Huguenot movement tried to strip the church of its pontifical airs, opulence and crowded cult of saints, and return it to the early virtues and simplicity of the early Roman Church when the Apostles of Christ ministered and walked the Earth.

The second takes us ahead to the French Revolution in the 1790s. Robespierre led a rebellion against the Catholic Church, seizing its lands and banishing the nuns and priests from churches and monasteries. He put a neo-pagan Cult of Reason in its place and established a Feast of the Supreme Being celebration to fill in the void left when the feast days of so many saints were nullified.

The third takes us into our own future in the early 21st century when the Catholic Church is pressured globally to reject its opulence and corruption and return to the humble virtues of the early Christian Church.

If, however, Nostradamus literally means a new religiousness to be forged in **Roman fashion** this may stand for the continued spread of today's neo-pagan and nature religions. Much of ancient Roman religion derived its **first and human laws** from the simple religion of the Etruscans. Theirs was more a worship of the godliness in Existence rather than of any particular deity or drove of demi-gods and goddesses. It was a celebration of life rather than a death cult of crucifixion and retribution in the afterlife for sins.

Quatrain Indexing Date: Q8 = 2008, the year when astrology's grand cosmic day (male-dominating influence) moves into cosmic night (female, intuitive dominance) for the following 35 years. This subtle change in the collective consciousness of humanity would be felt in a return to more feminine and nature-friendly religions.

2 Q9

Neuf ans le regne le maigre[1] en paix tiendra,	Nine years the rule of the slim one will hold in peace,
Puis il[2] cherra en foif fi fanguinaire:	Then he will fall into such a bloody thirst:
Pour luy[3] grand peuple fans foy & loy mourra,	On account of him a great people will die without faith and law,
Tué par vn beaucoup plus debonnaire.	Killed by one with a great deal more nobility.

[1]le maigre = the slim one, meager one, skinny, gaunt, etc.
[2]il = either he or it.
[3]luy = either him or it.

If we can target just who the **slim one** is we can unlock the secrets of this quatrain. Let's say that Nostradamus has the cycle of time correct; then Cheetham's interpretation could, successfully, make an interesting stretch that **slim** describes the vegetarian Adolf Hitler. He did have a nine-year run of spectacular political and military successes from 1933 through 1942, until the Allies dealt him his first serious military disasters at the battles of Stalingrad and El Alamein. But the stretch marks on the haunch of this interpretation will protest too much if Cheetham calls this nine-year reign a **peace**. World War II was already three years old and had harvested 15 million deaths by 1942.

One could salvage this interpretation if it proposed an alternative future that failed. It is well documented that Hitler told Mussolini during the late 1930s to be ready to start the war around 1942–43. Shortly after the Munich Pact in 1938 Hitler changed his mind and moved D-Day for world conquest up to the summer of 1939, to get the jump in the military modernization race on his adversaries. If Hitler hadn't changed his mind, his Third Reich would have known nine years of peace before the conflict.

In either case, the one with greater nobility who defeats Hitler is the aristocratic President Roosevelt of the United States, or the true and blueblooded aristocrat, the prime minister of Britain, Winston Churchill.

If Nostradamus is applying this description of **slim** to the broader-beamed Führer of the warring 1940s he does so with images he might have conjured of Hitler as an underfed tramp in the streets of Vienna in the early 1900s, and later during World War I as the wolfish lean-and-mean German soldier–messenger running the gauntlet of an artillery bombardment in the trenches.

A future application would have the thin man be President Clinton's current secretary of state, Warren Christopher. At the time of writing (May 1996) word has it that he would like to retire soon. But if he doesn't, his reign as peacemaker and shuttle diplomat will extend beyond two terms of President Clinton into the first year of a new democratic administration.

2 Q10

Auant long temps le tout ſera rangé,	**Before long everything will be**
Nous eſperons vn ſiecle bien ſeneſtre:	**organized,**
L'eſtat des maſques & des ſeuls[1] bien	**We await a very sinister century:**
changé,	**The lot of the masked and solitary**
Peu trouuerant qu'à ſon rang[2] vueille	**ones [the Clergy] greatly changed,**
eſtre.	**Few will be found who wish to stay in**
	their places.

[1]Old French allusion to celibate monks or the clergy.
[2]Row, line; order, class; rank.

The people of the 20th century have the dubious distinction of being numbered, recorded, categorized, mobilized, unionized, and institutionalized unlike people of any century before.

The foundations of Nostradamus' world – the unquestioned divine right of kings, rigid adherence to class distinctions, and the unassailable sanctity of the Church – have all been transformed, adapted, or swept away. God is either dead or is a woman; nuns want to be priests and priests want to marry. The once all-powerful royal houses of Europe are little more than museum pieces and targets of ridicule and contempt. All this is shadowed by the enormous expansion of technology. Historians estimate that in the past century we have made as many quantum changes in human civilization as the previous nineteen. The sounds and sights of our times must have left the prophet pulling his white beard in disbelief.

As Nostradamus' vision reaches our modern, cosmopolitan times, the future loses its focus on his native land and encompasses a world that has become, as he says in 1 Q63, *a small place*, in which the convulsions of history, for good or evil, affect everyone more completely than ever before.

Quatrain Indexing Date: 2 Q10 becomes 2 × 10 = 20th century.

2 Q11

Le prochain fils de l'aiſnier paruiendra,	**The following son will succeed the**
Tant eſleué iuſque au regne des fors:	**eldest son,**
Son aſpre gloire vn chacun la craindra,	**Such a great height as far as the**
Mais ſes enfans du regne gettez hors.	**realm of privileges:**
	His harsh glory will put everyone in
	fear,
	But his infants will be ejected from
	the realm.

This would make sense in relation to Edouard-Alexandre, Duc de Anjou (the future Henry III) if he had been the second son of Henry II – but it was Charles IX who came second. Anyway, Anjou was chosen king of Poland in 1573, through the country's notoriously careless and archaic *privileges* system. But the last two lines could just as easily describe his older brother Charles IX as they do Anjou during his reign as Henry III. Charles appeared to his people as **harsh** for acceding to pressure from his mother, Catherine de' Medici, and his advisors and ordering the massacre of Huguenots on St Bartholomew's Day. Henry III was less feared than reviled as an incompetent king. Neither brother left heirs to be ejected from the realm, unless the rumors of historical novelists are true that Charles IX sired bastard children in a secret marriage.

I imagine that Nostradamus is tying us up in a convolution of over-lapping brothers and generations of the House of Valois. If we return to line 1, we can conjure up the father of our first two subjects, Henry II, who was the second son in line to the throne until his elder brother, the Dauphin François, died of pleurisy in 1536. The dizzying pinnacle of kingship and its privileges were not expected by Henry II and, like his sons-to-be, he too was somewhat unprepared to succeed his father, Francis I, to the throne. Certainly Henry II waged wars against Charles V that could be characterized as **harsh** in their **glory**. Especially harsh was the catastrophic defeat of the French at St Quentin. His infant sons would be ejected from the realm – poetically at least. Death would carry off the three sons of Henry II, extinguishing the Valois.

An alternative to the Valois debacle could be argued for the heirs of Napoleon. Napoleon Bonaparte had at least two boy children. The first was an illegitimate child from his affair with the Polish princess Marie Walewska (note the notorious *privileges* link). The second was his legit-imate heir, the King of Rome, issuing from the Empress Marie-Louise, formerly a princess of Austria. Napoleon had a **harsh glory** as a conqueror and empire builder, and he did put the old "Boney" fear in every European Royalist during his 14-year reign. His infants would never rule. The bastard son grew up in Poland and the legitimate one returned with his mother to become a consumptive prince of Austria, dying at an early age.

Quatrain Indexing Date: Q12 = near miss for 1812, the year Napoleon made his first disastrous mistake and invaded Russia, ensuring that his infant son, the King of Rome, would never rule as Emperor of the French.

2 Q12

Yeux clos, ouuerts d'antique fantaſie,	Eyes closed, opened to antique fantasy,
L'habit des ſeuls ſeront mis à neant:	The habit of the solitary ones will be put to nothing:
Le grand monarque chaſtiera leur frenaiſie,	The great monarch will chastise their frenzy,
Rauir des temples le treſor par deuant.	Ravishing the treasure in front of the temples.

We return again to the Outlaw Master theme of Nostradamus' eight clues to a spiritual catalyst of a new religious revolution.

The priests of the mainstream religions hold in common their angry reactions to today's spiritual gurus and revolutionaries. Line 1 links us to 1 Q96 in which a new spiritual visionary comes with his eloquent criticisms of fossilized religious tradition to **harm the rocks** of dogma rather than **the people**. In the 21st century the hold of the priesthoods of many established religions on humanity will be shaken. Rebel mystics such as Osho, Krishnamurti, and Gurdjieff have predicted that within the next hundred years religions as we have known them will fade away because man will be simply man and not burdened with the separatist labels of Hindu, Muslim, Buddhist, or Christian. The **great monarch** could equally apply to the mysterious **man from the East** (2 Q29, 10 Q75). In Eastern mysticism a spiritual master is characterized as one who truly is a king or an emperor. They are known as the great monarchs of meditation, or as avatars, or even as Lords or Kings of the Full Moon. The treasure in front of the temples is the future youth of the world who will hear their message.

Quatrain Indexing Date: Q12 = 2012, the year the Mayan calendar predicts the end of time as we have known it. One of the tenets of the new religious revolution is to live in the eternity of the present, free of the bondages of past regrets and future woolgathering.

2 Q13

Le corps ſans ame plus n'eſtre en ſacrifice.	The body without soul no longer to be sacrificed,
Iour de la mort mis en natiuité:	Day of death put for birth:
L'eſprit diuin fera l'ame felice,	The divine spirit will make the soul happy,
Voyant le verbe en ſon eternité.	Seeing the word in its eternity.

Here is a rare glimpse at Nostradamus' view of the afterlife. With this quatrain one can understand why Nostradamus – encased in his swelling, aged body, was able to suffer the agony of the final stages of pulmonary edema and await death with serenity. Soon the body's pains and agonies would be cast off from the ascendant soul, the sacrifice of calumny and hard labors ended, his occult mission accomplished. Death's day, which some believed he had marked in his private ephemeris, would be a day of rebirth into the spirit (although one cannot help wondering if the wording of line 2 implies some understanding of reincarnation by the prophet). In 1554 Nostradamus foresees himself on his deathbed, biding his time with each faltering breath until that moment when the divine spirit he so arduously sought in prophetic trance would enfold his soul upon its release from corporeal existence. With the final death rattle, one of history's greatest time travelers is free of the past and the future to dwell in the eternity of the "now."

2 Q14

A Tours, Gien, gardé feront yeux penetrans,	At Tours, Gienne, watched over, the eyes will be keen,
Defcouuriront de loing la grand fereine:	They will discover from afar, the great serene lady:
Elle & fa fuitte au port[1] feront entrans,	She and her suite will enter the port,
Combat, pouffez, puiffance fouueraine.	Combat, thrusts, sovereign power.

[1]Either a **port** of a harbor or a city gate.

Tours and Gienne are both on the Loire. The **great serene lady** is the Queen Regent, Catherine de' Medici, who watches over her son and the realm with the keen eyes. Ten years after Nostradamus penned these words, watchmen on the walls of Salon, Provence, would glimpse her serene majesty **from afar** approaching the town to enter the gate of Avignon with a retinue of 800 nobles, courtiers, and soldiers on her Journey of Pacification. In the end, the journey pacified no one. The Wars of Religion would resume again, with the issue of **sovereign power** as much the cause for conflict between the royal houses of Valois, Bourbon, and Lorraine as the issue of religion.

2 Q15

Vn peu deuant monarque trucidé:	A short while before the Monarch is murdered,
Caftor, Pollux[1] en nef, aftre crinite:[2]	Castor, Pollux in the papacy, a bearded star:
L'erain[3] public par terre & mer vuidé,	Public treasure by land and sea is emptied,
Pife, Aft, Ferrare, Turin, terre[4] interdicte.	Pisa, Asti, Ferrara, Turin, property prohibited.

[1]Castor, Pollux: the Gemini twins, a classical metaphor for the twin-named popes John Paul I and II. The myth describes one twin as divine and the other all too human, implying that one of the two John Pauls was a divinely inspired mystic while the other is a political animal.
[2]Latin crinitus = bearded.
[3]Latin eranus = a fund contributed for mutual protection against want.
[4]Land, but in this case land as property.

In one complex verse Nostradamus describes and dates a sequence of events that perhaps relate to the Vatican Bank scandal. We see the murder of John Paul I, the rise of his successor, and the transit of Halley's Comet in 1986, when world attention about the Bank scandal reached a climax. **Castor** and **Pollux** is a good example of Nostradamus' using the classics to paint layers of meaning with very few words. The twins of Gemini may be a poetic description of two popes side-by-side with twin names (John Paul), who will run the papal ship of state. According to classical lore one twin was divine while the other was all too human and corrupt. Other prophecies might support the interpretation that Nostradamus views the second John Paul with disdain.

For now, the list of towns and the property prohibited in the final line is unclear. Most of the perpetrators of the Vatican Bank scandal were located in Rome and Milan. Perhaps we will see a future financial scandal involving the Vatican connected with banks in these Italian cities.

2 Q16

Naples, Palerme, Sicille, Syracuſes,	**Naples, Palermo, Sicily, Syracuse,**
Nouueaux tyrans, fulgures feux celeſtes:	**New tyrants, celestial lightning bolts,**
Force de Londres, Gand, Bruxelles, &	**explosions:**
Suſes,	**Forces from London, Ghent, Brussels**
Grand hecatombe, triomphe faire feſtes.	**and Susa,**
	Great slaughter, triumph to create
	holidays.

This represents the Allied invasions of Sicily and Italy in World War II. The **new tyrants** are Mussolini and Hitler, who wage Blitzkrieg (lightning war). The white-hot shells of German 88-mm guns crackling through the air at a low trajectory over Italian battlefields would certainly appear to the prophet as **celestial lightning bolts**. Line 3 describes some of the Allied contingents from Britain, Belgians fighting with the Free French contingents and, later, the Italian anti-Fascist units, represented by the synecdoche of **Susa**. To this day we celebrate the victory of 100 million Allied soldiers and remember the slaughter of 50 million people in two holidays: VE Day (Victory in Europe) and VJ Day (Victory in Japan).

2 Q17

Le camp du temple de la vierge veſtale,
Non eſloigné d'Ethne[1] & monts
   Pyrenées:
Le grand conduict[2] eſt caché dans la
   male,[3]
North[4] getez fleuues & vignes maſtinées.
	The campus of the temple of the vestal
	   virgins,
	Not far from Ethne and the Pyrenees
	   mountains:
	The great conduit is hidden, evil
	   within
	North blows up rivers and vineyards
	   bruised and destroyed.

[1]Either a) an anagram for Elne, a town in the foothills of the Pyrenees (Leoni); or b) Etna, volcano in Sicily.
[2]Old French *conduit* = conduit, duct, passage, tube, canal.
[3]Old French *malle* = trunk; or *mal* = evil. Alternative = **The great conduit is hidden within evil**.
[4]Perhaps *nord* = north; or a proper or enigmatic name – Lord North, Oliver North: take your pick.

Leoni believes this is another example of a "strictly local" quatrain "suggesting an event that Nostradamus once witnessed." We must uncover the ruins of a Roman temple to the hearth goddess Vesta, near the little town of Elne, which lies ten miles north of the Spanish border and ten miles south of Perpignan.

Line 3 is quite cryptic and doesn't fit well with the others, urging me to speculate that lines 3 and 4 are a completely different prophecy. One can describe *conduict* in different ways. It can be a conduit, duct, a tunnel, or tube. Perhaps it is the mountain pass over the Pyrenees. It could even be a water passage and therefore stand for the Midi Canal, which is around 38 miles north of Elne. To me the **great conduit** could be the Channel Tunnel, the great Eurotunnel between Calais (France) and Folkestone (England). *Dans la male* could have a double meaning for **evil within** and *within the trunk*, implying a bomb in a suitcase set to go off in a vehicle traversing a tunnel. North could be an anagram, a person's name, or even something a simple as a direction, to the **north**.

The Channel Tunnel has been described by one security expert as "a security nightmare – a prime terrorist target." Its creators pin their hopes on the new Sycoscan X-ray system, which can scan a container truck in two to five minutes. Another system is planned that will allow security guards to see three-dimensional images of a container's contents and determine the chemical composition of the materials inside a suitcase.

2 Q18

Nouuelle & pluie ſubite impetueuſe,
Empeſchera ſubit deux exercites:
Pierre ciel, feux faire la mer pierreuſe,
La mort de ſept terre & marin ſubites.
	New-fashioned and suddenly violent rain,
	Will suddenly impede the two armies:
	Celestial stone, discharges and
	   conflagrations make the sea gritty,
	The death of the seven suddenly by
	   land and sea.

The first two lines remind me of the first use of Stalin's top-secret Katyusha rocket launchers outside of Smolensk in 1941. The wailing phalanx of missiles falling from the sky caused the advancing German and Soviet forces to retreat. The last two lines could describe any number of naval battles and barrages from World War II. Nostradamus' gritty seas bring to mind oil slicks and the detritus of sunken battleships. The stones are artillery or naval shells. This time the **seven** are not the Valois children – they are the seven full members of the Axis Alliance: Germany, Italy, Japan, Finland, Hungary, Romania, and Slovakia.

2 Q19

Nouueaux venus lieu baſty ſans defence.	**Newcomers build a place without defense,**
Occuper la place par lors inhabitable:[1]	**Occupying a place [which] until then [was] inhabitable:**
Prez, maiſons, chãps, villes, prẽdre à plaiſance,	**Meadows, houses, fields, towns, to take at pleasure,**
Faim, peſte, guerre arpen long labourable.	**Famine, plague, war, extensive arable land.**

[1]Variant: uninhabitable. This could be another sainct/fainct (saint/false) wordplay: inhabitable (in English), or uninhabitable (if only the French meaning applies).

The newcomers are the Jewish survivors of the Holocaust who established their own state in the "Promised Land" of Palestine. Prior to the Holocaust the slow but steady colonization of Palestine by the Zionist movement gave rise to Jewish pioneers establishing communes (kibbutzim), which were always vulnerable to attack from hostile Arab neighbors; thus the term **without defense**. This early experience of vulnerability, compounded by the horrors of the Holocaust, has understandably deepened the Israeli feeling of being **without defense** in a hostile gentile world.

It can be argued that the cryptic phrase **until then [was] inhabitable** dates the creation of the Israeli state in 1948 as the beginning of a period when the Holy Land is in danger of annihilation. The Jewish state was achieved at the price of Palestinians' expulsion and, since its establishment, Arab–Israeli wars have raged in 1948, 1956, 1967, 1973, 1982; the Gulf War occurred 1990–91. As I am updating this (April 1996) yet another border clash has broken out with Hezbollah forces along the Lebanese border, the worst fighting since 1982. The quatrain's meadows, houses, fields, and towns taken with pleasure could be a criticism of Israel's policy of occupation in the West Bank, Gaza Strip, southern Lebanon, and the Golan Heights.

The final line of this prophecy could be a warning to a people once persecuted of the consequences of becoming persecutors themselves. It could signal the breaking point of a nation that, itself armed with a nuclear capability, will go to any lengths to prevent its neighbors from acquiring such power. The final line hints at horror and hope. Perhaps Nostradamus' apocalyptic sequence of *famine, plague, war* . . . will result from this regional doomsday arms race. If we are fortunate, a continued strengthening of global government and ethics, ensuring security and peace for Arab and Jew, will monitor the creation of a regional nuclear-free zone, creating a happy future of *extensive arable land* for all those living in the Middle East.

Famine, plague, war, extensive arable land is another of Nostradamus' litanies about a sequence of apocalyptic events. A great slaughter over disputed territories, perhaps those of the Middle East or any number of ethnic civil wars, is either endured, or it is prevented by new breakthroughs in agricultural genetics, creating a second Green Revolution that can feed the starving Middle East.

Quatrain Indexing Date: Q19 = 2019?

2 Q20

Freres & ſeurs en diuers lieux captifs,	**Brothers and sisters are captives in diverse places,**
Se trouueront paſſer pres du monarque:	**Will find themselves passing near the monarch:**
Les contempler ſes rameaux[1] ententiſz,	**They contemplate his attentive offspring,**
Deſplaiſant voir mẽton, front, nez, les marques.	**Unpleasant to see the marks on chin, forehead and nose.**

[1]branches, (poetic) for royal heirs.

In September 1557 a number of Huguenots, of high and low birth, were captured in a raid on the rue St Jacques in Paris. Accompanied by his children Henry II visited the prisoners. He was displeased to find so many of these heretics had been brutalized by their captors.

2 Q21

L'ambaſſadeur enuoyé par biremes,	**The ambassador sent as envoy by biremes,**
A my chemin d'incogneuz repoulſez:	**Halfway repulsed by unknown ones,**
De ſel[1] renfort viendront quatre triremes,	**Reinforced with salt will come four triremes,**
Cordes & chaines en Negrepont[2] trouſſez.	**Cords and chains packed up at Evvoia.**

[1]Old French *sel* = salt; (fig.) wit, pungency; or Greek for a kind of meteor, blaze, or light.
[2]Negroponte: Venetian name for the Aegean island of Euboea, their colony in Greece. Variant: the Black Sea (Old French *negre* = black, with Latin *pontus* = sea), giving us this alternative translation to line 4: *Ropes and chains packed up at the black sea.*

Biremes are galleys with two banks of oars, triremes with three banks. **Salt** is used a number of ways in *Les Propheties*, for anything from taxes to clever wit to even a meteorite strike. The latter application may be implied here. A number of quatrains could be descriptions of a meteorite crashing into the Aegean off the coast of the island of Evvoia, or Negroponte as it was named after the Venetian colony seized by the Turks in 1480.

Another translation of *Negrepont* gives us the *Black Sea*. This could make the quatrain a prediction for the Ottoman Turks' opening up the Bosphorus to Christian mariners. Or perhaps the galleys are a metaphor for the current dispute by the Russian Federation with Ukraine over divvying up the Soviet Black Sea Fleet. The packed-up ropes and chains are the mooring lines and anchors of mothballed Soviet warships.

2 Q22

Le camp Afcop[1] d'Europe partira,	**The aimless army of Europe will**
S'adioignant proche de l'ifle fubmergée:	**divide [break up],**
D'Arton[2] claffe phalange pliera,	**Collecting itself near the flooded**
Nombril du monde plus grand voix	**[submerged] island:**
fubrogée.	**The Arton fleet's ranks will fold up,**
	Navel [center] of the world by greater
	voice [vote] substituted.

[1]Nostradamian enigma: a) Greek *askopos* = aimless, obscure, incredible, imprudent or unseeing; b) Greek *Asopos* = Evvoia or Boeotia (Thebes).
[2] Greek *artos* = bread; anagram for NATO and/or Dayton.

The **aimless army** is the Warsaw Pact, which disbands as the Cold War comes to an end. Line 2 could be a play on words for Manhattan Island, New York, the international capital of the United Nations, which is seen here recovering after an earthquake or tsunami. The submerged (Manhattan) island could even describe New York by the 2020s, when the rising oceans expected as a result of the greenhouse effect will begin to flood the city.

D'Arton is both a near anagram for *D' Nato* (of NATO) and for Dayton, Ohio, home of the Dayton Accords, where the current adversaries in the Bosnian conflict finally agreed to a peace treaty, later officially signed in Paris toward the end of 1995. Nostradamus gives us an amazing double message, since NATO troops are pledged to enforce the peace of the Dayton agreement. I believe the success or failure of this experiment will have a significant influence on the future. If successful, the ethnic world war I foresee by the 2020s will be far less serious.

The poetic meaning of *nombril* (navel) is **center**, ie the capital of a new global government. This could still be the United Nations on the flooded island of Manhattan, negotiating solutions for the second great challenge of the near future – ecological disaster caused by overpopulation and overconsumption.

Quatrain Indexing Date: Q22 = 2022, the year NATO is retired?

2 Q23

Palais, oyſeaux, par oyſeau deschaſſé,	**Palace, birds, chased out by a bird,**
Bien toſt apres le prince paruenu:	**Very soon after the upstart prince:**
Combien qu'hors fleuue ennemi repoulſé,	**Although the enemy is repelled beyond the river,**
Dehors ſaiſi trait d'oyſeau ſouſtenu.	**Outside seized, dragged along, upheld by a bird.**

These **birds** symbolize a power struggle between monarchies of Europe between 1555 and World War I. They are the eagles of the Holy Roman Empire and Imperial Spain of Nostradamus' time. The eagle was also one of Henry II's emblems. Centuries later eagles would be used by the First and Second French Empires of the Bonapartes. Also worth considering are the double-headed eagles used by Russia and the Austrian Empire. But the **bird** could instead be a description of some future flying vehicle beyond the prophet's ability to describe. Perhaps a future leader is seized outside a palace and hoisted into the air into a helicopter.

On second thought, let us fly to the next quatrain.

2 Q24

Beſtes farouches de faim fleuues tranner,	**Beasts ferocious with hunger will cross the rivers,**
Plus part du champ encontre Hiſter[1] ſera.	**The greater part of the battlefield will be against Hiſtler.**
En caige de fer le grand fera treiſner,	**Into a cage of iron will the great one be drawn,**
Quand rien enfant de Germain obſeruera.	**When the child of Germany observes nothing.**

[1]Ister, archaic name for the River Danube.

Hiſter is probably the most famous enigmatic name coined by Nostradamus, encapsulating the name and childhood residence of Adolf Hitler in one word. Hiſter is the Latin name for the River Danube, near the shores of which Hitler grew up in Linz, Austria. In the original manuscript of Nostradamus' *Les Propheties* the s is written in the old Gothic form "ſ" – a spelling clue that makes the anagram resemble the German dictator's name more closely: Hister – Hi(ſ)ter – Hitler.

A total of over 100 million men from more than 50 nations were united against the Axis forces of Hitler and his allies, Italy and Japan. Using Europe's vast rivers as natural obstacles was a major part of Hitler's

Fortress Europe defense plan, especially on the Eastern Front. Titanic battles thick with the thunder and tumult of planes, tanks, and tens of thousands of artillery pieces were fought by the Soviets in crossing the Volga (Stalingrad, 1942), the Neva (Leningrad, 1943), the Dnieper (Kiev, 1943), the Danube (Budapest, 1944, and Vienna, 1945), and the Oder (Berlin, 1945). From the Western Front came the two great battles to cross the Rhine: Arnhem, 1944, and the Battle of the Rhine, 1945.

The third line most likely alludes to the fate of Mussolini, who actually was encaged (see 9 Q95). The final line is a coda to the madness of a Germany bewitched by the Third Reich. From its inception, most of its children were members of the Hitler Youth, which had as its major goal re-programming the minds of German children to dissociate them from many of the laws and ethics respected by peace-loving nations. Hitler even said that he wanted the children of Germany to become good "German Barbarians."

See Index: Hiſter.

2 Q25

La garde eſtrange trahira fortereſſe,	**The foreign guard will betray the fortress,**
Eſpoir & vmbre de plus hault mariage:	**Hope and shadow of a much higher marriage:**
Garde deceue,[1] fort prinſe dans la preſſe,	**The watchman deceived [and cut down], fort seized in haste,**
Loyre, Son, Roſne, Gar à mort oultrage.	**Loire, Saône, Rhône, Garonne, mortal outrage.**

[1]Either deceived or Latin *decisus* = cut down. Perhaps a double pun for a watchman being both deceived and cut down.

The defender of a fortress is General Bazaine, who in 1870 retreated to the fortress of Metz rather than press his advantage over the Prussians gained in a bloody battle at Gravelotte and St Privat. Bazaine would stay in Metz and effectively take out 170,000 desperately needed soldiers from the campaign. His indecisiveness allowed the German alliance to invade the heartland of France and win the Franco-Prussian War. Conspiracy buffs of the 19th century try hard to pin more than military incompetence on Bazaine's actions. Many Gauls vented their spleen at Bazaine during his court martial in 1872. Charges of treachery were made, and even a claim that Bazaine had received bribes from the Prussians, who promised him power and riches if he stayed put in Metz and let the Prussians encircle Napoleon III's forces at Sedan. This accusation was never proved; he was, however, charged with dereliction of duty and sentenced to life in prison.

One can poetically call François-Achille Bazaine a *foreign* guard, since he lacked the élan and the looks expected from a member of the officer class. Although he was personally brave, he was the spawn of low-class tradesmen, and his uniform strained and wrinkled over his swelling paunch as he rode hunched over in the saddle.

2 Q26

Pour la faueur que la cité fera,	**Because of the favor that the city will show,**
Au grand qui toſt perdra camp de bataille:	**To the great one who will soon lose the field of battle:**
Fuis le rang Pau Theſin verſera,	**Flying the Po position, the Ticino will pour forth,**
De ſang, feux mors noyés de coup de taille.	**The blood, fires, deaths, drowned by the blow of the blade's thrusting edge.**

I lean towards Prieditis' view that this concerns the final battles in the Italian campaign of World War II. I would add that the Po and Ticino rivers were forded in several places by the Allied forces. The overflowing of the Ticino could wax poetic for the overwhelming Allied attack on Mussolini's rump Fascist Republic at Salò. Milan is the city favored here as the scene mentioned in other quatrains of Mussolini's final indignity; his body was abused and mutilated, then hung upside down high over the angry mob for all to see.

See Index: death of Mussolini.

2 Q27

Le diuin verbe ſera du ciel frappé,	**The divine word will be struck from the sky,**
Qui ne pourra proceder plus auant:	**One who will not be able to proceed farther:**
Du reſerant[1] le ſecret eſtoupé,	**The revelation – the secret shut away,**
Qu'on marchera par deſſus & deuant.	**Such that they will walk over and ahead [of his dungeon].[2]**

[1]Latin *reserare* = to unlock, reveal.
[2]Le Pelletier commenting on line 4 said, "A man of whom one can say, *qu'on marchera par dessus et devant* is one who is found chained to the wall of the bottom of a dungeon . . . or buried at the foot of a wall."

Quatrains 2 Q27 through 2 Q29 return us to the theme of the eight clues to divining the founding father(s) of the 21st century's spiritual revolution from the East.

What follows is certainly not the only interpretation possible, but to me, line 1 implies the **divine word** of a spiritual teaching, or the utterer of these words himself, who is struck down from the sky. He is on a journey in a plane that either crashes or is **not able to proceed further** because it has been prevented from taking off from a runway. As strange and cryptic as this quatrain sounds, a recent event in the life of one contemporary spiritual rebel can be applied to every point in the quatrain.

In late October 1985 tensions were running high in the spiritual commune city of Rajneeshpuram. The cars of dozens of state and government agencies choked the parking lots of the downtown area. It was now becoming clear to the followers of Osho that these men, who had come initially to investigate the crimes committed against the citizens by one of their own, Ma Anand Sheela, were using this as an excuse to position themselves to freeze the assets of the commune and its citizens and close down the city itself. During Osho's long battle for his residential visa the Reagan administration had spent millions of dollars seeking evidence of his involvement in immigration fraud committed by over 100 foreign disciples. Charles Turner, the chief federal prosecutor in the immigration case against Osho, openly admitted to *The Oregonian* newspaper that their main objective was to use the law for political ends. The federal government wanted "the Bhagwan" out of America and his commune destroyed. Former Attorney General Ed Meese was quoted as saying that he wanted Osho isolated from his people.

An informant in the federal prosecutor's offices told Osho's lawyers that there was a secret indictment for his arrest. Turner denies it existed. Osho's lawyers say they tried to negotiate a peaceful transfer of Osho into custody but Turner would not discuss it. Rumors of public arrest and numerous death threats convinced Osho to fly out of Oregon.

One government plan in particular was confirmed by investigative reporter Max Brecher (author of *A Passage to America*), who interviewed and taped all the major players and National Guard generals responsible for preparing a Waco-style attack called Operation Serenity on Osho's commune. Brecher told me personally that Osho said that his flight across America was not an attempt to avoid justice and leave the country (he knew his Lear jet was not capable of international flight), but was his attempt to take his people out of harm's way. Given what Brecher has uncovered about Operation Serenity, the government's planned invasion of a city of 5,000 people by 8,000 national guardsmen with armored cars, supporting a helicopter attack on Osho's private residence in the center by special SWAT teams, would have made the immolation of David Koresh's Waco commune appear minor in comparison.

Once Osho's Lear jet was airborne it was tracked and communication was allegedly jammed. I have read Brecher's transcripts and listened to audiotapes of FAA controllers actually jamming the jet's radio transmissions. The radio messages from his lawyers advising him to reroute the jet back to Oregon are jammed, even though one is supposedly free to travel without interference until under indictment or warrant.

The jet lands in Charlotte, North Carolina, for refueling. Its occupants get a nasty surprise: They are immediately surrounded by dozens of guns pointing at them. US Marshals, yelling at the top of their lungs, arrest Osho and his attendants without a warrant, and his Miranda rights are not read to him. He is roughly treated, chained, and placed in a filthy holding cell smeared with blood and excrement below ground in the Charlotte County Jail.

Did Nostradamus see this modern mystic's persecution when he wrote this verse? Osho's passage over America is *struck from the sky*. Whether he did actually contemplate evading justice by flying to Bermuda or not will never be known. It is accurate to say that wherever he was planning to run he was not *able to proceed farther*. Osho and his spiritual *revelations* are *shut away* in a holding cell that is underground. Jailkeepers and disciples alike *walk over* his dungeon. For the next few days the world news broadcast images of Osho in leg and waist irons trying to raise his manacled hands pressed together in a namasté blessing to followers, reporters and jailers alike, serene and undisturbed by the harsh treatment. He endured 12 days of detention and persecution as he was flown across America from one secret (*underground*) cell to another until he reached Portland, Oregon, for a hearing, after which he was released on bail. For three of those 12 days, he had disappeared inside the American prison system. Not even his lawyers knew his whereabouts (*the secret shut away*). Osho later related that during the three "lost days," which it turned out he had spent in the Oklahoma City Jail, he had been forced to sign in under an assumed name, then thrown into a cell with a man dying from infectious herpes. Later, he was given bread with an odorless, tasteless spread, which he later assessed to be poisoned.

The final line may hide a more figurative message to Osho's disciples. They must *walk over and ahead* – that is, move on without their master's physical presence to guide them. Soon after Osho returned to Portland he was deported from America on an Alford Plea, which allowed him to maintain his innocence. Without his presence, the commune soon disbanded and its people scattered all over the world.

Within four years Osho was dead. After his 12 days in jail, Osho's health began a rapid decline. By January 1990 the 58-year-old seemed to have aged 20 years. His beard became as white as that of a man in his late seventies. Medical examinations by a number of noted physicians and toxicologists came to the same conclusion – that he had somehow been poisoned by heavy metals around the time he was under US custody.

During the first days of his incarceration in the Charlotte County Jail,

Osho was interviewed by Ted Koppel on ABC's *Nightline*. Osho claimed he was not fleeing the country and that he was "disappointed" with the US government. He called the "world's greatest democracy" a "hypocrisy."

2 Q28

Le penultiefme du furnom du prophete,	**Second to the last of the prophet's name,**
Prendra Diane pour fon iour & repos:	**Will take Diana's day as his day of silent rest:**
Loing vaguera par frenetique tefte,	**He will travel far and wide in his drive to infuriate,**
Et deliurant vn grand peuple d'impos.[1]	**Delivering a great people from subjection.**

[1]*impos* = Old French *impôt* = taxes; or Latin *impos* = not one's own master, powerless, subject.

Gautama the Buddha (560?–483? BC) proclaimed that the Wheel of Dharma – the dynamo for human spiritual evolution – would be turned once every 25 centuries by a world teacher to generate humanity's shift to a new state of consciousness. Another turn is due at the end of this millennium. Buddha used the Sanscrit word *dhyana* or *dhyan* for meditation, a name which corresponds to the French pronunciation of **Diana** used by Nostradamus. Diana is the goddess of the Moon. One of Nostradamus' main clues about the man who will initiate this turn of the Wheel concerns the decoding of his name. Apparently the world teacher's second, or middle, name means "moon." For instance, Osho – one of the candidates used – to be known as Bhagwan Shree Rajneesh; *Rajneesh* means "Lord of the Full Moon." In his full legal name – Rajneesh Chandra Mohan – the middle or **second to the last** name, Chandra, also means "moon."

Clue 5 (see Mars and Flame, EP104–105, EP139) also referred to a **people** linked to Hermes, the moon and meditation, and a teacher from the East coming to the West. Perhaps the teacher travels, or will travel, around the world. Perhaps his **drive to infuriate** (2 Q28) orthodox belief and his controversial message and actions will keep the teacher on the move. A number of the 20th century's most rebellious mystics from the East have used modern conveyances such as ocean liners, or have later become avid jet-setters throughout their *drive to infuriate* the status quo religions. Yogananda, Gurdjieff, and Meher Baba traveled by ocean liner from the East to Europe and America. Prabhupada flew to the West by plane; so did the Western-born mystic, Adi Da Santosha, when returning from sacred pilgrimages in the East. Osho and J. Krishnamurti are probably the most well-traveled gurus to date. Krishnamurti spent most of his long life sharing his concept of "witnessing" with tens of thousand of followers on six continents. In only six months, between November 1985 and May 1986, Osho flew from America to Cyprus, India, Nepal, Greece, France, Sweden, England, Ireland, Canada, Senegal, Uruguay, Jamaica, Portugal, and back to India.

Many of these eastern gurus claim to liberate their followers from the conditioned behavior that makes them mediocre cogs in society's machine. For example, Osho once said, "God is unknown. Truth is unknown. Beauty is unknown. Love is unknown. But the fearful mind always clings to the known. It does not go beyond the drawn line. It walks on the beaten track. The fearful person becomes mechanical, and he is no different from the drudge. Religions teach fear: fear of hell, fear of sins, and fear of punishment. Society teaches fear – fear of dishonor. Education teaches fear – fear of failure.

"Simultaneously there is greed attached – greed for heaven, greed for the fruits of virtue; greed for respect, position, reputation, success and rewards. All greed is the other side of the coin of fear. This way the consciousness of a person becomes full of fear and greed. The fire of jealousy and competition is aroused. The fever of ambition is created. There is no wonder if, in all these circular patterns, life is wasted.

"Such education is dangerous. Such religions are dangerous. Education is that which teaches fearlessness, stabilizes one in non-greed, gives energy to rebel, gives courage to accept the challenge of the unknown. Education should not teach jealousy and competition, but love; it should not encourage the insane speed of ambition, but the natural and self-inspired growth. But this can happen only if we accept the uniqueness of everyone's individuality."

2 Q29

L'Oriental fortira de fon fiege,	**The man from the East will come out**
Paffer les monts Apennins voir la Gaule:	**of his seat,**
Tranfpercera le ciel, les eaux & neige,	**Passing across the Apennines to see**
Et vn chafcun frappera de fa gaule.	**France:**
	He will fly through the sky, the rains
	and the snows,
	And strike everyone with his rod.

In two major quatrains about a man from the East there are allusions to the iron rod of Hermes. This rod is often interpreted to be a nuclear missile, a reading that makes the man an agent of the Antichrist. But interpreters should also remember the occult significance of Nostradamus' choice of vocabulary. The Hermes reference links the rod to the caduceus wand, the Western mystical symbol for enlightenment. The rod has the power to transform, liberating the truth inside the individual. This man from the East wields the rod like a Zen stick to jolt the world into waking from its illusions. From this we can infer that Nostradamus is describing an Eastern teacher who strikes out at the world and would therefore be unpopular with the mainstream culture. He might use unusual and unorthodox devices to stir people up, disturbing the "status codes" of social and religious behavior in our materialistic times.

During Osho's world tour he was expelled from Greece in early 1986 due to pressure from the Greek Orthodox Church and the American Embassy. It may be no more than an interesting coincidence that his flight plan closely matches Nostradamus' escape route four centuries before. Osho crossed the Apennine mountains of Italy to indeed *see France*. His Lear jet landed in Nice and was immediately surrounded by police with automatic weapons. After refueling, it was forced to take off at gunpoint to travel over the *rains* and *snows* of the Alps to Sweden.

Juliet Forman relates in her book *Bhagwan Shree Rajneesh: One Man Against the Whole Ugly Past of Humanity* (Rebel Publishing House), that once the harried guru left Nice, his attendant, Swami Dhyan John, remarked that Osho, in a makeshift bed, surveyed the snow-covered Alps bathed in morning sunlight rolling beneath his jet and a few moments later turned to Dhyan John and said, "Maybe if the world ended, existence would be better off and we could start again."

Flight pattern forecasts aside, several other Eastern mystics could vie for the title of Nostradamus' *man from the East*. Swamis Vivekananda and Yogananda were 19th- and early 20th-century pathfinders for Eastern mysticism, as is Jiddu Krishnamurti. Meher Baba and his European disciples traveled extensively through France and Italy during the late 1920s and made their way *across the Apennines*, though Nostradamus clearly implies a journey by air rather than by train or automobile.

Quatrain Indexing Date: Q29 = 1929, the year Krishnamurti held his milestone discourse in front of several thousand Theosophists at a retreat in Ommen, Holland, declaring that he was not the foretold Maitreya (Buddha's second coming) and that truth is a "pathless land."

2 Q30

Vn qui les dieux d'Annibal infernaux,	**One who the infernal gods of Hannibal,**
Fera renaiſtre, effrayeur[1] des humains:	**Will cause to be reborn, terror to all mankind:**
Oncq' plus d'horreur ne plus dire iournaulx,	**Never more horror nor the newspapers tell of worse in the past,**
Qu'auint viendra par Babel aux Romains.	**Then will come to the Italians through Babel.**

[1] Old French for terror. In this case, by extension, a *terror(ist) to all mankind.*

From the spiritual messenger from the East of the last quatrain, Nostradamus moves us to the other end of the spiritual spectrum introducing us again to the Third, and last, Antichrist. He appears to be a Middle Eastern or North African terrorist who might obtain enough nerve gas or plutonium to take the world hostage. The prophet supplies clues to this Antichrist over several quatrains. Here he hints at his place of birth, religion, military theater of operations, and throws in a tantalizing clue to his link with **Mabus** in 2 Q62.

A good place to start our prophetic detective work is by playing one of Nostradamus' favorite word games of factual hide-and-seek: the decoding of classical metaphors and ancient names to find their modern parallels. The Punic and Phoenician peoples worshipped an all-powerful God they called Baal, or Lord. Each region gave him a personalized name. Nostradamus may be hinting that the Antichrist comes from the modern-day region that, in former times, was a colony of the wide-ranging ancient Phoenician empire – an area that today includes Tunisia, Libya, Palestine, Lebanon, Israel, Iraq, and Syria.

Nostradamus' most famous doomsday prediction (10 Q72) warns future generations of a **King of Terror** descending from the skies in July 1999. This holy terror linked to Mabus and Hannibal's so-called **god** could point to an important location for the final Antichrist. Hannibal's Baal was called Hammon, the patron deity of Carthage. When Baal Hammon has been angered, he is described as a reigning **Terror from the skies** (10 Q72). The Romans had a custom of adopting the patron gods of a conquered nation and Latinizing their names. After the Romans had sacked the city of Carthage at the close of the Third Punic War in 146 BC, they built their own city over its ashes and renamed it Thurbo Majus. The enigmatic name M-A-B-U-S may stand as a classic anagram for "Majus," another link to the Antichrist and the *infernal gods of Hannibal*.

The chief headquarters of the Palestine Liberation Organization (PLO) lie just a few miles outside the ruins of Thurbo Ma(b)us' city. There still remain a few radical factions in the PLO dedicated to destroying Israel and establishing a Palestinian state over its remains, rather than along the West Bank of the Jordan river. These same freedom fighters (or Baal's terror-ists) have a reputation for considering any means to obtain their demands, from diplomacy to nuclear and chemical blackmail (*terror from the skies* [10 Q72]).

The idea of newspapers was inconceivable in the time of Nostradamus. This fact makes it clear to anyone reading today's newspaper stories about Saddam Hussein, Abu Nidal or Muhammar Qadaffi, or the bombing of the New York Trade Center, that these clues have contemporary relevance. In these quatrains Nostradamus may be hiding a warning of a future plague of world terrorism – mainly based in North Africa and the

Middle East. The worst scenario is of a handful of terrorist-sanctioning nations draging the world into nuclear war as early as 1999.

The final line links us to a series of disturbing quatrains warning of this Antichrist's leading a nuclear terrorist attack on Italy from a submarine. The Antichrist gets his support from **Babel**, an ancient name for modern Iraq.

See Index: Third Antichrist clues.

2 Q31

En Campanie le Caſſilin[1] fera tant,	In Campania the Volturno River of
Qu'on ne verra que d'aux les champs	Capua will do so much,
couuers:	That one will see only water covering
Deuant apres le pluye de long temps,	the fields:
Hors mis les arbres rien l'on verra de vert.	Before and after the long-lasting rain,
	Except for the trees one will see
	nothing green.

[1]Latin Casilinum = the ancient Roman name for Capua, on the Volturno river.

Here is another quatrain describing an era of floods followed by drought. This time waters overwhelm the banks of the Volturno river and the city of Capua is flooded. This may be another warning for humanity to become more ecologically sane; otherwise, terrible floods to come from the climactic disruptions in the 21st century will wash over the Earth.

2 Q32

Laict, ſang grenoilles eſcoudre[1] en Dalmatie,	Milk, blood, frogs prepared in Dalmatia,
Conflict donné, peſte pres de Balennes[2]	Conflict given, pest near Balennes
Cry ſera grand par toute Eſclauonie,[3]	The cry will be great from all of
Lors naiſtra monſtre[4] pres & dedans Rauenne.	Slavonia,
	Then will be born a monster near and
	inside Ravenna.

[1]Latin excudere = to forge, prepare, compose.
[2]Latin [Trebula] Balliensis = Treglia, north-east of Capua.
[3]Slavonia = a) Roman province that made up part of Pannonia (Hungary); b) Russia; c) Yugoslavia (land of the southern Slavs).
[4] Old French for a divine omen or a monster.

This may be a return to the Antichrist/nuclear terrorist theme from 2 Q30, or a warning about some future plague. Line 1 stands for chemical or biological warfare prepared on the Dalmatian coast (the Balkans). The conflict is either a resumption of the Bosnian struggle in the latter half of the 1990s or a new and wider Balkan war in the early decades of the 21st century. According to the superstitions of his day, Nostradamus foresees a grotesque baby animal or human being born in Ravenna, Italy, as a portent of the new Balkan war.

A wider interpretation of the great cry issuing from Slavonia would cite this as a prediction of either the Chernobyl nuclear disaster of 1986, or some future nuclear meltdown at a Russian or Eastern European reactor. It could also mark an outbreak of more extensive ethnic wars across the former Soviet Union, where germ and chemical warfare agents are widely used.

Monstre in Old French can mean monster, or a divine omen sent by the gods to a pagan seer through a (de)monstr(ation). Rather than a monster child, a divine omen or prediction will be **born** in the vision of some future clairvoyant in Ravenna.

If today's future-gazers often wax divine or monstrous in their descriptions of wonders to come 500 years in our future, how difficult must it have been for a man of the 16th century to describe weapons, machines, and plagues of the 20th and 21st century? Although it is popular among interpreters to divine biological or chemical weapons from the cryptic phrase **milk**, **blood**, **frogs**, it is also true that practitioners of folk medicine in Nostradamus' day often described lymphatic fluids and semen as **milk**, and **blood** was the vitality-giver or the immune system. Peasant healers blamed **frogs** for all viral diseases. With this in mind, the riddle of **milk**, **blood**, **frogs** becomes a description of the modern plague of AIDS (Acquired Immune Deficiency Syndrome), which infects the blood and lymphatic system chiefly through contact with semen or from intravenous drug use or tainted blood transfusions.

Quatrain Indexing Date: 2 Q32 = 2032, the year when there is either a nuclear disaster or an act of nuclear or chemical terrorism in the Balkans, Eastern Europe, or Russia. This may also be the year when AIDS or a new blood plague like the Ebola virus spreads across the planet.

2 Q33

Par le torrent qui defcent de Veronne,	**Through the torrent which descends from Verona,**
Par lors qu' au Pau¹ guidera fon entrée:	**About the time when the Pau [and Po rivers] will guide its entry:**
Vn grand naufrage, & non moins en Garonne,	**A great wreck [in Italy], and no less in the Garonne,**
Quand ceux de Gēnes marcheront leur contree.	**When those of Genoa will march [against] their country.**

¹Could be intended for both the *Po* and *Pau* rivers in Italy and France.

This may be part three of the grim future forecast for Italy and the Balkans during the 21st century and for global warming.

The torrent devouring Capua also overwhelms Verona. Other floods run down the Pau in France and the Po river valley in northern Italy. Videos made by survivors of the great floods in Provence and Genoa in the early 1990s convey the image of Mother Nature's naked and raging wave cascading down the Alpine valley in a frothing cloak of wreckage and crushed cars. Climatologists expect the storms producing such floods to be 50 percent stronger by the middle of the 21st century. Ecological breakdowns could lead to social breakdown. Perhaps we have a case here of Genoa seceding from Italy.

2 Q34

L'ire infenfee du combat furieux,	**The senseless wrath of furious combat,**
Fera à table par freres le fer luire:	**Will cause brothers to draw their swords at the table:**
Les defpartir, bleffé, curieux,	**They are separated, wounded, curiously,**
Le fier duelle viendra en France nuire.	**The proud duel will come to harm France.**

Mortal hatred has burned in the hearts of many a French prince in the last four centuries. The fratricidal intrigues of Henry III against his brother the Duc d'Alençon could be characterized as a duel or deadly competition, if not a literal duel with swords. This does not rule out a private incident seen through Nostradamus' magic but too far removed or repressed by courtiers of both young men to end up scribbled on the parchment of a contemporary historian.

2 Q35

Dans deux logis de nuict le feu prendra,	**Within two lodgings at night the fire will take hold,**
Plufieurs dedans eftouffez & roftis:	**Several within suffocated and roasted:**
Pres de deux fleuues pour feul il auiendra:	**Near the two rivers it will happen for sure:**
Sol, l'Arq,[1] & Caper[2] tous feront amortis.	**Sun, Sagittarius and Capricorn will all be exterminated.**

[1] Latin *Arquitenens* = Sagittarius the Archer.
[2] Latin *caper* = goat, thus *Capricornus*, the constellation of Capricorn.

Nostradamus promises a fire will take place in Paris (**near the two rivers** of the Marne and Seine) during the sun's transit of Sagittarius and Capricorn in November and December. One problem – the year isn't mentioned.

It is a stretch, but the closest I can come to the date is early October

1994, when a mass murder-suicide of a Christian doomsday cult known as the Order of the Solar Temple took place. Fifty-three charred bodies were found in the temple's two burned-out compounds, one in Granges-sur-Salvan, east of Geneva, Switzerland, the other in Chiery, a small village just north of Montreal, Canada. Montreal, like Paris, is a city near the confluence of two rivers, the Ottawa and St Lawrence.

2 Q36

Du grand Prophete les lettres feront prinfes,	**The letters of the great Prophet will be seized,**
Entre les mains du tyran deuiendront:	
Fraudes fon Roy feront fes entreprinfes,	**And will fall into the hands of the tyrant:**
Mais fes rapines bien toft le troubleront.	**His enterprise will be to deceive his King,**
	But his thefts will very soon trouble him.

James Randi (1990) speculates that in 1629 the aged son of Nostradamus was desperate to collect a selection of Latin letters of his father for safe-keeping, because a few of them betrayed open sympathy for the Protestants. The lines of this quatrain could record the sins of the father burdening the conscience of the son. César finally did recover the letters (which can be found translated into French by Jean Dupèbe in *Nostradamus – Lettres Inedites*). Perhaps if these letters had fallen into the hands of a contemporary Inquisitor instead of a modern debunker, César's life and reputation might have been threatened.

The last two lines may implicate César and his nephew, Vincent Seve, for creating a fake set of 58 Sixians (six-line poems) attributed to the hand of Nostradamus. The first edition of the Sixians was presented with a letter from Seve to Henry IV on 19 March 1605, at the Château de Chantilly.

In the letter Seve says the long-lost manuscript was presented to him by a certain Henry Nostradamus. There is no record of any Henry Nostradamus elsewhere in the prophet's papers or letters; Nostradamus, however, did have two brothers who may have sired this "Henry." Perhaps this deception of false prophecies and plagiarizing of his father (**his thefts**) weighed heavily on César. His father had made it clear in his Epistle to Henry II that his prophetic gift would not be transferred to his descendants. Perhaps this was a fact César secretly resented, and the hurt little boy hidden deep inside the subconscious of the old historian had guided his hand to forge some prophecies.

Another guilt-ridden myth-maker adequately described by the quatrain would be the Nazi astrologer and Nostradamian Karl Ernst Krafft, who was responsible for writing interpretations of Nostradamus for publication by Goebbels' propaganda ministry that predicted Hitler's victory over France. In 1941 Krafft's fortunes took a turn for the worse. In that year Rudolph Hess, Nazi Party official and follower of the occult, flew to England on a self-deluded errand of astrologically or psychically approved peace. Hitler instigated a purge of occultists and astrologers and Krafft was imprisoned. While in prison he was coerced by the Gestapo to continue his writing of National-Socialistically correct interpretations of Nostradamus. Krafft was sincere in his examination of the prophecies and his gift for astrology and interpreting Nostradamus had opened doors for him in the Reich. Now his inability to find a genuine prediction support-ing Nazi victory stretched him tight as a string. Finally he succumbed to a nervous breakdown and in January 1945 died from typhus while on his way to Buchenwald concentration camp.

2 Q37

De ce grand nombre que lon enuoyera,	*Of this great number that one will send,*
Pour fecourir dans le fort affiegez,	*To succor those besieged in the fort,*
Pefte & famine tous les deuorera,	*Plague and famine will devour them all,*
Hors mis feptante qui feront profligez.	*Except seventy who will be destroyed.*

Very general. At first glance it could describe a doomed relief force sent to a besieged fortress, who succumbs to the same pestilence and famine that is devouring the fortress defenders. However, on second examination this one may be the preface to the following quatrain's more modern-sounding forecast of the great loss of life in Russia and Eastern Europe when two rulers are **reconciled**.

2 Q38

Des condamnez fera fait vn grand nombre,	**A great number of people will be condemned,**
Quand les monarques feront conciliez:	**When the monarchs are reconciled:**
Mais l'vn deux viendra fi malencombre,	**But one of them will be so embarrassed and harmed,**
Que guere enfemble ne feront raliez.	**That they will hardly remain allies.**

The German–Soviet Non-Aggression Pact, signed in 1939, was a tacit agreement between the Nazi and communist dictators to postpone war between their two nations. It suited Stalin to believe in Hitler's promises, because it gave him time to start modernizing his backward armed forces. In Hitler's bible, *Mein Kampf*, he had made it clear that after France and England were sufficiently devastated he would turn his forces east and attack the Soviet Union in some Armageddonlike showdown between the Aryan master race and the "sub-human and godless" communists.

Like so many other world leaders, Stalin was content to believe that Hitler was bluffing when, in fact, he told had the truth. Stalin ignored intelligence reports of mass movements of German forces near the Soviet Union's western frontiers. Even after acquiring from a crashed German reconnaissance plane the plans of Hitler's imminent invasion of the Soviet Union, Stalin remained deluded that Hitler would not strike so soon.

But Hitler relentlessly proceeded with his plans in a way that even his general staff found difficult to believe. After defeating France and isolating England, and just two years after signing the non-aggression treaty, he hurled 3,800 tanks and three million men across the Russian border. In his memoirs, Nikita Khruschev relates how a chagrined Stalin, contemplating his greatest blunder and faced with catastrophic military losses, confided to Khruschev that they had turned Lenin's revolution "into shit" (*so embarrassed and harmed*).

As the prophecy states, many people would be condemned as a result of the German–Soviet Non-Aggression Pact. It paved the way for the rapid conquest of Poland by Germans from the west and Soviet troops invading from the east. Millions of Jews would be trapped. On 22 June 1941, Stalin's self-deception ended at the news of a surprise German offensive along a 1,000-mile front. Within the first year of combat he would lose 20,000 tanks, 15,000 planes; 6 million Soviet soldiers would be killed, wounded, or missing. Millions of Soviet POWs were condemned to death by starvation in German concentration camps. In three years of battle on the Eastern Front 2.5 million Germans and 21 million to 27 million Soviets would be killed, and vast numbers of Jews and Slavic peoples from that Eastern European war zone contained within the Hitler–Stalin Pact would die in Hitler's concentration camps.

Quatrain Indexing Date: Q38 = near miss for 1939, the year that saw Germany and the Soviet Union sign their non-aggression pact a few weeks before the start of World War II.

2 Q39

Vn an deuant le conflict Italique,	**A year before the Italian conflict,**
Germains, Gaulois, Heſpaignols pour le fort:	**Germans, French, Spanish for the fort:**
Cherra l'eſcolle maiſon de republicque,	**The school house of the republic will fall,**
Où, hors mis peu, ſeront ſuffoqué mors.	**Where, except for a few, they will be choked dead.**

This is about the burnout of hostilities in the Spanish Civil War just a short time before the outbreak of World War II in 1939. The **Italian conflict** is a synecdoche for the date Mussolini finally entered World War II,

June 1940. In the previous year Franco's Falangist forces, assisted by thousands of Italian Fascist soldiers, routed the Loyalist army and captured the fortified city of Barcelona on 26 January 1939. A number of Frenchmen fought on the Loyalist side in international brigades. Line 3 waxes poetic for the fall of the Loyalist government, which capitulated to Franco on 28 March 1939. Despite pleas by Britain and France for leniency, Falangist tribunals condemned thousands of loyalists to death by firing squad and by hanging.

Quatrain Indexing Date: Q39 = 1939, the year which saw the Spanish Civil War end while World War II began.

2 Q40

Vn peu apres non point longue interualle,	**Shortly afterwards, not a very long**
Par mer & terre sera faict grand tumulte:	**interval,**
Beaucoup plus grande sera pugne[1]	**A great roaring storm will be raised**
naualle,	**by land and sea,**
Feux, animaux,[2] qui plus feront	**The naval battles will be greater than**
d'insulte.	**ever:**
	Flames, creatures which will make
	more upheaval.

[1]Latin *pugna* = battle.
[2]Animals, creatures. Nostradamus often described modern machines as animals and monsters.

Marshal Foch, one of the finest French generals of World War I, was asked his opinion about the Treaty of Versailles when it was being drafted in 1919. "It is not a peace," he replied, "but an armistice of 20 years." It can be argued that the harsh terms it inflicted on Germany sowed the seeds for revenge, opening doors of opportunity for hate-mongers like Adolf Hitler. World War II followed exactly 20 years later in 1939. This brief interval left the victorious allies of World War I unprepared for the war of Nostradamus' Second Antichrist – the fearsome Hi*s*ter – who would unleash the **storm** of modern warfare and open the hell gates of concentration camps. His 16th-century mind could only identify the Stuka dive bombers, battleships and panzers as new **creatures**.

Quatrain Indexing Date: Q40 = 1940, the year which saw the fall of Nostradamus' France to the Nazis.

See Index: the Second Antichrist (Hitler).

2 Q41

La grand estoille par sept iours bruslera,	**The great star will blaze for seven days,**
Nuée fera deux soleils apparoir:	**The cloud will cause two suns to**
Le gros mastin toute nuict hurlera,	**appear:**
Quand grand pontife changera de terroir.	**The huge dog will howl all night,**
	When the great pontiff will change lands.

The collision of 21 fragments of the comet Shoemaker-Levi with Jupiter took place over a seven-day period in July 1994. The peak viewing time for the passing of the comet Hale-Bopp will be approximately one week in spring 1997. Because Hale-Bopp is ten times larger than Halley's Comet, one can expect the most significant light show since the great comet of 1812 foretold doom for Napoleon's Russian campaign. The second line can read either **two suns to appear** or *the sun to appear double*. Nuclear explosions have been described as double suns. The **huge dog** may have links to Nostradamus' **Great Dog and Dohan**, (EP98), his version of Ezekiel's Gog and Magog. The pope is forced to leave Italy. He is most likely the final pope of Nostradamus' and St Malachy's prophecies, Peter of Rome.

See Index: comet.

2 Q42

Coq, chiens & chats de fang feront repeus,	**Cock, dogs and cats will be fed with blood,**
Et de la playe du tyran trouué mort.	**And from the wound of the tyrant found dead.**
Au lict d'vn autre iambes & bras rompus,	**At the bed of one other, legs and arms broken,**
Qui n'auoit peur mourir de cruelle mort.	**He who had no fear of dying – cruel death.**

Pretty bloody and pretty obscure. Too obscure for me, but Leoni provides us with an interesting answer. The ancient Gallic cock symbolizes France. It appeared on the banners of the French Revolution. The **dogs and cats** sated in blood are the mobs standing at the guillotine executions led by Robespierre during the Reign of Terror. Between 12 July and 28 July 1794, the bloodthirsty mob watched the guillotine's blade slice the heads off 1,285 victims. Leoni adds that even the tyrant Robespierre "took fright at the horrors that were being perpetrated."

Leoni continues, "On 16 July he renewed the Committee of Public Safety. Too late; Robespierre was arrested, but freed by the troops of the Commune who took him to a strange bed in the Hôtel de Ville. The National Guard recaptured him and he was shot in the jaw, not limbs. After a long night of agony he was executed without further trial on 29 July at the Place de la Révolution, now known as the Place de la Concorde."

2 Q43

Durant l'eſtoille cheuelue apparente,
Les trois grans princes ſeront faits ennemis:
Frappés du ciel paix terre tremulente,[1]
Pau, Timbre vndans,[2] ſerpent ſus le bort
    mis.

During the appearance of the bearded
    star,
The three great princes will be made
    enemies:
The shaky peace on earth shall be
    struck from the skies,
The Po [or Pau], the winding Tiber,
    a serpent placed on the shore.

[1]Old French tremulente = trembling.
[2]vndans, from Latin undare, varients: to surge, overflow, inundate.

The orthodox interpretation would cite this quatrain for the great comet of 1577, the final year of the sixth War of Religion, when the **three great princes** would be Henry III, Henry de Navarre, and Henry de Guise. The concessions stipulated by the Peace of Bergerac were not honored by Henry III and the **shaky peace** was broken in a seventh War of Religion in 1580. The final lines do not support this slant as well as the first. This time the **serpent** cannot be Catherine de' Medici. There is no record of her being sent to Rome by boat.

A futuristic interpretation would see the **three great princes** as metaphors for leaders in the First, Second, or Third Worlds or, as we will examine in quatrains describing Armageddon, an alliance of three terrorist-sanctioning nations destined to fight amongst themselves. Peace being **struck from the skies** could link the **King of Terror** of 10 Q72 with the man of **evildoing** (3 Q60) commanding the submarine fleet. Perhaps a psychotic in the Abu Nidal organization can curry covert support from Libya or some future Islamic republic of Egypt. For a time in the early 1990s Nidal even had offices, plus tacit support by America's chief Arab ally, Saudi Arabia. The future may see a Libyan or Egyptian submarine, under cover of darkness, deposit a band of PLO commandos and their **serpent** – a metaphor for a stolen nuclear device or homemade atom bomb – off the Italian coast at the mouth of the Tiber river. Even a nuclear plant in northern Italy's Po river region could be the scene of a terrorist attack. One of Italy's two nuclear power plants is at Caorso, a town two miles south of the Po River near Cremona.

Another possibility would greet the new millennium dawn with a shaky peace on Earth. The next window for world war takes us into the 2020s, when ozone holes could open the way for deadly cosmic rays onto our grainbelts, killing off civilization's ability to feed itself. Add to this the exploding population of 8 billon to 10 billion hungry people and further climatic disruptions from a rising sea level caused by the greenhouse effect, and one would certainly see even the most solid peace agreements **struck**, as it were, *from the skies*.

See Index: Comet Hale-Bopp.

2 Q44

L'aigle poufée entour de pauillions,	**The eagle pushed back around the tents,**
Par autres oyfeaux d'entour fera chaffée:	**Will be chased there by other birds:**
Quand bruit des cymbres tube[1] & fonnaillons	**When the clash of the cymbals, trumpets and harness bells**
Rendront le fens de la dame infenfée.	**Will restore the senses of the senseless lady.**

[1]Latin *tuba* = trumpet.

Several times Nostradamus identifies Napoleon by the gilded eagles on his army's standards. He continues this play on birds in this reference to the chief forces opposing Bonaparte during the German campaigns of 1813, symbolized by the double-headed eagles of the Austrians, Russians, and the eagle standards of the Prussians. He was chased back into France by these birds, and he was forced to abdicate by April 1814. All Europe celebrated his defeat (**cymbals, trumpets, and . . . bells**). The **senseless lady** is Marianne, the symbol of republican France, brought back to her senses by the Bourbon restoration.

2 Q45

Trop le ciel pleure l'Androgyn procreé,	**Too much the heavens weep for the Androgyne procreation,**
Pres de ciel fang humain refpandu:	**Near the heavens human blood shed:**
Par mort trop tard grand peuple recreé,	**Because of death too late a great people re-created,**
Tard & toft vient le fecours attendu.	**Late and soon comes the awaited help.**

A rare prophecy of interplanetary war in our distant future? Within another century genetic engineering will allow humanity to branch off into different species. An androgynous "hu-womb-man" race will emerge . . . perhaps an off-world creation of future human societies dwelling on other planets or in deep space station colonies. There may be a war in space that exterminates this androgynous race of humans, but their genetic seed is preserved, allowing them to be **re-created** either through artificial insemination with other human species or with the aid of artificial womb technology beyond our current understanding.

Quatrain Indexing Date: Q46 = 2146, 2246, 2346, 2446, etc.

2 Q46

Apres grãd troche[1] humain plus grãd s'apprefte, Le grand moteur des fiecles renouuelle: Pluye, fang, laict, famine, fer[2] & pefte, Au ciel veu feu, courant longue eftincelle.	**After a great misery for mankind an even greater approaches.** **The great motor of the centuries is renewed:** **It will rain blood, milk, famine, iron and pestilence,** **In the sky will be seen a fire, dragging a trail of sparks.**

[1]Greek trukos = misery.
[2]Iron, steel; (poetic) the iron and steel of war weapons.

The first **great misery** for mankind is World War II. The next is World War III, expected to take place around the time the **great motor of the centuries is renewed**, at the millennium. Contrary to the hopeful signs for a new world order of peace that burgeoned at the end of the Cold War, collective prophecy down through history remains adamant that there will be a third world war either in the 20th century after Christ or at the beginning of the 21st. The fact that most casualties of a global nuclear war will come from starvation instead of blast and radiation effects has not been overlooked in Nostradamus' nightmare scenario of Armageddon, the final battle. Furthermore, a wave of global famine in the wake of gross overpopulation may be the cause of the war. The rain of blood could be rain choked with radioactive dust. Survivors of a chemical or biological weapons attack sometimes describe the detonation of warheads as a milky rain. The **fire dragging a trail of sparks** could be a double pun for the transit of either a great comet just prior to World War III or the missiles destined to be used in such a war. Halley's Comet in 1986 was a miss; Shoemaker-Levi's collision with Jupiter in 1994 also passed without a world war. This leaves the next comet calling card of Armageddon to the visitation of Comet Hale-Bopp in the spring of 1997, the closest cosmic omen so far to pass near the millennium, when the **motor of the centuries is renewed**.

In the year 1946 (Q46) America shipped a number of V-2 rockets, along with the scientists who created them, from Germany to the deserts of the American South-west for further testing and development. Perhaps we can yet avoid some near-future nightmare in which we destroy ourselves by lethal chemical weapons – whose action could be aptly described by 16th-century eyes as a rain of blood and milk. There may be still some time to forestall an aftermath of famine, war, and disease carried across the skies by the descendants of V-2 rockets, today's intermediate-range and intercontinental ballistic missiles.

Quatrain Indexing Date: Q46 = 1946, the year America shipped V-2 rockets and their creator, Dr Wernher von Braun, and his staff to America for further testing and perfecting of what later became the capital weapon of the Cold War, the Intercontinental Ballistic Missile (ICBM). On the positive side, 1946 was the birth year of the United Nations, a body dedicated to stop world wars.

See Index: Comets; missile themes.

2 Q47

L'ennemy grand vieil dueil meurt de poiſon,
Les ſouuerains par infiniz ſubiuguez:
Pierres plouuoir, cachez ſoubz la toiſon,
Par mort articles en vain ſont alleguez.

The grief-stricken, great old enemy dead from poison,
The sovereigns mastered by the infinite:
Stones rain, hidden under the fleece,
Through death articles in vain are unburdened.

A grieving enemy succumbs to poison during the time of a great meteor shower. This could be linked to the distant events of the final conflagration of Earth in AD 3755–3797 (see 10 Q67). The *sovereigns* in that case could be the future superhuman and spacefaring races that master the infinite void of space. The source of the meteor shower is the river of stars known as the Milky Way. The key to this stretch of an interpretation is to know how far Nostradamus takes poetic license with the word *articles*. A person can be called an article, or he could be indicating objects, or treaties being discarded. It could even be the jettisoning of cargo into space.

2 Q48

La grand copie[1] qui paſſera les monts,
Saturne en l'Arq[2] tournant du poiſſon Mars:
Venins cachés ſoubz teſtes de ſaulmons,
Leur chief pendu à fil de polemars.[3]

The great force who will pass the mountains,
Saturn in Sagittarius turning toward Piscean Mars:
Caches of venom [poison] under the heads of salmon,
Their chief hung with a yarn of twine.

[1] Latin *copia* = troops, army, force.
[2] Latin *Arquitenens* = Sagittarius.
[3] Greek *polemarchos* variant: one who leads the war.

Soviet forces were in the midst of their pullout from mountainous Afghanistan around the same time Saturn was in Sagittarius, and Mars was *turning* in and out of Pisces in May–July and October of 1988. Line 3 attempts to describe the fish-shaped shell of biological warheads used by the Soviet Air Force and artillery against the Afghan rebels and civilians. The former Afghan leader, Najibullah was hanged by Taliban fundamentalist guerillas in late 1996. The final line does not exclude a similar future fate for any number of warlords from rebel factions fighting over the rubble and scraps of Afghanistan, such as Ahmadshah Massoud or his arch-enemy, the blue-turbaned Heckmediyahr.

2 Q49

Les conſeilliers du premier monopole,	**The councilors of the premier**
Les conquerants ſeduits par la Melite:[1]	**monopoly [or conspiracy],**
Rodes, Biſance pour leurs expoſant pole,	**The conquerors seduced by the**
Terre faudra les pourſuiuans de ſuite.[2]	**inhabitants of Malta:**
	Rhodes, Byzantium on account of them
	exposing their sphere of influence,
	The pursuing noblemen will be
	needing land.

[1]Latin *Melita* = Malta.
[2]*Suite* = a) *fuite*, fleeing; b) *suite*, the rest, those that follow.

This all sounds like an account of the loss of Rhodes to the Ottomans during which the surviving Knights of Saint John evacuate to Malta. It could also cover the siege of Malta and the significance of the changing spheres of Ottoman and Christian influence in the Mediterranean.

2 Q50

Quand ceux d'Hainault, de Gãd & de	**When those of Hainaut, of Ghent and**
Bruxelles,	**of Brussels,**
Verront à Langres le ſiege deuant mis:	**Will see the siege laid before Langres:**
Derrier leurs flancz ſeront guerres	**Behind their flanks will be merciless**
cruelles,	**warfare,**
La plaie antique fera pis qu'ennemis.	**The ancient wound will do worse**
	than enemies.

The men of Hainaut, Ghent (the principle city of Flanders), and Brussels (the capital of Brabant) join forces with the Spanish troops attacking Langres on France's 16th-century frontier. Within two years of the prophet's death, these same men of Flanders, Brabant, and Hainaut would turn on their Spanish masters and begin waging an 80-year war to liberate the Spanish Netherlands.

2 Q51

Le ſang du iuſte à Londres fera faulte,	**The blood of the just will be demanded**
Bruſles par fouldres[1] de vint trois les ſix:	**at London,**
La dame antique cherra de place haute,	**Burnt by lightning fire in twenty-three**
Des meſme ſecte pluſieurs ſeront occis.	**the sixes [66]:**
	The ancient lady will fall from her high
	place,
	And many of the same sect will be killed.

[1]Old French *foudroyer* = to strike like lightning; to strike down severely, suddenly, stunningly, or with a loud noise and a dazzlingly bright light (Kidogo).

Many interpreters believe that **twenty-three the sixes** is an accurate though figurative prediction of the year of the Great Fire of London – 1666. Six in plural could be 66. The fire broke out on 1 September, in the *sixes*, which could alternatively target the correct decade, the 1660s. Nostradamus' love for complex verbal and numerical puns cannot, however, be ruled out, and *sixes* might mean the number of man and sin, "666."

The quatrain supports the date with details of the fire itself and continues elaborating on 2 Q53's **great lady** metaphor. This time it is the **ancient lady**, a personification of St Paul's Cathedral. The Church falling to Protestantism is symbolized in a more graphic warning: the roof of St Paul's will collapse from heat onto the faithful who seek shelter within its stone walls from the firestorm devouring their wooden houses.

This quatrain is Number 3 in James Randi's list of ten debunkable quatrains (see *The Mask of Nostradamus*, pages 189–93). He begins by splitting poetic hairs. The Benoist Rigaud edition does use *fouldres* (lightning strike) rather than *feu* (*fire*). Nostradamus, however, believed that plagues could be acts of God, that the poetic *fire* burning Protestant London could be a bolt from God (see the translation paragraph above).

It is true that English people never called St Paul's Cathedral the **old lady**; it is an Old French colloquialism for cathedrals, used by our old French prophet. Randi spins a shrewd new slant for lines 3 and 4, that the **ancient lady** stands for Queen "Bloody" Mary of England rather than for the Church or a cathedral. Mary ordained that England be purged of Protestants. She began burning them in neat groups of six on 22 January 1555. Randi correctly points to the publication of this quatrain in May 1555, four months after Mary begins her burnings, but this in itself does not objectively prove that Nostradamus was hiding a current event in a prophecy. We do not know when Nostradamus delivered his manuscript in the glacially paced mail of his day. We do know that he began writing the first three Centuries around April 1554. We are given speculation as evidence that Nostradamus would have known the intimate details of events in England, such as people being bundled for the fire in *sixes*.

This accusation by Randi hinges on the speed with which news traveled in the 16th century. An average journey from Paris to Salon, Provence, took three months — one month if the Queen sent news by Royal post to Nostradamus, which of course couldn't have happened because she was many months away from reading *Les Propheties* and even knowing he existed. The French ambassador to England might have sent his letters as fast as he could over the Channel to Paris, but mail is known to have taken one month to six weeks to travel that route. Now add another week for the news to spread through the court, a week for it to spread to the citizens of Paris and, finally, add three months for it to reach Nostradamus in Salon, and you get four months. For Randi's assumption to be right, the news would have had to reach Nostradamus four months before it happened! How else would he have enough time to write it in his manuscript and send it by bullock cart mail to his publishers in Lyons, who would then spend painstaking months typesetting and binding copies of his books to make the May 1555 release date?

I would not deny Randi's slant if it were the fulfillment of a near-future prediction. At the very least, scholars of Nostradamus have mistaken a near-future prophecy about the burning of 300 Protestants by Bloody Mary for a more distant future prophecy about the London Fire.

2 Q52

Dans plufieurs nuits la terre tremblera,	For several nights the earth will shake,
Sur le printemps deux effors fuite:	In the spring two great efforts together:
Corinthe[1], Ephefe[1] aux deux mers nagera,	Corinth and Ephesus will swim in two seas,
Guerre s'efmeut par deux vaillans de luite.	War set in motion by two valiant in combat.

[1]Corinth (Greece), Ephesus (Turkey). Earlier interpreters thought this was a classical synonym for England's war with Holland across the North Sea rather than the Aegean.

Interpreters usually apply this prophecy to the war between Holland and England in 1665–67. But since no superquake lasting several days occurred at this time, it may have a future connotation for Greece and Asia Minor. The Aegean region has experienced a dramatic increase of earthquakes; the 1980s registered 15 quakes measuring at least 6.5 or higher on the Richter scale. The last fatal quake took place in the Gulf of Corinth in June 1995. Ephesus has also suffered from severe earthquakes during its history.

Earthquakes can represent wars. Greece (Corinth) nearly waged war with Turkey (Ephesus) in 1995. Disputes over Aegean islands off the coast of Ephesus may result in armed conflict between them in the near future.

In early Christian times Ephesus was home of the first church of the Apocalypse. So **Ephesus** in a troubled state could also suggest that before too long the Apocalyptic view of Christianity will have an identity crisis, especially if doomsday does not take place between 1997 and 2001. Ephesus was also a province of Rome's Asia and could represent Asia in general by synecdoche as being in a troubled state or quaking.

Nostradamus was probably aware of the legendary seven sleepers who were supposed to have awakened after centuries to find Ephesus living under a Christian government. This might be a link to references to **the seven** or the **seventh** millennium in other quatrains, pointing to the year 2000 as a beginning of an era of religious renewal.

2 Q53

La grande peſte de cité maritime,[1] Ne ceſſera que mort ne ſoit vengée: Du iuſte ſang par pris damné ſans crime, De la grand dame par feincte n'outraigée.	**The great plague of the maritime city,** **Will not cease until there be avenged the death:** **Of the just blood, seized and condemned without a crime,** **The great lady is outraged by the pretense.**

[1]Maritime city can apply to London, Marseilles, and even Hong Kong.

Many Londoners thought the plague of 1665 was a punishment from God for Parliament's murder of Charles I (9 Q49). Whatever the true cause – divine retribution, mass suggestion, or simply bad sanitation – Nostradamus the royalist portrays the plague that carried off 68,596 Londoners as a scourge come to avenge an innocent king. The **great lady** is contemporary slang for either a Cathedral or the Catholic Church, who is **outraged** by the rise of Protestantism after the plague.

2 Q54

Par gent eſtrange, & Romains loingtaine Leur grand cité apres eaue fort troublee: Fille ſans trop different domaine, Prins chef, ferreure n'auoir eſte riblée.[1]	**Because of a foreign people, and remote from the Romans,** **Their grand city much troubled in the pursuit of water:** **Daughter without too much [of a] different domain,** **Captured chief, the lock not having been picked.**

[1]Old French *ribler* = to lead a wild life, rob, pillage, forage.

Wars in the next century may be fought over food and water rather than God and politics. Here we have Rome running out of water because of global pollution and overuse of Earth's dwindling fresh water sources. Rome (and by extension, the Vatican) is attacked by distant foreigners; who they are is unclear. According to the Manila-based Asian Development Bank, at least two-thirds of the world's urban population growth will occur in Asia. In China and India alone, some 800 million people will move into cities in the next 25 years. Exploding urban populations will certainly exceed water supplies in hundreds of Third World cities such as: Bejing, Mexico City, Calcutta, Bombay, Bangkok, and Lagos.

The second half of the quatrain is more obscure. Perhaps we have someone whose capture is more existential. He is a future pope or a global leader who has become a prisoner of circumstances beyond his control, such as overpopulation and the global water shortages. The **daughter** (whatever that means) suffers the same limitations.

Line 4 can also read *Captured chief, the ironworks not having been robbed*, or *. . . not having led a wild life*.

Quatrain Indexing Date: Q54 = 2054?

2 Q55

Dans le conflict le grand qui peu valloit,	**In the conflict the great man of little worth,**
A son dernier fera cas merueilleux:[1]	**Will commit an astonishing deed at his end:**
Pendant qu'Hadrie verra ce qu'il falloit,	**While Hadrie sees what is needed,**
Dans le banquet pongnale[2] *l'orgueilleux.*	**He stabs the proud during a banquet.**

[1]Old French variant: *exquisite*
[2]Old French *poiniard*, dagger; (poetic) to thrust the point of a sword.

The plague of French civil wars over religion would be concluded over an incident foreseen by Nostradamus 40 years before it happened. The Duc de Mayenne, Henry de Navarre's last rival for the French throne, feared the growing spread of *Les Seize*, or the Sixteen Parliamentarian movement, from Paris to other major cities. The Sixteen stands for the Catholic leaders of the sixteen quarters of Paris who had seized the capital to preserve the Catholic faith. With the assassination of Henry III this new leadership disrupted the old Catholic League and moved to fill the void left by the assassination of Henry de Guise, and to prevent Mayenne from taking the crown in the name of the Catholic League and the House of Lorraine. Radical elements of the Sixteen pressed even further, to overthrow the institution of royal rule itself.

Let us decipher this remarkable quatrain line by line. **In the conflict the great man of little worth, Will commit an astonishing deed at his end.** Mayenne planned a banquet for the entire People's Parliament to quiet their suspicions. He had them all murdered the following night. Nostradamus switches the sequence of events in the last two lines. Line 4 says: **He stabs the proud during a banquet**. Line 3 is the chronological end to this quatrain: **While Hadrie sees what is needed**. Again, **Hadrie** is an anagram for Henry de Navarre, who capitalizes on Mayenne's blunder by becoming a Catholic. "Paris is well worth a Mass," he declared, uniting France by simply changing his religious party label.

2 Q56

Que peste[1] & glaiue n'a sceu definer,[2]
Mort dans le puys[3] sommet[4] du ciel frappé:
L'abbé mourra quand verra ruiner,
Ceux du naufrage[5] l'escueil voulant
    grapper.[6]
	One whom rats and weaponry did not
	    know how to finish,
	Death on the hills of the Somme
	    struck from the sky:
	The abbé will die when he will see
	    ruined,
	Those of the wrecked [attack]
	    attempting to seize the obstacle.

[1]Pest, torment; vector of the plague, a rat.
[2]Old French definer = to die, finish, determine.
[3]Old French for mountains, hills.
[4]Either summit or a cryptogram for Somme, the scene of the great battle of World War I.
[5]Shipwreck; (fig.) wreck, wrecking.
[6]Old French for to seize.

The French *sommet* stands as a double pun for *summit* and the River **Somme**, where one of World War I's bloodiest trench battles was fought. On 1 July 1916, the British "Big Push" began after a thunderous artillery barrage. A hundred thousand men charged for the summit of the Thiepval Ridge, where they fell by the tens of thousands to German machine guns. The survivors who reached the hills were **struck from the sky** by German artillery. On that first day alone 19,000 British were killed out of a total of 60,000 casualties. By December they had pushed the Germans off the ridge, but no breakthrough was achieved. Five miles of penetration had cost the British 420,000 men, the French 195,000, and the Germans a shocking 650,000 men. The **abbé** may be one of any number of chaplains serving with the British Expeditionary Force that Nostradamus' prophetic eye has fixed itself upon. Perhaps the cleric dies shortly after watching the first disastrous attack.

2 Q57

Auant conflict le grand tombera,
Le grand à mort, mort trop subite &
    plainte,
Nay imparfaict: la plus part nagera,
Aupres du fleuue de sang[1] la terre tainte.
	Before the battle the great man will
	    fall,
	The great one to death, death too
	    sudden and lamented.
	Born imperfect, he will swim the
	    greater part of the way,
	Near the river of blood the ground is
	    stained.

[1]*Fleuue de sang* = river of blood, ie the Red River, near Dallas: a synecdoche for north Texas.

Perhaps these quatrains imply an alternative destiny for young Kennedy's Camelot, in which America never knew a Vietnam war or the social breakdown of the 1960s. President Kennedy was known for his **imperfect** moral conduct as well as a congenitally *imperfect* adrenal system and lower back. Perhaps if he had not been assassinated we would have also known him as the president who went the extra mile to end the Cold War, and who championed the black American advance toward equal civil rights to its completion. If JFK had lived, Senator Johnson would have fallen into political obscurity as a two-term vice-president, rather than become the slain President's successor and the captain of a failed administration overwhelmed by the debacle of Vietnam.

After John Kennedy's tenure in Camelot ended in 1968, the political dynasty would continue with Robert Kennedy. With the Cold War over, Robert's dream of bringing peace to the Middle East might have been realized by 1976. Maybe then, Senator Edward (Teddy) Kennedy would have had the time to mature and be a president through the tutelage of his living brothers, rather than struggle along as a psychological victim of assassination's tragedy.

President John F. Kennedy may have defined that murdered future when he once said, "What kind of peace do we seek? Not a *Pax Americana* enforced on the world by American weapons of war. Not a peace of the grave or the security of the slave. I am talking about genuine peace, the kind of peace that makes life on Earth worth living, the kind of peace that enables men and nations to grow and to hope and to build a better life for their children – not merely peace for Americans, but peace for all men and women; not merely peace in our time, but peace for all time." (*The Burden and the Glory*, Allen Nevins, ed.)

A longer lifespan for the two brothers would have given us all much more time during which the effort would have existed to bring about a Global Village by the 1990s. But their future was terminated and we now live with the ever clearer and always present danger that we will have to face Armageddon before the new millennium because the Cold War ended a generation too late!

---

2 Q58

Sans pied ne main dent ayguë & forte,	**With neither foot nor power, nor**
Par globe[1] au fort de port[2] & lainé nay:	**sharp and strong teeth,**
Pres du portail defloyal tranfporte,	**Across the globe in the fort of**
Silene[3] luit, petit grand emmené.	**port(land) and woolly native:**
	Near the front gate, foul transfer,
	Moon shining, little great one taken
	away.

[1]Latin *globus* = mass, crowd, throng; globe.
[2]Either a **port**, a door, a gate passage, or an apocope for Portland, Oregon.
[3] Greek *Seléné*, the Moon – either a symbol for Islam, or, more rarely, a clue to the name of a contemporary or near-future spiritual master from Asia.

This one is full of specifics but open to all kinds of interpretations. Cheetham thinks the **little great one taken away** is Napoleon. Fontbrune believes the myth that it is young Louis XVII busted loose from the Temple prison during the French Revolution.

The quatrain comes together if we apply it to the "Eight clues to a religious rebel" theme. Line 1 depicts an old or vulnerable spiritual leader who is captured without defense (Clue 1, outlawed teacher). Line 2 identifies someone who has traveled around the world extensively (Clue 7, infuriating traveler). The **moon shining** (Clue 8, his name) could also be a poetic description of his silent and spiritual demeanor.

The only Eastern guru (with bad teeth) who fits this interpretation is Osho, who was arrested in the United States in 1985 and shuttled for 12 days through the US penitentiary system. For three of those days his whereabouts were unknown to his followers and lawyers (**foul transfer**). Later it was proved that Federal officers at the Oklahoma County Jail tried to force him to log himself in under a false name. The jail records show a "David Washington" signed in someone else's handwriting above Osho's unique Sanscrit signature. Osho also claims to have been poisoned there while waiting to be transferred to jail in Portland (**foul transfer**).

He did arrive in Portland, where he was released on bail. American national television was filled with images of the little, frail, and beaming Indian mystic – chained in wrist, waist and leg irons – being hustled from one jail to the next. The Old French *lainé* comes from the Latin *lana*, meaning "wool"; the word *nay* (born) in Latin is *natus*, an extension of which is *nativus* or "born a native." In other words a *woolly native*. I can testify as an eyewitness that Osho, with his olive skin, trademark woolen cap and robes, and long, thick beard stretching down to his waist definitely looks like a *woolly native*. Before he was called Osho his name was Bhagwan Shree Rajneesh, which translates to "The Blessed One, Lord of the Full Moon."

2 Q59

Claſſe Gauloiſe par appuy de grande garde,	**French fleet through support of the**
Du grand Neptune, & ſes tridens ſouldars:	**great guard,**
Rongée Prouence pour ſouſtenir grand	**The great Neptune, and his trident**
band,	**soldiers:**
Plus Mars Narbon par iauelotz & dards.	**Prey upon Provence for the sake of**
	sustaining a large host,
	More war at Narbonne, from javelins
	and darts.

The **great Neptune** is not an Islamic invasion fleet in Nostradamus' time or in our future. This invasion happened in August 1944. **Neptune** stands for the 1,000 British and American vessels used to transport and sustain over a million men in their invasion of the French Riviera. Narbonne is farther south-west down the coast from the landings in Provence and did not see any significant action during the campaign. This does not rule out an alternative future potential never accessed by destiny, for fighting in the streets of that city.

2 Q60

La foy Punicque[1] en Orient rompue,
Grand Iud.[2] & Rofne, Loyre & Tag
   changeront:
Quand du mulet[3] la faim fera repue,
Claffe[4] efpargie, fang & corps nageront.

The Punic [Libyan] faith broken in
   the East,
Great Jordan and Rhône, Loire, and
   Tagus will change:
When the he-mule [the Democrat?]
   will be satiated,
Fleet sprinkled, blood and bodies will
   swim.

[1]The Punic faith = Old French (colloquial) for North African treachery.
[2]Abbreviation for the Jordan river region (Israel/Palestine/Jordan).
[3]Male donkey, the symbol of the American Democratic Party.
[4]Usually meaning *fleet* but sometimes army.

The day will come when the treachery of Libyan, Algerian, or North African terrorism will cease to cast its giant shadow over peace efforts in the Middle East. Line 2 uses rivers to symbolize the countries that will undergo great social and political changes when peace is finally a reality: Israel, Jordan, France, and Spain will change. The *he-mule* is the Democrat American President Clinton on the Jordan river signing the Palestinian peace accord in 1995 with Yasser Arafat of the PLO, Yitzhak Rabin of Israel, and King Hussein of Jordan. From this first step may issue either a millennium of peace or an unknown fleet or armed force sprinkled with chemical agents in a renewed war by 1999. Elsewhere there are references to a fleet being destroyed in the Arabian Sea or Persian Gulf (see 6 Q44). It is not clear whether the fleet is Western or Middle Eastern. The Punic treachery may link this to the "Baal Hammon" clue about the Third Antichrist (see 2 Q30, 2 Q62).

2 Q61

Euge,[1] Tamins,[2] Cironde & la Rochele,	Bravo! men of the Thames, Gironde
O fang Troyen![3] Mort au port de la flefche:	and La Rochelle,
Derrier le fleuue au fort mife l'efchele,	O Trojan blood [of France]! Killed at
Pointes feu grand meurtre fus la brefche.	the port by an arrow:
	On the other side of the river the
	ladder placed on the strongpoint,
	Points of fire great slaughter on the
	breach.

[1]Latin bravo! excellent!
[2]Syncope: Tamisiens, those of the Thames.
[3]fang Troyen = Popular 16th-century myth that the blood of Trojan royalty courses through the blood of French kings. Paris of Troy, meet Paris, France.

If we take the World War II slant, then here Nostradamus approves of Allied victory in Normandy. He mixes British, Americans, Poles, and Free French forces together as **men of the Thames**. Mention of the two towns on the south-western flank of Hitler's Atlantic Wall has little military significance unless this was an optional Allied invasion route never pursued. Indeed the Allies helped the Resistance cells in La Rochelle and around the Gironde so the Germans would think a diversionary invasion was imminent in the spring of 1944.

The **arrows** may be a few of Hitler's V-1 and V-2 rockets, which began falling on the French dock workers at Cherbourg and other French ports once the allies had liberated Normandy.

Line 3 tries to describe the ladderlike floating bridges extended across French rivers by the Allies. This specifically covers the climax to the Normandy campaign when the southern pincer of the US Army forded the Orne river and overwhelmed the German stronghold at Argentan during the battle of the Argentan–Falaise pocket. This allowed the Americans to link up with the British pincer grinding down from the north to trap over 60,000 German infantry and all the heavy equipment and armor of the German Seventh and Fifth Panzer armies. The final line describes the flash of artillery and tanks, and the lightning stingers of strafing allied planes inflicting great slaughter upon the German armor and infantry units choking the roads. Again and again frantic German units charged in human waves, trying to break through to the east, only to fall in heaps of dead before Allied machine gun positions (**great slaughter on the breach**). When it was over, the devastation was so great that an Allied officer said, "It was as if an avenging angel had swept the area, bent on destroying all things German." The Argentan–Falaise pocket saw more than 220 panzers, 860 artillery pieces, 130 antiaircraft guns and 7,130 vehicles destroyed, and 2,000 horses and more than 10,000 Germans slaughtered.

2 Q62

Mabus¹ puis toſt alors mourra, viendra,
De gens & beſtes vne horrible defaite:
Puis tout à coup la vengeance on verra,
Cent, main, ſoif, faim, quand courra la
*   comete.*

Mabus will soon die, then will come,
A horrible undoing of people and
**   animals,**
At once one will see vengeance,
One hundred powers, thirst, famine,
**   when the comet will pass.**

¹Unsolved anagram or enigmatic name most likely for the Third Antichrist or a weapon used by him. See commentary below.

Nostradamus' Third Antichrist has yet to be positively identified. In contrast with his certainty about Napoleon and Hitler, Nostradamus is less clear who this third tyrant is. Perhaps this is an example of his prophetic myopia that enabled him to be clearest about events of local or European history. When contemplating future events in more distant lands the prophet's vision tends to be cloudier. What does come through clearly is the fact that this Third and final Antichrist is not a prominent European leader. He may even be a minor player in a future conflict, an insignificant terrorist like Gavrilo Princip, the Serbian nationalist who assassinated Archduke Franz Ferdinand of Austria in Sarajevo, triggering World War I.

The man we know as **Mabus** may be some obscure future terrorist who, if he is not identified and retrained in time, will trigger World War III and the extinction of civilization as we have known it (see 2 Q30).

The time we have left to positively decode who or what **Mabus** is, and how to prevent the foretold terrible destiny, may already have passed. The final line could date the beginning of his legacy of terror around the time of the appearance of Halley's Comet in 1985–86; this, however, doesn't rule out a later appearance during the collision of the comet Shoemaker-Levi in July 1994, or the comet Hale-Bopp for the spring of 1997. The latter is expected to be ten times larger than Halley, making it a primary target for Nostradamus' dating, especially since it appears so close to the end of the millennium. (In fact, it appears right at the millennium in the Jewish lunar calendar.)

In 2 Q30 I proposed that **Mabus** is a cryptogram for Thurbo Majus, the classical Roman name given to the infernal god of Hannibal, an important clue to the Third Antichrist. Bardo Kidogo (1994), with his extensive etymological knowledge, moves along our detective trail from North Africa to Iraq and Iran. He sees **Mabus** as a cryptogram for Megabyzus. We will concentrate on only one of the two ancient Persians with this name cited by the Greek historian Herodotus. Gobrayas Megabyzus was one of several conspirators who overthrew a Zoroastrian priest (or magus) who had usurped the throne of Persia. Megabyzus wanted to disband the monarchy, but his co-conspirator Darius obviously talked him down from this lofty ideal, and he later helped Darius become Emperor of Persia. Later, as the Persian governor in Europe, Megabyzus showed himself to be a real tyrant with a flair for terrorism. His favorite modus operandi was to attack enemy states of Persia from within. He sired the notorious Zophyros (see RAYPOZ, 9 Q44), who betrayed Babylon to Darius.

An argument could be made that upon this classical foundation Nostradamus is building a prophecy for the near-future debacle of Saddam Hussein from within, by a Persian (or Iranian) ally. Tomorrow's **Mabus**/Megabyzus could successfully attack (those of Geneva = the West) with his RAYPOZ weapon in some act of nuclear terrorism.

I receive many letters each month asking if Saddam Hussein is the fearsome **Mabus**. I suggest a little experiment. Take a piece of paper and write "Saddam" backwards to get "Maddas." Now hold it in front of a mirror. If you are as dyslexic as I am you will soon see "Saddam" and wonder if Nostradamus spelled his approximated name backwards to get "Mabus." By following the rules of anagram, take one *d* out of "Maddas" to get "Madas," then reverse the second *d* to get a *b* for **Mabus**.

I also want to take the time to thank all those readers who keep me apprised of the career of the former governor of Mississippi (and former US Ambassador to Saudi Arabia), Raymond Mabus. At this time I don't sense anything malevolent about the ambassador, but this gives me the opportunity to look at yet another angle to the **Mabus** enigma. The ambassador may not be the Antichrist but a victim of such. Since the November 1995 car bombing of a US-run military training facility in Riyadh, Saudi Arabia has ended its long exclusion from terrorist acts. Ambassador Mabus had a dangerous assignment and I wish him well. I would not like to see him become the target of a future Gavrilo Princip and have his assassination trigger World War III.

And finally, the mysterious **Mabus** could be one of dozens of Saddam Hussein's more sophisticated Al Abbas versions of his Scud missiles. **Mabus** therefore becomes a weapon launched by the Antichrist in a surprise attack. It *will soon die* in the flames of its own successful explosion after its supersonic journey.

The Gulf War clearly demonstrated how Scuds or other intermediate-range missiles are perfectly designed for surprise in the compact theater of the Middle East. The chemical or nuclear extermination of just one of the region's capitals would result – as Nostradamus implies – in the sudden exposure of the Holy Land's ancient vengeances in a region-wide orgy or, as the prophet calls it, *a horrible undoing of people and animals*. World War III in miniature erases the land where Yéshua' walked and Muhammad drove his camels.

Quatrain Indexing Date: Q62 = 1962. Another quatrain with an Antichrist theme is numbered 63 (See 3 Q63, 5 Q63). Many psychics, among them American clairvoyant Jeane Dixon, predicted the birth of the Antichrist from the East for 1962.

2 Q63

Gaulois, Aufone bien peu fubiuguera,	*Southern Italy and Sicily will*
Pan, Marne & Seine fera Perme l'vrie:[1]	*subjugate very little,*
Qui le grand mur contre eux dreffera,	*Pau, Marne and Seine Parma will*
Du moindre au mur le grand perdra la vie.	*sink:*
	He who will erect the great walls
	against them,
	The great one will lose his life from
	the least at the wall.

[1]Latin *urere* = to burn, sting, consume; Latin *urinare* = to submerge in water.

The closest historical application would be the Maginot Line, built during the 1930s to satisfy the illusion of the French people that such a white-elephant fortification spawned from a World War I mindset could stop the mechanized German army of a modernized war machine. The best way to read this quatrain is backwards starting with line 4. The **great one** losing his life is poetic for the French leadership of the Third Republic, losing their political lives and reputation after the fall of France in 1940, when it became clear that the "impregnable" Maginot Line, with all its billions of dollars of siege guns, six-storied underground cement forts, and troglodyte armies, couldn't stop the breakthrough of even two modest German infantry attacks.

The rivers of line 2 represent France, which will sink in spirit and burn with defeat with the fall of the Maginot Line in the east and the invasion of the German panzers through the Ardennes and Flanders from the north-east. But revenge is promised in line 1, when the Free French and their Anglo-American allies invade Sicily and southern Italy in 1943.

2 Q64

Seicher de faim, de foif, gent Geneuoife,	*The people of Geneva to dry up with*
Efpoir prochain viendra au defaillir:	*hunger, and thirst,*
Sur point tremblant fera loy Gebenoife.[1]	*Hope near at hand will come to fail:*
Claffe au grand port ne fe peut acuillir.	*On the point of trembling will be the*
	law of the Cevennes.
	Fleet at the great port cannot be
	received.

[1]Latin *Gebenna* = the Cevennes mountain chain.

John Calvin, a native of Cevennes, established a Protestant Vatican of sorts in Geneva, Switzerland. His chief disciple, Théodore de Bèze, was born at Vézelay, also in Cevennes. This attack in prophecy could be aimed at Bèze, who had earned the prophet's ire for publishing the famous distech:

> Nostra damus cum falsa damus, nam fallere nostrum est;
> Et cum falsa damus, nil nisi nostra damus.

The Latin pun-ishment is mostly lost in the translation, which in bland English reads: *We give that which is our own when we give false things; for it is in our nature to deceive; And when we give false things, we give but our own things.* I would like to offer a more rogue-scholarly translation, one that attempts to return the spirit and poetry to Bèze's Nostradamus pun:

> Nostradamus comes false – Ah, damn us.
> When he "noses up" to damn us with his deceptions;
> For it is our nature – damn us – to note a damn falsehood!

None of Nostradamus' forecasts of imminent doom for Calvin's Geneva ever materialized. No siege took place requiring a fleet of boats coming from across Lake Geneva to victualize its citizens. Line 3 is accurate. Cevennes, the birthplace of Calvinism, suffered a full-scale revolt after the revocation of the Edict of Nantes in 1685.

---

2 Q65

Le parc enclin grande calamité,	*The sloping park, great calamity,*
Par l'Hefperie & Infubre[1] fera:	*Will be done through the land of the*
Le feu en nef pefte & captiuité,	*West and Lombardy:*
Mercure en l'Arc Saturne fenera.[2]	*The fire in the ship [the Papacy],*
	plague and captivity,
	Mercury in Sagittarius, Saturn's
	scythe will cut.

[1] The environs of Milan (modern Lombardy). A synecdoche for Italy in general.
[2] Latin *feneror* = to ruin; Old French *fener* = to cut the hay with a scythe.

Ever since the Northridge earthquake in Los Angeles, seismologists have made many disturbing discoveries of blind-thrust faults running under downtown Los Angeles. One of them is called the Elysian **Park** blind fault, which runs from Elysian Park right under the Dodger baseball stadium. This fact brings to mind the 6 Q88 **New City** earthquake prophecy in which a **theater** or stadium full of people collapses in a quake.

Line 2 further ties this quatrain to another frightening European temblor (described in 9 Q31) which inundates south-western England and shakes north-eastern Italy around Mortara (near **Lombardy**). Line 3 links us to 2 Q93, which tells the tale of Vatican destruction by fires and tidal waves during the papacy of the last pope.

Astrological Time Window

Wöllner believed the astrological aspects in line 4 to be the clearest dating of the destruction of the Vatican. Astrologer Dan Oldenburg thinks the "warning" may mean a conjunction. Saturn was in near-conjunction with Uranus while Mercury was in Sagittarius warning us of the onset of the first travails of the New Age in 1987, just a year after Halley's Comet visited Earth. Uranus conjunct Saturn is important because the two are co-rulers of the New Age of Aquarius. I would take Saturn's *scythe . . . cut* to describe the trajectory of its transit over Mercury in Sagittarius. This will happen again in late November 2015, late November 2017, and early November 2044. The last conjunction will be especially powerful, for Saturn and Mercury enter Sagittarius exactly at the same time.

Quatrain Indexing Date: Q65 = 1965. Quatrains numbered 65 from Centuries 2, 3, and 10 share the themes of schisms and scandals that threaten the future of the Catholic Church. Quatrain 66 of Century 6 (666), foretells the destruction of Rome and the birth of a new religion.

2 Q66

Par grans dengiers le captif eſchapé,	**The captive escaped through great dangers.**
Peu de temps grand a fortune changée:	**In a short time the great one has a change of fortune:**
Dans le palais le peuple eſt attrapé,	**In the palace the people are trapped,**
Par bon augure la cité aſſiegée.	**By a good omen, the city is besieged.**

This finishes Nostradamus' story of Napoleon's escape from Elba in 1815 (see 10 Q24). The little band of a few hundred sailors and 1,000 grenadiers had sailed through the Gulf of Genoa, hugging the coastline, and debarked at Cannes. On the road to Grenoble they were stopped by the Fifth Infantry regiment. Napoleon stepped in front of their pointed bayonets and said, "Soldiers of the Fifth, if you have come to shoot your Emperor, then here I am." The command to fire was given, but no one fired. Instead they broke ranks to join Napoleon (**The captive escaped through great dangers**). By the time his growing band reached Paris, Louis XVIII and his Bourbon supporters had fled. A triumphant Napoleon was carried up the stairs of the Tuileries into his bed. Journals of the day report that the crowds were so large that the gendarmes couldn't clear the Tuileries for many hours (**In the palace the people are trapped**).

But fortunes would change in a short time for the great Napoleon. Exactly 100 days after taking power he suffered his greatest defeat at Waterloo, bringing the armies of Europe into Paris for a second time in little over a year. For Nostradamus, the 16th-century monarchist, Napoleon's defeat at Waterloo is *a good omen*, for it anticipates the return to the throne of the royal house of Bourbon.

2 Q67

Le blonde au nez forche viendra commettre,	**The blond one to the forked-nosed one**
Par le duelle & chaſſera dehors:	**will come to confide,**
Les exilés, dedans fera remettre,	**Through the duel and will chase him**
Aux lieux marins commettant les plus fors.	**out:**
	The exiles, within will restore,
	Committing the strongest to the
	marine positions.

Definitely a restoration theme – but which one? Le Pelletier applies it to the restoration of Louis XVIII to the French throne after the fall of Napoleon in 1815. I tend to agree with Leoni, Cheetham, and David Pitt Francis, who believe it describes the showdown between James II (**the forked-nosed one**) and the **blond** Prince William of Orange for the British throne during the Glorious Revolution of 1688–89. In November 1688 William landed his army, unopposed, in south-western England. James, at the head of his own army, threatened a battle, but by this time his credibility and support was so low that the only blood spilled in their **duel** was from the severe nosebleed he suffered. From his strong **marine positions**, William methodically advanced to London. James II went into exile in France and William of Orange accepted Parliament's demands and became the first constitutional co-monarch of England, William III, with his wife Mary (James' daughter).

2 Q68

De l'aquilon[1] les effors feront grands,	**In the North, the efforts will be great,**
Sus l'Occean fera la porte ouuerte:	**Upon the Ocean will be the open**
Le regne en l'iſle fera reintegrand,	**window:**
Tremblera Londres par voille deſcouuerte.	**The kingdom of the Isles will be**
	restored,
	London will tremble by [the] cover
	exposed.

[1]Latin Aquilo = north wind, north.

Nostradamus continues his prophecy for the Glorious Revolution, which took place at the end of 1688, between two great northern wars fought by Sweden and Russia in 1655–60 and 1700–21. During the Glorious Revolution both the Tories and Whigs of Parliament allied against the extremely Catholic James II, who wanted to turn the clock back a hundred years by abolishing Anglicanism. A cross-section of Whig and Tory aristocrats discreetly invited the Dutch William of Orange to sail for England with a Dutch army to restore their religion and liberty. Although it was not written in their petition William took the hint and landed with his army to overthrow James II. Line 2 may blend events from two wars. In the Second Northern war Peter the Great fought Charles XII of Sweden to seize Baltic territory and gain a **window** to the West. He eventually won the war after 21 years of fighting and built the port of St Petersburg.

The blur of unborn events moves from Peter's fledgling Russian navy defeating the Swedes to William of Orange's navy landing on the English shore a decade earlier. Lines 3 and 4 return to England and the Glorious Revolution. **London** represents the members of Parliament who spent some sleepless nights waiting for William's invasion force to arrive before their secret petition for help was discovered. Also the rebels were concerned that James II could curry support against Parliament for having requested the help of a foreign invasion army. Although James tried to rally English patriotism, he could not trust his army of Protestant rank and file led by substandard Catholic officers and he fled into exile. William became King of England with his wife, the daughter of James II, as his co-ruler Queen Mary.

2 Q69

Le Roy Gaulois par la Celtique dextre,	**The French King through the Celtic right,**
Voiant diſcorde de la grande Monarchie:	**Beholding the discord of the great Monarchy:**
Sus les trois pars fera florir ſon ſceptre,	**Upon the three partners [or sides] will make his scepter flourish,**
Contre la Cappe[1] de la grand Hierarchie.	**Against the Cape[t] of the great Hierarchy.**

[1]Cryptogram for **Capet**, the ancient ancestors of the Bourbons.

Cheetham thinks this continues the Glorious Revolution theme. Le Pelletier pins it on Napoleon and the protests of the Bourbon hierarchy about Louis XVIII. I think it better suits the struggle of an earlier **Capet**, Louis XIII. Cardinal Richelieu, his chief of state, saw an opportunity to capitalize on the devastation and discord within the **great Monarchy** of the Holy Roman Empire. He entered France into the Thirty Years War transforming the conflict from a religious matter into a Habsburg–Bourbon struggle for European domination. France, Sweden, and Holland are the three allies (**partners**) pitted against Spain and the Holy Roman Empire. French military successes would award Louis XIII with Alsace and most of Lorraine (**his scepter** to **flourish**). **Capet** is the ancient name of the ancestors of the House of Bourbon, France's longest **hierarchy** of rulers.

2 Q70

Le dard du ciel fera fon eftendue,	**The dart from the sky will make its extension,**
Mors en parlant: grande execution:	**Deaths in speaking: great execution:**
La pierre en l'arbre la fiere gent rendue,	**The stone in the tree the proud people surrendered,**
Bruit humain monftre purge expiation.	**Clamor, human monster, purge expiation.**

Dolores Cannon's *Stone in the Tree* riddle for the mushroom (tree-like) cloud of an atomic blast is plausible, although *arbre* can also translate into *mast* or *shaft*. Given Cannon's slant Lamont had no idea that atomic attacks on Japan would end the war, yet he believed this quatrain foretold the defeat of Japan.

The **stone** – or *pierre* for Peter – in the mast could give us another Peter of Rome prophecy. In this case the final pope of doomsday is broadcasting from the Vatican's television tower when a missile knocks it out, killing the transmission (**deaths in speaking**). A **dart from the sky** is one of the invisible plague arrows of 16th-century lore, perhaps used here as a double pun for a nuclear missile and the plague of fallout it leaves behind. The atomic blast may be the nuclear weapon or **serpent** we see described in other quatrains that is deposited by terrorists on the Tiber river (2 Q43, 5 Q63).

The final line is another litany of the apocalyptic sequence of war and chaos followed by a new era (**expiation**).

2 Q71

Les exilés en Sicile viendront,	**The exiles will come into Sicily,**
Pour deliurer de faim[1] la gent eftrange.	**To deliver [them] from hungering [after] the strange nation.**
Au point du iour les Celtes luy faudront	**At daybreak the Celts will fail them**
La vie demeure à raifon: Roy fe range.	**Life resides by reason: the King joins.**

[1](Conventional) hunger; (fig.) intense desire, longing, thirst.

This is as general as they come. It could be about Henry II's hunger for Italian possessions and his numerous Italian intrigues and military escapades. But without more specific clues it could just as easily be about our times. In this case the **exiles** are Italian Mafia leaders deported to Sicily from the **strange nation**, or foreign land, the United States. They try to strike up an alliance with the French Mafia, but the French connection breaks down. As the prophet warns, **Life resides by reason**, so I will defer to the skeptics and stop my speculation.

2 Q72

Armée Celtique en Italie vexée,
De toutes pars conflict & grande perte:
Romains fuis, ô Gaule repoulſée,
Pres du Theſin, Rubicon pugne incerte.

Celtic army vexed in Italy,
On all sides conflict and great
  loss:
Romans fled, O France repulsed!
Near the Ticino, Rubicon uncertain
  battle.

This refers to the ill-fated French expedition during the closing stages of the Hapsburg–Valois War (1547–59). Henry II had sent an expedition to invade southern Italy in 1555 and that same year established a stronghold north of Naples. Promised support from Pope Paul IV never materialized (**Romans fled**). A French garrison at Siena capitulated to the Duke of Florence, precipitating a withdrawal of the French expedition from Italy by 1557. There is no record of a battle, certain or **uncertain**, near the Ticino or Rubicon rivers at this time.

2 Q73

Au lac Fucin de Benac[1] le riuaige,
Prins du Leman[2] au port de l'Orguion:[3]
Nay de trois bras predict bellique image,
Par trois couronnes au grand Endymion.

To Lake Fucino from the shore of
  Lake Garda,
Taken from Geneva to the port of
  Orguion:
Born with three arms the predicted
  warlike image,
Through three crowns for the great
  Endymion.

[1]Latin *Benacus* = Lake Garda.
[2]Latin *Lemannus* = Lake Geneva.
[3]Unsolved place name, possibly Orgon in southern France or Orgiano in northern Italy.

The Endymion myth is used to describe Henry II and his fawning love for Diane de Poitiers (whom he often had painted and sculpted in the classical likeness of the goddess Diana). Endymion was a young man cast by the goddess into a perpetual sleep, that she might caress him at her pleasure. Nostradamus predicts the **three crowns** of the pope's triple tiara will land on the king's brow. In other words, Henry II will achieve domination in the papal states, and in the Republic of Venice (represented by **Lake Garda**) and the two Sicilies (represented by **Lake Fucino**). These promises remained forever unkept due to Henry's jousting accident in 1559. **Orguion** remains an unsolved place name. It could be Orgon, a mere 20 miles from Salon, Provence. For the rest the symbolism is obscure. It could be a cryptic clue to some important coat of arms.

2 Q74
De Sens, d'Autun viendront iufques au
   Rofne.
Pour paffer outre vers les monts Pyrenées:
La gent fortir de la Marque d'Anconne,
Par terre & mer fuiura à grans trainées.

From Sens, from Autun they will
   come as far as the Rhône,
To pass further toward the Pyrenees
   mountains:
The people to sally forth from the
   Marsh of Ancona,
By land and sea it will be followed by
   great tracks.

Centuries after this is written the **great tracks** of trains will be laid on a line extending from Paris, south-east to Sens and Autun, and all the way down the Rhône river. Many a Frenchman, and a number of tourists like myself, can **sally forth** on the TGV high-speed train following this path from Paris to Nostradamus' Salon-en-Provence. Other lines carry one towards several destinations along the Pyrenees. Even the marsh of Ancona, where Nostradamus muddied himself genuflecting to a future pope, will enjoy its own **great track** for high-speed trains gliding along the Adriatic Sea. The final line implies that trains in our future will float on superconductive tracks set over the oceans.

2 Q75
La voix ouye de l'infolit[1] oyfeau,
Sur le canon de refpiral[2] eftage:
Si haut viendra du froment le boiffeau,
Que l'homme d'homme fera Antropophage.

The voice of the unusual bird is
   heard,
In the pipe of the breathing floor:
Bushels of wheat will rise so high,
That man will devour his fellow man.

[1]Unusual, unwonted, unprecedented.
[2]Old French for an air vent.

Line 1 may refer to the **strange birds** of the Epistle who visit the world as spiritual messengers just prior to the tribulations that will end humanity's childhood. Line 2 is some kind of device Nostradamus has difficulty describing. If one could see through the walls of a grain elevator one would observe grain being sucked down through a pipe in the floor, making it appear as if the device were a breathing thing. At the other end of the pipe stands a mountain of gold grain as one might witness in any number of grain storage compounds across North America, Europe, or Russia. It will not be long – in fact just a few years away – when those mountains of wheat kernels will be worth their weight in gold. In a world of increasing population and declining grain stocks, the day is not far off when the human race may be able to live only from one annual harvest to the next. In 1996 the global grain reserves had fallen to their lowest in history. If the global production of food were disrupted, we would have only enough food in reserve to feed the world for 49 days. Since the bumper crop of 1990 there has been zero growth in grain production, whereas the global population will have increased by 552.5 million by the publication of this book in March 1997.

In 1994 Lester E. Brown of the Worldwatch Institute predicted that by 2030 China alone will need to import virtually all the grain available for export in the world. In Nostradamus, *famine* is often followed by *war*. His astrology points to the 2020s and 2030s as the most likely time for a third world war to be fought over food. Brown and other globe watchers have stated that we have a window of less than 20 years to make revolutionary changes in the way we breed and use up the dwindling resources of the world.

His statement reminds me of a discourse series I attended in 1987 called *The Razor's Edge* given by Osho, an Indian mystic and, I might add, a rather strange bird in his own right. During the lecture he spoke on a number of life-negative habits humanity must shed if it is to survive. To cut overpopulation he suggested the world undergo an absolute moratorium on all births for "20 to 30 years." A hush fell upon the audience of ten thousand people. He paused for a moment, staring at the throng without as much as a blink and added, "It is not a question of democracy, because it is a choice between life and death. If the whole world is going to die, what are you going to do with your democracy? Democracy will be the rule then – for the graves, of the graves, by the graves – because people will have disappeared."

Quatrain Indexing Date: Q75 = 1975, a time of great famines and a significant increase in alternative spiritual movements (*strange birds* [EP212]). Or perhaps 2075, by which time food sustainability has collapsed or the message of the *strange birds* has been heeded in time to prevent the famine holocaust.

2 Q76

Foudre en Bourgongne fera cas portenteux,[1]	*Lightning in Burgundy will signify a portentous act,*
Que par engin oncques ne pourroit faire,	*That could never be done through genius [or trickery]:*
De leur senat sacrifte[2] fait boiteux,	*By their senate the sacristan is made lame,*
Fera sçauoir aux ennemis l'affaire.	*Will make the affair known to the enemies.*

[1]Latin *portentosus* = wonderful, revolting, portentous.
[2]Old French *sacriste* = sexton, sacristan; a priest.

At first I was tempted to agree with Cheetham's interpretation that the *sacristan . . . made lame* was Napoleon's version of Henry Kissinger, his grand chamberlain and diplomat, Charles Maurice de Talleyrand-Périgord.

Talleyrand was **made lame** as a child by a falling chest of drawers. He joined the priesthood and became Bishop of Antin in 1788, then renounced the priesthood during the French Revolution. But with all this said, line 3 clearly implies some priest being physically crippled or politically hamstrung by the actions of the Burgundian parliament when the victim is a full-grown man. This therefore cannot be Talleyrand.

2 Q77

Par arcs[1] feux poix[2] & par feux[3] repouſſés,	**Through Arcs, pitch, and repulsed by**
Cris hurlements ſur la minuit ouys:	**gunfire (and) conflagrations,**
Dedans ſont mis par les rampars caſſez,	**Cries, laments heard at midnight:**
Par cunicules[4] les traditeurs fuys.	**Within they are placed on the**
	smashed ramparts,
	The traitors fled through rabbit runs.

[1]Latin arcus = curve, ie bent bow; or Les Arcs, a town in Provence.
[2]Pitch, petroleum; Nostradamus makes an attempt to describe white phosphorus shells.
[3]Fires, burnings, combustions, conflagrations; discharge of fire-arms.
[4]Latin cuniculus = rabbit, as in rabbit passage, tracks or burrows.

Through his many travels Nostradamus would have known the town of Les Arcs well, since it sits in a picturesque valley along the main trade route from Salon through Aix-en-Provence to the seaport of Cannes. This quiet little town of the 16th century where Doctor Nostradamus refreshed himself between errands of mercy, would be the center of a vicious battle in the 20th century.

In the early morning hours of 15 August 1944, travelers of a different kind parachuted out of the sky and started picking their way through the steep hill tracks into the town of Les Arcs. Their reception turned out to be far more lethal than our Renaissance doctor would have experienced. In the sleepy square where he once watered his mule at the town well, four centuries later, 50 lost paratroopers of the 1st Battalion of the 517 Parachute Infantry, along with their Battalion commander, Major "Wild Bill" Boyle, stepped into a town garrisoned by 400 Germans! By dawn the little band was attacked from three sides by swarms of Germans laying down a hail of machine-gun and rifle fire. By mid-morning Wild Bill's men had managed to crawl out of the closing German trap, carrying their wounded through trails and sheep runs in the underbrush until they dug in to make a successful stand at a nearby farm house.

The following two days would see hundreds of American paratroopers seize Les Arcs in a full-scale attack launched by a barrage of 700 white phosphorus mortar rounds hurled into the German positions. On three occasions hundreds of German infantrymen tried to rally around the ramparts and platforms of the town's railway station, only to be scattered and set on fire by a renewed phosphorus barrage.

Nostradamus, ever sensitive to future man's new infernal weapons, is trying to describe in 16th-century terms the image of thousands of **pitch**-like phosphorus particles flying through the air upon detonation, raining down on the unprotected crouching men on the railway tracks and even flying through the open doors and windows of defensive positions in buildings. When released in the air a glob of phosphorus undergoes a chemical reaction with oxygen, making it burst into flame capable of burning a hole through clothing and skin. Pouring water on it only feeds the flames. The fire can only be smothered by dirt, and by the time a soldier is lucky enough to find the dirt to grind into the burning cauldron of his wound, he is beyond help.

2 Q78

Le grand Neptune du profond de la mer,
De gent Punique & fang Gaulois meflé:
Les Ifles à fang pour le tardif ramer,
Plus luy nuira que l'occult mal celé.

The great Neptune of the deep of the sea,
Of the Punic race and French blood mixed:
The Isles in blood, because of the tardy rowing,
More in fury will it do to him than the ill-concealed secret.

Jaubert applies this to Muslim naval intrigues in the second half of 1558, when the Turkish fleet promised Henry II it would aid the French in north-west Italy, but attacked Minorca instead. On 10 July they took Ciudadela, slaughtering or enslaving the entire population. Jaubert states that the **tardy rowing** was paid for with a bribe. No doubt the Habsburgs waged this weapon of wealth expecting the delay to completely demoralize the French.

2 Q79

La barbe crefpe & noire par engin,
Subiuguera la gent cruelle & fiere:
Le grand CHIREN[1] oftera du longin,
Tous les captifs par Seline baniere.

The man with the curly black beard through ingenuity,
Will subdue the cruel and proud people:
The great CHIREN will take from afar,
All those captured by the banner of the Turkish crescent.

[1]Anagram for HENRIC = Henry II. Variant: *Chyren.*

Nostradamus' warning in 1 Q35 to King Henry II not to participate in ritualized combat was echoed in every detail by a vision granted to Catherine de' Medici's own astrologer, Luc Gauricus. The prediction, like Jeane Dixon's famous President Kennedy prophecy, became well known years before the event. Less well known are this quatrain and 12 others describing an alternative destiny in store for Henry II of France if he had heeded the warnings of both prophets.

The predictions that might cover this unfulfilled life are linked by two enigmatic names, *Chyren* and *Selin*. Most interpreters agree that *Chyren* is an anagram for *Henryc*, the Old French spelling for "Henry". *Selin* stands for *seline*, from the Greek word for "moon", which was the device of Henry's mistress, Diane de Poitiers. Her family's heraldic crescent was added to the horizontal bar of the capital letter *H* of Henry's heraldic device.

Christendom's defeat of the Ottoman Turks at the naval battle of Lepanto is exhaustively detailed by Nostradamus in at least nine quatrains. For this first alternative-future entry, he could have been proposing that the skillful and curly-black-bearded commander of the Christian fleet, Don Juan of Austria, would have stood alongside Henry at Lepanto, had the latter lived past his 41st year to be present there in 1571. As it turned out, Don Juan of Austria earned the glory of commanding the Christian armada to victory and achieved the honor of freeing 15,000 Christian galley slaves from captured Muslim ships.

See Index: alternative future for Henry II.

2 Q80

Apres conflict du leſé l'eloquence,	After the conflict by the eloquence of
Par peu de temps ſe trame faint[1] repos:	the wounded one,
Point l'on n'admet les grands à deliurance,	For a short time brings a soft repose is
Des ennemis ſont remis à propos.	contrived:
	Not a single one of the great ones is
	allowed release,
	They are delivered to the enemies at
	the proper time.

[1]Old French a) lazy, easy, soft; b) false, feigned.

This one could be applied to just about anyone.

2 Q81

Par feu du ciel la cité preſque aduſte,	Through fire from the sky the city is
L'vrne[1] menace encor Ceucalion,[2]	almost burned by the sun,
Vexée Sardaigne par la Punique[3] fuſte,[4]	The urn menaces Deucalion once
Apres que Libra lairra ſon Phaëton.	again,
	Sardinia vexed by the Punic vessel,
	After that Libra will abandon her Sun.

[1]The **urn** of Aquarius, the water bearer – ie a metaphor for floods during the Age of Aquarius, or a terrorist bomb blast.
[2]Deucalion, the Greek Noah.
[3]Punic, ie Libyan/North African; in 16th-century Christian figures of speech, being **Punic** is synonymous with being treacherous.
[4]A low-oared galley, used elsewhere as potential code word for submarines.

Two future interpretations are possible.

New York, the Vatican, or some other city is burned from the sky by the atmospheric explosion of a nuclear missile, or by the detonation of a terrorist atom bomb concealed in a hijacked airliner. In the mid-1990s Algerian terrorists hijacked a jet airliner, and had they not been overwhelmed by security forces while refueling at Marseilles, they would have continued on to Paris and detonated the jet's 15 tons of air fuel in a huge fireball a few hundred feet over the center of the city.

The *urn* of the Aquarian water bearer, symbol of the New Age, menaces the Greek version of the Noah/Genesis myth. In other words, the first century of the Aquarian Age will see the oceans rise again through global warming. The stresses to ocean cities and flooded agricultural lands from a 1-to-3-foot rise in the Earth's oceans by 2050 could cause the kind of social breakdown that induces a new wave of global terrorism. The *urn* itself could be a terrorist bomb. The Libyan *fuste* could have a modern application as one of several diesel-powered attack submarines in today's Libyan fleet. A number of quatrains contain references that could indicate submarines from Libya or some other North African country carrying a terrorist group across the Mediterranean to launch an attack on the southern European coast. The Western democracies are often represented by the astrological symbol of Libra's balancing scales. They respond to a nuclear terrorist attack by unleashing their own *sun*, or atomic bomb.

The second future scenario returns us to the theme of a meteorite strike in the Aegean off the coast of Evvoia. The city burned by a fire from the sky is nearby Athens. Line 2 waxes poetic for the huge Genesis-like flooding resulting from an ocean strike. Scientist Bevan French, of NASA's Solar System Exploration Division inadvertently sides with the esoteric prophet Nostradamus in his expectation that such an impact from an asteroid 500 to 1,000 feet in diameter would immediately conjure a great sudden flood, or what French describes as "tidal waves hundreds of feet high, probably wiping out most cities on the nearest coast."

Around the time of the meteorite strike, unfortunate Sardinia is vexed by the Libyan submarine represented in the first interpretation. But the final line can either continue the theme of the West's overreaction to terrorism, or stand as a cryptic dating for the meteorite impact: when the sun finishes its transit of Libra, on any 22 October in the next 1,800 years.

Quatrain Indexing Date: 2 Q81 = 2081, the year the greenhouse effect causes a cascading meltdown of the Antarctic ice cap, causing a 20-to-200-foot rise in the sea level, or the year of a meteorite strike in the Aegean. A nasty splash either way.

2 Q82

Par faim la proye fera loup priſonnier,	**Through hunger the prey will make**
L'aſſaillant lors en extreme detreſſe,	**the wolf prisoner,**
Le nay[1] ayant au deuant le dernier,	**The assailant then in extreme distress,**
Le grand n'eſchappe au milieu de la preſſe.	**The [Marshal] Ney, having the**
	youngest men before him,
	The great one does not escape in the
	middle of the crowd.

[1]Le nay = a) possible corruption of l'aisné = elder; b) cryptogram for Marshal Michel Ney, Napoleon's second in command at Waterloo.

If we take nay to be a cryptogram for the fiery-red-and-hot-headed French Marshal, Michel Ney, the quatrain becomes clear. At Waterloo the indisposed Napoleon had relinquished most of his command of the battle to Ney, who valiantly but unwisely pitched his command in the saddle at the front of his troops, where he had little sense of the bigger picture. All day he had cast wave upon wave of French heavy cavalry against the Duke of Wellington's British squares on the ridge of Mont St Jean. Ney was like a hungry wolf exhausting itself, hurling his troops again and again at a well-armored prey. When Napoleon took back the initiative and sent his Imperial Guard in one last failed assault, the exhausted French broke and ran. Eyewitnesses recreated the pathetic picture of Marshal Ney, unhorsed for the seventh time, staggering about and waving a broken sword at the fleeing young men, cursing at them to reform (**the assailant . . . in extreme distress**). Napoleon himself would be swept off the battlefield by the stampede.

2 Q83

Le gros traffic d'vn grand Lyon changé,	**The vast trade of great Lyons changed,**
La plus part tourne en priſtine ruine.	**The larger part turns into a pristine**
Proye aux ſoldats par pille vendengé:	**ruin.**
Par Iura mont & Sueue bruine.	**Prey to the soldiers through a harvest**
	of plunder:
	Through the Jura mountains and
	Switzerland [a] misty rain.

During the French Revolution large sections of the old quarters of Lyons, the great commercial capital of southern France, were razed to the bare ground as a reprisal for a counter-revolution. The Epistle to Henry II will reveal that Nostradamus was aware of the new Revolutionary calendar, so he uses bruine to signify the month named Brumaire – the month of mists –- which is from mid-October to mid-November. The sack of Lyons took place in October 1793. Apparently the dating in the last line is spot-on.

2 Q84

Entre Campaigne, Sienne, Flora, Tuſtie,	**Between Campania, Siena, Florence,**
Six mois neuf iours ne ploura vne goutte:	**Tuscany,**
L'eſtrange langue en terre Dalmatie,	**Six months nine days without a drop**
Courira ſus vaſtant la terre toute.	**of rain:**
	The foreign tongue in the Dalmatian
	land,
	It will overrun: devastating the whole
	world.

Will future droughts stemming from the climatic stresses of the green-house effect trigger the next Balkan war in the 21st century? The drought spreads from central Italy over to the **Dalmatian land** of the Bosnian–Croatian Federation, where the **foreign tongue** of United Nations peace-keepers and nation builders is heard. The drought from the greenhouse effect has the potential to turn apocalyptic and fan out across the whole world.

See Index: droughts; global warming.

2 Q85

Le vieux plain barbe ſoubs le ſtatut ſeuere,	**The old full beard under the severe**
A Lyon faict deſſus l'Aigle Celtique:	**statute,**
Le petit grant trop outre perſeuere,	**Made at Lyons, over the Celtic Eagle:**
Bruit d'arme au ciel: mer rouge	**The little great one persists too long,**
Lyguſtique.[1]	**Noise of arms in the sky: the Gulf of**
	Genoa red.

[1]Latin Ligusticus = Ligurian.

Poetically speaking, the **old . . . beard** is Marshal Pétain, president of the Vichy government, a prisoner of the **severe statute** of the Nazi Armistice of 1940 and the new constitution that made Pétain little more than one of Hitler's flunkies. Nostradamus' calling the French Eagle **Celtic** might imply Pétain's political agenda to return France to its pre-Republican morality. He believed republicanism had brought France to disaster. The paternal old hero of the previous world war tried to lead his people towards earlier values of absolutism.

Line 4 describes the Allied bombings of Genoa and southern France in 1944–45.

2 Q86

Naufrage à claſſes pres d'onde Hadriatique,	**Wreck for the fleet near the Adriatic**
La terre tremble eſmeuë ſus l'air en terre	**waters,**
mis:	**The earth trembles, lifted into the**
Egypte tremble augment Mahometique,	**air, placed on the land:**
L'Herault ſoy rendre à crier eſt commis.	**Egypt quakes, Islam augmented,**
	The Herald surrenders himself [and]
	is commissioned to cry out.

At first glance this looks like another prophecy slotted for Nostradamus' near future: A Turkish fleet would be destroyed **near the Adriatic** at Lepanto in 1571. But no significant earthquake rocked Cairo for many centuries – until just recently, when in 1992 a temblor measuring 5.9 on the Richter scale shook the city for 40 seconds, killing 500 and injuring 6,500. The early 1990s also saw a dramatic rise in Islamic fundamentalism (**Islam augmented**) in Egypt, with a foreboding increase in assassinations and terrorist bombings by militants striving to overthrow President Hosni Mubarak's secular government.

The meaning of the final line may ring forth in our near future. It could imply that the **Herald** is either Mubarak (or his successor), forced to accede to fundamentalist pressure, or he is Sheik Abdel Rahman, who is purported by United States officials to be the mastermind behind the World Trade Center bombing a few months after the quake, in early 1993. Before the bombing the blind cleric was the loudest voice calling for the assassination of Mubarak. Now that he has been arrested, this **herald** of extremism faces deportation to Egypt. Will he be released from an Egyptian prison before facing execution because his followers succeed in overthrowing Mubarak? Will he be **commissioned to cry out** as the mouthpiece of a new Islamic Republic? Will the NATO fleet off Bosnia suffer a surprise terrorist attack? Other prophecies point to these potentials.

See Index: the Third Antichrist.

2 Q87

Apres viendra des extremes contrees,	Later will come from the remotest
Prince Germain, deſſus le throſne doré:	regions,
La ſeruitude & eaux rencontrees,	The Germain Prince, upon the golden
La dame ſerue, ſon temps plus n'adoré.	throne:
	The servitude and waters met,
	The lady in servitude, her time no
	longer adored.

Théophilus de Garencières (1672), in his archaic English, applies this to Gustavus Adolphus: "This Prophecy is concerning Gustavus Adolphus, King of Swedeland, who is called German Prince, because his Ancestors came out of Germany, he came out of a remote Countrey, that is Swedeland, he came upon a gilded throne, that is a Ship gilded, he shall make slavery and waters meet, because as soon as he was Landed he began to conquer, and to subdue that Lady (*viz.* Germanica) that was no more worshipped since as she was before."

I agree with Cheetham and think it is better applied to the accession in 1714 of George of Hanover to the English throne as George I. George was a German prince and a **Germain**, which means "cousin" in this case, of Queen Anne. The **lady in servitude** is Nostradamus' poetic characterization of the goddess Britannia, symbol of the British Empire. Upon Queen Anne's death, Parliament would have its Protestant ruler, George, the Elector of Hanover, bring an end to the era of Stuart rule.

2 Q88

Le circuit du grand faict ruineux,	The completion of the great and
Le nom septiesme du cinquiesme sera:	disastrous action,
D'vn tiers plus grand l'estrange belliqueux,	The name of the seventh will be that
Mouton, Lutece,[1] Aix ne garantira.	of the fifth.
	Of the third a greater, foreign
	warmonger,
	Sheep [Reims/Aries], Paris and Aix
	will not be kept in Aries.

[1] Old French Lutece, from Latin Lutetia = Paris.

This is clearly for the eighth War of Religion, also known as the War of the Three Henries (Henry III, Henry de Guise, and Henry de Navarre).

The name of the **seventh** is Valois – the seven children of Henry II and Catherine de' Medici. The **fifth** child would be the last Valois king, the notorious Henry III (**of the third**). The **foreign warmonger** is the future Henry IV (Henry de Navarre). At that time this Huguenot prince and province were not part of France. Henry IV, the best general of the three warring Henrys, began a long and protracted siege of Paris during the sun's transit of Aries (March–April 1590).

2 Q89

Vn iour seront demis les deux grands maistres,	One day the two great leaders will become friends,
Leur grand pouuoir se verra augmenté:	Their great power will be seen to increase:
La terre neufue sera en ses hauts estres,	The new land [America] will be at
Au sanguinaire le nombre racompté.	the height of its power,
	To the bloody one the number [is]
	reported.

As we shake ourselves awake from 50 years of Cold War eschatology, it is clear that Nostradamus and other seers share a collective vision that the Cold War scenario of MAD (mutual-assured-destruction) had little prophetic weight. A fresh look at prophecies beyond a doomsday standoff between Cold War superpowers returns prophecy to a third world war issuing from a conflict of biblical proportions in the Middle East. Moreover, the quatrains strongly suggest that such a war comes only after Russia abandons communism and has established a friendly relationship with the United States. The word used by Nostradamus for **friends** in the original text of line 1 is *demis*. This can stand for *d'amis* or **friends**, or for *demis* being *halved*, *split*.

The instigator of such a split-up could be the fearsome North African or Middle Eastern figure the prophet calls **Mabus** (2 Q62) and/or the Third Antichrist. Anytime between 1997 through 1999, or later between 2024 through 2038, this despot may use submarines based either in Libya or the Persian Gulf to trigger a terrorist event that undermines the precarious Russo-American friendship. At the present time, when the United States stands as the sole military superpower on Earth, there exists a very clear and present danger that the next Russian president after Boris Yeltsin could be an ultra-nationalist like Vladimir Zhirinovsky. A neo-Fascist dictator or a regurgitated neo-communist strongman could renew alliances with former Soviet allies like Saddam Hussein and Muhammar Qadaffi.

Line 4's **bloody one** could be the last Soviet president, Mikhail Gorbachev. Perhaps Nostradamus saw his trademark blood-splattered birthmark on his forehead and brow. The **number** reported is the agreed amount of an eventual 75-percent reduction of Soviet and American nuclear weapons after Gorbachev and US President George Bush signed START (the Strategic Arms Reduction Treaty).

Quatrain Indexing Date: Q89 = 1989. In my first book on Nostradamus (1986), I took the hint of the indexing of this quatrain to predict that the Cold War would end by the end of the decade.

2 Q90

Par vie & mort changé regne d'Ongrie,	**Through life and death the rule of Hungary changed.**
La loy sera plus aspre que seruice:	**The law will be more harsh than servitude:**
Leur grand cité d'vrlements, plaincts & crie,	**Their great city calls out with howls and laments,**
Castor & Pollux ennemis dans la lice.	**Castor and Pollux enemies in the arena.**

On 1 November 1956, as the people of Hungary struggle with another dreary winter of communist domination, their Premier Nagy sets off a brief flash-fire in the Cold War by declaring Hungary free of the Warsaw Pact Alliance with the Soviets. Three days later celebrations in the streets of Budapest are replaced by mobs hurling Molotov cocktails at invading Soviet tanks. **Castor and Pollux**, the twins of Greek mythology, do double duty meaning for pro-and anti-communist Hungarian brothers killing each other in the rubble of the "twin" city of Buda and Pest.

As fighting raged in the streets of Budapest, the Suez Canal crisis was gathering pace, leaving the United States, Britain, and France divided on what to do. Desperate calls from the Hungarian freedom fighters for Western assistance went unheeded. President Eisenhower would not wage nuclear war with Russia over Hungary. Once the rebellion was crushed, Imre Nagy and thousands of supporters of the uprising were shot, and Hungary would endure long decades of repressive Soviet-backed governments.

Nostradamus may have left a clue of hope for the Hungarians. Consider the indexing of this quatrain: number 90 could be intended for the time Hungary achieved democracy. Just two months prior to 1990 the Hungarian Communist Party was dissolved, and the Hungarian parliament passed legislation legalizing freedom of assembly and association. The year 1990 saw Hungary break away from communism to become a fledgling democracy. It was also the year that marked the beginning of the withdrawal of Soviet military forces from Hungary, a process completed by 19 June 1991.

Quatrain Indexing Date: Q90 = 1990.

2 Q91

Soleil levant vn grand feu l'on verra,	**At sunrise one will see a great fire,**
Bruit & clarté vers Aquilon tendants:	**Noise and light extending toward the North:**
Dedans le rond¹ mort & cris l'on orra,	**Within the earth death and cries are heard,**
Par glaiue, feu, faim, mort las attendants.	**Death awaiting them through weapons, fire, and famine.**

¹*rond:* figurative for the round orb of Earth.

The photograph of George Bush and Boris Yeltsin joyously waving the signed papers of the two nuclear disarmament START (Strategic Arms Reduction) treaties at the end of 1992 carries disturbing echoes of British prime minister Neville Chamberlain's brandishing his signed agreement with Hitler in 1938, a pact which he claimed meant "Peace in our time."

According to Nostradamus and the warnings of many other proven forecasters of future disasters, we could not be living in more dangerous times than these. The fulfillment of Armageddon is assisted by the ignorance or collective denial of some basic facts about both START I & II.

Before START II's 75 percent reduction can officially begin, the first treaty needs to be reratified by the new nuclear states that have arisen from the former Soviet Union. Even if the START treaties are ratified and proceed on schedule with a two-thirds reduction of weapons by the year 2003, 7,000 warheads will still be left in the US and Russian "peace" arsenals. These START treaties do not even begin to prevent nuclear proliferation in the Third World. Since China, North Korea, India, Iran, Iraq, Pakistan, Argentina, Brazil, Libya, and Israel will, no doubt, continue to pursue or enhance their nuclear capabilities into the next century, we can add another several thousand nuclear weapons to that new millennial arsenal.

Even if by the end of the 20th century a new age of "peace" cuts arsenals to a quarter of their doomsday bang, the START treaties will still allow an economically stressed United States, and a collapsing Russia ruled by some future ultra-nationalist dictator, to wield many thousands more intercontinental ballistic missiles and submarine-launched warheads in 2003 than existed in the Cuban Missile Crisis of 1962.

I believe this quatrain and the other terrifying Armageddon prophecies of Nostradamus were meant to remind those living in the latter days of the 20th century to remain constantly alert to the danger of relaxing into the illusion that we have passed Armageddon by. The following interpretations are intended to scare us out of making the new millennium as peaceful as a graveyard.

Here's how the world could end according to START. The treaties don't disarm doomsday, they just lessen the overkill. Mankind will have only twice the capacity for mass destruction, rather than its previous capability to destroy the world eight times over. If Russia and the USA launch an exchange of the thousands of megatons remaining after START II, the result will be a pall of darkness, reducing sunlight in the northern hemisphere to a few percent of normal within a few weeks. Surviving urban populations will suffer extreme cold, hunger, widespread radioactive pollution, and a complete breakdown of civil services. An estimated 1 billion will die from the initial effects of nuclear blasts and fire, and another 1 billion from untreated injuries and radiation sickness. In Nostradamus' apocalyptic litany of war, conflict is always followed by the shadow of *famine*, the greatest killing agent of a full-scale nuclear war.

Quatrain Indexing Date: Q91 = 1991, a near miss for the signing of START II by Russian president Boris Yeltsin and US President George Bush in 1992. Another possibility would frame a picture of the sunrise over Highway 8 stretching across the Iraq–Kuwaiti desert in February 1991. Hundreds of attack helicopters and jet bombers descend on the huge traffic jams of the retreating Iraqi army, strafing and dropping napalm in a rolling bombing pattern from the south to the north.

See Index: nuclear autumn.

2 Q92

Feu couleur d'or du ciel en terre veu,	**Fire color of gold from the sky seen on**
Frappé du haut nay, faict cas merueilleux:	**earth,**
Grand meurtre humain: prinſe du grād	**Struck by the high born, marvelous**
nepueu,	**deed done:**
Morts d'eſpectacles eſchappé l'orgueilleux.	**Great human slaughter, the great**
	nephew seized,
	Spectacular death, evades the
	arrogant one.

Le Pelletier fished just about every "nephew" quatrain out of the Centuries and put it in a tackle bag labeled "Napoleon III." Five years later, after Napoleon III was gone and his censors were out of a job, H. Torné-Chavigny confidently mongers his **nephew** slant for all to see on a gutting board called the Battle of Sedan (1–2 September 1870). The **fire color of gold** seen **from the sky** are German cannon shells mowing down thousands of the 100,000 French soldiers surrounded by the Prussians, in Napoleon III's version of a future French military disaster at Dien Bien Phu. The closest we can come to something striking in the proximity of a noble would be a bullet dusting the boot of the young Prince Imperial – showing great coolness under fire – while visiting the lines at Saarbrücken on 2 August 1870.

Lines 3 and 4 take us back to Sedan and can only be for the pathetic Napoleon III. On the last day of fighting when all hope of a breakout was dashed, he was seen in a number of places on the French battle lines sitting on his horse with both hands holding the saddle horn, in abject agony from a urinary infection, waiting for the Prussian artillery barrage to end his misery. Even though several officers were cut down at his side, no **spectacular death** would save his honor. He was captured with the rest of his army.

2 Q93

Bien pres du Tymbre[1] preſſe la Lybitine,[2]	**Very near the Tiber the goddess of**
Vn peu deuant grand inondation,	**death threatens,**
Le chef du nef prins, mis à la ſentine,[3]	**Shortly before the great flood:**
Chaſteau[4], palais[5] en conflagration.	**The head of the church will be taken**
	prisoner and put in the sewer,
	[Sant' Angelo] and the [Vatican] in
	flames.

[1]Tiber river; by extension, Rome and the Vatican.
[2]Latin *Libitina* = Goddess of death; the patroness of undertakers and morticians.
[3]Latin *sentina* = a) bilge water; b) dregs – ie rejected.
[4]In this case the *Castle* Sant' Angelo.
[5]*Palais* stands for the papal apartments of the Vatican.

Nostradamus' prophecies for the apocalyptic end of the papacy closely resemble the vision of St Malachy of Ireland for the final six popes before the Apocalypse. In 1138 this Irish priest, while on a pilgrimage to Rome, uttered 111 Latin phrases during an ecstatic trance. Each one stands as a prediction for one in the complete succession of 111 popes – from his contemporary pope, Celestinus II, unto doomsday. After John Paul II (whom he calls The Labor of the Sun, perhaps because he was born on the day of a solar eclipse), only two popes will follow, according to Malachy's list. Malachy's original manuscript was not discovered in the Vatican Archives until 1590 – 24 years after the death of Nostradamus – yet both men's prophecies give parallel clues to the harrowing life and times of the final pope.

Foreseeing the final Catholic Apocalypse St Malachy said:

> In the final persecution of the Holy Roman Church, Peter the Roman will occupy the See, who will guide his flock through numerous tribulations. These tribulations past, the town of seven hills will be destroyed and the terrible Judge shall judge the people.

One possible cause of the tidal waves destroying Rome is revealed in a foreboding set of quatrains predicting a meteorite strike in the Aegean Sea, which sets the great tub of the Mediterranean Sea sloshing back and forth over its coastlines in thousand-foot tsunamis.

Quatrain Indexing Date: Q93 = 1993, generally targeting our millennial times from his vantage point four centuries behind.

2 Q94

GRAND Pau grand mal pour Gaulois receura,	*Great Pau great evil will be received by the Gauls,*
Vaine terreur au maritin Lyon:	*Vain terror to the maritime Lion:*
Peuple infiny par la mer paſſera,	*Infinite people will pass by the sea,*
Sans eſchapper vn quart d'vn milion.	*A quarter of a million will not escape.*

Great Pau is an abbreviation of the anagram for Napoleon Bonaparte: Pau Nay Loron (Napaulon Roy (8 Q1)). Before the French people (**Gauls**) would lose millions of men in his wars of conquest, Napoleon was first brought to their attention for his bravery at the siege of Toulon in 1794 against the British (**the maritime Lion**). Nostradamus sometimes calls the French **infinite people**. Gallic pride aside, he adequately describes the French fleet crowded with Napoleon's soldiers setting sail for the Egyptian Expedition of 1798–99. Then our prophet makes a jump forward in time to the disastrous Russian Campaign of 1812, in which a quarter-million Frenchmen (let alone an equal number of non-French allies) would end their days buried under the snow.

Quatrain Indexing Date: Q94 = 1794, the year which saw the siege of Toulon.

2 Q95

Les lieux peuplez feront inhabitables,[1]	**The lands populated by humans will**
Pour chans[2] *auoir grande diuifion:*	**become uninhabitable,**
Regnes liurez à prudens incapables,	**Great disagreement and discord in**
Lors les grands freres[3] *mort & diffention.*	**order to obtain lands:**
	Kingdoms given to men incapable of
	prudence,
	Then for the great brothers death and
	dissension.

[1]Uninhabitable. This word keys in a similar theme of land disputes in the Middle East in 2 Q19.
[2]*chans* = misprint for *champs*, fields, (by extension) lands.
[3]The great brothers: a) of the north, Russia and the USA; b) of the Kennedy family, John and Robert Kennedy; c) of the House of Lorraine, the Duke and Cardinal de Guise, who were assassinated in 1588.

The ancient blood feud between the descendants of Abraham (the Arabs and Jews) may bring wars over territory to a head any time after the year 1995 through the 2020s. In other quatrains the **great brothers** seem to be the former superpowers who fought the Cold War (Russia and the United States). They begin fighting the final battle of Armageddon as allies but soon fall into dissension. Nostradamus does not give a good prophetic report card to today's latter-day world leaders.

The great brothers could also be the slain Kennedy brothers John and Robert. It can be argued that if John Kennedy had not been assassinated, and if Robert Kennedy had succeeded him as president, the Cold War of the **great brothers** of the north might have ended a generation earlier. Perhaps this would have taken the world down an alternative future track, avoiding the potential of a third world war from the breakup of the Soviet Union.

The **great brothers** can also include a more contemporary interpretation for Henry, Duc de Guise and Charles, Cardinal de Guise who were murdered by Henry III at Blois in 1588. Their **death** did cause great **dissension** between the Catholic royalists and Catholic Leaguers, causing a three-way civil war.

Quatrain Indexing Date: Q95 = 1995, the year when growing rifts between the Russian Federation and the United States begin a new era predicted by some Russia watchers – such as Professor Stephen F. Cohen of Princeton University – as the Cold Peace.

In my last Nostradamus book (1994) I made the following observation: "The ancient blood feud between the descendants of Abraham (the Arabs and Jews) may see their wars over territory come to a head by the year 1995."

The year 1995 saw the issue of Middle Eastern war or peace come to a head, but so far the momentum thereafter is tilting slightly toward peace. Yasser Arafat of the PLO and the Israeli leadership made major break-

throughs toward recognizing each other's right to exist and live as neighbors in peace. Although 1995 closed with the tragic assassination of
Yitzhak Rabin by Jewish extremists – and even though in the following
years Yasser Arafat may suffer the same fate from his own extremists –
there is hope that peace, rather than Armageddon, may be given a
chance in the Middle East.

2 Q96

Flambeau ardant au ciel soir sera veu,	A burning torch will be seen in the night sky,
Pres de la fin & principe du Rosne:	Near the end and the source of the Rhône:
Famine, glaiue: tard le secours pourueu,	Famine, weapons: the help provided [is] late,
La Perse tourne enuahir Macedoine.	When Persia turns to invade Macedonia.

A future Iranian Ayatollah seeks retribution against Saddam Hussein
through a nuclear attack.

There are several references in Les Propheties to a falling comet. These
comet descriptions, however, could also be the way a 16th-century man
would describe a falling Scud or intercontinental missile – in this case
one aimed at a target near the mouth of the Rhône river in southern
France. Macedonia could be a synecdoche for the Ottoman Turks
(modern-day Turkey), and also be a cryptic description of the coming
conflict between the Turks and Greeks caused by the potential eastward
spread of the Balkan ethnic wars.

Iran and Turkey are currently in political and religious competition to
draw the Central-Asian Muslim states into their respective spheres of
influence. In a worst-case interpretation of this quatrain, sometime in the
closing years of either this century, or the roaring and globally warmed
20s of the next, we will see Turkey bogged down in Balkan conflicts with
Greece over Macedonia. Iran will unleash a surprise attack on Turkey,
while nuclear terrorists attack southern Europe.

Quatrain Indexing Date: Q96 = 1996. Perhaps an attempt to pinpoint a
military incident between Turkey and Iran, who go to war over Kurdistan
in the late 1990s.

2 Q97

Romain Pontife garde de t'approcher,	Roman Pontiff, beware of approaching,
De la cité que deux fleuues arrouse,	Out of the city which the two rivers water,
Ton sang viendras aupres de là cracher,	In that place you will come to spit your blood,
Toy & les tiens quand fleurira la rose.	You and your friends when the rose will blossom.

This prophesies the death of Pope Pius VI, who was a prisoner of the French Directory. The city where two rivers meet is Valence, which is watered by the Rhône and the Isère. He was under house arrest in the town's citadel with an entourage of 32 priests (his *friends*). Pius VI died from an attack of acute gastroenteritis on 29 August 1799. Witnesses report that he was vomiting blood. The final phrase describes this event poetically.

Quatrain Indexing Date: Q97 is very close to the year of the Pope's death in 1799.

2 Q98

Celuy de fang reperfe le vifage,	**The one whose face is sprinkled with**
De la victime proche facrifiée,	**blood,**
Tonant[1] en Leo augure par prefage,	**Of the victim nearly sacrificed,**
Mis eftre à mort lors pour la fiancée.[2]	**Jupiter the Thunderer in Leo, omen**
	through presage,
	To be put to death then for the
	promise of romance.

[1]Latin *Jupiter Tonans* = Jupiter the Thunderer.
[2]*Fiancée* = a) marriage, bride; b) promise or assurance of romance.

This may have a connection with **the bloody one** of 2 Q89. I take it to mean the bloody birthmark marking the head and brow of Mikhail Gorbachev, the last Soviet president and the man responsible for the breakup of the Soviet Union. The **victim nearly sacrificed** is the communist experiment. The climax of Gorbachev's political career took place exactly within the transit of Jupiter through Leo, from 19 August 1990 through 11 September 1991.

In August 1990 Gorbachev is given virtual free reign to decontrol the Soviet economy. He moves slowly, but prices soar out of control. By October Germany reunifies as a consequence of Gorbachev's withdrawing military support to the East German leadership earlier in the year. Gorbachev gives official Soviet approval to the reunification. By the end of 1990 he has sided with the United States and the UN about sanctions against Iraq. He will allow the Gulf War to be waged against Saddam Hussein, a former ally, without Soviet intervention. In December 1990 Eduard Shevardnadze resigns as Soviet foreign minister, warning the Congress of the People's Deputies against "reactionaries"; Gorbachev ignores the warning.

Between 12 and 19 August, just as Jupiter moves through the final degrees – and therefore the most intense leg of its transit through Leo – an attempted coup by communist hardliners fails, thanks largely to the heroic efforts of Boris Yeltsin standing with a handful of loyal tank units and thousands of civilians at the Russian Parliament. The coup leaders flee. President Gorbachev returns to Moscow from his brief imprisonment, his credibility in tatters. Yeltsin becomes the new rising political star.

By 24 August Yeltsin suspends the Communist Party, bringing 74 years of communist rule in Russia to an end. On 5 September Gorbachev acquiesces, convincing the all-Soviet congress to give up its power. This wipes out any tenuous hold it still had over the constituent Soviet Republics. On the following day (just five days before Jupiter ended its transit of Leo) Gorbachev recognizes the independence of the three Baltic republics. Through his efforts he has all but dismantled the Soviet Union by mid-September.

In November 1990 Gorbachev warned that the Soviet Union might soon break up in "bloodshed and civil conflict." His statement to the world press was almost word-for-word what the Indian mystic Osho had predicted two years earlier, when Gorbachev was still the darling of the media and considered by many to be the man of the decade. Osho dictated and sent to the Russian President the following open letter, which was read before a gathering of ten thousand meditators in Pune, India, in December 1988.

> Instead of rejoicing over the failure of communism in Russia and boasting about the virtues of democracy, the Western leaders should be worrying about what will happen when the entire Soviet Union breaks down into civil war. President Reagan and the other Western leaders are urging Gorbachev to destroy communism, but they do not stop to consider that they are creating a recipe for disaster, with untold suffering for millions of people.
>
> If Gorbachev really wants to be a revolutionary, the only way is to bring meditation into the Soviet Union, not capitalism. If the Soviet Union turns into a country of capitalism, it will not only destroy itself, its dignity and power, it will destroy all the other small communist countries that are dependent on it. And bringing back the old organized religions is not going to change the economic status of the country. They are going to destroy whatever has been achieved in 70 years. Gorbachev's intentions are absolutely good – but with all good intentions, he is going in wrong and suicidal directions. Unfortunately all these things are going to happen.

Osho's **omen through presage**, if you will, was made over eight years ago. In 1997 the former Soviet states resemble the prophecy almost to a T. Because of Gorbachev's recklessness in dismantling the Soviet Union, the region – with its chronic food shortages, runaway crime, economic collapse, and ethnic and nationalistic rivalries – is already suffering from bloody civil wars. And they are spreading, along with the threat of neo-Fascism.

The final line intimates that Gorbachev himself, after returning to Russian politics, will eventually be killed for romancing with the Western capitalists and sending the Soviet experiment down the drain.

Astrological Time Window

Jupiter was last in Leo from 19 August 1990 through 11 September 1991. The next transit will be August 2002 through August 2003.

Quatrain Indexing Date: Q98 = 1998. A near miss for the notorious year 1999, when the friendship of the brothers of the north (the USA and Russia) begun by Gorbachev breaks down. The year 1998 may either mourn or celebrate Gorbachev's death or assassination.

2 Q99

Terroir Romain qu'interpretoit augure,	**Roman soil as that the augur interprets,**
Par gent Gauloyſe[1] par trop ſera vexée:	**Will be overly vexed by the Gallic people:**
Mais nation Celtique[2] craindra l'heure,	**But the French nation will fear the hour,**
Boreas,[3] claſſe[4] trop loing l'auoir pouſſée.	**North wind, the army having pushed too far.**

[1]Old French for French people.
[2]Celtique (poetic), the French.
[3]Latin = the north wind, north.
[4]Latin classis = fleet, army.

This is about French excesses and their retribution. The wide-scale persecution and plundering of Napoleon's Italian Campaigns between 1794–98 led the prophet to forecast divine retribution for a time in the future when Napoleon and his soldiers, lusting after plunder, advanced too far and tarried too long in Moscow (1812).

The first two lines describe his tough and tattered soldiers ransacking and plundering precious art and treasures of the papal states (**Roman soil**). In 1796, Napoleon forced Pope Pius VI to sign the Treaty of Tolentino, by which the pontiff surrendered his claims to Bologna, Ferrara, and the Romagna, and agreed to pay an indemnity of 30 million francs to add to the estimated 7 million francs worth of plunder already captured during the fighting.

Two years later the French seized the papal states and proclaimed a Roman republic. Pius VI was arrested by the French Directory and imprisoned in Valence, where he died in 1799. In that same year Napoleon returned from Egypt to become dictator of France, and, like the northern wind, descended one last time to vex Italy, crossing the St Bernard Pass to defeat the Austrians at Marengo in 1800. This gave him dictatorial rule over most of the Italian peninsula for the next 14 years.

But Nostradamus foresees retribution of biblical proportions for his First Antichrist. The final two lines jump ahead 12 years, using his **north wind** metaphor as a link from Marengo to Napoleon's catastrophic Russian campaign in which many a veteran of the summer plunder of the 1790s were to clutch their frozen hands in a death grip of the loot stolen during their winter retreat from Moscow.

Quatrain Indexing Date: Q99 = 1799, dating the death of the pope, and the beginning of the dictatorship of Nostradamus' First Antichrist, *Napaulon Roy* - Napoleon the King. It is likely that slotting this quatrain as Q99 is not by accident because Nostradamus correctly counts the years of Napoleon's tyranny in 7 Q13.

2 Q100

Dedans les ifles fi horrible tumulte,	**Within the isles such horrible tumult,**
Bien on n'orra qu'vne bellique brigue:	**Truly one will only hear a certain**
Tant grand fera des predateurs l'infulte,	**warlike faction:**
Qu'on fe viendra ranger à la grand ligue.	**So great will be the assault of the**
	plunderers,
	That their opponents will come to be
	drawn together in a great league.

The proximity to *Les Propheties'* publication date makes the siege of Malta – a decade after 1555 – the primary candidate here. Seven hundred knights of Saint John led by their doughty, a bit arthritic, 71-year-old Grand Master, Jean de la Valette, resist 40,000 Turks for five months until the siege is lifted by a Spanish force (**great league**) in September. The final line's **league** could also stand for the multinational Christian armada that would defeat the Turkish fleet at Lepanto.

A less likely interpretation would have the **isles** be Britain in the 1980s and 1990s. The **warlike faction** could be that of the hawkish Iron Lady prime minister, Margaret Thatcher, going to war with Argentina in 1982. The **warlike faction** could be the IRA and its plague of terror bombings in London. Imagine viewing these events from the 16th century, witnessing the glass-shattering explosions in the financial center of east London: one might think it was a war.

3 Q1

Apres combat & bataille nauale,	**After combat and naval battle,**
Le grand Neptune à ſon plus haut befroy:	**The great Neptune in his highest**
Rouge auerſaire de peur viĕdra paſle	**belfry:**
Mettant le grand Ocean en effroy.	**Red adversary will become pale with**
	fear
	Putting the great Ocean in terror.

Leoni posits that **Neptune** stands for the Ottoman Turkish navy and red symbolizes its Spanish adversaries in the battle of Lepanto in 1571. Rather than criticizing Nostradamus for getting the victory backwards (the Turks lost, not the Spanish), we should urge Leoni to move farther into the future to the Battle of Trafalgar in 1805.

The **great Neptune** is the slain victor of the battle, Lord Nelson, whose body was entombed with full military honors beneath the **highest belfry** in London, St Paul's Cathedral. The color **red** is more often used to symbolize French revolutionaries than Imperial Spain. The Spanish fleet, however, fought with the French at Trafalgar. Nelson's fleet routed both (the **red adversary will become pale with fear**).

Line 4 aptly describes the chaos and wreckage of the naval battle, with its blazing and exploding ships and hummocks of survivors clinging to masts and rigging, who roll with the first swells of a great gale that plagued both winners and losers after the battle.

3 Q2

Le diuin verbe donra à la ſubſtance,	**The divine word will give to the**
Cõprins ciel terre, or occult au laict	**essence, [that which]**
myſtique:	**Contains heaven and earth. The**
Corps, ame, eſprit ayant toute puiſſance,	**hidden gold in the mystic deed:**
Tant ſoubz ſes pieds comme au ſiege	**Body, soul and spirit having all power,**
Celique.	**All [is] beneath his feet as at the seat**
	of heaven.

This harks back to the occult confessions of Nostradamus in the Epistle to Henry II, wherein he describes what it is like to be embraced by a divinely inspired trance state before sitting down to prophesy. The **divine word**(s) are those secret incantations uttered by the prophet to fuel the inner **essence** of watchfulness. This essence is described elsewhere as that **slender flame** of awakened consciousness beyond judgements and mental

limitations required for a journey through the timescape of future potentials born of the present. This "essence" is the point of unity between the
worldly and the divine. It is what Eastern mystics call the witness, or that
still, small center of the cyclone of relentless thoughts and emotions. The
true alchemy happens only when the base metal of our egoistic mind and
persona is burned, destroyed, and transformed into the mystic's state of
"no-mind." In other words, one becomes the golden state of pure awareness that can bring the three main centers of human existence –the body,
mind, and soul – into harmony. The medium of prophecy, therefore,
attains union with heaven, which is godliness itself.

3 Q3

Mars & Mercure & l'argent ioint enfemble,	**Mars and Mercury and the silver [Moon] in conjunction.**
Vers le midy extreme ficcité:	**Towards the south there will be a great drought:**
Au fond d'Afie on dira terre tremble,	**From the bottom of Asia an earthquake will be reported,**
Corinte, Ephefe lors en perplexité.	**Corinth [Greece] and Ephesus [Asia Minor] then in a troubled state.**

Nostradamus' homeland in southern France and all of Africa will be
desiccated by a severe drought during a future conjunction of these
planets. Africa has the fastest-growing deserts in the world. The next 20
years will see an area the size of mainland United States devoured by
the Sahara. At the same time, Africa's population will double from 700
million to 1.4 billion people. Africa will be the first region to watch in
horror as its supersystems collapse. The **bottom** of Asia is the Indian subcontinent. During a conjunction of these planets in the autumn of 1993
the Killari-Latur earthquake in central India killed 10,000 people. Expect
the next astrological windows for these super-seismic events on 29 March
1998 and again at the turn of the millennium around 2 July and 1 August
2000. Political upheavals in Greece and Turkey may lead to war between
the two nations at this time.
    Quatrain Indexing Date: Q3 = 2003?

3 Q4

Quand feront proches le defaut des lunaires,	**When the failure of the lunar ones will be nigh,**
De l'vn à l'autre ne diftant grandement,	**From one another not extremely distant,**
Froid, ficcité, danger vers les frontieres,	**Cold, dryness, danger towards the frontiers,**
Mefme où l'oracle a prins commencement.	**Even where the oracle had its source.**

Jaubert believes line 1 targets the year when a solar and lunar eclipse occur closest to each other. The year 1556 did witness a solar eclipse on 1 November, followed by a lunar eclipse on 16 November. He quotes a certain Belleforest as confirming that there was no rain from April to August, and that a severe winter did visit France in December. The French frontier was threatened by the Spanish invasion of Picardy. Jaubert believes the final line refers to the Protestants at Salon who verbally threatened Nostradamus on the streets or the marketplace.

The real persecution of Nostradamus by heretics and Catholic fanatics alike didn't happen for another four years. Perhaps this quatrain is a personal prophecy reflecting Nostradamus' expectations of the first threatening reactions by his neighbors to *Les Propheties* in the autumn and winter months of the year following its publication.

3 Q5

Pres loing defaut de deux grands luminaires,	**Near, far, the failure of two great luminaries,**
Qui furuiendra entre l'Auril & Mars:	**Which will happen unexpectedly between April and March:**
O quel cherte! mais deux grans debonnaires,	**Oh, what a dear loss! but [for] two debonair great ones,**
Par terre & mer fecourront toutes pars.	**[Who] by land and sea will assist all parties.**

This probably is a continuation of the eclipse theme of the previous quatrain, but any clear meaning remains obscured by the shadow of its own eclipse.

3 Q6

Dans temple clos le foudre y entrera,	**Within the closed temple the lightning will pierce,**
Les citadins dedans leur fort greuez:	**The citizens within their fort injured:**
Cheuaux, bœufs hõmes, l'onde mur touchera,	**Horses, cooked-meat men, the tide will hit the wall,**
Par faim, foif, foubs les plus foibles armez.	**Through famine, drought, under the weakest armed.**

Could this be a 16th-century man struggling to describe an episode of a cement bunker being breached by a shell or a missile?

I believe his **temple** could represent the somber sanctuary of a cement shore battery along the Atlantic Wall. It could also be the reinforced bunker in the outskirts of Baghdad where hundreds of civilians sought sanctuary from American cruise missiles, only to watch helplessly as one of those frightful weapons cut through the reinforced steel and masonry and exploded in their midst (**the lightning will pierce**).

Whatever scene of carnage Nostradamus' roving third eye has uncovered, line 3 adequately pictures what happens to those trapped inside a tight place when a shell explodes: men become **cooked meat**. The reference to a **tide** hitting *the wall* is quite close to the wording of the *frightful amphibian* weapon of 1 Q29. The last line could describe wartorn Iraq and might paint a vision of the thousands of emaciated and half-naked Iraqi soldiers staggering out of the desert into captivity after 40 days' aerial bombardment with little food and water during the Gulf War of 1991.

3 Q7

Les fugitifs, feu du ciel fus les piques,
Conflict prochain des corbeaux s'esbatans,
De terre on crie aide fecours celiques,
Quand pres des murs feront les
   combatants.

The fugitives, fire in the sky on the pikes,
Next conflict will be that of the frolicking ravens,
From earth they cry for aid and heavenly assistance,
When near the walls [borders?] will be the combatants.

Bosnian refugees, NATO airstrikes, and missiles punctuate line 1. At the time of writing the Dayton Accords are holding and the terrible Balkan war of the 1990s may be coming to an end. Nostradamus does not believe this war of ethnic hatreds will be the last. He implicates Kosovo as the next flashpoint in the Balkans. This interpretation depends on the riddle **the frolicking ravens**. The city of Kosovo Polje is enshrined in every Serbian's nationalistic and religious programming as the center of Serbian faith and national pride. Kosovo Polje is also known as the Field of Blackbirds, where in 1389 the Ottoman Turks slaughtered an army of 26,000 Serbs, sending their nation into six centuries of obscurity. Today Kosovo's population is predominantly Albanian and the Serbian government rule is more like a military occupation. Many world watchers fear that once the Balkan boil of Bosnia cools, the abscess of Albania will erupt in a far wider and more uncontrollable Balkan war.

Line 3 aptly describes the plight of devastated Bosnia. The first **heavenly assistance** did come from American airdrops of food and clothing. The Old French *mur* (wall) can also mean "border" or "frontiers." One can only wonder if this bodes ill for the efforts of the IFOR (Implementation Force) troops to sustain the new demilitarized borders between the three Bosnian factions after 1998. If the millennium does pass without either a resumption of the Bosnian conflict or a new Kosovo crisis, expect the next serious Balkan war to break out in the 2020s, when ecological and overpopulation stresses could drag the entire world into a global civil war at the report of a second shot fired at Sarajevo.

3 Q8

Les Cimbres ioints auecques leurs voifins,	**The Cimbrians allied to their**
Depopuler viendront prefque l'Efpaigne:	**neighbors,**
Gens amaffez, Guienne & Limofins,	**Will come to ravage almost all of**
Seront en ligue, & leur feront compaigne.	**Spain:**
	People amassed in Guienne and
	Limosins,
	Will be in league, and will form their
	campaign.

The Cimbrians were an ancient tribe of Germany. Hitler and Mussolini used the Spanish tragedy as a testing ground to sharpen weapons and strategies for world conquest. Nazi and Italian armaments helped kill 600,000 Spanish between 1936 and 1939. The people amassed in south-west France are probably Frenchmen collecting together in the numerous international brigades that fought on the losing Republican side.

3 Q9

Bourdeaux, Rouan, & la Rochelle ioints,	**Bordeaux, Rouen, and La Rochelle**
Tiendront autour la grand mer Occeane,	**joined,**
Anglois, Bretons, & les Flamans	**Will hold around the great Ocean sea,**
conioints,	**English, Bretons, and the Flemings**
Les chafferont iufque au pres de Rouane.	**united,**
	Will chase them down as far as the
	approaches of Rouen.

Fontbrune makes an interesting stab at this one. He sees Bordeaux, La Rochelle, and Rouen **joined** by Hitler's Atlantic Wall and Nazi occupation. Following his drift, I would add that the Allied forces are represented by the double wordplay of the **Bretons** signifying the English as well as the men from Brittany fighting in the French Resistance. After the Normandy landings the Allied forces would push the Germans out of Normandy and beyond the **approaches of Rouen** where four years earlier the German Blitzkrieg had made deep penetrations into France through Flanders.

3 Q10

De fang & faim plus grande calamité,	**Greater calamity of blood and famine,**
Sept fois s'apprefte à la marine plage:	**Seven times it advances to the marine**
Monech de faim, lieu pris, captiuité,	**shore:**
Le grand mené croc en ferree caige.	**Monaco from hunger, place captured,**
	captivity,
	The great leader crushed in a metaled
	cage.

A dire future for the last Grimaldi ruling Monaco. A meteorite men-tioned in other quatrains strikes the Aegean Sea and sends tidal waves all the way up and down the Mediterranean. Proud Monaco is scoured down to its sandstone foundations by seven tidal waves hundreds of feet high.

But if you fear crapping out on this interpretation at the Casino de Monte Carlo, turn your attention with Lamont and Fontbrune back to World War II, when in 1943, German and Italian forces occupied Vichy France all the way to the principality of Monaco. Shortages of food and an abundance of bloodletting were quite common then.

Fontbrune's interpretation of seven flip-flops at Allied Command over planning and launching their French Riviera beach landings is a bit of a stretch. But he gets kudos from me for targeting Mussolini, rather than a Grimaldi prince, for the **great leader** crushed in a metal cage. Mussolini's corpse was hung upside down in the **metaled cage** of a bombed-out gasoline station in Milan on 29 April 1945. His face had been crushed by a man swinging a plank.

I would only add that some future Grimaldi trapped inside some future skyscraper (**metaled cage**) might meet his end when the meteorite's watery wall topples the building.

3 Q11

Les armes battre au ciel longue faifon,	**The weapons fight in the sky for a**
L'arbre au milieu de la cité tombé:	**long time.**
Verbine,[1] rongne, glaiue, en face tyfon,[2]	**The tree [has] fallen in the middle of**
Lors le monarque d'Hadrie[3] fuccombé.	**the city:**
	The sacred branch is cut by a blade
	in front of Tison,
	Then king Hadrie falls.

[1]Latin *verbena* = sacred bough. Alternative, *vermine*. As a negative pun the line could read: *The vermin is cut by a blade in front of Tison.*
[2]Brand, firebrand, revolutionary; internal conflict; Greek *tuphon* and Arabic *tufan* = typhoon (Kidogo).
[3]Anagram: *ad Henri* or *ad* = Latin *towards* or *to, Henri.* Leoni relates that many compared Henry IV to the Roman Emperor Hadrian (**Hadrie**).

After the catastrophic Wars of Religion had burned themselves out, Henry IV dedicated himself to guide France through 16 years of healing and rebuilding. But in 1610, while his coach was stuck in congestion in the rue de la Ferronerie in Paris, a red-haired wildman named Ravaillac jumped up on the wheel and stabbed him three times with a dagger.

According to Guynaud, a story that appeared in *Mercure Français* in 1619 described a phenomenon witnessed by several hundred people of a spectral army of up to 12,000 ghosts marching through the skies over Angoumois until sunset.

On page 154 of Jerry Dennis' book on weather phenomena entitled *It's Raining Frogs and Fishes*, he describes a rare atmospheric effect known as a Fata Morgana, named for King Arthur's sorceress half-sister, Morgan le Fay, who is said to have conjured images of castles reflected in the clouds. Temperature layering of the air does cause far-off images to appear "grotesquely magnified, elongated, and much taller than they are." A layer of cold air pressed between layers of hot air works like a magnifying glass to create a spectacular mirage. It is possible that the citizens of Angoumois did see actual columns of troops marching miles away, their reflections magnified in layers of atmosphere to make them appear like spectral armies.

It is with this omen of Henry's death – or a mere atmospheric phenomenon – that Nostradamus begins his prophecy: **The weapons fight in the sky for a long time**. Henry, the great powerhouse of a monarch, is then poetically described as a fallen tree.

He is the **sacred branch** of the Bourbon royal house, cut off from life by a fanatic's knife. On face value, Nostradamus the royalist calls him **sacred** because a king was believed to rule through divine right. A secret jibe from the anti-Huguenot prophet could also be hiding in the word *verbine*, which can also be a cryptogram for *vermine*. Rather than a **sacred branch** Nostradamus is saying that a *vermin* – in other words, a "rat" – is **cut** by Ravaillac's blade.

The rue Tison is not far from where Henry fell. Kidogo comes up with an intriguing word play on **Tison**, which can mean a firebrand or a revolutionary or internal conflict – and its Greek and Arabic cognates connect it with **typhoon**. The Hermetic mysteries tell us that Tiphon (Tison?) is the dragon representing ignorance, perversion, and unconsciousness. He is the devourer of souls. In prophecies concerning the French Revolution, Nostradamus uses the metaphor of a **whirlwind** to describe mindless rebellion. If he had foreseen a return to civil war after Henry IV's assassination had left a minor heir and another Medici (a distant relative of Catherine de' Medici) as queen regent, he is wrong. History granted France a far more modest outcome than it faced in the seer's own time with the sudden death of Henry II. The whirlwind of rebellion and war passed France by and visited central Europe in the apocalyptic Thirty Years War (1618–48).

3 Q12

Par la tumeur de Heb, Po, Tag, Timbre, & Rome,	Because of the agitation of the Ebro, Po, Tagus, Tiber and Rhône,
Et par l'eſtang Leman & Aretin:	And because of the pond of Geneva and Arezzo:
Les deux grands chefs & citez de Garonne,	The two great chiefs and cities of Garonne,
Prins mors noyez. Partir humain butin.	Seized, dead, drowned. Human booty divided.

A continuation of the global warming flood theme for the 21st century. The major river systems of Spain, Italy, south-west France, and Lake Geneva are marked for catastrophic flooding.

3 Q13

Par fouldre en l'arche[1] or & argent fondu,	**Through lightning in the box gold and silver are melted,**
De deux captifs l'vn l'autre mangera:	**Of the two captives one will eat the other:**
De la cité le plus grand eftendu,	**The greatest one of the city is overextended,**
Quand fubmergee la claffe[2] nagera.	**When the fleet travels under water.**

[1]Latin *arcus* = arc or arch; Old French *archée* = the principle of life from ancient physiology; (alchemy) the central fire; Latin *arca* = a box or ark. When the Ark of the Covenant was captured by the Philistines, they returned it because plagues broke out in every city into which they took it (Kidogo).
[2]Latin *classis* = fleet.

A conventional view would have the opening line be a description of some contemporary alchemical process. Is it a 16th-century man's attempt to describe the function of a modern submarine's atomic engines? This may be no less an act of wanton gibberish than are the attempts by modern visionaries to describe the future mechanics of warp drive and transporter beams. The first two lines could be the prophet's stab at the nuclear engines of submarines. The **lightning in the box**, or **in the ark**, may be a description of the electrical output produced by the implosion of atoms in a nuclear reactor, **captives** ("harnessed energies") that **will eat each other**. The third line may represent a future president of France, or a future pope in Rome, who has overextended his powers, be they political or military, when a submarine fleet travels underwater.

3 Q14

Par le rameau du vaillant perfonnage,	**Through the branch of the valiant personage,**
De France infime, par le pere infelice:	**Of lowest [infamous] France, because of the unhappy father:**
Honneurs, richeffes, trauail en fon vieil aage,	**Honors, riches, travail in his old age,**
Pour auoir creu le confeil d'homme nice.[1]	**For having had faith in the counsel of the inexperienced man.**

[1]Old French *nice* = simple, inexperienced, foolish.

This best fits the heir of Louis XIV – his great-grandson Louis XV. He came to the throne at age 5 in 1715. His grandfather had left France on the verge of bankruptcy. The **inexperienced man** is André de Fleury, the king's tutor and priest, who was already a spent and opinionated old man of 62 when he became Louis' mentor. Fleury would have a great influence over the king until the tutor's death in 1742. He managed to endow his liege with his own political naiveté, which only helped the Ancien Regime lurch ever closer to its doom-dealing date with the French Revolution at the end of the 18th century. The revolution of the mob **of lowest, (infamous) France** and resultant execution of Louis XV's grand-son and heir Louis XVI stemmed in part from the **unhappy** grandfather's economic excesses and political mediocrity.

3 Q15

Cœur, vigueur, gloire, le regne changera,	**Heart, vigor, in glory the kingdom will change,**
De tous points contre ayant ſon aduerſaire,	**On all sides having its adversary opposed,**
Lors France enfance par mort ſubiuguera,	**Then through death an infant will master France,**
Vn grand regent ſera lors plus contraire.	**A great regent will be then more contrary.**

This continues the Fleury/Louis XV theme. After the **heart, vigor** and **glory** of Louis XIV is extinguished by death at age 76, a mere infant – his grandson Louis XV – lands his five-year-old bottom on the august throne of France. The **contrary** regent is Philippe, Duc d'Orleans, whom the dying Sun King had chosen expecting a degree of greatness from his nephew that he failed to demonstrate. D'Orleans would be instrumental in the spread of corruption during the Ancien Regime that later led to the French Revolution.

Quatrain Indexing Date: Q15 = 1715, the year Louis XIV died, and Louis XV came to the throne.

3 Q16

Vn prince Anglois Mars à ſon cœur de ciel,	**The English Prince Mars in his heavenly heart,**
Voudra pourſuiure ſa fortune proſpere:	**Will want to seek his prosperous fortune:**
Des deux duelles l'vn percera le fiel,	**Of the two duels one will pierce his gall bladder,**
Hay de luy, bien aymé de ſa mere.	**Hated by him, well loved by his mother.**

Now to another plagued royal, one of our own time: the Prince of Wales. **Mars in his heavenly heart** could make Prince Charles an innocent bystander in the Eight Clues Theme. **Mars** is the symbolic color and energy of the new religious revolution foretold as coming to the West from Asia. The higher aspect of **Mars** in the occult scriptures is not that of a war god but of a Hermetic magician who changes base metals of human unconsciousness into the gold of enlightenment. **Mars** therefore could stand for a spiritual master coming from the East and link this quatrain to others in Nostradamus' Eight Clues to future spiritual teachers theme.

But how do we link Prince Charles to an Eastern guru? Though his royal cousin and friend, Prince Welf of Hanover. Welf was a grandson of the last German emperor. His mother was Princess Sophia of Greece, sister of Prince Philip of England, Charles' father. Welf's father, Prince George Wilhelm von Hanover, was the brother of Queen Frederika of Greece. The two cousin royals became friends early on during numerous royal holidays spent together. Charles and Welf studied at school together at Gordonstoun in Scotland. By the mid-1970s Prince Welf dropped out of his royal obligations to seek his spiritual path in the East. He wound up in Pune, India, taking on the orange robe of a sannyas (spiritual disciple) and the name Swami Vimalkirti, under the guidance of the controversial guru Bhagwan Shree Rajneesh (better known today as Osho).

Juliet Forman, who was a friend of Prince Welf, relates an intriguing story of a meeting between Prince Charles and Vimalkirti just prior to the latter's untimely death from a brain aneurysm. On pages 187–88 of her book *Bhagwan: The Buddha for the Future*, she writes:

> In December of 1980, Prince Charles arrived in Bombay; Kirti and Turiya [Princess Welf, Vimalkirti's wife] went to see him. Turiya remembers Charles as being somewhat envious of their freedom to do as they wanted with their lives. Warm and intelligent, with a healthy sense of humor, Charles had duties he felt obliged to honor. He wanted to remain open to the diversity of causes and approaches to life that he encountered in his work, so felt he could not ally himself to any one in particular. However, he took Kirti's locket in his hand at one point during their meeting, and, studying Bhagwan's photograph, commented on how intriguing his eyes were.

With this in mind, let us return to the quatrain. Line 1 sees the **English Prince** Charles meet his cousin Vimalkirti in Bombay. Kirti is dressed in a long red (**Mars**) robe as the disciple of a guru (the Magus of **Mars**). Kirti was a personal bodyguard of Osho while living at the ashram. He was well trained in the "martial" arts. Those who knew Kirti remembered his tall and graceful body and his soft, silent eyes. Those who loved him could easily characterize him as **Mars** with a **heavenly heart**.

There is a double meaning possible for **prosperous fortune**. In this case the fortune could be spiritual. Forman's account would strongly suggest that Prince Charles was tempted to follow his cousin's spiritual path. In later years he would be unfairly criticized by the press and the spiritually prejudiced for his mystical bent; there was something eccentric, they said, about the Prince of Wales' love of aloneness, silence, and meditation.

Charles' indecisiveness and eccentricities may stem from an ongoing spiritual crisis. He seems to be a man divided between fulfilling his duties as the heir to the British throne and following his mystical heart. Duty would require he marry. One could say that line 3's duel is more poetic than literal for his ill-starred marriage to Princess Diana. The piercing of his gall bladder might be figurative as well for the bile vented by both the Prince and Princess of Wales and mercilessly reported in Fleet Street tabloids, in what could be called one of the ugliest public breakups of the 20th century.

The second *duel* – between Charles and those who would not have him become King Charles III – may be yet to come if the reported meeting between Charles and the Rajneeshee Prince Welf is true. Charles, unlike his dominating mother, Elizabeth II, will grow to detest the politics and constraints of being a crowned head of Britain. The final line may give us a forecast of the reign of Charles III, characterizing him as the embittered – and perhaps last – king of Britain.

3 Q17

Mont Auentine bruſler nuict ſera veu,	**Mount Aventine will be seen to burn**
Le ciel obſcur tout à vn coup en Flandres:	**at night,**
Quand le monarque chaſſera ſon nepueu,	**The heavens obscured very suddenly**
Leurs gens d'Egliſe cõmettront les	**in Flanders:**
eſcladres.	**When the monarch will chase his**
	nephew,
	Then Church people will commit the
	scandals.

Aventine Hill is one of the seven hills of Rome. This could be another Destruction of the Vatican scenario (see 2 Q93) in which St Peter's Basilica and the papal enclave are destroyed by fire and tidal waves on doomsday. In several places Nostradamus speaks about a great solar eclipse that occurs just prior to the Apocalypse. The next total eclipse to obscure Flanders and Europe will be on 11 August 1999. The sun's shadow will cut a path through England, France, eastern Europe, and Turkey. It must be remembered that July of 1999 is slotted by the prophet for a significantly apocalyptic **terror** to descend on humanity *from the skies* (see 10 Q72).

Line 3 is obscure. Line 4, however, could call upon us to read the sequence of these lines backwards. In my previous book on Nostradamus I posed a theory that within the quatrains are three scandals foretold for the Roman Catholic Church that would lead to its self-destruction around the end of this millennium or sometime early in the next century.

In the first, the relationship between Fascism and the Papacy undermines the Vatican's spiritual integrity. The second scandal weakens this integrity further through the murder of a pope who is on the verge of revealing corruption in the Vatican Bank. This was Pope John Paul I. The third scandal decimates the Catholic clergy itself via a new kind of blood plague. This could be AIDS, Ebola, or a scourge from some other immunological breakdown caused by the depletion of the ozone layer and the global warming expected for the 21st century. With this reverse sequence in mind, line 4's scandals precipitate line 3's intrigues (yet to be revealed); then comes the total eclipse of 1999, followed soon after by Rome in flames.

See Index: papal scandals.

3 Q18

Apres la pluye laict assés longuette,	**After the rather long rain of milk,**
En plusieurs lieux de Reims le ciel touché:	**In several places in Reims the sky is struck:**
O quel conflict de sang pres d'eux s'appreste,	**Oh what a bloody conflict is prepared near them,**
Peres & fils Roys n'oseront approcher.	**Fathers and sons, Kings will not dare approach.**

The **long rain of milk** is mustard gas falling on the Western Front. For most of World War I Reims was a front-line city. Not only did it suffer from German bombardment for the bulk of four years, but it was further dev-astated by some of the war's greatest offensives: the First Battle of the Marne (1914), the Nivelle Offensive (1917), and the last-ditch German Ludendorff Offensive of 1918. Four years of war in the trenches of the Western Front in the Reims area saw over a million dead and twice that number maimed and gassed from both sides. Reims was not a safe city for man or king – definitely too close to the German guns and mustard-gas shells for a tour by George V of England or the Belgian King Albert I.

Quatrain Indexing Date: Q18 = 1918, the year of the final German offensive and the Franco-American counter-offensive that finally pushed the Germans beyond artillery range of Reims.

3 Q19

En Luques sang & laict viendra plouuoir,	**In Lucca it will come to rain blood and milk,**
Vn peu deuant changement de preteur:	**Shortly before the change of governor:**
Grand peste & guerre, faim & soif fera voir,	**Great plague and war, famine and drought will be seen,**
Loing où mourra leur Prince recteur.[1]	**Far from where their Prince rector will die.**

[1]Latin for leader, governor, instructor, ruler.

Who the protagonists are in this quatrain is unclear. The reference to a rain of blood and milk waxes chemical or biological for modern weapons of mass destruction. Line 3 is a powerful repeat of the apocalyptic sequence theme, making this more likely a prophecy of a toxic plague or, more metaphorically, a plague affecting the blood, such as Ebola or AIDS.

In Africa, AIDS is called Slim because it emaciates its victims. Perhaps the many parallel references to *plague* and *famine* stem from Nostradamus mistaking one for the other? In 16th-century medical language *blood* describes the vitality of a person's life force and health; in modern terms it signifies the immune system, and it is not only viruses that can disrupt the human immune system – the depletion of the Earth's ozone layer can weaken the immune systems of humans, and of the animals, and of the plants we eat. If we do not stop damaging our only umbrella against lethal cosmic rays, Nostradamus and other prophets see a global plague shadowed by an equally catastrophic worldwide famine.

Symptomatic of the global decline in human, plant and animal immunity to disease could be the mutation of common bacteria into more lethal antibiotic-resistant strains in the 21st century. Today, medical industries are behind in the race to find stronger antibiotics because funding in the last decade for research in the subject has been scarce. There will also be a plague caused by lethal pneumonia bacteria in the next 5 to 10 years. Add to this the sudden global increase of many other diseases that were once relatively controlled, such as tuberculosis, which are carried by the vector of our free-traveling global society, and we could have not one but several Black Deaths of global proportions between 1999 and 2050.

Quatrain Indexing Date: Q19 = 2019? Number 19 came up in an earlier Apocalyptic sequence prophecy in 2 Q19.

See Index: plague themes.

3 Q20

Par les contrees du grand fleuue Bethique,[1]	**Through the regions of the great river Guadalquivir,**
Loing d'Ibere au royaume de Grenade:	**Far from Iberia to the kingdom of Grenada:**
Croix repouſſees par gens Mahometiques,	**The Cross pushed back by the Islamic peoples,**
Vn de Cordube trahira la contrade.[2]	**One of Cordova will betray the country.**

[1]Latin *Baetis* = the Guadalquivir river, southern Spain.
[2]Provencal *contrada* = country.

In the early 1600s these regions of Spain were populated by the Moriscos (Christianized Moors). Philip III and the Spanish Inquisition began a systematic expulsion of the Moors from Spain in 1609–10; his pogrom would see Spain's culture and economy irrevocably weakened by the loss of its most educated and faithful subjects. Nostradamus may have reversed the truth by saying the Moors **pushed back** the cross. Actually, the Church authorities pushed the Moors out of Spain. However, many of the Moors who sailed to exile in North Africa would forswear the cross and return to Islam.

3 Q21

Au Cruſtamin[1] par mer Hadriatique,	In the Conca by the Adriatic Sea,
Apparoiſtra vn horrible poiſſon:	There will appear a horrible fish:
De face humaine[2] & la fin aquatique,	With a face [that is] human and its
Qui ſe prendra dehors de l'ameçon.	tail aquatic,
	Which will be taken without the hook.

[1]Latin *Crustuminus* = the river now known as the Conca, which runs into the Adriatic a few miles south of Rimini.
[2]Human; humane, benevolent.

The Conca river drains into the Adriatic ten miles south of Rimini. The **horrible fish** may be a submarine or any number of modern, or perhaps future, missiles with fins (**its tail aquatic**). The face of this "thing" is described here as either human, benevolent, or humanlike. Garencières lived long before the industrial age, so he thought it was a mermaid. In our age we might project (correctly or not) a technological image of a machine, as I have done. Or we might apply Nostradamus' image to some amphibian extraterrestrial making contact. A third possibility would create a distant future when humankind uses genetic engineering to branch out into different species. Some of those could be aquatic humans. Finally, this may be something more down to earth and closer to our times. How would you, as a 16th-century man, describe someone in a face mask, scuba gear, and flippers, coming out of the Adriatic after some deep-sea diving?

3 Q22

Six iours l'aſſaut deuant cité donné,	Six days the assault is made in front of
Liuree ſera forte & aſpre bataille:	the city.
Trois la rendront & à eux pardonné,	Freedom is attained in a strong and
Le reſte à feu[1] & ſang[2] tranche[3] traille.[4]	bitter fight:
	Three will hand it over, and to them
	pardon,
	To the rest fire, and bloody slashing
	and slaughter.

[1]*Feu* = Either the **fire** of war or the figurative **fire** of the hearth.
[2]*Sang* = Either the *blood* of war, or the figurative kindred *blood* of brother Semites – the Arab and the Jew in peace.
[3]*Tranche* = either to cut or slash, or to settle or solve an issue.
[4]Old French *treillis* = vine trellis, trawl net. Either the trawl net is poetic for sackcloth and mourning, or it stands for the fruit of the vine, the harvest of happiness and peace.

In 1967 Israel forestalled a planned invasion by Egypt, Syria, and Jordan by launching a lightning attack known as the Six Day War. Fierce fighting took place around the Old City of Jerusalem. Finally the Israelis retook the ancient platform where the Temple of Solomon once stood and where one of Islam's holiest shrines, the Dome of the Rock, stands today. The three handing over Jerusalem to the Israelis are Egypt, Syria, and Jordan. They are pardoned for past offenses. **Pardon** can also imply a lasting peace agreement in our near future. First Egypt and then Jordan came to officially accept the existence of Israel. In 1996, the Palestinian leader Yassir Arafat is pardoned, or recognized, by Israel as the legitimately elected president of the Palestinians. Even Syria may soon join with Jordan and Egypt in accepting the Jewish State. But the continued resistance of the other protagonists of Middle Eastern wars – Libya, Iraq, and Iran – to peace with Israel will only bring the *fire, and bloody slashing and slaughter* of a future war.

The final line is another example of Nostradamus' using a set of words that can point to completely opposite interpretations, depending on how you translate their literal and figurative meanings. He does this here to tell the people of the Middle East that they can still choose a positive alternative-future course by making the right responses in the present day. If they choose the familiar and negative course of war and revenge, the line translates as **To the rest fire, bloody slashing and sackcloth**. If they choose the unknown course of peace and reconciliation, the line can read *To the rest family, kindred, fruit on the vine*.

3 Q23

Si France paſſes outre mer lyguſtique,[1]	**If, France, you pass beyond the Ligurian Sea,**
Tu te verras en iſles & mers enclos:	**You will see yourself enclosed in islands and sea:**
Mahommet contraire, plus mer Hadriatique,	**Mahomet contrary, more so the Adriatic,**
Cheuaux & d'Aſnes tu rongeras les os.	**You will gnaw the bones of horses and asses.**

[1]Latin *Ligusticus* = Ligurian, the north-eastern Mediterranean Sea.

I believe Cheetham (in 1989) was on the right track when she wrote, "France will get into difficulties if it marches against Yugoslavia (across the Ligurian Sea)." The soldiers of modern France, bedecked in their blue United Nations berets and badges, have already risked their lives during the chaotic Bosnian civil war (1992–95). In 1996, *sans* blue berets, they continue to patrol the region as part of IFOR following the Dayton/Paris Peace Accords. Their region of operations covers part of the islands and irregular shoreline of the Dalmatian coast. A French carrier task force is currently stationed in the Adriatic. In a rare use of the intimate second person singular (*tu*), Nostradamus may be warning his beloved country-men to stay alert for future Islamic terrorist attacks coming from Arab terrorist advisors hiding in the ranks of the Bosnian army.

3 Q24

De l'entreprinfe grande confufion,	For the enterprise, great confusion,
Perte de gens, threfor innumerable:	Loss of people, innumerable treasure:
Tu n'y dois faire encore tenfion.[1]	You ought not attempt to expand
France à mon dire fais que fois	further there.
recordable.[2]	France, let what I say be remembered.

[1]Latin *tensio* = extension.
[2]Old French for memorable.

Nostradamus continues to use the familiar *tu*, and expands on the warn-ing in the last quatrain. Perhaps he fears the French of our day will get bogged down and bloodied by a widening guerrilla war in Bosnia – Europe's version of the Vietnam War.

On the other hand these lines are so general that one could even argue that Nostradamus is advising a different **France**: Prime Minister Pierre Mendès-France – Nostradamus is warning him to pull out of French Indochina before it is too late. Mendès-France's French soldiers would instead suffer a military disaster at the hands of the Vietminh at Dien Bien Phu in 1954. A French army would be completely surrounded and destroyed, losing all of its guns and equipment and suffering 2,293 killed, 5,134, wounded, and 10,000 captured.

3 Q25

Qui au Royaume Nauarrois paruiendra,	He who attains the kingdom of
Quand de Sicile & Naples feront ioints:	Navarre,
Bigore & Landes par Foyx loron tiendra,	When Sicily and Naples are allies:
D'vn qui d'Efpaigne fera par trop conioint.	He will hold Bigorre and Landes
	through Foix and Oloron,
	From one who will be too closely
	allied with Spain.

Sicily and Naples were allies only three times in history. Henry was crowned King of Navarre in 1572, coinciding with this rare alliance. The towns mentioned in the quatrain are in Navarre. Henry wisely disavowed Calvinism in order to survive the St Bartholomew's Day massacre, which was masterminded by the advisors of Charles IX, the one **too closely allied** to fanatically Catholic **Spain**. Henry's willingness to change religions at critical moments would later win him the French throne.

3 Q26

Des Roys & Princes drefferont
    fimulacres,[1]
	From Kings and Princes they will
	    raise imitations,

Augures, creuz efleuez arufpices:	**Augurs and empty prophets elevated:**

Corne,[2] *victime doree,*[3] *& d'azur,*
    d'acre,[4]
	Corn[ucopia], victim of gold, and of
	    azure, dazzling,

Interpretez feront les extipices.[5]	**Interpreted by the soothsayers.**

[1]Latin *simulacrum* = an imitation, pretense, fraud, sham; from Latin *simulare* = to simulate, copy.
[2]Horn; apocope for *corne d'abondance* = a cornucopia.
[3]Old French *d'oré*, gilded, of gold.
[4]Latin *acer* = dazzling.
[5]Latin *extispices* = inspectors of entrails, soothsayers.

I join forces with the crowd of other latter-day Nostradamians who take this one as a warning against a global economic collapse in our future. Nostradamus, as a coin-carrying Renaissance man, viewed paper money in less than positive terms. The closest thing we have today to a socially acceptable *augur* is a financial expert. I recall someone characterizing the trickle-down philosophy of Reaganomics in the 1980s as "voodoo economics." Rather than a promise of plenty (a **corn[ucopia]**), Reaganomics boosted America's national debt several hundred billion dollars faster than any president before him. The economic system as we have known it, is more in danger of a doomsday than ourselves. Take a capitalist philosophy that supports an unending increase of consumption and creation of new markets and hitch it on a uncontrolled population explosion of consumers, and I would bet on an economic Judgement Day any time down the road of the next 7 to 25 years.

Our **soothsayer**, Nostradamus, may be telling us that economics based on runaway greed, phony futurology, and a general lack of human values beyond the material, will lead us to disaster.

Shall we change ourselves and make him wrong?

3 Q27

Prince libinique puiffant en Occident,	**Libyan Prince powerful in the West,**
François d'Arabe viendra tant enflammer,	**The French will come to be so much** **enamored with the Arabian,**
Sçauans aux lettres fera condefcendant,	**Learned in literature, condescending** **he will,**
La langue Arabe en François tranflater.	**Translate the Arab language into** **French.**

In our day the drug of Libyan oil makes France and Europe politically – and possibly psychologically – dependent on unstable North African leaders. Maybe Nostradamus is recommending more caution so that extremists do not abuse the French fascination with things Arabic to gain power over them.

3 Q28

De terre foible & pauure parentele,	Of **weak land** and **poor parentage**,
Par bout & paix paruiendra dans l'empire:[1]	Through extremity, [she] will obtain
Long temps regner vne ieune femelle,	peace through the dominion:
Qu'oncques en regne n'en furuint vn	For a long time a young female will
fi pire.	rule,
	Never in the kingdom has arrived one
	so bad.

[1]Nostradamus may have intended **dominion** rather than *Empire* since he spells it with a lower-case *e*.

This entire prophecy is about Elizabeth I of England. Elizabeth's mother, Anne Boleyn, was of modest royal lineage (her father was Viscount Rochford and Earl of Wiltshire). The label of **poor parentage** may indicate parental skill rather than breeding. Anne Boleyn was executed on unsubstantiated charges of adultery, though Henry VIII was a notorious womanizer who went through six wives in his lifetime, Boleyn being the second. Elizabeth's childhood and youth were hard. Her mother was beheaded, as was her stepmother, Catherine Howard (Henry's fifth wife). As a young adult she suffered the ever-present threat of death as a Protestant princess in her stepsister's court. When Queen "Bloody" Mary died, Elizabeth, age 25, ascended to the English throne in 1558, made peace with France in 1559, and ruled as one of England's greatest monarchs for 45 years. In the final line, Nostradamus betrays his hatred of Protestants – and perhaps a wee bit too much Gallic arrogance - when he trashes Elizabeth.

3 Q29

Les deux nepueux en diuers lieux nourris,	**The two nephews reared in diverse**
Nauale pugne, terre peres tombez:	**places,**
Viendront fi haut efleuez enguerris,[1]	**Naval battle, fathers fallen [to the]**
Venger l'iniure ennemis fuccombez.	**ground:**
	They will come to be elevated very
	high for making war,
	To revenge the injury, enemies
	succumbed.

[1]Old French *enguerroier* = to make war (upon).

Look into the past 440 years and pick two nephews. Or worse, pick a couple due to arrive in the next few thousand years. Either way you go, no clear or definitive interpretation can be extracted. The most notable **nephews** of Nostradamus' day were those of Constable Montmorency:

Admiral Coligny, Cardinal Châtillon, and d'Andelot. With that said, nothing meshes.

3 Q30

Celuy qu'en luitte & fer au faict bellique,[1]	The one who in a contest with steel in a deed of war,
Aura porté plus grand que luy le pris:	Will have carried off the prize from one greater than he:
De nuict au lict fix luy feront la pique,	At night six will take the grudge to his bed,
Nud fans harnois fubit fera furprins.	Naked without his armor he will be suddenly surprised.

[1] Latin bellicus, of war.

In a **deed of war** – a joust – the Comte de Montgomery carried off the prize from Henry II. He fled Paris after Henry's death to lead Protestant forces in Normandy during the Wars of Religion. In further insult to the king's memory his battle flag bore the device of a broken lance. Catherine de' Medici no doubt identified Montgomery in this quatrain and may have tried to cook up her revenge (**grudge**) according to Nostradamus' prescient recipe, choosing six hand-picked men to steal the Huguenot prince from his bed (**without his armor**) and have him executed. The historical accounts of the swashbuckling Montgomery's end water down some of the dramatics of this quatrain, but it is generally accurate. In 1574, 20 years after Nostradamus wrote this prophecy, Montgomery (in his armor) and 150 men made a good show holding out against an army of 10,000 at Domfront. This makes the phrase without his armor more poetic and strategic than literal; with only a handful of men he was surprised by an overwhelming force. Catherine's preferred method of disposition was probably too risky. No one broke into his bedchamber; he was handed over to her forces through negotiation. He was promised the armor, if you will, of immunity, but Catherine made sure that was stripped. He was taken to Paris, condemned, and executed on June 27 (see 1 Q35).

3 Q31

Aux champs de Mede, d'Arabe & d'Armenie,	On the fields of Media [Persia], of Arabia and of Armenia,
Deux grans copies[1] trois fois s'affembleront:	Two great armies will assemble three times:
Pres du riuage d'Araxes la mefgnie,[2]	The host, near the bank of the Araxes,
Du grand Soliman en terre tomberont.	The earth trembles from the great Suleiman.

[1] Latin copia = forces, army.
[2] Old French mesnie = household, following host.

Throughout most of Nostradamus' lifetime, the Turkish Sultan Suleiman the Magnificent fought the Persians; the Battle of Araxes in 1514 was perhaps the pinnacle of their rivalry. This would seem to make the prophecy retroactive. Laver argued to the contrary that the quatrain is about another **Araxes**. He takes it to mean the Battle of Lepanto fought in the Gulf of Corinth in 1571, 16 years after this quatrain was published. The naval battle took place off Cape Papa, then known as Cape Araxum. It was there that Don Juan of Austria nearly destroyed the formidable fleet Suleiman had built during his lifetime. Upon the Sultan's death in 1566 it was handed over to his less-than-magnificent heir, Selin II. The soused son of Suleiman was also known as Selin the Sot.

3 Q32

Le grand Jepulchre du peuple Aquitanique,	**The great tomb of the people of Aquitaine,**
S'approchera aupres de la Tofcane:	**Will approach from the direction of Tuscany:**
Quand Mars Jera pres du coing Germanique,	**When Mars will be near the corner of Germany,**
Et au terroir de la gent Mantuane.	**And in the land of the people of Mantua.**

The military prowess of the Gascons in two different centuries is the subject of this quatrain. In the summer of 1557 the Gascon regiments were sent from Corsica to fight on the approaches to Rome under the command of François de Guise and Montluc. For line 3, Leoni supplies the Duke of Savoy's attempt to reconquer Mariembourg. For line 4, Jaubert tells us that the Duke of Ferrara had sent his son, Alfonso d'Este, to invade Mantua around the same time.

These locales do not limit us to a contemporary vision alone. Aquitaine signifies the warriors of Gascony. If we follow them down the dusty roads of Italy in the 1790s we see their bucklers, rapiers, and love of king replaced by a musket and bayonet and devotion to a shaggy general named Bonaparte. They are framed in parade formation, witnessing the surrender of General Würmser's 16,000 Austrians at Mantua. At the same time, the final two lines suggest other Gascons following the French Revolutionary War's other great general, Jean Victor Moreau, leading the Army of the Moselle across the Rhine in a renewed German campaign.

3 Q33

En la cité où le loup entrera,	*In the city where the wolf will enter,*
Bien pres de là les ennemis feront:	*Very near from there will be the*
Copie eftrange grand pays gaftera,	*enemy:*
Aux murs[1] & Alpes les amis pafferont.	*Foreign force, a great country will be*
	despoiled,
	At the walls and Alps the friends will
	pass.

[1]Old French borders, frontiers, or walls.

Hitler is the **wolf** seen in Paris after its fall in 1940. The great country is France, despoiled by the Nazis. But this time the final line might promise victory. The rest has Maginot Line possibilities. The key is divining who the **friends** are. I believe this quatrain could imply the ultimate success of the advance into Lorraine by American forces of Patton's Third Army alongside de Lattre de Tassigny's French forces in late 1944. By the spring of 1945 the American and French **friends** would **pass** the silent **walls** of the Maginot Line to plunge deep into Nazi Germany and seize final victory.

See Index: "Wolf" as double pun for Fascist Italy, or Hitler.

3 Q34

Quand le deffaut du Soleil lors fera	*When the eclipse of the Sun then will*
Sur le plain iour le monftre[1] fera veu:	*be*
Tout autrement on l'interpretera,	*The divine omen will be seen in the*
Cherté n'a garde nul n'y aura pourueu.	*plain daylight:*
	Quite otherwise will one interpret it,
	High price unguarded, none will have
	provided for it.

[1]Latin *monstrum* = divine omen, strange thing, scourge.

A total eclipse will occur over England, France, eastern Europe, and Turkey on 11 August 1999. It may be the same one mentioned in the Epistle and in other quatrains that heralds either Armageddon or a new millennium of peace. One cannot rule out that this *monstre* is some kind of extraterrestrial contact that signals doomsday for many of our spiritual dogmas and nationalistic ideas by proving once and for all that we are not alone in the cosmos. The solar eclipse expected in 2034 could be a divine omen of future economic collapse induced by the dog days of the greenhouse effect.

Quatrain Indexing Date: Q34 = 2034, when a total eclipse is expected on 20 March, just prior to the sun's transit from Pisces to Aries (the sign of wars, droughts, heat, or magical transformation).

3 Q35

Du plus profond de l'occident d'Europe,
De pauures gens vn jeune enfant naiftra:
Qui par fa langue feduira grande troupe,
Son bruit au regne d'Orient plus croiftra.

From the deepest part of Western
   Europe
A young child will be born to poor
   people:
Who by his speech will seduce a great
   multitude,
His reputation will increase in the
   Kingdom of the East.

Born in Braunau, Austria, Adolf Hitler – the child of a poor customs official – was destined to seduce the entire German nation through eloquent lies and half-truths. Imperial Japan (**the Kingdom of the East**) would join his Axis Alliance during World War II.

Quatrain Indexing Date: Q35 = 1935. A near miss for Germany and Japan's signing the Anti-Comintern Pact in 1936, a joint declaration that they would support each other in their opposition to international communism. This agreement led to Japan's induction into the Tripartite or Axis Alliance.

3 Q36

Enfeuely non mort apopletique,
Sera trouué auoir les mains mangees:
Quand la cité damnera l'heretique,
Qu'auoit leurs loix fe leur fembloit
   changees.

Put in a shroud not dead [but]
   comatose,
He will be found to have his hands
   [powers] eaten:
When the city will damn the heretic,
He who, it seemed to them, had
   changed their laws.

On face value this describes a comatose heretic mistaken for dead, but it works better as a poetic description of the aged general Pétain, the French hero of World War I who became the president of Vichy and France's greatest traitor in World War II. The key is hiding in the **hands**. The French *main* also means **powers**. When Hitler decided to occupy Vichy, Pétain's powers were gobbled up, as it were, by the Gestapo and German martial law. The dry and dour octogenarian may have gone rapidly senile under the pressure. The funeral shroud is figurative for the gathering gloom around him and his unpopular and collaborationist Vichy government as the war turned against Hitler. After the war Pétain would be damned as a political and national **heretic**. The final line returns to 1940 and the early days of Vichy after the defeat of France by the Germans. Pétain's administration of the unoccupied half of France began with a sense of deep relief. The paternal old man pledged to heal the country and created initial reforms that helped France far more than those of the stagnant Third Republic, which was blamed for the fall of France.

3 Q37

Auant l'aſſaut l'oraiſon prononcee,
Milan prins d'aigle par embuſches deceuez:
Muraille antique par canons enfoncee,
Par feu & ſang à mercy peu receus.

Before the assault the speech is
  delivered,
Milan taken by the eagle through
  delusive ambush:
Ancient rampart broken down by
  canons,
By fire and blood few receiving mercy.

We can only wonder if Nostradamus heard Napoleon Bonaparte make his now-famous first address to his motley new command, the Army of Italy: "Soldiers, you are ill-fed and half naked. The government owes you much, but it can do nothing for you. Your patience, your courage, do honor to you, but obtain for you neither advantage nor glory. I am going to lead you to the most fertile plains in the world; you will find there great cities, rich provinces; you will find there honor, glory and wealth. Soldiers of Italy, will you be wanting in courage?"

Apparently not. Their victories and exertions (as well as their plundering of Italian cities and their artworks) are legend. Napoleon's soldiers stormed Milan on 15 May 1796, and again on 2 June 1800.

3 Q38

La gent Gauloiſe & nation eſtrange,
Outre les monts, morts prins & profligez:
Au mois contraire & proche de vendange,
Par les Seigneurs en accord redigez.

The Gallic people and a foreign nation,
Beyond the mountains, dead,
  captured and killed:
By the contrary month and near the
  vintage time,
Through the Lords an accord is
  drawn up.

The month contrary to or opposite September (the month of the wine harvest) is March. Since in Provence harvest time might continue into October we can also include part of April. March 1559 ended with Pope Paul IV and Philip II of Spain compelling Henry II of France to sign the treaty of Cateau-Cambrésis (3 April), ending decades of war started by Charles V and the French over domination of Italy.

3 Q39

Les ſept en trois mois en concorde,
Pour ſubjuguer des Alpes Apennines:
Mais la tempeſte & Ligure[1] couarde,
Les profligent en ſubites ruines.

The seven in three months in
  agreement,
For subjugating the Apennine Alps:
But the tempest and Ligurian coward,
Destroys them in sudden ruins.

[1]Provencal ligur = leaguer; or abbreviation of Ligurien = Ligurian.

Nostradamus sees seven rulers in agreement on how to slice up Italian territory. Their arrangements are foiled by a cowardly Genoese (**Ligurian**) in their midst. Two Holy **Ligurian** Leagues were formed in the 16th century, the first in 1510, and a second 21 years after this quatrain was published.

Fontbrune applies **Ligurian coward** in a roundabout way to the Kingdom of Piedmont, which was betrayed by the cowardice of the Sardinian army which surrendered to Napoleon at Cherasco on 29 April 1796. Three months and three days later the Austrian army was defeated by Hoche and Moreau at the Battle of Löwen on 18 April 1797. This brought an end to hostilities in Italy among the **seven** armies of the Coalition against France.

A future scenario would have the **seven** be the Big Seven economic powerhouses of the developed world coming to the aid of Italy in the 21st century. The Ligurian region of north-western Italy will suffer some social or economic collapse. Perhaps this is caused by the great floods in that region foreseen elsewhere in the prophecies, caused by climate gone haywire from global warming. The coward in this case is a Genovese terrorist planting a bomb set to go off inside the meeting place of the Big Seven leaders (**destroys them in sudden ruins**).

3 q40

Le grand theatre ſe viendra ſe redreſſer,	**The great theater will come to be**
Les dez iettez & les rets ia tendus:	**made straight once more,**
Trop le premier en glaz[1] viendra laſſer,	**The dice thrown and the net already**
Par arcs proſtrais[2] de long temps ia fendus.	**stretched:**
	The premier person in tolling the
	death knell will become too
	fatigued,
	Laid low already for a long time by
	cleaved arches.

[1]Old French *glas* = knell, passing-bell, tolling; (figurative) tolling the death knell.
[2]Latin *prostratus* = overturned, ruined, destroyed.

I'll be very brief. This is a finely detailed obscurity.

3 q41

Boſſu[1] ſera eſleu par le conſeil,	**A crooked one will be elected by the**
Plus hideux monſtre en terre n'apperceu,	**council,**
Le coup voulant creuera l'œil,	**A more hideous monster not seen on**
Le traiſtre au Roy pour fidelle receu.	**earth,**
	The flying shot [or the desired blow]
	will pierce his eye,
	The traitor to the King received as
	faithful.

[1]Usually *hunchback* but in this case it is applied more poetically for a man's soul and character rather than his physical features.

The prophet's Catholic leanings paint the Huguenot Prince Louis de Condé as the **monster**. His description of Condé as a *bossu* (hunchback) may be intended for his crooked and scheming soul, since he was by all accounts a handsome figure of a man. Condé was shot dead by a soldier named Montesquiou at the battle of Jarnac in 1569 (14 years after this quatrain was published). Montesquiou discharged his pistol at Condé while the prince was pinned to the ground by his fallen horse. More than once Condé had negotiated himself out of execution for plots against Valois kings. He was forgiven by Francis II for his part in the Conspiracy of Amboise, and later pardoned with other Huguenot leaders by Charles IX for his part in the first War of Religion. But Condé was never faithful to the Catholic Valois.

3 Q42

L'enfant naiſtra à deux dents en la gorge,	**The infant will be born with two teeth in his throat [or mouth],**
Pierres en Tuſcie par pluye tomberont:	**Stones in Tuscany will tumble down with the rain:**
Peu d'ans apres ne ſera bled ni orge,	**A few years after, there will be neither wheat nor barley,**
Pour ſaouler ceux qui de faim failliront.	**For filling the stomach of those who will yield to famine.**

Here is another reference to a child born with two teeth, as in 2 Q7. It has been alleged that Louis XIV was born with two teeth already emerging from his gums. A severe famine is implied as well, not unlike in 2 Q7, but the Louis XIV/Man in the Iron Mask theme doesn't work so well here. There were no apocalyptic famines in Tuscany at any time during Louis' long 72-year reign, let alone any that could have been caused by a volcanic eruption (**stones . . . will tumble down with the rain**); there was, however, a significant eruption of Mt Etna in Sicily, which killed 20,000 people in 1669 (the 23rd year of Louis' reign). Perhaps Nostradamus misinterpreted Tuscany for Sicily. Nevertheless, a famine-dealing eruption covering the verdant fields and hills of Tuscany under several feet of ash could be waiting ahead in the future.

3 Q43

Gens d'alentour de Tarn Loth, & *Garonne,*	**People from around the Tarn, Lot and Garonne,**
Gardez les monts Apennines paſſer:	**Guard yourselves when passing the Apennine mountains:**
Voſtre tombeau pres de Rome & *d'Anconne,*	**Your grave near Rome and Ancona,**
Le noir poil creſpe fera trophee dreſſer.	**The black frizzled beard will set up a monument to victory.**

According to Le Pelletier, the Vatican recruited men from south-west France for their regiment of Papal Zouaves. The men of the Lot and Tarn river regions and those dwelling along the banks of the Garonne made the long journey to the papal states (represented here by Ancona). They would don the fez caps and baggy breeches of the exotic Zouave uniform and advance from Rome with the papal army over the Apennine mountains to seek and destroy the forces of the curly-black-bearded King Victor Emmanuel of the emergent Italian state. Battle was joined a few miles south of Ancona at Castelfidardo, where the papal army was routed and the Zouaves nearly annihilated.

3 Q44

Quand l'animal à l'homme domeſtique,	When the animal [is] tamed by man,
Apres grands peines & ſauts viendra parler,	After great efforts and difficulty, begins to speak,
De fouldre à vierge ſera ſi malefique,	The lightning so harmful to the rod,
De terre prinſe & ſuſpendue en l'air.	Will be taken from earth and suspended in the air.

Nostradamus tries his bewildered best to describe the 20th century's amazing inventions. The vision of cars, planes, and the mysterious powers of nature harnessed for our daily use strain his vocabulary and 16th-century conception. To him, the disembodied voice of mankind on the air waves is a tamed animal. The sights we pay little attention to, such as power lines, microwave transmitters, and even the future telecommunications media beyond our own time, must have fascinated him.

3 Q45

Les cinq eſtranges entrez dedans le temple	The five strangers entered in the temple,
Leur ſang viendra la terre prophaner:	Their blood will come to profane the land:
Aux Tholouſains ſera bien dur exemple,	To the Toulousans it will be a very harsh example,
D'vn qui viendra ſes loix exterminer.	Of one who will come to exterminate their laws.

Five persons enter the sanctuary in one of Toulouse's churches. They are killed by their pursuers, who will be tyrannizing Toulouse. The most likely candidates are Huguenots massacred by Catholics in the month following the St Bartholomew's Day massacre in August 1572. A second candidate would be an atrocity during the French Revolution. Toulouse was relatively quiet during this time. *The Chronicle of the French Revolution* mentions only one incident for 17 April 1791: three people were killed in clashes between patriots and troops of the Royalist St Barthélemy.

3 Q46

Le ciel (de Plancus la cité)[1] nous prefage,
Par clers infignes & par eftoilles fixes:
Que de fon change fubit s'aproche l'aage,
Ne pour fon bien ne pour fes malefices.

The sky (concerning Lyons) we presage,
Through clear signs and by fixed stars:
Suddenly the age of change approaches,
Neither for its good, nor for its evils.

[1]Lyons, founded by Lucius Manatius Plancus in 43 BC.

The last line hints that the Aquarian Age will be a time of true religious revolution, from Piscean-Age morality to the transmorality of the Aquarian Age (**neither for its good, nor for its evils**). In the next few hundred years Lyons and the world at large may experience a quantum leap in consciousness that could be called the revolution of the middle way – in which the only evil is unconscious behavior, the only good – awareness.

Astrological Time Window

The transit of Jupiter in Aquarius (January 1997) signals the beginning of the fixed-signed Aquarian Age. By January 1998, Jupiter, Uranus, and Neptune will be in the sign of Aquarius.

3 Q47

Le vieux monarque dechaffé de fon regne,
Aux Orients fon fecours ira querre:[1]
Pour peur des croix ploiera fon enfeigne,
En Mitylene ira par port & par terre.

The old monarch expelled from his realm,
Will go to the Orientals to seek assistance:
For fear of the crosses he will fold his standard,
To the Island of Lesbos he will go through port and by land.

[1]Old French for to look for, ask.

Take your pick of past, present, or future slants for an expelled Western leader who goes to the Asian (Middle-Eastern) camp for assistance. Fontbrune proposes the fall of the French state in World War II, with the **old monarch** Pétain on his departure east for the Nazi prison of Sigmaringen. But for this to work we must turn Mitylene into "island of mussels" rather than stay with the accepted Aegean island of Lesbos. This allows us to place Pétain in prison on the island of Yeu after the war. *Mitulus* is Latin for "mussel"; the main activity on the island is mussel- and shellfish-gathering. But what isn't noted is that Lesbos, which is situated much closer to the Turkish Orient, no doubt received the identical moniker for the same pastime.

3 Q48

Sept cens captifs eſtachez rudement,	**Seven hundred captives roughly**
Pour le moitié meurtrir, donné le ſort:	**bound,**
Le proche eſpoir viendra ſi promptement,	**For the half to be murdered, lots are**
Mais non ſi toſt qu'vne quinzieſme mort.	**drawn:**
	The approaching hope will come very
	promptly,
	But not so soon enough for fifteen
	dead.

The 700 captives could have met their misfortune any time after 1555. The number reminds me of the 700 PLO captives in Israeli prisons who were released in 1985 in a hostage switch for the passengers of a TWA airliner hijacked between Rome and Athens and diverted to Beirut by Amal militiamen. There were fatalities – but not fifteen. One off-duty US Navy Seal was chosen to be murdered by the terrorists after his armed service card and other papers were **drawn** for identification.

3 Q49

Regne Gaulois tu ſeras bien changé,	**French realm you will be greatly**
En lieu eſtrange eſt tranſlaté l'empire:	**changed,**
En autres mœurs & loix ſeras rangé,	**To a foreign place, the Empire is**
Roan, & Chartres te feront bien du pire.	**transferred:**
	With other morals and laws will you
	be governed,
	Rouen and Chartres will do their very
	worst to you.

Line 1 launches us towards a modern application as early as the fall of the Second Empire (1870), or later with the fall of France in 1940. In either case it is the *foreign* Germans to whom *the Empire is transferred*. The first switch of empires came as a consequence of France's defeat in the Franco-Prussian War. This allowed the German states to unite, forming the Second German Reich. The second transferal was made when the Third German Reich defeated France and placed her colonial empire under the puppet government of Vichy. Line 3 is another testament to the great changes in French behavior and civilization that must have confounded Nostradamus. Certainly Rouen was the scene of terrible fighting and destruction during 1940. In the end **Rouen and Chartres** may represent the region of Normandy in general, and therefore a correct interpretation of line 4 focuses on the outcome of the D-Day landings and the great summer land battles between the Allies and German Army Group B. By late August 1944 the Allied breakout from Normandy advanced on a wide front between Rouen and Chartres.

3 Q50

La republique de la grande cité,	The republic of the great city,
A grand rigueur¹ ne voudra confentir:	To the great austerity will not consent:
Roy fortir hors par trompette cité,	King to come forth summoned by
L'efchelle au mur, la cité repentir.	[the] trumpet's call,
	The ladder at the wall – the city
	repents.

¹Latin *rigor*= roughness, severity.

We may have three layers of a compound prophecy here. Paris, at least in Nostradamus' royalist point of view, will repent three times for its fatal attraction to Republican extremism.

The first repentance comes in 1588, when the leaders of the capital's 16 districts lead a popular rebellion against Henry III called the Day of the Barricades. The ultra-Catholic rebels quickly constructed barricades throughout the Left Bank districts, forcing the king's Swiss Guards and other units to retreat. According to our royalist prophet, the citizens of Paris suffer a terrible siege (**ladder at the wall**) laid by Henry IV in 1589 as a punishment for supporting the anti-royalist and proto-republican communards of the Sixteen.

Paris suffers a second bout of republican extremism during the French Revolution. The people rebel against the austerities and hardships forced upon them by the Ancien Regime. Republicanism devours thousands. Napoleon becomes dictator of the French, and after 2 million Frenchmen die (including a great number of Parisians), the trumpet calls for the return of the Bourbon monarchy. Paris repents again, suffering battles on its outskirts in 1814 plus two occupations by coalition forces in 1814 and in 1815 after they defeat Napoleon a second time.

The third brush with republicanism is the most extreme. The year 1871 opens with Paris falling in a siege by the Germans. This is precipitated by the defeat of a second Napoleonic dictator and a second empire spawned by a republican revolution in 1848. The fall of Napoleon III sees the new Third Republic agree to a dishonorable peace with the Second German Reich. Republicans in Paris blame the monarchist parliamentarians dominating the new government for the disagreeable terms, and form an independent republican government known as the Commune of Paris. French forces invade Paris and fight pitched battles with the Communards at the barricades in what has been called the Bloody Week (21–28 May 1871). Before the Communards were overwhelmed, they murdered their hostages, including the archbishop of Paris, and set fire to the Tuileries Palace, city hall, Palace of Justice and many other prominent buildings. Repentance came to the Parisians in the form of 17,000 summary executions, bringing the total death count to 30,000 people.

Quatrain Indexing Date: Q50 is a near miss for December 1851, when Louis Bonaparte (later Napoleon III) engineers a coup overthrowing the Third Republic. The following year sees him crown himself Napoleon III and establish the Second French Empire.

3 Q51

Paris coniure vn grand meurtre commettre,	**Paris conspires to commit a great**
Blois[1] le fera fortir en plain effect:	**murder,**
Ceux d'Orleans voudront leur chef	**Blois will ensure that it is fully**
remettre,	**carried out:**
Angiers, Troye, Langres leur feront vn	**The people of Orleans will want to**
meffait.	**replace their leader,**
	Angers, Troyes and Langres will do
	them a disservice.

[1]Château de Blois: (figurative) Henry III.

In two prophecies (this one and 1 Q85), Nostradamus describes with an economy of words the fateful murder of the two Guise brothers by Henry III and the repercussions of this act.

Paris conspires to commit a great murder. It is at the Louvre in Paris that Henry III reveals to his ministers his desire to kill Guise by feigning friendship and luring him to the Château Blois for a meeting with the Estates-General, France's parliament.

Blois will ensure that it is fully carried out. Blois is a double allusion – to Henry III and also to the place where the King's Mignons, his homosexual lovers and bodyguards, will inflict multiple stab wounds on Guise in his bedchamber on 23 December 1588.

The people of Orleans will want to replace their leader. D'Entraques, the leader Henry III sent to replace Guise as Governor of Orleans, met open rebellion on his arrival.

Angers, Troyes and Langres will do them a disservice. Nostradamus names the three pro-Huguenot towns that were scenes of the Catholic League's defeats.

Please turn to 1 Q85 for part two of this prophecy.

3 Q52

En la campaigne fera fi longue pluye,	**In the campaign there will be a very**
Et en la Pouille fi grande ficcité:	**long rain,**
Coq verra l'Aigle, l'æfle mal accomplie,	**And in Apulia a great drought:**
Par Lyon mife fera en extremité.	**Cock will see the Eagle, the wing ill**
	accomplished,
	By [the Lion] will it be put to the
	brink [or to the extreme].

Line 1 begins with a **campaign** vexed by bad weather, not the Italian province of Campania. No clear record exists of a notable drought in Italy during any of Napoleon's Italian campaigns. But it is a fact that the soldiers of his first Spanish campaign in 1808 suffered from extreme weather, especially when crossing numerous mountain passes. Napoleon made a fatal strategic error by not solidifying his hold on Spain in 1808 and instead turning his attention eastward to Austria and later Russia, relegating the Spanish theater (**wing**) of his operations to ill-conceived campaigns of his subordinates. Napoleon would lose his empire because he overextended himself in Spain and failed to check the successful campaigns of the British expedition (**the Lion**). The French *extremité* could be a play on the Spanish province Extremadura and acts as a good poetic description of the extreme brutality of the guerrilla warfare and lack of adequate supplies endured by the French in Spain.

3 Q53

Quand le plus grand emportera le pris,	**When the greatest one carries off the prize,**
De Nuremberg, d'Aufpourg, & ceux de Bafle	**Of Nuremberg, of Augsburg, and those of Basel:**
Par Agrippine[1] chef Frankfort repris,	**Frankfurt retaken by the leader of Cologne,**
Trauerferont par Flamant iufqu'eu Gale.	**He will go through Flanders right into France.**

[1]Latin *Colonia Agrippina* = Cologne.

Here is a sweeping overview of Hitler's political and military successes. Line 1 refers to his imperious performance before the Nuremberg rallies in 1933–34. **Augsburg**, **Frankfurt**, and **Cologne** (Köln) each act as a synecdoche for Hitler's seizure of the Rhineland in 1936. We can even speculate whether **Basel** is a synecdoche for a future trend never followed – a union of Swiss Germany with Hitler. Switzerland had a number of indigenous pro-Nazi movements. Hitler called the neutral country "an anachronism" and the Swiss people "renegade Germans." Had the war progressed in his favor, plans to incorporate Switzerland into the greater Reich might have been carried out. During the seizure of the Rhineland Hitler correctly concluded that the French didn't have the stomach to fight another war. He therefore invaded Poland with little fear that 45 French divisions stationed on his western borders near the Siegfried Line would dare attack him in the rear.

Long before the Nuremberg rallies sanctified the cult of Hitler, the French seer gives the impression that he could augur its catastrophic results, right down to the Panzer maneuvers. The first stage of Hitler's invasion of France started on 10 May 1940, with an western invasion of Holland and Belgium (**Flanders**) all the way to the French Channel coast at the Pas de Calais.

3 Q54

L'vn des plus grans fuira aux Eſpaignes,	**One of the greatest men will flee to Spain,**
Qu'en longue playe apres viendra ſaigner:	**Which will thereafter come to bleed from a long wound:**
Paſſant copies[1] par les hautes montaignes,	**Armies passing over the high mountains,**
Deuaſtant tout & puis en paix regner.	**Devastating all and then in peace to reign.**

[1]Latin *copia* = army, force.

Traditionally this can be applied to any invasion of Spain from France via the Pyrenees. The two major invasions occurred 1703–13 and 1808–13. Smaller incursions were made in the 1640s, 1794–95 and 1822.

Nostradamians of the latter-half of the 20th century believe the great one fleeing to Spain is General Francisco Franco. In 1936 he was exiled to the post of military governor of the Canary Islands by the socialist coalition ruling Spain. He would later fly back to Spain (**flee**) as the leader of a Nationalist insurrection against the Madrid government and form a military junta at Burgos. Once he had returned, the **long wound** of the Spanish Civil War raged over the mountainous Spanish countryside for the next three years, killing 600,000. The new Spanish dictator would rule a devastated and impoverished land and keep Spain out of World War II by declaring her neutrality.

3 Q55

En l'an qu'vn œil en France regnera,	**In the year that France has a one-eyed king,**
La court ſera à vn bien facheux trouble:	**The court will be in very great trouble:**
Le grand de Bloys ſon amy tuera,	**The great man from Blois will kill his friend,**
Le regne mis en mal & doubte double.	**The kingdom put into difficulty and double doubt.**

Line 1 is a descriptive dating for 1559, the pivotal year in French history when Henry II was on his deathbed, his left eye destroyed by the splintered shaft of the Comte de Montgomery (See 1 Q35). His premature death left the French court in chaos. The tenuous arrangement of Protestant and Catholic princes could not survive for long, and four decades of war lay ahead. In the second two lines Nostradamus jumps ahead to 1588, to describe the coming power struggle for the French throne. The dead king's third son, Henry III (*the great man from Blois*), will convene a meeting of the Estates-General in that year. There he will assassinate his chief rival, Duke Henry de Guise, by first feigning reconciliation with his old friend. The assassination splits the Catholic alliance in two (*double doubt*) and a three-way civil war ensues between Huguenots, the Catholic royalists, and the Catholic League.

3 Q56

Montauban, Nifmes, Auignon & Befier,	Montauban, Nîmes, Avignon and Béziers,
Pefte tonnerre & grefle à fin de Mars:	Plague, thunder and hail at the end of March:
De Paris pont, Lyon mur, Montpellier,	Of Paris bridge, Lyons wall, Montpellier,
Depuis fix cens & fept vingts trois pars.	Since six hundreds and seven twenties [score] three pairs.

War comes to southern France with all the iron **hail**, artillery **thunder**, and resulting plagues. This occurs at the end of some month of March in the future, or, as the line indicates, "in the wake" or "at the end of war." There are several possible readings for the date in line 4: 746 can become 1746, or you can count 746 years after 1555 to reach AD 2301. You can also take it as *six hundred and seven score three pairs*. This gives you 1653, or you can add 653 years to 1555, to get AD 2208.

We know of only one rough historical correlation. The Fronde rebellion in France was crushed in 1653 when Cardinal Mazarin returned to Paris after his exile the previous year. But none of the fighting took place in the towns and regions listed here. In the year 1746 France did fight wars in the Netherlands, but that far land is too far removed from the Rhône valley, Languedoc, and the French Riviera to be a link. Either that leaves a future event or this is a botched prophecy.

3 Q57

Sept fois changer verrez gent Britannique,	Seven times you will see the British nation change,
Taintz en fang en deux cens nonante an:	Dyed [or stained] in blood for two hundred ninety years.
Franche non point par appuy Germanique,	Not at all free from Germania's influence,
Aries doubt fon pole Baftarnan.[1]	Aries doubts the protector of Poland.

[1]Latin *Bastarnae* = the Bastarnians (inhabitants of southern Poland and the Ukraine).

The rise and fall of the British Empire is foretold in four brief lines that trace seven changes in royal blood over 290 years.

1. *Elizabeth I* (1558–1603)
Elizabeth I was the last Tudor monarch. On her death the throne passed to James I of the House of Stuart.

2. *Oliver Cromwell* (1649–1658)
The English Civil War brings bloody, violent change. The word *taintz* can mean **dyed**, indicating the famous red coats worn by English soldiers throughout the days of the empire. The coats were first seen on the backs of Cromwell's soldiers in the New Model Army, the restructured military force that brought him victory and later enforced his dictatorship as Protector of England. I see a second meaning to *tainz*. In a manner of speaking Charles I's defeat destined him to *stain* the headsman's block with his blood.

3. *Charles II* (1660–1685)
The ascension of Charles II to the throne in 1660 restores the royal House of Stuart.

4. *William III* (1689–1702)
The Glorious Revolution of 1688 sees William III of Friesland (Orange) take over the throne with his Stuart wife Mary (1689–1694).

5. *Anne* (1702–1714)
The House of Stuart continues with Queen Anne's ascent to the throne in 1702.

6. *George I* (1714–1727)
With the arrival of George I and the House of Hanover in 1714, German bluebloods take the throne warmed by Queen Anne.

7. *Adolf Hitler* (1933–1945)
Line 4 presages an end to royal blood-power from a more malevolent German influence. It foretells the World War II bloodbath that was set off when Hitler (Aries = god of war) ignored Britain's threat to go to war if the Nazis invaded Poland. Hitler also saw himself as the protector or overlord of the resource-rich Ukraine region. So obsessed was he with that prize that during Operation Barbarossa he made a strategic change in mid-campaign that lost him the war. Rather than take Moscow when it was vulnerable and ready to fall, he moved Army Group Center south to take the Ukraine region, thereby losing one month of good weather. After that his armies were stalled first by mud and later by blizzards as they faced a vastly reinforced Moscow salient.

Astrological Time Window

Aries is the god of war, but indicated here is the German Reich of Adolf Hitler, who was born on an Aries/Taurus cusp.

Quatrain Indexing Date: Q58 = 1958. The British Empire, for all intents and purposes, had ended by the late 1950s/early 1960s.

3 Q58

Aupres du Rhin des Montaignes Noriques,[1]
Naiſtra vn grand de gens trop tard venu:
Qui defendra Saurome[2] & Pannoniques,[3]
Qu'on ne ſçaura qu'il ſera deuenu.

Near the Rhine from the Noricum
   Mountains [Austria],
Will be born a great one of the people
   come too late:
One who will defend the lands of
   European Russia and the
   Hungarians,
One will not know what became of
   him.

[1]Latin *Noricum* = ancient Roman province, modern-day Austria.
[2]Latin *Sauromatia* = Sarmatia, a general name given by the ancient Romans to a vast area west of Scythia, extending from Europe to Asia, between the Baltic and Caspian Seas, including all of European Russia, Greater Lithuania and Poland.
[3]Latin *Pannonicus* = of the Pannonians, modern Hungarians.

Adolf Hitler was born in Braunau, Austria which, as an ancient Roman province, had once been called Noricum. Hitler believed he was Germany's savior. He arrived **too late** to make his chosen people, the "Aryan" Germans, aware of how abusive the Treaty of Versailles was to the Fatherland after its defeat in World War I. Hitler declared himself the Protector of Poland in 1939. His "protection" became an excuse to invade her, thus triggering World War II. The Hungarians (*Pannoniques*) were allied to Germany during the war. He would later meet disaster by forcing his generals to defend every foot of his conquests in European Russia, Hungary, and the rest of eastern Europe.

Mystery still surrounds the death of Hitler. For over 50 years after his suicide the Soviet KGB kept a secret Hitler Archive – File I-G-23, also known as the Operation Myth File. The Russians allowed investigative reporters Ada Petrova and Peter Watson to report its secrets in their book *The Death of Hitler* (W.W. Norton). It seems that Stalin became obsessed with confirming that Hitler's body had been positively identified because he wanted to be absolutely sure the Führer had not escaped punishment. There were disturbing rumors that Hitler had escaped Berlin in a plane or submarine and was still at large. Even when the KGB collected enough objective evidence to disprove this, it was decided to keep the Myth File secret and hold it in reserve just in case some pretender surfaced and claimed to be Hitler. Petrova and Watson found many surprising new details: the Führer's body and those of his mistress, Eva Braun, Josef and Magda Goebbels, and the Goebbels' children were buried in a secret gravesite in Magdeburg, East Germany, until 1970, when they were disinterred and cremated. The secret burial site and cremations were efforts by the Soviets to prevent their bones from becoming a rallying point for future neo-Nazi movements. Now all that remains of Hitler's corpse are a few skull fragments in the KGB file, one piece displaying the bullet hole from his suicide weapon.

3 Q59

Barbare empire par le tiers vſurpé,
Le plus grand part de ſon ſang mettre à
   mort:
Par mort ſenile par luy le quart frappé,
Pour peur que ſang par le ſang ne ſoit mort.

Barbarian empire usurped by the
   third,
The larger part of kindred he will put
   to death:
Through senile death the fourth
   stricken by him,
For fear that blood through the race
   not be stilled.

Théodore Bouys (1806) and Cheetham (1989) overlook the ticklish issue of portraying Bourbons as **barbarian**(s) – a label usually given to the Ottoman Turks – and cite this one for the French Revolution and the Third Estate. Leoni's view (1961) is more likely – that the prophecy is "entirely for Turkey: a third son will seize the throne in a palace coup, putting many of his brothers to death, in the best Ottoman tradition."

The closest historical match would be the Ottoman Civil War of 1559, four years after Nostradamus published this quatrain. Sultan Suleiman the Magnificent had three sons and a less than magnificent private life. Strong and invincible in war, he was easily influenced by the petty jealousies and intrigues of his harem, particularly those of his favorite wife, Roxelana. She had persuaded him to believe the falsehood that his eldest son Mustafa was plotting to take the throne. He had this most promising son from another wife beheaded in 1553. This left Roxelana's two sons, Selim and Bayazid, who upon her death in 1559 became fierce rivals. Bayazid raised an army to oppose Selim, whom Suleiman favored, but was defeated at the Battle of Konya. Suleiman later had him executed, leaving Selim the Sot heir to the Empire: **Barbarian** (Arab) **empire usurped by the third** [son]. Suleiman himself is the **fourth** stricken, by old age (**senile death**). The **him** of line 3 is unclear, since Nostradamus' grammar is purposefully scrambled. The **larger part** of Suleiman's male progeny are indeed put to death, leaving Selim, a mediocrity, as sole, sottish survivor. Perhaps Selim's dullness made Suleiman's guilt more excruciating and hastened his death in 1566.

Quatrain Indexing Date: Q59 = 1559! Right on target.

3 Q60

Par toute Afie[1] grande profcription,	Throughout Asia great prohibiting of

Par toute Afie[1] grande profcription,
Mefme en Myfie,[2] Lyfie,[2] & Pamphylie:[2]
Sang verfera par abfolution,
D'vn ieune noir remply de felonnie.

Throughout Asia great prohibiting of
outlaws.
Even in Mystia, Lycia and
Pamphilia:
Blood will flow because of absolving,
A young dark man filled with
evildoing.

[1]Afie = either Asia (China) or Asia Minor (Turkey).
[2]South central Turkey, Iran and Iraq. Together they give us modern Kurdistan.

In an interview held after Abu Abbas' successful attack on the Italian pleasure cruiser *Achille Lauro* in 1985, Abu Nidal redefined himself as well as his organization as a father (*abu*) of evil. He may be remembered yet as the King of Terrorism, or in other prophetic words of Nostradamus, the great **King of Terror** (10 Q72), the infernal God "Baal" Hammon (3 Q63). His operatives have secret bases in all the areas of the Middle East where that terrible ancient god had dominion. Asia Minor hosted many terrorist events during the Gulf War. Iraq and Iran provide the Abu Nidal organization with bases. The growing link between terrorist groups and the Kurdish war for independence against Turkey, Iraq, and Iran is also implied. The *young dark man* of evil could be Abu Nidal himself (if he is still alive) or one of his band of 100 to 200 young hit men.

A **great prohibiting of outlaws** could also describe a return to the harsher laws of the Islamic *Sharia* in the Middle East after a successful spread of the Islamic Revolution in the near future.

Asia could signify more than Asia Minor (Turkey) and hint at modern China, where many thousands of felons are annually marched out into fields or sports stadiums and publicly shot or hanged.

3 Q61

La grande bande & fecte crucigere,[1]
Se dreffera en Mefopotamie:
Du proche fleuue compagnie legere,
Que telle loy tiendra pour ennemie.

The great host and sect of the cross
[or the crusaders],
Will be massed in Mesopotamia:
Of the nearby river the fast company,
That such law will hold for the
enemy.

[1]Latin *crux-gerens* = cross-bearing: ie crusaders.

It could be said that Operation Desert Storm was the most recent Crusade of Christian armies in the Middle East; moreover, it starred the largest cast of Christian soldiers ever to fight in **Mesopotamia** in the 20th or any other century. Rick Atkinson in his book *Crusade: The Untold Story of the Gulf War* estimates that the West sent 4,000 tanks, 150 ships, and 600,000 soldiers (the vast majority from the Christian nations). The **nearby river** is the Euphrates during the rapid attack by the 101st Airborne Division cutting across Highway 8 next to the river. This action effectively cut Saddam Hussein's supply line to Kuwait during the 100-hour ground war. The final line may take us into the near future if we can define just which **law** holds in Iraq: Is it the brutal **law** of Saddam Hussein, or the sanctions of the United Nations? One could argue that the swiftness of the Allied encircling maneuver spearheaded by the 101st Airborne helped bring the conflict to an end before Saddam Hussein's Republican Guard divisions were destroyed. After the peace, he could use these relatively intact elite units to tighten his hold on Iraq.

3 Q62

Proche del duero par mer Cyrrene cloſe,[1]	**Near the Douro by the Bay of Biscay,**
Viendra perſer les grands monts Pyrenées:	**He will come to pierce the great**
La main plus courte & ſa percee gloze,	**mountains of the Pyrenees:**
A Carcaſſonne conduira ſes menées.	**The [power] shorter and his rabble,**
	To Carcassonne [he] will conduct his
	plots.

[1]*Cyrrene cloſe* or *percee gloze* (old French *perce* = stake, pole; opening); Leoni sifted through the etymological roots of the Phoenician and Basque languages to get the Bay of Biscay, rather than the Tyrrhenian Sea in the Mediterranean, since the Douro river is too far removed from the latter for the connection to make any sense.

Specific places warm a nest of obscurities. A leader will launch his invasion of France over the Pyrenees, starting from a point between the northern Spanish coast on the Bay of Biscay and the Douro river which marks the northern border of Portugal with Spain. The closest historical figure would be the Duke of Wellington during the Peninsular campaigns (1809–14). Napoleon had forced the British expedition of his predecessor, Sir John Moore, to evacuate Spain at La Coruña in 1808, a port near line 1's invasion source. Wellington would prosecute a successful campaign the following year, marching from Lisbon up the Tagus river into the heart of Spain, eventually crossing the northern Pyrenees to invade France. His final battle in the campaign was fought at Toulouse, which is 55 miles north-west of Carcassonne.

3 Q63

Romain pouuoir ſera du tout à bas,	**Roman power will be thoroughly abased,**
Son grand voiſin imiter les veſtiges:	**Following in the footsteps of its great**
Occultes haines ciuiles & debats,	**neighbor:**
Retarderont aux bouffons leurs folies.	**Hidden civil hatred and disputes,**
	Will postpone the follies of the
	buffoons.

Benito Mussolini, the founder of Fascism, led the way in his theatrical manipulation of the hysterical crowds, but Adolf Hitler soon outclassed him with even more sinister and histrionic public spectacles in his torch-lit rallies. Four centuries before, the prophet had described the two men as a couple of clowns.

Another interpretation replaces the buffoonery of the Fascist dictators with that of terrorist leaders like Abu Abbas and the more proficient Abu Nidal (his **great neighbor**). Sometimes Nostradamus hid the name of a perpetrator in an adverb. In French, **abased** is à bas. Certainly Italian international prestige was damaged first when the *Achille Lauro* was hijacked in October 1985 and later when Italian authorities allowed Abu Ab(b)as to leave the country and therefore to escape arrest.

Phonetically, this man's name comes closest to Nostradamus' **Mabus** enigma of 2 Q62. Abu Abbas = (M)abu (M)abbas (=Mabus). For years his PLF headquarters was in Tunisia, very close to the ruins of Carthage and the temples of Thurbo Majus (Mabus), the Romanized name of the **infernal god of Hannibal** (2 Q30) – another clue to the identity of the Third Antichrist. The *Achille Lauro* was hijacked one month before Halley's Comet became visible, a fact that reminds us of that quatrain which warns us that the fearsome Mabus will surface *when the comet will pass* (2 Q62).

Since 1986 the headquarters of Abu Abbas have been located in Baghdad. During the Gulf War (1991), as reported in **the journals** (2 Q30) and newspapers, he declared that his operatives would make good Saddam Hussein's threats to take the war to the West through terrorism. His scare tactics were so effective that worldwide security became tighter and more far-reaching than ever before. The psychological effect of Abu Abbas' threats was successful enough to spread terror, if not bloodshed.

Abu Abbas shows a flair for the theatrical that equals the histrionic egotism displayed by Adolf Hitler. Fortunately, Abbas has not, so far, been nearly as effective. It is hoped that his past crimes in the Mediterranean Sea against Italy will not be repeated or surpassed. In May of 1996 he was invited with other Palestinian leaders to the Gaza Strip for a national Palestinian conference. He told reporters that the *Achille Lauro* incident was a terrible mistake and was never planned by him in the first place.

Quatrain Indexing Date: Reverse 63 to read 39 and we date the creation of the Axis Alliance. Q63 = 1963, the year Ayatollah Khomeini was exiled from Iran, and his Islamic extremist movement bared its fangs for the first time. One might call him the George Washington of Terrorism – an inspiration to men like Abbas.

3 Q64

Le chef de Perſe remplira grande Olchade,[1]	**The chief of Persia will replenish the great Olchade,**
Claſſe Trireme contre gent Mahometique:	**The Trireme fleet against the Islamic people:**
De Parthe, & Mede, & piller les Cyclades,	**From Parthia, and Media, and the Cyclades to pillage,**
Repos long temps aux grand port Ionique.	**Rest for a long time at the great Ionian port.**

[1]Latin Olcades = a people living in Tarragona, near Cartagena in south-eastern Spain.

If this is past-oriented, it is a wild alternative-future failure. The Persians would not support the Spanish Moors (represented by the Olchade region of south-eastern Spain), nor would they send a fleet against the Turks in Greece. This is Nostradamus misreading his vision, putting ships and forces that did not exist into the hands of the Persians. He has made the same honest mistake as the modern Nostradamians who place the same impossible hardware and fleets under the dominion of Islamic states in an expected invasion of Europe in our near future.

3 Q65

Quand le ſepulcre du grand Romain trouué,	**When the great Roman's tomb [is] found,**
Le iour apres ſera eſleu Pontife:	**The day after a Pope shall be elected:**
Du Senat gueres il ne ſera prouué,	**The Senate [ie the Conclave] will not approve of him,**
Empoiſonné ſon ſang au ſacré ſcyphe.[1]	**His blood is poisoned in the sacred chalice.**

[1]Latin scyphus = chalice.

Here is a quatrain that may be trying to name the victim and relative date of a crime. In 1978 archaeologists claimed they had found the tomb of the first pope, the Apostle Peter, said to be buried beneath the Vatican. Pope John Paul I was indeed elected shortly afterwards by the Conclave (**Senate**) of Cardinals, a select body of several hundred cardinals who are called together from all over the world to elect a new pontiff when a pope dies. By tradition the Cardinals are sealed into their apartments as well as the common hall during voting and cannot leave until they have secretly and successfully elected a new pope. It is customary that their paper ballots are deposited in a golden chalice. In 1978, they elected Albino Luciani, the Patriarch of Venice, to the Papal See as Pope John Paul I.

According to the quatrain many of those in the Conclave would rue the votes they cast. Among the voters were some of the 12 cabinet ministers of the papal *curia*, led by Cardinal Villot, who would soon be deeply disturbed by the new pope's activism.

Immediately after his election, John Paul I demonstrated the new papal style – not to be autocratic and remote but down-to-earth and approachable. In his first speech he dispensed with the customary royal "we" to refer to himself and, in his papal inauguration, he rejected traditional pomp and ceremony. In place of the papal crown he wore a simple cap and, instead of being carried on the elaborate peacock-feathered throne designed for the ceremony, he chose to go on foot. In his first 30 days he paved the way for the reexamination of many traditional Church convictions. He once remarked that "God is not only your father, but your mother" – not a statement guaranteed to find favor with the existing Vatican hierarchy. He also angered the *curia* and worried Church conservatives with his support of women's rights and his readiness to take a new look at the Catholic Church's traditional, and rabid, conservative opposition to artificial means of birth control.

John Paul I was determined to examine the Vatican's financial affairs and to relocate several Vatican insiders who were major players in the operations known as Vatican Inc. His investigation would no doubt have uncovered the Vatican connections with the Mafia and with the right-wing Freemason's group known as P2. But before he could set plans for his investigation in motion, Pope John Paul I died suddenly of a heart attack.

John Paul always had a bottle of Effortil at his bedside to regulate his low blood pressure. Witnesses testified on the morning he was found dead in his bed that Cardinal Villot had the Effortil immediately cleared from the bedroom. Line 4's figurative description may imply that the heart attack was triggered by poisoning.

See Index: popes, poisoning of John Paul I.

3 Q66

Le grand Baillif d'Orleans mis à mort,	**The great Bailiff of Orléans put to death,**
Sera par vn de ſang vindicatif:	**He will be avenged by one of blood:**
De mort merite ne mourra, ne par ſort,	**By death deserved he will not die, not by fate,**
Des pieds & mains mal le faiſoit captif.	**His feet and hands sore he will keep him captive.**

Philippe d'Orléans played a vital role in the Revolution. He dropped his title of nobility to join the Revolution as Philippe-Egalité, and later, as a member of the National Assembly voted for the death of his own cousin, Louis XVI. It is the latter who is **avenged** in line 2 and 3 by our royalist-sympathizing prophet, when Philippe-Egalité himself is placed on the guillotine during the Reign of Terror by order of Robespierre.

3 Q67

Vne nouuelle fecte de Philofophes,	A new sect of Philosophers,
Mefprifant mort, or, honneurs & richeffes:	Scorning death, gold, honors and riches:
Des monts Germains ne feront limitrophes,	The German mountains will not be placed on the borders,
A les enfuyure auront appuy & preffes.	For a following they will have support and throngs.

Who are these unworldly **Philosophers**? Are they Lutherans of Nostradamus' day? German communists? Nazis? Could they even be skinheaded
neo-Nazis of our day? Whoever they are, they spread the contagion of
their heretical ways beyond the **German mountains** and find many adherents among the French people. In modern terms, line 3 could simply
be indicating that Europe will be without borders. Before doing a drastic
air-conditioning job on his head with a pistol, Adolf Hitler predicted
that something like Nazism would rise again "in a hundred years or so."
That means we should watch out for the graying-stubbled sons of today's
skinheads resurrecting Hitler's ghost in the 2030s and 2040s.

3 Q68

Peuple fans chef d'Efpaigne & d'Italie,	People without a leader in Spain and Italy,
Morts, profligez[1] dedans le Cherroneffe:	Dead, overcome within the peninsula:
Leur dict[2] trahi par legiere folie,	Their dictator betrayed by wanton folly,
Le fang nager par tout à la trauerfe.[3]	Swimming in blood everywhere in the traverse.

[1]Latin profligatus = overthrown, overcome.
[2]Old French dicteur = dictator.
[3]Crossing; that plies across; traverse; latitude (Leoni).

Both Italy and Spain constitute peninsulas. In contemporaries Benito
Mussolini and Francisco Franco they each had a notorious 20th-century
dictator. Both peninsulas were the scene of terrible battles, the Spanish
Civil War (1936–39) and the Allied Italian Campaigns of World War II
during 1943–45: Fascist Italy would end the final year of the war **without
a leader** since Mussolini was deposed in 1943 and was soon after reinstated as a puppet dictator by the Germans before he was killed by
Italian partisans. But Franco ruled Spain long after the war until his
death in 1975, making Nostradamus wrong or at least a chronicler of
a failed alternative future. Still, Mussolini aptly fits line 3's **wanton**
dictator. His military campaigns were a disaster. Even his expedition of
75,000 troops to support Franco gained him no political advantage and

drastically drained the Italian economy. The final line fits the mountainous terrain of either theater of war.

3 Q69

Grand exercice conduict par iouuenceau,	**Grand army led by a young lad,**
Se viendra rendre aux mains des ennemis:	**It will come to surrender itself into**
Mais la vieillart nay au demy pourceau,	**the hands of the enemies:**
Fera Chalon & Mafcon eftre amis.	**But the old one born to a half pig,**
	He will cause Châlon and Mâcon to
	be friends.

The half-pig occurs elsewhere (1 Q64 and as half-pig man in 8 Q44). Classical legend tells us that the city of Milan derived its name from the discovery of a creature that was **half pig** and half sheep. Napoleon occupied Milan in the 1790s while still a young general in the Revolutionary Wars. Mâcon and Châlon are in Burgundy. Perhaps they are a synecdoche for France in general.

On the other hand, old **one born to a half-pig** could be the son of an airman. This places the temporal window from the 1940s onward for the father. One could add 70 years for the **old** son and sight this event for the 2010s.

3 Q70

La grand Bretaigne comprinfe l'Angleterre,	**The great Britain including England,**
Viendra par eaux fi haut à inonder:	**Will come to be flooded very high by**
La ligue neufue d'Aufonne fera guerre,	**waters:**
Que contre eux ils fe viendront bander.	**The new league of Ausonia will make**
	war,
	So that against them they will come to
	tighten resistance.

Nostradamus calls England *great Britain*, a name she would not be known by for another 152 years. Line 2 might place this prophecy in the 21st century when the greenhouse effect could raise sea levels a minimum of 1 to 3 feet or as much as 16 to 20 feet if Antarctic ice begins to melt around the 2040s. **Ausonia** probably stands for Italy in general. Several quatrains may describe a terrible attack by nuclear terrorists on Italy, that might cause the creation of an alliance of Western powers set to obliterate the nations harboring these terrorists' bases. The last word, *bander*, could be an apocope for the Iranian naval harbor of *Bander* Abbas. Notice that *Abbas* rhymes with **Mabus**. Will Iran be the source of nuclear terrorism in Italy and will it encounter an overwhelming response in some future conflict of the mid-21st century?

3 Q71

Ceux dans les ifles de long temps affiegez,	*Those of the islands besieged for a long time,*
Prendront vigueur force contre ennemis:	*Will unleash great violence against their enemies:*
Ceux par dehors mors de faim profligez,	*Those outside [of Britain] overcome, die of hunger,*
En plus grand faim que iamais feront mis.	*By such starvation as has never been known.*

After the fall of France Britain fought virtually alone from the summer of 1940 through the summer of 1941, resorting to night bombing raids on German cities. The controversial strategy to indiscriminately bomb urban populations would escalate (**unleash great violence**) into the great fire-bombings of Hamburg and finally Dresden, where tens of thousands died in firestorms. An estimated 650,000 German civilians were killed by Allied bombing raids.

Starvation was one of Hitler's greatest weapons against what he labeled the "subhuman races" – those outside the protection of England. Over 13 million Russians, Poles, and Jews from all occupied countries were detained and willfully killed or starved to death.

3 Q72

Le bon vieillart tout vif enfeuely,	*The good old man shrouded and buried quite alive,*
Pres du grand fleuue par fauffe foufpeçon:	*Near the great river through false suspicion:*
Le nouueau vieux de richeffe ennobly,	*The new old man ennobled by riches,*
Prins à chemin tout l'or de la rançon.	*Captured on the road all the gold for ransom.*

We return to the theme of 3 Q36 and the fate of Pétain, the notorious leader of the Nazi puppet government of Vichy.

Line 1 has a poetic description similar to that in 3 Q36 of a man metaphorically shrouded and buried alive by events – an adequate description of Pétain's condition after the Germans occupied Vichy France. When the war came to its bloody conclusion the Gestapo released him from German prison and escorted the senile 89-year-old to the Swiss border. Two days after he crossed into Switzerland over a frontier road he was handed over to French officials. His trial took place in Paris, near the Seine river. The reference to riches does not apply literally. It poetically takes us back to the first days of the Vichy government when President Pétain was initially considered a heroic guardian of France's national values and identity after its humiliating defeat by the Nazis.

3 Q73

Quand dans la regne paruiendra le boiteux,	When in the realm the lame one will attain power,
Competiteur aura proche baftard:	The competitor will have a near relation [be a] bastard:
Luy & le regne viendront fi fort roigneux,	He and the realm will come to be so very mangy,
Qu'ains qu'il gueriffe fon faict fera bien tard.	That before it heals, it will be very late.

The key to unraveling this quatrain is defining which lame leader Nostradamus intended. Usually a French leader should limp to the front of the line, but I cannot completely rule out Hugh Allen's interpretation that it is the paralyzed American president Franklin D. Roosevelt. Allen is probably wrong in identifying Roosevelt's competitor as Al Smith, who ran for president in 1928 with Roosevelt as his vice-presidential nominee. Better to say it was Herbert Hoover, the man Roosevelt defeated in the 1932 presidential elections.

The last three lines of the prophecy focus on Roosevelt's greatest adversary, Adolf Hitler. The colon requires we assign the last two lines to Hitler's tattered and devastated empire at the close of the war.

3 Q74

Naples, Florence, Fauence & Imole,	Naples, Florence, Faenza and Imola,
Seront en termes de telle fafcherie:	Will come to terms of such vexation:
Que pour cõplaire aux malheureux de Nolle,	As to please the wretches of Nola,
Plainct d'auoir faict à fon chef moquerie.	Complaining of having mocked its chief.

Fafcherie may be play on the word "Fascist," making this some drama of sour grapes in the wine of Mussolini's Fascist Republic of Italy. On the whole this is a pretty obscure quatrain.

3 Q75

Pau, Verone, Vicence, Sarragouffe,	Pau, Verona, Vicenza, Saragossa,
De glaiues loings terroirs de fang humides:	Swords damp with blood from distant lands.
Pefte fi grande viendra à la grand gouffe,[1]	A very great plague will come with a great scab.
Proche fecours, & bien loing les remedes.	Relief near and the remedies far away.

[1]Shell, scab, husk, pod.

Nostradamus may have predicted the spread of AIDS through France, Italy, and Spain from the **distant lands** of Central Africa, the purported source of the plague. Scientists working in both the United States and at the Institute Pasteur in France were able to identify very quickly the retrovirus associated with AIDS. Photographs taken under the microscope reveal a virus chillingly close to the prophet's term *gousse* which can mean *scab*. Also one symptom of AIDS is a rare skin cancer – Kaposi's sarcoma – that covers the body in purple scabs.

All too often, interpreters of Nostradamus have overlooked the occult significance of his words. Nostradamus had to deal with a common superstition that armies of demons and angels descend from the skies to strike plague victims with invisible arrows and supernatural swords. **Swords** might therefore have been a poetic analogy for the spread of a plague. In the language of magic the sword is the symbol of the male phallus. Here the word may insinuate the misuse of male phallic energy and depict the male member as the chief vector for the spread of AIDS.

The early 1990s have witnessed a dramatic and more widespread incidence of the disease. Shocking estimates released in 1992 from Harvard University's School of Public Health suggest that the infection from AIDS will spiral out of control by the first decade of the next century and that 110 million adults and 10 million children will be infected by the year 2000.

There is no guarantee that even these numbers are correct, as the disease seems to be spreading faster than the data collectors can compute them. Since my last report on this quatrain in *Nostradamus: The New Revelations* (pages 170–71), the infection rate has risen from 5,000 to 13,000 people per day. South Asia continues to pull ahead of Africa and South-East Asia with the fastest spread of the plague. In Bombay's red light district, male laborers are contracting AIDS from the prostitute community and returning to their wives and families, exposing the vast population of rural India to the disease. With the highest infection rate in the world, when it has risen from 500 to 1,300 persons exposed to the virus every night, the Bombay red light district continues to be the plague's best staging ground for a huge explosion of AIDS in the Middle East, as many wealthier Arab clients, college students, and cheap laborers working in India carry the virus back to their wives and families at home. If these trends continue, by the early 21st century the situation in South Asia could parallel that of Uganda, in which 20 percent of the population have been exposed to AIDS. South-East Asia, North Africa and the Middle East could all go the way of Uganda by the 2020s.

In the deadly, rapid spread of AIDS and mankind's inability so far to cure it, the mathematics of a doomsday plague rise to meet Nostradamus' threat in the Epistle: that two-thirds of humanity will fall prey to this terrible scourge during the 21st century (see EPI 18).

Quatrain Indexing Date: Q75 = 1975. Medical researchers theorize that the first lethal strains of the AIDS virus began their spread in Central Africa around this time.

3 Q76

En Germanie naiſtront diuerſes ſectes,	**In Germany there will be born diverse sects,**
S'approchant fort de l'heureux paganiſme,[1]	**Vigorously approaching the blissful paganism,**
Le cœur captif & petites receptes,[2]	**The heart captive, the returns small,**
Feront retour à payer le vray diſme.	**They will return to pay the true tithe.**

[1]Paganism: a strange description Nostradamus often uses for the Protestant heresy of his time.
[2]Old French *revenues*, returns.

A failed prophecy set for the near future of Nostradamus' time. Protestant Germany would not return to the Catholic Church. A more modern interpretation works far better if the "new pagans" capturing the hearts of Germany are Hitler and the Nazis. With mass rallies and pageantry Hitler kept them under his hypnotic spell until it was broken, along with his Third Reich, with a pistol shot deep in the abyss of his Führer bunker during the Battle of Berlin.

3 Q77

Le tiers climat ſous Aries comprins,	**The third climate included under Aries,**
L'an mil ſept cens vingt & ſept en Octobre:	**In the year 1727, in October:**
Le Roy de Perſe par ceux d'Egypte prins:	**The Shah of Persia, captured by those of Egypt:**
Conflit, mort, perte: à la croix grand opprobre.	**Conflict, death, loss: great shame to the Cross.**

Here we have a rare example of a relatively unobscured quatrain, which clearly mentions the correct month and date of a major peace treaty concluded by Shah Ashraf and the Ottoman Sultan. The **climate** of **Aries** is war. **Egypt** is a synecdoche for the Turks and the Ottoman Empire, of which Egypt was a province at that time. Although the Shah of Persia was not captured, many historians agree that the peace arrangement was more advantageous to the Turks. The lands of Tauris, Emvan, and Hamadan were returned in recognition of Shah Ashraf's dynasty and the Shah recognized the Ottoman Sultan as legitimate successor to the Caliph.

The loss to Christendom reverberates to this day. Two great empires of Islam were strengthened as a result of this peace. The Ottoman Empire survived until the 20th century, and the stage was set for Nostradamus' second Arab Empire to become the drug pusher, as it were, of modern Christendom's oil addiction.

Robb on page 20 of *Nostradamus and the End of Evils Begun*, reports that he took this quatrain to a professor of mathematics at Columbia University to calculate the odds against its fulfillment being "merely a lucky hit." Robb takes the period of possible years to be those between 1555 and 3797 – 2242; we therefore have a 1:2,242 chance of getting the right year. Next, one has a 1:12 chance of getting the right month. The number of nations that exist in any year during a period of 2,242 years is variable. However, Robb tells us that even if only 15 nations existed in 1727 there would be 105 ways of selecting two of them. I would add that in 1727 over 500 Indian nations dwelled in North America alone. Add together all the Eurasian and African kingdoms and you get a number in the thousands. You would have a 1:tens-of-thousands chance to hit bingo by mentioning Persia, the Ottoman Empire or Egypt. You would get a 1:2 chance for picking the victor: the Shah or the Sultan. And finally another 1:2 to correctly foresee the consequences, ie **great shame to the Cross**.

Robb's professor calculated that the chance of a random lucky strike on all counts is $1:2,242 \times 105 \times 2 \times 2 = $ a 1:11,299,680 chance!

Now one sees why this is a quatrain no Nostradamus debunker the likes of Dr Edgar Leroy or Randi will tackle, because if they did it would mean the end of their skeptically righteous crusade.

3 Q78

Le chef d'Efcoffe auec fix d'Alemaigne,	**The chief of Scotland with six from Germany,**
Par gens de mer Orientaux captif:	**Made captive by people of the eastern sea:**
Trauerferont le Calpre[1] & Efpaigne,	**They will pass Gibraltar and Spain,**
Prefent en Perfe au nouueau Roy craintif.	**Present in Persia for the apprehensive new King.**

[1]Latin *Mons Calpe* = Gibraltar.

Odds would have it that this is about Nostradamus' time. Specific details are listed here. A Scottish leader with six German princes is captured in the eastern Mediterranean. They pass through the Strait of Gibraltar and Spain and are delivered to a new and apprehensive Persian Shah. The **eastern sea** could also be the Persian or Arabian Gulf.

There is great temptation to apply this one for our own times, but the pieces don't fit. The first shard would give us Bud McFarland and Oliver North leading a secret American diplomatic mission to Iran during in the mid-1980s to sell arms to the new and uncertain leader of Iran, Ayatollah Khomeini, who in return will release American hostages held by Iranian operatives in Beirut. A slightly more plausible wild shot would designate the chief of Scotland as the former British Prime Minister Margaret Thatcher giving permission for US F111 bombers to take off from Britain, so they could fly past Spain and through the Strait of Gibraltar to bomb Libya in 1986. This attack on Qadaffi's stronghold would make Khomeini **apprehensive** since Iran – not Libya – was the home base of the terrorists whose bombing of a Berlin discotheque triggered US retaliation. Either way, I feel this is just window dressing on a muddle.

3 Q79

L'ordre fatal sempiternel par chaisne,	**The fatal order and eternal**
Viendra tourner par ordre consequent:	**succession,**
Du port Phocen[1] sera rompue la chaisne,[2]	**Will come to turn by consistent order:**
La cité prinse, l'ennemy quant & quant.	**Of the port of Phocen the chain will**
	be broken.
	The city taken and the enemy at the
	same time.

[1]*Phocen* = a) Phocaeans, the founders of Marseilles; b) Phocis, central Greece; c) Phocaea, ancient Greek colony of west Anatolia, Turkey; d) Phoenician, general metaphor for modern-day Beirut, Lebanon, or other Phoenician centers along North Africa and the Middle Eastern coast.
[2]Chains were used to block off ports from attack. Marseilles had such a chain.

The mainstream interpretation sees the **fatal order** and **eternal succession** of war descending again on Marseilles as it is invaded by a sea attack that metaphorically breaks the **chain** across the harbor's mouth. The final line makes a queer separation between the city and the **enemy** inside being taken, as if the defenders are not French but occupiers who are captured. This fits best as an accurate prediction of the battle for the liberation of Marseilles in August 1944, where a German garrison of 16,000 commanded by Major General Hans Shaefer fought a chaotic eight-day battle in the streets with de Lattre's Free French divisions. Although no naval attack was made on the German garrison, de Lattre's men belonged to the Allied sea force that invaded the French Riviera. Shaefer surrendered the 7,000 survivors of his garrison on the thirteenth day of the landing.

A more eccentric interpretation of this quatrain hinges on a Middle Eastern translation of *Phocen*. Rather than a kenning for the French city of Marseilles – which in ancient times was originally colonized by the Ionians from the city of Phocaea in Asia Minor – we could expand the meaning to embrace Asia Minor itself to cover either modern-day Turkey or the Middle East.

The quatrain indexing and the poetic reference to the eternal cycle of fatality is more appropriate for the Phoenician homeland of modern Lebanon in the latter days of this century. Quatrain 79 = 1979, the year of a brief respite in the long Lebanese civil war between Muslims and Christian Phalangists in Beirut. The dating is also close enough to the early 1980s, a time of clashes between Israeli and Syrian-backed PLO and Hezbollah forces in the Bekaa valley. Perhaps the incursions of Israel into Lebanon in 1982 (**the city taken**) to destroy the PLO (**and the enemy at the same time**) are also implied. The return of peace to Lebanon in the late 1980s has remained in strength while artillery and Katyusha rocket clashes between Israelis and Islamic revolutionaries continue their evil cycle of death and reprisal along the Lebanese–Israeli security zone in southern Lebanon.

Quatrain Indexing Date: Q79 = 1979, or a new war in 2079?

3 Q80

Du regne Anglois l'indigne dechaſſé,
Le conſeiller par ire mis à feu:
Ses adherans iront ſi bas tracer,
Que le baſtard ſera demy receu.

From the English realm the worthless
**   one expelled,**
The counselor by ire put to the fire:
His adherents will go so low to efface
**   themselves,**
That the bastard will be half
**   received.**

I lean toward Pitt Francis' interpretation that the **worthless one** is Cromwell rather than his victim, Charles I, since Nostradamus' royalist sympathies would hardly bring him to call Charles I a **worthless one**, or a **bastard**. Leoni believes it can also be adequately applied to James II in 1688. Legally King of Britain but privately an unworthy bore, James would be chased from the throne by William III in the Glorious Revolution.

3 Q81

Le grand criat ſans honte audacieux,
Sera eſleu gouuerneur de l'armee:
La hardieſſe de ſon contentieux,[1]
Le pont rompu cité de peur paſmee.

The great crier, shameless (and)
**   audacious,**
Will be elected governor of the army:
The boldness of his contention,
The bridge broken [Pontrefact] city
**   and faint from fear.**

[1]Latin *contentio* = contention, controversy.

I imagine a few CNN trivia wags out there might tag the **great crier** as former CNN and current ABC anchorwoman Catherine Crier. But Jaubert cites Francis of Vendôme, who was designated Colonel of Infantry in 1557. His reasons, like his era, are too far removed for a modern understanding. Leoni tags a few more "rambunctious generalissimos" for the role, such as Wallenstein, the commander of the Imperial forces during the Thirty Years War. I would add to the confusion by translating *hardiesse* (**boldness**) as a play on the **Hadrie** anagram for Henry de Navarre: *Hardiesse* = *Hadrie*-like = Henry de Navarre.

Cheetham makes the most interesting stab. To her the key is understanding *pont rompu* (**bridge broken**). She gives us the rundown in a run-on sentence when she says, "It is a typical pun for the Latin *pons*, a bridge, and *fractus*, broken; it stands for the English city of Pontefract, the town famous for holding out for Charles I in two great sieges during the Civil War." Cheetham therefore believes that the **great crier** is Oliver Cromwell, the man responsible for the beheading of Charles I and not a man Nostradamus the royalist sympathizer would love.

A modern spin would take the broken bridge to be the old and picturesque stone bridge that once linked the Bosnian Muslim and Croatian quarters of Mostar. The destroyed bridge is a poignant symbol of ethnic war.

3 Q82

Friens,[1] Antibor,[2] villes autour de Nice,
Seront vaſtees[3] fort par mer & par terre:
Les ſaturelles terre & mer vent propice,
Prins, morts, trouſſez, pillés, ſans loy de
    guerre.
	Fréjus, Antibes, towns around Nice,
	Will be fiercely devastated by land
	    and sea:
	The locusts by land and by sea the
	    wind favorable,
	Capture, deaths, bundled and tucked
	    away, pillage without law of war.

[1]Cryptogram or misprint for *Fréjus*.
[2]Latin *Antipolis* = Antibes.
[3]Latin *vastatus* = devastated, ruined, destroyed.

American divisions of the US Seventh Army landed in the Gulf of Fréjus in August 1944, and fought two retreating German divisions all the way up the coast past Nice.

Line 2 describes the awesome power of 20th-century warfare and the destruction hurled on the French Riviera towns and country roads Nostradamus knew so well during his lifetime. The region around the Gulf of Fréjus took the brunt of the Allied bombing and naval gun barrages which reduced much of the beach front property into a lunar landscape. The swarms of blunt-nosed Allied gliders used in the large-scale paratroop landings might be described by the prophet as *locusts*. In the pre-dawn attack the Allied paratroopers jumped over a cloud-covered objective. If the *wind* hadn't been *favorable* a great number would have landed in the ocean and sunk like rocks because of their heavy gear. Only a handful suffered such a fate. The Old French *troussez* means "tucked up" or "bundled up." Did Nostradamus actually see the

paratroopers hastily gathering up their gear and parachutes in the drop
zones?

3 Q83

Les longs cheueux de la Gaule Celtique,	The long hairs of Celtic Gaul,
Accompaignez d'eſtranges nations:	Accompanied by foreign nations:
Mettront captif la gent Aquitanique,	They will make captive the
Pour ſuccomber à internitions.	Aquitainian people,
	For yielding to their intentions.

All the Bourbon kings could be called **long hairs**, especially Louis XIV,
who wore wigs that fell below the shoulders. Louis XVIII is the most
likely candidate since his return to the French throne depended on the
defeat of Napoleon by invading armies from a coalition of foreign monarchies. The generalities of the quatrain allowed Lamont in 1942 to
correctly predict life in post-war France, a time when Vichy collaborationists were prosecuted. He is wrong on the D-Day invasion route. Feint
attacks were considered but never launched against the southern end of
Hitler's Atlantic Wall.

3 Q84

La grand cité ſera bien deſolee,	The great city will be completely
Des habitans vn ſeul n'y demoura:	desolated,
Mur, ſexe, temple, & vierge violee,	Not a single one of the inhabitants
Par fer, feu, peſte, canon peuple mourra.	will remain:
	Wall, sex, temple and virgin violated,
	People will die through steel, fire,
	plague, [and] cannons.

Short of this being a future account of the destruction of Paris (see 1 Q55,
2 Q81), I would have to log this one for the final death agony of Hitler's
Nazi capital during the Battle of Berlin. By April of 1945 the city that
had already been pulverized by a year of 1,000 Allied bomber raids was
overwhelmed by a Soviet offensive of 1.2 million men. At the peak of
the street battle 12,000 guns and 21,000 multiple-rocket launchers
bombarded Soviet and German soldiers alike in a chaotic maelstrom of
street-to-street fighting. It is estimated that the month-long battle in
Berlin and along the Oder Front cost 400,000 German and 500,000
Soviet military casualties, plus an extra 200,000 civilians killed and
wounded. The victorious Soviet troops were known to have raped an
excess of 50,000 German women, as revenge for the deaths of 21 million
of their own people at the hands of the Nazis.

3 Q85

Le cité prinſe par tromperie & fraude,	The city taken by illusion and fraud,
Par le moyen d'vn beau ieune attrappé:	Entrapped by the means of a
Aſſaut donne Raubine pres de LAVDE,	handsome youth:
Luy & tous morts pour auoir bien trompé.	Assault given, Robine near the Aude,
	He and everyone dead for having
	thoroughly deceived.

The Robine is a tributary to the Aude, which was enlarged to make a canal in the Narbonne-Perpignan area. The city in question is one of these two. By writing *LAVDE* in capital letters Nostradamus is hinting – not too subtly either – at an anagram. *LAVDE* is probably a cryptogram for the general who crushed a Huguenot rebellion in this region in 1705–10. "LAVDE" slightly swiveled gives us "DEVLA," or De Villars. Replace the *v* with a *u* and you get the Latin derivative *laude*, "praise," a further link to de Villars, who is named outright and glorified by Nostradamus in P2. Line 4 aptly describes the Cevennes revolt (P2) in which hundreds of Huguenot towns and farms were burned to the ground and their inhabitants slaughtered.

3 Q86

Vn chef d'Auſonne aux Eſpaignes ira,	A chief of Ausonia will travel to Spain,
Par mer fera arreſt dedans Marſeille:	By sea he will make a stop within
Auant ſa mort vn long temps languira,	Marseilles:
Apres ſa mort on verra grand merueille.	He will languish a long time before
	his death,
	After his death one will see a great
	marvel.

An Italian leader will visit Spain, then make a stop in Marseilles, where he dies a slow death. The details are not specific enough to match any record of any seasick or otherwise ailing monarch who died there in the last four centuries.

3 Q87

Claſſe Gauloiſe n'approches de Corſegue,	Gallic fleet do not approach Corsica,
Moins de Sardaigne tu t'en repentiras:	Even less in Sardinia, you will repent
Treſtous mourrez fruſtrez de l'aide grogne,[1]	it:
Sang nagera, captif ne me croiras.	Every single one of you die frustrated
	[expecting] help from the cape,
	Swimming in blood, captive, you will
	not believe me.

[1] Old French *groing* = cape, promontory.

Part of the French fleet commanded by the Chevalier de la Ferrière was sunk in the Gulf of Lyons in 1566 while sailing past Sardinia and Corsica.

The Old French *grogne* is one of Nostradamus' concise double meanings. It stands for the *Cape* de Porceau (Cape Pig), which many of Ferrière's ships failed to reach before sinking. *Grogne* can also mean the snout of a pig. Also, *captif* stands for the fleet's chief navigator, Jean de Rian, who had once been a captured galley slave of Algerian pirates, in other words: *Captive-captain* Jean de Rian.

Nostradamus vents his frustration here. He knows this warning to his future countrymen about a naval disaster will go unheeded.

3 Q88

De Barſellonne par mer ſi grand armee,	**From Barcelona, by sea, a very great army,**
Toute Marſeille de frayeur tremblera:	**All Marseilles with terror trembles:**
Iſles ſaiſies de mer ayde fermee,	**Isles seized from the sea assistance is closed,**
Ton traditeur en terre nagera.	**Your traitor will swim on land.**

Le Pelletier believes this alludes to the twelve galleys sent by Philip II to assist the French Catholics during the Wars of Religion. Twelve little galleys hardly comprise the **very great army** envisioned by the seer, although Le Pelletier is right when he points out that the Spanish flotilla seized the isles of Château d'If and Rotonneau to shut off all help for Marseilles by sea. I would move this account four centuries forward to the large-scale commando attacks seizing islands all up and down the Riviera coast the night before the million-man Allied invasion of southern France in 1944. A few days after the landing, the German garrison at Marseilles dynamited the port facilities shortly before being overwhelmed by Resistance and Free French forces in street fighting throughout the city.

That said, Le Pelletier closes his interpretation with an intriguing argument. He cites the **traitor** of Marseilles as the consul, Charles de Casau, who conspired to deliver Marseilles to the Spanish flotilla. He was skewered by the rapier of Pierre Liberate, and the citizens of the city dragged Casau's body (**swimming**) through the gutters.

3 Q89

En ce temps là ſera fruſtrée Cypres,	**At that time there will be frustration (in) Cyprus,**
De ſon ſecours de ceux de mer Egee:	**Of its rescue by those of the Aegean sea (Greece):**
Vieux trucidez,[1] mais par meſles[2] & lyphres,[3]	**Old people massacred, but by cannon-balls and lamentation,**
Seduict leur Roy, Royne plus outragee.	**Their King seduced, Queen more outraged.**

[1]Latin *trucidatus* = slaughtered, massacred, destroyed.
[2]Old French *masles* = cannonballs.
[3]Greek *lypros* = in distress, lamentation, supplication.

During the Greek War of Independence Kutchuk Mehmed, the Turkish Governor of Cyprus, feared the rebellion on the mainland would spread to the island. He was reinforced from Istanbul with an extra 2,000 soldiers who he would use to disarm the island's Greek population. On a morning in July 1821 he invited the Metropolitan of Cyprus and all of his priests to his Nicosia palace on the pretext of getting them to swear an oath of loyalty to the sultan. Once the prelates were in the palace, the gates were closed; the governor's "guests" were manacled and a warrant for their arrest and execution read to them. Moments later the priests were beheaded. Kutchuk then ordered an island-wide confiscation of church property and the roundup and massacre of 450 prominent Greeks. The Ottoman Sultan Mahmud II had at first resisted Kutchuk's demand for a bloody purge of the Greeks and only agreed to it later because of the governor's persistence (*their King seduced*). No record exists of the opinion of the Sultan's chief wife.

3 Q90

Le grand Satyre & Tigre d'Hyrcanie,	**The great Satyr and Tiger of Hyrcania,**
Don prefenté à ceux de l'Occean:	**Gift presented to [by?] those of the Ocean:**
Vn chef de claſſe iſtra de Carmanie,	**A chief of the fleet will issue forth from Carmania,**
Qui prendra terre au Tyrren Phocean.[1]	**Who will take land at Tyrren Phocean.**

[1]*Phocean* = a) Phocaeans, the founders of Marseilles; b) *Phocis*, central Greece; c) Phocaea, ancient Greek colony of west Anatolia, Turkey.

Here we have the Caspian coast of Iran (once known as Hyrcania). A gift is given to *those of the ocean*, in other words, a great sea power such as Britain or the United States. Carmania is the ancient name for Iran's side of the narrow Strait of Hormuz. This is interesting. Who will *issue forth*, the Iranian fleet commander or the commander of a US flotilla? Iran will soon have a fleet of five modern Kilo-Class Russian submarines. Do they sail out from the Strait of Hormuz to rendezvous with other Islamic submarines in the Mediterranean?

Tyrren usually stands for the Tyrrhenian Sea, which has been mentioned in other "future Islamic submarine attack" themes. Phocean takes us to Marseilles, Greece or the Anatolian coast of Turkey as the targets for an attack. **Tyrren** includes the west coast of Italy – another candidate. I wonder if this has any connection with the man coming out of an *enclosed fish* in 2 Q5 who will make war?

3 Q91

L'arbre qu'eſtoit par long temps mort ſeché,	The tree which was limited for a long
Dans vne nuict viendra à reuerdir:	time by dormant dryness,
Cron[1] Roy malade, Prince pied eſtaché,[2]	In one night it will become green
Criant d'ennemis fera voile bondir.	again:
	The Saturnian King sick, Prince with
	a club foot,
	Dread of enemies will make his
	pretense bound.

[1]Greek Cronos = an old man – in this case his grandfather.
[2]Latin Saturn; Old French estache = stump.

Although Le Pelletier, in a fit of royalist projection, puts some stretch lines in the body of this prophecy to make it portray his Messiah, the Duc de Bordeaux, the savior foretold here may be someone far more significant and dangerous. Lines 1 and 2 overflow with Nazi poetics, alluding to the Teutonic Cult of the Tree, the myth of Tannhäuser, etc. – in short, many of the mottos and myths massaged by Hitler to stir the German people to his banner. And where does it lead? By 1945 Hitler is the epitome of a spiritually dead, black, moody Saturnian leader. He is pumped full of drugs, and ailing from chronic stomach cramps and perhaps the first twitchings of Parkinson's disease. Hitler's lightning-blue, fiery eyes, now dull, stare down his generals with a soulless pallor. After the disaster of Stalingrad in 1942 Hitler would make only two more public appearances, otherwise withdrawing to his cold, inhuman bunkers where he daily listened to reports of the progress of Allied armies devouring his Third Reich. The necessary public appearances were deferred to Josef Goebbels, his propaganda minister. Goebbels was born with a **club foot**.

If Goebbels is intended here, then voile is not a "sail" but figurative for the "veil" of his propaganda campaign – his **pretense** to keep the German fighting spirit alive to the bitter end. The last line could also read **the outcry of his enemies . . .** since the spelling of criant is ambiguous enough that it could stand equally for **outcry**. It could be safely said that to achieve his greatest propaganda successes Goebbels sublimated his fear of the approaching defeat in the closing years of the war. His powers of persuasion were equal to, and sometimes even transcended, the powers of Hitler to convince Germans not to give up hope for final victory, even as the Reich came crashing down from all sides.

3 Q92

Le monde proche du dernier periode,	**The world near the final period,**
Saturne encor tard ſera de retour:	**Saturn, again, will make a late return:**
Tranſlat empire deuers nation Brodde,[1]	**The empire is transferred towards the**
L'œil arraché à Narbon par Autour.	**Brodde nation,**
	The eye plucked out at Narbonne by a
	Goshawk.

[1] Old French *brode* = brown, black; feeble, decadent.

In the Preface the *final period* of Earth history is said to end in AD 3797, when the world is burned to a cinder by the final conflagration of the sun. Saturn making a long or *late return* must stand for the 2,000-year astrological Age of Capricorn (*circa* AD 4000– 6000) which sees humanity free of fried Mother Earth and dwelling on other star systems. The **Brodde nation** can characterize the dark-skinned people of Spain, or it can also mean the *brown*-skinned peoples of India, Africa and the Southern Hemisphere. Some prophets describe future humanity as the Race of Tan, because tomorrow's international society eventually will see all races intermarry. Space visionary Gene Roddenberry's *Star Trek* and *Star Trek, The Next Generation* television shows might do better to put a little more tan theatrical makeup on their predominantly white Anglo-Saxon starship crews. By the *final period* the real Captains Picard, Janeway and James T. Kirk might look more like green-eyed Polynesians or like actor-of-color Commander Sisko, in the TV spin-off *Star Trek: Deep Space Nine*.

The eye-plucking hawk in line 4 brings us down to earth again. At least falconry will still be a dangerous sport in the year 3797.

Quatrain Indexing Date: Q92 = a near miss for the year 3797.

3 Q93

Dans Auignon tout le chef de l'empire,	**In Avignon the chief of the empire,**
Fera arreſt pour Paris deſolé:	**Will make a stop because Paris is**
Tricaſt[1] tiendra l'Annibalique ire,	**desolated:**
Lyon par change ſera mel conſolé.	**Tricast will hold the Hannibalian**
	anger,
	Lyons will be sweetly consoled by the
	change.

[1] Either an anagram for a *multicast* television linkup; possibly Latin *Tricasses* = Troyes; or Old French *Tricastins* = natives of St Paul-Trois-Châteaux.

Because of its historical obscurity, line 1 may help us set the poetic stage for the rest. I believe this is for our near future, even though Avignon ceased to be ruled by a papal legate after 1791. The **Avignon . . . chief** is a broad synecdoche for the Catholic Church in general, and Rome in particular, since the Vatican is the place where the legates get their orders. Line 2 hints again of a future attack on Paris that makes it uninhabitable perhaps because of a biological or nuclear terrorist attack. Line 3's **Tricast** could be a television term: multicast, or a three-way TV linkup. It may also apply itself to a terrorist attack on the nuclear power plant at Tricastin near Lyons (see 1 Q99). Any mention of *Hannibal* draws our attention to 2 Q30's "North African Antichrist" theme. It seems the Third Antichrist will know how to manipulate the television media. Whatever the outcome, line 4 sees Lyons **sweetly** rewarded. But is it the French town or is this an abbreviated cryptogram for *sol Lionis*, the "sun lion" symbol of the great Mongol, Ghengis Khan? If so, we have a second link here to the "Third Antichrist/New Ghengis Khan theme" from the notorious "1999" quatrain (see 10 Q72).

Quatrain Indexing Date: Q93 = either a near miss for the end of the papal control of Avignon in 1791, or an approximate dating for the tribulation years leading up to Armageddon in 1999.

3 Q94

De cinq cens ans plus compte l'on tiendra,	*For five hundred years more they will take notice of him,*
Celuy qu'eſtoit l'ornement de ſon temps:	*Who was the ornament of his time:*
Puis à vn coup grande clarté donra,[1]	*Then suddenly a great revelation will be made,*
Que par ce ſiecle les rendra treſcontens.	*Which will make people of that century well pleased.*

[1]*Donnera* by syncope.

The obscurity of the grammar may make this quatrain a grammatical trap laid to expose the delusions of grandeur of most interpreters of Nostradamus to date. Nearly all scholars of the seer wave this quatrain around like some kind of banner of validation for their particular interpretation. The key to unlocking this quatrain's message is in how one deciphers which **people** of which **century** will be **well pleased** by their finest interpreter's commentary. On the other hand, all overt or covert self-delusion aside, the answer may be too obvious for the self-focused Nostradamian scholar to divine. The people and century could be that of Nostradamus' contemporaries. Counting five hundred years from the publication of *Les Propheties* gives us until AD 2055 to ponder on whose occult understanding of Nostradamus is right.

David Pitt Francis, on page 277 of his book *Nostradamus: Prophecies of Present Times?*, makes a good observation that Nostradamus may not have intended that we count 500 calendar years. But I disagree with his assumption that the end of the world and the Second Coming of Christ are expected by the year 2000; this would land Nostradamus' true interpreter and dispenser of revelations more than 55 years after the end of the world. Despite this rather Judeo-Christian prejudice for doomsday at the millennium, Francis makes a good point that Nostradamus, being a Christianized Jew, may have counted lunar rather than solar years, namely, years with 12 months of 29.3 days each for a total of 354.3 days. Five hundred lunar years equal 484.5 solar years.

"Calculating from Nostradamus' birth in 1503, this gives a terminating date of about 1987," says Francis. "The most appropriate date for an 'inspired' interpretation of the Centuries is therefore shortly *before* 1987–88, too late for the many claimants of the past, but just before Nostradamus' date for the end of the world." The lunar calendar dates Judgement Day for the year 1997. So, since this book is scheduled for release in the spring of 1997, and if you are still alive to read this, I guess Francis or Nostradamus got it wrong.

Quatrain Indexing Date: Q94 = 1994, perhaps an important year for some new revelation on Nostradamus? Maybe not.

3 Q95

La loy Moricque[1] on verra deffaillir,	**The law of More will be seen to**
Apres vn autre beaucoup plus feductiue:	**decline,**
Borifthenes[2] premier viendra faillir,	**Followed by one more pleasing:**
Par dons & langue vne plus attractiue.	**The Boristhenes [Dnieper] first will**
	give way,
	Through gifts and tongues more
	attractive.

[1]*Moricque* = a) Latin *mores* = custom, practice; b) Moor, Moorish, Muslim, etc.; c) the contemporary Sir Thomas More, author of *Utopia*, which was published in Latin in 1516 and was probably available at the library of Avignon when Nostradamus studied there; d) *moricque* = Armorique, either Armorica, Brittany, or America?
[2]Dnieper river region, Ukraine. A double pun for Russian President *Boris* (Yeltsin) and the *Boristhenes* (the Ukraine)?

Nostradamus was a contemporary of Sir Thomas More. There can be little doubt that our prophet read a Latin copy of More's *Utopia*, which was one of the first socialist manifestos ever written. This quatrain, along with 4 Q32 is a prophecy-in-progress concerning the fall of communism in Russia and its satellites. The two verses first predict the Czarist old order then communism itself replaced by a new and apparently more agreeable way of life.

Boristhenes is the 16th-century name for the Dnieper river and Ukraine region. Interpreters of this century have not been able to decipher the importance of the Ukraine in the downfall of communism. That was before the Chernobyl nuclear disaster of 1986 changed the lives of hundreds of thousands of Ukrainians and Belorussians who will live with the specter of radiation sickness for the rest of their lives. As a double pun **Boristhenes** can also stand for the first democratically elected president of Russia, Boris (Yeltsin), who is the catalyst for the modern Russian democracy movement that overthrew Gorbachev and communism. In size, military and industrial power, and population the Ukraine is the most significant former Soviet Republic to break away from the USSR. *Boris* (Yeltsin) became president of the Russian Federation at the same time the **Boristhenes** (the Ukraine) became an independent sovereign state.

The law of More can also indicate *the Moorish* or *Muslim law* will eventually give way to a new religiousness more attractive than the current fundamentalist extremes of today. The letters *Ar-* may have been dropped from *morique* to hide the connection of More's *Utopia* with America, which sometimes appears as *(Ar)morique* or *Americh* in the quatrains.

Quatrain Indexing Date: Q95 = 1995, either a near miss for the fall of Russian communism in 1991, or it targets the year of communism's resurgence in Russian politics in preparation for the Russian presidential elections in 1996.

See Index: America mentioned by seer.

---

3 Q96

Chef de Foſſan aura gorge coupee,	**The chief of Fossano will have his throat cut,**
Par le ducteur[1] du limier & leurier:	**By the guide [with the leash] exercising bloodhounds and greyhounds:**
La faict patré par ceux de mont Tarpee,	**The deed is executed by those of the Tarpeian Rock,**
Saturne en Leo 13. de Feurier.	**Saturn in Leo, 13th of February.**

[1]Latin *ductor* = leader, guide.

This is another prediction concerning the assassination of the Duc de Berri in 1820. In the town of Fossano, in Sardinia, is the palace of Marie Thérèse of Savoy, the Duc de Berri's grandmother, where he spent his vacations as Prince of Sardinia (**chief of Fossano**). On the night of 13 February 1820, the duke left the Paris Opera early because his wife was ill. As he helped her into the waiting carriage the duke was stabbed by Louvel, a republican fanatic employed in the royal stables. Although the stables had kennels for hunting and racing dogs, it is clear Louvel did not take care of the dogs. However, in his employment as a saddler he did make their leashes.

Nostradamus misses the mark regarding the area of the fatal wound, unless he can be excused by future potentials moving in a slightly less than predictable direction. Louvel didn't cut de Berri's throat, he stabbed him in the chest. The phrase **throat cut** could be another example of Nostradamus' poetic frenzies – Louvel as a *cut-throat*. The **Tarpeian Rock** symbolizes Louvel's republicanism. It was a term often used by the great revolutionary orator Marat in his impassioned speeches. He called for the French people to fling the Royalists off the Tarpeian Rock to their deaths, just as the republicans of ancient Rome had done with their enemies.

The planet Saturn was definitely not in Leo on the night of de Berri's assassination, but Louvel did murder the duke outside the Paris Opera on the night of 13 February 1820.

3 Q97

Nouuelle loy terre neufue occuper,	**A new law will occupy a new land,**
Vers la Syrie, Iudee & Palestine:	**Around Syria, Judaea and Palestine.**
Le grand empire barbare¹ corruer,²	**The great empire of the barbarian**
Auant que Phebés³ son siecle determine.	**will crumble,**
	Before the Century of the Sun is
	finished.

¹*barbare* = a) barbarian; b) Barbary Corairs of North Africa in Nostradamus' day; c) Libyans [Qadaffi?], Algerians or Tunisians of today; d) anagram from the French *Arabe* = Arabs.
²Leoni believes it is the Catalan *corroer*, to decay.
³*Phebés* = a) Phoebe, Roman moon goddess, associated with Diana. Also identified with the Greek goddesses Artemis, Hecate and Selene; b) Phoebus, the sun god, associated by the Romans with Apollo, the twin brother of Phoebe.

The quatrain is remarkably clear in giving us a positive alternative to doomsday by the millennium. The **new law** is either democracy or peace in the Middle East between Israel and its Arab neighbors. The play on *barbare* represents Nostradamus' pro-Christian bias against the Arab **barbarians**. It further hints that Islamic fundamentalist factions currently living in the regions once controlled by the Barbary pirates (Algeria, Tunisia [PLO headquarters], and Libya), are the source of Armageddon by the end of the 20th century (**the Century of the Sun**). But if peace efforts are successful, the push to establish an Arab empire based on vengeance and hate for the Jews will decay and crumble.

Quatrain Indexing Date: Q97 = 1997, which in the Jewish lunar calendar is the true millennium.

3 Q98

Deux royals freres si fort guerroyeront,	**Two royal brothers will wage war so**
Qu'entre eux sera la guerre si mortelle:	**fiercely,**
Qu'vn chacun places fortes occuperont,	**That between them the warfare will**
De regne & vie sera leur grand querelle.	**be so deadly:**
	That both will occupy fortified places,
	The realm and life will be [consumed
	by] their great quarrel.

Scholars have tried to pin this fratricidal duel on French royals, with little success. The verse best describes the civil war fought by the sons of Suleiman in 1559.

3 Q99

Aux champs herbeux d'Alein et du Varneigne, Du mont Lebron proche de la Durance, Camps de deux parts conflict ſera ſi aigre, Meſopotamie defaillira en la France.	**In the grassy fields of Alleins and Vernègues, Of the Lubéron mountains near the Durance, The armies on the two positions, the conflict will be so bitter, Mesopotamia will fail in France.**

Imagine, if you will, sitting in the safety and security of your local corner of Earth. Suddenly you see a future war superimposed upon the pastoral scene in your back yard. The battlefields described here are but a few miles away from the house where Nostradamus wrote his prophecies.

Alleins and Varnègues are two villages a few miles north-east of Salon. The Lubéron mountains sit on the north side of the Durance river. In 1944, Provence suffered bitter close-quarter fighting between the Allies and Nazis.

In other quatrains a **Mesopotamia . . . in France** refers to the Marne and Seine river region of Paris and the Ile de France district. In this case the **Mesopotamia** device may poetically depict Paris and the French people under their own Babylonian Captivity by the Nazis between 1940 and 1944.

3 Q100

Entre Gaulois le dernier honnoré, D'homme ennemy ſera victorieux: Force & terroir en moment exploré, D'vn coup de traict quand mourra l'enuieux.	**Between the Gauls the least one honored, Will be victorious over the man [who is his] enemy: Force and territory in a moment explored, A shot from an arrow, then the envious one will die.**

This is usually applied to any French general out of favor who rises to great power and prestige. General de Gaulle is the most recent subject, with his nemesis, the Vichy chieftain Admiral Darlan, the one assassinated (on 24 December 1942). This quatrain may be the coda to the Nazi occupation story of the previous quatrain.

Presages 1–14
from the Almanac of 1555

D'Efprit diuin l'ame prefage atteinte,
Trouble, famine, pefte, guerre courir:
Eaux, ficcitez, terre & mer de fang teinte,
Paix, trefue, à naiftre Prelats, Princes
  mourir.

**The soul touched from a distance by
  the divine spirit presages,
Trouble, famine, plague, war to
  hasten:
Water, droughts, land and sea stained
  with blood,
Peace, truce, prelates to be born,
  princes to die.**

This is the first of several bundles of quatrains from the annual almanacs of Nostradamus. They reveal a different writing style from that of *Les Propheties* – they are even more crabbed and halting. Either Nostradamus allotted less editing time to them to make his annual deadline or they suffer from editorial tampering by his disciple Chavigny, or by his son César Nostradamus.

Line 1 starts off with an occult confession similar to the one that launches *Les Propheties* in 1 Q1 and 1 Q2. The soul of Nostradamus becomes a medium for a divine spirit, or God, to presage the future. Whether that divine entity is another higher evolved spirit or simply the prophet's own Christ-consciousness is left open to speculation.

The rest is a general litany of apocalyptic one-word visions of misfortunes to haunt the year 1555, which ends in peace and truces between Catholics and Protestants all over Europe. The Peace of Augsburg, signed in September of that year, did cool down the hot winds of war, by granting Protestant princes freedom of worship and the right to introduce the Reformation into their territories (except for Calvinism). If **prelates to be born** is not meant literally, one could say the newly ordained pope, Paul IV, was *born*. The following year was inaugurated the future Pope Pius V, Bishop of Nepi and Sutri. At least one notable **prince** did **die** in 1555. King Henry II of Navarre was killed in a riding accident on 25 May.

P 2   *From the luminary Epistle on the said year* (1555)

La mer Tyrrhene, l'Occean par la garde,	**The Tyrrhenian Sea, the Ocean for**
Du grand Neptum et ſes tridents ſoldats:	**the defense,**
Prouence ſeure par la main du grand	**The great Neptune and his trident**
Tende,	**soldiers:**
Plus Mars Narbon¹ l'heroiq de Vilars.	**Provence secure because of the hand**
	of the great Tende,
	More Mars Narbonne the heroic de
	Villars.

¹Latin *Narbo Martius* = founder of Narbonne.

Here, Robb makes the best argument for a few of the presage quatrains that predict events far beyond the seer's times. He cites this one for Marshal de Villars, Comte de Tende, whose name and title are written outright. De Villars was one of Louis XIV's most trusted and valiant generals. (Some historians, like Pierre Goubert, would add that he was also one of the most vainglorious and contentious generals in Louis' monarchy.) Let us examine and expand upon the points Robb describes in his compelling line-by-line breakdown of the presage.

The Tyrrhenian Sea, the Ocean for the defense, the great Neptune and his trident soldiers. This is a reference to an English fleet lurking somewhere in the waters encircled by Corsica, Sardinia, Sicily and the west coast of Italy. The classical reference to Britannia, goddess of the ancient Britons, clearly indicates that the soldiers are English seafarers. She holds a trident symbolizing her rule of the oceans. By the first decade of the 18th century the English were well on their way to becoming the monarchs of the seven seas. Robb shows that the connection between the English and de Villars is evidenced in the marshal's own memoirs, in an account of his suppressing a Camisard peasant religious revolt in the Cevennes (1702–05). He writes, "The rebels had a respite because I was obliged to repair to the coast, which seemed menaced by a squadron of 45 vessels of the line which the English had brought into the Mediterranean. I was warned in time and took measures, so that neither the officers that landed nor those sent by the Duke of Savoy could enter the country."

Provence secure because of the hand of the great Tende. De Villars returned to pacify the revolt in the Cevennes. Louis XIV rewarded the general for this and for other victories against the English and Dutch by appointing him governor of Provence in 1712.

More Mars Narbonne the heroic de Villars. Nostradamus uses the classical name for Narbonne, *Narbo Martius*, and its environs to describe the Protestant peasant revolt of the Cevennes. Although Robb is correct about de Villars' instigating successful negotiations with the rebellion's leader Jean Cavalier, he overlooks a deeper double pun for **more Mars** (war) for **Narbonne**. The peace terms Cavalier had accepted were rejected by the Camisards and the rebellion dragged on into 1705. "More War" had also come from a papal bull of Pope Clement XI excoriating the Camisards. The bull urged Catholic peasants and de Villar's soldiers to show little clemency to the Huguenots. They razed over 450 Huguenot villages, burning and slaughtering most of the inhabitants. In the end de Villars, **heroic** as he was on the battlefields of the War of the Spanish Succession, was less than a hero in his treatment of Protestant civilians in the Cevennes. Still, de Villars is considered the last of the great military leaders of the French monarchy.

P 3   *January* (1555)

Le gros airain qui les heures ordonne,	**The big bronze one which regulates the time of day,**
Sur le treſpas du Tyran caſſera:	**Upon the death of the Tyrant it will be dismissed:**
Pleurs, plaintes et cris, eaux, glace pain ne donne,	**Tears, laments and cries, waters, ice bread does not give,**
V.S.C.[1] *paix, l'armee paſſera.*	**V.S.C.**[1] **[Philip II] peace, the army will pass away.**

[1]V.S.C., an acronym and anagram for <u>C</u>harles <u>V</u> <u>S</u>uccesseur: Philip II of Spain.

A tyrant dies at sunset in 1555. Two popes die in quick succession a few months later: Pope Julius II on 23 March, followed by Marcellus II on 30 April. No peace happened with Philip in January, but we might forgive our prophet for getting the event right but being 12 months off on the timing. In December of 1555, Charles de Guise, Cardinal de Lorraine, signed an agreement not with Philip II of Spain but against him. France and Pope Paul IV formed a new league to seize Milan, Sicily, and Naples from Philip and place French princes on these thrones with the pope as their suzerain (a feudal lord to whom fealty is due). The **tears, laments and cries** would come in the following year of French military and political disasters in Italy.

Prieditis applies V.S.C. to (V)inston Spencer Churchill, as a final victor in World War II. Hitler must therefore be the **Tyrant** in question – but he didn't die at sunset, nor was the sun poetically **dismissed** by a solar eclipse on the day he committed suicide around 3:30pm in the Führer bunker.

P 4   February (1555)

Pres du Leman frayeur fera grande,	Near Geneva terror will be great,
Par le confeil, cela ne peut faillir:	Through the counsel, that cannot fail:
Le nouueau Roy fait apprefter fa bande,	The new King has his league prepare,
Le ieune meurt faim, peur fera faillir.	The young one dies, famine, fear will cause failure.

In 1555 John Calvin's political foes, called the Libertines, were expelled from Geneva, and for the final six years of his life Calvin transformed Geneva into the Mecca of Protestantism, with him as its infallible Muhammad, so to speak. The identity of the **new King** or his band or **league** is not clear, and definitely not at the right time, if the seer pins February 1555 as the date for the creation of the Catholic League. This is either a failed prophecy or an unpursued quantum future potential in which the Duke of Savoy gathers together a league to march against Calvin and Geneva.

P 5   On March (1555)

O Mars cruel, que tu feras à craindre,	O cruel Mars, how you should be feared,
Plus eft la faux auec l'argent conioint:	More is the scythe [of Saturn] with the silver [Mercury or Moon] conjoined:
Claffe, copie, eau, vent l'ombriche craindre,	Fleet, forces, water, wind of shadow [and umbrage] to fear,
Mer terre trefue. L'amy à L.V. s'eft ioint.	Sea and land in a truce. The friend has joined [Martin] LV[ther].

The winds of war rustle in 1555, but no storm of religious wars is set to blow until 1562. War was not on France's dance card in that year, although a military adventure against Spanish possessions in Italy was in the planning stage. Perhaps Nostradamus had heard this in the rumor mill and took a 50-50 chance on a war prediction. The final line may be a continuation of the previous quatrain about Geneva and its theocratic ruler, John Calvin, who will **join** (equal) Martin Luther in stature as one of Protestantism's most influential leaders.

P 6   April (1555)

De n'auoir garde feras plus offenfé,	For not having a guard you will be more offended,
Le foible fort, Pinquiet[1] pacifique:	The weak fort, Pinquiet uneasy and pacific:
La faim on crie, le peuple eft oppreffé,	They cry "famine," the people are oppressed,
La mer rougir, le Long fier & inique.	The sea reddens, the Long one proud and iniquitous.

[1]Editorial error for Old French l'inquieté = iniquity, unrighteousness; evildoing, injustice.

The events are general. From this vantage point in the 20th century no clear case can be applied to events of April 1555. I am less critical than Leoni about Chavigny's theory, that these presage quatrains can be applied to other times. I do, however, believe they rarely target events more than a few months, years, or decades beyond the dates written in the Almanacs. Still, even I have given in to the temptation of earmarking one or two for events in the 20th century.

Renucio Boscolo's gives us an imaginative interpretation. He divines "Pinochet" from *l'inquiet* and with this he goes far to unlock the presage's obscurity, making a good though dubious interpretation. Boscolo speculates that Nostradamus knew Piedmontese dialect and would have noted that (Pin)quiet = (Pin)chet, which would signify Pinochet, the dictator who overthrew Chilean President Allende in 1973. **Pinochet . . . pacific** becomes *Pinochet* near the *Pacific*, namely Chile. The people are "pacified" but they are starving and oppressed by their new master. The reddened (pacific) sea stands for the revolution's bloodshed. Boscolo also gets *Allende* out of the French *offenſé*. I would make a further addition to this slant – that the **weak fort** symbolizes the battles fought around the presidential palace in Santiago, where Allende made a hopeless last-ditch battle.

P 7   May (1555)

Le cinq, ſix, quinze, tard et toſt l'on ſejourne,	**The five, six, fifteen, late and soon they remain,**
Le nay ſang fin: les citez reuoltees:	**The heir's bloodline ended: the cities revolted:**
L'heraut de paix vingt & trois s'en retourne,	**The herald of peace twenty and three return,**
L'ouuert cinq ſerre, nouuelles inuentees.	**The open-hearted five locked up, news invented.**

Line 1's numbers could be remixed to represent events in the year to follow 1555. Line 2 bespeaks revolts of the Huguenots and the end of the Valois bloodline. The **herald of peace** would therefore have to be Henry IV, after 23 years of war. Since the nine Wars of Religion ended in 1598, we count back 23 years to get 1575, the year the fifth War of Religion broke out. During that time Henry III, the last Valois, experienced a significant breach with his chief rival, Henry de Guise, which would later lead to Henry's death in 1588. Guise had rejected Henry III's Treaty of Monsieur because it gave too much religious freedom to the Huguenots. Guise would organize his own Catholic League and seek support from Philip II of Spain rather than from his own king. In effect Guise was challenging Henry III for the throne as well as fighting the Huguenots. In the end both men would fall to an assassin's blade, clearing the way for the Huguenot, Henry de Navarre, to reconvert to Catholicism, end the wars, and take the throne as Henry IV.

The last line is very specific but hard to place. Henry IV would become France's most popular ruler and some would say its most **open-hearted** one as well. The *five* who are **locked up** may be some of the sixteen leaders of the fanatic Catholic and anti-royalist rebellion known as the Paris Sixteen who were eventually killed or incarcerated by Guise's brother, the Duc de Mayenne.

P 8   June (1555)

Loin pres de l'Vrne[1] le malin[2] tourne arriere,	**At a distance, near the [constellation of] Aquarius, Saturn turns back,**
Qu'an grand Mars feu donra empeſchemens:	**That year great Mars will give [Aquarius] a fire opposition,**
Vers l'Aquilon[3] au midy la grande fiere,	**Towards the North to the south the great proud female,**
FLORA[4] tiendra la porte en penſement.[5]	**Florida in contemplation will hold the port.**

[1]Latin *Urna* = (Astrol.) the urn of Aquarius, the water bearer.
[2]*Le malin* = the wicked one, Saturn.
[3]*Aquilon* = a) Latin for the North, the North wind. Kidogo reminds us that Aquila is an autumn constellation of the Northern Hemisphere. It sits in the gap between the eastern and western branches of the Milky Way known as "the Rift." Ancient astronomers called it 'the eagle." I believe Nostradamus uses it here to describe the American "Eagle".
[4]*FLORA* = a) flora *flora* = flowers; b) abbreviation for Florence; c) an apocope for the Spanish *Florida*, the land of flowers. This is the American state where space launches take place at Cape Canaveral.
[5]Thought, pensive air, atmosphere.

Flora usually stands for Florence, Italy. In this presage I believe we have a rare jump out of Nostradamus' near-future time into a future far distant from our own. *Flora* is Florida; the **port** is not Miami but the space port of Cape Canaveral. The astrology dates a milestone in the human space effort as significant as the day Columbus set sail for the new world. A few hundred years from now, on a day when Saturn is in retrograde (*turns back*) either in Capricorn or Pisces, and when Mars is in Leo, opposed to Aquarius, humankind will launch its first interstellar mission to a new world in the constellation of Aquarius. We must wait a few centuries more to unravel the riddle of the **proud female**. Perhaps it stands for the name of the starship, or is a future name of the global Terran state that financed and built her. Will tomorrow's civilization be called *Gaia*, after the earth goddess of ancient Greece?

P 9   July (1555)

Huict, quinze & cinq quelle defloyauté
Viendra permettre l'explorateur malin:
Feu du ciel foudre, peur, frayeur Papauté,
L'occident tremble, trop ferre vin Salin.

*Eight, fifteen, and five what disloyalty
The evil spy will come to be
  permitted:
Fire in the sky, lightning, fear, Papal
  terror,
The west trembles, pressing too hard
  the Salty wine.*

Here is another number anagram for 1558. This is the first of many presage quatrains that probably detail events that are one year to a few decades ahead of their indexing. In that year Pope Pius IV devoted his energies to the Roman Inquisition (**papal terror**). The term **evil spy** might be one of many condemnations hurled by Pius at two of his prominent victims, Cardinal Giovanni Morone, who was imprisoned in Castel Sant'Angelo for heresy, and Reginald Pole, who was deprived of his legateship to England and died a broken man in 1558.

The **west** in this case is Spain. She would **tremble** from the political and strategic setbacks of that year when Philip II's hysterical wife, Queen Mary, died and the "Western" realm of England came under the control of Protestant Queen Elizabeth I. Many Englishmen viewed Mary's alliance to papist Spain as evil. The Old French meaning for *vin* (wine) can poetically stand for "passion." *Salt* can also refer to a "sharp" or "biting" disposition. The reference to **Salty** (and probably red) **wine** by poetic extension therefore gives us Queen Mary's notorious nickname, "Bloody" Mary, the first fanatically Catholic monarch to openly and passionately torture and burn Protestants by the hundreds.

P 10   August (1555)

Six, douze, treize, vingt parlera la Dame,
L'aifné fera par femme corrompu:
Dijon, Guyenne grefle, foudre l'entame,
L'infatiable de fang & vin repu.

*Six, twelve, thirteen, twenty will
  speak to the Lady,
The older one by a woman will be
  corrupted:
Dijon, Guienne hail, lightning makes
  the first cut into it,
The insatiable one of blood and wine
  satisfied.*

This may continue the Bloody Mary theme. Line 1 gives us a little background. After the death of Henry VIII of England and his sickly heir, Edward VI, Henry's daughter Mary Tudor was next in line for the throne in 1553. The number of petitioners mentioned here are members of Parliament, who were bound by Henry VIII's last will and testament to crown her queen.

Mary's rule was marred by her Catholic fundamentalist terror campaign against English Protestants. She married another intolerant monarch, Philip II of Spain. He is the **older one** somehow corrupted by her violence. Her zeal for hunting down and burning Protestants – though approved of by her husband – offended the limits even of his own legendary religious bigotry, putting him in the rare position of urging temperance.

The thunderstorms in Dijon and Guienne are the first lightning strikes from the human storms of religious strife raining down on France. The last line returns again to Bloody Mary (**the insatiable one of blood**) who in the first half of 1555 could be found wandering about her palace half naked and on the road to insanity, while 300 Protestants were being methodically burned at the stake in London in groups of six as per her commands.

P 11   September (1555)

Pleurer le Ciel a il cela fait faire?[1]
La mer s'apprefte, Annibal faict fes rufes:
Denys[2] moüille, claffe tarde, ne taire,
N'a fceu fecret, et à quoy tu t'amufes?[1]

The sky to weep for him, made to do
   that!
The sea is being prepared, Hannibal
   to plan his ruse:
[St] Denis [drops anchor], fleet
   delays, does not remain silent,
Has not known the secret, and by
   which you are amused
   [entertained]!

[1] ? is a misprint for !
[2] St Denis, the tomb of the House of Valois, therefore symbolizing Henry II.

The wording of the first two lines is similar to the Third Antichrist themes of 2 Q30 and 2 Q62, which caution Christendom against a terrorist submarine attack in North Africa in our future. If this is for 1555 it is some **Hannibal** or conqueror of the Barbary Corsairs like Dragut, preparing a feint attack of some kind.

St Denis snaps us out of the terrorist sub scenario and carries us back to the House of Valois and Henry II. The year 1555 cast its eyes upon Pope Paul IV and Henry fomenting diplomatic intrigues against Charles V. But Henry's Italian land and sea expedition was plagued by delays.

P 12   October (1555)

Venus neptune¹ pourſuyura l'entrepriſe,	**Venus Neptune will pursue the**
Serrez penſifs, troublez les oppoſans:	**enterprise,**
Claſſe en Adrie, citez vers la Tamiſe,²	**Pensive ones imprisoned, adversaries**
Le quart bruit bleſſé de nuict les repoſans.	**troubled:**
	Fleet in the Adriatic [or Fleet at
	Venice], cities towards the Thames,³
	The fourth clamor [of war], by night,
	the reposing ones wounded.

¹*Venus neptune*: In this case the classical metaphor represents Venice as god of the sea, the primary sea power of the Mediterranean.
²Thames? An enigmatic word: a) The River Thames is a synecdoche for London or England in general; b) La Tamise, a town in Flanders near Antwerp, therefore a synecdoche for the Spanish Netherlands.
³The line can also read: *Fleet at Venice, cities towards the Thames [England]*.

No naval or commercial enterprise of any historical significance was undertaken by **Venus** (Venice) in 1555. Nor is there any hint of Venetians inclining toward either England (**the Thames**) or the Spanish Netherlands (*la Tamise*).

This presage is better tailored to Philip's having amassed a Christian fleet in Messina (not Venice) in 1558 to recapture Tripoli. The fleet lowered anchor off the North African coast at the island of Jerba, disembarking land forces to fortify the island in preparation for their attack on Tripoli. Panic spread through the Christian encampment at the surprise of a large Turkish fleet on the horizon. The Turkish mariners bore down on the Christians as they were loading troops and equipment onto their galleys, many of which were sunk or captured.

P 13   November (1555)

Le grand du ciel la cape donra,	**The great one of the sky the cape will**
Secours, Adrie à la porte fait offre:	**give,**
Se ſauuera des dangers qui pourra,	**Relief, Adriatic [Venice] makes an**
La nuict le Grand bleſſé pourſuit.	**offer to the port:**
	He who will be able will save himself
	from dangers,
	By night the Great One wounded
	pursues.

This could be a continuation of the previous quatrain, with the Venetian fleet mistaken by the prophet for the Spanish and Italian naval expedition routed off Tripoli in 1558 by the Ottoman main fleet.

P 14   December (1555)

La porte exclame trop frauduleuſe &
  feincte,
La gueule ouuerte, condition de paix:
Rhoſne au criſtal, eau, neige, glace teinte,
La mort, mort, veut,[1] par pluye caſſé faix.

The port protests too fraudulently and
  false,
The maw opened, condition of peace:
Rhône in crystal, water, snow, ice
  stained,
The death, death, wind, through rain
  [the] burden broken.

[1]French vent = wind.

The port is probably Marseilles. The **Rhône** is expected to be frozen that winter with an apocalyptic spray painting of blood. This is followed by a sudden thaw flooding the Rhône river valley. None of this happened in December 1555.

1555 to 1556

Century IV

Cela du reſte de ſang non eſpandu,
Veniſe quiert ſecours eſtre donné:
Apres auoir bien long tēps attendu,
Cité liurée au premier cornet ſonné.

The remaining blood will not be spilt,
Venice seeks for help to be given:
After having waited for a very long
time,
The city is handed over at the first
call of the trumpet.

Venice, the Mediterranean Sea power, got little or no help from other Christian allies in its battles with Ottoman forces in Crete (1645–64) and in Cyprus. In Famagusta, the Cypriot capital, the Turks finally overwhelmed the starved defenders in 1573, after an interminable siege of 11 months.

Par mort la France prendra voyage à faire,
Claſſe par mer, marcher monts Pyrenées,
Eſpaigne en trouble, marcher gent
militaire,
Des plus grand Dames en France
emmenées.

Because of death France will
undertake a voyage,
Fleet by sea, marching over the
Pyrenees mountains,
Spain in trouble, military people
marching,
Some of the greatest Ladies led away
to France.

Because of the issue of death and succession, France would wave her bloody lace hanky as her fleets set sail for battle and her armed forces crossed the southern Pyrenees during the War of the Spanish Succession (1701–14). Charles II of Spain had declared his cousin, Louis XIV of France, his successor, triggering a wide-ranging war in Europe and North America between France and a grand alliance of Austria, England, Holland, Prussia, and Savoy. The **greatest Ladies** are Anne of Austria, daughter of Philip III of Spain, and Marie Thérèse, daughter of Philip IV. Their marriages into the French royal line caused the war. The former married Louis XIII, the latter took vows with Louis XIV.

4 Q3

D'Arras & Bourges, de Brodes grans enſeignes,	From Arras and Bruges, great banners from the Brodes,
Vn plus grand nombre de Gaſcõs battre à pied:	A greater number of Gascons fight on foot:
Ceux long du Roſne ſaigneront les Eſpaignes,	Those from along the Rhône will bleed the Spanish,
Proche du mont où Sagonte s'aſſied.	Near the mountain where Sagunto sits.

Brodes designates the olive-skinned Spanish infantry of Moorish descent. The French soldiers from Gascony distinguished themselves by holding off a sizable Spanish siege army surrounding Arras in 1654. This battle was immortalized in the writings of Cyrano de Bergerac, who was wounded at Arras. Lines 3 and 4 project a French invasion of Spain to follow, but here Nostradamus is compressing widely separated events in time into one. The French would invade Spain in the next century. Sagunto is on the east coast of Spain, about 20 miles north of Valencia on the spur of the Sierra de Espadán mountains. History records no battle of significance fought there, although Franco's Nationalist forces advanced through Sagunto to seize the Republican capital of Valencia at the end of the Spanish Civil War in 1939.

4 Q4

L'impotent prince faché, plaincts & querelles,	The impotent prince angry, groans and quarrels,
De rapts & pillé,[1] par coqz & par Libyques:[2]	Rape and pillage, by cocks and by Libyans:
Grand eſt par terre par mer infinies voilles,	Great it is by land, by sea infinite sails,
Seule Italie ſera chaſſant Celtiques.	Only Italy will be chasing the Celts.

[1]Old French *pille* = pillage, plunder.
[2]Latin *Libycus* = Libyan, African.

Many Nostradamians start with a discourse on an angered Charles V bemoaning the rape and pillaging of Elba by Barbary Corsairs. Unfortunately, this line of thinking loses a wheel in a prophetic pothole in line 4. If Nostradamus meant this one for his near future, it was almost immediately turned upside down by actual events. The Hapsburg–Valois Wars ended in 1559 with the French holding firm in Italy and meeting disaster in the northern theater at St Quentin.

With the help of a little dyslexia, one could make a new interpretation by reading the lines of the quatrain backwards. Line 4 attests to France's invading Italy in the closing days of the battle of France in 1940. Line 3 is general for the great naval battles of the Mediterranean between the Italians and British, and suggests the importance of shipping supplies to the combatants in North Africa. It describes the 1,000-ship Allied armadas invading Italy and the French Riviera after the defeat of the Afrika Korps. Libya is the scene of Italy's greatest military disasters during the North African campaign. The French – (**cocks**) in this case – are indirectly responsible for the poetic *rape and pillage* (rout) of Italians and Germans in North Africa, when French Vichy forces in Morocco and Algeria cross over to the Allied side, exposing the rear of the Axis armies to Allied attack. Line 1 reveals Mussolini to be the impotent, quarrelsome prince.

4 Q5

Croix, paix, ſoubz vn accomply diuin verbe,	**Cross, peace, under one the divine word accomplished,**
L'Eſpaigne & Gaule feront vnis enſemble:	**Spain and Gaul will be united together:**
Grand clade[1] proche, & combat trefacerbe,	**Great disaster near, and combat very sharp [and] bitter,**
Cœur ſi hardy ne ſera que ne tremble.	**No heart so fearless that it will not tremble.**

[1]Latin *clades* = disaster.

Few of Nostradamus' contemporaries could imagine a union of Spain with France; perhaps a military alliance is implied. Leoni thought the quatrain belonged to our own future in what he calls the "somewhat apocryphal era of the World Emperor and Antichrist."

Actually, the Antichrist he's looking for up ahead may already have fulfilled this prophecy in our past. This quatrain points to the first of Nostradamus' three Antichrists, Napoleon, who did technically seize Spain in 1808 and make it a French satellite of the First Empire by putting his brother Joseph on the Spanish throne. Lines 3 and 4 adequately describe the general uprising of the Spanish people against Joseph and the brutal guerrilla warfare that ensued against the French army of occupation. One need only look at the paintings and pen-and-ink drawings of Francisco de Goya to see just how savage the reprisals and counter-reprisals were. France lost 100,000 soldiers a year in Spain between 1808 and 1813, mostly from guerrilla attacks. The last jibe could be the prophet's accusation against someone as fearless even as Napoleon who, after his initial pacification of Spain in 1808, never returned to personally command his beleaguered soldiers and clean up the mess of his own Vietnam.

4 Q6

D'habits nouueaux apres faicte la treuue,[1]	**The new clothes after the discovery is**
Malice tramme & machination:	**made,**
Premier mourra qui en fera la preuue,	**Malicious conspiracy and**
Couleur venife infidiation.[2]	**machination:**
	The Premier [witness] will die who
	will prove it,
	Trap of Venetian rusty-red color.

[1]Old French *treuve* = discovery, find.
[2] Old French *insidiation* = snare, trap.

The **new clothes** are perhaps a clue yet to be understood. I leave it to the conspiracy buffs in our audience to unravel it. I would tag this generality to the John F. Kennedy assassination plot. The **Premier** one is his assumed assassin, Lee Harvey Oswald, who may also turn up in 6 Q37 as the innocent one **accused of the deed** and put to death. Oswald said he was a "patsy" – cheated, victimized, or framed to appear as Kennedy's assassin. Oswald is shot dead by an agent of the Mafia, Jack Ruby – another man with circumstantial connections to the assassination – so that Oswald cannot *prove* his contention and tell the truth about the conspiracy. The final line can also be translated as **the color of a Venetian trap** or a **Venetian treachery**. This might be Nostradamus implicating the Italian Mafia connection in the assassination. Check out the color of Venetian red. It is a rusty color quite similar to the notorious brick building in Dallas known as the Texas School Book Depository, where the first bullets of the assassin – whoever he was – were fired.

4 Q7

Le mineur filz du grand & hay Prince,	**The minor [youngest] child of the**
De lepre aura à vingt ans grande tache:	**great and hated Prince,**
De dueil fa mere mourra bien trifte &	**Will by leprosy be greatly marked at**
mince,	**the age of twenty:**
Et il mourra la où tombe cher lache.	**Of grief his mother will die very sad**
	and emaciated,
	And he will die [entombed] where
	falls the beloved's loose, cowardly
	flesh.

There is no record of a French king in his minority, or a youngest child in any French royal line dying of leprosy. Line 4 has a nice pun that uses both meanings of *tombe*, "(to) fall" and "tomb," as well as the double meanings possible for *lache*: "loose" and "cowardly." If I were a 16th-century Nostradamophile I would be impressed (or I'd be groaning at the pun-ishment).

4 Q8

La grand cité d'affaut prompt & repentin,
Surprins de nuict, gardes interrompus:
Les excubies & vielles fainct Quintin,
Trucidés gardes & les pourtrails rompus.

The great city by assault both prompt
  and swift,
Surprised at night, guards
  intercepted:
The guards and watchmen of St
  Quentin,
Massacred guards and the front gates
  broken.

This is definitely about the overwhelming assault of the Spanish against Coligny's tiny French garrison at St Quentin in 1557.

4 Q9

Le chef du camp au milieu de la preffe,
D'vn coup de fleche fera bleffé aux cuiffes:
Lors que Geneue en larmes & detreffe,
Sera trahie par Lozan & Souyffes.

The chief of the army in the middle of
  the crowd,
Will be wounded in the thighs by the
  shot of an arrow:
When Geneva was experiencing tears
  and distress,
Will be betrayed by Lausanne and the
  Swiss.

Another tirade against Calvin? Today, Geneva is no longer the Mecca of the Protestant movement as it was in Nostradamus' time, but the hub of diplomats and politicians dedicated to gathering present-day human civilization into a one-world global society. Since a 16th-century interpretation for this prophecy went foul, perhaps Nostradamus is alluding to some future political crisis when Switzerland will reject the efforts of diplomats of the United Nations to denationalize the world.

4 Q10

Le ieune prince accufé faulfement,
Mettra en trouble le camp & en querelles:
Meurtry le chef pour le fouftenement,
Sceptre appaifer: puis guerir efcrouelles.

The young prince falsely accused,
Will plunge the army camp into
  trouble and quarrels:
The chief murdered for his support,
Scepter to appease: then to cure
  scrofula [at the coronation].

Many tantalizing clues poke their heads out of the verbal underbrush of this quatrain, but they are too general to interpret. A commander of an army will falsely accuse a prince, lighting the fuse of a mutiny in the army camp. The commander is murdered for his accusation. The subjects can only be English or French, since their rulers are the only European monarchs who ever claimed to cure scrofula by their touch.

4 Q11

Celuy qu'aura gouuert de la grand cappe,[1]	He who will have government of the great cape,
Sera induict à quelque cas patrer:[2]	Will be led to execute in certain cases:
Les douze rouges viendront fouiller la nappe,	The twelve red ones will spoil the cover,
Soubz meurtre, meurtre se viendra perpetrer.	Under murder, murder will be perpetrated.

[1]Old French cape, cloak; usually the cape of the pope.
[2]Latin patrare = to perform, execute.

Leoni (1961) was unfortunately right on track with his interpretation about a pope who will be convinced on taking a drastic action that may be supported, but most likely opposed, by 12 hostile cardinals. They will kill the pope, then commit a string of murders in what Leoni calls a "sort of Papal Committee of Public Safety or Politburo." Events caught up with this interpretation in 1978, when a new pope did endeavor to drastically shake up the Vatican hierarchy. This upset the 12 conservative cardinals of the papal Curia, the Vatican's cabinet ministers. He was found dead the morning he had planned to start shuffling the leadership, and after his death murders were perpetrated on a number of lay bankers and associates of the Vatican Bank.

Nostradamus is talking about John Paul I, the revolutionary reformer whose activism and life was cut short by the **twelve red** cardinals of the Curia, who **spoil** his semi-secret investigation into the infiltration of the Mother Church by neo-Fascist elements of secret societies. The **case** of corruption in the Vatican would not be executed. Instead the pope, followed by many of the perpetrators and the investigators, would die.

4 Q12

Le camp plus grand de route mis en fuite,	The greater army on the road put to flight,
Guaires plus outre ne sera pourchassé:	Scarcely further will it be pursued:
Ost[1] recampé, & legion reduicte,	The expeditionary force reassembled, and the legion reduced,
Puis hors des Gaules du tout sera chassé.	Then they will be chased completely out of France.

[1]Old French ost = expedition, army, host.

This could be another compound vision of two modern invasions of France seen as one. First the World War I version.

In September 1914, during the first Battle of the Marne, the French forces were initially pushed back (**put to flight**) by the German Imperial armies, and for a time Paris was in danger. But a miscommunication prompted the German right wing to expose its flank to a French army, and the surprise attack forced the Germans onto the defensive. The BEF (British *Expeditionary Force*), initially repelled at Mons and other Belgian collisions with the Germans, did *reassemble* on a line between the Marne and Verres rivers and successfully checked the German advance at Coulommiers. After their failure in the first Battle of the Marne, the Germans never recovered the offensive initiative against the Allies. The war ground itself down into four long and bloody years of trench warfare, which finally swept them out of France by November 1918.

Now the prophecy jumps to the sons of the next generation of combatants, for the obscurity of the prophecy works nearly as well for the fall of France in 1940. The Allies believed that France had the most powerful army in the world to face the coming conflict with Hitler. But soon it was *put to flight*. The word *scarcely* describes the brief time it took Hitler's panzers to pursue and defeat the French. The Nazi blitzkrieg was launched in Holland and Belgium on 11 May. The BEF and French armies advanced into Belgium, allowing the powerful panzer armies of Rommel and Guderian to leap out of the forests of the Ardennes and trap the British army and half of the French in Belgium when they reached Calais nine days later on 20 May. By 3 June the BEF soldiers escaped to England, abandoning most of their equipment on the beaches of Dunkirk. With the British out of the picture, Hitler's armies turned west again to launch an offensive into France on 4 June. They brushed aside French armies, reaching the capital on 14 June, in *scarcely* seven days' time.

Line 3 even describes the next generation of the British Expeditionary Force reassembling in England after their evacuation from Dunkirk. A large number of French forces were also evacuated, but thousands of homesick soldiers returned after the fall of France rather than continue the struggle as part of General Charles de Gaulle's Free French forces (*the legion reduced*).

Line 4 promises the same bad end for sons of the German soldiers fighting in the First Marne. Exactly 30 years later their sons would be swept out of France by the Normandy Invasion of 1944.

4 Q13

De plus grand perte nouuelles raporté,	**Of the greater loss news is reported,**
Le raport fait le camp s'eſtonnera:	**The report will astonish the army:**
Bandes vnies encontre reuoltées,	**United troops against the revolters,**
Double phalange grand abandonnera.	**The double phalanx will abandon the great one.**

Garencières thought this applied to an incident in the 1580s during the Hundred Years War between Spain and the Dutch. A rumor of a great defeat spreading through the army of the Duke of Parma left his soldiers so demoralized that the Dutch succeeded in capturing Antwerp for a brief time. Garencières applies the **double phalanx** to Parma's Spanish infantry and cavalry. A phalanx is a classical Macedonian formation of 800 pikemen, 16 ranks deep and 50 across. Although armies of the 16th century employed large formations of pikemen, I believe the term is more poetic than literal. Nostradamus likes to call Philip II of Spain, Parma's liege, the Macedonian, comparing him to his namesake, the ancient Macedonian King Philip II, father of Alexander the Great.

4 Q14

La mort fubite du premier perfonnage,	**The sudden death of the leading personage,**
Aura changé & mis vn autre au regne:	**Will have changed and put another to rule:**
Toft, tard venu à fi haut & bas aage,	**Soon, but too late, [he] comes to high position, of young age,**
Que terre & mer faudra que on le craigne.	**It will be necessary to fear him by land and sea.**

This is general enough to fit any young and able king, leader, or president. Whoever he is, he comes to power as a young man and makes a big impact on the geopolitical stage early in his rule. Cheetham was the first 20th-century interpreter to pin this one on President John Kennedy, and since I am sometimes a creature of my century's projections, I do as well.

At age 43 Kennedy was the youngest person ever elected president. His masterful handling of the Cuban Missile Crisis in 1962 made him feared on land and sea by the Soviet Union. Nostradamus may be implying here that Kennedy would have become one of our century's greatest leaders if he had avoided assassination and finished his term.

4 Q15

D'où penfera faire venir famine,	**From where he thought to cause famine to come,**
De là viendra le raffafiement:	**From there will come relief supplies:**
L'oeil de la mer par auare canine,	**The eye of the sea watches like a greedy dog,**
Pour de l'vn l'autre donra huyle, froment.	**While one will give the other oil, and wheat.**

If certain actions committed in the present and past did not create their future reactions, history would have run down a different course and this riddle-filled quatrain might be just another bit of gibberish. The key to its secrets lies within the right interpretation of **greedy dog**. It represents groups of German U-boats, which hunted down cargo ships in what were called wolfpacks. The **eye of the sea** is the submarine periscope. The indexing may also apply this future vision to German submarines of World War I in 1915. In either conflict the strategic goal was the same – to cut off American military supplies, fuel, and food to Britain, starving her into submission. In both wars the German submarines failed.

Quatrain Indexing Date: Q15 = 1915, the year that saw the beginning of the German submarine campaign against the British Empire during World War I.

4 Q16

La cité franche de liberté fait ſerue,	**The free city of Liberty made servile,**
Des profligés & reſueurs faict aſyle:	**Made an asylum for corrupt ones and**
Le Roy changé à eux non ſi proterue:	**dreamers:**
De cent ſeront deuenus plus de mille.	**The King changed, to them not so**
	vehement:
	From one hundred [they] will become
	more than a thousand.

Europe had a number of free cities in the 16th century. If France is the lord here, the Dutch city of Orange may be the intended vassal, since it was subjugated by the French in 1713. During the Wars of Religion, Orange was a haven for Huguenot refugees from France, who Nostradamus condemns as corrupt, religious dreamers.

The **King changed** is either a successor to Henry II or the more religiously tolerant Louis XIV, who became the free city's new king after its incorporation into the French Empire.

Fontbrune thinks the reference to **more than a thousand** is a reason to take this quatrain into the 1860s and the Italian Wars of Unification. Garibaldi's little army of red-shirted rebels was known as the Thousand.

A number of modern interpreters see Washington DC as **the free city of Liberty** made servile by corrupt career politicians who are out of touch with the needs of the American people. I would add that President Reagan (1980–88) called himself an American Dreamer. American government has lost much credibility since the scandals of Watergate and the Iran-Contra affair.

Still, Nostradamus' Gallic focus would make Paris the most likely candidate for the **city of Liberty**, and his anti-republicanism would replace Republican Ronald Reagan with a corrupt French President of any one of five French Republics from 1791 to the year 2000.

4 Q17

Changer à Beaune, Nuy, Chalons &
  Dijon,
Le duc voulant amander la Barrée:
Marchant[1] pres fleuue, poiſſon, bec de
  plongeon,
Verra la queuë: porte ſera ſerrée.

To change at Beaune, Nuits, Châlon
  and Dijon,
The duke wishing to improve the
  Carmelite monks and nuns:
Merchant near the river, fish, beak of
  the diving bird,
To the queue, the gate will be closed.

[1]Old French for marchand = merchant; variant: marching.

Translating Barrée is the key to this quatrain. Either it stands for "motley" or "poor" people seeking alms, or it is the nickname of the holy order of Carmelite nuns and monks who were shut out of their monasteries during the French Revolution.

4 Q18

Des plus lettrés deſſus les faits celeſtes,
Seront par princes ignorans reprouués:
Punis d'Edit, chaſſez comme ſceleſtes,
Et mis à mort là où ſeront trouués.

Some of the most literate in the
  celestial arts,
Will be damned by the illiterate
  Princes:
Punished by Edict, driven out like
  criminals,
And put to death wherever they are
  discovered.

The closest thing to a pogrom against astrologers and astronomers took place in Hitler's Germany after the noted Nazi New-Ager Rudolf Hess flew to Scotland on his own half-baked errand for peace. He had consulted astrology to find the best date for his mission. This makes him one of Nostradamus' **illiterate Princes**, because the mission Hess thought was blessed by the stars ended in a complete fiasco. Upon landing he was immediately arrested as a prisoner of war. His declaration that Hitler had sent him to invite the British to cease hostilities and fight alongside Germany against the Soviet Union was viewed as the rantings of a star-bound lunatic. Perhaps someone more literate in astrology could have pointed out to Hess that he and the other Nazi **princes** were the obstruction to peace on Earth.

4 Q19

Deuant Rouan d'Infubres[1] mis le fiege,
Par terre & mer enfermés les paffages:
D'Haynault,[2] & Flãdres, de Gãd & ceux
  de Liege,
Par dons lænées[3] rauiront les riuages.

Before Rouen the Insubrians laid a
  siege,
The passages and crossings by land
  and sea cut off:
By Hainaut and Flanders, by Ghent
  and those of Liége,
Through cloaked gifts they will seize
  and ravage the shoreline by force.

[1]Lombards, by extension Italians.
[2]The Netherlands.
[3]Dons lænées: dons = gifts, pardons; Latin laena = cloak, mantle. Together they make cloaked gifts or a double pun "cloaked pardons."

The Italians never laid siege to Rouen, but their Axis allies, the Germans, did battle their way through the center of the city during the fall of France. The rest sounds like a description of the Nazi blitzkrieg through Holland, Belgium, and France, ending with a future image of Rouen's devastated Seine river shoreline in 1940.

4 Q20

Paix vberté long temps lieu louera,
Par tout fon regne defert la fleur de lys:
Corps morts d'eau, terre là lon aportera,
Sperants vain heur d'eftre là enfeuelis.

Peace and abundance for a long time
  the place will praise,
Everywhere in his realm, the fleur-de-
  lis, deserted:
Bodies dead by water, will [float]
  there by land,
Vainly awaiting the hour to be buried
  there.

Nostradamus returns again to the drowning of Royalist sympathizers at Nantes during the French Revolution. Where 5 Q33 depicts the atrocities of priests and women stripped and tied together to be drowned on sinking barges in the River Loire, this quatrain describes the aftermath of bloated bodies choking the river banks.

4 Q21

Le changement changera fort difficile,
Cité, prouince au change gain fera:
Cœur haut, prudent mis, chaffé luy habile,
Mer, terre, peuple fon eftat changera.

The change will be a very difficult
  change,
City, Provence will gain by the
  change:
Heart high, prudence placed, he, the
  clever [one] expelled,
Sea, land, people will change their
  country.

After the agony of the fall of France in World War II, Provence became part of Vichy, and the **city** of Paris remained part of the occupied portion of France after its defeat by Hitler in 1940. The new political landscape could scarcely be called a **gain**, unless Nostradamus is betraying a little more sympathy for the Vichy leader, General Pétain, than do his modern compatriots. It must be remembered that Pétain blamed French republicanism for all of France's disasters about as much as Nostradamus forewarned the same. Still, Pétain's high-minded beginning leads to a pitiable end as a prisoner of the Nazis, when they drag the puppet leader of Vichy by the strings, if you will, to a German prison after 1942. The defeat of the Third Reich brings a second change to Provence and France. The word *estat* can also mean a change in **state**, as in "condition," rather than a political change. Perhaps Nostradamus is trying to describe the transformation of Provence into a tourist haven from the agrarian society it was in his time.

4 Q22

La grand copie qui sera deschassée,	The great armed force which will be expelled,
Dans vn moment fera besoing au Roy,	In one moment it will be needed by the King,
La foy promise de loing sera faulsée,	The faith promised from afar will be falsified [and] broken,
Nud se verra en piteux desarroy.	He will be seen destitute and in pitiful disorder.

This is so general it could be applied to any king commanding any invading army that is expelled in a military disaster. It could be Napoleon in Russia or during the rout at Waterloo, or it is Hitler sacrificing the Sixth Army at Stalingrad. Odds would have it stand for Henry II losing his relief army in the military disaster of St Quentin.

4 Q23

La legion dans la marine classe,	The legion in the marine fleet,
Calcine,[1] Magnes[2] soulphre, & poix bruslera:	Lime, magnesium, sulfur and pitch will burn:
Le long repos de l'asseuree place,	The long rest in a secure place,
Port Selyn,[3] Hercle[4] feu les consumera.	Genoa, Monaco: fire will consume them.

[1]Provençal *calcine* = lime.
[2]*Magnes* = a) Latin *magnes* = magnet, loadstone; b) abbreviation for *Magnésie* = magnesium, a mineral used in Greek fire.
[3]*Port Selyn*, from Greek *seléné* = moon or crescent; either the port of Genoa or Istanbul.
[4]Latin *Portus Herculis Monoeci* = Monaco.

This is most likely about the same reduced **legion** of Free French mentioned earlier in 4 Q12. De Lattre's three Free French divisions were pulled off the Italian front to participate in Operation Dragoon, the Allied sea invasion of the Riviera, in August 1944. Nostradamus tries to describe the flame throwers of the Allied soldiers by listing the ingredients used in his time to make Greek fire, a primitive incendiary used by Byzantines to ignite enemy galleys.

The lightly defended docks and shipping yards of Genoa were bombed ferociously throughout 12–27 July 1944, in preparation for the Allied landings. Until 1944 Provence was a quiet backwater of the war. During Operation Dragoon, fighting raged up and down the coast from Marseilles to the approaches of Monaco.

4 Q24

Ouy foubs terre faincte dame voix fainte,
Humaine flamme pour diuine voir luire:
Fera les feuls de leur fang terre tainte,
Et les faincts tēples pour les impurs
    deftruire.

The soft voice of the sacred friend is
    heard under holy ground,
The human flame shines for the
    divine voice:
It will cause the earth to be stained
    with the blood of the celibate
    monks,
And to destroy the sacred [or false]
    temples of the impure ones.

Gautama the Buddha taught that the Wheel of Dharma – the teaching of truth – is like a great wheel which, 2,500 years after its first revolution, runs out of momentum. The next great world teacher – who is called Maitreya, meaning "friend" – is due to appear around the year AD 2000 and will restore momentum and power to all those seeking religious truth.

This quatrain predicts that organized religion will be destroyed by words of truth spoken by the **friend** through the **human flame** of a new religion – or better, a new religiousness that is individual and nondogmatic. In the original French the word **sacred** is represented by the word *saint* written in the archaic form with an *f* written for *s*, thereby implying that the "saint" is "faint," or false.

Quatrain Indexing Date: Q24 = 1924. Indian mystic and purported world teacher Meher Baba went into silence in 1925 and never spoke again, teaching through hand language and writing until his death 44 years later in 1969. Another candidate for Maitreya, Jiddu Krishnamurti, had his first *satori* (glimpse of enlightenment) in 1922.

4 Q25

Corps fublimés fans fin à l'œil vifibles:	**Sublime essence forever visible to the eye,**
Obnubiler[1] viendront par fes raifons:	**Come to cloud the conscious mind for reasons of its own:**
Corps, front comprins, fens chef & inuifibles.	**Body and forehead together, senses and the overseeing ego become invisible,**
Diminuant les facrees oraifons.	**As the sacred prayers diminish.**

[1]Latin *obnubilare* = to overcloud, obscure.

By evening one might find Nostradamus returning home from his meditations at evening mass at the nearby Church of St Michel in Salon. He passes through the heavy wooden front doors of his house and enters a courtyard where we watch him ascend the spiral stone staircase all the way to the top floor. He then enters a room with a timbered floor and stucco yellow walls, which has been transformed into a secret study; a portion of the roof has been removed to allow for the construction of an observatory. Once elevated above and beyond the petty pretenses of town life, he studies the sharp crystalline light of the stars appearing in the semi-arid and aromatic atmosphere of Salon's clear air. As the night descends upon the land we find his awestruck eyes bathed in the **sublime essence** of starlight as the cares of the day are lulled to sleep by a chorus of cicadas.

As midnight approaches, Nostradamus closes the heavy window of his study to block out the curious and the self-righteously challenged, and seats himself at his desk to study the parchment of forbidden books illuminated by the soft golden light of candles. Nostradamus turns to consult his ephemeris and plot the night's course on a horoscope. The stars and planets are points of reference to take our navigator to the other shores of higher consciousness to divine realms of future possibility. If the stars and their aspects on this warm summer evening warrant a wider sweep through the oceans of time, he will move across his study to sit upon the brass tripod set over a brass bowl filled with steaming water and pungent herbs. There he will empty himself of thought and care by reciting a sacred incantation. He will then slip into a trance of ecstasy, to hear and see the visions of his inner oracle projected in the mist rising in the aura of faint candlelight.

4 Q26

Lou grand eyſſame ſe leuera d'abelhos,[1]	**A great swarm of bees will arise,**
Que non ſauran don te ſiegen venguddos:	**But no one will know from whence**
Dēuech l'ēbouſq̃, lou gach[2] *deſſous las*	**they come:**
treilhos,[3]	**They ambush by night, the sentinel**
Ciutad trahido per cinq lengos[4] *non nudos.*	**under the vines,**
	The city handed over to five bribed
	babblers not naked.

[1]Provençal for the French *abeille* = bee. Symbolizes the bees on Napoleon's coat-of-arms. A symbol that was certainly never seen before on royal French livery.
[2]Provençal *gach* = a) sentinel; b) jay.
[3]Provençal *trelha* = vine. Le Pelletier applies it as a cryptogram of the French *treilles* = Tuil(l)eries.
[4]Provençal *lenguos* = babblers.

On 10 November 1799, inside the Hall of Mars in Saint Cloud, the 500 red-robed delegates of the Directory had just unanimously voted to have General Bonaparte, commander of the Paris garrison, arrested for encircling the building with troops. On the previous day he had begun from his headquarters at the palace of the Tuileries a coup d'état against the government on the pretext of quelling a supposed terrorist plot. The cheers were soon drowned out by the sound of drums beating the charge outside. Burly grenadiers cleared the hall. The delegates threw off their robes and jumped out of the windows in a panic. Nostradamus foresaw the empty Hall of Mars, like countless other halls throughout France, decorated with the bees of Napoleon's coat-of-arms, as a symbol of his coming Empire. The coup d'état was planned the night before. The *five babblers* are the Directory's executive counselors. Two of them had conspired with Napoleon; the other three were bribed to look the other way. Le Pelletier, who was the first to apply this to Napoleon's coup, makes a good argument that the Provençal word *treilhos* or *treilles* is a cryptogram for the palace of the Tuileries, in which Napoleon had set up his headquarters for the coup. However, the ambush on the Directory did not take place at night but in the afternoon. This is the only quatrain Nostradamus writes in his native Provençal tongue. Perhaps he did so to better mask Tuileries.

4 Q27

| Salon, Manſol,[1] Taraſcon de SEX. l'arc,[2] Où eſt debout encor la piramide: Viendront liurer le Prince Dannemarc, Rachat honny au temple d'Artemide. | Salon, Mausol, Tarascon of the arch of SEX, Where the pyramid is still standing: They will come to deliver the Prince of Annemarc, Redemption dishonored in the temple of Artemis. |

[1]Erratum for (St. Paul-de-)Mausole, a Roman monument named after a priory at Nostradamus' birthplace St Rémy. By the late 19th century it was an insane asylum where Van Gogh was confined shortly before his suicide in 1890.
[2]de SEX. l'arc: abbreviation for the inscription on the adjacent Roman arch. Together with the previous entry they both probably stand as a synecdoche for St Rémy.

Provence was the crossroads of many ancient peoples and empires. The valleys and hills were haunted by the forget-me-nots of ruins, and its people imprinted with the detritus of myths and legacies. One might picture Nostradamus as a boy on one of his many walks with his grand-father Jean, or later Pierre, through the surrounding, herb-spiced country outside the cluster of stone- and tile-roofed buildings of St Rémy. We might see the youth steadying the old physician in his stately robes and three-cornered cap as they picked their way along the uneven road out of town to walk in the nearby hills. After a time grandfather and grandson would hold their lessons on herbs, mythology and ancient history in the cool shade of two ancient Roman monuments just outside of town known as Les Antiques. One was incorrectly labeled **the pyramid** in Nostradamus' day and was mistakenly thought to be the mausoleum for a 4th-century hermit who once lived near by and later was named St Paul. Just by its side stood a crumbling arch of triumph with the abbreviated Latin inscription: SEX. L.M. JULIEI C.F. PARENTIBUS SUEIS.

Later in life Nostradamus would be one among many scholars to try his hand at filling in the entire inscription: Sextus Lucius Manlius Juliae Istam Columnam Fecit Parentibus Sueis. (James Randi incorrectly interprets this monument and its inscription as commemorating the victory of Julius Caesar "at the battle of Vercingetorix." Actually it commemorates Julius Caesar's victory over the Gallic chieftain Vercingetorix at the siege of Alesia in 52 BC.)

The last two lines do not seem to have any relevance to the monu-ments, except that the ancient structures are still standing when the enigmatic **Annemarc** comes to his deliverance.

For line 3, Randi makes the shallow observation that the enigma Prince Dannemarc stands for a "prince of Denmark" and pretty much brushes it off because he cannot furnish any record of a Danish royal ever being held for ransom near St Rémy. On the other hand, Leoni, with far more care and in-depth research into contemporary 16th-century events, gives a comprehensive historical overview of the quatrain (see page 624, *Nostradamus and His Prophecies*). He establishes that **Annemarc** (Anne's Lands) were the kingdoms of Hungary and Bohemia, which were part of the dowry of Princess Anne, wife of the heir to the Holy Roman Empire, Ferdinand, the brother of Charles V. The *Prince of Annemarc* would therefore be Maximilian, their son, who was 27 years old at the time Nostradamus wrote this verse. The prophet foresaw that Maximilian, the next heir-apparent to the Imperial throne, would become a Lutheran and put the succession into doubt.

Then Leoni reads far too much into the line. Those who **come to deliver** Maximilian from his heresy are not members of some relief army come to pry him free from incarceration. *They* could be the good council of family and priests who helped snap Maximilian out of his Protestant sympathies by 1560 so he could be elected King of **Annemarc** (ruler of Bohemia in 1562, and of Hungary in 1563, that is) and become Holy Roman Emperor by 1564.

Line 4 makes little sense for Maximilian. No doubt Nostradamus was a visitor at the ruins of a temple to Diana in nearby Nîmes, but the Emperor never set foot there, nor was he a prisoner among the ruins, Danish or otherwise. The Castle of Tarascon was frequently used as a prison, but with no apparent relevance to **Annemarc**.

---

4 Q28

Lors que Venus du Sol fera couuert,
Soubs l'efplendeur fera forme¹ occulte:²
Mercure au feu les aura defcouuert,
Par bruit bellique³ fera mis à l'infulte.

When Venus by the Sun will be covered,
Under the splendor will be a hidden form:
Mercury will have exposed them to the fire,
Through a warlike clamour will it be insulted.

¹Figure, configuration.
²Variant: occult, mystic, secret.
³Latin *bellicus* = of war; Bellona was the Roman goddess of war.

The light of Venus is covered by the sun twice a year when the two are in conjunction. A complete occultation of Venus by the sun (at 19 degrees Taurus) will take place on 9–10 June 2000 – a little over a month after the grand alignment of planets on 5 May 2000. At that time Mercury (which will be at 18 degrees Cancer) will rise in the pre-dawn sky, heralding the occultation. A peace will be broken (**insulted**) by war or an unspeakable terrorist act at that time, perhaps in the Middle East.

Astrological Time Window

The next complete occultation of Venus with the sun is New Year's Day 2026, within the next window for World War III during the transit of Neptune in Aries.

4 Q29

Le Sol caché eclipſe par Mercure,
Ne ſera mis que pour le ciel ſecond:
De Vlcan Hermes ſera faicte paſture,[1]
Sol ſera veu pur, rutilant & blond.

The Sun hidden eclipsed by Mercury,
Will be placed only second in the
**   heavens:**
The Vulcan Hermes will be
**   transmuted into pasturage,**
The Sun will be seen pure, shining
**   red and golden.**

[1]Old French *pâture* = food (for animals); pasturage; fodder.

Since the sun cannot be eclipsed by puny little Mercury (even during a rare transit of Mercury over the sun), Nostradamus may be using astrological metaphors for something else. Garencières (1672) thought this quatrain and 4 Q28, 4 Q30, 4 Q31, and 4 Q33 were all about the discovery of the "philosopher's stone," symbolizing the transmutation of base metals into gold. I would agree that this verse comes closest in the group to sounding alchemical in nature. The **Sun** therefore becomes "gold" and **Mercury** becomes either "silver" or the liquid metal of that name used in the alchemical process. A more esoteric slant would insinuate the "gold" of spiritual liberation and enlightenment hidden in the "silver" or "lunar" (feminine) technique of self-observation. In other words, the forgotten birthright of enlightenment is rediscovered through the technique of meditating on the self. Mystics from the East say there is a higher state than enlightenment that exists beyond description in dialectical language. Something that transcends mind and experience cannot be written about, only indicated. That might be why the **gold** of enlightenment is placed **second in the heavens**.

Whether we are talking about metal transformations, *moksha* or *Mahaparinirvana,* I have no idea how line 3 fits in. Turning **Vulcan Hermes** into fodder worthy for bovines (**pasturage**) has little to do with either metal or mental metamorphoses. My conceptual editor, Linda Obadia, suggests that because Hermes/Mercury stands for the god and planet of communication, maybe what is being transferred (the ineffable communication) serves as food for the soul.

In any case the **Sun** (enlightenment) will be seen in its pure state, shining **red and golden** (colors of Eastern mysticism, especially Tibetan). Perhaps this describes the shift in the spiritual axis of future civilization to Eastern mysticism.

4 Q30

Plus vnze fois Luna Sol ne voudra,
Tous augmenté & baiſſez de degré:
Et ſi bas mis que peu or on coudra,
Qu'apres faim, peſte, deſcouuert le ſecret.

For eleven more times the Moon will
    not want the Sun,
Both raised and lessened in degree,
And put so low that one will sew little
    gold,
That after famine and plague the
    secret will be revealed.

Astrological time window

This occult quatrain may be dating the number of Grand Astrological Lunar Cycles until the end of the world (354 years X 11). If we begin counting the cycles from the life of Christ we reach the year 3894, a little over a century past the dated destruction of Earth in 3797.

4 Q31

La Lune au plain de nuict ſur le haut mont,
Le nouueau ſophe[1] d'vn ſeul cerueau l'a
    veu:
Par ſes diſciples eſtre immortel ſemond,
Yeux au midy, en ſeins mains, corps au
    feu.

The Moon in the middle of the night
    over the high mountain,
The young sage alone with his mind
    has seen it:
His disciples invite him to become
    immortal
His eyes in the middle, his hands
    [folded] on his breast, his body in
    the fire.

[1]Latin sophus = wise man, sage.

We see Nostradamus describing the moment of awakening experienced by a young man who is alone at midnight. He has seen *it* – the truth of being – which transcends the dialectics of words and is beyond any duality.

The prophecy jumps into the future: the sage is no longer alone. He has many disciples who, by opening their hearts and minds, imbibe his existential truths. His body may die, but his essence, his immortality, lives on in his disciples. In some secret manner the sage will dissolve himself into them.

Two possible clues are hiding in the double pun of midy: either it means the sage faces south, in his temple or in meetings with disciples, or the word can mean "meridian" or "middle." One, therefore, can picture **the young sage** as a mystic from the East whose eyes move up toward the middle of his brow – his third eye – when he rises into a mystical ecstasy.

Line 4 could contain more complex layers of meaning, some that your author may have witnessed first hand when he was invited to participate in the funeral celebration and ritual cremation of one of this century's most controversial mystics, Osho.

On the evening of 19 January 1990, the body of Osho was brought into the public meeting hall at the Osho Commune International. Several thousand white-robed followers danced and celebrated in front of the flower-festooned bamboo bier, in the most unusual and happiest funeral I have ever experienced. There were certainly a lot of tears, but even in the midst of grief most of the faces in that hall were filled with a glow of gratitude and love for a man who for them was the most remarkable person they had ever known and loved.

After ten minutes the body was carried off on its final journey to the burning ghats, the simple funerary crematoriums one finds along Indian rivers. Chance would have it that I walked alongside his body all the way to the ghats. I could see him perfectly. Osho didn't look dead at all. Now I understand the stories about Zen disciples who resisted burning their master's body until they were sure he was really dead and not just playing a prank. Osho was just lying there. Very transparent, delicate, as if he were glowing from the inside. His was the most alive corpse I had ever seen. I couldn't believe he was actually dead until one of the pallbearers got a little carried away by the energy of the celebration and his dancing gait made Osho's head and neck bob about like rubber.

There were between 2,000 and 5,000 people in white at the ghats. I sat in the first row. I saw the man's peaceful face for the last time, bathed in the light of electric torches as the final logs and flowers were lowered onto the funeral pyre, to the sounds of musical instruments and thousands of voices singing a stirring devotional song. The verses warmed the cold and humid Indian night air with the words, "Step into the holy fire, walk into the holy flame, oh! Halleluia! Halleluia!" Soon a great flame leapt up from the funeral pyre. Osho's family was to my right. They were crying like children. His younger brother Amit, in particular, was sobbing with such innocence and beauty that I was carried into his sobs. But even as the tears came I sensed a presence, a heresy, growing inside me. "What are you crying for?" said the heresy (as if it could speak). I felt I was saying goodbye to someone who hadn't left – couldn't leave me. For the rest of the night this heresy grew, and along with thousands of others I could not contain my delight.

Let us look again at the quatrain.

Osho claims that his enlightenment took place in a park in Jabalpur, India, when he was alone, sitting under a malshree tree at midnight (*in the middle of the night*) on 21 March 1953. At the time he had just turned 21 years old (*the young sage*). He was born with five planets in the sign of Capricorn, which in occult astrology is symbolized by a *high mountain* cutting into the limitless sky. Osho describes enlightenment as a state of "no-mind," in which one lives in a ultimate state of freedom he also calls blissful **alone**ness. In the East the mind and the ego are to be witnessed as false phenomena outside of consciousness until one recognizes the truth of one's authentic being – which he often referred to as "It" (*The young sage alone with his mind has seen it*).

Osho often told his disciples that upon his death "I will dissolve into my people" in what he called the Buddhafield, the next stage in the evolution of human consciousness. This is a collective experience of enlightenment that all equally unique individuals can draw from. The days when people give up their responsibility to saviors are drawing to a close. Rather than the arrival of a Messiah in the 21st century, Osho predicted more of a collective awakening, or impersonal messianic experience. In other words, the Messiah is not coming – he is already hiding under our false egos and programmed behavior. The Messiah is within. Osho once said to Kurt Braun, the author of *Rajneeshpuram: The Unwanted Society*, that his people would become his autobiography (**His disciples** will **invite him to become immortal**).

Dr Amrito, Osho's personal physician, once told me that his patient experienced a strange physical phenomenon caused by his enlightenment – he felt constantly on fire inside. Osho was noted for keeping his room temperature at around 40 degrees to keep cool (**his body in the fire**). I can attest to the fact that he gave his daily discourses facing **south** in the Commune's meeting hall. He regularly could be seen with his eyes fixed **in the middle** of his brow in ecstasy. And his **body** on the funeral bier lay with its hands folded **in the fire** of the cremation pit.

Does this quatrain refer to the life and death of Osho? The one who knows lies buried in the wall of a Salonaise church.

Quatrain Indexing Date: Q31 = 1931. Osho was born on December 11, 1931.

4 Q32

Es lieux & temps chair au poiſſon donra lieu,	**In the places and times when flesh will give way [or a place] to fish,**
La loy commune ſera faicte au contraire:	**The communal law will be made in opposition:**
Vieux tiendra fort puis oſté du millieu,	**The old order will hold strong, then are removed from the scene,**
Le Pánta chiona philòn¹ mis fort arriere.	**Then communism put far behind.**

[1]*Pánta chiona philòn*: Greek *Panta* = all things; *koinos* = common, sharing; *philos* = friend, lover. In other words: one who loves to hold all things in common – i.e. a believer in communism.

This quatrain, along with 3 Q95, predicts the fall of communism in Russia and its former Soviet provinces. After the democratic revolution of the early 1990s the Communist Party was forced out of power, and is now running **in opposition** in democratic elections to various neo-Fascist, democratic and nationalist parties in the new political arena of post-Cold War Russia. The **old order** could either be the Czarist regime, which was overthrown by the Bolsheviks in 1917 after 1,000 years of rule, or it is the Bolsheviks and Communists themselves thrown out of power after hard-liners in the Politburo launched a failed coup against Gorbachev in August 1991. The last line of 3 Q95 says communism itself is supplanted by language and promises **more agreeable** – in other words, it is replaced by flowery and seductive promises of capitalism and democratic systems. So far the majority of Russians do not share the promise, but share the pain of dismantling seven decades of communism.

Edgar Leoni (1961) was definitely on the right track when he wrote at the peak of the Cold War, when the Soviet Union was a rising giant, not a collapsed colossus: "Another extremely fascinating quatrain, associated with 3 Q95 in predicting the decline of communism. Since there is no bizarre Ukrainian setting for this one, there exists the possibility of Nostradamus' foreseeing communist trends amongst some local and contemporary group, presumably one of the Protestant sects."

Clearly the connection between the Chernobyl nuclear disaster in the Ukraine and the decline of communism could not have been known by Leoni at that time. Newscasters at CBN (Christian Broadcasting Net-work), as well as secular reporters, continue to report on the significant rising tide of evangelical Protestantism in Russia during the 1990s. This makes Leoni's hunch remarkable, since a Nostradamus scholar living in 1961, the era of the Bay of Pigs fiasco and the building of the Berlin Wall, would find it hard to imagine that the empire of the **great Red**, which in 8 Q80 is destroying the churches, would see its people reopen them by the century's end.

4 Q33

Iupiter ioinct plus Venus qu'à la Lune,	**Jupiter joined more to Venus than to the Moon,**
Apparoiſſant de plenitude blanche:	**It will seem to appear in white fullness:**
Venus cachée ſouz la blancheur[1] Neptune,	**Venus hidden under the whiteness [innocence] of Neptune,**
De Mars frappée[2] par la grauée branche.[3]	**By Mars stricken by the white gravel.**

[1]*blancheur*: variant: cleanliness; (fig.) purity, innocence.
[2]*frappée*: variant: surprised, astounded.
[3]*grauée branche*: variant: Milky Way band of stars in the night sky.

This is the only quatrain in which Nostradamus comes close to rendering Neptune as an actual planet rather than using it as a classical metaphor for a sea power. This has made some interpreters believe he was foresee-ing the discovery of Neptune by the French astronomer Jean Joseph Leverrier and the German astronomer Johann Gottfried Galle, in 1846.

For such an assumption to be correct, a conjunction of Jupiter and Venus with a near-conjunction of a full moon must take place in the month of Neptune's discovery. This didn't happen. If we rewire Nostradamus' dyslexic description in line 3, we might get an occultation of Neptune by Venus rather than the other way around. Mars passes through the star band of the Milky Way (**the white gravel**) twice every two years, when it transits through Taurus and Gemini and again through Scorpio and Sagittarius. Mars **striking** Venus implies a detrimental aspect to such a square. Nostradamus could be referring to **Venus** (peace) being struck down by **Mars** (war). In that case **peace** is **hidden under Neptune**, which stands for a great sea power such as Britain thrust into war.

A third millennium application would suggest an alliance forged between human colonies on Jupiter and Venus, or, less likely, with cities on the Moon. The Martian colony suffers a surprise attack or comet collision from the direction of the center of the Milky Way galaxy.

4 Q34

Le grand mené captif d'eſtrange terre,	**The great one from a foreign land led captive,**
D'or enchainé au Roy CHYREN[1] *offert:*	**By gold-enchained offered to King Chyren:**
Qui dans Auſone,[2] *Milan perdra la guerre,*	**He who in Ausonia, Milan will lose the war,**
Et tout ſon oſt mis à feu & à fer.	**And all his army put to fire and sword.**

[1]CHYREN = anagram for Henryc = Henry II.
[2]Ausonia, which stands for the Kingdom of Naples in particular, as a French base during the Italian Wars, and for Italy in general.

Here again is another example of an alternative future for Henry II, dashed forever by his mortal wound in a tournament in 1559. If Henry II had forsworn jousting in his 41st year, Nostradamus expected him to break loose from the humiliating agreements of the Treaty of Cateau-Cambrésis and resume the Italian Wars, this time to victory. It seems that Nostradamus consoled his metaphysical self with a prophecy of French revenge to come in a battle that would follow the other accurately foreseen French disaster of St Quentin (which is still a few years beyond the penning of this quatrain).

The 1560s open with the French returning the favor to the Spanish near Milan, where the Spaniards and their allies also suffer the destruc-tion of an army and capture of their most notable generals. There's one extra bit of frosting to the sweet victory cake: either the Duke of Savoy or Philip II of Spain is captured and led back to Paris. Once there he is brought before Henry II in a victory parade, his hands chained with gold.

4 Q35

Le feu eſtaint, les vierges trahiront,	**The fire extinguished, the virgins will betray,**
La plus grand part de la bande nouuelle:	**The greater part of the new band:**
Fouldre à fer, lance les ſeulz Roy garderont,	**Thunderbolt from steel, lance the lone kings will protect,**
Etruſque & Corſe, de nuict gorge allumelle.[1]	**Tuscany and Corsica, by night throat cut.**

[1]Old French for blade, cutting edge.

The vestal **virgins** guarded the eternal flame of Vesta, goddess of the hearth to the Romans. This classical allusion points to a day when Italy will lose its vigilance against tyranny. The *fascia*, the bundle of sticks and axes symbolizing Ancient Rome, would be adopted by the Italian "Fascists" of Mussolini's new Rome. Line 3 might describe modern artillery, or it is yet another poetic allusion to Hitler's blitzkrieg (lightning-war) tactics. Corsica was abandoned by the Axis forces in 1943. Tuscany was the scene of heavy fighting in the final six months of the war.

4 Q36

Les ieux[1] nouueaux en Gaule redreſſés,	**The new sports to reform in Gaul,**
Apres victoire de l'Inſubre champaigne:	**After victory of the Lombard campaign:**
Monts d'Eſperie, les grands liés, trouſſés:	**The mountains of the West, the great ones tied and packed away:**
De peur trembler la Romaigne & l'Eſpaigne.	**Romania and Spain tremble in fear.**

[1]Variant: Old French *Jeux* =Jews.

Journals during the early years of the French Revolution commented on the new sporting crazes of public swimming in the Seine and the renaissance of classical Olympic sports such as track and field at the large-scale public celebrations and feasts outside Paris on the Champs de Mars. Napoleon Bonaparte prosecuted a victorious campaign in northern Italy (Lombardy) in 1798. In this case **the mountains of the West** are Spain. It is now ten years later, when Napoleon, as Emperor of the French, occupies that country and makes its Spanish Bourbon king a captive. This could also cover the French captivity of Popes Pius VI and VII during Napoleon's reign when Rome (the papacy) and Spain **tremble in fear**.

4 Q37

Gaulois par ſaults, monts viendra penetrer,	**By leaps the Gaul will come to**
Occupera le grand lieu de l'Inſubre:	**penetrate the mountains,**
Au plus profond ſon oſt fera entrer,	**He will occupy the great place of**
Gennes, Monech poußeront claße rubre.	**Lombardy:**
	His host will penetrate to the very depths,
	Genoa and Monaco will push the red fleet back.

Nostradamus continues on the future track of Napoleon. This time we move with him and the blue-coated, bayonet-tipped human snake of the Consular Army, winding its way down the switchbacks of the St Bernard Pass through the Alps on its way to the fertile Po valley of northern Italy. Napoleon seized Milan, the capital of Lombardy, on 2 June 1800. The port of Genoa was besieged by the Austrians and surrendered on 4 June. An armada from the British redcoats commanded by Lord Nelson frequently patrolled the seas of Genoa and Monaco at the time.

4 Q38

Pendant que Duc, Roy, Royne occupera,	**Depending which duke, king or queen will occupy,**
Chef Bizant du captif en Samothrace:	**The Byzantine chief with the captive in Samothrace:**
Auant l'aßault l'vn l'autre mangera,[1]	**Before the assault one will eat the other,**
Rebours ferré ſuyura du ſang la trace.	**The wrong-shodded, obstinate horse will follow the trail of blood.**

[1]Will eat; will squander; will run through (with a sword).

This is about the fall of the Ottoman Empire and the rise of modern Turkey during the Greco-Turkish war.

Mustafa Kemal, later known as Atatürk, is the **Byzantine chief. Samothrace** is a Greek Aegean island near the mouth of the strategic Bosphorus Strait. It stands as a near miss for the regions indicated in the verse – the Bosphorus, European Turkey and western Anatolia, all of which were seized by the Greeks after the collapse of the Ottoman Empire at the end of World War I. Between 1921 and 1922, Atatürk led an army from Ankara that threw the Greek army of occupation back into the sea. During their march on Ankara the Greeks had overextended their meager supply lines and were reduced to a starving rabble (**one will eat the other**). After a three-week battle on the Sakarya river they were forced to begin an agonizing year-long, 250-mile retreat (**the trail of blood**) toward Smyrna, which Atatürk captured after a three-day battle in September 1922.

Several thousand Greek prisoners and civilians were seized and slaughtered by the Turks. One could say that the Greeks' strategy and poor preparations were like a **wrong-shodded horse**, ready to throw the rider.

4 Q39

Les Rhodiens demanderont fecours,	**The people of Rhodes will demand relief,**
Par le neglect de fes hoyrs delaiffée:	**Abandoned by neglect of their heirs:**
L'empire Arabe reualera fon cours,	**The Arab Empire will assess its course,**
Par Hefperies la caufe redreffée.[1]	**Its cause revived again by the West.**

[1]Revived. In the 1970s, President Assad of Syria and Saddam Hussein of Iraq worked together as leading personages of the Arab Ba'athist (or Arab *Revival*) party, a political movement dedicated to uniting the Arab world into one Pan-Islamic superpower.

The generalities of the first two lines can either paint a historical background for Nostradamus' time or offer a prediction for the 20th century. First the historical slant. The conquest of Rhodes in 1522 by the Ottoman Turks required that Charles V move the Knights of Saint John to a new home on the island of Malta. In other words, the people of Rhodes are **neglected** by their knights, who under the terms of their surrender to the Sultan must leave the island. Now for the prophetic angle: the **heirs** of Rhodes, the Ottoman Turks, later lost this neglected island possession in a war with Italy in 1912.

The last two lines take us beyond our own time into the future of Pan-Arabism. Nostradamus' writings include prophecies that a fierce Muslim chieftain will invade the soft underbelly of Christian Europe. In the 16th and 17th centuries interpreters believed this Muslim would come with his hordes from the North African region of the Ottoman Empire. But the Turkish overlords and their "Barbare"/Libyan allies never made good these interpreted threats because the Arab Turkish empire began to crumble not long after Nostradamus' death.

Fast-forward to the 20th century and historical events that revitalize the prophetic debate. Here we have Nostradamus predicting that an Arab Empire would rise again. **Abandoned by neglect of their heirs: / The Arab Empire will assess its course, / Its cause revived again by the West.**

Oil has certainly revived the Arab Empire lost through the heirs of the 16th-century Ottoman Sultan, Suleiman the Magnificent. Furthermore, in the post-millenial world the West's hunger for Arab oil will swell to even more outlandish proportions. In 1993 it was reported that US dependence on foreign oil imports has risen to an all-time high of 50 percent. OPEC – rather than the Ottomans – will **revive again** as the demand for petroleum makes the dominant Arab wing of the oil cartel the power-brokers of energy for the developed world.

4 Q40

Les forteresses des assiegés serrés,
Par poudre à feu[1] profondés en abysme:
Les proditeurs seront tous vifs serrés,
Onc aux sacristes[2] n'aduint si piteux
    schisme.

The fortress of the besieged
    sealed,
And sunk to its depths by
    explosives:
The traitors will be entombed
    alive,
Never did such a pitiful division
    happen to the Saxons.

[1]poudre à feu = explosives.
[2]Old French sacriste, sexton; or Saxons, a synecdoche for eastern Germany.

The beginning and end of World War II are foretold in two quatrains numbered 40. They may be a message to France that the year of their greatest defeat, 1940, will be avenged. The second of the two quatrains describes Hitler's final moments deep inside his fortified Berlin bunker while bombardment and fighting rage on the surface.

Adolf Hitler, Nostradamus' Second Antichrist, shot himself two days after Mussolini's battered corpse was hung by its feet in Milan. The terrible war would end with eastern portions of Nazi Germany (**the Saxons**) divided from the rest of Germany by the Iron Curtain.

Quatrain Indexing Date: Q40 = 1940? See also 2 Q40

4 Q41

Gymnique[1] sexe captiue par hostage,
Viendra de nuit custodes[2] deceuoir:
Le chef du camp deceu par son langaige:
Lairra à la gente, sera piteux à voir.

The female sex captive as a hostage,
Will come by night to deceive her
    guards:
The chief of the army tricked by her
    language:
Will abandon [her] to the people. It
    will be pitiful to see.

[1]Coined by Nostradamus, or a misprint for gynique, from Greek gyne = female.
[2]Latin custodes = guards, guardians.

This is so general it could be applied to any hostage theme, so I will choose my favorite story. There's every chance it is not the one Nostradamus intended – unless the last line was a comment on the person's physical state at the end of my story.

Just prior to the Allied invasion of the Riviera, the Gestapo came pounding at the door of a certain Madame Fourcade of Aix-en-Provence. They demanded to know the identity of the man seen in her courtyard the night before. Fourcade replied that she had seen no one, that she was a simple homemaker who lived alone. The Gestapo officer was not

buying her story. He revealed that they already knew she had ren-
dezvoused with an important agent in the French Resistance, code-
named the Grand-Duc. When papers containing secret messages she had
sent to London were found under her sofa the Gestapo officer began slap-
ping her around, shouting "Confess, you're a terrorist! Confess! Where's
the Grand-Duc?" Fourcade reeled from the blows, her nose and mouth
bleeding. She had to clear her head and think fast. She wasn't just
another French terrorist; this petite woman was the mastermind and
founder of an extensive espionage network known as the Alliance of
Animals. The man they called the Grand-Duc was one of her co-leaders
in the spy network along the Côte d'Azur. Fourcade and this Grand-Duc
had met the previous evening to arrange the distribution of six tons of
ammunition, firearms and grenades, explosives, radios, and an assortment
of other supplies parachuted by the Allies at a secret drop zone a few
miles outside of Aix.

Fourcade had to stall the Gestapo in order to buy the Grand-Duc and
his men time to carry the supplies to safety. She suddenly remembered
that one of her contacts had seen the chief of the Gestapo at Aix leave
town the previous day. "I will talk only to your boss!" she said, glaring at
the underling in disgust. "You are too unimportant for me to bother
with."

The Gestapo agent dragged her out of the house by the hair and into a
waiting car. She was taken to Gestapo headquarters and thrown into a
cell. Sometime during the night Madame Fourcade made her daring
escape from jail. She stripped naked, squeezed her small frame through
the bars and dropped two floors to the ground, and ran into the night to
find shelter at the home of a fellow "Animal."

Quatrain Indexing Date: Q41 = 1941, a near miss for 1944.

4 Q42

Geneue & Lāgres par ceux de Chartres & Dole,	**Geneva and Langres by those of Chartres and Dôle,**
Et par Grenoble captif au Montlimard:	**And by Grenoble captured at Montélimar:**
Seyſett, Loſanne par fraudulente dole,	**Seysel, Lausanne through fraudulent deceit,**
Les trahiront par or ſoixante marc.	**They will betray them for sixty marks of gold.**

The locations in this quatrain are scattered across central and eastern
France and Switzerland. One could sniff out some Protestant or Calvinist
intrigue brewing here but little else, except that a *mark* was then the
equivalent of 8–8.6 ounces of gold.

4 Q43

Seront ouys au ciel les armes battre:	**Weapons will be heard fighting in the**
Celuy au meſme les diuins ennemis	**skies:**
Voudront loix ſainctes[1] iniuſtement	**In the very same year the divine ones**
debatre,	**enemies**
Par foudre & guerre bien croyans à mort	**They will desire unjustly to argue**
mis.	**over holy [or false] laws,**
	By lightning and war many believers
	are put to death.

[1]Old French *sainte* = holy; or *fainte* = false.

The description of aerial warfare places this one in the 20th century, most likely during World War II. The quatrain indexing may give us the year 1943, when the Allied powers sent their first 1,000-bomber air fleets over Berlin.

I would like to turn your attention to one of the greatest but least known aerial battles of the war, which took place on the Eastern Front at sunrise on 5 July 1943. A surprise attack of three Soviet air fleets of 2,500 bombers and escorts collided with 270 German fighters just as the German offensive on the southern flank of the Kursk salient was launched. The Soviets had timed their attack so they could bomb and strafe 1,500 German Stukas and bombers as they were taxiing for take-off on 16 airfields. The Soviets could not know that the Germans had new radar systems that alerted them to the attack in time to launch hundreds of fighters. The Soviet armada flying at 6,000 to 10,000 feet slammed into a hailstorm released from 19,000 heavy and light flak guns. In the first few seconds the German fighters shot 120 Soviet machines out of the sky. Dawn broke over the battlefields of Kursk with a million soldiers from both sides shaken by the thunder of the great air battle overhead. The rising sun reddened the smoke trails of hundreds of flaming aircraft. By the end of the day the score was 403 Soviet aircraft downed. The following day another 205 fell, making the total 608. At Prokhorovka, on 12 July the skies and earth reverberated with the sounds of a second titanic air battle that raged like a brawling swarm of godlike hornets over the greatest tank battle in history. Soviet Lieutenant-General Rotmistrov, crouched on a nearby hill, described the first collision of thousands of Soviet and German tanks in what may hopefully be the closest mankind will ever get to fighting the battle of Armageddon:

> The tanks were moving across the steppe in small packs, under cover of patches of woodland and hedges. The bursts of gunfire merged into one continuous, mighty roar. The Soviet tanks thrust into the German advance formations at full speed and penetrated the German tank screen. . . . There was neither time nor room to disengage from the enemy and reform in

battle order, or operate in formation. The shells fired at extremely close range pierced not only the side armor but also the frontal armor of the fighting vehicles. . . . Frequently, when a tank was hit, its ammunition and fuel blew up, and torn-off turrets were flung through the air over dozens of meters. At the same time over the battlefield furious aerial combats developed. Soviet as well as German airmen tried to help their ground forces to win the battle. The bombers, ground-support aircraft, and fighters seemed to be permanently suspended in the sky over Prokhorovka. One aerial combat followed another. Soon the whole sky was shrouded in the thick smoke of burning wrecks. On the black, scorched earth the gutted tanks burnt like torches.

If such modern war machines were viewed by Nostradamus, he might have described them as terrible winged gods. Many of the German tanks had the names of Nordic gods painted on their turrets. Even the new radar system that caught the Soviet air fleets by surprise on 5 July was named after a Nordic goddess, Freya. Line 3 could explain the equally fierce war of ideology on the Eastern Front: the true Nazi believers versus the true Marxist believers fought with a brutality not seen in other theaters of World War II. The final line can also be translated **By lightning war many believers are put to death.** Between 5 and 13 July, 70,000 Germans and 120,000 Soviets fell as the last Nazi blitzkrieg (lightning war) offensive in Russia ground to a halt.

Quatrain Indexing Date: Q43 = 1943, which also saw vast air battles over the German Third Reich.

4 Q44

Deux gros de Mende, de Roudés & Milhau,	***Two large ones of Mende, of Rodez and Milau,***
Cahours, Limoges, Caſtres malo ſepmano:	***Cahors, Limoges, Castres – bad week:***
De nuech l'intrado de Bourdeaux vncailhau,	***By night the entry, from Bordeaux an insult,***
Par Perigort au toc de la campano.	***Though Périgord at the peal of the bell.***

A centime for your prophetic thoughts, Monsieur Nostradamus. With this mishmash of French and Provençal phrases, your guess is as good as mine. It could be anything from an account of his fortunes and failures during his life as a roving medical student to a description of this interpreter's vacation in south-west France in August 1991.

4 Q45

Par conflit Roy, regne abandonnera,	***Through conflict [of a] King, the***
Le plus grand chef faillira au beſoing:	***realm will be abandoned,***
Mors profligés peu en rechapera,	***The greatest chief will fail in time of***
Tous deſtranchés vn en ſera teſmoing.	***need:***
	Dead, ruined, few will escape,
	All sliced up, [save] one who will be a
	witness to it.

Two possibilities vie for our favor here. The first is the Portuguese crusader King Sebastian I, who in August 1578 disembarked an army on the Moroccan coast, where it was annihilated by the Moors at Alcazarquavir. Sebastian's mangled body was never identified.

The second option would replace Sebastian with Napoleon III, who abandoned his Second Empire after being taken prisoner by the Prussians when he and 100,000 men were surrounded and captured at Sedan in 1870. One could say that before his capture the despondent French Emperor was a **witness** to the wreck of his army beset by cannon barrages from all sides. He had ridden his horse into the ranks of his men hoping that one of the shells slicing gaps through their serried ranks would dispatch him as well.

4 Q46

Bien defendu le faict par excellence,	***The deed well defended by excellence,***
Garde toy Tours de ta proche ruine:	***Guard yourself Tours from your near***
Londres & Nantes par Reims ſera defenſe,	***ruin:***
Ne paſſe outre au temps de la bruine.	***London and Nantes, through Reims,***
	will make a defense,
	Not passing further in the time of the
	mists.

The **deed well defended** is the network of trenches successfully held by the French and their Anglo-American allies against four long and bloody years of German attacks on the Western Front during World War I. Tours, being far to the south-east of the battle line, was spared the misery. This quatrain might point to an alternative future invasion of the Germans which failed to manifest earlier, or it is a temporal hiccup forwarding us to World War II when Tours was seized by the Aryan sons of those who fought in the first.

London is a synecdoche for Great Britain, with **Nantes** standing in for France in general. *Reims* suffered greatly as the largest French city on the front lines (**will make a defense**) between 1914 and 1918. By 1918 the German Hindenburg Line collapsed and the war was all but lost. In 1918 the Germans agreed to an armistice in November which the French call the **time of the mists**, bringing a halt to further Allied advances (**not passing further**).

4 Q47

Le noir farouche quand aura eſſayé,
Sa main ſanguine par feu, fer, arcs[1]
    tendus:
Teſtout le peuple ſera tant effrayé,
Voir les plus grans par col & pieds pendus.

The savage black [king] will have
    exercised
His bloody hand by fire, sword and
    trained [arquebus]:
All the people will be so terrified,
Seeing the great ones hanging by neck
    and feet.

[1]arcs = a) cryptogram for arquebus, a primitive matchlock musket with a hook-shaped stock;
b) Latin arcus = curve; (fig.) = bent bow.

Charles IX delighted himself by hacking off the heads of donkeys and pigs
with a single blow during royal hunts. He transferred his cruelty to
humans by sanctioning the St Bartholomew's Day Massacre two years
before his death from a cold in 1574, when he was 24. During the
massacre he was reported shooting fleeing Protestants from a balcony of
the Louvre with an arquebus matchlock musket.

4 Q48

Planure[1] Auſonne fertile, ſpacieuſe,
Produira taons ſi tant de ſauterelles:
Clarté ſolaire deuiendra nubileuſe,
Ronger le tout, grand peſte venir d'elles.

The fertile, spacious Ausonian plain,
Will produce so many gadflies and
    locusts:
The sunlight will become clouded,
Everything devoured, the great
    pestilence will come from them.

[1]Old French planure = plain.

A great cloud of locusts blots out the sun near Naples, Italy (**Ausonian
plain**). The extent of this plague places the event in our future. During
the mid-1980s North Africa suffered a series of widespread locust infesta-
tions. The newspapers of the day warned of the danger of locust invasions
carried by the hot Sirocco winds across the Mediterranean to Italy and
southern France, but the threat passed. The changes expected in our
climate over the next 50 years might well provoke a locust invasion in
the same area from Africa.

4 Q49

Deuant le peuple ſang ſera reſpandu,
Que de haut ciel ne viendra eſloigner:
Mais d'vn long temps ne ſera entendu,
L'eſprit d'vn ſeul le viendra teſmoigner.

Before the people, blood will be spilt,
It will not come far from the high
    heavens:
But for a long time it will not be
    heard,
The spirit of a single man will bear
    witness to it.

Few now believe that Lee Harvey Oswald was the true assassin, but according to Nostradamus, whoever actually killed Kennedy was seen by only one witness (**The spirit of a single man will bear witness to it**). On the day that President Kennedy's body lay in state, Jack Ruby – a Mafia man – killed Oswald in Dallas. Shortly afterwards, the Dallas chief of homicide declared the Kennedy assassination case closed.

Stephen J. Rivele, a noted investigative reporter on the Mafia, believes Corsican Mafia hit man Lucien Sartee was contracted to kill Kennedy. Sartee may be the man disguised in a policeman's uniform who is hidden in the **misty woods** – or wooded, grassy knoll of Dealey Plaza – in 6 Q37. Sartee was well known for taking the most dangerous hit jobs. His favorite ballistic signature for a kill was the dumdum bullet: hollow ammunition that shatters on impact, making horrible wounds like the one that ripped the president's head wide open. Sartee himself was shot dead a few years after the assassination.

Let's examine Nostradamus' **spirit** riddle in another way. Perhaps he is saying that conspiracy buffs of the future can do no better than wonder what tales the ghost of Sartee could tell about who really marked Kennedy for assassination. And then there is Jack Ruby who, before dying of cancer, admitted to a tantalizing tip of an iceberg of conspiracy when he made the following recorded statement to the Warren Commission: "The world will never know the true facts of what occurred because, unfortunately, the people who had so much to gain will never let the true facts come out, above-board, to the world."

4 Q50

Libra verra regner les Hefperies,[1]	**Libra will see the Western lands to govern,**
De ciel & terre tenir la monarchie:	**Holding the rule over the skies and the earth:**
D'Afie forces nul ne verra peries,	**No one will see the forces of Asia destroyed,**
Que fept ne tiennent par rang le hierarchie.	**Not until seven hold the hierarchy in succession.**

[1]Latin Hesperia = Land of the West; America?

At a time when the United States is the sole superpower, and a hierarchy, or Great Seven economic superpowers are gathered together, the menace from the East will be destroyed. The US is represented by Libra's scales of democracy and justice. Here again is the reference to Middle and/or Far Eastern alliances being destroyed, clearly placing this event in our near future.

America is portrayed in many prophetic traditions as the most fertile ground for the new religious teachings coming out of the East. The *seven* are the seven millennia in one of Nostradamus' time-track calculations that ends in AD 2000. This quatrain is Nostradamus' equivalent to Blavatsky's famous prophecies about a new spiritual teacher from the East. Madame Blavatsky (1831–91), one of the leading psychic seers of the 19th century, predicted that Maitreya (the Buddhist Messiah) would appear in Asia around the year 1950: "We are at the close of the cycle of 5,000 years of the present Aryan Kali Yuga, or Dark Age. This will be succeeded by an Age of Light . . . A new messenger of the spirit will be sent to the western nations. He is appearing in 1975."

In that year the teachings of Osho were spread westwards from the Indian subcontinent in a stream of publications. Interest in the leaders and teachings of the New Age/Human Potential Movement also burgeoned suddenly around 1975 and accelerated throughout the late 1970s. The teachings of Adi Da Santosha (Da Free John) and Sun Myung Moon also caught the attention of seekers in that period, although to a more limited degree.

Quatrain Indexing Date: Q50 = 1950, the year Blavatsky says a great religious master from the East, a catalyst for the next stage in human enlightenment, appears. The Egyptian Great Pyramid prophecies target the years 1953 through 2001 as the Age of Osiris, considered to be the time the Egyptian Messiah returns (see 1 Q56, 9 Q51.)

4 Q51

Vn Duc cupide ſon ennemy enſuyure,	A Duke eager to follow his enemy,
Dans entrera empeſchant la phalange:	Will enter within impeding the phalanx:
Haſtez à pied ſi pres viendront pourſuyure,	Hurried on foot they will come to follow so closely,
Que la iournee conflite pres de Gange.	That the day of battle is near the Ganges.

There is a French town called Ganges, in Languedoc, about 25 miles north of Montpellier, where Nostradamus earned his medical degree. This region was a Huguenot center during the Wars of Religion. No battle took place near Ganges during the nine wars, but this prohecy likely refers to the Camisard revolt of the Cevennes (1705–10).

The quatrain best fits the events of a battle fought in 1764 on the banks of the River Ganges at Buxar, India, between the rebel forces of Mir Kasim, the Nawab of Bengal, and Major Hector Monro's small army of British and native soldiers. Although greatly outnumbered, the British kept their cool and fired shattering volleys into the nawab's massed troops, then charged their line (**will enter within impeding the phalanx**).

Munro's men routed the superior force, inflicting heavy losses, and the British domination of Bengal was reestablished.

4 Q52

En cité obſeſſe[1] aux murs hommes & femmes,	**In the besieged city men and women to the walls,**
Ennemis hors le chef preſt à ſoy rendre:	**Enemies outside the chief ready to surrender:**
Vent ſera fort encontre les genſdarmes,[2]	**Wind will be strongly against the commanders,**
Chaſſez ſeront par chaux, pouſſiere, & cendre.	**They will be driven away by lime, flying dust, and ashes.**

[1]Latin obsessus = besieged.
[2]Armed policemen on horses; constables; (modern) commanders, viragos.

This prophecy promises victory to a city under a terrible siege. Paris, which suffered a siege in 1590 and in 1871, was not victorious against the besiegers either time, whereas the men and women of Leningrad (present-day St Petersburg), who suffered a 900-day siege (perhaps the greatest in history), were the clear victors against Hitler's forces. Line 4's use of **lime** begins a complex mixed metaphor for the substance people spread on the bodies of the dead before burial. One out of three Leningraders – 1 million people – died during the siege. **Lime, flying dust, and ashes** also describes the defeat of the Nazis in Russia: the **flying dust** of hot Russian summers impeded their advances; the white **lime** of ice and snow covered the corpses left behind in the northern bogs and barren steppes of Russian winters; and finally, **ashes** portrays the scorched-earth policies of Stalin who, during the initial Nazi advance in 1941, ordered his people to burn their houses and fields. Later, in early 1943, when the Soviets began their bloody three-year advance to Berlin, Hitler ordered his armies to destroy and burn everything left standing. The tracks of the German army's retreat were made in the ashes of that devastation.

4 Q53

Les fugitifs & bannis reuoquez,	**The fugitives and exiles dismissed,**
Peres & fils grand garniſſant les hauts puits:	**Fathers and sons, great garnishing of the deep well:**
Le cruel pere & les ſiens ſuffoquez,	**The cruel father and his own [people] suffocated,**
Son fils plus pire ſubmergé dans le puits.	**His most wicked son submerged in the well.**

This is too general to convey any definite prediction. Whenever I read it, the theme of Czar Nicholas I of Russia comes to mind.

A number of his generals and ministers on Czar Nicholas II's long list of dismissed personnel would become refugees of the Bolshevik Revolution. The Czar and his family were murdered and their naked and dismembered corpses were initially thrown down a flooded mine shaft (*deep well*). By using *garnissant*, Nostradamus might be saying that the Czar's blunders and atrocities had **prepared** his family's terrible end in the abandoned mine shaft. At first the Russians called the Czar their "little father" but his repressions and street massacres eventually earned him the name Bloody Nicholas. The final line implies that the body of Czarevich Alexis was also thrown down the mine shaft with his father, although forensic scientists dispute whether the remains found there or in other burial sites outside of Ekaterinberg include those of the Romanov heir.

4 Q54

Du nom qui onques ne fut au Roy Gaulois,	*Of a name never held by a Gallic King,*
Iamais ne fut vn fouldre ſi craintif:	*Never was so fearful a thunderbolt:*
Tremblant l'Italie, l'Eſpaigne & les Anglois,	*Italy, Spain and the English tremble,*
De femme eſtrangiers grandement attentif.	*[He will be] greatly attentive to foreign women.*

The **name never held by a Gallic King** is that of Napoleon Bonaparte, and with dreams of French royalty all but extinguished, it is doubtful anyone will alter this fact. Even his nephew, (Louis) Napoleon III, is just one of 20 French kings called Louis, the other republican *King* being Louis-Philippe, just one of seven with the name Philip. The name "Napoleon" is not true French but Corsican, and has deeper etymological roots in Italy than in France. Napoleon spoke fluent Italian and in his early days mangled his French with a thick Corsican dialect that only his first mistress, Josephine, could temper.

She would be the first of several important women in Napoleon's life who were, like himself, foreigners to France. Josephine, who later became his wife and Empress of France, was a Creole born in the French colony of Haiti. His paramour, opera singer Guiseppina Grassini, was one of Napoleon's early Italian conquests of the heart. She was called to sing regularly at his retreat at Malmaison. The ravishing Polish countess Maria Walewska was perhaps his most faithful mistress. She visited him during his first abdication and also bore him an illegitimate child. After Napoleon divorced Josephine he married Marie-Louise and crowned this daughter of Francis I of Austria as his second Empress. She bore him his first male heir.

Italy and Spain did **tremble** under the thunder and flash of Napoleon's cannons, and for long periods the English were isolated from Napoleonic Europe.

4 Q55

Quand la corneille ſur tout de brique ioincte,	When the crow on the tower put together by bricks,
Durant ſept heures ne fera que crier:	For seven hours will continue to squawk:
Mort preſagee de ſang ſtatue taincte,	Death presaged, by blood the statue is stained,
Tyran meurtry, aux Dieux peuple prier.	Tyrant murdered, and to the gods the people pray.

A prophecy as rich with images and omens as it is vague in implicating which tyrant is murdered at the cawing of a **crow**. This *raven*, as inscrutable as that conjured by Edgar Allen Poe, may cry "Nevermore . . ." to all of our questions.

When in doubt, an absurd interpretation is at least enjoyable: beware ye tyrant professors beneath the brick towers of *Corneille* – or better – Cornell University, in America – perhaps the crow squawks for thee. Of course this does not rule out a multitude of crows squawking on an equal number of brick towers around the world, "cawing" a curse at tyrannical teachers.

But all corny Cornell interpretations aside, we have a link – fragile as it is – to another reference to the Balkans. In 1389 the Christian forces of Serbian Prince Lazar were defeated by the Muslim army of Turkish Sultan Murad I at Kosovo Polje, the Field of Blackbirds (crows?) just outside Pristina. Today this battle is the rallying point for Serbian nationalism, which fact could allow us to apply this omen to the future death of a Serbian tyrant. Current candidates would be the disgraced General Ratko Mladic, self-styled Bosnian Serb President Radovan Karadzic, or Slobodan Milosovic, the made-over tyrant of what's left of Yugoslavia who, as tacit payment for bringing Bosnian Serbs to the peace table in the mid-1990s, may not face charges of war crimes.

See Index: Balkan war.

4 Q56

Apres victoire de rabieuſe[1] langue,	After the victory of the raving tongue,
L'eſprit tempté[2] en tranquil & repos:	The spirit tempered in tranquillity and rest:
Victeur ſanguin par conflict faict harangue,	The bloody victor makes harangues throughout the conflict,
Rouſtir la langue & la chair & les os.	Roasting the tongue and the flesh and the bones.

[1]Latin *rabiosus* = raving, fierce, mad; insane.
[2]Old French for tempered, moderate.

The power of Adolf Hitler's raging speeches makes him dictator of Germany. Eyewitness accounts describe how Hitler became possessed by some inner, almost orgasmic, force when he stood before the transfixed crowds. Some would even say that his relationship with a mass audience was like a man having sex with his mistress. Whenever Hitler left the podium, he was spent and dripping with sweat. Gone was the lightning-fire in his eyes; now that gaze had the soft glow of a man whose lust has just been satiated. After political campaigns during the early days Hitler would often rush to the tranquillity of his mountain retreat at Berchtes-garten. Later, as overlord of Germany, he considered the Bavarian chalet his official residence.

Line 3 is definitely about Hitler during the early successes of World War II, when the German people saw him making speeches or regularly heard him on radio. After the disaster of Stalingrad, Hitler made only two major speeches during the final years of the war. But the harangue never ceased. Now his generals at headquarters had to suffer a good roast-ing from Hitler's tongue for their defeats, right up to the final hours of his life. After he committed suicide, Hitler's tongue, flesh, and bones were burned in a shallow pit in the ruins of Berlin. Dr Faust Shkaravsky, the Chief Expert of Forensic Medicine with the First Belorussian Front, who performed the autopsy on Hitler's roasted skeletal remains, said, "The tongue was charred, its tip is firmly locked between the teeth of the upper and lower jaws."

4 Q57

Ignare enuie au grand Roy fupportee,	**Ignorant envy of the great king reinforced,**
Tiendra propos deffendre les efcriptz:	**He will propose forbidding the writings:**
Sa femme non femme par vn autre tentee,	**His wife, not his wife, tempted by another,**
Plus double deux ne fort ne criz.	**No longer will both couples shout their mouths off [so] loudly.**

This quatrain betrays Nostradamus' true feelings about Henry II and his mistress (**his wife, not his wife**), Diane de Poitiers. It implies that she was the first of a long line of Nostradamus debunkers whom the prophet con-demns as ignorant and envious of his gift. This quatrain may also be the closest we can come to Nostradamus' own account of his first meeting with the king and queen of France concerning his prophecies, a meeting he may have foreseen years before it happened. Censure of his writings and persecution by those **ignorant** and in **envy** of his prophetic gift always haunted the prophet. The first lines could imply that Nostradamus expected the king's cool reception. In other words, this prediction could be as much a case of common sense as prescient insight. Henry II was a most-royal jock who was not too interested in his wife's occult hysterics.

No documentation exists to prove whether at their meeting the king brought up the subject of censuring Nostradamus' prophecies. But since Nostradamus left the meeting a celebrity instead of a candidate for the stake, his power to please had clearly not failed him. Perhaps he countered the dire prediction of 1 Q35 with some of the 13 alternative prophecies displayed in *Les Propheties*. Where there is prophetic smoke there is often a burning heretic's fire. The Chyren-Selin predictions could be a seer's literary smokescreen. The king and his mistress would have certainly forbidden his writings had not a jousting lance ended the king's growing domination by the anti-Nostradamian *wife* who wasn't really his wife – his mistress, Diane de Poitiers. This is the same woman he honored on that eventful day at the tournament by wearing her heraldic colors into ritual combat rather than those of his queen.

4 Q58

Soleil ardent dans le gofier coller,	**To swallow in the throat the ardent Sun,**
De fang humain arroufer terre Etrufque:	**The Tuscan land soaked by human blood:**
Chef feille[1] d'eaue, mener fon fils filer,	**The chief bucket of water, to lead his son away,**
Captiue dame conduicte en terre Turque.	**Captive lady conducted into Turkish land.**

[1]*seille* = a) Old French for pail, bucket, jar; b) contraction of Old French *sëelle*, for *faucille* = sickle (Fontbrune). Fontbrune's future Soviet leader theme is remote but the sickle/crescent symbol can be applied to the Turkish flag, ie an Ottoman chieftain of the 16th–17th century or future Turkish leader.

This could be about anything from a future world drought to a nightmare version of the Mozart comic opera *The Abduction from the Seraglio*, which the composer thankfully never divined from reading Nostradamus. All irreverence aside, Tuscany falls underneath the same sunburnt line drawn across south-west France in the infamous 5 Q98. The events of this drought-laden prophecy, with its captive ladies and abducted sons, could therefore be set on the temporal stage of events in the globally warmed 21st century.

4 Q59

Deux affiegez en ardente ferueur,	**Two beset with ardent fervor,**
De foif eftaincts pour deux plaines taffes:	**Thirst extinguished by two full cups:**
Le fort limé, & vn vieillart refueur,	**The fort polished, and an old dreamer,**
Aux Geneuois de Nira monftra traffe.	**To the Genevans he will show the track of Nira.**

Common sense would require that I keep these prophecies from straying too far beyond Nostradamus' own time. That would make **Nira** an erratum for *Ivra* or the *Jura* mountains in Franche-Comté. With this in mind, and remembering that Geneva is the town of John Calvin, this quatrain could be part two of a wish-fulfilling prophecy about the capitulation of Geneva at the onset of a siege (see 1 Q33).

But **Nira** could also be an anagram for a modern state: *N-i-r-a* becomes *I-r-a-n*, and the Genevans represent the peacemakers of the United Nations rather than Calvin's theocratic city state.

Line 1 thus begins with the **ardent fervor** of Saddam Hussein versus Ayatollah Khomeini in the Iran–Iraq war of the 1980s. Line 2 is an occult metaphor. In tarot, the two of cups usually stands for the love between male and female, in the broadest sense. When afflicted it represents folly, dissipation, and waste – in other words, lovers becoming enemies in a war. While the war raged on, the Statue of Liberty perched over an old fort on Staten Island, in New York City, underwent major renovation (it was **polished**). In other quatrains, US President Ronald Reagan is called an **old dreamer**. He was proud of the nickname American Dreamer.

Reagan did have his tracks exposed to the United Nations peacemakers (in Geneva) and everyone else during the Iran–Contra conspiracy. Reagan declared before the world that he would not barter arms for American hostages held by Iran-based terrorists in Lebanon. Afterwards the Iranians proved him a liar by showing hard evidence that he did send emissaries to Iranian arms dealers in Switzerland and later to Iran itself. A shipment of several hundred US anti-tank missiles was traded in the hope of getting a hostage deal.

4 Q60

Les *ſept enfans en hoſtage laiſſés,*	**The seven infants left in hostage,**
Le tiers viendra ſon enfant trucider:	**The third will come to slaughter his**
Deux par ſon filz ſeront d'eſtoc percés,	**infant:**
Gennes, Florence, lors viendra encunder.[1]	**Two will be pierced by the rapier**
	because of his son,
	Genoa, Florence, then he will come to
	strike.

[1]Either Latin *inconditus* = confused, without order; Latin *incutere* = to strike against; or Latin *circumdare* = to envelop, encompass.

Le Pelletier hyperextended his reasoning facilities to make this a fit for the seven ill-fated Valois children. He gets *home* out of the Old French *hostage*, shredding every last tendon of credibility by saying it is a "Roman" word, *hostaige*, for "house." Neither I nor Leoni 35 years before me have found this Roman or Latin word. Without it, no interpretation for the Valois line can be hiding here. And anyway, Francis II was not killed by Henry **the third**, he died from illness when Henry was a child. Line 3 gives us the reason Le Pelletier tried so hard to make the theme fit, for it is true that Henry de Guise and his brother Cardinal Louis were both assassinated by multiple rapier thrusts in 1588. The reference to Genoa and Florence finally disposes of Le Pelletier's reasoning beyond any hope of recovery.

4 Q61

Le vieux mocqué & priué de ſa place,	**The old man mocked and deprived of**
Par l'eſtrangier qui le ſubornera:	**his position,**
Mains[1] de ſon filz mangées deuant ſa face,	**By a foreigner who will suborn him**
Le frere à Chartres, Orl.[2] Rouan trahyra.	**[or bribe him]:**
	The powers of his son are devoured
	before him,
	He who will betray his brother at
	Chartres, Orléans, and Rouen.

[1]Latin *manus* = hand; force, strength, power.
[2]Apocope for Orléans.

The purgatory of France under German occupation and Marshal Pétain's puppet Vichy government did not escape the attention of Nostradamus. By the summer of 1944, Hitler had stripped the sons of France and their leader – the **old man**, as Pétain was nicknamed – of all their powers. Pétain was then deported to Sigmaringen on 19 August, the same day the Allies (**brother**[s]), liberated **Chartres, Orléans, and Rouen**.

Quatrain Indexing Date: Q61 could be upside down for "19," giving us 19 August.

4 Q62

Vn coronel machine[1] ambition,	**A colonel will plot through ambition,**
Se ſaiſira de la plus grand'armée,	**He will seize the greatest part of the**
Contre ſon prince fainte[2] inuention,	**army,**
Et deſcouuert ſera ſoubz ſa ramée.[3]	**Against his Prince through a false**
	invention,
	He will be discovered under his
	branches.

[1]Latin *machina* = artifice, intrigue, ruse.
[2]Old French *fainte* = false.
[3]branches; arbor; green boughs, green arbor (by extension a green Bedouin tent, the green Libyan flag).

Garencières (1672), with the bad taste of Oliver Cromwell's civil war and rule still relatively fresh in his mouth, wrote, "I never saw the late Tyrant

Cromwell better painted to the life, than that in the three first lines."
Leoni reminds us that the rank of a **Colonel**-General of Infantry was
established in 1547, a century before Cromwell in France, and the post
was given to Admiral Coligny. Leoni makes a good case for the Catholic
point of view: Coligny is the ambition-bound usurper who became the
leader of the Huguenot armies. But both scholars draw a understandable
blank for the cryptic final line.

I propose that it stands for another **Colonel** – the desert mystic (or
madman), the Arab freedom fighter (or terrorist, depending on which
bread your bias is spread on) Muhammar Qadaffi.

In 1969 Colonel Qadaffi overthrew King Idris in the Libyan Revolution.
He seized the greatest part of the Libyan army's support in a secret coup
(*false invention*). The final line of the quatrain may cryptically relate
details of a notorious milestone in Qadaffi's life to be reached 17 years
later. On the night of 5 April 1986, when Halley's Comet was at the peak
of its transit of the skies, a terrorist bomb exploded in a Berlin disco,
killing two people, including a US serviceman. The Reagan government
chose to find evidence suggesting that the order for the bombing came
from Qadaffi. (Actually, other far more compelling evidence implicating
the Syrians and Iranians in the bombing was ignored by Reagan. But I
suppose an attack on the most vulnerable terrorist-sanctioning nation
would suit his political movie script better than a military attack on the
deep heartland of Islamic terrorism.) Nine days later, as the comet Halley
passed from sight – dating the moment Nostradamus' countdown to the
apocalypse began – US bombers attacked terrorist-related targets in
Libya. Bombs were also aimed at the Al Aziziya barracks in the desert
outside of Tripoli where, it is said, Qadaffi and his family sometimes
reside in a bedroom designed to look like a Bedouin tent. Qadaffi's two
sons were slightly injured by flying glass and his 15-month-old adopted
daughter, along with 100 people, were killed in what was clearly an assassination bombing mission. Qadaffi survived unscathed.

A translation of line 4 is difficult. In earlier books I had taken the
figurative meaning of *ramée* to deduce a green arbor or green flag symbolizing Qadaffi's Libya. A more down-to-earth translation of *ramée* as
branches might better describe Qadaffi the moment two bombs slammed
into his tennis court and another took out his front door. One might
have found him crouched beneath the branches (or legs) of his desk,
hiding his face from the flying glass.

Qadaffi, the son of a Bedouin shepherd, is still regarded in Libya as a
savior of Islam. Maintaining his pose as messianic visionary, he retains
eccentricities of character derived from his childhood in the desert. So
far, like his closest terrorist friend Abu Nidal, he has shown himself to be
a hardened survivor.

Quatrain Indexing Date: Q62 = 1962–63. Quatrains indexed either Q62 or Q63 often relate to significant years for a number of candidates in the lives of the Third Antichrist. As with Khomeini, this time was significant for Qadaffi. George Tremlett reports in his book *Gadaffi, The Desert Mystic* that our candidate here became a trainee officer at the military academy at Benghazi in 1963, where the commandant was assassinated later in the year. Many years later it was claimed (but never proven) that Qadaffi shot him.

4 Q63

L'armée Celtique[1] contre les montaignars,	**The Celtic army against those of the**
Qui feront fceuz & prins à la lipee:	**Mountain,**
Payfans frefz pouferont toft faugnars,[2]	**Who will be up high and snared with**
Precipitez tous au fil de l'efpee.	**a trick:**
	Peasants will soon give a fresh push
	to the grape presses,
	All hurled on the blade of the sword.

[1]Celtic, or a Royalist rebel army from Brittany.
[2]from Provençal *faugnar* = to press grapes.

Brittany and the Vendée regions fielded armies of Royalist counter-revolutionaries to fight the Republican forces of **the Mountain**, the higher seats of the National Convention in Paris. *Lipée* or **trick** could imply a ruse or decoy that causes someone **up high** or in command of the rebel forces to be lured into a trap.

This is exactly what happened to Henri de La Rochejaquelein, the heroic generalissimo of the White armies. While on a reconnaissance mission on 28 January 1794, "Monsieur Henri" galloped ahead of his companions to capture two republican stragglers for intelligence purposes. "Surrender, and I won't kill you!" he cried. The two bluecoats pretended to surrender; one of them even offered up his musket. Henry leaned down from the saddle to grab the barrel just as the man discharged the musket in his face, killing him instantly. Moments later Henry's companions rode down and butchered the two stragglers.

The death of Henri de La Rochejaquelein marked the turning point of the White rebellion. The Montagnards unleashed eight republican armies against the Royalist strongholds in the west. These so-called "infernal columns" were instructed to "devastate the Vendée." The orders from **the Mountain** read thus: "All brigands who are found with arms in their hands, or are convicted of having taken up arms, will be bayoneted to death. You will act in the same way with the women, girls and children who are in the same category. Nor will persons who are merely suspect be spared. All of the villages, towns, crops and everything else that can possibly burn will be consigned to the flames."

The devastation of the Vendée lasted from January though September of 1794. The final two lines poetically describe and date the bloodletting through the image of grape presses during the wine harvest, which happens in September.

4 Q64

Le deffaillant en habit de bourgeois,	**The defaulter in bourgeois garb,**
Viendra le Roy tempter de fon offence:	He will come to try the King with his offense:
Quinze fouldartz la plufpart Vftagois,[1]	Fifteen soldiers for the most part [bandits],
Vie derniere & chef de fa cheuance.	Last of his [low] life and [chiefly] of his fortune.

[1] Old French ustaige = pirate, corsair; and (by extension) bandit, outlaw.

Prieditis sees this for the **bourgeois** King Louis Philippe. Fontbrune conjures up a few more details to justify interpreting it as a bloody incident during the French Revolution of 1848 when a group of demonstrators (**bandits**) gathered on the Boulevard des Capucines and fired on units of the French National Guard. The latter returned fire, killing 15 and wounding 50. But this is so general that it could apply itself equally to some future defaulting king. Maybe it is for Britain's future Charles III or his heir.

4 Q65

Au deferteur de la grand forterefſe,	**To the deserter of the great fortress [Sedan].**
Apres qu'aura fon lieu abandonné:	After he will have abandoned his post:
Son aduerfaire fera fi grand prouefſe,	His adversary will display great prowess,
L'Empereur toft mort fera condamné.	The Emperor – soon to die – will be condemned.

This is an overview of the rise and fall of Napoleon III. On his ascent to power, Louis Napoleon was **condemned** to life detention in the (**great fortress**) of Ham. He escaped in 1846 to a castle (**fortress**) in England. Louis Philippe **abandoned his post** as king in the 1848 Revolution, thereby allowing Louis Napoleon to seize power and become Napoleon III. The French Emperor's **adversary** is the Iron Chancellor of Germany, Otto von Bismarck, who lays a political trap for the French with his demands for a resolution of the German unification question. Bismarck masterfully manipulated Gallic pride, baiting the Emperor to slap aside negotiations and charge into a war with the German states before France was prepared. Napoleon III was a poor emperor. Bismarck outmaneuvered him

politically and militarily. The luckless man was condemned by his countrymen for his capture at Sedan. The loss of power and the great shame of
his capitulation contributed to his rapid physical decline and death
shortly after the war.

4 Q66

Soubz couleur faincte de sept testes rasées,	**Under the false color of seven shaven heads,**
Seront semés diuers explorateurs:	**Will be sewn diverse spies:**
Puys & fontaines de poysons arrousées,	**Wells and fountains to water with poison,**
Au fort de Gennes humains deuorateurs.	**At the fort of Genoa, human flesh eaters.**

Leoni says the seven cropheads could be priests or cardinals. Cheetham
thinks one of them is the lucious-locked Oliver Cromwell, who commanded the close-cropped roundheads, and another is the cropheaded
Napoleon Bonaparte. But that leaves five bare- and brazen-headed
tyrants for us to trim off the list. Lamont believes they are the seven
dictators of the World War II period. He must mean the boneheaded
Mussolini of Italy, the stubble-topped Emperor Hirohito of Japan, buzz-
cut Francisco Franco of Spain, and the drafty-sided, shorn-naped and
raped-mustached Adolf Hitler of Nazi Germany. That leaves us with the
thick-and-oiled-at-the-top and short-on-the-sides hairdo of Josef Stalin
of the Soviet Union. Bringing up the rear, then, must be the cropheaded
dictators of Hungary, Romania and Turkey sporting anything from a
Prussian peach head to an Elvis Presley draft board cut.

The next three lines denote some espionage or terrorism afoot in
Genoa. This vision could extend beyond the Fascists of World War II:
the 1990s decade has its own crop of neo-Fascist cropheads involved in
acts of subterfuge and terror.

4 Q67

L'an que Saturne & Mars esgaux combust,[1]	**In the year when Saturn and Mars are equally fiery,**
L'air fort seiché, longue traiection:[2]	**The air is very dry, a long comet:**
Par feux secrets, d'ardeur grand lieu adust,[3]	**From hidden fires a great place burns with heat,**
Peu pluye, vent chault, guerres, incursions.[4]	**Little rain, hot wind, wars and raids.**

[1]Latin combustus = burned, consumed ruined, destroyed.
[2]Latin traiectio = shooting star, meteor, comet. In modern terms, a missile.
[3]Latin adustus = burned by the sun, tanned, scorched.
[4]Incursions, raids, surprise attacks or offensives. In modern terms a terrorist attack.

When Saturn and Mars are *equally fiery*, they are conjoined in a fire sign, preferably one of those most responsible for wars and raids: Aries or Leo. Many 20th-century wars and military offensives parallel this aspect. For example, in September through early November of 1917 Saturn and Mars were in Leo during the climax of several campaigns during the third year of World War I. This time window gave us a view of the Third Battle of Ypres, the first and second battles of Passchendaele on the Western Front, the eleventh Battle of Isonzo and the Battle of Caporetto on the Italian Front. In addition, Allenby's campaign in Palestine against the Turks was reaching its climax.

In World War II Saturn entered Aries at about the time Hitler's forces entered Warsaw in late September 1939, and was *equally fiery* with Mars in Aries all through the terrible Winter War between the Soviet Union and Finland in 1939–40.

Mars and Saturn were again together in Leo during the Indian Partition of autumn 1947, when over 10 million people were displaced and forced to wander over the dusty tracks of the dry months of autumn to find new homes in the newly divided countries of India and Pakistan. The two planets passed through Leo exactly during the same time period that the bloody riots and sectarian strife of the partition killed an estimated 1 million Hindus and Muslims. Mars joined Saturn in Aries at the onset of the Tet Offensive in January and February 1968, when Viet Cong and North Vietnamese troops made a surprise attack on 30 towns in South Vietnam, including the capital Saigon, and Hue.

Mars was in Leo and Saturn in Sagittarius during the great Iranian "human wave" offensive of early 1987 during the First Gulf War (Iran vs. Iraq). Saturn and Mars were in Aries in April of 1996, when hundreds of Katyusha rockets launched by Hezbollah rebels in southern Lebanon unleashed the greatest air, sea, and land bombardment by Israel since the Israeli invasion of Lebanon in 1982.

The next important transit of these planets in a fire sign was Mars in Sagittarius and Saturn in Aries in October 1997. During that year the comet Hale-Bopp will be in our skies. If armed conflict breaks out it will come as a reflection of the darker aspect of Sagittarius. Wars or terrorist raids inspired by, or reacting against, religious bigotry and a fanatic adherence to dogma and fundamentalism, would not be a surprise. There could be a crisis between the United States and China over Hong Kong's return to mainland China. A geological "war" is also implied by *hidden fires* so we could expect major earthquakes or a volcanic eruption at that time. Perhaps we will see a new eruption of Etna or Vesuvius in Italy, or another significant eruption in Martinique or at Mt Rainier in the Pacific North-west. Another wave of serious droughts, wars, earthquakes and eruptions is expected for the spring and early summer of 1998 when Mars and Saturn are together in Aries from March through April.

The phrase **hidden fires** could alternatively represent Deep Fire, the new US biological weapon, or another nuclear accident or future reactor meltdown (**hidden fires . . . burn with heat**). The **hot wind** and **long comet** or meteor might represent the new French stinger missile, the Mistral, named after the hot south wind that blows from Africa over Provence. The **hot wind** may cause the **wars and raids** of 1998 and others during other fiery transits of Mars and Saturn in the 21st century, as the planet Earth begins to heat up from global warming.

Quatrain Indexing Date: Q67 = 1967, a milestone year for Africa. It is the year that could have inaugurated a future global famine. According to the Worldwatch Institute, 1967 marked the beginning of the current disastrous decline of grain production in Africa: 1 million Africans starved to death in the Biafra famine that same year. It must be remembered that famines often trigger wars and raids in Nostradamus' prophecies. The seer numbers both of his famous world famine quatrains 67 (see 1 Q67, 4 Q67).

4 Q68

En l'an bien proche non eſloigné de Venus,	**In the year very near not far from Venus,**
Les deux plus grans de l'Aſie & d'Affrique:	**The two greatest ones of Asia and of Africa:**
Du Ryn & Hiſter[1] qu'on dira ſont venus,	**They are said to have come from the Rhine and from Hiſter,**
Crys, pleurs à Malte & coſté Liguſtique.	**Cries, tears at Malta and the Ligurian sea-coast.**

[1]Latin Ister = the Lower Danube area.

A clear prophecy for Hitler, the Axis Alliance, and early battles of World War II. Lamont cites 1939 in judicial astrology as the year of Venus. The **two greatest ones** are Axis allies of Nazi Germany. The first is Italy represented here by her extensive African colonies, the second is Imperial Japan, who would later join the two in the Tripartite pact in 1941. **Tears of blood** issue from concussion blasts of Axis bombing raids on the little island stronghold of Malta, which was of key strategic importance during the North African and Mediterranean campaigns. In other places Nostradamus records his vision of bombs falling on the Ligurian port of Genoa, a place he frequently traveled through. James Randi keeps his blinders on tight and makes an unconvincing argument that Hister is only about the River Danube and not a double pun for the river and the young boy, Adolf, who played on its riverbanks and dreamed up his terrible destiny.

4 Q69

La cité grande les exilés tiendront,
Les citadins morts meurtris & chaſſés:
Ceux d'Aquilee à Parme promettront,
Monſtrer l'entree par les lieux non traſſés.

The exiles will hold the great city,
The citizens dead, murdered and
   driven out:
Those of Aquileia will promise
   Parma,
To show them the entrance through
   the untrodden places.

Aquileia was an ancient Roman city that fell into decline in the early medieval period; by Nostradamus' time it was little more than a dilapidated village. Its close proximity to Venice makes it a classical device for that maritime powerhouse of the 16th century. The city-state of Parma, which belonged to the papacy as of 1511 and was made into a duchy by 1545, received some trade agreements from the Venetians. I read the last line's riddle of the **untrodden places** to mean that goods from Parma can be transported on Venetian merchant ships; since ocean travel leaves no footprints we therefore have an **untrodden place**.

4 Q70

Bien contigue des grans monts Pyrenees,
Vn contre l'aigle grand copie addreſſer:
Ouuertes veines, forces exterminees,
Que iuſque à Pau le chef viendra chaſſer.

Adjacent to the great Pyrenees
   mountains,
A man against the Eagle will direct a
   great army:
Veins opened, forces exterminated,
The chief will come to chase them as
   far as Pau.

The **chief** is Sir Arthur Wellesley (the Duke of Wellington); Nostradamus follows his progress of victories against the French in 1813–14. Losses incurred by Napoleon in Russia forced him to reduce the size of the French armies occupying Spain. Wellington took advantage of this and routed Marshal Jean Jourdan's army at Vitoria in June 1813. This sent most of the French army packing over the Pyrenees while Wellington relayed forces to lay siege to the remaining French garrisons at San Sebastián and Pamplona (**adjacent to the . . . Pyrenees**). Both strongholds fell to him between September and October (**forces exterminated**). Wellington crossed the Pyrenees into France with an army of more than 40,000 British, Portuguese, and Spanish troops. In early 1814 he pushed the French out of their fortified camp at Bayonne. He wheeled his army south along the eastern face of the Pyrenees, through the city of Pau, to clash with Soult's French army at Toulouse. With the abdication of Napoleon the following day, hostilities ended.

4 Q71

En lieu d'efpouſe les filles trucidées,	**Instead of a bride the daughters are**
Meurtre à grand faulte ne ſera ſuperſtile:[1]	**slaughtered.**
Dedans le puys veſtules[2] inondées,	**Murder of such wickedness, no**
L'eſpouſe eſtraincte par hauſte d'Aconile.[3]	**survivors to be.**
	The vestal virgins are drowned in the
	well,
	And the bride poisoned by a drink of
	Aconite.

[1]Old French survivor.
[2]Vestal virgins. Some photos of the Rubensesque Czarina surrounded by her sylphlike virgin daughters in their white, neo-classical ballroom gowns might appear to Nostradamus like a tableau of goddess Vesta and her virgin attendants.
[3]Misprint for *Aconite*.

Nicholas II of Russia and his entire family were shot by Red Guards in a town near the Ural mountains a few days before it was liberated by pro-Czarist forces. According to long-suppressed Bolshevik accounts, sometime after midnight on 17 July 1918, 11 members of the Czar's family and entourage were directed down into the basement of Ipatyev House in Ekaterinberg. There they waited in mounting tension, not knowing what would happen next. Soon a dozen executioners armed with pistols choked the doorway. The Czar stood up, the children clutched hold of each other. The basement air roared with gunfire for 20 minutes. Alexei and three of his sisters were still alive, groaning and writhing on the floor. The guards repeatedly stabbed them with bayonets, but the points hardly penetrated. Later, after stripping the corpses, they found that the women had sewn pearl necklaces, diamonds and gold coins into their undergarments. Their corsets had acted like flak vests, prolonging their death agony. The assassins took the jewelry and money, cut up and burned the remains, and threw them down a flooded mine shaft.

Nostradamus gives us little hope that any of the Czar's virgin daughters survived, yet his last centuries-old comment may support the newest evidence, uncovered in 1991, that supports the rumor that Anastasia was not dispatched by the hail of bullets shot by Cheka guards in the basement of Ekaterinberg. Exhumation of the remains from the muddy pit in a birch forest outside of town shows that Anastasia's was not among the skeletons.

According to William Maples, a biological anthropologist who heads the C.A. Pound Human Identification Laboratory in Gainesville,

Florida, none of the skeletons is young enough to have been Anastasia's or the Czarevich Alexei's. Nostradamus gives little support to those who believe that the late Anna Anderson, who claimed to be the Grand Duchess, is the real Anastasia. In fact, recent DNA tests have proved once and for all that she was a fraud. He seems adamant that the real Anastasia was poisoned (**by Aconite**).

There may, however, be more figurative meanings to **Aconite**. It may be interpreted as "dustless," "without raising any dust," from the Greek word *akonitos*, made up of *a* (without) + *konitos* (dusty), the latter element from *koniein*, "to raise dust" or "to thresh around." This may take the meaning beyond the deadly properties of monkshood herb and apply it to the Romanov murder mystery itself. In other words, all further investigation or exhumations, any search for a fire pit in the region, where forensic scientists believe Anastasia and Alexei were cremated, will raise no more "dust" and certainly no solutions. The mystery of Anastasia will remain *akonitos* – not worth the effort.

See Index: Romanov murders.

4 Q72

Les Artomiques[1] par Agen & l'Eſtore,	The Artomics through Agen and Lectoure,
A ſainct Felix feront leur parlement:	At St Félix will hold their parliament:
Ceux de Baſas viendront à la mal'heure,	Those of Bazas will come at an unfortunate time,
Saiſir Condon & Marſan promptement.	To seize Condon and Marsan promptly.

[1] *Artomiques*: A cousin anagram to D'Arton, standing for "those of NATO," see 2 Q22; b) anagram for Atomiques, the atomic ones.

The temptation is very strong among modern interpreters to give the enigma *Artomiques* a present-day application as **the Atomic ones** or **those of NATO**. The quatrain is on the whole better suited to Nostradamus' near-future time as an account of Huguenot centers in France. Garencières sifts his ingredients and takes the Greek *artos* for "bread," pulling from his interpretive oven *the bread-breaking ones*, since the Huguenots used unleavened bread in their Communion. All the towns mentioned are in southern and south-western France, and were centers of Huguenot activity. Some scholars believe this is a retroactive prophecy, returning us to the proto-Protestant rebellion of the Albigensians in 1167. I disagree. I believe Nostradamus is trying to warn his contemporaries of a widespread return in those regions to the Albigensian heresy in the guise of the Huguenots.

Quatrain Indexing Date: Q72 = a near miss for 1573, the year after the

St Bartholomew's Day Massacre only strengthened Huguenot resistance against Catholic France.

4 Q73

Le nepueu grand par forces prouuera,	**The great nephew by force will prove,**
Le pache[1] fait du cœur puſillanime:	**The crime [or treaty] committed by**
Ferrare & Aſt le Duc eſprouuera,	**the coward's heart:**
Par lors qu'au ſoir ſera le pantomime.[2]	**Ferrara and Asti the Duke will test,**
	When the comedy takes place in the evening.

[1]pache = a) Old French for treaty, agreement; b) peche = crime.
[2]pantomime = dumb show; or Latinized Greek for a stage performance featuring "everything (pantos) imitated (mimos)"; the nickname of the Paris Opéra.

The third de Berri assassination prediction (see 1 Q84, 3 Q96) accurately foresees Charles X stepping down during the revolution of 1830. The **great nephew** who eventually takes the throne is not of the Bourbons, nor of their successor, King Louis Philippe, but Louis Napoleon, the nephew of Napoleon Bonaparte. This quatrain is one of two numbered close to or exactly on the year of Louis Napoleon's death, 1873. It also correctly implies that he would best benefit from the assassination of the Bourbon heir, de Berri – who was stabbed outside the Paris Opéra on the night of 13 February 1820 (**when the comedy takes place in the evening**) – which would make destiny flow towards the reign of Louis Philippe. He in turn was destined to fall from power in a second revolution in 1848. Thanks in part to de Berri's assassin, Louvel, the Bonapartists were eventually able to seize power and elect Louis Napoleon as president of a Second Republic. The **nephew** of Nostradamus' First Antichrist, Napoleon Bonaparte, would become truly **great** by crowning himself in 1852 as Napoleon III, Emperor of the Second Empire.

   Quatrain Indexing Date: Q73 = 1873, the year Napoleon III died. In quatrain 74 of Century VI, the year of his death is mentioned outright as "three and seventy."

4 Q74

Du lac lyman & ceux de Brannonices,[1]	**Of Lake Geneva and those of Mâcon,**
Tous aſſemblez contre ceux d'Aquitaine:	**All assembled against those of Aquitaine:**
Germains beaucoup, encor plus Souyſſes,	**Many Germans, even more Swiss,**
Seront deffaicts auec ceux d'Humaine.[2]	**Will be routed with those of Humaine.**

[1]The people in the environs of Mâcon.
[2]ceux d'Humaine = either "those of humanity," or "those of Maine."

Mâcon is attacked by a Calvinist army marching out of Geneva 75 miles to the west. This polyglot force of German and Swiss mercenaries mixed with French Huguenots is defeated.

And now for what actually happened. During the Third War of Religion (1568–70), the Catholic forces and their Swiss sympathizers (rather than their enemies) won a victory against the Huguenots and their German mercenaries just north of Aquitaine at Montcontour in 1569. Montcontour is just 20 miles south-east of the department of Maine-et-Loire (*those of Maine*). Another clash took place the following year at Arnay-le-Duc, around 60 miles north-east of Mâcon.

Interpreters from the late 19th century through the early 20th could have used this quatrain to support the decision to build the Maginot Line against a threat of invasion from Switzerland.

Quatrain Indexing Date: Q74 = a near miss for 1575, the year which saw the Fifth War of Religion.

4 Q75

Preſt à combatre fera defection,	**Ready to fight he will desert,**
Chef aduerſaire obtiendra la victoire:	**The chief adversary will be victorious:**
L'arriere garde fera defenſion,	**The rear guard will make a defense,**
Les defaillans mort au blanc territoire.	**Those who falter dying in the white country.**

On the long road back from Moscow, Napoleon's Grand Army – now weary, demoralized and almost in rags – deteriorated into an undisciplined rabble. Many soldiers died in the freezing temperatures and gathering snow, while the tattered remnants of the once-great army fought off attacks by marauding Cossack bands. They received no help from their great commander, Napoleon, who callously left his soldiers to their fate, donned a disguise, and rode back to France on a sleigh, determined to rebuild his armies for the anticipated spring campaigns in Germany. The Grand Army of 20 nations and half a million soldiers that had crossed into Russia on a sunny June day in 1812 returned six months later as 20,000 sick, frozen, broken men.

4 Q76

Les Nictobriges[1] par ceux de Perigort,	**The people from the environs of Agen by those of Périgord,**
Seront vexez tenant iuſques au Roſne:	**Will be vexed holding as far as the Rhône:**
L'aſſocié de Gaſcons & Begorne,[2]	**The association of Gascons and Bigorre,**
Trahir le temple, le prebſtre eſtant au proſne.	**Betrays the [Huguenot] temple, the priest giving his sermon.**

[1] Latin *Nitiobriges* = the people in the environs of (what is now) Agen.
[2] An editorial mistake which has lasted the centuries. It should be *Bigorre*, which would rhyme.

All the places mentioned were hotbeds of Huguenot activity. The northern environs of Agen nestles against the ancient county of Périgord. Both are roughly 200 miles west of the Rhône river region between Dijon and Valence, where another large pocket of Huguenots lived. Gascony and Bigorre, in the extreme south-west of France, were subject counties of the Protestant kingdom of Navarre. This is Nostradamus hinting, sometime in 1556, that the seeds of a near-future civil war are being planted in the synods and temples of the Huguenots in these regions.

Quatrain Indexing Date: Q76 = 1576, the year closing the Fifth War and launching the Sixth War of Religion.

4 Q77

Selin monarque d'Italie pacifique,	**Selin king, Italy peaceful,**
Regnes vnis Roy chreſtien du monde:	**Kingdoms united by the Christian**
Mourant voudra coucher en terre	**king of the world.**
bleſique,[1]	**When he dies, he will want to lie in**
Apres pyrates auoir chaſſé de l'onde.	**Blois territory,**
	After having chased the pirates from
	the sea.

[1]Medieval Latin *Blesa* = Blois.

If King Henry II had listened to his Protestant jousting competitor, Comte de Montgomery, and called it a day . . . If Henry had led those assembled into the celebration of a happy double marriage rather than being carried from the field mortally wounded – who could say what course world history might have taken? Northern Italy might today be a part of France. No ruinous religious wars would have been fought between French Catholics and Protestants because Henry II would have united Christendom. The Bourbons might never have ruled, and the Palace of Versailles would not exist; instead, tourists would flock to the Château de Blois and the tomb of Henry II and Catherine de' Medici at St Denis. And interpreters like myself might be praising Nostradamus for clearly foreseeing Henry II sweeping the Mediterranean clean of Arab corsairs and Turkish navies.

Instead of writing this segment on alternative destinies I might be questioning why the great Henry II *didn't* die in a prophecy of ritual combat as proposed in 1 Q35. This interpreter might be sitting here over four centuries later listing scores of apparently failed quatrains that describe bloody religious civil war in France which obviously never took place because Henry lived until April 1577 (according to the quatrain's indexing) and was laid to rest at his beloved Château de Blois.

This scenario is an alternative future to rival any that the king might feverishly have dreamt as he lay on his deathbed, surrounded by his weeping family and courtiers – a prisoner of a sadder destiny long fore-warned and cruelly thrust home by a wooden splinter in his brain.

Quatrain Indexing Date: 1577 could have been the year of Henry II's death, at the age of 59, in this alternative future life.

4 Q78

La grand armee de la pugne[1] ciuile,
Pour de nuict Parme à l'eftrange trouuée:
Septanteneuf meurtris dedans la ville,
Les eftrangiers paffez tous à l'efpee.

The great army of the civil war,
By night Parma to the foreign one found:
Seventy-nine murdered inside the town,
The foreigners expired. All put to the sword.

[1]Latin pugna = combat, contest, battle.

The mention of **Parma** can give us either the city in Italy or the Spanish Duke of Parma, who fought the Dutch subjects of Spain in a bloody and protracted civil war in the Spanish Netherlands. The latter application suits the quatrain's details, since Parma's men on numerous occasions raided and burned Dutch villages, slaughtering their premier Protestant citizens along with Huguenot refugees (**foreigners**) from France.

4 Q79

Sang Royal fuis, Monhurt, Mas, Eguillon,
Remplis feront de Bourdelois les landes:
Nauarre, Bygorre poinctes & eguillons,
Profondz de faim vorer de liege glandes.

Blood Royal flees, Monheurt, (Le-) Mas(-d'Agenais), Aiguillon,
Replenished will be the Bordelais, the Landes:
Navarre, Bigorre weapon points and spurs,
Deeply hungry, to devour acorns of the cork oak.

We return again to the Wars of Religion in south-west France.

This one is much like 4 Q76; both are crammed full with place names, yet their meaning remains quite obscure. All the towns in line 1 are in the Agenais, west of Agen, and were probably points of call for the young doctor Nostradamus when he lived in Agen in the mid-1530s. The **Bordelais** peninsula has the city of Bordeaux at its base, another port of call for our doctor-prophet in his youth. The kingdom of Navarre (incorporating the ancient county of Bigorre) is in the extreme south-west corner of France.

The quatrain index may give us a dating for the subject of this Huguenot geography lesson, since it is a near miss for 1580. That was the year of the Seventh War of Religion, known as the War of the Lovers, since it had less to do with Catholic and Huguenot hostilities than the romantic escapades of King Henry de Navarre's lusty wife Queen Margot, the daughter of Catherine de' Medici. After the St Bartholomew's Day Massacre, Navarre and his queen escaped separately from near-house-arrest in Paris and returned to the Protestant south-west (**blood royals flee**). Their escape routes may be implied here, although they were both known to be hungry after something more erotic than gastronomic.

Quatrain Indexing Date: Q79 = 1579, a near miss for the year of the Seventh War of Religion, a six-month farce guided by the pikestaffs, darts, and – targets of more a lascivious kind – the romantic escapades of the beautiful Queen Margot and her equally promiscuous husband.

4 Q80

Pres du grand fleuue, grand fosse,[1] terre egeste,	**Near the great river, a vast trench, earth excavated,**
En quinze pars sera l'eau diuisee:	**It will be divided by water into fifteen parts:**
La cité prinse, feu, sang, cris, conflict mettre,	**The city taken, fire, blood, cries and battle given,**
Et la plus part concerne au collisee.[2]	**The greater part involving the collision [of forces].**

[1]Latin fossa = ditch, trench.
[2]Latin, collisio = clash, crash, shock. A number of French cities contain ruins of Roman coliseums. Most of these cities were conquered in the German invasion. Perhaps Nostradamus had a vision of Hitler's bronzed Aryan warriors after the Battle of France, picking about the coliseum ruins in nearby Arles on sight-seeing tours.

James Laver (1942) insists that Nostradamus' predictions were to become a key factor in French military policy before the war. He reminds us the 19th-century commentator Torné-Chavigny insisted that France build a huge fortification along her eastern frontiers with Germany and Switzerland to halt any future German invasions. During the late 1920s the French government planned to build a great defensive wall exactly as Torné-Chavigny prescribed along the eastern French frontiers, from Sedan all the way down to the frontier opposite Basel, Switzerland. The Maginot Line was built at the cost of 2 million dollars per mile (1930s value). This marvelous feat of engineering comprised a network of self-sufficient underground forts built in a vast trench seven stories deep into the earth, all interconnected by underground railways. The French government and its military advisors, convinced that the Maginot Line was impregnable, declared that France was safe from invasion. But its very existence led to a false sense of security, known throughout the 1930s as the Maginot mentality.

The quatrain is remarkably specific in detail. Half the fortifications faced the *great river* Rhine. The Maginot Line was broken in 15 places by rivers. No other eastern defensive trench in history can claim this feature.

Two years before the outbreak of World War II, Dr Max de Fontbrune, a noted scholar of Nostradamus, risked vilification on a national scale by declaring to French politicians and fellow countrymen that a vast redoubt of concrete fortresses and subterranean garrisons – a Gallic facsimile of a cement security blanket against future German invasions – would be a miserable failure in the coming war. The debate over Fontbrune's interpretations ended when Hitler and his generals had their snapshot taken at the Eiffel Tower. His disturbing interpretation turned out to be correct. The city in the quatrain is Paris, taken as a result of a sudden collision of battles fought by German panzers who sidestepped the Maginot Line to break through French and British forces in Belgium then plunge deep into France to seize the exposed French capital.

4 Q81

Pont on fera promptement de nacelles,
Passer l'armee du grand prince Belgique:
Dans profondrés[1] & non loing de Bruxelles,
Outre passés, detrenchés[2] sept à picque.

One will build promptly a bridge of
   boats,
To cross the army of the great Belgian
   prince:
Pouring forth into [Belgium] not far
   from Brussels,
Seven passed beyond [life], cut to
   pieces by pikes [weapons].

[1]Latin profundatus = poured forth.
[2]Old French detrancher = to cut in pieces, cut up.

Leoni reminds us that today the word **Belgian** does not cause much of a stir, but in the 16th century it was "as archaic as Lusitanian or Pannonian." We know that Philip II can be the only contemporary candidate, because he had been given this territory in 1554 by his father, Emperor Charles V. The quatrain accurately foresees an attack on northern France, which was launched few months after this quatrain was set down on paper. The invading army probably used a **bridge of boats** while passing over the Scheldt.

4 Q82

Amas s'approche venant d'Esclauonie,[1]
L'Olestant[2] vieux cité ruynera:
Fort desolee verra sa Romanie,
Puis la grand flamme estaindre ne sçaura.

A mass of men approach from Slavonia,
The Destroyer [Ne-apolluon] will
   ruin the old city:
He will see his Roman Empire quite
   desolated,
Then he will not know how to
   extinguish the great flame.

[1]Slavonia = Russia; the Slavs were a Sarmatian tribe which settled there in the 7th century.
[2]Destroyer. A Nostradamus coinate. Greek oles – combining form of ollumi = to destroy, plus possibly thanatos = death, death-dealing; thus "death and destruction," an apt description of Napoleon in Russia. See "ferocious name" links 1 Q76, 4 Q54, 8 Q1.

Napoleon's march to Moscow, which stretched his army's strength and supplies to the limit, was his greatest mistake. He had gambled everything on its success, but disaster awaited him in the great Russian capital. As the exhausted French soldiers camped in a deserted Moscow on the night of 14 September 1812, a handful of remaining Muscovites set their city of wooden buildings on fire. For three days and nights Moscow blazed. By the end only a fifth of the once-great city was left and Napoleon was forced to turn back and retrace his steps westwards.

4 Q83

Combat nocturne le vaillant capitaine,	**Nocturnal combat the valiant captain,**
Vaincu fuyra peu de gens profligé:	**Vanquished will flee, few people**
Son peuple efmeu, fedition non vaine,	**overthrown:**
Son propre filz le tiendra affiegé.	**His people stirred up, sedition not in**
	vain,
	Then his own son will hold him
	besieged.

Given the sad fact that the last 440 years have hosted over a thousand wars with night battles too numerous to count, this incident could fit any number of them.

4 Q84

Vn grand d'Auxerre mourra bien	**A great one of Auxerre will die very**
miferable,	**miserable,**
Chaffé de ceux qui foubz luy ont efté:	**Chased out by those who had been**
Serré de chaines, apres d'vn rude cable,	**under his [control]:**
En l'an que Mars, Venus, & Sol mis	**Locked in chains, at the end of a**
en efté.	**rough [and] grating cable,**
	In the year that Mars, Venus, and
	the Sun, are in conjunction in
	summer.

This could be a future French president from Auxerre who dies as a hostage of terrorists.

Astrological time window

The next conjunctions of the sun with Venus and Mars in Leo are in August 2000 and August 2019. Many wars in history begin when the planet Mars transits the constellation Leo. This takes place again in August–October 1998 and June–July 2006. For the 21st century I would expect the highest potential for war when Mars passes through Leo several times during a Saturn–Leo transit (August 2034–October 2036) while the planet Neptune is passing through the final degrees of its transit of Aries. During that time this rare conjunction of the sun, Venus and Mars in Leo will happen again in August 2032. This may be the year a future leader of France gets involved again in a wider war with a new pan-Arab superpower ruled by the **Arab prince** of 5 Q25. See also 1 Q15, 4 Q67, 4 Q84, 5 Q14, 5 Q91.

4 Q85

Le charbon blanc¹ du noir² sera chassé,	The white carbon of the king will be driven out,
Prisonnier faict mené au tombereau:	Made a prisoner taken in to the dung cart,
More³ Chameau⁴ sus piedz entrelassez,	His feet tied together like a rogue,
Lors le puisné sillera⁵ l'aubereau.⁶	Then the younger one will ravage the hobby falcon.

¹charbon blanc: wordplay for Bourbon blanc, white Bourbon – ie Louis XVI, whose cockade is white.
²Near anagram for roi = king.
³More: a) Latin mos, mortis = custom, practice; b) Leoni believes it is the Old French more = Moor (Maure); black; vigorous.
⁴Chameau = Camel; (fig) nasty, evil-minded, mischievous person. In other words a rogue who is customarily tied and bound.
⁵Will ravage, devastate, mortify, humiliate.
⁶Hobby falcon; (fig.) a squire.

The charbon blanc could be wordplay for **white Bourbon**. Noir is a near-anagram for **king**. This gives us Louis XVI, whose cockade and standard were white. Nostradamus is perhaps comparing a round piece of white charcoal to the flattened disk of a cockade.

On the cold morning of 21 January 1793, Louis was taken to the guillotine in a cheap coach. However, the hated Marie Antoinette was not spared the indignity of the multitudes staring at her in a two-wheeled dung cart, or tombereau, on the way to her execution later in October. She was not tied and bound, but her appearance, immortalized in a sketch by Jacques-Louis David, is that of a **rogue** with her long tresses jaggedly cut short to better expose her neck to the blade. The final line may be some cryptic message about their 11-year-old orphaned son Louis XVII, but it is impossible for me to decipher. He had been taken to another location in the Temple prison several months before her execution, where he was humbled by Simon the Cobbler – in other words, slowly abused and neglected to death.

4 Q86

L'an que Saturne en eau fera conioinct
Auecques Sol, le Roy fort & puiffant:
A Reims & Aix fera receu & oingt,
Apres conqueftes meurtrira innocens.

*The year that Saturn will be
conjoined in a water [sign]
With the Sun, the strong and
powerful King:
At Reims and Aix will be received
and anointed,
After conquests he will murder the
innocents.*

A new and powerful king will be crowned by tradition in Reims when the sun and Saturn are conjunct in a water sign (either Pisces, Cancer, or Scorpio). Saturn transits from one water sign to another roughly every 9.5 years. Latter-day Royalist interpreters of Nostradamus pin their hopes on the future coronation of Henry V, a messianic French blueblood yet to appear. He will rival the Sun King, Louis XIV, in his absolute power and rule. (How the French will ever support an absolute monarch as part of the European Union of the 21st century is beyond me, but many noted Nostradamians, including Jean-Charles de Fontbrune, Lamont, and Lemesurier are the apostles of this belief.) **Aix** stands for the German *Aachen*, where medieval German kings and later the Holy Roman Emperors were crowned. Henry V therefore will have to sweep aside all European Union (EU) agreements of the Treaty of Rome and all progress made over the last 50 years of European union to rule France *and* Germany as the new Charlemagne. Good luck!

If ever there was a chance for such an alternative future it has long passed by. Henry II was Nostradamus' favorite candidate for this Royalist gush. Louis XIV came the closest to being a second Charlemagne of the royal blood, and the very un-royal usurper, Napoleon Bonaparte, did rule an empire the size of Charlemagne's between 1807 and 1812.

My own favorite quixotic "Henry" candidate would have been "Monsieur Henri" de Vergier, Comte de La Rochejaquelein, general-issimo of the White Bourbon rebellion during the French Revolution. But a bullet in the forehead received a few weeks after his defeat at the battle of Le Mans ended his chances to become Henry V.

Astrological Time Window

For all of you wishing to toast a fifth Henry, your next astrological chances are 22 June 2003, November 2014, and 29 February 2024.

4 Q87

Vn filz du Roy tant de langues aprins,
A fon aifné au regne different:
Son pere beau[1] au plus grand filz comprins,
Fera perir principal adherant.

A son of the King very learned in
languages,
Different from his predecessor in the
kingdom:
His handsome father is understood by
the greater son,
He will cause the principal adherent
to perish.

[1]pere beau: handsome father; variant, beau-père = father or father-in-law.

Every line fits Henry III. He was fluent in several languages, unlike his twitchy brother Charles IX. He had a better understanding of kingship than Charles. One could say his mediocrity as a king was less than his predecessor's and almost equal to that of his **handsome father**, Henry II. Line 4 refers to his murder of the Guises in 1588.

4 Q88

Le grand Antoine du nom de faict fordide,
De Phthyriafe[1] à fon dernier rongé:
Vn qui de plomb voudra eftre cupide,
Paffant le port d'efleu fera plongé.

The great Antony by name by deed
sordid,
Riddled by lice [and consumption] to
his tormented end:
One who will want to be desirous of
the lead bullet,
Passing the port will be plunged
through by the elected one.

[1]Phthyriafe: a) Phthisis = consumption; b) Phthiriasis = suffering from lice, lousiness.

This prophecy may cut a bit too close to the codpiece for one of Nostradamus' contemporaries, Antoine de Bourbon, King of Navarre (1555–62). Phthiriasis, known today as pediculosis, is louse infestation – a pretty common ailment at a time when high- and low-born people bathed ten times or less a decade. There is no record of Henry de Navarre's father being a haven for lice, although Leoni cites sources declaring Antoine's royal neighbor across the Pyrenees, Philip II of Spain, was a louse-eaten monarch.

Antoine de Bourbon appears many times in Nostradamus' presage quatrains. Though not consumptive, he was a vacillating and easily manipulated man. After the death of Henry II he as much played the fool as was a key factor in the power struggle between François de Guise, the Cardinal de Lorraine and the Queen Regent Catherine de' Medici. As a grand noble he demanded more power and influence over the adolescent King Francis II, and tried to squeeze the lesser-noble Guise out of his position as Lieutenant-General of France and the closest advisor to the king. Catherine played Antoine de Bourbon against the Guise brothers in an attempt to hold on to her regency.

When civil war finally broke out in 1562, Antoine de Bourbon – a Protestant from birth – remained loyal to the Crown and led an army against his own brother, Condé, the leader of the French Protestant rebellion. Antoine de Bourbon was mortally wounded by a stray bullet while directing the siege of Rouen, near one of the city gates (**ports**). He lingered for six weeks, finally dying of blood poisoning the day the city fell.

4 Q89

Trente de Londres secret coniureront,	**Thirty of London will conspire**
Contre leur Roy sur le pont[1] entreprinse,	**secretly,**
Luy, fatalites la mort degousteront.	**Against their King, the enterprise on**
Vn Roy esleu blonde, natif de Frize.	**the sea,**
	He [and his] satellites will feel disgust
	for death.
	A fair King elected, native of
	Friesland.

[1]Latin *pontus* = the sea.

While Nostradamus lived, no Dutchman ever sat on the English throne (nor was it ever imagined) – let alone a Dutch prince specifically from Friesland. But the seer succeeds on all points in this daring quatrain numbered after the year William of Orange became King and co-ruler of England, 1689.

After the second wife of James II bore him a male heir, the Protestant British Parliament united together in rebellion against their fanatically Catholic king. A secret correspondence was passed over the Channel to William of Orange through his wife, Princess Mary who, until the birth of the king's son, had been next in line to inherit the English throne as one of James' two fully-grown (and Protestant) daughters from his earlier marriage. A petition was sent secretly from Parliament requesting her husband to set sail for England with an army of liberation. William wrote back, demanding that all the conspirators who wished him to lead their coup d'état put it in writing. Twenty-nine Lords signed (**thirty of London**). In response William set sail with his fleet (**the enterprise on the sea**).

The Duke of Marborough (one of his few allies, or **satellites**) deserted James and his court and brought the entire army over to William's camp. James II did not wish to die in the same manner as his grandfather, Charles I (**he . . . will feel disgust for death**), so he fled into exile in France. The Revolution was indeed Glorious because it was almost bloodless. The only bloodshed happened when the nervous James suffered a serious nosebleed during a march on the Dutch.

William of Orange was described as fair-skinned and blond in his childhood. His hair had turned a dusky brown by the time the British Parliament *elected* him king in 1689.

Quatrain Indexing Date: Q89 is right on target for 1689.

4 Q90

Les deux copies aux murs ne pourront ioindre,	**The two forces – at the walls – will be powerless to unite,**
Dans ceſt inſtant trembler Milan, Ticin:[1]	**In that instant Milan and Pavia to tremble:**
Faim, ſoif, doubtance ſi fort les viēdra poindre,	**Hunger, thirst, doubt will come to sting them very strongly,**
Chair, pain, ne viures n'auront vn ſeul boucin.	**No meat, bread, no victuals – no one will have a single mouthful.**

[1]Latin *Ticinum* = Pavia.

Milan and **Pavia** (which is 20 miles south of Milan) will both endure starvation and drought during a siege. Although Milan was occupied twice by Napoleon in the 1790s and also by the Allied armies of World War II in 1945, no siege has happened since this was written in 1555.

4 Q91

Au duc Gauloise contrainct battre au duelle,	**For the Gallic Duke coerced into fighting a duel,**
La nef Mollele[1] monech[2] n'approchera:	**The ship Melilla will not approach Monaco:**
Tort accuſé, priſon perpetuelle,	**Wrongly accused, perpetual prison,**
Son fils regner auant mort taſchera.	**His son will endeavor to rule before his death.**

[1]This looks like *Melilla*, the North African port.
[2]Latin *Portus Herculis Monoeci* = Monaco.

Jaubert directs this one to events of 1555–56. He believes it recounts the tale of some descendant of the great Duc de Nemours fighting a duel. Jaubert fights his own duel with the enigmatic barbarism *Mollele*. He changes it from *Mollele* to *Mole*, and explains that a timid Admiral de la Mole avoided bringing his fleet within range of the forts of Monaco during his campaign. In the 1940s, Roberts takes his turn on the literary mat with *Mollele*, pinning it down as Melilla, a Morroccan port occupied by Spain since 1490, but his connection leads nowhere in the context of this quatrain. One might just as well cite the Bay of Mellehia on the island of Malta. Cheetham and Leoni cry for assistance from 4 Q83, but its cloudy hints are similar and equally frustrating.

4 Q92

Tefte tranchee du vaillant capitaine,	**The head of the valiant captain cut off,**
Sera gettee deuant fon aduerfaire:	
Son corps pendu de fa claffe à l'antenne,[1]	**It will be thrown before his adversary:**
Confus fuira par rames à vent contraire.	**His body hung up on his fleet's antenna,**
	Confused it will flee by oars against the wind.

[1]Usually a yard-arm, especially a lateen sail-yard; in modern terms it is an aerial or antenna – in this case the fleet's main communications antenna.

In the melee of close combat during the naval battle of Lepanto (1571) the Muslim admiral, the valiant Ali Pasha, was struck in the face by a cannonball. A Christian knight seized the body, lopped off the head with his broadsword, and stuck it on a pike for all to see. The sight of their brave admiral's head is said to have started the Muslim rout.

A modern application would have some future admiral either dismissed or lose command of his fleet through death. Whatever the cause, the change of command is reported over the radio **antenna** to the rest of the fleet.

4 Q93

Vn ferpent veu proche du lict royal,	**A serpent seen near the royal bed,**
Sera par dame nuict chiens n'abayeront:	**Will be by the lady at night –**
Lors naiftre en France vn Prince tant royal,	**[watch]dogs will not bark:**
Du ciel venu tous les Princes verront.	**Then to be born in France a Prince so royal,**
	Come from heaven – all the Princes will see [him].

Line 1 could clue us in to Catherine de' Medici, who had a serpent added to her coat of arms after the death of her husband, Henry II, in 1559. But the rest fits better as an intimate and retroactive exposé of her private life as a new bride back in 1544 when Francis I – her father-in-law – ruled, and the long years of barrenness were broken by her first pregnancy.

Dogs guarding her bedchamber don't bark if the nocturnal visitor is her husband, the Duc d'Orléans (and future Henry II). The blessed event **come from heaven** is her first-born child, the future Francis II. I believe this quatrain was secreted into the prophecies to warm the heart of Nostradamus' beloved queen. The truth is, Francis II was an adolescent, royal wimp who died of the fainting sickness scarcely a year into his reign. But in the prophet's defense, had the royal father forsworn jousting and lived on into old age, perhaps his frightened boy would have had time to grow into manhood and make of himself a great king. If such an alternative future had transpired, his beloved Mary would have been Queen of Scots and of France.

4 Q94

Deux grans freres feront chaffez d'Efpaigne,	**Two great brothers will be chased**
L'aifné vaincu fous les monts Pyrenees:	**from Spain,**
Rougir mer, rofne, fang lemam	**The elder vanquished below the**
d'Alemaigne,	**Pyrenees mountains:**
Narbon, Blyterre,[1] d'Agath[2] contaminees.	**The sea to redden, Rhône, blood [in]**
	Lake Geneva from Germany,
	Narbonne, Béziers, by Agde (are)
	contaminated.

[1]Latin Baeterrae Septimanorum = Béziers.
[2]Latin Agatha = Agde.

This could be a continuation of the plague theme in Agde (see 8 Q21). **Narbonne, Béziers** and **Agde** are southern French ports near the Spanish border. Line 3 is another bloody dig at Calvin's Geneva by Nostradamus, to no historical effect. Our prophet unleashes a shotgun blast of predictions in four brief lines, none of which definitively hits the mark: We have the escape of two Spanish princes, with a defeat waiting for one of them at Roussillon; a Catholic German mercenary attack on Calvinist Geneva; a plague spreading to Narbonne and Béziers from ships hailing from Agde; and a naval battle turning the Mediterranean red with blood.

4 Q95

La regne à deux laiffé bien peu tiendront,	**The rule left to two they will hold for**
Trois ans fept mois paffés feront la guerre,	**a very short time,**
Les deux veftales contre rebelleront,	**Three years and seven months having**
Victor puis nay en Armorinque[1] terre.	**passed, they will go to war,**
	Their two vassals will rebel against
	[them],
	The victor is born on American soil.

[1]Either "American" or "of Brittany."

Quatrain 89 of Century II dates the year 1989 as the beginning of the end of the Cold War and the turn toward Russo-American friendship. Three years and seven months after formal friendship is acknowledged, they will go to war over the actions of rebellious regional allies (**vassals**). The American **vassal** could be Israel or any one of her many newfound Arab allies from the Gulf War of 1991. Even Iran was once a staunch American **vassal** before the rise of the submarine-packing Islamic fundamentalist regime in Teheran. Saudi Arabia is currently allied to America, but a shift in political and religious currents is brewing that could send the Saudis the way of the Iranians to become an anti-American Islamic state.

The Russian *vassals* would be any of her several Arab surrogates from the Cold War, such as Iraq, Syria, or the submarine-packing *vassals* of Libya, Egypt, or Algeria. One could also include former non-Russian Soviet states in Central Asia, Trans-Caucasia, or even the Ukraine as potential instigators of an ethnic war that drags the world down into the abyss of war.

The phrase **seven months** is the key for dating the time of the final breakup. The earliest window in time for Armageddon is 1999 and **seven months** (10 Q72). This targets January 1996 through July 1999 as the countdown time to global nuclear war.

January of 1996 does mark an important new milestone in post-Cold War Russo-American relations. It is the first time both nations have troops working side by side as *friends* enforcing peace in Bosnia as part of the IFOR (Implementation Force) of the Dayton Peace accords. July 1999 arrives exactly 3.5 years after the Russian and American units arrived in Bosnia.

If war comes, the American president of the time will be the victor. If I might digress for a moment, let me state for the record that I have been making presidential predictions since 1968 and I haven't missed yet. Since 1984 I've been lecturing and writing articles asserting that the American president in 1999 would be a Democrat finishing his second term in office. I declared Bill Clinton the winner ten months before the 1992 presidential elections. If I am correct about the president I hope I am very wrong about the crisis in 1999. If the world is on the verge of Armageddon by that time, it would be ironic if Clinton – who takes President Kennedy as a role model – could have to face the same terrible decision his idol faced during the Cuban Missile Crisis: to push or not to push the button of nuclear holocaust, that is the question.

Quatrain Indexing Date: Q95 = 1995, just one month shy of the countdown window of January 1996 through 1999.

4 Q96

La sœur aisnée de l'isle Britannique,	**The elder sister of the British Isles,**
Quinze ans deuant le frere aura naissance:	**Will be born fifteen years before her**
Par son promis moyennant verrifique,	**brother;**
Succedera au regne de balance.[1]	**Because his promise proves to be true,**
	She will succeed to the kingdom of the
	balance.

[1]*regne de balance* = the kingdom of Libra (the Balance). Leoni believes this applies to England, or in mundane astrology to Austria or Savoy. I believe the symbol of blind Justice holding the scales is also implied, making it a symbol for modern republican democracies in general and America in particular.

Britain's elder sister is a figurative description of the British Empire's 13 American colonies. With the help (*promise*) of an alliance with France (*her brother*), America will defeat Britain and eventually become an even greater republican democracy as *the kingdom of the balance*. The *balance* of the last line, with its possible allusion to the scales of Justice, refers to democracy.

Later, France would become America's *brother* in republicanism. Nostradamus accurately foresaw that the creation of the First Republic of France would occur 15 years after America asserted its liberty in 1776.

4 Q97

L'an que Mercure, Mars, Venus
  retrograde,
	The year when Mercury, Mars,
	  Venus [are] retrograde,

Du grand Monarque la ligne ne faillit:	*The great Monarch's line will not fail:*
Efleu du peuple l'vfitant[1] pres de Gagdole,[2]	*Elected by the Portuguese people near*
Qu'en paix & regne viendra fort enuieillir.[3]	*Cadiz,*
	One who will come to grow extremely *old in peace and reign.*

[1]Latin *Lusitani* = the Portuguese.
[2]*Gagdole* = a) Latin *Gades* = Cadiz; b) *Guarde*, for Guarda, a Portuguese city from which royal princes received the title Duke of Guarda.
[3]Old French *envieillir* = to grow old.

Prieditis says that Mercury, Mars, and Venus were retrograde when João IV was elected king in 1640, the year Portugal regained its independence from Spain. The founder of the Braganza royal line, João reigned for only 16 years, dying when 51 years old, but his capable administration restored Portugal to a respected position in Europe.

4 Q98

Les Albanois,[1] pafferont dedans Rome,	*The Albanians will pass into Rome,*
Moyennant Langres demipler[2] affublés:	*By means of Langres the multitude*
Marquis & Duc ne pardonnes à homme,	*are decked out grotesquely:*

Feu, fang, morbilles[3] point d'eau, faillir
  les bleds.
	Marquis and Duke will overlook no
	  man,

	Fire, blood, smallpox, no water, the *grain [crops] to fail.*

[1]Either the Albanians of Albania (in the Balkans) or an ancient Roman name for the people of modern Trans-Caucasia.
[2]Le Pelletier suggests Greek elements *demos-pleres* = mob-full or multitude.
[3]Old French *morbilles* = smallpox.

Scholars have tried to make the Albanians the soldiers of the Spanish Duke of Alva. The Duc de Langres mentioned in 7 Q4 is introduced to us here. Military maneuvers and a bevy of disasters are listed but shine no clear light on what this is all about. Titles like **Marquis** and **Duke** were code names for Resistance groups and leaders in southern France. If we take **Albanians** literally, they could be the tens of thousands of Albanian refugees who invaded Italy's shores in rusty ships in 1995. If one looks the other way and ignores **Langres** in line 2, then the ragged **multitude** are these jobless Albanians receiving aid from the Italian government.

The final line jumps ahead into the new century when the Albanian refugee problem will be far worse than it is today because of the strains put on food and water sustainability by overpopulation and global warming. The vision here is of refugees dying from want and disease in vast numbers when Albania, and the Balkans, possibly becomes the Rwanda of Europe in the early 21st century.

4 Q99

L'aifné vaillant de la fille du Roy,	*The valiant elder son of the King's*
Repouffera fi profond les Celtiques:	*daughter,*
Qu'il mettra foudres, combien en tel arroy,	*He will repel the Celts [French] so*
Peu & loing puis profond és Hefperiques.[1]	*very far:*
	He will launch thunderbolts – so
	many and in such an array,
	Near, and far, then deep into the
	West.

[1]from Latin Hesperia = Land of the West.

I have difficulty linking line 1 to Hitler's blitzkrieg into France in 1940. Perhaps the **elder** son of a king's daughter was meant for one of Hitler's generals. Rommel, Guderian, and Kleist have no family ties to the Kaiser's family – at least none that I could find. This prophecy may be yet another example of Nostradamus' viewing both German invasions of France during the 20th century as one event, when the Imperial German general staff did have direct links to the Kaiser. In both cases German forces penetrated deep into France. But line 3 steers us back to World War II and Hitler's blitzkrieg method of "lightning" mobile warfare. The successful strategy applied lightning speed coupled with pinpointed violence. It allowed the Germans to concentrate overwhelming forces of mechanized infantry, armor, and air power to strike like lightning against specific sectors of the enemy's line. Once the armored forces had broken through they raced on at breakneck speed, plunging deep into the enemy's rear areas, severing lines of communication and supply and causing great confusion. Normal infantry forces would pin down the enemy line long enough for the panzers to encircle and cut off entire enemy armies.

In other "lightning-war" quatrains, Nostradamus unsuccessfully warns his future countrymen of the secret route the German panzers would take through the forest of the Ardennes to break through the weakest part of the French line, at Sedan. And he correctly computes the time it would take for the panzers to seize Paris after the Allied defeat at Dunkirk – seven days.

4 Q100

De feu celeſte au Royal edifice,	Fire falls from the sky onto the royal building,
Quand la lumiere de Mars defaillira:	
Sept mois grãd guerre, mort gent de malefice,	When the light of war will weaken:
Rouen, Eureux au Roy ne faillira.	For seven months a great war, people dead through an evil spell,
	Rouen and Evreux will not fail the king.

The place in 16th-century Paris where tiles were kilned returns twice in Nostradamus' chronicle of future history. Perhaps when the prophet chanced upon the unassuming rows of kilns and piles of tiles during his visit to Paris in 1556, he had premonitions that the place of the Tiles, called *le Tuile*, would become the royal palace of Les Tuileries, the focal point for two future French revolutions. In 9 Q35 we will examine how *the* 500 Fédérés stormed the palace and humiliated King Louis XVI by forcing him to wear the **mitered** cap of the Revolution.

The quatrain above once more implies the Tuileries as the **royal building** destroyed by forces of the Paris Commune shortly after the end of the Franco-Prussian War (**war will weaken**). The palace was set on fire by artillery shells and incendiaries (**fire falls from the sky**). The war raged from July 1870 until February 1871 (**seven months**). The cause of death and grief was France's irresponsible military and political leaders, caught in the *evil spell* of war hysteria, who plunged the country into a military disaster. The people of Normandy (**Rouen and Evreux**) did wish to restore the monarchy through the National Assembly.

See Index: Tuileries palace.

Century V

Auant venue de ruyne Celtique,
Dedãs le tẽple deux parlementerõt,
Poignard cœur, d'vn mõté au courſier &
   picque,
Sans faire bruit le grand enterrerõt.

Before the Celtic ruination had
   come,
Within the temple two will parley,
Dagger to the heart, of one mounted
   on the charger and quarreling,
Without making a noise the great one
   will be buried.

Cheetham believes this metaphorical imagery describes the fate of young Louis XVII, who was separated from his mother and removed to another area of the Temple prison, where he was put into the care of the brutal Simon the Cobbler. She takes this quatrain to mean that Louis was buried at the Church of Ste Marguérite in 1795 as was officially announced.

Leoni takes a more modern interpretation for **Celtic ruin**. He thinks this quatrain spies on Molotov and von Ribbentrop inside the **temple** of the Kremlin in August 1939, as they drafted Hitler and Stalin's arrangements for a dual invasion and partition of Poland in the following month. With the Soviet–German Non-Aggression Pact signed, Hitler could hurl all his forces against the French in 1940, bringing on a **Celtic ruin**.

For me, the imagery comes closest to describing the death of the generalissimo of the White rebellion during the French Revolution, Henri Comte de La Rochejacquelein. The rebellion was strongest in the last outposts of the ancient Celts in France: in the Vendée, Brittany, and Normandy. Although "Monsieur Henri" did not meet his end in a church, Roman ruin, or a Huguenot "temple," he was **mounted on a charger and quarreling**, demanding the surrender of a Republican soldier; when the man offered up his bayonet-tipped musket, Henry reached down to grab it away, and the man discharged it in his face, killing him instantly. True – it wasn't literally a **dagger to the heart** but this may be intended metaphorically as an act of treachery.

Henry's companions were forced to disfigure his corpse so he could not be identified. Then they secretly buried him (**without making a noise**). With his death the tide had turned on the White counter-revolution. In the ensuing **Celtic ruin** eight republican armies known as "infernal columns" would methodically ravage royalist lands and massacre tens of thousands.

5 Q2

Seps coniurés au banquet feront luire,
Contre les trois le fer hors de nauire:
L'vn les deux claſſes au grand fera
    conduire,
Quand par le mail. Denier au front luy
    tire.

Seven conspirators at the banquet will
    cause to flash,
The swords [or iron] out of the ship
    against the three:
One will have the two fleets brought
    to the great one,
When through the [chain] mail. Into
    the last one's drawn brow.

If it weren't for the all the naval riddles this could easily parallel P57's account of Henry de Guise's private banquet where a toast to the death of his chief rival, Henry III, was brazenly offered. In other words, Guise and his cronies are **against the three** – Henry *le trois*. But as fate would have it, Henry III assassinated Guise first. The last line might describe the victim's surprise when he entered the king's bedchamber (foolishly, without bodyguards) for an audience and was pounced upon by a half-dozen men with drawn swords.

5 Q3

Le ſucceſſeur de la Duché viendra,
Beaucoup plus outre[1] que la mer de
    Toſquane:
Gauloiſe branche la Florence tiendra,
Dans ſon giron[2] d'accord nautique Rane.

The successor to the Duchy will
    come,
Very far beyond [Charles V] the sea of
    Tuscany:
Gallic branch will hold Florence,
The nautical Frog in his gyron by
    agreement.

[1] *plus outre*: a code for Charles V, since it is part of his famous salutation *plus outre Carlo Quint*.
[2] *giron*: a) a term for a heraldic device; b) lap; c) (fig.) bosom.

Nostradamus seems to be predicting that the relatives of Catherine de' Medici will end their rule of Florence and see their line replaced by a French prince. *Plus outre (Carlo Quint)* in line 2 alludes to Charles V, who kicked the Medicis out of Florence and twice reestablished them there. When the Medici bloodline died out in 1737, a descendant from the female line of the French throne, the Duke Francis de Lorraine, became Grand Duke of Florence. After he became emperor, the House of Lorraine became the House of Hapsburg-Lorraine. However, Tuscany continued to be ruled by the family until 1859, except for a brief interruption during the French Revolution and the Napoleonic Era. During the latter era Tuscany became the Kingdom of Etruria (1801–05), and was bestowed on an authentic **Gallic branch**, the Spanish Bourbons.

    Now to the cryptic **nautical Frog**. Le Pelleiter points to the myth in which Bacchus transformed the earliest inhabitants of Tuscany, the

Tyrrhenians, into frogs. Leoni believes the image represents the standard of the mythical Merovingian King Pharamond – three golden toads on a field of azure.

5 Q4

Le gros maftin de cité defchaffé,	**The great Mastiff driven out of the city [Paris],**
Sera faché de l'eftrange alliance:	**Will be angered by the alliance:**
Apres aux champs auoir le cerf chaffé,	**After having chased the stag to the fields,**
Le loup & l'Ours fe donront defiance.	**The wolf and the bear will defy each other.**

One can see from illustrations of the medieval English mastiff that its flat face does resemble the much smaller British bulldog of today. I cannot rule out that Nostradamus is applying the phrase **great Mastiff** to that famous British bulldog of World War II, Winston Churchill. When France was about to fall to Hitler in 1940, Churchill did make a last-minute flight to Paris to encourage the French leadership to keep fighting to the last. French defeatism was bad enough, but the alliance of Vichy France with Nazi Germany angered Churchill to the extent that he ordered an attack on French naval units anchored at Oran. Then the German **stag** was chased to the **fields** – or better, the Russian steppes – by its wolfish Führer. **Wolf** stands for Hitler himself, defying Soviet Russia. "Adolf" comes from the Old High German *Adoulf* "noble wolf," and "wolf" was Hitler's nickname. His command center for prosecuting the Russian invasion was also known as the Wolf's Lair.

5 Q5

Souz ombre faincte d'ofter de feruitude,	**Under the shady pretense of ousting servitude,**
Peuple & cité l'vfurpera luy mefme:	**People and city he will usurp [for] himself:**
Pire fera par fraux de ieune pute,[1]	**Far worse will he do because of the deceit of a young prostitute,**
Liuré au champ lifant le faux proefme.	**Book in the field reading the false poem.**

[1] Old French *pute* = prostitute.

Nostradamus continues on the Hitler theme. Line 1 characterizes a seductive Hitler saving Germany from the harsh terms (**servitude**) of the Versailles treaty and from "international Jewry." In line 2 the (German) people and their capital *city* of Berlin are usurped by Hitler. This may be a warning to the French people that they and their capital *city* of Paris will be next. The suicide of Hitler's niece and lover, Geli Raubal, hardened Hitler's heart. He admitted that she was the only woman he ever loved – if such an emotion was possible for him. Theirs was a co-dependent, controlling relationship. Her death defined his brutality. Line 4's **book in the field** makes little sense unless it is a cryptogram for *Mein Kampf* (Kamp[f] = *champ* = field [of battle]), Hitler's bible. It stands as the **shady pretense** or **false poem** of Hitler's dream of the Thousand-Year Reich.

5 Q6

Au Roy l'Augur¹ ſur le chef la main mettre,	**To the King, the Augur, putting his hand on the chief,**
Viendra prier pour la paix Italique:	**Will come to pray for the Italian peace:**
A la main gauche viendra changer le ſceptre,	**To the left hand will come a change of scepter,**
De Roy viendra Empereur pacifique.	**From King will come a pacific Emperor.**

¹Latin *Augur*, diviner, augur. In this case, apparently, the Pope.

Nostradamus the **Augur** figuratively rests his hand on Henry II, his candidate for the second Charlemagne. A pope will bestow the crown of Holy Roman Emperor on Henry so that he can restore peace in Italy. Henry II becomes king of France and Germany. It is enough to swell the head of any king; unfortunately Henry's brain lay swollen with an infection from a mortal lance wound in 1559, and he would never meet this lofty destiny.

5 Q7

Du Triumuir ſeront trouuez les os,	**The bones of the Triumvir will be found,**
Cherchant profond threſor ænigmatique:	**Looking for a deep enigmatic treasure:**
Ceux d'alentour ne ſeront en repos:	**Those around will not remain at rest,**
Ce concauer¹ marbre & plomb metallique.	**In this hollowing of lead and marble.**

¹Latin *concavare* = to hollow out.

Louis Philippe tried to enliven his faltering popularity by bolstering the growing French romance with the myth of Napoleon Bonaparte. In 1840, he ordered the return of Napoleon's corpse to France. The **Triumvir** is Napoleon, who in 1799 had been a member of a triumvirate of consuls ruling France. Napoleon's former aides Gourgaud and Bertrand sailed with the king's own son to make a positive identification of their long-dead master who had died 19 years earlier at the age of 52. They found the embalmed body in remarkable condition. Napoleon's face was similar to its appearance when he had seized power in 1799. His hair had grown to its youthful shoulder length. The ravages of cancer had burned away the fat, leaving the lean, Grecian face of his days of youth and glory.

His body was placed in a coffin of lead and marble and was shipped back to France, where it was drawn through the Paris streets on an ostentatious bier to its final resting place at the Hôtel des Invalides. The **enigmatic treasure** is the myth of France's lost glory. Louis Philippe tried hard to reawaken the romantic fever and transfer the national nostalgia to himself, but he never succeeded.

5 Q8

Sera laiſſé le feu vif, mort caché,	**There will be let loose living fire and**
Dedans les globes¹ horrible eſpouuentable,	**hidden death,**
De nuict à claſſe² cité en poudre laſché,	**Inside dreadful globes – horrible!**
La cité à feu, l'ennemy fauorable.	**frightful!**
	By night the city will be reduced to
	dust by the fleet,
	The city on fire, helpful to the enemy.

¹*globe* = a) a globe, sphere; the Earth; b) Latin *globus* = a crowd, a throng of men, a mob.
²Latin *classis* = a fleet: in this case it could be an air fleet.

This could be a vision of bombers releasing their dreadful cargoes over any number of cities: London in 1940, Dresden or Berlin in 1945, Hiroshima or Nagasaki in 1945, etc. Fontbrune reminds us of Virgil's phrase *globi flammarum* (whirlwind of flames). This may describe the great firestorms of Dresden or at Hiroshima after the first atomic attack. Or does this terrible prophecy wait in our future?

Hydrogen fusion is the **living fire** of the Sun. Radiation is its **hidden death**. Paris, therefore, may be destroyed by the one vector of doomsday the START treaties generally leave intact: missiles launched by submarine fleets. START's great pledges to dismantel the vast arsenals of land-based ICBMs could be at best a cosmetic device to mollycoddle us into thinking this planet is becoming a safer, non-nuclear place, while the real threat to our future lurks beneath the waves, and out of sight of our dreaming eyes.

Quatrain Indexing Date: Q8 = 2008?

5 Q9

Iuſques au fonds la grand arq demolue,	**The great arch will be demolished**
Par chef captif, l'amy anticipé:	**down to the foundations,**
Naiſtra de dame front face cheuelue,	**By the captive chief, his friend**
Lors par aſtuce Duc à mort attrapé.	**anticipated:**
	He will be born of a lady with hairy
	forehead and face,
	Then through guile the duke
	overtaken by death.

The Arc de Triomphe in central Paris may be threatened by a future terrorist attack. Hopefully the event foreseen here has already taken place, with far less dramatic impact than predicted. A bomb did explode at the Metro subway entrance near the Arc de Triomphe in 1995 as a reprisal for the French arrest of an Algerian terrorist leader. What to say about line 3? The terrorist bomber in question will have a very hairy mother? Is Nostradamus falling victim to a racial slur? Only his daemon knows!

If we derive "leader" from the original Old French meaning of **duke**, then this quatrain could be outlining the fate of some future terrorist leader who is deceived and assassinated.

Quatrain Indexing Date: Q9 = 2009?

5 Q10

Vn chef Celtique dans le conflict bleſſé,	**A Celtic chief wounded in the**
Aupres de caue voyant ſiens mort abbatre:	**conflict,**
De ſang & playes & d'ennemis preſſé,	**Near the cave seeing his [people] cut**
Et ſecourus par incognus de quatre.	**down by death:**
	Pressed by blood and wounds and
	enemies,
	And help from strangers [numbering]
	four.

More details may surface here concerning a future terrorist explosion that levels the Arc de Triomphe in Paris. This is to happen during an official gathering (perhaps Bastille Day, 14 July) when the French president and dignitaries are seated around the Arc de Triomphe. Or possibly the **cave** describes the location of the bomb sitting on one of dozens of plastic bucket seats attached to the walls of the Paris Metro station that is just underneath the arch. Line 3 describes the dead and injured, and the pandemonium following a bombing. The last line hints that the president's life is saved by four strangers.

5 Q11

Mer par ſolaires ſeure ne paſſera,	**Those of the Sun will not cross the**
Ceux de Venus tiendront toute l'Affrique:	**sea in safety,**
Lure regne plus Sol, Saturne n'occupera,	**Those of Venus will hold all of Africa:**
Et changera la part Aſiatique.[1]	**Their realm will no longer be**
	occupied by Sun [and]
	Saturn,
	And the Asiatic part will change.

[1]Usually Nostradamus applies "Asia" to the Far East, whereas the "Orient" usually stands for the Near or Middle East.

The Sun symbolizes Imperial Japan, which lost World War II because it could not adequately supply and reinforce its island fortresses when its maritime and naval fleet were sunk by American submarine and air power dominating the Pacific theater of war.

Venus links the subject of line 2 to Venice, a synecdoche for Mussolini's Italy. The Italians did have a number of colonies in Africa before the war, but certainly not *all* of the continent was in their hands. *Saturn* has a number of symbolic meanings, including Fascism. Saturn's color is black, the color of the German SS and the Italian Blackshirts. A Saturn cycle is 29.5 years, making this a partially successful attempt to date the beginning and end of Fascism in Italy. In March 1919 Mussolini founded the *Fasci de Combattimento* which officially became the Fascist Party in 1921. The last vestiges of it were overthrown in May 1945 after a 26-year reign.

5 Q12

Aupres du lac Leman ſera conduite,	**Close to Lake Geneva it [she] will be**
Par garſe eſtrange cité voulant trahir:	**conducted,**
Auant ſon meurtre à Auſpourg la grand	**By a young foreign girl desiring to**
ſuitte,	**betray the city:**
Et ceux du Rhyn la viendront inuahir.	**Before its [her] murder at Augsburg a**
	great retinue,
	And those of the Rhine will come to
	invade it.

Nostradamus tries a new angle for predicting the fall of Calvinist Geneva. He projects his bias again in a failed prophecy against John Calvin, rationalizing that some day the Lutheran kingdoms of Germany would invade and conquer Geneva. This of course never happened. One takes up this line of thinking from the clue *Augsburg*. In 1530, a year after Nostradamus received his doctorate at Montpellier, the Lutherans presented Charles V with the Confession of Augsburg at the imperial diet held in that city. The Peace of Augsburg which allowed all princes of free cities to choose Lutheranism, but not Calvinism, was ratified in September 1555. Nostradamus would have been aware of these occurences before this quatrain was published. Perhaps our seer had hoped the Lutherans would soon fall on the outcast Calvinists in Geneva.

The Peace of Augsburg repressed religious tensions in Germany for 63 years until the outbreak of the Thirty Years War. Geneva was never attacked during that war by Protestants or by Catholic armies. In fact, Geneva gained her independence from the Holy Roman Empire and Calvinism gained acceptance.

5 Q13

Par grand fureur le Roy Romain Belgique,	With great fury the Roman Belgian King,
Vexer vouldra par phalange barbare:	Will want to vex the barbarian with his phalanx:
Fureur grinsseant chassera gent Lybique,	Grinding fury, he drives out the Libyan people,
Depuis Pannons iusques Hercules la hare.[1]	From the Hungarians as far as the Pillars of Hercules.

[1]Latin ara = high seat, altar, monument.

Some interpreters believe the barbarians are German pikemen marching in a serried *phalanx* during the battles of the Thirty Years War. It would be a good call if the next line didn't clearly associate the barbarians with the Barbary tribesmen of Libya. This oversight directs our attention to who is standing in front of the phalanx of sharpened pikes, the Ottoman Turks and their Barbary allies. This is therefore more likely an account of the failed Turkish siege of Vienna, which took place in 1683, a few decades after the end of the Thirty Years War. The final two lines give us the long-term results. From this high-water mark in military actions against Christian Western Europe, the Turks and their Barbary vassals would see their empire pushed out of Hungary (Pannonia) in the following century, assuring a Gibraltar forever free of Muslim soldiers. Modern people take this freedom for granted, but Gibraltar's (and by extension southern Spain's) vulnerability to Corsair attacks was a hot issue in Nostradamus' time.

5 Q14

Saturne & Mars en leo Espaigne captifue,	Saturn and Mars in Leo, Spain captive,
Par chef Lybique au conflict attrapé:	Trapped by the Libyan chief in the conflict:
Proche de Malthe, Heredde[1] prinse viue,	Near Malta, Herod [Judea or Rhodes] taken alive,
Et Romain sceptre sera par coq frappé.	And Roman scepter will be struck down by the Cock.

[1]Le Pelletier believes *Heredde* is an anagram for Rhodes. I believe it stands indirectly for biblical Judea, which was ruled by Herod.

Napoleon's troops occupied both Spain and Portugal in 1808 during the Napoleonic wars (**Spain captive**). The British sent an army under Sir Arthur Wellesley (later to become the Duke of Wellington) to assist a general Spanish insurrection. By 1814, Wellington had swept the French out of Spain.

The quatrain takes a step backwards in time to the first stage of Napoleon's Egyptian expedition, the capture of Malta in 1798. The scruffy general (**the Cock**, symbol of France) would return from Egypt to seize France for himself. He oppressed and conquered the papal states, snapping up large portions of them for his Empire.

Herod is a cryptogram either for Rhodes or for Judea in honor of its notorious leader, King Herod. Napoleon did take his Egyptian expedition up through Palestine. The reference to a *Libyan chief* is unclear, unless Nostradamus is using the Latin *Libycus* for "North African" in general or a Mameluke horseman by extension, who might have envisioned trying to ride Napoleon down during the Battle of the Pyramids or at Aboukir.

Quatrain Indexing Date: Q14 = 1814, the year Wellington invaded France over the Pyrenees and brought a victorious end to his five-year campaign against Napoleon's forces in Spain. If the complete indexing 5 Q14 stands for "May 1814," then it comes close to dating the time Napoleon would lay down his own **scepter**. He signed his abdication on 11 April, just a few weeks shy of May.

Astrological time window

If this quatrain applies itself to our future, look for Saturn in Leo from July 2005 through September 2007, and again from August 2034 through October 2036.

5 Q15

En nauigant captif prins grand pontife,	**The great Pontiff seized while**
Grans apprets faillir les clercz tumultuez:[1]	**navigating,**
Second efleu abfent fon bien debife,	**The great one thereafter to fail the**
Son fauory baftard à mort tué.	**clergy in tumult:**
	Second one elected absent his welfare
	declines,
	His favorite bastard butchered to
	death.

[1]Old French *tumultuer* = to be in a tumult, with *tuez*, slain, butchered.

We continue the theme from the previous quatrain. At first glance it seems as though a pope is captured on the high seas. But this is the ship or Bark of St Peter steered unsuccessfully by a future pope sailing dangerous geopolitical waters. In this case it must be the **second** pope named Pius, suffering imprisonment by Napoleon. He is one of only two popes held in custody after 1555: Pius VI, his predecessor, who died in French captivity at Valence in 1799, and Pius VII, who was held under house arrest in Fontainebleau by Napoleon between 1809 and 1814. One could say the **second one**, Pius VII, was **absent** from the Vatican. The political power of the papal states never recovered from Napoleon's heavy-handed tactics.

Quatrain Indexing Date: 5 Q15 = May 1815, possibly a near miss for dating the papal persecutor's final defeat at Waterloo in "June" 1815.

5 Q16

A *ſon hault pris plus la lerme ſabee,*[1]	*The tears of the Sabines [no] longer at its high price,*
D'humaine chair par mort en cendre mettre,	*Changing human flesh into ashes through death,*
A *l'iſle Pharos par croiſars*[2] *perturbee,*	*At the isle of Pharos disturbed by [Christian] crusaders,*
Alors qu'à Rodes paroiſtra dur eſpectre.[3]	*Whereas in Rhodes there will appear a tough specter.*

[1]*sabee* = a) cryptogram for the Sabines, and by extension Fascist Italy; b) Latin *Sabaeus* = of Saba (the Arabian city famed for frankincense).
[2]*croiſars* - a) a play on Corsairs; b) Old French variant: *croisars*, cross-soldiers, crusaders; c) "cross-hairs."
[3]Provençal *espectre* = spectre, phantom.

Leoni assesses this one as part of the future "Christian crusade" theme. I lean towards Italy's involvement with Hitler's notorious crusade of the (Christian) Iron Cross against the Jews: **human flesh into ashes through death.** The island of Pharos forms part of the harbor of Alexandria. In December 1941, the harbor was in the "cross-hairs" (rather than Corsairs) of six Italian frogmen using manned torpedoes who crippled two British battleships in a daring commando raid. The Aegean island of Rhodes was part of Mussolini's empire at the onset of World War II. It was an import-ant naval and air base for the Germans and Italians. The **tough specter** could be the prophet's attempt to describe the unworldly shapes of German JU-88 bombers taking off for night raids on the harbor of Piraeus in 1941. On one such raid a British munitions ship was targeted; the explosion was comparable to that of a small atomic bomb.

5 Q17

De nuict paſſant le Roy pres d'vne Andronne,[1]	*Passing by night, the King near an alley,*
Celuy de Cipres & principal guette:	*The one of Cyprus and principal waylayer [or lookout]:*
Le Roy failly la main fuict long du Roſne,	*The king fallen, the hand flees the length of the Rhône,*
Les coniurés l'iront à mort mettre.	*The conspirators will set out to put him to death.*

[1]Andronne: a) Provençal *andronno* = narrow passage; b) Old French *androne* = alley.

This one could be linked to the assassination of Henry IV near the rue Tison, if it were not for the interpretive fly of **Cyprus** fluttering in the ointment. Little else is clear. Ravaillac was not a Cypriot, and, unlike the man described (who runs from the scene and is chased the length of the Rhône River), he was immediately caught. Ravaillac was a lone assassin and not the double-crossed hired killer pictured here.

See Index: Henry IV, assassination of.

5 Q18

De deuil mourra l'infelix profligé,	**The unhappy one will die, overcome by grief,**
Celebrera ſon vitrix¹ l'hecatombe:	**His conqueress will celebrate the sacrifice of many victims (hecatomb):**
Priſtine loy franc edict redigé,	**Pristine law, Frank edict drawn up,**
Le mur & Prince au ſeptieſme iour tombe.	**The wall and Prince to fall on the seventh day.**

¹Latin *victrix* = conqueress: in this case it stands for either the Goddess Britannia (for Britain) or Germania (for Imperial and/or Nazi Germany).

Nostradamus sometimes saw the clouded images of several events as one. This quatrain may superimpose two German offensives on Paris. The first is checked in 1918; the second is successful in 1940.

In June 1918 the German Imperial armies unleashed a series of powerful last-ditch offensives, first on the Lys canal and later (in early July) along the Aisne. The latter became known as the Second Battle of the Marne. The German infantry attacks bludgeoned their way 40 miles beyond the moonscapes and mud of the Western Front into the green fields of the French rear lines, reaching the Marne River a mere 37 miles from Paris. Their advance to Paris was finally checked by an attack of American doughboys in fierce fighting around Château Thierry.

Twenty-two years later, in June 1940, the sons of those mud-splattered German infantrymen sped past the very same Château Thierry inside armoured vehicles and clinging onto panzers on a successful drive to Paris. Once the Germans had thrown the British back over the Channel at Dunkirk, they wheeled their panzers westwards in Operation Red, the code name for the German offensive into France. The Blitzkrieg reached Paris in only seven days. Soon after the so-called impregnable **wall** of the Maginot Line was penetrated by German infantry, President Lebrun conceded defeat and asked for an armistice, and the Third Republic collapsed.

Quatrain Indexing Date: Q18 = 1918, the year of the Second Battle of the Marne. The prophecy indexing for Germany's successful conquest of France reverses 18 to 81 in 5 Q81.

5 Q19

Le grand Royal d'or, d'ærain augmenté,
Rompu la pache, par ieune ouuerte guerre:
Peuple affligé par vn chef lamenté,
De fang barbare fera couuerte terre.

The great Royal one of gold,
  augmented by brass,
The treaty broken, war set in motion
  by a young man:
People afflicted by a lamented chief,
The land will be covered with
  barbarian blood.

An obscure minefield of meaning. Step on and set off any interpretation you like. For me, it conjures up images of the "Antichrist as terrorist" theme. He is the **young man** filled with evildoing from 3 Q60. The final apocalyptic line fits well into the interpretation (reality hopefully being otherwise) that any North African country harboring a base for tomorrow's nuclear terrorists will be obliterated by overwhelming, even nuclear, retaliation. Western temptation for overkill is not so farfetched a danger. One need only look at the unveiled messages sent to Saddam Hussein by the United States during the Gulf War of 1991. The nuclear option was openly debated on the Senate floor. Diplomatic sources threatened Saddam Hussein with nuclear attack if even one of his chemical or biological warheads fell on coalition forces or upon Israel. He ignored all other warnings but even Saddam "Insane" took this threat seriously and kept the safety switch of his weapons of mass destruction cocked on.

5 Q20

Dela les Alpes grand armée paffera,
Vn peu deuant naiftra monftre vapin:
Prodigieux & fubit tournera,
Le grand Tofquan à fon lieu plus propin.

A grand army will pass beyond the
  Alps,
Shortly before will be born a monster
  scoundrel:
Prodigious and sudden will he
  turn,
The great Tuscan to his nearest
  place.

In 1859 the French **grand army** of Napoleon III crossed the Alps to engage the Austrians in northern Italy. Le Pelletier sees Garibaldi as the **monster scoundrel** because of his attempt to conquer the papal states. Where modern scholars search for a Middle-Eastern Antichrist, a 19th-century interpreter like Le Pelletier nominates the Red Italian revolutionary, Garibaldi. Line 4 circles backwards a few years to 1854, when Leopold II, the Grand Duke of Tuscany, was driven from Florence by Garibaldi's revolution. Being a Habsburg, Leopold retired to the **nearest** hospitable **place**, Austria.

5 Q21

Par le trefpas du monarque latin,
Ceux qu'il aura par regne fecouruz:
Le feu luyra, diuifé le butin,
La mort publique aux hardis incoruz.

By the death of the Latin monarch,
Those whom he will have assisted
   through his reign:
The fire will shine, the booty divided,
The public [and notorious] death to
   the daring ones who incurred it.

This is about the death of Mussolini. He and his mistress were shot trying to escape the collapse of Fascist Italy. Their bodies, along with those of other Fascist leaders, were abused by an angry mob in Milan. Mussolini and his mistress were hung by their feet on the metal girders of a bombed-out gas station. This notorious public spectacle is recorded elsewhere by Nostradamus.

Although some scholars consider Lamont's examination of Nostradamus second rate, in his defense, I reproduce here an interpretation of his that in itself is a successful prophecy. On pages 278–79 of *Nostradamus Sees All*, Lamont says: "The fall of Mussolini, the Fascist government of Italy as well as her allies is predicted in this quatrain. Also prophesied is the dismemberment of Fascist organizations and public death to Fascist leaders."

One must remember that these words were written in the late summer or early autumn of 1942, when Mussolini and Hitler were at the peak of their power. Hitler was hurling the Russians back towards the Caucasus and Stalingrad, Rommel and his Italian allies had thrown the British back into Egypt toward El Alamein, and Mussolini's forces had occupied the French Riviera. The Axis debacles of Stalingrad and El Alamein, and the collapse of Mussolini's government in 1943, were many months away.

Quatrain Indexing Date: Q21 = 1921, the year inaugurating Mussolini's Fascist dictatorship of Italy.

5 Q22

Auant qu'à Rome grand aye rendu l'ame,
Effrayeur[1] grande à larmée eftrangere:
Par efquadrons, l'embufche pres de Parme,
Puis les deux rouges enfemble feront chere.

Before, at Rome, the great one gives
   up the ghost,
Great terror for the foreign army:
By Squadrons, the ambush near
   Parma,
Then the two reds will celebrate
   together.

[1]Old French for terror, fright.

Two **red** revolutionaries (or two cardinals) celebrate together when a pope dies and fighting breaks out in **Parma**, in northern Italy. Conventional wisdom would place these events close to Nostradamus' time and make the victims of this ambush Spanish and Imperial troops. It is hard to confirm whether cardinals of the 16th century, or Italian communists of the 20th century, met when a pope died. If one equates rebels with both the Mafia and red cardinals of the Vatican Curia, they could have met in Parma or Milan and celebrated the death of John Paul I in 1978, which just occurred as he was about to blow the whistle on drug money laundering within the Vatican Bank and its financial contacts in northern Italy. Perhaps more information will become clear in the next quatrain.

5 Q23

Les deux contens feront vnis enfemble,	The two contented ones will be united together,
Quand la plufpart à Mars feront conioinct:	When for the most part they will be conjoined with Mars:
Le grand d'Affrique en effrayeur & tremble:	The great African in terror trembles:
DVVMVIRAT[1] par la claffe defioinct.	Duumvirate [the twin alliance] disjoined by the fleet.

[1]Latin *duum virum* = of two men; or *duumvir* = one of two co-equal magistrates. In ancient Rome a *duumvir* tribunal was appointed to investigate cases of high treason.

The **duumvirate** seems to be as much an alliance as an investigation into a terrorist act perpetrated by some North African source. In other words, the investigation by two countries scares the terrorist-harboring nations. Perhaps this has something to do with sanctions on Qadaffi's Libya for the bombing of Pan Am flight 301.

The grammar is foggy enough to make the cuumvirate a terrorist rather than an anti-terrorist alliance. It might be linked to the **triumvirate** alliance of terrorist nations set for our near future (see EP139).

This alliance will be broken by a fleet. This could apply to the submarine **fleet** themes of 5 Q62 and 5 Q63. Is it a fleet of North African submarines depositing terrorist commandos, or is it a fleet **melted and sunk** by the Trident submarines of the West? Could it also be the fleet **foundering** in the Persian or Arabian Gulf (6 Q44)?

5 Q24

Le regne & loy fouz Venus efleué,	The realm and law under Venus raised up,
Saturne aura fus Iupiter empire:	Saturn will have empire over Jupiter:
La loy & regne par le Soleil leué,	The law and realm raised by the Sun,
Par Saturnins endurera le pire.	Through the Saturnian ones it will endure the worst.

A modern Western, Judeo-Christian slant could view the **law** as an extreme interpretation of the Islamic Sharia, symbolized here by a crescent

Venus, rather than the moon. The **realm** could be any new Islamic state, that threatens the West. But it is most likely Iran, since **Saturn** might represent the black-robed mullahs of Iran around the turn of the millennium, when Jupiter and Saturn are in conjunction, in Taurus (also ruled by **Venus**).

In other quatrains the 20th century is called the **Century of the Sun** (2 Q10) that has risen over the resurgence of Islam. But as we enter the 21st century the fortunes of the Saturnian ayatollahs of Iran take a turn for the worse.

Prieditis warns of a time when Christianity will be supplanted either by Islam or a new pagan religion – when Christianity is under the influence of Saturn. I would add that Saturn (the co-ruler of the dawning Aquarian Age) influences the next 20 centuries. If the future is malefic, Saturn will bring on more religious Fascism and extremism in all mainstream religions, in reaction to the other, positive, aspects of Saturn as the Reality Checker. If the future falls in line with a positive Saturn aspect, the Aquarian Age will be more open to a scientific, less superstitious and dogma-bound religion.

Astrological time window

The next Jupiter–Saturn conjunction starts in Aries on 14 February and continues through 2 March 1999. It moves in and out of Taurus from 29 June through 24 October 1999 and back into Taurus from 15 February until 30 June 2000. A Saturnian crisis could bring Islamic fundamentalism to its climax as a threat to peace early in the next decade when Jupiter (*scepter*) is in aspect to bring world peace in June 2002: see 6 Q24.

5 Q25

Le prince Arabe Mars, Sol, Venus, Lyon,	**The Arab Prince, Mars, the Sun, Venus [in] Leo,**
Regne d'Eglife par mer fuccombera:	**The rule of the Church will succumb to the sea:**
Deuers la Perfe bien pres d'vn million,	**Inclined towards Persia very nearly a million men,**
Bifance, Egypte, ver. ferp.¹ inuadera.	**Byzantium, Egypt, the true serpent will invade.**

¹Apocope of Latin *vera serpens* = true serpent.

The long-lasting vendetta between Ayatollah Khomeini of Iran and Saddam Hussein of Iraq erupted in the Iran–Iraq war of 1980–88. This first Gulf War was the Middle East's bloodiest and longest to date. Over one million died in the bloodstained salt marshes and wastelands of the Tigris and Euphrates river delta of Mesopotamia.

In the summer of 1986 I warned incorrectly that Saddam Hussein might face defeat in the following year. I suggested this possibility in the light of the dating of a final Iranian offensive of almost one million men set to overrun Mesopotamia and defeat the **Arab Prince** (Saddam Hussein) in August of 1987. My interpretation gives us a chance to examine how the prophet's obscure grammar and an interpreter's prophetic bias can lead to conclusions that are only partly accurate.

Looking back at this interpretation, it can be argued that August of 1987 did prove to be a significant turning point in the war; it was not, however, in Iran's favor. By the end of July and through August, America's pro-Iraqi stance took a new twist when Kuwaiti tankers were reflagged under the American mast. In August 1987 the Reagan administration also began waging a secret war on Iran. For the next year numerous raids were made on Iranian gunboats and bases by US Navy Seals. Senior Pentagon officials state that US carrier-based airstrikes were authorized for Iranian Silkworm missile batteries on the Strait of Hormuz. American covert military actions between August of 1987 through July of the following year had the effect of turning the tide of the war in favor of Saddam Hussein's Iraq.

Although the Iranians had unleashed their initially successful final offensive of nearly a million men in the previous year (February 1986), and had seized the Faw Peninsula and fought their way to the approaches to the city of Basra by April 1987, my interpretation that they would overrun the Arab world all the way to the borders of Turkey and Egypt was a classic example of a prophet scholar's weakness for hyperbolic exaggeration.

At least for the present time.

With the information from intelligence reports on Iranian dispositions provided by the United States, Saddam Hussein was able to push his enemy out of the Faw Peninsula the following year. He could thus claim to be, if not the war's clear victor, the survivor who gained the greatest advantage. Ayatollah Khomeini died in 1988, to be replaced not by another black and angry Shi'ite mullah but by the more moderate Rafsanjani, who steered Iran away from direct confrontations.

Line 4 at least is clear on which region will suffer the greatest threat from the consequences of a future spread (invasion) of Islamic fundamentalism fanning out from Iran. Classical **Byzantium** and **Egypt** stand for the modern states of Turkey, Lebanon, Israel, the occupied West Bank and Gaza Strip, Syria, Jordan, Iraq, Egypt, and the rest of North Africa.

Astrological Time Window

The next conjunctions of the Sun with Venus and Mars in Leo will occur in August 2000, August 2019, and August 2032. The millennial conjunction in 2000 and the one in 2032 are the most likely candidates for the invasion of the **Arab prince**.

5 Q26

La gent efclaue par vn heur martial,
Viendra en haut degré tant efleuée:
Changeront prince, naiftre vn prouincial,
Paffer la mer copie aux monts leuee.

The slavish [Slavic] people through
   fortune in war,
Will become elevated to a very high
   degree:
They will change their Prince, one
   born a provincial,
An army raised in the mountains to
   cross over the sea.

Lines 1 and 2 predict the victory of the Soviet people over Nazi Germany. Line 3 foresees the **provincial** Nikita Krushchev from the Ukraine taking power after Josef Stalin.

Line 4 backtracks to 1942–44, when Soviet armies formed in the mountainous Caucasus battle sector were later carried by the Soviet navy across the Black Sea to retake the Crimean Peninsula in the second siege of Sevastopol.

A future slant to line 4 would turn the **army raised in the mountains** into the victorious Mujahideen rebels from the war in Afghanistan, seeking new battles and new jihads in the distant lands and seas of the Western powers and the Russian Federation.

5 Q27

Par feu & armes non loing de la marnegro,
Viendra de Perfe occuper Trebifonde:
Trembler Phatos Methelin, Sol alegro,
De fang Arabe d'Adrie couuert onde.

Through fire and arms not far from
   the Black Sea,
He will come from Persia to occupy
   Trabzon:
Pharos, Mitylene to tremble, Sun
   joyful,
The Adriatic Sea covered with Arab
   blood.

Although one cannot rule out Nostradamus' vain hope for an immanent collapse of the Ottoman Empire, this quatrain may tie in to 5 Q25's theme of a future spread of Islamic fundamentalist states from Iran (**Persia**) all the way to Turkey, the Middle East, and North Africa. There is fighting on the **Black Sea** coast of Turkey and the Iranians occupy **Trabzon**. The Egyptian port of Alexandria (**Pharos**) and **Mitylene** suffer either from earthquakes or from street fighting in an Islamic revolution. The melodramatic final line describes some future naval setback – either the Ottoman defeat on a **sunny** day at Lepanto in 1571 (near the **Adriatic**), or some defeat of the Arab submarine fleets in the same area in our near future.

5 Q28

Le bras pendu & la iambe liée,	**His arm hung and his leg bound,**
Vifaige pafle au feing poignard caché:	**Face pale, [and] in his breast a**
Trois qui feront iurez de la meflee,	**dagger hidden:**
Au grand de Gennes fera le fer lafché.	**Three who will be sworn in the fray,**
	Against the great one of Genoa blades
	will be drawn.

It is doubtful Nostradamus intended this one to refer to the assassination of an heir to the dukedom of Savoy, as Le Pelletier hoped back in 1867. King Humbert of Italy was assassinated 33 years later in 1900 by an unemployed smith named Acciarito. In Nostradamus' time **the great one of Genoa** was Andrea Doria, Grand Admiral of the Imperial Fleet and the despotic Doge of Genoa. Doria died of natural causes in 1560. In this alternative future that failed, his assassin was to have one arm in a sling, hiding the dagger.

5 Q29

La liberté ne fera recouuree,	**Liberty will not be regained,**
L'occupera noir fier vilain inique:	**It will be occupied by a black, proud,**
Quand la matiere du pont¹ fera ouuree,	**villainous and unjust man:**
D'Hifter, Venise fafchée la republique.	**When the matter of the Pontiff is**
	opened,
	The republic of Venice [Fascist Italy]
	will be vexed by Hitler.

¹Nostradamus shorthand for *Pontifex* = Pontiff, Pope.

The first line could depict the birth of the Nazi regime in 1933 spawned by the pretense of a national emergency that required the new German Chancellor, Adolf Hitler, to "temporarily" suspend individual civil rights (**liberty will not be regained**). But the **villainous** man in **black** could stand for any number of Italian Blackshirts and German Gestapo leaders, from black-clad Heinrich Himmler, commander of the SS, to the Italian dictator Mussolini. The quatrain identifies the future intrigues and tacit support of Mussolini and Hitler by the papacy of Pope Pius XII. The final line is not only a synecdoche for Mussolini's Fascist empire but also covers the many conferences between Hitler and Mussolini in Italy, giving the Old French *fafchée* (vexed) even more phonetic impact as "Fasch-ist."

The Axis Alliance would become a pact that bound the Italians body and soul to Hitler's self-destruction.

5 Q30

Tout à l'entour de la grande cité,	**All around the environs of the great**
Seront foldats logez par champs & villes:	**city,**
Donner l'affaut Paris, Rome incité,	**Soldiers will be lodged throughout the**
Sur le pont[1] lors fera faicte grande pille.	**fields and towns:**
	Paris to give the assault, Rome incited,
	Then great pillage will be inflicted
	upon the Pontiff.

[1]Possibly an apocope for *pontiff* rather than the Latin *pontus*, meaning bridge.

Rome was sacked twice by the French, in 1797 and 1808; the chief plunder was artwork carried to the museums of France. It was definitely not as severe as Nostradamus foresaw. He may have projected into the future what he knew of the terrible sack of Rome by Habsburg Imperial Forces in 1527. The **great pillage** might better represent the concessions of Pope Pius VI who was forced to relinquish part of the papal states in 1797. Later his successor Pius VII would helplessly watch the rest be incorporated into the French Empire by 1809.

5 Q31

Par terre Attique[1] chef de la fapience,	**Through the Attic land, source of all**
Qui de prefent eft la rofe du monde:	**wisdom,**
Pont[2] ruiné & fa grand preeminence,	**Which presently is the rose of the**
Sera fubdite & naufrage des vndes.	**world:**
	The Pontiff ruined, and his grand
	preeminence,
	Will be subjugated and a shipwreck in
	the waves.

[1]Attica, the ancient environs of Athens.
[2]Note this is the third quatrain in a row where *pont* is used for the Papacy rather than for a bridge or the ocean.

This is the third quatrain in succession to display a papal crisis. The *Attic land* refers metaphorically to Nostradamus' France (classical comparisons were all the rage at the court of Henry II, and again at the court of Napoleon centuries later). Napoleonic France nearly made the papacy – or Bark of St Peter – a **shipwreck**.

A future application is possible: the trials and tribulations of the Roman Catholic Church in the 21st century. Here we are privy to the final demise of the Vatican, which is replaced by a new Aquarian Age religiousness free of dogma and Piscean hierarchies. Our worldwide community becomes the new **Attic land**, a global democratic state equal in glory to the Golden Age of Greece. The mystic **rose** reference connects with Nostradamus' Eight Mystical Clues to the catalysts of a new spiritual revolution that will come in the 21st century.

Elsewhere in the prophecies Nostradamus hints that this new religious movement will be symbolized by the ocean. *Pont* relates to Latin *pontus*, "the ocean." This could hide a secret translation of line 3: **The pontiff ruined (by the oceanics).**

Quatrain Indexing Date: Q31 = either 1931 or 2031, years that may be important milestones in the creation of a new religiousness in the 21st century.

5 Q32

Où tout bon eʃt tout bien Soleil & Lune,[1]	**Where all is good, all well [in] Sun and Moon,**
Eʃt abondant ʃa ruine s'approche:	**Is abundant, its ruin approaches:**
Du ciel s'aduance vaner ta fortune,	**It comes from the sky to sift through your fortune,**
En meʃme eʃtat que la ʃeptieʃme roche.	**In the same state as the seventh rock.**

[1]*Soleil & Lune* = Sun and Moon: poetic allusion to gold and silver coins or a golden and silver standard.

There are several repeated and cryptic references in the quatrains to a catastrophe coming *from the sky* or to *fire from the skies*. Conventional 20th-century interpretations have attributed this disaster to nuclear war. Laver believed this quatrain stood for the sudden destruction of the abundant economy and life of the French Second Empire by the Franco-Prussian War. But this cannot apply, because the final line is a clear metaphor for the biblical Apocalypse. Our economy and wealth may indeed go to blazes in some future nuclear war, but one cannot rule out an interpretation of global warming as the catastrophe that descends with a different *fire*, to overtax the world's economies through super-hurricanes and rising oceans. The quatrain indexing could even stand for two different worldwide depressions, the first in the early 1930s. The more apocalyptic is set for the 2030s, the time many scientists and climatologists believe we will reap the uncontrollable fury of the greenhouse effect, if we do not curb our throwaway consumerism-unto-doomsday habits in the final years of this century.

Quatrain Indexing Date: Q32 = either the global economic depression *circa* 1932, or a future economic collapse due to overpopulation and global warming stresses in 2032.

5 Q33

Des principaux de cité rebellee,	**The premier citizens of the city in revolt,**
Qui tiendront fort pour liberté rauoir:	**Who will struggle hard to regain their liberty:**
Detrencher maʃles, infelice meʃlee,	**The men are cut up, unhappy mixture,**
Crys hurlemens à Nantes piteux voir.	**Cries, howlings at Nantes, piteous to see!**

The visions of future inhuman acts must have weighed heavily on the prophet, yet he continued to look, recording what he saw for the coming generations. Perhaps he was applying his skills as a doctor to treat human cruelty by exposing it to the open air like a wound so that it might heal, so to speak. In other words, publishing predictions of potential disasters and tragedies is like exposing a potentially serious wound to dry in the present so it maybe will not fester in the future.

One such failed case of forewarning concerns the atrocities committed in 1793 when victorious Republican forces occupied Nantes, the center of the Vendeean insurrection against the National Convention. General Carrier, a forerunner of men like Adolf Eichmann, collected all males from the wealthiest families – children and old men included – and put them on wagons heading for Paris and "Madame Guillotine" (**the men are cut up**). According to Le Pelletier, the phrase **unhappy mixture** describes the soldiers' macabre games of "Republican Marriage," played by the soldiers on the river docks. Monks and women were stripped of their clothes and bound together in couples. Then Carrier ordered them heaped onto barges to be taken out on the Loire river and sunk. The soldiers took turns shooting at the writhing, screaming targets drowning in the bloodstained water.

5 Q34

Du plus profond de l'occident Anglois,	**From the deepest part of western England,**
Où est le chef de l'isle Britannique:	**Where the chief of the British Isles is:**
Entrera classe dans Gyronde par Blois	**A fleet will enter into Gironde**
[or Blaye?],	**through Blois,**
Par vin & sel, feux cachez aux barriques.	**Through wine and salt, fires hidden in the casks.**

The **deepest** (farthest) western **part** of England is her American colonies, which in 1555 were little more than a dream of English explorers, for the foundation stones of the first English settlements were another half-century ahead. Some scholars believe Nostradamus foresaw a second Hundred Years War with England, and the return of English armies again to invade western and south-western France. Between 1559 and 1688 England and France were almost always at peace. Nostradamus seems to have dated here the English Glorious Revolution in 1689. He may have been aware of the consequences to Catholic France faced with the rising power of a now firmly Protestant England under William III and Mary.

Between 1689 and 1815, France and England fought seven major wars for European and maritime domination. One could call this the hundred year – or rather, 126-year – war. During that period the closest thing to a British invasion of south-west France was in 1814, when Wellington's Peninsular Army marched across the western Pyrenees to lay siege to

Bayonne and to Bordeaux, which is near the entrance of the **Gironde**. The last line is especially hard to fathom. **Salt** sometimes represents taxation. **Fires hidden in the casks** might be artillery rounds or incendiary shells used by Wellington's cannon on the fortifications of Bayonne or Bordeaux.

5 Q35

Par cité franche de la grand mer Seline,
Qui porte encores à l'eſtomach la pierre:
Angloiſe claſſe viendra ſoubs la bruine,
Vn rameau prendre, du grand ouuerte
    guerre.

For the free city of the great Crescent sea,
Which still carries in its stomach, the
    stone:
The English fleet will come under the
    drizzle,
To seize a branch, war opened by the
    great one.

The **Crescent sea** could describe the crescent-shaped coastline of Genoa on the Mediterranean or the great crescent sweep of the Bay of Biscay on the Atlantic. One cannot rule out Nostradamus' "Chyren-Selin" device as an alternative-future Henry II dominating the Mediterranean. There are those who would make the Persian Gulf that **great Crescent** (Islamic) **sea** and say this is about the recent Gulf War of 1991. In this case we have an American battleship *New Jersey* carrying the **stone** of cruise missiles deep in its hold.

With so many possibilities, it is time to shorten the list with a weather report. Intermittent **drizzle** punctuated the British Royal Navy's bombardment of Sword, Juno, and Gold Beaches during the Normandy landings, so D-Day on 6 June 1944 is one candidate, even though it is far north of the Bay of Biscay. (A feint attack on the southern end of Hitler's Atlantic wall was an option never taken by the Anglo-American forces.) One could forgive Nostradamus mixing his Anglo-Saxons in the Persian Gulf, since both American and British flotillas shelled Iraqi coastal defenses along occupied Kuwait – and it was **drizzling** during the final days of the war. The last line may be the best a 16th-century man can do to describe one of the *New Jersey's* cruise missiles taking out an Iraqi radar tower and command center – **seize a branch**.

5 Q36

De ſœur le frere par ſimulte faintiſe[1],
Viendra meſler roſee[2] en myneral:
Sur la placente[3] donne à vielle tardifue,
Meurt, le gouſtant ſera ſimple & rural.

The sister's brother through deceitful
    enmity,
Will come to mix dew with the mineral:
On the cake given to the slow old
    woman,
[Who] dies, tasting it – she will be
    simple and rustic.

[1] Old French *faintiſe* = deceit, dissimulation.
[2] *roſee* = a) Latin *ros*, dew; b) Latin *rosarius*. Leoni says alternatively that it is a poison extracted from the laurel rose.
[3] Latin *placenta* = a flat cake.

I cannot find much to add to this detailed yet obscure pharmacy/poisoning prophecy. Leoni in 1961 proposed that "since Nostradamus was a first-class pharmacist, some pharmacist may find a clue here."

No first-class pharmacist has come forward to unravel this mystery for 35 years, so it is most likely that the old woman hasn't nibbled yet.

5 Q37

Trois cents feront d'vn vouloir & accord,	Three hundred will be of one desire and accord,
Que pour venir au bout de leur attaincte:	In order to come to the end of their blow from a distance:
Vingts mois apres tous & records,	All after twenty months and records,
Leur Roy trahi fimulant haine faincte.	Their King betrayed simulating feigned hatred.

This one is a linguistic labyrinth. The key to unlock its secrets is the identity of those **three hundred**. Since we have roughly 300 religions on the planet Earth in our present day this could be about the near or even distant future. The **blow from a distance** could be poetic rather than literal. It is the blow all nations will feel when the first intelligent contact with another civilization is made. The day we have unquestionable proof of the existence of extraterrestrial civilizations on the planets of distant stars, we will know that it is time for the childhood of humanity to come to an end. Our divided civilization will suffer a blow to its 300 definitions of God, its nationalistic divisions, and any other dogma we have cherished. The reality of "others" out there will make it necessary for us to abolish all our divisions overnight and work as one family of hu-woman-ity.

The **King** or important world leader faking hatred may be a future American president who is forced by voters to **feign hatred** for inter-nationalism to gain votes; in his heart, however, he supports the dis-mantling of American national identity. This revelation reaches the press, and a great scandal ensues.

It will take 20 months – beginning on the date we receive incontro-vertible evidence (**records**) of alien life, and climaxing in the creation of a bona fide constitution of a United Nations of Earth – for the transfor-mation of our current civilization to be completed.

5 Q38

Ce grand monarque qu'au mort fuccedera,	He who will succeed the great monarch upon his death,
Donnera vie illicite & lubrique,	Will lead an illicit and debauched life,
Par nonchalance à tous concedera,	Through nonchalance he will concede to all,
Qu'à la parfin faudra la loy Salique.	So that in the end the Salic law will fail.

This one is right on target for Louis XV. His grandfather, Louis XIV, was actually called **the Great Monarch**. The great-grandson was far less a monarch and far more a playboy and spendthrift. The **Salic law** of French royal succession would later collapse because of Louis XV's Epicurean habits. He preferred to eat, drink, and be merry with his mistresses and let his successor, Louis XVI, deal with the disaster to come. For 20 years he allowed his mistress, Madame de Pompadour, to run the realm in his name, violating the **Salic law** barring women from ruling France. She was responsible for impoverishing the French economy through several ruinous wars of royal succession. He spent his final decades devoting all his time and energy to a new mistress, Madame du Barry, while France slipped ever deeper into debt. When informed of the misery and widespread discontent of the people, Louis XV was reported to have said, "After me, the deluge." Nostradamus gives us a variation of this famous statement in line 3.

5 Q39

Du vray rameau de fleur de lys iſſu,	**Issued from the true branch of the fleur-de-lys,**
Mis & logé heritier de Hetrurie:	**Placed and lodged as heir of Etruria:**
Son ſang antique de longue main tiſſu,	**His ancient blood woven by the drawn-out authority,**
Fera Florence florir en l'armoirie.	**Will cause the armorial bearings of Florence to flower.**

This quatrain is a paraphrase of 5 Q3. It correctly predicts the accession of a French royal to the throne of Tuscany. In 1737 Duke Francis of Lorraine (a descendant of French kings through his mother) became Grand Duke of Florence. From 1801 through 1805, Louis de Bourbon-Parma, a bona fide royal of the **fleur-de-lys**, sat on the throne in the Tuscan realm of Etruria having been placed there by Napoleon. In 1809, Napoleon used his **drawn-out authority** to incorporate Etruria formally into France. With **Florence** (the city of flowers) flowering, Nostradamus makes a few heraldic puns on Gallic pride in the final line. And why not, since it has become part of France, *mais non*? Perhaps he had a vision of blossoming fleur-de-lys in the Florentine armorial bearings.

5 Q40

Le ſang royal fera ſi trefmeſlé,	**The royal blood will be so very mixed,**
Contraint feront Gaulois de l'Hefperie:	**Constrained will be the Gauls by the lands of the West:**
On attendra que terme foit coulé,	**They will wait until his term has expired,**
Et que memoire de la voix foit perie.	**And that memory of his voice has perished.**

Cheetham makes a good call. She believes this quatrain takes us into the 20th century after the French royal bloodlines have mixed themselves into oblivion. Line 3 suggests someone in elected office rather than a royal. She reminds us that only one French President, Charles de Gaulle, intervened effectively in Western politics, especially when it came to the progress of European union. Once his term of office and influence ended with his resignation in 1969, and his death the following year, his no-saying policies to the European Common Market died with him.

Cheetham does not, however, notice the same fate overtaking the policies of another great French president, François Mitterand, who left office and died in 1995.

5 Q41

Nay Jous les vmbres & iournee nocturne,	*Born in the shadows and a dark day,*
Sera en regne & bonté Jouueraine:	*He will be sovereign in rule and goodness:*
Fera renaiſtre Jon Jang de l'antique vrne,	*He will cause his blood to be born again in the ancient urn,*
Renouuellant Jiecle d'or pour l'ærain.	*Renewing the age [century] of gold for that of brass.*

A total eclipse will be visible over much of Europe on 11 August 1999. Perhaps a great world leader or spiritual messenger will be born on this day? The poetry of line 3 and 4 clearly describes the advent of the Aquarian Age after the turn of the 20th century: Aquarius the Water-Bearer carries an **ancient urn**, and the 20th century has been called the **century of the sun (gold)** by Nostradamus (see 2 Q10).

Brass is an important metal in prediction and psychic mediumship.

5 Q42

Mars eſleué en Jon plus haut befroy,	*Mars elevated to its highest belfry,*
Fera retraire les Allobrox[1] de France:	*Will cause the Savoyards to be restored to France:*
La gent Lombarde fera ſi grand effroy,	*The people of Lombardy will cause very great terror,*
Au ceux de l'Aigle comprins Jouz la Balance.	*To those of the Eagle, included under the Balance.*

[1]Latin *Allobrox* = the classical inhabitants of Savoy.

When the times of war burn hot, Savoy will return to France. Nostradamus wrote this when Savoy was already a part of France (since 1535), making a bold prophecy between the lines that she would be lost again. Just a few years later the unthinkable happened. Henry II lost the Habsburg–Valois Wars and the dukedom was restored to the Holy Roman Empire through the treaty of Cateau-Cambrésis in 1559. Proud Savoy would not find itself under the dominion of France again for another 301 years. In 1860 the imperial eagle standards of a French army of the Second Empire, led by Napoleon III, invaded Italy to help the Savoyard King Victor-Emmanuel II defeat the Austrians (ie those astrologically **under the Balance** scales of Libra) to unite Italy. As a reward for his assistance, Victor-Emmanuel presented Savoy to Napoleon III.

5 Q43

La grande ruyne des facrez ne s'efloigne,	**The great ruin of the clergy is not far off,**
Prouence, Naples, Sicille, Seez[1] & Ponce:[2]	**Provence, Naples, Sicily, [Holy] Sées and Pons:**
En Germanie, au Rhin & la Cologne,	**In Germany, at the Rhine and Cologne,**
Vexez à mort par tous ceux de Magonce.[3]	**Vexed to death by all those of Mainz.**

[1]Sées = the seat of a bishopric in Normandy; or a double pun for the "Holy See" of the papacy and bishopric alike.
[2]Pons = a town 60 miles north of Bordeaux.
[3]Latin Maguntiacum = Mayence, most likely Mainz, in central Germany.

Nostradamus has mixed success with this one. The clergy would undergo religious persecutions in most of the places mentioned, but in widely diverse times and certainly not soon after the 1550s. The German Catholics in the regions of line 3 would suffer during the Thirty Years War of the next century. The clergy dwelling in the French areas of Normandy, south-west France, and Provence would be cast out of their churches and monasteries by the French Revolution in the early 1790s. The priests and two Popes would endure various degrees of indignity, pillage and incarceration under Napoleon's tyranny from 1797 through 1814.

The entire citizenry of Mainz, not just its clergy, was a victim of the general destruction and brigandage of the Thirty Years War. Between 1631 and 1635 Mainz lost around 25 percent of its dwellings, 40 percent of its population, and 60 percent of its wealth. Eyewitnesses William Crowne and the noted engraver Wenceslas Hollar describe the entire territory between Mainz and Frankfurt as desolate, and the people of Mainz so weak from hunger they could not even crawl out of their ruins to receive morsels of food offered by the two travelers.

5 Q44

Par mer le rouge ſera prins de pyrates,	On the sea the red [one] will be captured by pirates,
La paix ſera par ſon moyen troublee:	The peace will be troubled because of his plea:
L'ire[1] & l'auare commettra par fainct acte,	He will reunite anger [or Ireland] and greed through a false act
Au grand Pontife ſera l'armée doublee.	The army will be doubled by the great Pontiff.

[1]Either it is "the ire," "the anger," or it is a cryptogram for "L'Eire," Ireland.

Could *L'ire* be a play on "Eire," the Gaelic name for Ireland? If so, this is a wicked pun of a prophecy for a disastrous future unification of the Republic of Ireland with Northern Ireland. In the pun, this event will reunite *ire* (anger) as well as the Irish. The southern Irish army will swell in numbers to meet the Protestant north's rebellion (**red** being the universal color of rebels). Perhaps the militarization of Ireland is influenced by a future militant pope? Or maybe the capture of a **red** cardinal by Protestant terrorists has egged on the future **pontiff** to plead for the Irish Republican Army to re-**double** its repression?

5 Q45

Le grand Empire ſera toſt deſolé,	The great Empire will soon be desolated,
Et tranſlaté pres d'arduenne ſilue:[1]	And transferred near the forest of the Ardennes:
Les deux baſtards par l'aiſné decollé,	The two bastards will be beheaded by the oldest,
Et regnera Ænobarb,[2] nez de milue.	Aenobarbus will rule, the hawk-nosed one.

[1]*D'arduenne ſilue* = Latin *Ardvenna Silvae*, the Ardennes Forest.
[2]*Ænobarb* = Aenobarbus: Red- or Bronzebeard, an allusion to Hitler as the modern Barbarossa.

During the Battle of France, the Germans detected (as Nostradamus, apparently did centuries before) the fatal flaw in the French defensive plan that left the approaches to the Ardennes forest region near Sedan thinly defended by second-class troops. The French general staff could not believe that any large armored force might cross the thick-forested, hilly terrain (they had not read their Nostradamus). Here we have an unobscured reference to **the forest of the Ardennes** as the pivotal attack point of Hitler's invasion plan. The **great Empire** and colonies of the French would fall after a surprise attack that came out of the Ardennes at

Sedan. The French Ninth Army would be overrun by waves of panzers and Stuka dive-bombers.

The two men earning the prophet's condemnation as **bastards** could be the commanders of the French Ninth and Second Armies, Generals Corap and Huntzinger, respectively, who did not respond fast enough to prevent the Germans from crossing the Meuse river and splitting the French defensive line in two. The generals were not **beheaded**, but Corap was dismissed for incompetence and the able Huntzinger was given the painful dishonor of meeting Hitler in person to sign the armistice as the representative of the vanquished French. The most senior (**oldest**) French officer, Commander-in-Chief General Weygrand, tried in vain to stanch the flood of Germans breaching the French front. As a result Hitler occupied and ruled France. *Aenobarb*, as we will see in other quatrains, could be an enigmatic name for Adolf Hitler. Nostradamus may be metaphorically naming him after the medieval German King Frederick Barbarossa (Redbeard). The **hawk-nosed one** is Charles de Gaulle, the only French tank commander to briefly check the advance of Guderian's Panzer Corps, at Holnon Wood.

At the onset of the Battle of the Bulge four years later, Hitler said, "I prophesy that a great empire will be destroyed." He did not mean his own. Nostradamus continues to pinpoint the Ardennes Forest region of Luxembourg as the invasion avenue where the fortunes of two great empires would fail in the space of a few years. First the colonial empire of France is defeated by a German surprise thrust through the Ardennes in 1940. The quatrain can also apply equally to the Nazi empire's falling when the next German thrust through the Ardennes backfired in the Battle of the Bulge.

Quatrain Indexing Date: the quatrain is appropriately numbered 45 for the year the battle ended, and dates the Nazi empire's total annihilation down to the month = May (Century 5) of (19)45.

5 Q46

Par chapeaux rouges querelles &	**From the red hats quarrels and new**
nouueaux fchifmes,	**schisms,**
Quand on aura efleu le Sabinois:	**When they will have elected the**
On produira contre luy grans fophifmes,	**Sabine:**
Et fera Rome lefee par Albanois.	**They will produce great sophisms**
	against him,
	And Rome will be wronged by those of
	Albion.

Those of Albion are the British. The **red hats** belong to the pope's cardinals. During the late 1980s Pope John Paul II and the Archbishop of

Canterbury made the first tentative steps towards resolving a centuries-old schism between the Anglican and Roman Catholic Churches. What little progress was made will be lost when a future Archbishop of Canterbury snubs a successor of John Paul. This new pope may be St Malachy's foreseen Gloria Olivae or the last pope before the Apocalypse, Petrus Romanus, who is an Italian this time, a *Sabine* from an area north-east of Rome.

5 Q47

Le grand Arabe marchera bien auant,	**The great Arab will march well ahead,**
Trahy fera par les Bifantinois:	**He will be betrayed by the Byzantines:**
L'antique Rodes luy viendra au deuant,	**Ancient Rhodes will come forward to [meet] him,**
Et plus grand mal par auftre Pannonois.	**And greater evil through the Austrian Hungarians.**

Jochmans and Cheetham understandably pin this one on the recent Gulf War of 1991. In this case the **great Arab** is Saddam Hussein (see 5 Q25), betrayed by the Turks, who cut off Iraq's pipelines and join forces with the Allied coalition. **Rhodes** stands, by extension, for Greece, which lets the air out of the tires of Cheetham's interpretation, which she readily admits. There are two ways out of her dilemma.

The first places this event farther back in time during the many wars the Ottoman Empire fought first with the Holy Roman Empire and later with the Austro-Hungarian Empire. The struggles netted a gain, and later a loss, of its conquests in Hungary, Greece, and the Balkans. In this case the **great Arab** may be a non-Turkish general serving the Sultan, who is undermined by treachery from within by someone on his general staff.

The second alternative takes us beyond our own time to a near-future conflict between Iraq and Turkey over Kurdestan and water rights. All of Iraq's and Syria's water comes down the Tigris and Euphrates rivers from the Turkish mountains. Saddam Hussein, or his son Uday or some other heir to his dictatorship, might wage the war over water and initially penetrate deep into south-eastern Turkey. In the Bible, the prophet Ezekiel foresaw Armageddon on the day the Euphrates river runs dry and its cracked earthen bowels are crossed by armies.

While Iraq fights on one front, the Greeks attack Turkey from the west. The tensions between these two Aegean powers gave rise to a bloody war in the 1920s as well as a battle over Cyprus in the 1970s. War was narrowly avoided a third and fourth time during the 1980s and 1990s over disputed islands off the coast of Anatolia.

5 Q48

Apres la grande affliction du sceptre,	After the great affliction of the scepter,
Deux ennemis par eux seront defaicts:	Two enemies will be undone by them:
Classe d'Affrique aux Pannons viendra naistre,	The fleet from Africa will appear to rise up before the Hungarians,
Par mer & terre seront horribles faicts.	By sea and land horrible deeds will take place.

This may be a continuation of the three future tracks I described in the last prophecy. Leoni thinks the **great affliction of the scepter** is a reference to what he calls a "War of the Imperial Succession" theme. The nebulous line 2 can read either: **Two enemies will be undone by them**(selves) or . . . **will be undone by each other**. Other quatrains refer to fleets **plunging to the bottom** or **traveling underwater**.

Nostradamus often makes a North African or Arab connection to these submarine fleets who meet their showdown in the Adriatic, off the coast of what was once the Austro-Hungarian Empire and is now the broken shards of Yugoslavia. A fleet that will **appear to rise up before** its enemy clearly is one made up of submarines.

5 Q49

Nul de l'Espaigne mais de l'antique France,	Not from Spain but from ancient France,
Ne sera esleu pour le tremblant nacelle,	Will be elected for the trembling ship,
A l'ennemy sera faicte fiance,[1]	He will make a promise to the enemy,
Qui dans son regne sera peste cruelle.	Who will cause great plague during his reign.

[1] Old French for assurance, promise.

When the election for John Paul I's successor was under way, it was widely anticipated that the next pope might not be an Italian. There were several non-Italian candidates, including one from Poland and another from Latin America. The election ended in victory for the candidate from an area of south-west Poland that had once formed the outer frontier of Charlemagne's empire – **from ancient France**. The unsuccessful Latin American candidate is also referred to in line 1. In the time of Nostradamus Latin America was thought to be part of the Spanish Empire; hence the new pope is **not from Spain but from ancient France**. In his Epistle to Henry II Nostradamus had warned that, sometime in or near the period of this new non-Italian pope's tenure, the priests of the Catholic Church would be threatened by **plague**. Shortly after the election of Pope John Paul II, the world began to be aware of the great modern plague of AIDS. During the ensuing years churches have had to reassure their flocks that the disease cannot be passed through the sharing of a communion cup.

Since we do not yet know the origins of the AIDS virus, Nostradamus' *enemy* has still to be identified. Theories abound, including one that claims AIDS was some manufactured horror of the Cold War. However, if we examine a future pope who will *make a promise to the enemy* in the light of events that have occurred since the publication of my previous Nostradamus books, the Polish pontiff may be implicated as an accessory to a global drug-laundering scheme. The *promise* made by the pope of a future trembling theocratic state could be that of looking the other way as cash flows to feed the global plague of drug abuse. The evil tithe the Church gives to drug-money laundering through the Vatican Bank in part sustains the worldwide flow of poison up the needles in many an addict's arm – what Nostradamus in 10 Q65 calls the *pointed steel wounding all up the sleeve*.

A more positive interpretation would have John Paul II's promise be to the former *enemy* nations of the now-defunct Soviet Empire, which have forsaken communism. In 1989 the pope received a visit in Rome from Mikhail Gorbachev. The last leader of the Soviet Union gave the pontiff a tacit assurance that Ukrainian Catholics would be granted recognition by the outgoing communist regime. In the summer of 1993 John Paul II visited the former Soviet Baltic states.

Nostradamus sometimes calls Pope John Paul II **Pol**, a pun on his name and Polish origins, and **Mansol, the work of the sun**, possibly a designation that tallies with the medieval prophet St Malachy's description of John Paul II as "The Sun's Labor." Nostradamus frequently warns that John Paul II will be pursued by enemies and that his supporters will be captured and killed.

5 Q50

L'an que les freres du lys feront en aage,	**The year that the brothers of the lily will be of age,**
L'vn d'eux tiendra la grande Romanie:	**One of them will hold the great Romania:**
Trembler les monts, ouuert Latin paſſage	**The mountains to tremble, the Latin passage opened**
Pache[1] macher, contre fort d'Armenie.	**Pasha to march, against the fort of Armenia.**

[1]*Pache* = a) Old French *pache* = accord, agreement, treaty; b) *Pasha*: Turkish title for a governor.

Two countries have used the exact same fleur-de-lys device: Royalist France in the past and Bosnia in the present. It would be a stretch to say a Bosnian cleric will become governor of the Holy Roman Empire (*great Romania*). This quatrain is another alternative-future failure for Henry II as the Second Charlemagne, who unites France and the Holy Roman Empire and freely marches his armies over passes in the Alps to Rome. If Henry had lived, this prophetic fictional destiny could have made two of his sons Holy Roman Emperors while he ruled France. During this time a Turkish **Pasha** was to have invaded **Armenia**. No significant Armenian rebellion against their Turkish masters took place until 1879.

5 Q51

La gent de Dace, d'Angleterre & Polonne,
Et de Boëſme feront nouuelle ligue:
Pour paſſer outre d'Hercules la colonne,
Barcins,[1] Tyrrens[2] dreſſer cruelle
    brique.

**The people of Dacia, England and Poland,
And of Bohemia will make a new league:
To pass beyond the pillars of Hercules,
The Barcelonans and Tyrrhenians to mount a cruel brawl.**

[1]Latin *Barcino* = Barcelona.
[2]Latin *Tyrrheni* = ancestors of the Etruscans and Tuscans.

This could be about the changes in alliances during the latter days of World War II. Lines 1 and 2 describe the summer of 1944, when the Axis government of Romania (**Dacia**) collapsed under political pressure and the invasion of the Soviets. Romania later joined forces with the resistance forces of the Poles and Czechs (**Bohemia**) in fighting against the retreating German armies. English and American planes sometimes airdropped weapons and supplies to Eastern European resistance groups. Line 3 shows Nostradamus did not fail to see the great naval forces of the Allies streaming through the Strait of Gibraltar. But the final line's battle of Italians and Spanish (**Barcelonans**) is at best a failed quantum future, since the Spanish dictator Franco – although sympathetic to the Nazis – kept Spain neutral throughout the war. Sizable Polish units passed through the Strait of Gibraltar on English ships to fight in the Italian (**Tyrrhenian**) campaign.

5 Q52

Vn Roy ſera qui donra l'oppoſite,
Les exilez eſleuez ſur le regne:
De ſang nager la gent caſte[1] hyppolite,[2]
Et florira long temps ſoubs telle enſeigne.

**A King will be who will give opposition,
The exiles elevated over the realm:
To swim in blood the poor pure people,
And he will flourish for a long time under such a flag.**

[1]Late Latin *castus* = chaste, pure; (poetic license) castle, class (of people).
[2]Greek *hypolitis* = poor, mean, little.

Can a general quatrain find fulfillment in an application to the fall of the British Raj in 1947?

Although in his heart the British King George VI would have liked to retain his title as Emperor of India, by the mid-20th century British kings were little more than figurehead emperors of India, let alone figurehead constitutional monarchs.

The *exiles* are the leaders of the Indian Congress party, such as Nehru and Gandhi, who were frequently put in prison during their revolutions of civil disobedience. They became the new leaders of the Republic of India, the former *realm* of the British Raj. G*ent caste Hyppolite* could be translated into **the caste of the poor pure people**, a very close approximation to Mahatma Gandhi's euphemistic term for Indian untouchables – Harijans. The man in line 4 is the first prime minister of India, Jawaharlal Nehru, who remained in office from 1947 until his death in 1964.

5 Q53

La loy du Sol, & Venus contendens,	**The law of the Sun, and Venus in**
Appropriant l'esprit de prophetie:	** contention,**
Ne l'vn ne l'autre ne seront entendus,	**Appropriating the spirit of prophecy:**
Par Sol tiendra la loy du grand Messie.	**Neither the one nor the other will be**
	** understood,**
	Through the Sun will [be held] the
	** law of the great Messiah.**

This opens with an astrological metaphor; one cannot, therefore – as some Nostradamians do – take it merely at face value and contend that Christianity is here represented by the Sun, as if an English pun on **Sun** and **Son** were intended by a French-speaking prophet. Neither does **Venus** have a sufficient metaphorical relationship to Islam. But the first line could be a significant clue to the astrological makeup of one who Nostradamus believes will be a future prophet or enlightened spiritual catalyst for a worldwide revolution in consciousness in the 21st century.

The new spiritual teacher has Venus and the Sun conjoined in his natal chart. This aspect gives him a gift of prophecy. The **spirit** is the Christ-consciousness, the inner flame of his potential for divine awareness being fully awakened and remembered 24 hours a day. His mysticism, reflected in these astrological aspects, will not be understood by the masses. This has been true of all great spiritual catalysts of the past and present who most people call madmen or cult gurus. But in time these madmen of the present often become the respected Messiahs of tomorrow. Remember that cult guru Buddha, or that antisocial religious zealot called Jesus ransacking the moneychangers' stalls in the Temple of Solomon at Jerusalem? The final line may hide an important clue to the origins of the next world teacher. Classical metaphors hold the **Sun** as symbolic for the East, the land of the rising sun.

Quatrain Indexing Date: Q53 = 1953, the year in the Pyramid prophecy that inaugurates the era of Osiris, the time of the second coming of the Egyptian Messiah (1953–2001).

5 Q54

Du pont Euxine,[1] & la grand Tartarie,
Vn Roy ſera qui viendra voir la Gaule:
Tranſpercera Alane & l'Armenie,
Et dans Biſance lairra ſanglante[2] Gaule.[3]
	From the Black Sea, and great
	    Tartary,
	There will be a king who will come to
	    see France:
	[He] will penetrate through Russia
	    and Armenia,
	And in Byzantium [Istanbul] he will
	    leave his bloody rod.

[1]Latin *Pontus Euxinus* = the Black Sea.
[2]*sanglante* = bloody; bleeding; (figuratively) keen, biting, cutting, outrageous, gross.
[3]*Gaule* = a) switch, long stick; a rod; (figuratively) spiritually speaking, a Zen stick to whack one awake; b) nautical term for a flagstaff or flagpole of a ship; c) with an upper-case initial it could also be a play on "Gaul" for France.

This continues the "Spiritual Teacher from the East" theme. The prophecy parallels the journeys of one of the 20th century's most contro-versial and innovative spiritual masters, the Greek-Armenian mystic, George Ivanovich Gurdjieff (1877?–1949). Gurdjieff's ancestors were Greek colonists on the **Black Sea** coast. He was born in Alexandropol in Russian Armenia and was a precocious child who grew to be an indepen-dent and rebellious young man. For some 20 years Gurdjieff traveled throughout the most remote regions of Tibet, Central Asia (**Tartary**), and the Middle East in his obsession to understand the secrets hiding within life's mysteries. He began collecting disciples in Moscow just prior to World War I. However, his efforts to establish his mystery school were thwarted by the Russian Revolution. He and his disciples began their long exodus out of Russia by traveling south from St Petersburg and Moscow, crossing the Caucasus Mountains on foot to reach the **Black Sea** coast of Georgia. From there they sailed to Istanbul. By 1922, Gurd-jieff managed to purchase the Château du Prieuré, near Paris (ie he will **come to see France**), where he reopened his Institute for the Harmonious Development of Man.

Line 4 is rich with layers of subtle meanings for *sanglante Gaule*. **Bloody rod** can also become a ship's flag mast that **penetrates** the air when the ship sails. Gurdjieff and his disciples did sail from Georgia, passing along the Black Sea coast of Turkey to lay anchor in Istanbul (**Byzantium**) where they left the wind-cutting flagpole of their ship on the docks.

Sanglante Gaule can also translate into **cutting Gaul** or France, making this a multiple-layered pun for Gurdjieff's landing on the coast of France, and later using his **rod** of enlightened teachings to strike awareness into thousands of his "Gaullish" disciples.

It is my contention here and elsewhere that there are two final Antichrists presented to us by Nostradamus. One is an evil despot, and the other helps humanity transcend its addiction to Christian dogma. Rather than the latter being anti-Christ, he is anti-Christian. He will be a mystic from the East who inspires people to go beyond being merely followers of the great teachers, and to discover their own Christhood or Buddha-nature. In the hands of the evil despot, the **bloody rod** is a nuclear missile of the Third Antichrist, but for the teacher who awakens us to our sacred birthright, it is the rebelliously **red** rod of the Hermetic Magus, the caduceus wand of enlightenment. Since this man comes from the East, one might call his rod a Zen stick, striking the head of conventional religious morality and thought. An authentic spiritual catalyst for change must, by his very nature, be a rebel who disturbs the status quo. Gurdjieff, Osho, Meher Baba, Krishnamurti, and many other candidates from the 20th century have struck a blow at our hallowed and habituated opinions about human consciousness. (Please turn to 1 Q96 for further elaboration on the Antichrist/New "Christ" theme.)

Quatrain Indexing Date: Q54 = near miss for 1953.

5 Q55

De la felice Arabie contrade,	*In the country of Arabia Felix,*
Naiſtra puiſſant de loy Mahometique:	*There will be born one powerful in*
Vexer l'Eſpaigne, conqueſter la Grenade,	*the law of Mahomet:*
Et plus par mer à la gent Lyguſtique.	*To vex Spain, to conquer Granada,*
	And more by sea against the Ligurian
	[Genovese] people.

Someone born in Arabia who is **powerful** through following **the law** of the Islamic *Sharia* – perhaps a fundamentalist leader – will torment Spain and take back the Moorish stronghold of **Granada**. At this point the prophecy sounds more like an alternative near-future event for Nostradamus' era than a prophecy for our future. Raids of Islamic pirates along the Genovese coastline certainly happened in his time. Perhaps this great Muslim could have been the Corsair Barbarossa or his protégé Dragut, but neither man was born in Arabia. Barbarossa was born on the Aegean island of Lesbos, and Dragut was an Anatolian.

A number of 20th-century Nostradamians believe this is yet another warning of an invasion of Spain and southern Europe by Islamic armies in our near future. A dubious call, since today Islamic navies can boast of nothing more threatening than a handful of patrol boats. There isn't a single troop ship in any Arab navy to ferry even the modest armies of the North African nations across the narrow passage to Gibraltar from Morocco. If Saddam Hussein's army, once the largest force in the Middle East, lacked the supply trucks needed to sustain any more than a 70-mile plunge into Kuwait, how will the Arab hordes dreamed by my colleagues Lemesurier and Fontbrune transport their forces across 2,500 miles of potholed and sand-smothered North African roads to their staging areas in Morocco for a D-Day landing in Spain?

If we can draw any parallel in real historical fact, it is not the Arabs but the Nazis who come closest to vexing Spain in an alternative future option never realized. Hitler tried very hard to convince Franco to drop his neutrality and join the German war effort. Franco went as far as to allow the German Admiral Canaris, head of Nazi Intelligence, to send an espionage crew down through Spain to formulate an attack on the British base at Gibraltar. The planned attack was code-named *Felix*.

5 Q56

Par le tre∫pas du tre∫uieillart pontife,	**Because of the very aged Pope's death,**
Sera e∫leu Romain de bon aage:	**Will be elected a Roman of good age:**
Qu'il ∫era dict que le ∫iege debiffe,	**He will be accused of weakening the**
Et long tiendra & de picquant ouurage.	**Holy See,**
	And will last a long time, doing
	controversial work.

The succession of Pope Paul VI is implied in the first line. His tenure on the papal throne is described as one in which the Church is wracked with pressures to change. Pope Paul's conservative slant and anti-abortion policy did much to exacerbate the growing divisions in the Catholic Church during the turbulent 1960s.

However, it is also true to say that Pope Paul VI traveled more than any pope in history up to that time, and made more efforts to calm growing world tensions. A pope in radical contrast to his popular predecessor John XXIII, Paul VI was both more worldly and more politically astute. However, certain contacts with the darker corners of finance may have contributed to the weakening of the Holy See. During his papacy an old friend of his – a Sicilian banker with close ties to the Mafia – was engagd as financial advisor to the Vatican Bank. The activities of banker Michele Sindona, and of others involved in his schemes using Vatican money, led to a major scandal that was discovered in 1982. When a bank controlled by Sindona's group was found to be on the brink of collapse, a huge network of corruption, murder, and fraud was exposed. This network had been made possible and financed through Sindona's manipulation of the Vatican's enormous wealth.

5 Q57

Iſtra du mont Gaulfier¹ & Auentin,²	**There will go forth from mont**
Qui par le trou aduertira l'armée:	**Gaulfier and the Aventine,**
Entre deux rocs ſera prins le butin,	**One who through the hole will warn**
De S E X T. manſol faillir la renommee.	**the army.**
	The booty will be taken from between
	two rocks,
	The renown of Sextus the celibate will
	fail.

¹Montgolfier = the Montgolfier brothers, Joseph Michel and Jacques Etienne, constructed the first hot-air balloon in 1782. Its first manned flight was on 21 November 1783. It flew six miles at a height of 300 feet.
²*Aventine* = one of the seven hills of Rome.

Nostradamus sometimes scrambles his words and events like a mad cook concocting a seven-course meal in a blender. One clue, like a strong spice lost in this mess, can help bring out the original flavor of meaning. The riddle **through the hole** conjured many imaginative interpretations before 1794. One could assume it is a metaphorical hole rather than literal one – more like a peephole in the sky. Perhaps it represents the Montgolfier brothers, inventors of the hot-air balloon. They are perched in an unsteady wicker gondola beneath the hot-air hole of their balloon, signaling the Republican generals to indicate any **holes** in the enemy lines during the battle of Fleurus. **Aventine** stands for the Holy See in Rome. The Montgolfier's contemporary pope, Pius the Sixth (**Sextus**), would mourn the loss of the treasures (**booty**) of the Vatican stolen by victorious Revolutionary armies a few years after their victory at Fleurus.

This quatrain is the second in James Randi's list of ten debunkable quatrains (see *The Mask of Nostradamus*, pages 176–89). I found his interpretation to be a rather turgid exercise in literary smoke and mirrors. Randi hides the weakness of his argument by obsessing over a single point and piling one elaborate speculation on another. I was left in a quagmire of the same style of "torturously oblique and inventive" reveries he ascribes to Nostradamians who find themselves caught with their participles dangling over a weak interpretation. In the case of 5 Q57 he becomes obsessed with Old French semantics over the words *mont Gaulfier* and *Sext* and tries his best tricks to make them fit the enigmatic *Mansol, Tarascon de SEX* of 4 Q27. To validate his thinking process, his epic 13-page etymological merry-go-round demands that Nostradamus follow commonsense rules of French grammar. Such a demand stubbornly denies reality. Nostradamus made his own rules, and you have to conform your interpretations to them, not the other way around.

5 Q58

De l'aqueduct d'Vticenſe,[1] Gardoing,	**By the aqueduct of Uzès over the Gard,**
Par la foreſt & mont inacceſſible:	**Through the forest and inaccessible**
Emmy du pont ſera taſché au poing,	**mountain:**
Le chef nemans[2] & qui tant ſera terrible.	**In the middle of the bridge will be cut**
	off by the fist,
	The chief of Nîmes and who will be
	very terrible.

[1]Latin *Castrum Uceciense* = Uzès.
[2]Latin *Nemausus* = Nîmes.

Ruins of a Roman **aqueduct** in France extend from **Uzès** to **Nîmes**. The quatrain has been applied by Larmor (1925) and Boswell (1941) to a daring maneuver of the Duc de Rohan in September 1627. During a religious revolt Rohan's Calvinist brethren in Nîmes were besieged. The duke tried to assist them by moving artillery over the aqueduct. Line 3 is applied to his sappers who cut part of the supports of the bridge **over the Gard** to widen the path for the cannon. Rohan was made general or **chief** of the rebels upon his arrival at Nîmes.

5 Q59

Au chef Anglois à Nymes trop ſeiour,	**The chief of the English at Nîmes**
Deuers l'Eſpaigne au ſecours Aenobarbe:[1]	**tarries too long,**
Pluſieurs mourront par Mars ouuert ce	**Towards Spain Aenobarbe to the**
iour,	**rescue:**
Quand en Artois faillir eſtoille en barbe.	**Several [thousand or million] will die**
	by war opened that day,
	When in Artois a bearded star will fall.

[1]Latin *Aenobarbus* = Redbeard; also Nero's family name; Barbarossa.

It is a real stretch for a British **chief**, titular or actual, to be tarrying too long in Nîmes in the 16th century. But in the 20th century fewer stretch-marks are to be made on this poor prophecy, though they are still uncomfortably noticeable. One could stretch Nîmes to become a synecdoche for south France, a favorite tarrying ground for the Duke of Windsor, the deposed English **chief** Edward VIII. Then again, if this is a vision for the 16th century, Aenobarbe ("Bronzebeard") is Barbarossa the pirate – coming to aid Spain. Not!

The quatrain hyperextends belief far better if we stay in the 20th century, and Barbarossa the pirate turns into (Operation) Barbarossa, the code name for Hitler's invasion of Russia in 1941. Nostradamus uses *Aenobarbe* (Barbarossa) for Adolf Hitler, who did journey to the Spanish border just prior to the invasion for a meeting with Francisco Franco.

Hitler offered grain exports to **rescue** the war-devastated Spanish from starvation; in return Franco would join the Axis alliance. Franco remained coy and stayed neutral.

Artois makes a good stretch of this prophecy for either century your interpretation leans towards. During the late 16th century Artois was visited by war and mayhem, when it belonged to the southernmost province of the Spanish Netherlands. It was also often shelled (**star will fall**) and fought-over during both world wars of the 20th century.

5 Q60

Par teſte raſe viendra bien mal eſlire,	**By the shaven head[s] will come a very bad choice,**
Plus que ſa charge ne porte paſſera:	**Burdened with a load he will not be able to carry:**
Si grand fureur & raige fera dire,	**He will speak with great fury and rage,**
Qu'à feu & ſang tout ſexe trenchera.	**That to fire and blood he will cut (down) both sexes.**

Line 1 is usually thought to describe the roundheads of Cromwell or the cropped head of Napoleon. I would add Hitler because many of his followers, who made the ultimately **bad choice** of electing him Chancellor of Germany, had close-cropped, shaved heads. Hitler's speeches were notorious for their **fury and rage**. And his racial polices culled over 10 million Jews and Slavs of **both sexes** and threw them into death camps. Another 2 million German civilians of **both sexes** died in the final months of World War II, during the last onslaughts of Soviet armies into Eastern Prussia. Many **shaven heads** of the Catholic clergy of Pius XII were sympathetic to the Nazi anti-Communist and anti-Semitic cause.

Towards the end of the war, when Hitler was eating lunch one afternoon at his mountain retreat at Berchtesgarten, his longtime mistress Eva Braun regarded her rapidly aging and war-burdened Führer with concern. She tenderly asked him why he had been developing such a severe hunch in his back over the last few months. He looked up from his soup and said wistfully, "I carry very heavy keys in my pocket."

5 Q61

L'enfant du grand n'eſtant à ſa naiſſance,	**The child of the great one not by his birth,**
Subiuguera les hauts monts Apennis:	**He will subjugate the high mountains of the Apennines:**
Fera trembler tous ceux de la balance,	**He will make all those of the balance to tremble,**
Et des monts feux iuſques à mont Senis.	**And from the mountains fire [Vesuvius?] as far as Mt Cenis.**

The nearest son of a **great one**, but **not by birth**, is Eugène de Beauharnais, the son of Josephine and stepson of Napoleon. Beauharnais grew up to become one of Napoleon's best generals. Most of his victories came at the cost of the Austrian Habsburgs, again represented in political astrology by Libra (**the balance**). Beauharnais never fought a campaign in Spain, but his stepfather – the true conqueror of Italy – made him Viceroy of Italy.

5 Q62

Sur les rochers ſang on les verra plouuoir,
Sol Orient, Saturne Occidental:
Pres d'Orgon guerre, à Rome grand mal voir,
Nefs parfondrees & prins le Tridental.

One will see blood rain upon the rocks.
Sun in the East, Saturn [the Grim Reaper] in the West:
War near Orgon, a great evil seen near Rome,
The ships melted and sunk by the Trident.[1]

[1]Alternative: *The ships of the one who holds the Trident will be melted and sunk.*

The new START II agreement promises a two-thirds cutback in nuclear weapons by 2003. A majority of the remaining 7,000 nuclear devices will be on submarines (many of them are currently stationed on US Trident nuclear submarines). In World War II, air power decided the outcome of the war. In a Third World War, the outcome may be decided by submarine power.

In the not-too-distant future a surface fleet might be **melted and sunk** in the Arabian Sea, the Red Sea, or the Persian Gulf, most likely through nuclear attack by a submarine. As of this writing, Iran has received two of a fleet of five Kilo-class Russian-built submarines, the first two delivered in 1994. According to *Jane's Defense*, Libya has a fleet of six ex-Soviet Foxtrot attack submarines; Egypt has eight ex-Soviet Romeo-class submarines (which they seek to replace with more modern German-built Dolphin-class attack submarines); Algeria also has Kilo-class submarines; and Syria is planning to replace its three Romeo-class subs with Kilos. In a future conflict with the navies of the West, an Iranian submarine fleet might prevent a future coalition from steaming up the Arabian Sea past the Strait of Hormuz for a later-day crusade into the Islamic heartland. They will attempt to sink the Western fleets in the Red or Arabian Sea, or later, when they are bottled up in the Persian Gulf. The **ships melted and sunk** could also be the Iranian or any Arab submarine fleet that suffers a future nuclear retaliation by US Trident submarines. New satellite surveillance technologies that can electronically strip away the cloak of water concealing the location of enemy subs in any ocean may soon be in place.

Sun in the East, Saturn in the West is the astrological configuration dating all of the above events. Unfortunately, this opposition takes place once a year, making it impossible to pinpoint. The theme of a **rain** of **blood** is repeated several times in the quatrains, and seems to imply chemical weapons or radioactive rain.

Quatrain Indexing Date: Q62 = a near miss for 1963? One might hope that the October 1962 Cuban Missile Crisis was intended, with a quantum future that never happened: a full-scale US land, air, and sea invasion of Cuba tempted a Soviet field commander to launch a tactical nuclear weapon to sink the US fleet. We know now that President Kennedy and his Pentagon advisors were not aware that Soviet commanders down to brigade level had access to tactical nuclear missiles. In our alternative future scenario the Americans attack Cuba, and in the fog of battle a minor Soviet commander launches his nukes. The meltdown of the US invasion fleet triggers Armageddon.

Saturn was in opposition to the Sun during another international crisis exactly ten years later. In another October war, during the Jewish celebration of Yom Kippur in 1973, Soviet-backed Egypt and Syria unleashed a surprise attack on America's ally, Israel. When the Arabs were losing towards the end of the war, Soviet premier Leonid Brezhnev informed US president Richard Nixon that if he could not stop the Israeli advance across the Suez Canal, Soviet paratroopers would fly to Egypt's rescue. For nine hours Soviet and United States nuclear arsenals were on alert, poised to launch. Except for the Cuban Missile Crisis this was the closest brush with doomsday in the entire Cold War.

5 Q63

De vaine emprif e l'honneur indue plaincte,	From the useless enterprise of honor and undue complaint,
Galiotz errans par Latins froit, faim, vagues:	The small craft wandering about the Latins – cold, hunger, waves:
Non loing du Tymbre de ſang la terre taincte,	Not far from the Tiber river the land is stained with blood,
Et ſur humains ſeront diuerſes plagues.	There will be several plagues upon humankind.

We return to the vision of nuclear terrorists off the coast of Italy inside a North African submarine choosing its target – perhaps one of three nuclear power plants to be seized. One nuclear power plant is situated less than 40 miles down the coast from the mouth of the Tiber river at Latina. Another is under construction at Montalto di Castro, nearly 50 miles up the coast. A third reactor is planned on the banks of the Tiber near Rome.

Nothing in this quatrain directly hints at any reactors being seized by terrorists, but one can infer that some bloody calamity may happen at a

nuclear plant. As we will see in other quatrains, these images may be connected to an evacuation of southern Europe due to a plague of *false dust*
(5 Q90) – in other words, when there are *several plagues upon humankind*.

The *craft wandering*, tossed about or sunk may be the submarine fleet
already mentioned in 3 Q13. Perhaps Nostradamus is trying to describe
what for him would be strange-looking rubber boats or dinghies, full of
terrorist commandos paddling to shore. Are they detected and attacked?
The first line hints that the *enterprise of honor* is another empty gesture
in the legacy of stupid reasons that man slaughters his fellow man.

The quatrain numbers 62 and 63 often apply to prophecies related to
the Third Antichrist. Perhaps they stand for the date of a catalytic act
that launches the rise of Islamic fundamentalism. Ayatollah Khomeini
captured world attention in 1963 when his Iranian followers started their
Islamic revolution against the Shah. To this day, many of the prime
candidates for captain of the submarine fleet seek Iran as their haven and
staging ground for international terrorism.

Quatrain Indexing Date: Q63 = 1963. Other quatrains with an
Antichrist theme are numbered 62 and 63 (see 2 Q63, 3 Q63). This could
also refer to the year 2063.

5 Q64

Les aſſemblées par repoʒ du grand nombre,	*Those assembled by the tranquillity of*
Par terre & mer conſeil contremandé:	*a great number,*
Pres de l'Autonne[1] Gennes, Nice de	*By land and sea counsel*
l'ombre,	*countermanded:*
Par champs & villes le chef contrebandé.[2]	*Near Autonne Genoa, Nice in*
	shadow,
	Through fields and towns the chief
	"counterbanded."

[1]*Autonne*: unsolved proper noun. Possibly "Autumn" or a blend of geographical places within
the quatrain context for *Antibes* and *Mentone*.
[2]Old French *contrebander* = to revolt against law or ban.

The key to this quatrain is solving the meaning of *Autonne*. One might
settle on *au tonne*, or "nearly a ton," which goes nowhere. Or we can
replace the *u* with an *r* and swivel it around to get *en a(r)ton*, and slide "to
NATO". Now the line could read, "Close to NATO, Genoa, Nice in
shadow" With this in mind let us look at the prophecy again.

Line 1 gives us the *tranquillity* and security of the European Union.
Line 2 suggests that counsel or wisdom is canceled by land and sea – in
other words, a global upheaval. Is this another reference to the coming
ecological disasters of the 21st century that cause civilization to collapse
in a world war? In line 3 an event takes place near the southern command

center of NATO, which is in Naples, Italy. At the same time we see Genoa and Nice in shadow. This may allude to the great eclipse foreseen elsewhere by Nostradamus as an omen of Armageddon. The next total eclipse visible in this region of Europe is on 11 August 1999, a very important year in Nostradamus' prophecies (see 10 Q72). The **shadow** could be caused by the **plague of false dust** (5 Q90), which is either an ash cloud from an eruption of Vesuvius or Etna, or the residue from a nuclear terrorist attack, perhaps the same one that requires the evacuation of south-eastern Europe for nine months.

Line 4's *contrebande* has several possible translations. The **chief** here could be the commander of NATO, a terrorist leader, or even the president of the European Union, suffering a revolt ("**counterbanded**": being banded up against). Perhaps the word stands for smuggled goods that undermine this leader in some way – the contraband of smuggled nuclear or biological weapons from terrorists?

5 Q65

Subit venu l'effrayeur fera grande,	**Suddenly arrived, the terror will be great,**
Des principaux de l'affaire cachés:	**The principal players in the affair are hidden away:**
Et dame en braife[1] plus ne fera en veue,	**And the lady in the hot coals will no longer be in sight,**
Ce peu à peu feront les grans fachés.	**Thus little by little will the great ones be angered.**

[1]Variant: Old French *brasse* = brewing, mixing and mashing.

Very specific details drawn in the misty ink cloud of octopus poetry.

5 Q66

Soubs les antiques edifices veftaulx,	**Under the ancient vestal edifices,**
Non efloignez d'aqueduct ruyne:	**Not far removed from the ruined aqueduct:**
De Sol & Lune[1] font les luifans metaulx,	**The glittering metals are of the Sun and Moon,**
Ardante lampe Traian d'or burine.	**The ardent lamp of Trajan engraved with gold.**

[1]Latin *Luna* = the Moon, but in this case poetic for "silver."

Here we have one of Nostradamus' treasure-hunt quatrains. Garencières elaborates on Jaubert's interpretation, but both believe the treasure is located beneath the Convent of St Sauveur-de-la-Fontaine at Nîmes.

The convent was built on the ruins of a temple to the goddess Diana. Garencières claimed that the ruins of a basilica built by Hadrian and dedicated to his stepmother, the Empress Plotina, were still to be unearthed at Nîmes. Nostradamus therefore says that a lamp from the Temple of Plotina, made of gold and silver, was passed along to its final resting place near the Temple of Diana, where it will be dug up on some future date. Some scholars make the mistake of translating *ardante* literally as the "still-burning lamp," thinking this buried treasure is sprouting Vesta's eternal flame. They overlook the mystical truth – that the spirit of the goddess of the hearth is still alive. See a similar reference to the burning lamp in 9 Q9.

5 Q67

Quand chef Perouſe n'oſera ſa tunique	**When the chief of Perugia [the Pope]**
Sens au couuert tout nud s'expolier:	**will not venture his tunic**
Seront prins ſept faict Ariſtocratique,	**Sense to be covert stripped completely**
Le pere & fils mors par poincte[1] au colier.	**naked:**
	Seven will be taken [because of] the
	Aristocratic deed,
	The father and sons dead through a
	point [or a bullet] in the collar.

[1]Old French *pointe* = tip, head of an arrow; nose of a bullet.

Perugia was part of the papal states when Nostradamus wrote this, so it undoubtedly stands for the pope. Le Pelletier thought it stood for Sixtus V, for whom Nostradamus muddied a knee in reverence when the future pope was nothing more than a simple swineherd turned friar. Le Pelletier says, "When Sixtus V will not dare to excommunicate Henry III, for fear that the Church of Rome (already stripped, in 1534, by the schism of England) would be rendered entirely naked by a French schism, there will be an end to the posterity of Henry II, through a memorable event: Henry III will perish, as his father Henry II, through a thrust directed at the throat."

He is correct about the former Henry but quite wrong about the latter, who was stabbed in the belly. Since Le Pelletier wrote this in the 1860s he should have known better. I would clarify this oversight as an alternative future seen in Nostradamus' hydromantic mirror of the future. Perhaps he witnessed Brother Clement slashing the throat of Henry III. In Le Pelletier's defense, some scholars – such as Leoni – split hairs by saying Henry II's posterity didn't end with his son's death, since Marguérite de Valois lived on until 1615. This criticism overlooks the sexism of royal succession in France. Only the male heir matters.

5 Q68

Dans le Danube¹ & du Ryn viendra boire,	**In the Danube and the Rhine will come to drink,**
Le grand Chameau ne s'en repentira:	**The great Camel, [who] will not repent of it:**
Trembler du Rofne & plus fort ceux de Loire,	**Those of the Rhône to tremble, and even more so those of the Loire,**
Et pres des Alpes coq le ruinera.	**And near the Alps the Cock will ruin him.**

¹When Nostradamus uses *Danube* he means the river. When he uses the archaic name of the Danube, "Hister," he means Adolf *Hitler*, who grew up on the banks of that river.

Lines 1 and 2 are parallel futures never accessed. (1) The Ottoman Turks (described here by means of their long supply trains of camels) take Vienna in their siege of 1682 and get all the way to the Rhine, but are defeated by Christian forces led by France *near the Alps*. (2) The Asiatic hordes of the Soviet Union (whose Central Asian and Siberian units used camels as pack animals) would not only take Vienna in the closing months of World War II but push all the way to the Rhine.

Lines 3 and 4 may paint the picture of another failed quantum future during the Cold War years: the Blitzkrieg of the Warsaw Pact through West Germany. Those of the Rhône *tremble* because France becomes a front-line battleground for Armageddon. Some interpreters, such as Fontbrune during the 1980s, thought this would take place. I don't think he can support this interpretation now. However, he, Lemesurier and others see a 21st-century Islamic invasion (camels and all) up the Rhône and over the Rhine that is checked by a flank attack of the Western forces pouring out of their bases in the Alps. If my colleagues are correct, I'm willing to eat Nostradamus' four-cornered hat!

I believe Nostradamus was seeing alternative futures only for World War II. For instance, if Hitler hadn't slept in on 6 June, there would have been time for Rommel to get permission to bring his panzer armies right up to the Normandy landings and push the Western Allies into the sea. Had D-Day been an Allied disaster, the Allied landings on the Riviera would have taken on new significance. The advance up the Rhône river valley would have been far more difficult, and it is likely that the Soviets would have penetrated all the way from Vienna and Berlin to the Rhine before they linked up with the Anglo-American and Free French forces. If Hitler's Atlantic Wall had held, St Lô, Caen, Falaise-Argentan, Arnhem, and the Ardennes would have remained German rear areas in the battle of the Allied *south*-western front coming up from the French Riviera. Perhaps the Allies would have crushed the Nazi forces *near the Alps* in a showdown along the Rhône.

5 Q69

Plus ne ſera le grand en faux ſommeil,	*Never again will the great one be in a false sleep,*
L'inquietude viendra prendre repoʒ:	*The [state of] restlessness will come to replace [his] repose:*
Dreſſer phalange d'or, aʒur, & vermeil,	*To raise up a phalanx of gold, azure and vermilion,*
Subiuguer Affrique la ronger iuſques oʒ.	*[And] subjugate Africa – gnaw it to the bone!*

Le Pelletier applies this one to Louis-Philippe's attempt to bolster public support for his ever more unpopular reign with the conquest of Algeria in 1830–48. Le Pelletier gets the French Tricolor from line 3, by giving *phalange* an etymological makeover and turning it into "standard." Leoni says this is impossible, whereas Kidogo disagrees, declaring that *phalange* stands for the Greek **phalanx** which can mean "standard" as well as a unit of classical Macedonian pikemen.

5 Q70

Des regions ſubjectes à la Balance,	*The regions subject to the Balance,*
Feront troubler les monts par grande guerre:	*Will trouble the mountains with a great war:*
Captifʒ tout ſexe deu[1] & tout Biſance,	*Both sexes made captives, beholden to [their liberators] and all of Byzantium,*
Qu'on criera à l'aube terre à terre.	*So that at dawn they will cry out from land to land.*

[1]*deu* = a) Old French contraction of *de la* = *de*; b) past participle of *devoir* = to owe (money, thanks); c) compulsion, duty; (if followed by infinitive) to be obliged to, to be bound to, to have to.

This returns us to the current troubles in the Balkans and the future potentials for a wider ethnic war if the Dayton Accords fail.

The **regions subject** to the political, military, and economic influence of the United States (**the Balance**) include the nations of the EU and NATO alliance. Line 2 is a vision of the fighting between Serbian, Croatian and Bosnian armies drawing the firepower of a series of NATO airstrikes in 1995. A correct interpretation of line 3 requires the right translation of *deu*, a job made difficult by Nostradamus' gutted grammar. One way is to see the captives **beholden** to those allies who are **subject to the Balance**; in other words, the Dayton Accords allow the American forces along with their allies the French and British, to impose IFOR on the civilians of all sides in Bosnia. In effect they are **captives** of the agreement to demilitarize the region. Byzantium either stands for modern Turkey or is a general synecdoche for those Islamic nations (once within the extinct Ottoman Empire) that today are trying to arm the Bosniac Muslims in their fight against the Serbs.

The final line warns of a spreading global plague of ethnic wars if the Dayton Accords do not succeed in pacifying the Balkans. By the turn of the century ethnic wars could escalate, spreading east across the Balkans to include a Greco-Turkish conflict linked to Kurdish civil war in Turkey. The successful experiment in global peace enforcement represented by IFOR could flash a red light at further eruptions of wars in the Balkans and the former Soviet states (see 2 Q22)

5 Q71

Par la fureur d'vn qui attendra l'eau,	**By the fury of one who will wait for [or at] the water,**
Par la grand raige tout l'exercite eſmeu:	**By his great rage all the army [will be] stirred:**
Chargé des nobles à dixſept batteaux,	**Seventeen boats will be loaded with the nobles,**
Au long du Roſne, tard meſſagier venu.	**Along the Rhône, the messenger arrived [too] late.**

This is too general to interpret easily, but it is an easy prey to interpreters' projections. Many have tried to pin this on several wannabe conquerors of England, such as the Spanish Duke of Parma in the 16th century, Napoleon in the 19th, and Hitler in the 20th. But all these interpreters have our conquerors glowering over the wrong body of **water**, since the final line may place this prophecy in south France. Because little more than projection will get us anywhere with this prophecy let me reflect here that the waters are those of the Rhône, not the English Channel. The final line could bring us back to August 1944 and to the *sauer* visage of Major General Wend von Wietersheim viewing the late arrival of the 11th Panzer Division at the banks of the Rhône. They are too late to stem the Allied invasion of southern France.

5 Q72

Pour le plaiſir d'edict voluptueux,	**For the pleasure of the voluptuous edict,**
On meſlera la poyſon dans l'aloy:	**One will mix poison in the law:**
Venus ſera en cours ſi vertueux,	**Venus will be in a course so virtuous,**
Qu'obfuſquera du soleil tout à loy.	**That [it] will becloud the entire law of the sun.**

Some might consider this to be related to a "Sun, Venus/Messiah" prophecy, but it is most likely about the 1577 Edict of Poitiers. Pitt Francis is right when he says there was nothing **voluptuous** or associated with Venus about the edict, which granted toleration to the Huguenots. Some of Nostradamus' private letters hint at his real stance on the mainstream religions of his time (Catholic and Protestant), which could be as ambiguous one day as it was politically correct the next. Perhaps the clues in lines 1 and 3 require that we dig deeper into what is behind the words **voluptuous** and **of Venus**.

Our 20th-century definition of **voluptuous** might lead us to suspect that the prophet is calling the Huguenots a free-sex cult. That would be too vulgar an assessment. To be **of Venus** in the higher occult sense is to be for love and peace. One supports the feminine virtues of patience, reconciliation and forgiveness. This quatrain could therefore be Nostradamus' hint to the Huguenots to be more **of Venus** – to live and let live with their Catholic neighbors. Perhaps hiding in Nostradamus' ambiguity is the warning given elsewhere that in the future religion will evolve in surprising directions, directions that may even be repugnant to those who cling to limiting views. What may be hidden here is another hint that our prophet's intuition (if not his ego) sees Christian dogma as not truly religious, whether Catholic or Protestant. The pure essence of the message (**law**) of "the Son" will continue to suffer from the beclouded projections of dogmatic people who cannot tolerate the light of true clarity (**the sun**).

5 Q73

Perſecutee ſera de Dieu l'Egliſe,	**Persecuted will be the Church of God,**
Et les ſaincts temples ſeront expoliez:	**And the sacred [or false] temples will**
L'enfant la mere mettra nud en chemiſe,	**be plundered:**
Seront Arabes aux Polons raliez.	**The child will put his mother out**
	naked but for her chemise,
	The Arabs will be allied with the Poles.

The same theme continues but with broader strokes of geography and time. The question we must ask after seeing the obvious is: just what did Nostradamus mean by **Church of God**? Do we assume he is referring to the Catholic Church, or is that an obvious literary flytrap for the mediocre-minded to flutter against and remain glued to? When Jesus walked the Earth there were no popes, edicts or Vaticans. Christ was a real bull, not a paper or papal bull.

The same doubt surrounds the surface meaning of *ſainctz*, or **sacred**. Is he talking about the politically correct view of saints or is he mixing his Gothic ſ with f on purpose to hide the real meaning – not *saint* but **faint** or **false**?

It gets worse. Do the temples stand for the Vatican? The temples of the Huguenots and Protestants? Is the **child** in line 3 therefore the newborn Protestant Churches which are eventually to seize all the wealth of the Vatican **temple** and put their mother, the Roman Catholic Church, out in the streets in her 16th-century chemise? Or is this some new religious or neo-pagan movement in our own time that eventually eclipses mainstream religions of today, sending a dogmatic Mother Church out on the streets of the 22nd century in her slip?

Your guess is as good – or as bad – as mine. But help is on the way. The final line dates this blessed or bestial event for a time when Arabs are allied to Poles. With this in mind, it would be easy to shine a 20th-century reflection to the prophet's mirror, and see a Cold War slant, linking the **Poles** of the former Warsaw Pact with Soviet-sympathizing Arab nations like Iraq and Libya. One could extend the reverie even further and use the poor woman of line 3 as a metaphor for consequences visited on the Mother Church as a result of the Vatican Bank scandal of the 1980s – the unfortunate drug money laundering scheme during final climactic years of the Cold War, when a **Pole** was a pope, and Poles were allied to Marxist Arab states.

5 Q74

De ſang Troyen naiſtra cœur Germanique,	**Of Trojan blood will be born [a]**
Qu'il deuiendra en ſi haute puiſſance:	**German heart,**
Hors chaſſera gent eſtrange Arabique:	**Who will become so high a power:**
Tournant l'Egliſe en priſtine¹ preeminence.	**He will chase out the foreign, Arabic**
	people,
	Returning the Church to its
	fundamental preeminence.

¹Latin *pristinus* = former, original, pristine; (figuratively) fundamental, primitive.

Depending on whether this quatrain's moment in time has already passed, one could come up with a right-wing and Royalist interpretation to please the prejudices of Le Pen: poetic myths proclaim the French royalty to be direct descendants of the Trojans. Line 1 could describe the ultra-conservative leader of the National Front, Jean-Marie Le Pen. Many call this French right-winger a man with a **German** – or worse, neo-Nazi – heart. Line 2 tells us Le Pen or his successor will become the president of France after Jacques Chirac's seven-year term is finished, around 2002. This harsh nationalist will expel millions of Algerians and North Africans from modern France if he takes power, and he will lead a Catholic fundamentalist crusade on secular French culture.

5 Q75

Montera haut ſur le bien plus à dextre,	**[He] will rise high in wealth more to**
Demourra aſſis ſur la pierre quarree:	**the right,**
Vers le midy poſé à la feneſtre,	**[He] will remain seated on the**
Baſton tortu en main, bouche ſerree.	**[Peter] square:**
	Towards the South poised at the
	window,
	Crooked staff in hand, mouth sealed.

The slant of the last quatrain continues at the same angle, but instead of Jean-Marie Le Pen we could have here a future pope with right-wing sympathies. *Le bien* has many possibilities: the estate, mercy, benefit, the advantages, etc. Line 2 literally translates as *[H]e will remain seated on the square stone.* I cannot rule out a poetic coding for St Peter's *Square*, nor can I eliminate the possibility of a double pun for *pierre* (**Peter**) and "stone," making this another prophecy about the Vatican's final pope, Peter II. The pope's apartments face the southern and eastern walls of the Palazzo Vaticano overlooking St Peter's Square. The people below witness the new pope at the window, standing with his crooked staff and tight mouth. What secrets do those lips seal?

5 Q76

En lieu libere tendra ſon pauillon,	**In the open air will he pitch his tent,**
Et ne voudra en citez prendre place:	**And he will not want to take up**
Aix, Carpen. l'iſle volce, mont Cauaillon,	**residence in the cities:**
Par tous ſes lieux abolira ſa traſſe.	**Aix, Carpentras, the Isle(-sur-la-Sorgue), Vaucluse, Mont(favet), Cavaillon,**
	Throughout all these places he will abolish his trace.

All these places are near Salon. For me, I like to think that this verse paints a down-to-earth picture of Nostradamus as he journeys about the region. His private letters show he still made a number of trips around southern France as late as the early 1560s. Perhaps he is clueing us in to his camping habits. He prefers sleeping under the stars in the countryside to staying in the noisy, smelly, and often disease-ridden inns of the mentioned towns. In my reverie, I see him each morning taking care that he doesn't leave litter on the ground or the scar of a undoused and unburied fire pit upon the earth.

5 Q77

Tous les degrez d'honneur Eccleſiaſtique,	**All the degrees of Ecclesiastic honor,**
Seront changez en dial¹ quirinal:²	**Will be changed to Jupiter Quirinus:**
En Martial³ quirinal flaminique,⁴	**The priest of Quirinus to one of Mars,**
Puis vn Roy de France le rendre vulcanal.⁵	**Then a King of France will make him one of Vulcan.**

¹Latin *Dialis* = of Jupiter.
²Latin *Quirinalis* = of Quirinus.
³Latin: of Mars, the god of war and the classical Roman state. Classical metaphor used by Nostradamus for Napoleon.
⁴*Quirinal flaminique*: Latin *Quirinalis flamen* = priest of Quirinus, the God of the Classical Roman state.
⁵Latin: of Vulcan, Roman god, son of Jupiter and Juno; the smith god, lord of artificers, patron of crafts, known as Hephaestus in Greek mythology.

This quatrain has long puzzled interpreters. The keys to unlocking its secrets are hidden in its classical metaphors.

After excommunicating Nostradamus' First Antichrist, Pope Pius VII is arrested in his summer palace and secreted away to Savona, near Genoa, where he is held in virtual isolation, subject to Napoleon's whim. Napoleon arrested the pope in an effort to separate Church from state and keep the pope a purely religious leader. In his memoirs he writes: "I was in a position to exalt the pope beyond all bounds and to surround him with such pomp and ceremony that he would have ceased to regret the loss of his temporal power. I would have made an idol out of him."

In other words, Napoleon the **one of Mars**, ever modeling himself after the Roman Caesars, defines the pope's new role as god of a classical Roman state newly created by the **King of France** with Paris as the New Rome.

"Paris would have become the capital of Christendom," he writes, "and I would have become the master of the religious as well as the political world . . . my Church Councils would have been representative of all Christendom, and the popes would have been mere chairmen. I would have opened and closed these assemblies, approved and made public their decisions, as did Constantine and Charlemagne."

With an ingenious classical double pun Nostradamus mixes the subjective dream of the tyrant with objective facts. He calls Pius VII the **priest of Quirinus** after the French secret police arrest the pope at his summer palace, which is also called the *Quirinal*. Pius will be **one of** (or rendered by the patron of artificers) **Vulcan** – that is, a manufactured figurehead.

5 Q78

Les deux vnis ne tiendront longuement,	**The two will not remain united for**
Et dans treze ans au Barbare Satrappe:	**long,**
Au deux coſtez ſeront tel perdement,	**And within thirteen years [they give**
Qu'vn benira le Barque & ſa cappe.	**in] to Barbary [Libyan–Arab]**
	power.
	There will be such a loss on both sides
	That one will bless the Bark and cape
	[of the pope, of Peter].[1]

[1] Alternative: *That one will bless the bark [of Peter] and the cape [of the pope].*

A Libyan or Arab North African terrorist exerts the most influence in undermining future Russian–American international policies. The continued reference to the appearance of Halley's Comet as the event that trips the *Mabus* switch (2 Q62) puts the period of **thirteen years** exactly between 1986 and 1999! If Nostradamus was instead indicating the appearance of the great Hale-Bopp comet of 1997, the impact of the Third Antichrist is postponed until 2010. The latter case brings the 13-year countdown far closer to the end of time as we know it, as calculated by the most accurate timepiece in any ancient prophetic tradition, the Mayan calendar, which slates the end of the world for 2012.

The **bark [of Peter]** generally stands for the Vatican and the papacy. It may also imply that the millennial pope will be named **Peter**. The medieval Irish prophet St Malachy predicted the final pope – who is to reign until Judgement Day – would be called Peter of Rome.

5 Q79

Le ſacree pompe viendra baiſſer les aiſles,	**The sacred pomp will come to lower its wings,**
Par la venue du grand legiſlateur:	**At the coming of the great legislator:**
Humble haulſera vexera les rebelles,	**He will raise the humble, he will vex the rebels,**
Naiſtra ſur terre aucun æmulateur.	**None of his like will be born on [this] earth.**

This could open itself to an extraterrestrial slant. The **legislator** could be a human born in space or on an extraplanetary colony in our solar system, or a visitor from another star system. Perhaps the one who legislates is the great Messiah of the Aquarian Age, born in the 25th century, as foreseen by the British palmist and seer Count Louis Hamon in his book *Cheiro's World Predictions* (1931).

5 Q80

Logmion[1] grande Biſance approchera,	**Ogmios [Mercury?] will approach great Byzantium,**
Chaſſé ſera la barbarique ligne:	**The barbarian [Barbary] league [or line] will be chased away:**
Des deux loix l'vne l'eſtinique[2] lachera,	**Of the two laws the ethnic one will give way,**
Barbare & franche en perpetuelle brigue.[3]	**Barbarian and Frank in perpetual intrigue.**

[1]*L'Ogmion:* Ogmios was the Gaulish Celtic Hercules.
[2]Latin *ethnicus* = of a nation; of another nation; heathen, pagan.
[2]*brigne* = a) intrigue, underhand; b) tumult, brawl.

Ogmios was the god of eloquence and poetry to the Celts of Gaul. He is depicted as an old man armed with bow and club, attracting all kinds of people to himself by means of nets of amber and gold issuing from his mouth. Perhaps Nostradamus is hiding the identity of an important religious revolutionary under a metaphoric Gallic rock. Could he be indicating one coming to France from the direction of the East through Istanbul (**Byzantium**), perhaps Gurdjieff (see 5 Q54).

Nostradamus most likely intended this one for *Hercules* Duc d'Alençon, the youngest son of Henry II. When in 1555–56 *Les Propheties* were first published, the gurgling baby prince was many decades removed from the rakish adventurer and embarrassment he later became. But here he leads a crusade right into the heart of the Ottoman Empire, with mixed results. Either Nostradamus was completely off the mark, or this is not about a French crusade against the Turks but another Ogmios to come in our future. If so, the last three lines allude to current and near-future issues of ethnic wars, fighting between France and fundamentalist Algeria, and perhaps even the future of French troops in Bosnia.

5 Q81

L'oiseau royal[1] sur la cité solaire,	**The royal bird over the city of the sun**
Sept moys deuant fera nocturne augure:	**[Paris],**
Mur[2] d'Orient cherra tonnerre esclaire,[3]	**By night will prophesy warnings for**
Sept iours aux portes les ennemis à l'heure.	**seven months in advance:**
	The wall of the East will fall, thunder
	and lightning,
	In seven days the enemy directly at
	the gates.

[1]*oiseau royal* = royal bird, in this case the Nazi German eagle symbol of the Luftwaffe, painted on their planes and worn on their pilots' blue uniforms.
[2]Wall, frontier border; Kidogo reminds us that in the ancient and medieval world walls and borders were often viewed as synonymous.
[3]*tonnerre esclaire* = thunder and lightning, a metaphor for Hitler's Blitzkrieg (*lightning war*).

During a six-month lull in fighting after the fall of Poland, from December 1939 through April 1940, German planes flying over the Maginot Line and deep into French airspace dropped leaflets of Nostradamus' quatrains containing Karl Ernst Krafft's interpretations of French defeat. According to Boswell one German plane flew over Paris as early as 13 November 1939, rendering Nostradamus' prophecy of **seven months** applicable to the German eagles (**royal bird**) of the Luftwaffe.

Latter-day interpreters like to believe the **wall of the East** is none other than the Berlin Wall falling in 1990; this, however can work only if you ignore something crucial. When Nostradamus says **the city** or **the wall of the East**, it is taken for granted that these are French. The great eastern wall therefore is the Maginot Line, in which France sank its fortunes, hopes, and delusions of safety from a German invasion. Hitler's new brand of warfare called lightning war, or Blitzkrieg, made the Maginot fortifications strategically irrelevant. In the final days of the Battle of

France, two moderate sorties by German forces breached the fortifications and overcame their demoralized defenders.

Hitler's panzer corps skirted the Maginot Line, made lightning thrusts through Flanders, and sent his tanks and motorized infantry through the Ardennes in a surprise thunderstroke. They split the French and British forces in half. After the encircled British Expeditionary Force abandoned its heavy equipment on the beaches of Dunkirk, Hitler's Blitzkrieg turned south-west, breaking through French lines by directing an overwhelming force of arms, artillery and air strikes on small sectors. Once through, his mechanized forces advanced deep into the rear sectors. The slow-moving and generally unmechanized French armies were encircled. The final Blitzkrieg to Paris took only seven days!

5 Q82

Au conclud pache hors de la fortereſſe,	At the conclusion of the treaty outside the fortress,
Ne ſortira celuy en deſeſpoir mis:	He will not go, who, in despair, is placed:
Quand ceux d'Arbois, de Langres, contre Breſſe,	When those of Arbois, of Langres, against Bresse,
Auront monts Dolle, bouſcade d'ennemis.	Will have [in?] the mountains of Dôle an enemy ambush.

Arbois and Dôle are in Franche-Comté; Langres is in Champagne. The former was a dominion of the Spanish until 1678. Bresse was a part of Savoy until it became French in 1601. The stage of this quatrain is set for the eastern frontiers of 16th-century France. Fontbrune believes it describes the maneuvers and the defeat of Bourbaki's French eastern army during the Franco-Prussian War (1870–71).

5 Q83

Ceux qui auront entreprins ſubuertir,	Those who will have undertaken to subvert,
Nompareil regne puiſſant & inuincible:	An unparalleled kingdom, powerful and invincible:
Feront par fraude, nuictz trois aduertir,	Will act through fraud, three nights to warn,
Quand le plus grand à table lira Bible.	When the very great one reads his Bible at the table.

An obscure quatrain that best describes the assassination of Admiral Coligny, which launched the St Bartholomew's Day Massacre of Huguenots first in Paris and later across France. *Those who ... subvert* are Coligny and the Huguenot princes, whom Catherine de' Medici and the Catholic leadership have lured into Paris through a marriage of the licentiously inclined Henry de Navarre with Catherine's vixen daughter,

Marguérite de Valois. On the night of 23 August 1572, after the marriage festivities, Coligny (who was wounded two days before in a failed assassination attempt) was set upon by a band of Catholic soldiers, led by Henry de Guise, who burst into his apartments where it is said they found Coligny bandaged and in bed reading his *own* Calvinist Bible. They disemboweled him and then threw him out of the bedroom window while he was still alive. For the next three days and nights nearly 3,000 Huguenots – including many of the wedding guests – were slaughtered. The death toll across France in the next two months reached 50,000. This atrocity gained Catherine de' Medici praise from the pope, but it only strengthened Huguenot resistance.

5 Q84

Naiftra du gouphre & cité immefuree,	**He will be born of the gulf and unmeasured city,**
Nay de parents obfcure & tenebreux:	**Born of parents obscure and shadowy:**
Qui la puiffance du grand Roy reueree,	**He who the revered power of a great king,**
Voudra deftruire par Roüan & Eureux.	**Will wish to destroy through Rouen and Evreux.**

Rouen and Evreux are both in Normandy. We see them united together in 4 Q100, which concerns the fall of the Second French Empire in the Franco-Prussian War (1870–71). It is hard to tie this quatrain into the same theme. Many Nostradamians believe this one describes the third and final Antichrist in Nostradamus' evil trinity of despots – Napoleon and Hitler being the first two. Kidogo believes this is about the late Ayatollah Khomeini, who used Paris as his base of operations for the successful overthrow in 1978 of the Shah of Iran, the **great king**. I find Kidogo's synecdoche explanation of Rouen and Evreux standing for Paris a bit of a stretch. He says that Rouen is more than a metonymy for the seaport of Paris: "Rouen is a synecdoche for what is to be exported from France. In this case, and for which France produced the prototype, revolution."

Okay, but his etymological virtuosity hits a sour note with me when he turns **Evreux** into *Europe* because the "word-ending is adjusted in order to rhyme."

5 Q85

Par les Sueues & lieux circonuoifins,	**Through the Swiss and circumjacent places,**
Seront en guerre pour caufe des nuees:	**Will they be at war over the issue of the clouds:**
Gamp marins locuftes & coufins,	**Swarm of marine locusts and insects,**
Du Leman fautes feront bien defnuees.	**The mistakes of Geneva will be completely exposed.**

The Swiss reference stands for the location for the United Nations' second capital, Geneva. The theme here is not Calvinism but how the future international body will deal with the coming ecological crisis. A dire warning is made here so we of the present day can help the peace-makers of Geneva make this prophecy wrong.

A Third World War takes place in the 21st century over the issue of **the clouds** – in other words, the clouds of pollution and greenhouse gas emissions that bring on global warming and the depletion of Earth's ozone layer. One result of the climatic disruptions would be a vast cloud of locusts and insects, mentioned elsewhere in *Les Propheties*, that come to plague Italy and France. One might extend the meaning of **locusts** to include a 16th-century man's description of swarms of attack helicopter gunships in the next world war. The greatest **mistake** the international leaders at Geneva could make is not soldiering the world to fight a war against greenhouse emissions and overpopulation.

I am writing this in June 1996. Lester E. Brown of Worldwatch Institute estimates we have less than 20 years to change the course of our behavior as a species. Other prophecies point to the 2020s and 2030s as our second window for doomsday.

The following connection may only be coincidental, but one 20th-century Swiss prophetess named Emma Kunz made a prediction in 1938, nearly a half-century before anyone was aware of the danger of ozone holes: "There will be planes shaped like pencils that will take men into space and by so doing punch holes in the atmosphere, letting in lethal cosmic rays that will kill many millions."

5 Q86

Par les deux teftes, & trois bras feparés,	**Separated by two heads, and three arms,**
La cité grande par eaux fera vexee.	**The great city will be vexed by waters.**
Des grands d'entre eux par exil efgarés,	**The great ones among them led astray in exile,**
Par tefte perfe Bifance fort preffee.	**Byzantium hard pressed by the leader of Persia.**

Does line 1 describe a Hindu god, or is this Brahma-headed and Shiva-armed thing a machine? A great city – perhaps Paris or Bombay, if the Indian slant is correct – is overwhelmed by a flood. This could continue the previous quatrain's global warming theme. This time we are viewing the oceans rising in the 21st century and the resulting torment in a great city such as Calcutta or Bombay. Even Paris may suffer floods from the ocean pushing the flow of the Seine River back against the city. We also have references to a future war between Turkey and Iran in the next

century, as both jockey to seize political and economic power in the new
Muslim states of Central Asia forming since the fall of the Soviet Union.

5 Q87

L'an que Saturne hors de feruage,	**In the year that Saturn [is] out of**
Au franc terroir fera d'eau inundé:	**servitude,**
De fang Troyen fera fon mariage,	**In the Franch[e-Comté] territory he**
Et fera feur d'Efpaignols circundé.	**will be inundated by water:**
	Of Trojan blood will his marriage be,
	And he will be closely confined by the
	Spanish.

Franche-Comté belonged to the Habsburgs until 1674. The first line
gives the planetary configuration of Saturn passing out of the sign of its
detriment, which is Scorpio, an event that takes place too many times to
give a specific astrological time window here. A popular myth in Nostradamus' day bragged that the French royal bloodline descended from
ancient Troy. The Duke of Savoy, whom Nostradamus has *confined* by
alliances with Philip II of Spain, was married to the sister of Henry II. An
invasion of the French frontiers is implied. The Savoyard and his forces
will get bogged down in flooded territory. If Savoy is intended, lines 2 and
4 of this quatrain are a failed prediction.

5 Q88

Sur le fablon par vn hideux deluge,	**Through the hideous flood over the**
Des autres mers trouué monftre marin:	**fine sand,**
Proche du lieu fera faict vn refuge,	**A marine monster from other seas [is]**
Tenant Sauone efclaue de Turin.	**discovered:**
	Near the place will be made a refuge,
	Holding Savona, slave of Turin.

Here's another quatrain that reads better backwards – from the last line
to the first:
   Savona, 25 miles west of Genoa, belonged to the Republic of Genoa.
The latter did indeed become the **slave of Turin** in 1815, when it was
given to the House of Savoy. Lines 3 and 2 may tie us in to 2 Q43 and
5 Q63 in which a **serpent** is placed upon the shore near the Tiber river,
implying a terrorist commando group using an Arab submarine
(described as a hideous **marine monster**). Perhaps they find **refuge** somewhere on the Italian coast between Genoa and Savona. Finally, line 1 is
a mix of potentials. The ship/monster could be the detachable section of
the futuristic container submarines planned for the coming decade. It
slides through the breakers and deposits onto the shore a wheeled container
craft full of commandos.
   On the other hand, this prophecy may be about an oil tanker disaster.

Genoa is a major industrial port. Perhaps a tanker runs aground or collides with another ship, covering the beaches between Genoa and Savona with crude oil.

5 Q89

Dedans Hongrie par Boheme, Nauarre,	Inside Hungary through Bohemia, Navarre,
Et par banniere fainctes[1] feditions:	And by the banner of holy [or feigned] seditions:
Par fleurs de lys pays portant la barre,[2]	By the fleur-de-lys country carrying the bar,
Contre Orleans fera efmotions.	Against Orléans they will cause commotions.

[1]Another double pun in seeing the word "sacred" becoming "feigned."
[2]Barr, a town in Alsace; by extension, Alsace is intended here.

Nostradamus here points to centers of Protestant rebellion in the 16th and 17th centuries. Navarre and Bohemia were both centers of fervent Protestantism. A rebellion in Bohemia and Hungary in 1618 launched the Thirty Years War. The last two lines move the vision forward a generation beyond the end of this conflict, to the late 1680s. The Alsatian town of Barr is a few miles south-east of Strasbourg. Most of the region became a French possession by 1689 during the reign of Louis XIV. When he died in 1715 he was succeeded by his five-year-old great grandson. Louis XIV's brother, the Duc d'Orleans, became regent to the child king, although he came to be noted for his corruption and decadence.

5 Q90

Dans les cyclades,[1] en perinthe[2] & lariffe,[3]	In the Cyclades, in Perinthus and Larissa,
Dedans Sparte tout le Pelloponneffe:[4]	In Sparta, all of Peloponnesus:
Si grand famine, pefte par faux conniffe,[5]	A great famine – plague through false dust [fallout?].
Neuf mois tiendra & tout le cherroneffe.	Nine months it will last and through the whole peninsula.

[1]Aegean archipelago, including Chios.
[2]Thracian town in northern Greece.
[3]Thessalian town in Greece.
[4]Peloponnesus, the huge peninsula comprising southern mainland Greece.
[5]Either Greek konis = dust, ashes, or Latin connissus = exerted, striven against.

J. R. Jochmans theorizes that Nostradamus foresaw a nuclear disaster on the southern European coast of Italy between 1994 and 1996. It may be coincidental, but my own research indicates that a disturbing number of

Nostradamus' quatrains point to an Arab terrorist attack on a nuclear reactor in Italy or in the Balkans as the possible cause. The prevailing wind patterns of the Mediterranean during a reactor meltdown would form a radioactive cloud of dust extending over the regions mentioned above. It would be wise for Italy to continue its moratorium on the construction of nuclear plants, as well as to continue to keep their two existing reactors closed – forever.

Current objective evidence points to an even higher risk of a nuclear industrial accident in Eastern Europe and the Balkans, an accident that would cause the evacuation of south-eastern Europe for **nine months**. The six nuclear power plants in Bulgaria are notorious for their dilapidation and lax safety measures. At the time of writing, a Bulgarian nuclear reactor at Belene on the banks of the Danube is being atrociously mismanaged. The reactor stands without shielding of any kind beneath a simple warehouse roof. If it suffered meltdown, clouds of **false dust** would spread unimpeded. Since a nuclear accident or act of nuclear terrorism didn't happen in 1996, the next date for a **plague of false dust** for southern Europe would be July 1999.

The year 1996 is a crucial deadline for the revamping of the global nuclear industry. A number of atomic agencies have stated that many of the world's reactors were due to reach the end of their expected lifespan by 1996, especially some of those in Eastern Europe and Russia that are modeled after the archaic Chernobyl reactor design.

Quatrain Indexing Date: If Q90 was intended for 1990 this is a quantum future that is either dated incorrectly or was intended to indicate a terrorist attack during the buildup of Western forces for the Gulf War that has passed.

5 Q91

Au grand marché[1] qu'on dict des menſongiers,	**At the great market [European Community?] called that of the liars,**
Du tout Torrent & champ Athenien:	**Of all Torrent and the field of Athens:**
Seront ſurprins par les cheuaux legiers,	**They will be surprised by the light horsemen,**
Par Albanois Mars, Leo, Sat. vn verſien.	**By the Albanians – Mars is in Leo and Saturn in Aquarius.**

[1]*grand marché* = either a great market square, or the European Common Market (now the European Union).

Mars passed through Leo from 27 April through 23 June 1993 during Saturn's most recent transit of Aquarius. The **great market** could be the First World powers (the European Common Market), whose peace efforts were viewed as lies by those of every side in the Balkan fighting. Line 2 stands for Greece, which threatened the new state of Macedonia during that time.

The original French word *Albanois* can also be applied to modern-day Trans-Caucasia, which was named **Albania** by the ancient Romans. During April–June 1993 Armenian forces scored a major victory by grabbing Nagorno-Kharabach from Azerbaijan. As of the mid-1990s the Azeri-Armenian conflict remains stalled and the winds of war have moved to another region that was once part of what the ancient Romans called Albania. The terrible Russian-Chechnyian war, which began in 1994, has already killed over 50,000 people.

Greece and Turkey almost did fight another war over disputed islands near Asia Minor in 1995. On a more positive note, the sudden prospect of a Bosnian peace and the lifting of international sanctions against Serbia has put pressure on Greece to ease its blockade against Macedonia and restore the historically large and profitable trade relationship with Serbia via Macedonian transportation routes.

Certain astrological aspects (see 4 Q67) point to the danger of the Bosnian conflict's breaking out again in 1997–98 once the 60,000 peacekeepers of IFOR (Implementation Force) of the Dayton Accords agreement have left. However, other aspects might augur peace lasting in the region for another generation before a new Balkan war breaks out in around 2021.

Quatrain Indexing Date: Q91 = 1991, the year Yugoslavia broke up and several civil wars erupted between Serbs, Slovenes, and Croats. The following year the Bosnian war began.

Astrological Time Window

Saturn will not be in Aquarius again until March 2020 through March 2023. At that time Mars will transit Leo only once, in June–July 2021. This could be the next dangerous window in time for an outbreak of war in the Balkans or in Trans-Caucasia. This precedes the astrological window for a Third World War between 2024 through 2038, when the world's estimated 8.5 billion people will be fighting wars over dwindling water and food resources.

5 Q92

Apres le siege tenu dixsept ans,	**After the See kept for seventeen years,**
Cinq changeront en tel reuolu terme:	**Five completed terms will exchange**
Puis sera l'vn esleu de mesme temps,	**within [the Vatican]:**
Qui des Romains ne sera trop conforme.	**Then one will be elected at the same time,**
	Who will not be too conforming to the Romans.

This could be about modern popes. Pius XI ruled the Vatican for 17 years (1922–39). The five successors would be Pius XII (1939–58), John XXIII (1958–63), Paul VI (1963–78), John Paul I (1978), and the current pope, John Paul II. When he dies a new pope will be elected that will not please the Vatican status quo. Perhaps he will be as revolutionary as Pope John Paul I. On his prophetic papal list St Malachy has this new pope as the second to last to rule before doomsday. His name is *Gloria Olivae,* "the Glory of the Olive Branch," the symbol of a peacemaker.

5 Q93

Soubs le terroir du rond globe lunairé,	**Under the territory of the round lunar globe,**
Lors que fera dominateur Mercure:	**When Mercury will be dominant:**
L'ifle d'Efcoffe fera vn luminaire,	**The Scottish Island will form a luminary,**
Qui les Anglois mettra à defconfiture.	**Who will put the English into frustration.**

Interpreters usually believe Nostradamus foresaw at least the attempt, if not the reality, of Scottish king Charles I to restore Catholicism in England. His reign certainly did throw the English people into frustration and confusion. Rather than conquering the Protestant Parliament, he himself was conquered and beheaded in 1649.

Is the future of another King Charles possible here? Perhaps he meant the current Charles, Prince of Wales. Wöllner, taking his cue from Astrology's grand cosmic calendar, claims that Mercury was dominant between 1720 and 1756, and for another term beginning in 1972. If he is correct, expect this mystical and somewhat eccentric heir to the United Kingdom to one day leave his favorite retreat at Balmoral, Scotland, to be crowned King Charles III sometime before the period of Mercury domination ends in 2008.

5 Q94

Tranflatera en la grand Germanie,	**He will gather into Greater Germany,**
Brabant & Flãdres, Gand, Bruges, & Bolongne:	**Brabant and Flanders, Ghent, Bruges and Bologne:**
La traifue fainte, le grand duc d'Armenie,	**The truce feigned, the great Duke of Armenia,**
Affaillira Vienne & la Coloigne.	**Will assault Vienna and Cologne.**

Hitler's greatest gamble, the invasion of Soviet Russia, utterly failed. He could not shatter the Soviet Empire in eight weeks as planned. Stalin had enough time to harness Russia's vast manpower and industrial potential to bring total defeat to Hitler's empire. In a few words, this quatrain gives us a prophetic coda to Hitler's successes and catastrophes. First Nostradamus lists all the prewar successes: the occupation of the Rhineland, Austria, the Sudetenland, all of which Hitler would *gather* into his empire of *Grossdeutschland* (**Greater Germany**). Next, he lists the early Nazi conquests: the Netherlands, Belgium, Northern France. The Italian city of Bologna was occupied by Nazi forces later in the war when Mussolini's government collapsed.

Stalin and Hitler had a tacit understanding that their Non-Aggression Pact of 1939 was a postponement of the final battle to be waged between Fascism and Communism. In 1941 Hitler jumped the gun on Stalin and exposed the pact for what it was, a *feigned* truce. The title **great Duke of Armenia** is a synecdoche for Josef Stalin, who was born in Soviet Georgia and also spent many of his formative years in neighboring *Armenia*.

By 1945 the full consequences of Hitler's invasion of Russia were clear. Three years after facing near-defeat at the approaches of Moscow, the Russians had pushed the Nazis back into Europe and had themselves advanced as far as Berlin and Vienna.

Nostradamus' mention of Cologne remains either an interesting mistake or a future potential aborted. It implies the Allies may have faltered in the Normandy invasion or perhaps lost the Battle of the Bulge, leaving the Russians to completely overrun Germany. What a Cold War that would have caused!

---

5 Q95

Nautique rame inuitera les vmbres,	**The nautical oar will attract the shadows,**
Du grand Empire lors viendra conciter:	**Then will come to provoke the great Empire:**
La mer Aegee des lignes les encombres,	**In the Aegean Sea the encumbrances of wood,**
Empefchant l'onde Tirrene de floter.[1]	**Obstructing the diverted Tyrrhenian waves.**

[1]Latin *defluere* = to cease flowing, to be lost, to disappear.

Line 1 is cloaked in a riddle between *rame*, "oars", and *rane*, "frog," found similar to one in 5 Q3. This time the former meaning applies. The cryptic poetry paints an image of hundreds of Christian galleys gliding like great wooden water bugs with rolling arms of oars over the Tyrrhenian sea between Sicily and Tuscany. They are racing towards a rendezvous at Messina for a crusade against the Ottoman Turkish fleet. The clash did not happen in the Aegean, but at the mouth of the narrow Gulf of Corinth, at Lepanto, in 1571.

5 Q96

Sur le milieu du grand monde la roſe,
Pour nouueaux faicts ſang public eſpandu:
A dire vray on aura bouche cloſe,
Lors au beſoing viendra tard l'attendu.

Upon the middle of the great world –
the rose,
For new deeds public blood shed:
To speak the truth they will have
closed mouths.
Then at the time of need the awaited
one will come late.

Red or shades of **rose** are colors used symbolically by Eastern mystics and seekers to represent the fire of awareness, the sunset of the old world, and the dawning of the inner enlightenment, described by spiritual traditions as the Mystic Rose. A riddle **to speak** with **closed mouths** is almost a Zen koan, and may very well describe the 1990s worldwide interest in Eastern meditation techniques. In fact, there is more mainstream interest in meditation in these latter days of the 20th century than during the revolutionary 1960s.

The final line may be a poetic suggestion that, since spiritual truth is always ahead of its time, the **awaited** spiritual teachers may only appear to **come late** because the people do not easily accept or recognize authentic mystics. References to **red** (Eastern Mysticism) and **speaking the truth** with **closed mouths** (silence and meditation) link this quatrain to Nostradamus' theme of Eight Clues for the world's new religiousness. The new consciousness in the 21st century, catalyzed by the teachings of a handful of 20th-century mystics, will transcend current dogmas and religious hierarchies.

Among these catalysts Meher Baba (1894–1969) would be an important candidate. A master of the devotional path of Sufism, Meher Baba taught through silence from 1925 until his death 43 years later. He proclaimed to the world that he had come to sow the seeds of love in all hearts. His motto was: Don't worry, be happy. He taught through silence, fulfilling Nostradamus' prediction that the man to raise our consciousness would **speak the truth** through **closed mouth**.

Another mystic who redefined religion was J. Krishnamurti, one of the most prominent anti-masters of this century. He spent most of his long life sharing his concept of "witnessing" or "disidentification" with tens of thousands of followers on six continents.

The Indian mystic Swami Prabhupada flew west in the heyday of the spiritual rebellion of the 1960s to spread the message of Krishna Consciousness. One of the symbols of consciousness is flame, represented by the shades of red. The orange-robed Hare Krishnas seen on Western streets have angered and bewildered mainstream society, though generally at present the public has more of a sense of humor.

L. Ron Hubbard, author of *Dianetics* and founder of the Church of

Scientology, created Scientology to help people spiritually recover from psychic and mental traumas and restore a "clear" mental and spiritual state. His church uses a flaming volcano with red flames as one of its symbols.

Although the followers of Osho have ceased to wear their red colors in public, their ashram in India teams with tens of thousands of people wearing robes in shades of maroon (*rose* or "red" colors). One of Osho's meditation experiments was a technique called The Mystic Rose consisting of one three-hour session per day in a 21-day process. In the first week one laughs nonstop, every day for three hours. This loosens the psyche for the second week of crying for three hours. This is done to heal deep psychological and spiritual wounds. The final week is three hours a day of silent sitting and witnessing **To speak the truth they will have closed mouths**. The Mystic Rose meditation is one of several techniques regularly offered at their chief ashram in Pune, India.

Quatrain Indexing Date: the indexing may date the year 1996 as the beginning of a great political and theological struggle between the vested interests of orthodox religions and the new religiousness of the next millennium. Back in early 1994 I made the prediction that for the American presidential elections of 1996 the right-wing Christian faction of the Republican party would wage an all-out battle for the presidency. As I write this a month before the Republican Convention, I will say here that they will undermine their party's chances to win in November 1996. Clinton and Gore will be re-elected in a landslide, as I earlier predicted on radio and television back in July 1994. The two are sympathetic to many of the therapies and philosophies of the Human Potential Movement. If they can initiate reform and ecological responsibility in the United States, there is a chance we can all avoid the disasters to come in the 2020s.

5 Q97

Le nay defforme par horreur ſuffoqué,	The one born deformed suffocated by horror,
Dans la cité du grand Roy habitable:	In the habitable city of the great King:
L'edict ſeuere des captifs reuoqué,	The severe edict of the captives revoked,
Greſle & tonnerre, Condon ineſtimable.	Hail and thunder, Condom inestimable.

This is generally applied to the legendary Man in the Iron Mask. Believed to be either a great noble or the deformed twin brother of Louis XIV, he was forced to wear a cast-iron mask and live most of his life in a dungeon. Line 2 is applied to Paris, the city of the Sun King, Louis XIV. Line 3 describes Louis' revocation of the Edict of Nantes in 1685, which marked the end of Huguenot tolerance. Leoni, giving good tongue to his cheekiness adds, "Condom is a small town in Gurenne in the south-west, which, according to one theory, gave its name to a well-known rubber article."

5 Q98

A quarante huict degré climaterique,	**At a latitude of forty-eight degrees,**
A fin de Cancer[1] ſi grande ſeichereſſe:	**At the end of Cancer so great [is the]**
Poiſſon en mer, fleuue, lac cuit hectique,	**drought:**
Bearn, Bigorre[2] par feu ciel en deſtreſſe.	**Fish in the sea, river and lake boiled hectic,**
	[South-west France] in distress from fire in the sky.

[1]*fin de Cancer:* the sun ends its transit of Cancer every year around July 22.
[2]*Bearn, Bigorre:* these counties stand for the extreme south-west corner of France.

Scientists have traced the regularity of sunspot activity over the last billion years and relate it to 20-year cycles that coincide with periods of drought such as the one that created the famous Dust Bowl in the American farming belt during the 1930s. Sunspot activity is now entering a new phase that will continue up to the year 2000. The great planetary alignment in May of that year is expected to generate some of the greatest sunspot activity ever recorded.

Nostradamus warns us against creating a future drought of biblical proportions that will burn a swath across latitude 48 in the Northern Hemisphere. Drawing a line across that latitude on a map, we touch on nearly all the world's chief grain belts. Today's amber oceans of wheat stretching across North America and the Soviet Ukraine revert to prairies and inhospitable steppes in the next century.

Quatrain Indexing Date: Q98 = 1998? In my last Nostradamus book I correctly interpreted the increase in global warming after the mid-1990s when the dust from the eruption of Mt Pinatubo that slightly cooled the world had cleared the skies. With this interpretation in mind we can expect a wave of global droughts and heat waves by July 1998. From that time onward, global warming steadily kicks in, disrupting weather patterns, and the climate conditions needed to grow grain start to shift hundreds of miles north of where they are now.

5 Q99

Milan, Ferrare, Turin, & Aquillaye,	**Milan, Ferrara, Turin and Aquileia,**
Capne Brundis vexés par gent Celtique:	**Capua, Brindisi vexed by the Celtic people:**
Par le Lyon & phalange aquilee	**By the Lion and eagle's phalanx**
Quand Rome aura le chef vieux Britannique.	**When Rome will have the old British chief.**

Ancient **Aquileia** usually applies to nearby Venice. Along with all the other wide-ranging locales mentioned in the quatrain this covers all of Italy. The obvious application would be to some climactic turn of military fortunes favoring Henry II's domination of Italy. But this would never be. The French (**Celtic**) people **vexed** Italy during the French Revolutionary Wars 1792–99, and again in the Napoleonic wars in 1800–15. The last line makes marginally better sense if we jump from Napoleonic British redcoats to Tommies in camouflage in 1944–45. There we find them doing the bidding of their **old British chief**, Prime Minister Winston Churchill, as allies with the forces of the American *eagle*. The British Eighth Army advanced up the eastern Italian boot capturing Brindisi and Capua, Ferrara, and finally occupying Venice. By the war's end the American soldiers fought their way to Capua, Rome, Milan, and all the way to Turin.

5 Q100

Le boutefeu par ſon feu atrapé,	**An incendiary trapped in its own fire,**
De feu du ciel à Carcas & Cominge:	**Fire from the sky at Carcassonne and**
Foix, Aux, Maȝere, haut vieillart eſchappé,	**Comminges:**
Par ceux de Haſſe, des Saxons & Turinge.	**Foix, Auch, Maȝères, the exalted old**
	man escaped,
	Through those of Hesse, the Saxons
	[Germans] and Thuringia.

This could be describing the mechanics of a nuclear trigger. In a fission bomb, a hollow sphere of plutonium is surrounded by a second sphere of conventional TNT explosive. The entire outer sphere is ignited by an electrical charge that blasts inward from all sides at once, thus compress-ing – or, in the prophet's words, **trapping** – the plutonium in a critical mass. In hydrogen or thermal nuclear bombs a core of deuterium and tritium is ignited by the explosion of an atomic bomb. The radiation from the atomic bomb is focused on a styrofoam explosive surrounding the hydrogen bomb. The hydrogen **incendiary**, as in the fission process, is **trapped** and compressed by the surrounding atomic explosion, which raises the temperature of the deuterium-tritium core to around 20 million degrees Fahrenheit. By being **trapped in its own fire** the hydrogen bomb undergoes fusion and becomes a miniature sun as it explodes.

Though a future nuclear attack on southern France by terrorists or by a renegade North African nation with new ballistic missile technology is a viable interpretation, this quatrain can also apply to the fall of France in 1940, and later the fall of Pétain's Vichy government to German occupiers (**Hesse** . . . **Saxons** . . . **Thuringians**) in 1942.

6 Q1

Avtour des mõts Pyrenees grãs amas,	**Around the Pyrenees mountains a**
De gent eftrange fecourir Roy nouueau:	**great [H]amas,**
Pres de Garonne du grand temple du Mas,	**The foreign people to help the new**
Vn Romain chef le craindra dedans l'eau.	**king:**

Avtour des mõts Pyrenees grãs amas,
De gent eftrange fecourir Roy nouueau:
Pres de Garonne du grand temple du Mas,
Vn Romain chef le craindra dedans l'eau.

**Around the Pyrenees mountains a
great [H]amas,
The foreign people to help the new
king:
Near the Garonne from the great
temple of Le Mas,
A Roman chief will fear him under
the waters.**

I guess I'm falling victim to every interpreter's temptation to apply a quatrain to my own near future. This doesn't mean it isn't a correct application. The great **amas** collecting around the Pyrenees mountains could be a word-play for Hamas, the extremist Palestinian terrorist organization. Perhaps they have a secret base in south-western France. The rest is pretty vague. It seems that there is a submarine lurking in the Garonne estuary near Bordeaux, but the mention of **a Roman chief** may turn our attention once again to the numerous prophecies concerning a terrorist submarine attack near the **winding Tiber** (2 Q43) and Rome.

6 Q2

En l'an cinq cens octante plus & moins,
On attendra le fiecle bien eftrange:
*En l'an fept cens, & trois cieux en
tefmoings,*
*Que plufieurs regnes vn à cinq feront
change.*

**In the year five hundred eighty more
or less,
One will await a very strange
century:
In the year seven hundred, and three
the heavens bear witness thereof,
That several kingdoms – one to five –
will make a change.**

You would think that debunkers would be eager to tackle a dated quatrain such as this. Leroy and Randi remain silent. Probably for one good reason – Nostradamus got the events of 1580 and 1703 correct.

The year 1580 launched the strange and long century of French history referred to in this quatrain. The Seventh War of Religion – a short and eccentric affair that was less a test between Catholics and Huguenots than a battlefield for the romantic escapades of Queen Margot, the nymphomaniac and wife of the equally noted royal satyr, Henry de Navarre – began in that year. Nostradamus' long century ends in 1703 with France now a mighty empire under the authoritarian hand of Louis XIV, who was busy fighting the kings of Europe in the War of the Spanish Succession. The issue of the war is easy to uncloak in line 4. Spain was inherited by Louis XIV's grandson Philip V (or *to five*). **Several kingdoms** beyond Spain were incorporated into her empire: the kingdoms of Milan, the Two Sicilies, the Netherlands, and numerous colonies and holdings in Asia and South America. The political fate of one did **change**, by the war's end: the Treaty of Utrecht granted the Spanish Netherlands to the Holy Roman Empire.

6 Q3

Fleuue qu'efprouue le nouueau nay Celtique,	**The river that tests the newborn Celtic heir,**
Sera en grande de l'Empire difcorde:	**Will be in great discord with the empire:**
Le ieune prince par gent ecclefiaftique,	**The young prince, because of the ecclesiastical people,**
Oftera le fceptre coronel de concorde.	**Will take away the scepter of the crown of concord.**

Garencières explains that ancient Frenchmen would place a newly born French king on a target and make him swim on the surface of the Rhine, to determine whether he was legitimately begotten or not. The particular Celtic heir targeted here by Nostradamus, metaphorically at least, is probably Louis XIII or his son Louis XIV. Both royals were shaped and conditioned as young men by cardinals. The first had Cardinal Richelieu, and the latter Cardinal Mazarin, as mentor. The Rhine river region was the setting for many battles for both kings. Richelieu had drawn Louis XIII into the Thirty Years War; Mazarin's tutelage is indirectly responsible for Louis XIV's war lust. Concord and peace was often broken throughout his long reign, for Louis XIV's armies fought a number of battles along the lower Rhine during the wars of royal succession.

6 Q4

Le Celtiq fleuue changera de riuaige,	**The [French] river will change course,**
Plus ne tiendra la cité d'Agripine:	**And will no longer include the city of Agrippina [Cologne]:**
Tout tranfmué ormis le vieil langaige,	**All changed except the old language,**
Saturne, Leo, Mars, Cancer en rapine.	**Saturn in Leo, Mars [the god of war] plundering Cancer [in July].**

This could be a continuation of the theme in the previous quatrain. Line 1 might be a poetic metaphor for the changing current of France's political fortunes that brought on the unification of German states to form the Second Reich. The French have desired (and sometimes succeeded) in making the Rhine a **French river**. Both Charlemagne and Napoleon achieved it in empires past. The last line dates France's final loss of territory on the shores of the Rhine through the acquisition of Alsace and Lorraine by the Germans after the Franco-Prussian war.

Agrippina is a classical allusion to the city of Cologne on the western shores of the Rhine. The western Rhineland was the primal homeland of the Frankish tribes that later established France. All political allegiance was changed in Alsace and Lorraine but French (**the old language**) continued to be spoken and still remains the dominant language. The Franco-Prussian War began in the month of Cancer (July 1870). The constitution for the Second Reich was approved on 14 April 1871; according to mundane astrology, therefore, the German Empire was born under the sign of Aries, ruled by Mars – the god of war.

6 Q5

Si grand famine par vnde peſtifere,	So great a famine through a pestilent wave.
Par pluye longue le long du polle arctique:	[It] will extend its rain over the length of the Arctic pole:
Samarobryn[1] cent lieux[2] de l'hemiſphere,	Samarobryn, one hundred leagues from the hemisphere,
Viuront ſans loy exempt de pollitique.	[They] shall live without law, exempt from politics.

[1]Unsolved enigma with any number of translations from noted scholars: a) Leoni – Latin *Samarobriva* = Amiens? [doubtful; this does not fit the context]; b) Leoni – Sam R. O'Brien, some future astronaut ; c) Cheetham – from the Russian *samo* (self) *rabotin* (operating), for a Russian space station; d) Noorbergen – Latin *samara* = seed-pod, with verb *obire* = to wander, to travel or to encircle; e) Noorbergen – a *samara* is a seed from an ash, elm or maple tree and is composed of a central pod with either one or two projecting wings (just like a space satellite with solar panels).

[2]*cent lieux* = 100 leagues. In 16th-century Europe, the measure of a league varied considerably, from 2.5 miles to as much as 4.5 miles. Various scholars estimate Nostradamus' league to be 2.7 miles each, so that 100 leagues equals 270 miles.

The name *Samarobryn* has mystified interpreters of Nostradamus for years. According to the quatrain, whatever Samarobryn is, it is hovering some **hundred leagues** or 270 miles above us. However, experienced interpreters of Nostradamus often find that words or phrases, that have remained stubbornly obscure, are suddenly illuminated by the appearance of new words or names in our vocabularies. In effect, we are waiting for our world to catch up with Nostradamus' visions. This may be the case with the decoding of Samarobryn. For example, two early anti-AIDS test drugs, Suramin and Ribavrin, could be components of the word Samarobryn. An alternative reading is suggested by Erika Cheetham. She records an intriguing interpretation from one of her readers who thinks the word describes a Russian satellite: *samo* meaning "self" and *rabotin* meaning "operator" in Russia, hence self-operator. Samarobryn could then stand for the Russian space station Mir. René Noorbergen (1981) gives us an equally interesting image. Nostradamus, when faced with the images of a space station aloft over the limb of the earth, with solar wings outstretched, could only describe it in terms of the winged seed-pods of elm or maple trees, which are called *samara* in Latin. He then added the Latin *obire* to describe it "orbiting" the earth.

Samarobryn could be the source of a rare positive prediction of Nostradamus. As best as one can divine the wild poetry of Dr Nostradamus, this quatrain may give up some clues to consider in seeking the cure for AIDS. Unlocking this prophetic riddle may reveal a cure that comes from the skies themselves. Preliminary radical experiments infusing ozone into the bloodstream show promising potential for killing the AIDS virus. A more mainstream but no less farsighted alternative is research on new vaccines manufactured in zero gravity in a lab orbiting Earth. In the summer of 1992 one US space shuttle mission experimented with proteins in zero gravity to find a cure for AIDS. Scientific exploration of space-grown crystals may produce the cure for AIDS and many other diseases in our near future, negating most of Nostradamus' dire predictions of plague.

The cryptic double-talk of the final line that exempts those flying in space from law and politics may be positive in nature. To save our world from diseases the scientists in zero-gravity labs are working beyond the petty concerns of nationalism and politics.

6 Q6

Apparoiſtra vers la Septentrion,[1]	**There will appear towards the seven**
Non loing de Cancer l'eſtoille cheuelue:[2]	**stars of Ursa Minor and Polaris,**
Suze, Sienne, Boece, Eretrion,	**Not far from Cancer, the bearded**
Mourra de Rome grand, la nuict diſparue.	**star:**
	Susa, Siena, Boeotia, Eretria,
	Great Rome will die, the night having
	vanished.

[1]Latin *septentrio* = constellation of seven stars, near the Pole Star; Ursa Minor.
[2]*eſtoille cheuelue* = a bearded star, a comet.

This dire event may take place in July (the month of **Cancer**) 1999. The great comet is the omen warning the world to prepare itself for disaster or a great spiritual shift in consciousness. This comet is Hale-Bopp, which will cross the northern sky near the Big Dipper and the North Star in the spring of 1997, less than two years earlier. There will be a total eclipse passing the sun's shadow over Europe on 11 August 1999. Italy (**Susa,**

Siena) and Greece (**Boeotia, Eretria**) will witness this celestial event, as well as England, Flanders, France, Eastern Europe, and Turkey.

We will have to wait for the summer of 1999 to see whether **the night** of the eclipse has **vanished** along with the Vatican in some Catholic Apocalypse. The celestial configurations of line 1 may also represent the countries **the seven stars** shine over – the Brothers of the North – the United States (by grace of Alaska) and the Russian Federation. Elsewhere Nostradamus warns of the two going to war by summer 1999. We might hope that Nostradamus is speaking of the death of the long night of Catholic dogmas, and religious superstitions in general, which have caused so many wars and misunderstandings in history. In this more positive interpretation, the Brothers of the North undergo a religious revolution.

If nothing happens to Rome during the eclipse, a bearded star will appear at any time between the years 2000 and 3797, from a location between Polaris and Canis Major. It will fall in the Aegean Sea off Negrepont (the modern day island of Evvoia) where **Eretria** (now Aletria) is situated, east of **Boeotia**.

Quatrain Indexing Date: 6 Q6 = 66(6) the number of mankind living in sin, or better, unconsciousness. Or it is the year 2006, 2066, or even 3766.

6 Q7

Norneigre[1] & Dace, & l'ifle Britannique,	**Norway and Dacia and the British Isle,**
Par les vnis freres feront vexées:	**By the united brothers will be vexed:**
Le chef Romain iffu de fang Gallique	**The Roman chief issued from Gallic blood,**
Et les copies aux foreftz repoulfées.	**And the forces repelled back into the forests.**

[1]Probably a misprint for *Norvège* = Norway.

Norway, Romania, and Britain are sorely tested by the **united** Axis **brothers**, Hitler and Mussolini. Norway is conquered by the Nazis in 1940. Romania becomes an Axis satellite and is pressed into Hitler's invasion of Russia, suffering a disaster. Britain alone survives the initial onslaught of Hitler's conquest of Europe to become the base for the Allied landings that lead to final victory. The only distortions in this clear prophetic mirror reflect Mussolini incorrectly as having a French ancestor. The last line is vague. It could apply to the grudging withdrawal of German forces out of the woods of Luxembourg during the final weeks of the Battle of the Bulge. Nostradamus in 5 Q45 predicted the importance of the Ardennes forest in the fall of the French Colonial, and later the Nazi, empires.

6 Q8

Ceux qui estoyent en regne pour sçauoir,	Those who were in the realm for knowledge,
Au Royal change deuiendront apouuris:	By a royal change will become impoverished:
Vns exilez sans appuy, or, n'auoir,	Some exiles without support, or gold to possess,
Lettrez & lettres ne seront à grand pris.	The learned and learning will not be of high value.

One can read this two ways. First, we could see the further corruption of education – what is called in the United States the dumbing of America – by lax educational discipline and television's ever lower standards for intellectual stimulation. The second scenario sees the knowledge of facts – rather than an internal knowing – being discarded. This indeed is the challenge for the Aquarian Age. Am I to become a know-it-all or am I to take part in the coming spiritual revolution, and transcend my borrowed knowledge to become one-with-the-All, a wholistic human being? The change in education's course could begin as early as 2008 if the quatrain indexing is a date.

Elsewhere it is intimated that a *royal change* could make Charles, Prince of Wales, King Charles III by that time. Or the *royal change* is spiritual. The mystics tell us that consciousness is king, and the mind is its servant, not its master.

Quatrain Indexing Date: Q8 = 2008, the year in the Grand Cosmic calendar of Astrology when the 35-year cycle of cosmic day moves into a 35-year cosmic night; in other words, by 2008 the world's education systems may move from the rational, masculine **knowledge** and gravitate towards the more intuitive, the feminine **knowing**.

6 Q9

Aux sacrez temples seront faicts escandales,	In the sacred temples scandals will be committed,
Comptez seront par honneurs & louanges	They will be thought of as honors and praiseworthy
D'vn que on graue d'argent, d'or les medalles,	Of one of whom they engrave on medals of silver and gold,
La fin sera en tormens bien estranges.	The end will be in very strange torments.

Fontbrune believes this one is about Napoleon and the persecution of the Italian clergy in 1809. The quatrain indexing would support this. Napoleon did have his image engraved on gold and silver coins. In his final agonizing days of exile on the island of St Helena he suffered **strange torments** and delirious episodes while dying of stomach cancer.

In 1942, Lamont claimed that this quatrain forewarned the Catholic Church of a future scandal. I agree with him and target this one for the Vatican Bank Scandal and the purported murder of Pope John Paul I. It seems that the scandal's perpetrators will have continued success in avoiding justice, and their crimes may even come to be seen as noble acts. When Pope John Paul II took office he was briefed about the same revelations contained in the reports found spread across the bed of his dead predecessor. He did not, however, dismiss Bishop Paul Marcinkus, the man in charge of the Vatican Bank, a prime suspect for masterminding the scandal and participating in the conspiracy to kill the pope. Instead the new pontiff had him promoted to archbishop and kept him in firm control of the Church's finances throughout the rest of the 1980s. Marcinkus retired with honor after the longstanding threat by police authorities to detain him for questioning if he ever stepped outside of the Vatican was lifted.

The final lines may reprise the commentary on the long list of mysterious murders reverberating from the poisoning of the first John Paul (see 4 Q11 for the murder details).

Quatrain Indexing Date: Q9 = 1809, if Fontbrune's interpretation is correct, or it could stand for yet another terrible scandal involving the Vatican by 2009.

6 Q10

Vn peu de temps les temples de couleurs	In a short time the colors of temples
De blanc & noir des deux entremeſlee:	With black and white, the two will be
Rouges & iaunes leur embleront les leurs	intermingled.
Sang, terre, peſte, faim, feu, d'eau	The red and yellow ones will carry off
affollée.[1]	their possessions.
	Blood, earth, plague, hunger, fire,
	maddened by thirst.

[1]Old French *affollé* = maddened; murdered, crippled.

Most of this quatrain seems to describe, in halting 16-century terms, events of our own era. We see the intermingling of faiths and races. The **red and yellow ones** could stand for the retreat of Russian and Chinese Communism and the withdrawal of troops from satellite nations. Or it might even be applied to the diaspora of the Buddhist Lamas (who wear red and yellow) and the Tibetans. A third application would be watching the **red and yellow** native peoples preparing for the end of the white

man's world, collectively foreseen by their prophets as "the Great Purification by fire." The prophecy ends with one of Nostradamus' cryptic sentences describing the sequence of apocalyptic calamities: (*blood*) war and
AIDS; (*earth*) ecological disasters; (*plague*) toxic pollution, ozone holes
and AIDS; (*hunger*) the spread of global famine from crop failures and
overpopulation; (*fire maddened by thirst*) a double meaning representing the *fire* of global warming triggering the *fires* of war set by countries'
running out of water. In 1993, Sandra Postel, vice president of research
for the Worldwatch Institute, warned that scarcity of water would be to
the 1990s what oil embargoes and price shocks were to the 1970s. In her
book *Last Oasis: Facing Water Scarcity* (W.W. Norton, 1992), Postel
states that six of the nine Middle Eastern nations already face water and
food shortages and that their population will double by the end of the
20th century. At present nearly 40 percent of humanity depends on river
systems shared by two or more countries. Many upstream countries
believe they have absolute sovereignty over water inside their borders
and have little regard for nations downstream. Egypt's 62 million people
are hostage to Ethiopia's adherence to such a point of view. Ethiopia
wishes to dam off the headwaters of the Blue Nile and the Egyptian
government has made it painfully clear that they will go to war with
Ethiopia, Sudan, or any other country upstream that draws off too much
water from the Nile.

The same potential for wars **maddened by thirst** exists between the
Turks and their Arab neighbors, Syria and Iraq. Turkey's hydroelectric
projects threaten to cut off the flow of the Euphrates river. The biblical
prophecies of Eziekiel make it clear that such an act is the final omen
before the battle of Armageddon. A lion's share of Israeli water will come
from the aquifers underneath the future Palestinian state in the disputed
West Bank. A political breach between these neighbors would prompt
Israel to invade again.

Thus, future conflict in the region most augured to be the battlefield of
man's final catastrophic war may erupt due to disputes over ancient water
claims rather than ancient ethnic and religious feuds. Add the hotbed of
nuclear proliferation to the future cracked riverbeds of today's 100 developing nations currently disputing water rights with their neighbors,
and it is easy to see how a Third World War is more likely to result from
the stresses of overpopulation and ecological degradation than from
religious and political disputes.

Quatrain Indexing Date: Q10 = 2010, perhaps dating the end of the
first decade of the new century within Nostradamus' "apocalyptic
sequence" theme. We can expect blood-*plague* caused by ozone and
AIDS and Ebola-like diseases, in concert with food and water famines on
an overpopulated Earth.

6 Q11

Des sept rameaux à trois seront reduicts,	The seven branches will be reduced to three,
Les plus aisnez seront surprins par mort,	
Fratricider les deux seront seduicts,	Death will surprise the elder ones,
Les coniurez en dormans sesont morts.	Two will be attracted to fratricide,
	The conspirators while sleeping will be dead.

The **seven branches** reduced to **three** are the three surviving Valois children in 1574: Henry III, Queen Margaret of Navarre, and Hercules Duc d' Alençon. Henry and Hercules did engage in fratricidal war that ended when the latter died of a cold. Henry's chief rival for the throne, Henry de Guise, the commander of the Catholic League, did conspire to kill the king. Henry III moved first, inviting Guise to the Château Blois for a reconciliation and seducing him into a false sense of security; in other words, Guise was figuratively asleep or, in modern terms, he spaced it. He walked into the king's bedchamber without a bodyguard and was pounded and run through by a dozen of the king's bodyguards, at last collapsing at the foot of the king's bed. One could say that *dormans* (sleeping) is a double pun for the scene of his murder, the bedchamber, and Guise's strange lapse of awareness about the danger.

6 Q12

Dresser copies[1] pour monter à l'Empire,	To raise forces in order to ascend to the Empire,
Du Vatican le sang Royal tiendra:	
Flamans, Anglois, Espaigne auec Aspire,[2]	For the Vatican the blood Royal will hold:
Contre l'Italie & France contendra.	
	Flemings, English, Spain with Aspire,
	Against [the alliance] Italy and France will contend.

[1]Latin *copia* = forces, troops, army.
[2]Leoni believes it is a prosthesis of *Spire*, Speyer or Spires, an imperial city in the Palatinate. Or Germany, whose language is full of *aspirates*.

Napoleon raised many armies in his violent career. As a first-time commander of an army he transformed the motley forces of the French Revolutionary government to a fine-tuned conquering machine during his Italian campaigns (1794–98). He raised another expeditionary force to conquer Egypt in 1799. Then as First Consul of a new dictatorship, he formed the Consular Army to invade Italy over the Alps in 1800. As Emperor Napoleon I, he raised the Grand Army in 1804, first to invade England and later to conquer and dominate most of Western Europe by 1812.

In line 2 Fontbrune is influenced by the myth that the young Dauphin, Louis XVII, escaped from the Temple prison and was spirited away to the Vatican for his protection. But **will hold** could simply mean the Vatican stands firm in its support of the Bourbon succession of the Dauphin's uncle, Louis XVIII, after the downfall of Napoleon.

Line 3 lists a number of nations fighting in the coalition alliances against Napoleon. Nostradamus' use of **Flemings** as a synecdoche for the Belgians is daring because they were merely one of many subject peoples of the Spanish Netherlands. **Aspire** stands as a synecdoche for the patch-quilt of numerous German states in the Palatinate, first allied to and then against Napoleon. By 1809 he had incorporated most of Italy directly into the territory of the French Empire, so to say the coalitions were against **Italy and France** makes this prophecy too specific to be anything other than a vision of Napoleonic France.

6 Q13

Vn dubieux ne viendra loing du regne,	**A doubtful one will not come far from the realm,**
La plus grand part le voudra Souſtenir:	**The greater part will want to support him:**
Vn Capitole ne voudra point qu'il regne,	**A Capitol will not want him to rule at all,**
Sa grande charge ne pourra maintenir.	**His great burden he will not be able to maintain.**

This is Nixon. Nostradamus would not overlook a man who did so much to change the course of 20th-century history. But our prophet, ever the pessimist, had Nixon to "kick around" long before the controversial American president was born.

In line 1 Nixon is the **doubtful one** who is regarded warmly in France. Even the querulous Charles de Gaulle was an admirer. After Nixon's fall following the Watergate scandal, he could still find respect and honors during his visits to the **realm** of France. Perhaps Nostradamus is saying that Nixon is "not far" from being a Frenchman. In line 2 the **greater part** supporting Nixon during the 1968 presidential elections was what he called the Silent Majority. He declared himself the champion of nor-mal, middle-class Americans who were not represented in the turbulent political arena of the late 1960s. Line 3's **Capitol** represents Washington DC, and the Democrat-controlled Congress of the United States. Their fierce political rivalry with the Republican president finally led to their vote for his impeachment, forcing him to resign from office. Line 4 depicts a Nixon burdened with the cover-up over Watergate, unable to maintain power and fulfill his far-reaching geopolitical dreams to end the Cold War.

6 Q14

Loing de ſa terre Roy perdra la bataille,
Prompt eſchappé pourſuiuy ſuiuant prins,
Ignare prins ſoubs la doree maille.
Soubs fainct habit & l'ennemy ſurprins.

Far from his country a King will lose
the battle,
Promptly escaped, pursued,
subsequently captured,
Ignorant one taken under the gilded
mail.
Under false garb and the enemy
surprised.

Leoni makes a good argument for this quatrain, conjuring up some leads to a historical mystery yet to take place. In this case Nostradamus in 1555–56 is providing us with facts about the fate of a king of Portugal, a one-year-old at the time, who will be reported missing in action 23 years later.

In 1578 King Sebastian I of Portugal embarked on a crusade against King Fez of Morrocco. His army was massacred 60 miles south of Tangiers at the battle of Alcazarquivir. Official history says he was killed, but rumors of his survival continued, fostering a number of pretenders to the throne.

"This quatrain would thus tell that he had changed armor with a faithful friend, to be captured in his place," Leoni speculates. "Line 4 would suggest that the Moors discovered they had not killed the King, but preferred to let that impression prevail."

6 Q15

Deſſoubs la tombe ſera trouué le Prince,
Qu'aura le pris par deſſus Nuremberg:
L'Eſpaignol Roy en Capricorne mince,
Fainct & trahi par le grand Vvitemberg.

Under the tomb will be found the
Prince,
Who will be prized above Nuremberg:
The Spanish King in Capricorn slim,
Feigned and betrayed by the great
Wittemburg.

The prince **under the tomb** of the Führer bunker in Berlin is Adolf Hitler, who in happier days chose Nuremburg, the great medieval and Renaissance center of German culture and imperialism, for his Nazi Party rallies. The **Spanish King** is Francisco Franco. On 10 January 1941, he brushed aside Hitler's final demand that Spain enter World War II on the Axis side, replying that he had not received so much as a bushel of the grain promised by Hitler for his people, who after the Spanish Civil war were on the verge of starvation (**the Spanish king . . . slim**). The sun was **in Capricorn** on 10 January. Without Spain's help, Hitler (represented here by synecdoche as **the great Wittemburg**) could not proceed with his plan to seize Gibraltar from the British. This fact doomed all his campaigns to come in North Africa and the Mediterranean. One might imagine him in the last days of his life down in the sterile cavern of his bunker, brooding about opportunities missed and betrayal by the Spanish Fascist dictator.

6 Q16

Ce que rauy fera du ieune Milue,[1]	That which will be carried off by the young Kite,
Par les Normans de France & Picardie,	By the Normans of France and Picardy,
Les noirs du temple du lieu de Negrifilue[2]	The blacks of the temple of the spot in the Black Forest
Feront aulberge & feu de Lombardie.	Will make a public house and fire of Lombardy.

[1]Latin *milvus* = a kite or glede, a species of hawk.
[2]Latin, *silva nigra*, a black forest.

I would say this is about an incident from any one of the nine French civil wars of religion (1562–98). French soldiers from Normandy and Picardy will clash with Huguenots worshipping in their temple. Given the prophet's positivity and the religious tolerance of the time, the incident was a massacre. **The blacks of the temple** are Huguenots in their place of worship, which they called a temple. The color commonly worn by Huguenots was black. The Black Forest was an escape route for Huguenot refugees. A spread of religious warfare to Lombardy never happened.

6 Q17

Apres les limes bruflez les afiniers,	After the penance the priests [or the ass-drivers] burned,
Contraints feront changer habits diuers:	They will be compelled to change [into] diverse garbs:
Les Saturnins bruflez par les meufniers,	The Saturnians burned by the millers,
Hors la plufpart qui ne fera couuers.	Except the greater part who will not be covered.

This could be about anything since it is so obscure to us in our century. I would consider it to be a continuation of the incident, or atrocity, of the Wars of Religion in the previous quatrain, in which one Christian worshipper of Christ felt sanctioned by the Son of God to freely burn those of another sect of true believers in the Prince of Peace.

6 Q18

Par les phifiques le grand Roy delaiffé,	By the physicians the great King forsaken,
Par fort non art de l'Ebrieu eft en vie,	By fate, not by the Hebrew's art he remains alive,
Luy & fon genre au regne hault pousé,	He and his kindred pushed high in the realm,
Grace donnee à gent qui Chrift enuie.	Pardon given to the race which denies Christ.

A great monarch lies dying. So desperate is the hour that the Christian physicians must call a Jewish colleague to the rescue. Fate smiles on the Jewish doctor, the victim of his healing arts recovers, and great credit is showered on the doctor and his race. Some scholars believe this is retroactive rather than prophetic. Perhaps Nostradamus is smuggling in a comment on his past successes, or that of his grandfather, who may have once cured King René the Good of Provence (1409–80).

6 Q19

La vraye flamme engloutira la dame,	**The true flame will engulf the lady,**
Que voudra mettre les Innocens à feu:	**Who will want to put the Innocents to the fire:**
Pres de l'affaut l'exercite s'enflamme,	**Before the assault the army is inflamed,**
Quand dans Seuille monftre en beuf fera veu.	**When in Seville a monster in beef will be seen.**

Detractors of Nostradamus might complain that the only "bull" to be seen in this obscure quatrain is the forget-me-not that the **monster in beef** left behind for an interpreter to slip on; I do not intend, therefore, to wave my red flag too long or hard at this inscrutable bull of a quatrain.

I would instead flag this one for the Wars of Religion (1562–98) at a point just prior to the St Bartholomew's Day Massacre, in the summer of 1572. The **true flame** of righteousness inflames Catherine de' Medici to abandon her many attempts to sustain herself and her Catholic brethren in a life of Christian tolerance of their Huguenot neighbors. By Nostradamus' calling the Huguenots **Innocents** we get another hint of his secret support for religious freedom during his intolerant times. It is also true that Catherine's plan to assassinate only the leaders of the Huguenots got out of control, and many ordinary Huguenots, and even Catholic citizens, were caught and slaughtered during the massacres. Line 3 therefore could be any number of **assaults** by **inflamed** soldiers of the crown or Catholic League sanctioned by the promptings of Catherine de' Medici and the timid blessings of her son, Charles IX, which fueled the St Bartholomew's Day Massacre in August 1572.

Which leads me back to the bull.

Seville was a noted center for bullfights even in Queen Catherine's day. Perhaps hidden in some forgotten Spanish almanac is an account written between 1572 through 1589 of an unusually monstrous bull that could date these events. Short of this objective evidence, I run the danger of seeing this interpretation discarded as a waste product of another Nostradamian's fertile imagination.

6 Q20

L'vnion faincte[1] fera peu de durée,
Des vns changés reformés la plufpart:
Dans les vaiffeaux fera gent endurée,
Lors aura Rome vn nouueau liepart.[2]

The sacred union will be of short
    duration,
Some changed, the greater part
    reformed:
In the vessel will be the enduring race,
When Rome will have a new Leopard.

[1]L'vnion faincte = either "the false union" or "the sacred Union". It is another example of
Nostradamus' playing with the Old French sainct/fainct pun for sacred/false.
[2]Leopard. In heraldry the spotted, and sometimes winged, lion is called a leopard.

The family coat of arms of Pope John XXIII (1881–1963) was dominated
by a winged heraldic lion (which is a leopard). The prophet is also
accurate in his prediction of the short duration of John XXIII's papacy –
only four years. The **vessel** metaphor stands for two symbols: that of John
as the Patriarch of Venice and later that of him steering the **ship** of the
Holy See as Pope. In four short years John XXIII **changed** and **reformed**
the Catholic Church like no pope before him, launching the bark of the
Holy See into the modern era.

6 Q21

Quand ceux du polle artiq vnis enfemble,
En Orient grand effraieur[1] & crainte:
Efleu nouueau, fouftenu le grand
    tremble,
Rodes,[2] Bifance[3] de fang Barbare[4]
    taincte.

When those of the Northern pole are
    united together,
In the East will be great fear and
    dread:
The newly elected man is upheld – the
    great one trembles,
Rhodes, Byzantium will be stained with
    Barbarian [Libyan-Arab] blood.

[1]Old French for terror.
[2]Synecdoche for Greece.
[3]Byzantium, modern-day Turkey.
[4]Barbary Coast, modern-day Libya.

Greece and Turkey fought a bloody war back in 1921 and only narrowly
avoided a second full-scale encounter when Turkey invaded the island of
Cyprus in 1974. War was avoided again in 1988 and even as recently as
1995, when a dispute over an island (actually little more than a few
promontories) in the Aegean brought the two within a hairsbreadth of
military blows. This quatrain may warn of the next dangerous period for
a bloody Greco-Turkish conflict in our near future when the United
States and Russia (**those of the Northern pole**) are allies. In my last book
on Nostradamus I stated that the next threat of an outbreak of war could
take place around the time the United States and Canada ratified
NAFTA – putting this around the 1995 incident, which was fortunately
resolved in time by US diplomatic efforts.

The new man elected could be President Clinton, who in 1993 warned the North Korean leaders that if they used an atomic bomb they would see "the end of their country." Clinton will be **upheld** for a second term of office. After his 1996 re-election, a future Korean, Chinese, or Middle Eastern strongman will certainly tremble with fear, because I believe President Clinton is likely to carry out his threat if an Eastern nation uses nuclear weapons on its neighbors or supports the use of nuclear terrorism. The final line may link this war to an act of nuclear terrorism served up by a Libyan, Egyptian or Iranian submarine.

Quatrain Indexing Date: Q21 = 2021, the next date for a Greco-Turkish conflict?

6 Q22

Dedans la terre du grand temple celique,	**Within the earth of the great heavenly temple,**
Nepueu à Londres par paix faincte meurtry:	**Nephew at London – through a feigned peace – is murdered:**
La barque alors deuiendra scismatique,	**The bark [of the papacy] will then become schismatic,**
Liberté faincte sera au corn & cry.	**With horn call and cry, false Liberty will exist.**

There once existed a famous Roman temple to the god Apollo where the present-day Westminster Abbey now stands. The classical allusion therefore is to London and the British Empire. A royal nephew of the British crown will be invited to London and then murdered. At the same time a schism erupts in the Catholic Church. No murder of a royal in London has ever occurred. Le Pelletier tries to dress this obscurity with a Second Empire theme: Napoleon III, the **nephew** of Napoleon Bonaparte, is figuratively **murdered** by the ruinous terms of a trade treaty with Britain. The dress just doesn't fit.

6 Q23

D'esprit de regne munismes[1] descriées,	**Coins depreciated by the spirit of the kingdom,**
Et seront peuples esmeuz contre leur Roy:	**And people will be stirred up against their King:**
Paix, faict nouueau,[2] sainctes loix empirées,	**Peace, new saints, holy laws become worse,**
Rapis[3] onc fut en si tresdur arroy.	**Paris was never in such a harsh array.**

[1] from Latin *numisma* = coin; or Old French *munismes*, from Latin *munimines* = defenses, ramparts. The double pun being that from coins depreciated come the barricades of the French Revolution.
[2] *Faict nouveau*: complex pun for "new act/new falsehood/new saints."
[3] Anagram for *Paris*, using a play on the Latin *rapio* = I seize, snatch, tear away. This implies the chaos, rape and thievery of a future Paris.

In 1724 an anonymous detractor wrote that Nostradamus had composed this prophecy after the events of 1559, when the sudden death of Henry II left his heirs a royal coffer on the verge of bankruptcy. Certainly Paris was stirred to rebellion during the reign of the final Valois heir, Henry III, but the abuse of the holy laws by the Huguenots was modest in comparison to the complete trashing of Christian religion during the French Revolution.

The leaders of the Revolution, breastfed on the wit of Voltaire and the sincerity of Rousseau, rode the national wave of dissent over inflation and lack of bread to overthrow Louis XVI and the aristocracy in 1789. These writers became the *saints* of a new religion, the Cult of Reason, and the inspirational perpetrators of its counterpart, the Reign of Terror. It is possible that Nostradamus even names one of the more bloodthirsty leaders outright, *Saint*-Just, of the Committee of Public Safety, who said: "What constitutes a republic is the total destruction of the things opposing it." Saint-Just meant what he said – he became one of the main catalysts for the execution of thousands by guillotine.

6 Q24

Mars & le ſceptre ſe trouuera conioinct,	**Mars and the sceptre [of Jupiter] will meet in conjunction,**
Deſſoubz Cancer calamiteuſe guerre:	**A calamitous war under Cancer:**
Vn peu apres ſera nouueau Roy oingt,	**A short time afterward a new king will be anointed,**
Qui par long temps pacifiera la terre.	**Who will bring peace to the earth for a long time.**

Here we may see a promise of redemption for the world after the terrible natural disaster or war that brings terror down from the skies in July 1999 (*calamitous war under Cancer*). Wöllner targets this Mars/Jupiter conjunction for 21 June 2002 (the *JPL American Ephemeris* lists the conjunction in early April). The new king could be the long awaited Christian Messiah, or the Messiah of one of a half-dozen other religious traditions, who triggers Nostradamus' promised Millennium of Peace on Earth.

A few French Nostradamian royalists pray for the appearance of their long-awaited King Henry V of France.

Astrological Time Window

The next Jupiter/Mars conjunctions after April 2002 will be September–October 2004, December 2006 (in Sagittarius, which is ruled by Jupiter), February 2009 (in Aquarius), and April–May 2011 (in Aries, its closest conjunction to the Mayan calendar date for the end of time as we know it, in 2012).

6 Q25

Par Mars contraire fera la monarchie,	**By Mars contrary to the Monarchy,**
Du grand peſcheur en trouble ruyneux:	**Of the great fisherman will be in**
Ieune noir¹ rouge prendra la hierarchie,	**ruinous trouble:**
Les proditeurs iront iour bruyneux.²	**The young red [king] will take over**
	the government.
	The traitors will act on a misty day.

¹noir: cryptogram for roi.
²Old French bruineux = drizzly, misty.

Each line takes us a step closer to dating the month Napoleon seized power: **Mars**, with its color of war and revolution – ie **red** – overthrows the Bourbon monarchy, establishing that this quatrain concerns itself with the 18th century. Line 2 brings us to the late 1790s. The **great fisherman** is Pope Pius VI, already troubled by young Bonaparte's successful campaigns in Italy. Pius will soon suffer imprisonment and death in the year of the attempted coup, 1799. The **young red king**, of line 3 is Napoleon. He leads his fellow conspirators in the coup d'état in the month of November, much of which was known in the revolutionary calendar as Brumaire, "the month of mists" (**misty day**).

6 Q26

Quatre ans le ſiege quelque peu bien tiendra,	**For four years, the Seat will be held for some little good,**
Vn ſuruiendra libidineux¹ de vie:	**One will [then] accede to it who is more worldly.**
Rauenne & Pyſe, Veronne ſouſtiendront,	**Ravenna and Pisa, Verona will give support,**
Pour eſleuer la croix de Pape enuie.	**Desirous of elevating the Papal cross.**

¹Latin libidinosus = willful, arbitrary, capricious; worldly; lewd.

Nostradamus comes very close to predicting the four-and-a-half-year duration of Pope John XXIII's reign (28 October 1958–3 June 1963), and the new pope's popularity and attempts to help the Church move with the times (**elevate the cross**). The one who is **more worldly** depends on the translation of libidineux. The pure translation doesn't fit either man too well. Either the one who will **accede** is is down to earth and passionate rather than a remote and retreating priest, or **worldly** stands for one more cynically in sync with the corrupt, willful world of behind-the-door politicking. Pope John XXIII was known for his affability, knowledge of several languages, and his peasant's shrewdness and jovial humor when dealing with affairs of state. But his successor, Pope Paul VI, was a man whose urbane character and political sophistication was in great contrast to the humanity of Pope John. There are also rumors he had a homosexual lover.

It can be said that Paul VI had a complex and tortured personality; some contemporary cardinals described him as the Hamlet of the Vatican.

6 Q27

Dedans les isles de cinq fleuues à vn,	**Within the isles of five rivers to one,**
Par le croiſſant du grand Chyren Selin:	**Through the crescent of the great**
Par les bruynes de l'air fureur de l'vn,	**Chyren Selin:**
Six eſchapés, cachés fardeaux de lyn.	**Through the drizzles in the air the fury**
	of one,
	Six escape, hidden [in] loads of flax.

The **isles of five rivers** are metaphorical. Perhaps this alludes to 1 Q73's view of France threatened on five fronts by Charles V's son, Philip II of Spain. If so, these obscure details have something to reveal about the resolution of the Habsburg–Valois struggle for Italy after Henry II's disaster at St Quentin.

6 Q28

Le grand Celtique entrera dedans Rome,	**The great Celt will enter Rome,**
Menant amas d'exilés & bannis:	**Driving a mass of the exiled and**
Le grand paſteur mettra à mort tout	**banished:**
homme,	**The great Pastor [the Pope] will put to**
Que pour le coq eſtoient aux Alpes vnis.	**death every man,**
	Who was united at the Alps against [or
	for] the cock [of France].

The **great Celt** could identify another alternative future track for Henry II, or his heir Hercules Duc d'Alençon, defeating all Habsburg forces in Italy. It seems that the pope of that time will issue an order to put to death or excommunicate all imperialists.

Jaubert believes this one stands for the campaign of François de Guise in 1557, with its **mass of the exiled and banished** pouring out of Milan and Naples. He explains his way around line 3 by describing how Pope Paul IV protected all French allies from the forces of the Spanish Duke of Alva once Guise and his army were recalled to France. Line 4's ambiguous grammar can mean the pope **will put to death** the supporters **or** the enemies of France.

6 Q29

La veſue ſaincte entendant les nouuelles,	**The saintly widow hearing the news,**
De ſes rameaux mis en perplex &	**Of her offspring put in perplexity and**
trouble:	**trouble:**
Qui ſera duict appaiſer les querelles,	**He who will be instructed to appease**
Par ſon pourchas des razes fera comble.	**the quarrels,**
	By his pursuit of the shaven heads [they]
	will pile up beyond a full measure.

Catherine de' Medici was anything but a *saintly widow*, unless you prefer more aggressive types like St Elmo and St Michel. There's a better than 50-50 chance that Nostradamus intends this one for her. She was indeed a suffering widow, forced to bend an ear to the lamentations and troubles of her notorious sons. Upon the death of Charles IX, she summoned Henry III back from Poland to pacify the civil discord. Perhaps it would have been better if she had left Henry to rule in the Slavic backwater of Europe. Upon his return a three-way civil war would erupt between royalists behind Henry III (the Protestant claimant), Henry de Navarre, and the commander of the somewhat anti-royalist Catholic League of Henry de Guise and his brother the Cardinal de Guise. The cardinal (a *shaven head*) and his brother would be assassinated in 1588. The blade of another *shaven head* would add Henry III to the pile of slaughtered royals in the following year.

6 Q30

Par l'apparence de faincte faincteté,	**Through the appearance of faked sanctity,**
Sera trahy aux ennemis le fiege:	**The siege will be betrayed to the enemies:**
Nuict qu'on cuidoit dormir en feureté,	**In the night when they believed [they could] sleep in security,**
Pres de Braban marcheront ceux du Liege.	**Near Brabant will march those of Liege.**

This has something to do with the 80-year war for Dutch Independence fought in the Spanish Netherlands between Dutch Protestants and their Spanish masters. The city and bishopric of **Liège** is east of Brabant. There was no siege at **Liège**, but the Spanish failed in their siege of **Leiden** in 1574.

World War II buffs pin this one on Hitler's treacherous surprise invasion of neutral Holland in 1940.

6 Q31

Roy trouuera ce qu'il defiroit tant,	**The King will find that which he desires so much,**
Quand le Prelat fera reprins à tort:	**When the Prelate will be wrongly taken:**
Refponce au duc[1] le rendra mal content,	**The reply to the Duce will make him angry,**
Qui dans Milan mettre plufieurs à mort.	**It [the king's action] will put several to death in Milan.**[2]

[1]Duke: or in Italian, *Il Duce*, the nickname of Mussolini.
[2]Alternative: He in Milan will put several to death.

Nostradamus may have recorded the bloodless coup that precipitated Mussolini's execution when he said, **The King will find that which he desires so much . . . The reply to the Duce will make him angry.** King Victor Emmanuel III was no friend of the Italian premier, **Il Duce**. The Allied invasion of Italy in 1943 finally gave the king the political clout and the satisfaction to dismiss Mussolini in person. The result is related in the last line. This could presage Mussolini's execution of coup leaders, including his foreign minister, Ciano, after Il Duce's return to power. Or it is the death of Mussolini and his own lieutenants in Milan in 1945, the outcome of Victor Emmanuel's efforts to have Mussolini thrown out of power in 1943.

Quatrain Indexing Date: Q31 = 1931, when Mussolini was at the peak of his popularity in Italy – but this year marks the fatal rise of Hitler, who would be his undoing.

6 Q32

Par trahyſon de verges à mort battu,	**Beaten to death by rods for treason,**
Prins ſurmonté ſera par ſon deſordre:	**Captured he will be surmounted**
Conſeil friuole au grand captif ſentu,	**through his disorder:**
Nez par fureur quand Berich[1] viendra mordre.	**The odor of frivolous counsel exhaled at the great captive,**
	His nose in fury when Berich will come to bite it off.

[1] Anagram for *Reich* (after dropping the B), standing for the Holy Roman Empire.

Line 1 describes a form of ancient Roman execution for disobedient soldiers. Perhaps it is used here as a poetic device to describe the assassination of Wallenstein, the overbearing yet highly successful commander of the Imperial forces during the bloodiest phase of the Thirty Years War. By 1633 Wallenstein was ignoring the orders of Emperor Ferdinand and starting to pursue his own diplomatic offensive for a negotiated settlement with the Lutherans. In early 1634 the emperor issued a secret order to capture him for questioning. This was to be difficult for Wallenstein had exacted an oath of allegiance from his colonels, so the option to kill the emperor's finest general was approved with great reluctance. Nostradamus rails against this decision in line 3. At Pilsen the Emperor's hit men caught up with Wallenstein and his escort, who had stopped to rest on their flight towards Saxony, and brutally murdered them all. An Irish mercenary broke into Wallenstein's bedchamber and skewered the unarmed and half-dressed general with a pike. The mercenary then rolled the corpse up in a blanket and dragged it unceremoniously down the stairs (**surmounted in his disorder**).

Line 4 may blend a gruesome fad of those times with the anagram **Berich**. It was common practice to slice off the noses and ears of captives and string them together to dangle off the victor's broadrimmed hat. In colloquial terms, Nostradamus uses **nose** for one's sense or intelligence. By killing Wallenstein, the emperor of the First "Reich" (**Berich**) has cut off (**come to bite . . . off**) his best military commander. In other words he has cut off his **nose** to spite his own face.

6 Q33

Sa main[1] derniere par Alus[2] fanguinaire	*His power finally through bloody Alus,*
Ne fe pourra par la mer guarentir:	*He will be unable to protect himself*
Entre deux fleuues craindre main militaire,	*by sea:*
Le noir[3] l'ireux[4] le fera repentir.	*Between two rivers [he will] fear the*
	military hand,
	The black one will make the angry
	one repent of it.

[1]*main* = hand; (figuratively) one's power.
[2]Enigmatic proper name. Could be an anagram for "Saul."
[3]*noir* = black, or a near anagram for *roi* = king; thus black king.
[4]Old French *ireux* = angry, furious, irate.

The enigma *Alus* has links with 2 Q62's *Mabus* or (M)a(l)us.

The rest of the prophecy insinuates that, once sanctions against Iraq are lifted, Abu Nidal (*Mabus* operatives) may escalate terrorist activity on Saddam Hussein's behalf, using Iraq's worldwide embassy network. But this move will eventually bring apocalyptic consequences to both. The quatrain implies that Saddam Hussein (**the angry one**) is the man who is **unable to protect himself by sea** (his defenses proved useless against sea-launched cruise missiles both during and after the Gulf War of 1991). Saddam, the Mesopotamian leader **between two rivers** (the Tigris and Euphrates) who fears **the military hand** of the West, may also need to fear the **hand** or **power** of bloody **Alus**, the **black one**, who is someone other than Abu Nidal. He could be a future black-robed Ayatollah from Iran.

6 Q34

Du feu volant la machination,	*From the machine of flying fire,*
Viendra troubler au grand chef affiegez:	*It will come to trouble the besieged*
Dedans fera telle fedition,	*chief:*
Qu'en defefpoir feront les profligez.[1]	*Within there will be such sedition,*
	That the dissolute ones will be in
	despair.

[1]Latin *profligatus* = profligate, wanton, dissolute.

Line 1 describes an intermediate or intercontinental missile, smart bomb, or a low-flying cruise missile. In line 2 a **besieged** terrorist **chief**, perhaps Saddam Hussein of Iraq, faces a high-tech apocalypse as retribution for wars or acts of nuclear terrorism against the technologically dangerous armed forces of the Northern bloc.

Lines 3 and 4 picture the aftermath of sedition and civil war within the terrorist-harboring nation. This prophecy may have already been fulfilled during the Gulf War of 1991, when a *machine of flying fire* targeted every reinforced bunker suspected of protecting Saddam Hussein and his generals. The final line fits the account of Hussein during the month-long Allied bombing campaign, as he moved around the suburbs of Baghdad like a petty political exile, sleeping in safe houses. Unfortunately for the Iraqi people, their dictator survived the Allied onslaught and successfully crushed the two civil wars that followed in Kurdish Northern and Shi'ite Southern Iraq.

6 Q35

Pres de Rion[1] & proche à la blanche laine,	*Near the [Bear constellations] and*
Aries, Taurus, Cancer, Leo, la Vierge,	*near the "white wool" [the Milky*
Mars, Iupiter, le Sol ardra grand plaine,	*Way],*
Bois & citez, lettres cachez au cierge.	*Aries, Taurus, Cancer, Leo, Virgo,*
	Mars, Jupiter and the Sun will burn
	the great plain,
	Woods and cities, letters [or learning]
	hidden in the candle light.

[1]Probably a misprint or cryptogram for *Trion*, from Latin *Triones* = the constellations of Ursa Major and Minor.

Mars, Jupiter, and the sun passed through these constellations, sometimes in conjunction, from April through August 1987, and April through August 1991. The summer of 1987 hosted unprecedented drought and brushfires in Provence and the French and Spanish Riviera regions.

The comet Hale-Bopp will transit the northern skies in spring of 1997 near the **Bear constellations** of Ursa Major and Minor and through part of the Milky Way. A Mars–Jupiter–Sun conjunction will occur in March 1998. The three planets will be together in Aries in April 2011. We could expect a major drought from March through September of that year.

Quatrain Indexing Date: Q35 = 2035, which may see the apocalyptic droughts of global warming in full swing: see 3 Q34.

6 Q36

Ne bien ne mal par bataille terreftre,	*Neither good nor evil through*
Ne paruiendra aux confins de Peroufe:	*terrestrial battle,*
Rebeller Pife, Florence voir mal eftre,[1]	*Will reach the confines of Perugia:*
Roy nuict bleffé fur mulet à noire houfe.	*Pisa to rebel, Florence to see an evil*
	Being,
	King by night wounded on a he-mule
	with black saddle cloth.

[1]Old French *eftre* = to be; being, existence; creature.

The geographical stage is clearly set but the characters and action are obscure. Take your pick for the *evil Being* in Florence. The Old French meanings for *mal estre* can describe an evil state of being, felt inside one-self or hurled as a judgment at another. This *evil Being* may be the one who wounds a king in line 4. Nostradamus would have learned during his travels that Pisa was sold to Tuscany in 1405. Perhaps he saw a rebellion of Pisa in a future time near his own? It didn't happen.

With so little to go on, one cannot rule out the possibility that this *king* is to be taken not literally but as a metaphor for Nostradamus him-self. Perhaps he is giving us a historic rather than prophetic account of his travels in Italy during his self-imposed exile to avoid the Inquisition from 1537 through 1544. If so, maybe he runs into a rebellion of apothecaries and doctors in Pisa. Then he is slighted by someone in Florence, perhaps an Inquisitor, and we see him, heart wounded, escaping by night on his mule.

6 Q37

L'œuure ancienne Je paracheuera,	**The ancient work will be accomplished,**
Du toict cherra Jur le grand mal ruyne:	**And from the roof evil ruin will fall on**
Innocent faict mort on accuJera:	**the great man:**
Nocent caiché taillis[1] à la bruyne.	**They will accuse an innocent, being**
	dead, of the deed:
	The guilty one is hidden in the misty
	copse.

[1]Old French copse, a thicket of small trees and bushes.

Over four hundred years before President Kennedy's assassination in Dallas, Texas, in 1963, Nostradamus seems to be aware of the first few shots that may have come from Oswald's gun perched in a window on the sixth floor of the Texas School Book Depository Building. But he may have foreseen more than one assassin.

Over a dozen witnesses to the assassination in Dealey Plaza said they heard the fatal shot issue from the Grassy Knoll, a small grass-covered hill crested by a fence and trees which was in front and to the right of the passing motorcade. In the controversial documentary *The Men Who Killed Kennedy* (Bill Kurtis Production, 1988), a computer-enhanced version of a photograph taken in the direction of the Grassy Knoll 0.06 seconds after the fatal shot, dimly distinguishes a man dressed as a police officer aiming a rifle at the president. A puff of smoke is clearly displayed. A man stands to his left, presumably a spotter. The man standing on the grass to the right and in front of the gunman was later identified as Gordon Arnold, a soldier on leave. He testified to the FBI that he was concussed by the fatal bullet fired behind his ear and that he was assaulted by the mystery police officer, who threatened his life if he spoke of the incident. Arnold's testimony, along with those of dozens of other witnesses at the Grassy Knoll, was ignored both by the FBI and later by the Warren Commission, which was established to conduct an investigation. Within three years of President Kennedy's assassination, 17 witnesses testified that a shot had been fired from the direction of the Grassy Knoll. Others who refuted the Warren Commission's verdict of a lone gunman died in that same period. Two committed suicide, three died in car accidents, three suffered fatal heart attacks, six were shot, one had his throat cut, and one died from a karate chop to the throat. Only one death out of 17 was attributed to natural causes. An article in the London *Sunday Times* analyzed the odds in this bizarre sequence of deaths. The newspaper report concluded that the chance that 17 witnesses to the same crime would die within three years was one thousand trillion to one.

In 1988 Bill Kurtis found Gordon Arnold and showed him the computer enhanced blowup of the photograph. While on camera he positively identified the soldier as himself, as well as the policeman who had assaulted and threatened him. Thinking out loud he theorized why he had survived the strange rash of deaths while other witnesses on the Grassy Knoll had not. A few days after the assassination he had been shipped off to a remote Air Force base in Alaska. Perhaps the men who really killed Kennedy had lost track of him.

Nostradamus implicates a man other than Oswald as the real murderer of Kennedy. The accused may have been telling the truth when he claimed he was "a patsy." Line 4's Old French word *taillis* literally means **copse** or thicket of small trees and bushes. This comes even closer to the image of the mysterious figure aiming his rifle beneath the copse of trees on the Grassy Knoll. One can only wonder if the prophet had peered into the brass-bowl of prescient waters and conjured up this fuzzy, computer-enhanced photo of the real assassin *in the misty copse*.

See Index: Kennedy assassination.

6 Q38

Aux profligez de paix les ennemis,	*The enemies of peace, the dissolute ones,*
Apres auoir l'Italie superee:	*After having overcome Italy:*
Noir sanguinaire, rouge sera commis,	*The bloody black one, red, will be the commissioner,*
Feu, sang verser, eaue de sang couloree.	*Fire, blood to pour, water the color of blood.*

In a definitive interview held in 1985, Abu Nidal gave a new and more sinister meaning to his Arabic name, which in hip street language would be "the father who is real bad," as in cool. He kindled Western fears by proudly describing himself as "Abu Nidal, this evil spirit which moves around only by night . . . causing them nightmares," or as "more dangerous than an atomic bomb." He openly admits that his greatest dream is to "ignite a huge fire in the Middle East."

The identity of the Third Antichrist is obscured even more by the fact that Abu Nidal is the name of both the founder and the terrorist organization itself. Of all the candidates examined in the quatrains, Abu Nidal (man or organization) is the most likely to succeed in a future act of nuclear terrorism in Italy, if his psychotic threats are not taken seriously and prevented.

6 Q39

L'enfant du regne par paternelle prinſe,	**The infant of the realm through the**
Expolié ſera pour deliurer:	**capture of his father,**
Aupres du lac Traſimen l'azur prinſe,	**Will be plundered for the sake of**
La troupe hoſtaige pour trop fort	**delivering him:**
s'enyurer.[1]	**Near the Lake of Perugia the azure**
	captive,
	In order that the hostage troop gets
	too elated.

[1]Old French *eniurer* = to get intoxicated; (figuratively) to be elated.

This quatrain seems to be a retroactive preamble for Henry II during his Spanish captivity. The young Duc d'Orléans was sent as a hostage to replace his father Francis I, who had been captured by the Spanish at the Battle of Pavia in 1525. *Expolié* can also mean "deprived," a good description of the adolescent future Henry II, who never forgave his father or got over the bitterness he felt during his incarceration.

6 Q40

Grand de Magonce pour grande ſoif	**To quench the great thirst the great**
eſtaindre,	**one of Mainz,**
Sera priué de ſa grand dignité:	**Will be deprived of his great dignity:**
Ceux de Cologne ſi fort le viendront	**Those of Cologne will come to**
plaindre,	**grumble so loud,**
Que le grand groppe[1] au Ryn ſera getté.	**That the great rump will be jettisoned**
	into the Rhine.

[1]Low Latin *groppa* = haunches, rump.

Nostradamus predicts an event coinciding with the final dissolution of the Holy Roman Empire on 6 August 1806. The **great one of Mainz** would be the Archbishop of that city, who was one of the electors of the Empire. No archbishop of Mainz was forced to step down from his post during the 16th or 17th centuries. Certainly the men holding this position during the terrible days of the Thirty Years War had to abandon their throne to take cover from the numerous attacks and sackings visited on the city.

Events become clearer the farther forward we go. Mainz was occupied by the French Revolutionary armies in 1797, and was later parceled out by the Holy Roman Emperor to the French through a secret clause of the Treaty of Camporformio. Afterwards the Elector of Mainz continued to rule territory on the right bank of the Rhine, and remained in power until the Holy Roman Empire was formally abolished by Napoleon in 1806 – figuratively speaking, when Napoleon **jettisoned** the **great rump . . . into the Rhine** and replaced it with his German Confederation.

Leoni believes the **great thirst** is the desire of another German city state, during the final three years of the Imperium, to take on the title of Elector since this **great dignity** had been dropped by Mainz. The Elector and Archbishop of neighboring Cologne seems to be grumbling about the loss of the moribund Imperium. I believe that by abolishing the Electors and the First Reich, and bringing the German states together into a con-federation, Napoleon offered the first water to quench the **great thirst** in the region for a unification of Germany. He said as much while reflecting on his actions in exile on St Helena. In his memoirs Napoleon records a successful prophecy: that Germany would be united sometime in the 19th century. The Second Reich was formed in 1871, 50 years after his death.

6 Q41

Le second chef de regne d'Annemarc,	**The second chief of the realm of Annemark,**
Par Ceux de Frise & l'isle Britannique,	**Through those of Frisia [Holland] and [of] the British isle,**
Fera despendre plus de cent mille marc,	**Will spend more than one hundred thousand marks,**
Vain exploicter voyage en Italique.	**To exploit in vain the voyage to Italy.**

Annemark, the unsolved cryptogram, returns again (see 4 Q27). For a few brief years England and Frisia (a northern province of the Spanish Netherlands) were "ruled" by Philip II of Spain, thanks to his marriage to Queen Mary Tudor of England. Scholars usually try to contain the sub-ject of this quatrain within Nostradamus' time, but I have to agree with Cheetham that using the term **British isle** for England takes us beyond 1707, the year the kingdom of England was formally renamed Britain.

Line 2 definitely parallels the subject of 4 Q89 – William of Orange from Friesland (**Frisia**) sailing with his Dutch army across the channel to successfully invade England during the Glorious Revolution of 1688–89. Line 3 may be some future accounting of the expenses incurred by

William. But this still doesn't explain the mysterious **Annemark**. And William's fleet certainly didn't take a detour to Italy.

Cheetham thinks Annemark is Denmark, but this lead unwraps few answers. Leoni takes us back to Nostradamus' time because he thinks **Annemark** is the Holy Roman Emperor Maximilian II, the nephew of Charles V. Since Maximilian had Protestant sympathies, Leoni figures that Nostradamus expected him to be persuaded by Protestants in England and Holland to invade Italy from the north. This of course never happened.

6 Q42

A logmyon[1] fera laiffé le regne,	**To Hercules will be left the kingdom,**
Du grand Selin[2] qui plus fera de faict:	**The great Selin who will in fact do more:**
Par les Italies eftendra fon enfeigne,	**Throughout Italy will he spread out his banner,**
Regi fera par prudent contrefaict.	**It will be ruled by a prudent deformed one.**

[1] Apparent Nostradamus term for *l'Ogmion* = Ogmios, the Celtic legendary hero often equated with Hercules.
[2] Greek *selēnē* = moon or crescent; in this case an allusion to the monogram of Henry II which has the crescent of his mistress, Diane de Poitiers, hanging on the bar of his letter *H* to make (Chyren) Selin, *Henry Crescent*.

We return to the alternative future that never was. **Hercules** is the Duc d'Alençon, the youngest son of Henry II, who is left the kingdom. Before Henry II dies he will conquer all of Italy. The **prudent deformed one** is some viceroy that also apparently never was.

6 Q43

Long temps fera fans eftre habitée,	**For a long time will it remain uninhabited,**
Où Signe & Marne autour vient arroufer:	**Around where the Seine and the Marne comes to flow through:**
De la Tamife[1] & martiaux tentée,	**Tried by the Thames and soldiers,**
Deceuez les gardes en cuidant repoufer.	**The guards deceived in believing it repulsed.**

[1] A Nostradamus puzzle: a) the River Thames, used as a synecdoche for London, England; b) La Tamise, a town in Flanders near Antwerp.

The first two lines are a slight exaggeration, if applicable to Paris in the closing days of the Battle of France. By 10 June Paris was declared an open city. The Germans arrived to find it nearly deserted; over four-fifths of the population had fled. If the prophet foresaw the events in his roiling waters he would have witnessed streets devoid of people and the shutters

of nearly every shop and bistro closed. Those Parisians who had not abandoned the capital stayed indoors, waiting for the first units of Hitler's
legions to goose-step and um-pah-pah their way down the boulevards
with military pomp and sore heels. The day after the armistice, when
Hitler (the frustrated architect and artist) made his famous three-hour
whirlwind tour of the architectural sites of Paris, he experienced a similar
scene – as devoid of people as in his own watercolor paintings. The
populace abandoned the streets to slight the Führer.

Lines 3 and 4 move us a few years ahead to the British raids of Hitler's
Atlantic Wall around Dieppe and Calais in 1942. Because of these raids
the German **soldiers** and **guards** were deceived into believing the Allies
would target the Calais region, rather than Normandy, for their long-
awaited invasion.

Quatrain Indexing Date: 6 Q43 = 6 June (6th month) 1943; a near
miss for the Normandy Landings on 6/6/44.

6 Q44

De nuict par Nantes l'Iris apparoiftra,	**By night through Nantes the rainbow**
Des artz marins fufciteront la pluye:	**will appear,**
Arabiq goulfre grand claffe parfondra,[1]	**The marine arts will rouse the rain:**
Vn monftre[2] en Saxe[3] naiftra d'ours[4] &	**In the Arabian Gulf a great fleet will**
truye.	**plunge to the bottom,**
	A monster in Saxony will be born of a
	bear and a sow.

[1]The verb can alternatively imply a fleet being sunk.
[2]A monster, or a divine omen. In Nostradamus' time the birth of two-headed animals or
children was viewed as a divine omen of civil strife and disaster.
[3]Saxony, the eastern portion of Germany.
[4]Bear (the symbol of Berlin and of Russia).

We return to the theme of 5 Q62: a future threat of an Islamic submarine
attack on a Western fleet either in the Arabian Sea or the Persian Gulf
via the Strait of Hormuz. The riddle of meteorological magic taking place
off the French coast at the mouth of the Loire river, not far from Nantes,
remains to be solved. The imagery of line 1 reminds me of the computerized wizardry seen in a Prime Star satellite television commercial. Perhaps
in his nocturnal watch Nostradamus saw people sitting in front of our
magical, mysterious, and sometimes mind-draining TV boxes.

A man from the 16th century might describe a diving fleet of submarines as vessels that **plunge to the bottom.** Egypt is one Islamic nation
whose coastline encircles what could figuratively be called an **Arabian
gulf**, the Red Sea. The Mubarak secular government of Egypt is openly
seeking to replace its aging Soviet-built submarine fleet with the ultra-
modern Dolphin class attack submarines built by Germany (or **Saxony** by

synecdoche). Perhaps the **monster** is Nostradamus' attempt to describe this fantastically weird animal born in a Bremen dry dock. Monstrously deformed animals or children nearly always figure as omens for some military, social, or ecological disaster to come. If Mubarak's government is overthrown and Egypt becomes another fanatic Islamic state, a fleet of Dolphin submarines could be used to attack Western shipping.

6 Q45

Le gouuerneur du regne bien ſçauant,	**The governor of the realm – in the full**
Ne conſentir voulant au faict Royal:	**knowledge of [but],**
Mellile claſſe par le contraire vent,	**Not wishing to consent to the royal**
Le remettra à ſon plus deſloyal.	**deed:**
	The fleet [or army] of Mellilla
	through a contrary wind,
	Will deliver him to his most disloyal
	one.

Melilla is a Spanish possession on the Mediterranean coast of Morocco. One significant historical incident took place there that might have come to Nostradamus' attention. On 18 July 1936 conservative army chiefs at Melilla launched a revolt against the Spanish Republican government that soon spread to army garrisons across the Strait of Gibraltar into Spain. No fewer than three meanings are applicable here for Nostradamus' often-used word *classe*: the Greek *klassis*, for a fracture (in this case a "brake" from the government) by an *army* (Latin *classis*) commander. Their rebellion spreads poetically like a *fleet* (*classe*) sailing on *a contrary wind* from Spanish Morocco to Spain to launch the Spanish Civil War. The rebel military junta will deliver Francisco Franco from his exile to the Canary Islands to lead the invasion of the Spanish mainland.

6 Q46

Vn iuſte ſera en exil renuoyé,	**A just one will be sent back again into**
Par peſtilence aux confins de Nonſeggle,[1]	**exile,**
Reſponce au rouge le fera deſuoyé,	**Through pestilence to the confines of**
Roy retirant à la Rane[2] & à l'aigle.	**Nonseggle,**
	His response to the red one will cause
	him to go astray,
	King withdrawing to the Frog and the
	eagle.

[1]*Nonſeggle*: compound cryptogram made from the towns of *Mons*, Belgium, and *Riegel*, in the German Confederation, where Louis XVIII resided during both his first and second exiles from France: *Mons* = Nons + *seggle* = Riegel.
[2]Latin *rana* = a frog, symbol of the Merovingian kings of France – thus for Nostradamus a metaphor for any great or rightful French king of noble birth.

Lines 1 and 3 could target this for Louis XVIII during the 100 days he was sent back into exile because of his limpid *response* to the return of the former Jacobin *red* deposed French emperor, Napoleon Bonaparte. Louis sent his army in piecemeal confrontations to stop Napoleon's insignificant band of 1,000 soldiers who had escaped from the island of Elba.

Up to now, the enigma **Nonseggle** has remained an unsolved cryptogram. But I would apply it to towns or places of Louis XVIII's two exiles. It could be a compound of two cities, Mons in Belgium and Riegel in the German Confederation. Together they can make a classic cryptogram – **Nonseggle** from Mons-riegel. During his first exile Louis stayed in the German town of Riegel in 1796. He stayed twice in Mons (first in 1791, during his first exile, and again in June 1815).

The final line would imply his promised return by using animal metaphors to describe the French royal houses and their usurpers. Withdrawing from Belgium after Napoleon's defeat at Waterloo, Louis returns to reestablish the rule of the Bourbon monarchy, symbolized by the Merovingian frog metaphor usually applied by Nostradamus to rightful French royalty. Louis would be successful in blending Bonapartist (*eagle*) and Royalist (Merovingian *frog*) factions in a national reconciliation.

6 Q47

Entre deux monts les deux grans aſſemblés	**The two great ones assembled between two mountains**
Delaiſſeront leur ſimulté ſecrette:	**Will abandon their secret animosity:**
Brucelle & Dolle par Langres accablés,	**Brussels and Dôle by Langres overwhelmed,**
Pour à Malignes executer leur peſte.	**To execute their pestilence at Mechelen.**

Too many military maneuvers, truces, and wars have plagued the eastern frontiers of France and Flanders in the last four centuries for me to make a clear call. Still, I would say this stands for the Spanish Netherlands, and the portions of misery and bloodshed suffered by the Imperial possessions of Franche-Comté, Lorraine, and Burgundy during the final half of the Thirty Years War. **Mechelen** is a village five miles east of Maastricht, which suffered a siege in 1632. Dôle was also invested in 1636. Plagues (*pestilence*) within besieged cities were common.

6 Q48

La ſaincteté trop faincte & ſeductiue,	**Sanctity too false and seductive,**
Accompaigné d'vne langue diſerte:	**Accompanied by an eloquent tongue:**
La cité vieille & Parme trop haſtiue,	**The old city and Parma too hasty,**
Florence & Sienne rendront plus deſertes.	**Florence and Siena they will further render an uninhabited desert.**

This could cover the papal intrigues (and character) of Charles de Guise, Cardinal de Lorraine, leading up to the final Italian expedition of Henry II in 1557. The rest sounds retroactive. Or perhaps Nostradamus has fallen victim to history's repetitions. In this case the devastation visited on the environs of Florence and Siena during the earlier stages of the Hapsburg–Valois wars before 1555 was not repeated during the final French expedition in 1557, although the Duchy of Parma was threatened by the French.

6 Q49

De la partie de Mammer[1] grand Pontife,	Of the warlike party, the great Pontiff
Subiuguera les confins du Dannube:[2]	Will subjugate the frontiers of the
Chasser les croix par fer[3] raffe ne riffe,[4]	Danube:
Captifz, or, bagues plus de cent mille	To pursue the cross through the
rubes.	crooked cross of iron,
	Captives, gold, jewels, more than one
	hundred thousand rubies.

[1]Mammer = a) Mamers, Sabine name for Mars, the God of War; b) Mammertini, citizens of Messina, Sicily.
[2]This is one of the few times Nostradamus does not use the archaic Hister to describe the River Danube. The reason is that this is meant for the river, whereas the other applications are meant for Adolf Hitler.
[3]Iron, steel; pointed weapon.
[4]raffe ne riffe = Provençal de rifla ou de raffa = by hook or by crook: a pun blending the crooked staff of the pope with the crooked cross of the Nazi swastika.

In Nostradamus' time the Danube was also known by its Latin name, the Ister, sometimes spelled with a silent H. As we have seen in other verses the chief of **the warlike party** is said to be born on the banks of the Danube and named Hister (see 2 Q24, 4 Q68, 5 Q29, P15, and P31). Adolf Hitler was born in Braunau on the River Inn, near the Danube. He spent his early childhood and youth along its banks, in nearby Linz. Hitler would later subjugate those countries one could consider to be within the frontiers of the Danube. Czechoslovakia and Austria were swallowed up by Nazi Germany, and Hungary and Romania became Nazi satellites.

The swastika-symbol of the Nazi Party was commonly described as a **crooked cross**. The word *fer* in French can also mean **iron** giving the description another layer of visual meaning, as if Nostradamus had seen Hitler's image. Along with the swastika armband, Hitler wore the Order of the German Iron Cross on his jacket. The double meaning of **crooked** as evil is not missed by Nostradamus, who foresaw the vast crimes of the Nazis and the untold wealth they robbed from their victims. He points a damning finger at Pope Pius XII as an accessory to their crimes.

It is now widely acknowledged by historians that Pope Pius XII was sympathetic to the Fascist cause and that, by the time he became pope, he had a reputation for being able to deal successfully with Fascist governments. As Vatican secretary of state, he had played a major role in concluding a Vatican treaty with Nazi Germany in 1933. Despite world-wide pressure, the pope refused to excommunicate either Hitler or Mussolini during the war. In communications with his French and German clergy concerning the papal position on "just wars," his arguments were so cleverly constructed that the leading priest of these two opposing nations could each assure their governments that their military endeavors had the Church's blessing. In justification of his reluctance to condemn the German invasion of Poland, Pius XII said, "There are 40 million Catholics in the Reich. What would they be exposed to after such an act by the Holy See?"

It seems a certain prophet from Galilee, but not his representative on Earth, was ready to be crucified for his flock. We can only wonder what the Reich would have been exposed to if, after the invasion of Poland, Pius had excommunicated Hitler and Mussolini and ordered all Catholic citizens of Germany and its Axis allies to boycott their governments and desert their armed forces in peaceful acts of civil disobedience. Maybe World War II would have ended in the autumn of 1939 before it got under way.

It is also becoming clear the holy offices of the Vatican under Pius helped many Nazi war criminals escape from Europe after the war.

6 Q50

Dedans le puys feront trouués les oz,
Sera l'inceft commis par la maratre:[1]
L'eftat changé on querra bruict & loz,
Et aura Mars attendant pour fon aftre.

Inside the pit they will be found the bones,
It will be incest committed by the [stepmother]:
The state transformed, they will gather renown, rumor and praise,
And they will have Mars attending as their star and celebrity.

[1] *maratre* usually means "mother-in-law," but the incest theme would make "stepmother" more applicable.

Line 1 sketches the scene of White Russian soldiers and investigators roving the countryside outside of Ekaterinburg, Siberia, searching for evidence to support rumors that the remains of Czar Nicholas Romanov and his family were buried in the pit of an abandoned mineshaft. The use of *maratre* (mother-in-law) for **incest** is confusing. Perhaps **incest** is to be taken figuratively for the intrigues of the great pretender, Anna Anderson, who claimed to be the Archduchess Anastasia. Genetic testing of the remains uncovered at Ekaterinburg finally closed the case on her as a fraud. By line 3 Nostradamus gets back on track again. The Russian Empire was **transformed** into the Soviet Union, which became the staging area for the popular spread of Marxism around the world between 1920 and 1950. The final line describes the communist symbol of the red star.

6 Q51

Peuple aſſemblé, voir nouueau expectacle,[1]
Princes & Roys[2] par pluſieurs aſſiſtans:
Pilliers faillir, murs, mais comme miracle
Le Roy ſauué & trente des inſtants.

The people gathered to see a new spectacle,
Princes and Kings among many onlookers:
Pillars and walls fall, but as if by a miracle
The King and thirty of those present are saved.

[1]Prosthesis of *spectacle* = spectacle.
[2]*Princes & Roys* = Princes and Kings. Nostradamus either meant this literally or applied these titles to modern leaders. The latter application would include Nazi Party officials and government functionaries.

Karl Ernst Krafft, a Swiss citizen and a fervent believer in the Nazi Party, moved to Germany to offer his already well-known and respected astrological and intuitive services. While working for Himmler's Secret Service as an astrological consultant, Krafft submitted a paper at the beginning of November 1939 warning of an assassination threat hovering over Hitler's stars between 7 and 10 November. Horoscopes on the Führer were forbidden, so the paper was filed and locked away. On the evening of 8 November Hitler made his annual speech at the Munich Beer Hall, the scene of the 1923 Putsch. Mainstream historians say that pressing business forced him to cut short his speech. Hitler himself would relate to intimates that he felt a strong premonition to leave. Eight minutes after Hitler and a number of other key Nazi leaders left the hall, a time bomb hidden in a pillar behind the rostrum exploded, killing 7 and wounding 63. On hearing about the Führer's close brush with death, Krafft reminded Himmler's office of his forecast, and where it was filed. At this the Gestapo arrested him and brought him to Berlin. He was released to Josef Goebbels, who set him to work on the Nostradamus project as chief interpreter. It is said that the above quatrain helped Krafft pinpoint the time and place of the assassination attempt.

6 Q52

En lieu du grand qui ſera condemné,
De priſon hors ſon amy en ſa place:
L'eſpoir Troyen en ſix mois ioinct, mort nay,
Le Sol à l'vrne ſeront prins fleuues en glace.

In place of the great one who will be condemned,
Outside the prison his friend in his place:
The Trojan hope in six months joined, still-born,
The Sun in Aquarius, rivers will be frozen in ice.

The true fate of the young Dauphin, Louis XVII, is still an unsolved mystery. Official history says he died in the Temple prison from injuries and neglect in 1795. The X-Filers of the early 19th century believed he escaped and a deaf mute was substituted in his place. The **Trojan hope** is the Dauphin, for legend says the royal house of France is descended from ancient Trojan kings. This myth had its strongest support during the French Romantic movement of the early to mid-19th century. Soon after the last pretenders to the lost Louis XVII had petered out, Hector Berlioz staged his highly popular opera *Les Troyens*. Nicollaud (1914) believed that **Trojan hope** describes the means by which little Louis was spirited out of the Temple prison, in a wooden casket. You might say this was a reverse-Trojan-horse maneuver. Some believe he was taken to Rome where he lived under the care of priests in a secret hideout in the Vatican. Official records cite the death of the true Dauphin (or his substitute) on 8 June 1795. If the real Dauphin escaped, then according to Nostradamus he died in Rome six months later in January 1796, when *the Sun* is *in Aquarius*.

6 Q53

Le grand Prelat Celtique à Roy fufpect,	**The great Prelate of the Celts suspected by the King,**
De nuict par cours fortira hors du regne:	**By night by flight he will go out of the kingdom:**
Par duc fertile à fon grand Roy, Bretaigne,	**Through a fertile duke to his great King, Britain,**
Bifance à Cipres & Tunes infufpect.	**Byzantium to Cyprus and Tunis unsuspected.**

A French Cardinal gets into trouble with his king. Is it one of the de Guise family? Neither Charles de Guise, Cardinal de Lorraine, or Louis, Cardinal de Guise of the next generation, was forced to flee to England, where, according to Nostradamus, he would catch the first fast galley to Tunis via the Ottoman Turkish capital at Istanbul and Cyprus. This quatrain, like its subject, is sailing to nowhere.

6 Q54

Au poinct du iour au fecond chant du coq,	**At daybreak at the second crowing of the cock,**
Ceulx de Tunes, de Fez, & de Bugie:	**Those of Tunisia, of Fez, and of Bourgie:**
Par les Arabes captif le Roy Maroq,	**By the Arabs, the king of Morocco captured,**
L'an mil fix cens 7 fept, de Liturgie.	**In the year sixteen hundred and seven, of the Liturgy.**

Leoni makes a compelling argument that this one is a clear failure for the imminent collapse of the Ottoman Empire and the Barbary Corsairs, under Christian and Persian military pressures by 1607. He does not believe one can add years onto the word **Liturgy**, as it is used here only for scanning and rhyme and therefore is intended only for that year. Robb, Jochmans, and Noorbergen generally take the opposite view and count ahead to 1954 and the future overthrow of the Moroccan Sultan Sidi Mohammed ben Youssef.

Quatrain Indexing Date: Q54 = 1954. Between 1953 and 1955, ben Youssef was deposed and then reinstated after the French government recognized the independence of Morocco.

6 Q55

Au chalmé Duc, en arrachant l'esponce,[1]	**To the relaxed Duke, in drawing up**
Voile Arabesque voir, subit descouuerte:	**the contract,**
Tripolis[2] *Chio, & ceux de Trapesonce,*	**Arabesque sail seen, sudden**
Duc prins, Marnegro[3] *& la cité deserte.*	**discovery:**
	Triebolu, Chios, and those of
	Trabzon,
	The duke seized, the Black Sea and
	the city deserted.

[1]Provençal *esponcio* = promise, obligation.
[2]Either the Libyan port of Tripoli, or the modern-day Turkish port of Triebolu.
[3]*Marnegro*: Italian *Mare* (sea) + *negro* (black) = the Black Sea.

This could be a continuation of the theme from the preceding quatrain: a crumbling Ottoman Empire mistakenly forecast by Nostradamus for the early 17th century. The events could be right if this scenario unfolds a few hundred years later. The Ottoman Empire collapsed after World War I. The **Duke** could be Mustafa Kemal Atatürk, the father of the modern Turkish state, who drew up a constitution for Turkey. Line 2 is too general for a specific interpretation.

We might backstroke in time to Nostradamus' failed alternative future for 1607. A naval engagement takes place off the Turkish Black Sea coast between **Trabzon** and **Triebolu**. **Chios** is an island off western Asia Minor in the Aegean. Its importance in this story is difficult to ascertain. In a modern application this **Duke** could be a terrorist leader. His capture causes a catastrophe, requiring **Triebolu** (Tripoli) and **Trabzon** to be evacuated. In January 1996 a unit of Chechen guerillas captured a Russian ferry in the port of Trabzon. They intended to sail through the Bosphorus into the Aegean (near **Chios**) but surrendered while still in port.

6 Q56

La crainte armee de l'ennemy Narbon,
Effrayera si fort les Hesperiques:[1]
Parpignan vuide par l'aueugle darbon,
Lors Barcelon par mer donra les piques.

The dreaded army of the enemy
    Narbonne,
Will terrify so very much the
    Westerners:
Perpignan vacant through the
    sightless one of Arbon,
Then Barcelona by sea will supply the
    weapons.

[1]Hesperiques is usually used for Westerners or Americans, but in this case it is the Spanish.

The blind fellow from **Arbon** comes either from Lake Constance in Switzerland or the tiny village of Arbonne in southern France, but both are too far removed from the siege works around Perpignan, the capital of Roussillon which is the only possible subject of this quatrain. Narbonne is roughly 40 miles north of Perpignan. Barcelona is on the Spanish side of the Pyrenees, about 100 miles south of Perpignan. There was only one minor siege at Perpignan: in 1597, during the final years of the Wars of Religion. **Barcelona** was the **supply** hub for the Spanish expedition.

6 Q57

Celuy qu'estroit bien auant dans le regne,
Ayant chef rouge proche à la hierarchie:
Aspre & cruel, & se fera tant craindre,
Succedera à sacré monarchie.

He who was well advanced in the
    realm,
Having a red chief [a cardinal] near
    to the hierarchy [the Curia]:
Harsh and cruel, and he will make
    himself much feared,
He will succeed to the sacred
    monarchy.

A ruthless and ambitious cardinal well positioned **in the realm** of the Vatican will ascend to the papal throne. This could have happened a hundred times in the last four centuries. I will cast my chips in for a modern interpretation. Perhaps the successor to John-Paul II will be a well-soled papal politician and ideologue lurking in the Vatican's Curia. Perhaps he is even one of the **Twelve red ones** of the Curia Nostradamus may have linked to the poisoning of John Paul I in 1978 (see 4 Q11).

6 Q58

Entre les deux monarques esloignez,
Lors que le Sol par Selin clair perdue:
Simulté grande entre deux indignez,
Qu'aux Isles & Sienne la liberté rendue.

Between the two distant monarchs,
When the clear Sun is lost by Selin:
Great enmity between two indignant
    ones,
So that liberty is restored to the
    Islands and to Siena.

Here we have the royal feud between Philip II of Spain and Henry II of France, set for a climactic resolution. The **clear Sun** implies Philip's heraldic device of the sun of Apollo. The moon is Diana (Greek goddess of the moon), representing Diane de Poitiers (**Selin**). Had Henry avoided ritual combat he might have defeated the Spanish Habsburgs and even killed or captured his nemesis, King Philip. The final line promises that Henry will succeed in his conquest of Corsica by using bases in Siena.

6 Q59

Dame en fureur par rage d'adultere,	**The Lady in fury through rage of**
Viendra à ſon Prince coniurer non de dire:	**adultery,**
Mais bref cogneu ſera le vitupere,[1]	**She will come to her Prince to**
Que ſeront mis dixſept à martire.	**conspire, but not to tell him:**
	But soon will the blame be made
	known,
	So that seventeen will be put to
	martyrdom.

[1]*vitupere* = reprimand, blame, or perhaps "the culprit."

A general account of court intrigues. Perhaps a dangerous liaison will lead to seventeen executions. The closest event to this took place many years before Nostradamus wrote this verse, when Catherine Howard, the fifth wife of Henry VIII of England, was tried and beheaded for adultery in 1542 along with two of her alleged lovers.

6 Q60

Le Prince hors de ſon terroir Celtique	**The Prince outside of his Celtic**
Sera trahy, deceu par interprete:	**territory**
Rouan, Rochelle par ceux de l'Armorique[1]	**Will be betrayed, tricked by the**
Au port de Blaue deceus par moyne &	**interpreter:**
prebſtre.	**Rouen, La Rochelle through those of**
	Brittany [or America?],
	At the port of Blaye deceived by a
	monk and priest.

[1]Latin *Armorica* = Brittany. Variant: America (but not in this case).

A French prince far from his homeland is betrayed during negotiations. This fits well enough for Charles de Guise, Cardinal de Lorraine, who led the French delegation to the Council of Trent. **Rouen** is in Normandy; **La Rochelle**, just south of the Vendée, was besieged in 1625–28. Brittany, Vendée, and Normandy were battlegrounds for the White Terror during the French Revolution. **Blaye** is on the Gironde about 25 miles north of Bordeaux.

If Prieditis is correct and the harbor of Blavet in Brittany is intended rather than Blaye, then Henry IV is the prince outside of Brittany, the last Celtic stronghold of France which, in defiance of the terms of earlier treaties, had allowed foreigners and Catholic Leaguers to use the harbor of Blavet during the final War of Religion.

6 Q61

Le grand tappis plié ne monftrera,	The grand tapestry folded will not show,
Fors qu'à demy la plufpart de l'hiftoire:	But by halves the greatest part of [its?] history:
Chaffé du regne loing afpre apparoiftra	Chased far out of the realm he will appear harsh
Qu'au faict bellique chafcun le viendra croire.	So that everyone will come to believe in his warlike deed.

A cryptic quatrain. In medieval French the phrase *sur le tapis* means "on the carpet" or "on the table" and is figurative for the place where kings negotiate. In this case the negotiations fail. Line 2 could mean that the historical facts concerning the negotiation will be revealed over time. A king or leader fights from overseas to restore his power. With so little to go on this could just as well stand for anyone from Charles de Gaulle to the Iranian Ayatollah Khomeini. If it is for de Gaulle he is fighting to free France from the negotiated armistice that made her a puppet fiefdom of Hitler's Greater Germany. You could apply it equally to Ayatollah Khomeini and the breakdown of talks between the fundamentalist mullahs and the secular Shah of Iran during the early 1960s. In 1962 Khomeini was forced into exile, where he spent most of the next few decades in neighboring Iraq leading the fight for more Islamic freedom. In the late 1970s he was exiled to France where he led an open and bloody insurrection (**warlike deed**) that overthrew the Shah.

Quatrain Indexing Date: Q61 = 1961–62, the years of negotiations between Iranian Ayatollahs and the Shah of Iran on the issue of religious freedom.

6 Q62

Trop tard tous deux les fleurs feront perdues,	Too late both of the flowers will be undone,
Contre la loy ferpent ne voudra faire:	The serpent will not want to act against the law:
Des ligueurs forces par gallots[1] confondues,	The forces of the [Catholic] leaguers by the French confounded,
Sauone, Albinque par monech grand martyre.	Savona, Albenga, through Monaco great martyrdom.

[1]Old French or Breton for Gallic or French.

The two flowers are Catherine de' Medici's sons François II and Charles IX, while in their minority. After becoming a widow, Catherine had changed the main device in her coat of arms to a serpent clasping its own tail in its mouth. The ancient Salic law forbade any queen to rule France. Catherine's regency came the closest, but she never openly challenged the Salic law or seized the throne for herself, choosing instead to be peacemaker and a moderating element in the seesaw battles and bickering at court between the Huguenot Bourbons and the fanatically Catholic Guise. The latter were responsible for creating – and later controlling – the Catholic League. The leaguers were pledged to defend the faith against the Protestant heresy, but later were used to threaten the throne itself. They would be confounded when their greatest enemy, Henry IV, reconverted to Catholicism. The French people, tired of Catholic fanaticism and civil wars, generally abandoned the cause of supporting their new Catholic king. **Monaco**, an ally of the Spanish during the 16th and 17th centuries, was pledged by treaty to fight in her wars, even against France. **Savona** and **Albenga** were ports west of Genoa.

6 Q63

La dame ſeule au regne demeuree,	**The lady left alone in the realm,**
L'vnic eſtaint premier au lict d'honneur:	**Her unique [husband] first**
Sept ans ſera de douleur eploree,	**extinguished on the bed of honor:**
Puis longue vie au regne par grand heur.	**For seven years she will weep with grief,**
	Then a long life and good fortune for
	the kingdom.

Catherine de' Medici persevered as regent of a war-torn France through the reigns of her sons Francis II and Charles IX, at last losing power during the reign of her son Henry III. Her official mourning for her husband, Henry II, lasted seven years. She lived a long and courageous life, dying in 1589 at the age of 70. It is not enough to attribute long life solely to Catherine. The foggy syntax makes a promise to the kingdom of France in general: despite the troubles to come, the kingdom will flourish for exactly two more centuries after the year of her death – from 1589 until the French Revolution of 1789.

6 Q64

On ne tiendra pache aucune arreſté,	**They will not keep any peace agreement**
Tous receuans iront par tromperie:	**concluded,**
De paix & trefue, terre & mer proteſté,	**All the recipients will go on with**
Par Barcelone claſſe[1] prins d'induſtrie.	**[their] deceit and trickery:**
	The peace and truce, land and sea
	protest[ant],
	By Barcelona the fleet [or army]
	captured with ingenuity.

[1]Latin *classis* = fleet, or army.

I believe this one continues the Wars of Religion theme of the last three quatrains. It is a general commentary on the political treachery and the eight double-dealing peace agreements between the nine civil wars. Barcelona can fit into this quatrain, albeit somewhat incorrectly, only as a staging area for Spanish intervention in the ninth and final civil war. A Spanish army made a modest military demonstration into Roussillon in 1597, and for a short time laid siege to Perpignan. But no fleet or army of Barcelona was captured.

This does not rule out a stretch to a more modern time – 1938–39, during the last campaigns of the Spanish Civil War. The Republican Army made its last stand around Barcelona. From time to time a few Soviet cargo ships carrying munitions and advisors sailed from the Black Sea to lay anchor in its harbor, but this could hardly be called a *fleet*. Nor was any ship bombed. Barcelona, however, was captured by six Nationalist armies. After the civil war Franco broke his promise of leniency to Republican supporters and ordered many shot (**they will not keep any peace agreement**).

6 Q65

Gris & bureau demie ouuerte guerre,	Gray and brown half-opened war,
De nuict feront affaillis & pillez:	By night they will be assaulted and
Le bureau[1] prins paffera par la ferre,[2]	pillaged:
Son temple ouuert, deux au plaftre grillez.[3]	The brown captured will pass through
	the [prison] lock,
	Two behind bars in the plaster [of his
	prison window], his temple opened.

[1]Old French *burel* = brown.
[2]Old French for lock; (figuratively) prison.
[3]Old French *griller* = grilling, grilled window; to put behind bars.

A play on colors could pit the **brown** revolution of the National Socialist Party against the field-**gray**-coated soldiers of the Weimar Republic during Hitler's failed Munich Putsch. His coup is **half-opened** due to poor coordination. Hitler's brown-shirted soldiers advanced on the city center and were shot down by German military police. Later that night many **brown** revolutionary leaders were rounded up (**assaulted and pillaged**). Hitler was arrested and later sent to Landesburg Prison.

Nostradamus has played with temple/prison puns before, and he's doing it here. Hitler turned his prison cell into a comfy temple where he gave birth to his bible of Nazism, *Mein Kampf*. One can imagine the seer using his porthole in time to look through the bars of the prison window and witness the author and his scribe, Rudolph Hess, working away on the Nazi bible.

6 Q66

Au fondement de la nouuelle Jecte,	**At the founding of the new sect,**
Seront les oz du grand Romain trouués,	**The bones of the great Roman will be**
Sepulchre en marbre apparoiſtra couuerte,	**found,**
Terre trembler en Auril, mal enfouez.	**The sepulchre covered by marble will**
	appear,
	The earth trembles in April, badly
	buried.

Nostradamus dates the appearance of a new sect to correspond with the discovery of St Peter's authentic tomb.

For the **Roman** is St Peter, whose bones, Nostradamus tells us, will be found beneath the Vatican at the time of a cataclysm. We cannot rule out the interpretation of another future trend expressed in other quatrains – that the tomb was to be found in 1978, the year a dramatic influx of interest in the teachings of Osho, Hubbard, Moon, and Adi Da Santosha. It can be assumed, therefore, that the **new** religious **sect** has already appeared. The indexing of 6 Q66 could, on closer inspection, hide the biblically symbolic number 666, which represents man and the Antichrist. If this is a correct interpretation, Nostradamus does not make it clear whether the number stands for the new sect or is intended as a jibe at the Roman Catholic Church as un-**Christ**-tian. Certainly all the candidates explored are, to varying degrees, considered threats to the orthodox Christian view of the universe.

6 Q67

Au grand Empire paruiendra tout vn	**Quite a different man will attain to**
aultre	**great Empire,**
Bonté diſtant plus de felicité:	**Distant from kindness, more so from**
Regi par vn iſſu non loing du peaultre,[1]	**happiness:**
Corruer regnes grande infelicité.[2]	**Ruled by one coming a short time**
	from his bed.
	The kingdom falls to the ground,
	great wretchedness.

[1] Old French for bed, a prostitute's pallet.
[2] Latin infelicitas = unhappiness, misfortune, bad luck.

Emperor Napoleon I was a brooding, lonely man. "Friendship is only a word. I care for nobody," he once said. Of the many women who loved him, only Empress Josephine was his true confidante. The common people believed she was his good-luck charm. In more psychological terms, she knew the workings of his mind. It is said that she was an avid reader of Nostradamus, but we can only speculate whether she recognized the cryptogram *Pau-Nay-Loron* as her life's love. Napoleon's fortunes faded after he divorced Josephine to marry a more fertile Marie-Louise of Austria. "Not another Austrian!" murmured the common French folk. Marie-Louise was the grand-niece of Marie Antoinette. An unlucky omen, indeed! It is a fact that Josephine was dead set against Napoleon's invasion of Russia. But her counsel was disregarded. By the disastrous year 1812 another woman – a rather simple-minded little breeder – was coming *a short time* from the Emperor's bed.

6 Q68

Lors que ſoldatz fureur ſeditieuſe,	**When the soldiers in a seditious fury,**
Contre leur chef feront de nuict fer luire:	**Against their chief will cause steel to**
Ennemy d'Albe ſoit par main furieuſe,	**flash by night:**
Lors vexer Rome & principaux ſeduire.	**The enemy of Alva being in a**
	powerful fury,
	Then to vex Rome and seduce the
	principal ones.

Jaubert applies this to events of 1556, when Pope Paul IV refused to recognize the abdication of Charles V or the inheritance of Ferdinand II. He persecuted the Spanish delegations in Rome and scraped together a papal army that was easily trounced by the Spanish forces of the Duke of Alva stationed in northern Italy. The Spanish army overran the papal states and forced the pope to accept Alva's generous peace terms. The duke's balancing act of military demonstrations and seductive diplomacy would strongly influence a papal change in course, away from the French toward the Spanish political camp. Nostradamus also has Alva suppressing a revolt of Spanish troops and auxiliaries. In this case we move a few years ahead to the early stages of the Dutch revolt in the Spanish Netherlands.

6 Q69

La pitié grande ſera ſans loing tarder,	**The great pity will exist before long,**
Ceux qui dõnoient ſeront contrains de prẽdre,	**Those who gave will be constrained to take away,**
Nudz affamez de froit, ſoif, ſoy bander,	**Naked, starving, they resist the cold and thirst,**
Les monts paſſer commettant grand eſclandre.	**To pass over the mountains committing great scandal.**

This is general enough to be a penury theme pointing to a time when the generous are later forced to beg for their survival. The final lines could stand for any group of outcasts, political or religious, or any number of starving refugees crossing the mountains. Elsewhere Nostradamus has accurately foreseen the future destitution of the Catholic clergy during the French Revolution. In 1792 they were forced out of their churches and monasteries, stripped of their wealth and even their religious clothing (**naked**), and sent packing. Priests who had hoarded great wealth under the guise of Christian charity were themselves forced to beg for food and clothing. Many of these outcasts could be seen trudging over the Alps to take refuge in friendlier climes and Catholic states in Italy. Tattered bands of beggar priests roving the streets of Rome tarnished the Church's image.

6 Q70

Au chef du monde le grand Chyren[1] sera,	**The great Chyren will be chief of the world,**
Plus oultre[2] apres aymé, craint, redoubté:	**After [Charles V] loved, feared and dreaded:**
Son bruit & loz les cieux surpassera,	**His fame and praise go beyond the heavens,**
Et du seul titre victeur fort contenté.	**And [he will be] greatly satisfied with the sole title of victor.**

[1]Anagram for *Henryc* = Henry II.
[2]*Plus oultre*: PLVS VLTRA CAROL' QUINT. The device of Charles V.

If ever there was a quatrain to boost the ego of a king living in fear because of an anti-jousting prediction, this is the one. Nostradamus elevated Henry to the top of the list of power-mongering kings of Christendom. Even Charles V, the unquestioned master of the 16th-century (European) world – King of Spain, protector of the Netherlands, and Holy Roman Emperor – is relegated to a complimario part in future history. It is a fact that Henry II's weakness for gushing flattery equaled Nostradamus' need to survive the Inquisition.

Quatrain Indexing Date: 1570? If the indexing of these prophecies is a device for dating, then a number of them pinpoint the 1570s as the time when Henry, the Chyren-Selin, will make his mark as the second Charlemagne.

6 Q71

Quand on viendra le grand Roy parenter,	**When they come to give the last rites to the great king**
Auant qu'il ait du tout l'ame rendue:	**Before he has completely given up the ghost:**
Celuy qui moins le viendra lamenter,	**He who will come to lament over him the least,**
Par Lyons, d'aigles, croix, couronne vendue.	**Through Lions, of [monarchies], [Christianity afflicted], crown betrayed.**

After 6 Q70 comes the alternative negative future trail Henry II did follow down the annals of history. Line 1 invites us to tarry at the king's bedside. We see the bandaged head of the delirious monarch roll fitfully to the sonorous payers of the last rites. Line 2 refers to Coligny and the other Protestant leaders gathered around his bed shoulder to shoulder with their Catholic rivals during the ten-day death watch. One could also find them in the hallways on their breaks, plotting their schism even before Henry was dead. Line 4 brings us back to the events of 1 Q35 when the **young** Protestant **lion** Comte de Montgomery failed to lower his lance and mortally wounded his king. Although Henry forgave him before he slipped into a coma, the rest of Catholic France would not. The prophecy ends with figurative references to the coming nine Wars of Religion which pitted the monarchies of Protestant Navarre against the Catholic Valois. The French crown itself would be betrayed by the Catholic Leaguers of Henry de Guise in a three-way struggle for the French throne.

6 Q72

Par fureur faincte d'eſmotion diuine,	**Through feigned fury of a divine**
Sera la femme du grand fort violee:	**emotion,**
Iuges voulans damner telle doctrine,	**The wife of the great one will be**
Victime au peuple ignorant immolee.	**violated:**
	The judges wishing to condemn such
	a doctrine,
	The victim sacrificed to the ignorant
	people.

Grigoriy Rasputin, the controversial monk and faith healer, is claimed to have healed the young Czarevich Alexis of serious hemophilia attacks. This healing power gained him great influence over the boy's mother, the Czarina Alexandra. Rasputin also had a reputation for seducing many Russian princesses, perhaps even the Czarina herself, with his hypnotic powers. Eventually the aristocrats, angry at his domination of the Czar's family, conspired to murder him. Around Christmas 1916 they lured Rasputin to a party in St Petersburg, promising an evening of debauchery. Late in the party, as a phonograph played *Yankee Doodle*, Rasputin's hosts plied him with cyanide-laced drinks. When the poison had no effect, they shot, stabbed, and bludgeoned him. Still Rasputin survived. Finally, they threw him bound and chained into the Neva river through a hole in the ice. When his body was recovered it was clear he had died from drowning.

Rasputin, like Nostradamus, had the gift of future sight. In his last letter to the Czarina he predicted his murder would take place before New Year's Day, 1917. He promised that if he were killed by peasants (**ignorant people**) the Czarina and her family would flourish, but if the murderers were princes, she and all her family would be killed within two years by the peasants. Nostradamus backed up Rasputin's either-or prediction over 350 years before Czar Nicholas II and the Czarina (*wife of the great one*) were imprisoned and shot by the Bolsheviks (judges) and *sacrificed to the ignorant people*.

6 Q73

En cité grande vn moyne & artiſan,	**The great city a monk and artisan,**
Pres de la porte logés & aux murailles:	**Lodged near the gate and the walls:**
Contre Modene[1] ſecret, caue diſant,	**Speaking secretly against [the]**
Trahis pour faire ſouz couleur	**modern, [in the] theatre seats,**
d'eſpouſailles.	**To betray for acting under the pretext**
	of nuptials.

[1]Usually means Modena, Italy, but in this case I prefer "modern."

I don't know what in blazes this episode is about, so I'll reveal a secret to you that no respectable Nostradamus scholar has dared admit so far. When the warped wordplay is too tangled to untussle, and one's brain begins to burn, one must conjure the great Daemon Monty Python, for an answer. This is what Monty told me: "This quatrain is about a cleric and an artist whose spate of spit exchange in the back seats of a movie theater has been rudely interrupted by the less-than-satisfactory avant-garde performance of a honeymoon scene in a movie entitled: *Intercourse of the Penguin*."

See Index: Penguin – good luck.

6 Q74

La deſchaſſee au regne tournera,	**She who is driven from the reign will**
Ses ennemis trouués des coniurés:	**return,**
Plus que iamais ſon temps triomphera,	**Her enemies found among conspirators:**
Trois & ſeptante à mort trop aſſeurés.	**More than ever her time will**
	triumph,
	Three and seventy, to death assured.

Empress Eugénie was Napoleon III's chief confidante. She played Josephine to his Bonaparte. The empress exerted a powerful influence on her husband's policies and had her fair share of enemies at court, chiefly among his procession of mistresses. When the emperor was deposed by the National Assembly after his capture at Sedan, she followed him into exile to live at Chislehurst, England. Line 4's *three and seventy* may be a dating for the death of Napoleon III in 1873. In no other century in the year "73" has a great French leader's death coincided with the end of a French Empire. This quatrain, number 74, cannot be ruled out as a further hint in dating the event. The general slant of this prophecy points to the year Napoleon III died while undergoing surgery. The former empress lived a long and fulfilling life (**her time will triumph**) and finally passed away in 1920. Though driven out by her people in 1871, Eugénie often returned to her adopted homeland, and she purchased apartments overlooking the open garden space at the end of the Louvre where her previous residence, the Tuileries, had once stood.

This quatrain is number 10 in James Randi's list of ten debunkable quatrains (see *Mask of Nostradamus* pages 215–18). To me, his logic is clear. He must find a way to make this either sound retroactive, or be an "accurate" prophecy about an event that took place in the same year the quatrain was published. Only this could support his view that Nostradamus was cheating whenever he sounds accurate (see 2 Q51, Randi's debunking argument number 3). He ascribes to Charles A. Ward's interpretation that 6 Q74 must be about the life of the English Queen Elizabeth I. Neither Ward nor Randi seems to be aware that Elizabeth was never **driven from the reign** to **return** – in other words, this is clearly about a queen already in power who is exiled, and later returns. Although Randi is correct to criticise Ward and others for making "three-and-seventy" stand for Elizabeth at age 70 dying in the year 03 of the 17th century, he is handicapped by an incomplete study of history which makes him completely overlook other candidates, such as Empress Eugénie, and the importance of "73," see below.

Quatrain Indexing Date: Q74 = 1874, a near miss for the death of Napoleon III in 1873. However in line 4 Nostradamus does say **three and seventy** (see 4 Q73).

6 Q75

Le grand pilot par Roy ſera mandé,	**The great pilot will be sent for by the King,**
Laiſſer la claſſe pour plus haut lieu attaindre:	**To leave the fleet for a higher post to attain:**
Sept ans apres ſera contrebandé,	**Seven years later he will be in revolt,**
Barbare armée viendra Veniſe craindre.	**The Barbarian army will come to terrify Venice.**

The ambitious Gaspard de Coligny rose to the rank of Admiral of France (**great pilot**) in 1552. He commanded the doomed garrison at St Quentin in 1557, and while imprisoned by the Spanish converted to Protestantism. Upon the death of Henry II he resigned his post and attained a much **higher post** as the head of the Calvinist Party. During the first War of Religion in 1562, he was made the first Lieutenant-General of the Huguenot armies. Coligny was one of the chief instigators of truces and civil wars, and remained so until his brutal murder during the St Bartholomew's Day Massacre in 1572. During this same period Venice and her Mediterranean possessions were menaced by Sultan Suleiman the Magnificent and Selim II. The latter's forces would overwhelm the Venetian colony on Cyprus in 1570.

Quatrain Indexing Date: Q75 = a near miss for events from the early 1570s mentioned above.

6 Q76

La cité antique d'antenoree[1] forge,	**The ancient city forged by Antenor,**
Plus ne pouuant le tyran supporter:	**No longer being able to support the**
Le manchet fainct au temple couper gorge,	**tyrant:**
Les siens le peuple à mort viendra bouter.	**The false one-armed man in the**
	temple to cut a throat,
	The people will come to drive back his
	followers to death.

[1]Latin *Antenoreus* = of Antenor, the legendary Trojan founder of Padua.

The city of Padua, in northeastern Italy, once belonged to the Republic of Venice. The tyrant is a Venetian Doge who will be assassinated by a *false one-armed* man. The people of Padua will rise up and slaughter his chosen city magistrates. An alternative future that never happened.

6 Q77

Par la victoire du deceu fraudulente,	**After the victory of the fraudulent**
Deux classes vne, la reuolte Germaine:	**deception,**
Le chef meurtry & son filz dans la tente,	**Two fleets [made] one, the German**
Florence, Imole pour chassés dans Romaine.	**revolt:**
	The chief and his son murdered in the
	tent,
	Florence, Imola, eagerly pursued into
	Romania.

A number of German revolts could fit here. Those taking place during the Thirty Years War in the 17th century are the most likely. **German revolt** was a phrase commonly applied to any general rebellion of Protestants against the Imperial Catholic authorities.

6 Q78

Crier victoire du grand Selin croissant,	**To cry victory of great Selin growing**
Par les Romains sera l'Aigle clamé,[1]	**crescent,**
Ticcin, Milan, & Gennes n'y consent,	**By the Romans will the Eagle be**
Puis par eux mesmes Basil[2] grand reclamé.	**clamored for,**
	Pavia, Milan, and Genoa will not
	consent to it,
	Then by themselves the great king
	reclaimed.

[1]Old French *clamer* = to demand, from Latin *clamare* = to proclaim.
[2]Greek *basileus* = king, prince, lord, captain.

Here is the great (Chyren) **Selin**, Nostradamus' comic-book-hero version of his mediocre contemporary, Henry II. The papacy will clamor for assistance from the (French) **Eagle** – a symbol also used by Henry II. In other alternative-future tracks Philip II of Spain is captured. (Dream on, Nostradamus!) The three provinces fall to Henry after **the great king** is **reclaimed** by Spain.

6 Q79

Pres du Tefin les habitans de Loyre,	**Near the Ticino the inhabitants of the**
Garonne & Saonne, Seine, Tain, &	**Loire,**
Gironde:	**Garonne and Saone, Seine, Tain and**
Outre les monts drefferont promontoire,	**the Gironde:**
Conflict donné Pau[1] granci,[2] fubmergé	**Beyond the mountains they will erect**
onde.	**a promontory,**
	Conflict given, [Na]Pau[lon]
	snatched, submerged in water.

[1]In this case it is an apocope for Nonstramus' famous cryptogram for Napoleon: *Pau Nay Loron = Napaulon Roy.*
[2]*granci* = Tuscan *grancito* = snatched, seized, hooked.

In the battle of Lodi (10 May 1796) young Bonaparte led an attack against the Austrians on a bridge over the River Adda. His excited men pressed on too hard and shoved the little general off the bridge into the river (**submerged in water**). Some quick-thinking soldiers **snatched** him out of the water before he drowned.

6 Q80

De Fez[1] le regne paruiendra à ceux	**From Fez the kingdom will reach out**
d'Europe,[2]	**to those of Europe,**
Feu leur cité, & lame trenchera:	**Their city blazes, the sword will**
Le grand d'Afie[3] terre & mer à grand	**slash:**
troupe,	**The great man of Asia by land and**
Que bleux,[4] pers,[5] croix, à mort	**sea with a great troop,**
dechaffera.	**So that blues, Pers[ians], the cross,**
	will be driven out to death.

[1]*Fez*: in modern terms North Africa.
[2]The European Union.
[3]*Le grand d'Afie*: this could be the new Ghengis Khan of 10Q 72.
[4]"blues" stands for the blue-capped soldiers of the United Nations.
[5]Persians, or Iranians.

In an insecure, multi-polarized 1990s world, China appears to be heading for an open, alliance with many of the more aggressive Islamic states. Although the United States is the world's foremost arms dealer – followed by Russia and the democracies of Germany, France, and Britain –

China supplies the greatest number of regional ballistic missile delivery systems, plus the reactors, know-how, and fissionable materials for the nuclear arms programs of North Korea, Iran, Libya, Pakistan, and India. In 1993 China supplied Iran with 20 billion dollars' worth of conventional weapons and the means to build two nuclear reactors that can produce enriched uranium for warheads. US Intelligence believes China is Iran's principal source for the latter's secret nuclear weapons project.

If the United Nations cannot quickly and effectively redefine itself and ensure the supremacy of international law over national law, and if fairness is not sustained in the peace efforts in the Middle East, China will by default become the defender of Arab and Islamic rights and have great political influence over the supply of oil to the West. She may become the new safe haven and training camp for the Jihad of terrorism. In a worst-case scenario, China – whether communist or not – may find herself under the dictatorship of a future Genghis Khan. She fulfills a biblical and Nostradamian nightmare as the linchpin of a new regional Sino-Pan-Islamic alliance against Europe, Russia, and America in a nuclear Third World War between 1999 and 2020.

6 Q81

Pleurs, crys & plaincts, hurlement effraieur,	*Tears, cries and laments, howls, terror,*
Cœur inhumain, cruel, noir & tranſy:	*Inhuman heart, cruel, black and [making one] shudder with fear:*
Leman, les iſles de Gennes les maieurs,	*Geneva, the isles, of Genoa the superiors,*
Sang eſpancher, frofaim[1] à nul mercy.	*Blood to be shed, hunger for bread and cheese – to none mercy.*

[1] Apparently a coinage by Nostradamus from *froment-faim* = cheese-hunger.

One can picture the sounds of Armageddon rising from the shivering waters of the brass bowl. The prophet hears cries that make him **shudder with fear**. Perhaps he sees the Third Antichrist. If only we could peek over the seer's shoulder and see the face of this cruel man so we might forestall his evil destiny. The **black one** is back again. Is it Abu Nidal or someone belonging to the Abu Nidal terrorist group? **Geneva** stands as the capital of internationalism and peace negotiations. It is here that efforts will be made to bring about the next step in civilization, a global society. Geneva is attacked. Does she fall victim to Raypoz (9 Q44), the fierce weapon of the Antichrist? Images shift again and the prophet sees Genoa attacked. Does he witness the clouds of **false dust** (5 Q90) from a nuclear terrorist bombing that causes her evacuation? The visions in the waters boil together in a thick clot of misery.

6 Q82

Par les defers de lieu, libre, & farouche,
Viendra errer nepueu du grand Pontife:
Affommé à fept auecques lourde fouche,
Par ceux qu'apres occuperont le cyphe.[1]

Through the wilderness of unguarded and sullen rank,[2]
The nephew of the great Pontiff will come to wander:
Beaten to death by seven with a heavy staff,
By those, who afterwards will occupy the Chalice.

[1]Latin scyphus = chalice, cup, goblet.
[2]Literal translation: Through the wildernesses of free and wild places, or, After Libra has been desolated and abandoned (Jochmans).

This one is open to any time and any interpretation. If one agrees with Jochmans (Rolling Thunder, pages 99–100), then this continues the apocalyptic theme of the previous quatrain. We are told of future trials, tribulations, assassinations, and evacuation themes for the last popes during the destruction of Rome in the battle of Armageddon. In this case Jochmans believes that after a future pope is murdered a new one will evacuate to America. Once he is there, American clergymen will eliminate the office of the papacy as sole ruler of the Church.

Although Jochmans says Libra stands as the astrological sign of the Roman Catholic Church, the French libre (free) and the scales of Libra the Balance apply also to the United States. It may be America and not the Vatican that is **desolated and abandoned**.

6 Q83

Celuy qu'aura tant d'honneur & careffes,
A fon entree de la Gaule Belgique:
Vn temps apres fera tant de rudeffes,
Et fera contre à la fleur tant bellique.

He who will have much honor and caresses,
At his entry into Belgian Gaul:
A while after he will act so rudely,
And he will act very bellicose to the flower.

A number of scholars believe this quatrain was fulfilled twice in the 16th century. Upon Charles V's abdication in 1555, his son, Philip II, was embraced by his Protestant Dutch subjects in the Spanish Netherlands as their new lord. Philip, however, soon betrayed his self-righteous and intolerant Christian values and had a rebellion on his hands by 1568. Thus began the 80-year War for Dutch Independence. Philip would also vent his bigotry on Protestant Henry de Navarre and wage wars with the "lilies" of France, in 1589–98.

6 Q84

Celuy qu'en Sparte Claude ne peut regner,	**The lame one who in Sparta could not rule,**
Il fera tant par voye feductiue:	**He will do much through seductive means:**
Que du court, long, le fera araigner,	**So that by the short and the long of it he will be accused,**
Que contre Roy fera fa perfpectiue.	**Of making his perspective opposed to the King.**

Leoni makes a good guess. The **lame** leader is Franklin D. Roosevelt, since he was "one of the most famous cripples in history." But I believe this prophecy better fits the clubfoot of another famous cripple of World War II: Josef Goebbels, Hitler's propaganda minister. By using some of the quatrains to falsely foresee a Nazi victory he became the man most responsible for making Nostradamus a world-famous prophet. Goebbels was occasionally at variance to Hitler on how to wage propaganda wars. For example, Goebbels was critical of Hitler's vulgar cinematic comparisons of Jews with stampeding rats in the gutters in a notorious Nazi docudrama. It is said the movie was so horrifying that even the wives of Party members fainted in their seats. Goebbels preferred a more subtle and seductive anti-Semitic-cineramic theme such as that of the highly popular historical drama *Jüde Suss.*

6 Q85

La grand cité de Tharfe par Gaulois	**The great city of Tarsus by the Gauls**
Sera deftruite, captifz tous à Turban:	**Will be destroyed, all the Turbaned ones captured:**
Secours par mer du grand Portugalois,	**Relief from the sea from the great one of Portugal,**
Premier d'efté le iour du facre Vrban.	**The first day of summer, Saint Urban's day.**

Tarsus was never destroyed by Nostradamus' Rambo version of Henry II– *Chyren Selin.* And the only event remotely close to the location in line 1 happened in the first week of the Gulf War against Iraq in 1991, when US naval commanders programmed their Tomahawk missiles to fly over the mountains of southern Turkey to bear down on targets in northern Iraq. With this said, Tarsus was not destroyed, though it may have suffered a rattling of its windows from supersonic flights of coalition jets using Turkish airbases.

Line 3 has us backtrack a few centuries to a time favored by Nostradamus for the collapse of the Ottoman Turks in 1607 (6 Q54). Portugal at the time was at best a faltering naval power. Certainly no Portuguese galleons laid anchor in a Christian-conquered city of Tarsus (it is ten miles inland from the sea); nor did they lay anchor at the nearby port of Mercin (Içel) – unless Nostradamus has mixed Portuguese wooden man-o'-wars with metal United States military container ships used in the Gulf War.

One St Urban has his feast day on 7 April; another's is 5 September. Pope Urban I's feast day is 25 May. Then there is St Urban, Bishop of Langres, who is fêted on 23 January. Summer starts on 21 June. Only someone in the Southern Hemisphere could celebrate the feast day of St Urban of Langres on the **first day of summer**. Unless a reader can inform me of a clearly documented commemoration date for the gaggle of twelve St Urbans remaining on the list, there's no dating this quantum future failure.

6 Q86

Le grand Prelat vn iour apres ſon ſonge	**The great Prelate one day after his**
Interpreté au rebours de ſon ſens:	**dream**
De la Gaſcogne luy ſuruiendra vn monge,	**Interpreted as the contrary of its**
Qui fera eſlire le grand Prelat de ſens.	**meaning:**
	From Gascony a monk will drop in
	unexpectedly,
	Who will cause the great Prelate of
	Sens to be elected.

Maybe Nostradamus is relating the outcome of an ancient prophecy (*circa* AD 600) fulfilled in his time. Sens was one of the first of twelve prelatures, or archbishoprics, of Gaul. Nostradamus may have been aware of a prophetic dream experienced by the original archbishop. In it the prelate foresaw the future election of an archbishop during the 1550s, as well as a monk from Gascony who is able to interpret the vision to those that would elect him.

6 Q87

L'eſlection faite dans Frankfort,	**The election made in Frankfurt,**
N'aura nul lieu Milan s'oppoſera:	**Will be annulled, Milan will be**
Le ſien plus proche ſemblera ſi grand fort	**opposed:**
Que outre le Rhyn és mareſchz chaſſera.	**The closest follower will seem so very**
	strong
	That he will drive him out into the
	marshes beyond the Rhine.

Nostradamus believed the inheritors of Charles V's partitioned empire would go to war. As we have already seen, Charles V's son, Philip II of Spain, received all Spanish New World holdings, a collection of Italian dukedoms, and the Spanish Netherlands. Philip's uncle, Ferdinand II, received the Holy Roman Empire. His election as emperor took place a few years after this was written in 1558.

Apparently Nostradamus believed Philip II's inheritance of the Duchy of Milan would be opposed by Ferdinand, which would send them off to war. Philip will win a decisive victory against Imperial forces near the Rhine River and thereby win back Milan. All very clear – yet none of it happened.

6 Q88

Vn regne grand demourra defolé,
Aupres del Hebro fe feront affemblees:
Monts Pyrenees le rendront confolé,
Lors que dans May feront terres tremblees.

A great kingdom will remain desolate,
Near the Ebro they will be gathered
  in assemblies:
The Pyrenees mountains will console
  him,
When in May [spring] there are great
  earthquakes.

To start with, one could cite a Spanish Civil War slant: Falangist forces gather on the Ebro in preparation for their final successful offensives against the last Spanish Republican strongholds in Catalonia. By 1939 hundreds of thousands of refugees would flee north over the Pyrenees into France. In the following year the French themselves would be made desolate by the earth-shaking German tanks and the bombs of Stuka dive-bombers during the Nazi Blitzkrieg of May 1940.

If *earthquakes* literally mean temblors, this quatrain is the first of several references to a series of superquakes, in some future **May** [*spring*], or even a shift of the Earth's rotational axis.

On 5 May 2000, the new moon will align with Earth, the sun, Jupiter, and Saturn. Five planets will pull away from us on the opposite side of the sun. We do not yet know how this gravitational tug-of-war will affect the increased rotational wobble predicted for the Earth at that time. Solar activity is expected to increase 20 percent due to the near-exact alignment of Jupiter and Saturn with the Earth and the sun. This could further aggravate the next great drought that is forecast for the late 1990s. The planet Uranus lines up with the sun on a near-right-angle to the alignment of Saturn, Jupiter, the sun and the moon, all pulling away from Earth.

In 1959 Dr R. Tomaschek of Munich reported on a 43-year study he had made on earthquakes. His research results, summarized in the geophysics section of *Nature* magazine, indicated a remarkably consistent pattern in Uranus' position when earthquakes occurred. Of the 134 earthquakes with a magnitude of seven and three-quarters or greater examined by Tomaschek, a significant number had occurred when Uranus was within 15 degrees of its upper or lower transit of the meridian of the epicenter. In Tomaschek's opinion Uranus is responsible for

influencing three of the 20th century's most devastating earthquakes: in
Tokyo 1923, Honshu (1933), and Assam, India (1950).

Uranus was at or near a perfect right-angle to the Earth's position for
much of the latter half of 1993 through January 1994. During that time
India suffered one of its worst killer quakes in decades, the Killari-Latur
quake in September 1993. Then western Los Angeles and the heavily
populated San Fernando Valley were severely shaken on 17 January 1994
by a quake that toppled or severely damaged more than 20,000 structures
and buildings, made the huge Los Angeles Coliseum stadium unsafe, and
crippled several freeways.

When Uranus once again returns to a position 90 degrees from Earth
during the grand alignment of planets in May 2000, in the worst-case
scenario the friction of Uranus would give enough energy to the invisible
gravity line of Saturn, Jupiter, the sun and the moon to topple Earth off
its polar axis. What is more likely, however, is a series of superquakes
throughout the year, primarily in the spring. These will be remembered as
the greatest killer temblors in history.

It is important to stress that this quake could be more subjective than
literal. For instance, if by the spring of 2000 the world were to be shown
unquestionable proof of the existence of extraterrestrial intelligence, the
earthquake to our religious, moral, and political values would bring
about a spiritual and social "axis shift" as far-reaching as any physical one.

See Index: Axis shift in spring.

6 Q89

Entre deux cymbes piedz & mains eftachés,	**Between two boats feet and hands are**
De miel face oingt & de laict fubftanté:	**tied,**
Guefpes & mouches, fitine[1] amour fachés,	**With honey the face anointed and**
Poccilateur[2] faucer, Cyphe[3] tempté.	**with milk sustained:**
	Wasps and flies, fatherly love vexed,
	Cup bearer [Russia-bearer] to falsify,
	Chalice tested.

[1]Greek *phitus* = father.
[2]Latin *pocillator* = cup-bearer.
[3]Latin *scyphus* = chalice, cup, goblet.

A quatrain choking on data overload in the throat of obscurity. I give up,
– but Le Pelletier has not. He says, "Napoleon, after having been consecrated as Emperor of the French by sovereign Pontiff Pius VII, will be
chained doubly at the isles of Elba and St Helena [*between two boats*]."
(Actually, I find it hard to call an island a boat. Le Pelletier would do
better to say "the *two boats* sending Napoleon twice to island exile.")
"The Emperor, in despair after the refusal of the Allied sovereigns to
ratify the treaty by which he consented to abdicate in favor of his son,

will try in vain to kill himself, during the night of 12 or 13 April 1814, in taking a poison prepared badly by his surgeon."

In fact, Napoleon's packet of poison had been around his neck for years and had no doubt lost its potency with time. The first half of the word *Poccilateur* remotely resembles the cyrillic letters for "Russia," one of Napoleon's victorious enemies. And *wasps* could be an allusion to the bee symbol on Napoleon's imperial livery.

6 Q90

L'honniſſement puant abhominable	**The stinking and abominable disgrace**
Apres le faict ſera felicité,	**After the deed he will be**
Grand excuſé, pour n'eſtre fauorable,	**congratulated,**
Qu'à paix Neptune ne ſera incité.	**The great excuse for not being**
	favorable,
	That Neptune will not be encouraged
	toward peace.

This could be about any murderer, assassin, or terrorist getting away with a terrible crime. Pick your projections. Fontbrune sees Hitler's skullduggery in the Munich Pact of 1938, which allowed the Western allies to dismember Czechoslovakia in the fateful appeasement of the sabre-rattling Führer. **Neptune** usually stands for a great sea power; here it is either the Ottoman Turks or the British Navy.

6 Q91

Du conducteur de la guerre nauale,	**Of the commander of the naval war,**
Rouge effrené, ſeuere horrible grippe,	**The unbridled red, severe, horrible**
Captif eſchappé de l'aiſné dans la baſles:	**quarrel,**
Quant il naiſtra du grand vn filz Agrippe.	**Captive escaped from the elder one in**
	the ball:
	When there will be born a son to the
	great Agrippa.

This one could be about the naval battle of Lepanto fought in 1571 at the mouth of the Gulf of Corinth. Nostradamus is never one to overlook a classical comparison. In this case Don Juan of Austria, commander of the Christian fleet, is compared with the great Roman admiral Marcus Agrippa at the battle of Actium, which was fought 100 miles northwest of Lepanto back in 31 BC. The one in the **ball** and chains could be any of 15,000 Christian slaves freed from the holds of captured Turkish galleys. Certainly a few of them were nobles whose families were too impoverished to pay a ransom for their release. **Ball** might also describe the cannon shot that killed Ali Pasha, the admiral of the Muslim fleet.

6 Q92

Prince de beauté tant venuſte,	Prince of beauty so graceful,
Au chef¹ menee, le ſecond faict² trahy:	Led to the head, made second to betray:
La cité au glaiue de poudre face aduſte,	The city to the blade, the face burnt by gunpowder,
Par trop grand meurtre le chef du Roy hay.	Because of too great a murder the head of the King hated.

¹chef = chief, commander, principal; (figuratively) the head.
²faict = made; variant: deed, so the line could read: . . . a second deed to betray.

Most scholars believe Louis XVI is the **prince of beauty** represented here. History gives Louis a mixed review on his "comely" and somewhat corpulent "beauty." I imagine that Bouys, Le Pelletier, and Robb were influenced to pin this one on Louis because of what follows line 1. Nostradamus the royalist, however, may have been lauding the inner beauty of this mild-mannered and somewhat mystical man. In the rest of the prophecy Nostradamus plays on the literal and figurative meanings of *chef* (Louis' head and Louis as head of state):

Led to the head. In 1774 Louis XVI is led to the altar of the cathedral at Reims for his coronation.

Made second to betray. The Revolution reduced him in rank (**made second**) making him a constitutional monarch. He made an oath to maintain the liberties of the people and promised never to leave France to lead a counter-revolution. He betrayed both pledges when he and his family made their famous flight to Varennes (see 9 Q20).

The city of the blade. A *glaive* is a one-edged blade similar to that of the guillotine. Louis' betrayal led to his execution and the general purge of all traitors to the Revolution by the National Committee. After Louis and Queen Marie Antoinette met their end, thousands more felt the heavy slice of the guillotine upon the nape of their necks during the Reign of Terror.

The face burnt by gunpowder,/Because of too great a murder the head of the King hated. Sanson the executioner held Louis' severed head aloft, a trophy for the cheering, bloodthirsty mob. Later his head and body were thrown into a grave coated with quicklime powder so his hated remains would dissolve.

Quatrain Indexing Date: Q92 = 1792, the year Louis XVI was convicted of treason. It could also stand as a near miss for his execution in January 1793. This is the second time a remarkably accurate prophecy on the fate of Louis XVI reveals an accurate dating (see 9 Q20).

6 Q93

Prelat auare d'ambition trompé.	**The avaricious Prelate by ambition deceived.**
Rien ne fera que trop viendra cuider:	**He will come to believe nothing [for him] is too great:**
Ses meffagiers, & luy bien attrapé,	**He and his messengers completely entrapped,**
Tout au rebours voir, qui le bois fendroit.	**He who cut the wood sees all in reverse.**

This describes a greedy and self-righteous priest, blinded by ambition, who meets his end.

6 Q94

Vn Roy iré fera aux fedifragues,[1]	**A King will be angry with the See-breakers,**
Quand interdicts feront harnois de guerre:	**When forbidden will be arms for war:**
La poifon taincte au fuccre par les fragues	**The poison tainted in the sugar for the strawberries**
Par eaux meurtris, mors, difant terre terre.	**Murdered by waters, dead, saying: "land, land."**

[1]*sedifragues:* possibly for Latin *sedem-frangere* = to break a seat; thus any of several possible translations: seat-breakers; (Holy) See-breakers.

Out of a pool of generalities and obscurities jumps a Christian "fish" of a different etymological color. This is a prophecy damning the Holy **See-breakers**, the Protestants, but little more can be divined except a reference to tainted desserts and drownings. The image reminds me of the ironic painting by the 17th-century Dutch artist Van de Venne. On both sides of a river are a collection of hundreds of notables from the two main religious persuasions. In the water scantily clad Rubenesque men and women swim around boatloads of Protestant ministers and Catholic priests trying to net the potential cavorting converts out of the water.

A different baptism by water was waiting for victims of the Wars of Religion in the 16th century and the Thirty Years War in the 17th, when Christians with drawn swords – rather than Bibles – did unto other Christians as they were done by, casting their slaughtered victims into the rivers of France and Germany.

6 Q95

Par detracteur calumnié à puis nay.	By the detractor calumny [lodged]
Quand iſtront faicts enormes & martiaux:	against the younger born.
La moindre part dubieuſe à l'aiſnay,	When enormous and warlike deeds
Et toſt au regne ſeront faicts partiaux.[1]	will go on:
	The least part doubtful for the elder one,
	And soon in the kingdom there will be partisan deeds.

[1]Old French *partial* = partisan, ie of the French Resistance.

Leoni conjures up a cadet who is either a younger brother or from a younger branch of a royal family. Fontbrune believes it refers to the court martials held by the Republican government after the Paris Commune, as well as to the rift between the Orléanists and Legitimists in 1871. It isn't a bad try, but the quatrain is so general it could stand equally for the trials of Vichy leaders in 1945, the victims of the Paris Seize in 1588–89, or even the Nuremberg War Trials.

6 Q96

Grande cité à ſoldatz abandonnée,	Great city abandoned to the soldiers,
Onques n'y euſt mortel tumult ſi proche,	Never was there ever a mortal tumult so near,
O quelle hideuſe calamité s'approche,	O what a hideous calamity approaches,
Fors vne offence n'y ſera pardonnée.	Except one offense nothing will be pardoned.

General! Apply it to the sacking of the city of your choice. Some might say this is for the devastation of Paris during the bloody repression of the Paris Commune in 1871. The fury charging Nostradamus' writing makes me choose the final stages of the Battle of Berlin in 1945. The first three lines describe close-quarter fighting and the enormous casualties among civilians. Soviet reports released after the Cold War indicate the battle casualties from friendly fire were the highest in history. One can imagine the lethal barrage experienced by the 500,000 men of two Soviet army groups hurling themselves into street battles under a crossfire of 33,000 guns and multiple rocket launchers. During the final week of fighting the German and Soviet military casualties and civilian deaths approached an estimated 2,000 an hour.

It is hard to know what the one pardoned offense in line 4 could be. Perhaps Adolf Hitler's final offense, his own suicide, can be pardoned, since the Führer's death would finally put an end to the slaughter and savaging that his World War had perpetrated on humanity.

6 Q97

Cinq & quarante degrés ciel bruſlera,	**At forty-five degrees [latitude], the**
Feu approcher de la grand cité neufue,	**sky will burn,**
Inſtant grand flamme eſparſe ſautera,	**Fire approaches the great new city,**
Quand on voudra des Normans faire	**Immediately a huge, scattered flame**
preuue.	**leaps up,**
	When they want to have verification
	from the Normans [the Northern
	Bloc].

The sky ignites into flames on the latitude near New York City. Such an attack is quite conceivable after the year 2003, when START II fulfills its promises.

Another interpretation sees the **new city** of Novi Byelograd (New Belgrade), a suburb of Belgrade, the Serbian capital, being destroyed (perhaps by nuclear terrorism) in 1997. Whereas most interpreters believe Nostradamus got his latitudes wrong and this quatrain is for New York, it must be acknowledged that New Belgrade is the only city in the world that sits almost right under latitude 45. In August 1993 Bosnian Serb military leaders were the first Balkan combatants to threaten reprisals against their neighbors or the West through nuclear terrorism.

A more conventional doomsday interpretation sees this blaze in the sky as the greenhouse effect causing an interminable series of droughts beginning as early as 1997. (We know that in 5 Q98 fire descends from the skies over latitude 48, which draws a line across most of the Northern Hemisphere's grain belts.) If a new city is destroyed by a nuclear disaster, it is more likely to be one of the many new nuclear towns and cities with decrepit Chernobyl-style Soviet reactors. These sit along this latitude in Eastern Slovakia, in the cities of the Donets Basin in southern Ukraine, and Rostov (in southern Russia).

Quatrain Indexing Date: Q97 = 1997, the year I expect a new wave of global droughts and famines to begin.

6 Q98

Ruyne aux Volſques de peur ſi fort	**Ruin for the Volcae [of Languedoc]**
terribles,	**with fear so very terrible,**
Leur grand cité taincte, faict peſtilent:	**Their great city [Toulouse] stained,**
Piller Sol, Lune & violer leurs temples:	**pestilential deed:**
Et les deux fleuues rougir de ſang coulant.	**To plunder Sun, Moon and violate**
	their temples:
	And the two rivers to redden with
	gushing blood.

This is part one of a three-part treasure hunt using times past and the game of prophecy. Part one begins in a distant classical setting (see 8 Q29, 8 Q30).

The **Volcae** were the legendary Gallic tribe purported to have conquered and pillaged most of southern Europe and part of Anatolia in the late 4th and early 3rd centuries BC. They are said to have hoarded a treasure trove of plundered gold and silver (*sun and moon*) inside their temples at **Toulouse**. Classical karma knocked on the door of the Volcae when Toulouse was torched and sacked by a Roman army under Consul Caepio in 106 BC. The bloodshed from Toulouse drained into the Garonne, near the confluence of the River Touch and the tributary of Hers.

Part two will focus on Caepio's plunder of Toulouse.

6 Q99

L'ennemy docte ſe tournera confus,	**The erudite enemy will turn around**
Grãd camp malade, & de faict par	**confused,**
embuſches,	**The great army enfeebled, and**
Mõts Pyrenees & Pœnus[1] luy ſerôt faicts	**defeated through ambushes,**
refus,	**The Pyrenees and Pennine**
Proche du fleuue deſcouurât antiques	**mountains will be refused to him,**
oruches.	**Near the river discovering the ancient**
	urns.

[1]Latin *Alpes Poeninae* = Pennine Alps.

Generally obscure, but my call makes Napoleon the **erudite enemy**. He was well read, a novelist in his own right, and possessed an IQ estimated at around 143. But all of his intellectual gifts could not save him from the bleeding ulcer the guerrilla war in Spain would become to his Empire. While Napoleon fought in person in the German campaigns in 1813, the decimated French army of Marshal Jourdan retreated over the Pyrenees mountains after their sound defeat by the Duke of Wellington at Vitoria. The Pennine Alps, which run between the St Bernard and St Gothard passes in Switzerland, seem irrelevant in the context of the closing years of Napoleonic France. The St Bernard pass did become a rocky welcome carpet for Napoleon on happier days, when he led an army into Italy to defeat the Austrians at Marengo in 1800.

Perhaps Nostradamus is playing with the clues just to see how erudite the *interpreter* can be. If **Pennine** is an abbreviation for "Appennine," then perhaps this stands for the passes **refused** to Napoleon's brother-in-law, Jochim Murat, when his army was routed by the Austrians at the battle of Tolentino in 1815. The last line's reference to ancient artifacts does little to help matters, because all potential areas referred to here are rich in archeological debris.

Quatrain Indexing Date: Q99 = 1799, a near miss for Napoleon's invasion of Italy over the Alps in 1800.

6 Q100

| LEGIS CANTIO CONTRA INEPTOS CRITICOS. | INCANTATION OF THE LAW AGAINST INEPT CRITICS. |

Quos legent hofce verfus maturè cenfunto,
Profanum vulgur, & infcium ne attrectato:
Omnesq; Aftrologi Blenni,[1] Barbari procul
*   funto,*
Qui alter facit, if ritè, sacer esto.

May those who read this verse
**   consider it profoundly,**
Let the profane and ignorant herd
**   keep away:**
And all Astrologers, Idiots and
**   Barbarians stay far away,**
He who does otherwise, let him be
**   subject to the sacred rite.**

[1]Greek *blennos* = simpleton, blockhead.

Here we have the famous incantation against crusading debunkers, dilettantes, Nostra-channelers, nitpicking critics, and read-at-a-glance know-it-alls. Leoni is surprised to find **Astrologers** included on the list. During the 16th century an astrologer was viewed as a mere soothsayer, whereas a "celestial scientist" or "Astrologue," was not. In his Preface and Epistle narratives Nostradamus makes redundant efforts to characterize his cosmic calculations as above those of a mere astrologer.

Contrary to popular interpretation line 4 need not be taken literally as a curse. There is no hex coming from Nostradamus; rather, the curse of the projections we already harbor are reflected back to us by Nostradamus' mirror into the future. For example, if you are a debunker who has crammed Nostradamus up your own preconceived conclusions before even entering into a serious study of the quatrains, your writings will reflect this prejudice to others. If you take the other extreme and believe anything you see in his verses to be the one and only truth, Nostradamus' mirror will equally reflect all your manic and mediocre projections. Authors who conjure books – and a fast buck – out of his prophecies by publishing pot-boilers like *Nostradamus on women, love, money, your pet's future*, etc., often find their books bending the shelves of remainder clearing houses. In other words, shallow intentions and amateurish research into the prophet will be reflected in the author's interpretations and his or her pocketbook.

After 20 years of study, I conclude that the **sacred rite** has something to do with how the mirrorlike qualities of Nostradamus' word games reveal the curses I hide from myself. The **sacred rite** is initiated by my attempt to discover in his tangled verses the projected hopes, fears, expectations – and occasionally prophetic insights – I spread over his dark mirror like dust. If I can become aware of my dusty projections, I am blessed. If not – well, no one is cursing me but myself.

6 Q100dp

Fille de l'Aure, afyle du mal fain,	**Daughter of the breeze, asylum of the**
Ou iusques au ciel fe voit l'amphitheatre:	**unhealthy,**
Prodige vu, ton mal eft fort prochain,	**Where on the horizon the**
Seras captiue, et des fois plus de quatre.	**amphitheatre is seen:**
	Prodigy seen, your evil is very near,
	You will be captive, and more than
	four times.

This is the first of 8 duplicate quatrains scattered through Centuries 6, 8 and 10. Their discoverer is most likely Nostradamus' self-proclaimed chief disciple, Chavigny. Their authenticity is suspect, although I am of the opinion that they are, for the most part, authentic if somewhat overedited originals.

Several towns in Provence are noted for their hot Mistral winds and ancient Roman amphitheatres. Le Pelletier believed it was Orange, but tourists picking through the ruined amphitheaters of Nîmes, Arles, and Fréjus can also enjoy a breath of hot summer breezes during late afternoons of Provence.

Le Pelletier makes a good argument for Orange, since it was captured four times before the 19th century. The city property rights were owned by William the Silent. When this was written between 1557 and 1560, he is the **prodigy seen** who in 1668 would lead the Protestant revolt in the Spanish Netherlands. During the forthcoming Wars of Religion, Orange was taken by the Calvinists in 1561, recovered by the Catholics in 1562, and seized yet again in 1573 by a mercenary named Glandage. In March 1660 Louis XIV forcibly razed its fortifications to prevent further Huguenot rebellions. One could also say the fourth capture took place in 1701, when the claim of ownership for Orange was resolved by the death of William III and the extinction of the House of Orange. Louis XIV settled a disputed claim by awarding the city to Francis Louis de Bourbon-Conti, who gave the city to France in 1731.

7 Q1

L'Arc du threſor par Achilles deceu,	**The Ark of the treasure through**
Aux procreés ſceu la quadrangulaire:	**Achilles cut off,**
Au faict Royal le cõment¹ ſera ſceu	**In the documents, the quadrangular**
Corps veu pẽdu au veu du populaire.	**known:**
	By the royal deed the comment will be
	known
	Body seen hung in the sight of the
	populace.

¹Latin *commentum* = invention, contrivance; comment (Robb).

Robb makes one of his finest arguments for the veracity of Nostradamus' second sight (*Prophecies on World Events by Nostradamus*, pages 11–12). It concerns the killing of Concino Concini, Chief Minister of France in 1617, by order of the 16-year old Louis XIII. Concini and the Queen Regent, Marie de' Medici, had together drained the royal treasury and squandered on themselves the hard-earned national savings collected by the late Henry IV. By 1617 Concini had bought himself the highest powers of France. Even the protests of the Estates General, summoned in 1614, had not the power to see him dismissed. Garencières tells us that by this time Concini had purchased the royal title. He adds, "The Maréchal d'Ancre was first complained of for his malversations by Achilles de Harlay, President of Paris." De Harlay's attacks resulted in Concini's cash cow, the **Ark** of the royal treasury, being **cut off** for the time being.

Though checked, the corrupt Florentine remained all-powerful. He was still Chief Minister of government and of finance, as well as Constable of the French armed forces. He had powerful friends in his pocket, among them de' Medici herself. Only death could stop him. Unfortunately for Concini, he did not have the young king on his side. Louis XIII detested him and was easily convinced by his new favorite, an army officer named Albert de Luynes, to order a coup.

On 24 April 1617, when Concini sauntered into the broad public square of the Louvre known as the Quadrangle, a band of the king's bodyguards blocked his path. Monsieur Vitri, the captain of the Guard, read the royal order for Concini's arrest in the name of the king. Concini saw the pistols held at the ready under their cloaks, turned and ran and was shot down trying to escape.

Louis had given the order for his arrest and execution (**the royal deed**). When he heard that Concini was dead, he made the now-famous comment, "Now I am king!" (*the comment will be known*). According to Sir Richard Lodge, Concini's body was hung in sight of the populace. After he was buried the mob dug him up and hung him by the feet off the Pont Neuf before they dragged his swelling corpse through the dirty streets to be burned (*Body seen hung in the sight of the populace*). Robb reminds us that Concini's bought title means "Marshal of the Anchor." He believes line 1 hides this title since an anchor has an *Ar(c)*-shaped curve.

Quatrain Indexing Date: 7Q1 backwards is 17 = 1617.

7 Q2

Par Mars ouuert Arles de donra guerre,	**Opened by Mars Arles will not give war,**
De nuict feront les foldartz eftonnés:	**By night will the soldiers be astonished:**
Noir, blanc à l'inde diffimulés en terre,	**Black, white to indigo concealed on**
Souz la faincte vmbre traiftres verez[1] & fonnés.	**land,**
	Under the sacred [or feigned] shadow you will see traitors and ring [the alarm].

[1]*verez* = a) Old French *verrer* = to sweep; b) *verrez*, 2nd person plural, future tense, of *voir* = you will see.

I could support my 20th-century bias and say this is too obscure for me to unravel. It would be more honest to say that I don't have enough information to write anything definitive. Obscurity isn't always Nostradamus' fault. Often the clues become clearer when we move closer to a prophecy's time for fulfillment. I can only give a hunch, for what it's worth, that this might represent the fighting around Arles during the inland advance of Franco-American forces after their sea landings on the French Riviera.

In other places, Mars stands for a militant Germany. Line 2 adequately pictures the general confusion behind German lines when thousands of Allied paratroopers descended from the skies the night before the landings. Line 3 could be the prophet's attempt to describe the landing beacons and flares guiding the paratroopers to the drop zones. Perhaps he saw French collaborators ring the alarm to their German masters quartered in Arles.

7 Q3

Apres de France la victoire nauale,	**After the naval victory of France,**
Les Barchinons, Saillinons,[1] les Phocens,[2]	**The Barcelonians, Saillinons, those of Marseilles,**
Lierre d'or, l'enclume ferré dedans la bafle,	**Robber of gold, the anvil shut within the ball,**
Ceux de Ptolon au fraud feront confens.	**Those of Ptolon will be a party to the deception.**

[1]Nostradamus' name for the inhabitants of environs of Salon. Le Pelletier claims *Saillien* represents the classical Ligurian tribe, the Salians, which once lived in the Salon area.
[2]*Phocens* = Latin *Phocaeans*, founders of Marseilles.

This is about Operation Anvil (otherwise code-named Dragoon), the Allied invasion of southern France in 1944.

The only fly in the cloudy wine of this interpretation is line 2, which again places Barcelona in the Riviera landings. **Saillinons** stands for the environs of Salon, where troop movements and a few skirmishes between American and retreating German units did take place. Marseilles was a major battle zone three days after the landing. The cryptic line 3 could be about French Resistance operations leading up to Anvil. Perhaps it describes in poetic obscurity the intrigues of FFI forces or the plundering of banks by the Nazis prior to the invasion. The **ball** could be a bomb, or Nostradamus' attempt at describing one of the numerous ocean mines laid by the Germans along the Riviera.

Ptolon in line 4 stands for Ptolemy, the classical allusion to Hellenistic Egypt. During World War II Egypt was the chief British base of operations in North Africa. It is from there that the Axis armies suffered their first catastrophic defeat in the Mediterranean war zone at El Alamein in 1943. This defeat eventually led to the French Riviera landings of 1944.

7 Q4

Le duc de Langres aſſiegé dedans Dolle,	**The Duke of Langres besieged in Dôle,**
Accompaigné d'Oſtun & Lyonnois:	**Accompanied by Autun and those of Lyons:**
Geneue, Auſpour, ioinct ceux de Mirandole,	**Geneva, Augsburg, joined with those of Mirandola,**
Paſſer les monts contre les Anconnois.	**To pass over the mountains against those of Ancona.**

Well, what to say about this net made of many geographical locations, cast over a large body of obscure possibilities? To start with, **Langres** is in Champagne on the eastern frontier of France. It has no **duke** but there is a bishop. This post was held from 1528 to 1561 by Claude de Longwy, Cardinal de Givry. Since **Duke** François de Guise, and later his son Henry, were the hereditary seneschals of Champaigne, perhaps Nostradamus intends either scion of the House of Lorraine in this prophecy.

Now for another geography lesson, in lines 2 and 3: **Dôle** was in Franche-Comté and remained a Spanish outpost until 1678, long after the House of Lorraine was reduced to irrelevance. To the west of Franche-Comté lies **Autun** in Burgundy. **Lyons** lies south of Burgundy. **Geneva** was an independent state and Calvinist Mecca in Switzerland. **Augsburg** was a bishopric in southwest Germany, but is better known as the scene of the Diet that produced the Augsburg Confession, as well as the Treaty of Augsburg, which pacified the Protestants in central Europe until the 17th century. Now we march east and south to sunny Italy, toward the independent Italian principality of **Mirandola**; then we travel farther south to the papal possession of **Ancona** on the Adriatic.

One wonders if we will find purpose for our prophet's geographic wanderings. This quatrain could stand as an alternative future never accessed. The forces of Guise and Burgundy find themselves besieged at Dôle by the Spanish while the papal states are invaded by Imperial troops. If we drop our Guises, we do get from the prophetic labyrinth a siege of Dôle, the capital of Spanish-held Franche-Comté, in 1636 during the Thirty Years War. By the autumn the Imperial forces pushed the French out of the region, but no battles took place in Italy at this time.

7 Q5

Vin ſur la table en ſera reſpandu,
Le tiers n'aura celle qu'il pretendoit:
Deux fois du noir de Parme deſcendu,
Perouſe à Pize fera ce qu'il cuidoit.

Wine on the table some will be
   spilled,
The third will not have that which he
   [it?] claimed:
Twice descended from the black
   [king] of Parma,
Perugia will do to Pisa that which he
   [it?] believed.

Nostradamus might have traveled leisurely through the narrow streets of **Parma** on a mule. I saw it pass by my train window between a few black blinks of a train tunnel on my way to Florence to produce my first Nostradamus book in 1986. Be that as it may, the prophecy describes the succession of blue- and bastard-bloods in Italian principalities. In Nostradamus' time the papacy possessed Perugia, and Pisa was a property of the Prince of Tuscany. Parma was pieced together into a Duchy by Pope Paul III in 1545 to pacify his bastard son Pierluigi Farnese. Now this has little relevance to the prophecy unless Nostradamus means **twice descended** to chronicle the two families holding the dukedom from 1545 through 1859. Once the Farnese seed had petered out, Parma passed to the princely Bourbons from 1731 through 1859.

Who cares!

7 Q6

Naples, Palerme, & toute la Secille,
Par main barbare[1] ſera inhabitee,
Corſicque, Salerne & de Sardeigne l'iſle,
Faim, peſte, guerre fin de maux intemptee.

Naples, Palermo and all of Sicily,
Will be uninhabited through
   barbarian hands,
Corsica, Salerno, the island of Sardinia,
Hunger, plague, war, the end of
   extended evils.

[1]barbare = a) barbarian; b) Barbary Corairs of North Africa in Nostradamus' day; c) Libya (Qadaffi?), Algerians or Tunisians of today; d) cryptogram from the French Arabe = Arabs, or Arab terrorists.

This is the thirteenth and final quatrain displaying an apocalyptic sequence of hunger, plague, and war leading to the end of extended evils and a new era of peace. In this quatrain a number of disasters are hinted at: First, a nuclear reactor meltdown, triggered by an act of nuclear terrorism, which causes the evacuation of everyone on the islands of Sicily, Corsica, Sardinia, and the southern half of the Italian peninsula. The prevailing winds of a terrorist attack on French nuclear reactor plants in the Rhône river valley could be the source. Winds carrying clouds of chemical or biological agents across the Adriatic from some future Balkan War or nuclear disaster are another possibility. In 5 Q90 a plague of **false dust** requires the evacuation of southeastern Europe for nine months. If this plague comes through terrorism, the culprits are fingered by a Nostradamian cryptogram of *barbare* for either North Africans or North African-based Arab terrorists.

Lest we become overwhelmed by these imminent travails, it is important to remember that what is fighting and dying – the **extended evils** of the old humanity – will be replaced by something much more life-affirmative. The creative process is always inherently destructive to the old order. Michelangelo's *David*, for example, emerges from the chaos that destroyed the original form of rock from which it is sculpted. According to many traditions of prophecy, we are now living through the final chaotic and violent stages of the world as we have known it for the past 10 millennia. Our world, moving towards the birth of a new humanity, is like that rock being chiseled away by a great sculptor's strokes. We may despair at seeing the detritus of old and hallowed traditions, ecosystems and social systems fly off into oblivion. We are bound to feel anguish at what is being forever lost and fear for what is yet to come.

For Nostradamus, the mysterious and divine sculptor is the cosmos. The stars and planets are its language. Through them, the prophet sets before us dates that mark the final tribulation-strokes leading to the Millennium and the revelation of a new humanity.

7 Q7

Sur le combat des grans cheuaux, legiers,	**Upon the struggle of the great light horses,**
On criera le grand croiſſant confond.	**They will proclaim the Islamic resistance is overwhelmed.**
De nuict tuer monts, habits de bergiers,	**To kill by night, in the mountains, dressed in shepherd's clothing,**
Abiſmes rouges dans le foſſé[1] profond.	**Abysmal Reds in the deep valleys.**

[1]Ditch, drain, trench; moat.

Much of this prophecy could be attributed to the Afghanistan War (1979–88). The struggle of the great **light horses** could describe the

Afghan guerrillas making their way through the mountain passes on horses and pack animals. One can get **Islamic resistance** out of line 2's *le grand croissant* (the great crescent). Most of the Mujahideen were dressed in shepherd's clothing. The **abysmal Reds** are the Soviet occupation forces that systematically destroyed and gassed hundreds of Afghani villages and towns, killing over one million civilians *in* **the deep valleys** of mountainous Afghanistan.

7 Q8

Flora fuis, fuis le plus proche Romain,	**Florence flee, flee the nearest Roman,**
Au feſulan ſera conflict donné:	**At Fiesole will conflict be given:**
Sang eſpandu, les plus grans prins à main,	**Blood shed, the greatest ones captured by hand,**
Temple ne ſexe ne ſera pardonné.	**Neither Temple nor sex will be spared.**

One of the ways to enjoy the vista of Florence is to travel to the little fortress town of Fiesole perched high over the Arno valley. Sitting on the high hills and looking down on the meandering Arno as it draws its blue line through tiled-roofed forget-me-nots of the Renaissance, I have a hard time imagining Nostradamus' dire warnings about this town coming true. Perhaps they are only the detritus of his own fears projected on the waters of his oracle, and not a future that will be. The past few centuries assure us that the story within this quatrain of a battle at Fiesole, and the slaughter of all its men and women, is a future that never happened. May it never happen.

7 Q9

Dame à l'abſence de ſon grand capitaine,	**The Lady in the absence of her great captain,**
Sera priee d'amours du Viceroy,	**Will be invited to make love with the Viceroy,**
Faincte promeſſe & malheureuſe eſtraine,	**Feigned promise and unlucky success in love,**
Entre les mains du grand prince Barroys.	**Between the hands of the great Prince of Bar.**

Some believe the Lady of this quatrain is the mistress of Henry II, Diane de Poitiers, shortly after his death in 1559. But if you could peek into the bedchamber and see the spent Diane de Poitiers resting in the bed, you would find a woman already well into her hot flashes and fifties at the writing of this quatrain. Stop, retrace your narrative steps, click on "virtual reality" and drag down the name of the person this quatrain is actually about, Marguérite de Valois, better known by her many lovers as *la Reine Margot*. It is said she was Nostradamus' favorite of the seven

Valois children whose horoscope he drew at Blois in 1556. But the events of this prophecy capture our petite Margot long past puberty. She is now a fetching beauty and, some wags would add, a fetchable nymphomaniac.

Though initially repelled by the pungent Protestant, Henry de Navarre, Marguérite later saved his life during the St Bartholomew's Day Massacre and became his confidante. On occasion – after getting used to his Protestant ways and his garlic breath – she also behaved as his wife in the biblical sense.

A **Viceroy** would be comparable to a Constable or Lieutenant-General of France. That leaves us the old and crotchety Anne de Montmorency, the Constable of France, as one of Margot's strange bedfellows (definitely not her type) or the dashing and virile **Viceroy** (or Lieutenant-General) of the Catholic leaguers, Henry de Guise.

Line 3 is definitely Margot; she had numerous frivolous love affairs and a handful of deep though tragic liaisons, such as with Le Molle, who was beheaded. Line 4 aptly describes the more significant object of her pleasure and passion, Henry de Guise, who just so happened to be born in the Castle of **Bar**. Just what did Nostradamus see in the little child's stars, that he prudently kept secret from her mother, Catherine de' Medici? Did he witness the baby of François de Guise and her daughter in their dangerous liaisons of the coming decades?

7 Q10

Par le grand prince limitrophe du Mans,	**By the great Prince bordering Le Mans,**
Preux & vaillant chef de grand exercite:	**Gallant and brave chief of the great**
Par mer & terre de Gallotz[1] & Normans,	**army:**
Cafpre paffer Barcelone pillé ifle.	**By land and sea with Gallot-speaking**
	Bretons and Normans,
	To pass Gibraltar and Barcelona the
	isle pillaged.

[1] Old French *Gallot* = what the Breton-speaking inhabitants of Brittany call the French-speaking Bretons.

Le Mans is the chief city of Maine in northwest France. Neighboring Mayenne is the next. It belonged to the Guises of the House of Lorraine. In Nostradamus' day François de Guise's brother Claude was the Marquis of Mayenne, Duc de Aumale, and Governor of Burgundy (1526–73). He fought a number of significant battles during the Wars of Religion. But what a future he might have had if his liege, Henry II, had not died in a jousting accident in 1559 and instead had become the second Charlemagne of Nostradamus' dreams. No battles with Protestants at Dreux, St Denis, and Montcontour would have happened. Instead the Marquis de Mayenne would lead an invasion of Spain and North Africa. He could have tagged one of the Balearic Islands onto his titles.

7 Q11

L'enfant Royal contemnera la mere,
Oeil, piedʒ bleſſés, rude, inobeiſſant,
Nouuelle à dame eſtrange & bien amere,
Seront tués des ſiens plus de cinq cens.

The infant Royal will despise his
    mother,
Eye, feet wounded, rude, disobedient,
Strange and very bitter news to the
    lady,
Her followers will be killed, more
    than five hundred.

I believe this is about Concini's assassination (see 7 Q1) and has nothing to do with the death of Napoleon III's son, the Prince Impériale, during the Zulu Wars in South Africa in 1879.

The **infant Royal** is Louis XIII, who hated his free-spending and decadent mother, Marie de' Medici. Upon reaching age 16, he ordered his household guards to murder her favorite, the highly unpopular and corrupt chief minister of the realm, Concini. Concini resisted arrest (**rude, disobedient**) and was shot several times in the quadrangle of the Louvre (**eye, feet wounded**). Louis rejoiced at the news, declaring "Now I am a king!" but Marie grieved the loss of her chief companion in draining the royal treasury. Her days of buying friends and extravagant gifts were over. Garencières claims that more than 500 of Marie de' Medici's followers were killed. One was the sorceress wife of Concini, who was convicted as a witch and beheaded. Her body was publicly burned.

7 Q12

Le grand puiſné fera fin de la guerre,
Aux dieux aſſemble les excuſés:
Cahors, Moiſſac iront long de la ſerre,
Reffus Leſtore, les Agenois raʒés.

The great younger brother will make
    an end to war,
Before the gods the exiles assemble:
Cahors and Moissac will go far from
    the prison,
Refusal at Lestore, the people of Agen
    cut down.

Most scholars agree that since the **younger brother**, or descendant of the younger brother, of a ruler is called a cadet, any scion of the Guise would be considered cadets of the House of Lorraine. This doesn't rule out other cadets in French history, such as the youngest brother of Louis XVI, the Duc de Artois, who later became Charles X. **Cahors, Moissac**, and **Agen** are all in southwestern France. This prophecy would better parallel the civil wars fought by the Guise during the Wars of Religion. Artois didn't lead White Bourbon armies in that region during the royalist counter-revolution, which saw most of the fighting in Brittany, Normandy, Lyonnais, and mainly in the Vendée.

7 Q13

De la cité marine & tributaire,	From the marine and tributary city,
La *fefte raze prendra la fatrapie:*	The crophead will take the seat of government:
Chaffer fordide qui puis fera contraire,	To chase the sordid one who will then be against him,
Par quatorze ans tiendra la tyrannie.	For fourteen years he will hold the tyranny.

After becoming First Consul of France, Napoleon, the hero of Toulon *the marine and tributary city*, shaved off his long locks to resemble his favorite ancient Roman dictator, Julius Caesar. Nostradamus dates the exact length of time Napoleon would hold power in this new image – fourteen years (from 9 November 1799 to 13 April 1814).

There have been many attempts to identify the *sordid one* Napoleon must *chase*. I would say it is Napoleon's chief military rival for glory during the French Revolutionary Wars, General Moreau, who later turned against Bonaparte and was exiled (chased *out*) when Napoleon became a dictator. He offered his services to the Allied Coalitions fighting to restore Bourbon rule to France. Moreau was killed by a lucky shot from a French cannonball at the Battle of Dresden in 1813.

Quatrain Indexing Date: Q13 = 1813. The German Campaign and the Battle of Nations, which broke Napoleon's Empire. The year 1813 just misses for the year of his abdication, 1814, but his abdication occurred on 13 April 1814.

7 Q14

Faux expofer viendra topographie,	They will come to expose the false topography,
Seront les cruches des monumens ouuertes:	The funeral urns and monuments will be opened:
Palluler fecte faincte philofophie,	Thus multiplies the philosophy of the sacred [or false] sect,
Pour blanches, noires, & pour antiques vertes.	Blacks for white, and sour [grapes] for the ancients.

In Nostradamus' day the massive eight-towered fortress of the Bastille lay on the outer defense perimeter of Paris. By July 1789 it was made into a prison. It quickly became a much-hated symbol of the Ancien Régime, an island in a sea of tenements of the poor. After it was seized by the Paris mob, the Bastille was demolished. Perhaps line 2's poetry implies the demolition of the Bastille as well as the numerous desecrations of graves and tombs across France during the Revolution. Robespierre and his henchmen would later abolish the Church and put in its place the Cult of Reason. Line 4 waxes poetic with *sour [grapes]*: we learn that our royalist prophet views the new order of France with sour grapes.

Quatrain Indexing Date: 7 Q14 = Bastille Day, 14 July (7th month) 1789. This is the second time a quatrain is numbered 14 that probably applies to the French Revolution.

7 Q15

Deuant cité de l'Infubre[1] contree,	**Before the city of the Insubrian**
Sept ans fera le fiege deuant mis:	**region,**
Le trefgrand Roy y fera fon entree.	**The siege will be laid for seven years:**
Cité puis libre hors de fes ennemis.	**The very great King will make his**
	entry.
	City then free away from its enemies.

[1]Lombardy, of which the capital city is Milan.

A detailed prophecy of a seven-year siege of Milan that never happened. The King is presumably the Charlemagne who never was, the great *Chyren Selin*, Henry II. He liberates **Milan** and the Lombards from the yoke of Spanish Imperialism so that they can instead enjoy the new Imperialism of the French. The closest this quatrain comes to fulfillment is through the usurpation of Milan by the arrival of a most unroyal and un-*Chyren* tyrant, Napoleon Bonaparte. Milan, and by extension, Lombardy, did suffer a seven-year war with the French from 1793 through 1800, which ended with Napoleon's triumphal entry into Milan on 2 June 1800.

7 Q16

Entree profonde par la grand Royne faicte	**The deep entry made by the great**
Rendra le lieu puiffant inacceffible:	**queen**
L'armee des troys lyons fera deffaite,	**Will render the place powerful and**
Faifant dedans cas hideux & terrible.	**inaccessible:**
	The army of the three lions will be
	defeated,
	Causing within a hideous and terrible
	event.

In 1985, Indira Gandhi, the Prime Minister of India, was gunned down by Sikh separatists who had infiltrated her bodyguards. The murder was in retaliation for her ordering the Indian Army's bloody attack of Khalistani guerrillas holding out within the holiest shrine of the Sikhs, the Golden Temple in Amritsar. The **great queen** could be Mrs Gandhi or her granddaughter, Priyanka, who is being groomed for power by the Congress Party. The **army** of **three lions** is the Indian Army (the Republic of India has **three lions** huddled together in its federal device). If

Nostradamus is not alluding to this incident, perhaps he is implying some future defeat of a descendant of Gandhi in a war over Jammu-Kashmir and the Punjab. The final line could describe a breakdown of Indian society in the wake of sectarian violence after the defeat. Or perhaps *within* something worse. Maybe our prophet is warning of a plague from *within* – in other words, a radiation scourge caused by a nuclear disaster at the atomic plant near Mumbai (Bombay), or from a nuclear bush war with Pakistan sometime between 1996 and 2026.

7 Q17

Le prince rare de pitié & clemence,	**The prince rare in pity and clemency,**
Viendra changer par mort grand cognoiſſance:	**Will come to change through death great knowledge:**
Par grand repos le regne trauaillé,	**Through great tranquillity the kingdom fashioned,**
Lors que le grand toſt ſera eſtrillé.	**When the great one soon will be fleeced.**

Jochmans in *Rolling Thunder* (page 208) claims this describes events in AD 9000, near the Age of Scorpio, when humanity experiences a spiritual and physical death and regeneration. Later in *Nostradamus Now* (page 222) he sharpens his view a bit upon an Antichrist-or-Avatar theme, saying the teacher will be a comforter, peacemaker, and revealer to humanity.

I might add that these changes may come far sooner than AD 9000. However, real spiritual catalysts never actually behave in the way we project on them. When Jesus walked the Earth, the Jewish people dreamed of a militant savior in the Age of Aries mode. But Jesus was a master of the softer, more mystical and abstract Piscean era. Now, as the age of the "fish man" draws to a close, it would be good to become aware of Piscean projections we place on the Aquarian Age spiritual masters we condemn today. The new always challenges the known. The truth never fits with the dream. And those who can change the course of human consciousness are usually downright disturbing to our egos and our dreams.

Quatrain Indexing Date: Q17 = 2017, 2117, 2217, etc.

7 Q18

Les aſſiegés couloureront leurs paches,	**The besieged will color their pacts,**
Sept iours apres feront cruelle iſſue	**Seven days after they will make a cruel attack**
Dans repoulſés feu, ſang. Sept mis à l'hache	**Driven back inside fire, blood. Seven put to the ax**
Dame captiue qu'auoit la paix tiſſue.	**The Lady who had woven the peace captive.**

Obscurity is the mother of many speculative children. Some will grow up to be entertaining, others embarrassing. Here is a collection of interpretive progeny born from the filmy womb of Nostradamus' verse.

Cheetham (from Leoni) adds this to the long list of brow-scratchers: "A treacherous enemy will pretend to sue for peace while under siege." Leoni says he will make a savage attack seven days later; Cheetham says he will fall into the hands of disaster while making a daring escape. Both agree on the retroactive sense of line 4, which is redolent of the "Ladies Peace" of 1529, as the Peace of Cambrai was known, since it was negotiated by the mother of Francis I and the aunt of Charles V. When in doubt, Lamont casts his vote for France's surrender in World War II and the inept Vichy government that followed. Prieditis raises his hand for the Soviet–German Non-Aggression Pact of 1939. And last but not least, Jochmans gives a "dam" for *dame* as an abbreviation for "Saddam" Hussein, the **peace captive** of the Gulf War of 1991.

Prieditis' call is the most plausible call since Hitler and Stalin's pact was signed seven days before the outbreak of World War II. The seven metaphorically **put to the ax** are the seven neighbors of Nazi Germany soon to be overrun: Poland, France, Russia, Holland, Belgium, Yugoslavia, and Greece. The **Lady** is Marianne, symbol of the Third French Republic, made **captive** by the fall of France in 1940.

7 Q19

Le fort Nicene ne ſera combatu,	**The fort of Nice will not be fought against,**
Vaincu ſera par rutilant metal	**It will be vanquished by shining metal**
Son faict ſera vn long temps debatu,	**Its reality will be a long time debated,**
Aux citadins eſtrange eſpouuantal.	**To the citizens strange and frightful.**

This is a mystery in shining metal. Perhaps the city fathers of Nice are being bribed by the **shining metal** of money. Leoni says this may have been fulfilled once after 1555–56.

In a modern application, the fort of Nice is vanquished without a fight by the shining metal of a missile. But one could push this poor prophecy over the edge of a shiny metal UFO whose sighting will be *a long time debated*. Jacques Vallee records a UFO sighting in the little village of Biot, just a few miles outside of Nice (*Passport to Magonia*, page 228, case #253). While riding home from his job as a municipal employee on 14 October 1954 (whether on a bicycle, motorbike or car is not made clear in Vallee's report), José Casella sighted an oval-shaped aluminum object. It was about 5.5 meters in diameter and 1 meter high. When he stopped, the object sprang into the sky at a high speed. Several other witnesses confirmed the sighting. They describe the disk as gray, supporting a dome, and emitting a soft whistle. Apparently it took off when Casella was only 6 meters away.

7 Q20

Ambaſſadeurs de la Toſcane langue,	**Ambassadors of the Tuscan language,**
Auril & May Alpes & mer paſſer:	**April and May, the Alps and sea to**
Celuy de veau[1] expoſera l'harangue,	**pass:**
Vie Gauloiſe ne venant effacer.	**The one of the calf will deliver the**
	harangue,
	[About] not wanting to erase the
	French way of life.

[1]Le Pelletier believes this is a play on *Vaud*, the Swiss canton.

Initially this one hinges on **veau** standing for the Calvinist stronghold of the Vaud, whose chief city is Lausanne. Nostradamus' nemesis, Théodore de Bèze, was a professor of Greek there from 1549 to 1558. Lee McCann, writing during World War II, feels compelled to make the **one of the calf** Adolf Hitler bleating his **harangue**, because the Führer was born a Taurus on the cusp of Aries (April 30). He conquers France in 1940 and pledges not to erase the French way of life. Leoni, ever the Astrophobe, thinks McCann's calf/Hitler idea is absurd. He makes Tuscany a synecdoche for Fascist Italy. Now our **calf** is the bull-necked Mussolini, promising peaceful intentions for the French between 1938 and 1940, while preparing his own entry into World War II with 32 divisions during April and May of 1940. He did attack France over the Maritime Alps on 20 June. The French navy and the RAF made a sortie on the Italian coast six days later.

7 Q21

Par peſtilente inimitié Volſicque,[1]	**By the pestilential enmity of**
Diſſimulee chaſſera le tyran:	**Languedoc,**
Au pont de Sorgues ſe fera la traffique,	**Dissimulated the tyrant chased out:**
De mettre à mort luy & ſon adherant.	**On the bridge of Sorgues will be made**
	a trade,
	To put to death him and his
	adherent.

[1]Latin *Volcae* = classical inhabitants of the territory corresponding to Languedoc.

Here we have an incident on the bridge at **Sorgues**, a town in Vaucluse, between Avignon and Carpentras. **Languedoc** had a number of Huguenot strongholds during the Wars of Religion. Perhaps a hostage or prisoner was exchanged at the bridge, later leading to the execution of a Huguenot fanatic and his disciple. But this could apply equally to a similar event on the bridge of Sorgues during the Royalist counter-revolution in 1792–93. Or perhaps Vichy collaborationists are turning over a French Resistance leader and his companion to the German Gestapo. Without any evidence from the townspeople of Sorgues to the contrary, this remains a castle prophecy in the clouds.

7 Q22

Les citoyens de Mefopotamie,[1]
Yrés encontre amis de Tarraconne,[2]
Ieux, ritz, banquetz, toute gent endormie
Vicaire au Rofne,[3] prins cité, ceux
    d'Aufone.

> The citizens of Mesopotamia,
> Angry against the friends of
>   Wormwood,
> Games, rites, banquets, the whole
>   population put to sleep
> Vicar at Rome, city taken, those of
>   Ausonia [southern Italy].

[1]Either modern Iraq; the Venassin enclave between the Rhône and the Durance at Avignon; or, Paris between the Seine and Marne.
[2]Tarraconne = a) Latin Tarroca = Tarragona in Catalonia, Spain; b) Tarragon = wormwood = Chernobyl in Ukrainian (Kidogo).
[3]Either Rome or the Rhône River.

The citizens of Iraq after the Gulf War of 1991 are angry at their former Soviet allies, the Russians, represented here by **Wormwood** (Chernobyl in Ukrainian). Line 3 carries us north to the former Red Square, where we see the renaissance of Communist Mayday celebrations between 1996 and 1999. The Communist Party is put back in power by a Russian people tired of the harsh capitalist realities and chaos of democracy. They desire to return to the blissful sleep of Marxist slogans and impossible proletarian dreams. The final line clearly logs this during the times of the final pope when Rome is seized or destroyed in either an ecological or military holocaust in the 21st century.

7 Q23

Le Royal fceptre fera contrainct de prendre,
Ce que fes predecefeurs auoient engaigé:
Puis que l'aneau on fera mal entendre,
Lors qu'on viendra le palays faccager.

> The royal scepter will be constrained
>   to take,
> That which his predecessors had
>   pledged:
> Because they will pretend not to
>   understand about the ring,
> When they will come to sack the
>   palace.

Detailed leads going nowhere specific very fast. I sense a reference to a king inheriting not only the **scepter** but the bankrupt royal treasury of his predecessor. The crown jewels and the palace go on the block. The mobs of the French Revolution did **sack** the Tuileries **palace**. In a less likely application, a British royal of the 21st century might be obliged to sell off jewels and downsize the Crown's number of palaces to make ends meet.

7 Q24

L'enseuely sortyra du tombeau,	**The one put into a shroud will come out from his tomb,**
Fera de chaines lier le fort du pont:	**He will cause the fort of the bridge to be tied in chains:**
Empoysonné auec œufz de Barbeau,[1]	**Infected with the spawn of a pimp,**
Grand de Lorraine par le Marquis du Pont.[2]	**Great One of Lorraine by the Marquis du Pont.**

[1]*Barbeau* = a) blue-bottle or cornflower; (slang) pimp; b) *barbel* = a European freshwater fish with barbels on its upper jaw (Leoni).
[2]*Marquis du Pont*: the younger son of the House of Lorraine had the title of Marquis du Pont à Mousson.

Lines 1 and 2 depict someone incorrectly declared dead. Once out of his tomb he will cause the Marquis du Pont (à Mousson) to be put in chains. A Barbeau can be either a blue flower or a pimp. If **Barbel** is intended, the fry of a European freshwater fish is implied, perhaps as some metaphor for a person or coat-of-arms. If this is for Nostradamus' near future, the **Great One of Lorraine** is young Charles III being taken to the French court by the Marquis du Pont à Mousson for his education. Leoni reminds us that the title **Marquis du Pont** was awarded to the man ruling a sovereign principality created by Emperor Charles IV under the Duc de Bar. This second title, which was given to youngest sons of the Duc de Lorraine, was borne by the heir to the Duchy of Bar which passed to the House of Lorraine in 1431.

So who is the one struggling out of his shroud? The Duc de Lorraine is poisoned by his youngest son, the young marquis. A specific prophecy about an event that never happened.

7 Q25

Par guerre longue tout l'exercite expuiser,	**Through long war all the forces exhausted,**
Que pour souldartz ne trouueront pecune:	**So that they will not find money for the soldiers:**
Lieu d'or d'argent, cuit on viendra cuser,[1]	**Instead of gold and silver, they will come to coin leather,**
Gaulois ærain, signe croissant de Lune.	**Gallic brass, sign [of the] crescent moon [stamped upon it].**

[1]Latin *cudere* = to stamp out (coins), to mint money.

After a ruinous war, no money remains in the treasury to pay the mercenary soldiers.

This sounds as if it could be a near-future prediction of Henry II's financial difficulties in paying mercenaries after the debacle of St Quentin and his loss of the Hapsburg-Valois Wars by 1559. Line 3's idea of **leather** money may be more poetic than literal for the collapse of the economy. A number of Nostradamians pin this event on the economic depressions after World War I. McCann gives us a good reason to do so. An illustration in the *Extrait du Jour* (Georges Lachapelle, *Les Finances de la IIIᵉ République* [2/26/1937]) displays a series of French coins that were minted in 1914 and were in the form of a full moon; those of 1918 are only a half moon. They shrank to a quarter moon in 1936, and finally to thin crescents in 1937. Leather money metaphors aside, this could therefore be a prophecy illustrating the devalued French franc in the final decades of the Third Republic.

7 Q26

Fuſtes & galees autour de ſept nauires,	Foists and galleys around the seven ships,
Sera liuree vne mortelle guerre:	They will deliver a deadly war:
Chef de Madric receura coup de vires,[1]	The Chief of Madrid will receive a thrust from arrows,
Deux eſchapees & cinq menees à terre.	Two escaped, and five brought to land.

[1] *vires* = arrows; alternative: *virer* = to attack (in a nautical sense).

A contemporary slant gives us seven Spanish galleons beset by the galleys of Barbary Corsairs in the Mediterranean. In 1571 Don Juan of Austria, the half-brother of Philip II, set sail from Messina to engage the Ottoman Turkish fleet. He commanded a Christian armada of 200 galleys from Spain, Monaco, the papal states, and Venice, including 6 galleasses. The latter were larger and more heavily armed than anything yet seen in the Mediterranean. They would act like floating wooden fortresses, raining down deadly fire upon the Turkish galleys in their effort to help the Christians win the Battle of Lepanto. The commander of the Spanish galleys was not killed by **arrows**, but Barbarigo, the commander of the Venetian galleys, died instantly from a shot through the eye by an arrow, just as his galleys had run the Turkish left wing aground on the coast and were chasing their fugitive crews inland for the final slaughter.

7 Q27

Au cainct[1] de Vaſt la grand caualerie,	At the wall of Vasto the great cavalry,
Proche à Ferrage empeſchee au bagaige:	Near to Ferrara hindered by baggage:
Prompt à Turin feront tel volerie,	Suddenly at Turin they will commit such robbery,
Que dans le fort rauiront leur hoſtaige.	That inside the fort they will ravage their hostage.

[1] Old French for belt or waist. Possibly used here to mean "encircling".

Nine villages, a monastery near Arras, and a port near Cherbourg, all in northern France, are named after St Vast, but the focus here is in Italy. **Turin** in Savoy spent much of the 16th century in French hands. A reference to the city walls of **Vasto** would direct us far away to the south of **Turin** and Ferrara, near Chieti, in the Kingdom of the Two Sicilies. The sacking and general chaos in Turin could just as well describe the final stages of the Italian Campaign of World War II, when Italian partisans fought elements of the retreating German Army (**hindered by baggage**) and Italian Fascists of the Salò Republic in the streets of Turin.

7 Q28

Le capitaine conduira grande proye,
Sur la montaigne des ennemis plus
proche,
Enuironné, par feu fera tel voye,
Tous efchappez, or[1] trente mis en
broche.

The captain will conduct the great herd,
On the mountain much nearer to the enemy,
Surrounded, by fire will he cut such a path,
All escaped except for thirty put on the spit.

[1]Misprint for hors = without, except for.

Clearly a military theme of breaking out of a surrounded position and running the gauntlet of enemy fire. **Put on the spit** can also describe running someone through with a sword.

7 Q29

Le grand Duc d'Albe fe viendra rebeller
A fes grans peres fera le tradiment:
Le grand de Guife le viendra debeller,
Captif mené & dreffé monument.

The great Duke of Alva will come to rebel,
He will betray his great forebears:
The great one of Guise will come to conquer him,
Led captive and a monument erected.

In the city of Nancy, the capital of the royal House of Lorraine, try searching for a monument erected to celebrate the rout of the Duke of Alva by François de Guise, circa 1557. If you find it in the town square you'll probably need to check which parallel universe you are in, because such a monument does not exist in our universe. This is a very specific prophecy of a quantum future failed.

7 Q30

Le ſac s'approche, feu, grand ſang eſpandu	The sack approaches, fire, great shedding of blood,
Po, grands fleuues, aux bouuiers l'entreprinſe,	Po, great rivers, to the idiots the enterprise,
De Gennes, Nice, apres long attendu,	Of Genoa, Nice, after a long wait,
Fouſſan, Turin, à Sauillan la prinſe.	Fossano, Turin, the capture at Savigliano.

Although clear in its details concerning a potential future for the Italian towns and cities of modern-day Piedmont, the time is hard to establish. Line 1 sounds too modern to apply to struggles over Piedmont during the Italian Wars (1494–1559) between France and the Holy Roman Empire. Through future goggles we might see a great **sack** of the region as part of a Third World War and a general breakdown of civilization in the 21st century due to overpopulation and global warming. It is more likely, however, that this reflects the final days of World War II, when Allied forces had shattered the final line of German defenses and swept north and northwest across the Po river valley in April 1945. Italian partisans staged large-scale urban insurrections in **Genoa** and **Turin** to overthrow what was left of Mussolini's puppet fascist Republic of Salò. If **the capture** is of Mussolini at Savigliano, in south central Piedmont, it is off by 120 miles. He and his mistress were making a run for the Swiss border when they were taken up by Italian communist partisans outside the village of Dongo.

7 Q31

De Languedoc, & Guienne plus de dix,	From Languedoc, and Guienne more than ten,
Mille voudront les Alpes repaſſer:	Thousand will want to pass again over the Alps:
Grans Allobroges marcher contre Brundis	The great Savoyards to march against Brindisi
Aquin & Breſſe les viendront recaſſer.	Aquino and Bresse will come to drive them back.

Nostradamus puts his arms around a large chunk of territory to stage these events. **Languedoc** and **Guienne** cover southwest France, while **Bresse** drags in territory north of Lyons. To catch up with the conquering soldiers of Savoy we must bend down all the way to touch the Italian boot at **Brindisi** and **Aquino** and find ourselves equally exposed to an attack from the rear from **Bresse**, which causes the **Savoyards** to retreat.

A satisfactory description of something that never happened. Nothing close to this occurred unless you see the French towns listed here as a synecdoche for France taking over the Kingdom of Savoy in 1610.

Fontbrune makes a sterling effort to conjure Garibaldi and his rebel band, known as the One Thousand. He points to their conquest of Sicily and Naples, the second Naples campaign and Savoy's cession to France, *circa* 1859–60. But his translation of *more than ten* as the estimate of the French contingent, and his application of **Alps** as a synecdoche for Genoa are a bit weak. Garibaldi's thousand-man force never "passed over the Alps," nor desired to. The numbers implied in lines 1 and 2 could be **ten/thousand** leaving interpreters to imagine Garibaldi's **thousand** applies when in fact Nostradamus ran into a rhyme and meter problem when composing this quatrain.

7 Q32

Du mont Royal naiſtra d'vne caſane,[1]	**From a little rural domain [he] will**
Qui caue, & compte viendra tyranniſer	**rise to the royal mountain,**
Dreſſer copie de la marche Millane,	**One who will tyrannize over the vault**
Fauene, Florence d'or & gens eſpuiſer.	**[of finances]**
	To raise a force in the region of
	Milan,
	To drain Faenza, Florence of gold and
	men.

[1]Alternative: late Latin *casana* = bank; the line can therefore read: *Of a bank of the royal mount will be born . . .*

Lamont and Robb believe this is a prophecy for the rise of Mussolini and Italian Fascism. He would rise from humble origins to climb the **royal mountain,** as it were, through an invitation by King Victor Emmanuel III to form a government as Italy's *Duce*, or prime minister, by 1922. His famous running march on Rome, which brought him to power in that year, was organized in **Milan.** The towns in the final line stand as a synecdoche for his military adventures in Ethiopia (1935–36), the Spanish Civil War (1936–39), and later the disastrous expeditions to Russia and North Africa (1941–43), which together would exhaust Italy's treasury and kill hundreds of thousands of her sons.

7 Q33

Par fraude regne, forces expolier,	**Through fraud the kingdom – forces**
La claſſe obſeſſe, paſſages à l'eſpie:	**stripped away,**
Deux fainctz amis ſe viendront rallier,	**The fleet blockaded, passages for the**
Eſueiller hayne de long temps eſſoupie.	**spy:**
	Two false friends will come to stand
	into the land,
	To awaken hatred for a long time
	dormant.

This best describes one of the darkest and most dishonorable days in the British Royal Navy. With France fallen in 1940, British Task Force H under Sir James Sommerville was ordered by Winston Churchill to shell the French fleet while it lay peacefully moored in the Algerian port of Mers-el-Kebir, at Oran. It must be remembered that the French Navy was the fourth largest in the world at that time. Hitler could have incorporated this armada (*forces stripped away*) to augment his modest surface fleet for the planned invasion of England. Sommerville stationed his 6 capital ships and 11 destroyers a few miles outside of the harbor, training his guns on two French battleships and several cruisers anchored in a line. He radioed an ultimatum to French Admiral Marcel-Bruno Gensoul: Mutiny against their new government and join the Royal Navy or be scuttled. Gensoul, feeling that the ultimatum made a *fraud* out of their one-time alliance against the Germans, refused. Sommerville then unleashed a ferocious 10-minute barrage, supported by naval torpedo aircraft, killing 1,297 French sailors and crippling and sinking all but the battleship *Strasbourg*, which sailed out of the harbor unscathed.

The incident drew new blood out of ancient wounds harbored by the French for the English. Eyewitnesses describe the French sailors burying their dead and openly damning the English. One sailor was so bitter that he took a straight razor and sliced a tattooed Union Jack off his arm.

7 Q34

En grand regret fera la gent Gauloife,	**In great regret will the Gallic people be,**
Cœur vain, legier croira temerité:	**Vain and wanton of heart, they will**
Pain, fel, ne vin, eaue: venin ne	**trust in reckless boldness:**
ceruoife,	**Bread, salt, no wine, water: venom, no**
Plus grand captif, faim, froit, neceffité.	**ale,**
	Greater captivity, hunger, cold, and want.

Here we have the dark days of the Nazi invasion and occupation of France (1940–44). One can feel Nostradamus' disgust for the lack of French leadership of that future day, and for the failure of its generals in the 1940 campaign. The phrase **they will trust in reckless boldness** describes the Maginot mentality, France's belief that the ruinously expensive and outdated fortifications of the Maginot Line could keep out Hitler's modern panzer armies. During later stages of the occupation the people of France were on the verge of starvation. This was especially true of Paris.

7 Q35

La grand pefche viendra plaindre,	**The great fish will come to complain,**
plorer	**and weep**
D'auoir efleu, trompés feront en l'aage:	**For having [made] the choice. Deceived**
Guiere auec eux ne voudra demourer,	**will they be about the age:**
Deceu fera par ceux de fon langaige.	**Scarcely at all will he want to remain**
	with them,
	Deceived will he be by those of his own
	tongue.

Le Pelletier taps Henry III as King of Poland for this one, on the basis that *peſche* (fish) stands for the reckless way Polish nobility would *fish* for a new king. This odd practice came into being when Henry III abandoned his Polish throne to return to France upon the death of Charles IX in 1574. About which Le Pelletier says: "Poland will complain and weep of having elected, in the person of the Duc de Anjou, a King whose unexpected arrival on the throne of France, after the premature death of Charles IX, will destroy the calculation which it had made on the respective ages of the two brothers; he will not remain long with the Poles. This prince will perish of a violent death at the hands of his countrymen."

7 Q36

Dieu, le ciel tout le diuin verbe à l'vnde,	**God, the heavens, all the divine words in the waves,**
Porté par rouges ſept razes à Bizance:	**Carried by seven red shaven-heads [cardinals] to Byzantium:**
Contre les oingz trois cens de Trebiſconde,	**Against the anointed three hundred from Trabzon,**
Deux loix mettront, & l'horreur, puis credence.	**Will set forth two laws, first horror then trust.**

The first line could be a 16th-century attempt to describe the widespread use of modern telecommunications by all religions. The rest could chronicle the peace efforts of a future pope. This may be another example of Nostradamus' vision of the Holy See paralleling that of St Malachy. In the 12th century the Irish prophet called the second-to-last pope before Judgment Day *Gloria Olivae* (Glory of the Olive Branch, ie Glory of Peace). A number of seers believe the pope after John Paul II will be very active in Middle Eastern peace efforts. Perhaps here we examine a prediction of that next pope sending **seven** cardinals to Turkey as peace envoys.

The reference to the **three hundred** from the Black Sea Turkish port of **Trabzon** remained obscure until Chechen terrorists hijacked a Turkish ferry carrying 300 passengers from the port of Trabzon on 16 January 1996. It is safe to say the hostages were **anointed** at least with good luck. Their hijackers decided to release them and give themselves up without a fight. The Chechens had seized the ferry as a gesture of protest against what they considered the Russian government's insincere efforts for peace in Chechnya. The cryptic final phrase could promise that the horror of war will be replaced by a new peace settlement sometime before the Millennium.

7 Q37

Dix enuoyés, chef de nef mettre à mort,	*Ten envoys, the captain of the ship*
D'vn abuerty, en claſſe guerre ouuerte:	*put to death,*
Confuſion chef, l'vn ſe picque & mord,	*Warned by one, in the fleet there is*
Leryn, ſtecades[1] nefz, cap dedans la nerte.[2]	*open war:*
	Confusion, the chief and another
	prick and bite each other,
	Leryn, the isles of Hyères, ships, prow
	into the darkness.

[1]Latin *Stoechades* = Isles of Hyères.
[2]Old French for blackness; or Greek *nerthe* = beneath, (from) underneath.

The Isles of Lérins are off the southern coast of France between Cannes and Antibes. The Isles of Hyères are east of Toulon. American and French commandos did guide their landing craft under cover of darkness to attack German batteries stationed on the Hyères Islands the night before the Allied landings on the French Riviera in 1944. Line 3 could be used to describe the fracas between two American commanders. Admiral Spencer S. Lewis, commander of the task force landing the US 36th Division, was forced to redirect his troops to a neighboring beach because their objective had not been adequately bombed and shelled. He did this without consulting General Dahlquist, the commander of 36th division, who couldn't be reached because he was already on shore. This communications breakdown and unauthorized change in the tactical plan could have thrown the Allied landings into confusion and disaster. Dahlquist and a number of Allied top brass commanders initially were furious with Admiral Lewis, but his action turned out to be correct. He certainly did not lose his command or his head, as implied by Nostradamus.

7 Q38

L'aiſné Royal ſur courſier voltigeant,	*The elder Royal upon a prancing*
Picquer viendra, ſi rudement courir:	*steed,*
Gueulle, lipee, pied dans l'eſtrein pleignant	*Will spur it so roughly that it bolts:*
Trainé, tiré horriblement mourir.	*Mouth, lips, foot complaining in the*
	grip [of the stirrup]
	Dragged, pulled, horribly to death.

First Chavigny, then Jaubert, and finally Le Pelletier apply this to an accident in which a royal pulled the reins so tight on a mettlesome horse that its mouth was cut, upon which the maddened horse threw the prince, who was dragged by the stirrups to a horrible death. Clear enough on the incident – but you would be surprised to see how many candidates there are for the prince stuck in the stirrup. Jaubert thought it was Henry

II of Navarre, who died in an equestrian accident on 15 May 1555, a short while after Nostradamus drafted this quatrain. Le Pelletier applies it to Crown Prince Ferdinand, the eldest son and heir of Louis-Philippe, who was killed by his maddened horse on 13 July 1842. Leoni reminds us to consider a third possibility, the heir of the Prince de Bourbon-Roche-sur-Yon, who was killed in 1560 "under somewhat similar circumstances."

7 Q39

Le conducteur de l'armée Françoife,	**The commander of the French army,**
Cuidant perdre le principal phalange:	**Expecting to lose the principal**
Par fus paué de l'auaigne & d'ardoife,	**phalanx:**
Soy parfondra par Gennes gent eftrange.	**Upon the pavement of oats and slate,**
	The foreign people will undermine
	themselves through Genoa

This is too general for a specific interpretation. Fontbrune believes it stands for Napoleon's sacrifice of Massena's French garrison under siege at Genoa in 1800. Massena's **principal phalanx** (a force of 15,000 men) tied down enough Austrian regiments to gain his master some advantage when facing Melas at the battle of Marengo. It is said that the besieged and emaciated French garrison was forced to consume a disgusting blend of oats and bean bread before they surrendered.

7 Q40

Dedans tonneaux hors oingz d'huille &	**Within casks anointed outside with oil**
greffe,	**and grease,**
Seront vingt vn deuant le port fermés,	**There will be twenty-one ports closed**
Au fecond guet par mort feront prouef fe:	**in front of him,**
Gaigner les portes & du guet affommés.	**At the second watch through death**
	they will perform a feat:
	To gain the gates, and by watching,
	be knocked on the head.

The traditional interpretation proposes another Trojan horse ruse, this time used to capture a seaport. The interlopers succeed in entering the town, only to be knocked out by the port's guards.

A more radical projection-cum-potential-prophecy can be conjured if one searches history for a man denied entry in **twenty-one ports** or national borders. The only man who fits this description was the controversial Indian mystic Bhagwan Shree Rajneesh (Osho) during his spiritual world tour of 1986.

The **casks** of line 1 could be a 16th-century man's take on the luggage heaped in a Lear jet rented by Osho and his small entourage of disciples.

As they flew from one air *port* to the next, they were sometimes shadowed by a US Air Force plane, whose dark-suited occupants manage to arrange the revocation of one entry visa after another for the little band of Rajneeshees. From November 1985 through May 1986, Osho had his visitor's visa inexplicably canceled and his person forcibly expelled from Greece, Jamaica, Nepal, and Portugal. His residence visa for Uruguay was revoked through pressure put on President Sanginetti by American President Ronald Reagan. Osho was denied legal entry to the United States, Antigua, Barbuda, Holland, France (at gunpoint), Fiji, Sweden, Switzerland, Britain, Italy, West Germany, Ireland, Canada, Uruguay, Jamaca, and Spain. He was forced to return to his homeland of India – the one place he couldn't be denied entry.

There he re-established his spiritual headquarters in Pune, 100 miles inland from Bombay. This had been the location of his first spiritual ashram and meditation campus, in the 1970s. But even in Osho's own country, the United States government of the Christian right-leaning Reagan administration put diplomatic pressure on India to deny entry visas to suspected followers. The US Attorney General, Ed Meese, openly admitted that the government wished to isolate "the Bhagwan" from his people. This effort failed, and today Osho Commune International is considered one of the fastest-growing spiritual campuses in the world, with as many as 10,000 people from all over the globe teaching and studying meditation and therapy techniques there.

Followers of Osho call the second Pune commune "Pune Two" – or in Nostradamus' words, the *second watch* of witnessing seekers experiencing Osho's meditations in a unique socio-spiritual milieu.

When Osho died in January 1990, quite possibly of complications from poison administered while he was jailed in the United States, his death celebration was reported by 700 newspapers and television news shows around the world. One could say the *feat* performed was a celebration exuding gratitude, joy and a festiveness one doesn't expect at a funeral of a dead spiritual leader. On each anniversary of Osho's death, thousands of disciples enjoy a huge week-long Mardi Gras festival.

The final line describes the black-painted wooden doors of the "Gateless Gate," which open to let anyone enter Osho's 60-acre mediation campus in Pune. If you were to go there to learn the science of self-witnessing or *watching*, you might find yourself sitting in the Vipassana group along a glass-enclosed and air-conditioned marble walkway running through the late Osho's tropical garden. There you'd sit with eyes closed, watching the movement of mind and emotions. If your watchfulness should wander, you can expect an attendant to walk past and gently tap you on the head with a Zen stick, or in Nostradamus' words: *by watching, be knocked on the head.*

7 Q41

Les oz des piedz & des mains enſerrés,	The bones of the feet and the hands shut in [or locked away],
Par bruit maiſon long temps inhabitee:	Because of the noise, the house long uninhabited:
Seront par ſonges concauant deterrés,	Digging in dreams, they will be unearthed,
Maiſon ſalubre & ſans bruyt habitee.	House healthy and inhabited without noise.

Here Nostradamus is an exorcist of a haunted house. He suggests a technique of meditation to help the victims find the bones of the dead and give them a proper burial. It has been my experience as well, during my own investigations of hauntings (to be described in detail in future books), that we feed spectral phenomena with our thoughts and dreams. I discovered that once the subject of a haunting used self-observation techniques to go **digging** in their own **dreams**, as it were, the very understanding of their part in feeding the phenomenon exorcised the ghost.

7 Q42

Deux de poiſon ſaiſiz nouueau venuz,	Two newly arrived in possession of poison,
Dans la cuiſine du grand Prince verſer:	To pour out in the kitchen of the great Prince:
Par le ſouillard tous deux au faict congneuz,	Through the scullion both caught in the act,
Prins qui cuidoit de mort l'aiſné vexer	Seized [is the one] who thought to vex the elder one with death.

A clear and graphic description of a foiled political assassination attempt by poisoning, which Nostradamus keeps safely obscure by giving no clue about which great prince is to be poisoned or when the deed will be done. Numerous assassination attempts were made on the leaders of both sides during the Wars of Religion. For instance the **great Prince** Henry de Navarre (later Henry IV of France) survived twenty-three known assassination plots before a lone murderer, Ravaillac, knifed him to death in a Paris traffic jam in 1610.

7 Q43[1]

Lorsqu'on verra les deux licornes,	When one will see the two unicorns,
L'vne baiſſant, l'autre abaiſſant,	The one grazing, the other lowering,
Monde au milieu, plier aux bornes	World in the middle, to fold to the boundaries
S'enfuyra le nepueu riant.	The nephew will run away smiling.

[1]The next six quatrains are considered by some scholars to be surviving examples of the missing second half of Century 7.

All Nostradamus has to do is write the word **nephew** and Le Pelletier will rope Louis Napoleon to the quatrain. This time the nephew of Napoleon Bonaparte is caught abandoning his Italian allies by signing the Treaty of Zurich, in 1859. His reasons didn't wash with Leoni 35 years ago, and they get even less respect from me in 1996. The two unicorns refer to a common device found in too many coats-of-arms of too many noted nephews to solve this mystery. Only one thing is certain: these point-tipped horses don't belong to Louis Napoleon's heraldry.

7 Q44

Alors qu'vn bour fera fort bon,[1]
Portant en foy les marques de iustice,
De fon fang lors portant long[2] nom
Par fuite iniuste receura fon fupplice.

When the Bour' is very "bon"
Bearing in himself marks of justice
Then bearing the oldest name of his
   blood:
Through flight he will unjustly
   receive his punishment.

[1]bour fera fort bon = Bour(bon) is very good.
[2]Long; length; extent (in years): long is missing in some editions.

In the mid-1860s Le Pelletier commented that "when a very good Bourbon will sit on the throne of France, bearing the hand of justice and a name longer than that of any other King of his line, this Prince, because of his flight to Varennes, will be unjustly condemned to the extreme penalty." Louis XVI is indeed a man with a long and illustrious name, as the 16th king with that appellation. Although historians attribute the French Revolution to the weakness of Louis XVI, Nostradamus reveals great affection for the hapless king. Opposed to violence, Louis appeared to lack leadership qualities, making him an ineffectual ruler of a great nation. But perhaps Nostradamus sensed the humanitarian in him; he wrote one quatrain that may foresee Louis offering equal rights to Jews, an action which would have greatly endeared him to Nostradamus.

Forced by the revolutionaries to surrender his power to the new constitutional monarchy, Louis also had to exchange his royal name, Bourbon, for Capet, the **oldest name of his blood**. Virtually imprisoned with his family in the Tuileries, Louis made plans to escape, but the ill-fated venture was doomed to failure. Louis reached only as far as the frontier town of Varennes in northeastern France. But the prophecy Nostradamus wrote about this **flight** will extend his fame for a thousand years or more (see 9 Q20).

7 Q73

Renfort de fieges manubis[1] et maniples[2]	**Reinforcement of sieges, plunder and**
Changez le facre et paffe fur le profne,	**platoons**
Prins et captifs n'arrefte les preztriples	**The sacred changed and the sermon**
Plus par fond mis efleué, mis au trofne.	**passed over,**
	Taken and captives it does not stop
	the priesthood
	Put into the lowest depths, raised,
	put on the throne.

[1]Latin *manubiae* = plunder.
[2]Latin *manipulus* = maniple, a subdivision of an ancient Roman legion consisting of 60 or 120 men.

Line 1 draws the curtains over Nostradamus leaded mirror to find the French Revolutionary armies laying siege at Toulon and later plundering Italy. In both cases they are led by the ratty-haired, lean and mean Napoleon Bonaparte. Line 2 recounts the National Committee's persecution of the clergy. The Catholic *sermon* is **passed over** for the absurdities of Robespierre's Cult of Reason. Line 3 hints that the clergy will successfully endure the Revolution and the Child of the Revolution: the tyrant Napoleon. First they go underground to conduct their masses; later, Napoleon returns them to the pulpit in an attempt to make the Church a puppet of his policies. Line 4 returns to General Bonaparte in the early days. In 1794 this underfed artillery officer was thrown in jail under suspicion of being a Jacobin sympathizer. But no guillotine was made to slice his long, scraggly locks and little neck. His fortunes would change, and from the depths of a dungeon he would rise to become dictator in 1799, and later Emperor of France in 1804. By 1800 he would also hire a better barber and sacrifice his split ends to history.

7 Q80

L'Occident libre les Ifles Britanniques	**The West free the British Isles**
Le recognu paffer le bas, puis haut	**The recognized one to pass low, then**
Ne content trifte Rebel corss.[1] Efcotiques	**high**
Puis rebeller par plus et par nuit chaut.	**Discontented, melancholy Rebel**
	Scottish corsairs
	Then to rebel much more and by
	warm night.

[1]Apocope for *rebelles corsaires*.

The **West** is the thirteen American colonies of Great Britain who gain their independence after the American Revolution (see 4 Q96). The last three lines focus on John Paul Jones and his checkered career as one of America's first naval heroes. Jones was born in Scotland and later became a merchant mariner. He served as chief mate in a slave brigantine for two years until he returned to merchant shipping. On a voyage to Scotland the master and mate of his new ship died and he took command, sailing the vessel safely into port. For his service he was given command of his own merchant ship, and he began trading in the West Indies. At Tobago, in 1773, Jones killed the ringleader of a mutinous crew and escaped to America. The English thereafter considered him a pirate and an outlaw.

The American Revolution in 1775 raised his fortunes again. He was given a commission in the new Continental Navy. Over the next three years he commanded three American raiders. Jones is the **Scottish corsair** responsible for numerous raids on British home ports and for the destruction of many vessels. He continued to serve in the American navy after the war, then became a military advisor to Czarina Catherine the Great of Russia. Nostradamus was correct in foreseeing Jones as a **melancholy** and **discontented** man. Throughout his naval career this military visionary suffered the envy and resistance of his peers. Rivals in Catherine's court conspired to have him dismissed. He died in Paris, a burnt out and frustrated man.

Quatrain Indexing Date: Q80 a near-miss for 1779, the year John Paul Jones commanded the *Bonhomme Richard* and won a sanguinary naval engagement with the British man-of-war *Serapis*. Early in the battle, the British commander severely raked his ship with gunfire and asked if Jones wished to surrender, to which he uttered his immortal reply, "I have not yet begun to fight!" With his own ship sinking, Jones and his men boarded the British warship and captured her crew after a bitter hand-to-hand fight.

7 Q82

Le ſtratageſme ſimulte ſera rare	**The stratagem, enmity will be rare**
La mort en voye rebelle par contrée:	**The death en route, rebellion in the**
Par le retour du voyage Barbare	**country:**
Exalteront la proteſtante entrée.	**On the return from the Barbarian**
	voyage
	They will exalt the Protestant entry.

This is the only time the word **Protestant** appears in the prophecies. We have here a meeting between Protestants and either Algerian corsairs or Muslims (ie Ottomans, North Africans and Arabs). Perhaps its purpose is to forge a strategy that will subvert their mutual enemy, the Catholics. Someone in the Arab/Corsair delegation dies en route to the gathering. Rebellion **in the country** of France is implied, giving us as temporal target the French Wars of Religion (1562–98). As of writing I have found no evidence of such an aborted meeting between Muslims and Huguenots.

7 Q83

Vent chaut, conſeils pleurs, timidité,	**Warm wind, counsels, tears, timidity,**
De nuit au lit aſſailli ſans les armes:	**The night in bed assailed without**
D'oppreſſion grande calamité,	**arms:**
L'epithalame conuerti pleurs et larmes.	**Great oppression, calamity,**
	The nuptial song converted, weeping
	and tears.

Initially this sounds like Act III, scene two, of Wagner's *Lohengrin*. All whimsy aside, the timing and real participants to this surprise visit of attackers to a bedside on some **nuptial** night is open to anyone's interpretation.

1556 to 1559

Presages 15–23
from the Almanac of 1557

P 15   January (1557)

L'indigne orné craindra la grande fornaiſe,	The shocking and infamous armed one
L'eſleu premier, des captifs n'en retourne:	will fear the great furnace,
Grand bas du monde, L'Irale[1] non alaiſe,[2]	First the chosen one [the Jews], the captives not returning:
Barb. Iſter, Malte, Et le Buy ne retourne.	The world's lowest crime, the Angry Female Irale not at ease,
	Barb[arossa], Hitler, Malta. And the Empty [soulless] One does not return.

[1]Possible cryptogram for Israel.
[2](F)a(i)laise = Failaise: the Battle of the Falaise–Argentan pocket, Normandy campaign, August 1944 – a catastrophic German defeat in a battle of encirclement which marked the beginning of the end of German resistance on the Western Front. Non alaiſe = not at ease.

We now leap four centuries ahead to Hitler's Final Solution.

For the 16th-century Western European mindset, cremation was the most disgraceful act one could inflict upon the dead. In this often-over-looked prophecy Nostradamus, the Christianized Jew, forewarns us of the Holocaust and its perpetrator's ultimate defeat.

The **infamous one** is Hitler, who drew his power from manipulating people's fear. He sanctioned the German SS commander Heinrich Himmler to apply German technology in the creation of an efficient **great furnace** for burning millions of Jewish corpses. No order was written for the final solution, as Hitler feared leaving behind any incriminating evidence. The Nazis succeeded in influencing many Jewish community leaders to calm their people with false hope that their stint as modern Babylonian **captives** in concentration camps was only temporary. But those who passively left the ghettos of Eastern Europe in the endless trains of cattle box cars never returned. Mother Israel is still not **at ease** in a world that continues to betray signs of anti-Semitism.

The final line, naming the strategic disasters that caused Hitler to lose the war, leaves no doubt that this quatrain foretells the fall of the Second Antichrist, and not some Barbary Corsair of the 1550s.

Barb is another allusion to the medieval German ruler Barbarossa, Hitler's favorite German king after Frederick the Great. From this reference we may infer that Nostradamus is drawing a parallel with Hitler's obsession with conquering and colonizing the East in a great crusade. Operation **Barb**arossa was the code name for Hitler's disastrous Russian Campaign.

Malta was the linchpin for Hitler's military catastrophes in the south. He never grasped the strategic importance of conquering that small Mediterranean island. Throughout the North African campaigns, ships carrying supplies to Rommel's Afrika Korps were sunk by Allied ships and planes based on Malta. Thanks to Malta, Rommel could not sustain his offensives or capitalize on his remarkable victories in the desert, and he could not defeat the British and seize the Middle Eastern oilfields for Germany. At the same time, German forces were overextended in Russia and were unable to reach the Baku oil fields. Hitler would lose the war because he could not cut off the flow of oil to the Allied war effort or sustain his own oil supplies. He is **the empty one**, the inhuman messiah of fear no longer able to fuel his world conquest. Hitler's Final Solution was defeated and the Christianized Jewish prophet promises Israel that such evil will not return.

P 16   May (1557)

Conioint icy, au ciel appert[1] depefche,	**Conjoined here, in the sky the dispatch opened,**
Prife, laiffée, mortalité non feure:	**Taken, left behind, mortality not certain:**
Peu pluye, entrée, le ciel la terre feche,	**Little rain, entry, the sky and earth dries,**
Defait, mort, pris, arriué à mal-heure.	**Undone, death, caught, arrived at a bad hour.**

[1]Latin *apertus* = open, manifest.

Line 1 is very futuristic. A telecommunications message could be said to **open** or make itself **manifest** on one's TV or console from a signal out of the sky. Maybe we can stretch this one farther ahead to a time when telecommunication is obsolete and messages literally materialize at their intended destination. The rest of this presage is quite specific and quite open to even more wild speculation.

P 17   June (1557)

Victor naual à Houche,[1] Anuers diuorce,	**Naval victor at Hoek, Antwerp divorce,**
Né grand, du ciel feu, tremblement haut brule:	**Great heir, from the sky fire, trembling high woods:**
Sardaigne bois, Malte, Palerme, Corfe,	**Sardinian wood, Malta, Palermo, Corsica,**
Prelat mourir, l'vn frappe fur la Mule.	**Prelate to die, strikes the one on the Mule.**

[1]Either Hoek, Belgium, or the Hook of Holland (Hoek-van-Holland).

Fontbrune starts off well by placing line 1 for the French victory against an English invasion force at Antwerp on 24 December 1809. Napoleon's divorce from the Empress Josephine took place shortly after, on 12 January 1810. The generalities recorded in this presage could apply themselves equally to the discord in the Spanish Netherlands of Nostradamus' time.

Sardinian wood was used to build galleys for the many naval battles of the Mediterranean during the late 1550s. Malta would endure a Turkish siege in 1565. Corsica and Palermo would be raided by Barbary Corsairs off and on during the 1550s and 60s. The man **on the Mule** has been seen before. He could be Nostradamus himself. The Prelate might be a cardinal who persecuted the seer in his travels and who is scheduled in the prophet's ephemeris to die in June 1557.

P 18   July (1557)

L'heraut errant du chien au Lyon tourne,	**The errant herald turns from the dog to the Lion,**
Feu ville ardra, pille, prife nouuelle:	**Fire will burn the town, pillage, new prize:**
Decouurir fuftes,[1] Princes prins, on retourne,	**To discover foists, Princes taken, they return,**
Explor.[2] pris Gall.[3] au grand iointe pucelle.	**Spy taken Gaul, to the great one joined to the virgin.**

[1]*fuftes* = a) a low, oared galley; b) English "foist", to pass off as genuine; Dutch dialectical *vuisten* from *vuist* = fist.
[2]Apocope of Latin *explorator* = spy.
[3]Latin *Gallia* = Gaul; France.

The first line is cloudy except for a number of clues pointing to action between France and England (**the Lion**). A town is bombarded and taken. If this is meant for the seizure of Calais in July by the French in August 1558, it is one and a half years early. The use of **foists** is not clear less they stand for a sneak attack unrecorded by history (the Dutch dialectical word for **foist** is *vuist* = "fist"). If it is a play on the English to "foist off" or "to impose something that isn't wanted," then the foist is used to smuggle a spy from England to France. The **Princes taken** must be the English commanders and noblemen captured at Calais, Dunkirk, and Thionville between 1557 and 1558. The capture of Calais gave Henry II the political clout to demand and receive the hand of young Mary, Queen of Scots (**the virgin**), for his son, the Dauphin (**to the great one joined**).

P 19   August (1557)

De la grand Cour banni. conflit, bleffé,	**From the great court banished, conflict, wounded,**
Efleu, renduë, accufe, mat.[1] mutins:	**Elected, delivered, accused, cunning mutineers:**
Eu feu cité Pyr.[2] eaux, venins, preffé,	**And fire on the Pyrenees city, water, venoms, pressed,**
Ne voguer onde, ne facher les Latins.	**Not to travel by water, not to anger the Latins.**

[1]Apocope of *matois* = cunning, crafty, sly.
[2]*cité Pyr.* = Perpignan.

The first two lines take us back to 1557. The military disaster of St Quentin (fought in August) engendered a search for scapegoats at the French court. There were rallies in the streets of Paris against Anne de Montmorency, Constable of France, with a sea of placards condemning him as one of the authors of the national disaster. Although he was in the royal doghouse for pushing the king too hard to make war, he was not banished from court. The true scapegoat for St Quentin was Gaspar de Coligny, **elected** by the king to command the defeated French army at Calais. One could say he was technically banished, since he was taken prisoner (**delivered**) and held incommunicado in the Spanish-held fortresses of Lille, Sluys, and Ghent. The rest of the presage phases out of 1557 and moves into the future. No attack on Perpignan (which at the time was a Spanish stronghold) took place that year, although the French laid siege to it 40 years later during the final phase of the French Wars of Religion.

P 20   September (1557)

Mer, terre aller, foy, loyauté rompuë,	**Sea, land to go, faith, loyalty broken,**
Pille, naufrage, à la cité tumulte:	**Pillage, wreck, tumult in the city:**
Fier, cruel acte, ambition repeuë,	**Proud, cruel act, ambition sated,**
Foible offenſé: le chef du fait inulte.	**Weakling offended: the perpetrator of the deed unpunished.**

This could easily be applied to the French debacle of St Quentin and its repercussions. The disaster forced Henry II of France to sue for peace with Philip II of Spain, resulting in the Treaty of Cateau-Cambrésis, which ended the Habsburg-Valois Wars. France gave up all her conquests (**land to go**) except Metz, Toul, and Verdun, effectively ending all French claims to Italian territory. St Quentin broke the faith the French people had in Henry II's advisors, such as Montmorency and Coligny. The defeat of France triggered much soul-searching. For many, like Coligny, this led to an open rebellion against the French crown for its disastrous intrigues with the pope. It also resulted in a complete break in France between Protestantism and the Catholic faith.

Line 2 describes St Quentin itself, bathed in flames. We see the wreck of the French defenders and the rape and pillage of the town by Spanish and English mercenaries, which lasted for two days. One could apply Coligny to line 4 as **the weakling** who, when explaining himself to avoid captivity, blamed the penetration of the Spanish over the city's walls on the desertion of one company. It was a flimsy excuse, for the Spanish had broken through the city's defenses in seven places.

P 21   October (1557)

Froid, grand deluge, de regne dechauſſé,
Nieʒ,[1] diſcord, Trion,[2] Orient mine:
Poiſon, mis ſiege, de la cité chaſſé,
Retour felice, neuue ſecte en ruyne.

Cold, great flood, expelled from the
  kingdom,
Idiot [nephew], discord, Ursa Major
  and Minor, source [in the]
  East:
Poison, siege laid, expelled out of the
  city,
Happy return, new sect in ruins.

[1] Old French nieʒ = nephew, grandson; idiot.
[2] Latin Triones = the constellations of the Great Bear and the Little Bear; Nostradamus sometimes uses constellations to hide countries – in this case it is Russia.

Although he is slightly off on the timing, Nostradamus successfully forecasts a war on the remote fringes of Europe for the end of the year. The Livonian War (1557–82) involved Russia, Poland, Sweden, and Denmark in a dispute over the possession of Livonia (present-day Estonia and Latvia).

Line 1 may relate to local French events. The expulsion of Coligny and other nobles into Spanish captivity after St Quentin is followed by a forecast of an unseasonably cold winter. Line 2 moves the focus to the Baltic region and Russia, depicted here sitting under the constellations of Ursa Major and Minor in the northern skies. In other words we have the "Big Bear" of the Duchy of Muscovy, ruled by Ivan the Terrible, and the twelve lesser Russian principalities, "the small bear(s)" which are incorporated into his expanding empire. Ivan the Terrible (a closer translation from the Russian is "Ivan the Awe-inspiring") started the wars in early 1558 by invading Poland.

Line 3 may allude to the consequences of the invasion when the war turned against Ivan in the late 1570s. Livonian and Polish forces expelled the Russians from many of their cities and besieged the Russian towns of Polotsk and Pskov. **Poison** was one of Czar Ivan's weapons against his enemies, although its entry here might apply to the agent of his own death in 1584, two years after the end of the war.

The final line, which brings us back to France and the **happy return** of ransomed noblemen captured from St Quentin, provides an alternative future for the destruction of the Huguenot movement. This didn't happen until the next century, but was certainly considered and tentatively planned for by Henry II after the Treaty of Cateau-Cambrésis of 1559 turned his attention from the distractions of foreign expeditions and placed it on the growing cancer of Protestantism in his own realm.

P 22   November (1557)

Mer cloſe, monde ouuert, cité[1] renduës,	Sea closed, world opened, city exhausted,
Faillir le Grand, eſleu nouueau, grand brume:	The Great One to fail, the newly elected, great mist:
Floram patere,[2] entrer camp,[3] foy rompuë,	Florence to be open, campus to enter, faith broken,
Effort fera ſeuere à blanche plume.	Stress will be severe to the white plume.

[1]cité stands for Paris.
[2]Latin flora(m) patere = the flower to lie open; Florida?.
[3]campus; party.

The first three staccato phrases set the stage for post-St Quentin, France: Spain's victory closes the Atlantic to the French and opens the New World to wider exploitation. Paris – and by extension France – is at least financially **exhausted**. Five decades of Hapsburg–Valois Wars have all but emptied the royal coffers, and France will face bankruptcy in the following year. The **great one** who failed is the Constable of France, Montmorency, whose failure to relieve Coligny at St Quentin led to the slaughter of his relief force and his own capture.

Nostradamus makes a near miss for events that were supposed to occur in the misty month of November, but which actually took place in October, when François de Guise was **newly elected** as Lieutenant-general of the realm. Florence was not occupied by a French expeditionary army in the following few years, so this is an unfulfilled wish. The stressed-out ruler is Henry II, who, at 38, is shocked out of his immaturity by St Quentin and at last takes more direct responsibility for ruling France.

P 23   December (1557)

Tutelle à Veſte, guerre meurt, tranſlatée,	Tutelage on Vesta, war dies, transferred,
Combat naual, honneur, mort, prelature:	Naval combat, honor, death, prelacy:
Entrée decez, France fort augmentée,	Death come in, France greatly augmented,
Eſleu paſſé, venu à mal-heure.[1]	Elected one passed, come to a bad end.

[1]unhappy hour, evil moment.

It would be wrong to apply this presage to our times. I believe it clearly stands for the events of 1557–59, the aftermath of St Quentin, and the peace following the Treaty of Cateau-Cambrésis. The classical allusion to **Vesta** stands for the "Motherland" of France. The treaty agreement **transferred** almost all the conquests of the Valois from the prior 50 years back to the Spanish. France was geographically and politically **augmented** or "changed."

The newly elected Lieutenant-General of France, François de Guise, who starred in the previous presage, is the subject of the last line. Accurately forecasting Guise's rise to power as the King's right-hand man in P22, Nostradamus also foresees the consequences of his tragic end, which occured by assassination before the siege of Orléans in 1563, at the close of the First War of Religion.

The Epistle to Henry II

Before we ride the wild rapids of this famous dedication letter to Henry II of France, a few observations.

We return to Nostradamus' prose writing style. As with the Preface, a white-water rapids metaphor is fitting, but with a few variations. Now the river finds the easiest routes around the "stones" or subjects of discourse. The thoughts stuck in the flow of his dissertation are little more than the rocks his rushing stream-of-consciousness style needs to make the white water babble. In other words, the collision of elements is more important than the meaning.

Once his racing waters have well soaked our battered sensibilities and have pushed us over the edge of a cataract that splashes in all directions, Nostradamus presents us with a most peculiar prophetic narrative. After the fall, the waters of his words will surge in random and unpredictable currents of time and future vision. We will bob backwards and forwards in the undertow of the time continuum. Just when we are about to drown, Nostradamus will pull us back into the calmer, cloudier waters of his double-talking digressions before again sending us back down more prescient cataracts into pools of simultaneous time travel.

The seer's time machine kayak will run amok. Prepare yourselves to be rolled over rocks of past, future, and alternative futures. Often Nostradamus' river of words will change time directions in mid-sentence and mix eras together. Do not try to grab hold of any rocky subject or predicate that passes by. Do not grow too attached to the direction a linking verb may push you. Where the Preface was a single river, the Epistle is a raging river delta – a labyrinth with many course changes in terms and tenses. In the Epistle, what is said is far less important than what reading it digs loose from the riverbed of your subconscious mind.

As with the Preface I have turned the translation back towards its original irrational stream-of-consciousness format.

For better enjoyment and understanding, I suggest you use the reader's meditation technique described in the opening of the Preface.

Now to my commentary:

EP1 *EPIſTRE*
À L'INVICTISSIME
TRES-PVISSANT, ET
tres-chreſtien
Henry Roy de France ſecond;
Michel Noſtradamus ſon
tres-humble, tres-obeiſſant ſeruiteur & ſubiect, victoire & felicité.

EPISTLE
TO THE MOST INVINCIBLE,
MOST POWERFUL, AND
Most Christian
Henry King of France, the Second:
Michael Nostradamus, his
very humble and very obedient servant
and subject, wishes Victory and Happiness.

EP2 *Povr icelle ſouueraine obſeruation que i'ay eu, ô tres-chreſtien & tres victorieux Roy, depuis que ma face eſtant long temps obnubilee ſe*

Because of the royal audience that I had, O most Christian and most victorious King, ever since my long-beclouded face

EP3 *preſente au deuant de la deité de voſtre Maieſté immeſuree, depuis en ça i'ay eſté perpetuellement esblouy, ne deſiſtant de honnorer & dignement*

first presented itself before the immeasurable deity of your Majesty, I have remained perpetually dazzled – not desisting to honor and justly

EP4 *venerer iceluy iour que premierement deuant icelle ie me preſentay, comme à vne ſinguliere maieſté tant humaine.*

venerate that day when I first presented myself before so singular a Majesty and so humane.

EP5 *Or cherchant quelque occaſion par laquelle ie peuſſe manifeſter le bon cœur & franc courage que moyennant iceluy mon pouuoir euſſe faict*

Now in searching for some occasion on which I would be able to manifest the good heart and frank courage, by means of which I should be able to have made

EP6 *ample extenſion de cognoiſſance enuers voſtre ſereniſſime majeſté.*

ample extension to the knowledge of your most Serene Majesty.

EP1-6 Nostradamus begins with a turgid bit of buttering-up! But then, it may be unfair of me to project my 20th-century bias on our prophet. In his day reading and writing were still a novelty. People tended to spice and oversweeten their verbiage. Royal personages like Henry II (who were big on show and action, and intellectually challenged), probably loved the musicality and length of the salutation as much, if not more, than the content. Nostradamus was a successful author because he knew how to communicate with his audience. The nobility's need for a good boot-licking by those of lower birth is well-known, and Nostradamus provides the proper diplomatic and literary devices of his times to gain the king's attention.

He reminds the king of their previous royal audience in 1556 and diplomatically avoids any mention of how displeased he was with the paltry sum the king offered for his journey, which had been paid from his own pocket and cost him a small fortune. But more pressing issues require that he cover this wound with the sugar and spice and nothing but nice preamble **good heart** . . . **frank courage**, ad nauseum, to obtain the king's blessing for printing the final three volumes of *Les Propheties*. A royal endorsement meant that more people would read his prophecies and be exposed to their treasures and secrets.

EP7　*Or voyant que par effects le declairer ne m'eftoit poffible, ioint auec mon fingulier defir de ma tant longue obtenebration & obfcurité, eftre*

But perceiving how in effect it is not possible for me to declare myself, together with my singular desire to take a break from my very long-beclouded obscurity and be

EP8　*fubitement efclarcie & tranfportee au deuant de la face du fouuerain œil, & du premier monarque de'vniuers, tellement que i'ay efté en*

suddenly transported toward the presence of [your] sovereign gaze – that of the premier monarch of the universe. I have also been

EP9　*doute longuement à qui ie viendrois confacrer ces trois Centuries du reftāt de mes Propheties, paracheuant la miliade, & apres auoir*

long in doubt as to whom I would dedicate these three remaining Centuries of my Prophecies completing the thousand [planned]. And after having

EP10　*eu longuemēt cogité d'vne temeraire audace ay prins mon addreffe enuers voftre majefté, n'eftant pour cela eftōné, comme raconte le grauiffime*

cogitated for a long time upon [my] rash audacity, I have presumed to address your Majesty, as one not having been astonished – as those mentioned by that most grave

EP11　*aucteur Plutarque en la vie de Lycurgue, que voyant les offres & prefens qu'on faifoit par facrifices aux temples des dieux immortels d'iceluy*

author Plutarch, in the life of Lycurgus – who on seeing the offerings and presents made as sacrifices in the temples of the immortal gods of that

EP12　*temps & à celle fin que l'on ne s'eftonnaft par trop fouuent defdictes fraiz & mifes ne s'ofoyent prefenter aux temples.*

era, and that they attributing too often an importance to such donations did not dare present anything at all inside the temples.

EP13　*Ce nonobftant voyant voftre fplendeur Royalle, accompagnee d'vne incomparable humanité ay prins mon adreffe, non comme aux Roys de*

Nevertheless, seeing that your royal splendor, [is] accompanied by an incomparable humanity, I have paid my address to it and not as if to those Kings of

EP7   Nostradamus' work (with all its magic and obscurity implied here) makes him unable to deliver this dedication in person.

EP8   More suspense and sugar to quicken the king's interest: Who will Nostradamus choose to dedicate his prophecies to.

EP9   This line implies that during his private audience with the king and queen in 1556 Nostradamus must have told them he planned to write 1,000 quatrains. Some scholars believe this reference to only ten Centuries puts the authenticity of the fragmentary Centuries XI and XII in doubt. I would have agreed with them if the letter had been written six years later when the fragments were composed. Can't a prophet change his plans?

EP10 At last! The king must be smiling with pleasure now. Here comes the **rash** request that Henry receive this dedication to his final three Centuries of *Les Propheties*.

EP11 And look here! Marvelous! The strange old petitioner has used a classical metaphor (so in vogue at court) that compares the King with ancient rulers of yore. The good doctor compares himself to the Greek and Roman pilgrims in Plutarch's *Life of Lycurgus* who bestowed presents or burnt offerings to their divinely born king in his **temple**.

EP12 Nostradamus is our pilgrim at the steps of the royal residence, offering to God's chosen monarch of France his final three Centuries as his sacrifice. Nostradamus' genuflecting pen compares his inability to enter St Germain-en-Laye in person, with the timidity of the worshippers of classical gods who placed so much importance on their donations that they did not dare to present anything inside the sanctity of a god's temple. If you wash off the metaphorical molasses, you might find the true Nostradamus shuddering at the idea of funding a second royal visit to Paris himself. The first journey had cost him tens of thousands of dollars.

EP13 More adulation suited to an easily flattered King. Nostradamus dedicates his last three Centuries to the aura of the king's **incomparable humanity**, which the seer obviously feels from afar, etc., etc.

EP14 *Perſe, qu'il n'eſtoit nullement permis d'aller à eux, ny moins s'en approcher.*

Persia whom one could neither be permitted to stand before, nor to approach.

EP15 *Mais à vn treſprudent, à vn treſſage Prince i'ay conſacré mes nocturnes & prophetiques ſupputations, compoſees pluſtoſt d'vn naturel*

But it is to a most prudent and most wise Prince that I have dedicated my nocturnal and prophetic calculations – composed rather out of a natural

EP16 *inſtinct, accompagné d'vne fureur poëtique, que par reigle de poëſie, & la plus part composé & accordé à la calculation Aſtronomique,*

instinct, accompanied by a poetic frenzy, than according to the rules of poetry – and for the most part composed in accordance with astronomical calculations,

EP17 *correſpondant aux ans, moys & ſepmaines des regions, contrees, & de la pluſpart des villes & citez de toute l'Europe, comprenant de l'Affrique,*

corresponding to the years, months and weeks of the regions, countries, and the majority of towns and cities of all Europe, also including Africa,

EP18 *& vne partie de l'Aſie par le changemẽt des regions, qui s'approchẽt la plus part de tous ces climats, & compoſé d'vne naturelle faction:*

and part of Asia, through the changes that will transpire in a majority of all these regions – and composed as by a natural faculty.

EP19 *reſpondra quelqu'vn qui auroit biẽ beſoin de ſoy moucher, la rithme eſtre autant facile, comme l'intelligence du ſens eſt difficile.*

Someone will answer – who would do well to blow his [snotty] nose – that the [poetic] rhythm is as easy as the comprehension of the meaning is difficult.

EP20 *Et pource, ô tres-humaniſſime Roy, la plus part des quatrains prophetiques ſont tellement ſcabreux, que l'on nÿ ſçauroit donner voye*

And that, O most humane King, is because most of the prophetic quatrains are [made so] rough and ticklish that one would not know how to make way

EP14   Nostradamus finally puts a cork in it with a classical flourish about the exotic Persian potentates who were so remote from their subjects – in comparison to the more enlightened and **humane** Henry.

EP15   Now begins a long dissertation on his prophetic techniques.

EP16   His nocturnal and poetic calculations are composed out of **natural instinct** and intuition accompanied by **poetic frenzy**. Here Nostradamus is stating for the record that he is well aware of how wild and seemingly incomprehensible his poetry appears.

EP17   With this said, he makes the same declarations we saw back in the Preface – that his subjectivity, ecstasies, and divinely inspired trances are translated into the mundane language of dialectics and linear time by means of astronomical calculations. The nuts and bolts of his math are not explained, of course.

EP18   Here is the clearest exposition in any of his writings about the prophecies' geographical reach. Any scholar or dilettante outside of these regions, such as in Japan and the Americas, should take note. As Nostradamus' second sight moves farther away from his native France, it finds fewer and fewer events in other geographical areas, and the prophecies become less detailed. In the 625 geographical references I found in his prophecies the distribution is as follows:

France 270; Italy and surrounding islands 113; Spain and Portugal 34; Germany and Central Europe 43; Britain, Belgium, Holland, and Scandinavia 26; Greece and Eastern Europe 63; North Africa and the Middle East 55; North and South America 11; and the stars of the Northern Hemisphere (including potential space colonies) 10.

EP19-20   Nostradamus acknowledges the criticism of his writing style and then leaves it hanging in the air. Nor does he explain why his writing is so obscure and convoluted. No answer is his answer.

He now maneuvers the narrative away from such concerns and brings the king back to something more objective about his prophecies. He won't explain *what* they are but will address *why* they were written. In his letter and the remaining 300 quatrains his goal is to provide – albeit obscurely – clues to the chronological overview that begins with the near future after March 1557 and expands all the way past the seventh millennium.

EP21   *ny moins aucuns interpreter, toutesfois eſperant de laiſſer par eſcrit les*
ans, villes, citez, regions où la plus part aduiendra, meſmes de l'annee
1585.

through them, nor even less interpret them. However, I was hoping to
leave a written record of the years, towns, cities, regions in which most
of the events will come to pass, even those of the year 1585

EP22   *& de l'annee 1606. accommençant depuis le temps preſent, qui eſt le 14.*
de Mars, 1557. & paſſant outre bien loing iuſques à

and of the year 1606, beginning from to present time, which is the
fourteenth of March, 1557, and passing far beyond to

EP23   *l'aduenement, qui ſera apres au commencement du ſeptieſme millenaire*
profondement ſupputé, tãt que mon calcul aſtronomique & autre

the coming advent which will be after the commencement of the seventh
millennium, profoundly reckoned, as far as my astronomical calculation
and other

EP21-22　　The mid-1580s through 1606 would indeed witness the climax of the Wars of Religion and the beginning of the reconstruction of France under a new royal family, the Bourbons.

EP23　　The Preface and quatrains already indicate successful forecasts for the *advent* of revolutions by **the common** (vulgar) *people* (PF17) against the rule of British kings in America (4 Q96), French kings in France (1 Q14), and the overthrow of the Czarist and Mandarin rule in great communist revolutions in Russia and China (1 Q54, 3 Q95, 4 Q32).

The quatrains themselves point to the coming golden age at the opening of the seventh millennium around the year 2000; the Epistle, however, offers two alternative time tracks. One launches the seventh millennium all the way back in 1224; a second time track sets the **commencement** in 1826. The latter date sits closest to the **common** advents of revolutions in France and Europe between 1789 and 1848.

It makes me wonder if Nostradamus' confounding **calculations** follow a pliable system akin to the computations of Chaos theory. In other words, did he use a system in which the numbers change according to the time track born out of events in the present?

Any student of the occult knows that the exact beginning of an age is not something you can find on a train schedule and expect to see roaring up on time to the station platform of the present. An age begins influencing the collective destiny of humanity like the squalls that transform a drought-afflicted landscape. The influences of a new age sometimes fall as a drizzle; at other times they pour down like a thunderstorm. The showers come and go, and the trees and grass slowly turn green. Can you find one date in an ephemeris that pinpoints the particular moment all the trees and grass turned green?

The advent of a new era is a gradual phenomenon, but the speed can be influenced by history's collective choices, and even the action of one powerful man. Take, for instance, the recipient of this Epistle. In a little less than two years, Henry II will make a choice to compete against Gabriel de Lorge, the Comte de Montgomery, and get himself killed. This action will set history walking down a future track that eventually brings the House of Bourbon to the French throne.

The Bourbons dominated European destiny for exactly two centuries, and their excesses triggered the French Revolution. The revolution created the circumstances for Napoleon Bonaparte to dominate Europe and spread the concept of the revolution across the continent to the common people. Napoleon set

EP24 *ſçauoir s'a peu eſtēdre, où les aduerſaires de Ieſus Chriſt & de ſon egliſe, commenceront plus fort de pulluler, le tout a eſté cōposé &*

knowledge has allowed me to extend, when the adversaries of Jesus Christ and his Church will begin to multiply greatly. The whole [of my predictions] I have composed and

EP25 *calculé en iours & heures d'election & bien diſpoſees, & le plus iuſtemēt qu'il m'a eſté poſſible.*

calculated on well-appointed and well-disposed days and hours and as accurately as was possible to me.

EP26 *Et le tout Minerua libera, & non inuita, ſupputant preſque autant des aduentures du temps aduenir, comme des eages paſſez, comprenāt de*

All when Minerva was free and not unfavorable [to one's natural abilities], calculating almost as many future events as have already passed, including the

EP27 *preſent, & de ce que par le cours du temps par toutes regiõs l'on cognoiſtra aduenir tout ainſi nommement comme il eſt eſcrit, n'y meſlant*

present, and out of which through the course of time, they will know through all regions what is to happen, all exactly as it is written, with

EP28 *rien de ſuperflu, combien que l'on die: Quod de futuris non eſt determinata omnino veritas.*

nothing superfluous, although some may say: Concerning the future there can be no entirely determined truth.

the stage for the revolutions of the 19th century, Marxism, and the Bolshevik revolution. He also was responsible for launching the eventual unification of Germany. The Second Reich gave us World War I. The defeat of the Second Reich sets the stage for Hitler's Third Reich and World War II. The victors of World War II waged the Cold War, which finally led to the post-Cold War world of today.

Perhaps this track in history and all its tributaries would not have happened if Henry II had decided *not* to joust with Montgomery. If the Valois line had flourished, the Bourbons would have remained petty kings of little Navarre. The people responsible for leading the world to the French and Russian Revolutions, to Napoleon, and to the World Wars and Cold War would not, thanks to a shattered lance, have been in power. That does not mean that these revolutions would never have taken place. Of course many factors besides one man's mistake influence the flow of history. But these might have been delayed in the same manner as rains can be delayed by unexpected meteorological changes.

One can speculate that Nostradamus calculated three time tracks for the seventh millennium in accordance with potential changes in future history's inclinations.

EP24 He gives the king the first of several warnings about the coming dangers for the Church. This is an important – and potentially dangerous – theme for Nostradamus to broach.

EP25 One of the *few* consistencies in this letter is the balancing of controversial statements with the defense that his work is based on astrological calculations sanctioned by the Church. He hastens to admit, however, that his all-too-human limitations may be responsible for some inaccuracy.

EP26 He performs his astronomical machinations either on holy days of the Church or, more likely, on days with positive astrological configurations for divining the future. (Minerva was the Roman goddess of wisdom and sound advice.)

EP27 Next comes the immodest declaration that all things predicted in his Epistle will be known in **all regions**. This reads a little like the snake-oil salesman pitch in his medicinal books. On the other hand, the claim is not completely without merit. Although in 443 years few of Nostradamus' controversial prophecies have revealed **what is to happen** in all regions, it is true that his prophecies are more widely read **through all regions** in and beyond Christendom than any other Judeo-Christian prophet.

EP28 Here comes Nostradamus the spin doctor. If there is **nothing superfluous** in his prophecies, then he's found an adequate hiding

EP29   *Il eſt bien vray, Sire, que pour mon naturel inſtinct qui m'a eſté donné par mes auites ne cuidant preſager, & preſager adiouſtant & accordant iceluy*

It is quite true, Sire, that with my natural instinct which has been given to me by my ancestors, [and without] believing in predicting, [but] adapting and reconciling this

EP30   *naturel inſtinct auec ma longue ſupputation vny, & vuidant l'ame, l'eſprit, & le courage toute cure, ſolicitude, & facherie par repos & tranquilité de l'eſprit.*

natural instinct by uniting it with my long calculations, and [by] emptying my soul, mind and heart of all care, solicitude and vexation through [a state of] tranquillity and stillness of mind and spirit.

EP31   *Le tout accordé & preſagé l'vne partie tripode æneo.*

All of these are brought into harmony and predicted partly by means of the brass tripod.

EP32   *Combien qu'ils ſont pluſieurs qui m'attribuent ce qu'eſt autant à moy, comme de ce que n'en eſt rien, Dieu ſeul eternel, qui eſt perſcrutateur*

Although there are some who would attribute to me that which is as much mine as that which is not mine at all, Eternal God alone – who is the thorough searcher

EP33   *des humains courages pie, iuſte, & miſericordieux, en eſt le vray iuge, auquel ie prie qu'il me vueille defendre de la calumnie des*

of human hearts, pious, just and merciful – is the judge of the matter, and it is to him I pray to defend me from the calumny of

place behind this Latin quote. His declaration **Concerning the future there can be no entirely determined truth** implies that we are such changeable beings that at any moment we can reset the course of history through a single action or opening of awareness. By extension one could say that truth cannot be entirely adapted to one's beliefs. Each of us will have to decide which is more **superfluous**, Nostradamus' obscurity or the projections we make upon it.

It would be good for all code-breaking Nostradamians like V. J. Hewitt and Peter Lorie to meditate on the declaration above. If the future cannot be entirely determined, how could Nostradamus have set his prophecies in one all-encompassing secret code?

EP29   Nostradamus returns to another convoluted explanation of how he predicts the future, assuring us that he does his best to balance his natural prophetic instinct with rational calculations. Tidied up, his statement might read, "I didn't rely on blind belief but reconciled and adapted my instincts in union with astronomical calculations."

EP30   He lets us in on a few secrets, describing his use of meditation to still the mind, body and emotions to bring these centers into silent harmony. This makes him an empty vessel capable of receiving prophetic visions.

EP31   Sometimes his viewing screen into the future is the brass bowl of the Brachidae oracular tradition. In other words, he practices hydromancy (water gazing – see PF93; I Q1-2).

EP32   No doubt he can feel the glare of Church authorities peeking over Henry II's shoulder as the king reads this Epistle. So Nostradamus pens a qualifying statement: Don't attribute to me any divine powers – these messages are coming from God and not from my ego. God alone is my judge.

EP33   Nostradamus' natal chart shows the moon in Scorpio in a grand water (emotional) trine. He is someone who takes any criticism – warranted or unwarranted – close to heart. Others' opinions of him really pushed his buttons, as we would say today. I don't think he ever resolved his hurt or understood how identified he became with the **calumny** of others. I feel compassion for his difficulty. It is a strange and giddy experience to walk into a bookstore, pull a newly released Nostradamus book off a shelf, and find within its pages an entire chapter about yourself, your character and your work. It pains the heart to find self-righteous and peevish attacks mixed in with constructive criticism. Nostradamus deferred resolving such attacks to God and Judgement Day. Thankfully, I don't have this luxury since I am not imprisoned

EP34   *meſchants, qui voudroyent auſſi calumnieuſement s'enquerir pour*
quelle cauſe tous vos antiquiſſimes progeniteurs Rois de France ont guery
des

evil men, who would likewise calumniously want to inquire by what
means all your ancient progenitors, the Kings of France, have cured
the

EP35   *eſcrouelles, & des autres nations ont guery de la morſure des ſerpens, les*
autres ont eu certain inſtinct de l'art diuinatrice, & d'autres cas

scrofula, and how [the kings of] other nations have cured the bite of
serpents, how yet others have had a certain instinct for the art of
divination, and many other cases

EP36   *qui ſeroyent longs icy à racompter.*

which would be [too] long to recite here.

EP37   *Ce nonobſtant ceux à qui la malignité de l'eſprit malin ne ſera comprins*
par le cours du temps apres la terrenne mienne extinction, plus ſera

Notwithstanding those who cannot contain the malignity of evil spirit as
time elapses after my earthly extinction,

EP38   *mon eſcrit qu'a mon viuant, ce pendant ſi à ma ſupputation des ages ie*
faillois ou ne pourroit eſtre ſelon la volonté d'aucuns.

my writings will have more [impact] than during my lifetime; however,
should I have made errors in my calculation of the ages, or prove not to
be able to please according to everybody's whim,

EP39   *Plaira à voſtre plus qu'imperialle maieſté me pardonner, proteſtant deuant*
Dieu & ſes Saincts, que ie ne pretends de mettre rien

may it please your More Than Imperial Majesty to pardon me –
protesting before God and His Saints that I have no pretensions toward
putting anything

EP40   *quelconques par eſcrit en la preſente epiſtre, qui ſoit contre la vraye foy*
Catholique, conferant les calculations Aſtronomiques, iouxte mon ſcauoir:

in the writing of the present Epistle, that might be against the true
Catholic faith, while consulting Astronomical calculations contiguous to
my knowledge.

by Christian mythologies. In my experience there is no need to bug poky old God about those professional debunk-sayers who judge my work as skullduggery and strive to give me a piece of their skull-buggering. They are free to do as they like. It is their problem and their pleasure.

EP34-36 Nostradamus curries sympathy by comparing his plight to that of the king, who himself suffers the darts of detractors who deny his ancestral healing powers. A popular myth ascribes to the kings of France the God-given power to heal those suffering from scrofula, a now rare but once fairly common condition in which the lymph nodes of the neck and face were affected by tuberculosis, causing unsightly swelling and scarring. As part of the traditional coronation ceremony at Reims Henry II, like other French kings before and after him, was obliged to bestow his blessings on a multitude of sick children and their parents waiting outside the cathedral for him.

EP37-40 But if we cut through all the tricky and self-righteous man-euvering about calumny, we discover that our seer has made one claim that cannot be refuted. The future *has* been his judge, and his prophecies are having more and more impact the farther we move forward from the time Nostradamus walked this earth. Yes, he is obscure. Yes, he is a flatterer in this letter. And yes, he avoids rebutting his critics which – in my opinion, is rather cowardly. Despite his many failings, however, no one can deny that Nostradamus as a prophet – or even as a prophetic quack – has had more impact on the world after his death. In fact, no Judeo-Christian prophet is more widely read or discussed in both the Christian and non-Christian societies of the world than Nostradamus.

That controversial declaration required another temporizing remark about his prophetic technique. His calculations are not those of an astrological soothsayer, he assures us, but are prosecuted in a spiritually correct fashion, according to God's will.

EP41-50 The narrative moves down an altogether new direction. This will be the first of two forays we will take into the past, beginning from the year of the Creation to AD1557. The date of Creation, according to Nostradamus Time, is arrived at through an eccentric calculation that apparently relies as much on emotion and intuition as on mathematics. His number-crunching is purposefully confusing, and the reason for this is not made clear. Most pre-Darwinian bible-bashers set God's Creation of the world at 4004 BC. Nostradamus designates 4758 BC. He vaguely cites one source for his countdown – Eusebius, an early Christian

EP41 *car l'eſpace de temps de nos premiers, qui nous ont precedez ſont tels, me remettant ſous la correction du plus ſain iugement, que le*

For the distance of time since our primeval [ancestors], who preceded us is such – I submit myself to correction by the most sane judgment – that

EP42 *premier homme Adam, fut deuant Noë enuiron mille deux cens quarante deux ans, ne computant les temps par la ſupputation des Gentils,*

first man, Adam, lived 1,242 years before Noah –- not reckoning the time by the calculations of the Gentiles

EP43 *comme a mis par eſcrit Varron: mais tant ſeulement ſelon les ſacrees Eſcriptures, & ſelon la foibleſſe de mon eſprit, en mes calculations Aſtronomiques.*

as set in the writings of Varro but solely and totally according to the Holy Scriptures, as best my feeble understanding and my astronomical calculations can interpret them.

EP44 *Apres Noë, de luy & de l'vniuerſel deluge, vint Abraham enuiron mille huictante ans, lequel a eſté ſouuerain Aſtrologue, ſelon aucuns, il inuenta*

After Noah, and the universal flood, came Abraham – about 1,080 years later – who was a superlative Astrologer [and] according to some, he invented

EP45 *premier les lettres Caldeiques: apres vint Moyſe enuiron cinq cens quinze ou ſeize ans, & entre le temps de Dauid à Moyſe, ont eſté cinq cens ſeptante ans là enuiron.*

the Chaldean alphabet. After that came Moses – about 515 to 516 years – and between the time of David and of Moses there were around 570 years.

EP46 *Puis apres entre le temps de Dauid, & le temps de noſtre ſauueur & redempteur Ieſus Chriſt, nay de l'vnique vierge, ont eſté (ſelon aucuns*

Then after that, between the time of David and the time of our Savior and Redeemer, Jesus Christ, born of the matchless Virgin, have elapsed (according to some

EP47 *Cronographes) mille trois cens cinquāte ans: pourra obiecter quelqu'vn cette ſupputatiõ n'eſtre veritable, pource qu'elle differe à celle d'Euſebe.*

chronographers) 1,350 years. It could be objected that this calculation cannot be right, because it differs from that of Eusebius.

theologian and fellow renegade calculator of creation-based timelines, who fell in, out, and into favor again at the Council of Nicaea in AD 325–27.

In this timeline the current seventh millennium starts in AD 1242, more than three centuries before Nostradamus wrote this Epistle. This matches up with his statement in the Preface that *we are now in the seventh millenary* (PF87). But for some mysterious reason a second, vastly divergent, timeline for the history of the world is waiting for us later in the Epistle – one in which the seventh millennium begins in 1826.

The first Epistle timeline inserted here reads almost like a ragged rough draft for the next which is only slightly more plausible. For centuries commentators have jumped (or fallen) into these two tiger-traps of calculation, crawling out of their studies with an assortment of scratched and moth-eaten master-cipher number theories. I don't feel like wasting anyone's time with a rundown of all the theories – except one. Nostradamus claims in EP26 to have predicted that the same number of events will occure after the birth of Christ as from Creation to his birth (4,758 years). Taking this tack, we subtract 1,557 (for the year 1557) to arrive at a balance of 3,201 years of future history remaining in his prophetic account (that's 2,758 years left after AD 2000). That means his prophecies should cover events 961 years beyond the final conflagration of the Earth in AD 3797 – all the way to AD 4758. But with all that said, he returns to waffling and nebulous declarations about his calculations. He claims they may not be *good and valid for all nations*, and his math is founded on divining the trajectory of stars through an *emotion infused* into him by his *ancient progenitors*. This, in effect, makes Nostradamus the only man who can tame the tiger of his mathematical codes.

EP48   *Et depuis le temps de l'humaine redemption iufques à la feduction detestable des Sarrazins ont esté six cens vingt & vn an, là enuiron,*

And from the time of human redemption to the detestable seduction by the Saracens, have elapsed 621 years, or thereabouts,

EP49   *depuis en çà l'on peut facilement colliger quels temps font passez, si la miéne fupputation n'est bonne & valable par toutes nations, pource que*

from which one can easily add up the amount of time gone by – although my calculations are not good and valid for all nations because

EP50   *le tout a esté calculé par le cours celeste, par affociation d'efmotiõ infufe à certaines heures delaiffees, par dèfmotiõ de mes antiques progeniteurs:*

the total has been calculated by the celestial courses, in association with the emotion infused – at certain hours of solitude – by the emotion of my ancient progenitors.

EP51   *Mais l'iniure du temps, ô fereniffime Roy, requiert que tels fecrets euenemens ne foyent manifeftez, que par ænigmatique*

But the injustice of the times, O Most Serene King, requires that such secret events [or rituals?] should not be made manifest except in enigmatic

EP52   *fentence, n'ayant qu'vn feul fens, & vnique intelligence, fans y auoir rien mis d'ambigue n'amphibologique calculation: mais pluftoft fous*

sentences having, however, only one sense and meaning, without having nothing of ambiguity put in nor any amphibological calculation [ie having more than one meaning]; but rather [should they be] kept under

EP53   *obnubilee obfcurité par vne naturelle infufion approchant à la fentence d'vn des mille & deux Prophetes, qui ont esté depuis la*

a cloudy obscurity, with a natural infusion approaching the sentence of one of the 1,002 Prophets, who have existed since the

EP54   *creation du monde, iouxte la fupputation & Chronique punique de Ioel,* Effundam fpiritum meum fuper omnem carnem & prophetabunt filij veftri, & filiæ veftræ.

creation of the world, together with the calculation of the Punic Chronicle of Joel: I will pour out my spirit upon all flesh and your sons and daughters shall prophesy.

EP51 And his apologies to the king make it clear that he will not reveal the *secret* mathematical rituals of his ancient ancestors because of the *injustice* – or better, the religious intolerance – *of the times*.

EP52, 53 His notorious poetic obscurity is underscored with a claim that can rub one's face in one's own judgements about our prophet's writing style. In it he disclaims all the criticisms of his prophecies that, at least on the surface, appear true. They are ambiguous, layered with many meanings, and open to all kinds of interpretations. Actually he could be implying here that no matter how cloudy these prophecies appear they each have only one meaning. How Nostradamus gets his number of **1,002 Prophets** is beyond me.

EP54 As with the Preface, Nostradamus reveals to the king the basic formula of his prophetic process: a natural birth-given capacity to be a divine medium, anchored in some kind of secret and purportedly objective calculation, then shared at large in writing cloaked in premeditated obscurity.

There is nothing **Punic** or Phoenician/Carthaginian about the Hebrew prophet Joel, unless Nostradamus is drawing this translation from some Greek or Phoenecian text. **Calculation** is used when "opinion" or "insights" or "thinking" of Joel would make better sense. The quote implies that God has poured his spirit on Nostradamus' family for many generations.

EP55 *Mais telle prophetie procedoit de la bouche du ſainct Eſprit, qui eſtoit la*
ſouueraine puiſſance eternelle, adioincte auec la celeſte à d'aucuns

But such Prophecy proceeded from the mouth of the Holy Ghost who has
been the sovereign and eternal power, in association with the celestial
[power], [by which] some

EP56 *de ce nombre ont predit de grandes & eſmerueillables aduentures:*

of this number have made predictions of great and marvelous events.

EP57 *Moy en ceſt endroict ie ne m'attribue nullement tel tiltre. Ia à Dieu ne*
plaiſe, ie confeſſe bien que le tout vient de Dieu, & luy en rends

As for myself, I by no means would ever assign such a title to myself –
God forbid, indeed – I readily confess that all emanates from God, and to
him is rendered

EP58 *graces, honneur, & loüange immortelle, ſans y auoir meſlé de la*
diuination qui prouient à fato: mais à Deo, à natura, & la pluſpart

thanks, honor and undying praise, without having mixed therein any
divination proceeding from fate, but to God, and to nature, and for the
most part

EP59 *accompaignee du mouuement du cours celeſte, tellement que voyant*
comme dans vn miroüer ardent comme par viſion obnubilee, les grands

accompanied by celestial movements and orbits, just like looking into a
burning mirror, with clouded vision – great

EP60 *euenemens triſtes, prodigieux, & calamiteuſes aduentures qui*
s'approchent par les principaux culteurs.

events, sad, prodigious, and calamitous happenings that approach
toward the principal worshippers.

EP61 *Premierement des temples de Dieu, ſecondement par ceux qui ſont*
terreſtrement ſouſtenus s'approcher telle decadence, auecques mille autres

First, upon the temples of God, secondly, upon those who, sustained by
the earth, approach such decadence, with a thousand other

EP62 *calamiteuſes aduentures, que par le cours du tẽps on cognoiſtra aduenir:*

calamitous happenings that through the course of time will be known in
the future.

EP55, 56   I believe his deference to the prophetic powers of the 1,002 seers is a veil to confuse the Church censors. What he'd like to declare is that he uses none other than the Holy Ghost of the Christian Trinity as his spirit messenger. In other words, the same spiritual and celestial conduit of God that poured its seed into the Virgin Mary impregnates Nostradamus with a divine vision of tomorrow.

EP57   Skeptics of Nostradamus might say that his redundant disclaimers that nothing spiritually incorrect is being practiced here and that he is "not a prophet" is akin to Nixon proclaiming, "I am not a crook." But even the hint that he is inspired by the Holy Ghost "itself" does require another genuflection to the Inquisitors. This time his bottom line is: "I don't have the powers of a biblical prophet, but God uses me sometimes because I use only rituals that are those sanctioned by the Church and religiously correct."

EP58   His predictions are therefore not the soothayings of witches, Christ-killing Jews, God-hating Satanists, Cabalists, or Calvinists, all of whom fix their fulminations on the fickle finger of *fate*. Not in the least! O ye of racks and blazing stakes, Nostradamus is not deviating from any of your esoteric, officially sanctioned bigotry and intolerant views. Our diviner is a humble and hereditary instrument of God.

EP59, 60   He does add a new tool to his arsenal of augury – the magic mirror. Maybe he is describing what initiates experience: images issuing from its dark unlit and leadened surface cascade out of rings of pulsing flames not dissimilar to those conjured by the retinas of meditators or who find their eyes drawn like magnets upward to the brow.

Thus, our prophet views – framed in flames of mysterious fires – the shadows of the sad and wondrous adventures of the future to befall Christendom.

EP61, 62   First in priority are visions that, on the surface, concern the future evolution of man's religions but actually relate to humanity's evolution toward higher consciousness and the eternity of God. The secondary visions at first seem to describe the destinies sustained and nurtured by the people and their secular civilizations. But underneath them is a message about the evolution or devolution of human unconsciousness – that nightmare of habitual, mechanical, conditioned behavior that fuels negative futures and dooms us to be so predictable.

EP63   *car Dieu regardera la longue ſterilité de la grand dame, que puis apres*
conceura deux enfans principaux: mais elle periclitant, celle qui luy

For God will look upon the long sterility of the great dame, who shortly
afterwards will conceive two principal infants: but she being in peril,
[and] she who to him/her

EP64   *ſera adiouſtee par la temerité de l'aage de mort periclitant dedans le*
dixhuictieſme, ne pouuant paſſer le trente-ſixieſme qu'en delaiſſera trois

will be adjoined by the temerity of the era being in danger of death in her
eighteenth [year], and will be unable to live beyond her thirty-sixth
[year] when she will leave three

EP65   *maſles, & vne femelle, & en aura deux, celuy qui n'en eut iamais d'vn*
meſme pere, des trois freres ſeront telles differences, puis vnies &

males and one female, and of these two will not ever have had the same
father; between the three brothers there will be great differences, then
[such] unity and

EP66   *accordees, que les trois & quatre parties de l'Europe trembleront; par le*
moindre d'aage ſera la monarchie Chreſtienne ſouſtenue, augmentee:

cooperation, that the three and four parts of Europe will tremble; the
youngest in age will sustain and augment the Christian Monarchy [of
France/Papacy?]:

EP67   *ſectes eſleuees, & ſubitement abaiſſees, Arabes reculez, Royaumes vnis,*
nouuelles Loix promulguees: des autres enfans le premier

The elevated sects [will be] suddenly abased, Arabs will retreat, Kingdoms
will be united, and new Laws promulgated. Of the other infants the first

EP68   *occupera les Lions furieux coronnez, tenants les pattes deſſus les armets*
intrepidez.

will occupy the fierce crowned Lions [India?], holding their paws upon
the intrepid armorial bearings.

EP69   *Le ſecond ſe profondera ſi auant par les Latins accompaigné, que ſera*
faicte la ſeconde voye tremblante & furibonde au mont Iouis deſcendant

The second, accompanied, will penetrate so far into the Latins that the
second trembling path will be made and the ferocious one [Napoleon] to
the St Bernard Pass descending

EP63 The prose prophecy begins in a real muddle. A couple of slants are possible. In the first the **great dame** could be Catherine de' Medici, and the two principal infants her children Francis II and Henry III.

EP64 But for this to work we would have to substitute Francis II for Catherine, since he was the one who died in his 18th year.

EP65 The next few lines could describe the destinies (and questionable lineage) of some of her other children: Elizabeth (queen of Spain), Charles IX, Henry III, and Hercules (Duc d'Alençon). I have difficulty making any sense of it. The babbling current of his narrative seems to follow the "Valois children" slant. After the death of Francis II, the three surviving and quarrelsome brothers are Charles IX, Henry III, and Hercules Duc d'Alençon. Perhaps this flip-flop from sibling rivalry to unity was meant as an enthusiastic proposal rather than a prophecy to Henry II that his sons would unite or dominate most of Europe.

EP66 Still, Nostradamus could be forecasting an alternative destiny here – one that has a slim chance only if the father avoids his jousting accident and manages to guide his young sons to adulthood. Alençon (**the youngest** [son] **in age**) definitely did not live up to this lofty prediction. He died of a cold and is remembered as a laughingstock bumbling about in his effort to woo Elizabeth I.

EP67 In an alternative future Nostradamus promises Henry II that the new Hercules Duc d'Alençon will work miracles. He will undermine the Huguenots and Protestants: the Corsairs and Turks (**Arabs**) will abandon Christian waters and be driven out of Eastern Europe. New religious edicts will be promulgated, Christian kingdoms united under the Mother Church. All quite miraculous – and not a single one of these dreams was fulfilled.

EP68 Now we make the first of many temporal shifts to centuries ahead. The three surviving sons of Henry II are mistaken by the prophet or overlaid with visions of the three Antichrists: Napoleon, Hitler and Mabus. Napoleon's cherished dream to conquer India (symbolized by the three-headed lion, which is one of India's symbols) was never fulfilled either by **the first son**, Charles IX, or by Bonaparte.

EP69 The image of **the second** child as a mature Henry III leading troops over the Alps to conquer Italy is washed away by his father's poor choices and premature death. In his place appears Antichrist Number One, Napoleon (the man with the **ferocious name** [1 Q76]), leading his armies into Italy over the St Bernard Pass two and a half centuries later.

EP70 *pour monter aux Pyrennees, ne ſera tranſlatee à l'antique monarchie, ſera
faicte la troiſieme inondation de ſang humain, ne ſe trouuera de*

**to climb the Pyrenees which will not [however], be transferred to the
ancient monarchy [of France]. [Finally] the third one will cause an
inundation of human blood, and [one] will not find**

EP71 *long temps Mars en careſme.*

Mars fasting for a long time.

EP72 *Et ſera donnee la fille par la conſeruation de l'Egliſe Chreſtienne, tombant
ſon dominateur à la paganiſme ſecte des nouueaux infideles,*

**And the daughter will be given for the preservation of the Christian
Church, her lord falling into the pagan sect of the new infidels,**

EP73 *elle aura deux enfans, l'vn de fidelité, & l'autre d'infidelité par la
confirmation de l'egliſe catholique.*

**she will have two children: one faithful, and the other unfaithful by the
sanction of the Catholic Church.**

EP74 *Et l'autre qui à ſa grande confuſion & tarde repentance la voudra ruiner,
ſeront trois regions par l'extreme difference des ligues, c'eſt*

**And the other, who to his great confusion and later repentance, will
want to ruin her, will have three regions with extremely different
boundaries, namely**

EP75 *aſſauoir la Romanie, la Germanie, l'Eſpaigne, qui feront diuerſes ſectes
par main militaire, delaiſſant le 50. & 52. degrez de hauteur, & ferõt*

**Rome, Germany, and Spain, which will [consist of] diverse sects by
military force – leaving behind the 50th and 52nd degree of latitude –
and will**

EP70   Napoleon – not Henry III – would cross the Pyrenees in 1808, at the head of 200,000 men, to occupy Spain. The Spanish would not relinquish their power to the usurper from France or to any Bourbon king (**ancient monarchy**) before or after Napoleon.

It is hardly possible that this **inundation of human blood** on a vast scale could be the creation of the **third** (son) of Henry II. The guy better suited to the gory poetry is the **third** Antichrist.

EP71   This is most likely an astrological metaphor rather than a date for a period when Mars will not be in major aspect during Lent. It means that the god of war will celebrate his Fat Tuesday, or his "mardigore," without temperance for many years.

EP72   Just when our prophet seems to be wetting his pen to chronicle the Third Antichrist, he backtracks through time to the early 1570s when Henry II's daughter, Marguérite de Valois, gets married off to that **infidel** Henry de Navarre who, as a Huguenot, falls victim to one of Nostradamus' neo-pagan put-downs for the new Calvinist sect. The marriage was arranged in part to unite the Valois and Bourbon bloodlines and preserve peace between the embittered sects of French Christians.

EP73   But Marguérite, though quite promiscuous, would not have any children by Henry de Navarre. So the story of **two children** – one growing up in the Catholic faith and the other against it – is at the very worst a dream of our prophet, or perhaps just a quantum future unfulfilled by actual events and therefore forever dangling out of time. Is that clear? Don't worry, it gets worse.

EP74   The heretic child sprouting from Marguérite's womb (and Nostradamus' imagination) will grow up desiring to ruin his mother. How he does this is lost to us, washed away by a flood of new images that take us on another temporal detour to deposit us at the threshold of **three regions**.

EP75   Ah, but in what time reality is our psychedelic seer framing Italy, Germany and Spain? Are these three regions broiled in the religious wars of the First Reich during the the Thirty Years War (1618–48)? It seems more likely that Nostradamus' time-tripping has landed us smack in the middle of the Fascist realms of Italy (**Rome**), Nazi **Germany**, and Franco's Fascist **Spain** from 1941 through 1942. This is when military forces of various Fascist sects from all three were sent north and east to fight on the Russian Front. The Spanish, though officially neutral, sent an entire division of Fascist volunteers along on Hitler's crusade against Bolshevism. Mussolini sent an entire army to fight on the flank of the German Sixth Army at the Battle of Stalingrad. By the way, the Italian Eighth Army was overwhelmed by a dozen Soviet armies that

EP76   *tous hõmaige des regions loingtaines aux regions de l'Europe de Septentrion de 48. degrez d'hauteur, qui premier par vaine timidité*

all render homage to the remote [ancient?] regions [misprint: religions?] of Europe and of the Russian north from 48 degrees latitude; the first by vain timidity

EP77   *tremblera, puis les plus occidentaux, meridionaux & orientaux trembleront, telle ſera leur puiſſance, que ce qui ſe fera par concorde & vnion*

will tremble, but afterwards those of Western lands, the southern and the [middle] Eastern will tremble – such will be their power, that what will be forged in concord and union

EP78   *inſuperable des conqueſtes belliques.*

[will be] invincible to warlike conquests.

EP79   *De nature ſeront eſgaux: mais grandement differentz de foy.*

In nature they will be equal, but [they will be] extremely different in faith.

EP80   *Apres cecy la dame ſterile de plus grande puiſſance que la ſeconde ſera receuë par deux peuples, par le premier obſtiné par celuy qui a eu*

After this the sterile Dame, of greater power than the second, will be received by two peoples [nations]: by the first made obstinate by those who have had

EP81   *puiſſance ſur tous, par le deuxieſme & par le tiers qui eſtẽdra ſes forces vers le circuit de l'Orient, de l'Europe aux Pãnons l'a profligé &*

power over all; by the second and by the third which will extend its forces toward the circumference [sphere?] of Eastern Europe where, in Pannonia it will be overwhelmed and

EP82   *ſuccombé & par voyle marine fera ſes extenſions à la Trinacrie Adriatique, par Mirmidons & Germaniques du tout ſuccombé, & ſera la*

overcome, and by marine sail it will come to extend [their forces] to Sicily, the Adriatic through the Balkans and the Germans having wholly succumbed, and it will cause the

pushed them back from a defensive line that happened to inter-
sect the **50th** parallel!

EP76   The first **ancient religion** is the pagan state religion of Adolf
Hitler's Third Reich to which his Axis allies, poetically at least,
rendered homage. The Battle of Stalingrad turned the tide on the
Eastern Front against Hitler. The city sits exactly in between the
48th and 49th parallels.

EP77   It is difficult to ascertain upon whom this **timidity** comes. It
seems Nostradamus is saying that of the two **diverse** and **remote**
sects (EP75–77) of Fascism and Communism the first **will tremble**
at the 48th degree (the parallel over Stalingrad). This implies its
eventual destruction by the second sect **remote** from God – the
atheistic communists.

But **afterwards** – or better, after Stalingrad – the fighting will
eventually spread westwards. The Soviets push the Axis alliance
back into the **Western lands** of Europe and the Anglo-American
alliance sweeps the Axis out of North Africa (the **southern**
lands) and defeats the **Eastern** land of Imperial Japan.

EP78   Indeed, the Allies – Britain, the Soviet Union, and the United
States – were invincible in their **warlike conquests**. Together
with their lesser allies, they fielded forces of over 50 million men
against Hitler.

EP79   The Western Christian democracies cohabiting with communist,
atheistic Russians in their alliance against the Axis Powers would
make the **nature** of their union **extremely different in faith**.

EP80   It appears that EP80 through 83 describe the routes of Allied
victories against the Axis in World War II. The **sterile Dame**
could be metaphorical for the goddess Germania, representing
Hitler's Third Reich. The **second** then becomes Mussolini's Italy,
which is **received** or delivered by the British and American forces
(the **two peoples**) invading Italy from North Africa in 1943.

EP81   The **third** nation is that of the Soviets – pushing Germania's
forces (the **first** nation) out of Russia and **Eastern Europe**. Hitler
did suffer some of his last large-scale defeats on the Eastern front
when he squandered his last panzer tank reserves during his final
offensive push to relieve Budapest (**in Pannonia**) in early 1945.

EP82   We return to 1943, and visions of the great Allied fleets in the
Mediterranean putting down fire and lowering landing craft at
Sicily. Nostradamus also forecasts Allied landings along the
labyrinth of islands and sunny beaches of the Dalmatian coast
(**Balkans**). The latter never happened, but was Winston
Churchill's first strategic choice for an invasion of southern
Europe. In 1944 he pressed his case very hard with Roosevelt and

EP83   *ſecte Barbarique du tout des Latins grandement affligee & deſchaſſee.*

Barbarian sect to be greatly afflicted and driven out of all the Latins [states].

EP84   *Puis le grand empyre de l'Antechriſt commencera dans la Atila & Zerſes deſcendre en nombre grand & innumerable; tellement que la*

Then the great empire of the Antichrist will begin – where [once] Attila['s empire] and Xerxes descended [Central Asia and Persia] – in numbers great and countless, so many that the

EP85   *venue du ſainct Eſprit, procedant du 48. degré fera tranſmigration, deſchaſſant à l'abomination de l'Antechriſt, faiſant guerre contre le*

coming of the Holy Ghost, proceeding from the 48th degree [of latitude], will make a transmigration, driving out the abomination of the Antichrist [who is] making war against the

EP86   *royal qui ſera le grãd vicaire de Ieſus Chriſt, & contre ſon egliſe, & ſon regne per tempus, & in occaſione temporis,*

Royal [Pope] who will be the great Vicar of Jesus Christ, and against his Church, and his reign for a time and to the end of time.

the Allied commanders but was overruled. The main invasion route through southern Europe was switched to the coast of Nostradamus' native Provence. Eventually the **Germans** succumbed to total defeat.

EP83 The **Barbarbian** *sect* is that of the Nazis. **Barbarian** could be a decoy word for "Barbarossa," which Nostradamus may apply elsewhere in the quatrains as a code name for Adolf Hitler. The *sect* of Hitler is *driven out* of Italy.

EP84 Now the stream of visions pitches forward toward a time ahead of our own, and sees the war of the Third Antichrist. Nostradamus uses classical allusions to describe a new **empire**, or Pan-Islamic superstate, that includes the newly independent states of former Soviet Central Asia (**Attila's empire**), united with modern day Afghanistan, Syria, Iran, Iraq, Pakistan, Trans-Caucasia, and Turkey (**Xerxes**). The eastern potentates of Attila and Xerxes were notorious for their attempts to invade and conquer Western civilization; the same allusion therefore is applied to a future Asian or Middle Eastern potentate of an Islamic superstate who has designs to do the same.

Efforts to unite the Islamic world into one state are not new. The unity of language, culture, and religion makes this theoretically more feasible than uniting the various religions, cultures, and language groups of Europe into a European Union. Fear and prejudice of Christendom against Islam has prompted the West to do its utmost to keep the Islamic world divided. These efforts will eventually fail in the early decades of the next millennium.

EP85 Nostradamus waxes biblical and paints a picture of a vast Asian horde assembled to do battle with the Christian West. They are routed by the transmigrating **Holy Ghost**, who issues from someplace on latitude 48 degrees. Earlier in the Epistle this latitude related to the Battle of Stalingrad. The references to latitudes 45 and 48 appear in quatrains for what some believe is either the bombing of New York (6 Q97) or a catastrophic drought in the 21st century grain belts of the world on latitude 48, that brings on a global famine (5 Q98).

A more abstract reading of the descent of the **Holy Ghost** could suggest that the holy spirit of love and consciousness awakens in the hearts of human beings to such an extent that the forces of unconsciousness that fuel the "antichrist" – or better, "anti-consciousness," in humanity – are driven out of our hearts.

EP86 The Antichrist – whether he is literally an Islamic potentate or a force of human unconsciousness – is attacking a future pope in the 21st century. Other references in *Les Propheties* to this attack

EP87   *& precedera deuant vn eclypſe ſolaire le plus obſcur, & le plus tenebreux, que ſoit eſté depuis la creation du monde iuſques à la mort &*

And this will be preceded by a solar eclipse more obscure and more dark [and mysterious], than any since the creation of the world except for the death and

EP88   *paſſion de Ieſus Chriſt, & de là iuſques icy, & ſera au moys d'Octobre que quelque grande tranſlation ſera faite, & telle que l'on cuydera la*

passion of Jesus Christ, from that time till now, and there shall be in the month of October some great movement and transference [of the globe] and it will be such that one will think that

EP89   *peſanteur de la terre auoir perdu ſon naturel mouuement, & eſtre abiſmee en perpetuelles tenebres, ſeront precedans au temps vernal & s'en enſuyuant apres d'extremes changemens, permutations de regnes, par*

the Earth has lost its natural [gravitational] movement, and that it will be plunged into the abyss of perpetual darkness; there will be initial omens in the spring, and extraordinary changes in rapid succession thereafter, reversals of kingdoms

EP90   *grands tremblemens de terre, auec pullulation de la neuſue Babylonne fille miſerable augmentee par l'abomination du premier holocauſte, &*

and mighty earthquakes, with the increase of the new Babylon, the miserable daughter, augmented by the abomination of the first Holocaust, and

of the Antichrist make a spiritual battle within the Church itself equally possible. In a more down-to-earth interpretation, the future pope and the Roman Catholic Church are victorious against the Eastern, pan-Islamic fundamentalist invasion. But one must be careful here and note how difficult it is for even the finest, most self-observant prophets not to project their hope that their religion is victorious over all others.

EP87 There are many references in prophecy to either a long-lasting solar eclipse or the sun being blacked out all over the world for three days by either volcanic or nuclear ash. You can even find references to a comet or meteorite strike causing such a cloud to cover the Earth. In a less doom-laden interpretation, *and this will be preceded by a solar eclipse* could mean that these events will begin after the reign of Pope John Paul II, who was born under a solar eclipse. In St Malachy's prophecy of the succession of popes unto doomsday, John Paul is called *De Labore Solis*, which means "the Sun's Labor," a medieval poetic phrase applied to solar eclipses. After the passing of John Paul II only two popes will follow, according to St Malachy's list. A total eclipse will occur in much of Europe on 11 August 1999.

EP88 Many prophetic traditions share the theme of Mother Nature's ultimate revenge for the abuse of this planet by humankind. Nostradamus' account is one of the most terrifying. He dates the slow apocalyptic rock and roll starting perhaps in October 1999 and continuing through May 2000.

EP89 In 6 Q88, 9 Q31, 9 Q48, and 9 Q83, Nostradamus refers to sudden violent natural phenomena occurring in spring – particularly during the month of May. No allusion is made to the year of these events, except for one prediction concerning a vast hail-storm in AD 3755. In the other four quatrains Nostradamus may well be giving us descriptions of the cataclysm to come during the next grand alignment of planets on 5 May 2000.

I personally lean towards the interpretation that the upheaval that will undermine civilization as we know it will be caused by a spiritual shift in consciousness rather than a physical jolt. The discovery of intelligent life on other planets might topple the axis of our religious and political moralities on their ears, might it not? The existence of "others" out there would end nation-ism overnight (*reversals of kingdoms*). When faced with unkown intelligences in the cosmos, our world would make *extraordinary changes* and unite as one.

EP90 We appear to step back in time through the gates, of Auschwitz to the *first Holocaust* – of the Jews in the 1940s. A second holocaust

EP91 *ne tiendra tant feulement que feptante trois ans, fept moys, puis apres en fortira du tige celle qui auoit demeuré tant long temps*

it will last no less than 73 years and 7 months, thereafter one will issue forth from the stock which had for so long remained

EP92 *fterile, procedant du cinquantiefme degré, qui renouuellera toute l'eglife Chreftienne.*

sterile – one proceeding from the 50th degree, one who will renew the whole Christian Church.

EP93 *Et fera faicte grande paix, vnion & concorde entre vng des enfans des frons efgarez & feparez par diuers regnes, & fera faicte telle paix*

And then great peace will be established, union and concord between the children of the frontiers who have been gathered and separated by diverse reigns; and such will be the peace established

EP94 *que demeurera attaché au plus profond baratre le fufcitateur & promoteur de la martialle faction par la diuerfité des religieux & fera*

that he [Satan] who was instigator and promoter of military factions, born of the diversity of religions, will remain chained to the deepest pit, and

spawned by the machinations of a **new Babylon** (in modern terms, Saddam Hussein's Iraq) is implied in our near future.

EP91   The threat from the new Babylon will last for 73 years and seven months. But as usual Nostradamus doesn't tell us when to start our countdown, except if **seven months** refers to 10 Q72's **In the year 1999 and seven months.** For all we know, Nostradamus could be talking about the length of the Babylonian threat to the state of Israel. In that case the number 73 indicates the years from 1973 through 1999 which embrace the timespan of Nostradamus' 25-to-27-year war of the Third Antichrist (8 Q77). Perhaps we can count 73 years and seven months from the inception of the Israeli state – from 1948 through 2021 – which gets us close to the best astrological time window for the Third World War in the 2020s. Finally, one might even say that **73** stands for July of 1973 or 2073, when a great spiritual master who is the catalyst for changing the direction of human consciousness and spiritual evolution will appear.

EP92   Anyway, the general drift can blow us, on the one hand, towards terrible tribulations of ecological, geological, and social catastrophes, accompanied by the rise of religious intolerance and the Third Antichrist. On the other hand, we can look toward a counterbalancing force – a spiritual revolution that will arise again from a mysterious source of human enlightenment, **which had for so long remained sterile**, bringing humanity out of childishness and into maturity for a golden age of peace.

EP93   On the secular level we can anticipate a new international governing body. Perhaps it is a born-again United Nations. **Union and concord** will be forged between those who fought each other in the Third World War. The references to gathering and separation by **diverse reigns** is interesting because it implies that national and religious divisions must fade away before a millennium of peace can happen. If there are no nations, who will start a war? How can organized religions preach their monopoly on God and virtue if people come to understand that religious labels and dogmas cut and divide them from an intimate divine experience and from each other? Perhaps out of one last paroxysm of suffering, people of the 21st century will learn that the nature and essence of God dwells in every heart, and dogma and politics are the real Antichrist.

EP94   **Satan** therefore represents our unconsciousness, our "sin". If the childhood of humankind comes to a close after the new millennium, Satan will be thrown, like a junked nuclear weapon, into that metaphorical pit. The biblical implication is that Satan will

EP95   *vny le Royaume du Rabieux qui contrefera le ſage.*

the kingdom of the Rabid one, who acts against the wise one, will be united.

EP96   *Et les contrees, villes, citez, regnes, & prouinces qui auront delaiſſé les premieres voyes pour ſe deliurer ſe captiuant plus profondement*

And the countries, towns, cities, kingdoms, and provinces who will have abandoned their old ways to gain liberty, [but who will in fact have] enslaved themselves still more profoundly,

EP97   *ſeront ſecrettement fachez de leur liberté, & parfaicte religion perdue, commenceront de frapper dans la partie gauche, pour tourner à la*

causing them to secretly let go of their liberty, and lose faith in their perfect religion, they will begin to strike to the left, only to return to the

EP98   *dextre, & remettant la ſaincteté profligee de long tẽps auec leur priſtin eſcrit, qu'apres le grãd chien ſortira le plus gros maſtin, qui*

right, and replacing the sanctity overcome long ago with their pristine scriptures; thereafter the great dog will send forth the largest of mastiffs, who

remain chained in the abyss for 1,000 years. So we could expect
the return of Satanic – ie unconscious – human behavior after AD
3000.

EP95 The **kingdom of the rabid one** is that of Nostradamus' three
Antichrists: Napoleon, Hiſter and the Third yet to come. A
biblical reference to Satan's being locked away in the abyss or
chained within a pit follows the poetic theme that fits with the
prophecy of Hitler's Führer bunker (4 Q40). It may yet mold itself
around one of the chief candidates for the Third Antichrist,
Saddam Hussein, who has his own subterranean "Führer" bunker.
It would take a direct hit from a nuclear bomb to destroy
Saddam's shelter.

EP96, 97 After Armageddon the world is one, and its peoples live in
earthly paradise for 1,000 years. In time a subtle loss of that
perfect consciousness (**religion**) begins. The Hindus believe that
the momentum of enlightenment during a golden age suffers its
own entropy. Slowly, imperceptibly, year after year the light of
consciousness and love fades, and the world returns to its old
unconscious and divisive ways. After the year 3000 the fall may
take as long as seven centuries. But Nostradamus assures us in the
Preface that the end of the world – the "real" end, that is – takes
place in a final conflagration of the sun in the year 3797.

If unconsciousness dictates that humanity returns to its predictable habits, something similar to the Atlantian myth may
beset our godlike descendants 1,800 years hence. The wicked
mainstream society somehow tampers with natural forces, causing
the sun to destroy the Earth. Those ever-present secret societies
that keep the flame of true consciousness and enlightenment
alive in any era – whether it is an age of golden wisdom or a
period as intolerant and as dark as iron – see what is coming and
decide to abandon Earth and its people to their insanity. They
travel through space and time to distant worlds to start a new
Garden of Eden. Perhaps they travel to those constellations
referred to by our prophet, the stars of Aquarius and Cancer.

EP98 The **great dog** could be Nostradamus' version of Ezekiel's Gog
and Magog from the Old Testament, but the time frame is
unclear. Are we thrown backwards from the 3700s to an
Armageddon that explodes at the turn of the 20th century and
continues through the 2020s? Or is Nostradamus still taking us
down a far distant-future track to the era of humanity's galactic
explorations, when a "dog-faced" race of extraterrestrials threatens our existence? Instead of the 1990s he could be pointing to
the 3790s, the final years of Mother Earth. Are the Dogam (see

EP99　*fera deſtruction de tout, meſme de ce qu'au parauant ſera eſté perpetré,*
ſeront redreſſez les temples comme au premier temps, & ſera

**will cause [the] destruction of all, even of what had in the beginning
been perpetrated. Temples will be set up again as in ancient times, and**

EP100　*reſtituté le clerc à ſon priſtin eſtat, & comme˜cera à meretricquer &*
luxurier, faire & commettre mille forfaicts.

**the priest will be restored to his original position, and he will begin his
whoring and luxury and will commit a thousand offenses.**

EP101　*Et eſtant proche d'vne autre deſolation, par lors qu'elle ſera à ſa plus*
haute & ſublime dignité ſe dreſſeront de potentats & mains

**And on the eve of another desolation, when she [the perverted Church]
will be at her most high and sublime dignity, potentates and military
powers**

EP102　*militaires, & luy ſeront oſtez les deux glaiues, & ne luy demeurera que les*
enſeignes, deſquelles par moyen de la curuature qui les attire,

**will confront her, and take away the two swords, and leave her only the
insignia, whose curvature attracts them.**

EP115) responsible for tampering with the fusion furnace of our sun, causing it to rapidly age and expand into a red giant that devours our Earth? Or are these canine-faced entities attacking the outposts of our star-trekking voyagers who are colonizing stars in the constellation of Aquarius? In the Preface Nostradamus implies that our colonies there will come to grief, whereas the mission to the constellation of Cancer will be an unrivaled success.

EP99, 100 The vision of some galactic Armageddon in Nostradamus' prophetic waters shivers out of focus and is replaced by the viscous liquidity of potential events 700 years earlier, around the end of the third millennium. Perhaps he beholds the beginning of man's descent from the golden age of peace. It seems that a new paganism and hedonism arise in the 2990s. But before events can come into focus, the tides of the prophetic waters flow farther backwards in time, and the voice of the spirit lurking at the bottom of his brass bowl becomes none other than the daemon screech of heavy-metal vocalists of the 1990s. Perhaps now we are looking over his shoulder to view our own times of religious discord, licentiousness, and the pretentious whining of the irresponsible.

EP101 We enter the unfolding drama of our millennium's spiritual battle between old and new religious thinking. Certain mainstream Christian interpreters of prophecy say that when Christianity dominates the world, the end-times are near. What is not said, but is understood by the esoteric wings of every religion, is that when a living religion goes mainstream, its dogma becomes crystallized. The established faith is like a flower that has faded, soon to go to seed. It is natural that it pass away so new flowers of religiousness can grow out of its rotting remains.

EP102 Nostradamus' obscurity is calculated to allow Church Inquisitors (and this interpreter) to project their own judgements on these harsh words. With this in mind I interpret **she** to mean the chief religion dominating the world at our time – the churches and sects of Christianity. *She* will be threatened by new **potentates and military powers** from the East. China is destined to become a superpower in the next ten years. But it is mentioned in other non-Christian prophetic traditions that the Christian-dominated West's overreaction to the rising power of the East and the Pacific Rim nations is more dangerous than the Easterners themselves. However, this doesn't rule out a vicious and extremely fundamentalist minority of Eastern terrorists who might steal two nuclear missiles (**two swords**) and leave only the insignia or national emblems behind. The curvature of the swords implies

EP103 *le peuple le faiſant aller droict, & ne voulant ſe condeſcendre à eux par le*
       bout oppoſite de la main aygu touchant terre voudront ſtimuler

The people will make him go to the right and will not wish to submit
themselves to those of the opposite extreme with the hand [power in]
sharp [position], touching the earth, and will want to spur on

EP104 *iuſques à ce que naiſtra d'vn rameau de la ſterille, de long temps, qui*
       deliurera le peuple vniuers de celle ſeruitude benigne & volontaire,

until there will be one born from a branch long barren, who will deliver
the people of the world from a meek and voluntary slavery

EP105 *ſoy remettant à la protection de Mars, ſpoliant Iupiter de tous ſes*
       honneurs & dignitez, pour la cité libre, conſtituee & aſſiſe dans

and place them under the protection of Mars, stripping Jupiter
[America?] of all his honors and dignities, and will establish himself in
the free city which is situated in

EP106 *vne autre exigue* mezopotamie.

another tiny Mesopotamia.

EP107 *Et ſera le chef, & gouuerneur iecté du milieu, & mis au haut lieu de l'ayr*
       ignorant la conſpiration des coniurateurs, auec le ſecond traſibulus,

And the chief and governor will be cast out from the middle and hung in
the air, ignorant of the conspiracy of the plotters with the second
Thrasibulus,

EP108 *qui de long tēps aura manié tout cecy,*

who for a long time will have directed all this.

the scimitar of the Muslims.

EP103 This line could describe the pressure placed on future Western leaders by their constituents to swing towards right-wing political and religious extremes during the transit of Pluto through Sagittarius during the early 21st century. Sagittarius also rules the higher mind and religious free thinking. As the world undergoes tremendous changes many will tenaciously hold on to fundamentals of what they know. Fortunately many more will accept the challenge to change and adapt themselves to the new and unknown revelations of the coming millennium. Some people will cling to the fossilized religious and political values of the past, while many others will want to discover and explore new forms of political and religious science.

EP104 In this statement regarding **voluntary slavery**, the 16th-century prophet addresses the cornerstone of all major religions today – belief. This is a somewhat poetic reference to freeing people from their belief structure (**voluntary slavery**), which has been so often abused by religious leaders to entrap their followers into obedience.

EP105, 106 The phrase **place them under the protection of Mars** remains a riddle until we look at the occult connection between Mars in its higher form and Hermes, the bearer of the enlightened rod. Mars rules the astrological sign Aries, a fire sign. Both are represented by the color red as described in clue four of the Eight Clues to Spiritual Catalysts. Eastern mystics wear red or orange. Higher Mars is represented by the Hermes the Magician holding the caduceus (rod) of enlightenment. The philosophical similarities between Hermetic teachings and those of Eastern Tantra, which is the essence of Eastern philosophies, seem to imply that this new religion is not like the old, judgemental religions, but perhaps teaches an acceptance of life.

A reference to a **free city** is unclear, but it seems not to be Baghdad (**Mesopotamia**). It could be Paris, France, or some experimental spiritual city or campus in the United States that is an affront (**stripping . . . honors and dignities**) to mainstream American religious values: America is sometimes represented by the planet **Jupiter**. In astrology Jupiter rules religious expansiveness, and its negative aspects are religious self-righteousness and bigotry.

EP107 In classical Greek history Thrasibulus was known as the People's Friend because he restored the Athenian democracy. Apparently a **second Thrasibulus** is behind a conspiracy to overthrow a political leader who is centrist in his views (**from the middle**).

EP108 Perhaps Nostradamus – who as a royalist is not so keen on

EP109   *alors les immundicitez, les abominations feront par grande honte obiectees*
& manifeftees aux tenebres de la lumiere obtenebree,

Then the impurities and abominations will to great shame be brought to
the surface and made manifest in the gloom of the obscured light;

EP110   *ceffera deuers la fin du changement de fon regne, & les chefs de l'Eglife*
feront en arrìere de l'amour de Dieu, & plufieurs d'entre eux

[it] will cease toward the end of a change in his reign, the leaders of the
Church will be backward in their love of God, and several of them

EP111   *apoftatferont de la vraye foy, & des trois fectes, celle du milieu, par les*
culteurs d'icelle fera vn peu mis en decadence.

will apostatize from the true faith, and of the three sects, the one in the
middle [the Catholic], because of its own partisan worshippers, will be
somewhat thrown into decadence.

EP112   *La prime totallement par l'Europe, la plus part de l'Affrique exterminee*
de la tierce, moyennant les pauures d'efprit, qui par insēfez efleuez par

The first one [the Protestants?] will be entirely undone in all of Europe
and part of Africa by the third [the Islamics?], by means of the poor in
spirit who, aroused by madmen [terrorists?], will through

EP113   *la luxure libidineufe adultereront.*

worldly luxury [oil] commit adultery.

EP114   *La plebe fe leuera fouftenant, dechaffera les adherans des legiflateurs, &*
femblera que les regnes affoiblis par les Orientaux

The supporting mob will rise up and chase out the adherents of the
legislators, and it will seem that the realms weakened by the Easterners

democracy – views this *second Thrasibulus* as a vulgar right-wing populist fanning the passions of the masses against a more meritorious leader who is cast out and lynched, either literally or politically.

EP109 Nostradamus confides to his king and to future generations his vision of the end of the 20th century, when global conflicts over faith and ethnicity are overshadowed by the greatest plague of history. The *impurities and abominations* float to the surface of a decadent society *towards the end of a change in its reign* – perhaps implying the change in British "reign" when Elizabeth II gives way to Charles III or Charles to his son, William V. The *change in ... reign* could also imply one of the two successors remaining on Nostradamus' and St Malachy's lists of popes after John Paul II.

EP110 In the two thousand years since the living Yeshua walked the Earth, the Messiah has his name decimated – or rather de-Semited – into Jesus, and the living organism of his religious movement is turned into a huge organization and industry based on dogmas and policies. To be *backward in love of God* means that religious politics, rather than prayer, run the hierarchy of the Vatican. But Nostradamus is impartial with his barbs. He stabs all the Western mainstream religions.

EP111 First he shoots his augured arrows at the *decadence* and *partisan differences* of the Catholics. Since the 1960s Vatican I and II have caused a schism between the orthodox and liberal worshippers, and the Catholic Church has undergone a split that may eventually turn out to be greater than during the Reformation and Counter-Reformation of Nostradamus' time.

EP112 Now he shoots a foreboding message that is perhaps aimed at the Protestant-dominated governments of the United States and Britain, which have had such a negative influence over the Arab world in the 20th century. A reckoning may be at hand, and by the direction of a resurgent Islam.

EP113 But our consistently anti-Islamic seer reserves his hardest slam for the Arabs. The renaissance of Arab power foretold in the quatrains spurs from a new source of *worldly* wealth: oil (1 Q53). Although mainstream Islam does not support its extreme elements, these factions hold a lot of power and influence when they use the weapon of terrorism against their own moderate leaders and against the West. They are past masters at stirring up the impoverished and poor majorities of the Arab world with their brand of intolerant religious populism (which is another negative aspect of Jupiter).

EP114 The tide of Islamic fundamentalist revolutions has already over-

EP115   *que Dieu le createur aye deſlié ſatan des priſons infernalles, pour faire*
naiſtre le grand Dog & Dogam, leſquels feront ſi grande fraction

that God the Creator has loosed Satan from the prisons of hell, to give
birth to the great Dog and Dogam [Gog and Magog?], who will make
such a great and abominable breach

EP116   *abominable aux Egliſes, que les rouges ne les blancs ſans yeux ne ſans*
mains plus n'en iugeront. Et leur ſera oſtee leur puiſſance

in the Churches that neither the reds nor the whites without eyes
[perception] nor without hands [powers] will any longer give judgment
over them, and their powers will be taken away from them.

EP117   *alors ſera faicte plus de perſecution aux Egliſes, que ne fut iamais,*

Then will commence such a persecution of the Churches as never before
seen.

EP118   *& ſur ces entrefaictes naiſtra la peſtilence ſi grande, que des trois pars du*
monde plus que les deux defaudront.

And in the meantime there will appear so vast a plague that more than
two-thirds of the world will fail and decay.

thrown King Idris of Libya for Muhammar Qadaffi in 1969 and the Shah of Iran for Ayatollah Khomeini in 1978–79. The inference is that Islamic extremists will incite the impoverished mobs to topple secular and moderate Islamic governments across Turkey, North Africa, and the Middle East. By the early 21st century much of the Arab world will unite in a pan-Islamic alliance or as a religious super-state based on a narrow view of the Koran.

EP115 Biblical prophecy gives lurid accounts of tomorrow's most likely installment of nuclear bush warfare. Both the Old and New Testaments promise that the final battle of mankind will be fought by the Israelis against an Arab coalition allied to mighty Northern powers called Gog and Magog (see EP98). Could they be Russia (Gog) and America (Amagogica)? Perhaps **Gog** and **Magog** parallel the mysterious "Brothers of the North" theme (EP141).

EP116, 117 Nostradamus returns to the decadent Churches. The vested interests of the world's established religions will have neither the *perceptions* nor the *powers* to initiate new religious understanding. In other words, the natural entropy of religions sets in. I would like to proffer a very different interpretation of *persecution of the Churches*. They are persecuted, or rejected, because they are no longer in harmony with the times. One could say that Jesus and his followers "persecuted" or attacked the established religion of Israel 2,000 years ago when he came to reject the laws of Moses and create a new testament. The same was done by Muhammad to the animist and established pagan religions of his time; by Buddha, who rejected Hinduism; and so on.

EP118 Whether the visions of EP104–118 describe a Satanic antichrist or a religious revolt against the archaic anti-consciousness of established religions is open to debate. One thing is certain: Nostradamus presents a potential nightmare vision for the end of the 20th century and the early decades of the third millennium. Looming behind fierce global conflicts over faith and ethnicity is the dark shadow of the greatest plague humankind will ever experience. If we do not curtail our global population explosion by setting up a stringent global policy of birth control in the next ten years, Mother Nature will visit us with immunological and blood diseases similar to those that devastate out-of-control rodent populations. The question each of us must ask is, Do we choose *now* to use our human reason and change our ways, or do we go on behaving instinctively, like animals? Will we choose life or continue to overpopulate and pollute our range and die like rats in the 21st century? By 2020 the estimated population of the

EP119   *Tellement qu'on ne ſe ſçaura ne cognoiſtra les appartenans des champs &*
maiſons, & naiſtra l'herbe par les rues des citez plus haute que les
genoulx.

**So many [die] that no one will know or be able to determine the true
owners of fields and houses, and the weeds in the city streets will come
up higher than the knees,**

EP120   *Et au clergé ſera faicte totalle deſolation, & vſurperont les Martiaulx ce*
que ſera retourné de la cité du Soleil de Melite, & des iſles Stechades,

**and for the Clergy there shall be total desolation, and the warlords will
usurp what is returned from the City of the Sun, from Malta and from
the Isles of Hyères,**

EP121   *& ſera ouuerte la grãde cheyne du port qui prend ſa denomination au beuf*
marin.

**and there will be opened the great chain of the port that takes the name
of the marine ox [Marseilles].**

human race will be eight billion. Nostradamus foresees **more than two-thirds** of that number, or over 5.3 billion people, failing and decaying from a future plague at that time.

EP119 We still have time to prevent the global catastrophes caused by overpopulation. But it will take courage. It will take radical changes in the way we view our lives on this Earth. One solution would call us to initiate a voluntary moratorium on births for 30 years. I would suggest that as many people as possible seal this moratorium, as I have done, with a surgeon's scalpel and get sterilized. This would mean that only those infants currently being born can have children, when they reach the age of 30. Moreover, they should have the understanding to replace themselves with only one child per parent. A 30-year moratorium would eliminate the unsustainable addition of an estimated 100 million children burdening the planet each year during the 21st century times 30 years. The birth rate will plunge to meet the natural death rate eliminating the expected population increase of three to four billion people by the 2030s.

To many this proposal will sound drastic, even draconian. It is. But as we enter the next century and start feeling the disastrous effects our numbers will have on civilization, more and more people will understand that preventing the birth of a child is more humane and loving than delivering a newborn into a world that cannot sustain its quality of life. The eradication of this suffocation of Earth's ecosystem may forestall the Third World War that so many prophetic traditions (examined in my book *The Millennium Book of Prophecy*) warn will be caused by famine, thirst, and a breakdown of society's supersystems and infrastructures due to overpopulation. Instead of eight to ten billion, the world population by 2030 could be a few billion less than the 5.8 billion people burdening the Earth in 1997. This equates to more wealth, room, and resources for a higher quality of life for everyone on our planet.

EP120 Now back to the prophecies. Nostradamus withdraws from the early decades of the third millennium to deposit us on the shores of the French Riviera in August 1944. The Allied landings of Operation Dragoon would deliver the **City of the Sun** (Paris) back to the French. Malta was attacked by Axis air forces but remained in Allied hands. Free French and US commando units began the Allied invasion of the Riviera by launching amphibious attacks on German gun positions on the **Isles of Hyères**.

EP121 Three days later **Marseilles** was liberated by American and Free French forces.

EP122 *Et ſera faite nouuelle incurſiõ par les maritimes plages, vollant le ſault Caſtulum deliurer de la premiere repriſe Mahumetane.*

And a new incursion will be made through the maritime shores, with the intention of delivering Sierra Morena from the first Muslim recapture.

EP123 *Et ne ſeront du tout leurs aſſaillemens vains, & au lieu que iadis fut l'habitation d'Abraham, ſera aſſaillie par perſonnes qui auront en*

And their assaults will not all be in vain, and the place which was once the abode of Abraham will be assaulted by persons who will hold the

EP124 *veneration les Iouialiſtes.*

Jovialists in veneration.

EP125 *Et icelle cité de Achem ſera enuironnee & aſſaillie de toutes parts en treſgrande puiſſance de gens d'armes.*

And this city of Achem will be surrounded and assaulted on all sides by a most powerful force of warriors.

EP126 *Seront affoiblies leurs forces maritimes par les occidentaulx,*

Their maritime forces will be weakened by the Westerners.

EP127 *& à ce regne ſera faicte grande deſolation, & les plus grandes citez ſeront depeuplees, & ceux qui entreront dedans, ſeront comprins à la*

And great desolation will fall upon this realm, and its greatest cities will be depopulated and those who enter within will fall under the

EP128 *vengeance de l'yre de Dieu.*

vengeance of the wrath of God.

EP129 *Et demeurera le ſepulchre de tant grande veneration par l'eſpace de long temps ſoubz le ſerain à l'vniuerſelle viſion des yeulx du ciel, du*

The sepulcher, an object of such great veneration for the space of a long time, will remain in the open, exposed to the universal vision of the gaze of heaven, of the

EP130 *Soleil, & de la Lune,*

Sun and of the Moon.

EP122 Nostradamus crosses his prescient wires of perception to conjure a false image of Spain either invaded by the Allies or used as a base for the Allied invasion of Southern France. He may have thought Spain would end up a victim of an Ottoman Turkish invasion in his near future, not ours.

EP123, 124 The vision fluctuates and beams us down to the final decade of the 20th century. We see a Protestant leader (the **Jovialist/** American) such as Protestant American president George Bush directing a Western and Arab coalition against Saddam Hussein's Iraq (the ancient **abode of Abraham**) during the Gulf War of 1991. Maybe a second Gulf War with Iraq is implied here for the late 1990s or early 21st century.

EP125 If we take **Achem** literally and not as an anagram, we must go back to the formidable Allied forces that fought in the German city of Achem in late 1944. This was the first German city to fall to Allied forces on the Western Front.

EP126, 127 The **maritime forces** are those of Japan and Germany, which were weakened and devastated in the great naval battles of the Pacific and the battles of the Atlantic. Continuing the inclination towards the World War II interpretation, I would say the **desolation** here adequately describes images sent by Nostradamus' angelic messengers of vast stretches of gutted blocks and rubble-filled empty streets of Berlin, Hamburg, Dresden, or the flattened wastelands of Hiroshima and Nagasaki.

EP128 Guided by the ethereal hand of his angelic emissary, Nostradamus might step into a vision of a city street of Hiroshima and interpret the shadows of its vaporized inhabitants burnt into the rubble by the atomic flash as the **wrath of God**.

EP129, 130 His emissary from the continuum may propel him forwards to the turn of the millennium and so to parallel 9 Q84's cryptic vision of the tomb of a great Roman (most likely St Peter), somewhere beneath the Vatican, which will be opened after the obliteration of Rome.

EP131 Or perhaps Nostradamus wipes the latter-day doom from his feverish eyes and continues along time's path through the devastation of post-World War II Germany. He describes the burnt-out churches filled with the draft animals and soiled fodder of the Soviet occupation forces from the East. Maybe he sees the Asiatic Muzhiks looting holy relics.

EP132–134 It is not clear which time track Nostradamus is treading – that of World War II or III. If what he foresaw has already happened, the Eastern leader who suffers a **calamitous affliction** is Emperor Hirohito of Japan in the closing weeks of World War

EP131   *& sera conuerty le lieu sacré en ebergement de troupeau menu & grand, & adapté en substances prophanes.*

The holy place will be converted into a stable for a herd small and large and adapted for profane substances.

EP132   *O quelle calamiteuse affliction sera par lors aux femmes enceintes, & sera par lors du principal chef oriental la plus part esmeu par les*

Oh what a calamitous affliction will then befall pregnant women, and then [befall] the principal Eastern chief and the majority of his agitated people [who]

EP133   *septentrionaulx & occidentaux vaincu, & mis à mort, profligez, & le reste en fuite & ses enfans de plusieurs femmes emprisonnez,*

[will be] vanquished, and put to death, overwhelmed, and the survivors scattered by the Northerners and Westerners; and his children, offspring of many women, imprisoned.

EP134   *& par lors sera accomplie la prophetie du Royal Prophete, Vt audiret gemitus compeditorum, vt solueret filios interemptorum,*

And by then the prophecy of the Royal Prophet will be accomplished: Let him hear the groaning of the captives, that he might deliver the children of those doomed to die.

EP135   *quelle grande oppression que par lors sera faicte sus les princes & gouuerneurs des royaumes, mesmes de ceux qui seront maritimes &*

What a great oppression then will fall upon the princes and governors of kingdoms and especially of those that are near the sea and

EP136   *orientaux & leurs langues entremeslees à grande societe, la langue des Latins & des Arabes par la cõmunication punique, & seront tous ces*

eastward, their language intermixed in a great society [of nations]; the language of the Latin nations and of the Arabic intermixed via the North African interchange. And all these

EP137   *Roys oriẽtaux chassez, profligez, exterminez, non du tout par le moyẽ des forces des Roys d'Aquilon, & par la proximité de nostre*

eastern Kings will be driven away, beaten and annihilated, not altogether by means of the forces from the Kings of the North – and by the proximity of our

II. Hirohito accepted the offer of unconditional surrender to the Western Allies after the Soviet **Northerners** unleashed a million-man invasion that crushed Japanese armies in Manchuria. The delivered **children of those doomed to die** might describe the re-education of Japanese and German children taken from the arms of their war-criminal parents. But if he is not moving along a World War II time track then the **Eastern chief** is the leader of the Sino-Islamic alliance waging Armageddon in the 21st century against a Northern and Western alliance of America, Europe, and Russia.

Nostradamus' vision of the affliction befalling pregnant women echoes a prophecy of Matthew 24:19, in which Jesus is purported to have said, *How dreadful it will be in those days for pregnant women and nursing mothers*. Both seers' warnings will be borne out in our near future if overpopulation continues unabated into the 2020s.

EP135-139   Nostradamus steps back to paint us a broader picture of what appears to be World War III alliances. Sides will be drawn seven years before the end of the 20th century, or the war will be fought sometime after 1999 and will last for seven years. A triumvirate of **eastern Kings** will secretly unite, using ambushes and anarchy as their main weapons against their chief nemeses, the **Kings of the North** – possibly America, the EU, and Russia. Language **intermixed in a great society of nations** places this prophecy in modern times. Note the **North African** allusion to Tunisia, the head-quarters of the PLO. Libya's close ties with France and Italy through oil are also inferred. Because Nostradamus usually defines all points beyond Greece as Asia, this Eastern alliance has every chance of being a Middle-**Eastern** and even North African Axis alliance.

I can only assume from continual references throughout the Bible, and the auguring of Nostradamus and other prophetic giants such as Edgar Cayce and Cheiro, that the three most likely combinations for candidates for this triumvirate are Libya, Syria, and Iran; Egypt, Syria and Iran; or even Sudan, Libya and Iran. Elsewhere in the quatrains we have already examined references to **Mesopotamia** – Iraq – playing a primary role in the greater war to come. Operation Desert Storm may be no more than an early episode in a long pan-Islamic war with the West that will make some of America's staunchest Arab coalition allies, like Syria and Egypt, into greater enemies than the Iraqis. Whoever the Middle-Eastern **triumvirate** finally turns out to be, they will find support from some greater **eastern King**, implying the leader of the

EP138 *ſiecle par moyen des trois vnys ſecretremēt cerchāt la mort & inſidies par
embuſches l'vn de l'autre, & durera le renouuellement de*

**century, by means of three united secretly in seeking death by ambushes
[terrorism], one against the other; and the renewal of**

EP139 *triumuirat ſept ans, que la renommee de telle ſecte fera ſon eſtendue par
l'vniuers & ſera ſoubſtenu le ſacrifice de la ſaincte & immaculee*

**the Triumvirate shall last for seven years; yet, the fame of such a sect
will spread the world over, and will uphold the sacrifice of the holy and
immaculate**

EP140 *hoſtie, & ſeront lors les Seigneurs deux en nombre d'Aquilon victorieux
ſur les orientaux, & ſera en iceux faict ſi grand bruict &*

**host, and then will the lords, two in number of the North [bloc?], be
victorious over the Eastern ones and there shall be made a great noise
and**

EP141 *tumulte bellique, que tout iceluy orient tremblera de l'effrayeur d'iceux
freres non freres Aquilonaires.*

**warlike tumult that all the East will quake with fear of those two
brothers of the North who are yet not brothers.**

EP142 *Et pource, Sire, que par ce diſcours ie metz preſque confuſeement ces
predictions & quand ce pourra eſtre & l'aduenement d'iceux, pour le*

**And therefore, Sire, through this discourse I present these predictions
almost in confusion, and [especially as to] when and in what order they
will take place. For the**

EP143 *denombrement du temps que s'enſuit, qu'il n'eſt nullement ou bien peu
conforme au ſuperieur, lequel tant par voye aſtronomique que par*

**chronology of time which follows, conforms very little, if at all, with that
which has been set forth, although it was determined by means of
Astronomy, and [determined] by**

EP144 *autre, meſme des ſacrees eſcritures, qui ne peuuent faillir nullement, que
ſi ie voulois à vn chacun quadrin mettre le denombrement du temps*

**other sources, even including the Holy Scriptures, and thus cannot err.
If I had wanted to give each quatrain its dating in time,**

People's Republic of China or North Korea.

The Arab triumvirate and its Eastern ally, China, suffer the mother of all massacres through the overwhelming firepower of the great Northern powers. If by the **proximity of our century**, Nostradamus means that Armageddon is at hand, he is as inaccurate on dating the final battle as St John of Revelation was in the 1st century AD, when he slotted the Second Coming of Christ in his own near future.

EP140, 141   Nostradamus, like many of history's greatest prophets, shares a collective vision that the Cold War scenario had little prophetic weight. If there is to be a Third World War, it will come from a conflict of biblical proportions in the Middle East. And the quatrains strongly suggest that such a war comes only *after* Russia drops communism and becomes **brothers**, or friends, with the United States. But beware: the brotherhood is premature. When Nostradamus says they are **yet not brothers**, he makes a word-play link to 2 Q89's two great *friends* who are **halved**. Nostradamus uses *demis*, which can be the French *d'amis* ("of friends") or the Latin *demi-* ("halved" or "split" apart). The instigator for this split could be **Mabus** (2 Q62) and/or the Third Antichrist, who may use submarines based in either Libya or the Persian Gulf to trigger a terrorist event so horrendous that it undermines the Russo-American alliance.

EP142   **Almost in confusion?** That's putting it euphemistically, Nostradamus!

EP143, 144   Now he jettisons his Armageddon theme to gird up his literary loins for a very lengthy digression. He begins by making the immodest claim that he could have calculated and dated every prophecy if he wanted to. Upon this suggestion, I have made the lengthiest examination of the quatrain indexing anyone has done so far, positing that these numbers sometimes hide dates. I have found some correlation, but uncovered no order or code that would unlock the dating in all quatrains.

EP145   Apparently the king didn't order Nostradamus to put his math where his mouth was.

EP146   Nostradamus takes one more swipe at his critics and **calumniators**. Then, in his strange math he sends us marching down the second of two timelines which is calculated differently from the one we saw earlier in EP42–49.

EP145 *ſe pourroit faire: mais à tous ne ſeroit aggreable, ne moins les interpreter, iuſques à ce, Sire, que voſtre majeſté m'aye octroyé ample*

I could have done so. But it would not have been agreeable to all, least of all to those interpreting them, [and was not to be done,] Sire, until Your Majesty granted me sufficient

EP146 *puiſſance pour ce faire, pour ne donner cauſe aux calũniateurs de me mordre.*

power to do so, lest calumniators be presented with the opportunity to carp at me.

EP147 *Toutesfois comptans les ans depuis la creation du monde, iuſques à la naiſſance de Noë, ſont paſſez mille cinq cens & ſix ans, & depuis la*

Anyway, counting the years from the creation of the world up to the birth of Noah as being 1,506 years, and from the

EP148 *naiſſance de Noë iuſques à la parfaicte fabrication de l'arche, approchãt de l'vniuerſelle inondation, paſſerent ſix cens ans ſi les*

birth of Noah up to the complete construction of the Ark, near the time of the Great Flood, as 600 years – let the

EP149 *dons eſtoyent ſolaires ou lunaires, ou de dix mixtions. Ie tiẽs ce que les ſacrees eſcriptutes tiennẽt qu'eſtoyent Solaires.*

[information] given be solar, or lunar, or a mixture of the ten [actually he means "two"] – I hold that the sacred scriptures use Solar [years].

EP150 *Et à la fin d'iceux ſix cens ans, Noë entra dans l'arche, pour eſtre ſauué du deluge, & fut iceluy deluge vniuerſel ſus la terre, & dura vn an & deux mois.*

And at the end of these 600 years, Noah entered inside the Ark, to be saved from the deluge – and this universal deluge over the Earth lasted one year and two months.

EP147–159	Timeline I (EP42–49)	Timeline II (EP142–158)	Real Time?
God creates Adam	4758 BC	4174 BC	c. 4 million BC
Noah born	–	2668 BC	(evolution creates man?)
The flood ends	3516 BC	2067 BC	c. 12,000 BC
Abraham born	2436 BC	1772 BC	(according to various
Isaac born	–	1672 BC	Atlantis/deluge myths)
Jacob born	–	1612 BC	
Jacob into Egypt	–	1400 BC	c. 1650 BC
"Time of Moses"	1920 BC	–	c. 1275 BC
Exodus	[ditto?]	970 BC	c. 1225 BC
David born	1350 BC	–	c. 1040 BC
King Solomon	–	494 BC	c. 961 BC
First Temple built	–	490 BC	c. 950 BC
Seventh Millenary begins	AD1242	AD1826	c. AD 2000

A number of good scholars have consigned a great deal of gray matter to the muddle of Nostradamus' math. Nostradamus readily admits to calculating two different timelines in the same letter for the same history of the world. The Seventh Millennium, by the way, can start back in AD1242, in AD1826, or even around our own millennial period of AD 2000.

At this stage it seems appropriate that a scholar named Bardo would offer one of the most down-to-earth explanations of the Epistle's confusing creation-based dates. (See pages 95–97 and 149–50 of Bardo Kidogo's *The Keys to the Predictions of Nostradamus*.)

Kidogo reminds us that all countdowns require a "year one" (technically called an "emergent year") for reference. In this case Nostradamus suggests the date of his Epistle, 14 March 1557. But our prophet often changes his mind and calculations in mid-thought. Kidogo gives us a number of wide-ranging estimates of just when "year one" was – varying from Bishop Ussher's 4004 BC to 5200 BC suggested by the 4th-century bishop of Caesarea, Eusebius. It seems that Nostradamus employs the bias of the latter's mathematics. Since Nostradamus mentions Eusebius as his source (EP47), I will cut to the quick and tell you that Kidogo believes the year AD 325 is Nostradamus' base number for a creation countdown system, since the bishop declares that the first Ecumenical Council at Nicaea convened in that year dates the official birth of the Christian Church.

EP151 *Et depuis la fin du deluge iusques à la natiuité d'Abraham, paßa le nombre des ans de deux cens nonante cinq.*

And from the end of the deluge up to the birth of Abraham, 295 years elapsed.

EP152 *Et depuis la natiuité d'Abraham iusques à la natiuité d'Isaac, paßerent cent ans. Et depuis Isaac iusques à Iacob, soixante ans, dés l'heure qu'il*

And from the birth of Abraham up to the birth of Isaac, 100 years elapsed. And from Isaac up to Jacob 60 years elapsed; from the time he

EP153 *entra dans Egypte, iusques en l'yßue d'iceluy paßerent cent trente ans.*

entered into Egypt up to when he left, 130 years passed.

EP154 *Et depuis l'entree de Iacob en Egypte iusques à l'yßue d'iceluy paßerent quatre cens trente ans.*

And from the entry of Jacob into Egypt up to the Exodus 430 years passed.

EP155 *Et depuis l'yßue d'Egypte iusques à la edification du temple faicte par Salomon au quatriesme an de son regne, paßerent quatre cens octante ou quatre vingt ans.*

And from the Exodus out of Egypt up to the building of the Temple by Solomon in the fourth year of his reign, there elapsed 480 years.

EP156 *Et depuis l'edification du temple iusques à Iesus Christ selõ la supputation des hierographes paßerent quatre cens nonante ans.*

And from the building of the Temple up to [the time of] Jesus Christ, according to the calculations of the Hierographs, there passed 490 years.

EP157 *Et ainsi par ceste supputation que i'ay faicte colligee par les sacrees lettres sont enuiron quatre mille cent septante trois ans, & huict moys, peu ou moins.*

And so, by this calculation that I have made, derived from the sacred writings, there are around 4,173 years and eight months, more or less.

EP158 *Or de Iesus Christ en ça par la diuersité des sectes, ie le laiße, & ayant supputé & calculé les presentes propheties, le tout selon l'ordre*

Kidogo proposes that if AD 325 is the starting date of this system, all dates included within it must fit the events described in
their verses. He cites one example, Quatrain 49 of Century 1, in
which we find the year 1700. He says: "To this is added 325, the
date of the Council of Nicaea, producing 2025. With this we
turn to the Julian calendar, because that was the one in use in
Nostradamus' time. Julius Caesar introduced it in 46 BC. And
2025 minus 45 – not 46, because there is no 'year zero' – gives
1980."

He translates the quatrain thus: "Well before the moves in
1980, those of the East will take important captives. With Islamic
fervor they will almost get rid of the Northern presence." His
twists of the old languages to get the Ayatollah of Iran banishing
the Northern or American influences out of Iran by 1980 is certainly plausible. But I found that the grammar and syntax could
equally place this quatrain literally in the year 1700, at the beginning of the Great Northern War between Charles XII, Peter the
Great of Russia, and for a brief time the Ottoman Turks (**those of
the Moon** [1 Q49]).

Listed below are all the precise dates one can find for events
that are past and can therefore be examined carefully.

Quatrain #	Year quoted	Kidogo's year	Successes or failures
6 Q2	1580	1860	No political map of European or Islamic realms changed in 1580. In 1860 Italy is united and the southern states of the US move towards secession. Two out of the predicted five "kingdoms" do change.
8 Q71	1607	1887	Some Nostradamians insist that astrology was censored by a Council of Malines in 1607. But I have not found any edict, bull, or other paper condemning astrologers in this or any other year of Pope Leo XIII's reign. A failure for Kidogo's theory.
6 Q54	1607 of the liturgy	1887	The Ottoman Empire did not fall in 1607, neither did it collapse in the year 1887. This is a failure for Nostradamus and Kidogo's theory on both counts.

Now, on the subject of Jesus Christ, in that there is such a diversity of sects, I leave it behind; and having reckoned and calculated the present prophecies, all according to the order

EP159   *de la chayſne qui contient ſa reuolution, le tout par doctrine aſtronomique, & ſelon mon naturel inſtinct, & apres quelque temps &*

of the chain which contains its revolution [cycle], all by astronomical doctrine, and according to my natural instinct; and after a while and

EP160   *dans iceluy comprenant depuis le temps que Saturne qui tournera entrer à ſept du moys d'Auril iuſques au 25. d'Aouſt, Iupiter à 14. de Iuin iuſques au 7.*

within this comprising the time when Saturn will turn to enter on 7 April till 25 August, Jupiter on 14 June till 7

EP161   *d'Octobre, Mars depuis le 17. d'Auril iusques au 22. de Iuing, Venus depuis le 9. d'Auril, iuſques au 22. de May, Mercure depuis le 3. de Feurier, iuſques au 27. dudit.*

October, Mars from 17 April till 22 June, Venus from 9 April, till 22 May, Mercury from 3 February till the 27th.

EP162   *En apres du premier de Iuing iuſques au 24. dudit, & du 25. de Septembre iuſques au 16. d'Octobre, Saturne en Capricorne, Iupiter en Aquarius, Mars*

After that, from 1 June till the 24th, and from 25 September till 16 October, Saturn in Capricorn, Jupiter in Aquarius, Mars

EP163   *en Scorpion, Venus en Piſces, Mercure dans vn moys en Capricorne, Aquarius & Piſces, la lune en Aquarius, la teſte du dragon en Libra: la*

in Scorpio, Venus in Pisces, Mercury about a month in Capricorn, Aquarius and Pisces, the Moon in Aquarius, the head of the Dragon in Libra: its

EP164   *queue à ſon ſigne oppoſite ſuyuant vne conionction de Iupiter à Mercure, auec vn quadrin aspect de Mars à Mercure, & la teſte du dragon*

tail in its opposite sign following a conjunction of Jupiter and Mercury with a quadrain aspect of Mars and Mercury, and the head of the Dragon

Quatrain #	Year quoted	Kidogo's year	Successes or failures
10 Q91	1609	1889	Some scholars declare that officials at the Paris court and at the Vatican expected Pope Paul V to die in 1609. He lived until 1621. Pope Leo XIII lived until 1903. In both cases no new pope was elected in either year. A failure for Nostradamus and Kidogo's theory on both counts.
10 Q100dp	1660	1940	Louis XIV did ascend to the throne the following year (1661). Hitler, though he was to die, is clearly not the Merovingian king implied here by the **toads** that are to rule the world in 1940. Because Hitler had designs to dominate the world, one could say a fragment of Kidogo's theory is dubiously fulfilled.
1 Q49	1700	1980	This applies equally to the great Northern War of 1700 or the Islamic Revolution in 1980. A tie for Kidogo, but no sure success.
6 Q2	1703	1983	Both Spain and the Ottoman Empire change rulers, making a total of **five** kingdoms **changed** as written in this quatrain. A success for Kidogo's theory.

In the end there's only one clear success for Kidogo's theory – in 6 Q2. There is a 50–50 chance for success in his example from 1 Q49, and a mere fragmentary coincidence for 10 Q100dp.

We could examine many other dating theories, but space requires we move on. Suffice it to say that, at least in my opinion, Kidogo's system had the best chance of being objectively verified.

EP160-166   I believe this is Nostradamus' astrological preamble to the French Revolution. He catapults us down the calendar, taking us through the age of Christian civil war and the breakdown of the faith, via the years 1558 through 1792. Indeed the seed of religious wars between French Protestant and Catholics would erupt on the death of Henry II in the jousting accident Nostradamus tried so hard to forewarn the king about in writing (and

EP165 *ſera auec vne conionction du Soleil à Iupiter, l'annee ſera pacifique ſans eclipſe, & non du tout, & ſera le commencement comprenant ce de ce que*

will be with a conjunction of the sun with Jupiter; the year will be peaceful without an eclipse. But not everywhere. And then will be the commencement of what

EP166 *durera & commençant icelle annee ſera faicte plus grande perſecution à l'egliſe Chreſtienne que n'a eſté faicte en Affrique, & durera ceſte icy*

will long endure, and beginning this year will be a greater persecution of the Christian Church than it has ever experienced in Africa, and this will last

EP167 *iuſques l'an mil ſept cens nonante deux que lon cuydera eſtre vne renouation de ſiecle: apres commencera le peuple Romain de ſe*

till the year 1792, which they will believe to mark [marks] a new Age. After this the Roman people will begin to

EP168 *redreſſer & deſchaſſer quelques obſcures tenebres receuant quelque peu de leur priſtine clarté non ſans grande diuiſion &*

re-establish themselves, and to chase away some obscure shadows, recovering a bit of their ancient splendor – but not without great division and

EP169 *continuelz changemens.*

continual changes.

EP170 *Veniſe en apres en grande force, & puiſſance leuera ſes ayſles ſi treshault ne diſtant gueres aux forces de l'antique Rome,*

Venice, after that, in great force and power will raise its wings so very high, not much less than the might of ancient Rome.

EP171 *& en iceluy temps grandes voyles Biſantines aſſociees aux liguſtiques par l'appuy & puiſſance Aquilonaire donnera quelque*

And at that time great Byzantine sails associated with the Genovese, and through the support and power of the North will hinder

EP172 *empeſchement que des deux Cretenſes ne leur ſera la Foy tenue.*

them so [greatly] that the two Cretans will be unable to retain their Faith.

no doubt in person during his audience in 1556). The death of Henry did cause the crisis that led to nine civil wars from 1562 through 1598. The plague of religious wars spread to the Spanish Netherlands (1568–1648) and erupted in the Thirty Years War across the Holy Roman empire (1618–48) and the English Civil War between Puritans and Catholic-leaning Royalists (1642–46). The wars of and against religion became more subtle in the following 144 years, as the scientific leanings of the Aquarian Age began influencing and challenging Piscean-Age religious faith systems. The year 1792 marked the abolition of Catholic religion in France and the establishment of a new calendar and the Cult of Reason.

EP167 The persecution of the Church during the Revolution had only begun in 1792; however, Nostradamus had accurately foreseen the year the revolutionaries created a new calendar to mark the dawn of a new age.

EP168, 169 Now begins the second and final roller-coaster ride through the future. Nostradamus' prose jerks, flutters, and piles images on us much like the fictional donut-shaped time porthole known as the Guardian of Forever in Harlan Ellison's *Star Trek* episode "Journey to the Edge of Forever."

From the French Revolution we jump ahead to the unification of Italy in 1860, then take another spring forward to the neo-Roman empire of Mussolini in the 20th century.

EP170 One can imagine the air fleets of Italy stretching their wings over the Mediterranean – to attack Libya in 1925, and later Somalia and Ethiopia in 1935–36.

EP171, 172 The thunderclouds of World War II gather. The non-aggression pact Hitler signs with the Soviet Union (**the North**) encourages Mussolini and Fascist Italy (**the Genovese** by synecdoche) to begin the first stage of their conquest of the Mediterranean to create a modern Imperial Rome.

EP173 Though cryptic and vague, the narrative might describe the Eastern Mediterranean theater in 1941, when Hitler's overwhelming might descends through the Balkans. Here he rescues the Italians and overwhelms Greek and British naval and land-based forces, first in Greece and later through naval (**arks** [ships] . . . **Neptune**) and aerial assault of the island of Crete.

EP174, 175 Many unions and treaties were **split apart** on or near these dates. In 1936 the Treaty of Versailles was broken by the Nazi occupation of the Rhineland, and in 1938 by the occupation of Austria. Full-scale war broke out between China and Japan in 1937; the Nazi usurpation of Czechoslovakia broke the Munich

EP173 *Les arcz edifiez par les antiques Marciaux s'accompagnerõt aux vndes de Neptune,*

The arks [arches?] built by the ancient warriors, will accompany them to [into?] the waves of Neptune.

EP174 *en l'Adriatique fera faicte difcorde grande, ce que fera vny fera feparé, approchera de maifon ce que parauant eftoit & eft grande cité*

In the Adriatic [Italy, Yugoslavia and Greece] there will be great discord, and that which is united will be split apart; to a house will be reduced that which formerly was, and is, a great city,

EP175 *comprenãt le Pempotam la mefopotamie de l'Europe à quarante cinq, & autres de quarante vng, quarantedeux, & trentefept,*

including England and France in [the year] '45 and other [broken unions] of '41, '42 and '37.

EP176 *& dans iceluy temps & en icelles contrees la puiffance infernalle mettra à l'encontre de l'Eglife de Iefus Chrift la puiffance des*

And at this time and in those countries the infernal power will employ against the Church of Jesus Christ, the power of the

EP177 *aduerfaires de fa loy, qui fera le fecond Antechrift, lequel perfecutera icelle eglife & fon vray vicaire par moyen de la puiffance des Roys*

adversaries [against] the [holy] law, which will be the second Antichrist, who will persecute that Church and its true Vicar, by means of the power of temporal Kings,

EP178 *temporelz, qui feront par leur ignorance feduitz par langues qui trancheront plus que nul glaiue entre les mains de l'infenfé:*

who in their ignorance will be seduced by tongues which will cut more sharply than any sword [if placed] in the hands of the madman.

EP179 *le fufdit regne de l'antechrift ne durera que iufques au definement de ce nay pres de l'aage & de l'autre à la cité de Plãcus accompagnez de l'efleu*

The said reign of the Antichrist will last only to the determination of him who was born near the age [the time?], and of the other one of the city of Lyon, accompanied by the elected

Pact of 1938; the British saw their alliance with the French split asunder with the defeat of France in 1940. The next union to crumble through Hitler's invasion of Russia in 1941, was the notorious Soviet-Nazi Non-Aggression Pact. Long-standing trade agreements between Japan and America were broken in 1941 with the Japanese attack on Pearl Harbor. The Second Antichrist's union of Japan, Italy, and Germany was finally destroyed with the total defeat of the Axis alliance in 1945.

EP176–178   The Vatican's location in the heartland of the Axis alliance did pose an unusual set of problems for the Catholic Church. Pope Pius XI and later Pius XII had to walk a tightrope: they were activists for the rights of Catholics persecuted by the Nazis, who were at the same time surrounded by *the infernal power* of the Second Antichrist's chief ally, Mussolini. It is believed that Pius XII was in some measure sympathetic to the Nazis. The pope made the controversial decision to abandon defending the rights of one set of Catholics, the Poles, to save another set of Catholics who represented half the population of Germany.

The devices of evil applied by the Second Antichrist, Hiſter, are described. The first is persecution of the Holy Church by means of *temporal kings* (secular leaders); the second uses the powers of the Second Antichrist himself to persuade the Axis masses. With the sharp tongue of propaganda, he cuts down resistance to his will far better than any other weapon could have done. Hitler skillfully mixed truths with lies into a seduction. His powers of persuasion were compelling: the German people could not break his spell until this *madman* lay dead and burning in a gasoline bath in a shallow pit surrounded by the smoldering ruins of Berlin.

EP179   The reign of the second Antichrist is determined by one born *near the* (same) *age*. Hitler's date of birth – and even more, his date of death – closely parallel those of Mussolini and the American Allied leader, Franklin Delano Roosevelt. Hitler was born in 1889, Mussolini in 1883, and Roosevelt just one year earlier in 1882. All of them died in the same month: April 1945. Roosevelt died first, from a cerebral hemorrhage on 12 April, followed by Mussolini, who was shot by partisans on 28 April, and finally Hitler, two days later on 30 April.

The *other* leader is relatively easy to guess. He is not a governor of the French city of *Lyon* but the Prime Minister from the city of the British "Lion" – Winston Churchill of London, Great Britain.

EP180   *de Modone Flucy par Ferrare maintenu par liguriens Adriaticques & de la proximité de la grande Trinacrie.*

one of Modone Flucy, through Ferrara, maintained by the Venetians, and of the proximity of great Sicily.

EP181   *Puis paſſera le mont Iouis.*

Then the mountains of Jupiter [the great St Bernard] will be passed.

EP182   *Le Galique ogmium, acompagné de ſi grand nombre que de bien loing l'Empire de la grand loy ſera preſenté & par lors & quelque temps*

The Gallic Mercury [or Hercules], accompanied by a great number that from great distances [in] the Empire of the great law, will be presented, and then and for some time

EP180 Here is an uncanny prophecy about the final month of the Allied Italian campaign. It pinpoints the area where Anglo-American forces penetrated the Ghengis Khan line – the last in a long and bloody series of fortified defense lines laid across the Italian peninsula by the Germans. The cryptogram **Modone Flucy** has two meanings. In the first, **Modone** corresponds to the region of "Modena" and **Flucy** represents the Greek word *phulë* ("tribe"), implying an area claimed "by the tribe of Modena." It was in fact Modena where American forces made a rapid breakthrough of the Ghengis Khan line in April 1945. At the same time the British Eighth Army made its breakout exactly **through Ferrara**, rolling back the routed German forces all the way up the Adriatic coastline past Venice! **Sicily** is mentioned somewhat retroactively, no doubt to ensure we understand that this is indeed about the Allied Italian campaign that began with the invasion of Sicily in 1943.

Let us return to the cryptogram **Modone Flucy** to unravel the mystery of who this **elected one** from **Modone Flucy** is. He must be the humbled and deposed Mussolini who in 1943 is liberated from prison by Hitler's paratroopers. Hitler later **elects** him to rule the puppet northern Italian Fascist state called the Salò Republic, which by synecdoche contains **Ferrara** and **Modena**. But more specifically, **Modone** could also hide a word play on Meldola or Modigliana, the two towns a few miles from Mussolini's birthplace, the little village of Predappio.

EP181 The **mountains of Jupiter** is a classical allusion to the St Bernard Pass. In the closing days of World War II, American armored units raced across the Po valley to block the exit of German units trying to escape Italy by seizing all the Alpine passes.

EP182 But now someone has kicked Nostradamus' prophetic TV screen and time's focus has gone topsy-turvy. The images are in shadow and the lines of static of many eras are running into each other. The image of Nostradamus' impossible destiny for Henry II's last son flutters and rolls past our view. It makes little sense in relation to what he's yet to recount, unless the **Gallic Mercury** is none other than Charles de Gaulle, the leader of the Free French. If so, then at least my interpreter's twist of the TV rabbit ears has given me a clearer signal from Nostradamus' show. Now our prophet turns his future gaze on his own native France during the Nazi occupation and the source of the troops coming to its deliverance heralding **from great distances**. This would be the armies of Americans crossing the Atlantic to liberate first distant North Africa, then Italy, and finally France herself. Also coming

EP183   *apres ſera eſpanché profuſeement le ſang des innocens par les nocens vng peu eſleuez, alors par grãds deluges la memoire des choſes*

thereafter the blood of the innocents will be spilled profusely by the guilty ones recently elected; then because of great floods, the memory of things

EP184   *contenues de telz inſtrumens receura innumerable perte meſmes les lettres: qui ſera deuers les Aquilonaires par la volonté diuine & entre*

contained in such instruments [TV? or computer chips?] will suffer incalculable loss, even letters [and learning] – this will happen to the Northern People by the will of the Divine, and in the meantime

EP185   *vne foys lyé ſatan.*

Satan will be bound.

EP186   *Et ſera faicte Paix vniuerſelle entre les humains: & ſera deliuree l'egliſe de Ieſus Chriſt de toute tribulation, combien que par les Azoarains*

And there will be established universal peace among humans, and the Church of Jesus Christ will be delivered from all tribulation, although the Philistines

from that far-off American land is a new kind of **Empire of the great law**, the international law of the United Nations. One wonders if Nostradamus viewed its birth in San Francisco in the closing years of the war and saw France's champion speaking beneath its banner. Perhaps Nostradamus later saw the UN's international capitol building rise on the shores of New York City.

EP183 Now it seems his linear perception of the future slips on a temporal banana peel, as he staggers back and forth between flickering horror visions typical of the widescale persecution and slaughter of civilians during the 20th century. Perhaps it is the Holocaust of the Jews, or maybe he sees the countless faces and hears the cries of the children drawn, quartered and slaughtered by the tens of millions during World War II and during the post-war "peace."

Or is Nostradamus' vision sliding forward upon the blood of those innocent victims of our population explosion in the 21st century?

EP184, 185 Nostradamus bewails the break from the past traditions that will come after the new millennium. The leaders democratically elected by their mob-ocracies fail to satisfy our royalist prophet's bias. Their instruments of communication – perhaps our TVs, CDs and computers – will minimalize and sound-byte real knowledge and investigation down to the bone in a future world that moves far too fast for even our usually progressive prophet to follow. This loss of learning will mainly fall on the **Northern People** of the developed nations. But lest this dark vision overwhelm our pessimistic prophet, we can take heart in the reassurance that our near-future times, with their disruptions of society and learning, are the darkest hours before the dawning of a millennium of peace. Perhaps he is seeing what other collective visions of our times have described as our civilization's collective nervous breakdown on a global scale between 2000 and 2030. This is a twilight time between a black era and a golden age, in which we must face what is false, uncreative, and life-negative about our religious, political, economic, and social traditions. The passage through the valley of humanity's wake-up call will be painful, but such a nervous breakdown – or should I say "nervous breakthrough"? – can shock us out of our slumber and give birth to a new sense of humanity.

EP186 Only when we undergo the loss of the past and its fossilized traditions (what Nostradamus calls **letters**) and suffer the planetary disaster of global warming and rising oceans that will defy our out-of-control birthrate, can we confront for the first time what is collectively Satanic (ie, robotic, repressed, and unconscious) in man. The promise of **universal peace** indicates that Nostradamus,

EP187   *voudroit mesler dedans le miel du fiel, & leur pestifere seduction, & cela sera proche du septiesme millenaire que plus le sanctuaire de*

would like to mix the honey of bile, and their pestilent seduction; and this will be near the seventh millenary [millennium], when the sanctuary of

EP188   *Iesus Christ ne sera conculqué par les Infideles qui viendront de l'Aquilon, le monde aprochant de quelque grande conflagration,*

Jesus Christ will no longer be trodden down by the Infidels who will come from the North. The world [will be] approaching a great conflagration,

EP189   *combien que par mes supputations en mes propheties, le cours du temps aille beaucoup plus loing.*

although, according to my calculations in my Prophecies, the course of time runs much further.

EP190   *Dedans l'epistre que ces ans passez ay desdiee à mon fils Cæsar Nostradamus, i'ay assez appertement declaré aucuns poincts sans presage.*

In the Epistle that some years ago I dedicated to my son César Nostradamus, I declared some points openly enough, without presage.

EP191   *Mais icy, ô Sire, sont comprins plusieurs grands & merueilleux aduenemens, que ceux qui viendront apres le verront,*

But here, O Sire, are included several great and marvelous events which those who will come after will see.

EP192   *& durant icelle supputation Astrologicque conferee aux sacrees lettres la persecution des gens Ecclesiastiques prendra son origine*

And during this astrological computation, conferred with the sacred scriptures, the persecution of the Ecclesiastical people will have its origin

EP193   *par la puissance des Rois Aquilonaires vnis auecques les Orientaux,*

in the power of the Kings of the North, united with the Easterners.

in a rare moment of positivity, foresees that we will make the changes that an encounter with the "satanic" will bring, and those habits which make us a miserable and frightened race will be bound and hidden away for a thousand years.

EP187 Nostradamus' notorious mudpie mathematics aside, the **seventh millenary** must be the year 2000 because so many of his quatrains parallel the visions of other great prophets around the globe targeted for that time.

Here we have a reference to the coming showdown between right-wing Christendom and righteously winged Islamic fundamentalism, represented here by **the Philistines**. The biblical allusion is a link to the Third Antichrist, who in 2 Q30, is described as the infernal Phoenician and Philistine **God of Hannibal**, Baal Hammon. This quatrain, along with 2 Q62, leads us down the trail of clues for the Third Antichrist, who is known as **lord of the skies** or a **king of terror** when he makes his appearance in the famous 1999 Armageddon quatrain of 10 Q72.

EP188 The Millennium of Peace sees the essence, if not the dogmas, of Christianity victorious over the northern **Infidels**. Depending on your political or religious persuasions, they could be the EU and America (Gog and Amergogica?) More likely it is the Russian Federation backpedaling towards a return to communism, only to be overthrown before the millennium's end by a neo-Czarist or neo-Fascist dictatorship.

Nostradamus remains obscurely coy about the time when we will feel the heat of the great conflagration approaching.

EP189 There are several interpretations of this compound prophecy; one – or all of them – may have been intended by our continuum-conscious prophet. Perhaps he blends together near and far-future visions of conflagration. The first is the greenhouse effect in the early 21st century. The second is a far more catastrophic version of global warming expected seven centuries into the ninth millennium – during the real doomsday of AD 3797, when the Earth is consumed by the sun's fire (see PF80, 81).

EP190, 191 He takes a breath in the narrative while loading up for another barrage of **marvelous events** to come. It is intimated here that what follows leans toward the distant-future predictions of the Preface. We can also infer that, except for one or two temporal twitches back to World War II, our prophet is commenting upon events starting in the latter days of the 20th century and plunging far beyond the year 2000.

EP192, 193 He begins with our times, when the authority of the priesthoods of every religion will be questioned. From 1996 through July 1999 we may see the creation of a new political alliance

EP194 *& celle perfecution durera vnze ans quelque peu moins, que par lors defaillira le principal Roy Aquilonaire, lefquels ans accomplis*

And this persecution will last for eleven years, or somewhat less, for then the principal King of the North will fail [or default]. These years accomplished,

EP195 *furuiendra fon vny Meridional, qui perfecutera encore plus fort par l'efpace de trois ans les gẽs d'eglife, par la feduction apoftatique*

his southern ally will arise, who will again persecute with greater severity the people of the Church for the space of three years through apostatising seduction

EP196 *d'vn qui tiendra toute puiffance abfolue à l'eglife militante, & le fainct peuple de Dieu, obfervateur de fa loy, & tout ordre de religion*

by one who will hold absolute power in the Church militant, and the holy [or false] people of God, keeping to his law, and the whole order of religion

EP197 *fera grandement perfecuté & affligé, tellement que le fang des vrais ecclefiaftiques nagera par tout, & vn des horribles Rois temporels,*

will be persecuted [to the extreme] and afflicted, in such a measure that the blood of the true ecclesiasts will flow everywhere, and one of the horrible temporal Kings

EP198 *par fes adherans luy feront donnees telles loüanges, qu'il aura plus refpandu de fang humain des innocens ecclefiaftiques, que nul*

will be so highly praised by his adherents [simply] because he will have shed more human blood of innocent ecclesiasts than

between Russia (one of the **Kings of the North**) and China. The latter may already have an alliance with a pan-Islamic confederation of states that are attempting to become a supernation similar to that of the European Union or North American Free Trade Association (NAFTA) in the Western Hemisphere. Actually this Sino-Russian alliance may have already happened a half-century earlier when Stalinist Russia and Red China were once allied during the Cold War.

EP194, 195 The following 11-year time window also has parallels to this breakdown described in 5 Q78, of Russo-American relations through an act of North African terrorism within 13 years. The **King of the North** is most likely Russia rather than America because Russia is geographically closer to Nostradamus' remote viewing and has been prone to persecuting the Christian Church. In 5 Q78 I pinpointed Gorbachev's rise to power in the year 1986 as the time to start counting the 13-year time window from 1986 through 1999. If we count the Epistle's window of **eleven years, or . . . less**, we get the crisis in Russia erupting any time after the pivotal Russian election campaign year (June 1995 through June 1996), Boris Yeltsin, riddled with alcoholism and heart disease, staggered to victory in 1996. Perhaps he is the **principal King of the North** who **will fail** from heart failure any moment now (August 1996). Once the strains of Chopin's funeral dirge fade and the catalyst for Russian democracy is sealed inside the Kremlin wall, there is great danger of a new Fascist leader becoming dictator. Perhaps the new Russian president will re-establish ties with a former Cold War Arab vassal (**southern ally**) like Algeria, Libya, or Iraq. There is even more of a danger that a future US president will overreact to this development of a new "Cold Peace" with Russia. The North African leader, or the Third Antichrist (**southern ally**), will wage religious persecution – in this case against Christians and moderate Muslims. But he will also fail or be overthrown.

EP196 Whatever the timing, during this period the Mother Church will be in great peril. The pope to follow John Paul II may be an ideologue for a return to Catholic fundamentalism. He will lead a militant Church that is against Islamic fundamentalists and New Agers. In fact either the next pope or the one to follow him unto doomsday could end up being a former Jesuit or a protégé of the Catholic populist and anti-Eastern-religion campaigner Cardinal Ratzinger.

EP197, 198 The collision of extremists commanding the militant Christian and Islamic sides of the religious question will see blood of authentic servants (**true ecclesiasts**) of religious truth and love shed in martyrdom.

EP199 *ne ſçauroit auoir du vin, & iceluy Roy commettra de forfaicts enuers l'egliſe incroyables, coulera le ſang humain par les rues publiques &*

anyone else know to have [spilled] of wine: and this King will commit incredible crimes against the Church, human blood will flow through the public streets and

EP200 *temples, comme l'eau par pluye impetueuſe, & rougiront de ſang les plus prochains fleuues, & par autre guerre naualle rougira la mer, que*

temples like water after driving rain, reddening with blood the nearby rivers, and through another naval battle he will [also] cause the ocean to be reddened, such

EP201 *le rapport d'vn Roy à l'autre luy ſera dit: Bellis rubuit naualibus æquor.*

that one King will say to another: Naval battles have caused the sea to blush.

EP202 *Puis dans la meſme annee & les ſuyuantes s'en enſuyura la plus horrible peſtilence, & la plus merueilleuſe par la famine precedente, & ſi*

Then, in the same year, and in those following there will ensue the most horrible pestilence, and made more stupendous by the famine which preceded it, and such

EP203 *grandes tribulations que iamais ſoit aduenue telles depuis la premiere fondation de l'Egliſe Chreſtienne, & par toutes les regions*

great tribulations that will never have occurred since the first foundation of the Christian Church, and covering all the regions of the

EP199 The bloodthirsty king in question may be Nostradamus' third and final Antichrist who slaughters the Christian clergy.

EP200, 201 Nostradamus cloaks his obscurities in fire and brimstone prose that shows us how bloodthirsty this fellow will be. A climactic naval battle has **caused the sea to blush**. Perhaps this refers to those quatrains that describe a fleet **plunging to the bottom** or **foundering in the Arabian Gulf** (6 Q44), or **ships melted and sunk by the Trident** (5 Q62). One cannot rule out a compound vision of several timelines that mix the Battle of Lepanto in 1571 with naval engagements in the Mediterranean during World War II. These are somehow blended over a temporal double exposure combining future engagements of Western fleets with Arab and Iranian submarines in the Persian Gulf, Red Sea, or Arabian Sea. I would not rule out naval battles fought with nuclear weapons in the Arabian Sea between Pakistan and the formidable Indian navy in some nuclear bush war in the early 21st century.

EP202 **A most horrible pestilence** will emerge from the breakdown of human, plant, and animal immune systems due to toxic pollution and lethal doses of cosmic rays pouring through ozone holes. This will precede or exacerbate a global famine after the collapse of Earth's ecosystem due to overpopulation. All it would take is the slight disruption of the growing seasons through global warming to initiate a series of droughts that devastate the grainbelts of the northern hemisphere (see 5 Q98). A rise of just one foot (30 centimeters) in sea level would flood much of the Asian rice crop destroying 90 percent of Asia's source of food. If North America stopped exporting grain, more than 100 countries around the world would starve. In two years Africa could lose a half-billion people to the famine. Without food, the starving nations would throw aside all treaties and wage war with their more advantaged neighbors. Even if today's tinderbox regions such as the Middle East can resolve their differences by the millennium and live for a generation in peace, their current exploding birth and consumption rates could mean fresh water will run out by the 2020s and 2030s. Armageddon, therefore, will be waged over water rather than religion and politics. You can add to this a Chinese superpower of the 2020s going to war simply because it cannot feed its starving billions.

EP203 The global famine triggers global warfare. In desperation, the poorer nations who have no military capability to openly fight the technologically superior military forces of the West will turn to terrorism. Food-rich countries will become the hostages of starving nations. Most likely nuclear and biological weapons will be used, or civilian nuclear reactors will be seized and destroyed,

EP204   *Latines. Demeurant par les veſtiges en aucunes contrees des Eſpaignes.*

Latins [the modern-day Mediterranean region and the Balkans, etc.] leaving vestiges of its effect in some countries of the Spanish [modern North and South America included].

EP205   *Par lors le tiers Roy Aquilonaire entendant la plaincte du peuple de ſon principal tiltre, dreſſera ſi grande armee, & paſſera par les deſtroits*

At this time the third King of the North, hearing the cries of the people of his principal title, will raise a very mighty army, and will pass through the straits

EP206   *de ſes derniers auites & biſayeux, qui remettra la plus part en ſon eſtat, & le grand vicaire de la cappe ſera remis en ſon priſtin eſtat,*

of his predecessors and ancestors, and will recoup most of it into his possession, and the Great Vicar in the cap will be returned to his original state.

EP207   *mais deſolé & puis du tout abandonné, & tournera eſtre Sancta ſanctorum, deſtruicte par paganiſme, & le vieux & nouueau teſtament*

But desolated, and then abandoned by all, he will turn to find the Holy of Holies [Rome] destroyed by Paganism, and the Old and New Testaments

causing a series of Chernobyl-sized disasters in the West. Although it seems hard to believe in the 1990s, it is not impossible to countenance nuclear missiles from the Arab world or from China striking as far afield as Paris, London, New York, and San Francisco in the next 10 to 30 years. The West will retaliate with overwhelming force, and entire nations will be wiped off the face of the Earth in the twinkling of an eye. Thus, the plague Nostradamus envisions that kills the enigmatic Mabus and **both animal and man** (2 Q62) descends *from the skies* (10 Q72).

EP204 According to Nostradamus the coming global famine and pestilence will be the greatest tribulation in the memory of the world since Christ walked upon it. Even the Western Hemisphere will feel the effect (Nostradamus would have included regions of the New World [North and South America] as part of *some countries* ruled *of the Spanish* in his day.)

EP205 One can only wonder if the repetition of human unconsciousness has gathered all three world wars into one ghastly collage of temporal cutouts in the prophet's magic mirror. Still, the next lines imply a future world war beyond the mid-1990s.

The **third King of the North** is America hearing the cry of the British, their ancestral or **principal** people. But what straits are we talking about here? Are these the Straits of Gibraltar and do we have here GIs huddled in battleships and troop carriers on their way to the beaches of Sicily, Salerno, or the French Riviera? Or are we witnessing the old battle wagons, such as the USS *New Jersey*, remodeled with their lethal new arsenals of cruise missiles, heading down the Strait of Hormuz? Do we witness them launching their smooth and frightful missiles under midnight's cloak to reflect their trail of fire upon Persian Gulf waters on their way to Baghdad? Or shall we wander further into tomorrow, beyond the Gulf War of 1991, and see the fleets of the West passing the Strait of Hormuz to launch a new generation of smart bombs tipped with nuclear weapons over the lands of our biblical ancestors? Baghdad and Teheran, and perhaps even the Islamic state of Saudi Arabia, are leveled in a flash of Satan's fiery eye.

EP206 The West is saved once again by the overwhelming force of arms. I pray we have passed these events and it is World War I or II that Nostradamus is envisioning here, not the destruction and misery of a world war yet to come.

EP207 The clouds of war and tomorrow's obscure potentials clear for a moment and Nostradamus' narrative recalibrates his movement through time to witness the devastation of Rome and the holy scriptures abolished and burned.

EP208   *feront dechaffez, & bruflez, en apres l'antechrift fera le prince infernal,*
encores par la derniere foy trembleront tous les Royaumes de

will be thrown out and burned. After that the Antichrist will be the
infernal prince. Again for the [third and] last time, all the Kingdoms

EP209   *la Chreftienté, & auffi des infideles, par l'efpace de vingt cinq ans, &*
feront plus grieues guerres & batailles, & feront villes, citez,

of Christianity, and even [those] of the infidels, will tremble for the
space of 25 years, and there will be more grievous wars and battles, and
there will be towns, cities

EP210   *chafteaux, & tous autres edifices bruflez, defolez, deftruits, auec grande*
effufion de fang veftal, mariees, & vefues violees, enfans

chateaux [citadels?] and all other buildings burnt, desolated and
destroyed with a great effusion of virgin blood, the raping of married
women and widows, and suckling children

EP211   *de laict contre les murs des villes allidez, & brifez, & tant de maux fe*
commettront par le moyen de Satan prince infernal, que prefque

dashed to pieces against the walls of towns, and so many [other] evils
will be committed under the aegis of Satan the infernal Prince, that
almost

EP212   *le monde vniuerfel fe trouuera defaict & defolé, & auant iceux*
aduenemens, aucuns oyfeaux infolites crieront par l'air. Huy, huy, &

the entire world will be found undone and desolate. Before these events
many rare birds will cry in the air, "Now! Now!" and

EP208 Now dawns the reign of Nostradamus' third and final Antichrist who is characterized as being far worse than Hitler on his worst days. His war will last either 25 years or, as 8 Q77 states, 27 years.

When will he appear? On what year do we pin the beginning of his 27-year war? I'm aware of two views. In one of these, which I have examined in other books, the year 1999 is the climax to the war of the Antichrist; therefore we would start counting from 1972–73. In this period there was in fact a dramatic rise in Arab power and terrorism. We witnessed the slaughter of Israeli athletes at the Munich Olympic Games of 1972. Israel nearly lost the war of Yom Kippur (1973). And the Arab oil embargo in 1974 taught the world that OPEC and its Middle Eastern members were a power to be reckoned with. But no Antichrist figure has clearly emerged in the manner of the previous two, Napoleon and Hitler.

Other quatrains augur the Third Antichrist's appearance during the transit of a comet. The comet Kohoutek did appear in our skies around 1972–73, but it proved to be one of astronomy's biggest anticlimaxes. The next chance for number three's appearance happened around 1985–86, with Halley's Comet. Another anticlimax without an antichrist. Then there was Shoemaker-Levi's collision with Jupiter in 1994. Definitely a significant event and, as we've seen elsewhere, it seems to have been predicted by Nostradamus, but no clear figure for the Third Antichrist has stepped forward out of the numerous Middle Eastern candidates I have. The Hale-Bopp comet is significantly larger than Halley's and is expected to be the greatest celestial light show of the 20th century when it flames its tail over the northern skies in the spring of 1997 (when this book first reaches the bookstores).

If the Third Antichrist doesn't appear between 1997 and 1999, we might happily celebrate Nostradamus' most notable prophetic red herring. But we must consider an interpretation proffered at the end of what is so far one of the best documentaries yet filmed on the prophecies of Nostradamus, *The Man Who Saw Tomorrow*, hosted by the late Orson Welles. In the documentary, the year 1999 is not the end of the war of the Antichrist but the beginning. Count 25 or 27 years ahead and the climax of his war shifts to between 2024 and 2026. Astrologically speaking, this brings us into the next and most volatile period in human history, best suited for the eruption of a Third World War. If 1999 passes without an Antichrist, rather than easing our awareness we should sharpen it and use this reprieve from Armageddon to make the right decision today to forestall Armageddon in the 21st century.

EP213 *feront apres quelque temps efuanouys,*

sometime later will vanish.

EP214 *& apres que tel temps aura duré longuement fera prefque renouuelé vng*
autre regne de Saturne, & fiecle d'or, Dieu le createur dira entēdant

And after this has endured for a long time, there will be almost renewed
another reign of Saturn, and the golden age [Age of Aquarius]: God the
Creator, hearing the

EP215 *l'affliction de fon peuple, Satan fera mis & lyé dans l'abifme du barathre*
dans la profonde foffe, & adoncques commencera entre Dieu & les hommes

affliction of his people will command that Satan be cast into the abyssal
depths of the bottomless pit, and be bound there; and then will
commence between God and men

EP216 *vne paix vniuerfelle & demeurera lyé enuiron l'efpace de mille ans, &*
tournera en fa plus grande force la puiffance ecclefiaftique, & puis tourne
deflié.

a universal peace, and for around the space of a thousand years [Satan]
will remain bound – and the Ecclesiastical [spiritual] power will evolve
into its greatest energy – and then [Satan is] turned loose.

EP217 *Que toutes ces figures font iuftement adaptees par les diuines lettres aux*
chofes celeftes, vifibles, c'eft affauoir par Saturne, Iupiter &

All these figures represent the just adaptations of the holy scriptures
with visible celestial bodies, namely, Saturn, Jupiter and

EP218 *Mars. & les autres conioincts comme plus à plain par aulcuns quadrins*
lon pourra veoir.

Mars and others conjoined, as can be seen more fully in some of the
quatrains.

EP219 *l'euffe calculé plus profondement & adapté les vngs auecques les autres.*
Mais voyant, ô ferenifs. Roy, que quelcuns de la cenfure

I would have calculated more profoundly and adapted them even more,
one with the other, but for the fact, O Most Serene Highness, that some
given to censure

EP220 *trouueront difficulté, qui fera caufe de retirer ma plume à mon repos*
nocturne. Multa etiam, ô rex omnium potentiffime præclara & fanè

I'm all for making the Third Antichrist into that prophetic red herring by applying political pressure to lower the birth rate, clean up pollution, and prevent the circumstances that could fuel his evil destiny. Remember, had the victorious powers of World War I treated Germany fairly, the circumstances of social breakdown in the Weimar Republic would not have nurtured the rise of the last Antichrist, Adolf Hitler.

EP209–212   A destiny of global war is described here as something like a worldwide rash of civil wars and social breakdown, a Balkanization of human civilization. Ethnic cleansing is a plague that could infect continents with the pustulous boils of war. The effectiveness with which the Western and Russian leaders handle the growing crisis in the Balkans and Trans-Caucasia between 1996 and 1999 is crucial to the shape of things to come. Depending on their action, the ethnic plague could be either cauterized or spread worldwide. The spark that ignited World War I at the beginning of the 20th century could light the nuclear fire of a Third World War on its centenary anniversary (2014–18).

EP213   Nostradamus used animal riddles in his messages. Perhaps the birds mentioned here somehow describe a symbol or aspect of the religious visionary who will help to stave off the dire events described in the rest of this passage. That message may be anti-prophetic. The key to avert disaster may come from dropping the outmoded past and turning away from obsessions with a tomorrow that never comes. Humanity must gather its genius, energy, and love and pour it onto the present. One can only respond to life's challenges in the present moment.

EP214, 215   And after the travail of the early 21st century a new humanity is born. The "old man" represented in the Bible by sin (forgetfulness) and Satan (unconscious habits) is replaced by *Homo Novus*, the new humanity, that recognizes the equality of men and women and the right of each person to be equally unique. Human evolution embarks on a new journey at the dawn of the Aquarian Age (ruled by **Saturn** in Nostradamus' time). The nightmare of unconsciousness (**Satan**) is chained and cast away for 1,000 years.

EP216   The forces of unconsciousness will give us a break until the dawning of the next millennium in AD 3000. In the meantime humanity will become a meeting of godliness and earthliness until the natural cycle of epochs guides those future descendants to take for granted what they have achieved and slip once again into a new age of endarkenment.

would raise difficulties, therefore I withdraw my pen to [seek] my nocturnal repose: For many events, O most powerful king of all, both ordinary and extraordinary,

EP221 in breui ventura, ſed omnia in hac tua epiſtola innectere non poſſumus, nec volumus, ſed ad intelligenda quædam facta, horrida fata, pauca

are to transpire soon, but we neither could nor would be able to bring them all together into this epistle; nevertheless, in order to comprehend certain horrible utterances of divine fate, a few

EP222 libanda ſunt, quamuis tanta ſit in omnes tua amplitudo & humanitas homines deóſque pietas, vt ſolus ampliſsimo & Chriſtianiſſimo regis

must be set forth. So great is your grandeur and humanity before men, and your piety before the gods, that you alone are worthy of the great title of Most Christian King,

EP223 nomine, & ad quem ſumma totius religionis auctoritas deferatur dignus eſſe videare.

and of being the one to whom the highest authority in all religion should be deferred.

EP224 *Mais tant ſeulement ie vous requiers, ó Roy treſclement, par icelle voſtre ſinguliere & prudente humanité d'entendre plus toſt le deſir de*

But I shall only beseech you, O Most Clement King, by this your singular and prudent humanity, to understand rather the desire of

EP225 *mon courage, & le ſouuerain eſtude que i'ay d'obeyr à voſtre ſereniſſime Maieſté, depuis que mes yeux furent ſi proches de voſtre ſplendeur*

my heart, and the sovereign zeal I have to obey your Most Serene Majesty, ever since my eyes approached your solar

EP226 *ſolaire, que la grandeur de mon labeur ne attainct ne requiert*

splendor, [rather] than the grandeur of my labor can [by itself] attain or acquire.

EP227 *De Salon ce xxvij de Iuing, Mil cinq cens cinquante huit.*

From Salon, this 27th of June, 1558

EP228 *Faciebat Michaël Noſtradamus Salonæ Petræ Prouinciæ.*

Written by Michael Nostradamus of Salon-de-Crau, Provence.

EP217-228 Nostradamus winds down with one more claim of religious correctness for his astronomy. He earnestly declares that the only reason he did not extend his prophecies further was because *some given to censure would raise difficulties*. Then he ends the Epistle with a lavish fusillade of Latin tributes to Henry II and the smoke of humble platitudes, as was expected of a good subject to the king. The final date marks the passing of a year and three months since the date, 14 March 1557, mentioned in EP22.

8 Q1

PAV, NAY, LORON¹ plus feu qu'à ſang
    ſera.
Laude² nager, fuir grand aux ſurrez.³
Les agaſſas⁴ entree refuſera.
Pāpon, Durance⁵ les tiēdra enſerrez.

PAU, NAY, LORON⁶ *will be more of*
fire than of the blood.
To swim in praise, the great one to
flee to the confluence.
He will refuse entry to the Piuses.
The depraved ones and the Durance
[France] will keep them
imprisoned.

¹anagram for NAPAULON ROY, Napoleon, King.
²Old French for praise
³Greek *surrhous* = confluence, flowing together (Latin *Confluentes* = Coblenz? Latin *Confluens* = Münster?).
⁴Provençal *agassa* = magpie. A synonym for the French spelling, *agace*, is *pie*, which is also French for "Pius" (Leoni).
⁵cryptogram for France.
⁶Three towns clustered together in southwest France in ancient Béarn; however, the subject is a person and not places.

The anagram Pau Nay Loron swiveled once becomes Nay Pau Loron, and twice, Napaulon Roy = Napoleon, King. The spelling for Napoleon in Corsican style, Napauleone, is even closer to the anagram. In a more sinister decoding, one drops an *N*, reverts the *u* phonetically to *y*. The anagram then forms a version of the Greek horror of the Apocalypse, Apollyon, the angel of the abyss from Revelations 9:11 or, in this case, the Corsican horror Apaulyon Roy or "King Destroyer." This is the man with the **ferocious name of destroyer** from 1 Q76.

The quatrain also describes him as a man of war-**fire** more than of royal **blood**. Napoleon's father, Carlo Buonaparte, was a minor Corsican noble. Napoleon, a passionate man, born under the **fire** sign of Leo, was well tested and distinguished in the **fire** of combat. The French spelling for the Provençal *agassa* is *pie*, which is French for Pius, the name of two popes terrorized and imprisoned by Napoleon during his reign: Popes Pius VI and Pius VII. Pius VI died in captivity in Valence, on **the confluence** of the rivers Isère and Rhône in 1799. **Durance** is a cryptogram for France.

This quatrain is #7 in James Randi's list of ten debunkable quatrains (see *Mask of Nostradamus* pages 207–12). Once again Randi expects Nostradamus to follow the logic of French grammar. His common sense fools him into believing the city of Pau and the lesser towns of Nay and Oloron cannot be turned into an anagram for Napoleon. I could agree with this if I too ignored that the other 23 words correlate with these three as a person rather than as places. To tackle Nostradamus one must have an unbiased and open mind with an innate sense of poetic license, hitched to a thorough knowledge of Old French and world history. More than a few years of study of his odd grammar is required to get acquainted with his peculiar and impulsive syntactical habits. I doubt Randi has spent 20 years on this; in my opinion his expectations and perceptions, delivered in a flashy and authoritarian tone, reveal a lack of under-standing to anyone who has spent a few decades on this subject of Nostradamus' rules of anagrammar.

Quatrain Indexing Date: (1)81(0) = a play on 1810 or 1811? If so, these are the peak years of Napoleon's dominance of Europe, just prior to his disastrous campaign in Russia in 1812.

8 Q1dp

Seront confus plufieurs de leur attente,	**Several will be confused in their waiting,**
Aux habitants ne fera pardonné:	**To the inhabitants pardon will not be**
Qui bien penfaient perfeuerer l'attente,	**given:**
Mais grand loifir ne leur fera donné.	**Those who thought well of persisting in the waiting,**
	But not much spare time will be given them.

This is the first of six duplicate quatrains that shadow the "official" 8 Q1 through 8 Q6. Leoni believes they are too clear and straightforward to be above suspicion. Either they are heavily doctored Nostradamus originals or blatant forgeries. Leoni, along with Lamont, believes they are best applied to European history between the world wars.

Leoni calls this duplicate quatrain a vision of "Sitzkrieg" and "Blitzkrieg," the long nine-month lull on the Maginot/Siegfried Line during the winter of 1939–40 that ended in the sudden violence of Hitler's lightning panzer invasion of France in May 1940. Lamont, writing two years after the fall of France, targets this one a little earlier, back to the peace and confusion of the post-World War I years and the failure of the Versailles treaty and the League of Nations to contain Hitler and prevent World War II.

8 Q2

Condon & Aux & autour de Mirande	**Condon and Auch and around Mirande**
Ie voy du ciel feu qui les enuironne.	**I see fire from the sky which encompasses them.**
Sol Mars conioint au Lyon puis marmande	**Sun and Mars conjoined in Leo, then [at] Marmande**
Fouldre, grand grefle, mur tombe dans Garône.	**Lightning, great hail, wall falls into the Garonne.**

Condom, Auch, and Mirande are all in southwest France in the department of Gers; Marmande is close by, about 50 miles up the Garonne from Bordeaux. The falling wall may detach itself from a number of towns along the Garonne, such as Bordeaux, Agen, or Toulouse. The tenor of this quatrain is definitely apocalyptic, but whether it is ecological or military in nature is open to interpretation. Often Nostradamus speaks of a *fire from the sky* besetting southwest France during a future greenhouse drought. The *fire* could also be set by enhanced lightning storms in a warmer climate. In 1994 Geomet (the world weather service) reported a 20 percent increase in lightning strikes in the United States, mainly in the central Mississippi valley and the Eastern seaboard.

Nostradamus and other seers present us with an either/or choice: the fires of spiritual awakening or the flames of global warming and nuclear war. It depends on us which aspect of Mars we access by our actions – the Mars of War or the magician of enlightenment. Emil Ruir sides with the Magus and refers this quatrain to the period of global transformation. G. Gustaffson (1956) targets the Sun/Mars conjunction in Leo expected on 22 August 2113.

Astrological Time Window

Many wars in history begin when Mars transits the constellation of Leo. This takes place again in August–October 1998 and June–July 2006. In the 21st century I would expect the highest potential for war when Mars passes through Leo several times during a Saturn–Leo transit (August 2034–October 2036).

8 Q2dp

Plufieurs viendront, et parleront de paix,	Several will come, and will speak of peace,
Entre Monarques et seigneurs bien puiffans:	Between Monarchs and very powerful lords:
Mais ne fera accordé de fi pres,	But it will not be accorded so soon,
Que ne fe rendent plus qu'autres obeiffants.	As they no longer render themselves as obedient as the others.

The second 8 Q2 is not inordinately lucid to be a forgery. However, it is open to a number of failed peace negotiation themes. The generalities can allow one to include among these the attempts by Catherine de' Medici to appease and repress the rising power of Huguenot princes and the Guise during the 1550s and 1560s. One could also go forward four centuries to the failed peace efforts made by the monarchies of Europe before their power was destroyed by the slaughter of World War I.

8 Q3

Au fort chaſteau de Viglanne & Reſuiers	In the sturdy castle of Vigilanne and Resviers
Sera ſerré le puiſnay de Nancy:	The younger born of Nancy will be shut up:
Dedans Turin ſeront ards les premiers,	Within Turin the first ones will be burned,
Lors que de dueil Lyon ſera tranſy.	When Lyons will be shuddering with grief.

Here is another wild goose chase through European geography. Line 1 suggests numerous combinations for **Vigilanne and Resviers** which are located in Italy. Nancy is the capital of Lorraine. The royal cadet (**younger born**) could be the father-in-law of Henry III, Nicholas, Comte de Vaudemont and Duc de Mercœur, a noted contemporary of Nostradamus who lived until 1577. Nostradamus intends this quatrain for either the Duc de Mercœur or the Guise cadet, Charles III, Duc de Lorraine. Either one becomes a prisoner in an Italian dungeon on the isle of Garda (which is between San Vigilo/**Vigilanne** and the French Riviera/ **Resviers**). But this alternative destiny is a complete failure. Neither man was burned at the stake. Turin was occupied by the French when Nostradamus wrote this between 1555 and 1556.

8 Q3dp

Las quelle fureur! helas quelle pitié,	Alas what fury! Alas what a pity,
Il y aura entre beaucoup de gens:	Will there be between a great many people:
On ne vit onc vne telle amitié,	Never did one see such a friendship,
Qu'auront les loups à courir diligents.	As the wolves will have in liking to run.

This one is as vague for me as it was for Leoni 35 years earlier. He makes a good call that line 4's **wolves** are Hitler and Mussolini's Axis alliance pitted against the legendary **friendship** of American President Franklin Delano Roosevelt and British Prime Minister Winston Churchill. I would add only that such an interpretation supplies the reason for the doubly wolfish pun of the final line. The two **wolves** are the predatory Axis dictators. Adolf in Old High German means "noble wolf", and Mussolini was the leader of a resurgent Fascist Rome, symbolized by a wolf suckling the founders of ancient Rome, Romulus and Remus.

8 Q4

Dedans Monech le coq ſera receu,	**Inside Monaco the cock will be received,**
Le Cardinal de France apparoiſtra	
Par Logarion Romain ſera deceu	**The Cardinal of France will appear**
Foibleſſe à l'aigle, & force au coq naiſtra.	**By the Roman Legation will he be deceived**
	Weakness to the eagle, and strength for the cock will grow.

Charles de Guise, Cardinal de Lorraine, returns again. His cross-signaled negotiations with the pope in 1557 resulted in Henry II strategically damaging his Italian adventure north of Naples. This left him exposed to a Spanish attack on his northern front with his finest troops stationed in Italy doing next to nothing. Henry sent a second-rate army to relieve St Quentin, only to lose both the garrison and the relief army in a military disaster. Because of a **Cardinal of France**, Henry II was forced to relinquish almost all French conquests from 50 years of Italian wars with the Holy Roman Empire. It is the Imperial **eagle** and not the French **cock** that is strengthened, unless Nostradamus is speaking of the long-term outcome far beyond the humiliating peace terms of Cateau-Cambrésis (1559). In the coming two centuries France would grow stronger while the Holy Roman Empire faded away.

8 Q4dp

Beaucoup de gens voudrons parlementer,	**Many people will want to come to terms,**
Aux grands Seigneurs[1] qui leur feront la guerre:	**With the great world leaders who will bring war upon them:**
On ne voudra en rien les eſcoulter,	**They will not want to hear anything of their message,**
Helas! ſi Dieu n'enuoye paix en terre.	**Alas! If God does not send peace to the Earth.**

[1] *grands Seigneurs* = (old application) Great Lords; (modern) great world leaders.

The straightforwardness of the language in this quatrain makes it suspect as a forgery. Nonethelesss, it is a plea worth heeding, especially in our own times.

It is an invitation for all individuals to break out of the mob psychology and slip out from under the influence of their shepherds – the political and religious leaders. For me, this prophecy is a universal call for a spiritual rebellion against the mindset implanted and sustained down through history: to toe the line and not think for ourselves. Individuals who are independent and integrated do not make good subjects, docile-and-dumb citizens, or slaves of our leaders.

Alas! If God does not send peace to the Earth. Can't Nostradamus, or his forger, see the obvious problem with this supplication? Can they not see that surrendering their responsibility to someone else, whether a Messiah or a Führer, only sinks them deeper into the mess Earth has become? Perhaps God doesn't answer our prayers because we are his hands, his eyes, his heart.

Our consciousness is His intelligence at work. Our forgetfulness and mechanical habits are his "sin."

8 Q5

Apparoiſtra temple luiſant orné,	There will appear a gleaming ornate temple,
La lampe & cierge à Borne & Bretueil.	The lamp and candle at Borne [river] and Bretueil.
Pour la lucerne le canton deſtorné,	For the Canton of Lucerne turned aside,
Quand on verra le grand coq au cercueil.	When one will see the great Cock in his coffin.

Some ancient Roman or Celtic temple miraculously appears. There are two places called **Breteuil**, both in northern France: one is in Normandy, about 20 miles southwest of Evreux; the second is 10 miles west of Montdidier. A Borme river flows in the French Alps 10 miles southeast of Geneva. Line 3 forecasts the overthrow of Calvinism in the Canton of Lucerne, making this another one of Nostradamus' wish-fulfilling prophecies against the contemporary Protestant "heresy." This unfulfilled event is scheduled to take place around the time a great French king dies.

Fontbrune, who is an equally passionate French royalist in our century, as Nostradamus was in his, promotes the wish if not the reality of this prophecy by saying, "The Catholic Church will be seen shining and honored; masses will be said in Holland and Picardy . . . ." Fontbrune later implies that Switzerland will become entirely Catholic around the time his royalist messiah, the future Henry V, passes away.

8 Q5dp

Pluſieurs ſecours viendront de tous coſtez,	Some help will come from all sides [coasts],
De gens loingtains qui voudront resiſter:	From distant people who will want to resist:
Ils ſeront tout à coup bien haſtez,	Suddenly they will be much hurried on,
Mais ne pourront pour cette heure aſsister.	But they will be unable to assist at that hour.

This could be a continuation of the World War II theme of the previous duplicate quatrain. Leoni applies it to the United States prior to its entry into the war, shipping military equipment to the British in their

Lend-Lease program (**help . . . from all coasts**). The Japanese attack on Pearl Harbor **suddenly** hurried the Americans into the global conflict, but they were unable to openly assist the British in what Winston Churchill called "their finest hour," the Battle of Britain, in which the might of the German Luftwaffe was defeated by a few hundred British, Polish, Canadian and South American fighter pilots.

8 Q6

Clarté fulgure à Lyon apparante	**Brightness, lightning at Lyons are seen**
Luyfant, print Malte fubit fera eftainte,	**Shining, Malta is seized, and will**
Sardon, Mauris traitera decepuante,	**suddenly be extinguished,**
Geneue à Londes à coq trahyfon fainte.	**Sardon, Maurice will negotiate deceitfully,**
	Geneva at London to the Cock feigned treason.

Lightning storms in Lyons in the year 1565 were to have warned of the imminent conquest and annihilation of the little island state of Malta, ruled by the Knights of St John. That did not happen. Le Pelletier believed **Sardon** stood for Sardinia. He claims St Maurice was the patron saint of Sardinia and Savoy. Leoni splits hairs, asserting that Maurice wasn't *the* patron saint of Sardinia. (It depends on which saint cult you ask.) Since Sardinia was not part of Savoy until 1720, the events of this prophecy clearly must extend beyond 1565.

I believe it has something to do with Sardinia's fate in the political maneuvering and negotiations surrounding the treaties of Utrecht (1713), and Rastatt and Baden (1714) which brought an end to the long and costly European war over dynastic and national rights known as the War of the Spanish Succession. The Treaty of Utrecht passed off Sardinia to Austria. Then Austria swapped it with Savoy for the Kingdom of Sicily in 1720. Once united with Piedmont and Savoy, Sardinia became the nucleus of the kingdom of Italy by the 19th century.

During the French Revolution, **Lyons** witnessed the lightning flash of cannons lined up in the town square to execute the leaders of a Royalist rebellion. General Bonaparte, on his way to Egypt, seized tiny Malta in 1798. He fared far better than the Ottoman Turks: they lost more than 20,000 men – only two of his were killed.

8 Q6dp

Las quel désir ont Princes eftrangers,	**Alas, what desire foreign Princes have,**
Garde toy bien qu'en ton pays ne vienne:	**Guard you well lest they come into your country:**
Il y aurait de terribles dangers	**There would be terrible dangers**
Et en maintes contrees, mefme en la Vienne.	**And in many countries, even in Vienna.**

Although *Vienne* most often indicates the village in Dauphiné départe-ment of France, this warning is for the people of Vienna, Austria, to guard against the desires of Adolf Hitler. On 11 March 1938 Hitler crossed the Austrian border with his army and occupied Vienna. The prophet's warning against Hitler's insatiable appetite for other people's lands was unheeded again by Daladier and Chamberlain, who, to appease Hitler, signed away the Sudetenland in the Munich Pact, only to see him gobble up the rest of Czechoslovakia by March in the following year. Many more countries would soon feel the jackboot of Nazi occupation.

8 Q7

Verceil, Milan donra[1] intelligence,	**Vercelli, Milan will give information,**
Dedans Tycin ſera faite la paye.[2]	**Within Pavia the wound [or plague]**
Courir par Siene eau, ſang, feu par	**will be made.**
Florence.	**To run through the waters of the**
Vnique choir d'hault en bas faiſant maye.	**Seine, blood, fire through Florence.**
	Unique one falling from high to low
	[calling] "Help me!"

[1]Syncope for *donnera* = will give.
[2]Wound; plague.

At first blush this quatrain warms to the old theme of France and the Habsburgs in their centuries-old tug-of-war for possession of the Duchy of Milan (**Vercelli, Milan**). But line 3 embraces a wide-ranging area from the Seine river, symbolizing Paris, all the way to **Florence** and Tuscany. By the time Nostradamus wrote this, the Habsburg–Valois wars were winding down, so I would place this farther ahead to the French Revolution and Napoleonic era (1789–1814). But since combat was not waged in Florence during any of Napoleon's Italian campaigns, I cannot rule out a World War II application. Florence and Tuscany were seriously visited by war in the final stages of the Italian Campaign in 1944. Also in that year, the **waters of the Seine** were forded by the advancing Anglo-American forces in late August 1944. The **unique one falling from** a high position of power is therefore not Napoleon but Benito Mussolini, who at the time ruled Milan and its environs as a figurehead of a shrinking puppet Fascist republic in northern Italy controlled by the Nazis.

8 Q8

Pres de l'interne dans de tonnes fermez,	**Near Focia enclosed within the barrels,**
Chiuaz fera pour l'aigle la menee,	**Chivasso will plot for the eagle,**
L'eſleu caſſé luy ſes gens enfermez,	**The elected one driven out, he and**
Dedans Turin rapt eſpouſe emmenee.	**his people shut up,**
	Within Turin abducted spouse taken
	away.

The theme of Italian wars returns again, this time focusing on the near contemporary struggles of the French occupation of Turin during Nostradamus' time. "Linternum" (*l'interne*) is the ancient Roman name for the village of Foce de Patria, northwest of Naples. A French expedition camped there in the late 1550s. **Chivasso** is a few miles northeast of Turin, and was occupied by the French. The prophet warns of a Habsburg plot conceived there, but the ringleader (apparently some elected city magistrate) and his co-conspirators are locked up, and he is exiled.

8 Q9

Pendant que l'aigle & le coq à Sauone	*While the eagle [is] with the cock at Savona*
Seront vnis Mer Leuant & Ongrie,	
L'armee à Naples, Palerne, Marque d'Ancone	*The Eastern Sea and Hungary will be united,*
Rome, Venise¹ par Barb' horrible crie.	*The army at Naples, Palermo, the marches of Ancona*
	Rome and Venice – a horrible outcry by the Barb.

¹Venice: in the modern, World War II application as a synecdoche for Fascist Italy.

Except for the fact that American (*eagle*) and French (*cock*) forces were not present to liberate **Savona**, Italy, the quatrain adequately describes Allied advances during the final weeks of the war in 1945. By that time the Soviets had completely liberated Hungary and the Black Sea region from the Nazis. At the same time Allied forces were marching up the Northern Italian peninsula past Ancona, as a result of their successful victories of 1943 in Sicily (**Palermo**) and southern Italy (**Naples**). Rome could stand for the Vatican, which gave substantial tacit support to Mussolini's Fascist Empire (symbolized by **Venice**). The **horrible outcry** from **Barb**(arossa) comes from Hitler in the last days of his life, which were noted for the Führer's rabid outbursts against the German people's betrayal of his Third Reich.

8 Q10

Puanteur grande fortira de Laufanne,	*A great stench will come out of Lausanne,*
Qu'on ne fçaura l'origine du fait,	*Such that one will not know the origin of the deed,*
Lon mettra hors toute la gent loingtaine	*They will put out all the distant [and remote] people*
Feu veu au ciel, peuple eftranger deffait.	*Fire seen in the sky, foreign people defeated.*

Nostradamus turns up his Gallic nose at his greatest contemporary intellectual rival, Théodore de Bèze, John Calvin's chief disciple, who taught

Greek at **Lausanne** and was responsible for writing vicious essays against the prophet. No doubt Bèze earned Nostradamus' epithet *beste* (beast) to repay Bèze for calling him *Monſtredamus* (Monsterdamus). Here the prophet promises Bèze's and Calvin's exile from Switzerland when omens in the heavens manifest. Rare aurora borealis appearances aside, Nostradamus would not be satisfied by history. Bèze, the **distant . . . people** from France, would leave the Swiss Canton of Vaud after the death of John Calvin in Geneva not as an exile but as an apostle of Calvinism. He would preside over the synods of French Huguenots held at La Rochelle in 1571 and at Nîmes in 1572, and would live until 1605, dying at the age of 86.

8 Q11

Peuple infiny paroiſtra à Vicence	**The infinite people [the French] will appear at Vicenza**
Sans force feu bruſler la Baſilique	
Pres de Lunage deffait grand de Valence,	**Without force, fire to burn the Basilica**
Lors que Veniſe par more[1] prendra pique.	**Near Lunage the great one of Valenza defeated,**
	When Venice through More will take up the quarrel.

[1]*More* = a) possible misprint for *mort* = death; b) the law of Sir Thomas *More* (3 Q95), a contemporary of Nostradamus; c) the "Moors" or Muslims in an invasion.

Vicenza was in the Venetian Republic. In the Italian context **Valence** could be Valenza in the Habsburg Duchy of Milan rather than Valence, the French town at the confluence of the Rhône and the Isère. Another candidate would be Valencia in Spain, which was the final capital of the Republicans during the Spanish Civil War of 1936–39, but I think the latter leads to a dead end. It is a historical fact that Napoleon Bonaparte's Army of Italy tramped more than once through the valley of Lunigiana in eastern Liguria. He would march from Verona to capture Venice via Vicenza in 1797.

8 Q12

Apparoiſtra aupres de Buffalorre	**He will appear near to Buffalora,**
L'hault & procere entré dedans Milan,	**The high and tall one entered into Milan,**
L'abbé de Foix auec ceux de ſaint Morre	**The Abbot of Foix with those of St Maur**
Feront la forbe abillez en vilan.	**Will perform trickery dressed up as serfs.**

Here is another recounting of Nostradamus' travels. Perhaps the clues he leaves here are meaningful only to those guilty ones he personally contacted.

Buffalora is a village west of Milan so unremarkable that Nostradamus himself must have known about it only because he slept there. St Maurus was the misidentified founder of a Benedictine monastic order in Gaul; that makes **those of St Maur** Benedictine monks. It is possible Nostradamus spent some time with Augustinian monks at the 9th-century Abbey of St Volisianus, at **Foix**.

8 Q13

Le croifé frere par amour effrenee	**The crusader brother through**
Fera par Praytus Bellerophon mourir,	**unrestrained love**
Claffe[1] à mil ans la femme forcenee	**Will cause Bellerophon to die through**
Beu le breuuage, tous deux apres perir.	**Proetus,**
	Army for a thousand years the woman
	passionate,
	The potion drunk, both of them
	afterwards perish.

[1]Latin *classis* = fleet, but in this case figuratively for army.

The first leg of Napoleon's journey to his final place of exile, the island of St Helena, was upon the decks of the HMS *Bellerophon*. Nostradamus appears to be blending the classical myth of Bellerophon with the fate of Napoleon. Antea, the wife of *Proetus*, king of Argos, sent Bellerophon to kill the Chimaera, a half-winged dragon, half-ram headed monster. He was an innocent youth who prayed to Athena (also the goddess of tactics) for advice. In a dream she told him where to find a winged horse known as Pegasus. When he awoke he found a golden bridle on the bed. Bellerophon bridled and tamed the winged horse, and with the help of Athena's knowledge of tactics, successfully rode Pegasus out of the sun to dive-bomb and kill the Chimaera.

Bellerophon would win many more battles but would lose his innocence and become arrogant and vain. Like Napoleon he didn't know when to stop. One day he decided to ride Pegasus as high as Mount Olympus, the home of the gods, to boast of his deeds. While he ascended, Zeus sent a gadfly to bite the haunch of Pegasus, who threw Bellerophon. The youth fell from great heights, as Napoleon and the Chimaera did. He was not killed but passed the rest of his days as a lame beggar.

Poetically speaking, Napoleon fell from the heights of being an overlord of Europe to become master of the mediocre Longwood Estate on the rocky desert island of St Helena. Liver ulcers and stomach cancer would eventually cripple him in earnest. In his diaries General Bertrand describes the once all-powerful emperor begging for a spoon of coffee, "How many thoughts on so great a change! Tears came into my eyes as I watched this man, who was so terrible, who gave his commands so proudly, so absolutely, pleading for a spoonful of coffee, begging leave and obeying like a child, asking again and being refused, harking back and never succeeding, never resenting it . . . . Now he had the docility of a child. This was the great Napoleon: pitiful, humble."

The quatrain could be a vague chronicle of Napoleon's unbridled love affairs. Even while slowly dying by inches at Longwood, he managed to make two women his mistresses, Mesdames Bertrand and Montholon. The latter bore him a bastard daughter, Napoléone. Line 3 could blend the legacy of his armies (lasting *for a thousand years*) with the chief object of his carnal passions, the Empress Josephine. The *potion* in this case is poetic for the ups and downs of their co-dependent romance, which at times swung from the sweetness of a love philter to a chalice of bitterness and poison.

The final line implies that Napoleon may have been slowly poisoned by the British on St Helena, a myth he desperately wanted to believe. Or it implies his own suicide attempt in 1814 prior to his first abdication. Somehow the layers of future events become entangled in Nostradamus' vision, and Napoleon's failed suicide attempt is woven together with the death of Josephine from pneumonia two and a half months later.

Quatrain Indexing Date: Q13 = 1813, a near miss for 1814, the year Napoleon attempted suicide and Empress Josephine died.

8 Q14

Le grand credit d'or d'argent l'abondance	**The great credit of gold and**
Fera aueugler par libide[1] l'honneur	**abundance of silver**
Sera cogneu d'adultere l'offence,	**Will cause honor to be blinded by**
Qui paruiendra à son grand deshonneur.	**lust**
	The offense of the adulteress will
	become known,
	Which will occasion to her great
	dishonor.

[1]Latin *libido* = lust, passion; unlawful, excessive desire.

This could be another economic crash prophecy. The adulterous lady may be the symbol of a libidinous and corrupted Marianne, the symbol of the French Revolution. The prophet's derogatory descriptions of adultery and financial greed may be directed toward what in other quatrains is the United States – the **adulterous lady** (8 Q70) is symbolized by the Statue of Liberty. A third application would take the biblical slant that she is Lady Babylon, or modern-day Iraq under Saddam Hussein. Since the Gulf War (1991) he and his family have been living in opulence while the people of Iraq suffer under the crushing economic pressure of international sanctions.

8 Q15

Vers Aquilon¹ grands efforts par hommaſſe
Preſque l'Europe & l'vniuers² vexer,
Les deux eclypſes mettra en telle chaſſe,
Et aux Pannons³ vie & mort renforcer.
	Towards the Northern land great
	      exertions by the mannish woman
	Nearly all of Europe and the world to
	      vex,
	The two eclipses she will put to utter
	      rout,
	And to the Pannonians life and death
	      to reinforce.

¹Latin *Aquilo* = the north wind, the northern land.
²Old French usage would interpret as "all the world" rather than the modern "all the universe."
³Latin *Pannonius* = a Pannonian, inhabitant of classical Hungary.

This is vague enough to ensure that no interpretation made thus far is completely satisfactory. A woman leader, who can be as aggressive as a man when she wants to be, makes great diplomatic exertions to Russia (or she is making those exertions *from* Russia). In either case she will vex Europe and the world. A modern application would have the Iron Lady herself, Margaret Thatcher, as the one resisting communist Russia and putting a political monkey-wrench into the process of European Union.

A more likely candidate would be Catherine the Great of Russia (1729–96). The two total eclipses in France might date her life. She was born five years after an eclipse that cast a shadow across Normandy, Paris, and Venice on 22 May 1724. The second eclipse threw its shadow over Brussels, Paris and La Rochelle on 1 April 1764. Catherine had ascended to the throne as Empress of All the Russias two years earlier. At that time Russia was an ally of the Austrian Empire (**Pannonians**) during the Seven Years War, which ended in 1763, a year before the second eclipse.

8 Q16

Au lieu que HIERON¹ *feit ſa nef fabriquer,*
Si grand deluge ſera & ſi ſubite,
Qu'on n'aura lieu ne terres s'atacquer
L'onde monter Feſulan Olympique.²
	At the place where Jason had his ship
	      built,
	There will be such a great and so
	      sudden a flood,
	That one will not have a place or
	      lands to fall on
	The wave mounts the Olympic
	      Fesulan.

¹cryptogram for IESON or JASON of the Argonauts.
²*Feſulan Olympique*: Leoni makes this a composite word for the Greek Mt Olympus and the Italian town of Fiesole.

This is the last of several quatrains outlining the catastrophic effects of a future flood caused by a meteorite strike in the Aegean.

The initial splash could send the sea over 10,000 feet high, a good several hundred feet over Mt Olympus. The tidal waves would boil back and forth and roil again over the coastlines of the Mediterranean. For instance, the citizens of Fiesole, Italy, perched high above the Arno Valley (900 feet above sea level) would watch helplessly as neighboring Florence – a town noted for its art and catastrophic floods – is consumed by the Arno River for the last time. The runoff would not come from the Appennines but from a new and terrible retrograde flood of sea water.

Quatrain Indexing Date: Q16 = 2026, 2116 . . . 2816, ad infinitum.

8 Q17

Les bien aifez fubit feront defmis
Par les trois freres le monde mis en trouble,
Cité marine faifiront ennemis,
Faim, feu, fang, pefte & de tous maux le
    double.

Those at ease will suddenly be cast
    down
The world put into trouble by three
    brothers,
The enemies will seize the marine
    city,
Famine, fire, blood, plague, all evils
    doubled.

This may return us to the near future and those prophecies warning of a triumvirate of three terrorist-sanctioning nations (***three brothers***) taking the whole world hostage.

The hi-tech rout of one of the Third World's largest conventional armies during the Gulf War of 1991 may force politically radical states to switch to more covert tactics in the future. At present the northern states appear to have terrorists and their supporters under control. However, future demagogues of the south may be waiting patiently for more advantageous times, when an economic depression early in the 21st century, makes the United States more isolationist. At that time we might see a new sequence of apocalyptic events arising from the actions of the three secretly allied ***Eastern*** or terrorist nations mentioned in the Epistle.

London, Marseilles, or Hong Kong could each be characterized as a ***marine city***. One would hope this catastrophic forecast was already fulfilled by the street battles of Marseilles in August 1944, when the *three* **brothers** could have been the Fascist dictators Hitler, Mussolini, and Franco.

A near-future scenario would unveil a world crisis after the 1997 transfer of Hong Kong to China. A terrorist threat to London is also possible.

Quatrain Indexing Date: Q27 = 2027?

8 Q18

De Flora iſſue de ſa mort ſera cauſe,
Vn temps deuant par ieuſne & vieille
 bueyre
Par les trois lys luy feront telle pauſe,
Par ſon fruit ſauue comme chair crue
 mueyre.

From Florence [the] cause of her
 death will be issued,
Once before by young and old to
 drink,
For the three lilies will give her such
 a pause [to reflect],
Through her offspring safe as raw
 meat [is] dampened.

Florence is the capital of the Medici Duchy of Tuscany. The symbol of the three lilies of France narrows the possible candidates of this verse to the two Medici Queens of France, Catherine de' Medici or Marie de' Medici. I believe Nostradamus is speaking of the former candidate.

The Medici legacy of poisoning of their enemies is implied with a double pun for the death-dealing medium. *Flora* in line 1 stands for both Florence and the Latin *flora* for flowering plants, some of which, in this case are poisonous. Controversy surrounds Catherine de' Medici in later life for using poison to dispense with her enemies. Line 3 is all too true for the tribulations of Catherine during the difficult years as Queen Regent and later as Queen Mother during the latter half of the Wars of Religion. She witnessed the premature deaths of two sons, Francis II and Charles IX, certainly giving her **pause**. In 1588, while she herself was dying of pneumonia, Catherine could reflect upon the coming end of her favorite, Henry III, who would also be assassinated. She was well aware of the prophetic warnings made by Nostradamus and Ruggieri of disasters to befall the House of Valois. Yet she soldiered on, ever the Italian fatalist. The riddle of line 4 can be clarified. **Raw meat** is **dampened** by blood – a pretty gruesome coda. In other words, her offspring will never be safe. All but one of her seven children (Marguérite de Valois) would die unnatural and premature deaths, most at the hand of violence.

8 Q19

A ſoubſtenir la grand cappe[1] troublee,
Pour l'eſclaircir les rouges marcheront,
De mort famille ſera preſque accablee.
Les rouges rouges le rouge aſſomeront.

To sustain the great troubled Cape[t],
To solve it the reds will march,
A family will be almost overcome by
 death.
The red red ones will strike the red
 one on the head.

[1]Old French for cloak; possibly "Capet" for "Citizen Capet," the name Louis XVI was forced to bear after the French Revolution.

We return to the Reign of Terror and the fate of citizen **Capet**. The debate in the National Convention over the king's punishment becomes a full-fledged power struggle between the moderate Girondins (**reds**) and the radical Jacobins (the **red red ones**). The moderate reds tried to save the king, but their political strategies and street marches were disorganized. The doubly-red Jacobins overwhelmed them as predicted, sending most of the Girondins to the guillotine. Three out of four members of the immediate royal family would also die: Louis XVI, Queen Marie Antoinette, and their son, the Dauphin.

8 Q20

Le faux meſſaige par election fainte	**The false message about the rigged election**
Courir par vrben rompue pache arreſte,	**To run through the city the broken pact stopped,**
Voix acheptees, de ſang chapelle tainte,	**Voice bribed, by blood [the] chapel [is] stained,**
Et à vn autre l'empire contraicte.	**And to another one the empire contracted.**

This is probably about the Thirty Years War and a breakdown in the Imperial Electors' system due to bribery and scandal. A Holy Roman Emperor is elected through the purchased **voices** of a key elector. A civil war ensues and the illegal emperor is overthrown. The Thirty Years War was launched in 1618 by a revolt in Bohemia, when its citizens elected the Protestant elector Frederick V of Palatine instead of the Catholic Habsburg Emperor, Ferdinand II, to the throne of Bohemia. In the following year forces of the Catholic League and Imperial troops under Tilly routed a Bohemian army at the Battle of Weisser Berg (White Mountain). Soon Catholic troops would indeed **run through the city** of Prague and reimpose Catholicism and Ferdinand II rather than Palatine as the heir to the Bohemian throne (**to another one the empire contracted**).

8 Q21

Au port d'Agde trois fuſtes entreront	**To the port of Agde three foists will enter,**
Portant d'infect non foy & peſtilence	**Carrying the infection and pestilence, and not the faith**
Paſſant le pont[1] mil milles embleront,	**Passing [over] the sea they will carry off a thousand thousands,**
Et le pont[1] rompre à tierce reſiſtance.	**And the bridge broken by the resistance of the third.**

[1]Usually Latin *pontem* = bridge, and at other times Latin *pontus* = sea. In both instances (in lines 3 and 4) the meaning intended for *pont* could be either.

This could be a continuation of the plague theme in Agde (see 4 Q94), wherein a conflict in Nostradamus' near future along the southern French ports of Narbonne, Béziers, and Agde leads to a pestilence starting on plague-infested ships limping into Agde after a naval battle with the Spanish in the Mediterranean.

A million deaths from the plague in Agde would be a gross exaggeration for the 16th century. It is tempting to look beyond our times for another invasion and pestilence. Perhaps a ship carrying radioactive waste or biological weapons is hijacked by terrorists and enters the port of Agde. The terrorists threaten to unleash their cargo into the atmosphere if their political demands aren't met. A *foist* is a long galley that lies low in the water, similar to a submarine. Perhaps this is another "terrorist submarine" scenario, but this time the victim is France rather than Italy.

Fontbrune bends the grammar of line 3 to get a million Islamic soldiers invading France through Agde. Where he imagines such a horde will get the estimated 1,000 warships and transports to cross the Mediterranean is beyond me; they must be hiding in the cellar of some castle in the clouds. But in his defense, perhaps this is an invasion prophecy that went wrong. A million men on a thousand ships did land in southern France a few hundred miles up the coast in the Gulf of Fréjus in 1944 during the Anglo-American invasion called Operation Anvil/Dragoon.

8 Q22

Gorſan,[1] Narbonne,[2] par le ſel aduertir	**Gorsas and Narbonne by the salt to warn**
Tucham, la grace Parpignan[3] trahye,	**Touching pardon the Paris [pledge] betrayed,**
La ville rouge n'y vouldra conſentir	**The red city will not wish to consent to it**
Par haulte vol drap gris vie faillie.	**By flight gray drape's life is ended.**

[1]Antoine Joseph Gorsas (1752–93), deputy, journalist; founder of *Courier de Paris à Versailles*.
[2]Count Louis Marie Jacques de Narbonne (1755–1813), minister, moderate revolutionary.
[3]Robb cites Larmor who believes *Parpignan* stands for "Paris-born" and is a deliberate misspelling to make it only appear to be the city of Perpignan. He adds that Larmor's Latin is a bit lax since *pignus* (in Paris-*pignan*) means "pledge."

Gorsas (**Gorsan**) was a moderate journalist who, with Count Louis de Narbonne, tried to send a message hidden inside a salt shaker (**by the salt to warn**) to Louis XVI in the Temple prison. The king had promised never to leave Paris before his flight to Varennes (**Paris pledge betrayed**). *Red* Paris wanted him dead for his *flight* disguised in a *gray drape*, or cloak of a Carmelite monk.

8 Q23

Lettres trouuees de la royne les coffres,[1]	*Letters found in the Queen's cabinet,*
Point de fubfcrit fans aucun nom d'autheur	*No signature, without any name of the author*
Par la police[2] feront cachez les offres,	*The offers will be hidden by the police,*
Qu'on ne fçaura qui fera l'amateur.	*So that they will not know who the beneficiary is.*

[1]Nostradamus' description is archaic for the cupboards and cabinets used two centuries later, during the French Revolution.
[2]Old French *police* = a) government; b) ruse.

Fontbrune's exhaustive study of the legal transcripts of the trial of Louis XVI conjures up an interesting answer for this prophecy. This may predict an episode in the trial of Louis XVI concerning rumors (fanned by yellow journals of the day) of a secret iron cabinet that hid an inventory of the king's finances.

The president of the tribunal asked the king to examine a set of compromising unsigned letters, plus a written contract for police protection, all purported to be written in the king's hand. To his best recollection, the monarch could not remember ever writing them. The president then asked, "Did you cause to be built in one wall of the Tuileries palace a cabinet with an iron door, and keep papers therein?" The king shook his head. " I know nothing about that, nor about the unsigned paper."

The defense lawyer, Louis de Sèze, went on to explain that no inventory of these sealed letters was made in his presence by the defendant. It would be easy for enemies of the king to slide malicious papers under the seal, or remove those letters that might help in the king's defense. It must be remembered that Louis' apartments were broken into, cabinets were broken open, and papers were scattered. Some of them no doubt were lost or stolen.

During his cross-examination the king repeated his denial: he knew nothing about an iron cabinet or the papers inside, and in any case, he pointed out, the most important documents would have found their way into a satchel entrusted to Queen Marie Antoinette's lady-in-waiting, Madam Campan (**letters found in the Queen's cabinet**).

8 Q24

Le lieutenant à l'entree de l'huys,	**The lieutenant in the doorway,**
Affommera la grand de Perpignan,	**Will knock down the great one of Perpignan,**
En fe cuidant fauluer à Monpertuis.	**In thinking to save himself at Monpertuis.**
Sera deceu baftard de Lufignan.	**The bastard of Lusignan will be deceived.**

In Nostradamus' time **Perpignan** in southwest France was in Spanish
Roussillon. **Lusignan** is 280 miles to the northeast, about 20 miles south-
west of Poitiers. In medieval times Lusignan was ruled by a family of
nobles that included Crusader kings of Jerusalem and rulers of Cyprus.
The French family tree expired in 1308, whereas the Middle Eastern
branch passed its titles on to the House of Savoy in 1485. This points to
the House of Savoy as Nostradamus' **bastard of Lusignan**, especially
when we remember that Nostradamus' patron, the Comte de Tende,
Governor of Provence, was the son of the Grand Bastard of Savoy. Lusignan therefore is only referred to here as a description of royals involved
in the predicted conflict in Roussillon.

Montpertuis is most likely the Perthus Pass in the Pyrenees, south of
Perpignan. Nostradamus believes Tende will seize Perpignan from the
Spanish in Roussillon. Flushed with victory he advances towards the
pass, only to be trapped in the mountain terrain on the Spanish border by
a Spanish relief army.

There was only one minor siege at Perpignan, in 1597, during the final
years of the Wars of Religion. The Perthus Pass would be the supply and
invasion route for the Spanish. Later, in 1640, Louis XIII invaded
Catalonia through the pass. The next notable Comte de Tende would be
de Villars (1653–1734). But he never fought in Roussillon or Spain.

8 Q25

Cœur de l'amant ouuert d'amour fertiue	*Heart of the lover opened by furtive love*
Dans le ruyſſeau fera rauyr la Dame,	*Will ravish the Lady in the brook,*
Le demy mal contrefera laſſiue,	*The wanton woman will fake being*
Le pere à deux priuera corps de l'ame.	*half hurt,*
	The father will deprive the body of
	each of its soul.

A princess and her secret lover make for the nearest creek to cool their
ardor. The wanton wench is roundly satisfied in a violent sexual liaison,
but will later fake being ravaged and sic her father on her lover. This
copulating couple of the stream had better hope there is such a thing as
reincarnation, because papa is slated to put to death both lusty libertines.

8 Q26

De Caton es[1] trouues en Barſellonne,	*The bones of Cato found in Barcelona,*
Mys deſcouuers lieu terrouers & ruyne,	*Placed, discovered, place found and*
Le grãd qui tient ne tient vouldra	*ruined,*
Pamplonne.	*The great one who holds and does not*
Par l'abbage de Montſerrat bruyne.	*hold [them?] will want Pamplona.*
	By the Abbey of Montserrat [there is]
	drizzle.

[1]Probably misprint for *os*, bones, because Old French *es* (planks) is out of context.

No, this is not a prophecy about Kato Kalen! But I expect some tabloid will try to make more mischief by squeezing an O. J. Simpson prophecy out of Nostradamus. In this case they'll have to report that the bones of Kato will be found outside of Barcelona, near the Abbey of Montserrat, the same cavernous and ornate pile of masonry that German composer Richard Wagner modeled for interior scenes of his opera *Parsifal*.

But all absurdities aside, Leoni reminds us that none of the ancestors of the great Roman orator had their bones entombed in Barcelona or Montserrat. Well, true, but the grandson of Cato (C. Porcius Cato) died in Spain, in neighboring Tarragona, a mere 40 miles down the Spanish Riviera coast. In Nostradamus' defense against Leoni's scholastic hair-splitting, the prophet might be using a 16th-century legend about the old bones to spice up his prophecy.

Fontbrune in turn reminds us that in the 16th-century *cato* was used as a mocking term for those outwardly earnest or soft-spoken types who were in reality rebellious and vicious by nature. With this in mind he believes it stands for the undisciplined Spanish army that invaded and pillaged Roussillon in 1640, and Louis XIII's counter-attack, in which he invaded Catalonia, occupied the Duchy of Montserrat, and laid siege on Barcelona.

8 Q27

La voye auxelle l'vne fur l'autre fornix[1]	*The auxiliary path, one arch upon the other [an aqueduct]*
Du muy defer hor mis braue & geneft,[2]	*Of the move deserted except for the brave to be born,*
L'efcript d'empereur le fenix[3]	*The writing of the Emperor, the phoenix*
Veu en celuy ce qu'à nul autre n'eft.	*Beheld by the one, which to none other is.*

[1]Latin *fornix* = a) arch; b) brothel.
[2]Old French *genest* = a) Genista, the broom plant; b) *genet* or Jennet, a Spanish horse; c) from the Greek for "generating" life: to be born.
[3]*fenix*: Latin *phoenix* = a) Phoenician; b) the Phoenix, 500-year-old bird.

Nostradamus is describing the arches of an aqueduct, although Cheetham thinks a translation of the ancient French would turn the arches into those of a brothel. Line 2's *muy* and *genest* are also open to many different interpretations. Either it is: **Of the move [or advance] deserted except for the brave** . . . or it can also read **Of Le Muy deserted, except for the brave** . . . .

Line 3 is ambiguous too. It could be "the writing of the Phoenician Emperor"– thus an Emperor of North Africa and the Middle East, like the Turkish sultan – or "Phoenix Emperor." In the latter case he is some potentate who rises from the ashes of a disaster to rule again. We have known enough emperors in history who fit this description to make line 4 impossible to interpret unless we are talking about an object rather than a person.

In 1994, *World Press Review* reported that Norwegian shipping-line owner Knut Utstein Kloster was planning to construct the *Phoenix*, a floating high-tech "world city" combining business and cultural activities. If it is built, the 1,320-foot ocean liner will be three times larger than any previous passenger ship. It will carry 5,600 passengers and contain three giant hotels, office space, convention facilities, shops, a concert hall, and an athletics arena.

8 Q28

Les simulachres d'or & argent enflez,	**The imitations of gold and silver [will**
Qu'apres le rapt au lac furent gettez	**become] inflated,**
Au defcouuert eftaincts tous & troublez.	**Which after the rape [are] thrown**
Au marbre efcript prefcripz intergetez.	**into the burning lake**
	After discovering all is exhausted and
	dissipated by the debt,
	All scrips and bonds are wiped out.

The prophecy has been fulfilled only in part, but stands every chance of complete realization in the near future. It has relevance to both the stock market crash of 1929 and to a future day of reckoning when America's huge deficit goes out of control.

In Nostradamus' day there was no paper money, only coins. His description of **imitations of gold and silver** is, therefore, a triumph of foresight. The quatrain number, 28, could be a near miss for the actual year of the stock market crash.

The last two lines may foretell the outcome of today's global inflation and America's national deficit – a kind of economic Judgment Day. The efforts of political prophet Ross Perot, Republican Party revolutionary Newt Gingrich, and President Clinton to conjure economic reform may have come too late to stem the karmic results of extending credit for credit. Despite the promising improvements of the US economy during Clinton's administration, the national, not to mention global, deficit continues to grow, and prophetic warnings predict a drastic return to inflation by the new millennium as a consequence of stresses put upon the global economy by overpopulation and ecological disasters. If the United States does not support the call for a fundamental change in its economic world view, its paper money may not be worth the wood (taken via the **rape** of the earth and exhausted) to burn it any time from 1997 onward.

Quatrain Indexing Date: Q28 = 1928, a near miss for the stock market crash of 1929.

8 Q29

Aut quart pillier lon ſacre à Saturne.	**At the fourth pillar [pillage?] the one**
Par tremblant terre & deluge fendu	**dedicated to Saturn.**
Soubz l'edifice Saturnin trouuee vrne,	**By earthquake and flood demolished**
D'or Capion rauy & puis rendu.	**Under the Saturnian edifice an urn**
	[Aquarius?] found,
	Of gold carried off by Caepio and then
	restored.

This is part two of Nostradamus' treasure hunt. We return to the devastated temples of the ancient Volcae, a tribe of plunderers themselves pillaged by the Romans at Toulouse in 109 BC. Line 1 plays on **pillar** and **pillage** to obscure the first clue to the secret hiding place of a great Gallic treasure hoard. Cayla Paviot's *Histoire de Toulouse* says the current Church of St Saturnin-du-Taur was built over the site of the "secret lake" where, according to legend, a great heap of silver and gold lies beneath a cavern lake's surface. As a young vagabond doctor, Nostradamus lived for a time in Toulouse and must have heard the tale. Decades later, sitting in his secret study – his own figurative cavern – Nostradamus entertained himself by blending projection with prophecy to predict the treasure's location and discovery. **A pillar . . . the one dedicated to Saturn** is a wicked pun implying that the treasure is buried directly under the Church of St Saturnin.

Leoni finds it difficult to understand why a church would be dedicated to Saturn. Here again this fine scholar overlooks the occult poetry and pun-ishments of the prophet. Saturn's color is black, and Nostradamus sometimes uses the term to describe the black clothing (and in his opinion the "black" and pagan heresy) of the Huguenots. Toulouse was a major center of Protestant rebellion. In line 4 Nostradamus mixes his myths and pillagers. **Caepio** sacked Toulouse and apparently seized the **urn** full of gold and silver buried under the fourth pillar of a temple later razed and rebuilt as a church during the early Christian era. By some miraculous event, the gold will be **restored** to its hiding place. Some scholars suggest that Caepio himself was robbed of the treasure while passing through Marseilles. I tend to think he returned it himself, for reasons the following quatrain will explain.

8 Q30

Dedans Toloze non loing de Beluezer	**Within Toulouse not far from Beluezer**
Faiſant vn puy long, palais d'eſpectacle	**Making a deep pit, palace of spectacle**
Treſor trouué vn chacun ira vexer,	**Treasure found will come to vex everyone,**
Et en deux locz tout & pres del vaſacle.	**And in two places and near the Bazacle.**

[1]*Beluezer* = a) Provençal *belousar* = to dig; b) *beluze* = in central France a rock formation known in English as a schist.

Part three of Nostradamus' Treasure in Toulouse story takes us forward in time to its future discovery.

Bazacle was the name of a castle that protected the bridge and main city gate of Toulouse; it is also the name of the city's milling quarter. In these locales someone will find a buried treasure near a formation of schist rock, which is common in central France, and is called *belousar* (**Beluezer**) in the Provençal language. Line 2 implies that ancient riches will be unearthed during an excavation for building a **palace of spectacle**. Perhaps this is Nostradamus' way of describing a movie house of today or a virtual reality pavilion of tomorrow. The unearthing triggers an ancient hex that will bedevil Toulouse. Perhaps the future Toulousians will learn the hard way why Caepio **restored** the gold to its hiding place. As with nasty dogs it is better to let sleeping and hexed treasures lie.

8 Q31

Premier grand fruit le prince de Pefquiere	**The first great fruit [of] the prince of Peschiera**
Mais puis viendra bien & cruel malin,	**But then will come a cruel and evil man,**
Dedans Venife perdra fa gloire fiere	**Within Venice he will lose his proud glory**
Et mys à mal par plus ioyne Celin.	**And put to evil by the younger [Chyren?] Selin.**

Another Henry II-as-*Chyren Selin* quatrain. Hercules Duc d'Alençon is implied in other places as his successor (6 Q42) as well as conqueror of Italy and supressor of proud Venice. This prophetic pipe dream couldn't be more off the mark for the brutish prince, who turned out to be the nervy and nerdy Valois version of Jim Carrey (during his quieter moments) in a dark comedy.

8 Q32

Garde toy Roy Gaulois de ton nepueu	**Guard yourself, Gallic King, of your nephew**
Qui fera tant que ton vnique filz	**He who will do so much that your unique son**
Sera meurtry à Venus faifant vœu,	**Will be murdered [while] making a vow to Venus,**
Accompaigné de nuict que trois & fix.	**Accompanied at night by three and six.**

A prophecy for the Venetian Republic, which contained Verona and Vicenza in Nostradamus' day. Verona and Vicenza, respectively, are 65 and 40 miles due west of Venice. A French king's son is threatened by 36 conspirators. My hunch tells me this is another *Chyren-Selin*/Henry II, *Ogmios*/Hercules Duc d'Alençon prophecy. In this case the latter may be assassinated. That is, of course, if he heeds this warning from a prophecy about Henry II's alternative future that was never accessed.

8 Q33

Le grand naiſtra de Veronne & Vincence,	**The great one will be born of Verona and Vicenza,[1]**
Qui portera vn ſurnom bien indigne,	**Who will bear a very unworthy surname,**
Qui à Veniſe vouldra faire vengeance,	**He who at Venice will desire to take vengeance,**
Luy meſme prins homme du guet & ſigne.	**He himself is taken [by a] man of the watch and the sign.**

[1]Both cities are a synecdoche for northern Italy.

Mussolini was born in northern Italy. His surname means "muslin-maker," a lowly profession in Nostradamus' time. Mussolini and Hitler's first meeting in **Venice** in 1933 was a flop. Hitler, dressed in shabby civilian clothes, stood next to Il Duce who was resplendent in military uniform. A diplomat watching Hitler deplane at Lido Airport said, "I was fascinated to watch the expressions on their faces. Beneath the obligatory cordiality I found I could see an expression of amusement in Mussolini's eyes and of resentment in Hitler's." Hitler could not understand Il Duce's florid German and Mussolini could not follow Hitler's sharp Austrian accent. Few witnesses at the time could imagine that a few years after that Venetian comedy, Hitler would forge an Axis pact with Mussolini. Hitler, the man *of the sign* (the swastika), would get his revenge by turning Mussolini and his regime into a puppet satellite of Nazi Germany.

Quatrain Indexing Date: Q33 = 1933, the year Hitler came to visit Mussolini for the first time.

8 Q34

Apres victoire du Lyon au Lyon	**After the victory of the Lion at Lyon**
Sus la montaigne de IVRA Secatombe[1]	**Upon the mountains of Jura a great slaughter**
Delues[2] & brodes[3] ſeptieme million	**Floods and dark-skinned ones seventh million**
Lyon, Vlme[4] à Mauſol mort & tombe.	**Lyons [Lion?], Ulm at Mausole [Mausoleum at St Rémy?) death and the tomb.**

[1]Misprint for *Hecatombe*.
[2]Latin *diluvies* = flood; desolation; destruction.
[3]Old French *brode* = black; brown; decadent; (figuratively) Spanish.
[4]*Vlme* = Ulm, or possibly a play on Latin *ulmus* = elm.

There are many possibilities for *Lyon au Lyon*: You can have a **victory** of the (British) "Lion at Lyons," "over the Lion by Lyons," "of the Lion into Lyons," etc. Nor can one clarify this muddle by applying the theme of the young lion against the old Lion of 1 Q35, since the location of this prophecy is in southern Germany. In 1805 Napoleon outmaneuvered and captured Mack's Austrian army of 72,000 men at Ulm. Unfortunately that doesn't tie in with other clues in this quatrain, such as a lion's victory at Lyons, the slaughter in the Jura mountains in Franche-Comté, and the assembly or loss of seven million of the **dark-skinned ones** (which could be an army from the brown or black races or the olive-skinned soldiers of Spain). An army numbering seven million is too large for this event to take place before the 20th century. *Vlme* could also be the die at the Roman Mausoleum outside Nostradamus' birthplace at St Rémy, Provence (see 4 Q27).

It does sound remotely familiar to the alternative future failure seen in 5 Q87 – an invasion by either Savoy or the Habsburgs into Franche-Comté through Alsace.

8 Q35

Dedans l'entree de Garonne & Bayſe	**Within the entry of the Garonne and**
Et la foreſt non loing de Damazan	**Baïsse**
Du marſaues[1] gelees[2], puis greſle & bize	**And the forest not far from Damazan**
Dordonnois gelle par erreur de mezan.[3]	**Discoveries from the frozen sea, then**
	hail and the dry and cold north wind
	The people of Dordogne frost through
	error of the month.

[1]Old French *mar* = sea; *save* = discovery.
[2]Old French *gelée* = frost.
[3]Metathesis of Latin *mensis* = month, changed to preserve the rhyme.

A meteorological quatrain. A severe winter hits southwestern France where the Baïsse river joins the Gélise (hidden in a double-pun for frost: *gelées/Gélise*) to flow into the Garonne at Aiquillon, a few miles east of Damazan. A severe frost besets the Dordogne river valley. This could cover any severe winter. The worst winter on record closest to the publication of this prophecy was seven years later in 1564–65. This doesn't rule out Nostradamus' foreseeing the advent of a second ice age in our near future.

8 Q36

Sera commis conte oingdre aduché	**It will be committed against the**
De Saulne & ſainct Aulbin & Bell'œuure	**anointed brought**
Pauer de marbre de tours loing eſpluché	**From [Lons-le-]Saulnier and St Aubin**
Non Bleteram reſiſter & chef d'œuure.	**and [the] beautiful work**
	To pave with marble taken from
	distant towers
	Not to resist Bleteram and [his]
	masterpiece.

Lons-le-Saunier, St Aubin, and Bletterans are clustered together in Franche-Comté. The **beautiful work** is a marble paved floor or pathway, made from **marble taken from** a nearby Roman ruin or plucked from the **towers** of some conquered city. This bit of 16th-century trivia must have meant something to Nostradamus' contemporaries.

8 Q37

La forteresse aupres de la Tamise	*The fortress near the Thames*
Cherra par lors le Roy dedans serré,	*Will fall when the king is locked up*
Aupres du pont sera veu en chemise	*inside,*
Vn deuant mort, puis dans le fort barré.	*He will be seen in his shirt near the*
	bridge
	One confronting death then barred in
	the fort.

Lines 1 and 4 bracket the execution of Charles I of England in the story of a captured king being taken to Windsor Castle (**fortress**) near the Thames. On 30 January 1649, Charles was led to the scaffold at Westminster, there to be stripped to his shirt for beheading. Later, Garencières relates, his bloodstained shirt was hung on a pole from London Bridge two miles from the place of execution (**near the bridge**).

8 Q38

Le Roy de Bloys dans Auignon regner	*The King of Blois in Avignon to rule*
Vne autre foys le peuple emonopolle,[1]	*Once again the bloodthirsty people,*
Dedans le Rosne par murs fera baigner	*In the Rhône he will make to bathe*
Iusques à cinq le dernier pres de Nolle.	*by the walls*
	Up to five the last one near Nolle.

[1] *emonopollet* = a) Greek *haima* = blood, + *pole* = pole or rod – ie bloody rod; b) Le Pelletier has *haimapnoos*, bloodthirsty, or *haimatopotes*, blood-drinker.

Here's a real head-scratcher. A king residing in the Château Blois must be a Valois. Henry III is usually described as **one from Blois**. The papal enclave at **Avignon** will come under a Valois king in Nostradamus' near future. Leoni believes **Nolle** is either an anagram for Oulle, a village near Avignon, or a play on "Yule"/Christmas, the time when five men are executed through drowning in Lyons. One thing is certain: no Valois seized Avignon, and this execution is too general to be easily solved.

8 Q39

Qu'aura esté par prince Bizantin,	*He who will have been for the*
Sera tollu par prince de Toloze.	*Byzantine prince,*
La foy de Foix par le chef Tholentin,	*Will be taken away by the Prince of*
Luy faillira ne refusant l'espouse.	*Toulouse.*
	The faith of Foix through the chief of
	Tolentino,
	Will fail him, not refusing the bride.

One hopelessly obscure quatrain deserves another. Usually a Byzantine prince is a Turkish sultan, a high-ranking general, or a Barbary Corsair like Barbarossa or Dragut. Toulouse has princes of the Montmorency clan as its source of hereditary governors; unless we are talking about a spiritual "prince" of Toulouse – the Archbishop of Toulouse. Now we hop over half the Mediterranean Sea to the chief, prince, or archbishop of Tolentino, a town 25 miles southwest of Ancona, in the papal states. We can assume that this *chief* is the pope by synecdoche. The pope will find the Huguenots of **Foix** (a synecdoche for Navarre), of little religious *faith*, even though they are *not refusing the bride*. The woman in question must therefore be Henry de Navarre's future queen, the Catholic Marguérite de Valois, who would be forced to marry the Huguenot king in 1572, fourteen years after this was written.

8 Q40

Le ſang du Iuſte par Taurer la daurade,	**The blood of the Just for Taur and La Daurade,**
Pour ſe venger contre les Saturnins	**In order to avenge himself against the Saturnians**
Au nouueau lac plongeront la maynade,[1]	**In the new lake they will plunge the servants,**
Puis marcheront contre les Albanins.	**Then they will march against those of Alva.**

[1]Provençal *mainada* = a) band; b) child, people, servants.

The Protestants of Toulouse will revolt. The town is represented here by its two churches: St Saturnin-du-Taur and that of Ste-Marie-de-la-Dorade. Saturn's color is black; therefore **the Saturnians** probably refers to the black-clad Huguenots or Calvinists who have committed heresies at these Catholic churches. The **new lake** returns us again to the legends of 8 Q29–30, where Caepio's treasure lies hidden in an urn in a subterranean lake. It seems the Huguenots have drowned the **servants** of the Church of Saturn before they march off to do battle with the Albanian mercenaries of the Spanish Duke of Alva.

Pieces of this puzzling vision were fulfilled. Toulouse did attract Huguenot revolts and atrocities during the Wars of Religion, but nothing that specifically matches these clues. The Spanish did make token penetrations into southwestern France during the last War of Religion. One might have seen Toulousians marching against the Spanish, but not against Alva. A few pieces of this broken pot of a prophecy do not hold water.

8 Q41

Efleu fera Renard ne fonnant mot,	**The fox will be elected without**
Faifant le faint public viuant pain d'orge,	**speaking a word,**
Tyrannizer apres tant à vn cop,[1]	**Playing the public Saint, living [on]**
Mettant à pied des plus grans fus la gorge.	**barley bread,**
	Afterwards he will suddenly become a
	tyrant,
	Placing his foot on the throats of the
	greatest.

[1]Old French syncope of *coup*, to preserve the rhyme.

To his revolutionary contemporaries Robespierre was known as **the fox** for his ruthless and cunning methods of ensnaring and exterminating his enemies. Two centuries before he was born Nostradamus also chose to describe him as a fox. By 1793, after having eliminated most of his opposition in the Assembly, Robespierre functioned as a virtual dictator of France. As high priest of the Cult of Reason, he played the **public Saint** at a celebration marking the birth of the new republican religion, held in a crowd of uneasy spectators in the Champs de Mars.

The words **barley bread** may describe more than his austere and puritanical character. Robespierre tried to avoid the guillotine by shooting himself but succeeded only in shattering his jaw. At his trial in the offices of Public Safety, the dictator – his self-inflicted wounds bandaged and bleeding – was seated on a box of army bread samples.

At the height of his power Robespierre had decreed that "Any individual who usurps the nation's sovereignty will be immediately put to death by free men." The legal machinery he had perfected led to his execution in 1794. His death ended the Reign of Terror.

8 Q42

Par auarice, par force & violence	**Through avarice, through force and**
Viendra vexer les fiens chiefz d'Orleans,	**violence**
Pres faint Memire[1] *affault & refiftance.*	**The chief of Orléans will come to vex**
Mort dans fa tante diront qu'il dort leans.	**his supporters,**
	Near Saint Memire assault and
	resistance.
	Dead in his tent they will say he
	sleeps within.

[1]Coinage by Nostradamus: no St Memire exists. Le Pelletier divines the Church of St Méri out of it; however an anagram is possible.

By the year 1848 the avaricious Louis Philippe was universally disliked. He spent the revolution mostly asleep in his canopied bed (**tent**). The fighting in the streets started near the Rue de St Merri (perhaps in cryptogram *Memire*). Philippe did not die in the revolution; Robb, however, believes that the word **dead** may be figurative for his psychological death. Witnesses describe him emerging from his bedroom looking more dead than alive. He stood before members of his cabinet in a nightcap and soiled nightshirt, with a two-day-old growth of beard. In this condition he officially signed his abdication.

Nostradamus makes a pungent French rhyme of line 2's *Orléans* and line 4's *dort leans*, but in English (*leans* = lying down) the impact is reduced to a literary gelding. One might restore its vitality by saying Philippe is a Duke of Orléans who leans closer to being a king, and is found either lying down on the job or lean-ing when the council come for his signature of abdication.

Quatrain Indexing Date: (1)842 = 1842: a near miss for 1848?

8 Q43

Par le decide[1] de deux choſes baſtars	**Through the fall of two bastard things**
Nepueu du ſang occupera le regne	**The Nephew by blood will occupy the**
Dedans lectoyre[2] feront les coups de dars[3]	**realm**
Nepueu par peur pleira l'enſeigne.	**Within Lectoure there will be the blows of arrows**
	The Nephew through fear will fold his standard.

[1]Latin *decidere* = to fall.
[2]Anagram for *Le Torcy*, a suburb of Sedan.
[3]Arrows: he means artillery shots but uses the more figurative *dars*/arrows instead to preserve the rhyme in lines 1 and 3: *bastars . . . dars*.

Here is another debunker's nightmare. It stands not only as an unquestionably fulfilled prophecy, but also as a documented example of a Nostradamus scholar making an accurate interpretation years before an event took place or could even be imagined. Le Pelletier logged the following interpretation in 1867, when the Second Empire of Napoleon III was at its peak. The French military disaster at Sedan and the collapse of the empire from the Franco-Prussian War was still three years off.

Le Pelletier writes: "Following the overthrow of the two illegitimate governments of Louis-Philippe of Orléans and of the National Assembly of 1848, Napoleon III, the great-nephew of the founder of the Napoleonic dynasty, will mount the throne of France. At a later date there will be, within Lectoyre, a battle in which the imperial Nephew because of fear will have the standard [of France] folded."

Le Pelletier is on the right track, but he backtracks – or better, covers his tracks – with a few turgid apologies to the emperor (and to Imperial censors who might confiscate his books for making objectionable references to the fall of the empire). First he says in the footnotes that "this epoch is indeterminate and nothing now [1866] makes it foreseeable."

Then he tackles the enigma *lectoyre* in line 3: "The name of Lectoure, a town in the department of Gers, comes naturally to mind. Nevertheless, the word *lectoyre* might, in one of the many tongues familiar to Nostradamus (Hebrew, Greek, Latin, Celtic, Provençal, Spanish and Italian) have a connotation not yet perceived, and which will be revealed after the event itself, as happens in a number of predictions."

After he tries to lay a smokescreen of classical allusions to direct attention away from his politically incorrect call, Le Pelletier gets down to business and concludes: "There are thus grounds for believing this refers to the imperial nephew, who will cause the banner of his enemies to be folded by the terror of his arms. It could nevertheless mean the contrary, and the calculated ambiguity of the text has as its object to veil, until its realization, a check to the fortunes of the imperial arms."

A little over three years later the veil on this prophecy and the anagram of *lectoyre* would be lifted to reveal Napoleon III and the French Army of the Meuse, numbering 100,000 men, surrounded by the Prussians and Bavarians at the fortress city of Sedan. *Lectoyre* easily stands as an anagram for Le Torcy, which was a pivotal sector in the French city's defenses during the battle. Leoni has found an interesting observation by Colonel Maude in his commentary on the battle published in *Encyclopaedia Britannica* : "The only part which Sedan's defenses played, or might have played, in the ensuing battle lay in the strategic possibilities of the fine and roomy bridgehead of Torcy, covering an elbow bend of the Meuse whence the whole French army might have been hurled between the German III and Meuse armies, had there been a Napoleon to conceive and execute this plan."

The inept nephew of the great general was hardly one to conceive such a plan, nor did any of the equally inept commanders of the surrounded army do so. Prior to the battle Napoleon III had been stripped of his empire, titles and command of the army, and was relegated to traveling in the train of the general staff. On the second day of the battle, after trying unsuccessfully to get himself killed by a stray Prussian artillery round, Napoleon III finally reasserted himself and persuaded Generals Ducrot and Wimpffen to hoist the white flag over the citadel of Sedan. The official surrender of the emperor and 82,000 survivors took place at the Castle of Bellevue in Conchéry, about two miles west of Le Torcy.

8 Q44

Le procreé naturel dogmion,[1]	The natural offspring of Ogmios,
De sept à neuf du chemin destorner	From seven to nine to turn aside from the road
A roy de longue & amy aumi hom,	To the King of long and friend to the half-man,
Doit à Nauarre fort de PAV prosterner.	Owes it to Navarre to lay low the fort of Pau.

[1]dogmion = of Ogmios, the Celtic hero often equated with Hercules.

Ogmios, the Celtic deity comparable to Hercules, is implausibly applied by Nostradamus to Henry II's brutish youngest son, Hercules, in an equally implausible alternative future in which the father is King of the French and Emperor of the Holy Roman Empire. It appears that if Henry had not died in his jousting match, a quantum future awaited him: He and Catherine de' Medici would have had three more children (**from seven to nine** Valois descendants). Henry II would have lived a long life, and befriended the **half-(hu)man** Protestant ruler of Navarre. Pau is the capital of Navarre and the seat of the Bourbon royal house. The **fort** is the famous Castle of Pau, where Henry de Navarre was born. In Nostradamus' alternative future the castle of his birth is razed to the ground by Henry II or his heir, **Ogmios**, and he never becomes Henry IV of France.

8 Q45

La main escharpe & la iambe bandee,	His hand in a sling and his leg bandaged,
Longs puis nay de Calais[1] portera	Leading-reins the younger one will carry from Calais/the palace
Au mot du guet la mort sera tardee,	At the word of the watchman his death will be delayed,
Puis dans le temple à Pasques saignera.	Then he will bleed in the Temple at Easter.

[1]Calais = a) Pas-de-Calais, the French seaport, and one of the final English possessions in France during Nostradamus' day; b) cryptogram for (P)alais = palace.

Leoni and Boswell get bogged down in a "mind-field" of historical muddles when they interpret Calais as the sea port and do not follow the cryptogram (P)alais. The latter does unlock the quatrain's obscurities to reveal a clear account of the destiny of Louis XVII.

The fate of the son and heir to the royal house who would have become Louis XVII is still a mystery, but it may be that Nostradamus' visionary powers enabled him to see what actually happened to the young prince.

Taken from his mother, Marie Antoinette, the 11-year-old prince was placed in the care of Simon the Cobbler, who was instructed by Stenart, the procurer of the Commune, to "humble" the boy. Stenart hinted there was no reason to either kill him or keep the Dauphin alive. That the cobbler took Stenart at his word and maltreated him is confirmed by the report of a Dr Harmand, who examined him in December 1794. He noted tumors on his left arm and unsightly swellings on his knees. In June 1795 Louis' death was announced to the Committee of General Security by Achille Sevestre, who stated that the cause of death was complications arising from a severe swelling of his left wrist and knee which, over the past few months, had required frequent dressing and bandaging (*hand in a sling and his leg bandaged*). The commissioners later visited the Temple prison where they viewed a body claimed to be that of young Louis. It was lying under a sheet stained with blood and was so badly disfigured that positive identification was impossible. The words of Nostradamus, written two centuries earlier, suggest that Louis bled from a cruel beating at Easter, and that his injuries were so terrible that they led to his death in the summer of 1795. The truth of this mysterious incident can probably never be verified.

8 Q46

Pol¹ menſolee² mourra trois lieuës du Roſne,³ *Fuis les deux⁴ prochains taraſc⁵ deſtrois:* *Car Mars fera le plus horrible throſne,* *De coq & d'aigle de France freres trois.*	**Paul the Celibate will die three leagues from Rome,** **The next two [Popes?] fled the oppressed Tarascan monster:** **For Mars will make the most horrible throne,** **Of the Cock and of the Eagle of France, [the] three brothers.**

[1]*Pol:* a) either Paul or an abbreviation of *Pollone* = Poland. In this case, Paul the Pole.
[2]*menſolee* = a) derivative of the Latin word for celibate; b) medieval Latin *mens solis* = the astrological meridian: noon – the point at which the sun reaches its highest position.
[3]*Rosne* usually stands for the Rhône river, but the clues here direct us to see *Rosne* as a cryptogram for Rome.
[4]*les deux:* if "the two" are popes, then this applies to John Paul I and II.
[5]*taraſc* = a) Tarascon: the town is named after a monster, the Tarasca; b) (Kidogo:) *Tarragon*, or wormwood, is a bitter herb from the plant *Artemisia dracunculus*, a native of Eastern Europe and also of southern Russia, in which its name, in Ukrainian, is *Chernobyl*.

Three popes have had the name Paul since 1555: Paul IV (1555–59), Paul V (1605–21), and Paul VI (1963–78). Only the last died six leagues from Rome at the papal summer residence at Castel Gandolfo. Nostradamus may be making an ironic jibe at Pope Paul VI's piety when he calls him *the Celibate*. It was widely rumored that the pope had a homosexual lover.

Fontbrune and Kidogo offer an intriguing interpretation. *Pol menſolee* stands for the Polish Pope John Paul II. First, *Pol* stands for *Pollone*, the ancient French word for Poland or, in this case, Paul the Pole. Then one adds an *a* to m(a)nſolee (*celibate*) signifying John Paul II. This is another of Nostradamus' parallels to the earlier prophecies of St Malachy. Second, Fontbrune thinks Nostradamus invented the compound word *mansol* out of the Latin *manus*, (= hand, thus manual work, travail, labor, etc.), and *sol* (the sun). Kidogo refines the compound word to get the medieval Latin *mens solis*, the astrological meridian over which the sun reaches its highest position at noon time. Both interpretations link *Pol menſolee* to St Malachy's prediction that John Paul II would be called *De Labore Solis*, or the Sun's Labor, since he was born during a solar eclipse.

Nostradamus could be telling us that the pope in office at the time of writing this (April 1996) will also end his days at Castel Gondolfo, outside of Rome. **The next two** popes would then be the last two on St Malachy's list before doomsday, whom he calls *Gloria Olivae*, the Glory of the Olive, and *Petrus Romanus*, Peter of Rome. They both flee the Tarascon monster, a creature Kidogo interprets as "wormwood," which in Ukrainian is *Chernobyl*. One decade ago in April 1986, humankind suffered the worst nuclear disaster in history when the Chernobyl nuclear power plant exploded and disgorged radiation around the world. This quatrain may warn of a worse nuclear disaster to come during the reign of the next two popes, perhaps from the surviving three reactors at the Chernobyl site. As I write this on the tenth anniversary of the disaster, a minor reactor leak at Chernobyl is being reported.

Line 3 uses wording similar to the famous Mabus/Third Antichrist prophecy of 2 Q62: **horrible throne/horrible undoing**.

The final line seems to be a general dating for modern France in the latter half of the 20th century. The three brothers are US President John F. Kennedy and US president hopefuls Senators Robert and Edward Kennedy.

8 Q47

Lac Treſmenien portera teſmoignage,
Des coniurez ſarez dedans Perouſe:
Vn deſpolle contrefera le ſage,
Tuant Tedeſq[1] de ſterne[2] & minuſe.

The Lake of Perugia [Trasimene] will bear testimony,
Of the conspirators locked up within Perugia:
A fool will imitate the sage,
Killing German destroyed and cut to pieces.

[1]Old French *Tudesque* = Teutonic, German.
[2]Old French *esterner* = to destroy, overthrow, rout.

This could be a World War II German occupation theme, since the only German army of any significance stationed near the Lake of Perugia after this prophecy was written was that of von Kessering. This army occupied Italy in 1943 and defended the Trasimene Line in June 1944. The *fool who will imitate the sage,* may be Nostradamus' dig at either the Nazi astrologer Karl Ernst Kraft or his boss, Josef Goebbels, Hitler's propaganda minister, for trying to misuse Nostradamus' predictions to persuade the world that the Nazis could win the war. Line 4 predicts the gruesome end for the *killing German* Adolf Hitler.

8 Q48

Saturne en Cancer, Iupiter auec Mars,	**Saturn in Cancer, Jupiter with Mars,**
Dedans Feurier Chaldondon[1] faluaterre:[2]	**In February, Chaldean soothsayer at**
Sault Caftallon[3] affailly de trois pars,[4]	**Salvatierra:**
Pres de Verbiefque conflit mortelle guerre.	**Sierra Morena mountains assailed**
	from three sides.
	Near Verbiesque conflict, mortal war.

[1]Enigma: possibly Latin *Chaldaeus* = Chaldean, soothsayer.
[2]From Latin *salva terra* = safe land – or the name of a place. There are three places in Spain, one in Mexico, and two in Portugal with the name Salvatierra.
[3]Probably Latin *Saltus Castulonensis* = Sierra Morena.
[4]Old French for sides.

Every time Saturn was in Cancer during the 20th century, the world was in the midst of a global war. *Jupiter* was *with Mars* in Taurus while *Saturn* was finishing its transit through *Cancer* in May–June 1917, during the massive Anglo-French offensive at Messines. Taurus rules the earth and soil. Just two days after Mars (god of war) joined *Jupiter* (god of the advance when at war) in Taurus, the French and British detonated 20 massive land mines dug under the German trenches, sending a wall of earth thundering into the air. Thousands of Germans were obliterated.

July and August 1944 saw Jupiter and Mars in Leo while Saturn was in Cancer. This time a German Army Group Center on the Eastern Front was obliterated by a titanic Soviet offensive overlooked by most Western historians because of their historical bias toward the Normandy campaign, which took place at the same time. If one is in accord with Boswell's concept that *Verbiesque* stands for Serbia, then one can see this quatrain as a description of the battles that raged near Serbia during the Slovak uprising against the Germans, and Soviet armies steamrolling into Bulgaria and Romania in August 1944.

The Sierra Morena mountain range divided Spanish Nationalist and Republican forces during the early campaigns of the Spanish Civil War. Although Mars and Jupiter were together in Capricorn in October 1937, Saturn was not yet in Cancer. Still, in October 1937 the Nationalists did mop up Republican resistance in the Sierra Morena region after sending three offensives out of the mountains to reduce the Republican strongholds of Merida, Lopera, and Cordoba.

There are three Salvatierras in Spain. Strangely enough, February 1937 saw the Nationalists building up for a big push scheduled for 31 March against Republican strongholds in the Basque towns of Bilbao, Guernica and Durango. Durango is only 20 miles northeast of a Basque town called Salvatierra, putting it right in the war zone. The identity of the *soothsayer* is harder to come by.

Astrological Time Window

This rare aspect threatens war again with Jupiter and Mars in the same sign with Saturn in Cancer in August–November 2004 and October–November 2033. The latter transit falls right in the middle of the next terrible window of global conflict described elsewhere in terms of other astrological aspects.

8 Q49

Satur. au bœuf ioue en l'eau, Mars en fleiche,	**Saturn in Taurus, Jupiter in the water [sign], Mars in Sagittarius,**
Six de Feurier mortalité donra:	**Sixth of February will give death:**
Ceux de Tardaigne à Bruges ſi grand breche,	**Those of Sardinia at Bruges so great a breach,**
Qu'à Ponteroſo chef Barbarin[1] mourra,	**That at Ponteroso [Red Bridge?] the Barberini chief will die.**

[1]Old French *Barbarin* = barbarian, or the Barberini, an influential Roman noble family which included Pope Urban VIII.

A number of details point nowhere fast with this prophecy. Neither the Sardinians nor the people of Soissons ever attacked Bruges, in Belgium. There is a Ponterosso about eight miles north of Genoa, where Nostradamus expects the Baraberini, an Italian noble house, to mourn the passing of its last heir on 6 February of a year when Saturn is in Taurus, Jupiter is in a water sign, and Mars is in Sagittarius. A specific and rare configuration indeed.

It just so happens that the last representative of the Barberinis died in 1738. The day is not known, but the planetary configurations described by Nostradamus did take place in February of that year. And since they won't arrange themselves like that again until long after the world's destruction in 3797, it is safe to say that Nostradamus got this prophetic fragment right on target.

8 Q50

La peſtilence l'entour de Capadille,[1] | The pestilence around Capellades,
Vne autre faim pres de Sagont[2] s'appreſte: | Another famine takes hold near to
Le cheualier baſtard de bon ſenille, | Sagunto:
Au grand de Thunes fera trancher la teſte. | The bastard knight of the good old man,
 | He will cause the great one of Tunis to cut off his head.

[1]Latin Capillada = Capellades, a town 30 miles northwest of Barcelona.
[2]Sagunto, about 25 miles north of Valencia, Spain.

Don Juan of Austria is **the bastard knight** and son of Charles V – described here as **the good old man** enjoying his retirement at the time this quatrain is being written. Two years after his victory at Lepanto, Don Juan recaptured Tunis from the Algerian Corsairs in 1573 for his legitimate half-brother, Philip II of Spain. It can be assumed that Don Juan beheaded the ruler who had been installed by the Algerians. Although no record exists of a famine at Sagunto, it is a well-documented fact that Spain suffered several outbreaks of plague between 1570 and 1574. All in all, a successful prophecy.

8 Q51

Le Bizantin faiſant oblation, | The Byzantine making oblation,
Apres auoir Cordube à ſoy reprinſe: | After having taken Cordoba to himself again:
Son chemin long repos pamplation, | Long rest [on] his path, vines cut down,
Mer paſſant proy par la Colongna[1] prinſe. | At sea the passing prey taken by the Pillars of Hercules.

[1]From Colonnes d'Hercule, the Pillars of Hercules – ie the Strait of Gibraltar.

Noted and amateur interpreters alike use this as supporting a "Future Arab Empire" theme. They overlook near-future events in 1558, when the Turkish fleet and its Algerian vassals will score a major rout of a Spanish expedition that lands on the island of Jerba off the coast of Libya. By consequence of the Arab victory Philip loses a string of outposts along the North African coast, excluding Oran. The Turkish corsairs row past the Strait of Gibraltar to lay anchor in the Canary Islands and establish a base for raiding Spanish treasure ships sailing home from the New World.

Nostradamus, writing this quatrain in early 1557, could not have been aware of the Spanish expedition that took place in the latter half of 1558. He correctly sensed the Arab advance into the Western Mediterranean, and perhaps his projected fears added more ambitious Arab conquests to his vision that then actually happened. Not only do they seize treasure ships (**passing prey**) in the Strait of Gibraltar (which did happen), but he has them landing in southern Spain to retake Cordoba, which was once a Moorish stronghold (Sorry, Nostro, no brass alchemist's ring for this one). In his vision the tea-toting Muslims can be seen **making oblation** to Mecca and hacking down the vineyards of reconquered Spain.

8 Q52

Le Roy de Bloys dans Auignon regner,	**The king of Blois to rule in Avignon,**
D'Amboiſe & ſeme[1] viendra le long de Lyndre:	**From Amboise and the Seine, [he]** **will come the length of the Indre:**
Ongle à Poytiers ſainctes æſles ruyner,	**Talon at Poitiers, sacred wings to**
Deuant Bony.	**ruin,**
	Before Boni.

[1]Possibly seme is an erratum for seine; or Old French seme = weak.

Line 1 is an exact repetition of the first in 8 Q38. Amboise is 25 miles down the Loire from Blois. The Indre flows into the Loire another 25 miles downstream from Amboise, below Tours. Poitiers is 75 miles to the south. Seme could be a double-pun for the Old French seme ("weak") blended with an erratum for the Seine river (representing Paris). In other words seme could mean "weak Paris." Line 4 has been dismembered by the censors.

The geographical clues allude to the Conspiracy of Amboise in March 1560, when a band of Protestant nobles attempted to capture the adolescent king Francis II, who was resting at the Château d'Amboise after a hunting vacation. Two days before the attack the Comte de Sancerre was patrolling the Loire outside of Tours when he came across a band of armed Huguenots led by Baron de Castelnau. Sancerre tried to arrest the brigands but they were too numerous, and he fled. After acquiring reinforcements he traced the Huguenots' trail to the Château de Noizay, just a few miles outside of Amboise, and arrested the band. This incident was one of many that exposed the Protestant plot and led to its ignominious and bloody end. "Weak/Seine/Paris" might represent the impotence of the Catholic capital, which could not protect the young king with arms but later waged a war with pamphlets against the Huguenots.

8 Q53

Dedans Bolongne voudra lauer ſes fautes,	**Within Boulogne [or Bologna] he will** **want to wash away his faults,**
Il ne pourra au temple du Soleil:	**He will not be able to [go?] in the** **temple of the Sun:**
Il volera faiſant choſes ſi hautes,	**He will fly away doing things so** **exalted,**
En hierarchie n'en fut oncq vn pareil.	**In the hierarchy there was never one** **to equal him.**

Bouys, Le Pelletier, and Robb make a compelling argument that this quatrain is about the French port of Boulogne on the English Channel rather than the Italian city of Bologna. Ancient London once had a temple to Apollo (**temple of the Sun**), which was destroyed in an earthquake in AD 154. Westminster Abbey was built over its ruins. The man who cannot go there is Napoleon Bonaparte, who had marshaled his new Grand Army of 200,000 men at Boulogne in 1804. He was preparing to cross the Channel and invade England when he was forced to march the army eastwards (**he will fly away**) to stave off a Russian–Austrian invasion in 1805. The resulting continental campaigns of 1805–07 against Austria, Prussia and Russia would contain some of Napoleon's greatest military triumphs (**doing things so exalted**): Austerlitz, Jena, Eylau, and Friedland. Line 3's poetry aptly describes Napoleon as **flying** rather than marching, because he is often represented in the prophecies as the eagle reflected in the standards of his army.

Some scholars have difficulty applying **hierarchy** to Napoleon, since it usually stands for a religious succession of the popes. The habitual response is to drag this quatrain from Boulogne to the 16th-century papal possession of Bologna and prop it up for the glorious ascension of a future pope. I believe Nostradamus used **hierarchy** rather than **reign** or **succession** as a calculated obscurity, to lead interpreters away from the obvious Napoleon theme. Certainly no other French emperor or king was equal to his military genius.

8 Q54

Soubs la couleur du traicte mariage,	**Under the color of the marriage treaty,**
Fait magnanime par grand Chyren felin,	**Magnanimous deed by great Chyren Selin,**
Quintin, Arras recouurez au voyage,	**[St] Quentin and Arras recovered on the journey,**
D'eſpaignols fait ſecond banc macelin.[1]	**Of the Spanish a second [butcher's] bench made.**

[1]Latin *macellum* = meat market, or by context the "butcher's" bill from a great military slaughter.

Nostradamus probably wrote these lines after the humiliating loss of St Quentin and Arras to the Spanish in 1557. At the time Henry II's daughter, Elizabeth, was considered for marriage by Philip II's son, Don Carlos. But Philip's hysterical wife, "Bloody" Mary Tudor, is soon to die, so he decides to take the young Elizabeth for himself in 1559. It is less a prophecy and more a projection of promised revenge to please his king, who will see his enemies butchered in some future victory. In other "Chyren Selin" themes, by missing a date with the shattered lance of Comte de Montgomery, Henry II lives to avenge St Quentin in a battle in Italy in which Philip II of Spain, and/or his protégé, the Duke of Savoy, are captured after their army is annihilated.

8 Q55

Entre deux fleuues ſe verra enſerré,
Tonneaux & caques vnis à paſſer outre,
Huict ponts rompuz chef à tant enferré,
Enfans parfaicts ſont iugulez en coultre.

Between two rivers he will find
  himself enclosed,
Casks and barrels joined to cross
  beyond,
Eight bridges broken, chief so many
  times run through,
Perfect children have throats
  strangled [sliced] on a knife.

Many important battles fought in the last four centuries used pontoon bridges. This quatrain might apply to the Battle of the Berezina in 1812, when pontooniers of Napoleon's retreating army were forced to stand up to their chins in icy waters to tack together two flimsy bridges across the Berezina river so Napoleon's forces could cross before they were surrounded and destroyed by three Russian armies. The **two rivers** refer to the Berezina and the human **river** of the Grand Army, which was little more than a tattered rabble of stragglers by this time. At a third bridge upstream at Borisov a French division was annihilated in a holding battle with a Russian army staged to make them believe the main crossing would occur there. The two bridges at the actual crossing area were severed by cannon shots and ice floes; perhaps they were repaired **eight** times. Once Napoleon's effectives had cut their way through the mobs to cross the bridges, the Russian columns soon appeared in the east. The pontooniers then set the bridges ablaze, stranding over 10,000 terrified stragglers and camp followers (including many women and children) on the eastern bank. Many risked being burned alive and ran over the flaming wooden planks, while others staggered and hopped over the ice floes, only to drown. Many children died in the stampede or were dispatched by a Cossack's knife.

8 Q56

La bande foible le terrre occupera
Ceux de hault lieu feront horribles cris:
Le gros troppeau[1] d'eſtre[2] coin troublera,
Tombe pres D. nebro[3] deſcouuers les
  eſcris.[4]

The feeble group will occupy the earth,
Those of the high place will make
  horrible cries,
The large flock of the outer corner
  will cause trouble,
It falls near D. nebro the calling
  papers discovered.

[1] Flock, herd, drove.
[2] In this case, rather than the verb "to be", probably Old French *estre* = outer.
[3] D. *nebro* = a) possibly a cryptogram for the star Deneb, 1,600 light years from earth in the constellation of Cygnus the Swan – at magnitude −7.1 it is one of the brightest stars in the Milky Way Galaxy; b) the Scottish city of Edinburgh.
[4] Old French *escris* = cries, shouts, callings, announcements; an erratum for *escripts* (*écrits*).

We take another rare plunge into the distant future of humanity, when Earth is inhabited by a genetically and culturally spent civilization. *Those of the high place* in the heavens, members of a human colony on another star system, fall into conflict either with other alien races or with the Terran home world.

Nostradamus may be using bird metaphors here to describe the space-faring humanity of the high Aquarian Age. A spacecraft carrying important information about such a rebellion crashes on a planet in the star system orbiting **D. nebro** (Deneb, by cryptogram) in the Cygnus constellation. References in the Preface describe a stellar expedition from Earth to stars in the neighboring constellation of Aquarius. Attempts to colonize the quadrant apparently fail.

The last line may hide a double meaning. *Escris* comes from the Latin root for **writings**, **papers**, or the Old French word for *cries*. Perhaps Nostradamus is trying to describe a form of communication that blends thought, sound, and writing into one organic medium.

See Index: Cancer and Aquarian space colonies.

8 Q57

De ſouldat ſimple paruiendra en Empire,	**From simple soldier he will attain to Empire.**
De robbe courte paruiendra à la longue:	**From the short robe he will attain to the long:**
Vaillant aux armes en egliſe ou plus pyre,	**Brave in arms or the very worst towards the Church,**
Vexer les preſtres comme l'eau fait l'eſpōge.	**He will vex the priests as water does the sponge.**

An interpreter's tug-of-war has been raging between Garencières and Bouys and Le Pelletier concerning who the **simple soldier** is. According to Garencières, one of the first men to translate *Les Propheties* into English, that soldier is Oliver Cromwell: "I never knew nor heard of any body to whom this Stanza might be better applied, than to the late Usurper, Cromwell, for from a simple soldier, he became to be Lord Protector, and from a student in the University he became a graduate in Oxford, he was valiant in Arms, and the worst Churchman that could be found; as for vexing the priest, I mean the Prelatical Clergy, I believe none went beyond him." (Note that punctuation and grammar is in its original form.)

In the following centuries a better candidate appears: the usurper Napoleon Bonaparte. His contemporary, Bouys, and later Le Pelletier promote the current and temporally correct interpretation I will elaborate below.

Napoleon was a shaggy, underfed artillery officer during the Revolution.

The rigid division of class was dissolved by the fall of the aristocracy, creating a situation for promotion that was both dangerous and advantageous. Napoleon gambled on his merit and made a meteoric rise to become the Revolution's brightest general. The people of France, tired of years of chaos, accepted this new law-and-order dictator. Five years after the death of Robespierre Napoleon overthrew the Directory and proclaimed himself First Consul of France in 1799. By December 1804 he had discarded the **short** consular robe for the **long** ermine train of an emperor, when he was crowned by a blackmailed Pope Pius VII in Nôtre Dame Cathedral in Paris. Both Pope Pius VI and Pius VII (*the priests*) knew nothing but grief and imprisonment during the years of Napoleon's domination of Europe. Napoleon tried to end the temporal powers of the Catholic Church. He desired to make the second pope move the Vatican to Paris from where he could pull the papal strings.

8 Q58

Regne en querelle aux freres diuiſé,	**Realm in quarrel divided between the brothers,**
Prendre les armes & le nom Britannique:	
Tiltre Anglican ſera tard aduiſé,	**To take the arms and the name of Britain:**
Surprins de nuict mener à l'air Gallique.	**The Anglican title will be advised too late,**
	Surprised by night leading into the French air.

Between 1557 and today, no brothers have quarreled over the British throne, let alone triggered a civil war. Perhaps Nostradamus has his genealogy wrong. Rather than brothers it is James II and his son-in-law, William of Orange, fighting over the English crown in November–December 1688 in what later became known as the Glorious Revolution, since the only blood spilled was from James' most royal proboscis, which was prone to bleeding when he was stressed.

James had taken the throne in 1685, and did everything in his power to suppress Parliament and return England to Catholicism. By 1687 he had even arrested the Archbishop of Canterbury and six other prelates. Parliament secretly invited the Dutch Prince William of Orange, who was married to James II's Protestant daughter, Mary, from a previous marriage, to invade England and restore order. William landed his army in November 1688. The conspiracy against James was so complete that his own army marched over to join the Dutch camp. A few months prior to the revolution James made a gesture to reconcile his differences with the bishops of the Anglican Church, but they held firm against him, seeing that his concessions would be forgotten if they relaxed their resistance. But the game was up by early December. James fled into exile in France (*into the French air*) rather than suffer the fate of another Stuart ruler, Charles I.

8 Q59

Par deux fois hault, par deux fois mis à bas,[1]	**Two times put high, two times put low,**
L'orient aussi l'occident foyblira:	**The East also the West will weaken:**
Son aduersaire apres plusieurs combats,	**Its adversary after several battles,**
Par mer chassé au besoing faillira.	**Driven out by sea will fail at a time of need.**

[1]*mis à bas* = put low. But *mis à bas* could also hide the name of a terrorist leader named M(is)abas = Mabus, or (mis) Abas (see 2 Q62, 3 Q63).

A general account of East–West tensions of the 20th and perhaps the early 21st centuries. In other prophecies Nostradamus speaks of his contemporary Arab–Turkish empire collapsing but rising again because of a new source of wealth – this can only be petroleum. Line 1 forecasts the new empire will also be **put low**. This quatrain may stand for the Arab OPEC nations in our near future following the lead of the European Union and creating a Pan-Islamic superstate in the coming 20 years.

The last two lines may detail events of the next world war (or better, free-for-all) breaking out any time between 1999 and the 2020s. The foggy grammar makes it unclear which adversary is vulnerable to water attack. Other quatrains imply it will be the Arab leader named Mabus, or Alus Sanguinaire who will **fear the sea** (6 Q33) because of ocean launched cruise missiles.

8 Q60

Premier en Gaule, premier en Romanie,	**The premier of France, the premier of Romania,**
Par mer & terre aux Angloys & Paris:	**By sea and land for the English and Paris:**
Merueilleux faits par celle grand mesnie,[1]	**Marvelous deeds by that great troop,**
Violant[2] *terax perdra le NORLARIS.*	**Violating [or violent] monster will be denied Lorraine.**

[1]Old French *mesnie* = household, followers, troops.
[2]Violating, or possibly an error for *violent*.

NORLARIS is a fairly obvious cryptogram for Lorraine, which France lost to the German Empire in her humiliating defeat in the Franco-Prussian War (1870–71). The **premiers** or leaders of France and Romania were allied with the British (**English**) against the Germans and the Austro-Hungarian Empires in World War I. In 1915 an Anglo-French expedition (**the English and Paris**) landed in Greece at Salonika and checked a Bulgarian advance into Serbia. They were intended to support Romania, which would soon enter the war. Actually, they did little to help Romania, which was crushed by the Germans in 1916. The expeditionary force in Greece had swollen to half a million men by 1918 and was used successfully to hurl the Bulgarian armies out of Macedonia and much of Serbia (*marvelous deeds . . . great troop*) Nostradamus is not only ranting with Gallic pride, he is accurate when he describes the German soldiers as *violating/violent* monsters for their many atrocities against defenseless Belgian and French civilians throughout the war. By the war's end, the Versailles Treaty forced the German Empire to relinquish Alsace and **Lorraine** to the French.

8 Q61

Iamais par le decouurement du iour,	**Never by the exposure of daylight,**
Ne paruiendra au figne fceptrifere,	**Will he attain to the scepter-bearing**
Que tous fes fieges ne foyent en feiour,	**[royal] sign,**
Portant au coq don du TAG amifere.	**Until all his sieges are at rest,**
	Bringing to the Cock [the] gift of the
	body of armed soldiers.[1]

[1]TAG = a) abbreviation for the Tagus River; b) *tagma* = body of soldiers or legion. With this in mind the line could also read: Bringing to the Cock [France] the gift of the armed Tagus [River].

Interpreters have applied this to different candidates for the French crown who cannot openly attain it by royal blood line or divine right. Le Pelletier (a royalist) tried to pull the Imperial robe over the eyes of his contemporary, Emperor Napoleon III, when he said, "Never will a Napoleonic Emperor reach the throne openly and in direct line. Every time will he take his first steps in the shadow of the republican flag, and he will scarcely conceal his aim, acknowledging that he owes his position to the love of battle with which he had inspired the French people."

Le Pelletier's republican theme applies better to Napoleon III's uncle, Napoleon Bonaparte, who stepped out of the shadow of republicanism to become First Consul of France after his coup d'état against the Directory in 1799. He did not crown himself Emperor until the Revolutionary wars (*all his sieges*) were over in 1802 and the survivors of the British **siege** against his Egyptian expeditionary army were allowed to return home. Then Napoleon usurped the crown of French Emperor in 1804. The first sketch made by the painter Jacques Louis David for his famous panorama of the coronation at Nôtre Dame shows Napoleon acting like a commoner, snatching the crown out of the pope's hands and putting it on his own head.

In the last line the *gift* is an omen of dangers to come for Napoleonic France when French armies in 1809 attempted to retake Portugal with a failed invasion down the valley of the Tagus to conquer Lisbon. **Armed Tagus** aptly describes the ambitious fortifications Sir Arthur Wellesley's British and Portuguese forces built to block all possible invasion routes to Lisbon.

8 Q62

Lors qu'on verra expiler le fainct temple,	**When one sees the holy [or false]**
Plus grand du Rofne leurs facrez	**temple robbed,**
prophaner:	**The greatest one of [Rome?]**
Par eux naiftra peftilence fi ample,	**profaning what is sacred to them:**
Roy fuit iniufte ne fera condamner.	**Through them will be born a**
	pestilence so widespread,
	The King is unjust and will not have
	them condemned.[1]

[1] The line can also read: **The King flees the unjust**, or **The King flees unjustly, [so that] he will not be condemned.**

A general description of the desecration of holy property, tacitly approved of by a heretic king. Fontbrune thinks it is a future sack of the Vatican, which forces a pope from the Catholic capital to the Rhône river region. Lamont in 1942 saw a revolution in Italy after the fall of Mussolini that would threaten the Church. Actually, in Italy's first post-war election the Communist Party almost took power. Kidogo (*Keys to the Predictions of Nostradamus* page 162) bends the meaning of several words and the laws of synecdoche to the extreme, wrestling from them future agricultural fraud in the Common Market, that will go unpunished. Certainly the obscurity of this quatrain can support his interpretation, but it can support just about anyone else's as well.

8 Q63

Quand l'adultere bleffé fans coup aura	**When the adulterer wounded without**
Meurdry la femme & le fils par defpit,	**a blow will have**
Femme affoumee l'enfant eftranglera:	**Murdered his wife and [his] son out**
Huict captifs prins, s'eftouffer fans refpit.	**of spite,**
	Wife beaten to death, the child he
	will strangle:
	Eight captives taken, to choke
	without respite.

This story of adultery, family violence, a hostage situation and murder sounds like any nightly local news broadcast on US television during the 1990s, but its generality leaves it open for any time in the past between now and 1555, if not the next 1,800 years to AD 3797. The wound **without a blow** is obviously an effect on the adulterer's ego, which triggers madness and mayhem. Choked **without respite** could point to a mass murder by strangulation, or perhaps as the result of tear gas shot into the killer's holdout, choking him and his eight hostages.

8 Q64

Dedans les Ifles les enfans tranfportez,	**Within the Isles the children [are] transported,**
Les deux de fept feront en defefpoir,	**Two out of seven will be in despair,**
Ceux du terrouer¹ en feront fupportez,	**Those of the land will be supported by it,**
Nom pelle prins des ligues fuy l'efpoir.	**Nom pelle taken, the hope of the leagues fails.**

¹Old French *terrouer* = soil, land, ground.

At the beginning of World War II as many as two million British children were evacuated from the cities and the coastal regions along the Channel and North Sea. Roughly two out of seven children under the age of 14 had to leave their homes. One can imagine the scene of despair reflected in Nostradamus' watery portal into the future: tots and their parents saying tearful farewells at the railway and bus stations of London, a city spotted with the shadows of barrage balloons stretching their lines taut, waiting for the Luftwaffe. The majority of English adults supported the harsh measure because it freed many parents to sustain the weapons-manufacturing and agriculture industries during the darkest years when England stood virtually alone against Hitler's Reich. The evacuations no doubt saved many innocent lives during the Blitz in 1940–41 and the V-1 and V-2 rocket attacks of 1944–45.

The enigma **nom pelle** draws our attention to southern France in the year 1942, when cities that had avoided German occupation saw the jack-booted invaders appear in their streets with the fall of the Vichy government. **Nom pelle** could be a cryptogram for "Mon(t)pell(i)e(r)." If Nostradamus has masked the meaning of **league** by putting it in plural, then the fallen **league**(s) must therefore be the League of Nations, which could not sustain Peace on Earth as has been hoped.

8 Q65

Le vieux fruftré du principal efpoir,	**The old one frustrated in his principal hope,**
Il paruiendra au chef de fon empire:	**He will attain to the head of his empire:**
Vingt mois tiendra le regne à grand pouuoir,	**Twenty months he will hold the realm with great power,**
Tiran, cruel en delaiffant vn pire.	**Tyrant, cruel in giving way to one worse.**

Nostradamus' portal stays trained on Vichy France. On 10 July 1940 Marshal Pétain, the 83-year-old hero of World War I, held a rump session of the French Assembly. It granted him absolute powers until a new constitution should be created. Twenty months later the aged president relinquished most of his powers to his sinister vice-premier, Pierre Laval, who was a far more passionate Nazi collaborationist. Pétain, the **old one**, had a long list of frustrated aspirations for the new *État français*. He wanted to turn the clock back to the days prior to the French Revolution when clericalism, authoritarianism, and paternalism reigned in a traditionalist France. Pétain envisioned Vichy as a regime above republican politics around which all French people of goodwill could rally. The doddering old man's dream had little to do with Vichy's reality. Pétain's Utopia became one of the most viciously partisan governments in French history. After 20 months he was little more than a powerless figurehead with the tyrannical Laval pulling his strings.

8 Q66

Quand l'efcriture D.M.[1] trouuee,	**When the inscription "D. M." [is] found,**
Et caue antique à lampe defcouuerte:	**And the ancient cave is discovered with a lamp:**
Loy, Roy, & Prince Vlpian efprouuee,	**Law, King and Prince Ulpian tried,**
Pauillon Royne & Duc fous la couuerte.	**Pavillion, Queen and Duke under the blanket.**

[1]Latin abbreviation for *Diis Manibus* = At the Hands of the Gods, an equivalent in epitaphs of the inscription "Here lies . . ."

"D.M." stands for the ancient Roman inscription *Diis Manibus* (At the Hands of the Gods), which one finds starting most epitaphs. Many commentators from Chavigny on have woven fantastic and far-fetched interpretations for the ancient lamp-lit cave. To them, "D.M." is not what it seems. Some thought it stood for the resting place of Nostradamus' original drafts of *Les Propheties* or is a hidden stash of decoding instructions for unlocking the prophet's obscurity. Renuncio Boscolo is convinced it stands for a place in his home town of Turin called Domus Morozzo, where Nostradamus is purported to have left an inscription on a marble plaque.

He cites only one source for the existence of this inscription, a Professor Ben Audi Segre of Jerusalem who had read one of his books. The professor was informed of the current location of this plaque by his aunt. Boscolo and Professor Segre found it in a Turin office building just where she said it would be and, lo and behold! what synchronicity! The office building is right next to the bookstore where Mr Boscolo bought his first

Nostradamus book! Because of this discovery Boscolo waxes Virgin Mary-like about the Holy Ghost of the prophet impregnating his inter- pretations. He declares that a "new light would shine upon the darkness of the quatrains." He adds that we should expect political changes at the same time (as if something as ubiquitous as political changes don't happen at any other time). Boscolo claims to have found the inscription in 1975, the same year Spanish dictator Francisco Franco died and King Juan Carlos ascended to power. He makes an unconvincing argument that the **Ulpian** noble family name can be applied to **Prince** Juan Carlos' parents conceiving him **under the blanket** somewhere in Rome, where the future king was born.

One can find two photos of Boscolo's plaque on pages 56, and 57 of his book *Nostradamus: Key to the Future*. I am puzzled by it. For one thing "D.M." is not to be found anywhere on the inscription. We have only the unnamed aunt of Professor Segre as a witness that it was once tacked on the wall of Domus Morozzo. No interview with the aunt is offered by Boscolo.

Now, I could make my own far-fetched claims about "D.M." based on accidental coincidences. In the summer of 1986, I was overseeing the final design of my first Nostradamus book in a lovely villa 20 minutes out- side of Florence that was once owned by the opera singer Enrico Caruso. Over on the next hill sat a cluster of mausoleums which are known in Italy as a city of the dead. I toured this village of tombs one day and saw many "D.M." inscriptions. What a remarkable coincidence! Does this make me *the* Nostradamus scholar? Should I get all excited about being in Caruso's villa because I too happened to be a professional opera singer for six years prior to my writing career? Golly!

I would like to alter Boscolo's statement. Rather than "shine a new light upon the darkness of the quatrains," we interpreters and debunkers alike more often use the darkness of the quatrains to reflect the light of our egos.

8 Q67

PAR. CAR. NERSAF[1], *à ruyne grãd difcorde,*	**Paris, Carcassone [and] France, to**
Ne l'vn ne l'autre n'aura election,	**ruin, great discord,**
Nerfaf du peuple aura amour & concorde,	**Neither the one nor the other will**
Ferrare, Colonne[2] grande protection.	**have an election,**
	Nersaf will have the love and concord
	of the people,
	Ferrara, Colonna great protection.

[1]PAR (apocope for Paris) CAR (ditto for Carcassonne) NERSAF (near-anagram for France).
[2]Either the Roman family Colonna, or Cologne (*Colonia Agrippina*).

It is pretty difficult to tie all these far-ranging places together and make some sense out of this quatrain. It seems to be a blend of the French Wars of Religion and the Habsburg-Valois War. First off, Carcassone is in Languedoc, and was a gathering point for Huguenots. Paris would suffer a popular rebellion and siege (**great discord**). Many sieges and battles would punctuate three decades of general social and religious turmoil throughout France.

The final lines may clue us in to the principal subject. The Italian locations are at least figurative leads to a protagonist. Ferrara was a duchy belonging to the House of Este. The Duc d'Este was father-in-law of the man who, it could be said, lit the match that started the Wars of Religion, François de Guise. The Duc d'Este was the commander-in-chief of the Franco-Papal forces fighting the Spanish in 1557 during the Habsburg-Valois Wars. The Colonna family of Rome was pro-Spanish, but this fact has little relevance unless **Colonna** stands for the German city of Cologne. I can't see much more by waving my hands in the smoke of this prophecy.

8 Q68

Vieux Cardinal par le ieufne deceu,	**The old Cardinal deceived by the**
Hors de fa charge fe verra defarmé,	**young one,**
Arles ne monftres double foit apperceu,	**Outside of his office, he will see**
Et Liqueduct[1] & le Prince embaufmé.	**himself disarmed,**
	Arles do not show that the double is
	perceived,
	And [borne by water] both he and the
	Prince embalmed.

[1]Nostradamus' compound word, possibly for *ille aquae ductus*, "he who is driven [or led] by water." Reynaud-Plense thinks it hides a more vulgar meaning, the Latin verb *liqueducere* = to rot away into liquid form.

Here is another extremely accurate prophecy. In 1642 Cardinal Richelieu was at 57 already an old man and close to death. He was obliged to travel through France in a purple-canopied barge pulled along the riverbank. His 22-year-old disciple, Cinq-Mars, had double-crossed him out of most of his powers and command of the army (**outside of his office . . . himself disarmed**), but Nostradamus sees one last gesture of power for the man who actually ruled France behind the ineffectual Louis XIII. Le Pelletier (1867) gives us the best interpretation of any: "Old Cardinal Richelieu will be unseated by the young Cinq-Mars, his former protégé, who will cause him to lose the favor of Louis XIII and to resign his office; but he will receive, some time afterwards, from the town of Arles, a copy of the treaty negotiated by Cinq-Mars on 13 March 1642, with Spain, in the name of Monsieur, the brother of Louis XIII; and he will have this treaty shown to the King, who will recall the Cardinal at once. Richelieu will then travel up the Rhône, from Tarascon to Lyons, sick and lying on his bed, on a boat, leading with him as prisoners Cinq-Mars and de Trou; then he will go down the Seine, in the same manner, from Fontainebleau to Paris, where he will die two months after, on December 4, 1642. On the following 14 May Louis XIII will die also, and both will be embalmed, according to ancient custom."

8 Q69

Aupres du ieune le vieux ange baiſſer,	Beside the young one the old angel falls,
Et le viendra ſurmonter à la fin:	And he will come to surpass him in the end:
Dix ans eſgaux au plus vieux rabaiſſer,	Ten years equal to most, the old one to fall again,
De trois deux l'vn huictieſme ſeraphin.	Of three two one eighth Seraphim.

This seems to be a more general take of the previous quatrain. Nostradamus, with tongue in cheek, calls a political creature like Richelieu an **old angel** falling from favor with Louis XIII and supplanted by his double-dealing protégé, Cinq-Mars. Line 2 is accurate. The protégé would be arrested as a conspirator and Richelieu would return to favor. History would see him **surpass** all his rivals as the man who de facto ruled France during the reign of Louis XIII. When the old cardinal and his king died within months of each other, a new **angel** in cardinal's robes would pull the strings while his charge, Louis XIV, was in his royal minority. Louis XIV was four years old when Cardinal Mazarin became regent. Technically speaking Louis' minority lasted exactly **ten years**. This would now make Mazarin the **old one** falling out of favor. Around the time Louis XIV was 14, Mazarin would be exiled from France twice (**fall again**) because of his intrigues with the Prince de Condé against the French Parliament in 1551 and later during the civil war of the Fronde in 1652. With all this said, the final line is possibly a puzzling reference to the monks of the **Seraphim** Order more popularly known as the Franciscans.

8 Q70

Il entrera vilain, meſchant, infame,	He will enter, wicked, unpleasant, infamous,
Tyranniſant la Meſopotamie:[1]	Tyrannizing over Mesopotamia [Iraq]:
Tous amys faits d'adulterine d'ame,	All friends made by the adulterous lady,
Tertre horrible noir de phiſonomie.	The land dreadful and black of aspect.

[1]Greek meso-potamios, between rivers, in this case the Tigris and Euphrates rivers, specifically the delta region in the southern portion of Iraq, where Saddam Hussein is methodically exterminating the marsh Arabs at this time.

The modern land of post-war Iraq fits these apocalyptic adjectives. It is a dark and unpleasant place ruled by a dictator who has become infamous worldwide for ruthless oppression, particularly of the Arab Shi'ites of Mesopotamia and the Kurds in northern Iraq.

The Second Gulf War left Kuwait covered in a shroud of oil ash (*the land dreadful and black in aspect*). Another dreadful legacy is the coalition bombers and guided missiles unloading over 100,000 tons of bombs on Kuwait and Iraq, killing 20,000 to 50,000 Iraqi troops and wiping out enough of Iraq's civilian infrastructure to cause a breakdown of its water purification system. As a result of the war within a year an estimated 170,000 Iraqi children may have died from gastrointestinal diseases complicated by malnutrition. After five years the death estimate has risen to 500,000 children.

Iraq is poised to break up any time between now and the millennium. By that time Iran will have quietly amassed an armed force to match that of Saddam Hussein's prior to Operation Desert Storm and may yet fill the political void by uniting with the Shi'ite Iraqi Arabs to form a new pan-Shi'ite state. Although increasing numbers of ayatollahs are supporting radical Shi'ite fundamentalism, the moderate Rasmanjani still remains in power at the time of writing.

If a Third Gulf War should take place between 1996 and 2000, Iran's priests of the Jihad will show the world they have learned lessons from Saddam Hussein's blunders: Do not take the border-dispute bait before you have achieved the means to arm your regional ballistic missiles, your super-guns, and your bombers with nuclear weapons.

In the third and final Gulf War waged at a time of dreadful astrological aspects, a **black and angry** (6 Q33) ayatollah could sweep across the Middle East to the sound of jet engines and nuclear-tipped missiles to do battle with Israel and the forces of the West led by the United States.

8 Q71

Croiſtra le nombre ſi grand des aſtronomes, | **The number of astronomers will grow**
Chaſſez, bannis & liures cenſurez, | **so great,**
L'an mil ſix cens & ſept par ſacre glomes,[1] | **[That they will be] driven out,**
Que nul aux ſacres ne feront aſſeurez. | **banished and their books censured,**
| **The year 1607 by the [Catholic]**
| **assemblies for the consecration,**
| **So that none will be safe from the**
| **priests.**

[1]Latin, *glomus* = body of people, assembly.

This is a second dated failure for the year 1607. No specific papal bull came from Pope Paul V permitting persecution of astrologers by the

Inquisition in that year. Some Nostradamians say this was fulfilled when astrology was censored by a Council of Malines in that year. This council is a figment of some Nostradamian's imagination, sustained by lazy research down through the centuries. It seems that some commentator made this fact up, and was thereupon copied by successors. No such council convened in that year. A similar persecution-of-astrologers theme arises in 4 Q18, but I believe it centers on the purge of soothsayers in the Third Reich in 1941–42.

8 Q72

Champ Perufin d'lenorme deffaite,
Et le conflit tout aupres de Rauenne:
Paffage facre lors qu'on fera la fefte,
Vainqueur vaincu cheual manger la venne.

[On the] Perugian field, Oh! what an
  enormous defeat,
And the conflict very close to
  Ravenna:
Sacred passage then they will
  celebrate the feast,
Vanquisher vanquished, the horse's
  flesh to eat.

In Nostradamus' day Perugia and Ravenna were in the papal states. There is 100 miles of territory between Ravenna and Perugia. An earlier reference to fighting near Lake Perugia (Trasimene) fits well with the Allied breakthrough of the German Trasimene Line in June 1944. But nothing here either makes or refutes any clear link to anything. Prieditis also believes this could represent the final engagements in northern Italy during World War II. The British Army broke through the last German defensive line at Ravenna, then began its sweep across the eastern Po river valley. In 1724 an anonymous critic of Nostradamus declared this quatrain to be a retroactive prophecy for the victory of Gaston de Foix at Ravenna in 1512.

8 Q73

Soldat Barbare le grand Roy frappera,
Iniuftement non eflogné de mort,
L'auare mere du fait caufe fera,
Coniurateur & regne en grand remort.

The barbarian soldier will strike the
  great King,
Unjustly not far away from death,
The avaricious mother will be the
  cause of the deed,
Conspirator and realm in great
  remorse.

Jochmans' interpretation published in 1993 is worth quoting: "Saddam [Hussein] is here predicted to be assassinated, or he will carry out a daring terrorist act to assassinate the prime minister of Israel. Either occurrence will take place during an important banquet or dinner gathering, or celebration" (*Nostradamus Now* page 193).

A number of points were fulfilled in late 1995, when Israeli Prime Minister Yitzhak Rabin was gunned down in Jerusalem a few minutes after leaving a festive rally celebrating the Middle East peace effort. The assailant, however, was not an agent of Saddam Hussein or an Arab sympathizer but a Jewish fundamentalist. Nevertheless, it could be said that his assassination served the designs of Saddam Hussein by putting Binyamin Netanyahu in Rabin's place as prime minister. It remains to be seen whether the hawkish Netanyahu can make peace with the Arabs.

There is still time to find out if Jochmans' first alternative future – an assassination of Saddam Hussein at a rally – will take place. I would add another potential scenario: the assassination by Islamic terrorists of a US president who will be elected in the year 2000. Perhaps the *Barbare* assassins come from Libya or Algeria. The next Jupiter–Saturn conjunction in Taurus in the year 2000 sets destiny's stage for another American president to either die or be killed while in office. Be very watchful of the vice-presidential candidates in that election. One will probably be a woman, and she could become president.

8 Q74

En terre neufue bien auant Roy entré,	A king entered very far into the new land,
Pendant ſubges luy viendront faire acueil,	While his subjects will come to bid him welcome,
Sa perfidie aura tel rencontré,	His perfidy will have such an effect,
Qu'aux citadins lieu de feſte & recueil.	That for the citizens a cause for a festival and reception.

Just how do we translate *terre neufue* (new world)? It depends on what intimate historical details or imaginings an interpreter prefers. The theme is clear enough. A king or leader enters deep inside a new territory; his subjects come to welcome him as some kind of liberator. The odd twists of phrase in line 4 reveal that perfidy is in the eye of the beholder. To his followers the king's controversial actions and statements are cause for a celebration. I therefore read between the lines that to the mainstream public he is thought as perfidious (or maybe Nostradamus feels insulted by the future leader's alien values). Nostradamus rarely speaks of the **new land** of America directly. And I can't rule out a distant future theme for some trouble between a new human space colony and its native alien neighbors occupying a "New Earth."

Because a number of quatrains concerning spiritual **kings** coming from the East are indexed with the numbers 74, 75, 76, I can't rule out the following exotic interpretation:

Nostradamus rarely missed a world newsmaker. It is doubtful he missed the controversial Bhagwan Shree Rajneesh (Osho), a mystic from the

East who left India to stay in America from 1981 through 1985. By the mid-1980s images of the little man with the knit cap and long, flowing white beard, dancing behind the wheel of one of his 94 Rolls-Royces to the music of his red-clad followers on his daily drive-bys were broadcast on televisions and printed in newspapers all over the world. His experimental commune Rajneeshpuram (which means "Vision of the Lord [king] of the Full Moon") became world famous. An entire spiritual city of 5,000 citizens and 20,000 guests was created from scratch, flourished, and became a ghost town all within four tumultuous years.

The raison d'être of Osho's passage to America has been the subject of many debates (and will be the subject of a forthcoming book from me). Whether his commune in Oregon, which so plagued and pushed the buttons of the Christian political right and Ronald Reagan's administration, was just a circus, an evil fraud, or one of history's most significant religious experiments remains to be understood. For the present matter, this quatrain could be a prophecy about Osho, represented here as a spiritual master or **king** who has **entered very far into the new land** of the United States. If one is coming **from the east** as Nostradamus implies this foreseen spiritual teacher will do, settling in Oregon on the west coast of America is indeed a deep penetration.

It is documented by video cameras that upon his arrival at the new commune city, Osho was greeted by his followers with dancing, singing and general celebration. In the following year, the press was abuzz with the gathering of 15,000 to 20,000 followers at the first of four annual World Celebrations. The celebrants convened on the 88,000-square-foot linoleum floor of a huge greenhouse converted into a meditation hall. Anyone watching television during the summers of 1983 through 1985 could not miss the image of an ocean of red-clothed people dancing ecstatically around the podium of their spiritual master. I myself will never forget the sight of 20,000 people yelling, jumping and dancing to the rhythms of what the Rajneeshees called Dynamic Meditation, a brilliantly designed form of structured catharsis that Osho claims can clear the way for authentic meditation.

What would Nostradamus make of such a vision of hopping youngsters in red bikinis and robes shaking the waters in his brass bowl? Was their guru a charlatan exploiting their innocence? Or were Nostradamus' ideas of religion being confronted as were the Christian sensibilities of President Reagan's righteously-winged administration which exerted political and legal pressures to destroy the Indian mystic's visionary city? What is certain is that every seemingly outrageous device of Osho, such as "free sex" and the Rolls-Royces, or his witty and devastating criticisms of politics and the world's religions, only provided a platform on which his disciples celebrated with more totality.

Were they brainwashed followers?

Are we brainwashed followers of our society?

Quatrain Indexing Date: Q74 = 1974? A number of seers such as Madame Blavatsky predicted a sudden influx of interest in Eastern mysticism in America for the mid-1970s. Moreover, quatrains describing this event are indexed in the mid-70s of a number of Nostradamus' Centuries. See also 10 Q74 and 10 Q75.

8 Q75

Le pere & filz feront meurdris enfemble,	**The father and son will be murdered together,**
Le prefecteur[1] dedans fon pauillon:	**The count within his pavilion:**
La mere à Tours du filz ventre aura enfle.	**The mother at Tours will have her belly swollen with a son.**
Caiche[2] verdure de feuilles papillon.[3]	**Herb chest with little leaves of paper.**

[1]late Latin praefectius = Count, but equivalent also to many other offices.
[2]Provençal caicha = chest, box, coffer.
[3]Old French papillon = small bit of paper.

More than any other interpreter, Leoni has done his homework to ascertain whether this specific prophecy came close to fulfillment. Here's the test: A count within his tent or pavilion must murder the king and dauphin together. At the same time the pregnant wife of either the king or prince will be at Tours. As Leoni says, "The odds against this joint assassination with a pregnant widow at Tours must run into the millions."

So far in the history of royalty in France or royalty of any other country, beginning in 1558, no monarch and his heir have been murdered at the same time as the expectant mother of either man's seed is living or visiting Tours. "Of the sixteen French monarchs (fourteen kings and two emperors) since 1557," Leoni says, "only five died in any fashion resembling murder (Henry II, III and IV and Louis XVI and XVII). Only in the case of Louis XVI and Louis XVII was there any proximity in the time of the 'murders' (twenty-nine months)." One can argue that Nostradamus is vague enough to make the murdered king and dauphin any murdered political leader and protégé. But no matter how you slice it with your guillotine, no murder of important leaders has left a pregnant widow in Tours in the last 440 years.

Perhaps this is an alternative-future failure for the notorious papers of the iron chest of Louis XVI, the unsubstantiated evidence used in court to convict him of treason. King and dauphin did die fairly close together in time. The problem is, Marie Antoinette was neither pregnant nor in a dungeon in Tours, unless Nostradamus meant the **towers** of the Temple prison in Paris.

8 q76

Plus macelin que Roy en Angleterre,	**More a butcher than a King of England,**
Lieu obfcur nay par force aura l'empire:	**Born of obscure rank he will gain**
Lafche fans foy, fans loy faignera terre,	**Empire through force:**
Son temps s'approche fi pres que ie	**A coward without faith, without law,**
foufpire.	**he will bleed the land,**
	His time approaches so near that I sigh.

Le Pelletier was the first to attribute this verse to Oliver Cromwell (1599–1658), the soldier, statesman, enthusiastic Puritan, and denier of the divine right of kings who played a decisive part in winning the English Civil War (1642–51) for the Puritans. He was declared Lord Protector in 1653 and established excellent links with Protestant countries in Europe.

For a prophet who could look perhaps 7,000 years into the future, the birth of Oliver Cromwell, the man who made England a republic, might well have seemed very near indeed. Nostradamus the Catholic and royalist had little love for the fiery Puritan leader of the Roundheads, describing him as a man who would **butcher** a King and **bleed the land**, but he does not begrudge him his key role in making England a world power. Perhaps too, Nostradamus' visions showed him the real Cromwell who, despite his public claims to divine protection, was *a coward without faith*, removing his armor only behind the safety of a bolted door and living in daily fear of assassination.

8 q77

L'antechrift trois bien toft annichiliez,	**The Third Antichrist very soon**
Vingt & fept ans fang durera fa guerre:	**annihilated,[2]**
Les heretiques morts, captifs, exilez,	**Twenty-seven years his bloody war will**
Sang corps humain eau rogie grefler[1] terre.	**last:**
	The heretics [are] dead, captives
	exiled,
	Blood-soaked human bodies, and a
	reddened, icy hail covering the earth.

[1]French *grêler* = to hail; to ravage, ruin, or spoil by hail. Kidogo cites *grêlé* = pock-marked; airborne pollution, contamination, or in this case chemical or biological weapons.
[2]Variation: **The Antichrist very soon annihilates the three [brothers].** This might imply a general dating for these events around the time the three Kennedy brothers are killed by the forces of the Antichrist. A common oversight is to assume that the last living brother of the slain President Kennedy, Senator Edward Kennedy, is the third brother targeted for assassination by the anti-Christian forces. The Kennedy patriarch, Joseph Kennedy, had earmarked the oldest brother, Joseph Jr, as the number-one choice for the presidency. Young Joe was killed while fighting "anti-Christian" Nazi forces in World War II. Interesting theories abound that implicate the pro-war and "anti-Christian" forces of the Cold War military industrial complex as well as the Mafia in the assassination of John and Robert Kennedy. It can be argued that Edward Kennedy, the youngest brother, was never part of the prophecy.

If 10 Q72 gives us July 1999 as the ending to the Third Antichrist's 27-year war, one must count back 27 years to find the war's beginning, 1972. (Note the reversal of "2" and "7," perhaps we have a link through a numbers game.) The following year the Yom Kippur conflict precipitated the Arab oil embargo of 1974. Clearly the early 1970s observed a new pan-Arab economic empire starting to flex its global military and economic muscles. After 1973 Western industrial survival became ever more dependent on Middle Eastern oil. The surviving superpower of the Cold War, the United States, now relies on the Middle East for over 50 percent of its oil. The region that fuels modern civilization is the forewarned millennial battlefield of Armageddon.

The START (strategic arms reduction treaties) I and II will still allow Russia and America to wield 7,000 intercontinental ballistic missiles and submarine-launched warheads. That is almost six times the number of nuclear arms that existed during the Cuban Missile Crisis in 1961 – poised to destroy the world.

Nostradamus is one of many prophets down through history who warns us to be most vigilant against Armageddon when it appears – and let me repeat "appears" – that peace is at hand. Currently Russian and US missiles are not targeting each other's cities, but don't fall into that millennial dream of peace too quickly. Yeltsin has a serious heart condition. The world is one missed heartbeat away from a new Russian government of communist hard-liners, or worse, neo-Fascists. It would take only a few days, if not a few hours, to retarget all the missiles again.

New computerized climate models show that a nuclear exchange of 7,000 warheads between Russia and the United States can still create enough debris and smoke from 7,000 cities to create a nuclear winter. In fact, it would take no more than the obliteration of several hundred cities to thrust enough dust, oil, and smoke into the upper atmosphere to spread the funeral cloud of nuclear winter across the Northern, and even the Southern Hemispheres. The lack of sunlight and the climatic disruption would severely damage or kill off most plant life in the coming year. The human food chain may never adequately recover. Without the grain and rice baskets of the Northern Hemisphere, two to three billion people could die from starvation the following year.

The detonated weapons could rapidly increase the degradation of Earth's ozone layer, allowing direct ultraviolet radiation (10 Q72's *terror ... from the skies*) to bake Earth's surface – and the survivors – once the dust clouds of Armageddon vanish.

The last line assigns an ironic potential destiny to today's inadequate gestures of disarmament. Rather than a full-scale nuclear winter, the climax to the Third Antichrist's terrible war will be reached as the northern kings unleash only enough nuclear mayhem to annihilate the three Middle Eastern kings of the terrorist triumvirate. The tons of smoke and dust damaging Earth's atmosphere and food chains will be enough to create a mere nuclear "autumn." We will look out of our windows and find not radioactive snows but a dust-reddened ice rain falling over the entire planet.

8 Q78

Vn Bragamus[1] auec la langue torte,
Viendra des dieux le ſanctuaire:
Aux heretiques il ouurira la porte,
En ſuſcitant l'Egliſe militaire.

A broadsword [or a soldier of fortune]
   with his twisted tongue,
Will come to the sanctuary of the gods:
To the heretics he will open the gate,
Thus arousing the militant Church.

[1]Old French bragamas = broadsword. Derivative: Provençal Braimanso = a soldier of fortune.

The European armies of the 16th and 17th centuries relied primarily on the broadsword and pike of mercenaries. In most cases these soldiers came from the many kingdoms of Germany, where the **twisted** blade of a Bragamus sword was invented. The verse gives us a sweeping overview of nearly a century of Protestant and Catholic strife across Europe, starting in 1562 with the onset of the French Wars of Religion and through till 1648 with the end of both the Dutch eighty-year War for Independence and the Thirty Years War. We see a vision of mercenary soldiers breaking down the doors of churches, and the counter-attack of the Catholic armies. Nostradamus blames one man in particular for all this brouhaha, but he doesn't name him outright. Perhaps **he** is a Holy Roman Emperor who mollycoddled Lutheran Imperial electors, giving them license to seek independence from Imperial power, triggering the Thirty Years War in 1618. Or perhaps this is Philip II of Spain, coercing the Dutch population of the Spanish Netherlands into a full-fledged revolt by 1568. A French culprit is the most likely choice of Nostradamus. And for once he may have gotten a prophecy right about his nemesis, John Calvin, whose extreme Protestantism was a major cause of the Catholic Church's militancy during the Counter-Reformation.

8 Q79

Qui par fer pere perdra nay de
   Nonnaire,[1]
De Gorgon ſur la ſera ſang perfetant,[2]
En terre eſtrange fera ſi tout de taire,
Qui bruſlera luy meſme & ſon enfant.

He who by steel will lose his father
   born of Virgo,
From Gorgon [thereupon] will be blood
   conceiving again while pregnant,
On an alien Earth he will do
   everything to keep silent,
He who will burn himself and his child.

[1]Medieval Latin nonneria = nunnery.
[2]Apheresis of Latin superfetans = conceiving again (while pregnant).

If *Nonnaire* is figurative for the constellation of Virgo the Virgin, this otherwise hopelessly obscure quatrain could make some sense as a eugenics experiment conducted centuries from now.

If one paints this in the colors of science fiction, we have here a man born in a space colony in the constellation of Virgo, who will lose his father from an injection (*steel* syringe). This man will genetically bond with a hideous extraterrestrial woman comparable to the mythical **Gorgon**, one of three snaky-haired sisters whose ugliness turned the beholder to stone. Perhaps Nostradamus, with his archaic ideas of beauty can describe future alien races only as monsters or repulsive. Anyway, a genetically transformed humanoid or alien with unusual gynecological abilities has her ovum impregnated in an artificial laboratory womb while she carries another baby to full term in her own womb. The **alien Earth** could be a colony on any number of planets in our own solar system, or upon planets orbiting stars in the constellations of Cancer and Aquarius, as implied elsewhere by Nostradamus. The eugenics experiment is a disaster. The mixture of two humanoid races produces a monstrous child so repulsive that the father immolates himself and the child.

8 Q80

Des innocens le ſang de veſue & vierge,	**Blood of the innocent, of the widow and**
Tant de maux faits par moyen ſe grand	**virgin,**
Roge:	**So many evils committed by means of**
Sainctz ſimulacres trempez en ardant	**the great Red.**
cierge,	**Holy Icons placed over burning candles.**
De frayeur crainte ne verra nul que boge.	**Terrified by fear, none will be seen to**
	move.

Thousands of Russian Orthodox churches were systematically dynamited and countless religious icons burned by order of the early Bolshevik government of Lenin and later by the **great Red** of all communist dictators, Josef Stalin, whose reign of terror over his own subjects was the greatest of the 20th century. Stalin liquidated at least 10 million Soviets, and an equal number disappeared or died in Siberian labor camps. The first line can be applied to the vicious execution of the last Czarina and her virgin daughters, or it is a general description of those numberless vulnerable victims of Stalinism.

8 Q81

Le neuf empire en deſolation,	**The new empire in desolation,**
Sera changé du pole aquilonaire:	**It will be changed by the northern pole.**
De la Sicile viendra l'eſmotion,	**From Sicily the commotion will come,**
Troubler l'empriſe à Philip tributaire.	**To trouble the enterprise tributary to**
	Philip.

The **Philip** here probably refers to no one more enigmatic than our prophet's contemporary, Philip II of Spain. Nostradamus foresees a Habsburg civil war between Philip and Uncle Ferdinand over the division of Charles V's empire. A great insurrection against Philip's authority apparently starts in Sicily. This would bring desolation to his **new** Spanish Empire.

Nothing like this happened, but one cannot rule out an alternative future destiny avoided by some correct action of Philip II. If the name **Philip** had been replaced by "Hister" or "Duce," every scholar of the post-World War II period would have said, "Gee, Nostradamus got it right again. Both Hitler's and Mussolini's **new empires** began to collapse when Allied forces invaded Sicily in 1943."

Of course this does not rule out a future world leader named **Philip** coming to grief in the 21st century. Will the **new empire** be the European Union or the United States (both **northern pole** super-nations)? Quatrain 92 of Century 3 also speaks of a great empire in desolation. It is forced to move south. This could signify a migration of survivors from some cataclysmic event, either from the devastation of a Third World War or from lethal ozone holes developing over the Northern Hemisphere by 2020.

8 Q82

Ronge long, ſec¹ faiſant du bon valet,	**Lean, slow, wrinkled, playing the good valet,**
A la parfin n'aura que ſon congie,	**In the end he will have nothing but his dismissal,**
Poignant poyſon & lettres au coulet,	**Acute poison and letters in his collar,**
Sera ſaiſi eſchappé en dangie.	**He will be seized, escapade in danger.²**

¹Dry, arid; withered; lean, gaunt; emotionally barren.
²Alternative: *He will be seized, escaped into dangers.*

Here is another instance of a quatrain predicting local or personal events concerning Nostradamus and his immediate circle. A creaking old butler is dismissed. A letter of poisonous words hidden in his collar? Maybe the butler failed as a messenger (**escapade in danger**) or has escaped into the arms of danger.

Prieditis believes this is a veiled prophecy against the 18th-century French philosopher, Jean Jacques Rousseau, who started life as a butler for several families of nobility. Far from **wrinkled**, he was a young valet with a **lean**, **slow** energy and dry heart. He was eventually dismissed by all his employers and took on a highly successful writing career, becoming one of the most cherished philosophers of the French Revolution. On the other hand, his writings are viewed by Nostradamus as **poison**, for they are later adopted by some of the Revolution's worst tyrants, such as Robespierre, to inflict bloodshed and terror.

8 Q83

Le plus grand voile hors de port de Zara,	*The greatest sail out of the port of Zara,*
Pres de Bifance fera fon entreprinfe:	*Near Byzantium will he manage his*
D'ennemy parte & l'amy ne fera,	*enterprise:*
Le tiers à deux fera grand pille & prinfe.	*Separation of enemy and friend will*
	not take place,
	The third will impose great pillage
	and capture upon both.

Zara is the Venetian name for the legendary Dalmatian seaport that is now Dubrovnik. Venice held it when Nostradamus composed this verse, which I and a number of other Nostradamians down through the centuries suspect is either a retroactive prophecy or a historical aside describing how Venice acquired Zara in the infamous Fourth Crusade of 1202.

Venice had agreed to transport the Crusaders to Egypt for 85,000 marks and half the booty. When the Crusaders reached into their chain-mail pockets, and found themselves short on cash, they made a deal with the Venetian Doge: to first sieze from the Hungarians the coveted port of Zara for Venice, in exchange for half the Islamic booty and transport to the Middle East. When the soldiers of the Cross sacked and butchered their Hungarian brethren at Zara, Pope Innocent III excommunicated the entire army of the Fourth Crusade, from their commander Boniface III, Duke of Montferrat, down to the rattiest Christian-killing soldiers for Christ. The Crusaders, ever faithful to the Doge and the almighty god of pillaging, went on to capture and sack Constantinople, the greatest medieval Christian city in the world, in 1204. Boniface established **Romania,** or a Latin Empire of the East, and advanced no further to harm even a hair of an infidel.

8 Q84

Paterne orra de la Sicile crie,	*Paterno will hear the cry from Sicily,*
Tous les aprefts du gouphre de Triefte:	*All the preparation in the Gulf of*
Qui s'entendra iufque à la trinacrie,[1]	*Trieste,*
De tant de voiles, fuy, fuy, l'horrible pefte.	*Which will be heard as far as Sicily.*
	So many sails, flee, oh flee the
	dreaded pestilence!

[1] Latin *Trinacria* = poetic term for Sicily because as a roughly triangular island it has 3 peninsulas.

We return to the alternative future track of 8 Q81. A revolt in Sicily spreads through the Spanish possessions of Philip II in southern Italy.

Paterno could stand for a number of places, such as a town 10 miles northwest of Catania, Sicily, or for the ancient Roman city called Paternum, in southern Italy, on the Gulf of Taranto. Apparently the rebellion against the Spanish reaches Venice, for the **Gulf of Trieste** implies the northernmost end of the Adriatic. Venice belonged to the Imperial Habsburgs while the Kingdom of the Two Sicilies belonged to the Spanish. Nostradamus predicts a major naval expedition planned against Philip by Venice. The **dreaded pestilence** sounds more like a description of the invasion than a disease, unless the Venetians succumb to a plague infesting their galleys while en route to the naval engagement. A specific quatrain for a future that never panned out.

8 Q85

Entre Bayonne & à fainct Iean de Lux,	**Between Bayonne and St Jean-de-Luz,**
Sera pofé de Mars la promotoire:	**Will be laid [at] the promontory of**
Aux Hanix¹ d'Aquilon Nanar² hoftera lux,	**Mars:**
Puis fuffocqué au lict fans adiutoire.	**For the unconquerable Northerner**
	Nanar will take away the light,
	Then suffocated in bed without
	assistance.

¹Greek cryptogram for *aniketos* = unconquerable; or Latin *Hamaxaeci* = the nomads of northeastern Europe; or Latin *annixus* = having made an effort.
²Possibly Latin *nonaria* = prostitute.

This is yet another accurate prediction for the fall of Napoleon beginning with events in the year 1814, when the Duke of Wellington's Anglo-Spanish army invaded France over the Pyrennees in 1814 and made its camp at St Jean-de-Luz. From there he advanced to besiege Marshal Soult's forces encamped at Bayonne. Napoleon's capital is described poetically here as the **promontory of Mars** god of war, beset by advancing armies of the allied coalition. The battle for Paris was fought near the **promontory** of Montmartre.

Fontbrune believes *Nanar* is an abbreviation for *Napoleon Bonaparte*. Well, could be – but what about his vanquisher, the great **Northerner** Czar Alexander I of Russia? The latter would make more sense. It is Alexander who demands and receives Napoleon's abdication. In other words, he and the Russian armies are most responsible for Napoleon's greatest defeats in Russia in 1812, and at the Battle of Nations in Leipzig in 1813. Alexander also had a hand in many of Bonaparte's greatest defeats during the French campaign of 1814. It is the Czar who will **take away** Napoleon's **light** or glory. I would agree with Fontbrune that the final line aptly describes Napoleon on his deathbed in 1821, dying by inches from ulcers on his liver and from stomach cancer.

8 Q86

Par Arani tholofer ville franque,	**Through Ernani, Tolosa and Villa franca,**
Bande infinie par le mont Adrian:	**Infinite band through the mountain of Adrian:**
Paffe riuiere, Hurin[1] par pont la planque,	**It passes the river, combat over the plank [for] the bridge,**
Bayonne entrer tous Bihoro criant.	**Bayonne will be entered, all crying, "Bihoro!"**

[1]Old French Hurin = dispute, combat, struggle, hostility.

I agree with Leoni. This is probably a miss for the Wars of Religion and not about the Spanish Civil War. It is certainly not about a future-farcical invasion of southwest France from Italy through Toulouse and Bayonne. Bayonne is in the extreme southwest corner of France. Ernani, Tolosa and Villafranca, and Mt Adrian are clustered together in Spain, southwest of Bayonne over the western edge of the Pyrenees. The storming of a bridge could therefore only take place on one built across the Bidassoa river, since it is the only river north of the Pyrennees between these Spanish locations and Bayonne. "**Bihoro**" is the war cry of soldiers of Navarre, whether from the Spanish or French side of the Pyrenees. Nostradamus foresees an invasion of Spain by the **infinite band**, which usually means the French. The battle cry would pin this one as a failed alternative near-future prediction for Nostradamus' time, since neither Henry de Navarre nor France staged an invasion over the Bidassoa in the 16th century. And after that Navarre as an independent state of France or Spain becomes insignificant.

8 Q87

Mort confpiree viendra en plein effect,	**The death conspired will come into full effect,**
Charge donnee & voyage de mort:	**The charge given and the journey to death:**
Efleu,[1] creé, receu par fiens deffait,	**Elected, created, received by his own and undone,**
Sang d'innocence deuant foy par remort.	**Blood of the innocent before faith in remorse.**

[1]Old French form of modern élu = elected.

Nostradamus, the avowed royalist, could have written this postscript after seeing a vision of the hapless Louis XVI bound like a common criminal, rumbling along in a cheap carriage on his way to his execution on 21 January 1793.

The **death conspired** by the deputies of the National Convention comes to **full effect** on that day. The **charge** of death by guillotine is passed. The king makes his final **journey** between two ranks of National Guards cutting a passageway through a silent crowd. The last two lines offer one- to two-word ephitets for the final years of his life. He was raised to kingship, **elected** or appointed by the National Convention to be their **created** constitutional puppet king. He is **received** by his own people, who judge him and condemn him to death. But to Nostradamus, the blood soaking the blade is that of an innocent, sacrificial lamb.

Louis tried to address the crowd while on the scaffold. Before the drum roll drowned him out, he was heard to say: "People, I die an innocent man! I pardon the authors of my death! I pray to God that my blood shall not fall on France."

8 Q88

Dans la Sardeigne vn noble Roy viendra,	Into Sardinia a noble King will come,
Que ne tiendra que trois ans le royaume,	Who will hold the kingdom for only
Plufieurs coulleurs auec foy conioindra,	three years,
Luy mefmes apres foin fomeil marrit fcome.	He will join several colors with him,
	He himself after care [and] sleep [by]
	scorn afflicted.

The concept of a **King** from Sardinia had little relevance until the early 18th century when the island realm was transferred to Austria from Spain in 1713 and later incorporated into the Duchy of Savoy in 1720, making the Savoyard Duke the titular king of Sardinia. Only once in history has Sardinia had its own resident king. He was Charles-Emmanuel IV, and he ruled for only three years, between 1798 and 1802. Here is Le Pelletier's (1867) observation: "Charles Emmanuel IV, King of an old line, despoiled by the French Republic of his continental possessions, will retire to the isle of Sardinia, where he will reign three years (1798 to 1802); then he will abdicate in favor of his brother Victor Emmanuel I, and after many worries, he will go to live an obscure, sad and humiliating existence at Rome, where he will die in 1819, as a Jesuit."

8 Q89

Pour ne tumber entre mains de fon oncle,	In order not to fall into the hands of
Qui fes enfans par regner trucidez,	his uncle,
Orant[1] au peuple mettant pied fur Peloncle,	Who slaughtered his children in order
Mort & traifné entre cheuaux bardez.	to rule:
	Arguing with the people, putting his
	foot on Peloncle,
	Dead and dragged between barded
	[armored] horses.

[1]orant = Latin orans = speaking, arguing, pleading, praying.

A man called **Peloncle** by anagram is drawn and quartered between **barded** (armored) **horses**. Ravaillac, the assassin of Henry IV, was executed in this way, but there is no connection, since he acted alone.

8 Q90

Quand des croiſez vn trouué de ſens trouble,	**When one of the crusaders [is] found with his senses troubled,**
En lieu du ſacre verra vn bœuf cornu:	**In place of the holy one will see the horned ox:**
Par vierge porc ſon lieu lors ſera comble,	**Through the virgin pig its [her/his?] place then will be full,**
Par Roy plus ordre ne ſera ſouſtenu.	**By the King order will no longer be maintained.**

Robb (1984) reminds us that the **horned ox**, like the horned lamb in Revelation, represents the power of Islam, but he incorrectly applies this prophecy to an impossible vision of an Arab military occupation of France in our near future. It may be the Arab occupation by Saddam Hussein of Arab Kuwait.

Quatrain Indexing Date: 8Q90 = August (8th month) 1990, which saw Iraq invade Kuwait.

8 Q91

Frymy les champs des Rodanes[1] entrées,	**Entered amidst fields of the Rhodes [or Rhône] people,**
Ou les croyſez feront preſque vnys:	**Where the crusaders will be almost united:**
Les deux braſſieres[2] en piſces rencontrées,	**The two leading strings [Mars and Venus?] met in Pisces,**
Et vn grand nombre par deluge punis.	**And a great number punished by flood.**

[1]Latin *Rhodanus* = the Rhône, or (by metonymy) dwellers by the Rhône. Or *Rhodius* = of Rhodes, Rhodians, the people of the Aegean island.
[2]Straps, strings. A classical allusion to the lead strings forged by Vulcan and used by Mars to bind Venus.

The Christian colony on the island of Rhodes was conquered by the Turks in 1523. It remained their possession until the Turko-Italian War of 1912. The Italians delivered it to Greece in 1945. If this is about the people of the **Rhône** river valley region, they can expect a great flood on that river when Mars and Venus are in conjuction. The problem is, this conjunction happens every year in winter or spring.

8 Q92

Loin hors du regne mis en hazard voyage,
Grand oft duyra pour foy l'occupera,
Le Roy tiendra les fiens captif oftrage,
A fon retour tout pays pillera.

Far distant from the realm, sent on a
dangerous journey,
He will lead a grand army and will
keep it for himself,
The King will hold his nation
hostage,
He will plunder the whole country on
his return.

A number of exploitative rulers could stand in a royal queue and lay claim to this prophecy. Prieditis and Gustafsson make a good argument that this quatrain is for Charles XII of Sweden, during the Great Northern War (1700–21). After his defeat by Peter the Great of Russia at Poltava (1714), Charles escaped to Turkey, where he stayed as a captive guest of the Ottoman Sultan. He made the dangerous journey back to Sweden in 1715 and immediately set to work stripping the country of men and wealth to create another powerful army.

Napoleon Bonaparte would be my second candidate. The French Directory permits him to lead an expeditionary force into Egypt in 1799; he makes them his own personal army of conquest. He abandons his men to return to France and become its dictator. For the next 14 years he bleeds the economy and the blood of 2 million Frenchmen in his wars of conquest. In 1812, as Emperor Napoleon, he loses a half-million-man army (known as the Grand Army) along with 100,000 horses in distant Russia. Upon his return to France after a harrowing journey by sleigh, he strips the country bare of every available horse, cannon, French franc, and male teenager to muster a second half-million-man **Grand Army**, which he throws away in the carnage of the coming German Campaigns of 1813.

My third candidate would be Mao Tse Tung. In the early 1930s Chiang Kai-Shek's Nationalist forces tried to encircle and annihilate the Chinese Red Army. Mao Tse Tung heroically led the communists on a 6,000-mile journey through the Chinese hinterlands to safety during what is popularly called the Long March. Later he kept the hardened Red Army for himself, at last defeating the Nationalist Chinese in 1949. In the 1960s, the aging demigod of Communist China threw the world's most populated country into the destructive catharsis and social turmoil of the Cultural Revolution, during which an estimated 20 million people died from liquidation by Red Guards or from famine.

8 Q93

Sept moys ſans plus obtiendra prelature,
Par ſon deces grand ſchiſme fera naiſtre:
Sept moys tiendra vn autre la preture,
Pres de Veniſe paix vnion renaiſtre.

No more [than] seven months will he
hold the office of prelate,
Through his death a great schism will
arise:
Seven months another will hold the
prelacy,
Near Venice peace, union reinstated.

This could be about what goes on behind the sealed doors of the Vatican during a Conclave of Cardinals. It may even predict an election crisis of that august body as soon as the death of John Paul II requires the nomination of a new pope. Several popes have sat in the papal throne seven months or less before dying. In fact in 1558, the year Nostradamus dedicated this and the other final 300 quatrains of *Les Propheties* to Henry II, there were three popes. This happened again in 1590, when Urban VII was elected after the death of Sixtus V, only to die after two weeks. Then Gregory XIV was elected, dying within ten months. The last time three popes reigned in one year was fairly recently, in 1978, when Paul VI was replaced by John Paul I, who died within a month and was replaced by the current pope, John Paul II. No rift in the Church resulted from the first two instances. As we have seen elsewhere a potential schism started between John Paul I and his Curia, but his death suddenly – or perhaps, conveniently – ended the threat. Albino Luciani was the Patriarch (or **prelate**) of Venice before he became John Paul I. As we know, St Malachy's list of popes unto doomsday is down to two more candidates after John Paul II. It is possible that he may live to see the millennium, but he might be quickly succeeded by two candidates.

8 Q94

Deuant le lac ou plus cher fut getté,
De ſept mois, & ſon oſt deſconfit:
Seront Hiſpans par Albannois gaſtez:
Par delay perte en donnant le conflict.

Before the lake where most of the
treasure was cast,
Of seven months, and its host
frustrated:
The Spanish will be plundered by
those of Albions:
By delaying giving battle.

Skill in seamanship in both peace and in war established England's long domination of the waves. When Nostradamus wrote this quatrain Spain and England were allies. It refers to an English attack on Spanish treasure galleons to take place in 37 years. In 1590, 40 Spanish treasure galleons laden with gold from South America sailed through the narrow mouth of the Bay of Cadiz to lay anchor after a seven-month voyage. The bay of

Cadiz received its name from the Punic word **Gaddir**, meaning "enclosed place" (perhaps a **lake**). Shortly after midday, the Spanish spotted the sails of English raiders on the horizon. The Spanish were not too concerned. No sane mariner would enter the narrow opening of the bay to give battle. To the captains of the 13 Spanish man o'war escorts it was unthinkable to sail to tackle the English raiders until they had enjoyed a good siesta. That was their mistake.

While the Spanish dozed, the English rode the wind straight into the harbor and raked the treasure fleet's escort with deadly cannonades. To keep the gold out of English hands, the Spanish were forced to set fire to the entire fleet.

Nostradamus calls the English **those of Albion**, after the Latin name given to the British mainland by the Romans. The quatrain indexing, 94, could be a near miss for 1590, the year of the attack.

8 Q95

Le feducteur fera mis en la foffe,	**The seducer will be placed in the ditch,**
Et eftaché iufques à quelque temps:	**And will be tied up for some time:**
Le clerc vny le chef auec fa croffe,[1]	**The theologian joins the chief with his cross,**
Pycante droite attraira les contens.	**The sharp right will attract the contented ones.**

[1]Either cross, or Old French *crosse* = abbey.

This could be a prophetic coda to the end of the Reagan years, when his presidency suffered (**tied up for some time** and **placed in the ditch**) through political scandals like Iran-Contra. Reagan will also be remembered as a strong advocate for right-wing Christian fundamentalism. He was proud of the title American Dreamer, and his "feel-good-with-the-flag" sentiments satisfied the American public's collective need during the 1980s to wax patriotic and restore pride whenever possible to a country traumatized by the Vietnam war and the Watergate Conspiracy.

Quatrain Indexing Date: Q95 = 1995. The Gingrich–Dole Republican Congress was in its heyday in 1995; however, I will hold to the prediction I made in 1983 that a two-term democrat will sit in the US presidency between 1992 and 2000 (I write this on 21 April 1996).

8 Q96

La fynagogue fterile fans nul fruit,	**The sterile Synagogue without any fruit,**
Sera receue entre les infideles:	**Will be received by the infidels:**
De Babylon la fille du pourfuit,	**Of Babylon the daughter is pursued,**
Mifere & trifte luy trenchera les aifles.	**Miserable and sad they will clip her wings.**

The first two lines build a foundation in history. Even in Nostradamus' day the Temple of Solomon at Jerusalem was considered a *sterile* ruin of the Jewish Diaspora. Without the *fruit* of the lost Ark of the Covenant it has become a mere platform for the Golden Temple of the Muslims (*received by the infidels*).

Lines 3 and 4 build a future vision on the foundation of the past. But as usual, the structure of Nostradamus' writing is pliable enough to give us an either-or fudge. They can also read: *Those of Babylon [Iraq] will pursue [and persecute] the daughter [Israel?]. Misery and sadness will clip her wings.*

Nostradamus, who foresaw the Holocaust of Hitler, warns his people of a future holocaust coming from Babylon (modern-day Iraq and Syria). *The daughter* is the Israeli state, whose wings of peace are clipped – from within by a new right-wing government of Netanyahu, and from without by Iraq coming forward again to lead the Arab extremist cause.

Quatrain Indexing Date: Q96 = 1996. A new Israeli right-wing Prime Minister, Binyamin Netanyahu, officially took office the day I entered this interpretation on 18 June 1996. On this day the Arab world held its breath. Would he continue the Middle East peace efforts or derail them between now and 1999? Nostradamus' prophecies indicate two destinies for Israel – peace by the new millennium or a second and wider-ranging war in the Middle East.

8 Q97

Aux fins du VAR *changer le pompotans,*[1]	**At the end of the Var to change the**
Pres du riuage les trois beaux enfans	**all-powerful,**
naiftre:	**Near the bank the three beautiful**
Ruyne au peuple par aage competans,	**children to be born:**
Regne ay pays changer plus voir croiftre.	**Ruin to the people by [the time they**
	are of] competent age,
	Kingdom and country to change and
	seen to increase.

[1]Compound of Greek *pan* = all, and Latin *potens* = powerful, thus "All-powerful." (See 10 Q100).

Some interpreters think *pompotans* is the enigmatic *Pempotans* of 10 Q100, whom Garencières believes are the **all-powerful** English. But the link does not succeed here. The River Var flows into the Mediterranean between Cannes and Nice. When Nostradamus wrote this, the Var was the eastern boundary of France's border with Savoy. The following year, in October of 1559, Nostradamus received a royal visitor at his door – none other than Emmanuel-Philibert, Duke of Savoy, who was stopping in Salon on his way home to Nice. The duke was paying his respects to the man who had made several well-known and documented predictions in *Les Propheties* of Savoy's victory against the French forces at St Quentin.

The Duke of Savoy stayed at the Castle of the Emperi at Salon for several months until a wave of pestilence safely passed from his realm. In December he summoned Princess Marguérite to come to enjoy the dry winter climate with him there. It must be remembered that this sister of the late French King Henry was one of the brides on the ill-fated wedding day that fulfilled quatrain 35 of Century 1. Still, according to all reports she did not bear Nostradamus any ill will for his prophecy. In his history of Provence, César relates that the princess "entertained him a long time and did him much honor."

Nostradamus may have hidden a prophecy here that describes the eventual incorporation of Savoy into France at a time when three children are born either to the contemporary Duke and Duchess of Savoy or to their descendants. One of the three beautiful children could be Amadeus II of Savoy (1675–1732). During his reign the Savoyard people suffered much devastation from invading French forces after Amadeus abandoned the Grand Alliance of Louis XIV and switched sides in 1704 to join with the Austrians during the War of the Spanish Succession. Savoy became part of France in 1860.

8 Q98

Des gens d'Eglise sang sera espanché,
Comme de l'eau en si grand abondance:
Et d'vn long temps ne sera restanché,
Ve ve[1] au clerc[2] ruyne & doleance.

Of the Church people blood will be poured out,
In as great abundance as water:
And for a long time it will not be suppressed,
Woe, woe to the clergy ruin and grief.

[1]Latin *vae* = alas, woe.
[2]Old French for clerk, scholar, cleric.

A general prophecy for the Catholic Apocalypse, with possible links to 10 Q65: **O vast Rome, your end draws near.** Or perhaps this connects with EP118's description of the clergy's being utterly destroyed by a vast plague that kills two-thirds of humanity. In both instances the source of death is some disease weakening the blood, possibly AIDS or some other attack on the immune system through pollution, biological weapons, or from a depletion of the ozone layer during the 21st century.

Quatrain Indexing Date: Q98 = 1998, possibly the beginning of the final tribulation of the Catholic Church.

8 Q99

Par la puiſſance des trois Rois temporel,
En autre lieu ſera mis le ſainct ſiege:
Où la ſubſtance & de l'eſprit corporel,
Sera remis & receu pour vray ſiege.

Through the power of the three
 temporal Kings,
The sacred See will be put in another
 place:
Where the substance of the spirit and
 the body,
Will be restored and received as the
 true See.

The prophecy of the Catholic Apocalypse continues. Nostradamus and many other seers describe the final pope and his surviving cardinals escaping the devastation of Rome, which is utterly destroyed either by terrorism or a natural disaster. In any case three world leaders could be helping them move their headquarters elsewhere to start a new and revamped Catholic Church. But this is not the only interpretation possible. This prophecy could support the vision of Catholic seers such as Gioacchino de Fiore (1130–1202), who foresaw doomsday as the end of orthodoxy and dogma, a time when people become mature enough to have a direct relationship with God – or better, godliness – without a Church or Bible between them. The final two lines also embrace a similar vision of de Fiore and many non-Christian shamanic and Eastern seers who predict the coming of a new mankind that will restore a harmony between the spiritual and physical dimensions of life (**the substance of the spirit and the body**).

Quatrain Indexing Date: Q99 = 1999? The indexing may be yet another indication that the darkly beclouded year 1999 has a silver lining. It doesn't have to be a date with doomsday; we could make it a date with "bloomsday" – the flowering of a new spiritual revolution unlike any ever seen in human history.

8 Q100

Pour l'abondance de larme reſpandue,
Du hault en bas par le bas au plus hault:
Trop grande foy par ieu vie perdue,
De ſoif mourir par habondant deffault.

For the abundance of the tears shed,
From high to low through the low to
 the highest:
Too great a faith through sport – a life
 lost,
To die from thirst through abundant
 absence.

This is obscure enough to work for anything. A recent tragedy for the Grimaldi Royal house of Monaco could be applied here, if we read the lines from 4 to 1. Princess Caroline lost her husband in a boat-racing accident. Line 4 is the odd line out, since it describes someone dying of thirst rather than drowning. Perhaps this is an alternative-future failure?

The daredevil had **too great a faith** in his abilities to cheat death. In this case his boat flipped over and he was knocked out by the impact and drowned. Lines 2 and 1 describe the sad state funeral, which was given great attention by the magazines and press in Europe. One saw the Grimaldi clan in black; the shattered princess leaning on her father's arm, her beautiful face beneath the veil twisted with grief; the entire principality from the highest to the lowly born, in tears. First her mother, Princess Grace, and now her husband. The myth of the Grimaldi curse strengthened.

9 Q1

Dans la maiſon du traducteur de Bourc,	In the house of the translator de [la]
Seront les lettres trouuees ſus la table:	Bourc,
Borgne, roux, blanc, chanu tiendra de	The letters will be found on the table:
cours,	One-eyed, red-haired, white, hoary-
Qui changera au nouueau conneſtable.	headed will hold the course,
	Which will change for the new
	constable.

Bourc is used here to direct our attention to the environs of Bordeaux, where a rebellion was brutally suppressed by Anne de Montmorency, the Constable of France. In 1548 the incident inspired one of France's most noted 16th-century scholars, Etienne de la Boétie, to write his classic on tyranny entitled *La Servitude Volontaire* (known in English as *Anti-Dictator*). It appears that Nostradamus hides in *de Bourc* an inference to *de la Boétie* as well, for he was aware of the great controversy the idealistic young author caused at the French court. Montmorency tried to have the book suppressed, and it was not published until both men were dead.

Looking ahead from 1558 Nostradamus foresaw the Constable's successor, Henry de Montmorency, sustaining the feud until the satisfaction of cold-steeled revenge was attained. This didn't happen. Boétie died four years before Anne de Montmorency was killed in battle in 1567. The feud died with the elder Montmorency, and the manuscript was finally published in 1570. It is considered one of the most important essays on democracy.

9 Q2

Du hault du mont Auentin voix ouye,	From the top of the Aventine hill, a
Vuydez vuydez de tous les deux coſtez:	voice is heard,
Du ſang des rouges ſera l'ire aſſomye,	Evacuate, evacuate all of you on both
D'Arimin Prato, Columna debotez.	sides:
	By the blood of the red ones will the
	anger be appeased,
	From Rimini and Prato, the Colonna
	expelled.

Lines 1 and 2 evoke a classical episode used for future prophetic purposes. The **Aventine** is one of the Seven Hills of Rome. At one time all the members of the plebeian wing of the Roman Senate retreated to the Aventine hill to protest Patrician tyranny. Thus we have the current Italian

political phrase "withdrawing to Aventine," which means breaking off all
negotiation and discourse until demands are met. So we could have here
any number of modern Italian governments suffering a boycott, or a vote
of no-confidence. I agree with Fontbrune that the clearest possibility is an
assessment of the political climate of Italy just after Mussolini took
power, when in 1924 the Socialist deputy Matteoti was kidnapped and
killed by Fascists. The opposition deputies left the Chamber in protest –
in other words, they retreated to the Aventine hill.

The anger against Fascism would be appeased in the blood spilled by
Italian **red** communist partisans in April 1945, when Mussolini, his
mistress, and a number of Fascist functionaries were executed. Mussolini
is poetically described here through a reference to the Colonna family
clan, who fought a legendary battle with their rivals the Orsini to be First
Family of Rome. Mussolini, like the Colonna of old, had the Vatican in
his corner. Nostradamus, who in other places makes it clear he is aware
of Fascism undermining the virtues of the Roman Catholic leadership,
correctly promises Mussolini's fall from power. By the way, Mussolini was
born near **Rimini and Prato**.

9 Q3

La magna vaqua[1] à Rauenne grand trouble,	**The great cow at Ravenna in great trouble,**
Conduicts par quinze enferrez à Fornafe:	**Led by fifteen shut up at Fornese:**
A Rome naiftre deux monftres à tefte double,	**At Rome two monsters with double heads will be born,**
Sang, feu, deluge, les plus grands à l'efpafe.[2]	**Blood, fire, floods, the greatest ones [escape].**

[1]Latin *magna vacca* = great cow. Magnavacca is the name of a valley and tiny port (renamed
Porto de Garibaldi) between Ravenna and Ferrara, and also the name of a former canal in the
same area.
[2]Space, room – in this case to gain distance from their pursuers to make an escape.

Two-headed monsters might imply a latter-day symbol of the Austrian
Hapsburgs, who dominated Italy (represented by **Rome**) through the
middle of the 19th century. Magnavacca (Great Cow) is the name of a
small port between **Ravenna** and Ferrara at the mouth of the Po river,
renamed Porto de Garibaldi after the Italian revolutionary who effected
the unification of Italy. It was at Magnavacca that Garibaldi and his
followers made a daring escape by boat from an Austrian and papal police
dragnet. Just as the Austrians entered the town of Cesenatico, they made
their escape in thirteen (rather than **fifteen**) vessels. They were intercepted near the Marches of Comacchio by an Austrian gunboat. Refusing
to surrender, they were pursued under fire around the Cape of Magnavacca. One by one the boats were splintered and sunk by gunfire, and

their occupants drowned (***blood, fire, floods***). Only three boats and 30 men (including Garibaldi) made landfall. The Austrian police blocked every road to Venice, so the survivors retreated to Ravenna, a noted haven in the papal states for Italian patriots.

9 Q4

L'an enfuyuant defcouuerts par deluge,	**The year following discoveries out of a flood,**
Deux chefs eſleuz le premier ne tiendra:	**Two leaders elected the first one will not hold:**
De fuyr vmbre à l'vn d'eux le refuge,	**For one of them refuge from fleeing a shadow,**
Saccagee caſe qui premier maintiendra.	**Plundered [will be] the house which [the] first will maintain.**

This is dated for a time when discoveries of a treasure occur one year after a flood. We can link this quatrain to either the three-part Toulouse treasure hunt of 6 Q98, 8 Q29, & 8 Q30, or to 6 Q66, in which a tomb of the **great Roman** is uncovered in the ruined Vatican after Rome is destroyed by fire and tsunamis.

The two leaders may be popes, perhaps a reference to the twin-named popes of our times, John Paul I and II. The first one died within a month of his election (***the first one will not hold***). Line 3 pictures the second John Paul poetically ***fleeing a shadow***, perhaps out of guilt about the purported murder of the first John Paul, conspiracies during his reign such as the Vatican Bank scandal (***plundered***), or the infiltration of neo-Fascist organizations like P2 and the Mafia into Vatican affairs (see 4 Q11). In the end, the ***house***-hold of the pope in the Vatican will hold fast to its secrets until some great natural catastrophe or act of God descends on Rome.

9 Q5

Tiers doit du pied au premier ſemblera,	**The third toe of the foot will appear like the first,**
A vn nouueau monarque de bas haut	**To a new monarch from low height:**
Qui Piſe & Lucques Tyran occupera,	**He who will occupy Pisa and Lucca as Tyrant,**
Du precedent corriger le deffaut.	**To correct the fault of his predecessor.**

Deformed feet and interpretations are afoot in this obscure prophecy of Italian intrigues. Le Pelletier (1867) may have a toe-hold on something: "The National Assembly of 1848 [the second Third Estate] – a copy of the National Convention of 1792 [first Third Estate] – will be trampled by a new Emperor, Louis-Napoleon Bonaparte raised, like the first one, from low to high, by vote of the people. This Prince, the same one who in his youth [1831] will have led the revolutionary movement of Tuscany, in mounting the throne will take the name of Napoleon III, in order to make up for the deficiency of the son of Napoleon I (Napoleon II, Duke of Reichstadt), dead at Vienna on July 22, 1832."

9 Q6

Par la Guyenne infinité d'Anglois,	A countless number of Englishmen in Guienne,
Occuperont par nom d'Anglaquitaine:	Will occupy it under the name Anglaquitaine:
Du Languedoc Ispalme[1] Bourdelois,	In Languedoc, Ispalme, Bordelais,
Qu'ils nommeront apres Barboxitaine.[2]	Which they will later name Barboxitaine.

[1]Enigmatic place name.
[2]Ditto. Possibly Barbe-Occitanie, "Barbe" being the enigmatic Aenobarbe and "Occitanie" the medieval name for Languedoc or the whole French Mediterranean coast.

The first two lines are better applied retroactively to the long centuries of English domination of southwestern France. Lamont (1942) saw this as an English invasion of another king and the future influx of English settlers visiting south and southwestern France. The European Union has brought about the purchase of many French farms by English families as summer cottages, and the trend can only increase as the borders of Europe fade away. In the 21st century native French people will continue to sell their houses and villas to wealthier ecu-coined Europeans.

9 Q7

Qui ouurira le monument trouué,	The man who opens the tomb when it is found,
Et ne viendra le ferrer promptement:	And who does not close it promptly:
Mal luy viendra & ne pourra prouué,	Evil will come to him that no one will be able to prove,
Si mieux doit eftre Roy Breton ou Normand.	It would have been so much better to be a Breton or Norman king.

When Nostradamus was living in Salon he was pursued one day by a Caban peasant gang, who cursed and threatened him. Eventually, Nostradamus turned on them with his cane, roaring at them to be off. As they fled from the prophet he shouted after them, "You will never put your filthy feet on my throat while I'm alive or after I'm dead."

Nostradamus made good his threat. During his last illness he gave his wife instructions concerning his burial. She was to have his body entombed in the wall of the church of the Cordeliers in Salon and, most important of all, it was to be placed upright so that no craven fool could put his foot on the grave. Throughout the centuries that followed, stories circulated about Nostradamus' last resting-place, including the traditional tale that the prophet had buried with him a secret document containing the key to all his prophecies. Sometime either a half-century after his death, or even as late as the year 1700, the city fathers of Salon decided to move the body of their illustrious citizen to a more prominent wall of the church. They took a quick, careful look inside the coffin. It contained no paper of any kind. But there was one surprise. It is claimed that around the skeleton's neck hung a medallion inscribed with the date of the exhumation. It would have amused Nostradamus to see how the leading citizens of Salon responded to the practical joke he had devised some 134 years before. Reverently the city fathers resealed the coffin and installed it, again upright, in its new location; for many years it rested in peace.

But in 1791, during the turbulence of the French Revolution, some national guards from Marseilles broke into the church on a drunken looting raid, armed with picks and shovels. They smashed the eight-foot marble slab concealing the prophet's coffin and began to ransack its contents. When the noise of their vandalism and singing aroused the neighborhood, a certain M. David, the mayor of Salon, hurried to investigate the commotion. He arrived at the church to find a macabre dance of death in progress, with soldiers and townspeople tossing the prophet's bones in the air. In the center of this grisly scene a shaggy guardsman was drinking wine from Nostradamus' skull. The peasants, believing that drinking blood from the skull would give you the prophet's powers, had dared the guardsman to drink. Wine seemed an acceptable substitute for the blood and may also have helped the soldiers blot from their minds Nostradamus' warning that a quick and violent death would be visited on anyone who dared to desecrate his grave.

Faced with the prospect of Salon's most illustrious bag of bones being carried off as souvenirs, and mindful of the prophet's warning, the mayor had to act quickly. He explained to the soldiers that Nostradamus had predicted the French Revolution and was thus a hero to be revered. He soon had them collecting the bones they had scattered in their drunken riot and later made sure that the prophet's remains were safely reinterred.

Two possible destinies are recorded for the soldier. One reports that Mayor David had him hanged the following day. The second story is more interesting. By the next morning the guardsmen were on their way back to Marseilles. On the road from Salon they were ambushed by Royalist sympathizers, and the soldier who had used the prophet's skull as a wine glass suffered a quick and violent death from a sniper's bullet.

Quatrain Indexing Date: 9Q7 = 1797, perhaps a near miss for 1791.

9 Q8

Puiſnay Roy fait ſon pere mettre à mort,	*The younger son made King will put his father to death,*
Apres conflit de mort tres inhoneſte:	*After the conflict [a] very dishonest death:*
Eſcrit trouué ſoubſon donra remort,	*Inscription found, suspicion will produce remorse,*
Quand loup chaſſé poſe ſus la couchette.[1]	*When the wolf chased out lies down on the bunk.*

[1]Bunk or bedcover.

The first two lines are clear enough. After a war, a younger prince kills his aging father, the king. The other lines are meant to give us more definite leads. At a time when the escaped **wolf** (perhaps the young son) is resting, an inscription (perhaps evidence of the order to murder the king) is found by someone suspicious of foul play.

There is not much more I can say except that **wolf** can apply itself in two ways: either as an animal symbol for Italy or, to a lesser degree, as the nickname for Adolf Hitler. *Adolf* is the old High German word for "noble wolf" ("wolf" is *loup* in French). The latter "wolf" application is a long shot. To make it credible one needs to find an instance in which a young prince who is a Nazi sympathizer might have secretly had his father killed to bring the country in line with Hitler. King Alexander I of Yugoslavia was assassinated by Croatian terrorists in Marseilles in October 1934, leaving his cousin, the 11-year-old Peter, on the throne with Alexander's brother, Crown Prince Paul, as Regent. Paul's sympathy for the Nazis only caused more rebellion in the realm.

A third **wolf** candidate is the Chechen terrorist-cum-battlefield commander Shamil Basayev, who is also called a lone wolf. He has threatened to wage full-scale terrorism against Russia, and the whole world, if Chechnya is not granted independence from the Russian Federation.

9 Q9

Quand lampe ardente de feu , inextinguible	*When the lamp burning with an inextinguishable fire,*
Sera trouué au temple des Veſtales:	*Will be found in the temple of the Vestals:*
Enfant trouué feu, eau paſſant par trible,	*Infant found fire, water passing through the sieve,*
Perir eau Nymes, Tholoſe cheoir les halles.	*Nîmes, Toulouse perish [in] water, the market to collapse.*

Could this be a flood and economic collapse caused by the goddess of the hearth Vesta on the warpath of global warming and floods in southwest France? The eternal flame flickering from a gold and silver treasure lamp of the Roman earth goddess has surfaced before – back in 5 Q66. Jaubert and Garencières believe this buried lamp lies somewhere near the ruins of the temple of Diana at Nîmes. A terrible flood in Nîmes is predicted in line 4. Leoni, ever the comprehensive researcher, tells us that such a flood occurred on 9 September 1557 as a result of a cloudburst that lasted from 1 to 8 pm. The *History of Nîmes* (Menard, 1874) describes the water reaching six feet in some places and even cites this quatrain in connection with the flood. Roman monuments were exposed, but apparently no lamp of Vesta was found.

Thus we wait for another meteorological catastrophe to visit Nîmes (and Toulouse 140 miles to the northwest) that will uncover the vestal lamp. A more abstract interpretation of all this finds Vesta's **fire** and floods to be the result of a runaway greenhouse effect in the 21st century. Such floods and ecological disruptions from global warming could threaten the European Common **market** with a **collapse**, perhaps as early as 2009, if the indexing is meant as a date.

Quatrain Indexing Date: 9Q9 = either [19]99 or 2009, or even 2099.

---

9 Q10

Moyne moyneſſe d'enfant mort expoſé,	**The child of a monk and nun exposed**
Mourir par ourſe & rauy par verrier:[1]	**to death,**
Par Fois & Pamyes le camp ſera poſé,	**To die by a she-bear, and carried**
Contre Tholoſe Carcas, dreſſer forrier.	**away by a boar:**
	[Near] Foix and Pamiers the army
	will be camped,
	Against Toulouse Carcassone, the
	forager to pitch a tent.

[1]Latin *verres*= boar, or Old French *verrier*= glazier.

An imaginative mess of scandal and animal symbols. This soap opera is set in southwest France, and the locations draw a line north by northwest, perhaps giving us a clue to the direction in which our boarish interloper ran off with his human suckling prey.

From Foix the boar moves 20 miles north to Pamiers, then 50 miles north to Toulouse. Then it circles back to Carcassone, which is 50 miles down the Canal du Midi from Toulouse. This quatrain probably describes the movements of some Huguenot or Catholic abductee during the Wars of Religion.

9 Q11

Le iufte à tort à mort lon viendra mettre,
Publiquement & du millieu eftaint:
Si grande pefte en ce lieu viendra naiftre,
Que les iugeans fouyr feront contraint.

**They will come to put a just man to
wrongful death,
In public [he is] extinguished in their
midst:
So great a pestilence will come to
arise in this place,
That the judges will be coerced to
flee.**

Here we have a clear example of Nostradamus' strong belief that plagues
were a punishment from God falling upon cities and countries that publicly kill their kings. A great pestilence did befall the citizens of London
16 years after they thronged to see the public beheading of Charles I, in
1649. No plague descended to punish the assembled Parisians after the
execution of Louis XVI on 21 January 1793. While on the scaffold, Louis
XVI made a rather prophetic final statement: "I pray to God that my
blood shall not fall on France." History records that his execution
triggered the plague of bloodshed called the Reign of Terror. Almost all
of his judges, such as Robespierre and Saint Just, would share his fate:
public execution by guillotine.

9 Q12

Le tant d'argent de Diane & Mercur,
Les fimulacres au lac feront trouuez:
Le figulier cherchant argille neufue,
Luy & les fiens d'or feront abbreuez.

**The great amount of silver of Diana
[the moon] and Mercury
[Hermes],
The images will be seen in the lake
[the mind of meditation]:
The sculptor looking for new clay,
He and his followers will be soaked in
gold.**

This is another occult quatrain. References in other quatrains to **silent
rest,** (2 Q28), **images will be seen in the lake** (9 Q12), and **alone with his
mind** (4 Q31) describe the universal tenets of the inner science of meditation. They imply the silence and distance from thoughts one experiences
while watching the constant movement and flux of life, the mind, and the
emotions. The Pali words *dhyana* and *dhyan*, which correspond to the
French pronunciation of "Diane" used by Nostradamus, were used by
the Buddha to mean "meditation." Again, fire and Hermes make a link to
the Eight Clues to the founders of the coming Spiritual Rebellion.

Quatrain Indexing Date: Q12 = 2012, the last year on the Mayan
calendar, when time and the world as we know it come to an end. It is
said by mystics that meditation takes one out of time to dwell in the

reality of the present. Perhaps the worldwide spread of meditativeness will collectively change the way humanity views time. Rather than an end of time, we may see a world beyond 2012 that ends its fixation on time. A timekeeper from ancient Central America might, therefore, have misread the future, and thought the world would come to an end in 2012.

9 Q13

Les exilez autour de la Soulongne,	**The exiles around Sologne,**
Conduis de nuict pour marcher à Lauxois:	**Conducted by night to march into**
Deux de Modene truculent[1] de Bologne,	**Auxois:**
Mys defcouuers par feu de Burançois.	**Two of Modena ferocious for Bologna,**
	Introduced, discovered by the fire of
	Buzançais.

[1]Latin *truculentus*, = ferocious, harsh, sadistic.

Nostradamus is on another geographical goose chase to no clear end. Two men from Modena, Italy, who are bullish about Bologna, are discovered at Buzançais, which is just south of the Sologne, a region on the southern bank of the Loire between Orléans and Blois. The place names imply they are contemporary agents of the papal states. Perhaps they were caught snooping around the favorite Château playgrounds of the Valois. The two are exiled from Sologne and conducted by guards 100 miles east to Dijon.

9 Q14

Mys en planure chauderons d'infecteurs,	**Put on the flat surface of the dyer's**
Vin, miel & l'huyle, & baftis fur forneaux:	**cauldron,**
Seront plongez fans mal dit mal facteurs,	**Wine, honey and oil, and built over**
Sept. fum extaint au canon des borneaux. [1]	**furnaces:**
	They will be plunged, labeled as
	malefactors without [saying] evil,
	Seven smokes extinguished in the
	cannon from Bordeaux.

[1]Possibly cryptogram for Bordeaux.

Although Leoni (1961) calls this just another bit of "gibberish . . . and a strong competitor for the title of most obscure," his observation reflects any Nostradamian's understandable frustration. So many intimate events of history are lost to us that could make hundreds of Nostradamus quatrains lucid. Traitors (**malefactors**) being executed by cannon – sounds quite similar to a real atrocity, dealt by the Republican repression of Royalists in Lyons during the French Revolution.

9 Q15

Pres de Parpan[1] les rouges detenus,
Ceux du milieu parfondrez menez loing:
Trois mis en pieces, & cinq mal ſouſtenus,
Pour le Seigneur & Prelat de Bourgoing.

Near Perpignan the reds detained,
Those of the middle completely
  ruined, led far off:
Three cut in pieces, and five badly
  sustained,
For the Lord and Prelate of
  Burgundy.

[1]Syncope for Parpignan (Perpignan).

Although Perpignan was a center for French communist political activity, the **red** described here is the red color of Imperial Spain. Perpignan was the capital of Roussillon, which belonged to the Spanish until 1659. Some Franco-Spanish struggle near the Pyrenees seems to be involved. Leoni thinks line 4 refers to the Governor of Burgundy in Nostradamus' day. The post was held by the brother of François de Guise, Duc de Aumale, from 1550 until his death in 1573. Since Burgundy has four bishoprics, Nostradamus may have François' brother Charles, Cardinal de Lorraine, in mind as the **Prelate of Burgundy**. No military action in Roussillon took place before his death or the murder of his clerical successor, Louis, Cardinal de Guise in 1588, although a minor siege of Perpignan was launched in the final War of Religion. The other details are too remote from the 20th century to conjure even speculation.

9 Q16

De caſtel Franco ſortira l'aſſemblée
L'ambaſſadeur non plaiſant fera ſchiſme:
Ceux de Ribiere ſeront en la meſlee,
Et au grand gouffre deſnieront l'entree.

From Castille, Franco will bring out
  the assembly,
The ambassador will not agree and
  cause a schism:
The people of Rivera will be in the
  crowd,
And they will refuse entry into the
  Gulf.

The Spanish dictator Francisco Franco and his predecessor, Primo de Rivera, are mentioned outright. Prior to the Spanish Civil War, Rivera was dismissed and exiled to Paris, where he died in 1930. His son, José Antonio Primo de Rivera, formed the quasi-fascist Falange movement (**the people of Rivera**) to vindicate the memory of his father. José Antonio became one of its earliest martyrs. Franco would later take on the party's mantle of power.

In 1936, the leftist-leaning Republican government had Franco exiled to the Canary Islands. He later returned through Spanish Morocco, to Spain and organized a military junta at Burgos. With the **assembly** of a

Nationalist government sworn to defeat Republican administration in Madrid, Spain lurched into the **schism** of a full-scale civil war.

Franco survived World War II by remaining neutral. Adolf Hitler pressured him hard to allow Axis troops overland access for an attack on the British base at Gibraltar. With Gibraltar conquered, Hitler would control the mouth of the Mediterranean – called a **Gulf** here. Franco would deny Hitler permission (**refuse entry into the Gulf**). This strategic loss was one Mussolini and Hitler's forces in North Africa could not compensate for.

Robb in 1941 documented a successful interpretation of this quatrain by reading "Riviera" for **Rivera**. He was able to forecast a meeting with Franco and the Axis powers on the French Riviera several months before it happened. He also confidently and correctly predicted that the meeting would not bring Franco over to the Axis alliance, nor would he grant them access to attack Gibraltar (**refuse entry into the Gulf**). A daring interpretation for a time when conventional wisdom deemed Hitler unstoppable after his forces had conquered most of Western Europe and isolated England.

---

9 Q17

Le tiers premier pis que ne feit Neron,	**The third one first does worse than Nero,**
Vuidez vaillant que fang humain refpandre:	**Vacant [soulless?] [and] valiant, how much human blood flows:**
R'edifier fera le forneron, [1]	**He [or it] will cause the oven to be rebuilt,**
Siecle d'or, mort, nouueau Roy grand efclandre.	**Golden Age, dead, new King, great scandal.**

[1]Literally "baker's boy," used here figuratively for an oven.

Nostradamus stuffs a lot of accurate prophecies into this quatrain about the French Revolution. The *Tiers* (*État*) or Third Estate (**third one**) convenes in 1789 and effectively reduces Louis XVI to a figurehead role as constitutional monarch. It is implied here that this action will soon unleash the bloodthirsty genie out of the bottle of repressed collective passions built up after centuries of royal rule, making Paris equal in decadence and violence to the capital of Nero. Like Rome, Paris will host a public orgy of executions, such as was seen in the bowels of the ancient Coliseum. By 1793 the Third Estate will become the tyrannical Committee of Public Safety, which cooks up its own version of "bread and circuses" by entertaining the Paris mob with thousands of public executions at the guillotine during the Reign of Terror. Line 3 indirectly describes the ovens and furnaces of *Le Tuile* – "the place of the Tile kilns" – where the Palace of the Tuileries would stand two centuries after Nostradamus' day. It was there that a number of significant incidents in more than one French revolution took place (see 4 Q100, 9 Q35). In line 4 Nostradamus the royalist describes the Ancient Regime as a **Golden Age** killed by Louis XVI. He is the ineffectual **new King** whose credibility with his people was twice destroyed by **scandal** – first by the diamond necklace scandal and later by breaking his pledge never to attempt an escape from France. The first scandal helped bring on the Revolution; the second led to his execution for treason and brought on the Reign of Terror.

Quatrain Indexing Date: Q17 = 1917? Nostradamus draws close parallels in his prophecies to the French and Russian Revolutions (see 1 Q14).

9 Q18

Le lys Dauffois portera dans Nanſy,	**The Lily of the Dauphin he will carry to Nancy,**
Iuſques en Flandres electeur de l'empire:	**The Elector of the Empire as far as Flanders:**
Neufue obturee[1] au grand Montmorency,	**A new prison for the great Montmorency,**
Hors lieux prouez deliure à clere[2] peine.[3]	**Outside the usual place delivered up to famous punishment [clere peine].**

[1]Late Latin *obturatum* = stopper: figure of speech for "prison."
[2]Old French *cler* = illustrious, celebrated.
[3]Old French *peine* = punishment, penalty; pain.

Once again Nostradamus transmits detailed futures in very few words. In the first two lines he identifies the next and future French ruler, Louis XIII, who would use the title **Dauphin** before coronation. He also mentions the city of **Nancy**, which was liberated in 1633 by the same king. Line 2 tells us the reason: to free Philip Christopher von Sötern, the **Elector** of the Holy Roman Empire, who was imprisoned near **Flanders** in Brussels.

Lines 3 and 4 take a retroactive look at the execution in 1632 of the Constable of France and the popular governor of Lanquedoc, Henry de Montmorency. Nostradamus calls him **the great**, the epithet for this popular hero who was tricked by Cardinal Richelieu into supporting Louis' idiot brother in his claim for the throne. Montmorency was condemned to die at the newly constructed Hôtel de Ville. The prophet correctly calls it a **new prison** and **outside the usual place** for execution.

Louis' punishment of Montmorency was indeed famous at the time. Even the Queen of England and the pope pleaded for leniency on his behalf, but to no avail. The original words for **famous punishment** are *clere peine*. The swordsman who beheaded the governor was named

Clerepeyne! All this was seen by Nostradamus over 75 years before it happened.

9 Q19

Dans le milieu de la foreſt Mayenne,	**In the middle of the forest of**
Sol au Lyon la fouldre tombera,	**Mayenne,**
Le grand baſtard yſſu du grand du Maine,	**Sun in Leo, the lightning will fall,**
Ce iour fougeres pointe en ſang entrera.	**The great bastard issued from the**
	great one of Maine,
	On this day a point will enter the
	blood of Fougères.

Mayenne was in the province of Maine in northwest France. It was a possession of the House of Guise. Part of the vast forest of Mayenne stretches between Fougères and the city of Mayenne, about 25 miles to the east. From 1552 through 1576 Maine was the territory of Edouard-Alexandre, Duc d'Anjou (later Henry III). The **great bastard** may be a figurative rather than literal condemnation by the prophet for the great Catholic troublemaker during the Wars of Religion, Charles, Duc de Mayenne (1554–1611), the second brother of Henry de Guise. Little clear context can be salvaged from this quatrain unless the lightning strike of an assassination in the month of Leo (August) is implied here. Anjou as Henry III would be stabbed by the **point** of an assassin's blade in August 1589 – not at Fougères or during a hunt in the forest of Mayenne, however, but in his bedroom at Saint-Cloud.

9 Q20

De nuict viendra par la foreſt de[1] Reines,	**By night he will come by the forest of**
Deux pars[2] vaultorte[3] Herne[4] la pierre	**Reines,**
blanche:	**Two couples, devious route, Queen,**
Le moine noir[5] en gris dedans Varennes,	**white stone:**
Eſleu[6] cap.[7] cauſe tempeſte feu, ſang	**A monk-king in gray in Varennes,**
tranche.	**Elected Cap, causes tempest, fire,**
	and bloody slicing.

[1]Grammatical error: *foreſt de(s) Reines*.
[2]Old French *pair, par* = couple.
[3]Compound word: Old French *volte* = route, and *tort* = detour.
[4]Near-anagram for *Reine* = Queen (drop the H, move the r = *rene*; add the i= *reine*).
[5]Anagram for *roi* (if you drop the n).
[6]Old French for elected.
[7]Apocope for (Louis) Capet, ie Louis XVI.

On the night of 20 June 1791 the royal family, disguised as servants of Baroness de Korff, left Paris in a heavy covered carriage to journey north to the border and freedom. Traveling throughout the night and the next day, they arrived at the town of Varennes just before midnight in search of rest and refreshment. The town's mayor, a man called Sauce, invited the weary travelers into his grocery store to take a glass of wine and, while they drank, he and his wife asked them about themselves and their journey. Sauce was suspicious of the couple – the nervous man dressed in a monkish gray hat and cloak and the woman who, although clad in a plain white dress, was betrayed by her manner and bearing as a lady of noble birth.

When an interested listener standing near by recognized the royal couple, Sauce sent him to alert the town garrison. In desperation Marie Antoinette, tears streaking her face, begged Madame Sauce to let her family continue their journey. She was unmoved by the royal tears. "I love my King, but I love my husband as well and would not have him lose his head." Louis and his family were returned to Paris as prisoners.

Over two centuries before this doomed escape attempt and its tragic consequences were played out, Nostradamus had foreseen it all.

This quatrain is startlingly accurate in every detail. It is numbered 20 for the date of the attempted escape – 20 June 1791. The royal family's road to freedom took them past the **forest of Reines** but the coach was eventually forced, by the poor road and lack of replacement horses, to make a detour. **Devious** thus describes a detour, the secrecy and their disguise. Witnesses who reported seeing the pair during their escape described them as a **married couple** and Louis as a **monk**. The town of **Varennes** was the scene of their discovery. **Queen, white stone** gives in only three words a perfect description of Marie Antoinette's appearance and emotional state. She wore a white dress, and some said that shock and distress turned her hair white overnight. **White stone** could be a double-pun alluding to both her hardness of heart towards the lower classes and lack of personal warmth, and to the notorious diamond necklace scandal. **Elected Cap**, is Louis Capet, formerly the supreme ruler Louis XVI, now elected monarch of the new constitutional government, whose death will spark a counter-revolution (**causes tempest**), that will be suppressed by the Republicans with the guillotine (**bloody slicing**).

This quatrain is #4 in James Randi's list of 10 debunkable quatrains (see *Mask of Nostradamus* pages 193–99). It is true that a significant chronicler of the events of the flight of Varennes is Mme Campan. We can be critical of those few Nostradamians who make her a participant in the flight, but this should not be used to steer the reader away from the credibility of her account, which she openly declared was "from the queen and from the other persons who witnessed her return."

Randi says he has made exhaustive research to find "other eyewitnesses" who attest that Marie Antoinette was wearing a gray dress with a black cape. I think he would do a great service to the study of Nostradamus if he would cite their names, list the resource materials, etc. He hops over the more uncomfortable hits of Nostradamus: that Louis was dressed in gray, that **Queen, white stone** is at least poetic and metaphorical, and that her severe attitude to the lower classes is implied in **stone**, as is the diamond **stone** necklace scandal. It is true in the literal sense that Louis' entourage didn't take a **devious route** from that usually taken by the post relays to Metz through Varennes. **Devious** is descriptive of the fact that his escape was secret, and in contradiction to the king's promise to the Revolutionary government that he would never leave Paris.

Louis XVI was indeed **elected**, or "chosen," to the position of constitutional monarch by the new Republican government. In the *Larousse Dictionnnaire de l'ancient Français*, the adjective *eslu* means "elevated," or "lifted in rank and dignity." But all bandying of semantics aside, the Revolutionary council elected to "raise" Louis XVI to his new position as a constitutional monarch. It suits Nostradamians to translate *cap.* as Capet because it is a fact that the new constitutional monarch was addressed by the name Citizen Capet as a snub of the more royal Bourbon surname. The **Cap** description is a key to other quatrains, making the analogy stronger.

Randi is right: Louis' entourage did not go **through** the Forest of Reines, the line reads <u>par</u> *le foreſt de Reines* or <u>by</u> *the forest of Reines*. To come <u>by</u> the forest doesn't always mean you pass **through** it. Nostradamus scholar Théodore-Claude Bouys, a contemporary of Louis XVI, in his *Nouelles considérations puisées dans la clairvoyance*, published in 1806, claims that a *Fôret des Reines* existed at that time. The road to Varennes passed right through it. One reason why Randi can't find it on a map is that this forest, like so many others in modern times, has been chopped down and forgotten. And finally, Randi avoids comment on the synchronicity of quatrain 20 matching the date of the escape 20 June.

Quatrain Indexing Date: Q20 = 20 June, 1791. It is possible that Century "9" is intended to be turned upside down, rendering it as 6 for June.

---

9 Q21

Au temple hault de Bloys ſacre Solonne,	At the high temple of St Solenne at Blois,
Nuict pont de Loyre, prelat, Roy pernicant:[1]	Night, bridge of the Loire, prelate, King killing outright:
Curſeur[2] victoire aux mareſtz de la lone,[3]	The mark of victory in the marshes on the Olonne,
Dou prelature de blancs à bormeant.[4]	Whence the prelacy of the whites – destruction.

[1]Latin *pernecans* = killing or slaying outright; or *pernix* = swift.
[2]Old French *curseur* = runner, messenger; or, Old French *cuiseur* = deep imprint, mark, impression.
[3]Provençal *lona* = pool, pond (any body of still water).
[4]À *bormeant* = a) Latin *aboriri* or *abortare* = to miscarry. b) Provençal *abouriment* = destruction.

Scholars great, mediocre, and royalist alike believe the *king of Blois* is the messianic future king of France, Henry V. But to me, it is painfully obvious that the king in question who prays in the Cathedral of St Solenne at Blois is the very un-Christlike Henry III. In the nearby Château Blois he will commit his most dastardly act. Henry III is the king **killing outright** his chief rivals, Henry de Guise and the Cardinal de Guise, in 1588. Nostradamus adds that a battle will be fought in the marshes outside the city of Blois. This never transpired. The **prelacy** of the Cardinal de Guise is certainly destroyed by the rapiers and knives of the king's henchmen.

Quatrain Indexing Date: Q21 = a near miss for 22 December 1588, the day Henry III had the Guise brothers murdered at Blois.

9 Q22

Roy & ſa court au lieu de langue halbe,	**The King and his court in the place of**
Dedans le temple vis à vis du palais:	**a cunning tongue,**
Dans le iardin Duc de Mantor & d'Albe,	**Within the temple facing the palace:**
Albe & Mantor poignard langue & palais.	**In the garden the Duke of Mantor**
	[Mantua] and of Alba,
	Alba and Mantor rapier-tongue and
	palace.

Cheetham (from Leoni) makes the mistake of thinking this continues the intrigues at Blois from the previous quatrain. The key to unlock this one lies in the translation of *Mantor* and *Albe*. The Duchy of Mantua (Mantor) and the Marquisate of Montferrat (which includes the town of Alba) are the most likely choices. Both were ruled by Guilielmo Gonzaga between 1550 and 1587. A plot to kill Gonzaga was unsuccessfully pursued at Casale, the capital of Montferrat. The reference to a (French) **King and his court** has little relevance to these Italian intrigues. Perhaps Nostradamus is simply reporting on the procession of images in the waters of his oracle, shifting his view from Blois to another location.

9 Q23

Puiſnay iouant au frech deſſous la tonne,	**The younger son playing outdoors**
Le hault du toict du milieu ſur la teſte,	**under the arbor,**
Le pere Roy au temple fainct Solonne,	**The top of the roof in the middle over**
Sacrifiant ſacrera fum de feſte.	**his head,**
	The father King in the false Temple
	is solemn,
	Sacrificing he will consecrate the
	festival smoke.

After their return from a failed attempt at escaping Revolutionary France, Louis XVI and the royal family wasted away in the Temple Prison in Paris. Louis occupied a solitary, gloomy cell in the tower keep. From his tower he could look down on his son playing in the prison gardens under the watchful eyes of the guards. Two hundred years before, Nostradamus shared this view and, almost as if he were peering over Louis' shoulder, wrote: *The younger son playing outdoors under the arbor . . . The father King in the false Temple is solemn.*

9 Q24

Sur le palais au rochier des feneſtres,	**Upon the palace at the stone balcony of the windows,**
Seront rauys les deux petits royaux:	**The two little royals will be carried off:**
Paſſer Aurelle,[1] Luthece.[2] Denis cloiſtres,	**To pass Orléans, Paris, Saint Denis cathedral,**
Nonain, mallods[3] aualler verts noyaux.	**Nun, wicked flies gulp down the green pits [cores].**

[1] Latin *Aurelianum* = Orléans.
[2] Latin *Lutetia* = Paris.
[3] *mallods* = a) Old French *malots* = flies; b) *malois* = wicked, detestable; c) Latin *malum* = apple.

We continue with the story of the sad fate of Louis' children at the Temple Prison. Nostradamus adds some fuel to the conspiracy theories by claiming the Dauphin will be spirited away from prison. The succession of cities is placed backwards on purpose. Young Louis XVII is removed first to St-Denis, then through Paris to Orléans. The final line, quite strange, can also read **Nun, to swallow cores of green apples.** It could be some detailed observation by the prophet of an incident during the journey when there was little food to eat. Perhaps the Dauphin escaped with the help of nuns. Some believe he was taken to a hiding place in the Vatican, where he died soon after his escape. History claims the first-born **little royal** Marie Thérèse escaped execution and was swapped for Republican prisoners held by the Austrians. She later married her cousin the Duc d'Angoulême. All escape theories aside, this second-born **royal** is said to have died in the Temple Prison in 1795.

9 Q25

Paſſant les ponts venir pres des roſiers,	**Passing the bridges to come near the rosebushes,**
Tard arriué pluſtoſt qu'il cuydera:	**Arrived late, sooner than he will think:**
Viendront les noues eſpaignols à Beſiers,	**The new Spaniards will come to Béziers,**
Qui icelle chaſſe emprinſe caſſera.	**So that this chase will break the enterprise.**

Béziers is on the path of the traditional Spanish invasion route into France from Roussillon; thus a **new** Spanish invasion is predicted. Béziers remained a frontier town until Roussillon was incorporated into France in 1659. *Des rosiers* could implicate any number of French towns named Rosiers or similar. The closest candidate would be Rosières in the Massif Central.

9 Q26

Nice fortie fur nom des lettres afpres,	**Leaving Nice under the name of the harsh letters,**
La grande cappe fera prefent non fien:	**The great [Pope] will present a gift not his own:**
Proche de vultry aux murs de vertes capres,	**Near Voltri at the walls with green capers,**
Apres plombin le vent à bon effien.	**Beyond Piombino the wind in good earnest.**

Voltri is on the Mediterranean coast between Genoa and Savona. Piombino is down the Italian coast opposite the island of Elba. After his first abdication in 1814 Napoleon was exiled to Elba, where the Congress of Vienna permitted him to rule the little island. But a toy empire could not satisfy for long his hunger for power. In late February 1815 he set sail with a band of 1,500 men in a little flotilla, evading the British cruisers off Piombino and hugging the coast near Genoa all the way to a landfall in France near Cannes. Napoleon is the man elsewhere described by a **ferocious name** (1 Q76); in this case Napoleon is **the name of the harsh letters**. In 1817, Pope Pius VII, who Napoleon tormented and imprisoned at Savona, requested the British lessen his hardships during his final exile on St Helena.

9 Q27

De bois la garde vent cloz rond pont fera,	**The guardian of the woods, the wind will be close round the bridge,**
Hault le receu frappera le Dauphin:	**The received one high will strike the Dauphin:**
Le vieux teccon[1] bois vnis paffera,	**The old craftsman will pass the woods with company,**
Paffant plus oultre du Duc le droit confin.	**Passing far beyond the rightful confines of the Duke.**

[1]*Teccon* = a) Old French *tecon* = a game like soccer; b) Greek *tektõn* = carpenter, craftsman, which is more likely here.

A quatrain dense with details. Laver applied it to Dubois and therefore to the reign of Louis XV. Cheetham (from Leoni) sees it as another example that Nostradamus foresaw the escape of Louis XVII from the Temple

Prison. Other quatrains, however, confirm history's claim that he died in prison in June 1795. *Plus oultre* could be part of the motto Nostradamus uses for Charles V (*Plus outre Carlo Quint*), putting this event somewhere – and somewhat retroactively – between 1555 and 1558.

9 Q28

Voille Symacle[1] port Maffiliolique,	**Allied sail [fleet], port of**
Dans Venife port marcher aux Pannons:	**Marseilles,**
Partir du gouffre & finus Illirique,	**In the port of Venice to sail to the**
Vaft à Socile, Ligurs coups de canons.	**Pannonias:**
	To part from the gulf and bay of
	Illyria [the Adriatic Sea],
	Destruction in Sicily, Genoa, cannon
	shots.

[1]Greek *symmachos* = allied, auxiliary.

During World War II Churchill, ever the anti-communist, lobbied hard for an Allied sea invasion of the Balkans. He hoped to seize Yugoslavia, Hungary, and Czechoslovakia and march on Nazi Germany from the south, to forestall the occupation of much of Eastern Europe by the Soviets. An invasion of the Riviera took place instead. The RAF and US Eighth Air Force bombings of Genoa and the Anglo-American campaign in Sicily are implied by line 4.

9 Q29

Lors que celuy qu'à nul ne donne lieu,	**When the one who gives place to**
Abandonner voudra lieu prins non prins:	**none,**
Feu nef par faignes,[1] bitument à Charlieu,	**Will want to abandon the place**
Seront Quintin Balez[2] reprins.	**captured yet not captured:**
	New fire through swamps, bitumen at
	Charlieu,
	St Quentin [and] Calais will be
	recaptured.

[1]Old French *saigne* = marsh, swamp: there are marshes around St Quentin.
[2]*Balez*: cryptogram for Calais.

François de Guise, the Lieutenant-General of France, recaptured Calais from the English on 6 January 1558. St Quentin was returned to the French in the general settlement of Cateau-Cambrésis in 1559. The latter fact makes this a bona fide prophetic success. Whether Nostradamus actually foresaw the capture of Calais is arguable. It depends on the honesty of Nostradamus, for the prophecy was fulfilled before special copies of the Epistle and the last 300 quatrains reached the printers.

9 Q30

Au port de PVOLA & de fainct Nicolas,	At the port of Pola and of San Nicolo,
Perir Normande au gouffre Phanaticque:[1]	A Norman will perish in the gulf of
Cap.[2] de Bifance raues crier helas,	Quarnero,
Secours de Gaddes[3] & du grand Philipique.	[Pope's cope] in the streets of
	Byzantium cries, "Alas!"
	Help from Cadiz and the great Philip.

[1]Latin Sinus Flanaticus = Gulf of Quarnero.
[2]Usually stands as apocope for Capet, but in this case it is the "cape" (the cope) of a pope.
[3]Latin Gades = Cadiz.

All the place names put this one entirely in former Yugoslavia. Clearly it is not a modern-day prophecy but a failed alternative future. No large-scale Christian crusade by Spanish and Imperial forces was launched against the Turks in the Balkans during the 16th or any other century. Apparently Philip II was meant to use the great Spanish port of Cadiz as the main supply center for the Balkan crusade.

9 Q31

Le tremblement de terre à Mortara,	The trembling of the earth at
Caffich fainct George[1] à demy perfondrez:	Mortara,
Paix affoupie, la guerre efueillera,	The tin islands of Saint George are
Dans temple à Pafques abyfmes enfondrez.	half sunk:
	Drowsy with peace, war will awaken,
	In the temple abysses ripped open at
	Easter [spring].

[1]Caffich faint George = Greek Cassiterides, the tin islands (the name given to Cornwall and the Scilly Islands) of St George (the cross of St George has been the standard of England from the times of the Crusaders).

Nostradamus predicts a tremendous quake will submerge half of England under the Atlantic Ocean. If the reference is not a synecdoche for England, the prophecy applies to the Scilly Islands off Cornwall. England's southwestern region will sink when a quake rocks a wide region of Europe from Cornwall all the way to Mortara, Italy, in the Po valley. Leoni believes a statue of St George in Mortara (with tin inside it) is involved. Great seismic activity is predicted in several quatrains for the spring or around **Easter**. If May 2000 is implied, then the war is World War III (1999) and the temple perhaps represents the Vatican destroyed by fire and tidal waves. This scenario is chronicled in other quatrains as part of future tribulations that face the last pope.

In AD 592 the Irish missionary St Columba (or Columbcille) saw a vision that Ireland would be sunk under a sudden overwhelming flood seven years before Judgement Day. According to the modern seer Edgar

Cayce, the British Isles and the west coast of northwestern Europe will be changed by quakes and inundations in the "twinkling of an eye." If we assume that Judgement Day comes with the new millennium and count back seven years, we reach 1993. Southern England did not sink in that year, but the region was *half-sunk* in the wettest rainy season on record. Perhaps prophetic scholars can now file this shared vision away under "history's prophetic exaggerations."

Quatrain Indexing Date: Q31 = 1931. Between 1931 and 1984 the north magnetic pole has shifted 480 times to the northwest, while the south magnetic pole is racing into the Indian Ocean. Scientists are disturbed by the accelerated shifts in the 1990s of the true and magnetic poles of Earth. Leading experts believe we are already undergoing a new axis shift. The north pole has moved ten feet between 1960 and 1968 – eight times faster than in the previous 60 years.

9 Q32

De fin porphire profond collon trouuee,	**A deep column of fine porphyry found,**
Deſſoubs la laze[1] eſcripts capitolin:[2]	**Under the base inscriptions of the**
Os poil retors Romain force prouuee,	**Capitol:**
Claſſe agiter au port de Methelin.	**Bones, twisted hair, Roman force**
	proved,
	Fleet to stir at the port of Mitylene.

[1]Greek *laz* = foot, base.
[2]Latin *Capitolinus* = pertaining to the Capitol, of ancient Rome in particular.

Mitylene is the name of the ancient capital town on the Aegean island of Lesbos, off the west coast of Asia Minor. Roman inscriptions in line 2 may indicate the location of some tomb. Perhaps it is that of the Apostle Peter. Larmor (1925) reports that in 1588 "an enormous obelisk of rose granite" was found by workmen in the Basilica of St Peter in Rome. "At this date," Larmor adds, "a Venetian squadron invaded the isle of Lesbos and its capital."

9 Q33

Hercules Roy de Rome & d'Annemarc,[1]	**Hercules King of Rome and of**
De Gaule trois Guion[2] ſurnommé:	**Annemark,**
Trembler l'Italie & l'vude de ſainct Marc,	**Three [times] one surnamed de**
Premier ſur tous monarque renommé.	**Gaulle will lead France.**
	Italy and the one of St Mark [Venice]
	to tremble,
	First monarch, renowned above all.

[1]Leoni sees this as a clever enigma: *the Mark of Anne.* The kingdoms of Bohemia-Moravia and Hungary became a Habsburg *mark* or frontier province in 1526, through the marriage to the Emperor-designate Ferdinand of their heiress, Anne.
[2]Old French *Guion* = Guide, chief, leader.

Nostradamus starts off on the wrong foot with line 1. It is chock-full of ambitious visions for the infant son of Henry II, Hercules, later Duc d' Alençon. He is made **King of Rome** (the Holy Roman Empire) and also King **of Annemark**, which would mean king of Hungary and Bohemia. A striking prophecy, since it is strikingly wrong. Line 2 restores some equilibrium. We are moved far into the future to another Herculean French leader. In 1940 Charles de Gaulle distinguished himself by leading France three times – first as head of the Free French forces, then as the leader of the provisional post-World War II government until 1946, and again in 1958 during the Algerian crisis, during which he gained voter approval to become the first president of the newly established French Fifth Republic. Line 3 stands for Fascist Italy, which did tremble with the shot and shells of units of de Gaulle's Free French fighting alongside their British and American allies.

Many royalist-leaning Nostradamian scholars believe the **first monarch** of renown is a future French King Henry V. However, I believe this reference could apply equally to de Gaulle, since Nostradamus doesn't seem to differentiate between presidents, chiefs, or kings when speaking about our times. During his long presidency (1958–70) the imperious de Gaulle proved himself to be the most significant French leader in the 20th century.

9 Q34

Le part ſoluz mary[1] ſera mittré,[2]
Retour conflict paſſera ſur le thuille:
Par cinq cens vn trahyr ſera tiltré,
Narbon[3] & Saulce[4] par coutaux auons
  d'huille.

**The husband, alone, afflicted, will be
  mitered,
Return, conflict will take place at the
  Tuileries:
By the five hundred one betrayer will
  be ennobled,
Narbonne and Saulce we have oil for
  our blades.**

[1] Old French marir = to be afflicted, to be vexed.
[2] The miter actually represents the cap of Mithras, the ancient Persian god of light in the Zoroastrian tradition, who wages constant war with the forces of darkness. Mithraism became a highly ritualized religion very popular with soldiers of ancient Rome. The cap was adopted by French revolutionaries as Roman or eastern classical attire was in vogue.
[3] Either the town of Narbonne, or Louis Marie Jacques Narbonne, moderate French revolutionary.
[4] Either Salces near Narbonne, or an Old French spelling of Sauce, surname of the mayor of Varennes (see 9 Q20).

The mayor of Varennes is named outright. The quatrain also anticipates two violent incidents at the Tuileries – the abuse of the king and the massacre of his Swiss Guard. The **husband** links this quatrain to the Varennes prophecy's **married couple** (9 Q20). Louis, separated from his family, will face a murderous mob at his Tuileries apartments and be forced to put on the revolutionary cap; he is thus described by Nostradamus as *mittré* because the cap (miter) resembled those worn by the ancient priests of Mithras.

Le Thuille, the word used in *Les Propheties* for the Tuileries, means "place of the tiles." When Nostradamus visited Paris in 1556, the site on which the palace was later to be built contained tile kilns. In August 1792 the Tuileries was ransacked in a bloody attack led by the 513 Fédérés, better known as the Five Hundred Marseillaise for their song, which later became the French national anthem.

The enobled betrayer is *Sauce*, spelled with an *l* in the archaic form; *Narbon* is Narbonne, a moderate revolutionary who tried to persuade the National Assembly to pardon the king. Nostradamus couples the names of Sauce and Narbon to pit radicals and moderates against each other over line 4's cryptic play on words: **we have oil for our blades**. As a grocery store owner, Sauce would also have been an oil merchant. In figurative terms his role in the king's arrest oiled the blade that was to sever not only the king's head but Sauce's own, in the Reign of Terror to come.

This is #5 in James Randi's list of ten debunkable quatrains (see *Mask of Nostradamus* pages 199–205). It suits Randi to judge the parts while ignoring their connection to the whole. He thinks *Par cinq cen(t)s* does not mean **by the five hundred** because Nostradamus would have been a bad poet not to follow the poetic laws to make *cens* into *censura* to keep the syllables in sync with line 2. The fact remains that Nostradamus *is* a bad poet: moreover he is purposely intending to become even worse. In hundreds of instances Nostradamus gets the gender of his nouns wrong, and makes all kinds of wild spelling errors and rhythmical barbarities of verse. Some of this is done for occult effect. I doubt Randi ever actually studied at the feet of mystics. If he had had an authentic master he would know from direct experience that they sometimes play the fool and use cloudy devices to push one's bias button. He might come to understand that an egoistic, programmed-to-be-mediocre personality superimposed over our true nature must ever find justification for itself to survive. A mystic will sometimes write in a way to expose this egoism. Those of us who are identified with our ego will be satisfied that the mystic is a charlatan and will walk away; whereas those who have the courage to dis-identify with their point of view may continue hurtling over these obstacles to experience something beyond the foolish behavior of the mystic and their own hair-splitting, conditioned mind.

Randi makes an elaborate literary sleight-of-hand over the tile kilns/ Tuileries issue. He says that since Catherine came to visit Nostradamus in 1565 (wrong! it was 1564), she would have made him aware of the

Tuileries project, which was under construction in 1564. Of course no documentation of this is provided by Randi. And anyway, how does this relate to a prophecy published in 1558? Well, if you isolate this point and ignore all the others in the quatrain you could say that Nostradamus was hedging his bets that eventually the tile kiln factories he passed in 1556 would later be replaced by the palace. But this still doesn't explain how Nostradamus saw the palace attacked by around five hundred revolutionaries. How would he know about a king being **mitered** with the Mithras cap in that palace? How did he know the names of two major figures in the French Revolution, Narbonne and Sauce? If you have a predatory mind you can isolate each point and find ways to undermine it, just as you can dissect each part of a flower until you conclude that a flower never existed.

9 Q35

Et Ferdinand blonde ſera deſcorte,
Quitter la fleur ſuyure le Macedon:
Au grand beſoing defaillira ſa routte,
Et marchera contre le Myrmidon.

And Ferdinand the fair will be
    stripped bare,
To abandon the flower, to follow the
    Macedonian:
In the great need his course to fail,
And he will march against the
    Myrmidon [Macedonians?].

King Ferdinand of Bulgaria was brown haired, but this is the only mistake Nostradamus makes in this quatrain. He was brought up in France and was a passionate Francophile. But World War I forced him to abandon France and join with Germany, for the Kaiser had promised to help Bulgaria regain Macedonia, which was predominantly populated by Bulgarians. He had twice failed to achieve this dream against the Turks, in the First Balkan War of 1912–13 and against his former allies the Serbians, Greeks, and Romanians, who cheated him of Macedonia in the Second Balkan War of 1913. The Serbian treatment of Bulgarians in Macedonia was far worse than at the hands of the Turkish Sultan.

The **Myrmidon** are the soldiers of Thrace who went to Serbia. During World War I Ferdinand's armies attacked Thrace and Serbia. By 1915 a French expeditionary force along with the British army had landed in Greece. Once again Ferdinand was betrayed by an ally. The Germans drastically reduced their forces in Bulgaria in 1918 for their final push on the Western Front. This allowed his beloved Frenchmen to aid his Serbian enemies to sweep the Bulgarian army out of Macedonia in the battle of the Vardar river. At the end of the war Bulgaria was indeed **stripped bare**. The Versailles Treaty reduced her to a mere 30,000 square miles and a population of 5 million, and demanded that she pay a reparations burden of 2.25 billion gold francs. Resentment was so great among his exhausted subjects that Ferdinand fled Bulgaria in 1918. He was succeeded by his son, King Boris III.

9 Q36

Vn grãd Roy prins entre les mains d'vn Loyne,[1]	**A great king captured by the hands of a young man,**
Non loing de Paſque confuſion coup cultre:[2]	**Not far from Easter, confusion, incision of the knife:**
Perpet.[3] captifs temps que fouldre en la huſne,	**Everlasting captives, times when the lightning is on the top,**
Lors que trois freres ſe bleſſeront & mutre.	**When three brothers will be wounded and murdered.**

[1]Misprint for Old French joine = young man.
[2]Latin culter = plowshare; razor, knife, (modern) scalpel.
[3]Apocope of Latin perpetualis = everlasting, perpetual.

On 30 March 1981, 20 days before Easter Sunday, President Reagan was shot by William Hinckley Jr while exiting the VIP door of the Washington DC Hilton Hotel. Along with the bewilderment and trauma felt in America on that terrible day, there was confusion about how badly the president was injured. As six shots rang out the president had immediately been shoved into a waiting limousine by Jerry Parr, the senior secret service agent on the scene. The car made for the White House and a few critical minutes passed before Parr or the president knew he was seriously wounded. Reagan assumed the pain he felt under his arm and the shortness of breath were caused by the security agent's shove. Then he coughed bright red blood, indicating a serious lung wound, and Parr immediately ordered the car to drive to George Washington University Hospital. At the hospital the president's natural vitality continued to work against him, concealing the seriousness of the wound. He walked unaided into the emergency room, but he had already lost three pints of blood from internal bleeding. The bullet had ricocheted off the limousine, entered Reagan's left side under the arm, and bounced off the rib, puncturing and collapsing a lung and lodging an inch above his heart. Two hours of surgery were required to pull the president out of danger.

The final two lines could define the general time window for the Reagan assassination attempt: the turbulent latter half of the 20th century (**when three** [Kennedy] **brothers will be wounded**). The **everlasting captives** might represent the 63 American hostages held in Iran for **444** days, released minutes after President Reagan was sworn into office. The phrase can also double for the next seemingly **everlasting** hostage crisis in Lebanon plaguing Reagan's two terms. **Lightning on the top** works well as a description of the aerials televising both the Kennedy assassination and the attempt on Reagan's life.

9 Q37

Pont & molins en Decembre verſez,	Bridge[s] and [wind]mills overturned
En ſi haut lieu montera la Garonne:	in December,
Murs, edifices, Tholoſe renuerſez,	The Garonne [river] will rise to a
Qu'on ne ſçaura ſon lieu auant matronne.[1]	very high place:
	Walls, buildings, Toulouse overturned,
	So that none will know his place
	before [the] midwife.

[1]Matron or midwife.

A vision of a great flood on the Garonne overwhelming Toulouse in southwest France, and another warning of the coming climatic disruptions in the 21st century. The last two lines imply that the floods will unravel the social fabric of society. The final cryptic statement about knowing one's place before a **midwife** could apply to our near future. In the first half of the 21st century everyone will experience a break with the past and all its outmoded morals and traditions. The collective prophetic message of many seers underscores a new birth for all humanity, which requires letting go of everything one knows from before. This at face value looks horrific to the ego, but if one takes it as a spiritual metaphor, then this phrase promises a new start for all humankind, such as that foretold by Isaiah 65:17: "Behold, I will create new heavens and a new Earth. The former things will not be remembered, nor will they come to mind."

See Index: global warming.

9 Q38

L'entree de Blaye par Rochelle & l'Anglois,	The entry at Blay for La Rochelle and
Paſſera outre le grand Æmathien:[1]	the English,
Non loing d'Agen attendra le Gaulois,	Will pass beyond the great Macedonian:
Secours Narbonne deceu par entretien.	Not far from Agen [he?] will wait for
	the French,
	Help [from] Narbonne misled by a
	conference.

[1]Latin Emathia = poetic synonym for Macedonia (or Thessaly).

Philip II is usually **the great Macedonian** after his classical namesake, Philip II of Macedon, father of Alexander the Great. But Le Pelletier conjures a better meaning, applying Aemathien to the name of a mythological figure who opened the gates of morning to the Sun. Thus we have the Sun King Louis XIV.

I don't see this as another failed quatrain on a future Hundred Years War with the English; the change of characters here makes the prophecy work far better for the events of 1702–04: "Louis the Great will feel at ease when he will have constructed, in 1689, the Pate de Blaye, to close the entrance of the Gironde to the English, who are allied with the French Calvinists of La Rochelle against the Revocation of the Edict of Nantes. As for the Camisards, in revolt in the Cevennes, they will await the help from Agen and Narbonne promised them by their co-religionists: relief that will be rendered impossible after the submission in 1704 of Jean Cavalier, their principal leader, following a conference at Nîmes with Marshal Villars."

9 Q39

En Arbiſſel à Veront & Carcari,	**In Albisola to Veront and Carcara,**
De nuict conduits pour Sauonne atrapper,	**Conducted by night to entrap Savona,**
Le vifz Gaſcon Turby, & la Scerry,	**The quick Gascon La Turbie and**
Derrier mur vieux & neuf palais gripper.	**L'Escarène,**
	Behind the wall old and new palace to
	pounce upon.

A palace on the Riviera between Genoa and Savona is raided by a Gascon pirate. La Turbie and L'Escarène are north of Monaco. The raider's haven is therefore in the Duchy of Savoy. Albisola, **Veront** (probably Vorazzo or Voragine), and the mountain pass of **Carcara** were all in the Republic of Genoa. I am unable to verify if any raid of this kind took place.

9 Q40

Pres de Quintin dans la foreſt bourlis,	**Near [St] Quentin in the forest of**
Dans l'abbaye ſeront Flamens ranches:	**Bourlis,**
Les deux puiſnays de coups my eſtourdis,	**In the Abbey the Flemish will be**
Suitte oppreſſée & garde tous aches.	**butchered:**
	The two younger sons half-stunned
	from blows,
	The rest crushed and the guard all
	hacked to pieces.

Quite obscure. Jaubert believes it describes the preliminary moves of the Spanish army prior to its siege of St Quentin in 1557, making this quatrain slightly retroactive. He also believes **Bourlis** is a proper name for the Abbey of Vermandois, in the forest of the same name, which was captured by the Spanish. Leoni views Jaubert's interpretation as a "combination of conjecture and downright falsification."

9 Q41

Le grand Chyren ſoy ſaiſir Auignon,	**The great Chyren will seize Avignon,**
De Rome lettres en miel plein	**From Rome letters [written] in a honey**
d'amertume:	**full of bitterness:**
Lettre ambaſſade partir de Chanignon,	**Embassy letter to leave from Chanignon,**
Carpentras pris par Duc noir rouge	**Carpentras taken by a black duke with**
plume.	**a red plume.**

This is the future Nostradamus promises his king if he only can leave temptation behind and refuse to fight just one more match with Montgomery in ritual combat. Rather than lying half blinded and bloodied in his deathbed, he could be riding down a different path on which the Venaissin papal enclave of Avignon (including Carpentras) falls to his sword, and the embittered and vanquished pope is forced to anoint Henry's face with **honey** during his coronation as a new Holy Roman Emperor *and* King of France.

Chanignon could be a cryptogram for Chantonnay, the Spanish ambassador to France between 1557 and 1560. This is the only fulfilled prediction in this quatrain. It seems Nostradamus already knew that three years later the ambassador's letters concerning his prophecies would find their way to Philip II of Spain.

9 Q42

De Barſelonne, de Gennes & Veniſe,	From Barcelona [Spain], from Genoa and Venice,
De la Secille peſte Monet vnis:	From Sicily, pestilence allied with Monaco.
Contre Barbare claſſe prendront la viſe,	They will take their aim against the Barbary fleet,
Barbare, pouſſe bien loing iuſqu'à Thunis.	The barbarian driven very far, as far back as Tunis.

The Papal and Venetian fleets rendezvous at Messina with Spanish galleys (including contingents from **Monaco** and **Genoa**) to form the Christian armada commanded by Don Juan of Austria. They crush the combined Turkish and Algerian Barbary fleet in the Gulf of Lepanto – the present-day Gulf of Corinth – forever ending Muslim dominance of the Mediterranean. The quatrain also chronicles the immediate strategic results of Lepanto, Don Juan's invasion and conquest of Tunis in North Africa.

9 Q43

Proche à deſcendre l'armée Crucigere,[1]	Near the point of landing the Crusader army,
Sera guettee par les Iſmaëlites:	Will be ambushed by the Ismailites:
De tous coſtez batus par nef Rauiere,	Struck from all sides by the ship Raviere,
Prompt aſſaillis de dix galeres eſlites.	Promptly attacked by the elite galleys.

[1]Latin *crucem-gerens* = bearing a cross, thus a crusader.

Either this is a future crusade in the Persian Gulf or the Gulf War from our recent past (1991) is implied here. The planned landing of the Coalition forces on the shores of Kuwait was little more than a ruse to tie down Iraqi forces on the coast. In a future Middle Eastern war the United States and her allies may not have the luxury of Saudi Arabian ports and airfields for a slow build-up of forces, especially if Saudi Arabia herself becomes a fanatic Islamic state allied against the West and Israel. The West may be forced to make a landing on hostile shores in the 21st century.

A number of ships in the US Navy have had the name USS *Paul Revere*. A warship with this name will play an important role in the next Gulf War.

9 Q44

Migres migres de Genefue treftous,	**Leave, leave Geneva everyone!**
Saturne d'or en fer fe changera,	**Saturn will change wealth to**
Le contre RAYPOZ[1] *exterminera tous,*	**weapons,[2]**
Auant l'a ruent de ciel fignes fera.	RAYPOZ **will exterminate all the**
	opposition.
	Before the invasion the heavens will
	show signs.

[1]Cryptogram for: Zopyros, the Babylonian betrayer; b) (phonetic) cryptogram: RAIPOS = OSIRAP, in which replace P with R to get OSIRAK, site of the former Iraqi nuclear weapons reactor outside of Baghdad.
[2]Alternative: **Saturn will change itself from gold into iron.**

At first glance previous interpreters have applied this one to the Geneva of Nostradamus' day, warning its citizens to beware of a religious witch-hunt launched by John Calvin. He is RAYPOZ, a cryptogram for Zopyre (Zopyros), the notorious betrayer of Babylon to the Persians, who cut off his nose and ears and generally mutilated himself to play a limping fugitive from Persian barbarity. While in Babylon he gained many influential and sympathetic friends whom he used to deliver the city into the hands of Darius.

Until recently no one found reason to revise this interpretation; then Babylon rose again as a significant newsmaker in the guise of Saddam Hussein's Iraq. Rather than Calvin being a Zopyros reincarnated, the new threat to Geneva — and what it currently represents on the world stage — comes from a modern Zopyros of Babylon who figuratively cut off his nose to spite his face in the Gulf War of 1991, and is currently seeking sympathy and enough influential friends to develop an atomic bomb.

In addition to its role as the United Nations' second capital, the city of Geneva also stands as a general synecdoche for the peaceful or destructive uses of the atom. In August 1955 representatives of 72 countries gathered in the city for a first meeting to exchange information on the peaceful uses of atomic power. Some countries, misusing the knowledge acquired at this meeting, were later able to develop into today's Third

World nuclear powers. In the following decades the name "Geneva" became synonymous with efforts by Russia, the United States, and the United Nations to negotiate nuclear arms control and stem the tide of ethnic wars.

The quatrain clearly implies that the diplomats of Geneva have something to fear from this Nostradamian riddle. Deciphering the right meaning for the enigmatic word, RAYPOZ, could help the peacekeepers forestall Armageddon.

Take this interpretation of RAYPOZ as a biblical anagram for "Zopyros," and you get a modern parallel in Saddam Hussein of Iraq (Babylon). He is betrayed by the Reagan and Bush administrations (actively involved in diplomatic missions to Geneva); although they tacitly supported his war against Iran during the 1980s, the Bush Administration turned on him in August 1990 when he invaded Kuwait. The resulting siege of Iraq by the Western and Arab coalition forces required Saddam to relinquish all the military and political gains he had made in the Iran–Iraq war.

Rescrambling the letters of RAYPOZ, while following the Nostradamian rules for decoding anagrams, supports this interpretation. Then RAYPOZ represents not only Zopyros but also an actual location called Osirak outside of Baghdad. If we spell RAYPOZ phonetically (RAYPOS) we get OSIRAP. Follow the rule of replacing one letter (P) with another (K) and we have OSIRAK. This was the name of the place, not far from the site of the ancient city of Babylon, where the French built an experimental reactor. In 1981 the reactor was bombed by the Israelis, who were convinced that Iraq was using it to build the first Islamic atomic bomb. Since that attack Saddam Hussein has dedicated himself –with little concern for the blood and suffering of his people and the self-mutilation of Iraq via wars and sanctions – to take revenge, both on Israel and, ultimately, on the northern powers – the EU and the United States.

If we are following the correct path in this interpretation, RAYPOZ stands as an anagram for the weapons of mass destruction Saddam Hussein or his heirs will use to take future revenge on America and the West. Despite the devastation of his country's infrastructure and the dismembering of his conventional armies in the Gulf War, disturbing evidence mounts against Saddam. It is hard to imagine him ever honoring his obligations related to UN sanctions on his country; beating his biological and chemical weapons into plowshares and smashing his nuclear weapons into pruning hooks does not appear to be on his program. Large stockpiles of chemical warheads with hundreds of Scud missiles to carry them aloft are still unaccounted for. A flow of weapons-grade plutonium smuggled out of the former states of the Soviet Union finds its way to Baghdad. The CIA estimates that once UN sanctions are lifted, Iraq could produce nuclear weapons within five to seven years, restock its chemical weapons within a year, and reactivate its biological agents in only a few weeks.

The final line encourages us to examine some of the major astrological *signs* that date an invasion of RAYPOZ in our near future. Astrologers point to the conjunction of Uranus and Neptune on 24 October 1993 as one of the most significant cosmic **signs**. It dates the beginning of a fire of awakening consciousness spreading over the world, or a fire of world war stretching across the planet in a rash of ethnic and Middle Eastern conflicts. From 1993 through 1996, the number of wars raging throughout the world began to climb to levels experienced during the Cold War: 37 to 45 conflicts.

Another important celestial event is Saturn's transit from Aquarius to Pisces in late January 1994. The two-year transit of Saturn through Pisces was meant to force us to face our spiritual attitudes. This encounter brings to the surface collective issues of human denial, our insistence on ignoring the need to drop fossilized religious beliefs, dead social traditions, and dogmatic political policies. Becoming fundamentalist about any or all of these could drag us into a Third World War. From an astrological and esoteric point of view, these issues should have been positively dealt with during Saturn's transit of Pisces; otherwise many more wars will break out during its transit of Aries beginning on 7 April 1996, through 10 June 1998. This is the most dangerous near-future period for RAYPOZ to inflict its revenge in an act of nuclear terrorism. If the Third Antichrist does not sabotage our future during this time window, many of Nostradamus' references to terrorists attacks and plagues of **false** (or atomic) **dust** will threaten us again in the 2020s (see 5 Q90).

9 Q45

Ne fera foul iamais de demander,	**There will never remain a single one**
Grand Mendofus[1] obtiendra fon empire	**to ask,**
Loing de la cour fera contremander,	**Great Mendosus will obtain his empire**
Pymond, Picard, Paris, Tyrron[2] le pire.	**Far from the court he will cause to be**
	countermanded,
	Piedmont, Picardy, Paris, Tuscany
	the worst.

[1]*Mendofus* = a) Latin *mendosus* = full of faults, erroneous; b) cryptogram for Vendôme, the House of Bourbon, which ruled Navarre and won the French throne under Henry IV (of Navarre) in 1594.
[2]Latin *Tyrrheni*, Etrurians (thus Tuscan, Florentine).

Mendosus is a clever anagram for Henry IV. He would become king of France (**will obtain his empire**) after a long, hard struggle with Henry III and the Catholic Leaguers during the Wars of Religion. He would win over the Catholics by changing (**countermanded**) his oath to become a

Protestant. Later he would wage war with the House of Savoy (**Piedmont**). The mention of **Picardy**, the northernmost province of France, has little relevance to the time of Henry's reign, though Picardy was later to be an avenue of invasions and the scene of several sieges during the latter half of the Thirty Years War. Henry clearly never embarked on any Italian adventures as the Valois had.

9 Q46

Vuydez, fuyez de Tholofe les rouges	**Vacate, flee from Toulouse the reds**
Du facrifice faire expiation,	**To make expiation, for the sacrifice**
Le chef du mal deffouz l'vmbre[1] des courges	**The chief of evil beneath the shadow [unconsciousness] of imbeciles**
Mort eftrangler carne omination.[2]	**Death to smother carnal prognostication.**

[1]Shadow; shade; obscurity; (figuratively) unconsciousness; being in the dark.
[2]Latin *carne ominatio* = divination through flesh (raw meat).

Reds stands universally for cardinals or revolutionaries. The most likely application would be a double-pun for **red** Republicans persecuting **red** cardinals and priests in Toulouse in the purge of the Catholic Church during the French Revolution. Another application describes Wellington's British **red** coats fighting the French **reds** of Napoleonic France at the Battle of Toulouse in 1814. Other than that, the details of this verse remain hopelessly cryptic.

9 Q47

Les foulz fignez d'indigne deliurance,	**The undersigned to the infamous deliverance,**
Et de la multe[1] auront contre aduis,	**And from the mob having contrary advice,**
Change monarque mis en perille pence,[2]	**Monarch's change of mind puts him in peril,**
Serrez en caige fe verront vis à vis.	**Locked up in cages they will see each other face to face.**

[1]Latin *multus* = many, multitude; a throng.
[2]Double pun: pennies/pence or thought, mind.

Jaubert takes a swipe at applying this to François II (1559–1660) but I would place it one year earlier as a introduction to Henry II's notorious jousting accident foretold in 1 Q35.

Line 1 is a dig at the marriage contract signed by Henry II with Philip II for the marriage by proxy of Henry's daughter Elizabeth. Our prophet uses **infamous deliverance** to describe the humiliating peace terms heaped on Henry II for losing the Italian Wars after the French rout at St Quentin. In other words, by promising never to threaten Italy Henry is *delivered* from a disastrous string of wars that have left the royal coffers on the verge of bankruptcy.

Line 2 describes the crowds gathered for the tournament at the rue de St Antoine. Maybe the crowds were starting to leave after the official final bout ended in a draw – but they flocked back to the lists when word was passed around that the king asked for yet another try at Montgomery.

Line 3 has a wicked double-pun. The French word for "thought" rhymes (at least in the spelling) with the English "pence" or pennies. In other words, money is where Henry's mind is. The threat of national bankruptcy was never far from his thoughts during his final days on Earth. The last line gives us another interesting *cage* riddle. Moments before the king makes his fateful run at Montgomery, the prophet takes us into his helmet to see his adversary through the gilded cage of his visor. That same gaze will be half-blinded a second later when a large splinter from Montgomery's lance pierces the *cage*.

9 Q48

La grand cité d'Occean maritime,	**The great city of the maritime ocean,**
Enuironnee de maretz en criſtail:	**Surrounded by a swamp of crystal:**
Dans le ſolſtice hyemal & la prime,	**In the winter solstice and the spring,**
Sera temptee de vent eſpouuental.	**Will be tested by a terrible wind.**

The all-glass façades of the world's newest skyscrapers transforming the face of cities like New York and Hong Kong could be described by a 16th-century man as swamps of crystal destroyed by thousand-mile-an-hour winds.

This *swamp of crystal* could represent the abstract, crystal shard-like skyscrapers of Pudong, the new financial section of Shanghai scheduled for completion by the year 2000. Pudong is expected to outstrip Hong Kong as the financial capital of Asia. The *terrible wind* could whip through Shanghai, Hong Kong or any number of futuristic high-rise cities in the middle of the next century that meet up with a greenhouse-enhanced typhoon or hurricane. Worldwatch Institute estimates that the world's warming oceans will feed killer hurricanes that will exceed the ferocity of today's storms by 50 percent. It is not inconceivable that even skyscrapers could topple from the impact of such deadly winds.

9 Q49

Gand & Bruceles marcheront contre Enuers	**Ghent and Brussels will march against Antwerp**
Senat[1] du Londres mettront à mort leur roy,	**The Senate of London will put to death their king,**
Le ſel & vin luy feront à l'enuers,	**The salt and wine will overthrow him,**
Pour eux auoir le regne en deſſarroy.	**To have them will put the realm in disarray.**

[1]Nostradamus means Parliament.

In 1648 the Spanish grew exhausted with their 80-year war against the Dutch. They ceded the Scheldt to Holland resulting in the financial ruin of Antwerp. A year later the English Parliament executed Charles I. **Salt and wine** is a 16th-century figure of speech standing for taxation as well as strength and wisdom. Its first meaning aptly describes the king's unpopular tax levies used to sustain his rule of England without Parliament, which he had abolished. The second meaning describes Charles' legacy of poor decisions based on the rotten advice he received from his ministers and supporters throughout his reign.

This quatrain is #6 in James Randi's list of ten debunkable quatrains (see *Mask of Nostradamus* pages 205–07). Randi relies on a "quick perusal of history books" to pull attention away from 1648 and the final stages of the Eighty-Year War in the Spanish Netherlands. He places line 1's events in the Spanish Netherlands of 1555 where, he says, there was "much activity going on in the area of Ghent, Brussels and Antwerp." But as usual he doesn't specify *what* activity. It certainly was not seditious forces of Ghent and Brussels marching against Antwerp. If it had been, I'm sure Mr Randi would have loudly declared so. Understanding Nostradamus requires more than a quick perusal of history, his grammar, and his occult background.

The rest of Randi's essay avoids encountering the other important successes of this quatrain. Instead he tries a strategy of placing all the events retroactively, or fetching a few historical bromides about Nostradamus' obscurity making his verses open to interpretation. To me it is what Randi doesn't say in his argument that shouts loud and clear. Where is his rebuttal to the ceding of the Scheldt to Holland in 1648, and the consequent ruin of Antwerp? The Dutch revolt in the Spanish Netherlands created a division between the southern (Belgian) and northern (Dutch) halves of that Spanish-administered realm. Poetic license allows for a economic **march** against Antwerp.

Randi avoids the correlations that make line 2 more than mere coincidence. For instance: how many times in history have events in the Spanish Netherlands coincided with an English Parliament putting its king to death in the following year? How many times between 1555 and the present has a King of England been executed by Parliament? Furthermore, the quatrain indexing is 49 (the year of the execution was 1649). **Salt and wine** represent taxes and general financing. Something more substantial than a light read of history will show that it was Charles I's inability to economically support his Royalist government and military campaigns that led to his undoing. So, in review, how many economically challenged English kings were executed by order of Parliament during the division of the Spanish Netherlands around the year 1649? Is this mere chance, or are we keeping our heads in the sand?

Quatrain Indexing Date: Q49 = 1649, the year Charles I was executed.

9 Q50

| Mandoſus[1] toſt viendra à ſon hault regne
Mettant arriere vn peu de Norlaris: [2]
Le rouge blaiſme, le maſle à l'interregne,
Le ieune crainte & frayeur Barbaris.[3] | Mendosus will soon come to his
　exalted reign
Putting behind a little the Norlaris:
The pale red one, the male in the
　interregnum,
The apprehensive youth and Barbaric
　terror. |

[1]Latin *mendosus* = full of faults, erroneous; or a crytogram for the House of Vendôme, the Bourbons.
[2]Cryptogram for *Lorraine*.
[3]*Barbare*, altered to make the rhyme.

Line 1 and 2 are a clear prophetic success for the ascent of Henry IV (**Mendosus**) to the French throne in 1594 – 36 years after this was written. He belongs to the greater noble family of Bourbon, and therefore any claims by lesser-noble families such as the House of Lorraine are set aside according to the Salic law of French royal succession. This includes any claims to the throne by the old Cardinal de Bourbon (**the pale red one**), the Duc de Mayenne, the Lieutenant-General of the realm, who took on this title from his murdered brother, Henry de Guise during the **interregnum**. The epithet **Barbaric terror** is applied by Goudoulet to the Marquis de Pont-à-Mousson, later Duc de Lorraine, another wannabe candidate for the throne. *Barbaris* may be the only flaw in this prophecy. **Barbaric** usually characterizes "Arabic" terrors or Barbary Corsairs. Perhaps if we twisted the cryptogram towel tight enough we could squeeze Marquis out of "Barbaris." To do so one would replace B with an M and reverse and turn the second *b* upside down to make a *q* to get "Marqaris"; then, drop the redundant *r* and replace the second *a* with a *u* to get "Marquis."

9 Q51

| Contre les rouges ſectes ſe banderont,
Feu, eau, fer, corde par paix ſe minera,
Au point mourir, ceux qui machineront,
Fors vn que monde ſur tout ruynera. | Against the red sects religions will
　conspire,
Fire, water, steel, the [ac]cord
　through peace to weaken,
On the point of dying, those who will
　contrive,
Except one who above all the world
　will ruin. |

Most interpreters of Nostradamus believe his references to the color red relate to revolutionaries. But perhaps these revolutionaries are not those from Russia or France, who spring most readily to mind. Using the world *secte* makes this less likely a prophecy against communism. Moreover the *red* cardinals of the Roman Catholic Church do not belong to a sect, but to a mainstream religion. A *red sect*, therefore could point to the red clothes worn by the followers of Osho during the 1970s and 1980s. The controversial Rajneesh movement gained the ire of all the world's main-stream religions. Those *who will contrive* are the mainstream religions who are *on the point of dying* and will be replaced in the coming cen-turies by one or a number of today's current cults.

Rajneeshees, Moonies, and New Agers going mainstream?! This inter-pretation is not as radical as it seems. All great religions began as cults or *sects*. Such terms are the four-letter words traditional religions use to describe the new religious movements that threaten their status-quo. Line 4's grammar is twisted enough to describe two possible destinies. One sees the old dying religions succeed in destroying one of the new religions before they themselves pass away. Or worse, the leaders of one of the old religions will convince their followers to hold on to fossilized moralities long enough to destroy the world. The current old-religious leader who comes to my mind is Pope John Paul II, who tenaciously fights against contraception in a world groaning with overpopulation. It is more than likely that people of the mid-21st century may look back at John Paul as a criminal against humanity, because he used his power to keep the world from bringing down the birth rate in time to save billions of lives.

Quatrain Indexing Date: 9Q51 = 1951? Prophecies from the ancient pyramids to 19th-century mystic Madame Blavatsky target 1950 through 2001 as the pivotal moment in human history, or a gestation period, if you will, that gives birth to a new humanity.

9 Q52

La paix s'approche d'vn cofté, & la guerre	**Peace approaches on one side, and war**
Oncques ne fut la pourfuitte fi grande,	
Plaindre hõme, femme, fang innocent par terre	**Never was the pursuit [of it] so great,**
Et ce fera de France à toute bande.	**To begrudge men, women, innocent blood on the land**
	And this will be throughout the whole of France.

Both Jaubert and Le Pelletier apply this one to the Peace of Cateau-Cambrésis (1559). In this case the French people will turn away from fighting the Spanish and begin quarreling amongst themselves in nine civil wars of religion. Line 3 hints of the coming massacres of men, women, and children at Vassy and the nationwide Huguenot pogroms after St Bartholomew's Day in 1572.

9 Q53

Le Neron ieune dans les trois cheminees	*The young Nero in the three chimneys*
Fera de paiges vifs pour ardoir getter,	*Will cause living pages to be thrown*
Heureux qui loing ſera de telz menees,	*to burn,*
Trois de ſon ſang le feront mort guetter.	*Happy who will be those far away*
	from such happenings,
	Three of his blood will have him
	ambushed to death.

The noted historical novelist Rafael Sabatini wrote of a young page being thrown into a fireplace by an enraged Italian prince of the Renaissance. Garencières said, "This fact savoureth so much of bestial cruelty that I cannot believe any Christian Prince can ever be guilty of it."

A modern application would frame the three towering chimneys of Auschwitz emitting the smoke of uncounted thousands of Jewish and Slavic boys, by order of the infernal Nero of the 20th century, Adolf Hitler.

9 Q54

Arriuera au port de Corſibonne,	*There will arrive at Porto Corsini,*
Pres de Rauenne qui pillera la dame,	*Near Ravenna, he who will plunder*
En mer profonde legat de la Vlisbonne	*the lady,*
Souz roc cachez rauiront ſeptante ames.	*In the deep sea the legate from Lisbon*
	Hidden under rock they will carry off
	seventy souls.

If you find yourself in the right century, on the right lonely stretch of Italian coastline near Porto Corsini, about eight miles northeast of **Ravenna**, you might come across the subject of this quatrain. If you do meet this interloper, can you ask him for the rest of us just who the lady is who is primed for plundering. And while you're at it, kindly inquire why a cardinal or papal **legate** from Portugal is involved?

9 Q55

L'horrible guerre qu'en l'Occident	*The horrible war which is being*
s'appreſte	*prepared in the West*
L'an enſuiuant viendra la peſtilence,	*The following year the pestilence will*
Si fort horribles que ieune, vieulx, ne beſte,	*come,*
Sang, feu, Mercure, Mars, Iupiter en	*So very horrible that young nor old,*
France.	*nor animal [may survive]:*
	Blood [plague?] fire, Mercury, Mars,
	Jupiter in France

It has been customary to apply this quatrain to the outbreak of Spanish influenza of 1918 following World War I. In our own times, however, it is more easily related to several current plagues of blood. AIDS is the obvious first choice, but a second blood disease, caused by the highly contagious Ebola virus, could eventually rain on us from the air through the breath of its victims if it spreads around the world from its isolated pockets in the African rainforests of Zaire.

Astrologer Dan Oldenburg says this conjunction of planets takes place every two to three years on average. The conjunction provides a window for terrible, explosive spreads of plague and war or a positive break-through against disease and war. The last time this conjunction occurred was in December 1995. By the end of that year it was painfully apparent that India would become the worst affected AIDS region between 1995 and the year 2000. The National AIDS Control Organization estimates 1.62 million of India's 850 million population are infected with AIDS, up 60 percent from 1993. Worldwatch Institute reported between 20 to 26 million people infected worldwide with HIV by 1995. An estimated 5 million to 9 million of them have already developed full-blown AIDS, and nearly 90 percent of these AIDS victims have died thus far. Experts project that the number of people carrying the virus could double between 1995 and 2000. The November/December issue of *Worldwatch* magazine also reported a plague of 34 wars raging on Earth – and the number is on the rise. There is also a new trend in the post-Cold War era in which "increasing numbers of violent civil wars or internal collapses such as those in former Yugoslavia, Somalia, Cambodia, and the Chechnyan region of Russia."

One positive development during this conjunction of planets was a breakthrough in AIDS vaccine research in Sydney, Australia, where eight Australian HIV survivors offer hope for an effective vaccine that can prevent infection altogether. These scientists are performing genetic splicing of the HIV virus, removing a negative gene and adjacent sections of genetic material to make HIV its own vaccine. In a *Time* magazine article titled *AIDS Mystery Solved* (20 November 1995), researcher Nicholas Deacon declared, "Not only have the recipients and the donor not progressed to disease for 15 years, but the prediction is that they never will."

Dan Oldenburg cites the next window in time for this conjunction's spread of good or bad news about plagues of war and disease as 23 February 1998, when Mercury and Jupiter conjoin the Sun at five degrees Pisces with Mars at 23 degrees Pisces. This conjunction has extra malefic strength because it is squared by Pluto at eight degrees Sagittarius. The Moon joins this conjunction on 27 February. The next windows for major global plague events will be in July 2002 and September 2004.

A **blood (plague)**, (see also 8 Q17) however, need not be caused by AIDS or Ebola alone. These conjunctions could also date the coming of a second immuno-deficiency plague, perhaps caused by pollution creating holes in the atmosphere's protective ozone layer. The **invisible swords** (3 Q75) of such a plague are ultraviolet radiation waves that will cause **scabs** [ibid.] of skin cancer, and cataracts, and break down the immune systems of human, vegetable and animal life on Earth.

Astrological Time Window

War was not **prepared** in 1918; in fact it was coming to an end the last time this conjunction of planets took place, during the swine flu epidemic. This discrepancy opens the door to the possibility that this is a prophecy for our near future. If we squeak by the potential of a terrible war that is **prepared** but never launched around 1999, the next conjunctions of Jupiter, Mars and Mercury after 2004 are February 2009 (in Aquarius), April–May 2011 (in Aries, its closest conjunction to the Mayan calendar's date for the end of time as we know it, in 2012), and December 2011 through January 2020 (in Capricorn).

9 Q56

Camp pres de Noudam[1] paſſera Gouſſan ville,	**The army near Houdan will pass Goussainville,**
Et à Maiotes[2] laiſſera ſon enſeigne,	**And to the eager soldiers they will leave its ensign,**
Conuertira en inſtant plus de mille,	**They will convert in an instant more than a thousand,**
Cherchāt les deux remettre en chaine & legne.[3]	**Searching for the two to put them back in chains and wood.**

[1]Misprint for Houdan
[2]*Maiotes* = a) an enigmatic place name or an erratum for the town of Mantes; b) Greek *memaotes* = those eager for something (Le Pelletier).
[3]Provençal *legna* = firewood.

Houdan and Goussainville are both west of Paris. The latter was little more than nine miles northeast of Dreux, where the Huguenot and Royal armies clashed in the First War of Religion in 1562. The battle began with a collision of Huguenot and royalist cavalry. The commander of the royalist army, Anne de Montmorency, the constable of France, was captured along with several dozen troopers and some cavalry standards (**ensign**). The Huguenot cavalry led by Admiral Coligny sought to exploit its advantage with a counterattack but was repulsed by Catholic infantry. Line 3 hints that either 1,000 Huguenots will be killed (**converted instantly** from life to death in the failed attack), or they will be captured and will later request conversion to Catholicism. The final line paints a picture of Huguenot troopers with chained and manacled hands held fast by heavy wooden stocks (**chains and wood**).

9 Q57

Au lieu de DRVX vn Roy repofera,	*In the place of Dreux a King will repose,*
Et cherchera loy changeant d'Anatheme,	*And will search for a law changing Anathema,*
Pendant le ciel ſi tresfort tonnera,	*While the sky so very loudly will thunder,*
Portee neufue Roy tuera ſoymeſme.	*[At] the new gate the King will kill himself.*

In the following year (1563) after the royalist victory at Dreux, the Queen Regent Catherine de' Medici – acting in the name of her pubescent son, Charles IX – cooled the passions of the first civil war by issuing the Edict of Amboise, which granted freedom of worship to the Protestant nobility and gentry. This arrangement satisfied neither Huguenot nor Catholic (**Anathema** to both sides). The thunder of cannon and arquebus would rend the air in eight more civil wars.

Charles IX never committed suicide. One could say, metaphorically at least, that such edicts were suicidal to his future. History records that nine years later the 23-year-old king, physically and emotionally exhausted, died of a cold in 1574. It is believed the sensitive nervous system of Charles IX broke down from guilt over being bullied by his mother into ordering the St Bartholomew's Day Massacre two years earlier.

9 Q58

Au coſté gauche à l'endroit de Vitry,	*On the left side at the site of Vitry,*
Seront guettez les trois rouges de France:	*The three reds of France will be waylaid:*
Tous aſſoumez rouge, noir non murdry,	*All those who are red felled, black not murdered,*
Par les Bretons remis en aſſeurence.	*By the Bretons, confidence restored.*

There are several Vitrys in France. But I agree with Fontbrune's imaginative interpretation of Vitry-le-François, which is a short distance northeast of Valmy. Here the French republican forces won their first victory against the Coalition forces during the French Revolutionary Wars. Fontbrune thinks those of the **left** are the many lawyers such as Tronchet or le Chapelier, who founded the **Breton** club (which would later become the Jacobin Club). Ambitious men within the Jacobins form less **red** and more extreme **red** revolutionary factions. One was a triumvirate (**three reds**) of Adrien du Port, Charles de Lameth, and Barnave, who opposed la Fayette and Mirabeau. The latter two supported a constitutional monarchy. The insatiable appetite of Jacobin extremism would devour

Mirabeau and other moderates, and finally most of the Jacobin leaders themselves during the purges and counter-purges of the Reign of Terror.

9 Q59

A la Ferté prendra la Vidame,	**At La Ferté-Vedame he will seize,**
Nicol tenu rouge qu'auoit produit la vie:	**Nicolas held, the red one who had**
La grand Loyſe naiſtra que fera clame,	**produced life:**
Donnant Bourgongne à Bretons par enuie.	**The great Louise – who acts secretly**
	– one will be born,
	Giving Burgundy to the Bretons
	through envy.

La Ferté-Vidame is about 25 miles southeast of Dreux, which was the scene of the first significant battle of the Wars of Religion in 1562. There is only one Nicholas of note who lived in Nostradamus' day: Nicholas of Lorraine, Comte de Vaudemont and Duc de Mercœur, uncle of young Charles III of Lorraine, who was kinsman to the Guise. Nicholas of Lorraine had a daughter named Louise, born in 1553, who was destined to marry Henry III. Line 3 stands as a failed alternative future. Louise never gave birth to a bastard child. Her marriage to the final Valois king was also childless.

Quatrain Indexing Date: Q59 = 1559, the fateful year when both Louise and Henry III were mere children, and the splinter of a jousting lance that penetrated the gold visor of Henry II killed the king and set their destinies on a course towards marriage.

9 Q60

Conflict Barbar[1] en la Cornere noire,	**Conflict! Barbarian in the black**
Sang eſpandu trembler la d'Almatie:	**Headdress,**
Grand Iſmaël mettra ſon promontoire,	**Blood shed, Dalmatia to tremble:**
Ranes trembler ſecours Luſitanie.	**Great Ishmael[2] will set up his**
	promontory,
	Frogs to tremble, aid [to] Lusitania
	[Portugal].

[1]cryptogram for Arab or the Barbary Coast (Modern Algeria, Tunisia or Libya).
[2]Ishmael = son of Abraham and Hagar, the grand ancestor of the Arab people; patriach of Shi'ite Muslims.

Line 1 may describe the black headdress of an Arab terrorist stationed in North Africa or Libya. Line 2 warns the West to stop the flow of Arab advisors and arms to the Balkans. The tenuous peace of the Dayton Accords could break down in a future Balkan war pitting Bosnian Muslims against their Croatian allies rather than against the Serbs. *Ishmael* may be the first name of the "Great Arab" or Third Antichrist, who exploits the Bosniacs and the new war to establish a base in Europe (*its promontory*). A terrorist base in the Balkans is viewed by all Christian-dominated governments of the EU as a real danger. **Frogs** are either a poetic allusion to France (via Merovingian "frogs" as a symbol of ancient French royalty), or Nostradamus is using the colloquial or vulgar description of his future countrymen who, like other wealthier members of the EU are obligated to provide aid to newer members of the union, such as Portugal.

9 Q61

La pille faite à la cofte marine,	**The [acts of] plunder made upon the sea coast,**
La cita noua & parens amenez:	
Plufieurs de Malte par le fait de Meffine,	**The città nova [new city] and relations brought forward;**
Eftroit ferrez feront mal guerdonnez.	**Several of Malta through the deeds of Messina,**
	Will be closely shut up, sweetly rewarded.

During the siege of Malta in 1565, several hundred Knights of the Maltese Cross withstood a sustained attack of 40,000 Turks between May and August 1565. Before the Turks departed, three-quarters of the invasion force was killed by combat and the plague. Six years later the Knights of Malta sent four galleys to join the gathering Christian naval forces at Messina. (Malta was a protectorate of the Habsburg Kingdom of the Two Sicilies, of which Cittanova and Messina were part.) The Maltese would overall be **sweetly rewarded**, although they shared the Christian armada's total victory against the Turkish navy at Lepanto, in the bay of Corinth. Here the Turks and Barbary Corsairs lost over 230 galleys sunk and captured.

Quatrain Indexing Date: 61 = possibly a near miss for the siege of Malta in 1565. But it is a stretch.

9 Q62

Au grand de Cheramon agora,	**To the great one of [or at] Cheramon agora,**
Seront croifez par ranc tous attachez,	
Le pertinax Oppi, & Mandragora,	**The crusaders by rank will all be attached,**
Raugon[1] d'Octobre le tiers feront lafchez.	**The long-lasting Opium and Mandrake,**
	Raugon will be released on the 3rd of October.

[1]*Raugon* = Greek *rogas* = split, rent, cleft.

Cheramon agora ("the flat area in the dell") was the name of an ancient Greek town in Asia Minor, currently the Turkish town of Usak. One could make a cryptogram for Amer(i)ch-Nago(y)a, or America and Japan. Kidogo applies his etymological skills to turn **Cheramon** into "Common," as in the Common Market or EU. He also conjures a compound word constructed from *chercher*, to seek; *chère* as in *la bonne chère*, good living; *chèr*, dear, and *commun* for common (Market). This implies some future economic difficulties for the new Europe. The **crusaders** theme has been applied to the recent "crusade" of Western forces in the Gulf War of 1991. One could say that EU **crusader** allies attached themselves to the American military horde of Operation Desert Storm. Japan sent medical and logistic assistance – the first time since World War II the nation sent military units abroad.

Opium and mandrake were included in herbal compounds used in many magical practices. Leoni thinks the enigmatic **Raugon** stands for the Rogonis river or the modern Bender-rik. But this quatrain is vague enough to allow "Raugon" to be the US President Ronald "Reagan." A terrorist bombing of the US Marine barracks in Lebanon on the 23rd rather than the **3rd** of **October** 1983 worked public opinion to effectively release Reagan from the quagmire of peacekeeping in Lebanon. He withdrew the marines from Beirut and put them on US warships offshore in February 1984.

9 Q63

Plainctes & pleurs crys & grands vrlemens,	**Lamentations and tears, cries and great howls,**
Pres de Narbon à Bayonne & en Foix:	**Near Narbonne at Bayonne and in Foix:**
O quel horrible calamits changemens,	**Oh what horrible calamities and changes,**
Auant que Mars reuolu quelques fois.	**Before Mars has made several revolutions.**

Line 1 sets the stage for the general pandemonium and violence of the French Revolution. Nostradamus directs our attention to three cities on the French side of the Pyrenees. Bayonne is on the Atlantic on the western end, Narbonne on the Mediterranean on the eastern end, and Foix is about 77 miles west of Narbonne. The porthole in time takes our prophet down the narrow cobblestone streets of these towns to plague his disbelieving eyes with visions of peasant mobs ransacking the homes of the aristocracy and pillaging graveyards and churches. Monks and nuns are stripped of their holy vestments and forced to live like beggars in the streets. A ripple in the timescape propels him forward into the closing years of the Napoleonic Wars. He sees great columns of smoke rising from the English cannonade of Bayonne in 1814. The smoke issues from the earthen martial altar of artillery redoubts, who dedicate their shrapnel and iron to Mars, the god of war.

The planet Mars makes one revolution around the sun every 687 Earth days. The French Revolution lasted a little more than ten years, from the storming of the Bastille on 14 July 1789 to Napoleon's coup d'état against the Directory on 10 November 1799: this would allow five revolutions of Mars. Nostradamus may intend a double-meaning for **revolutions**, seeing the French Revolution as waves of several successive outbreaks of explosive and violent change. During the first revolution of Mars the initial rebellion against the absolute power of the king in 1789 leads to the overthrow of the constitutional monarchy and the formation of the First Republic in 1791; the second revolution of Mars ends with the outbreak of a Royalist counter-revolution in the Vendée and the Reign of Terror by 1793; by 1795, the second counter-revolution known as the White Terror ends and the Directory is established. In 1797, the Directory weathers another Royalist threat when a party of Monarchists are voted into its ranks in the general election. By the end of the final revolution of Mars in 1799, an economic crisis and general corruption in the Directory sowed the seeds of a new wave of martial revolution. The final **horrible** . . . **change** in Nostradamus' eyes would be the usurper Napoleon, his Second Antichrist, becoming First Consul of France.

9 Q64

L'Æmathion paſſer monts Pyrenées,	**The Macedonian to pass the Pyrenees**
En Mars Narbon[1] ne fera reſiſtance,	**mountains,**
Par mer & terre fera ſi grand menée.	**In Narbonne will not offer resistance,**
Cap.[2] n'ayant terre ſeure pour	**By sea and land he will manage so**
demeurance.	**great an intrigue.**
	Cap. having no land safe to stay in.

[1]Latin *Narbo Martius* = Narbonne.
[2]Probably apocope of *Cap*et or Capetian.

Macedonian usually stands for Philip II of Spain in particular, and the Spanish in general. Philip II, however, did not undertake any major invasion over the Pyrenees to seize Narbonne, so either our prophet is wrong or he is mixing up his Spanish Philips. That at least is what Le Pelletier (1867) believes. He takes the second meaning for *Aemathion* as "sun god" and turns this prophecy around to become an invasion of Spain by Louis XIV (also known as the Sun King) during the War of the Spanish Succession. It is now Philip V of Spain, Louis' **Cap**etian grandson, who is forced into exile by French attacks by land and sea. He never was exiled on account of the French, although he did lose his campaign to retain the succession to the French throne for his family. Four years after the war, in 1724, Philip V did abdicate in favor of his son Louis, but resumed the crown nine months later after his son's untimely death.

9 Q65

Dedans le coing de Luna viendra rendre,	He will come to take himself to the
Ou sera prins & mis en terre estrange,	corner of the Moon,
Les fruicts immeurs seront à grand	Where he will be taken and placed on
esclandre	alien land,
Grand vitupere à l'vn grande louange.	The unripe fruit will be the source of
	great scandal,
	Great blame, to the other great praise.

In a 16th-century Europe dominated by the Church it would have been heresy to suggest that Earth was not the center of the universe. Yet in this time of limited scientific understanding and widespread superstition, Nostradamus dared to propose that, one day in the future, men would be able to walk upon another planet.

Even at the beginning of the 20th century the idea that, within 70 years, men would be able to travel in a man-made vehicle through space to *Luna* was unimaginable. Closer examination of the word *dedans* opens the interpretation further for a return of man to the moon in the 21st century. After man has taken himself **to** the moon he will later take himself **within the corner of the Moon**, where he will construct a permanent underground lunar base.

The last two lines could bring us back down to earth to the Challenger disaster. The American space program was castigated for sending their astronauts on the **unripe fruit** of faulty rocket boosters prematurely approved to fit the budget. At the time of the Challenger disaster, however, the Soviet space program was running smoothly with the complete support of its government and people (**to the other great praise**) (see 1 Q81).

Quatrain Indexing Date: Q65 = 1965, a near miss for the Apollo 11 moon landing in 1969; or the year 2065, when mankind will build a permanent base on the moon.

9 Q66

Paix, vnion sera & changement,	There will be peace, union and change,
Estats, offices bas hault, & haut bien bas:	Estates and offices [that were] low
Dresser voyage le fruict premier torment,	[are] high, those high [made] very
Guerre cesser, ciuil proces debats.	low:
	To prepare for a journey torments the
	first [child],
	War to cease, civil processes, debates.

This could represent any post-cataclysmic or postwar period. An occult interpretation of line 3 identifies the *first* as the children of a new mankind, who are about to embark on a new era of exploration of space and the inner exploration of the soul.

Quatrain Indexing Date: Q66 = 2066?

9 Q67

Du hault des monts à l'entour de Lizer,
Port à la roche Valen. cent affemblez:
De chafteau neuf pierre late en donzere,
Contre le Creft Romans foy affemblez.

From the height of the mountains
    around Isère,
At the entrance of the rock of Valence,
    one hundred are assembled:
From Châteauneuf, Pierrelatte, [and]
    in Donzère,
Against Crest, Romans faith assembled.

These are guerrillas of the Catholic faith most likely preparing to attack the Huguenots in Nostradamus' time. The seer gives us quite a wide range of geographic theaters, starting with the department of Drôme, where Valence is a town on the confluence of the Isère and Rhône rivers. Romans is roughly 10 miles northeast of there, and Crest is 15 miles to the southeast. We store away our rucksack of reasoning and follow these 100 guerrillas 45 miles down the Rhône from Valence until we enter the town of Pierrelatte.

After enjoying some wine and cheese we leave Pierrelatte, marching south about five more miles until nature calls at Donzère. At this point some of our guerrillas might ask, "How in blazes can we find Châteauneuf on the road to Pierrelatte – it is way down south, near Avignon!" And we might ask why a plains town like Donzère is in this quatrain at all mixing with Crest, Romans, and Pierrelatte in the mountainous country of Valentinois.

Well, if Nostradamus had been there with us, lacing his hiking boots, sharing our trail mix, and imparting clearer instructions, we would know where this band of heretic hunters were going.

9 Q68

Du mont[1] Aymar[2] fera noble obfcurcie,
Le mal viendra au ioinct de Saone &
    Rofne:
Dans bois cachez foldats iour de Lucie,
Qui ne fut onc vn fi horrible throfne.

From montainard Amar the noble will
    be obscured,
The evil will come at the junction of
    the Saône and Rhône:
Soldiers hidden in the woods on St
    Lucy's Day,
When never was there so horrible a
    throne.

[1]mont: abbrevation for a) The Mountain, an extreme Jacobin faction commanding the higher seats of the National Assembly; b) a montainard, a member of The Mountain.
[2]Surname of Jean Babtiste Amar (1755–1816), a powerful orator, deputy of the National Assembly, or Leoni: Mont Aymar = a cryptogram for Montélimart, or "Mountain of Slaughter." It makes for a rich double pun, since Amar and the other montainards gave the orders for some of the Revolution's bloodiest massacres.

The execution of King Louis XVI of France triggered an orgy of blood-letting known as the Reign of Terror. The men responsible – those of the most *horrible* . . . *throne* – are most likely the members of the National Assembly, who were known as The Mountain. The Jacobin-dominated government made Paris *the city of the blade*, as Nostradamus describes it in another quatrain. Using the old style of spelling, he names Jean Babtiste Amar (Aymar), the speaker of the bloodthirsty Committee of Public Safety, whose members were responsible for voting the king's execution (*the noble* . . . *obscured*). Amar's fiery words stirred the montainard delegates into ordering a quick and ruthless reprisal for the pro-Royalist city of Lyons, which sits on the *junction of the Saône and Rhône* rivers. Sixteen hundred houses owned by counter-revolutionaries were demolished, as well as the city fortifications and most of the Bourgneuf quarter. Many thousands were shot or guillotined. Some citizens of Lyons were tied to a wall and shot point blank by cannons. Whatever mangled mess remained alive was dispatched by sabers.

The Royalist guerrilla army in the Vendée was defeated in the battle of Le Mans on 13 December 1793 (*St Lucy's Day*). The Republican forces shattered the Royalists' defensive line drawn along the edge of a wood covering the approach to the town. No quarter was given. At least 15,000 Royalists were shot by the sanction of The Mountain.

9 Q69

Sur le mont de Bailly & la Brefle	**On the mountain of St Bel and L'Arbresle**
Seront caichez de Grenoble les fiers,	**The proud people of Grenoble will be hidden,**
Oultre Lyon, Vien. eulx fi grande grefle,	**Beyond Lyons and Vienne on them a very great hailstorm,**
Langouft[1] en terre n'en reftera vn tiers.	**Lobster on the land not a third will remain.**

[1] Old French *langouste* = locust; lobster in modern French.

The people of Grenoble hid in their cellars as US and German artillery and small-arms fire echoed through the narrow French alpine valleys during the summer of 1944 when Germans fought a delaying action through the alpine valleys before Grenoble. Around the same time in the Rhône river valley, we also have a *very great hailstorm*. This describes the savaging of the German columns by Allied forces during its retreat through the mountainous bottleneck known as the Montélimar Gap, which is between 65 and 80 miles down river from Lyons and Vienne, respectively. Once again Nostradamus uses crustaceans or "land lobsters." to describe German panzers, Allied tanks, and armored cars. The Germans lost two-thirds of their vehicles to Allied gunfire in the Montélimar Gap. *St Bel* and *L'Arbresle* are roughly three miles apart on a mountainside 12 miles northwest of Lyons. Their connection to Grenoble makes little sense, although one might have used binoculars at their vantage point to see the retreating remnants of the German Nineteenth Army pulling out of Lyons in September 1944.

9 Q70

Harnois trenchant dans les flambeaux cachez	Sharp-edged weapons hidden in the torches
Dedans Lyon le iour du Sacrement,	In Lyons the day of the Sacrament,
Ceux de Vienne feront treftous hachez	Those of Vienne will be all hacked to pieces
Par les cantons Latins Mafcon ne ment.	By the Latin cantons Mâcon does not lie.

Nostradamus continues his account of the German retreat through Vienne and Lyons. Line 1 could describe the flames of artillery discharging sharp-nosed shells from mortar tubes, tanks, or gun barrels. After being mauled at the Montélimar Gap the Germans fought a delaying action through Vienne and abandoned Lyons in early September 1944. Line 3 better describes the fighting in and around Vienna (**Vienne**) in the closing days of the war, when it was captured by the Soviets. The reference to the Latin cantons of southeast Switzerland makes little sense in this context, but **Mâcon**, which is 42 miles up the Saône river from Lyons, was the next major destination in the German retreat.

The **day of the Sacrament** is understood as Corpus Christi, the first Thursday after Trinity Sunday, eight Sundays after Easter. Perhaps Nostradamus is using Christian holidays to pinpoint the end of World War II in the European theater. Easter Sunday was on 1 April 1945. The Third Reich officially capitulated between 8 and 9 of May (the Soviets celebrate the latter date). Corpus Christi was celebrated 22 days later on 31 May 1945.

9 Q71

Aux lieux facrez animaux veu à trixe,[1]	At the sacred places animals are seen with wool,
Auec celuy qui n'ofera le iour:	With him who will not dare the day:
A Carcaffonne pour difgrace propice,	At Carcassone for propitious disgrace,
Sera pofé pour plus ample feiour.	He will set for a more ample abode.

[1]Greek *thrix* = hair, wool.

Here we have another oddity. Except for the location of the drama, *Carcassone*, this story of a reclusive, shamefaced fellow, and sheep grazing in churches, is hopelessly obscure. Fontbrune's oracle has put his astral foot into an unlikely interpretation. The fellow who can't show his face in daylight is some informant for the Russian soldiers who will occupy Carcassone in World War III.

I am in alignment with Garencières' view: "Whether the author [Nostradamus] understands himself here I know not, I am sure I do not."

9 Q72

Encor feront les faincts temples pollus,	**Again will the holy temples be polluted,**
Et expillez par Senat Tholosfain,	**And plundered by the Senate of**
Saturne deux trois cicles reuollus,	**Toulouse,**
Dans Auril, May, gens de nouueau leuain.	**Saturn two, three cycles revolved,**
	In April, May, people of the new
	leaven.

We can pin this one on the Huguenots in the city parliament of Toulouse disputing with Catholics over the Holy Eucharist during the Wars of Religion.

Here we have an attempt to predict the rise and fall of French Protestant fortunes by using Saturnian cycles. Finding out where Nostradamus' religious allegiances lie depends on which way we read the sequence of the quatrain's lines. First off, a revolution of Saturn takes 29.5 Earth years. I would suggest the sequence be read backwards starting with line 4. The reference point is 13 **April** 1598 when Henry IV signs the Edict of Nantes, which gives Huguenots limited freedom of religion. Louis XIV's revocation of the Edict of Nantes in 1685 comes 87 years later. Three cycles of Saturn comprise just under 88.5 years! The Senate of Toulouse is plundering the disbanded Huguenot temples. This makes the first (and in this reading, the final) line a subtle hint of Nostradamus' Huguenot sympathies, since the papists are polluting the holy temples and not the other way around, as is usually interpreted.

9 Q73

Dans Fois entrez Roy ceiulee[1] Turbao,	**In Foix the blue Turbaned King**
Et regnera moins reuolu Saturne,	**entered,**
Roy Turban blanc Bizance cœur ban,	**And he will reign less than a**
Sol, Mars, Mercure pres la hurne.	**revolution of Saturn,**
	The white Turban King Byzantium
	heart banished,
	Sun, Mars, Mercury near the urn
	[Aquarius].

[1]Latin caeruleus = dark blue, sea green.

Turbans are usually associated with oriental tyrants. A Muslim army invades southwestern France and occupies Foix and remains entrenched there for 29.5 years (one revolution of Saturn). Meanwhile the white-turbaned Sultan of the Ottomans has his **heart banished** (his feelings are repressed, for reasons Nostradamus does not make clear). Since no occupation of Muslims in southwest France has taken place – and little military infrastructure exists in Muslim states to mount such an invasion in our future – another possibility would have this blue-turbaned king sent into exile at Foix without an army. Foix could be a synecdoche for France.

Astrological Time Window

The Sun, Mars, and Mercury were in Aquarius on 1 February 1979, the day the **black**-turbaned Ayatollah Khomeini flew into Iran from France, after 15 years of exile, to become the new Islamic Republic's religious leader.

Quatrain Indexing Date: Q73= 1973, a pivotal year in the 27-year war of the Third Antichrist (see 8 Q77).

9 Q74

Dans la cité de Fertʃod¹ homicide,	**In the city of Fertsod homicide,**
Fait & fait multe beuf arant ne macter,	**Arrange and arrange [again] many**
Retour encores aux honneurs d'Artemide,²	**oxen [for] plowing, no sacrifice,**
Et à Vulcan corps morts ʃepulturer.	**Return again to the honors of**
	Artemis,
	And to Vulcan bodies to bury.

¹*Fertsod*: cryptogram – *Fert* = Latin *fertus* = rich, fertile; or Old French *fer* = iron, steel; *sod* = Sodom; or the city of "Iron Saddam" = Bagdad.
²Greek goddess of human fertility therefore strongly associated with the moon, identified by the Romans as their goddess Diana; used by Nostradamus as a metaphor for the cresent moon of Islam.

All kinds of interpretative booby traps are possible for the enigma *Fertsod*. Torné-Chavigny made it an anagram for Paris ("Rich Sodom"). The "Sodom and Gomorrah" theme could place this quatrain in our times and a little closer to its biblical home. If you take *fert* as an abbreviation of the Old French word *ferté*, which means "stronghold", then *Fertsod* becomes *Ferté Sodom*. This makes the line read **in the city of the stronghold of Saddam**, which is modern Baghdad, the capital of Iraq.

One can take line 2 figuratively as a biblical parable for hard times when one cannot afford to make sacrifices to the ancient bull gods of classical Iraq and must use every animal to plow the fields. This could apply itself well to the effects of crushing sanctions and embargoes against Saddam Hussein's regime after the Gulf War of 1991. Saddam Hussein brushed aside offers from the United Nations to allow Iraq to export oil for food and humanitarian needs, bringing terrible hardship and the danger of famine to his people. The riddle *arrange and arrange* [*again*] fits well with the constant back-and-forth negotiations between Iraqis and the United Nations over lifting the sanctions.

In line 3 Nostradamus is applying a classical metaphor of Artemis, the Greek goddess, to the Islamic crescent and the future of Saddam Hussein. Artemis is a huntress, and the arrow hitting its mark is one of her symbols. In other quatrains Nostradamus uses the arrow metaphor for modern-day cruise missiles. After the era of sanctions Iraq could suffer a third Gulf War and the return of missiles and smart bombs attacking the concrete bunkers (strongholds]) of Saddam Hussein.

The classical metaphor of **Vulcan** in the last line implies a horrific future either for the Iraqi people or for Saddam and his lieutenants. They are all commended to the fire sacrifice of Vulcan, god of the forge, smithing, and mechanical inventions. It must be remembered that Vulcan forged the thunderbolts of the god Jupiter. In other quatrains "Jupiter" sometimes becomes a metaphor for the United States. In short, *Fertsod* becomes a target of Jupiter's steel and fire thunderbolts (American missiles). Perhaps the Vulcanale of global warming is the cause of a conflict between Iraq and Syria against Turkey (a NATO ally) over water rights to the Tigris and Euphrates rivers. Finally, the Vulcan metaphor could predict a successful conventional or nuclear-cruise-missile attack incinerating Saddam Hussein, his heirs and his relations in the underground stronghold of his own command bunker underneath Baghdad.

9 Q75

De l'Ambraxie & du pays de Thrace,	**From Ambracia [Arta] and from the country of Thrace,**
Peuple par mer mal & ſecours Gaulois,	**People by sea, evil and aid from the French,**
Perpetuelle en Prouence la trace,	**Perpetual [is] the trace of them in Provence,**
Auec veſtiges de leur couſtume & loix.	**With vestiges of their custom and laws.**

Ambracia (Arta) and **Thrace** represent the western and northeastern corners of Greece, and by extension stand for Greece herself. The ancient Greeks colonized Provence, and traces of their culture remain in Nostradamus' homeland. He foresees a time when the Greek people will call and receive **aid** and **evil** from Provence, or by extension, France. France, along with Britain and Russia, did come to the aid of the Greeks in their successful war of independence against the Ottoman Turks (1821–32).

After **aid** in the 19th century, the 20th century started with France and her allies giving **evil**. During World War I, a Franco-British expeditionary force landed uninvited in neutral Greece. To ensure her continued neutrality they seized control of the telegraph and postal systems as well as the Greek navy and large stores of armaments from the army, and blockaded the coast.

9 Q76

Auec le noir*¹* Rapax*²* & ſanguinaire, Yſſu du peaultre*³* de l'inhumain Neron, Emmy deux fleuues, main gauche militaire, Sera murtry par Ioyne chaulueron.*⁴*	**With the black/king Rapax** **[Rapacious] and bloodthirsty,** **Issued from the pallet of inhuman** **Nero,** **Between two rivers the military power** **[on the] left,** **Will be murdered by the Young bald** **one.**

¹Double pun and near-anagram of *noir* = black, and *roi* = king. An evil king.
²Latin for rapacious.
³Old French *peaultre* = pallet; brothel.
⁴Variant: *chau(t)veron* = young hothead.

This describes the downfall of either Saddam Hussein or a future Iranian tyrant, by means of a **bald** political or military adversary in his own court, or by a future **bald** general of another global coalition. Jochmans thinks the **bald one** is General Schwartzkopf, theater commander of Operation Desert Storm during the Gulf War of 1991.

He tells us that "Schwartzkopf" means "smooth-head"; however, it is my understanding that it means "black head" in German or, by extension "black commander." Neither the theatre commander, Schwartzkopf, or his commander, General Colin Powell, are bald men though their hair is short-cropped. Too bad Nostradamus didn't use *noir teste* (*noir tête* in modern French); then we would have had a match for the black overall commander, Colin Powell.

9 Q77

Le regne prins le Roy conuiera,*¹* La dame prinſe à mort iurez à ſort, La vie à Royne filz on deſniera, Et la pellix*²* au fort de la conſort.*³*	**The realm taken [it] will convict the** **King,** **The Queen sent to death by jurors** **chosen by lot,** **They will deny life to the Queen's son,** **And the prostitute shares the fate of** **the consort.**

¹*conuiera* : a) Old French *convier* = to invite, to bid, (figuratively) to urge; b) variant: *convicra*, from Latin *convicior* = to rail at; *convicium*, a violent reproach; (Robb) to convict.
²Latin *pellex* = concubine, mistress.
³*conſort(e)* = a) consort, a companion; b) (in the negative sense) an accomplice in crime.

Nine months after the execution of her husband, Louis XVI, Queen Marie Antoinette was herself led to the guillotine, on 16 October 1793.

Her archrival, Madame du Barry, mistress to the king's grandfather, suffered the same fate on 22 December and is considered by some to be **the prostitute** involved. Some scholars have criticized the stretching of **consort** into "wife" – hence Marie Antoinette. I don't have a problem with the poetic license. In Old French the word has its root in the Latin *consors*, meaning "one who shares fate," thus "companion," or (in the negative sense) "an accessory or an accomplice in crime." From the point of view of the Committee of Public Safety, du Barry and Marie Antoinette were traitors. Perhaps Nostradamus is punning with us again?

He mentions the fact that the jurors for the Queen's sham trial were chosen by lot, a practice that was rarely used. Her son, the 11-year-old Dauphin (Louis XVII) was torn away from her three months before her execution and spirited away to another cell in the Temple prison to be placed under the charge of the brutal Simon the Cobbler. There he would die of beatings and neglect. The revolution would **deny** life to her son, and the throne.

9 Q78

La dame Grecque de beauté laydique,[1]	**The Greek lady of beauty [like that of] Lais,**
Heureuſe faicte de procs innumerable,	**Made happy by innumerable suitors,**
Hors tranſlatee au regne Hiſpanique,	**Transferred out of the Spanish kingdom,**
Captiue prinſe mourir mort miſerable.	**Taken captive to die a miserable death.**

[1]Latin *Laidis* = of Lais, the most beautiful woman of Corinth, or the Nostradamian alternative of *laid*, or *lait* = ugly.

Lamont believed the **Greek lady** stands for democracy, so he applies the quatrain to democracy's death in Spain beginning in 1936 at the onset of the Spanish Civil War. In the previous decade Larmor (1925) identified her as Marie de' Medici because her curvaceous charms were "comparable to that of the Greek courtesan Lais." In 1631 she was exiled to Brussels in the Spanish Netherlands. The queen, who was notorious for draining the royal French treasury during her glory days, died a pauper in Cologne in 1642 (*a miserable death*).

9 Q79

Le chef de claſſe par fraude ſtratageme,	**The chief of the fleet through fraud and stratagems,**
Fera timides ſortir de leurs galleres,	**Will make the timid ones come out of their galleys,**
Sortis murtris chef renieur de creſme,	**Having come out, murdered is the chief renouncer of the holy oil,**
Puis par l'embuſche luy rendront les ſaleres.	**Then through ambush they will render him his wages.**

This is about Admiral Coligny, the **chief renouncer** of the chrism – holy oil – of Catholicism. The marriage of Henry de Navarre to Marguérite de Valois was used as bait by Catherine de' Medici and the Catholic leadership to lure the **timid** Admiral Coligny and the Huguenot leaders to the royal wedding in the lion's den of ultra-Catholic Paris. The night after the wedding reception Coligny was wounded by an assassin hired by Medici. Her plan was to slaughter only Coligny and the chief Huguenot leaders on St Bartholomew's Day (23 August 1572), but the bloodletting of Huguenots, no doubt quickened by a particularly severe heat wave, soon spread out of control across Paris. By the time the wave passed 50,000 Huguenots had been massacred across France.

9 Q80

Le Duc voudra les fiens exterminer,	**The Duke will want his followers exterminated,**
Enuoyera les plus forts lieux eftranges,	**He will dispatch the strongest ones [to] foreign places,**
Par tyrannie Pize & Luc ruiner,	**Through tyranny Pisa and Lucca to ruin,**
Puis les Barbares fans vin feront vendanges.	**Then the Barbarians without wine will gather the vintage.**

Here we have another **Duke**/ Il **Duce** Mussolini prophecy. By 1941–42 Mussolini had dispatched his best generals and strongest armed forces to distant foreign fronts in Russia, Ethiopia, and North Africa, where they met with disaster. Once the Germans occupied Italy in 1943 and returned Mussolini to power, he had his foreign minister, Ciano, and many other close associates executed for treason.

Pisa and Lucca suffered from strategic bombing and Allied ground attacks as the right-hand extremity of the German Arno defense line in 1944. The **Barbarians** are probably Algerian Muslims prohibited by the Koran from drinking alcohol (**without wine**). The only time one could picture them gathering a wine harvest would be in the 1930s and 1940s, when modern tea-totalling Algerians tended the grapes of their colonial French masters.

9 Q81

Le Roy rufé entendra fes embufches,	**The sly King will understand his ambushes,**
De trois quartiers ennemis assaillir,	**From three fronts the enemies assail,**
Vn nombre eftrange larmes de coqueluches,	**A strange number, tears from the hooded men,**
Viendra Lemprin[1] du traducteur faillir.	**The brilliance of the translator will come to fail.**

[1]Greek *lampros* = brilliancy, grandeur, splender.

Ambush is a word used more than once to describe something similar to guerrilla wars or the terrorist attacks of our day. They attack or are attacked by SWAT teams from three sides. The **hooded** terrorists weep from tear gas canisters thrown into their hideout. The brilliant attempts of negotiators to convince the terrorists to surrender fail. Hopefully this is only a forecast of the failure of myself and other **translators** of Nostradamus to get the quatrain right.

9 Q82

Par le deluge & peſtilence forte,	**By the flood and virulent pestilence,**
La cité grande de long temps aſſiegee,	**The great city for a long time**
La ſentinelle & garde de main morte,	**besieged,**
Subite prinſe, mais de nul outragée.	**The sentinel and guard dead by hand,**
	Sudden capture, but none outraged.

General and apocalyptic. The **great city** usually stands for Paris. There are other visions of Paris. A future beset by flood. The **virulent pestilence** could be AIDS or some sort of Ebola blood plague virus, or even a plague of the immune system caused by the 21st century's enlarged ozone holes. If this is still to come and not a failed prediction of the past, the 21st century will have its wars and sieges just like every century before, unless we break from the habits and the stupidity of the past in time to forestall the plagues and ecological challenges that await us.

9 Q83

Sol vint de Taurus[1] ſi fort terre trembler,	**The sun in 20 degrees Taurus there**
Le grand theatre rempli ruynera,	**will be a great earthquake,**
L'air, ciel & terre obſcurcir & troubler,	**It will ruin the great theater that is**
Lors l'infidelle[2] Dieu & ſaincts voguera.	**full up,**
	Darkness and trouble in the air, on
	the sky and land,
	When the infidel calls upon God and
	the saints.

[1] *Sol vingt de Taurus* = May 10.
[2] Infidel, non-Christian; the unfaithful.

Interpretation of this quatrain has become a great controversy among Nostradamus scholars of the past 50 years. It is generally agreed that it forecasts an earthquake that will destroy a major theater or perhaps a stadium at the time of ecological troubles (**air** . . . **sky** . . . **land**). The final line could reveal a 16th-century theist's expectation that the ferocity of the earthquake, perceived to be an expression of divine wrath, would be so great that even unbelievers would return to God.

During the spring of 1988, a majority of published Nostradamus scholars declared that Los Angeles would suffer the long dreaded Big One – the killer quake lurking in the tension of the San Andreas Fault – in May of that year. At that time I wrote many published press releases and even appeared on the Los Angeles television show *Eye on LA* to declare that my colleagues' interpretations were flawed, and that Asia and California would be at risk in 1989 and the early 1990s.

May 1988 came and went with a fanfare of hysteria in Los Angeles. Unfortunately my 1986 interpretations of Nostradamus' astrology had been correct regarding October 1989. A series of six powerful earthquakes rocked northern China's Shanxi province, 160 miles west of Beijing, and the tremors were felt in suburbs of the Chinese capital. The now famous Loma Prieta quake of San Francisco also took place in October of that year. The quake measured 7.0 on the Richter scale, making it the city's most significant temblor since the Great Earthquake of 1906.

With this quatrain Nostradamus sets the stage for interpretive mischief by clearly giving us the date of the quake but not the year. I think this event has the best chance of taking place between the 5th and 10th of May 2000. It will most likely result from the gravitational stresses caused by the great planetary alignment of that period.

9 Q84

Roy expoſé parfaira l'hecatombe,	**The King exposed will complete the slaughter,**
Apres auoir trouué ſon origine:	**After having found his origin:**
Torrent ouurir de marbre & plomb la tombe,	**A torrent to open the tomb of marble and lead,**
D'vn grand Romain d'enſeigne Meduſine.[1]	**Of a great Roman with the Medusine device.**

[1]Leoni gives us Latin *Medusaeus*, for "of Medusa" whose serpent-topped head turned all onlookers to stone. Lee McCann believes it is an anagram of *Deus in Me*, the motto of St Peter. I would add that the name Peter, or *pierre* in French, means "stone." The *Medusa* that can turn people into stone may be Nostradamus' nasty description of the final pope of the foretold apocalypse, who he claims elsewhere will be named "Peter."

Great natural disasters are predicted by Nostradamus and other seers to take place perhaps as soon as spring of the year 2000, when the tomb of St Peter will be uncovered in the ruins of the Vatican after the flood. The **great Roman** is interpreted as St Peter since **Medusine** is an anagram of *Deus in Me*, Peter's motto. In 1138 the medieval Irish St Malachy predicted that the last pope of the Vatican during the apocalypse would be named Peter. According to the timing of his prophecies, this might place the final pope on his prophetic list around, or shortly after, the dawning of the new millennium.

Medusine could tie us in to 2 Q4's serpent weapon placed on the shores of the Tiber. This weapon may be some nuclear device terrorists intend to smuggle up the river to Rome.

9 Q85

Paſſer Guienne, Languedoc & le Roſne,	**To pass Guienne, Languedoc and the Rhône,**
D'Agen tenans de Marmande & la Roole:	**From Agen holding Marmande and the Réole:**
D'ouurir par foy p¹ Roy Phocē² tiêdra ſõ troſne,	**To open by faith through the king the Phocean will hold his throne,**
Conflit aupres ſainct Paul de Mauſeole.	**Conflict after St Paul-de-Mausole.**

[1]Incomplete word – p(ar) Roy: a) through the king; b) Old French parroy = the seashore; c) parroi = wall, partition.
[2]Phocaeans, the founders of Marseilles.

Guienne once was a large province of southwest France. Languedoc is farther east, between Guienne and the Rhône. Agen, Marmande, and La Réole are on the Garonne in Guienne. Marseilles is farthest east of the other locations on the French Riviera. Line 4 stands for conflict in St Rémy, Nostradamus' birthplace, which is about 40 miles northwest of Marseilles. Other than this, little more can be gleaned, except that all these areas could have undergone civil strife during any or all of the Nine Wars of Religion 1562–98.

9 Q86

Du bourg Lareyne paruiêdrõt droit à Chartres,	**From Bourg-la-Reine they will reach straight to Chartres**
Et feront pres du pont Anthoni penſe,	**And they will pause near Pont d'Antony,**
Sept pour la paix canteleux comme martres,	**Seven for peace, as crafty as martins,**
Feront entree d'armée à Paris clauſe.	**Will make an entry with the army to a closed Paris.**

During Napoleon's final gamble for power known as the Hundred Days he faced a coalition of seven European powers: Britain, Austria, Prussia, Russia, Sweden, Spain, and Portugal. Le Pelletier applies the quatrain to the second capitulation of Paris, on 3 July 1815.

"The general of the seven nations in coalition against Napoleon, under the pretense of re-establishing peace, but secretly desirous of weakening France, will, by virtue of the capitulation, enter a Paris stripped bare of troops and evacuated by the French army, which will retreat to Chartres, to take up positions beyond the Loire, passing on the way Bourg-la-Reine and Pont d'Antony, beneath which it was encamped."

9 Q87

Par la foreſt du Touphon eſſartee,
Par hermitage ſera poſé le temple,
Le Duc d'Eſtampes par ſa ruſe inuentee,
Du mont Lehori prelat donra exemple.

In the forest of Torfou, cleared,
By the hermitage the temple will be
placed,
The Duke of Étampes through the
ruse he invented,
Will make an example of the prelate
of Monthéry.

Monthéry is less than 20 miles southwest of Paris, and Étampes is another 10 miles farther. Three royal mistresses held the title of d'Estampes: Anne de Pisseleu, Diane de Poitiers, and Gabrielle d'Estrées. Other than this we have a trail of intimate details that can at best only be objects of conjecture. History does not easily document the more successful secret royal trysts, especially if they were carried out with discretion. It seems the forest of Torfou was cleared centuries before Nostradamus wrote this prophecy. The **hermitage** may or may not have existed, but the **temple** could be something like a gazebo constructed for Diane de Poitiers or else be her favorite bedroom for liaisons. Étampes itself was considered by her lover Henry II for a temple to the goddess Diana, after her favorite alias. Perhaps lines 3 and 4 allude to some dangerous liaison set to aggravate a celibate cardinal.

9 Q88

Calais, Arras ſecours à Theroanne,
Paix & ſemblant ſimulera l'eſcoutte,
Soulde d'Alabrox deſcendre par Roane,
Deſtornay peuple qui deffera le routte.

Calais, Arras aid for Thérouanne,
Peace and semblance will simulate
the spy,
The remainder from Savoy to descend
through Roanne,
The people dissuaded who yield the
route.

Interpreters from Jaubert to Leoni have implied that Nostradamus was cheating in the first two lines, since the events in lines 1 and 2 could be applied to 1557. At that time Calais, the English stronghold, had Philip II of Spain as its titular king through marriage to Mary Tudor. Arras and the ruins of Thérouanne (which was leveled by Charles V in 1553) lie to the southeast in the province of Artois, which was a full-fledged Spanish possession. To avoid cheating his readers with a retroactive prophecy, Nostradamus would have had to pen this quatrain during the beginning of the Truce of Vaucelles (February 1556) and the Anglo-Spanish attack that came from Artois to rout the French garrison and relief army at St Quentin (10 August 1557).

The last two lines clearly augur future events. The Treaty of Cateau-Cambrésis in 1559 awarded Savoy the French territory of Bresse, which brought their frontier within 35 miles of Roanne. The statement **Savoy to descend through Roanne** may warn of a near-future Savoyard invasion via this route. The final line applies to actual historical events over four decades later, when Savoy was forced to yield this potential invasion route through Bresse to Henry IV in 1601.

9 Q89

Sept ans ſera Philip. fortune proſpere,	*For seven years fortune will favor Philip,*
Rabaiſſera des Arabes l'effort,	*He will beat down the exertions of the Arabs,*
Puis ſon mydi perplex rebors affaire,	*Then in the middle [of his reign], a perplexing and paradoxical affair,*
Ieuſne ognyon abyſmera ſon fort.	*Young Ogmios will destroy his stronghold.*

The French grew restless under the Bourbon King Charles X. He was deposed in the 1830 revolution by Louis Philippe, Duc d'Orléans. He too was deposed in the even bloodier Europe-wide rash of revolutions in 1848. Both Louis Philippe and his successor, Louis Napoleon, feature prominently in Nostradamus' prophecies

Louis Philippe's first seven years were a era of prosperity and domestic peace. The successful conquest of Algeria during that time brought added glory, both to France and to its royal house. But things began to sour midway in his 14-year reign. By 1838 riots were erupting in Lyons, Grenoble, and Paris over the limited right to vote. The new Bonapartists rallied around the dead emperor's nephew, Louis Bonaparte (poetically described by the prophet as **Ogmios**, after the Celtic hero-god of eloquence and poetry). Louis Philippe had him imprisoned, but to no avail. The French people persisted in their perplexing, paradoxical love affair with Napoleon's dictatorship and, in time, this would precipitate Louis Philippe's downfall.

Another interpretation places the event closer to Nostradamus' time. Philip II of Spain loses a fortress, or even his empire, to the Celtic Hercules, who could be the matured son of Henry II, Hercules, the Duc d'Alençon. If this is the correct application, this prophecy is either pathetically wrong or just another alternative future unaccessed. Instead of dying in a joust, Henry II lives long enough to guide his youngest son to be a powerhouse of European rulers, rather than become its most notable blue-blooded buffoon.

9 Q90

Vn capitaine de la grand Germanie,	A Captain of Greater Germany,
Se viendra rendre par simulé secours,	Will come to deliver false help,
Vn Roy des Roys aide de Pannonie,	A King of Kings, support from Pannonia,
Que sa reuolte fera de sang grand cours.	So that his revolt will cause a great shedding of blood.

Nostradamus wrote this commentary on the mid-20th century catastrophe that was World War II. The quatrain contains many clues to support this interpretation. **Greater Germany** was the name Hitler used for his Nazi empire *Grossdeutschland*. Hitler in his madness saw himself as a self-appointed messiah (**King of Kings**) of the "Aryans." **Pannonia** stands for the Axis ally Hungary, which sent 300,000 soldiers to fight alongside the Germans against the Soviet Union. Hitler promised the German people that if they supported his dreams of conquest they would become masters of the world, but if they failed he would take them and the world into the abyss. After 12 years of his tyranny, and 50 million killed in World War II, the Germans had nothing, and were left trying to survive in the smoke and rubble of his **false** dreams and delusions.

9 Q91

L'horrible peste Perynte & Nicopolle,	The horrible plague Perinthus [Eski Eregli] and Nicopolis [Prevenza],
Le Chersonnez tiendra & Marceloyne,	The Peninsula [Peloponnesus] will it cling to and [also] Macedonia,
La Thessalie vastera l'Amphipolle,	Thessaly it will devastate [and] Amphipolis [Salonika],
Mal incogneu & le refus d'Antoine.	An unknown evil and the refusal from Anthony.

All these locations are in Greece and Macedonia. This may be related to the great plague of **false dust** described in 5 Q90. **Anthony** may yet appear as a leader by that name in the near future. Or Nostradamus could be using a saint as a metaphor: Anthony of Egypt (AD 251–356) was a widely revered saint during the medieval and Renaissance period. He was known as a great healer of people and animals. In other quatrains Nostradamus talks of a great war or plague that kills both people and animals (2 Q62). Perhaps he believes a plague comes to future humanity because of a wickedness so intractable that even the saint will refuse to apply his healing powers to it.

Quatrain Indexing Date: Q91 = 1991? Note the similar indexing to the "plague of false dust" quatrain (5 Q90). Could Nostradamus be trying to date this event for the 1990s? One cannot rule out the 2090s for both prophecies.

9 Q92

Le Roy voudra dans cité neufue entrer,
Par ennemis expugner lon viendra:
Captif libere faux dire & perpetrer,
Roy dehors eſtre, loing d'ennemis tiendra.

The king will want to enter the new
city,
Through its [his] enemies they will
come to subdue it [him]:
Captives liberated to speak and act
falsely,
King to be outside, he will keep far
from the enemy.

As vague as this is, lines 1, 2, and 4 can be applied retroactively to Henry II, who is physically far removed from the stalemates and military disasters drawing the Habsburg–Valois wars to a close in 1559. In other quatrains **new city** stands for either Cittanova or Neapolis (an archaic form of Naples). A French expeditionary army had an encampment north of Naples in 1557–58. Henry II had always wanted to sail to Naples and personally lead his own forces to glory. This would never happen.

The syntax of line 2 is open to switching **its** with **his** so it can read, **Through its enemies they will come to subdue** him. He cannot leave France to move his stalemated armies in the north and south of Italy. He must remain in Paris while Montmorency marches off to relieve Coligny's French garrison at St Quentin. Both forces are destroyed by the Spanish, and their commanders captured. Henry II, by proxy, is sufficiently **subdue**d by his enemies, Philip II of Spain and Emmanuel Philibert of Savoy. Only line 3 can be called a prophetic statement beyond what Nostradamus already knew by late 1557, and it is a good prediction. Before their liberation from Spanish captivity, Coligny and Montmorency would be used by the Spanish as negotiators to arrange the humiliating peace treaty of Cateau-Cambrésis in 1559. To Nostradamus the patriot, their negotiations are false and craven, whereas history sees their efforts as practical and realistic attempts to end 50 years of French–Spanish tensions.

9 Q93

Les ennemis du fort bien eſlongnez,
Par chariots conduict le baſtion,
Par ſur les murs de Bourges eſgrongnez,
Quand Hercules battra l'Hæmathion.[1]

The enemies from the fort very far,
In chariots conducted [to] the bastion,
From above, the walls of Bourges
reduced to pieces,
When Hercules will strike the
Macedonian.

[1]Haemathion = a) Latin Emathius = Macedonian; b) thus Philip II, after his classical namesake, Philip II of Macedon; c) Aemathion = a sun god or possibly the "Sun King" Louis XIV.

Here again is a quantum future for Hercules Duc d'Alençon. The battered **Macedonian** is Philip II of Spain. A mobile siege of weapons is used to pulverize the walls of Bourges, a city in central France. Le Pelletier uses the second interpretation of *Haemathion* to get the Sun King Louis XIV, and he ignores a few difficult verbs like *battra* ("will strike") when he describes Vauban's new earthen fortifications around Bourges which cause the old city walls to fall into disrepair in 1651. Le Pelletier flips over a noun on his grammatical skillet to make an adjective so that *Hercules* can become the Herculean effort of Louis XIV "in digging the canal of Languedoc, destined to join the Mediterranean to the Atlantic."

9 Q94

Foibles galleres feront vnies enfemble,
Ennemis faux le plus fort en rampart:
Faible affaillies Vratiflaue tremble,
Lubecq & Myfne tiendront barbare[1] part.

Weak galleys will be united together,
False enemies the strongest on the
rampart:
The weak assailed, Bratislava
trembles,
Lübeck and Meissen will take the
barbarian side.

[1]*Barbare* = a) Barbary or Libyan; b) Barbar(ossa), code name for Hitler's invasion of Russia in 1941; by extension, Adolf Hitler.

This could be about the dismemberment of Czechoslovakia in 1938–39 by the Munich Pact. In this case *barbare* is another allusion to Adolf Hitler as Barbarossa. Nazi Germany made Slovakia an Axis satellite. Lübeck and Meissen are German towns on the Baltic that obviously stand with Barbarossa as part of Nazi Germany. Fontbrune believes **barbarian side** foresees the disembarkation of Rommel's Afrika Korps at Tripolitania in February 1941.

9 Q95

Le nouueau faict conduira l'exercite,
Proche apamé iufques aupres du riuage,
Tendant fecour de Milannoife eflite,
Duc yeux priué à Milan fer de cage.

The new fact will command the army,
Almost cut off up to near the shore of
the river,
Help from the Milanais elite holding
out,
Duce loses his eyes in an iron cage in
Milan.

The fall of Nazi Germany is described from the point of view of her Italian Allies. We begin with the Russian Front, November 1942. The **new** and terrible **fact** is that Stalingrad falls, exposing the Italian Eighth Army to encirclement (**cut off**). Their defensive lines are overwhelmed **near the** western **shore of the** Don **river**. By 28 April 1945 the Axis forces were routed on all fronts. Hitler remained in Berlin, scraping together his last reserves for a final stand against the Soviet steamroller. The same day,

Mussolini and his mistress, Clara Petacci, fell into the hands of communist partisans in northern Italy. After a few words in a mock trial they were gunned down in the street and their bodies hauled to Milan to be strung upside down from the charred steel frame of a bombed-out gas station (*in an iron cage in Milan*). The gathering crowd vented years of repressed rage at Il **Duce**'s body by throwing stones and shooting. Women even urinated on the corpses. One man pummeled Mussolini's face beyond recognition (*loses his eyes*) with a board.

9 Q96

Dans cité entrer excercit defniee,	**The army denied entry into the city,**
Duc entrera par perfuafion,	**Duce will enter through persuasion,**
Aux foibles portes clam[1] armee amenee,	**To the weak gates the army is secretly conducted,**
Mettront feu, mort de fang effufion.	**They will put it to fire and sword – effusion of blood!**

This is vague enough to apply to any theme of an army denied entry to a besieged city.

9 Q97

De mer copies[1] en trois parts diuifees,	**The sea forces are divided in three parts,**
A la feconde les viures failleront,	**The second one will be lacking [exhaust?] the supplies,**
Defefperez cherchant champs Helifees,	**Giving up all hope, searching for the Elysian Fields,**
Premier en breche entrez victoire auront.	**The first ones entering the breach will have victory.**

[1]Latin *copia* = troops, forces, army.

Universally cited as obscure. Latter-day scholars try to squeeze a Third-World-War invasion of Europe out of it via the Muslims theme. I, however, will call this one for the Battle of Trafalgar in 1805.

On our watery stage we have three belligerent fleets (*sea forces in three parts*): the French and Spanish fleets versus Lord Nelson's British Fleet. The Spanish vessels were poorly equipped and supplied, and morale and belief in the French cause was low. Obscurity helps the third line fit for either naval commander. If Nelson is meant it might describe the first moments of anguish he and his officers felt as he was shot through the spine by a sharpshooter at the peak of the battle. Or maybe it stands for the French commander, Villeneuve, who witnesses catastrophe and capture all around him and, wishing he were dead, searches for the peace and rest of heaven represented here in the classical description of the **Elysian Fields** (the paradise of Greek mythology).

Leoni is right to scratch his head over the use of a military term for land maneuver (*entering the breach*) during a naval battle. I would suggest that this is just the thing Nostradamus would do to stimulate our curiosity to look for a naval engagement that entailed a maneuver similar to a **breach** of a battle line. And that is why Trafalgar calls to me, since it is noted in the annals of naval history for Lord Nelson's daring maneuver and seamanship in leading his entire fleet, in tandem, cannons blazing, right through the lines of Spanish and French ships – in effect smashing a huge breach into their formation.

9 Q98

Les affligez par faute d'vn feul taint,	**The afflicted ones stained through the fault of a single one,**
Contremenant à partie oppofite,	
Aux Lygonnois mandera que contraint	**The contravener in the opposite party,**
Seront de rendre le grand chef de Molite.	**To those of Lyons he will send word that obliged by force**
	They will give [themselves] up to the great chief of Molite [war].

This is about the repression of the Royalist rebellion in Lyons in October 1793. Royalists had rioted against the re-election of Nivière Chol, their draconian Republican mayor who was earlier forced to resign because of his nocturnal police raids on Royalist households (*the fault of a single one*). Barère of the Committee of Public Safety is the one ordering the repression of the Lyonnais (*obliged by force*). Sixteen hundred houses owned by Royalist families were razed along with all the city's fortifications. As a final punctuation to their barbarity the Republican soldiers constructed a liberty column over the ruins of the Bourgneuf quarter with the inscription: "Lyons waged war on Liberty, Lyons is no more."

Quatrain Indexing Date: Q99 = 1799, a near miss for the actual sacking of Lyons in 1793.

9 Q99

Vent Aquilon fera partir le fiege,	**Northern wind will cause the siege to be raised,**
Par murs geter cendres, chauls, & poufiere,	
Par pluye apres qui leur fera bien piege,[1]	**Over the walls to throw ashes, lime chalk and dust,**
Dernier fecours encontre leur frontiere.	**Through rain afterwards, which will do them much harm,**
	Meanest assistance against their frontier.

[1]Provençal *piegi* = worse.

The wording is similar to 4 Q52 so this could be part two of a prophecy for the Soviet breakout from the siege of Leningrad, described here as a **northern wind**. In January 1943, the Germans in their frozen foxholes and machine gun positions on the right bank of the River Neva saw the black human waves of Soviet infantry coming out of Leningrad, pouring over the white glare of the frozen river. The brittle air was shattered by the roar of thousands of voices emitting icy spray as they yelled "Urrah! Urrraahh!!" The Germans held their fire until the wave of men began to bear down on their side of the river bank. Suddenly the cracked lips of a hundred officers cried "Feuer!" The first wave slammed into a wall of flying steel, finding themselves boiling and collapsing in bloody ruin on the river bank. A second wave broke over their bodies, then a third, a fourth, a fifth. Soon the ice was black with the choked and bloody flotsam of shattered human waves. But no man can stop the sea. And on that day an ocean of Soviet soldiers fell, retreated, and crashed again upon that shore until their roaring flood mounted the river bank and crashed over the German foxholes to break the siege of Leningrad.

My historical reveries aside, this could have a near-future application for the Bosnian peace-enforcing efforts of IFOR and the lifting of another legendary siege of another Slavic town in our times, Sarajevo. Perhaps we can divine the events that are set to unfold when the tour of peacekeepers is completed. Line 1 sees the great "Northern" superpower of the United States landing troops in Bosnia in the dead of winter (**Northern wind**) in January 1996. Line 2 could describe the war crimes of the Serbs, who shot and buried tens of thousands of captured Bosnian men in lime-filled mass graves. Line 3 may report the harsh weather conditions plaguing combatants and peace enforcers alike in this mountainous region.

The final line recounts the long years of neglected assistance to the Bosnian Muslims. It might also hint that these new demilitarized frontiers separating the former warring sides will prove of little help if IFOR's commanders remain rigidly on schedule and pull out by early 1997. Nostradamus may be cautioning us that the commitment to peace should last for a generation (30 years) rather than a paltry 12 months. Until the collective mindset towards ethnic cleansing is deprogrammed from the new generation, history will repeat itself again in a new and ferocious Balkan war by 1999 or the 2020s.

Quatrain Indexing Date: 9Q99 = September (9th month) 1999? Turn "999" upside down to get 666, the biblical number for man living in sin (ie forgetfulness).

9 Q100

Naualle pugne nuict fera fuperee,	Naval battle [at] night will be subdued,
Le feu aux naues à l'Occident ruine:	The fire in ships, to the West ruin:
Rubriche neufue la grand nef coloree,	New code, the great ship colored,
Ire à vaincu, & victoire en bruine.	Anger to the vanquished, and victory in a drizzle.

After a week of sparring with English squadrons, the 130 ships of the Spanish Armada lay at anchor in the exposed harbor of Calais on 7 August 1588. They hoped to rendezvous with Parma's Army of Flanders and ferry them across the Channel to attack England. The morale of the Spanish and Portuguese crews was low, and nerves were aggravated by rumors of the English preparing floating mines and explosive-packed hulks to be guided along with the night tide, into their tightly packed harbor. Shortly after midnight the watchmen in a hundred crow's nests atop a forest of Spanish masts cried out a warning, "Fire ships!" Along the ghostly wall of English sail in the open waters outside of Calais first one, then two, and finally eight columns of fire blossomed on the waves bearing down with the tide on the Armada. The Spanish ships unfurled their sails and scattered to sea. Some of them were dragging anchor lines, while the majority cut their lines and left on the bottom of Calais harbor a fortune in lost anchors. At dawn the English squadrons under the command of Sir Francis Drake pounded the disorganized Spanish with every round they had, sinking several galleons. A gale swept up the channel, carrying the Armada into the North Sea. The Spanish commander, the Duke of Medina-Sidonia, gave up all hope of his rendezvous with Parma and ordered the fleet to sail around the British Isles back to Spain. This decision would mean losing half his ships and men to the gales and rocks off Ireland (see 10 Q2).

Century X

10 Q1

A l'ennemy, l'ennemy foy promiſe
Ne ſe tiendra les captifs retenus:
Prins preme mort & le reſte en chemiſe,
Dãné le reſte pour eſtre fouſtenus.

By the enemy, the enemy faith
  promised
Will not be sustained, the captives
  retained:
Captured, one near death and the rest
  in their shirts,
Damned are the rest for being
  supported.

First off, this one is nebulous enough to apply to any number of wars during which POWs and refugees are betrayed or abused. Lamont cites this for the unfairness of the Versailles Treaty to Germany. Leoni throws in his lot for the Vichy regime, when the Nazis made collaboration a one-way street with Hitler as the turgid Teutonic traffic cop. I'll only add that this applies itself equally well to the plight of Soviet POWs, who were offered the choice of either dying from starvation and exposure by the millions in open fields surrounded by barbed wire, or joining the SS as auxiliary legions to fight the communists as part of the Russo-German Army of Liberation. A large contingent was formed, nominally commanded by one of Stalin's brightest former generals, Lieutenant General Andrei Vlasov, who himself was a prisoner of the Germans. The Russian POW's new German masters had promised they would fight in Russia in a combined army but Hitler distrusted Russians and the majority of these men were scattered in small groups amongst German units on the Eastern Front. Whole battalions went to quiet areas in the Western theater, where one could find Ukrainians and Russians in jackboots and German field-gray helmets and uniforms, patrolling lonely roads in Nostradamus' native Provence. When the war was over thousands of these men rushed westward to surrender to the British and Americans. They pleaded with their Western captors for asylum, but Stalin demanded their return. A total of 800,000 had served in German units throughout the war. By the war's end most found themselves back where they had started – as half-naked minions of the damned, behind barbed wire. They had escaped death in Nazi concentration camps to fight for Hitler, only to perish in Stalin's concentration camps because they had done so. Even Vaslov, the man Heinrich Himmler had called the Russian de Gaulle, was hanged by Stalin's henchmen.

10 Q2

Voille gallere voil de nef cachera,	**Veil of the galley, the sail of the ship**
La grande claſſe viendra ſortir la moindre:	**will hide,**
Dix naues proches le tourneront pouſſer,	**The great fleet will come to leave the**
Grande vaincue vnies à foy ioindre.	**smaller one:**
	Ten ships near will turn to drive it back,
	The great one vanquished, to join those
	united in faith.

This continues the vision of galleons from the Spanish Armada (9 Q100) swerving to avoid collisions with each other as they escape the tight confines of the harbor at Calais to dodge a blazing line of eight English fire ships bearing down on them. Not a single galleon caught fire. Equally surprising, there was only one collision of Spanish ships in the midnight chaos of 130 vessels cutting their anchor lines and scattering in all directions. Although Nostradamus is off by two ships, the infernal vessels did **drive** the Spanish Armada **back** to Spain. The smoking **veil** of eight English vessels had flushed the Spanish into the open waters in a state of hopeless disarray. First the guns of Sir Francis Drake's smaller but more numerous men-o'-war pounded the Armada. Then a sudden blast of winds from a Channel gale sent the Spanish up the North Sea on their fateful journey around Scotland and down past the storm-plagued, treacherous west coast of Ireland. There many a shipwrecked Spaniard crawled ashore, only to have his throat cut by Irish brigands. The **great one vanquished** is Philip II of Spain who, upon receiving the report from the tattered and crestfallen Duke of Medina-Sidonia, commander of the Armada, resigned himself to God's will. The means by which he could depose the Protestant Queen Elizabeth I and return England to the **united . . . faith** of the Catholic fold lay shattered in abandoned hulks on the lonely reefs of Ireland.

10 Q3

En apres cinq troupeau ne mettra hors vn,	**After the fifth will not put out a flock,**
Fuytif pour Penelon[1] l'aſchera:	**A fugitive for Penelon [Poland?] he**
Faulx murmurer ſecours venir par lors,	**will turn loose:**
Le chef le ſiege lors habandonnera.	**To murmur falsely, help to come by**
	then,
	The chief will then abandon the siege.

[1]An enigma: Le Pelletier twists it into a near-anagram for *Polone*, Poland.

Penelon may stand as an anagram for Poland. This unknown who arrives on the scene after a succession of five rulers, or five kings with the same name, could be the heir to the messianic future king of France, Henry V. But this is hopelessly obscure.

10 Q4

Sur la minuict conducteur de l'armee,	At midnight the commander of the army,
Se fauuera, fubit efuanouy:	Will save himself, suddenly vanished:
Sept ans apres la fame non blafmee,	Seven years after his fame [is] unblemished,
A fon retour ne dira oncq ouy.	To his return they will say naught [but] "yes."

Since 1891 most interpreters have followed Ward's lead and pinned this one on England and Charles II's defeat at the Battle of Worcester (1651). Charles II was one of the few survivors of the massacre. He put on a disguise and underwent a harrowing nine-week escape to France via Scotland. With the last Scottish resistance crushed it would appear that Cromwell's English republic was assured. But exactly seven years later in 1658 Puritan fortunes would change with the death of Oliver Cromwell and the rising public tide of nostalgia for the return of royalty. Two years after Cromwell's death Charles II would again sit on the English throne, his reputation – and that of royalty itself – unblemished as he launched the Restoration.

10 Q5

Alby & Caftres feront nouuelle ligue,	Albi and Castres will form a new league,
Neuf Arriens Lisbon & Portugues,	New Aryans, Lisbon and the Portuguese,
Carcas, Tholoufe confumeront leur brique,	Carcassonne, Toulouse will destroy and consume their intrigue
Quand chief neuf monftre[1] de Lauragues.	At the time of the chief new monster, the Lauragues.

[1]Monster, or a divine omen delivered by a daemonic messenger.

All the places were in Languedoc. The Portuguese connection to this region and the **new Aryans** can only make some sense if this is a description of underground espionage routes used by Nazi (**Aryan**) and Allied spies during World War II. Southwestern France was a hotbed of Resistance activity. Couriers, refugees, and escaped prisoners of war were frequently shuttled over the French–Spanish border. Lisbon, in neutral Portugal, was the capital of espionage traffic for both sides during the war. Le Pelletier translates the final line as **when the new chief will go out**. This could be a new Resistance leader traveling from the environs of Castelnaudary (the *pays* or ancient department or county of Lauragues), near **Albi**, **Castres** and **Toulouse** on his clandestine journey to Lisbon.

10 Q6

Sardon[1] Nemans[2] ſi hault desborderont,	*The Gardon will flood Nîmes so high,*
Qu'on cuydera Deucalion[3] renaiſtre:	*That they will believe Deucalion*
Dans le coloſſe la plus part fuyront,	*reborn:*
Veſta ſepulchre feu eſtaint apparoiſtre.	*Into the colossus [amphitheater] the*
	greater part will flee,
	Vesta's sepulchre fire appears
	extinguished.

[1]Possible erratum for the Gardon (or Gard) river.
[2]Latin *Nemausus*, = Nîmes.
[3]*Deucalion*: the Greek Noah.

This resumes the flood theme of 9 Q9. As noted earlier Nîmes was flooded on 9 September 1557. Jaubert adds that this combined with a flood of the Gardon, although historical reports do not support this. The torrents of rain uncovered the foundations of ancient Roman buildings, but no lamp of Vesta was unearthed. Nostradamus most likely penned this quatrain shortly before the event, and the manuscript was probably in the ink-blackened hands of his Lyonnais printer when thunderclouds darkened the skies over Nîmes the day of the flooding rain. One can hope that a future flood of that city caused by global warming is not foretold here, for it would be so severe that citizens of 21st century Nîmes would be forced to rush into the ruins of the famous Roman amphitheater to escape the mounting waters.

10 Q7

Le grand conflit qu'on appreſte à Nancy,	*The great conflict that they are*
L'æmethien dira tout ie ſoubmetz:	*preparing at Nancy,*
L'iſle Britanne par vin, ſel en ſolcy,	*The Macedonian will say "I*
Hem. mi deux Phi. long temps ne tiendra	*subjugate all,"*
Metz.	*The British Isle in anxiety over wine*
	and salt,
	Hem. mi two Phi. Metz will not hold
	for long.

Le Pelletier's lumbering account has merit. He once again takes *Aemathien* to mean the Sun King (Louis XIV), placing the window in time between the end of the Thirty Years War and the rise of Louis XIV as the fully matured monarch of France:

"The Treaty of Westphalia, concluded with the Emperor in 1648, under the reign of Philip IV, King of Spain, and before the War of the Spanish Succession, an enterprise in the interests of Philip V, grandson of Louis XIV, will cede Metz to France and cause it to surely lose its ancient title of imperial city. [In other words, the actions of **two Phi**{lips} are described here.]

"England, a prey to the horrors of [the Civil War], will decapitate its legitimate King, Charles I, in 1649, who will have lacked strength and wisdom [*wine and salt*] in the government of his state.

"Nancy will be taken in 1660 by the French, who will drive out its Duke, Charles IV, raze its fortifications and incorporate it into France.

"It will be then [1661] that Louis XIV, relieved of the tutelage of Mazarin, will begin to rule himself, and will put into effect his famous maxim, 'The State, that's me.'"

10 Q8

Index & poulſe parfondera le front,	**With index finger and thumb he will moisten his forehead,**
De Senegalia le Conte à ſon filz propre:	**The Count of Senigallia to his own son:**
La Myrnarmee par pluſieurs de prinfront,	**The Mynarmians**[1] **through several in short order,**
Trois dans ſept iours bleſſes mors.	**Three in seven days wounded dead.**

[1]Latin *Mimnermia* = (a title of) Venus; (figuratively) the Venitian Republic next to Urbino.

Senigallia was once a fiefdom up the Adriatic coast from Ancona in the papal states. In 1474 it was incorporated into the possessions of Giovanni della Rovere, by order of Pope Sixtus IV, his uncle. The della Roveres ruled Senigallia and the Duchy of Urbino until 1624. However, their rule died with a whimper, not violently as predicted here.

10 Q9

De Caſtillion figuieres iour de brune,	**In the Castle of Figueras on a misty day,**
De femme infame naiſtra ſouuerain prince:	**From an infamous woman will be born the sovereign prince:**
Surnon de chauſſes perhume luy poſthume,	**Surname of breeches [stockings?] on the ground [will make him] posthumous,**
Onc Roy ne feut ſi pire en ſa prouince.	**Never was a King so very bad in his province.**

Lamont pairs this one with the Spanish Civil War but does little to elaborate why. So to help him along I will add that **Figueras** is on the Spanish side of the Pyrenees near the Mediterranean and was the last Loyalist capital in 1939. The **Castle** San Fernando is an 18th-century citadel where many loyalists and republican prisoners spent their days locked inside, wasting away as victims of Francisco Franco's dictatorship. The **prince** with a surname in Spanish, Basque or French for **breeches** or **stockings** is executed by the evil **King**, which possibly is Franco.

10 Q10

Tafche de murdre enormes adulteres,
Grand ennemy de tout le genre humain:
Que fera pire qu'ayeulx, oncles, ne peres,
En fer,[1] feu, eau, fanguin & inhumain.
	Stained with murder, enormous
	    adulteries,
	Great enemy of the entire human
	    race:
	One who will be worse than his
	    grandfathers, uncles or fathers,
	Hell, fire, water, bloody and
	    inhuman.

[1]En fer: = a) Hell; b) in iron.

One of the harshest quatrains Nostradamus ever wrote. Leoni tells us that the Venetian ambassador Morenigo applied the epithet of line 2 to Napoleon – Nostradamus' First Antichrist. One could also apply it to Adolf Hitler or the Third Antichrist yet to appear. One of the current candidates for the Third Antichrist is Saddam Hussein of Iraq. Line 3 might imply that fearsome as the Iraqi dictator is, his descendants could be far worse. His pathologically cruel son, Uday, is being groomed to take his place in the 21st century.

A distant-future interpretation would make the **inhuman** one the leader of an alien race threatening the existence of our own.

10 Q11

Deffoubs Iouchere du dangereux paffage,
Fera paffer le pofthume fa bande,
Les monts Pyrens paffer hors fon bagaige,
De Parpignam courira duc à tende.
	Below Junquera, at the dangerous
	    passage,
	The posthumous one will have his
	    group cross,
	To pass the Pyrenees mountains
	    without his baggage,
	From Perpignan the Duce will rush to
	    Tende.

Franco's victory in the Battle of the Ebro River broke Republican resistance in Catalonia in early 1939. The **posthumous one** of 10 Q9 returns as Dr Juan Negrín, the communist prime minister of the Loyalist government. He gathers his cabinet for the ascent from Junquera over the Perthus Pass across the Pyrenees to sanctuary in France. Calling Negrín **posthumous** is the prophet's way of saying his cause is already lost, even though he would return to the final Republican stronghold near Valencia, via France, to continue the fight. The last two lines shift the timescape forward a few years. In the place of Negrín's haggard refugee government in southern France comes a worried Il Duce to plead with Franco for one last time to enter World War II on the Axis side. Their meeting place was on the French Riviera, near Tende. Mussolini would be just as unsuccessful at Hitler. According to Franco, he bluntly asked him, "Duce, if you could get out of the war, would you?" Mussolini started to laugh, raised his arms to the sky, and cried, "If only I could, if only I could."

10 Q12

Efleu en Pape, d'efleu fera mocqué,	**The one elected Pope will be mocked by his electors,**
Subit foudain efmeu prompt & timide:	**This enterprising and prudent person will suddenly be reduced to silence:**
Par trop bon doux à mourir prouocqué,	**They cause him to die because of his too great goodness and mildness,**
Crainte eftainte la nuict de fa mort guide.	**Fear, extinguished [in] the night, [they will] lead [him] to his death.**

When Albino Luciani became Pope John Paul I on the death of Paul VI (1978), the world was surprised and delighted. His beaming smile and warm, approachable manner were worlds away from the kind of steely political maneuvering that usually accompanied a rise to the papal throne. He counted cardinals throughout the world as his friends and had made a great success of a tenure in Venice. But the candidates in the papal election included a number of Vatican insiders, so it was to his great surprise – and that of many experienced Vatican watchers – that he emerged victorious.

A born reformist, Pope John Paul I immediately enraged the conservatives in the Curia and threatened those who had secretly abused the privileges of power. On the night before his death, he had given a list to Cardinal Villot, the papal secretary of state. It ordered many dismissals and a complete reshuffle of the staff in the power structure of the Vatican. The night before the pope planned to start his reformation of the Vatican Bank and make changes in other key posts, he retired for bed at 9:30 pm His servants found him at 4:45 am dead in his bed, with the papers listing who was to be dismissed scattered over the covers and the floor. As soon as Cardinal Villot was summoned to the bedroom he pocketed the papers, along with the pope's last will and testament (which had been in the desk in his study). Then he issued false statements to the police and the press about the circumstances surrounding the death of the pope. The controversial list has never been publicly disclosed.

In Florence, Cardinal Benelli emerged for a press conference on the morning the pope's death was announced. With tears in his eyes he said, "The Church has lost the right man for the right moment. We are very distressed. We are left frightened."

10 Q13

Souz la pasture d'animaux ruminant,	**Beneath the pasture of ruminating**
Par eux conduicts au ventre herbipolique:	**animals,**
Soldats cachez les armes bruit menant,	**Conducted by them to the belly of the**
Non loing temptez de cité Antipolique.	**herb-selling city:**
	Soldiers hidden, their weapons bringing
	sedition,
	Tried not far from the city of Antibes.

Leoni's exhaustive research uncovers an interesting interpretation from Leroux (1710). Leoni says, "He devotes page after page to the drama of soldiers hidden in a hay wagon on the way to a market in Antibes, and their adventures en route." Leoni, tongue in cheek, reminds us that with enough historical data stuffed in one's head, one can glean from a Nostradamian quatrain all the intimate details of a future episode, be it famous or irrelevant. Then again, perhaps Leroux's grasp of local Provençal folk history is superior to that of other quatrain un-crunchers.

10 Q14

Vrnel Vaucile sans conseil de soy mesmes	**Urnel Vaucile without a plan of his own**
Hardit timide par crainte prins vaincu,	**Daring, timid through fear captured**
Accompaigné de plusieurs putains blesmes,	**and vanquished,**
A Barcellonne aux chartreux conuaincu.	**Accompanied by several ghastly whores,**
	At Barcelona in the Carthusian
	convent, convicted.

This could be another anecdote from Nostradamus' travels through southern Europe, masquerading as a prophecy (see 10 Q14, 10 Q29, 10 Q41).

The best setting for the verse's confused protagonist, who we see staggering with a train of bargain-price whores, would be the town of Urgel in Catalonia. There is a Carthusian monastery at Monte Allegro, several miles west of Barcelona, and our hero, who is an acquaintance of Nostradamus, ends up there. The various translations of *convaincu* allows it to mean either **convicted** for his vices or **convinced** by the monks that he should live a more pious life.

10 Q15

Pere duc vieux d'ans & de soif chargé,	**Father duke old in years and burdened**
Au iour extreme filz desniant les guiere	**by thirst,**
Dedans le puis vif mort viendra plongé,	**On his last day his son denying him the**
Senat au filz la mort longue & legiere.	**jug**
	Into the well plunged alive, will come
	up dead,
	Senate by son, the death long and
	trifling.

A cruel son denies his dying father's last wish, a drink of water. Instead he throws the old man down a well, where he drowns. The city parliament orders death by hanging. Every city in France had a parliament, so its very hard to document this crime and punishment. I will have to ask the criminologists among my readers to enlighten us about any misdeed that matches the vision recorded here.

10 Q16

Heureux au regne de France, heureux de vie	Happy in the realm of France, happy in life
Ignorant ſang, mort fureur & rapine,	Ignorant blood, death, fury and plunder,
Par non flateurs ſera mys en enuie,	For a flattering name [Flatterers for his name?] he will be envied,
Roy deſrobé trop de foy en cuiſine.	The King protected [for his security], too much faith in the kitchen.

Le Pelletier (1867) applies this well to Louis XVIII.

"Happily restored on the throne of France, and happy during his life, Louis XVIII will not die a violent death and, unlike his brothers, he will not be the victim of criminal outrages. He will be given the flattering surname of *Désiré*. This prince will be guilty of not occupying himself enough with public affairs and of loving good cheer (wine and drink) too much."

Le Pelletier avoids Louis' less-flattering surname used by the common people: a wicked pun in Old French for *Louis Dix-huit – Louis de suette*. No longer Louis "Eighteen" he is now Louis "of Feverish Sweats". Courtiers recount how the corpulent king used to gorge himself so passionately that he perspired heavily.

10 Q17

La royne Ergaſte[1] voyant ſa fille bleſme,	The penitentiary queen seeing her daughter wasting away,
Par vn regret dans l'eſtomach encloz,	Because of the regret in her breast enclosed,
Crys lamentables ſeront lors d'Angoleſme,	Lamentable cries will come then from Angoulême,
Et au germain mariage fort clos.	And the marriage to the cousin foreclosed.

[1] *Ergaſte* = a) Latin *ergastulum*, = workhouse, penitentiary; b) Latin *ergastulus*, = a convict.

While enduring the personal and national tragedies of 1559 and 1560, Catherine de' Medici remained gravely concerned for the health of her favorite daughter, Elizabeth, Queen of Spain. One can see in their correspondences that the 15-year-old had become a confessor to her grieving mother, who must have felt imprisoned by a fate that killed her husband in a jousting accident that pushed her sickly child, Francis II, onto the throne. Francis showed every indication that his succession to the throne would be painfully short. To top all of this, as Francis began his last battle to live, letters from Madrid arrived reporting that Elizabeth was fighting an attack of smallpox. One can imagine the queen alone in her apartments, dressed in widow's weeds, sobbing, nursing regrets. Apparently the extra bad news predicted as coming from Angoulême did not find a space on her writing desk. Although Francis would die, as predicted in 10 Q39, Catherine would later receive the good news from Elizabeth's own recovered hand that she had survived the pox.

Le Pelletier (1867) cannot brush aside Angoulême as I. He writes: "Marie-Antoinette, a prisoner and reduced to working with her hands like a slave, will see [her daughter] La Madame Royale, pale with grief caused by the misfortunes of her family. There will then be, in the Temple prison lamentable cries from the young princess who will be Duchess of Angoulême through a marriage in name only with Louis-Antoine de Bourbon, Duc d'Angoulême, her first cousin, to whom she will have been engaged in 1787."

Madame Royale would be traded for Republican prisoners. She would eventually marry Angoulême in 1799 and return home after Napoleon was permanently exiled from France in 1815.

10 Q18

Le ranc Lorrain fera place à Vendofme,[1]	The House of Lorraine will make way for Vendôme,
Le hault mis bas & le bas mis en hault,	
Le filz d'Hamon[2] fera efleu dans Rome,	The high put low and the low put high,
Et les deux grands feront mis en deffault.	The son of Hammon will be elected in Rome,
	And two great ones will be put at a loss.

[1]Vendôme, a Duchy established in 1515 by François I for Charles of Bourbon, Henry IV's grandfather. He bestowed the title of Duc de Vendôme on one of his sons by Gabrielle d'Estrées.

[2]Hamon: a) Amon is a major ancient Egyptian sun god, a pun on Henry IV, being a "Sun King", a title immortalized by his grandson Louis XIV; b) King Amon of Judah, son of Manasseh, aped the blasphemies of his father and was assassinated by his own servants, implying here that Henry IV, aping the Catholicism of his predecessor, will be assassinated by a servant of Catholicism, the fanatical Ravaillac (see 3 Q11).

The chief scion of the House of Lorraine, Henry de Guise, was the charismatic and popular leader of the Catholic League, sworn to defend the throne against the Protestant Huguenots. Guise, along with the help of his brothers, Cardinal Louis and Charles, Duc de Mayenne, aspired to seize the throne from Henry III. All three brothers would come to grief through Henry III's completion of **the great and disastrous action** mentioned in 2 Q88 – the murder of Henry and Louis de Guise.

The brothers Guise of the House of Lorraine lose all to Henry IV, also known as the Duc de Vendôme. *Hamon* is an anagram for the Egyptian sun god Amon, who got respect from the Romans after he was merged with their chief god, Jupiter. Nostradamus plays with anagrams and mythology to compose an accurate parallel with Romans of the Vatican who would accept a heretic Huguenot Prince **Hammon** as their own. The two losers are the Duc de Guise and his brother, the Duc de Mayenne.

10 Q19

Iour que fera par royne faluee,	**The day that she will be hailed as Queen,**
Le iour apres le falut, la priere,	**The day after the benediction, the prayer,**
Le compte fait raifon & valbuee,	**The reckoning is right and reasonable,**
Par auant humble oncques ne feut fi fiere.	**Once humble never was one so proud.**

Pick any good and **proud** queen on her coronation day. Thanks to the obscurity we have centuries of queens to choose from. The first candidate would be Elizabeth I of England, who was newly crowned after the death of the childless Queen "Bloody" Mary. Our prophet, however, rarely had anything good to say about Mary's Protestant successor. Today's Elizabeth II could just as well be crowned with this flattering prophecy.

10 Q20

Tous les amys qu'auront tenu party,	**All the friends who will have belonged to the party,**
Pour rude en lettres mys mort & faccagé,	**For the rude in learning sacked and put [to] death,**
Biens publiez par fixe grand neanty,	**The public goods through fixed [price] the great one annihilated,**
Onc Romain peuple ne feut tant outragé.	**Never were the Roman people so outraged and wronged.**

Post-World War II scholars, by the grace of hindsight, ascribe this one to post-Fascist Italy. Lamont (1942) had the foresight to say it described the "fate that is in store for those in power in Italy." It must be remembered that 1942 in Italy, Fascism was a year away from collapse. Hitler was still advancing into southern Russia, and Italian armies there and alongside Rommel's Afrika Korps were pushing into Egypt.

10 q21

Par le despit du Roy soustenant moindre,	For spite of the King sustaining the lesser one,
Sera meurdry luy presentant les bagues,	He will be murdered presenting the jewels to him,
Le pere au filz voulant noblesse poindre	The father wishing to impress nobility on his son
Fait comme à Perse iadis feirent les Mague:	Does as the Magi did in the Persia of old.

This one is beyond me. Fontbrune sees **Persia** and thinks it has something to do with the fall of the Shah of Iran in 1979 and his abdication to his son. I am unconvinced by Fontbrune's assertion that the white-robed ancient Persian **Magi**, or priests of the Zoroastrian religion, represent the black-robed Ayatollahs of today's Iran.

10 q22

Pour ne vouloir consentir au diuorce,	For not wishing to consent to the divorce,
Qui puis apres sera cogneu indigne,	Which afterwards will be recognized as unworthy,
Le Roy des Isles sera chassé par force	The King of the Isles will be driven out by force
Mis à son lieu que de roy n'aura signe.	One is put in his place who will have no mark of kingship.

Nostradamus presents us with a modern concept far beyond the 16th-century mind: an English king who abdicates the throne for a twice-divorced commoner, not wishing to remain in his social **place** without the woman he loved.

The Prince of Wales was considered one of the most eligible bachelors of the 1930s. But in Parliament and the higher echelons of London society, many disapproved of his nightclub outings, first in the company of an attractive, dark-haired American socialite and her English husband, then later without the husband. The prince's father, King George V, was dying of cancer and soon Edward would be king. He was also to become the moral defender of the Anglican faith, which required that he marry a girl of suitable blood and moral integrity. When, as King Edward VIII, he continued to see divorcée Wallis Simpson, Parliament sent him an ultimatum: drop Wallis or relinquish the crown. Millions heard the king announcing his abdication on the radio – Nostradamus' **tamed animal** (3 q44). Edward declared he could not continue his responsibilities of office without the woman he loved. After his abdication he was given the title "Duke of Windsor" and left England for a life of exile. As soon as she had finalized her second divorce he married Wallis Simpson (see 10 q40).

10 Q23

Au peuple ingrat faictes les remonſtrances, *Par lors l'armee ſe ſaiſira d'Antibe,* *Dans l'arc Monech feront les doleances,* *Et à Freius l'vn l'autre prendra ribe.*[1]	**To the ungrateful people are made the** **remonstrations,** **By then the army will seize Antibes,** **In the arch of Monaco they will make** **piteous cries,** **And at Fréjus the one will take away** **the shore from the other.**

[1]Provençal *riba* = bank, shore, edge.

This is about Operation Dragoon! Line 1 gives the Vichy collaborators' view of the Resistance saboteurs in their midst. Antibes is less than 20 miles up the coast from the main American beach landings in the Gulf of Fréjus. The US Seventh Army rolled the German 157th and 148th Divisions up the coast through Antibes and beyond Monaco to Menton.

10 Q24

Le captif Prince aux Italles[1] *vaincu* *Paſſera Gennes par mer iuſqu'à Marſeille,* *Par grand effort des Forens*[2] *ſuruaincu*[3] *Sauf coup de feu barril liqueur d'abeille.*[4]	**The captive prince conquered in Elba** **He will pass Genoa by sea as far as** **Marseilles,** **Through great effort overcome by the** **foreigners** **Safe [from] gunshot, a barrel [of]** **bee's liquor.**

[1]Either Italy or Latin *Aethalia* = Elba.
[2]*Forens* Old French *forains* = foreigners.
[3]*ſuruaincu*, from Latin *supervinco* = to conquer, overcome.
[4]Bee: Napoleon had bees on his Imperial livery.

When Napoleon abdicated in 1814 the Congress of Vienna exiled him to the Mediterranean island of Elba. The following year he escaped to gather forces for a return to France. His route may have been known by Nostradamus over 240 years before. The little squadron sailed through the Gulf of Genoa hugging the coastline, debarking at Cannes, 100 miles south of Marseilles. This makes Marseilles at best a mere alternative future landfall, or worse, a failed prediction. Line 4's cryptic description could be an attempt to describe Napoleon's return to Paris. He is the one safe from gunshots, for Louis XVIII has fled France. He is the metaphorical **bee** of his own imperial livery, hoisted like a barrel of liquor on the shoulders of a joyful crowd as they carry him up the stairs into the Tuileries.

Line 3 ends the prophecy. Napoleon would be forced to abdicate again after foreign armies defeated him at Waterloo.

10 Q25

Par Nebro ouurir de Brifanne paffage,
Bien eflongnez el tago fara mueftra,
Dans Peligouxe[1] fera commis l'outrage
De la grand dame affife fur l'orcheftra.

Through the Ebro to open the
    Bézenas passage,
Very far away the Tagus will make a
    demonstration,
In Pelligouxe will the outrage be
    committed
By the great lady seated in the
    orchestra.

[1]Enigmatic place name: perhaps *Pellegrue*, a town 35 miles east of Bordeaux?

If *Brisanne* stands for Bézenas, a town north of Narbonne, then we have
the traditional Spanish invasion route into France. The Ebro river in
northeastern Spain was the setting of the largest battle of the Spanish
Civil War. Fighting also transpired on the headwaters of the Tagus in
central Spain. But what to do about silly line 4? Garencières (1672) gave
it a try: "Here once more I lost my Spectacles, and could not see through,
therefore I had rather be silent than coin less, I shall only tell you, that
'Orchestra' in Latin is the seat wherein noble Personages sit at the
beholding of Stage-plays."

10 Q26

Le fucceffeur vengera fon beau frere,
Occuper regne fouz vmbre de vengeance:
Occis oftacle fon fang mort vitupere,
Long temps Bretaigne[1] tiendra auec la
    France.

The successor will avenge his
    beautiful brother [or: brother-in-
    law],
He will occupy the realm under the
    shadow of vengeance:
Obstacle slain, his blood[line?] dead
    to reprimand,
For a long time will Britannia hold
    with France.

[1]Latin *Britannia* = name of the Roman province of Great Britain; (poetic) the female personification of the British Empire; Brittany, France.

What might Robert Kennedy have done if he hadn't been assassinated in
1968 and had gone on to win the American presidential election against
Richard Nixon? The alternative future he never followed may be hidden
in the first two lines: he would take the seat once occupied by his slain
brother, John F. Kennedy, and avenge his death. Conspiracy theories
about who killed JFK abound; one says he was assassinated by Mafia
elements in the United States government as a way to put his brother
Robert, the United States Attorney General, out of business. With his
brother dead, the campaign Robert waged against organized crime was
shelved because the Kennedy administration was replaced by President

Johnson, who did not care for Robert Kennedy. But if Robert had returned to the White House, this time as president, tantalizing hints in this quatrain indicate that he would have resumed his full-scale legal war against the Mafia and taken his revenge.

Line 3 gives us the quantum future that did unfold. The Mafia, nervous about the threat of a Robert Kennedy presidency (**obstacle**), conspired to have him assassinated at the Ambassador Hotel in Los Angeles after making a victory speech at the California primary. Both the avenging brother and his reprimand are made, in effect, **dead**.

For the final line, Leoni had a hard time in 1961 imagining a union between France and England of significant duration. Such a bond through the European Union exists today in the 1990s.

10 Q27

Par le cinquieme & vn grand Hercules,	**Through the fifth one and a great Hercules,**
Viendront le temple ouurir de main bellique,	**They will come to open the temple by the power of war,**
Vn Clement, Iule & Afcans recules,	**One Clement, Julius and Ascanius put back,**
Lefpe,[1] clef, aigle n'eurent onc fi grand picque.	**The sword, [papal] key[s], eagle never once felt so great a quarrel.**

[1] Old French *L'epée* = the sword.

Depending on how you interpret **fifth** and **Clement** you might think, as Leoni believes, that Nostradamus plugged the gaps of his history of the future with retroactive prophecies. He believes we have moved backwards in time over 30 years to 1527, when Charles V (**the fifth one**) was at war with Pope Clement VII and an imperial army composed mostly of Lutheran German mercenaries, under the command of the Duc de Bourbon, sacked Rome. For this to work **Hercules** must stand for the renegade duke. **Clement** is obvious enough, but Leoni adds that the other two names in line 3 represent the pope. The papal **keys** stand for the Vatican; the **eagle** standards and the unsheathed **sword** of the rampaging Imperial army apply to the sack of Rome, which rivaled the ransacking of Rome by the Vandals in ancient times. The **temple** pried open by the soldiers is the Vatican.

It all fits quite well, and if you agree with Leoni's interpretation you have fallen into Nostradamus' clever trap. The retroactive aspects of this verse are inserted to take your attention away from its application over 30 years beyond the time it was written. Elsewhere Nostradamus has described Henry III as the **fifth** Valois child of Henry II and Catherine de' Medici. **Hercules** is the first name of Henry III's younger brother, the

Duc d'Alençon. Nostradamus incorrectly ascribes to him a far more important role in history than accessed. The **temple** returns to its usual application by Nostradamus for the Huguenot temples opened in defiance of Catholic edicts during the Wars of Religion. The Dominican Friar Jacques **Clement** assassinated Henry III at Saint-Cloud in 1589. (**Julius** may be a near miss for Jacques.) Clement killed him with a dagger thrust rather than a **sword**, although the Old French *l'espe* can imply the plunge of sharp cold steel into a victim by sword or by dagger. In any case the weapon is in the hands of a representative of the Holy Church (**keys**), and **eagle** is also the symbol of the Valois monarchy.

10 Q28

Second & tiers qui font prime muficque,	**Second and third which make first-**
Sera par Roy en honneur fublimee:	**class music,**
Par graffe & maigre prefque demy eticque,	**By the King it/he will be sublimated**
Raport de Venus faux rendra deprimee.	**in honor:**
	Through thick and thin almost half-
	consumptive,
	Report of Venus [is] false – to be
	debased.

Leoni says this is far too obscure for a reasonable interpretation. Well, one person's reason is another person's rhyme. But like Leoni, I surrender the chore to others. Prieditis thinks it is for the Third Republic after the Franco-Prussian War and the rivalry between Orléanists and Legitimists. He also thinks it signifies the untimely death in combat of Napoleon III's son, who was fighting alongside the British in the Zulu Wars in South Africa.

10 Q29

De Pol MANSOL[1] *dans cauerne caprine,*	**Of St Paul-de-Mausole in the cavern**
Caché & prins extrait hors par la barbe:	**of goats,**
Captif mené comme befte maftine,	**Hidden and seized, [the goat?] pulled**
Par Begourdans amenee pres de Tarbe.	**out by the beard:**
	Captive led like a mongrel dog,
	By the Biggore people brought near to
	Tarbes.

[1]*Pol* MANSOL = synecdoche for St Rémy, Nostradamus' birthplace.

Century 10 is full of odd and unprophetic insertions. It seems our man was running out of prophetic steam. What to say? Nostradamus has got my goat with this detailed but equally obscure anecdote about a whiskered ungulate, utterly disconsolate about being pulled out of some cave near the prophet's birthplace of St Rémy. A childhood story perhaps? Maybe the goat was a mischievous pet, shipped off by the family *like a mongrel dog* and bound and tied to his new home 250 miles away in the southwestern corner of France. Tarbes was the capital of Protestant Navarre. If there's a connection to Antoine de Bourbon or Henry de Navarre it fails to bleat clearly.

10 Q30

Nepueu & ſang du ſainct nouueau venu,	**Nephew and blood of the newly**
Par le ſurnom ſouſtient arcs & couuert:	**created saint,**
Seront chaſſez mis à mort chaſſez nu,	**Through the surname sustaining the**
En rouge & noir conuertiront leur vert.	**arches and roof:**
	They will be chased out, naked, put
	to death,
	Into red and black will they convert
	their green.

The **nephew** is Louis Napoleon, whose uncle, Napoleon I, was honored (or better, placated) by a desperate Pope Pius VII when his birthday, 15 August, became the feast day of St Napoleon, an early Christian martyred by Diocletian. You will not find his feast day listed in most books on saints, but during the Napoleonic Wars many French soldiers worshipped him as the patron saint of warriors. He was sometimes represented in the likeness of the emperor himself. The rest of the quatrain is usually applied to the presidency and reign of the **nephew** Napoleon III.

10 Q31

Le ſainct Empire viendra en Germanie,	**The holy empire will come into**
Iſmaëlites trouueront lieux ouuerts:	**Germany,**
Anes voudront auſſi la Carmanie,	**The Ismaelites will find open places:**
Les ſouſtenans de terre tous couuerts.	**Asses will also want Carmania,**
	The supporters all covered by earth.

Erika Cheetham, reading the early edition of my first book *Nostradamus and the Millennium*, made the following observation: "Hogue interprets the first line of this quatrain as 'The Russians will enter Afghanistan.' I cannot follow his train of thought."

I can't follow it either, Ms Cheetham, because I never wrote that interpretation. It was inserted into the early edition without my permission by my first publisher, Philip Dunn (aka Peter Lorie). He also took a few other contractual liberties such as throwing in a fraudulent Sixian under my name. I was not made aware of these additions until *Millennium* was already printed and waiting for shipment to the booksellers. I managed to get most of his spurious insertions and editorial errors out of the next editions.

With that said, I am at last able to give Ms Cheetham and the rest of you my interpretation of this quatrain.

I agree with Cheetham: line 1 is clearly about the **holy** Roman **empire**, of the first German Reich. The syntax is odd, since the German states were already a part of the Imperium, unless this moves us forward to the 17th century during the Thirty Years War, when Imperial armies invaded the Protestant kingdoms of central and northern Germany to bring them back into the Empire. The **Ismaelites** could stand for Muslims, Arabs in general, or the Ottoman Turks plotting to take advantage of the great Christian civil war of that day. Actually in the century following the death of Suleiman the Magnificent (1566–1666) the Ottoman Empire passed a relatively quiet period in their western theater. They neither had the will nor the energy to conquer exposed Christian realms, nor did they suffer a threat of reconquest by the embattled Christians. By 1683 the Ottoman **Ismaelites** were on the warpath again, advancing into the **open** plains before Vienna, where they would fail a second time to take the Holy Roman Empire's capital.

Carmania is definitely not part of Afghanistan; it is a Persian territory on the northern shore of the Strait of Hormuz. Since Nostradamus wrote this, nothing historically significant has taken place in Carmania or in the Strait of Hormuz until recent times.

The derogatory reference to **asses** could describe protagonists in the recent Iran–Iraq War (1980–88). The shores of Carmania were used by the Iranian fleet of hundreds of motor-boat raiders attacking tankers bound for Iraq in the Persian Gulf. By 1987 the United States was again playing favorites with tyrants and gave Saddam Hussein tacit support in the war by guarding Kuwaiti oil tankers in the Persian Gulf. For the next year a secret war was fought by America with Iran. One could depict the taunting of the little motor boats in the Iranian fleet as asinine. Two-thirds of these boats were destroyed in American commando raids. Covert US support helped Saddam Hussein gain an edge against Iran. It might have led this particular ass of a dictator to think he could later attack Kuwait with impunity in 1990. Line 4 poetically describes the sad outcome. Tens of thousands of Iraqi dead were hastily buried by the allied forces during their 100-hour land offensive in 1991, ending the Gulf War in an Iraqi rout.

10 Q32

Le grand empire chacun an devoir eſtre,	**The great empire each year is obliged to be of [greatness],**
Vn ſur les autres le viendra obtenir:	**One will come to obtain power over the others:**
Mais peu de temps ſera ſon regne & eſtre,	**But for a short time will his realm and life continue,**
Deux ans aux naues ſe pourra ſouſtenir.	**Two years in his ships he will be able to sustain himself.**

Lamont believed this stood for the future of Hitler and Germany after 1942. He correctly predicted that Hitler would create a great empire, but that his might would last only until the end of 1943. Lamont wrote this around September 1942, when the German offensive to take Stalingrad reached its greatest fury. At the time Hitler was still winning the war and capturing large tracts of land. His forces were plunging deep into the Caucasus territories of Soviet Russia and threatening their oilfields at Mozdok and Baku. Nearly all of Europe and half of European Russia was under the jackboot of his Third Reich, save for neutral (and sympathetic) Portugal and Spain, plus neutral Sweden and Switzerland. Rommel's Afrika Korps had pushed the British deep into Egypt and was preparing for another plunge to the Nile from their positions outside of El Alamein.

But for a short time his Reich and his **life** would **continue**. By the end of 1943 Hitler's fortunes had dramatically changed. Soviet Armies rolled back his Stalingrad, Caucasus, and Kursk offensives. Rommel's Afrika Korps had surrendered in Tunisia. Sicily and Italy were invaded. Mussolini's regime had collapsed. Hitler would fight on for nearly two more years. His U-boats (**ships**) would participate in some of the last actions of the war on the day of the German surrender.

Lamont has a very interesting indirect premonition of alternative future potentials. He speculates on a chance of internal disintegration in the Reich that would aid the Allied war effort and perhaps end the war earlier, thus avoiding the tremendous expenditures of blood and money. In other words, the war might be unexpectedly cut short because of a coup against Hitler. Hitler miraculously survived the bombing of his situation room at his Eastern Prussian headquarters in late July 1944. It is a well known fact that a majority of the casualties and property damage in the World War II European theatre took place in the nine months remaining. Had Hitler died, a provisional government supported by the German high command would have sued for an armistice and saved 20 million lives.

10 Q33

La faction cruelle à robbe longue,	**The cruel faction of the long robe,**
Viendra cacher ſouz les pointus poignards:	**Will come to hide underneath the**
Saiſir Florence le Duc & lieu diphlongue,[1]	**sharp daggers:**
Sa deſcouuerte par immurs & flangnards.	**To seize Florence the Duke and the**
	double-sounding place,
	Its discovery by the lawless and the
	flatterers.

[1]Misprint for *diphtongue* = (a word) with two syllables.

Some sense can be salvaged from line 3. The **double-sounding place** must be the Florentine suburb of Fiesole, a town sitting on a promontory with a marvelous view of Florence, in the Arno valley. The verse may describe a cruel Medici duke of Florence. A coup is uncovered by the Duke's corrupt yes-men.

10 Q34

Gaulois qu'empire par guerre occupera,	**The Gauls who will hold an empire through war,**
Par fon beau frere mineur fera trahy:	**By his minor brother-in-law will he be betrayed:**
Par cheual rude voltigeant trainera,	**By a rebellious, stunt-riding stallion, he will draw along,**
Du fait le frere long temps fera hay.	**The deed of the brother[-in-law, and in arms] will be hated for a long time.**

Robb (1942) applied this one to Napoleon Bonaparte and his brother-in-law, the dashingly costumed and politically fickle Joachim Murat, King of Naples. The French under Napoleon sustained an empire through 14 years of wars and more than 40 major battles. Murat, one of the greatest cavalry leaders of the Napoleonic wars, was married to Napoleon's younger sister, Caroline. As the French empire began to collapse the parvenu king abandoned his post and betrayed Napoleon in 1814. The emperor had this to say about the treacherous dandy: "The conduct of the King of Naples is infamous, and that of the Queen [Caroline] has no word to describe it. I hope to live long enough to take vengeance, for myself and for France, on such ingratitude." (**The deed . . . will be hated for a long time.**)

Ever the man of passion and impulse rather than political scruples, Murat switched sides again during the Hundred Days campaign of 1815. Napoleon warned him not to engage his meager forces in a major battle. The rebellious king of Naples ignored his advice and flung his Italian army in a foolhardy attack against the Austrians at Tolentino. Nostradamus paints a picture of the daredevil horseman, who was already a legend for his exploits under fire, being carried off the field in a river of his own fleeing soldiers. He would return to France and be shot on 13 October 1815. His last request to the firing squad was that they should aim for his heart and not shoot up his handsome face.

10 Q35

Puifnay royal flagrand d'ardant libide,	**The younger son of the king flagrant in ardent lust,**
Pour fe iouyr de coufine germaine:	**To enjoy his first cousin:**
Habit de femme au temple d'Arthemide:[1]	**Female attire in the temple of Artemis:**
Allant murdry par incognu du Maine.	**Going to be murdered by the unknown one of Maine.**

[1]Greek goddess of human fertility, closely associated with the moon, here symbolizing Diane de Poitiers.

A royal scandal at French court is implied here. At the time Nostradamus wrote this, the younger sons of Henry II, the future Charles IX and Henry III, were children. Neither prince had a flagrant randiness for a first cousin. It is more likely they lusted after their sister Marguérite. The murderer is a noble from Maine or a Duc de Mayenne. Claude, the brother of François de Guise, was governor of Burgundy and son-in-law of Diane de Poitiers, Henry II's moon-goddess-fixated mistress. Upon Claude's death in 1573, his nephew Charles became Duc de Mayenne and the arch-enemy of Henry III and Henry IV. And if that isn't clearing things up, the youngest son of Henry II, the Duc d'Alençon, could be the *one of Maine*: the town of Alençon is in that province. Any way you look at it, Nostradamus gets an F for a failed prophecy.

10 Q36

Apres le Roy du foucq guerres parlant,	**After the King of the stump speaking of wars,**
L'ifle Harmotique le tiendra à mefpris:	**The United Isle [Britain] will hold him in contempt:**
Quelques ans bons rongeant vn & pillant,	**For several good years one gnawing and pillaging,**
Par tyrannie à l'ifle changeant pris.	**Through tyranny in the isle prices changing.**

One can be easily stumped by the number of potential interpretations for the *King of the stump*. Mainstream interpretations make him the titular king of England, Philip II of Spain, rattling his sabre at English governmental authorities after his wife, Mary Tudor, dies childless in 1558, effectively canceling his claims to England. Although line 3 adequately describes any number of British sea-dogs raiding Spanish treasure ships in the ensuing decades, calling England, Wales, and Scotland a *United Isle* doesn't fit the times.

This brings us ahead four centuries to 1938–39, when countless radios in the United Kingdom of Britain and Northern Ireland occasionally hear the gruff and growl of Adolf Hitler's stump speeches as he threatens world war if his territorial demands on Czechoslovakia and Poland are not met. The first three years of the war granted his legions a string of victories (*several good years*). Hitler's henchmen exploited the conquered lands of Europe like pirates. The austere price controls and rationing of basic goods during the U-boat siege of the British Isles could be characterized as a tyrannical-though-necessary evil.

10 Q37

L'affemblee grande pres du lac de Borget,	*The great assembly near the lake of Bourget,*
Se ralieront pres de Montmelian:	*They will rally near Montmélian:*
Marchans plus outre penfifs feront proget,	*Traveling further afield the thoughtful ones will draw up a plan,*
Chambry, Moraine combat fainct Iulian.	*Chambéry, St Jean-de-Maurienne, St Julien, combat.*

All locations were in the Duchy of Savoy. Larmor (1925) believes this was fulfilled by the Battle of St Julien fought sometime in the closing years of the Ninth War of Religion (1589–98). The Duke of Savoy gathered his forces at Montmélian for an invasion of France, but was defeated just a few miles south of Geneva by Henry IV at St Julien. According to Larmor, Henry then captured Chambéry and St Jean-de-Maurienne.

10 Q38

Amour alegre non loing pofe le fiege,	*Light love lays the siege not far away,*
Au fainct barbar feront les garnifons:	*The barbarian saint will be at the garrisons,*
Vrfins Hadrie[1] pour Gaulois feront plaige,	*The Orsini and Hadrie will provide a guarantee for the French,*
Pour peur rendus de l'armee aux Grifons.	*For fear rendered by the army of the Grisons.*

[1]cryptogram for the Adriatic, or for Henry de Navarre/Henry IV?

Amour alegre has been applied as an approximation of the popular epithet for Henry IV. He laid siege to Paris in 1590. The Huguenot king is characterized here as a **barbarian saint** of Protestantism. Nostradamus sees him behind the siege works among his soldiers, many of them Protestant German and Swiss (**Grison**) mercenaries. Line 3 jumps to Italy and the powerful Orsini clan, who usually sided with the French in Italian intrigues. Nostradamus implies that they supported Henry (**Hadrie**) when he signed the Franco-Swiss treaty granting the French right of passage through the strategic Valtelline Pass. Fearful of losing the important route to a Franco-Swiss (**Grison**) alliance, the Spanish seized the pass in 1609.

10 Q39

Premier fils vefue malheureux mariage,	*The first son, a widow, an unfortunate marriage,*
Sans nuls enfans deux Ifles en difcord,	*Without any children. Two islands [plunged] into discord,*
Auant dixhuict incompetant eage,	*Before eighteen years, still a minor,*
De l'autre pres plus bas fera l'accord.	*For the other one betrothal happens while even younger.*

Shortly after Henry II died from his wounds in a tournament, as predicted in 1 Q35, courtiers began to take *Les Propheties* even more seriously, especially the above quatrain. They believed line 1 told of Henry's heir, the timid, sickly adolescent Francis II, and his unfruitful marriage to the Scottish princess Mary Stuart. The widow was the grieving queen regent, Catherine de' Medici. In the ensuing years more of the quatrain's secrets were revealed. Mary Stuart (**without any children**) returned to Scotland and became queen. This threw the two island kingdoms (England and Scotland) **into discord** over a power struggle between Mary and the childless Queen Elizabeth I of England. Charles IX, the heir to the French throne and betrothed at the age of 11 to Elizabeth of Austria, is **the other one** mentioned in line 4.

10 Q40

Le ieune nay au regne Britannique,
Qu'aura le pere mourant recommandé,
Iceluy mort LONOLE[1] donra topique,
Et à son fils le regne demandé.

The young heir to the British realm,
Which his dying father had recommended to him,
When the latter is dead, London will dispute [with him],
And from his son, the realm is demanded back.

[1]Erratum for *Londres* = London.

Two quatrains foretell the abdication of Edward VIII of England in 1936. Parliament and high society could not tolerate their king, the defender of the Anglican faith, marrying an American divorcée, Wallis Simpson, and for his part Edward could not bear ruling without the woman he loved. After he abandoned the throne, his brother, the Duke of York, next in line, succeeded him.

Nostradamus' opinion of George VI is not flattering. Perhaps he disliked the new king's stutter, which he heard in his visions. It was believed – particularly by George VI's wife, Queen Elizabeth – that the king was unprepared for the stressful job and consequently, suffered a premature death. We may therefore infer from Nostradamus that a different and better future for the British royal line would probably have come from Edward VIII. As the prophet saw it, the pressure to force abdication upon him would later be viewed as **unworthy** (10 Q22).

If Edward's love had been accepted by Parliament, he might have ruled until his death in the early 1970s. This alternative future might not have prevented Elizabeth II from becoming Queen of England, since Edward and Wallis never had children. As first in the line of succession Elizabeth, daughter of the Duke of York, might have ascended the throne in middle age in the early 1970s, and we would have never enjoyed the magical images in the 1950s of the fetching beauty receiving her crown.

Quatrain Indexing Date: Q40= 1940, a near miss for 1936?

10 Q41

En la frontiere de Cauſſade & Charlus,	*On the frontier between Caussade and Caylus,*
Non guieres loing du fonds de la vallee,	*Not very far from the bottom of the valley,*
De ville Franche muſicque à ſon de luths,	*From Ville Franche music in the sound of lutes,*
Enuironnez combouls & grand mittee.[1]	*Surrounded by [the sound of] cymbals and great fiddling.*

[1]Possibly Greek *milos* = a stringed instrument.

All the locations are roughly 50 miles east of Agen, where Nostradamus once lived and fell in love with his first wife. Perhaps this is another anecdote from Nostradamus' travels that would be recognized only by those who enjoyed the music of the intimate party.

10 Q42

Le regne humain d'Anglique geniture,	*The human realm of Angelic offspring,*
Fera ſon regne paix vnion tenir:	*Will cause its [or his] realm to hold in peace and union:*
Captiue guerre demy de ſa cloſture,	*War captive halfway inside its [or his] enclosure,*
Long temps la paix leur fera maintenir.	*For a long time peace will be maintained for them.*

This has off-world and distant-future potential. Space-faring humanity will genetically bond with an extraterrestrial humanoid race. This union will eventually bring a lasting peace on Earth – and any new Earths colonized by our distant descendants. Many extraterrestrialists believe humanity is a spiritual and genetic experiment.

10 Q43

Le trop bon temps trop de bonté royalle,	*Too many good times, too much of royal goodness,*
Fais & deffais prompt ſubit negligence:	*Ones made and unmade, prompt, sudden, [by] negligence:*
Legier croira faux d'eſpouſe loyalle,	*Lightly will he believe in the unfaithfulness of his loyal spouse,*
Luy mis à mort par ſa beneuolence.	*He is put to death through his benevolence.*

Here is a good example of interpreters' foresight and hindsight. Garencières (1672) logged the following foresight: "This is concerning another King, who through his too much goodness, simplicity and negligence, shall make and unmake those about him, and being fickle, shall believe false reports, made concerning his own wife; and at last by his too much goodness, shall be put to death."

Le Pelletier's contribution of hindsight is written 195 years later. He makes a compelling argument for this being the tragic epilogue Nostradamus wrote for Louis XVI: "[He] will be put to death because he will have applied himself too little (because of his mediocrity) to the affairs of State, because of his weakness, his indecisiveness, the untimely irascibility of his character, his negligence, the lightness with which he will have put faith in the calumnious reports against the honor of the Queen, and above all, because of his excessive kindness, which will leave him defenseless before his enemies."

10 Q44

Par lors qu'vn Roy ſera contre les ſiens,	**When a King will be against his subjects,**
Natif de Bloys ſubiuguera Ligures:	**A native of Blois will subjugate the Genoese:**
Mammel, Cordube & les Dalmatiens,	**Mammola, Cordoba and the Dalmatians,**
Des ſept puis l'ōbre à Roy eſtrēnes & lemures.	**Of the seven then the shadow to the King, New Year's money and ghosts.**

Nostradamus usually calls Henry III **Blois** after his country residence, Château Blois, the scene of his notorious murder of Henry de Guise. After Guise's murder the Catholic League and much of Catholic France rebelled against their king, forcing him to seek asylum with his enemy, Henry de Navarre. Century 10 is full of quatrains with renegade lines, such as line 3, which seem to be visionary spikes disturbing Nostradamus' radio signal from the future. Mammola is in southern Italy, Cordoba is in Spain, and the Dalmatian coast runs along the Balkan side of the Adriatic Sea. None of this has any relevance to Henry III. Line 4 turns the dial back to catch a clearer signal. The **seven** are the Valois children of Henry II and Catherine de' Medici. The line alludes to the spectral destiny of the dying Valois line. Henry III kills Guise a few days prior to New Year 1589. The **shadow** or **ghost** of Henry III, the last Valois king, would be released by the assassin's blade later that year. The reference to **ghosts** returns us to the Valois tomb in 1 Q10, where the spirits of the royal line bewail the end of their kind.

10 Q45

L'ombre du regne de Nauarre non vray,	The shadow of the realm of Navarre not true,
Fera la vie de fort illegitime:	It will make life one of fate illegitimate:
La veu promis incertain de Cambray,	The vow made in uncertainty in Cambrai,
Roy Orleans donra mur legitime.	King Orléans will bestow a legitimate border.

A number of interesting tangles in this verse. Lines 1 and 2 could be applied to two contemporary kings of Navarre, Antoine de Bourbon and his son, Henry de Navarre: Jaubert explains that their kingdom was **not true** since the real Kingdom of Navarre was in Spain. I, however, believe this applies to the shadow of doubt cast on Navarre by Antoine de Bourbon over the issue of royal succession after the untimely death of Henry II in 1559. This issue of greater noble houses demanding more control of the regency of Francis II, and later of Charles IX, dominates the presage quatrains from the early 1560s. Line 3 ties itself around another fragment of thought that brings us back to the Treaty of **Cambrai** in 1529, in which Francis I made a **vow** to abandon his claims to Naples, Artois, and Flanders. His son, the Duc d'Orléans, later Henry II, broke the agreement in 1556, only to accede to even harsher terms after his defeat at St Quentin in 1557.

10 Q46

Vie fort mort de L'OR vilaine indigne,	Life, fate, death from gold, infamous slut,
Sera de Saxe non nouueau electeur:	He will not be a new Elector of Saxony:
De Brunfuic mandra d'amour figne,	From Brunswick he will send for a sign of love,
Faux le rendant au peuple feducteur.	The false seducer delivering [Brunswick] to the people.

Sexual debauchery may be used here for the wheeling and dealing of those universal "strange bedfellows" – the politicians of any era. In this case we zero in, rather indiscriminately, on the closed-door deliberations of an Imperial Elector of Saxony. Who it is is not made clear, but we can plot our time window for the early 1600s, when Christian II of Saxony resisted pressure to support the Protestant Union of principalities with the Netherlands. The Duchy of Brunswick, to the northeast of Saxony, did not play an important role until the opening phase of the Thirty Years War, when another Christian – Duke Christian of Brunswick-Wolfenbüttel – espoused the Protestant Palatine rebellion of Frederick of the Palatinate. I suppose the **sign of love** was Brunswick's support of Frederick of the Palatinate against the Imperial armies of the Holy

Roman Emperor. Brunswick's army was defeated by Tilly at Höchst on the Main in 1622. Frederick was ready to make peace with the Catholic Imperials, and as a gesture of reconciliation, dismissed the zealous Brunswick and retired to await the outcome of the negotiations. One might call Frederick a *false seducer* of Brunswick. Peace talks broke down and the fighting resumed, Brunswick and his mercenary army pitching their support directly with the Dutch. The *infamous slut* is, in Nostradamus' pro-Catholic eyes, the Babylonian whore of Protestantism.

10 Q47

De Bourze ville à la dame Guyrlande,	From Burgos town to the Lady of Giurlaine,
L'on mettra fus par la trahifon faicte:	They will impose [a severe punishment] for the treason committed:
Le grand prelat de Leon par Formande,	The great prelate of Léon through Formentera [of the Balearic Islands],
Faux pellerins & rauiffeurs defaicte.	False pilgrims and ravishers undone.

This is about the Spanish Civil War. In 1936 Franco's military junta was established in **Burgos** and Nationalist columns from Vallodolid and Salamanca captured Alto de **Léon** Pass (northwest of Madrid) in the first of several pitched battles to take the Spanish capital. Republican forces invaded the Balearic Islands, capturing Ibiza and **Formentera**. After Franco defeated the Republicans in 1939, the junta sent hundreds of thousands of Republican leaders and collaborationists to prison *for the treason committed*. The prelate's role in all of this is unknown, but the Republicans could be characterized as the *false pilgrims* of leftist and communist politics *undone* by the Nationalist victory.

10 Q48

Du plus profond de l'Efpaigne enfeigne,	From the depths of Spain, banners,
Sortant du bout & des fins de l'Europe,	Coming out from the ends of Europe,
Troubles paffant aupres du pont de Laigne,[1]	Troubles passing near the bridge of the Aisne,
Sera deffaicte par bande fa grand troupe.	Its great troop will be routed by bands.

[1] L'Aisne river, near the Spanish route of invasion leading to the Battle of St Quentin.

The battle of St Quentin (10 August 1557) was still a few weeks or months in the future the night Nostradamus viewed the events with his magical devices. First he sees the legions of Spain marching 40 miles out of the Spanish Netherlands and passing the Aisne river on their way to besiege Admiral Coligny's little garrison in the fortress city of St

Quentin. As often happens with prophets, Nostradamus incorrectly reads the impressions in his watery porthole and reports the opposite outcome of the battle. His warning of a Spanish invasion near the Aisne is correct, but it is the French relief army that is routed and Coligny's garrison that is overwhelmed, rather than the Spanish.

Some skeptics, such as Randi, believe that to enhance his reputation Nostradamus either covered his mistakes or wrote fake prophecies from current events by having his editors in Lyons tinker with his manuscript in the months before the publication date. If that were true, why wasn't line 4 changed to "the great French troop will be routed"?

10 Q49

Iardin du monde aupres du cité neufue,	**Garden of the world near the new city,**
Dans le chemin des montaignes cauees:	**In the path of the hollow mountains:**
Sera ſaiſi & plongé dans la Cuue,	**It will be seized and plunged into the Vat,**
Beuuant par force eaux ſoulfre enuenimees.	**Drinking by force the waters poisoned by sulfur.**

Twentieth-century interpreters have pinned this one on a future attack on New York City. The good news is, it may have already been fulfilled with the Arab terrorist attack on the World Trade Center (26 February 1993) and it may also describe a second, more deadly terrorist bombing plot foiled by FBI agents later that year.

New Jersey is known as the Garden State (**Garden of the world**). This would make neighboring New York City the **new city**. The **hollow mountains** are Nostradamus' description of the two cavernous skyscrapers of the World Trade Center. In February 1993 a rental truck filled with explosives was driven over from the Garden State and abandoned in the underground parking lot beneath the complex. Minutes later a tremendous explosion killed six and injured 1,000 people. The truck bomb was positioned in such a way as to undermine one of the towers so that it would collide with its neighbor and send both towers, and their 50,000 occupants, cascading into the Hudson river.

In line 3 Nostradamus, the consummate recipe-maker, is trying to describe the terrorists at work, mixing liquid chemicals and volatile fertilizers together in the **Vat** (which in this case were large yellow plastic containers) to make a rudimentary bomb. Line 4 might describe an alternative future thankfully forestalled several months later when FBI agents, tipped off by an informant, raided a second bomb factory in Queens. They rushed into the building to find five men described by the agents as Muslim fundamentalists hunched over 55-gallon barrels, swirling wooden spoons to mix fertilizer and diesel fuel into an explosive paste. Their plan was to set off several huge explosions around New York

City just prior to the 4th of July. The bombs were meant to level the offices of the United Nations and a skyscraper housing FBI offices. Two truck bombs would target the Holland and Lincoln Tunnels under the Hudson river. If a 500-pound (227-kilogram) fertilizer bomb exploded in the Holland Tunnel during rush hour, dozens of people and cars would be crushed flat by the violent pressure of the blast. Thousands of cars would jam on their brakes in a huge chain reaction. Seconds later thousands of trapped motorists would gape in horror at the wall of flames and smoke heading their way. If the ventilation systems did not survive the explosion, hundreds, even thousands, might be burned alive or die in the suffocating smoke. Experts doubt such an explosion would be strong enough for the Hudson river to come flooding in; Nostradamus, however, may differ, when he describes people in their cars drowning in the forceful wave of sulfurated water.

10 Q50

La Meufe au iour terre de Luxembourg,	**The Meuse by day in the land of Luxemburg,**
Defcouurira Saturne & trois en lurne:	**It will discover Saturn and three in the urn:**
Montaigne & pleine, ville, cité & bourg,	**Mountain and plain, town, city and borough,**
Lorrain deluge trahifon par grand hurne.	**Flood in Lorraine, betrayal by the great urn.**

The Meuse was an important geographic obstacle in both World War German invasions of Belgium and France. By early September 1914 the Moon, Jupiter, and Uranus were in Aquarius (*the urn*) when the French and British forces started their great retreat off the Meuse front to regroup around Paris for the First Battle of the Marne. French counter attacks did *flood* into the German-occupied province of Lorraine. No such astrological aspect occurred on 13–14 May 1940 when, a generation later, German panzer armies raced out of the Ardennes forests on the Luxembourg-French frontier to seize a bridgehead on the Meuse at Sedan.

A more obvious interpretation would picture a great flood of the Meuse river near Lorraine when Saturn joins three other planets in the sign of Aquarius.

Astrological Time Window

At the end of the last transit of Saturn through Aquarius (December 1993/ January 1994) when the Sun, Mercury, and Venus were in Aquarius, northwestern Europe had the worst flooding in decades along the Meuse (Maas) in the Netherlands, and over a wide area of eastern France and low-lying ports of Germany and Belgium. Further continent-wide storms dumped more than a month's worth of rain during a single day in parts of France. The next transit takes place in February 2021, when the planets Mercury, Venus, and Jupiter will join Saturn in Aquarius.

10 Q51

Des lieux plus pas[1] du pays de Lorraine,	**Some of the lowest places in the**
Seront des baſſes Allemaignes vnis:	**country of Lorraine,**
Par ceux du ſiege Picards, Normans, du	**Will be united with the Low Germans:**
Maiſne,	**Through those of the [Holy] See**
Et aux cantons ſe feront reunis.	**Picards, Normans, [those] of**
	Maine,
	And they will be reunited with the
	cantons.

[1]Misprint for *bas*.

Lorraine became part of Germany twice: in 1871–1919 and later in 1940–44.

The **cantons** of Switzerland and the Holy **See** of the Vatican may eventually merge into the European Union sometime in the early 21st century.

10 Q52

Au lieu où LAYE[1] & Scelde ſe marient,	**At the place where the Lys and the**
Seront les nopces de long temps maniees:	**Scheldt become as one,**
Au lieu d'Anuers où la crappe[2] charient,[3]	**Will the nuptials be arranged for a**
Ieune vieilleſſe conſorte intaminee.	**long time:**
	At the place in Antwerp where the
	crap is carried,
	Young, aging consort unsullied.

[1]LAYE: the Flemish spelling of the River Lys.
[2]Old French *crappe* = filth, chaff, excrement.
[3]Old French *charier* = to convey, carry, travel, go, proceed.

Ghent is where these two rivers converge. The subject is not made easily clear unless we take as many liberties in the translation as Fontbrune has done. If *nopces* (nuptials) becomes "alliances" and the s of *consort* is replaced with an f to get *conforer* ("to sustain"); and if we add "by combat" to the end of line 4, then we get at best an overview of Ghent's role as a town where many alliances and treaties were signed down through the centuries. He also translates *crappe charient* into "muddy rains" to come up with the great floods of 1914.

A more literal translation foresees the tedious engagement of an aged suitor and his blushing young bride finally end with the old fellow on his honeymoon in Antwerp. They are performing a less-than-satisfactory job between the folds of the nuptial bed. The old man's virginity is left un-sullied. Perhaps a better outcome could be had if the old fellow didn't rent a room with a river view overlooking the refuse heaps.

10 Q53

Les trois pellices de loing s'entrebatron,	**The three concubines will quarrel for a long time,**
La plus grand moindre demeurera à l'eſcoute:	**The greatest one will remain the least to listen:**
Le grand Selin[1] n'en fera plus patron,	**The great Selin will no longer be her patron,**
Le nommera feu pelte[2] blanche routte.	**She will call him fire shield, white route.**

[1]Greek = Selēnē, moon, crescent; Sultan Suleiman; Sultan "Selim" his successor.
[2]Latin pelta = a small shield used by the Thracians, very similar to those used by Turkish Janis-saries at the siege of Malta in 1565.

There are two possibilities for this cryptic prophecy. Either it is one last pampering alternative prophecy for Henry II as the all-conquering **Chyren Selin**, or it is for the **Great Crescent** leader of the Ottoman Turks, Suleiman the Magnificent. I lean towards the latter.

Suleiman in his old age found comfort and council from Mihrimah, the daughter of his favorite wife, the late Roxelana ([he] **will no longer be her patron**). In the 1660s Mihrimah lobbied hard for him to seize the strategic island of Malta from the Knights of St John. Her words were echoed in the chorus of indignant concubines in the Seraglio, following the capture by the knights of a large merchant ship en route from Venice to Istanbul. The ship had carried a valuable cargo of luxury goods postmarked for the harem. The last line is hard to define, but the general tone sounds like a young woman's praise swelling the ego of an old warrior into action. At 70 he was too old to lead the attack on Malta, but he sent an expedition under Piale and Mustafa Pasha and Dragut to invade the island to – as the Turkish Corsair, Dragut, said – "smoke out this nest of vipers."

The siege of Malta was a failure.

10 Q54

Nee en ce monde par concubine fertiue,	**Born into this world of a furtive concubine,**
A deux hault miſe par les triſtes nouuelles,	**The two raised high by the sad news,**
Entre ennemis ſera prinſe captiue,	**She will be taken captive among enemies,**
Et amené à Malings & Bruxelles.	**And brought to Malines and Brussels.**

A specific account of the child or children of a royal French concubine. The two daughters of Diane de Poitiers may be intended. One was married to the Duc d'Aumale (a brother of François de Guise), another to the

Duc de Bouillon. Neither girl suffered capture or incarceration at Malines and Brussels.

10 Q55

Les malheureuſes nopces celebreront	*The unhappy marriage will be celebrated*
En grande ioye, mais la fin malheureuſe:	*In great joy but the end unhappy:*
Mary & mere nore deſdaigneront,	*Husband and mother will scorn the*
Le Phybe mort, & nore plus piteuſe.	*daughter-in-law,*
	The Apollo dead and the daughter-in-
	law more pitiful.

Certainly the current Prince of Wales and his mother, Elizabeth II, scorn her ex-daughter-in-law Princess Diana. And if this is intended for her – and I must stress again "if" – her future and that of the British royal family looks dismal. Her princely Apollo of the wedding ceremony is now the toad of her dead romantic dreams. In the 21st century Princess Di becomes a pitiful survivor of the shipwreck that was the British monarchy. Yet it seems she will survive her ex-husband who may be the last king of England.

10 Q56

Prelat royal ſon baiſſant trop tiré,	*The royal prelate his bowing too low,*
Grand fleux de ſang ſortira par ſa bouche,	*A great flow of blood will come out of*
Le regne Anglicque[1] par regne reſpiré,	*his mouth,*
Long temps mort vif en Tunis côme	*The Anglian reign, by the realm to*
ſouche.	*breathe again,*
	For a long time dead as a stump of
	wood living in Tunis.

[1]*Anglicque* = a) angelic; b) Anglian (of England).

A prelate of royal standing bows down and suffers a hemorrhage; or worse, he has bowed his head down upon the chopping block of the headsman. *Anglicque* can stand for "angelic" as well as "Anglian." Whatever the case, either the beatific or the British realm is brought to life again from the prelate's misfortune after a long dormancy. Pretty vague.

10 Q57

Le ſubleué ne cognoiſtra ſon ſceptre,	*The uplifted one will not know his*
Les enfans ieunes des plus grands honnira:	*scepter [royal authority],*
Oncques ne fut vn plus ord[1] cruel eſtre,	*The young children of the greatest ones*
Pour leurs eſpouſes à mort noir bannira.	*will be dishonored:*
	Never was there a more filthy and
	cruel being,
	For their wives the black king will
	banish them to death.

[1]Old French *ordurier* = filthy, ribald, lewd.
[2]Near-anagram *roi/noir* for a black or evil king.

Some Nostradamians believe this one is about the Third Antichrist. Indeed the dark doings of this family apply themselves well to the dysfunctional clan of Saddam Hussein. This may bode evil ruin and dark death for the near relations of the man whom Nostradamus may have already condemned for setting fire to the Kuwaiti oilfields and turning the land of Mesopotamia (Iraq) into a black wasteland (8 Q70).

In 1995 the Iraqi dictator's sons-in-law defected, seeking asylum, along with their wives, in Jordan. Hussein Kamel al-Majid, who was once the Iraqi minister of armaments, and his brother, believed they could curry favor with the West by divulging Saddam's secret weapons program. Six months of disappointing negotiations and putting up with nagging, homesick wives consequent on such disappointment proved too much for the al-Majid brothers. They returned home in February 1995, gambling that their wives' appeals for clemency would soften the heart of their father-in-law. Hardly! Like daughters, like father. They immediately filed for divorce upon returning to Baghdad. The Iraqi News Agency said the brothers, their father, and a young sibling had been killed in a gun battle when angry clansmen stormed the family residence, declaring that their "blood should be shed because of their treason to the homeland."

In my previous book (1994) I noted Kamel al-Majid as well-positioned to take power, but as line 1 implies, his serious miscalculations in the following year assured he would never **know his scepter** (figurative for authority) as Iraq's new tyrant.

10 Q58

Au temps du dueil que le felin monarque,	**At the time when mourning the feline**
Guerroyera le ieune Æmathien:[1]	**monarch**
Gaule banfler, perecliter la barque,	**Will make war upon the young**
Tenter Phoſſens[2] au Ponant[3] entretien.	**Macedonian:**
	Gaul to stagger, the bark [of St Peter]
	to be in jeopardy,
	To try Marseilles in the West
	entreaty [negotiations].

[1]Latin *Emathius* = Macedonian.
[2]Phocaeans, the founders of Marseilles.
[3]The West or Occident, as opposed to the Levant; applied here (like Hesperique) for either Spain or the United States.

If we apply this one to our own future, by prescient invitation we attend the funeral of a world leader born under the *feline* sign of Leo the Lion. Although we could apply this to many Leonine leaders, I would hypothetically move us forward in time to the 2020s or 2030s to a wooded cemetery in Arkansas, where we hear the future president of the United States make an impassioned eulogy over the flag-draped coffin of the long-retired two-term president, Bill Clinton. His (or her) watch at the White House will place this president in the middle of the next time window for a threat of worldwide warfare, caused by food shortages and population strains on the planet's ecological balance.

The new president asks the assembled dignitaries to remember the legacy of President Clinton, who forestalled warfare in the 1990s by placing peacekeepers in Macedonia. Perhaps "she" reminds them of the shortsightedness of a succession of presidents after Clinton who pulled peacekeepers out of the Balkans too hastily and set the stage for the current crisis. Now she has no choice but to send US troops back to Macedonia not as peacekeepers but as combatants put in harm's way to help the hardpressed French to contain the spread of a global ethnic war in the Balkans.

The war threatens to topple the Roman Catholic Church of the final pope which Nostradamus and St Malachy both call Peter of Rome (in Nostradamus' case he is helmsman of **the bark** of St Peter). Marseilles may be the site of peace negotiations to stop the next Balkan war.

10 Q59

Dedans Lyon vingt cinq d'vne halaine,	***Within Lyons twenty-five of the single***
Cinq citoyens Germains, Breſſans, Latins:	***breath,***
Par deſſous noble conduiront longue traine,	***Five citizens, Germans, Bressans,***
Et deſcouuers par abbois de maſtins	***Ladin [-speaking Grisons]:***
	Under a noble they will conduct a
	long train,
	And discovered by the barks of mastiffs.

Jaubert (1656) declares this one fulfilled on 5 September 1560 by a Calvinist plot under Condé. To be more specific, the events parallel those written in P53: Maligny, a surviving Protestant leader of the Conspiracy of Amboise, led a band of 4,500 men out of Dauphiné to seize Lyons. His force was routed by the city's alert royal garrison – personified here as vigilant Catholic **mastiffs** – guarding the city against the Protestant predators. Nostradamus incorrectly foresaw foreign elements in Maligny's band, such as German mercenaries and Bressans from Savoy. He seems to hear the hushed commands in the Ladin- or Romansch-speaking Grisons, from a canton in southeastern Switzerland.

10 Q60

Ie pleure Niſſe, Mannego, Pize, Gennes,	***I weep for Nice, Monaco, Pisa, Genoa,***
Sauone, Sienne, Capue, Modene, Malte:	***Savona, Siena, Capua, Modena, Malta:***
Le deſſus ſang & glaiue par eſtrennes,	***For the above, blood and sword***
Feu, trembler terre, eau, malheureuſe	***through a New Year's gift,***
nolte.[1]	***Fire, the earth to tremble, water,***
	unhappy nolition [unwillingness].

[1]Latin *noluntas* = nolition, unwillingness (the opposite of *voluntas* = volition, voluntariness, will).

For years Malta was continually bombed by the Luftwaffe. Siena, Savona, and Genoa suffered Allied aerial bombing runs. Nice and Monaco endured the Allied landings in the Riviera in 1944. Siena, Capua, Modena, and Pisa struggled in the wake of battles fought during the latter stages of the Italian campaign. The **New Year's gift** is given several times to the Allied cause. Around New Year 1943 Hitler's forces capitulate at Stalingrad, bringing an end to his conquests. The new year in 1944 begins with Allied landings at Anzio near Rome. New Year 1945 celebrates the last German offensive at the Battle of the Bulge checked and soon pushed out of the Ardennes.

The last line's **unhappy nolition** or **(unwillingness)** aptly describes the citizens of all the towns mentioned. The French towns were under German occupation. The citizens of the Italian towns were never eager to stand by Hitler and go to war with the whole world. By 1943 when the war came home to Italy, they were unwilling to support Mussolini and he was overthrown. Within two weeks of the coup the inhabitants of these towns discovered a new and darker level of **unhappy unwillingness** to serve their former allies, as German forces occupied the country and all Italians were forced to pledge allegiance to Mussolini as a puppet dictator of the Salò Fascist Republic.

---

10 Q61

Betta,[1] Vienne, Emorte,[2] Sacarbance,[3] Voudront liurer aux Barbares[4] Pannone: Par picque & feu, enorme violance, Les coniurez defcouuers par matrone.	**Betta, Vienna, Emorte, Sopron, They will want to deliver Pannonia to the Barbarians: Through pike and fire, enormous violence, The conspirators discovered by [a] matron.**

[1]*Betta* = a) Latin *Baetis* = the Guadalquivir; b) Latin *Baetica* = one of the Roman provinces of Spain.
[2]*Emorte* = a) *Augusta Emerita* = Merida.
[3]Sopron, a town 30 miles southeast of Vienna.
[4]In this case *Barbares* is a loose reference to the Ottoman Turks rather than specifically Barbary, or Arab, forces, since the Turks invade the "holy" Roman Empire using the classical route of barbarians who sacked the ancient Roman Empire.

This and the next quatrain are a generally correct prediction of the Austro-Turkish War of 1683–99. But first let's throw out the non-sequitur entries of *Betta* and *Emorte* from line 1. They stand for the Guadalquivir and Merida River regions of southern Spain. The Spanish played no part in this war. Line 2 describes the Christian Holy League of Imperial troops, Poles, and Venetians relieving besieged Vienna (1683) and participating with the Russians in the subsequent sweep of the Turks (**the Barbarians**) out of Sopron, Buda, and the rest of Hungary (**Pannonia**).

Line 3 characterizes the great battles of Christian pikemen fighting in close quarters with Turkish jannisaries at the walls of Vienna, or later soundly thrashing the Turkish forces at the battle of Senta (1697). This defeat cost them Hungary, Transylvania, Croatia, and Slavonia, as finalized in the Treaty of Karlowitz in 1699. The last line makes little sense, unless it tries to frame the intrigues of peace negotiators swapping territory.

10 Q62

Pres de Sorbin[1] pour aſſaillir Ongrie,
L'herault de Brude les viendra aduertir:
Chef Biſantin, Sallon de Sclauonie,
A loy d'Arabes les viendra conuertir.

Near Sorbia [Saxony] in order to
   assail Hungary,
The herald of Buda[pest] will come to
   warn them:
Byzantine chief, Salona of Slavonia,
He will come to convert them to the
   law of the Arabs.

[1]Synecdoche for the Electorate of Saxony: using a historical reference to the medieval Sorbian March, against the Slavic Sorbs, in Saxony around Leipzig.

Nostradamus has events backwards. It is the Christians who will convert Hungary and much of the Balkans in the Austro-Turkish War of 1683–99. In 1683, 150,000 Turks invested the 15,000-man garrison of Vienna. A relief force of 45,000 Germans (from the Electorate of Saxony) and Austrians converged with a Polish relief army of 30,000 men led by King John III Sobieski to relieve Vienna. (**Sorbia** and "Sobieski" make a close match.) Perhaps our prophet was trying to name one of the liberators of Vienna. Three years later the Christian forces of Poland, the Holy Roman Empire, Venice, and the Duchy of Moscow formed a Holy League blessed by Pope Innocent XI. This crusading alliance swept over Hungary and Transylvania, taking Buda, the Turkish capital of Hungary. Sultan Suleiman II is the **Byzantine chief** Nostradamus incorrectly predicts will counterattack and return Hungary and Dalmatia (**Salona**) to Islam. Actually, the Sultan did not live to see the war reach its disastrous finale at the battle of Senta. The treaty of Karlowitz gave Salona, the ancient capital of Dalmatia, to the Venetians. Slavonia became part of Austria.

10 Q63

Cydron, Raguſe, la cité au ſainct Hieron.[1]
Reuerdira le medicant ſecours:
Mort fils de Roy par mort de deux heron,
L'arabe Ongrie feront vn meſme cours.

Cydonia [Canea], Ragusa [Dubrovnik],
   the city of Stridon [Bosnia],
To grow green again with healing help:
The son of the King dead because of
   the death of two heroes,
Arabia and Hungary will take the
   same course.

[1]Stridon = previously known as St. Heiron.

At first this looks like part three of the Austro-Turkish War prophecy, but it could also be a general overview of the succession of Turkish possessions eventually lost to the Ottoman Empire in the centuries after the war. Initially the Turks lost much of the Dalmatian coast to Venice. Stridon went to the Austrians, as did most of Hungary. **Cydonia** represents Crete, which remained a Turkish possession until the Greek War of Independence ended in 1832. Arabia wasn't freed from Turkish domination until the end of World War I.

10 Q64

Pleure Milan, pleure Lucques, Florance,	**Weep Milan, weep Lucca and**
Que ton grand Duc sur le char montera,	**Florence,**
Changer le siege pres de Venise s'aduance,	**As your great Duc [Mussolini]**
Lors que Colonne à Rome changera.	**mounts the four-wheeled vehicle,**
	To change the seat [of government] it
	advances near to Venice,
	When at Rome the Colonna will
	change.

The fall of Mussolini's government in Rome was declared in the Piazza Colonna in September 1944. All three towns of line 1 following Il Duce have a lot to weep for: During World War II, Milan is severely bombed. Lucca, which sits astride the the German Arno Line, encounters front-line combat. Florence and the Arno valley are the scene of heavy fighting in the closing stages of the protracted and bitter Italian Campaigns of 1943–45. The British wing of the final Allied push into northern Italy took Venice in the closing weeks of the war.

Rather than "chariot", *char* could stand for a four-wheeled vehicle like the truck used by Mussolini and his mistress, Clara Petacci, on their final dash to the Swiss border. The truck was stopped at a checkpoint run by Italian communist partisans. The fugitives were discovered and summarily shot.

10 Q65

O vaste Rome ta ruyne s'approche,	*Oh vast Rome, your ruin draws near,*
Non de tes murs de ton sang & substance:	*Not that of your walls but of your*
L'aspre par lettres fera si horrible coche,	*lifeblood and substance:*
Fer poinctu mis à tous iusques au manche.	*The harsh one of letters will make so*
	horrid a notch,
	Pointed steel all wounding up the
	sleeve.

As we have already seen, Nostradamus was a firm believer in divine retribution. He was sincerely convinced, for example, that London suffered plagues and fire as a holy reprisal for the execution of King Charles I. His harsh view of the future of the Church may, therefore, be not so much anti-Catholic as pro-Christ. The plague of which he speaks may be a multi-faceted attack on the spiritual blood and substance of Christ's teachings by profane alliances of Fascists and drug-money launderers. The final line may be the prophet's attempt to describe the plague of intravenous drug use (*pointed steel wounding all up the sleeve*).

The **harsh one of letters** is the investigator(s) into Vatican conspiracies. Revelation of these will expose the corrupt custodians currently destroying the spiritual substance of the Church. In my opinion, David Yallop will be remembered as a prime candidate for that **harsh** though uncompromisingly brave **one of letters** who risked his life to expose the extent of drug-money laundering by the Vatican Bank.

If Nostradamus is talking divine retribution here, he may be suggesting that the first two corruptions – of Fascism and drugs – will lead the Catholic clergy toward a literal plague affecting the blood in their veins. The **lifeblood** or vitality of the body could be, in modern terms, the human immune system. Towards the end of this century several plagues of the blood will decimate the clergy; the one that springs readily to mind is AIDS. This disease could be spread via their ranks through intravenous drug use or homosexual acts. Current estimates by homosexual activist priests, such as AIDS-sufferer Father Robert L. Arpin, indicate that over 40 percent of the Catholic priesthood are practicing homosexual behavior.

Quatrain Indexing Date: Q65 = 1965. The mid-1960s began the great schism of today's Catholic Church.

10 Q66

Le chef de Londres par regne l'Americh,
L'ifle d'Efcoffe tempiera par gelee:
Roy Reb[1] auront vn fi faux antechrift,
Que les mettra treftous dans la meflee.

The chief of London through the rule
   of America,
Will burden the island of Scotland
   [Britain] with a cold thing:
Roy Reb will have so false an
   Antichrist,
As to bring them all into the conflict.

[1]*Roy Reb*: enigmatic name: Reb the King; Rebel the King; Reagan the King?; variant spelling for Rob Roy, the 18th-century Scottish rebel. The gist of the quatrain better supports the Cromwell or Reagan interpretations.

In 1672 Garencières wrote the following, adamant that this quatrain could only apply to his century: "I conceive this Prophecy can be appropriated to no body better than Oli. Cromwell, who is called here the *Chief of London* by *Reign* of America, that is, by Reign of confusion, whose projects and treasons were all brought to naught, by the victorious Mars of the ever renowned General Monck, who came with his army from *Scotland* to London in the Winter time, he is called a false Antichrist, because he was an enemy to King, and Reb, that is Respublican or Commonwealth."

I am equally adamant that this applies to the 20th century:

During the late 1950s Harold Macmillan, the British prime minister, conceded to American wishes by establishing the first ballistic missile bases in Great Britain. In the 1980s, Prime Minister Margaret Thatcher's government allowed the Americans to station another *cold thing* – the new Pershing II intermediate nuclear missiles – in the British Isles.

Roy Reb may be an enigmatic phrase for Ronald Reagan. The former president made clear his Christian faith and his view of the Soviet Union as the Evil Empire. And his get-tough foreign policies against anti-Christian communism and terrorist leaders like Libya's Colonel Muhammar Qadaffi did increase world tension. The final line could also be an unheeded warning to the Reagan administration and those administrations to follow not to continue the US Middle Eastern policy that succors and strengthens one dictator to destroy another. This happened with the arming of Saddam Hussein against the Ayatollah Khomeini during the Iran–Iraq conflict of 1980–88. Reagan and his cabinet opened themselves to further conflict by the bombing of the Marine barracks in Lebanon and the notorious "arms for hostages" policy, which led to the Iran-Contra scandal. This scandal was to damage the credibility of President Reagan and his successor, George Bush (*bring them all into the conflict*).

Quatrain Indexing Date: 10 Q66 = the year 1066: the delivery of Pershing II missiles on British soil. Note the ironic and retroactive coincidence in the quatrain numbers dating the Norman victory at the Battle of Hastings in 1066, the last time England was successfully invaded and conquered.

10 Q67

Le tremblement fi fort au mois de May,	**A very mighty quake in the month of May,**
Saturne, Caper,[1] Iupiter, Mercure au beuf:	**Saturn [in] Capricorn, Jupiter and Mercury in Taurus:**
Venus auffi Cancer, Mars, en Nonnay,[2]	**Venus also in Cancer, Mars in Virgo:**
Tombera grefle lors plus groffe qu'vn euf.	**At that time hail will fall greater than an egg.**

[1]Latin *caper* = goat, for Latin *Capricornus* = Capricorn.
[2]Nun, virgin, Virgo.

This rare astrological configuration takes place 42 years before Nostradamus' predicted end of the world in AD 3797. When the sun expands into a red giant the Earth will experience tremendous gravitational and climatic stresses. The reference to **May** could tie this quatrain in with those that resemble descriptions of great earthquakes in California or the shift of Earth's axis. Rather than scaring Californians every May with prophetic cries of "Wolf!" interpreters might consider the Big One hitting LA or San Francisco not in May 1997, 1998, 1999 or 2000 but during **May** over 1,800 years hence, in the spring of AD 3755.

10 Q68

L'armee de mer deuant cité tiendra,
Puis partira fans faire langue alee:
Citoyens grande proye en terre prendra,
Retourner claffe, reprendre grande emblee.

The army of the sea will stand before
  the city,
Then it will leave without making a
  long passage:
A great flock of citizens will be seized
  on land,
Fleet to return, to retake the great
  robbery.

Clear enough. A fleet holds its position in the ocean next to, or within the harbor of, a city. Armed crews land ashore and in short order surprise and capture a multitude of citizens for ransom. Then the fleet sails home with purloined people and pillage. Too many raids by pirate fleets have been recorded in the last four centuries for me to be more specific.

10 Q69

Le fait luyfant de neuf vieux efleué
Seront fi grand par midy aquilon:
De fa seur propre grande alles leué.
Fuyant murdri au buiffon d'ambellon.

The luminous deed of the old one
  exalted anew,
They will be very great through the
  South and North:
By his own sister raised, great crowds,
Fleeing, murdered in the bushes of
  Ambellon.

Leoni thinks the wooded village of Ambel near Grenoble is intended, and leaves it at that. This area is quite close to an important battle fought by maquis guerrillas of the French Resistance around Vercors in the wooded mountains southwest of Grenoble in the alpine Isère region.

The **luminous deed of the old one** takes us back to 1940, when the aged Marshal Pétain came out of retirement to lead France after its humiliating defeat by the Germans. In the early days of the Vichy government many Frenchmen looked up to the hero of World War I as their savior. He soon turned out to be nothing more than a doddering figurehead of a collaborationist regime. The Resistance grew very strong in German-occupied northern France and the unoccupied southern portions of Vichy France. Line 3 is specific in detail but hard to fathom in this context. Perhaps it describes the efforts of a woman maquisard in the Resistance to raise support for their cause.

The battle for the Vercors Plateau (9 June–24 July 1944) pitted 950 maquis guerrillas against 20,000 German SS paratroopers and infantry in a vicious mountain battle. The fighting cost the lives of 750 maquisards. There were a number of Nazi atrocities. In one case 50 seriously wounded marqisards managed to crawl into the underbrush. They were found by a troop of SS and beaten to death one by one (*fleeing, murdered in the bushes*).

10 Q70

L'œil par obiect[1] fera telle excroiſſance,[2]	**The eye, through an object will be like a swelling outgrowth,**
Tant & ardante que tumbera la neige,	**Burning so much that the snow will fall,**
Champ arrouſé viendra en deſcroiſſance,	**The fields watered will come to decrease,**
Que le primat ſuccombera à Rege.	**As the primate succumbs at Rege.**

[1]Variant: thing, article.
[2]Excrescence; an abnormal, disfiguring outgrowth or enlargement; a swelling (tumor, etc.).

The first line sounds to me like a 16th-century physician trying to describe someone's eye seen under a futuristic magnifying glass. Could a vision of a visit to a 20th-century optometrist have wiggled its way between the momentous and dire events usually crowding Nostradamus' hydromantic porthole to the future?

The traditional interpretation links this obscure surgical and climatological augury to the death of the archbishop (or *primate*) of Reggio in the toe of the boot of Italy. Since I don't find anything is definitive, nothing stops me from kicking this obscure scrying far into our own future as a candidate for an off-world interpretation. *Rege* could be part of the name of a new world orbiting some star system. Our primate is not an archbishop by that time: hopefully he isn't a monkey but a human being. Line 2 is Nostradamus' best attempt at aping the absurdities of that old American folk song *Oh Susannah*: ". . . the sun's so hot, I froze to death / Susannah don't you cry . . ." Perhaps he is observing a doctor using liquid hydrogen to burn off someone's wart.

10 Q71

La terre & l'air geleront ſi grand eau,	**The earth and air will freeze a very great water,**
Lors qu'on viendra pour ieudy venerer:	**When they come to venerate Thursday:**
Ce qui ſera iamais ne fut ſi beau,	**That which will be, never was [it] so fair,**
Des quatre pars le viendront honorer.	**From the four quarters they will come to honor it.[1]**

[1]Variant: He who will be, never was there one so fair . . . to honor him.

Line 1 is figurative for a large body of water – a lake or perhaps an ocean frozen by a record-breaking winter storm. Thanksgiving is a national quasi-religious American holiday held the fourth Thursday in November. Too many severe cold snaps and early blizzards have been recorded during a few centuries' worth of Thanksgiving Day feasts to spook up a clear incident. Unless, that is, Nostradamus is predicting the first celebration of prayer and thanksgiving by the New England colonists at Plymouth Rock after bringing in the first harvest in 1621 – an event to take place a full 64 years after he wrote this verse. The pilgrims had indeed survived a terrible winter the year before, with the help of the "pagan" Indians (whom they would later decimate with genocide and disease). In that first year, however, these devout Christians shared their table with the red men. Perhaps Nostradamus also sees images of two centuries of emigration to the ethnic melting-pot of the United States by people from every corner of the world. America is unique in history as a promised land for the religiously, politically, or economically downtrodden.

10 Q72

L'an mil neuf cens nonante neuf ſept mois,	In the year 1999 and seven months [July],
Du ciel viendra vn grand Roy d'effrayeur.	A great King of Terror will come from the sky.
Reſuſciter le grand Roy d'Angolmois.[1]	He will bring back the great King Genghis Khan.
Auant apres Mars regner par bon heur.	Before and after Mars rules happily.

[1]Old French Mongolois = of the Mongols.

Nostradamus' most famous doomsday prediction warns future generations of a **King of Terror** descending from the skies in July 1999. This holy terror could be linked to the Third Antichrist who may be the fearsome **Mabus** of 2 Q62 or the North African terrorist from 2 Q30 who is from the land of the infernal Hannibal's God. Hannibal's God or "Baal" was called "Hammon," the patron deity of Carthage – and a name that can mean "Lord of the Sky." When Baal Hammon is angered he is described as a real reigning **terror** from the skies. As we have noted earlier, the ruins of Carthage are quite close to the former headquarters of the Palestinian Liberation Organization during its most radical period, implying that a candidate for the Third Antichrist may have been trained there in his formative years. By 1999, this terrorist from the land of "Baal" might wage war on Israel or its Western allies *from the sky*, either with a nuclear missile or a jet which is loaded with plutonium dust or chemical weapons that is detonated over a city.

Many interpreters have tried to understand the prophetic significance of Nostradamus bringing back to life the *Roi d'Angolmois* (the great King of the Mongols) by the last July of this millennium. Genghis Khan united the Mongolians of the Central Asian steppes into an all-conquering army that forged the largest land empire in history. By 1279 the empire stretched from the east coast of Asia to the Danube river in Europe, and from the Siberian steppes to the Arabian Sea. Sixteen years later the Mongol Empire became the world's first Sino-Islamic super-power. The vast Islamic western wing of his empire included modern-day Iraq, Iran, Pakistan, and the Central Asian republics of the former Soviet Union.

Genghis Khan was one of history's greatest kings of terror. Tens of millions died in the bloody conquests initiated by the warlord and his successors, and his record of destruction, devastation and genocide is appalling. According to the prophet, Genghis Khan and his empire are now returning: the warlord has been brought back to life.

In 1990 in a major propaganda campaign designed to uphold the virtues of totalitarian role models and condemn democratic dissidents, the leaders of the People's Republic of China restored Genghis Khan to his "rightful" place in Chinese history.

Our First Antichrist, Napoleon Bonaparte – who appears to have had some prophetic powers – is said to have coined the famous warning: "China? There lies a sleeping giant. Let him sleep! For when he wakes he will move the world."

The recent rehabilitation of the Mongol warlord responsible for China's greatest imperial glory corresponds with a new awakening of Chinese world influence. It is forecast by many prophetic traditions that China will awaken from her long, slumbering isolation to assume a position of great influence in human history and culture, or she will be the prime mover in unleashing the mayhem and violence of Armageddon. For either destiny, the die will be cast in the final years of the 20th century. The good or evil consequences of China's rise to superpower stature will, however, depend largely on how other nations help or hinder her great destiny. China will become either the spokesman or the armory for the non-aligned nations of the Third World.

At the present time (July 1996) the aging communist leadership remains in power, and the Chinese economy continues to grow. The ever mounting stresses of food sustainability and employment for the world's most populous nation continue to stretch her ability to maintain social and political stability. The return of Hong Kong in the summer of 1997 could trigger an international crisis later in the year. Perhaps it will also trigger another popular movement towards democracy, which could bring on further repression by the hard-line leadership. The death of Deng Xiaoping or other elder hard-liners is expected to bring on a serious internal power struggle between now and 1999. The possibility exists that China may become more reactionary and militant by the century's end. Although the United States remains the world's foremost arms dealer, China supplies the highest volume of regional ballistic missile delivery systems, plus the reactors, know-how, and fissionable materials for the nuclear arms programs of North Korea, Iran, Libya, Pakistan, and India. United States Intelligence believes China is Iran's principal source for their secret nuclear weapons project.

The possibilities flowing from the present moment tempt me to believe that 1999 is not the end of the **27-year war of the Third Antichrist** (8 Q77) but its beginning. Between 1999 and 2026, if the United Nations cannot become the unquestioned world parliament and if international law does not have greater weight and fairness than national law, peace will not be restored to the Middle East, and the Arab and Islamic nations will look to China, the new superpower, as their defender against US domination.

By the 2020s, oil and food will be the new weapons of geopolitics. By that time China will require *all* the current world export of grains of 1996 to survive. America will import two-thirds of its oil from the Arabs. China may be forced to counter America's politics of food with a Sino-Islamic alliance that allows her to curb America through the politics of oil. If a new Sino-American Cold War takes place, China will become the new safe haven and training camp for the jihad of terrorism. In a worst-case scenario China – whether communist or not – may find herself under the dictatorship of a future Genghis Khan. She fulfills a biblical and Nostradamian nightmare as the linchpin to a new regional Sino-pan-Islamic alliance against Europe, Russia, and America in a nuclear Third World War by the mid-2020s.

The final line makes a cryptic reference to Mars. A consideration of the occult meaning of this planet which, in conventional wisdom, represents the god of war and mayhem, opens up the possibility of a positive outcome in the future. The phrase **before and after Mars rules happily** can be interpreted to mean that the higher aspect of Mars, as the god of magic and spiritual transformation, **rules happily** in the new millennium. The rise of China as a superpower to match the United States could bring balance and stability to the world. The quality of effort, courage, and skill that the leaders of both great nations employ to effect the change from nationalist to internationalist government before and 27 years after 1999 will determine which aspect of **Mars** will **rule** – bloody war or benign enlightenment.

Quatrain Indexing Date: Q72 = a near miss for 1973. Count back 27 years from 1999 and you get the beginning of Nostradamus' 27-year war of the Antichrist. If we move safely past July of 1999, perhaps the destiny of the Third Antichrist will have been effectively neutralized.

10 Q73

Le temps preſent auecques le paſſé,
Sera iugé par grand Iouialiſte:
Le monde tard luy ſera laſſé,
Et deſloyal par le clergé iuriſte.

The present time together with the
past,
Will be judged by the great man of
Jupiter:
The world too late will be tired of him,
And disloyal through the oath-taking
clergy.

For once, Nostradamus slams John Calvin with a little less force. He is the chief "Jovialist" – the label Nostradamus gives to the Huguenots and Calvinists, defining them as neo-pagans. Our prophet is a little less identified with his ire and almost stills his judgments and emotions enough to see the future of John Calvin's movement. Nostradamus may be finally surrendering to the fact that Calvin would die from old age, with the seed of his heresy still intact and spreading. The world would not tire of Calvin in time to burn him at the stake while he lived. Calvin died a few years after this was written and not before the growing momentum of Calvinism was secure.

With this said, a modern or future application is also possible for some controversial neo-pagan guru or New Age healer of our own day. Perhaps this applies itself to Nostradamus' **Man from the East** (see 2 Q29, 10 Q75).

10 Q74

An reuolu du grand nombre ſeptieſme,
Apparoiſtra au temps ieux d'Hecatombe:
Non eſloigné du grand eage millieſme,
Que les entrés ſortiront de leur tombe.

The year the great seventh number is
accomplished,
Appearing at the time of the games of
slaughter:
Not far from the age of the great
millennium [2000],
When the dead will come out of their
graves.

During the Second Gulf War, US pilots talked about airstrikes as if they were plays in an American football game. In a quatrain set for a future time when people treat the ultimate human tragedy of war with new lows of banality, it is a promise of hope that humankind will transcend its ancient tomb of fossilized traditions that have sustained endless cycles of war and rape, and be reborn into a new millennium of peace.

The **seventh number** is that of the seventh millennium, the source of much contention and confusion amongst Nostradamus scholars, because the prophet counts us down to the date of doomsday or bloomsday with different starting dates. Either it comes in this millennium or in AD 3242 – or even AD 3826.

If before the year 2000 man can reject political power games in favor of a new awakening, the world may survive into the third millennium after Christ.

10 Q75

Tant attendu ne reuiendra iamais,
Dedans l'Europe, en Afie apparoiftra:
Vn de la ligue yffu du grand Hermes,
Et fur tous Roys des orients croiftra.

Long awaited he will never return.
He will appear in Asia [and be] at
   home in Europe:
One who is issued from great Hermes,
And over all the Kings of the East will
   he grow.

We return to Nostradamus' last quatrain in the Eight Clues to Spiritual Catalysts theme. It is an all-too-predictable habit that we seek a new world teacher who will satisfy what we know rather than trust those who shatter all we *think* we know with their new spiritual message. Most people in Judea 2,000 years ago wanted a military commander and felt short-changed by Jesus Christ. We need to be aware of projecting a Jesus Christ image on the spiritual catalysts walking (and globetrotting) the Earth today. Nostradamus has made it clear that the next great spiritual masters are coming from the East. Clearly he had to cloak his revelation so as not to be burned as a heretic. But if one gets the message between the lines of dozens of prophecies, it is clear that he is warning us not to look for the Second Coming of some gentile made-over blond and blue-eyed Hollywood Jesus, nor should we expect some dark-haired and kosher man from Galilee named Y'shua.

The **long awaited** projection of Jesus Christ we have created **will never return**.

The new world teacher will be from India or the Far East. He will issue from the non-dualistic teachings of Hermes. The Hermetic message is very close to the Eastern Tantric path, which teaches "As above, so below; all is divine." In the Hermetic and Tantric paths there is no Hell to fear or Heaven to pine for. These are childish illusions. No God exists outside of you. Without your awakened eyes and heart, God cannot perceive or love his universe. Without your understanding transcending judgments and conditioning, there is no transcendental state of God. Without your enlightenment, God is as fast asleep as you are. In short, the Hermetic and Tantric visions propose that your existence is either a paradise or a hell of your own making, and no savior will be coming to carry your burdens. The Aquarian Age is about impersonal messianic phenomena. No sheep, no shepherds, no bleeding messiahs. The masters of the future point the way, but it is your life to live and your universe to travel.

Jesus said of his own return that he would come under a new name as a "thief in the night." Nostradamus describes this world teacher to be in the manner of Hermes, who was also worshipped as a god of thieves.

Such a master (or masters) is born in Asia, but he, like so many other masters from the East, are like seeds blown westwards to fertilize and flower in Europe and the Western Hemisphere. By the end of the last century we began to see many gurus and rishis walking among Europeans and North Americans. We have seen Vivekananda's orange turban towering over the throngs of New York City in the Gay Nineties. And in a 1924 photo of George Gurdjieff's we see his inscrutable gaze, as he stood on the deck of the SS *Paris* viewing the United States for the first time on his arrival in New York. Outside of Paris one could find his spiritual communards rehearsing their sacred dances in a château outside of Avon. If one was climbing the cliffs off Capri in the 1930s one could find the silent Meher Baba leading his disciples over the rocks with hand signs. You could observe Krishnamurti quite at home in Europe speaking to thousands at Ommen, Holland, or decades later at Saanen, Switzerland. In the 1960s the sadhus of TM were *at home* in Europe and America. The orange dancing flowers, the Hare Krishnas, spruced up the drab-clothed multitudes from LA to London.

By the 1970s Western free spirits began returning home to establish new religious movements that had a decidedly Eastern slant. There was L. Ron Hubbard's Buddhist-inspired Scientology. And we had the blissful Franklin Allen Jones, flying over the Appennines and France, returning to America from his pilgrimage to India creating the Free Daist Communion. He would later teach thousands of followers under many new names from "Bubba" and Da Free John to Adi Da Santosha.

In the 1980s Sun Myung Moon would declare himself Christ returned and shock people to attention. And later a man from the East would land in the western United States to establish a spiritual city of 20,000 people "to provoke God," smack-dab in Reagan's born-again America. A guru of the Indian dirt footpaths collided with Western materialism: Osho drove in 94 Rolls-Royces to provoke the inherent greed of the Reagan yuppie era, as well as make a break from thousands of years of religious tradition that made spiritualism synonymous with poverty.

Whether such men are charlatans or true shamans of a new religiousness is still unknown. What is certain is that seeds of a century of Eastern teachers have been planted in Western hearts and minds. We await their full flowering in the 21st century.

Quatrain Indexing Date: Q75 = 1975, the year Madame Blavatsky predicted for a "messenger to come to the west in 1975."

See Index: Eight clues to the catalysts of the coming spiritual revolution.

An Assessment of the Twelve Candidates

SWAMI PARAMAHANSA YOGANANDA
(1893-1952)
Indian mystic, and founder of the Self-Realization Fellowship

Nostradamus' references to a man from the East, colors of flame, teachings flowering in the West, intensive travel and revolutionary ways of teaching yoga can be applied to Yogananda. However, Yogananda's desire to synthesize the beliefs of the established religions of the world make him unlikely to be the one against whom *religions will unite* (5 Q96). So far, Yogananda's followers have not been universally rejected by the mainstream religions.

MEHER BABA
(1894-1969)
Indian Sufi mystic

Meher Baba was indeed a rebel, but a peaceful one: his teachings were neither inflammatory nor designed to unsettle the established religions – he was no infuriating traveler (2 Q28)! Although his philosophy did include the concept of living in the **Now** (EP212), it contains no bird symbolism, no moon aspect – either symbolic or actual – (1 Q56, 2 Q28, 2 Q59, 4 Q31, and 9 Q12), and no mention of either the color red (5 Q31, 5 Q96, 9 Q5), or of flames (EP104–105).

SWAMI PRABHUPADA
(1896-1978)
Founder of the Hare Krishna movement

Though his chanting and dancing followers, the orange-robed Hare Krishnas, have angered and mostly puzzled many Westerners, it cannot be said that mainstream society views their existence as a dangerous threat to organized religious thinking. Moreover, Prabhupada's teachings, although new for people in the West, are based on ancient Hindu-Vedic scriptures, and he encourages his Western disciples to adopt the lifestyles prescribed by those traditional texts. In addition, the movement has not significantly grown in size since the mid-1980s and seems to have passed its peak.

L. RON HUBBARD
(1916-1986)
Author of Dianetics™, Founder of the Church of Scientology

The ideas of the Scientology movement, which Hubbard drew mainly from Hinayana Buddhism and mainstream psychology, are basically traditional. Although his teaching is essentially Eastern in its source, Hubbard does not come *from the East* (2 Q29, 10 Q75), was not born under Mars (EP104–105), has no moon connection (EP212), and does not follow a Hermetic tradition (2 Q29).

'ABDU'L-BAHÁ
(1844–1921)
Leader of the Bahá'i faith

Despite the fact that the Bahá'í movement and its founding masters are Eastern (Iranian), have provoked controversy, and have been the catalyst for the 20th-century's new openness to the interrelation of different faiths, the movement is not universally rejected as a cult by orthodox faiths, except fundamentalist Islam. There are millions of Bahá'ís the world over, and their message of peaceful rebellion through diplomacy has great merit, but the movement does not conform to all of Nostradamus' eight clues.

G. I. GURDJIEFF
(1877–1949)
Master of the "Fourth Way"

His written teachings are still steady sellers and Gurdjieff study groups exist all over the world. But the generally exclusive quality of his mystery schools, notwithstanding their great merit, do not indicate any significant worldwide spread of his band of "religiousness" to the mainstream. Nor do the orthodox religions unanimously consider his teachings a particular threat.

J. KRISHNAMURTI
(1891–1986)
Indian philosopher and meditator

Krishnamurti was opposed to any "guru" concept and any religion created in his name. As a consequence, his insights were never directed or challenging to the status quo. Since his death there has been no upsurge in proponents of his teaching.

SWAMI SATYA SAI BABA
(1925–   )
Siddi Yogi

His teachings, primarily Hindu-fundamentalist, are not highly controversial in nature. There is no Hermetic aspect to his work (2 Q29). Of the living masters, Satya Sai Baba has one of the largest followings, but his movement is confined mainly to India. Though his teachings do not constitute any threat to international authorities, an assassination attempt was made on his life in June 1993 by former disciples with connections to extreme Hindu fundamentalist groups. Since 1986 no significant change in his status has taken place, and there are signs that outside India his movement is gradually losing momentum.

S U N   M Y U N G   M O O N
(1 9 2 0 –)
Founder of the Unification Church

Moon has antagonized many people with his claims that he is Jesus Christ returned. He has also angered families and members of the general public by the apparent disruption that adherence to his Church causes in the family lives of his followers. He has traveled extensively and his symbol is a red rising sun in the east. He is an arch anti-communist (**delivering a great people from subjection** [EP104–105]).

Since my first book on Nostradamus (1986) Moon, now released from jail, has gone significantly mainstream in the right-wing Christian fundamentalist movement in the US Republican Party. He has been embraced by mainstream evangelist leaders such as Jerry Falwell. Evidence supports the contention that Moon's Unification Church has been a major supporter of the Reaganites and former president George Bush. Though Moon resembles more Nostradamian clues than any other teacher examined thus far, he appears to be turning into a politically correct religious insider rather than a spiritual rebel. No connections with Hermes (2 Q29) are evident, and his name, at least phonetically, parallels the English word "Moon", requiring Nostradamus to mean the English word for Moon. Perhaps most significant, claiming himself as the messianic successor to the founder of one of the major orthodox religions does not make him the foretold catalyst of a new religion.

O S H O   (F O R M E R L Y   K N O W N   A S   B H A G W A N   S H R E E   R A J N E E S H)
(1 9 3 1 – 1 9 9 0)
Indian philosopher

Osho's teachings lean towards Tantra, the Eastern religious discipline related, as we have seen, to Hermetic teachings (2 Q29). Tantra also contains the meditative concept of living in the present – the **Now** (EP212). The Osho movement was symbolized in the 1980s by two flying birds; its current symbol is a lone swan flying free from the bonds of Earth and into the cosmos (EP212).

Fitting quite closely Nostradamus' Eight Clues, his full legal name – Rajneesh Chandra Mohan – has two connections with *moon*. *Rajneesh* means "Lord of the Full Moon," and his mid or **second to last name**, *Chandra*, means "moon" (2 Q28).

Although his followers have ceased to wear their red colors in public, their main headquarters at an ashram in India teems with thousands of people wearing robes in shades of maroon (**red/rose** *color*: 5 Q96, EP104). Despite his death in 1990, Osho's movement continues to flourish: Erich Folath of *Stern* magazine reported in 1993 that attendance at Osho's commune was up by 40 percent from the previous year. In 1995 their commune reported their biggest increase of attendance ever; interestingly, 60 percent never knew the guru while he was alive.

Osho's links with Nostradamus' eight provided clues seem to match extremely well. We do not know, of course, that the prophet intended his quatrains to imply one religious leader – there could be several: *Many rare birds will cry in the air, "Now! Now!"* EP212.

ADI DA SANTOSHA
(1939–)
American mystic

Adi Da is not from the East (2 Q29, 10 Q75), although he was a disciple of masters in India and his teachings have Eastern origins. He does, however, claim to be the reincarnation of Swami Vivekananda, an early Eastern mystic catalyst (1863–1902) who visited Europe and America in the 19th century. Adi Da has traveled extensively and lived in India as a disciple prior to his self-realization. His teachings are unquestionably related to the Eastern flame (5 Q96) and the symbolic Martian red (EP104–105). No significant relationship exists to birds: the Free Daist movement uses as its symbol the Dawn Horse, a prehistoric variant of Kalki, the White Horse of Hindu prophetic tradition.

The mid-1990s have seen another transformation of Adi Da's name and teaching style. But the scope of his movement is limited compared with the burgeoning increase in the followings of Maharishi Mahesh Yogi or Osho. The situation could change.

SWAMI MAHARISHI MAHESH YOGI
(1911–)
Founder of the Transcendental Meditation movement

TM (Transcendental Meditation) has taproots in the ancient Hindu Vedic scriptures and seems now to have been largely accepted by orthodox religions as representative of the New Age movements. It was taught in Western colleges until 1977.

As of 1996 the Maharishi and the TM movement is continuing to hold its own as a likely candidate. But the Maharishi's generally diplomatic integration with the religious mainstream does not bode well for fulfilling Nostradamus' forecast of the new Messiah being one who will shake down the dogmas of fossilized religious thought.

This is the last quatrain entry of the Eight Clues theme, and it seems appropriate to remind ourselves that we are still not far enough down the line to draw precise conclusions as to the identity of the man or men whom Nostradamus and many other prophets saw as the instruments of the birth of the new "religiousness." As the prophecies unfold into reality, it remains to be seen just what new revelations we can hope to understand in the coming New Age.

10 Q76

Le grand Senat difcernera la pompe,[1]
A l'vn qu'apres fera vaincu chaffé:
Ses adherans feront à fon de trompe,
Biens publiez, ennemis defchaffez.

The great Senate will discern the parade,
For the one who afterwards will be driven out, vanquished:
His adherents will be there at the sound of a trumpet.
Their possessions for sale, the enemies driven out.

[1]Latin *pompa* = (triumphal) parade.

During 45 May Day celebrations in Red Square, the **great Senate** of the United States took note of the military pomp and ponderous anthem of the Soviet Union strutting its Cold War clout before world television. Then the Berlin Wall and communism came down with a crash. Today many of the Soviet military hats and greatcoats, pieces of the wall, and an assortment of Lenin statues are sold in the West as souvenirs. A more serious development is the bargain sale of Soviet conventional, chemical, and nuclear weapons on the world's black markets.

10 Q77

Trente adherans de l'ordre des quiretres:
Bannis leurs biens donnez fes aduerfaires:
Tous leurs bienfaits feront pour defmerites,
Claffe efpargie deliurez aux corfaires.

Thirty adherents of the order of Quirites [citizen warriors?]:
Banished, their goods given their adversaries:
All the good things they did will be taken as misdeeds,
Fleet scattered, delivered to the Corsairs.

We continue with a augury for the end of the Cold War. **Quirites** stands for citizen warriors, or better, a people's army. This might be the way a 16th-century seer describes the red martial star on Soviet soldiers' caps. Now one sees these tokens in hock shops around the world. Boris Yeltsin **banished** the Communist Party after the last Marxist coup tried to overthrow democratic reform in August 1991. The party has since risen again to unsuccessfully challenge Yeltsin in the presidential elections of 1996. They curry support from older Russians and former apparatchiks of the Soviet bureaucracy who are disenfranchised by the runaway capitalism of the 1990s. The new Russia has stripped many elderly Marxists of their privileges and benefits. Long before the breakup of the Soviet Union the Soviet navy began selling their cast-off submarines and naval vessels to modern-day Algeria, Tunisia, and Libya (lands of the 16th-century Corsairs). Now many of their prime vessels are on the block at bargain prices.

10 Q78

Subite ioye en fubite triftesse,	**Sudden joy into sudden sadness,**
Sera à Rome aux graces embrassees:	**Will be at Rome for the graces embraced:**
Dueil, cris, pleurs, larm. fang excellent liesse	**Grief, cries, tears, weeping. Blood, excellent mirth**
Contraires bandes furprinfes & troussees.	**Contrary groups surprised and trussed up.**

A vision of the contradictory images fluttering on modern Italian television? Who knows. This could describe any number of instances of sudden joy and sadness felt by people waiting for news of survivors from some ship or airplane accident.

10 Q79

Les vieux chemins feront tous embellys,	**The old paths will be all improved,**
Lon passera à Memphis fomentree:	**One will travel [to a place] similar to Memphis:**
Le grand Mercure d'Hercules fleur de lys,	**The great Mercury of Hercules, fleur-de-lys,**
Faifant trembler terre, mer & contree.	**Causing to quake land, sea and country.**

As far as I know, the authors of cheap-thrills Nostradamus articles in the tabloids have yet to make hay over line 2 of this quatrain: FLASH! Nostradamus predicts Elvis sighting!

The new king from **Memphis** probably isn't the King of Rock. As flashy as his sequined costumes were, I never saw any with fleur-de-lys designs. But all levity aside, a snarling and sexy King of another song and dance is meant here. The great **Hercules** of the lilies can only be a king of France. The references to home improvements in the first two lines are not intended for the new driveway at Graceland. They are better applied to the public works of Louis XIV during the period of 57 peaceful years when the rocks of the stonemasons rolled to finish the Palace of Versailles. "Thank-yah-v'ry-much."

10 Q80

Au regne grand du grand regne regnant,	In the great reign of the great reign reigning,
Par force d'armes les grands portes d'airain:	Through force of arms the great gates of brass:
Fera ouurir le Roy & Duc ioignant,	Will he cause to open, the King and Duke joining,
Port demoly nef à fons iour serain.	Port demolished, ship to the bottom, day serene.

Too many seaports have been devastated in the past four centuries to conjure up a specific case in this verse. Take your pick from the most recent hell-raisings – from the brass gates of Catherine the Great's gutted winter palace near the harbor of Leningrad to the three devastations of Sebastopol in 1856, 1942 and 1944; or even pass your way through the strafed and bombed port of Pearl Harbor in 1941.

10 Q81

Mis tresor temple citadins Hesperiques,	Treasure [is] placed [in a] temple [by] Western citizens,
Dans iceluy retiré en secret lieu:	Withdrawn therein to a secret place:
Le temple ouurir les liens fameliques,	The temple opened by hungry bonds,
Reprens rauis proye horrible au milieu.	Recaptured, ravished, a terrible prey in their midst.

This is pretty cryptic but we might return to the "collapse of the Soviet Union" theme from 10 Q76–77, with a chilling warning. The Communist Party could rise again with a vengeance between 1996 and 1999. The Communist candidate for president, Gennady Zuganov, lost his 1996 bid to become president and turn the clock back to the old Soviet Union. Could this be a prophecy of civil war after the collapse of Russian capitalism and the cut-off of **Western** financial aid?

10 Q82

Cris, pleurs, larmes viendront auec coteaux,	Cries, weeping, tears will come with knives,
Semblant fouyr donront dernier assault:	Seeming to flee they will deliver a final assault:
Lentour parques planter profonds plateaux,	Around the parks; they will set up vast platforms,
Vifs repoussez & meurdris de prinsault.	Violently repelled and murdered instantly.

Lines 1 and 2 sound very much like the pandemonium of the retreating battered French troops of Napoleon at the Battle of Marengo, in 1800, near Alessandria, Italy. Here we observe their pursuit by the slow, serried ranks of Austrian infantry whose bayonets glint in the late-afternoon sun. But the Austrian columns soon stepped into the shattering volleys and cavalry charges of a fresh French corps commanded by General Desaix. Although he is shot and killed in the first attacks, Desaix's men repel the Austrians. Line 3 shows the tables turned; now it is the Austrians who are sent reeling back up the road to their encampments and artillery parks in a rout. At this point my own interpretation flees in a rout from Nostradamus' puzzling phrase, *they will set up vast platforms*. Unless I can make *profons plateaux* stand for an Austrian defensive line in an earthen fortification set around their camp, I cannot vouch for platforms being overwhelmed by the victorious French at Marengo, because that didn't happen.

This quatrain is really a universal generality for any last-ditch counter-attack that snatches victory from defeat and hurls the routed attackers back into their own defensive lines, where they are overwhelmed and slaughtered. It could equally be applied to a hundred battles on the Eastern or Western Front during both World Wars. One might hope the potential for this event ends with the World Wars of the 20th century and will not raise its specter again in a World War for the 21st century.

10 Q83

De batailler ne fera donné figne,	**The signal to fight will not be given,**
Du parc feront contraint de fortir hors:	**They will be obliged to go out of the**
De Gand lentour fera cogneu l'enfigne,	**park:**
Qui fera mettre de tous les fiens à morts.	**Around Ghent the banner will be**
	recognized,
	Of him who will put all his followers
	to death.

This seems to continue the theme of the previous quatrain and narrows down the arena of battle to Flanders. If it applies to the fighting of Nostradamus' time, we have here the battles fought in the Spanish Netherlands during the 80-year War of Dutch Independence (1568–1648). If it is for our times, these are the shattered artillery parks of the Belgian and British forces in the early stages of the Imperial German invasion of Belgium during World War I; or it is a repetition of abandoned British artillery parks during the Nazi German Blitzkrieg into Belgium in 1940. And if we move four years ahead we find the Germans themselves abandoning their equipment during their battles with the British in the Scheldt estuary (near Ghent) in late 1944.

10 Q84

La naturelle à ſi hault hault non bas,
Le tard retour fera marris contens:
Le Recloing ne ſera ſans debats,
En empliant & pendant tout ſon temps.

The natural girl so high, high, not
  low,
The late return will make the grieved
  ones contented:
The reconciled One will not be
  without debates,
In employing and losing all his time.

This is completely obscure and open to all kinds of interpretations.

10 Q85

Le vieil tribun au point de la trehemide,
Sera preſſee captif ne deſliurer,
Le vueil non vueil le mal parlant timide,
Par legitime à ſes amis liurer.

The old tribune on the point of
  trembling,
He will be pressed not to deliver the
  captive,
The will will-less, speaking the timid
  evil,
To lawfully deliver to his friends.

Many details supporting a vague subject. Modern scholars apply this one to the octogenarian premier of Vichy France, Marshal Pétain, and his negotiations with the Germans between 1940 and 1943 for the release of 1 million French prisoners of war from slave labor.

10 Q86

Comme vn gryphon viendra le Roy
  d'Europe,
Accompaigné de ceux d'Aquilon,
De rouges & blancs conduira grand
  trouppe,
Et iront contre le Roy de Babylon.

Like a griffin will come the King of
  Europe,
Accompanied by those of the North,
The reds and whites led in a great
  troop,
And they will go against the King of
  Babylon.

This is either about the Gulf War of 1991 against Saddam Hussein of Iraq (**the King of Babylon**), or it augurs a future Gulf War in which the leader of the European Union, accompanied by the United States (**those of the North**), return to the oilfields of the Middle East in a second, far more violent clash with Saddam Hussein.

Nostradamus may use the mythical **griffin** (a beast with the wings of an eagle and the body of a lion) to describe the US (**eagle**) F-16s, the black-skinned and macabre-shaped Stealth fighter-bombers, the sleek dragonfly bodies of Apache helicopters with their tiger-shark-teeth decals, terrorizing all Iraqi airspace alongside the British (**lion**) Tornado and Jaguar fighter-bombers of Operation Desert Storm.

Reds and whites could stand for a number of things. I tend to lean toward the signal colors of Coalition battle units. The American 1st Division (known as the "big red one") spearheaded the 7th Corps, plunged into Iraq to outflank Iraqi forces in Kuwait.

10 Q87

Grand Roy viendra prendre port pres de Niſſe,
Le grand empire de la mort ſi en fera
Aux Antipolles poſera ſon geniſſe,
Par mer la Pille tout eſuanouyra.

The great king will come to take the port near Nice,
The death of the great empire will be completed
In Antibes will he place a heifer,
By sea the pillage will completely vanish.

Nice is near the port of Fréjus, where Allied landings slammed ashore in August 1944.

The **death of the great empire** describes the imminent and total defeat of Nazi Germany nine months later (see 5 Q45, the "Battle of the Bulge" quatrain). As so often happens in the quatrains of Centuries 9 and 10, the last two lines devolve into the cryptically idiotic. I am not aware of any Nazi or Allied division that had a cow as their symbol. And I doubt this is Nostradamus using an ungulate to describe some futuristic machine or vehicle entering Antibes during the Allied advance. One might apply the lame poetics of line 4 to the end of the Nazi occupation and exploitation of France through an Allied invasion **by sea**.

10 Q88

Pieds & Cheual à la ſeconde veille,
Feront entree vaſtient tout par la mer:
Dedans la poil[1] entrera de Marſeille,
Pleurs, crys, & ſang, onc nul temps ſi amer.

Foot and Horse at the second vigil,
They will make an entry devastating all by sea:
He will enter the port of Marseilles,
Tears, cries, and blood, never times so amer[ican].

[1]Leoni reminds us that Le Pelletier sees this as an eratum for port; Garencières gives it as port.

A few days after the Allied landings near Fréjus, French forces dressed and equipped in American uniforms and armaments were fighting the Germans in the streets of Marseilles. Amer can mean "bitter." But it could be an interesting double-pun: "Amer"-ican. It could be argued that the United States gained the greatest advantage by winning World War II, for she became the leader of the Free World.

10 Q89

De brique en marbre feront les murs reduits,	The walls will change from brick to marble,
Sept & cinquante annees pacifiques:	Fifty-seven peaceful years:
Ioye aux humains renoué l'aqueduict,	Joy to humans, the aqueduct renewed,
Santé, grands fruict ioye & temps melifique.[1]	Health, abundant fruit, mellifluous times.

[1]Latin *mellificus* = honey-making.

Louis XIV once said, "Since there must be war, it is better to wage it against my enemies than against my children." Though he would fight wars throughout his long reign, he kept his promise and France enjoyed domestic peace – a period of stability that Nostradamus accurately predicted 100 years before in 1557.

After the Battle of the Dunes in 1657, France didn't have another war inside its borders for the next 57 years of life remaining for Louis XIV. His reign is characterized by innovative building: the Palace of Versailles was constructed at his command, and a network of canals (**aqueduct**s), notably the Midi connecting the Atlantic to the Mediterranean Sea, was laid.

10 Q90

Cent fois mourra le tyran inhumain,	A hundred times will the inhuman tyrant die,
Mys à fon lieu fçauant & debonnaire,	His place taken by a wise and debonair man,
Tout le fenat fera deffoubs fa main,	The entire senate is in his hand,
Faché fera par malin temeraire.	He will be vexed by a malicious scoundrel.

"I still don't understand why I lost," Napoleon often remarked during his slow fade into history and tropical siestas on St Helena. "I should have died at Waterloo!" Here we may have an augury of Napoleon's inner torture at being out of the loop of history; he is a workaholic fighting and losing the battle against his two greatest enemies, time and inactivity. Dying *a hundred times* could also be a pun that dates the time of his final bid for power in what historians call the Hundred Days, the three-month period between his triumphal return to Paris on 20 March and his defeat at Waterloo (18 June 1815).

Replacing him on the French throne is Louis XVIII, who was nicknamed *Le Débonnaire*. The new French Parliament pledged itself to their new king, but ardor for the new monarchy soon cooled with the crowning of his brother, Charles X, a few years later. Charles X is the quatrain's **vexed** man, tormented by a Republican fanatic who kills his son, Charles, Duc de Berri, the legitimate heir to the throne of France.

10 Q91

Clergé Romain l'an mil fix cens & neuf,
Au chef de l'an feras election:
D'vn gris & noir de la Compagne yffu,
Qui onc ne feut fi maling.

Roman clergy, in the year of 1609,
At the beginning of the year you will
hold an election:
Of one gray and black from Campania
will come forth,
Never was there one so wicked as he.

A pope will be elected in the year 1609. He will have been born in the southern Italian province of Campania. Either he comes from the **gray**-robed order of the Franciscans or he shuffles about the Conclave of Cardinals in the **black** robes of a Dominican friar. Never was there so wicked a pope that never was. Nostradamus misses completely. In his defense, it could be said that the waves of future destinies took a different course. If such an evil Campanian monk lurked about the Vatican, he did so under the watchful gaze of Pope Paul V, who ruled the Holy See from 1605 to 1621.

10 Q92

Deuant le pere l'enfant fera tué,
Le pere apres entre cordes de ionc,
Geneuois peuple fera efuertué,
Gifant le chief au milieu comme vn tronc.[1]

Before the father the child will be slain,
The father afterwards between ropes
of rushes,
Genevan people will have exerted
themselves,
The chief's headless trunk lying down
in their midst.

[1]Latin *truncus* = trunk (without branches), torso (without head or limbs).

Geneva was the Protestant Mecca ruled by John Calvin, its Protestant Muhammad. Nostradamus once again displays his own human failings rather than delivering an accurate prophecy. His hatred of John Calvin begs his inner daemon to reveal a false vision of Calvin being decapitated and ripped apart limb by limb, by an angry mob.

10 Q93

La barque neufue receura les voyages,
Là & aupres transfereront l'empire:
Beaucaire, Arles retiendront les hoftages,
Pres deux colomnes trouuees de prophire.

The new bark [of St Peter] will
accept voyages,
There and near by they will transfer
the Empire:
Beaucaure, Arles will retain the
hostages,
Near where two columns are found
[made] of porphyry.

The **bark** of a new **St Peter** might bring us back to the St Malachy–Nostradamus' parallel prophecy for the final pope of doomsday, Peter II.

He will continue the globe-trotting tradition of Paul VI, John Paul II, and his successor, whom St Malachy calls Glory of the Olive ("the branch of peace"). The cryptic phrase **transfer the Empire** has appeared before, in 3 Q92. In both cases it may refer to a swing of geopolitical power during the 21st century from the industrial northern nations to the overpopulated and developing Southern Hemisphere countries. The **empire** transferred may refer to Peter II's new papacy being forced to leave a devastated Rome (see 2 Q93). The new home of the papacy may be Beaucaire in southern France, a few miles up the Rhône from Arles. Two columns made of porphyry will be discovered near by. Perhaps they are part of an ancient Roman ruin yet to be uncovered by archaeologists.

10 Q94

De Nifmes, d'Arles, & Vienne contemner,	**From Nîmes, from Arles and Vienne, scorn,**
N'obey tout à l'edict Hefpericque:	**Not at all to obey the Western edict:**
Aux labouriez pour le grand condamner,	**To the tormented for the great one condemnation,**
Six efchappez en habit feraphicque.	**Six escaped in seraphic [Franciscan?] garb.**

An invasion force marches north from the direction of Nîmes in Languedoc and Arles in Provence, advancing up the Rhône river valley to Vienne, which is about 20 miles south of Lyons. *Hespericque* implies either a Spanish invasion scheduled for Nostradamus' near future or an invasion by some **Western** alliance. The former never happened; the latter could be a slightly inaccurate plotting of the attack route followed by the Anglo-American and Free French forces of the **Western** alliance during their invasion of the Riviera in 1944. The advance began from landings near Fréjus, then swept westward through Toulon and Marseilles, swinging north around Arles up the 140 miles of the Rhône river valley past Vienne to Lyons.

Interestingly enough, the crack 11th Panzer Division stationed around Bordeaux raced hundreds of miles across France with the intention of blocking the Allied advance. They paused for a time in Languedoc and rumbled through Nîmes. But their rough-and-ready commander, General von Wiedersheim, was too late. His staff heard him complain bitterly about the Wehrmacht policy which allowed armored units to move only under personal orders from Hitler (**for the great one condemnation**). Because of Hitler's indecision the 11th Panzer cooled their panzer engines too long in Languedoc for them to push the Allied landings back into the sea. The odd final line is difficult to apply to either invasion scenario.

10 Q95

Dans les Espaignes viendra Roy trespuissant,	Into Spain will come a very powerful King,

Dans les Eſpaignes viendra Roy
   treſpuiſſant,
Par mer & terre ſubiugant or midy :
Ce mal fera rabaiſſant le croiſſant,
Baiſſer les aiſles à ceux du vendredy.

Into Spain will come a very powerful
   King,
By sea and land subjugating [the
   golden?] South:*
This evil will cause the humbling of
   the crescent,*
A lowering of the wings of those of
   Friday [the Muslims].*

By 1808 Emperor Napoleon I had occupied Spain and subjugated most of the principalities and kingdoms of Sardinia, Sicily, and Italy into his Empire. Less than ten years earlier, one sees him as the younger and leaner general of the Revolutionary Wars, astride his horse within the flaming walls of French musketry sputtering death from the square formations in the shadow of the pyramids. His French Expeditionary Army of Egypt **humbled** the Muslim cavalry armies of the Mamelukes at the Battle of the Pyramids outside Cairo in 1799. A few months later French bayonets and cannons drove a Turkish army – **crescent** banners and all – into the sea at Aboukir.

10 Q96

Religion du nom des mers vaincra,
Contre le ſecte fils Adaluncatif,
Secte obſtinee deploree craindra,
Des deux bleſſez par Aleph & Aleph.[1]

The Religion named for the oceans
   will overcome,*
Against the sect of the son
   Adaluncatif,*
The obstinate, deplored sect will be
   afraid,*
Of the two wounded by Alif and Alif.

[1]*Aleph*: Hebrew name for the first letter in their alphabet; adopted by the Greeks (*alpha*) and used by them as the name of their (different) letter A. Variant: *Alif*, the first letter of the alphabet in Arabic.

The anagram **Adaluncatif** has baffled interpreters for the past half century. I take it to be a riddle about Qadaffi and the consequences of the bombing of Pan-Am flight 301 in 1988. If my interpretation of the index numbering of this quatrain is correct, in 1996 the controversy is in some way resolved, or Libya's relations with the West will worsen. At the time of writing (May 1996) the United States is warning Libya to dismantle its nearly completed underground chemical and biological weapons facilities. Another overt or covert surgical military attack on Libya is implied.

    There are two translations for "oceanic." The term "Oceanic religion" could be somewhat awkwardly describing Qadaffi's bed on the night of the US bombing raid on his home in 1986. Author and former British

Parliament member George Tremlett has been one of the few Westerners invited into Qadaffi's house in the center of a military barracks outside of Tripoli. The bombed bedroom is enclosed in glass, like a shrine, without one shard of shrapnel or piece of broken masonry disturbed since the night of the bombing. Tremlett's book *Gaddafi: The Desert Mystic* contains a photograph of the bed; at the head we see an illuminated and vividly colored panoramic photo of ocean waves crashing on the rocks.

The "oceanic" religion probably stands for a new religious movement dated to spread in the mid-to-late 1980s. Only one new sect supports this interpretation, the Rajneesh movement, whose spiritual leader, the late Bhagwan Shree Rajneesh, changed his name to Osho in 1990. He explained that the new name is derived from William James' word "oceanic," which means dissolving into the ocean. Oceanic describes the experience, he says, but what about the experiencer? For that he instructed his followers to use the word "Osho." This name is also used as a Zen salutation that can essentially be translated as "oceanic consciousness." The Osho movement continues to gain international momentum and thousands of new followers each year despite the death of its founding guru in 1990, making it one of the most important and fastest-growing new religious sects of the New Age.

Adaluncatif is one of the prophet's classic anagrams. Reshuffle the letters and they form "Cad(t)afi Luna." Allowing for phonetic spelling changes, it is possible to get "Qadaffi Luna," "Qadaffi of the Moon," or "Qadaffi of the Crescent of Islam."

The laws of anagram can also divine Abu Nidal out of **Adaluncatif**. Remove "A(dal)u(n)cat(i)f" and we get Nidal. Drop the *c* and the remaining letters *a-u-a-t-f* can phonetically spell "fatau," for Fatah, the militant branch of the Palestinian Liberation Organization. Now the trick is to decode just what the Hebrew letter Aleph or the Arabic Alif stands for in this context.

If this is indeed a quatrain predicting a new religious movement overcoming pressures from the Islamic extremism of "Qadaffi Luna," who are the **two wounded** men responsible for a crime so heinous that it eventually brings destruction upon their whole terrorist sect? This quatrain could be predicting the 1988 bombing of Pan-Am Flight 103 over Lockerbie, Scotland. Western intelligence sources believe that Colonel Qadaffi and Abu Nidal together ordered the bombing as a retaliation for the Iranian airliner accidentally shot down by the USS *Vincennes* at the end of the First Gulf War (1980–1988).

Who then are the two men *Aleph/Alif*?

Apparently, these Hebrew and Arabic letters are not the same as our letter A. Instead they correspond not to the vowel sound "a" but to the glottal stop that precedes it. With that said, one cannot rule out that

Nostradamus the obscurer would lead the seeker off the trail with his or her logic and knowledge of etymology. Perhaps he was more interested in the spelling of the word in Roman letters rather than its sound?

If so, then the first *Alif* could be (A)hmed Jibril, head of the terrorist group Popular Front. The CIA suspects Jibril received Qadaffi's blessing and support to avenge the downing of the Iranian airliner by US forces. The second *Alif* is either (A)bu Nidal or his business partner Monzer (a)l-Kassar, the notorious Syrian arms and drug peddler (also in the employ of the CIA) who worked for Iran-Contra conspiracy figure Oliver North. United States officials believe Monzer was involved in planting the bomb and that he informed his US intelligence connections about the deed.

Aleph and Alif might also stand for one man: (A)li (F) (a)l-Megrahi, one of two Libyan terrorist operatives widely believed to have set the bomb in a suitcase on a connecting flight to Pan-Am 301. Libya is currently suffering under UN economic sanctions for not surrendering Ali al-Megrahi and his colleague, Lamen Kh(alif)a Fhimah, for prosecution.

The information possessed by these two sets of men may yet be the cause of some or all of them being shot (*wounded*) – Qadaffi fears the consequences to Libya if any of them go to trial.

Quatrain Indexing Date: Q96 = 1996, the year when Libya's relations with the West will worsen.

10 Q97

Triremes pleines tout aage captif,	*Triremes full of captives of all ages,*
Temps bon à mal, le doux pour amertume:	*Times good to bad, the sweet for the bitter:*
Proye à Barbares trop toſt ſeront haſtifs,	*Prey to the Barbarians hasty they will be too soon,*
Cupid de voir plaindre au vent la plume.	*Greedy to see the feather [plume of smoke?] wail in the wind.*

The Muslim and Christian navies of Nostradamus' time used captured prisoners and civilians as slaves to row their galleys, although neither side possessed galleys with three stacks of oars. Line 2 describes the galley slaves themselves, who lost their freedom and now suffer bitterly. They appear to be Muslims stuck in the stinking hold of a Christian galley that has suddenly become prey to Barbary Corsairs, who might make a foolhardy and badly planned attack. One interpretation of line 3 finds the slaves' hope for liberation *hasty*. The Muslim galley slaves gaze at the Barbary Pirate ship through the portholes, hopeful to see the first plume of smoke and hear the cannonball's scream across the bow of their ship. But the wind is not in their favor and their Christian masters hoist sail and outdistance the pirate.

10 Q98

La ſplendeur claire à pucelle ioyeuſe,
Ne luyra plus, long temps ſera ſans ſel:[1]
Auec marchans,[2] ruffiens loups odieuſe,
Tous peſle meſle monſtre[3] vniuerſele.

The bright splendor for the merry
    maid,
Will shine no longer, for a long time
    will she be without [zest]:
With merchants, ruffians, odious
    wolves,
All pell-mell, the universal monster.

[1]Salt; (figuratively) zest, wit.
[2]Old French *marchant* = either merchant or mercenary.
[3]Either monster or divine omen.

Garencières (1672) sets the stage: "This is concerning a famous beauty, who in her latter age shall prostitute herself to all comers." Le Pelletier, ever the biased royalist, transforms the **merry maid** Marianne, symbol of the French Revolution (and the Statue of Liberty in New York City) into the sagging harlot of the Third Republic, which was deposed by Napoleon III.

I would add that this general quatrain could just as easily be applied to the future of the Fourth or even the current Fifth Republic of France. Line 3 adequately applies itself to the merchants-turned-malcontents during the trucker rebellions of the early 1990s, when French produce transporters blocked roads and buried them in piles of produce. They protested the new EU laws that took a deep bite into French agricultural protectionism. The **universal monster**-cum-divine omen could be the result of a battle: human greed and nationalistic short-sightedness versus the coming globalization of society. Here my own view is very close to Jochmans'. If nationalism is not transcended soon, ecological and earth catastrophes will be triggered by the negative, short-sighted actions of nationalists and protectionists.

10 Q99

La fin le loup, le lyon, bœuf, & l'aſne,
Timide dama ſeront auec maſtins:
Plus ne cherra à eux la douce manne,
Plus vigilance & cuſtode aux maſtins.

The end of the wolf, the lion, bull and
    the Ass,[1]
Timid deer will be with the mastiffs:
No longer will fall upon them the
    sweet manna,
More vigilance and guarding for the
    mastiffs.

[1]In this case a symbol of Palestine, after Pales, the (Latin name for the) Phoenician ass-headed androgynous god of that region.

At first sight this appears to foretell the extinction of even these common animal species if we do not become responsible stewards of Earth.

In the quatrains animals often symbolize countries: the **wolf** is Italy; both the **lion** and the **mastiffs** are Britain; the **bull** is Spain; the **ass** represents Palestine; the **deer** is Germany. In one interpretation for this collection of animals, they represent the loss of their national identities in the coming 21st century as the world evolves, for better or worse, towards internationalism.

The wolf can also signify two allusions for the First and Second Antichrist: *loup* in French, or "Adolf" from Old High German, which means "noble wolf" (for Adolf Hitler). The Third Antichrist may also have the nickname "lone wolf" as does one guerrilla leader in Chechnya, who in 1995–96 threatened Russia with nuclear terrorism.

Nationalism, xenophobia, and Führer-worship is the **sweet manna**, if you will, for the ego of an Antichrist, whether he is a Napoleon, Hitler, or one yet to surface. The breakdown of nationalistic identifications will signify the end of humankind's long and bloody modern era of national-ism, which started with the Napoleonic wars of the 19th century and climaxed with the World Wars of the 20th. The once ferocious wolves of the Nazi empire have become the timid **deer** of a peaceful and prosperous Germany, which is today closely allied economically and militarily to Great Britain as a co-member in the EU. It seems that Nostradamus calls upon Britain, the future state within Europe, to apply **more vigilance** against the rise of Fascism and tyranny in Europe.

I believe Garencières has the best interpretation for the closing two lines: "This signifieth that the Europeans shall be fed no more with Manna, as the Jews were in the Desert, but shall pass to the Land of Promise, that is of peace and quietness."

Once there are no more nations, most wars will cease. Humankind in the 21st century will at last have matured and will be ready to face the next challenge of transcending the second cause of wars and division – dogmatic and fossilized religions. A number of collective visions of tomorrow, which I compiled in *The Millennium Book of Prophecy* (Harper-Collins), tell us that in the Aquarian Age humankind's spiritual evolu-tion will move us away from blind faith to a more scientific outlook. These collective visions promise us that once the religions have faded away around the end of the next century, their void could be filled by another wing of science, the subjective science of self-observation – meditation.

Quatrain Indexing Date: Q99 = 1999. In this case a more positive outcome to the fearsome "1999" prophecy of 10 Q72.

10 Q100

Le grand Empire ſera par Angleterre,
Le pempotam[1] des ans plus de trois cens:
Grandes copies paſſer par mer & terre,
Les Luſitains n'en ſeront pas contens.

A great empire will be for England,
The all powerful one through the sea
    for more than 300 years:
Great forces will pass by land and
    sea,
The Portuguese will not be satisfied.

[1]From Greek pan = all, and the Latin potens = powerful, we get "the all powerful one", or Greek potamos = river (rarely, sea), thus a double pun for all-seas and the metaphorical "river" of English merchant marines and man-o'-wars which flowed upon them.

When Nostradamus wrote these words, England was a minor sea power. It would have seemed impossible then that this small island kingdom would eclipse great 16th-century powers, such as Portugal, to become a world empire through its domination of the seas. Yet this is exactly what Nostradamus predicts. But from what date does Nostradamus begin to count his 300 years? We know the British Empire seriously declined after World War II and that, by the late 1950s, the British had acceded to the American **empire**'s request to position nuclear missiles on British soil. By the early 1960s the British Empire was almost completely dismantled. If we define this period as the end of the empire, the beginning, according to Nostradamus' time scale, would be towards the end of Oliver Cromwell's time. After the English Civil War, Cromwell's reforms had indeed assisted England to move towards world-power status, and the English Navigation Act of 1661 prompted both the rapid growth of her merchant marine fleet and economic domination of international shipping lanes.

10 Q100dp

Quand le fourchu ſera ſouſtenu de deux
    paux,
Auec ſix demiycorps et ſix ſizeaux ouuerts:
Le tres puiſſant Seigneur, heritier des
    crapauds,
Alors ſubiugera, ſous soy tout l'Vniuers.

When the fork will be supported by
    two columns,
With six half-bodies and six open
    scissors:[1]
A very powerful lord, heir of the toads,[2]
Will then subjugate the whole world
    to himself.

[1]Jaubert claims that this quatrain was doctored in earlier editions to yield the year 1593 rather than the correct 1660. It seems the propagandist from the earlier edition wanted a Protestant "toady" on the throne, such as Henry de Navarre.
[2]Jaubert replaces the forgery "The great King of the toads will rout his enemies" to the above.

In 1656 Jaubert interpreted this duplicate quatrain in these words: "By this quatrain the King of France would appear to be Emperor of the World in 1660. One may indeed hope for this, but it does not seem likely to be accomplished; however, the true Nostradamus seems to predict that he ought to be Emperor soon. May God will it for the maintenance of his Church, and of this very Christian Kingdom."

It is thought that a reading of this interpretation may have prompted Louis XIV, then King of France, to visit the prophet's tomb at the beginning of 1660, in the company of the queen and his mentor, Cardinal Mazarin. The quatrain opens with a riddle: *When the fork will be supported by two columns, With six half-bodies and six open scissors*. This should be interpreted according to the structure of Roman numerals. The fork – V – supported by two columns becomes M. Six half-bodies – Cs – and six open scissors – Xs – spell out MCCCCCCXXXXXX. This gives us the year 1660, when the prophet says: *A very powerful lord, heir of the toads, Will subjugate the whole world to himself*.

At 22 Louis XIV, the future Sun King of France, had an opinion of himself that matched Nostradamus' lofty prediction. He became sole ruler of France in 1661 after the death of Cardinal Mazarin. He was destined to subjugate his people and prove himself a worthy descendant of the ancient Merovingian kings, who bore toads as a heraldic device.

✦✦✦

Presages 24–33
from the Almanac of 1558

✦✦✦

P 24   January (1558)

Puiſné Roy fait, funebre epithalame,
Sacrez eſmeus, feſtins, iceux, ſoupi
   Mars:
Nuit larme[1] on crie, hors on conduit la
   Dame,
L'arreſt & pache rompu de toutes pars.

The young King makes a funeral
   wedding song,
Holy one stirred up, feasts, of the
   said, Mars dormant:
Night tears they cry, they conduct the
   lady outside,
The arrest and peace broken on all
   sides.

[1]*Larme* = tears. Le Pelletier believes this should be *l'arme* = the arms, or *aux armes* = of arms.

Line 1 opens the year with a blend of near and distant-future outcomes for the limpid young Dauphin of 14 years. This is the near-future Francis II, who was married to the 15-year-old Mary, Queen of Scots in April of 1558. At the time of his marriage Francis' sickliness was already a major concern. The riddle ties a wedding song with a funeral dirge, adequately foreseeing the unconsummated marriage to be. In little over two years the honeymoon of these genuinely in-love royals would come to an unconsummated end with the Dauphin's death from a number of physical complaints. It is believed his physical maturity was so stunted that he was still pre-pubescent at his untimely death at 18.

P 25   March (1558)

Vaine rumeur dedans à Hierarchie,
Rebeller Gennes, courses, inſults,
   tumultes:
Au plus grand Roy fera la monarchie,
Election, conflit, couuerts, ſepultes.

Vain rumor within the Hierarchy,
Genoa to rebel: courses, offenses,
   tumults:
For the greater King will be the
   monarchy,
Election, conflict, covert burials.

Although Genoa was dominated by its powerful neighbors, France and Piedmont, it had no reason to rebel against them in 1558 or in any other year before or after 1797, when it lost its independence and became part of the puppet Ligurian state during the French Revolutionary and Napoleonic eras. So this one is a miss or a failed quantum future. Fontbrune would have us change the word *Gennes* from a version of "Genoa" to the Latin word *genus* for "a class" of people – in this case the prole-tariat. This would give a class struggle, fitting his interpretation of this presage for the Bolshevik Revolution of 1917.

We are offered enough details to satisfy at least the projection of such a prophecy. The **Hierarchy** is the Russian aristocracy. The people of Russia rebel against the Czar and the aristocracy because of their outrages (**offenses**). The greater king could be Lenin, or by extension the greatest autocrat of them all, Stalin, who admitted he wanted to best Ivan the Terrible in all ways. The last line stands for the democratic elections to come in the 1990s, which will end the communist era. The **conflict** and **covert burials** indicate the mystery surrounding the secret location of the bodies of the slaughtered Czar and his family.

P 26   April (1558)

Par la difcorde defaillir au defaut,	**Through discord in the absence [the Guises?] to fail,**
Vn tout à coup le remettra au fus:	**One suddenly will put him back on top:**
Vers l'Aquilon feront les bruits fi haut,	**Towards the North will be noises so loud,**
Lefions, pointes à trauers, par deffus.	**Lesions, points to travel, above.**

Montmorency's absence during his Spanish captivity helped restore the king's fondness for the old constable, and the political blunders of François de Guise and his brother, the Cardinal de Lorraine, only made Henry II desire his return and restoration (**put him back on top**). Nostradamus may again be a year ahead of himself if he is describing the rehabilitation of Montmorency. The constable played an influential role as go-between, for Philip II and Henry II in negotiating the Treaty of Cateau-Cambrésis in April of 1559 rather than 1558. The last two lines may stand as further references to the Livonian War between Ivan the Terrible of Russia and an assortment of Baltic states.

P 27   May (1558)

La mer thyrrhene de differente voile,	**On the Tyrrhenian Sea, of different sail,**
Par l'Occean feront diuers affaults:	**On the Ocean there will be diverse assaults:**
Pefte, poifon, fang en maifon de toile,	**Plague, poison, blood in the house of canvas,**
Prefults[1] Legate efmeus marcher mer haut.	**Prefects, Legates stirred up to march [sail] high seas.**

[1]Latin *praesul* = president, prefect; public dancer.

Another successful prophecy concerning the disastrous Spanish expedition against the Barbary Corsairs at the island of Jerba (see P12). By orders of Philip II of Spain, Christian galleys head across the Tyrrhenian Sea in the latter half of 1558, to rendezvous at Messina and then cross the wider waters of Mediterranean (**Ocean**) to recapture Tripoli from the Muslims. A large Ottoman fleet surprised the Christian navy and its encampment on the beaches of Jerba, an island off the coast of Tripoli. The Christian fleet made a rapid retreat, stranding thousands of its soldiers, who waged a fighting retreat through the **house of canvas** of their tent encampment around the island's fortress. The capture of all the island's wells by the Turks leaves us imagining the scene implied here by the seer: dwindling reserves of tainted water and the plague-like fevers suffered by the Christian garrison as it slowly dies of thirst. Their surrender, and further conquests of Spanish strongholds in western North Africa would stir Christian prefects and holy legates alike to prepare firepower and faith in a resumption of the Mediterranean naval wars from 1559 through 1572.

P 28   June (1558)

La où la foy eſtoit fera rompuë,	**There where the faith was it will be broken,**
Les ennemys les ennemys paiſtront:	**The enemies will feed upon the enemies:**
Feu Ciel pleuura, ardra, interrompuë,	**Fire rains [from the] Sky, it will burn, interrupted,**
Nuit entrepriſe. Chef querelles mettront.	**Enterprise by night. Chief will make quarrels.**

A continuation of the previous presage, with more attention on the horrors suffered by the abandoned Christian garrison on the island of Jerba. Cannibalism may be implied by line 2. The hot North African sun **rains** down to bake the thirsty men. The prophet might have foreseen a discussion of a night raid, perhaps a last ditch attempt at a breakout through the Turkish trenches to a moored galley and freedom. But the garrison commander votes it down.

P 29   July (1558)

Guerre, tonnere, mains champs depopulez,[1]	**War, thunder, forces [upon the] fields, depopulated,**
Frayeur & bruit, aſſault à la frontiere:	**Terror and noise, assault on the frontier:**
Grand Grand failly, pardon aux exilez,	**Great Great One fallen, pardon for the exiles,**
Germains, Hiſpans,[2] par mer Barba.[3] banniere.	**Germans, Spaniards, by sea the Barbarian banner.**

[1] Latin depopulatus = depopulated, laid waste.
[2] Latin Hispania = Spain.
[3] Apocope for Barba(re) = Barbary Corsairs.

This could continue the story of the Spanish debacle at Jerba or it could tell a tale of the massing of Spanish troops on the frontiers of France, prior to the close of the Italian Wars in 1559. A number of Germans worked for Spain as mercenaries in their Italian provinces, so one could also imagine the picture of German Landsknechts and Spanish Conquistadors standing shoulder to shoulder on the parapets of the abandoned Christian garrison of Jerba, gazing feverishly at the forest of Islamic sails and banners of the Ottoman galleys and Barbary Corsairs. Line 3 sticks out as a forecast for something more locally French that will take place in the following year after the signing of the Treaty of Cateau-Cambrésis; perhaps it is the return of those captured at St Quentin. Peace brought a pardon from captivity for Montmorency, Coligny, and other architects of the military disaster.

I would not rule out a modern application for *Barba*. It could stand for the code name of Hitler's Armageddon in the steppes of Russia, Operation Barbarossa, the greatest invasion in history. On 22 June 1941, the thunder of 8,000 artillery pieces and 2,000 planes roared across a thousand miles of Soviet frontier. Three million Germans, Romanians, Hungarians, and Italians, along with a division of Spanish Fascists, completely surprised the Soviet army. At this time the Barbarossan banner of Hitler's swastika flew from the standards of U-boats that inflicted catastrophic losses on the British merchant marine, during their early convoy runs to Murmansk to supply the Soviet Union with much-needed arms. In three years' time the Soviet Union would suffer a vast depopulation of 20 million to 27 million people, with 25 million wounded and injured.

P 30   *August* (1558)

Bruit ſera vain les defaillans trouſſez,	**The noise will be vain, the faltering**
Les Razes[1] pris: eſleu le Pempotan:	**ones bundled up,**
Faillir deux Rouges & quatre bien croiſez,	**The Shaven Ones captured: the all-**
Pluye empeſchable au Monarque potent.	**powerful One elected:**
	The two Reds and four true crusaders
	to fail,
	Rain [that is] troublesome to the
	powerful Monarch.

[1]*Razes* usually targets shaven heads for Catholic priests, but sometimes it can be applied to the Roundheads of the English Civil War who shaved off their locks.

At face value this could describe the English Civil War because *Pempotan* usually stands for England. But that doesn't rule out a quantum future failed concerning the real desire of François de Guise, the Lieutenant-General of France, to use his recent conquests of Calais, Dunkirk, and Thionville as bases for an invasion of England.

P 31   October (1558)

Pluye, vent, claffe¹ Barbare Ister,²
   Tyrrhene,
Paffer holbcades,³ Ceres, foldats munies:
Reduits bienfaits par Flor. franchie Siene,
Les deux feront morts, amitiez vnies.

Rain, wind, forces, Barbarossa
   Hitler, the Tyrrhenian Sea,
Vessels to pass Orkneys and beyond
   Gibraltar, grain and soldiers
   provided:
Retreats too well executed by
   Florence, Siena crossed,
The two will be dead, friendships
   joined.

¹Latin *classis* = fleet, army, forces.
²*Barbare Ister* = Barbarossa Hitler.
³*holbcades* = a) Latin *Olcades*, a tribe residing in southeastern Spain; b) *Orcades* = the Orkney Islands.

One must start with the 16th-century potentials of this presage. Line 1 can give us the far-ranging geographic and strategic situation for the Ottoman Turks if you apply the arcane name of the River Danube, the *Ister*, to delineate the westward extent of Ottoman expansion into Europe. After the Christian debacle at Tripoli, the Turks and Barbary Corsairs conquer every Spanish port in North Africa except Oran by 1559. Their galleys sailed past southwestern Spain (known in ancient times as the land of the Olcades) and ventured out into the Atlantic through the Strait of Gibraltar to reach the Canary Islands. But the last two lines make the 16th-century slant fall flat.

We must move forward in time to World War II to pick up the prophetic thread with a different translation for *holbcades* and *(H)ister* – they stand for the Orkney Islands and Adolf Hitler.

Because he lost 1,100,000 men in 1941 (230,000 from frostbite alone), Hitler could not resume his Russian Campaign along the entire front. The *Tyrrhene* stands for the southern and western Italian coastline around the region of the Mediterranean Sea – site of the successful Allied landings at Sicily, Salerno, and Anzio. Line 2 maps the major convoy routes from America through the North Atlantic and Gibraltar that eventually supplied the Allies with enough food, fuel, and soldiers to win. Nostradamus' original word for "Orkneys" or "Orcades" in line 2 could also stand as a spelling pun for the Greek variant for transport ships – *holkadoi*. The word is used to describe the Allied convoys themselves as well as the islands they passed. It could also be a classical synecdoche for Gibraltar, since the area belonged to the tribe of Spanish Gauls called Olcades. By the end of 1944 both Siena and Florence were liberated by the Allies (**crossed**). The Germans did withdraw to the previously con-structed Gothic line (**retreats too well executed**) outside of Florence, which for a brief time checked the Allied advance during the final winter of the war. The final line relates the fateful Axis alliance of Nostradamus' Duce and Hiſter joined in friendship and death.

P 32   November (1558)

Venus le belle entrera dedans FLORE.[1]	**Venus the beautiful will enter Florence.**
Les exilez ſecrets lairront la place:	**The secret exiles will leave the place behind:**
Veſues beaucoup, mort de Grand on deplore,	**Many widows, they deplore the death of the Great One,**
Oſter du regne, le Grand Grand ne menace.	**To remove from the realm, the Great Great One does not threaten.**

[1]Latin *Flora* = flowers, apparently used for Florence.

Most of this is too obscure for my 20th-century mind to untangle, except for the hint that the **death of the Great One** might indicate Pope Paul IV, though that occured the following year. The **Great Great One** may represent Charles V who did die in 1558, but it was two months earlier, in September.

P 33   December (1558)

Jeux, feſtins, nopces, mort Prelat de renom.	**Games, feasts, nuptials, dead [the] Prelate of renown.**
Bruit, paix de treſue pendant l'ennemy mine:	**Noise, peace of truce while the enemy threatens:**
Mer, terre & ciel bruit, fait du grand Brennon,	**Sea, land and sky noise, deed of the great Brennus,**
Cris or, argent, l'ennemy l'on ruyne.	**Cries gold, silver, the enemy they ruin.**

Sometime in the previous year Nostradamus wrote a description of the wedding celebrations for the Dauphin and Dauphine, Francis II and Mary, Queen of Scots, although he records them a few months late. Once again he tags another omen of death onto the end of the wedding party. The renowned **Prelate** is the former vice-legate to Bologna, Giovanni Angelo de Medici, who became Pope Pius IV after the death of Paul IV in 1559 (and not at the end of 1558 as marked here). Line 2 is correct; peace would follow the truce between Spain and France. The **enemy** that **threatens** could be the Corsairs and Ottoman Turks, but most likely it is the Spanish, who would hold much power over France after the Treaty of Cateau-Cambrésis in 1559.

Line 3 falls back on a classical metaphor. **Brennus** was a Cisalpine Gallic chieftain who conquered Rome in 390 BC It seems Nostradamus is beating around the classical underbrush again with his magic wand, trying to chase out a wish-fulfilling tiger of a prophecy that his own great Brennus, Henry II, will conquer Rome and banish the Spanish from Italy. This, like all other prophetic promises of Henry II resuming his military adventures in Italy, would remain unfulfilled. Nostradamus' prophetic bias has him misinterpreting his signs and portents of the successful conquest of Italy and Rome by Napoleon over 235 years later.

Presages 34–46
from the Almanac of 1559

P 34 *On that said year* (1559)

Pleur, glas grand pile, paffer mer, croiftre regne,	**Lament, knell, great pillage, to pass the sea, the realm to increase,**
Sectes, Sacrez outre mer plus polis:	**Sects, holy ones more polite beyond the sea:**
Pefte, chaut, feu, Roy d'Aquilon¹ l'enfeigne,	**Plague, warmth, fire, banner of the King of Aquilon [the North],**
Dreffer trophée, cité d'HENRIPOLIS.²	**To erect a trophy, city of Henripolis.**

¹Latin, *Aquilonaris* = of the North, of the North Wind; northern; Russia.
²*Henripolis,* Greek *polis* = City of Henry.

We begin with general forecasts for the entire year of 1559. Line 1 describes the dangers to come when Barbary Corsairs raid French ports in the Mediterannean, as well as those Christian ports along the Algerian coast soon to be overwhelmed by the Turkish fleets. The **realm** of France did not increase in size, unless he means an upswing in her financial situation which at best was very modest after facing near-bankruptcy in 1557. Line 2 comments on the status of Huguenot **sects**, and their Catholic brethren being more cordial outside of the city of Paris. This was true since Paris was a Catholic bastion and therefore not too pleased to play the host for the Huguenot courtiers and nobility, whose numbers were way out of proportion to the national population (1 in 15 million Frenchmen were Huguenots, but two-fifths of the nobility). Line 3 gives us the annual plague and weather report, then jumps to a commentary on Russia and the Livonian conflict. Our prophet's fascination with symbols makes him unable to resist mentioning the new emblem Ivan the Terrible has created for monarchic Russia: a double-headed eagle. The year ends with a **trophy** erected in the city of Henry II, Paris. The statement by itself is harmless enough, but the prophecies of *Les Propheties* imply, at least poetically, that the trophy is the shattered lance that killed the king (see 1 Q35).

P 35   January (1559)

Plus le Grand n'eftre, pluye, au char[1] le
  criftal,
Tumulte efmeu de tous biens abondance:
Razez, Sacrez, neufs vieux efpouuental,
Efleu ingrat, mort, plaint, joye, alliance.

The Great One to be no longer, rain,
  in the chariot, the crystal,
Tumult stirred up, abundance of all
  goods:
Shaven ones, Holy ones, new ones,
  old ones frightful,
Elected ingrate, death, lament, joy,
  alliance.

[1]Variant: a four-wheeled vehicle.

Very general, but the **Great One to be no longer** could stand for the death of a major head of state. As we know, Pope Paul IV and Henry II died in 1559. The crystal chariot could be an attempt to describe the glasslike finish of some modern or future automobile.

P 36   February (1559)

Grain corrompu, air peftilent, locuftes,
Subit cherra, noue nouuelle naiftre:
Captifs ferrez, legers, haut bas, onuftes,[1]
Par fes os mal qu'à Roy n'a voulu eftre.

Grain corrupted, air pestilent, locusts,
Suddenly it will fall, new pasturage to
  be born:
Captives put in irons, light ones,
  high-low, loaded,
Through his bones evil which he had
  not wished to be to the King.

[1]Latin onustus = loaded, burdened, full.

General local themes one might have seen forecast in an almanac. February must bring rains that corrupt the stored wheat of the previous harvest. The air, humid and swampy because of the rains, will therefore be pestilent, as was popularly believed in those days. But an early spring thaw is implied, and with it the return of green pastures. People are captured who may have had high station or jobs and are put low. Pretty vague! But if this stands for the notable captives Montmorency and Coligny, it is retroactive. The last line might imply the prophet himself. Our arthritic seer feels **through his bones** what is going to happen; he intuitively sees the coming evil he wishes would not be – a vision of the king's forthcoming death through a jousting accident

P 37   March (1559)

Saifis au temple, par fecte longue brigue,
Efleu rauy au bois forme querelle:
Septante pars naiftre nouuelle ligue,
De la leurt mort, Roy appaifé, nouuelle.

Seized in the temple, through a sect's
  long intrigue,
Elected, ravished in the woods, forms
  a quarrel:
Seventy pairs new league to be born,
From there their death, King
  appeased, news.

An incident in a Huguenot church (*temple*) is forecast for March. Nostradamus seems to join in the McCarthyism of his own troubled times. Rather than the red communist scare of the Cold War, we get the 16th-century Protestant heretic scare, wherein all spying and intrigues are blamed on the cult minority of that time. The rest of the prophecy is open to interpretation. It seems the Huguenot spy, perhaps a woman follower, is caught and ravished. Out of this *seventy pairs* (perhaps seventy Huguenot couples?) are executed, and King Henry II is appeased. As usual, none of this can be substantiated beyond the general record of growing atrocities against Huguenots during 1559.

P 38 *April* (1559)

Roy ſalué Victeur,[1] Imperateur,[2]	**King hailed as Victor, and Emperor**
La foy fauſſée, le Royal fait cogneu:	**[Master],**
Sang Mathien.[3] Roy fait ſuperateur,	**The faith broken, the Royal deed known:**
De gent ſuperbe humble par pleurs venu.	**Macedonian blood, King made**
	conqueror,
	The arrogant people come to humility
	through tears.

[1]Variant: conqueror.
[2]Latin *Imperator* = Master, Emperor.
[3]Nostradamus' pet word *Æmathien* = Macedonian, or Philip II of Spain, a classical allusion to the father of Alexander the Great who was also known as "King Philip II."

This is less a prophecy and more a political commentary on the mood of the French people after they lost the Hapsburg–Valois Wars and sign the Treaty of Cateau-Cambrésis, which took place in April 1559.

Line 1 hails the victor, Philip II of Spain, though Nostradamus is incorrect to call him an *Emperor*, as the title of Holy Roman Emperor was given by Philip's father, the retiring Charles V, to his uncle, Ferdinand I, the year before. Charles awarded Philip the dominions of the Spanish empire, making him de facto emperor, but it was a title he never used. Philip in this case is the *Macedonian* king, in a classical word-play for the father of Alexander the Great, also called Philip II. He is characterized as similar to the Barbarian *Macedonian* conqueror of the proud, superior, and *arrogant* culture of Greece, who in this quatrain stand for the humbled people of France.

P 39 *May* (1559)

Par le deſpit nopces, epithalame,	**Through spite nuptials, wedding song,**
Par les trois parts Rouges, Razez partis:	**For the three parts Reds, Shaven ones**
Au ieune noir[1] remis par flame l'ame,	**divided:**
Au grand Neptune Ogmius conuertis.	**For the young black/king through fire**
	the soul [is] restored,
	To the great Neptune Ogmios converted.

[1]Near-anagram for *noir/roy*, black king.

A number of fulfilled and dead-end leads may be planted here concerning the future consequences for the sons of Henry II.

The *spite* might describe the mood of many French nobles (especially Huguenots) who do not wish to consort with the Spanish victors of St Quentin or see Philip II forge blood ties to the French throne. This speaks of the double wedding (*nuptials*) scheduled for the summer between Philip's protégé, the Duke of Savoy, and Henry's sister, Marguérite, as well as the forthcoming marriage of Philip himself to Henry's daughter, Elizabeth. The wedding guests will be spectators at the tournament that mortally wounds Henry II.

Line 2 is obscure. It could be an attempt to describe the three-to-two ratio at court of Catholic nobles – represented by the red-robed and shaven cardinals – to the Protestant Huguenots. It could also indicate the plots to annihilate the Huguenots discussed out of earshot of the festivities. The cardinals (**Shaven ones**) and the **Reds** (the Spanish in this case) confer here with Catholic French nobles, behind closed doors, the Spanish pressuring the French Catholics to be more ruthless and kill off the Huguenots in the same way Torquemada eradicated the Moorish and Jewish "vermin" in the last century. There are a number of possible leads for **Ogmios** the Celtic Hercules, but if this is a 16th-century presage, as the vast majority are, then it is a goof for Henry II's youngest son, Hercules, the future Duc d'Alençon, who might become a Protestant.

P 40   *June* (1559)

De maiſon ſept par mort mortelle ſuite,	From the [Royal] house seven through death in mortal succession,
Greſle, tempeſte, peſtilent mal, fureurs:	Hail, tempest, pestilent evil, furies:
Roy d'Orient d'Occident tous en fuite,	King of the East all the West in flight,
Subiuguera ses iadis conquereurs.	He will subjugate his former conquerors.

A rapid and far-ranging overview of events. Line 1 starts with the seven children of the House of Valois, correctly implying that they are succeeded only by death and the end of the Valois line. Line 2 is generally apocalyptic. Line 3 may stand for Suleiman the Magnificent of the Ottoman Turks, putting the Christian forces in flight. Nostradamus would have been aware of this because in the previous year a number of Spanish fortress ports in North Africa were conquered. This would continue throughout 1559. The last two lines correctly see Suleiman turn eastward to at least check, if not *subjugate*, the Turks' ancient *former conquerors*, the Persians. In 1559 the feud between Suleiman's favorite son, Selim, and his younger brother, Bayezid, reached its climax. With his father's reinforcements Selim defeats Bayezid at Konya. Bayezid will escape to Persia, where the Shah tries to exploit his important hostage to get Suleiman to return Mesopotamian lands conquered in Suleiman's earlier campaigns. But no fatherly heart beats for Bayezid, who languishes in captivity. In an abstract way Suleiman does **subjugate** the Shah by forcing him to bow to his supremacy. No lands are returned, and he compels the Shah to have his son strangled on Persian soil. The only compromise allowed is that the executioners are allowed to strangle his son with a bowstring made by Turks.

P 41   July (1559)

Predons[1] pillez chaleur, grand fechereffe,	Pirates pillaged, heat, great drought,
Par trop non eftre, cas non veu, inouy:	Through too much not being, event
A l'eftranger la trop grande careffe,	not seen, unheard of:
Neuf pays Roy l'Orient efblouy.	For the foreigner the too great
	endearment,
	New country King, the East
	fascinated.[2]

[1]Latin *praedo* = plunderer robber.
[2]Variant: *New country, King of the Orient fascinated.*

The presage is logged in for the time of Henry II's fatal accident. It starts with what might be a local prediction, perhaps in Salon itself, of pirates or plunderers being robbed by their own kind during an unusually hot and dry summer. The honor among thieves allows no evidence of the robbery to be revealed to investigating magistrates. No one knows about, sees, or has heard of the crime.

The second half of the presage expands the focus to include world events. The **foreigner** who is too affectionate could be Nostradamus' cynical description of Philip II of Spain, who will marry Henry II's daughter, Elizabeth Valois, by proxy. **New country King** is a good example of special grammatical enigmas one finds in the writing style for the presages. Does it mean a king will come from the countryside, or a king will come from a newly formed country? Or has a comma and the qualifying "and" been removed so that it should read: **New country** [and] **King**? Nostradamus may have made the phrase ambiguous to protect himself and his family. By July of 1559, France would become a new country with all the suddenness and finality of the crack of a splintering wooden lance on a field of ritualized combat. She would have a new king, the immature Francis II. In one stab of a wooden splinter through his father's eye comes a new and dark era. At once the virile and newly matured King, who was beginning to take full control of the country from his self-centered and backbiting advisors, is replaced by a sickly and terrified boy delivered to the Montmorencys and the Guises, who behave more like a pack of power-hungry wolves.

The *East* is *fascinated* by all this. The "Oriental" Ottoman Sultan in far-off Istanbul would find the news of the political chaos in France fascinating. A discordant France could only nurture his ambitions for further expansion into the Christian half of the Mediterranean.

P 42 August (1559)

L'Vrne trouuée, la cité tributaire,	*The Urn found, the city tributary,*
Champs diuifez, nouuelle tromperie:	*Fields divided, new delusion:*
L'Hifpan blef̄é faim, pefte militaire,	*Spain wounded famine, military plague,*
Moq. obftiné, confus, mal, refuerie.	*Mockery obstinate, confused, evil, reverie.*

A presage stuffed tight with details that only a local contemporary of Nostradamus could decipher. This may be a link to other treasure themes of *Les Propheties*. Toulon has been referred to in 7 Q13 as a city **tributary** to Marseilles. The town of Charlieu, which is about 40 miles from Lyons, could be called a tributary city as it is on the Sornin river, a tributary of the Loire. Perhaps the **Urn** in question is to be found within the walls of the famous old abbey of Charlieu near Besançon. Spain would not be directly wounded or suffer famines and plagues in 1559. The year was glorious for Spain in her European theater; she reveled in political and military victories over France and won almost complete control of Italy after 50 years of conflict. If Spain was at all **wounded** it came from the Ottoman Turks, who followed up their success at a battle for the island of Jerba by establishing control over most of North Africa, starting in 1558 and continuing through the early 1560s.

P 43 *September* (1559)

Vierges & vefues, vofltre bon temps s'approche,	*Virgins and widows, your good time approaches,*
Point ne fera ce que l'on pretendra:	*Not at all will it be that which they will pretend:*
Loin s'en faudra que foit nouuelle approche,	*Far it will be necessary that the approach for it be new,*
Bien aifez pris, bien remis, pis tiendra.	*Very agreeable situation taken, completely restored, it will hold worse.*

For better or worse, the best I can do to unravel this plague of obscure and contradictory messages is to use a variation on the famous nursery rhyme, *Ring Around the Roses*:

> Ring around the virgin dames,
> A pocket full wordy games
> Speculate, speculate,
> We all fall down!

P 44   October (1559)

Icy dedans ſe paracheuera,	**Here within it will be completed,**
Les trois Grands hors le BON-BOURG*[1]*	**The three Great ones outside, the**
ſera loin:	**Bourbon will be far:**
En contre deux l'vn d'eux conſpirera,	**Against the other two one of them will**
Au bout du mois on verra le beſoin.	**conspire,**
	At the end of the month they will see
	the necessity.

[1]Near-anagram for *Bourbon*, in this case standing either for Antoine de Bourbon, King of Navarre, or the Prince de Condé.

The seer assures us "it" will be completed within the month of October. The three great ones could be François de Guise, his brother, the Cardinal de Lorraine, and the Queen Regent, Catherine de' Medici, who as Catholics and the guardians of the minority rule of Francis II are **outside** of the Huguenot-leaning Antoine de **Bourbon**, the King of Navarre. Antoine de Bourbon maintained that the king was too young to govern and was incompetent to bestow to his uncles, the Guises, the authority they assumed. Antoine believed that tradition dictated this right belonged to princes of the greater nobility (**Great ones**) – those of the royal blood, like himself. The usurpation of power by lesser nobility such as the Guises put French sovereignty in danger.

In October 1559 an anonymous pamphlet defending Antoine de Bourbon's view appeared throughout Paris. The Guises found it necessary to reply with their own pamphlets by the end of October (**end of the month**). Thus began a barrage of words between supporters of the Guises and those of Antoine de Bourbon that would make any commie-condemning McCarthy or Newt Gingrich blush at the mean-spirited and libelous attacks. It could be said this war of words presaged the civil war of fire and bloodshed to come three years later.

P 45   November (1559)

Propos tenus, nopces recommencées,	**Talks held, nuptials recommenced,**
La Grande Grande ſortira hors de France:	**The Great Great woman will go out of**
Voix à Romagne de crier non laſſée,	**France:**
Reçoit la paix par trop feincte aſſeurance	**Voice in Rome not fatigued from**
	crying out,
	Receives the peace through too false
	[an] assurance.

Generally on target for 1559, if not for the month of November. The doubly great woman is the daughter of Queen Catherine de' Medici, Elizabeth, on her way with her entourage to Spain after her marriage by proxy to Philip II in the summer. Of all Catherine's daughters she showed the most potential for rule, but died in 1568 while giving birth at the age of 22. The unfatigued voice in Rome is that of the new Medici pope, Pius IV. Pius would reverse his predecessors' anti-Hapsburg foreign policies and embark on friendly relations with Philip II of Spain, a move that our anti-Spanish prophet from Salon believes is based on false assurances.

P 46   December (1559)

La joye en larmes viendra captiver Mars,
Deuant le Grand feront efmeus Diuins:
Sans fonner mot entreront par trois parts,
Mars affoupi, deffus glas toutent[1] vins.

Joy in tears will come to captivate Mars,
Before the Great one the Divines will be stirred up:
Without uttering a word they will enter from three sides,
Mars made drowsy [quieted?], upon ice run the wines.

[1]Provençal *troutar* = to run.

A presage rich with symbolism set for the beginning of winter, 1559. Mars, the god of war, will be crying in his wine, if you will. In other words, after all the hot and hasty words between Huguenots and Catholics in the Paris print shops in the autumn during the war of the pamphlets, there will be no civil war in the winter.

1560 to 1567?

Century XI

11 Q91

Meyſnier, Manthi, et le tiers qui viendra,
Peſte et nouueau inſulte, enclos troubler:
Aix et les lieux fureur dedans mordra,
Puis les Phocens[1] viendront leur mal
   doubler.

Meysnier, Manthi, and the third one
   that will come,
Plague and a new insult, to trouble
   the enclosure:
Aix and the places thereabouts the
   fury within will bite hard,
Then the Phocens [those of
   Marseilles] will come to double
   their evil.

[1]Phocens: a) Phocaeans, founders of Marseilles; b) those of Phocis, central Greece; c) Phocaea, ancient Greek colony of west Anatolia, Turkey; d) (poetic) Phoenician metaphor for modern-day Beirut, Lebanon.

The enigmatic **Meysnier** and **Manthi** are people not places. The *enclosure* could be anything. What first comes to my mind is the papal legation of Avignon. This might make Meysnier and Manthi Huguenot leaders out to insult the pope's officials. The last two lines clearly put this event in Provence. Aix suffers civil unrest, perhaps as a result of the many thousands of small incidents between Huguenots and Catholics that history overlooks. The *fury* of religious intolerance and righteousness makes people judge others. The final line may reveal our prophet's discordant relationship with Marseilles as he gives it another prophetic poke. One wonders what ego bashing went on between him and the local apothecaries and doctors to make him so bitter.

A World War II application would have **Meysnier** and **Manthi** stand for two French Resistance fighters, or double agents, who compromise the espionage cell in some way (**trouble the enclosure**). Gestapo sweeps are then doubled in Marseilles.

In a present-day or future application **Meysnier** and **Manthi** could be cryptograms for leaders in the Marseilles Mafia. Their *enclosure* becomes a safe house for hitmen on the run. The last line tells us that Mafia activities in Marseilles will increase in the 21st century.

It must be noted that **Phocens** need not always stand for Marseilles. The setting could be Greece, Turkey, or even Lebanon.

11 Q97

Par villefranche, Maſcon en désarroy,	**Through Villefranche, Mâcon in disarray,**
Dans les fagots ſeront ſoldats cachés:	**Within the bundles soldiers will be hidden:**
Changer de temps en prime pour le Roy,	**Times to change in the spring for the King,**
Par de Chalon et Moulins tous hachés.	**In Châlon and Moulins all hacked to pieces.**

Moulins is about 70 miles west of Mâcon. Villefranche, Mâcon and Châlon-sur-Saône are all on the Saône river north of Lyons. They were part of a major escape route for prisoners of war fleeing Germany during World War II. The French Resistance often hid escapees in cargo trucks and boats on their way down the Saône and Rhône rivers. It seems the escaped soldiers meet an unlucky end. But this is all speculation because the prophecy, king and all, is quite vague. Times did change in the spring of 1945 for **king** Hitler – the Nazi empire collapsed in defeat.

Century XII

12 Q4

Feu, flamme, faim, furt,¹ farouche, fumée,
Fera faillir,² froiſſant fort, foy faucher:
Flis³ de Denté toute Prouence humée,
Chaſſé de regne, enragé ſans cracher.

Fire, flame, famine, furtive, ferocious,
   fumes,
Foreseen to fail, forcibly flagellated,
   faith falsified:
For the arrow [Son?] of Denté all
   Provence sucked in,
Chased out of the realm, enraged
   without spitting.

¹Old French for secretly, furtively; robber.
²Fera fallir: (literal translation) "It will cause to fall...".
³Old French flis = arrow. Le Pelletier thinks it an erratum for fils.

This is one of those rare times when the English language can dance with Nostradamus' irrational rhyme. The first two lines give us the most complex alliteration in Les Propheties; therefore it is a little suspect. Still, one wild whack at an alliteration – whether willful, whimsical or warranted – is possible in his polemic prose or prophecies. (Phew!)

The enigma **Denté** could be for Renaissance poet Dante Alighieri (1265–1321), author of The Divine Comedy, as the first lines hint at Danté's Inferno. Some infernal con man suckers all of Provence. He is discovered, thrown out of the Provençal realm (or by extension, out of France). But **Denté** keeps his temper under control and doesn't spit at his victims. Very strange. A wide variety of people could be implied. I'm sure Nostradamus debunkers would like to project this on the future of the prophet himself, whereas believers with a bias to put everything he says into the future might finger some Marseilles Mafia kingpin being thrown out of Provence. Many translations are possible for **enraged without spitting**. With a more violent bent, it could mean "enraged blood to spurt."

I find this a bit too flashy for Nostradamus. It sounds like César or Chavigny trying to spice him up. Perhaps they edited the original? Leoni believes its style betrays it as a leftover from the Almanacs. If so, there's more garlic spicing the grammar than usual.

12 Q24

Le grand secours venu de la Guyenne,	*The great relief come from Guienne,*
S'arrestera tout auprès de Poictiers:	*Will halt quite near Poitiers:*
Lyon[1] rendu par Mont Luel et Vienne,	*Lyons [or the Lion] surrendered*
Et saccagez par tous gens de mestiers.	*through Montluel and Vienne,*
	And plundered everywhere by the
	men of arms.

[1]Either the city of Lyons or the British "Lion."

A very intriguing failed prediction, if the **great relief** was intended for an Allied invasion of Hitler's Atlantic Wall on its southwesternmost flank. The forces of the British **Lion** come ashore in June of 1944 and advance through the southwest province of Guienne, but Rommel's panzers out-flank them, and with only aircraft-carrier air support the British advance grinds to a stop near Poitiers. I suppose this will sound like a stretch to many of you, but it is no worse than the interpretation of modern Nostradamians Lemesurier and Fontbrune, who think the Atlantic in-vasion of southwest France is a counter-attack sometime in our very near future against vast (and nonexistent) Muslim navies and armies that have occupied Spain, Western Germany, and France.

If we take **Lyons** to mean the city and not the British Lion, the last two lines drop out of quantum future reverie and parallel what did happen to German forces retreating up the Rhône river valley after the second Allied landing in southern France in August of 1944. **Montluel** and **Vienne** were the escape routes of the shattered German Nineteenth Army after it abandoned Lyons, with a loss of 20,000 captured.

12 Q36

Assault farouche en Cypre se prepare,	*A ferocious assault is being prepared*
La larme à l'œil, de ta ruyne proche:	*in Cyprus,*
Byzance classe, Mortisque si grande tare,	*Tear in my eye, for your approaching*
Deux differents, le grand vast[1] par la roche.	*ruin:*
	Byzantine fleet, very great Moorish
	loss,[2]
	Two different ones, the great
	devastation by the rock.

[1]Low Latin *vastum* = devastation, annihilation.
[2]Variation: **Byzantine and Moorish fleet very great loss.**

Lemesurier applies this one yet again to a future Asiatic invasion. He wins the Asiatic Muslim Invasion sweepstakes against Fontbrune and Noorbergen with a grand total of over 450 applications! At least Font-brune does not tack this one to the future; he touts a past Muslim inva-sion, the capture and sack of Cyprus by the Turks in 1571.

12 Q52

Deux corps, vn chef, champs diuifés en deux, *Et puis repondre à quatre non ouïs:* *Petits pour grands, apertius[1] mal pour eux,* *Tour d'Aigues[2] foudre, pire pour Euffouis.[3]*	**Two corps, one commander, fields divided in two,** **And then reply to the four unheard:[4]** **Little ones for great ones, clear evil for them,** **At the Tower of Aiguesmortes, lightning, the worse for Essoyes.**

[1]Latin *apertus* = open, clear.
[2]*Tour d' Aigues* = the tower of Aigues. Either a place or poetic "The Tower of Fevers", an occult metaphor for the tower card in the Tarot (the Tower of Agues and Death). Nostradamus therefore uses a double occult pun on the town of Aiguemortes as pivotal in some future disaster. *Ague* in Old French means "sharp fever."
[3]Leoni believes it could be a cryptogram for the town of *Essoyes* in Champagne.
[4]Variant: **And then reply to the unheard quarters.**

Aiguesmortes is located on the western mouth of the Rhône. It was a noted medieval seaport, from which Louis IX embarked on his Crusades. The town of **Essoyes** comes closest to the enigma *Eussouis*, but it takes us all the way beyond the Rhône river valley to Champagne around 25 miles southeast of Troyes.

The two far-ranging towns mark the theater of operations of a 20th-century crusade. The crusaders aren't sailing from the environs of Aiguesmortes but landing there with a fleet of 1,000 warships, 3,000 planes, and 1 million men in Operation Dragoon, in August 1944. The German order of battle positioned the LXXXV and LXII corps of Wiese's Nineteenth Army along the French Riviera. The bulk of the latter corps was situated right over the site of Aiguesmortes and the western mouth of the Rhône. The initial Allied landing barrage has been referred to before as **lightning**. Indeed, anyone who has seen such shellings from afar would agree with such a description for the thunder and flash of heavy guns. The Allied advance did pass through the Troyes/Essoyes region that autumn, and did face stiffening resistance as the Germans regrouped with their backs against their own border. The northeast borders of France saw some of the least noted and most vicious battles of the Allied Western Front (**worse for Essoyes**).

12 Q55

Triftes confeils,[1] defloyaux, cauteleux, *Auis mechant, la Loy fera trahye:* *Le peuple efmeu, farouche, querelleux,* *Tant bourg que ville, toute la paix haye.*	**Sad Soviets, disloyal, cunning,** **Evil advice, the Law [of More?] will be betrayed:** **The people stirred up, ferocious, quarrelsome,** **So much that in borough as in town, the entire peace hated.**

[1]French for "Councils", or "Soviets" in Russian.

This one could be about the future consequences of Mikhail Gorbachev's dismantling of the Soviet Union. In the short term it brought an end to the Cold War, but in the long run the chaos and breakdown of Russian society may beckon a future Fascist or neo-Czarist dictator onto the scene. Like Germany after World War I, Russia could get its own Adolf Hitler who can cause another world war. Often Nostradamus has joined the chorus of modern and ancient prophets who admonished that a more prudent and patient easing of the Soviet system into capitalism would forestall Armageddon.

The **sad Soviet** hard-liners try a coup in 1991. The communists learn their lesson, just as Hitler did in his Munich Putsch. Like Hitler, they become cunning enough and think they are in a position to subvert the democratic system by using it. They make a bid to win back power in the 1996 elections, and fail.

Gorbachev is seduced by the capitalist US presidents Reagan and Bush (**evil advice**). His lack of leadership causes the communist system to collapse, undermining the Soviet experiment to create the first classless, communist society (**the Law** [of More] **will be betrayed**). The final lines foretell the coming civil wars in Russia that threaten the world and spread the sale of former Soviet nuclear weapons to terrorists. Thanks to Gorbachev, the Cold War is replaced by the chaos and horrors of a Cold Peace.

12 Q56

Roy contre Roy et le Duc contre Prince,	**King against King and the Duke against Prince,**
Haine entre iceux, diſſenſion horrible:	**Hatred between them, horrible dissension:**
Rage et fureur ſera toute prouince,	**Rage and fury will be in every province,**
France grande guerre et changement terrible.	**In France great war and terrible changes.**

The last five quatrains of fragmentary Century XII roll out a series of Wars of Religion predictions.

We start with Protestant Henry de Navarre against either Charles IX or Henry III as the Catholic King of France. At the same time lesser nobles like the Duc de Guise fight a blood feud with the Protestant Prince de Condé. A homicidal hatred boiled between Protestants and Catholics, high- or low-born. All attempts to negotiate a settlement always collapsed into horrible dissension. The religious civil wars did spread to every province. Although the actual battles were not numerous and there were long interludes of intrigue, truces, and negotiations between them, the history books fail to convey the day-to-day social strife, beatings, robberies, and petty crimes perpetrated by those righteous Catholics or

Huguenots who believed Jesus told them to punish the wicked heretics. A number of these incidents would escalate into full-scale massacres of Huguenots and Catholics in the large towns and cities of Paris, Angers, Saumur, Albi, Bourges, Rouen, and Troyes. Historians also overlook the atrocities inflicted in dozens of smaller villages and lonely farms or on the roadsides across the land. Contemporary chroniclers put the death toll of innocent victims in the hundreds of thousands.

12 Q59

L'accord et pache fera du tout rompuë:	**The accord and peace will be**
Les amitiés pollues par difcorde:	**completely broken:**
L'haine esueillie, toute foy corrompuë,	**The friendships polluted by discord:**
Et l'efperance, Marfeille fans concorde.	**Hatred aroused, all faith corrupted,**
	And hope; Marseilles without
	concord.

A continuation of the last quatrain's litany of grief and violence due to befall France in the Wars of Religion. Nostradamus wrote these extra Centuries XI and XII around the time of the first outbreak of civil war in the early 1560s. The final quatrains of Century XII could be as much a local account for Salon as a national prophecy.

12 Q62

Guerres, debats, à Bloys guerre et tumulte,	**Wars, debates, at Blois war and**
Diuers aguets, adueux inopinables:	**tumult,**
Entrer dedans Chafteau Trompette,	**Diverse watches, unexpected avowals:**
infulte,[1]	**To enter into Château Trompette,**
Chafteau du Ha, qui en feront coulpables.[2]	**affront,**
	Château du Hâ, those who will be to
	blame for it.

[1]Latin *insultum* = a leaping out at, sudden rude attack.
[2]Latin *culpabilis* = culpable, worthy of blame, criminal.

The Château Trompête and Château du Hâ were both at Bordeaux. Blois is 210 miles northeast of Bordeaux. It was the chief residence of the Valois kings during the civil wars. Nostradamus is using these geographical locations to set the stage for the Third War of Religion (1568–70). Out of Blois comes the unsuccessful plot to kidnap the Huguenot leaders, the Prince de Condé and Admiral Coligny, triggering the conflict. Charles IX is bullied by his mother, Catherine de' Medici, to send forth the Catholic army into southwest France under his brother, the Duc d'Anjou (the future Henry III). Anjou surprises and defeats the Huguenots at the battle of Jarnac on the approaches to Bordeaux. Condé is killed; however, Anjou would rather exult in his victory than pursue the surviving

Huguenots or seize Bordeaux (synecdoche: **Château du Hâ**). The seer implicates Anjou and the Catholic leadership as **those who will be to blame** for losing the initiative not only at Jarnac, but also eight months later at the battle of Montcontour.

12 Q65

A tenir fort par fureur contraindra,	**To hold the fort by fury, he will coerce,**
Tout cœur trembler. Langon aduent terrible:	**All hearts to tremble. Langon, terrible arrival:**
Le coup de pied mille pieds ſe rendra,	**The kick will return a thousand kicks,**
Guirond. Guaron, ne furent plus horribles.	**Girond, Garonne, never more furious or more horrible.**

This continues the theme of the Third War of Religion (1568–70).

The Wars of Religion were noted for their small-scale but fierce sieges against Huguenot châteaux, especially along the Dordogne river basin. I cannot find a clear historical record of a skirmish or siege in or around Langon, 25 miles upstream from Bordeaux. Either it is a quantum future avoided, or the incident is far too intimate a clash for historians of the 20th century to cite.

12 Q69

EIOVAS[1] proche eſloigner, lac Leman,	**SAVOY near to – [but] put farther away – [from] Lake Geneva,**
Fort grands appreſt, retour, confuſion:	**Very great preparations, return, confusion:**
Loin des nepueux, du feu grand Supelman,[2]	**Far from the nephews, of fire great Supelman,**
Tous de leur suyte.	**All of their following.**

[1] Anagram for Savoie (Savoy).
[2] *Superman?* Leoni believes this is simple Latin *super* = super. He then cites Roquefort's three etymological theories for *man*: a) that *mann* or *man* came into the Old French vocabulary through the Germanic roots of the Normans; b) that *mann* is an ancient Celtic word; c) and finally, the word *mann* is derived from Latin *manens* = one inhabiting, thus an inhabitant.

At face value this could forecast one more of many attempts of Nostradamus' astrological client and friend, the Duke of Savoy, to regain Geneva which the House of Savoy had lost in 1522. Circumstantial evidence supports the theory that Nostradamus lobbied hard for the Duke to reconquer the city of his bugbear, John Calvin. A closer examination uncovers a dual prophecy. The first two lines defers an attack on Geneva to the next generation. *Evoias* the *Supelman* decoded is "Savoy the Great Superman" the duke's son, Charles-Emmanuel the Great. On the night of 11 December 1602 he ordered a daring 1,000-man raid on Geneva, which was repelled and routed by its inhabitants. Most interpreters have tried unsuccessfully to fit the last two lines into this scenario. It can't be done because the **nephews** belong to another prophecy, which is hidden in the second cryptic meaning of *Supelman*.

Leoni collected an interesting etymological history and offered a persuasive argument supporting the theory that *Supelman* stands for "Superman." I would add that one could apply the law of anagram and drop the *p* to get "Suleman" then add an *i* to get "Sulieman" the Turkish sultan of Nostradamus' time. Perhaps the Christian censors cut the final passage because the last two lines foretell too clearly some military disaster inflicted on Christendom by Suleiman the Magnificent or his nephews.

12 q71

Fleuues, riuieres de mal feront obftacles,	**Rivers, streams of evil will be obstacles,**
La vieille flamme d'ire non apaifee:	**The old flame of anger unappeased:**
Courir en France; cecy comme d'oracles,	**To run in France; this as of oracles,**
Maifons, manoirs, Palais, fecte rafee.	**Houses, manors, Palace, shaven sect.**[1]

[1]Catholic priests.

The last surviving quatrain of Century XII finishes the main body of Nostradamus' prophetic works with what is most likely one parting warning about the Wars of Religion.

Presages 47–57
from the Almanac of 1560

P 47   January (1560)

Iournée, diete, interim, ne concile,	**Day's journey, diet, interim, no council,**
L'an paix prepare, peſte, faim ſchiſmatique:	**The year peace is being prepared, plague, schismatic famine:**
Mis hors dedans changer Ciel, domicile,	**Put outside inside, sky to change, domicile,**
Fin du congé,[1] reuolte hierarchique.	**End of holiday, hierarchical revolt**

[1]*Fin du congé*, cryptogram variation: *Fin du Condé* – end of Condé: turn the g upside down to get a d for the Bourbon Prince de Condé.

Here is a cluster of predictions on the Conspiracy of Amboise (P47–P49). Lines 1 and 2 cover attempts by the Queen Regent, Catherine de' Medici, François de Guise, and the Cardinal de Lorraine to convene the first Estates-General since 1484, primarily to put a stop to the growing opposition against royal centralized power after Henry II's death; and secondly, to find a way to pay the royal debt and end growing strife over the legal rights of Huguenots, who also challenged the power and profits of the crown. Line 3 is a tricky one but **outside inside** could be a riddle for the precarious political state of Coligny and Condé, the masterminds of the conspiracy of Amboise (set for March), which was an attempt to abduct or "liberate" the adolescent king Francis II from his Guise advisors. The Catholic leadership judged them traitors (**outsider**s), but Catherine prevented their execution and pardoned them because she needed their support (or **insider**s) to counterbalance the ambitious and powerful Guises.

Line 4 moves ahead to events at Amboise when the young king was ending his hunting holiday along the Loire river. Turn the g in *congé* upside-down and you get a d for "Condé," the ringleader for the conspiracy of Amboise. This is aptly described as a hierarchical revolt between greater and lesser nobles: the blood-royal Bourbons, who wanted to succeed to the French throne, versus the petty-royal House of Guise, which had usurped power as the minor king's guardians and teachers. The French Huguenots, led by the Bourbon Prince de Condé, with foreign support by other Protestant leaders, Queen Elizabeth I of England and

John Calvin in Geneva, had planned an expedition to abduct the young King Francis at the Château of Amboise and arrest the Catholic leaders around the Ides of March. Condé also advised his men that Guise and his brother the cardinal were to be given a similar coup de grace à la Julius Caesar if they resisted arrest.

P 48   February (1560)

Rompre diete, l'antiq. facré rauoir,	**Diet to break up, the ancient sacred**
Deffous les deux, feu par pardon	**one to recover,**
s'enfuyure:	**Under the two, fire through pardon to**
Hors d'armes Sacre: long Rouge voudra	**result:**
auoir,	**Consecration without arms: the tall**
Paix du neglect, L'Efleu le Vefue[1] viure.	**Red will want to have,**
	Peace of neglect, the Elected One,
	the Widow[er], to live.

[1]Vefue, a Nostradamus coinage to make le Vefue (for la Veuve, the widow) to rime with L'Efleu (the chosen, or elected one) for reasons unknown to me. Perhaps it's a play on meaning for the newly elected Pope Pius IV, who has the same name, Medici, as the widow Catherine although historians tell us they were not related. The gender ambiguity has a hidden message. The widow Catherine must rule like a **Widower**, like a man. Even though the French Salic law forbade queens of France from ruling, Catherine came closer than most to reigning over France like a king.

The first line establishes the background. The delegates leave the Imperial Diet held in Augsburg in 1555. Their convention was called the Religious Peace of Augsburg since it intended to settle the religious question in Germany and be a model for Protestants and Catholics all over Christendom to follow. The motto at Augsburg was: "There should be concluded and established a continual, firm, and unconditional peace, lasting forever." In the abstract view the ancient and sacred one **to recover** is religious tolerance itself. But events starting with the Conspiracy of Amboise would ensure that the fragile thread of tolerance would soon snap in France.

The **two** are Condé and Coligny, the ringleaders of the Conspiracy of Amboise scheduled for the following month. François de Guise is alerted to their coup. The two are arrested and 56 of their co-conspirators are executed. The crenelations of the Château Amboise will be decorated with their mangled bodies. As stated earlier, Catherine de' Medici pardons Condé and Coligny to counterbalance the power of the Guises. Ever since the death of Henry II she had been compelled to play a dangerous game of counterbalancing her allegiances of the Regency against three rival aristocratic factions (Bourbons, Montmorencys, and Guises), who were all vying for control of the throne in the royal minorities of her sons, Francis II and Charles IX. Eventually her plan to pardon Coligny and Condé would see them unleash the fires of civil war later on. If Catherine had allowed both men to be executed at Amboise, Coligny would not have been around in

1572. As it happened, Catherine ordered his assassination on St Bartholomew's Day in that year and triggered the nationwide massacre of Huguenots, which only widened the civil wars out of anyone's control.

The **tall Red** could represent the red-robed Cardinal de Lorraine, Charles de Guise, and his half-hearted attempts to make peace with the Huguenot nobility.

Out of the grammatical ambiguity of **elected . . . widow** walks the widow Catherine. She is indeed **elected** or appointed as Queen Regent over Francis II in 1560, and her shrewd pardons and counterbalancing maneuvers compel both the Guise and Bourbon factions to put some teeth into her regency.

P 49   March (1560)

Fera paroir eſleu de nouueauté,	**To be made to appear elected with**
Lieu de iournée, ſortir hors dès limites:	**novelty,**
La bonté feinte de changer cruauté,	**Place of day-labor [the historic day?],**
Du lieu ſuſpect ſortiront treſtous viſtes.	**to go beyond the boundaries:**
	The feigned goodness to change to
	cruelty,
	From the suspected place quickly will
	they all go out.

This is set for the month of the Conspiracy of Amboise. Line 1 continues the story from the last Presage. Catherine's appointment as Queen Regent gave her a lot more power than any mother of an adolescent French king before her. The Huguenot leaders Condé and Coligny feign **goodness** and plan an assassination of the Guise to "liberate" the young king from their influence. The plot is chosen for the same **historic day**, on which the Roman dictator Julius Caesar was assassinated – the Ides of March. But the hideout of their small band of co-conspirators is already known by François de Guise. Their coup is **suspected** even as the band begin their ride to Amboise. Soon they are captured and many are executed.

P 50   April (1560)

Du lieu eſleu Razes n'eſtre contens,	**With the place chosen, the Shaved**
Du lac Leman conduite non prouuée,	**Ones will not be contented,**
Renouueller on fera le vieil temps:	**Led from Lake Geneva, unproven,**
Eſpeüillera[1] la trame tant couuée.	**They will cause the old times to be**
	renewed:
	They will expose and frighten off the
	plot so well hatched.

[1]Eſpeüillera = a) Old French espewirer = to frighten; b) Provençal espelhar = to strip, despoil; c) espeüillera is a composite word for both actions of exposing and frightening.

This returns to the preliminary secret meetings held prior to the Conspiracy of Amboise between French Protestant plotters and John

Calvin in Geneva. Perhaps the meeting is placed out of time sequence on purpose to protect the prophet. The **old times** . . . **renewed** plays with the Nostradamian theme that Protestantism is a neo-pagan cult. The last line, if applied to the actions at Amboise, accurately foresees François de Guise exposing and frightening off the plot to abduct the king.

P 51   May (1560)

Pache Allobrox[1] fera interrompu,	*Savoy peace will be broken,*
Derniere main[2] fera forte leuée:	*The last hand [power] will cause a*
Grand coniuré ne fera corrompu,	*strong levy:*
Et la nouuelle alliance approuuée.	*The great conspirator will not be*
	corrupted,
	And the new alliance approved.

[1]Latin *Allobroges* = inhabitants of classical Savoy.
[2]Latin *manus* = hand, strength, authority, power, force.

Maybe this is a little note to the Duke and Duchess of Savoy, friends of Nostradamus. This would have been written the year he visited them possibly making some of the events recorded here retroactive. Savoy under Duc Emmanuel-Philibert, protégé of the Spanish King Philip II, wars with France (**peace broken**). The riddle **last hand** – or better, the **final power** – points to the Duke of Savoy, the champion of the battle of St Quentin. Here he routed a hastily collected and second-rate army of levies and German mercenaries commanded by the Constable of France, Anne de Montmorency. Perhaps Nostradamus is being sarcastic when he calls it **strong**; otherwise he is pumping up the ego of his friends and astrological clients, the Duke and Duchess of Savoy, by calling the French levy **strong**.

The last two lines may tune us into an accurate view of the good works and single-pointed virtues of the Duke. He would restore the broken prosperity of Savoy and do away with the Austrian and French factions. The **new alliance** is not clear. Perhaps it is a wishful propagation rather than prophecy. Our prophet would like Savoy to be allied with France. This of course would not be. The Duke of Savoy's son, Charles-Emmanuel the Great (1580–1630), would fight long and hard against France throughout his reign.

P 52   July (1560)

Longue crinite lefér le Gouuerneur,	*A long comet to wrong the Governor,*
Faim, fiéure ardante, feu & fang fumée:	*Hunger, burning fever, fire and reek*
A tous eftats Iouiaux[1] grand honneur,	*of blood:*
Sedition par Razes allumée.	*To all estates Jovial Ones*
	[Huguenots?] in great honor,
	Sedition by the Shaven ones, ignited.

[1]*Iouiaux* = followers of Jupiter. Nostradamus uses classical allusion to the Huguenot heresy as being some new cult of neo-pagans.

The one governing France during Francis II's minority may stand for the Lieutenant-General of France, François de Guise. The **long comet** is an occult metaphor for an evil omen. In the final days of August (not July) at the Assembly of Notables, it became evident that pressure from the Huguenot nobility had worked to confound Guise's plans to forestall convening the Estates-General. He knew the nobility of France would gang up against him, perhaps even set the stage for a coup. To add insult to conspiracy, suspicious correspondences were found on a messenger named La Sargue, who under torture implicated Antoine de Bourbon, the Prince de Condé, and a number of other notables in a new conspiracy plot. Perhaps line 2 describes La Sargue manacled to the dungeon wall, being tortured. The last line chronicles the ire of the devoutly Catholic priests who are angry with Guise for letting the Huguenots get away with too much.

The next notable comet sighting was 17 years later: the great comet of 1577. In that year Henry III defeats the Huguenots in the Sixth War of Religion and disbands the Catholic League, which at the time had Henry de Guise, the son of François de Guise, as its wronged **governor**.

P 53   *August* (1560)

Peſte, faim, feu & ardeur non ceſſée,	**Plague, famine, fire and ardor incessant,**
Foudre, grand greſle, temple du ciel frapé:	**Lightning, great hail, temple[1] struck from the sky:**
L'Edict, Arreſt, & grieue loy caſſée,	**The Edict, arrest, and grievous law broken,**
Chef inuenteur ſes gens & luy hapé.	**The chief inventor his people and himself snatched up.**

[1]What Huguenots called their place of worship.

The weather of high summer is in harmony with the mood of the land. The entire left bank of the Rhône river valley, Provence, Languedoc, Guyenne, Périgord, Poitou, and Limoges was seething with latent civil war. It had already broken out in Dauphiné. From there Maligny, a surviving leader of the conspiracy of Amboise, will lead an army of 4,500 in August to seize Lyons, the financial capital of France. The **lightning** bolt, figuratively, does hit the Huguenot **temple**. In early September Maligny's army is discovered and routed by the city's royal garrison after a hot fight. François de Guise puts the country on a war footing and mobilizes the royal regiments. The Edict of Amboise, which gave lip-service to Huguenot religious freedoms, is forgotten. By command of Guise hundreds of seditionists are arrested and the regiments of the king go on a campaign throughout the land to crush any signs of revolt.

Another lightning bolt against Huguenot leaders was hurled at the King of Navarre by Francis II in the form of a letter commanding him and

his brother, Prince de Condé, to appear in court and explain themselves
– "or else." The two were circumvented by the military demonstrations
and repressions of Guise and forced once again to seek protection from
the Queen Regent in her balance-of-power tightrope act to contain the
ambitions of the Guise.

P 54 September (1560)

Priuez feront Rafes de leurs harnois,	**Deprived will be the Shaven Ones**
Augmentera leur plus grande querelle:	**[the Roundheads?] of their arms,**
Pere Liber[1] deceu fulg.[2] Albanois,[3]	**It will augment their quarrel much:**
Seront rongées fectes à la moëlle.	**Father Liber [Bacchus, god of wine?]**
	deceived lightning Albanians,
	Sects will be gnawed to the marrow.

[1]Late Latin *Liber*, the Italian deity associated with Bacchus as god of wine. Or Bacchus
himself. Possibly the implication is that someone is being made drunk.
[2]*fulg.*: apocope of Latin *fulgur* = lightning.
[3]Either Albanians, "those of Alba," or classical Albania, the modern-day Trans-Caucasian
region.

It seems our prophet is frantically turning the dial of time to find the right
station in the future. The presage might better fit an English civil war of
the next century. But just as we seem to have a clear signal the dial slips
from armed Roundheads of Oliver Cromwell to squeal and whine farther
forward into tomorrow's many interpretations of **Albanians**. Take your
pick which Albanians are intended here. Are they contemporary Spanish
mercenaries of the Duke of Alva? Are they the people of Albion, the
ancient name of the English? Could they be Albanians in any one of
a half dozen Balkan conflicts in the last four centuries, including in the
1990s? Maybe they are Nostradamus' other classical **Albanians** in modern-day Trans-Caucasia. If so, his dial is working around the time station
of either the Chechen War or the Armenian–Azeri conflict of the 1990s.

Father Liber is another word-bender. Is he Father Liberty, ie the
United States, or an Italian wino of a deity associated with Bacchus? And
what is our divinely all-American democratic or deified drunken
metaphor doing to deceive the **lightning** Albanians?

All this is beyond me. When in doubt, let's start with an interpretation
for the present. The lightning of the Albanians could be their sudden terrorist strikes on the United States from the Caucasus region. Another
Albanian connection may swing closer to the 17th-century sudden
attack by the English on the Dutch during their many naval disputes in
that era. We can turn the dial of time farther back to 1588 and get Alva's
successor, the Duke of Parma, assembling an invasion army against
England in the Spanish Netherlands. While he is waiting to be ferried
across the Channel by the Spanish Armada, Parma's invasion is foiled by

a **lightning** night attack of the English fleet. They guide flaming hulks into the multitude of Spanish galleons, scattering the Armada.

P 55 October (1560)

Sera receuë la requeſte decente,	**The modest request will be received,**
Seront chaffez & puis remis au ſus:	**They will be driven out and then**
La Grande Grande ſe trouuera contente,	**restored on top:**
Aueugles, ſourds ſeront mis au deſſus.	**The Great Great woman will be found**
	content,
	Blind ones, deaf ones will be put
	uppermost.

We move back to 1560, to be presciently present at the much-awaited meeting of the young king with Antoine de Bourbon and the Prince de Condé at Orléans. The two must explain themselves in the face of evidence pointing to their involvement with the Huguenot conspiracies of the summer. It is hard to say what is **modest** about the request of the king for the meeting. Perhaps our seer is being sarcastic. At first the meeting revealed how the immature King Francis II could sound decisive when properly coached by the Guises and banishment for Antoine de Bourbon and execution of Condé seemed possible. But Catherine de' Medici (**the Great Great woman**), seeing the Bourbons at the mercy of their enemies, could use maternal pressure to deflect the danger by undermining the king's passion for severe punishment. Soon a new development would silence the high-pitched rattling voice of Francis castigating the Bourbon princes. He fell seriously ill after a session of violent horse-riding and exercise. His eventual death in December would pave the way for the two Bourbons to be restored and pardoned (**restored on top**). Catherine could at least content herself with her enhanced role as Queen Regent of yet another and far younger son in his royal minority, Charles IX. Her bluffs also succeeded in persuading Antoine de Bourbon to formally renounce any claim to the regency. The final line reveals the seer's general repugnance for the leadership of France, knowing full well, from his seer's vantage point, that the bloody civil wars and reigns of the last Valois were still to come.

P 56 November (1560)

Ne ſera mis, les nouueaux dechaſſez,	**He will not be placed, the New Ones**
Noir[1] & de LOIN[2] et le Grand tiendra fort:	**expelled,**
Recourir armes. Exilez plus chaſſez,	**Black king [from afar] and the Great**
Chanter victoire, non libres reconfort.	**One will hold hard:**
	To have recourse to arms. Exiles
	expelled further,
	To sing of victory, not free, consolation.

[1]Near anagram for *noir/roy*, black king.
[2]Capitals may indicate word play for *Lion, Lyon* (lion or Lyons), or *Loing de* = from afar.

This continues the overview of events from the royal audience in Orléans in the autumn to the new regency of Charles IX. The Bourbon leaders, Antoine de Bourbon, King of Navarre, and the Prince de Condé, **will not be placed** as regent. The second line gives us the *noir-roi* cryptogram Nostradamus uses as a device for Charles IX. The adolescent king who gave our prophet honors in 1564 is characterized as a **black king** because of the evils he will bring to France as the weak and malleable neurotic who gives permission for the nationwide massacres of Huguenots during the coming St Bartholomew's Day massacre. The **Great One** is François de Guise, who for a few years more will hold tenaciously to his power both as Lieutenant-General of France and as the boy-king's chief advisor. Line 3 is a general commentary on the national emergency and the continued persecution and repression of the Huguenot minority. Thousands sought safety in Protestant Geneva and other principalities. For many it was the second exile (**expelled further**) within a few years. The Guises and Catherine can **sing of victory** at suppressing the second Huguenot rebellion before it broke out, but the Bzyantine quality of French royal politics and the large minority of Huguenots prevent complete freedom of action. Therefore, once again **consolation** rather than conflict is proffered.

P 57   *December* (1560)

Les duels laiſſez, ſupremes alliances,	**The mourning left behind, supreme alliances,**
Razes grand mort, refus fait à l'entrée:	**Great Shaven One dead, refusal given at the entrance:**
De retour eſtre bien fait en oubliance,[1]	**Upon return kindness to be in oblivion,**
La mort du iuste à banquet perpetrée.	**The death of the just one perpetrated at a banquet.**

[1]Old French *oubliance* = oblivion, forgetfulness.

Rather than chronicling the death of Francis II for December, this presage seems to hiccup forward in time 14 years to the final days of 1574 and the foreseen death of Charles de Guise, Cardinal de Lorraine (**Great Shaven One**). He died at age 49 from catching a cold from walking barefoot while leading a holy procession of flagellating monks. His death was given little official notice. Even his bitter rival, Catherine de' Medici, hearing the news when sitting down for dinner, was at pains to make a post-mortem statement which had little weight. After a few perfunctory reflections that had no effect on her guests, she hissed loudly, "Today has died the wickedest of men!" and attacked her dinner with gusto. But his ghost is said to have haunted her. A week later, while at dinner, Catherine let out a cry and dropped her wine glass. She swore she had seen the cardinal's ghost. For weeks afterwards she passed through a strange state of mourning. Unable to stop thinking about him, she suffered that per-verse and intimate loss that only those who have survived the death of a lifetime enemy can feel. Catherine's mourning would be **left behind** and replaced with foreboding for her favorite son, Henry III, soon to be crowned king of France. He was emotionally high-strung and quickly dis-couraged. He had returned from Poland already chafing to get out from under the domination of his mother, who wanted to wage a fifth civil war with the Huguenots. By December 1574 he had decided to negotiate with the Protestant Confederacy and make peace (**supreme alliances**). Time shifts forward once again and the final two lines move us ahead to the last months of 1588. Their chilling poetry gives us a view of how Henry III would later seal his end by plotting to assassinate his chief rival, the petty-royal Henry de Guise. In fairness to the king – who, all faults aside, Nostradamus acknowledges as the *just* blood royal to be sitting on the throne – Guise's desire to assassinate him was mutual. An Italian actor acting as the king's informant was present at a dinner given by Henry de Guise's brother, the Cardinal de Guise. A toast was proposed to Henry de Guise: that he should become the next King of France (**death . . . perpetrated at a banquet**). The king would **return** the **kindness** upon Henry de Guise and the cardinal when they returned to the king's coun-try residence at Château Bois, and have both men assassinated. This deed would precipitate his own assassination in the following year.

P 58 *On the said year* (1561)

Le Roy Roy n'eftre, du Doux[1] la pernicie,[2]
L'an peftilent, les efmeus nubileux:
Tien' qui tiendra[3] des grands non leticie,
Et paffera terme de cauilleux.

The King, King not to be, destruction
  by the Clément one,
The year pestilent, the beclouded
  stirred up:
For the great nobles every man for
  himself, no joy:
And the term of the mockers will pass.

[1]Latin *dolcis*, Old French *doux*: mild, gentle; Clément.
[2]Latin *pernicies* = destruction, ruin, disaster, calamity. Le Pelletier was the first to argue that *Doux la pernicie* is the key to decoding line 1 for the assassination of Henry III (King of Poland and France – "King, King") by Jacques Clément.
[3]*Tien' qui tiendra*: Le Pelletier suggests this is from Latin *teneat qui tenebit*, let him hold onto (what) he may grasp or "every man for himself."

Nostradamus detains us in the 1580s, giving us a prophetic coda to a quatrain published back in 1555: the famous prophecy of the assassination of Henry III in 1 Q97. The **King, King not to be** is Henry III who, before he ascended the French throne was King of Poland. He met a pernicious end, leaning close to hear a whispered message from a seemingly agreeable and gentle Dominican friar, Brother Clément, who then stabbed him with a concealed dagger. The year **beclouded** and **pestilent** is not 1561 but 1589. With Henry III's murder the House of Valois has fallen, leaving the greatest nobles, Mayenne of Guise and Henry de Navarre, to fight a free-for-all battle for the French throne. The **mockers** are the fanatic Catholic and anti-royalist leaders of the Paris "Sixteen," who would be ruthlessly overthrown by Mayenne.

P 59 *March* (1561)

Au pied du mur le cendré cordigere,[1]
L'enclos liuré foulant caualerie:
Du temple gors Mars & le Falcigere,[2]
Hors, mis, demis, & fus la refueruie.

At the foot of the wall the ashy
  Franciscan,
The enclosure delivered, the cavalry
  trampling:
Outside the temple Mars and the
  Scythe of Saturn,
Outside, to divide the friends, and
  upon the reverie [musing].

[1]Medieval Latin *Cordiger* = Franciscan.
[2]Latin *falciger* = one who carries a scythe – a symbol of Saturn.

We return to the time track of March 1561. The vindictive and weak Antoine de Bourbon is pressed by the English to exert his legitimate claims to the throne and lead France into the Protestant camp, since he is next in blood line for the crown after the nervy and immature boy king, Charles IX.

Line 1 is a riddle I can't crack. Line 2 is poetic for the unchastened Prince de Condé, who took his acquittal for the conspiracy of Amboise as a favor and turned around to marshal troops in March. **Temple** is the name for a Huguenot house of worship; thus the **temple Mars** represents the Huguenots more in the mood for war-ship than worship. This mood will bring on a rebellion of the Grim Reaper, **Saturn** (Nostradamus' symbol of evil revolutions). Saturn's color is black, and many Huguenots adopted black clothing to set themselves apart from what they viewed as the more decadent opulent attire worn by Catholics.

The Huguenots will become defiant and militant in this year. The issue of religion will divide thought (**musings**) and **divide** friend against friend in bloody civil wars. The moment this prophecy hit the bookstands, Nostradamus was already divining images and composing quatrains for the first of several civil wars to begin in 1562.

P 60   April (1561)

Le temps purgé, peſtilente tempeſte,	**The times purged, pestilential tempest,**
Barbare inſult, fureur, inuaſion:	**Barbarian insult, fury, invasion:**
Maux infinis par ce mois nous appreſte,	**Infinite evils for this month [are] prepared for us,**
Et les plus Grands, deux moyns, d'irriſion.	**And the Greatest Ones, two less, of mockery.**

Line 1 gives a general apocalyptic overview of the deepening conflicts over religion that kept staining the fabric of life in France. This line can be the prophet's personal account of disturbances in Salon itself, with its roving gangs of Catholic hoods (Cabans) assaulting anyone who is different or well-to-do, let alone Protestant. Small and numerous raids (**invasions**) along the French Riviera by Barbary Corsairs (**Barbarian insult**) were almost endemic during the early 1560s.

Line 3 demonstrates Nostradamus' consistent ability to predict the near future through astrology. April 1561 in particular was noted for religious agitation across the length and breadth of France, culminating in religious riots in Paris. April also hosted the preliminary assemblies around France that chose representatives for the scheduled meeting of the Estates-General. These assemblies gave foreboding indications that Catherine's regency of the minor King Charles IX would be contested.

Line 4 is pretty cryptic. I would guess that the **two less** to be mocked by the Catholic leadership would be the Huguenots Antoine de Bourbon and the Prince de Condé, who were by now a real threat.

P 61 May (1561)

Ioye non longue, abandonné des fiens,	**Joy not long, abandoned by his followers,**
L'an peftilent, le plus Grand affailly:	**The year pestilent, the Greatest One**
La Dame bonne aux champs Elyfiens,	**assailed:**
Et la plus part des biens froid non cueilly.	**The good Lady in the Elysian Fields,**
	And the greater part of the cold goods
	not gathered.

By saving his skin more than once, Catherine de' Medici had tried to make it clear to Antoine de Bourbon that his authority was only nominal to hers with regard to the regency of Charles IX. But this *joy* or satisfaction she felt from outwitting Antoine de Bourbon was not long lived. By May nearly all court watchers at home and abroad understood that she was a Queen Regent who could be intimidated. The pestilential dissension and political maneuvers of 1561 continued to infect the land with more discord. In the spring of 1561 the amnesty of Condé scandalized the Catholics and encouraged the Protestants to commit illegal acts of public assembly and reopening of their temples. The **Greatest One** could be Charles IX in his minority, who was crowned in Reims on 15 May. It was a ceremony noted for its lack of opulence, for the kingdom was on the verge of bankruptcy. It is recounted that the crown placed upon the boy's head was so heavy that after standing through the hours of ritual he was seen to weep silent tears of pain.

Although I cannot find a clear reason for it, the general drift of the presages makes me speculate that the **good Lady in the Elysian Fields** may be offering another homage to Catherine de' Medici. This is the second time I find Nostradamus using this device for someone searching for the peace and rest of heaven, represented here in the classical description of the Elysian Fields (the paradise of very early Greek mythology), see 9 Q97.

Line 4 is obscure. Perhaps it describes a local account of a bad crop? It could be some cryptic poetry for the Huguenots themselves (**cold goods**) not being gathered up and incarcerated.

P 62 June (1561)

Courfes de LOIN,[1] *ne s'appreſter*	**Incursions of the Lion [Lyons?], not to**
conflicts,	**prepare for conflicts,**
Trifte entreprife, l'air peftilent, hideux:	**Sad enterprise, the air pestilent, hideous:**
De toutes parts les Grands feront afflicts,[2]	**From all sides the Great Ones will be**
Et dix & fept affaillir vingt & deux.	**afflicted,**
	And ten and seven to assail twenty and
	two.

[1]Double-pun for Old French *Loing* (afar) and *Lion*, or *the English Lion from afar.*
[2]Old French *aflit*, afflicted, thrown down.

Incursions of the Lion is an allusion to English pressure on the King of Navarre, Antoine de Bourbon, to seize the crown from the regency of Catherine de' Medici. The *sad enterprise* could be the delusions of François de Guise, who was busy forming a coalition of Catholic leaders, ostensibly to protect the faith but in reality to propel him to the throne. On 5 June Guise would lead the procession of the Fête-Dieu through the crowded streets of Paris. To his ears and eyes the loud ovations and waving arms of thousands of Catholic Parisians were a consecration of his cause. He seemed not to care that he was escorting the Catholic child-king and the Protestant King of Navarre, who were riding a few paces behind.

The *Great Ones . . . afflicted* will be the Catholic Triumvirate of François de Guise, the Constable of France, Anne de Montmorency, and the Maréchal de St André, who had buried their own legendary rivalries to create an alliance of Catholic nobles against the Huguenots. This would lead to the formation of the Catholic League, and later, to civil war.

Here are some interesting possibilities for the cryptic numbers of the last line: It took 23 days (*twenty and two*) of deliberation for the fanatically Catholic Assembly of Parliament to pass a verdict canceling all concessions made to the Huguenots. This effectively cleared the way for a return to the old methods of persecution and repression. Their verdict became the basis for Catherine de' Medici's Edict of July (7th month?), a provisional edict that required ratification in the upcoming National Council. A document of calculated obscurity rivaling the nebulous writing of our prophet was intended by its authors to cool the Assembly's religious Catholic extremism and pacify the Huguenots. Catherine understood that the new Catholic Triumvirate could be as much of a menace to the throne as the growing religious discord throughout the country.

P 63   *July* (1561)

Repris, rendu, efpouuanté du mal,
Le fang par bas, & les faces hydeufes:
Aux plus fçauans Pignare efpouuantal,
Pefte, haine, horreur, tomber bas la
    piteufe.

Retaken, surrendered, terror-stricken
    by the evil,
The blood far inferior [below?], and
    the faces hideous:
To the most knowledgeable ones the
    ignorant one frightful,
Plague, hatred, horror, the piteous
    female to fall low.

The first two lines could almost describe some terror machine, or a group of lowly born ruffians (*blood far inferior*). Maybe these are Cabans taunting the prophet in the streets of Salon.

Line 3 could take us back to the National Council in Paris, which began on the last day of July 1561. History also calls this the Colloquy of Poissy. Théodore de Bèze, John Calvin's right-hand man, had been invited by Catherine de' Medici to travel all the way from Geneva to speak before the cardinals and Catholic leadership (*the most knowledgeable ones*). All went well enough until Bèze made a heretical remark concerning the Holy Eucharist. Catherine's experiment was a failure. She tried to save her reputation by calling Bèze's visit a success, explaining that she had intended to expose and discredit the Protestant doctrine by luring Bèze before the National Council to vent his heresies (*the ignorant one frightful*).

The gamble backfired. **Plagues, hatreds** and the **horror** of religious civil war would follow. Catherine de' Medici is the **piteous female** who gambled and lost credibility at Poissy. She suffered bitter criticism from Rome during her audience with the Jesuit General Lainez. He lectured her severely about temporal rulers meddling in religious affairs. She said nothing in her defense; tears welled up in her eyes. Her **fall** could be more subjective than literal. Ralph Roeder in his book *Catherine de Medici and the Lost Revolution* (page 293) gives us a good definition of her main character flaw: "She had the invincible quality of never knowing when she was vanquished, because she had the inveterate defect of not understanding why she had failed."

P 64　August (1561)

Mort & faifi, des nonchalans le change,[1]	**Dead and seized, the nonchalant ones [of] the exchange,**
S'elongnera en s'approchant plus fort:	**They [it] will go far away in approaching more strongly:**
Serrez vnis en la ruyne, grange,	**United ones locked up in the ruin, barn,**
Par fecours long eftonné le plus fort.	**Through long help the strongest one astonished.**

[1]Either change, or exchange.

Here Nostradamus leads us forward in time to see how the seeds sown at Poissy will bring a harvest of wrath by early 1562.

On 1 March François de Guise, with his family and an armed troop of 200 men, was passing through the town of Vassy. A tolling church bell caught his attention. He was told a congregation of Huguenots were assembling for worship. At first he thought to observe their service, but then remembered it was Sunday and decided to attend mass instead. As it turned out, the Catholic church was next to the local grange (**barn**) where the Huguenots were congregating. Their singing was loud enough to drown out Guise's devotions. Servants were sent next door to admonish them. There was some pushing and shoving. When Guise appeared someone threw stones at him. His escort unsheathed their swords and charged the barn. Thirty Protestants were slaughtered and 130 wounded.

Line 1 gives us a picture of how easy it was (**nonchalant**) for the bodyguards of Guise to lose control and inflict carnage at the barn in a violent **exchange**. Line 2 recounts the travel itinerary of Guise before the incident at Vassy. First his entourage would cross the Rhine to visit the Duke of Würtemburg at Saverne (**far away** from his own lands of Lorraine). Upon returning to France he journeyed again to his estates in Nanteuil, which are closer to his home base of Orléans, (**approaching much more**). The **one astonished** could be Guise in a state of shock at the end of the massacre. Soon the news of the event would astonish people across France and launch the First War of Religion.

P 65   October (1561)

Gris, blancs & noirs, enfumez,[1] *&* *froquez,*[2]	**Gray, whites and blacks, hidden, and broken,**
Seront remis, demis, mis en leurs sieges:[3]	**They will be put off, divided, put in their sieges:**
Les rauasseurs se trouueront mocquez,	**The ravishers will find themselves mocked,**
Et les Vestales serrées en fortes rieges.[4]	**And the Vestals [virgins?] confined behind strong bars.**

[1]Old French *enfumer* = to disguise, hide; (figuratively) to create a smoke screen.
[2]Provençal *frocar* = to break, to be put out of combat.
[3]Either seats, or sieges.
[4]Provençal *riege* = grill, bars, grating.

As we have seen from the last quatrain, the vision of future events has jumped ahead six to nine months to 1562. This is a general description of what was to come in the nine French Wars of Religion, which included a number of sieges, since the Huguenots and Catholics relied on their fortified towns for security. In addition to an occasional full-scale battle thousands of smaller skirmishes, forays, raids, and pillaging punctuated the struggle. Heap on top of this the usual brutality of religious wars in which the righteous of both sides seem to think that the same God and his Son sanction their mass rapes and massacres of the other, and you have the weary, centuries-old justification for killing one's fellow man.

Presages 66–78
from the Almanac of 1562

✤✦✤

P 66   On the said year (1562)

Saiſon d'hiver, ver bon, ſain, mal eſté,	*Season of winter, good spring, sound, bad summer,*
Pernicieux autone, ſec, froment rare:	*Pernicious autumn, dry, wheat rare:*
Du vin aſſez, mal yeux, faits, moleſté,	*Of wine enough, bad eyes, deeds, molested,*
Guerre, mutin, ſeditieuſe tare.	*War, mutiny, seditious waste.*

The first three lines could be a general view of any year, but the final line is right on target for the **war** and mutinies of early 1562 that led to the first of nine Wars of Religion.

P 67   January (1562)

Deſir occulte pour le bon paruiendra,	*The hidden desire for the good will succeed,*
Religion, paix, amour & concorde:	*Religion, peace, love and concord:*
Lepitalame du tout ne s'accordra,	*The nuptial song will not be completely in accord,*
Les hauts qui bas, & haut mis à la corde.	*The high ones, who [are] low, and high, put to the rope.*

This accurately foretells Catherine de' Medici's highest moment in diplomacy, the creation of the Edict of January. This was her last chance (**hidden desire**) to bring peace to Catholics and Protestants by legalizing the co-existence of two religions in one state. But Nostradamus' hopeful poetry begins to snag by the third line, with a perverse euphemism that this new marriage of religions was not **completely in accord**. In fact France was a powder keg ready to explode. The last line leaves no doubt that such desires were doomed. Indeed many nobles (**high ones**) from both sides who gave peace one last chance would later be hanged or slaughtered when civil war broke out a few months later. Taking the **rope** metaphor one poetic step further: in the aftermath of the massacre of Protestants at Vassy (see P64) the perpetrator, François de Guise, sent for the justice of the peace of Vassy to rebuke him for allowing Protestants to assemble. The magistrate reminded Guise of the Edict of January, at which Guise brushed him off, saying, "The sword will soon cut the knot of the edict." Cut the knot it would, and leave many a citizen of France in the curve of the hangman's rope because of their religious beliefs.

P 68 February (1562)

Pour Razes Chef ne paruiendra à bout,	For the Shaven Ones the Chief will not reach the end,
Edicts changez, les secrets mis au large:	Edicts changed, the secret ones set at large:
Mort Grand trouué, moins de foy, bas debout,	Great One found dead, less of faith, low [in] standing,
Dissimulé, transi frappé à bauge.[1]	Dissimulated, shuddering, wounded in the boar's lair.

[1] Old French for hut; wretched abode, boar's lair.

Here the assassination of fiery François de Guise is set for the beginning of 1562, though it should be placed for early 1563. This presage works best if you read it backwards from line 4 to line 1. Guise – who, it could be said, started the war with his massacre at Vassy – did all he could to keep the conflict going until there was a clear Catholic victory. He was the last obstacle to peace; leaders on both sides were ready to call it a draw so they could join forces and eject the English, who had seized the ports of Le Havre and Dieppe. On the day before Guise planned his final all-out assault on the city of Orléans, he was riding down a lane with several companions when an assassin hiding behind a hedge shot him dead.

Perhaps Nostradamus foresees the Duke's final moments as his body shudders in a heap on the lane. The phrase **in the boar's lair** can make an interesting poetic description for the assassin, crouching in his lair in the hedge, taking aim at Guise.

Line 3 is Guise's obituary: **less of faith** (indeed, he was more pugilistic than pious, a man of holy war, not holy wafers) **low [in] standing** (he was a usurper, a lesser royal, and his rise to the highest posts next to the king had irked the greater noble houses like the Bourbons).

Lines 2 and 1 give us the dénouement. With his death Huguenots and Catholics sign the Peace of Amboise, which will grant Huguenots limited toleration (**edicts changed**) but which doesn't satisfy the Huguenots, who believe the Catholic leaders are sending spies abroad (**secret ones set at large**) to plan an international Catholic conspiracy against them. As time passes the Catholic leaders and the priesthood see Guise as the martyr of their cause. He was the chief of the Holy League who, because of his assassination cannot achieve his cherished objective (**will not reach the end**): the annihilation of the Huguenots.

P 69 March (1562)

Efmeu de LOIN, de LOIN[1] pres minera,	Moved by [the English] Lion, near [the
Pris, captive, pacifié par femme:	English] Lion he will undermine,
Tant ne tiendra comme on barginera,	Taken, captive, pacified by a woman:
Mis non paffez, ofter de rage l'ame.	He will not hold as well as they will
	waver,
	Placed unpassed, to oust the soul
	from rage.

[1]LOIN . . . de LOIN: either the English Lion or the city of Lyons. The latter translation of the line would read: **Moved by Lyons, near Lyons he will undermine.**

It would seem the obvious thing to tag this presage for events in Lyons. If this, however, is an accurate forecast for events in 1562, we must replace "Lyon" with the "Lion" of England. Elizabeth I sent troops to the Normandy ports of Le Havre and Dieppe, ostensibly to support French Huguenots (**pacified by a woman**).

The riddle of line 2 aptly describes the battle of Dreux, which was fought in north-central France, near the ports seized by the English (**near [the] Lion**). The Huguenot cavalry under the command of Gaspar de Coligny, Admiral of France, and the Prince de Condé repelled the weaker royal cavalry attack led by the commander of the Catholic Forces of the King and the Holy League, Anne de Montmorency, the Constable of France. The Catholic cavalry was no match for the hymns, hue, and cry of the fanatic Protestant troopers. The Catholic horsemen wavered and Montmorency was captured. Next the Huguenot cavalry pursued the retreating Catholic army and found themselves equally repulsed by the serried ranks of Catholic infantry. This time Coligny was captured. Thus, as Nostradamus puts it: **He** [Coligny] **will not hold as well as they** [the Catholic cavalry] **will waver**.

The last line's riddle could imply that in captivity the two leaders eventually negotiated the Peace of Amboise through which, at least for a short time, the **souls** of French Hugenots and Catholics were prohibited by a peace arrangement **from** acting on their **rage**. In other words this awkward moral, set in the worst kind of Nostradamian convolutions of grammar, means: any peace arranged by generals is just another time of preparation for the next civil war.

P 70 April (1562)

De LOIN[1] viendra fufciter pour mouuoir,	From Lion (England) he will come to
Vain defcouuert contre peuple infiny:	arouse to move,
De nul cogneu le mal pour le deuoir,	Vain discovery against infinite people:
En la cuifine trouué mort & finy.	Known by none the evil for the duty,
	In the kitchen found dead and finished.

[1]Either the English Lion or the city of Lyons.

I would again use **Lion** for the Lion of England rather than Lyons. The occupation of the ports of Dieppe and Le Havre by the English did not sit well with either Huguenots or Catholics. Nostradamus often describes the French as the *infinite people*. They see the support of the English for the Huguenot cause as vain and exploitative of all French people. After the Treaty of Amboise, Catholic and Huguenot patriots evict the English from these ports.

I can't untangle the last two lines. I suppose someone is poisoned. A food taster perhaps. All seriousness aside, given the hygiene of the times I wonder why there aren't more prophecies of bucolic botulism in the kitchen broth.

P 71   May (1562)

Rien d'accordé, pire plus fort & trouble,	**Nothing in accord, worse and more severe trouble,**
Comme il éstoit, terre & mer tranquiller:	**As it was, land and sea to quieten:**
Tout arresté, ne vaudra pas vn double,	**All arrested, it will not be worth a double,**
Dira l'iniq, Conseil d'annichiler.	**The iniquitous one will speak, Counsel of annihilation.**

A general comment on the First War of Religion. Nothing is in accord between the Catholic and Huguenot leaders, who after the death of Henry II move from bad relations to worse, until the powder keg of Christian love and toleration explodes with an all-out test of who's "bad" in the love of the Lamb. Take your pick for which *iniquitous* Huguenot or Catholic leader Nostradamus is tapping. Most likely our prophet means François de Guise, who was the most vocal of those in the Holy League, here counseling *annihilation* of Protestants in France.

P 72   June (1562)

Portenteux fait, horrible & incroyable,	**Portentous deed, horrible and incredible,**
Typhon[1] fera esmouuoir les meschans:	**Typhoon [Tison/rash one?] will make the wicked ones move:**
Qui puis apres souftenus par le cable,[2]	**Those who then afterwards supported by the cable [communication?],**
Et la plufpart exilez fur les champs.	**And the greater part exiled on the fields.**

[1]*Typhon* = a) Old French *typhon* = rash, bold; b) *Tison* = brand, firebrand, revolutionary; c) Greek *tuphōn* and Arabic *tufan* = typhoon (Kidogo); d) Hermetic for *Tiphon*, the Dragon representing ignorance, perversion, unconsciousness, the devourer of souls.
[2]A thick cord; (poetic) communication.

To all intents and purposes, this is about the First War of Religion, but an application farther ahead to the early 1600s is possible. **Typhoon** can stand for the rue Tison, the street in Paris close to the assassination site of Antoine de Bourbon's son, Henry de Navarre (the future Henry IV of France) 48 years hence in May of 1610 (a month earlier than targeted here). But lest we forget how prone these presages can be to other interpretations, I am tempted to jump ahead 379 Junes into the future to 22 June 1941, and Hitler's invasion of Russia.

The **portentous deed** is Hitler's launching the greatest offensive in history: 3,000,000 men, 3,580 panzer tanks and armored vehicles, 600,000 other motorized vehicles, 1,830 planes, 7,184 guns, and 750,000 supply horses make a surprise attack on the Soviet Union along a thousand-mile front. Hitler himself commented on the day of the offensive that "the world will hold its breath." The invasion of Russia is an incredible deed, since Hitler had signed a Non-Aggression Pact with Stalin just a few years before. Hitler's final push for Moscow was code-named Operation **Typhoon.** The **wicked ones** are the extreme ideologues fighting on both sides, who made the Eastern Front World War II's most savage arena of battle. The Soviet communists ignored the Geneva Convention and the Nazis were instructed to view the Slavs as subhuman, destined to be culled by the tens of millions to fulfill Hitler's dream of **Lebensraum** (living space) for the Ayran master race. Line 3 could be a 16th-century man's attempt to describe the radio and telephone cables used by the signal corpsmen in a modern war. The final line is another way of describing the millions captured by both sides who were forced to tend the fields of slave labor camps. A total of 2 million German and nearly 5 million Soviet soldiers were captured in three years of fighting.

P 73   July (1562)

Droit mis au throſne du ciel venu en France,	**Right put on the throne come into France from the sky,**
Pacifié par vertu l'Vnivers:[1]	**The whole world pacified by Virtue:**
Plus ſang eſpandre, bien toſt tourner change,	**Much blood to scatter, sooner change to come,**
Par les oyſeaux, par feu, & non par vers.[2]	**By the birds, and by fire, and not by vers.**

[1]Vnivers = a) universe; b) Old French usually applies it to "the whole world."
[2]Latin vir = man; vers. Serpens = motto of Catherine de' Medici.

We return to the events of 1562 and find Nostradamus promising divine intervention on the side of the Catholic throne of France. Then the civil wars will end and peace will descend on the world.

As if . . . !

This starts as a hopeful but hopelessly wrong prophecy by one who is burdened with the visions of war. But our prophet recovers his apocalyptic equilibrium in the final lines. The Peace of Amboise would last a mere four years. Peace is indeed *for the birds*. The *fire* for war is kindled, not the peace as desired by **Vers** Serpens, the cryptic title for the serpentine coat of arms of Catherine de' Medici who, in her own warped way, tried harder than any other leader of the time to reconcile Huguenots and Catholics in France.

P 74   August (1562)

Les coulorez, les Sacres malcontens,
Puis tout à coup par Androgyns alegres:
De la pluſpart voir, non venu le temps,
Pluſieurs d'entr'eux feront leurs ſoupes
    maigres.

*The colored ones, the Sacred
    malcontents,
Then suddenly through the happy
    Androgynes:
Of the greater part to see, the time
    not come,
Several amongst them will make their
    soups weak.*

This is a macabre presage. If it centers on the year 1562, we have nothing clearly historical to latch onto. Perhaps the riddles of the first two lines represent hermaphroditic priests or nuns of some Christian order who cook a weak soup that upsets the tummies of an entire monastery or nunnery.

Maybe this is a monastery of another kind. I would not rule out the possibility that the **Androgynes** could be Rajneeshees in their Indian ashram in the late 1970s, where both frolicking sexes wore robes and both men and women grew the long tresses.

I meditated there in 1980–81, and can tell you that the soup was thick and delicious.

But finally, I have to partly agree with the projected reveries of Jochmans, that this could be about an androgynous humanity in the distant future preparing for the next step in human evolution. Regretfully, I have to warn you all that the future will see a marked de-evolution of *soups*.

P 75   September (1562)

Remis ſeront en leur pleine puiſſance,
D'vn point d'accord conioints, non
    accordez:
Tous defiez, plus aux Razes fiance,
Pluſieurs d'entr'eux à bande debordez.

*They will be returned to their full
    power,
Conjoined at one point of the accord,
    not in accord:
All defied, more promised to the
    Shaven Ones,
Several amongst them outflanked in a
    band.*

They could be anyone, but if we have returned to the First War of Religion of 1562, **they** are probably the two opposing commanders at the inconclusive and bloody Battle of Dreux, the Huguenot Prince de Condé and the Constable of France, Anne de Montmorency, leader of the Catholic forces. In the following year the two prisoners negotiated the Peace of Amboise, which awarded measured religious toleration for the Huguenots. The latter half of the presage forebodes doom for this accord that is **not in accord**. A second civil war would break out in 1567 when the Huguenot leaders, Condé and Coligny, would lead a band of 1,500 horsemen in an attempt to abduct the royal family. They believe the young king Charles IX is becoming involved in an international Catholic conspiracy backed by Rome. In other words, **the accord** is **not in accord** because of the rumored perfidy of the **Shaven Ones** – the Catholic priests and their pope. The Huguenot abduction runs afoul when it is **outflanked** by Catholic units at Meaux.

P 76   October (1562)

Par le legat du terreftre & matin,	**For the legate of terrestrial and [at] dawn,**
La grande Cape[1] à tout s'accommoder:	**The great Cape [Capet/Pope?] will accommodate himself to all:**
Eftre à l'efcoute tacite LORVARIN,[2]	**Tacit LORRAINE, to be listening,**
Qu'à fon aduis ne voudra accorder.	**He whose advice they will not want to agree with.**

[1] *La grand Cape* = usually *the great cape* (or cope) of the Pope.
[2] Cryptogram for LORRAINE, ie François de Guise, head of the petty-royal house of Lorraine.

One interpretation would return us to the autumn of 1562 and the closing months of the First War of Religion. **Tacit LORRAINE** could be the Cardinal de Lorraine, the brother of François de Guise, who headed the French delegation at the Council of Trent in Rome. There one might find him **listening** to Pope Pius IV, but Pius and a majority of the representative legates did not agree with the Cardinal de Lorraine's view that bishops should have more autonomy from Rome.

P 77   November (1562)

D'ennemy vent empefchera la troupe,	**The enemy wind will impede the troop,**
Le plus grand point mis auant difficil:	**For the greatest one advance put in difficulty:**
Vin de poifon fe mettra dans la couppe,	**Wine with poison will be put in the cup,**
Paffer fans mal de cheual gros fouffil.	**To pass the great gun without horse-power.**

The **enemy wind** sounds like something modern, such as a variation on the Kamikaze (divine wind) attacks in World War II. The right interpretation depends on which way the wind blows. We might have to step forward five years to grab a thread of meaning. The Battle of St Denis was fought in November of 1567 during the Second War of Religion. Catherine de' Medici's biographer, Ralph Roeder, described the Huguenot cavalry attacks as "cyclonic onslaughts . . . flinging themselves again and again on the enemy . . ." but there is no record of windstorms impeding the advance of either army. The third line is a typical account of poisoning, unless **the cup** is some futuristic biological weapon. The last line is definitely futuristic: if the prophet is trying to describe armored mobile artillery, this could stand for anything from Hitler's Panzerjägers to the self-propelled artillery of the Coalition forces in Operation Desert Storm. A desert "storm" could be described as an ***enemy wind***.

P 78   *December* (**1562**)

Par le criſtal[1] l'entrepriſe rompuë,
Ieux et feſtins, de LOIN[2] *plus repoſer:*
Plus ne fera pres des Grands ſa repuë,
Subit catarrhe l'eau beniſte arrouſer.

Because of [through the?] crystal the
    enterprise is broken,
Games and feasts, in LYONS *to repose*
    more:
No longer will he take his repast with
    the Great Ones,
Sudden catarrh, blessed water, to
    bathe him.

[1]*Par le cristal*: either "because of," or "through the" crystal.
[2]In this case it is Lyons, not the English "Lion."

Too obscure for me to interpret clearly. The cryptogram *Loin* concerns actions in the city of **Lyons** rather than the sports and feasts of the English. Some notable (perhaps an acquaintance of the prophet) who dines with the nobility (**Great Ones**) either sees his favorite crystal table-ware broken, or his enterprise is broken because of the **crystal** of winter ice. We can even infer this man's enterprise is broken because at some fête he caught a bad winter cold, followed by the rapid onset of pneumonia (**sudden catarrh**). In the end his body is bathed in holy water before it is dressed for the funeral.

Presages 79–91
from the Almanac of 1563

❦❦

P 79 *On the said year (1563)*

Leuer ſain, ſang, mais eſmeu, rien d'accord,	To raise health, blood, but stirred up, nothing in accord,
Infinis meurtres, captifs morts, preuenus:	Infinite murders, captives deaths, anticipated:
Tant d'eau & peſte, peur de tout, ſonnez cors,	So much water and plague, fear of all, horns sounded,
Pris, morts, fuits, grands deuenir, venus.	Captures, deaths, flights, to become great, come.

Now begins the overview for the coming year of 1563 that Nostradamus composed around spring and summer of 1562, when the First War of Religion was just getting started. The general tenor of this presage is pessimistic about there being any end in sight for the war by the new year. The war's greatest battle was fought at Dreux on 19 December 1562, and the new year ushered in fighting and skirmishes that continued in a number of places while the bloody siege of the Huguenot stronghold of Orléans ground on. The Peace of Amboise (it should be called a truce) was still three months away. And further conflicts would be waged to eject the English out of Dieppe and Le Havre.

P 80 *January (1563)*

Tant d'eau, tant morts, tant d'armes eſmouuoir,	So much water, so many deaths, so many arms to rouse,
Rien d'accordé, le Grand tenu captif:	Nothing in accord, the Great one held captive:
Que ſang humain, rage, fureur n'auoir,	What human blood, rage, fury, has not [happened],
Tard penitent, peſte guerre, motif.	Late repentance, plague, war, the motif.

One feels the prophet's lamentation of the death and destruction wrought by the first of nine civil wars. With his greater vision of tomorrow, he must view the continued nightmare and hypocrisy of each new gesture of reconciliation as little more than a break to replenish forces and politically maneuver for the next war. It is possible this Almanac went to the printers before Nostradamus would have known of the Battle of Dreux, where the Constable of France, Anne de Montmorency, was captured.

P 81   *February* (1563)

Des ennemis mort¹ de langue s'approche,	The bite of the enemy's tongue approaches,
Le Debonnaire² en paix voudra reduire:	The Debonair one to peace will want to reduce:
Les obſtinez voudront perdre la proche,	The obstinate ones will want to lose the kinswoman,
Surpris, Captifs, & ſuſpects fureur nuire.	Surprised, Captives, and suspects fury to injure.

¹Old French for bite rather than *mort* = death.
²Debonair; of good stock, noble born.

Le Debonnaire surfaces here again, but it is doubtful it is intended for Louis XVIII way off in the far-distant 1800s (see 10 Q90). But this epithet is hard to tag on the players on the scene in early 1563. It cannot be François de Guise, since he was dead set against making peace, and at this time was leading methodical and bloody attacks on Huguenot bastions around the city of Orléans. That leaves the two prisoners – the Huguenot leader Gaspar de Coligny, or Anne de Montmorency the Catholic – as candidates for **le Debonnaire** holding negotiations while in captivity. The obstinate ones are those fanatical Catholics allied to the war-mongering Duc de Guise who see the pacifist Queen Regent, Catherine de' Medici, as an obstacle to continued warfare. Catherine considers the deadlock on the battlefield justification for her policies of peace and tolerance. In the end Nostradamus forecasts correctly that a surprising development of peace would come through the negotiation of the **captive** nobles. The last phrase introduces the next crisis for Coligny, who was implicated by the captured assassin of the Duc de Guise, the double-spy Poltrot de Méré, as the one who ordered the Duke's death. Even though Poltrot made the admission under torture and later retracted it, this revelation was food for Catherine de' Medici's suspicions against Coligny. The investigation of the admiral, however, did not substantiate Poltrot's claim. Coligny asked Catherine to delay the trial until he could confront Poltrot in person and restore his honor, but while Coligny was on his way to Paris Poltrot was executed, leaving the accusation alive to fester at Court.

P 82   March (1563)

Peres & meres morts de deuls infinis,	Fathers and mothers dead of infinite sorrows,
Femmes à deul, la peſtilente monſtre:	Women in mourning, the pestilent she-monster:
Le Grand plus n'eſtre tout le monde finir,	The Great One to be no more, all the world to end,
Soubs paix, repos, et teſtous à l'encontre.	Under peace, repose and every single one in opposition.

Here is a presage slated for what would be a significant month in French history. Did Nostradamus correctly foresee the Peace of Amboise, signed on 19 March 1563? First he launches into a general lamentation for the dead and the sorrows of the survivors of France's first of nine Wars of Religion. The *pestilent she-monster* is not his occult disciple, Catherine de' Medici, but the Protestant Queen Elizabeth I of England. The **Great One** who is no more is François de Guise, whose assassination at the siege of Orléans removed the last obstacle to peace. The fiery duke's world did come to an end with death. After all the fighting and loss the Amboise agreement only brought France full circle, back to what was basically the same unsatisfying terms of toleration that comprised the Edict of January promulgated in 1562.

P 83   April (1563)

En debats Princes & Chreſtiens eſmeuë,	**Princes and Christendom stirred up**
Gentils[1] eſtrangers, ſiege à Christ moleſté:	**in debates,**
Venu treſmal, prou bien, mortelle veuë,	**Foreign nobles, Christ's See molested:**
Mort Orient peſte, faim, mal traité.	**Become very evil, much good, mortal**
	sight.
	Death in the East, plague, famine,
	evil treaty.

[1]Old French for noble; gentile.

Nostradamus remains exactly on track for the atmosphere of Europe after the Treaty of Amboise. With the first pause in the Wars of Religion came renewed debate over religious rights throughout Europe. There were *foreign nobles* in France. Two Protestant English armies occupied Dieppe and Le Havre. The papacy did feel molested by these encroachments and others by Protestantism in southwestern France. Pope Pius IV had bankrolled much of the Catholic war effort in France. He was not at all happy with the Treaty of Amboise. Nor was Philip II of Spain who, along with the pope, secretly pressured the Catholic leaders of the new French government to reject the *evil treaty* of reconciliation and wage a holy war to annihilate the Huguenot plague before it was too late. The *death in the East* may be the only failure of the presage, as it may stand for the death of the Turkish sultan Sulieman the Magnificent, who would live for another three years.

P 84   May (1563)

Terre trembler, tué, prodige, monſtre,	**Land to tremble, killed, wasteful,**
Captifs ſans nombre, faire defaite, faite:	**monster,**
D'aller ſur mer aduiendra malencontre,	**Captives without number, to do,**
Fier contre fier mal fait de contrefaire.	**undone, done:**
	To go over the sea misfortune will occur,
	Proud against the proud evil done in
	disguise.

An essentially successful forecast, if a little too melodramatic, for the ejection of the English at Le Havre. The campaign began the following month and took the bulk of the summer to complete. The English garrison was shipped over the Channel, but no misfortune or gale arrived to devastate the fleet. The last line continues the blood feud of Coligny and the House of Guise throughout the summer (**proud against the proud**). After the execution of Poltrot, Coligny could not face his accuser and clear his name. Therefore **evil** is **done in** the **disguise** of killing a traitor.

P 85   June (1563)

L'iniuſte bas fort l'on moleſtera,
Greſle, inonder, threſor, & graué marbre:
Chef de ſuard[1] peuple à mort tuëra,
Et attachée ſera la lame à l'arbre.

The unjust one lowered, they will molest him fiercely,
Hail, to flood, treasure, and engraved marble:
Chief of Persuasion people will kill to death,
And attached will be the blade to the tree.

[1]Latin *Suada* = abstract female deity representing Persuasion; or *Suardones* = inhabitants of classical Brunswick, Lüneburg, or Hanover.

Perhaps Nostradamus here represents Admiral Coligny as the **unjust one** whose reputation is **lowered** by the suspicions that he ordered the assassination of François de Guise. On the day Poltrot was dismembered at the Place de Grève in Paris, a multitude of supporters of François de Guise assembled at Notre Dame to view the remains of their fallen hero. In death the duke became a martyr for the Catholic cause, while Huguenots rallied around their beleaguered admiral, making his innocence their cause. The **Chief of Persuasion** may be the late duke's brother, Charles de Guise, Cardinal de Lorraine, who would return to France at the end of the year after a 15-month absence while leading the French delegation at the Ecumenical Council of Trent. He would fill the void of leadership for the House of Lorraine. The long-term consequences would be more civil war (**people will kill to death**).

The clues in the final line will require one more locally positioned in Nostradamus' time to unravel. It might describe the wooden shaft of pikes and halberds used to dismember Poltrot.

P 86   July (1563)

De quel non mal? inexcufable fuite,	**Of what not evil? inexcusable result,**
Le feu non deul, le Legat hors confus:	**The fire not double, the Legate**
Au plus bleffé ne fera faite luite,	**outside confused:**
La fin de Iuin le fil coupé du fus.[1]	**Against the worse wounded the fight**
	will not be made,
	The end of June the thread cut by
	firing.

[1]Old French for firing (a weapon); a wooden shaft, a spindle.

This might work for the trials and tribulations of Charles de Guise, Cardinal de Lorraine, while he led the French delegation at the Holy See's Council of Trent during the summer of 1563. The cardinal was Catherine's best **Legate** to negotiate some papal concessions for religious toleration for her Huguenot citizens. She used him to cut off the hot words fueling the fires of civil war at their source, the Vatican. The cardinal's efforts were dragged down into the morass of the daily routines of the Council (*the legate outside confused*). The line also applies to his reaction when news of the assassination of his brother reached Trent. This loss brought to an end the intimate relationship that was the key to his power and his passion for life. He would make one more rebound in the negotiations, but when his closest allies, the Jesuits, abandoned his cause, he was deeply wounded and returned to court. Catherine declined to execute the decrees of the Council of Trent, which she strongly believed would only make tensions between Huguenots and Catholics far worse.

In a poetic fashion line 4 foretells the consequences of such intolerant papal edicts. The fragile **thread** of peace would be **cut**, not at the end of June 1563 as implied here, but exactly three years ahead in June 1566, when nuns and monks were massacred by Protestants at Pamiers, near Toulouse.

P 87   August (1563)

Bons finement affoiblis par accords,	**Fine bonds enfeebled by accords,**
Mars & Prelats vnis n'arrefteront:	**Mars and Prelates united will not**
Les grands confus par dons incidez corps,	**stop:**
Dignes, indignes bien indeus faifiront.	**The great ones confused by gifts [of]**
	mutilated bodies,
	Dignified ones, undignified ones will
	seize the well endowed.

A general commentary about the **fine bonds** of law and peace weakened throughout the latter half of the year by newly formed provincial Catholic leagues. Poetically speaking Mars, the god of war, will be allied to the cardinals in the spreading practice of local governments financing local armies to fight regional crusades against their Huguenot neighbors. The religious civil wars became an escalating contest of great noble families to general civil war. The last lines are obscure. Perhaps they record some atrocity during the Wars of Religion.

P 88   *September* (1563)

De bien en mal le temps ſe changera,	**From good to the evil times will change,**
Le pache d'Auſt,[1] des plus Grands eſpérance:	**The peace in the South, the expectation of the Greatest Ones:**
Des Grands deul Luis[2] trop plus trebuchera,	**The Great Ones grieving Louis too much more will stumble,**
Congnus Razez pouuoir ny connoiſſance.	**Well-known Shaven Ones have neither power nor understanding.**

[1] Apocope for Latin *Australis* = south.
[2] Prince **Louis** de Condé (1530–69), brother of Anthony of Navarre, uncle of Henry IV, Huguenot leader killed in 1569 at the battle of Jarnac.

The good times of peace quickly change. War threatens the land, especially in the southern provinces, where the Huguenot population was large. The presage seems to trip forward a few years to the Third War of Religion. We have two sets of **Great[est] Ones**, the first are the Catholic noble families, who have an expectation of peace in the Protestant-dominated south. The second set of **Great Ones** are families of the Huguenot nobility, grieving the loss of Louis, Prince de Condé, at the battle of Jarnac in 1569. From his writing desk in the year 1562, Nostradamus implies that Condé will stumble along making military and political blunders until the day he is killed years later at Jarnac (**too much more will stumble**). One might apply **stumble** to the details of his death. He was pinned under his fallen horse when a Catholic soldier ran him through. The French priesthood (**Shaven Ones**) had little Christian love for their Huguenot neighbors, who in turn returned the infernal gesture. The final line indicates that this lack of understanding is as grievous in the case of the Third War of Religion as it was for the first two.

P 89   *October* (1563)

Voicy le mois par maux tant à doubter,	**This is the month[2] for evils so many as to be doubled,**
Morts, tous ſaigner peſte, faim, quereller:	**Deaths, plague to drain all, famine, to quarrel:**
Ceux du rebours d'exil viendront noter,	**Those of the reverse of exile will come to note,**
Grands, ſecrets, morts, non de contreroller.[1]	**Great Ones, secrets, deaths, not to censure.**

[1] Old French to criticize, to censure.
[2] October 1563.

Nostradamus is pretty close on the mark, give or take a week. In the end of September the entire Guise clan, dressed in black, met the king at Melun and renewed their petition to prosecute the case against Admiral Coligny. The king agreed, but the Guises demanded that the trial be held in Parliament. Coligny refused to acknowledge parliament's or the court's jurisdiction to prosecute, as they were both hotbeds of Catholic bigotry. Coligny had it within his powers as Admiral of France to reserve judgement of the case to himself. Starting in October he studied it for three months. His finding? Well, with little concern for the "double-evil" of his flagrant conflict of interest, Coligny decided to adjourn from any acquittal or arrest of himself, suspending the investigation for three years (*secrets, deaths, not to censure*).

An outbreak of *plague* was reported in Lyons and Salon by the winter of 1563.

P 90   November (1563)

Par mort mort mordre, conſeil, vol,
    peſtifere,
On n'oſera Marius[1] aſſaillir:
Deucalion[2] vn dernier trouble faire,
Peu de gens ieunes: demy mort treſſaillir.
	**Through death death to bite, counsel,
	    robbery, pestiferous,
	They will not dare to attack the
	    Marines:
	Deucalion a final trouble to make,
	Few young people: half-dead to give a
	    start.**

[1]Possible misprint for Marines.
[2]The ancient Greek mythological survivor of the great flood. Deucalion is used here as a figure of speech for a flood in France for the end of the year.

A plague of bad government, bad social behavior, and the recorded outbreak of the pestilence that did hit the Rhône valley and reach down to Provence itself, starting at the end of 1563. Flooding often hastened the visitations of the plague, and it is safe to say that this prediction of heavy winter rains is probably a viable one, though I do not possess the historical report of a flood in this year. The attack considered upon the **Marines** is not clear unless it was intended for the English mariners and garrison at Dieppe.

P 91   December (1563)

Mort par deſpit fera les autres luire,
Et en haut lieu de grands maux aduenir:
Triſtes concepts à chacun viendront nuire,
Temporel digne, la Meſſe paruenir.
	**Dead through spite he will cause the
	    others to shine,
	And in an exalted place some great
	    evils to occur:
	Sad concepts will come to harm each
	    one,
	Temporal dignified [one?], the Mass
	    to succeed.**

Unclear – unless Nostradamus has logged a premonition of the death of someone he hated the most, John Calvin, who would die in 1564. If this is the right interpretation, Nostradamus pens yet another failed prediction of evil Calvinism and its leaders falling before the success of the Catholic masses. This prediction probably pleased the majority of his readers, who were Catholics.

Presages 92–104
from the Almanac of 1564

P 92   On the said year (1564)

L'an fextil pluyes, froment abonder, haines,
Aux hommes joyes, Prince Roys en divorce:
Troupeau perir, mutations humaines,
Peuple affoulé:[1] et poifon fous l'efcorce.

The sextile year rains, wheat to
    abound, hatreds,
Joy to men, Princes [and] Kings
    divorced:
Herd to perish, human mutations,
People oppressed: and poison under
    the surface.

[1]Old French affouler = to drive mad; to step on, oppress, vex, murder.

The presage gives us a general and unspecific review for the coming year, during which Nostradamus would reach the pinnacle of respect. A sextile year is one more astrologically harmonious than the last (which in general was true for him). A good harvest is promised, as is a further harvest of hatreds, but this does not lead to another civil war for 1564 as predicted. I know of no divorces among royalty in this year. Some unlucky farmer is going to lose his herds to the predicted **rains** of line 1, and it seems that new freaks of human nature will be born. These **mutations** were always a great horror and entertainment for the peasants. An omen of coming evils is also implied, but these seem to be reserved for another year. The last line definitely captures the mood of the country folk during the fragile peace between civil wars.

P 93   January (1564)

Temps fort diuers, difcorde defcouuerte,
Confeil belliq, changement pris, changé:
La Grande n'eftre, coniurez par eau perte,
Grand fimulté, tous au plus Grands rangé.

Times very diverse, discord discovered,
Council of war, change taken in,
    changed:
The Great Woman not to be,
    conspirators through water lost,
Great hostility, for the great one all
    steady.

Very general. There was no council of war in 1564, though there would be a council met to discuss Queen Regent Catherine de' Medici's plans to take the court on a tour of the realm called the Journey of Pacification. She could be the **Great Woman not to be**, for her expedition, which started with such good intentions to help bring peace to the land, would fail.

P 94   February (1564)

Deluge grand, bruit de mort conſpirée,
Renoue ſiecle, trois Grands en grande
    diſcord:
Par boutefeux la concorde empirée,
Pluye empeſchant, conſeils malins d'accord.

Great deluge, noise of death conspired,
The era renewed, three Great Ones
    in great discord:
Through fire-brands the concord
    made worse,
Rain hindering, malignant counsels of
    accord.

Here again is a jump forward by a generation into the 1580s and the Eighth War of Religion, better known as the War of the Three Henries (**three Great Ones**): Henry III, Henry de Guise (son of François de Guise), and Henry, King of Navarre (son of Antoine de Bourbon). As stated before, the accords attempted between Catherine de' Medici's last son and the new master of the House of Guise were notorious for their mutual treachery (**the concord made worse . . . malignant counsels of accord**). It must be noted that Henry de Guise was murdered by the king's bodyguards at the Château Blois during a driving rainstorm (**rain hindering**).

P 95   March (1564)

Entre Roys haines on verra apparoiſtre,
Diſſentions & Guerres commincer:
Grand Changement, nouueau tumulte
    croiſtre,
L'ordre plebée on viendra offenſer.

Between Kings hatreds one will see
    appear,
Dissensions and Wars to commence:
Great Change, new tumult to
    increase,
They will come to offend the plebeian
    order.

Nostradamus continues his overview of the War of the Three Henries. War did **commence** in 1585–89 and a Henry would take the French throne. The **Great Change** indicates the dramatic reversal of fortunes in which Henry III murders his hated rival Henry de Guise, ending the latter's claim to the throne. Then Henry III is murdered, bringing Henry de Navarre forward to claim the throne by rightful succession as Henry IV. This leaves one surviving Guise, the Duc de Mayenne, to make a Catholic claim to the throne and stir up **new tumult** in a ninth and final War of Religion (1589–98). We also see the Paris "Sixteen" Parliamentarians (**plebeian order**) taking over the capital. Both Mayenne and Henry IV would **come to offend** the plebeians. The latter would lay siege to Paris, and Mayenne would have many of the Sixteen assassinated. One more **Great Change** is required of Henry to negate Mayenne's claim to the throne and end the civil wars. He re-embraces Catholicism in 1593.

P 96 April (1564)

Secret coniur, confpirer populaire,	**Secret conspiracy, the common rabble**
La defcouuerte en machine[1] efmouuoir:	**to conspire,**
Contre le Grands, *[2]	**The discovery in the machine to move:**
Puis trucidée & mife fans pouuoir.	**Against the Great Ones, ***
	Then slaughtered and put [in a state]
	without power.

[1]Latin, *machina* = machine; (figuratively) artifice, intrigue, ruse; malevolent preparations, machination.
[2]The asterisk may represent a passage censored by the Church authorities in the 1605 edition.

We move ahead 24 years to 1588 and the rebellion of the Seize (Sixteen) Parliamentarians, the sixteen city notables of Paris, who plotted to expel Henry III from the capital. In May 1588 (note the near miss for April) the king found himself terrified of the potential coup and popularity of Henry de Guise who conspired to take his throne. When Guise arrived outside of Paris, the king ordered eleven Swiss and four French detachments around the Louvre and the Latin quarter. In response to the army of occupation, the citizens (**common rabble**) moved into action with surprising efficiency, setting up barrel barricades at 50-meter intervals all through the Latin quarter. The rebellion of the common Catholic people against the unpopular Henry III and the royalists (**the Great Ones**) spread across France. But the head of the rebellion was eventually cut off, so the body fell. Henry de Guise was killed, and his brother, the Duc de Mayenne, turned against the Sixteen and conspired to have most of the notables assassinated (**slaughtered**). Then their chief Huguenot adversary, Henry de Navarre, converted to Catholicism, making the rebellion irrelevant or **without power**.

This presage could have links to another people's rebellion centuries later, during the French Revolution – the extreme right-wing Jacobin terrorists who conspired to assassinate their former party member, Napoleon Bonaparte, after he became dictator of France, in 1800. The Jacobins called their failed plot the Infernal Machine.

P 97 May (1564)

Temps inconftant, fieures, pefte, langueurs,	**Times inconstant, fevers, plague,**
Guerres, debats, temps defolé fans feindre:	**languors,**
Submerfions, Princes à mineurs rigueurs,	**Wars, debates, times desolated**
Felices Roys & Grands, autre mort	**without feigning:**
craindre.	**Submersions, Princes to minors**
	austerities,
	Happy Kings and Great Ones
	[nobles], other death to fear.

A litany of generalities that could be applied to any of the nine Wars of Religion or the inconstant intervals of peace between them.

P 98   June (1564)

Du lieu feu mis la peſte & fuite naiſtre,	*Where fire [is] placed the plague and*
Temps variant, vent, la mort de trois	*flight will arise,*
Grands:	*Times variable, wind, the death of*
Du ciel grands foudres, eſtat des Razes	*three Great Ones:*
paiſtre,	*From the sky great lightning bolts, to*
Viel pres de mort[1] bois peu dedans	*feed upon the estate of the Shaven*
vergans.[2]	*Ones,*
	Old One near death, wood scarce and
	in decline.

[1]*Viel pres de mort*: this describes Nostradamus himself.
[2]*vergans* = a) Old French *vergon* = twig; b) (poetic) the royal "branch" of the Valois, in decline at the same time as Nostradamus is approaching death.

A general account best targeted for the climactic days of 1588–89 and the assassination of Henry de Guise, the Cardinal de Guise, and Henry III (***death of three Great Ones***). The last two lines seem to be personal prophecies for Nostradamus, with a veiled critique on the sorry state of the Valois royal line hidden behind a phrase about thinning greengrowth (***wood scarce***).

P 99   July (1564)

En peril monde & Roys feliciter,	*In peril the world and Kings to*
Razes eſmeu par conſeil ce qu'eſtoit:	*thank,*
L'Egliſe Roys pour eux peuple irriter,	*Shaven Ones stirred up by counsel*
Vn monſtrera apres ce qu'il n'eſtoit.	*[about] what was:*
	The Church Kings for them people to
	irritate,
	One will show [divine omens]
	afterwards what he was not.

Here is Nostradamus' condemnation of French kings, whether Valois or from Navarre. Real leadership could have tempered their factions and guided them to pursue tolerant policies. Instead, most of the time they are caught pouring fuel on the passions of religious warfare. Nostradamus' stuttering grammar aside, this traffic jam of statements in the last three lines could give us a prediction of the priests and monks (***Shaven Ones***) converting Father Clément from a meek and mild monk to the murderer of Henry III.

P 100 *August (1564)*

Deluge pres, peſte bouiue, neuue,	Flood near, bovine plague, new.
Secte flechir, aux hommes ioye vaine:	Sect to bow, for men vain joy:
De loy ſans loy, mis au deuant pour preuue,	Of law without law, placed in front for proof,
Apaſt, embuſche: et decens couper veine.	Bait, ambush: and duped into cutting a vein.

It is difficult to confirm the floods or mange plagues logged for August, but exactly one year later, in 1565, Catherine's Journey of Pacification found the royal court pitching its tents along the French border with Spain at Bayonne. The Spanish queen (Catherine's daughter Elizabeth) would meet her with the Catholic fanatic Duke of Alva as her shadow. Catherine had so wanted to negotiate directly with Philip II of Spain and soften his extremist demands on her to get lethal with the Huguenots in her realm. Being a reclusive and closed man, he feared a direct negotiation eye-to-eye with the Queen Regent. He also made matters worse by demanding that no Huguenot prince be present at meetings with the Spanish queen as they would be an insult to her piety. Catherine was forced to **bow** to pressure and exclude the leadership of the Huguenot **sect**. Whatever good Catherine tried to create through the conference by submitting to the Spanish King's unfair demands was practically drowned out by the Huguenot leaders' view that their exclusion at the Conference of Bayonne was more proof of the rumors of an international Catholic conspiracy against them. Later that year when Huguenot leaders were summoned to the Council of Moulins for a reconciliation, the cancer of suspicion would taint all efforts to reform the laws of the land (**law without law**). This phrase could also stand for the forced reconciliation of the Guises and Admiral Coligny staged at Moulins. Charles XI was coached to pronounce judgment before the Council. He completely exonerated the Admiral. This perfunctory act of **law** was performed more to quell the private feud that was undermining public order than to prove the Admiral's guilt or innocence, and therefore was generally viewed as hypocritical (in other words, **law without law, placed in front for proof**). The final act of the farce required adversaries to publicly embrace the admiral. Henry de Guise, the teenage son of the murdered François de Guise, abstained from embracing Coligny.

Line 4 moves us eight years ahead when Henry de Guise – now a grown man – will have the admiral killed in the St Bartholomew's Day Massacre. Guise and other Catholic fanatics use the invitation to the wedding of the King of Navarre and Marguérite Valois as the **bait**, to dupe the admiral and the Huguenot leadership to spill their blood (or open **a vein**) in an **ambush** that night after the wedding ceremony.

P 101   September (1564)

Tout inonder, à la Razée perte,
Vol de mur, mort, de tous biens abondance:
Efchappera par manteau defcouuerte,
Des neuf & vieux fera tournée chance.

To flood all, to the Shaven Female, loss,
Flight from the wall, death,
    abundance of all goods:
He will escape through a mantle of
    coverings,
Of new and old ones the hazard will
    turn.

Very detailed, but difficult to unravel from my vantage point in the latter half of the 20th century. It is a historical fact that the Rhône was flooded the following month. This seems to be about a theft of holy objects belonging to a Mother Superior of a convent during a time of flooding. The thief's escape route and his disguise is described.

P 102   October (1564)

La bouche & gorges en feruides puftules,
De fept Grands cinq, tous diftilante nuire:
Pluye fi longue, à non mort tourment bulles,
Le Crand mourir, qui treftous faifoit luire.

The mouth and throat in burning
    pustules,
Of seven Great Ones, five, the
    distillant to ruin all:
Rain so long, blisters torment not to
    death,
The Great One to die, he who made
    all to shine.

There does not seem to be any reference to the royal visit of the Queen Regent and King Charles XI to Nostradamus in Salon which took place in October 1564. The **seven** could be the Valois children. At this time only **five** children would have been present when Nostradamus redrew their horoscopes. Elizabeth was reigning in Spain at the time and Francis II was dead. Nostradamus would be summoned for a second audience at Arles because the court's progress was delayed at Arles by the flooding of the Rhône (**rain so long**). No great monarch died in October. Pope Pius IV died in December 1565; Sultan Suleiman the Magnificent of the Ottoman Empire in September 1566; and last but not least, the great occult one himself, our prophet, left this world in 1566.

P 103   November (1564)

Par bruit de feu Grands & Vieux defaillir,
Pefte affoupie, vne plus grande naiftre:
Pefte de l'Ara, foin caché, peu cueillir,
Mourir troupeau fertil, ioye hors preftre.

Through noise and fire Great Ones
    and Old Ones to fail,
Plague suppressed, a greater woman
    to be born:
Plague of the Altar, hidden hay, to
    gather little,
The fertile flock to die, joy beyond the
    priest.

A cryptic forecast of the Huguenot rebellion against mainstream Catholic dogma? *Through noise and fire* of war the nobles and the **Old Ones** fail. "Old Ones" was a term used throughout Europe for pagan worshippers. Nostradamus compares the Huguenots with Jovialists (worshippers of Jupiter); therefore Protestantism becomes the **plague** at the altar. The pagan/classical slant continues . . . This plague of evil at the altar of sacrifice is responsible for the gods' blighting the herds and fields of those who seek holy **joy beyond** (the dispensation of) **the priest**. Perhaps Nostradamus is applying his belief that plagues and crop failures have their source in impiety.

P 104   December (1564)

Alegre point, douce fureur au Sacre,	**Cheerful point, sweet fury at the Consecration,**
Enflez trois quatre & au cofté mourir:	**Swelled up three four and on the hillside to die:**
Voye defaillir, n'eftre à demy au facre,	**Road to fail, not to be by half at the consecration,**
Par fept & trois, & quinte courir.	**For seven and three, and the fifth to run.**

We have a repugnant image of swollen bodies lying in the sun on a hill. The rest is hard to decipher. The final line's **seven and three** is on track with 6 Q11's **seven branches reduced to three** prophecy about the Valois children. We move forward and find Henry III, his bumbling brother the Duc d'Alençon, and Queen Marguérite de Navarre during the first ten years of Henry's reign, ending with the death of the duke in 1584. The **fifth to run** is the fifth Valois child born to Queen Catherine de' Medici, Henry III who, after having Henry de Guise murdered at Blois, is forced to run from his own Catholic camp into the embrace of his enemy, Henry de Navarre.

P 105   *On the said year (1565)*

Pire cent fois c'eſt an que l'an paſſé,
Méſme au plus Grands du regne & de
l'Egliſe:
Maux infinis, mort, exil, ruyne, caſſé,
A mort grande eſtre, peſte, playes & bille.[1]

A hundred times worse this year than
  the year passed,
Even for the Greatest Ones of the
  realm and of the Church:
Infinite evils, death, exile, ruin,
  smashed,
To death great woman to be,
  pestilence, plague sores, and bile.

[1]Bile, (venting) spleen, gall, anger. It would have to be *bise* (dry north wind; kiss; or *biser* = to spoil) if it were to rhyme with *Eglise*. *Bille* can also mean: billard ball, marble, taw; log; noddle; etc.

A foreboding future but not very accurate for 1565. Although times were bad enough, the undercurrents of religious war never broke through the dam of control until after the Queen Regent finished her Journey of Pacification in May the following year. It is doubtful that the **great woman** is Catherine, since other quatrains clearly and accurately forecast a long life of service for France. The great female must be some other queen who dies of pestilence. Perhaps it is intended for Elizabeth I, who did suffer an attack of the pox early in her reign. She did not die, however.

P 106   *January (1565)*

Neiges, roüilleures, pluyes & pluyes
  grandes,
Au plus Grand ioye, peſtilence in opie:
Semences, grains beaucoup, & plus de
  bandes,
S'appreſteront, ſimulte n'amortie.

Snow, rustiness, rains and great
  rains,
Even for the Greatest Ones joy,
  pestilence sleepless:
Seeds, plentiful grains, and more of
  bands,[1]
They will prepare themselves, enmity
  unallayed.

[1]In this case bands of thieves, Cabans.

The weather forecast for January is dismal and the crops are due for a plague of rust fungus. But Nostradamus in his presages is often unspecific about his weather forecasts. I would take more notice of them if he said things like: "great rains in Lyons while Normandy is dry." What we do know from historical records is that the following winter was severe.

I have a suspicion this presage has been re-edited. Such contradictory phrases as *joy, pestilence sleepless* are too abrupt for even Nostradamus' crabbed style. Perhaps Chavigny or César wrote these lines. If this is the hand of Nostradamus, the generalities forecast for 1565 are plausible, except for the *plentiful* harvest. Line 4 refers to the bands of Cabans and small armies of Catholics that were conscripted by local parliaments. France was indeed preparing herself for a second civil war.

P 107 *February* (1565)

Entre les Grands naiftre grande difcorde,	**Between the Great Ones a great discord will arise,**
Le Clerc procere¹ vn grand cas braffera:	**The noble Cleric will plot a great event:**
Nouuelles fectes mettre en haine &	**New sects to place in hatred and discord,**
difcorde,	**All people will strive for war and change.**
Tout peuple guerre & change offenfera.	

¹Latin *procer* = noble; *procerus* = tall.

No great discord beyond the endemic plague of distrust and maneuvering for advantage erupted within the traveling court during the Journey of Pacification. The **great discord** came later in the year, when the Queen Regent conferred with her daughter, the Queen of Spain, at the Conference of Bayonne. The Huguenot princes were not invited to the proceedings, and that did cause great discord throughout the land. The **noble Cleric** is the Cardinal de Lorraine, Charles de Guise, who would plot something politically significant in early 1565: he would appropriate for the House of Lorraine the idea of Catholic Leagues by putting his political clout behind the first League, established in Guienne.

Regional Catholic leagues were as much of a threat to the central authority of the crown as they were to the Huguenot communities. By supporting these new Catholic leagues – or **sects** as Nostradamus calls them – the cardinal's plotting and maneuvering planted the seeds for the future outbreaks of three-way civil wars between the forces of the Crown, the Catholic Leagues, and the Huguenots. Around February the cardinal was hatching schemes to gain Spanish military assistance in fighting the Huguenots. Later at the Conference of Bayonne, he openly bounced this idea around in official meetings with the Spanish Ambassador, the Duke of Alva.

P 108   March (1565)

Secret coniur, changement perilleux,	Secret conspiracy, perilous change,
Secrettemeut conspirer factions:	Factions to conspire secretly:
Pluyes grands vents, par orgueilleux,	Rains, great winds, for arrogant ones,
Inonder fleuues, peſtifere actions.	Rivers to overflow, pernicious actions.

This continues the theme of the Cardinal de Lorraine's plots within plots to bolster the Catholic Leagues and test the political waters, both national and international, for foreign military assistance against the Huguenots. Nature metaphors again parallel the excesses of France's war fever.

P 109   April (1565)

Pulluler peſte, les Sectes s'entrebatre,	Plague to multiply, the Sects to quarrel with each other,
Temps moderé l'hyver peu de retour:	Times moderated, winter, little return:
De meſſe & preſche grieuement foy debatre,	Of mass and [Protestant] meeting house grievously to debate,
Inonder fleuues, maux, mortels¹ tout autour.	Rivers to overflow, evils, deadly [ones] all around.

¹mortels: this is a play on the noun and adjectival meanings. Either it means "deadly ones" or "ones doomed to death" because they are heretics. In those days being a heretic meant you were choosing eternal death rather than the eternal life in Christ awarded to those who followed the spiritually correct dogmas of the Catholic Church.

In the first half of the year new Leaguers and royalists quarreled with words, not weapons. Although the winter was not as bad as the one to come the following year, the general breakdown of French society, compounded by even an average winter meant **little return** of food. Crop failures and famine were common throughout the mid-1560s. At this time debates and arguments heated up Catholic Churches and neighboring Huguenot meeting houses. To Nostradamus the weather's vagaries paralleled the excesses of feeling and intolerance of the French people. Perhaps he believed in the popular superstition that people's good and bad feelings influenced the weather.

P 110   May (1565)

Au menu peuple par debats & querelles,	To the people of lower class in debates and quarrels,
Et par les femmes & defunts grande guerre:	And through the women and defunct ones great war:
Mort d'vne Grande, celebrer eſcrouëlles,	Death of a Great Woman, to celebrate the scrofula [the coronation],
Plus grandes Dames expulſées de terre.	More great Ladies expelled from the land.

This continues the themes of the previous presages with the only addition that Nostradamus foresaw (perhaps firsthand at his own church meetings in Salon) how the emotional displays of hysterical women, and the mediocre-minded fanned the negative passions of the debate beyond talk into open aggression. Maybe line 3 is another failed attempt to predict the death of Elizabeth I from her bout with smallpox, or some future pestilence. On the other hand, this may be a failed prediction of the death of Mary, Queen of Scots and the exile of her ladies-in-waiting from **the land** of England. In early 1565 Elizabeth did give permission to Lord Darnley to journey to Scotland and visit her royal rival. For Queen Mary it was love at first sight. Her marriage to Lord Darnley began a series of events that would lead to her fall from the Scottish throne, her long incarceration by Elizabeth, and at the last her beheading.

P 111   June (1565)

Viduité tant maſles que femelles,	**In widowhood as many males as females,**
De grands Monarques la vie pericliter:	**The life of great Monarchs to be in jeopardy:**
Peſte, fer, faim, grand peril peſte meſle,	**Plague, steel, famine, great peril pell-mell,**
Troubler par changes, petits Grands conciter.	**Troubles through changes, lesser Nobility to incite.**

A good overview of the catastrophes to come in future civil wars, although Nostradamus does not correctly target the time. By June the court had proceeded from the Riviera through Languedoc to Guyenne. Nostradamus is not wrong in his comments on what evils would later result from the controversies of the late spring and early summer of 1565. The Catholics in Guyenne were a minority in a Protestant-dominated region. Their efforts to create a Catholic League with its own army of protection was supported by the Cardinal de Lorraine, as we have mentioned earlier, and set a precedent for a three-way civil war in the coming years. As we know, the House of Guise was viewed by blood royals and the Queen Regent as a gaggle of upstarts and usurpers of powers that are not traditionally granted to those belonging to the **lesser Nobility**. But since no faction in court was strong enough to dominate the French Crown, the lesser-royal Guises and Montmorencys, and the greater royal Bourbons and Valois, were compelled again and again to affix the mask of reconciliation and collaboration with blood enemies, while biding their time for the right moment to thrust in the dagger and step over their rivals and take the throne.

P 112   July (1565)

Grefle, roüilleure, pluyes & grandes playes,	**Hail, rust, rains and great plagues,**
Preferuer femmes, feront caufes du bruit:	**To preserve women, they will be the**
Mort de plufieurs pefte, fer, faim par hayes,	**cause of the noise:**
Ciel fera veu quoy dire qu'il reluit.	**Death of several [through] plague,**
	steel, famine, through hatreds,
	The heavens will be seen, which is to
	say that it will be re-lit.

The rust blight foretold back in the first general presage for this year has a clear target date in July, but the accuracy or inaccuracy of this grange prophecy is forever protected by its generality.

Line 2 has a few possible applications. The Catholic Leagues were established for general protection but took a special pride in shielding their womenfolk from being ravaged by their heretic neighbors in Christ, the Huguenots. In July Philip II of Spain made it clear to Catherine de' Medici that the Conference of Bayonne scheduled for the following month would not go forward if Protestants were present at the meetings with the Spanish delegation. A man noted for his intractable religious bigotry, Philip believed the honor and sensibilities of the Queen of Spain and her entourage would be threatened by the presence of heretics.

Catherine staked her entire Journey of Pacification on a face-to-face meeting with Philip. She reluctantly agreed to terms arranged to **preserve women** of the Spanish delegation.

Equal to Philip's bigotry was his ruthless political calculation. He must have known that by excluding the Huguenot leadership he would cause enough **noise** of rumor and conspiracy-mongering to ensure another civil war and force Catherine to let Spain assist (and dominate) Catholic France. As it came to pass, the rumor of conspiracy did trigger the Second War of Religion in 1657, and Spanish forces actively participated in the Eighth and Ninth Wars of Religion in the 1580s and 1590s.

The last line is a riddle about an omen in the sky. It is impossible to say for sure if it alludes to the 3 Q11 omen of marching armies that were seen prior to the assassination of Henry IV.

P 113   August (1565)

Point ne fera le grain à fuffifance,	**Not at all sufficient will be the**
La mort s'approche à neiger plus que blanc:	**grain,**
Sterilité, grain pourri, d'eau bondance,	**The death approaches to snow more**
Le grand bleffé, plufieurs de mort de flanc.	**than white:**
	Sterility, grain rotted, the water
	abundant,
	The great one wounded, several put
	to death on the flank.

Very general and impossible to apply to this year. Famine did cover much of France in 1566. Winter was severe and crop failures were common. But the military tone of the last line might push us forward in time to the Battle of St Denis in late 1567. Montmorency led a successful cavalry attack on the Huguenot flank but was killed (**the great one wounded**). Thus we see the end of the life of the great Constable of France who Nostradamus first met face to face at his hotel lodgings when our prophet was summoned to court in 1556.

P 114   *September* (1565)

Guerre de fruits ny grain, arbres & arbriſſeaux,	**War, of fruits nor grain, trees and scrub-brush,**
Grand volataille, procere ſtimuler:	**Great volatility, noble to spur on:**
Tant temporel que prelat leonceaux,	**As temporal as the young-lion-like prelate,**
TOLANDAD vaincre, proceres reculer.	**D'ANDELOT to conquer, noble ones to draw back.**

Decoding the near-anagram TOLANDAD gives us the Protestant leader d'Andelot, the brother of Admiral Gaspar de Coligny. Once again the actual time frame is farther in the future than specified here and may accurately chronicle d'Andelot's leadership in Picardy as well as his participation in the battles and sieges of the Second and Third Wars of Religion.

P 115   *October* (1565)

De tout changé, perſecuter l'vn quatre,	**Everything changed, one to persecute four,**
Hors maladie, bien loin mortalité:	**Outside malady, morality very far:**
Des quatre deux plus ne viendront debatre,	**Of the four two more will not come to debate,**
Exil, ruyne, mort, faim, perplexité.	**Exile, ruin, death, famine, perplexity.**

If this isn't some personal drama in the household of Nostradamus, or an account of persecution or criticisms by his neighbors, then pinning this on a specific event in October or any year is difficult. Jumping ahead to the Council of Moulins early the following year, we could have the official and insincere reconciliation foisted on the Guises by the Queen Regent in an effort to quell the blood feud between them and Admiral Coligny before it disrupted public governing of the realm. The **one to persecute** is Admiral Coligny and **the four** are the murdered François de Guise (his purported victim), his wife the Duchesse de Guise, his brother the Cardinal de Lorraine, and his son Henry de Guise. The **two** who will no longer **come to debate** the Admiral's guilt or innocence are the cardinal and duchess, who publicly embrace Coligny at Moulins. The adolescent Henry de Guise would abstain from hugging Coligny and was even more impolite as a grown man in issuing the order that resulted in throwing Coligny out of an upper floor window at Henry's feet during the St Bartholomew's Day Massacre.

P 116   November (1565)

Des grands le nombre plus grand ne sera tant,	*Of the great ones the greater number will not be so many,*
Grands changements, commotions, fer, peste:	*Great changes, commotions, steel, plague:*
Le peu deuis: pressez, payez, contant,	*The small estimate: lent, paid, content,*
Mois opposite gelée fort moleste.	*Opposite month [the] frost molests severely.*

The first line reports that the population of higher-born nobles will continue to dwindle due to violence. Line 2 is another case of premature timing for future warfare. Line 3 may be personal. Line 4 is a weather report.

P 117   December (1565)

Fort gelée, glace plus que concorde,	*Severe frost, ice more than concord,*
Vesues matrones, feu, deploration:[1]	*Widows, matrons, fire, lament:*
Ieux, esbats, ioye, Mars[2] citera discorde,	*Games, frolic, joy, Mars to incite discord,*
Par mariages bonne expectation.	*Through marriages good expectation.*

[1] Old French for a bard's lament.
[2] Astrology: lower vibration of Mars = the god of war; or, higher aspect = the Magus, god of alchemy and positive, innocent, and creative transformation.

Very obscure and general. One would expect **severe frost** somewhere in France during any December. Widows mourn their fallen men from the First War of Religion, and now they can lament the ache of punishing frosts. Nostradamus finally gets his meteorological prophecy right – the winter of 1565–66 was terrible. The scene of **games** and **frolic** could be Moulins, where the court is holed up to wait out the winter during the closing months of Catherine's Journey of Pacification. Catherine made every motherly effort to ease religious tensions by creating a court full of charm and entertainment. She invented what was called a Flying Squadron of 35 fetching maidens and ladies, picked from the first families of France, who supplied the entourage with the charms she lacked. At Moulins one might expect a regular schedule of sports events and pageantry (both are ruled in astrology by Mars). But the baser vibrations of Mars (the god of war – and of short tempers and impulsive emotions) would later *incite* discord. After public reconciliation with Coligny at Moulins, the widowed Duchesse de Guise would soon remarry and become Madame de Nemours. This match, along with the reconciliation, was received with hope (***good expectations***) by Catherine.

Presages 118–129
from the Almanac of 1566

ﾟﾟﾟﾟ

P 118   On the said year (1566)

Aux plus grands mort, iacture d'honneur
& violence,
Profeſſeurs de la foy, leur eſtat & leur ſecte:
Aux deux grandes Egliſes diuers bruit,
decadence,
Maux vioſins querellans ſerfs d'Egliſes ſans
teſte.

**For the greatest ones death, loss of
honor and violence,
Professors of the faith, their estate
and their sect:
For the two great Churches diverse
noise, decadence,
Evil neighbors quarreling serfs of the
Church without a head.**

Le Pelletier believes this to be the last authentic presage: numbers 119 through 141, the final presages, are forgeries in his eyes. Many of the remaining presages do reveal suspicious divergences from Nostradamus' narrative voice (as peculiar as it is); however, in my opinion the majority do not sound any stranger than usual.

The ailing Doctor Nostradamus was certainly aware that his time and energies were running out. As a candle increases its glare just before it is snuffed out, he may have extended his prophetic reach to write presages that would eventually fill one and a half almanacs after his death.

It is safe to speculate that his rapid decline after 1564 allowed Nostradamus to write only a handful of authentic drafts for the almanacs (including presages that comment on his final days). His signature during this time was so infirm that Chavigny may have transcribed the prophecies himself. One cannot rule out even the possibility that Chavigny was secretly allowed to fill in the holes and edit the authentic drafts under Nostradamus' guidance before the prophet's death in early July 1566. The Almanac of 1567 may even include a few presages aped by Chavigny, to make a complete set.

This first presage for 1566 may be authentic. It takes us back once again to the Livonian conflict that pitted Ivan the Terrible of Russia against the Poles over the issue of the Baltic states. In 1564 the tide had turned in favor of the Poles and Ivan was occupied with a brutal repression of the Boyars.

One needs to read the lines backwards to get a clear and potentially retroactive prophecy about the Boyars Revolt of 1564. News of Moscovy traveled very slowly and was clothed in the sketchiest of details, so the accuracy of details about the uprising in a region so remote from Provence cannot be attributed to anything other than Nostradamus' prophetic powers.

Russia was gripped in a war with its western neighbors over control of the Baltic principality of Livonia. The Metropolitan of Moscow (**professors of the faith . . . Church without a head**), fearing a serf's revolt in favor of Ivan the Terrible, agreed not to interfere with the Czar's witch-hunt of state enemies and surrendered to him near-autocratic powers. The two great Churches are the Russian Orthodox versus the Catholic Church during the Livonian War. In line 2 Ivan uses his new powers to form a state police that hunt down and nearly liquidate the entire Boyar class of Russian noble families. In other words, the Metropolitan surrenders his leadership (**Church without a head**) to the tyrant, who brutally kills, imprisons and plunders the fortunes of the Boyars (**their estate and their sect . . . for the greatest ones death, loss of honor and violence**).

P 119   January (1566)

Perte, iacture grande, & non sans violence,	**Waste, great loss, and not without violence,**
Tous ceux de la foy, plus à religion,	**All those of the faith, more for religion,**
Les plus Grands perdront vie, leur honneur & cheuance	**The Greatest Ones will lose their life, their honor and fortunes**
Toutes les deux Eglises, la coulpe à leur faction.	**Both the two Churches, the sin in their faction.**

This presage is suspect because Nostradamus does not usually call the Protestant religion or its place of worship a Church. He calls Huguenots Jovial Ones in keeping with his favorite metaphor for them as a new pagan cult of Jupiter, and he consistently calls their place of worship a "temple." I don't recall the Catholic and Protestant Churches ever being described together as **the two Churches**.

With that said, this presage does apply itself moderately well to events starting in January 1566 that would lead to a second civil war by 1567. The new year began with Catherine de' Medici summoning the Huguenot nobility to court, which was residing temporarily at Moulins. After their exclusion from the Conference of Bayonne (June–July 1565) the Huguenot nobility expected a trap, and no official reassurance from court could ease their suspicions of an international Catholic conspiracy.

The most dangerous rumors are those perfumed with a splash of fact. At Bayonne Catherine had done her best to include the Huguenots, but the Spanish would not be seen in the same tent with "heretics," so she excluded them in the hope of salvaging the conference. It is true the

Spanish ambassador, Alva, would have liked Catherine to kill off the Huguenots, and he had made enough innuendoes to this fact. One of them was heard by the boy of 12 – the young Henry, King of Navarre, who was pursuing his education by traveling along with Catherine's mobile court. No adult expected him to understand the proceedings, but Henry was a very inquisitive child. He was present at one audience between Alva and Catherine at which he picked up on at least one allusion even a child could understand. Alva had said, "The head of one salmon is worth a thousand frogs." The child later told his mother and she immediately alerted Condé and Coligny, who took it to mean that Catherine and the Spanish planned to decimate the Huguenot leadership.

Which brings us back to the approaches of Moulins in January 1566, with the clank and rattle of the Huguenot nobility fully armed and surrounded by a small army of bodyguards arriving at court. Before official business could begin, Catherine provoked a final reconciliation between Coligny and the Guises over the unsubstantiated claim that the admiral had ordered the assassination of François de Guise. At the hearing the Cardinal de Guise made a foreboding statement in his address to Charles IX: "All such accords will last, and can last, only as long as the power lasts which imposes them. They offer no security to the accused party (Coligny) and no satisfaction to the injured one (the House of Guise), and in the course of time such agreements would not prevent my brothers and my nephews or, in lieu of them, those who are related to me by blood from killing the Admiral, whenever they might find him, and from shedding their last drop of blood for this purpose . . ."

After seven days a reconciliation was acted out. The audience, consisting of Catherine, the king, and the Royal Council, sat down to watch the performance of the cardinal and admiral embracing. From stage left came the Duchesse de Guise to perform the same gesture. Next was the official reconciliation of the Montmorencys with the Guise. But one Guise missed his cue and was not available to receive the admiral's hug. Young Henry de Guise could not bring himself to embrace the man whom he fervently believed had ordered his father's death.

Thus the presage of January works as a prediction of the consequences to come. After the performance of reconciliation, the Council of Moulins remained in session. Its revolutionary reforms to the French government and local parliaments would be a *waste*. They would not stop local parliaments from levying armies and escalating the civil wars from a fight of nobles into a national obsession.

Line 2 tells us that people will put more energy into the dogma of religion than into searching their hearts for the faith and forgiveness taught by religion. This sin of dogma over religiousness is a cancer in both Churches. It will cause the deaths of many a great noble, and the exhaustion of the honor and fortunes of the Houses of Guise, Montmorency, and the Royal House of Valois in the wars to come. Montmorency and Condé die in battle. Coligny will be killed by the order of the same adult Henry who as a young boy could not bear his embrace. Finally, Henry de Guise dies at the hands of Henry III, who is extinguished by the blade of a monk, thus destroying the House of Valois.

P 120   March (1566)

A deux fort Grandes naiſtres perte pernitieuſe,	*For the two very Great Ones pernicious loss to arise,*
Les plus Grands ſeront perte, biens, d'honneur, & de vie,	*The Greatest Ones will cause loss, goods, of honor, and of life,*
Tant grands bruits couriront, l'vrne trop odieuſe.	*As much great noises will run, the urn very odious,*
Grands maladies eſtre, preſche, meſſe en enuie.	*Great maladies to be, [Protestant?] meeting-house, mass in envy.*

This continues the theme of the sham of reconciliation between the great noble houses of France. The fact that it almost apes the previous quatrain makes it suspect as a regurgitation by Chavigny. The two **Great Ones** are Coligny and young Henry de Guise, who would both be drowned in the maelstrom of blood feuds and religious feuds of the coming civil wars. The **Greatest Ones** are the greater-noble houses of Bourbon and Valois, which will send hundreds of thousands to their deaths in their struggle for the throne in eight more civil wars of religion. The **great noises** of pledged reconciliation are metaphorically toasted with wine goblets made of funeral urns, spilling blood. The Council of Moulins will not stop the maladies of the intolerant praying in the Protestant meeting-houses or taking communion in Catholic masses.

P 121   April (1566)

Les ſeruants des Egliſes leurs Seigneurs trahyront,	*The servants of the Churches will betray their Lords,*
D'autres Seigneurs auſſi par l'indiuis des champs:	*Of other Lords also by the undivided of the fields:*
Voiſins de preche & meſſe entr'eux querelleront,	*Neighbors of meeting-house and mass will quarrel amongst them,*
Rumeurs, bruits augmenter à mort pluſieurs couchans.	*Rumors, noises to augment, to death are several lying.*

A suspect presage. Nostradamus rarely mimics a prior quatrain so completely.

P 122   May (1566)

De tous biens abondance terre nous produira,	*Of all blessings abundance, the earth will produce for us,*
Nul bruit de guerre en France, horſmis ſeditions:	*No din of war in France, seditions put outside:*
Homicides, voleurs par voye en trouuera,	*Man-slayers, robbers one will find on the highway,*
Peu de foy, fiéure ardente, peuple en emotion.	*Little faith, burning fever, people in commotion.*

This one is definitely written by Nostradamus; it is partly incorrect and I doubt Chavigny was cunning enough to have inserted a glaring goof retroactively. It recalls the statement Nostradamus made to Catherine de' Medici during her visit to Salon: that general peace would settle on Europe in 1566. True, there wasn't a war raging in France, but **seditions** being **put outside** is going a little too far. Lines 3 and 4 may be the first inkling of Nostradamus describing his final days, beginning with his last journey to the Royal Embassy at Arles. Although he predicts the danger of meeting brigands on the road, there is no record of our prophet being robbed or assaulted. The last line conjures a vision of our old and fever-ridden Doctor in Ordinary in his coach, taking in the peaceful country-side and passing the unpeaceful villages and people seething with religious hatred rather than basking in the faith in God's grace and forgiveness.

P 123   June (1566)

Entre peuple diſcorde, intimitié brutale,	*Between people discord, brutal enmity,*
Guerre mort de grands Princes, pluſieurs pars d'Italie:[1]	*War, death of great Princes, several parts [of Italy]:*
Vniverselle playe, plus fort occidentale,	*Universal plague, more strong [in the] West,*
Tempore bonne et pleine, mais fort ſeche et tarie.	*Times good and full, but very dry and exhausted.*

[1] *d'Italie* – not in all editions.

Although later editions add "of Italy" to line 2, I believe this better chronicles events in France, either retroactively as a Chavigny addition or prophetically as Nostradamus' view of 1566. This year did see the death of one **great Prince**, if you could call Suleiman the Magnificent of the Ottoman Empire such. The **universal plague** of religious hatreds may be implied here. And it was worse towards the west of Provence in the Huguenot-dominated regions of the French southwest. I would say the last line is the seer commenting on his own life. His final days were emotionally peaceful, and the spring and summer months around Salon de Provence are known to be some of the driest in the land. By the time he enjoyed his last June days on Earth, Nostradamus was physically burned out and **exhausted** by his eventful life.

P 124   July (1566)

Les bleds trop n'abonder, de tous autres fruits force,	**The grains not to be plentiful, in all other fruits, plenty,**
L'Efté, printemps humides, hyver long, neige, glace:	**The Summer, spring humid, winter long, snow, ice:**
En armes l'Orient, la France fe renforce,	**The East in arms, France reinforces herself,**
Mort de beftail prou miel, aux affiegez la place.	**Death of beasts much honey, the place to be besieged.**

Nostradamus is right about the lack of plentiful grains; France suffered a famine in the spring of 1566. But the view that other **fruits** (which would include vegetables) are in plenty cannot be substantiated by the facts, unless the general famine had less impact in his locality. After the general weather report he tells us something most French people could easily guess, that the Turks (**the East**) were in a military mood. During the previous summer Sultan Suleiman the Magnificent had suffered his first major defeat by the Christians at the siege of Malta. But the prophet may have sensed something his countrymen didn't know – that Suleiman was at the head of a vast army setting forth on a campaign against the Hungarians. France, indeed, was rearming itself, not against the hordes of Islam but against internal divisions. June was the official end of Catherine de' Medici's two-year Journey of Pacification. Her circuit of the realm to foster peace had fallen victim to a vicious circle of Protestant and Catholic hatreds. There were no sieges in France during 1566; however, the Turks laid siege to the Croatian fortress of Sziget.

No mention of Nostradamus' death is made in this presage.

P 125   August (1566)

Par peftilence & feu fruits d'arbres periront,	**Through pestilence and fire fruits of [the] trees will perish,**
Signe d'huiie abonder. pere Denis non gueres:	**Signs of oil to abound. Father Denis not scarce:**
Des grands mourir, mais peu d'eftrangers faillirõt,	**Some great ones to die, but few foreigners will sally forth in attack,**
Infult, marin barbare, & dangers de frontieres.	**Offense, Barbarian marines, and dangers at the frontiers.**

Here we have a forecast of tree blight, which one might expect to find in a prophecy for an almanac. But the buds of spring and summer promise a good olive oil crop for the fall. As we know the Turkish sultan did die in his tent bed on 5 September just before the final victorious assault on Sziget. If Nostradamus means *few foreigners* sallying forth against France, he is right. But during this time Suleiman the Magnificent had amassed the mightiest Ottoman army to date and hurled it against the Christian states in the Balkans. Raids by corsairs along the Riviera were endemic so it is easy to predict such *offenses* from Barbary pirates (*Barbarian marines*) landing onshore and carrying off people and loot. If anyone feared *dangers at the frontiers* of France it was the Huguenots, who believed the Spanish were plotting with French Catholics to wipe them out. I render the task of disclosing who Father Denis is to anyone more familiar with French Provençal history than myself. I'll only speculate that the good **Father** is the Cardinal de Lorraine working for the House of Valois, symbolized by their sepulchre at St **Denis**.

P 126   September (1566)

Pluyes fort exceſſives, & de biene abondance,	**Rains very excessive, and of blessings abundance,**
De beſtial pris iuſte eſtre, femme hors de danger:	**The cattle price to be just, women outside of danger:**
Greſles, pluyes, tonnerres: peuple abattu en Frãce,	**Hail, rain, thunder: people depressed in France,**
Par mort trauailleront, mort peuple corriger.	**Through death they will work, death to reprove people.**

The general daily soap opera and meteorological vagaries of life in France in the high summer of 1566. A safe prediction, whether it was written by the now-expired and entombed prophet or pieced together by Chavigny in his name.

P 127   October (1566)

Armes, playes ceſſer, mort de ſeditieux,	**Armes, plagues to cease, death of the seditious ones,**
Le pere Liber grand non trop abondera:	**Great Father Liber [the god of vines] will not much abound:**
Malins feront ſaiſis par plus mallcieux,	**Evil ones will be seized by more malicious ones,**
France plus que iamais victrix triomphera.	**France more than ever victorious will triumph.**

This one just doesn't sound authentic to me. But even if it is a forgery, it plays safe by describing the usual rhythms of the land. Plagues generally tapered off in the high summer, and of course one would expect a report in September on the wine harvest. This time the take isn't so good. And there doesn't seem to be a record to test the prediction's veracity. Line 3 does not give up any specifics, such as who the *evil ones* and the *more malicious ones* are. So many minor civil and religious incidents between Catholic and Huguenot neighbors went unrecorded during this time that applying this to domestic strife is impossible. The last line is completely wrong for the latter half of 1566, whether it is forged or penned by Nostradamus.

P 128   November (1566)

Iufqu'à ce mois durer la fechereffe grande,	Up to this month the great drought will endure,
A l'Itale & Prouence, des fruits tous a demy:	For Italy and Provence all fruits to half:
Le Grand moyns d'ennemis prifonnier de leur bande,	The Great One less of enemies prisoner of their band,
Aux efcumeurs, Pyrates, & mourir l'ennemy.	For the scroungers, Pirates, and the enemy to die.

I could not find a record of a drought ending in October 1566. But if I were forging a presage, I could count on a 50-50 chance of being "a great prophet" if I predicted the rains' return to Provence and Italy in October. According to dead Nostradamus' ghostwriter, Chavigny, those pesky Barbarian/Barbary **Pirates** from North Africa get their comeuppance in an October raid.

P 129   December (1566)

L'ennemy tant à craindre retirer en Thracie,	The enemy so much to be feared to retire into Thrace,
Laiffant crys, hurlemens, & pille defolée:	Leaving cries, howls, and pillage desolated:
Laiffer bruit mer & terre, religion nutrie,[1]	To leave noise on sea and land, religion murdered,
Iouiaux[2] mis en route, toute fecte affoulée.	Jovial Ones put on the road, every sect to become angry.

[1] Possibly from Old French *mutre* = murder.
[2] Jovial Ones usually stand for Protestants, less often for pagans.

This could be Nostradamus – or it is Chavigny on a rare good day of writing. The theatre is the Balkans. After the death of Suleiman the Magnificent, the Ottoman army did withdraw gradually to the Turkish frontiers. This wasn't even near Thrace; the border was closer to modern-day Belgrade in Serbia. The last lines seem to return us to France and French waters, and the same old religious wars theme of the other presages.

P 130   On the said year (1567)

Mort, maladie aux ieunes femmes, rhumes,
De teſte aux yeux malheur marchands de
    terre:
De mer infauſt, femmes mal, vin par
    brumes,
Prou huile trop de pluïe, aux fruits moleſte
    guerre.

**Death, malady for young women,
head colds,
From the head to the eyes a wretched
deal of land:
By sea misfortune, seeds bad, wine in
mists,
Much oil too much rain, molests the
fruits, war.**

This is a fake presage. It is most likely from Chavigny with writer's block.

P 131   January (1567)

Priſons, ſecrets: ennuis, entre proches
    diſcorde,
La vie on donnera, par mal diuers
    catarrhes:
La mort s'en enſuyura, poiſon fera
    concorde,
Frayeur, peur, crainte grande voyageant
    lairra d'arres.

**Prisons, secrets: annoyances, discord
between neighbors,
They will give life, through evil
diverse catarrhs:
Death will ensue, poison will cause
concord,
Terror, fear, great dread traveling
will release from guarantees.**

Ditto.

P 132   February (1567)

Priſons par ennemys occults & manifeſtes,
Voyage ne tiendra, inimitié mortelle:
L'amour trois, ſimultez ſecret publiques
    feſtes,
Le rompu ruyné, l'eau rompra la querelle.

**Prisons for enemies hidden and
manifested,
Travel will not hold, mortal enmity:
Love three, secret hostility, public
festival,
The broken ruined, the water will
break the quarrel.**

A third aping of Nostradamus.

P 133   March (1567)

Les ennemys publics, nopces & mariages, La mort apres, l'enrichy par les morts: Les grands amys ſe monſtrer au paſſage, Deux ſects iargonner, de ſurpris tards remords.	The public enemies, nuptials and marriages, Death after, he grown rich through the deaths: The great friends will show themselves in the passage, Two sects to jabber, from surprise remorse later.

Perhaps this is Chavigny beyond writer's block, but it is still bogus.

P 134   April (1567)

Par grandes maladies, religion fachée, Par les enfans & legats[1] d'Ambaſſade: Don donné à indign, nouuelle[2] loy laſchée, Biens de vieux peres, Roy en bonne contraue.	Through great maladies, religion offended, Through the infants and gifts of the Embassy: Gift given to a worthless one, new law relaxed, Goods of old fathers, King in good country.

[1]Old French *legat* = legacy, gift.
[2]Either *nouvelle* = new, or *nulle* = no.

Okay, now we have something here that, for me at least, has the musical cadences of Nostradamus' poetic barbarisms (discordant as they are). Granted, this could be Chavigny finally becoming a worthy parrot of his master. As with P122 we may begin to see Nostradamus predict the final months of his life, as well as his death. What is equally possible is the beginning of a long and dubious legacy of others successfully writing and projecting themselves behind the name of Nostradamus.

The final presages concern some cryptic **gift** or treasure Nostradamus is charged to deposit at the regional Parliament at Arles. Whether this treasure is worldly or occult isn't made clear; only we know that he is obliged to do this deed as a royal representative of the young King Charles IX. The recipient in Arles is deemed **a worthless one**.

Or worse, the judgment is aimed at Charles IX himself. This presage either continues the thread of Nostradamus' authenticated quatrains that tag Charles as the *noir/roi* or the black-evil-king of the St Bartholomew's Day Massacre to come, or Chavigny is scribbling here and covering his tracks by hiding behind his master's implied interpretation for Charles IX. The **new law** could be against religious intolerance proscribed by the Treaty of Amboise. If vigilance against intolerance is **relaxed** then war is near. In any case Nostradamus with foresight – or through his parrot disciple's hindsight – has accurately tagged 1567 as the start of the second War of Religion.

P 135   May (1567)

Du pere au fils s'approche: Magiftrats dits seueres,	From the father it [he] approaches the son: Magistrates called severe,
Les grands nopces, ennemys garbelans:[1]	The great nuptials, enemies mangling:
De latens mis auant, par la foy d'improperes,[2]	The concealed put in front, through the faith of reproaches,
Les bons amis & femmes contre tels groumelans.	The good friends and women against such grumblings.

[1]Low Latin garbellare = to sift, hence by usage to mangle, mutilate.
[2]Latin improperus = slow; improperium = taunt, reproach.

Line 1 could have something to do with César pleading for his dying father to change his last will and testament and bequeath to him the cherished astrolabe. But the rest reads as too brazen a contradiction for me to say it is completely original. Weird wordings, yes!, but where does one see such glaring and contradictory vulgarities as **faith of reproaches** in *Les Propheties*?

P 136   June (1567)

Par le threfor, trouué l'heritage du pere:	Through the treasure, found – the heritage of the father:
Les Roys & Magiftrats, les nopces, ennemys:	The Kings and Magistrates, the nuptials, enemies:
Le public mal veillant, les Iuge & Maire,	The public malevolent, the Judge and Mayor,
La mort, peur & frayeur: & trois Grands à mort mis.	The death, fear and terror: and three Great Ones put to death.

The first three lines could be about Nostradamus.

The **treasure** could be Nostradamus' legacy to his son, or an intangible gift discovered through use of some occult tool, book, or instrument (such as his astrolabe) cryptically concealed here as **the treasure**.

The reference to **nuptials** could transport us a few years ahead to 1572, during the stifling hot dog days of August in Paris, when King Charles IX gave the sweating hand of his sister, Marguérite de Valois, to the garlic-perfumed paw of Henry, King of Navarre. The people of Catholic Paris were in a malevolent, muggy mood, and thanks to the schemes of Catherine de' Medici and Henry de Guise, their mutual rival, Admiral Gaspar de Coligny, would be assassinated along with thousands of Marguérite's Huguenot wedding guests on the night of **death, fear and terror** – St Bartholomew's Eve. As a consequence of this massacre the **three Great Ones** are put to death in the coming decades of civil war: Henry III,

Henry de Guise, and much later, Henry de Navarre after he takes the French throne as Henry IV of France. I would caution the reader that this authentic final line may have been stolen and repeated here by the forger.

P 137 July (1567)

Encor la mort s'approche, don Royal & Legat,	**Again the death approaches [him], Royal gift and Legacy,**
On dreſſera ce qu'eſt, par vielleſſe en ruyne:	**He will prepare what is, through old age in decay:**
Les ieunes hoirs de ſoupçon nul legat,	**The young heirs in suspicion of no legacy,**
Threſor trouué en plaſtres & cuiſine.	**Treasure found in plasters and kitchen cookery.**

Another possible reference to personal accounts of Nostradamus' impending death, but it is almost too clear and obvious to be an original. Still, even if it is a bogus prophecy the details may be based on facts known by Chavigny and Nostradamus' family about his final days. Line 1 implies that he had been close to death more than once in his final months (*again the death approaches*). This seems to have happened just after his return from a 50-mile round-trip by springless coach to the regional parliament at Arles. Perhaps this was one exhausting journey too many for our vagabond seer, and it brought on the final illness. Line 2 is pretty self-explanatory: he is preparing himself for death.

Line 3 returns us again to the family crisis surrounding the distribution of his valuables. The young heirs are his gang of children. Perhaps the *suspicion of no legacy* is just a case of sibling – rather than sibylline – rivalry. The final line gives us another clue that *the treasure* is more worldly. Grandma might hide her money in a mattress, but our aging prophet hides his stash of gold coins *in plasters*. The word could mean either some plaster container, or a nook hidden by a plaster wall. *Cuisine* can mean the treasure is hidden in the kitchen or in some special cooking pot. The *legacy* is something more abstract: it is the knowledge the master confiture-maker leaves to his daughters for cooking up remedies, aromatic cosmetics, and healing balms.

P 138 August (1567)

Les ennemys ſecrets ſeront empriſonnez,	**The secret enemies will be imprisoned,**
Les Roys et Magiſtrats y tiendront la main ſeure:	**The Kings and Magistrates will hold there a sure hand:**
La vie de pluſieurs, ſanté maladie yeux, nez,	**The life of several, healthiness, malady [in the] eyes and nose,**
Les deux grands s'en iront bien loin à la male heure.	**The two great ones will go away very far at the bad hour.**

An obscure and cryptic presage that may be hiding a more personal theme of foreseen revenge against Nostradamus' **secret enemies**. The choice of words might lead us to think this is a more general presage about the doings and undoings of French royalty in the next civil war. The last two lines could be a prophecy about his children and their future health maladies. In this case the **two great ones** may refer to favorite children or family members, such as his brother Jean and eldest son César, leaving home at the wrong time, perhaps at the moment of his death.

P 139 September (1567)

Longues langueurs de tefte nopce, ennemy,	Long debility in the head, nuptial, enemy,
Par prelat & voyage, fonge du Grand terreur:	Through Prelate and journey, dream of the Great One terror:
Feu & ruyne grande trouué en lieu oblique,	Fire and ruin, great one found in the oblique place,
Par torrent defcouuert fortir noues erreurs.	By torrent discovered, new errors to come out.

More grist for the mill of speculation about Nostradamus' final days. Perhaps he tried to arrange a marriage for one of his daughters with someone at the Embassy in Arles. Or maybe he gave his last psychic reading there, concerning a client's marriage plans. Perhaps he interpreted a terrifying dream of the Archbishop of Arles. We can speculate further and see Nostradamus having some final visionary dream of God or his divine spirit medium showing the prophet a vision of his oncoming death. He sees a vision of his body, buried upright in the wall of a church (**in the oblique place**) being desecrated in the distant future.

The last line seems to be missing enough commas to open it to several applications. We could envision some treasure or Nostradamus' tomb discovered or opened after a torrent or flood; or the **torrent** could be poetic for a storm or flood of revolution similar to the "whirlwind" applications he used for the French Revolution. In both cases the coming centuries will give birth to many a naked legend about his grave, further cloaked in the nebulous swaddling cloths of old wives' tales. From legends of medallions and secret code books hidden amongst the prophet's moldy bones, to the claims of modern-day mediums who channel Nostradamus sandwiched between cetacean and extraterrestrial spirit messengers, more misunderstandings, projections, and errors will certainly be made in His-stories of Nostradamus.

P 140   October (1567)

Les roys Magiſtrats par les morts la main mettre, *Ieunes filles malades, & des grands corps enfle:* *Tout par langeurs & nopces, ennemys ſerfs au maiſtre.* *Les publicques douleurs, le compoſent tout enflé.*	**The Kings and Magistrates through the deaths, the hand [power] to place,** **Young girls sick, and of the Great Ones [the] body swells:** **All through languors and nuptials, enemy serfs for the master.** **The public sad, the Composer[1] all swelled up.**

[1]The Author (Nostradamus).

Nostradamus' final days? The data implied here could have historical merit, even though it is inserted as a false prophecy, most likely by Chavigny.

Line 1 begins with a general prophecy of the deaths of great magistrates and future kings of France. Line 2 implies that his young daughters, still children, also were sick and needed care during his final illness. Pulmonary edema, or dropsy as it was known then, made Nostradamus' body swell. Despite the suffering and debilitation, he manages to arrange his last will and testament (perhaps masked here by *nuptials* for the will does categorize in great detail the dowries of his daughters). The reference to *enemy serfs* (peasants) pestering the master is one last jibe at the Catholic hoods, the Cabans, who bullied the seer. But the last line contends that they are in the minority, for most of Salon's citizens, are sad to see their illustrious doctor – the composer of the greatest history of the future yet written – suffer and swell up with dropsy.

P 141   November (1567)

Du retour d'Ambaſſade, don de Roy; mis au lieu *Plus n'en fera: Sera allé à Dieu:* *Parens plus proches, amis, freres du ſang,* *Trouué toutmortprez du lict & du banc.*	**On his return from the Embassy, the King's gift put in place.** **He will do nothing more. He will be gone to God.** **Close relatives, friends, brothers by blood,** **[Will find him] completely dead near the bed and the bench.**

Nostradamus' last prophecy describes his approaching death.

In June 1566, shortly after his return from the Embassy at Arles as the king's representative from Salon, Nostradamus had a severe attack of gout. He sensed his approaching death and had a last will and testament made on the 17th. His fortune was recorded to be 3,444 crowns – a substantial sum for his day. Leoni collected a list of speculations from different historians: 3,444 crowns equaled 500,000 francs in 1920; or 11,000 US dollars in 1940. But Leoni gives us the best measure of value when he says that a room in a good house in Paris during Nostradamus' time "could be rented for four crowns a year."

Nostradamus arranged for the money and his worldly possessions to be distributed to his wife, three sons and three daughters. Every possibility was covered in the will. His wife, Anne, was pregnant, so he made contingencies for twins. He also made arrangements for the possible death before marriage of any daughter.

Tearful lobbying by his two favorite siblings, first-born Madeleine and César, compelled him to summon the notaries back to his bed on 30 June to add a codicil to the will that granted César possession of his astrolabe and large gold doctor's ring just after his death (a wait of little more than 72 hours). Madeleine was to receive two walnut chests with all the jewels, clothes, and ornaments they contained, for her immediate enjoyment, rather than wait the long years until the chests were opened on her wedding day.

During his final days Nostradamus had his bed moved to his beloved upstairs study, and a special bench was built so he could maneuver his disabled body throughout the room and prop up his ulcerated leg. Around 25 June 1566, Dr Nostradamus diagnosed that his gout had deteriorated into dropsy (in modern terms a mixture of kidney failure and pulmonary edema that causes the body to swell painfully). Witnesses report that he remained alert and serene to the end in spite of his acute suffering.

Father Vidal, the Superior of the Franciscan monastery of Salon, was called on 1 July to hear Nostradamus' final confession and perform the last rites. Chavigny, who claims to be the last man to see him alive, gives the following account: "The day before he exchanged this life for a better, after I had spent many hours with him, and late at night was taking leave of him until the following morning, he said, 'You will not see me alive at sunrise.'"

At sunrise the next morning Chavigny carefully led family and friends up the spiral stairs to the study. They found Nostradamus, a prophet to the last, his lifeless body sitting peacefully in bed, with his gout-enflamed foot propped on the bench.

Select Bibliography

The Earliest Principal Edition of Nostradamus' Ten "Centuries" Used in this Book

LES PROPHETIES DE M. MICHEL NOSTRADAMVS. Dont il y en a trois cens qui n'ont encores iamais esté imprimées. Adioustées de nouueau par ledict Autheur. A Lyon, par Benoist Rigavd. 1568. Auec permission.
LES PROPHETIES DE M. NOSTRADAMVS. Centuries VIII. IX. X. Qui n'ont encores iamais esté imprimées. A Lyon, par Benoist Rigavd.

The first volume contains the Preface and 642 quatrains; the second contains the Epistle and 300 quatrains. The copy can be found at the Musée Arbaud, Aix-en-Provence, France.

Source of Duplicate Quatrains from Centuries 6, 7, 8, and 10 and Fragmentary Centuries 11 and 12

PREDICTIONS ADMIRABLES pour les ans courans en ce siecle. Recueillies des Memoires de feu M. Michel Nostradamvs, vivant Medecin du Roy Charles IX., & l'vn des plus excellens Astronomes qui furent iamais. Presentées au tres-grand Inuincible & tres-clement Prince Henry IIII, vivant Roy de France & de Nauarre, Par Vincent Seue de Beaucaire en Languedoc, dés le 19. Mars 1605, au Chasteau de Chantilly, maison de Monseigneur le Connestable de Montmorency.

Although the printer's name and locality is not entered, Edgar Leoni posits that Pierre Duruau of Troyes is the source because of its striking similarity to later editions under that name published in 1626 and 1629. The 1605 edition includes 4 of the 12 duplicate Century VII quatrains and all 6 of VIII from the Ménier editions of 1589; one extra quatrain for VI and one for X; 2 for XI and 11 for XII as well as 141 Presages and 58 (fraudulent) Sixains. One can find a copy in the Harvard Library, U.S.A.

The Presages

Edgar Leoni points out that in *Bulletin du Bibliophile* (1862), page 784, Buget states that they originally surfaced in Chavigny's *Janus Gallicus* of 1594 (*see* Chavigny *below*)

Better-known Commentaries on Nostradamus

THE AUTHOR'S RATING

✍ ✍ ✍ ✍ ✍ Excellent scholarship. Innovative and open-minded interpretations, and a good balance of metaphysical theory and skepticism. A grade of A to B+.

✍ ✍ ✍ ✍ For the most part a solid examination, though generally less brilliant and compelling than the best. A grade of B to B–.

✍ ✍ ✍ Moderate to poor scholarship. An uneven grasp of the prophecies, although not always without merit. A grade of C+.

✍ ✍ The work suffers from a clear and prejudiced agenda to sing homilies to Nostradamus, trash him, or exploit interest in the subject for profit. A grade of C to D.

✍ Amateurish research. At best a work by a dilettante. At worst a book burdened with biased and somewhat unconvincing (and at times downright loony) New Age theories. A grade of F (fail).

✍ ✍ ✍ Boscolo, Renucio, *Nostradamus, Key to the Future.* Abbot Press, Burlingame, CA, 1984

✍ ✍ ✍ ✍ Brennan, J. H., *Nostradamus, Visions of the Future.* Aquarian Press/ HarperCollins, London, 1992

✍ Cannon, Dolores, *Conversations with Nostradamus, Volume One,* Ozark Mountain Publishers, Huntsville, AR, 1989

✍ ——, *Conversations with Nostradamus, Volume Two,* Ozark Mountain Publishers, Huntsville, AR, 1990

✍ ——, *Conversations with Nostradamus, Volume Three,* Ozark Mountain Publishers, Huntsville, AR, 1992

✍ ✍ ✍ Cheetham, Erika, *The Prophecies of Nostradamus,* Capricorn Books/G. P. Putnam Sons, New York, 1974

✍ ✍ ✍ ✍ ——, *The Further Prophecies of Nostradamus, 1985 and Beyond,* A Perigee Book/Putnam Publishing Group, New York, 1989

✍ ✍ ✍ ——, *The Final Prophecies of Nostradamus,* A Perigree Book/Putnam Publishing Group, New York, 1989

✍ ✍ ✍ ✍ Fontbrune, Jean-Charles de, *Nostradamus, Countdown to Apocalypse,* Henry Holt and Company, New York, 1983

✍ ✍ ✍ ✍ ——, *Nostradamus 2, Into the Twenty-First Century,* Henry Holt and Company, New York, 1984

✍ ✍ ✍ ✍ Francis, David Pitt, *Nostradamus, Prophecies of Present Times?* Aquarian Press, Wellingborough, Northamptonshire, 1986

✍   Hewitt, V. J. (with Peter Lorie), *Nostradamus, The End of the Millennium. Prophecies: 1992 to 2001*, Simon & Schuster, New York, 1991

✍   Hewitt, V. J. *Nostradamus, His Key to the Centuries. Prophecies of Britain and the World 1995–2010*, Heineman, London, 1994

✍ ✍ ✍ ✍   Jochmans, Joseph Robert, *Nostradamus Now, Prophecies of Peril and Promise for the 1990s – And Beyond*, Sun Books/Sun Publishing, Santa Fe, NM, 1993

✍ ✍ ✍ ✍ ✍   ——, *Rolling Thunder, The Coming Earth Changes*, Sun Books/Sun Publishing, Santa Fe, NM, 1980

✍ ✍ ✍ ✍ ✍   Kidogo, Bardo, *The Keys to the Predictions of Nostradamus*, Foulsham, London, 1994

✍ ✍ ✍   Lamont, André, *Nostradamus Sees All*, W. Foulsham Co., Philadelphia, 1942

✍ ✍ ✍ ✍ ✍   Laver, James, *Nostradamus; or, The Future Foretold*, Penguin Books, London, 1942 (and 1950 in paperback)

✍ ✍ ✍   Lemesurier, Peter, *Nostradamus, The Next 50 Years*, Berkeley Books, New York, 1993

✍ ✍ ✍ ✍ ✍   Leoni, Edgar, *Nostradamus, life and literature*, 1961. (Reissued) *Nostradamus and his Prophecies*, Wings Books, New York, 1982

✍ ✍   Lorie, Peter, *Nostradamus, The Millennium & Beyond: Prophecies to 2016*, Simon & Schuster, New York, 1993

✍ ✍ ✍   McCann, Lee, *Nostradamus, The Man Who Saw Through Time*, Greenwich House/Crown, New York, 1984

✍ ✍ ✍ ✍   Prieditis, Arthur, *The Fate of the Nations: Nostradamus' Vision of the Age of Aquarius*, Llewellyn Publications, St. Paul, MN, 1982

✍ ✍   Randi, James, *The Mask of Nostradamus*, Charles Scribner's Sons, New York, 1990

✍ ✍ ✍ ✍ ✍   Robb, Stewart, *Prophecies on World Events by Nostradamus*, Liveright Publishing Corporation, New York, 1961

✍ ✍ ✍   ——, *Nostradamus and the End of Evils Begun*, Longmeadow Press, Stamford, CT, 1991

✍   Roberts, Henry C., *The Complete Prophecies of Nostradamus*, New York, 1947 and 1949

✍ ✍   Voldben, A., *After Nostradamus*, Citadel Press, New York, 1974

✍ ✍   Ward, Charles A., *Oracles of Nostradamus*, London, 1891, Reprinted by Dorset Press, London, 1986

Other Commentaries on Nostradamus

Here is a partial list of works of other noted interpreters, commentators and debunkers from the last 443 years referred to in my text.

Allen, Hugh Anthony, *Window in Provence*, Boston, 1943

Bonnot, Jean de, *Les Oracles de Michel de Nostredame dit Nostradamus*, annotated by Anatole le Pelletier and Serge Hutin, 1976, 2 vols

Boswell, Rolfe, *Nostradamus speaks*, 1941

Bouys, Théodore, *Nouvelles considérations sur les Oracles et particulièrement sur Nostradamus*, Desenne, Debray, Paris, 1806

Chavigny, A. de, *Les Pléiades du Sieur de Chavigny, Beaunois, divisées en VII livres, prises et tirées des anciennes prophéties et conférées avec les oracles du tant célèbre et renommé Michel de Nostradame, jadis conseiller et médecin de trois Rois très chrestiens. Où est traté du renouvellement des siècles, changement de l'Empire et advancement du nom Chrestien*, Pierre Rigaud, Lyon, 1604

——, *Commentaires du Sieur de Chavigny sur les Centuries et Prognostications de feu Michel de Nostredame du Breui*, Paris, 1596

——, *La première Face du Janus français extraite et colligée des Centuries de Michel Nostradamus, par les héritiers de Pierre Roussin*, Lyon, 1594 (BMA)

Fontbrune, Dr Max de, *Les Prophéties de Nostradamus Dévoilées. Lettres à Henry Second*, Adyar, 1937

——, *La Prédiction mystérieuse de Prémol*, Michelet, Sarlat, 1939

Garencières, Théophilus, *The True Prophecies or Prognostications of Michael Nostradamus*. London, 1672

Gustafsson, G., *Europas framtid enligt Nostradamus*, Stockholm, 1956

Jaubert, Etienne, *Eclaircissement des véritables quatrains de Nostradamus et Vie de M. Nostradamus*, Amsterdam, 1656

Krafft, Karl E., *Nostradamus prezice viitorul Européi*, Bucharest, 1941

Larmor, A. Colin de, *Les merveilleux quatrains de Nostradamus*, Nantes, 1925

Le Pelletier, Anatole, *Les Oracles de Nostradamus, astrologue, médecin et conseiller ordinaire des rois Henry II, François II et Charles IX*, Le Pelletier, 40, rue d'Aboukir, Paris, 1867, 2 vols

Leroux, Jean, *La clef de Nostradamus . . . Par un solitaire*, Paris, 1710

Leroy, Dr Edgar, 'Les origines de Nostradamus', *Mémoires de l'Institut historique de Provence*, vol. 18, Marseille, 1941

Noorbergen, Rene, *Nostradamus Predicts the End of the World*, Pinnacle Books/Windsor Publishing Corp., New York, 1981

Reynaud-Plense, Charles, *Les Vraies Centuries et Prophéties de Michel Nostradamus. Colligées des premières éditions imprimées à Lyon en 1558–1605 et, à Troyes en 1611, et à Leyde en 1650, avec sa Vie, et un Glossaire Nostradamique*. Salon, 1940

Ruir, Emile, *Le Grand Carnage d'après les prophéties de Nostradamus de 1938 à 1947*, Ed. Medicis, Paris, 1938

——, *L'Ecroulement de l'Europe, d'après les prophéties de Nostradamus*, Paris, 1939

——, *Nostradamus, ses Prophéties, 1948–2023*, Paris, 1948

——, *Nostradamus: Les Proches et Derniers Evénements*, Ed. Médicis, Paris, 1953

Torné-Chavigny, H., *Réédition du livre de prophéties de Nostradamus*, 1862 edition, expanded in 1872

Wöllner, Dr Christian, *Das Mysterium des Nostradamus*, Leipzig, 1926

Magical and Metaphysical Studies

Barker, Stan, *The Signs of the Times: The Neptune Factor: America's Future and Past as Seen Through Planetary Cycles*, Llewellyn, St Paul, MN, 1986

Eisen, William, *The Universal Language of Cabalah, The Master Key to God Consciousness*, DeVorss & Co., Marina Del Rey, CA, 1989

Green, Jeff, *Pluto, The Evolutionary Journey of the Soul*, Llewellyn, St Paul, MN, 1993

Gibson, Walter B. and Litzka R., *The Complete Illustrated Book of Divination and Prophecy*, Arrow Books, London, 1989

Hall, Angus, *Signs of Things to Come*, Danbury Press/Aldus Books, London, 1975

Hall, Manly P., *The Secret Teachings of All the Ages: An Encyclopedic Outline of Masonic, Hermetic, Qabbalistic and Rosicrucian Symbolical Philosophy. Being an Interpretation of the Secret Teachings concealed within the Rituals, Allegories and Mysteries of all Ages*, The Philosophical Research Society, Inc., Los Angeles, CA, 1977

Iamblichus (Thomas Taylor, Tr.), *Iamblichus on The Mysteries of the Egyptians, Chaldeans, and Assyrians*, Wizards Bookshelf, San Diego, CA, 1984

Mathers, S. Liddell MacGregor (Tr.), *The Key of Solomon the King (Clavicula Salomonis)*, Samuel Weiser, Inc., York Beach, ME, 1972

Parise, Frank, (ed.), *The Book of Calendars*, Facts on File, Inc., New York, 1982

Roussat, Richard, *Livre de l'Estat et Mutation des Temps*, Lyons, 1550

Weed, Joseph J., *Complete Guide to Oracle and Prophecy Methods*, Parker Publishing Co., New York, 1971

Wilson, Colin, *Mysterious Powers*, Danbury Press/Aldus Books, London, 1975

Studies on General Prophecy Related to Nostradamus

Forman, Henry James, *The Story of Prophecy in the Life of Mankind*, Tudor Publishing Company, New York, 1940

Gattey, Charles Neilson, *Visionaries and Seers*, Prism Press, Dorset, 1977

——, *Prophecy and Prediction in the 20th Century*, Aquarian Press, Wellingborough, Northamptonshire, 1989

Greenhouse, Herbert B., *Premonitions: A Leap into the Future*, Bernard Geis Associates, 1971

Haich, Elizabeth, *Initiation*, Seed Center, Garberville, CA, 1974

Hall, Manly P., *Sages and Seers*, The Philosophical Research Society, Inc., Los Angeles, CA, 1975

Kert, Christian, *Nostradamus, Le mage de Salon*, Salon-de-Provence, Editions Les Centuries

Mann, A. T., *Millennium Prophecies, Predictions for the Year 2000*, Element, Shaftesbury, Dorset, 1992

Parker, Bonnie, *Napoleon's Book of Fate*, Aquarian Press/Thorson Publishing Group, Wellingborough, Northamptonshire, 1988

Pennington, Bruce, *Eschatus: Future Prophecies from Nostradamus' Ancient Writings*. Paper Tiger/A Dragon's World Book, Surrey, 1976–77

Rajneesh, Bhagwan Shree (Osho), *The Razor's Edge*, Rebel Publishing House Gmbh, Cologne

Reader's Digest, *Strange Stories Amazing Facts: Stories that are bizarre, unusual, odd, astonishing, and often incredible*, Reader's Digest Association, Inc., Pleasantville, NY, 1977

Wallechinsky, David, *The Book of Predictions*, William Morrow & Co., Inc., New York, 1980

General History and Miscellaneous Studies

Aarons, Mark, *Unholy Trinity: The Vatican, The Nazis, and Soviet Intelligence*, St Martin's Press, New York, 1991

Ardagh, John, *Cultural Atlas of France*, Facts On File/Andromeda Oxford, New York, 1991

Aron, Robert, *France Reborn, June 1944–May 1945. The History of the Liberation*, Charles Scribner's Sons, New York, 1964

Ashley, Maurice, *The English Civil War*, St Martin's Press, New York, 1990

Atkinson, Rick, *Crusade: The Untold Story of The Persian Gulf War*, Houghton Mifflin Company, Boston, 1993

Attwater, Donald, *The Penguin Dictionary of Saints*, Penguin Books, Harmondsworth, Middlesex, 1965, New York, 1983

Auchincloss, Louis, *Richelieu*, Viking Press, New York, 1972

Bailey, Ronald H., *World War II: Prisoners of War*, Time-Life Books, Alexandria, VA, 1981

Bayly, Dr Christopher, *Atlas of the British Empire*, Facts On File/Hamlyn, New York, 1989

Bierman, John, *Napoleon III and His Carnival Empire*, St Martin's Press, New York, 1988

Black, Greengrass, Howarth, Lawrance, Mackenney, Rady, Welch, *Cultural Atlas of The Renaissance*, Prentis Hall/Andromeda Oxford, New York, 1993

Blumenson, Martin, *World War II: The Liberation*, Time-Life Books, Alexandria, VA, 1978

Botting, Douglas, *World War II: The Second Front*, Time-Life Books, Alexandria, VA, 1978

Braudel, Fernand, *The Mediterranean and the Mediterranean World in the Age of Philip II*, Harper Collophon, New York, 1966

Brecher, Max, *A Passage to America: A Radically New Look at Bhagwan Shree Rajneesh and a Controversial American Commune*, Book Quest Publishers, Bombay, 1993

Breuer, William B., *Operation Dragoon, The Allied Invasion of the South of France*, Airlife, Shrewsbury, Shropshire, 1988

Burke, John, *An Illustrated History of England*, Collins, London, 1974

Burman, Edward, *The Inquisition: Hammer of Heresy*, Dorset Press, New York, 1984

Carr, John Laurence, *Life in France under Louis XIV*, Capricorn Books, New York, 1966

Carr, Raymond, *The Spanish Civil War: History in Pictures*, W.W. Norton, New York, 1986

Cartwright, Frederick F., *Disease and History*, Dorset Press, New York, 1972

Castleden, Rodney, *World History: A Chronological Dictionary of Dates*, Shooting Star Press, New York, 1993

Chadwick, Henry, *Atlas of the Christian Church*, Facts On File/Andromeda Oxford, New York, 1989

Chapman, Guy, *The Dreyfus Trials*, Palidin/Granada, Frogmore, 1974

Chronicle Publications, *Chronicle of the French Revolution 1788–1799*, Chronicle Communications, London, 1989

Clarke, Arthur C. *2061: odyssey three*, Del Rey/Ballantine, New York, 1987

Cooke, Donald A., *The Life & Death of Stars*, Crown Publishers, New York, 1985

Cooke, Jean, *History's Timeline: A 40,000 Year Chronology of Civilization*, Crescent Books, New York, 1981

Cornell, Tim, *Atlas of the Roman World*, Facts On File/Andromeda Oxford, New York, 1992

Coveney, Peter (and Roger Highfield), *The Arrow of Time*, Fawcet Columbine, New York, 1990

Crankshaw, Edward, *Bismark*, Viking Press, New York, 1981

Dennis, Jerry, *It's Raining Frogs and Fishes, Four Seasons of Natural Phenomena and Oddities of the Sky*, HarperCollins Publishers, New York, 1992

D'Orliac, Jehanne, *The Moon Mystress, Diane De Poitiers, Grant'Sénéchalle de Normandy*, J. B. Lippincott Company, London, 1930

Dunn, Richard S., *The Age of Religious Wars, 1559–1689*, W.W. Norton & Company, New York, 1970

Durby, George (Ed.), *A History of Private Life: Revelations of the Medieval World*, The Belknap Press of Harvard University Press, Cambridge, MA, 1988

Eggenberger, David, *An Encyclopedeia of Battles: Accounts of Over 1,560 Battles from 1479 B.C. to the Present*, Dover Publications, New York, 1985

Elliott, J.H., *Imperial Spain: 1469–1716*, St Martin's Press, New York, 1964

Elson, Robert T., *World War II: Prelude to War*, Time-Life Books, Alexandria, VA, 1978

Evslin, Bernard, *Gods, Demigods & Demons: An Encyclopedia of Greek Mythology*, Scholastic Book Services, New York, 1975

Farmer, David Hugh, *The Oxford Dictionary of Saints*, Oxford University Press (third edition), New York, 1992

Fernandez-Armesto, Felipe, *The Spanish Armada: The Experience of War in 1588*, Oxford University Press, New York, 1988

Fodor, Denis J., *World War II: The Neutrals*, Time-Life Books, Alexandria, VA, 1978

Forman, Juliet, *Bhagwan: The Buddha of the Future*, Rebel Publishing House, Poona, India

——, *Bhagwan: One Man against the whole ugly Past of Humanity*, Rebel Publishing House, Poona, India

Fraser, Antonia, *Cromwell, The Lord Protector*, Dell, New York, 1973

——, *Mary Queen of Scots*, Delacorte Press, New York, 1978

Geison, Gerald, *The Private Science of Louis Pasteur*, Princeton University Press, Ewing, NJ, 1995

Gleick, James, *Chaos: Making a New Science*, Penguin, New York, 1987

Goubert, Pierre, *Louis XIV and Twenty Million Frenchmen*, Vintage Books/Random House, New York, 1966

Greengrass, Mark, *France in the Age of Henri IV*, Longman, New York, 1984

Griffiths, Richard, *Pétain: A biography of Marshal Philippe Pétain of Vichy*, Doubleday & Co., New York, 1972

Groden, Robert J., *The Killing of a President*, Penguin Books, New York, 1994

Ground Zero, *Nuclear War, What's in it For You*, Pocket Books/Simon & Schuster, New York, 1982

Hamlyn, Paul, *The Life and Times of Louis XIV*, Hamlyn Publishing Group Ltd., Middlesex, 1968

Hardman, John, *Louis XVI*, Yale University Press, New Haven & London, 1993

Herold, J. Christopher, *The Age of Napoleon*, American Heritage Publishing Co./Harper & Row, New York, 1963

Herzog, Chaim, *The Arab-Israeli Wars*, Random House, New York, 1982

Hibbert, Christopher, *The House of Medici: Its Rise and Fall*, William Morrow & Co., New York, 1975

Hughes, Robert, *Barcelona*, Alfred A. Knopf, New York, 1992

Inglis, Brian, *Abdication: The first full account of Edward VIII's agony and crisis—the grueling test of a nation and its prince*, The Macmillan Company, New York, 1966

Jones, George Hilton, *Convergent Forces: Immediate Causes of the Revolution of 1688 in England*, Iowa State University Press, Ames, Iowa, 1990

Keegan, John (Ed.), *The Times Atlas of the Second World War*, Harper & Row, New York, 1989

——, *Barbarossa, Invasion of Russia 1941*, Ballantine, New York, 1970

Kelly, J. N. D., *The Oxford Dictionary of Popes*, Oxford University Press, New York, 1986

Kennedy, Paul, *The Rise and Fall of the Great Powers: Economic Change and Military Conflict from 1500 to 2000*, Fontana Press/Random House, New York, 1988

Kinross, Lord, *The Ottoman Centuries, The Rise and Fall of the Turkish Empire*, Morrow Quill Paperbacks, New York, 1977

Kohn, George C., *Dictionary of Wars*, Anchor Books/Doubleday, New York, 1986

Lange, Nicholas de, *Atlas of the Jewish World*, Facts On File/Andromeda Oxford, New York, 1992

Leslie, Peter, *The Liberation of the Riviera, The Resistance to the Nazis in the South of France & the Story of its heroic Leader Ange-Marie Miniconi*, Wyndham Books, New York, 1980

Levi, Peter, *Atlas of the Greek World*, Facts On File/Andromeda Oxford, New York, 1993

Lister, R. P., *Genghis Khan*, Barnes & Noble Books, New York, 1960

Livesey, Anthony, *The Historical Atlas of World War I*, Henry Holt Reference Book, New York, 1994

Loomis, Stanley, *The Fatal Friendship: Marie Antoinette, Count Fersen and the Flight to Varennes*, Doubleday & Co., New York, 1972

Mackenney, Richard, *Sixteenth Century Europe: Expansion and Conflict*, St Martin's Press, New York, 1993

Mansel, Philip, *Louis XVIII*, Blond & Briggs, London, 1981

Massie, Robert K., *Nicholas and Alexandra*, Atheneum, New York, 1968

Matthew, Donald, *Atlas of Medieval Europe*, Facts On File/Andromeda Oxford, New York, 1992

Mellenthin, Maj. Gen. F.W. von, *Panzer Battles: A Study of the employment of Armor in the Second World War*, Ballantine Books, New York, 1971

Milner-Gulland, Robin, *Cultural Atlas of Russia and the Soviet Union*, Facts On File/Andromeda Oxford, New York, 1991

Moore, James, *Gurdjieff: The Anatomy of a Myth*, Element, Shaftesbury, Dorset, 1991

More, Sir Thomas, *The Utopia of Sir Thomas More*, Roslyn, Walter J. Black, Inc., New York, 1947

Morford, Mark P. O., *Classical Mythology*, Longman, (third edition), New York, 1985

Mitford, Nancy, *Madame de Pompadour*, Harper and Row, New York, 1968

Neff, Donald, *Warriors at Suez: Eisenhower Takes America into the Middle East*, Linden Press/Simon & Schuster, New York, 1981

Noone, John, *The Man Behind the Iron Mask*, St Martin's Press, New York, 1988

Nostradamus, Michel, *Traité des Confitures* (first edition 1557), Imp. sur les presses des Imprimeries Réunies de Senils pour le compte de Gutenberg Reprint, 1979

Nostredame, César de, *Histoire De Provence*, Montpellier/Laffite Reprint (first edition 1614)

Parker, Geoffrey, *The Thirty Years' War*, Barnes & Noble, New York, 1987

Robinson, Francis, *Atlas of the Islamic World since 1500*, Facts On File/Andromeda, Oxford, New York, 1992

Roeder, Ralph, *Catherine de' Medici and the Lost Revolution*, Garden City Publishing, New York, 1939

Rotmistrov, R, "The Speed of Attack of a Tank Army," in *Voyennoistoricheskiy zhurnal*, No. 6, 1964

Rutherford, Ward, *Blitzkrieg 1940*, Gallery Books, New York, 1979

Schama, Simon, *Citizens: A Chronicle of the French Revolution*, Vintage Books/Random House, New York, 1990

Schevill, Ferdinand, *A History of the Balkans, From the Earliest Times to the Present Day*, Dorset Press, New York, 1991

Seale, Patrick, *Abu Nidal, A Gun for Hire*, Random House, New York, 1992

Seward, Desmond, *Napoleon and Hitler, A Comparative Biography*, A Touchstone Book, New York, 1988

Smith, Denis Mack, *Mussolini, A Biography*, Vintage Books/Random House, New York, 1982

Speer, Albert, *Inside the Third Reich*, Collier/Macmillan, New York, 1970

Stewart, Bob, *Barbarossa, Scourge of Europe*, Firebird Books, Dorset, 1988

Toland, John, *Adolf Hitler*, Doubleday & Company, New York, 1976

Tremlett, George, *Gadaffi: The Desert Mystic*, Carroll & Graf Publishers, New York, 1993

Vallee, Jacques, *Passport to Magonia: on UFOs, Folklore, and Parallel Worlds*, Contemporary Books, Chicago, 1969

Vallee, Jacques, *Confrontations: A Scientist's Search for Alien Contact*, Ballantine Books, New York, 1990

Wallace, Robert, *The Italian Campaign (World War II)*, Time-Life Books, Alexandria, VA, 1978

Wernick, Robert, *World War II: Blitzkrieg*, Time-Life Books, Alexandria, VA, 1978

Williams, Neville, *Henry VIII and His Court*, Cardinal, London, 1971

Yallop, David A., *In God's Name: An Investigation into the Murder of Pope John Paul I*, Bantam Books, New York, 1985

Index

G

M

DEDICATION

To the witness, the Blessed One within.

ACKNOWLEDGMENTS

With this book I end a journey into Nostradamus' prophecies which has spanned over two decades. I wish to thank John Bole (wherever he may be) for turning me onto the subject; my mother Irene Hogue, for her tireless contributions and assistance; to my dear friend and fellow traveler, Nadine Joyau, and her mother, Janine, for contacting various scholars and museums in France; to my agent and friend, Ronald S. Tanner, who had the faith and fortitude to help me complete, in record time, this largest book ever written on Nostradamus; to my publisher Michael Mann, his secretary, Sue James, my project manager, Grace Cheetham, Roger Lane, the production director, Cath Haslam, the editorial manager, Mike Darton, the copy-editor, and all the people at Element Books Ltd for burning the midnight oil to see this book through to the printers in time.

No modern-day commentator or critic of Nostradamus could write a thorough study on this subject without standing on the shoulders of the great scholar and commentator Edgar Leoni, who was the last man to write a complete examination of the prophet over 36 years ago. We modern interpreters are all too indebted to him and mention his name all too little. Other notable commentators who deserve (but rarely receive) our thanks are Stewart Robb, James Laver and Anatole le Pelletier.

I also wish to thank Linda Obadia for her conceptual editing, spiritual support and friendship; Arpana Greenwood for her translating assistance; Janine and Marcel Joyau for their generous hospitality (and great cooking!); Marc and Béatrice "Biche" Joyau for our tours through the French countryside; and a big hug to my father, "Bud" Hogue.

I also wish to personally thank Jacqueline Allemand, directress of the Maison de Nostradamus (Salon-en-Provence) for helping me obtain rare manuscripts and almanacs of Nostradamus; M Morel, Director of the Academie des Sciences, Agriculture Arts et Belles-Lettres d'Aix (Musée Paul Arbaud, Aix-en-Provence) for copies of the Benoist Rigaud 1568 edition of the prophecies of Nostradamus; Dr Louis Turi; Dan Oldenburg for his astrological insights; and finally Hans Holzer of the New York Committee for the Investigation of Paranormal Occurences for his encouragement and guidance.